INTERNATIONAL HANDB(
ECONOMICS OF EDUCATI(

International Handbook on the Economics of Education

Edited by

Geraint Johnes

Professor of Economics, Lancaster University Management School, UK

Jill Johnes

Lecturer in Economics, Lancaster University Management School, UK

Edward Elgar Publishing Ltd

Cheltenham, UK • Northampton, MA, USA

Published by
Edward Elgar Publishing Limited
Glensanda House
Montpellier Parade
Cheltenham
Glos GL50 1UA
UK

Edward Elgar Publishing, Inc.
136 West Street
Suite 202
Northampton
Massachusetts 01060
USA

A catalogue record for this book
is available from the British Library

Library of Congress Cataloguing in Publication Data

International handbook on the economics of education/edited by Geraint
  Johnes, Jill Johnes.
    p. cm. — (Elgar original reference)
  Includes bibliographical references and index.
  1. Education—Economic aspects. I. Johnes, Geraint, 1958– II. Johnes,
Jill, 1962– III. Series.

  LC65.I59   2004
  338.4'737—dc22   2004047118

ISBN 1 84376 119 X (cased)

Printed and Bound in Great Britain by MPG Books Ltd, Bodmin, Cornwall

Contents

Contributors

Susan L. Averett, Department of Economic and Business, Lafayette College, Easton, PA, USA.

Steve Bradley, Department of Economics, Lancaster University Management School, Lancaster, UK.

Sarah Brown, Department of Economics, University of Leicester, UK.

Elchanan Cohn, Department of Economics, Moore School of Business, University of South Carolina, USA.

Samuel T. Cooper, Webster University, Greenville, USA.

Peter J. Dolton, University of Newcastle upon Tyne and London School of Economics, UK.

David Greenaway, Department of Economics, University of Nottingham, UK.

Michelle Haynes, Nottingham University Business School, UK.

William H. Hoyt, University of Kentucky, Lexington, Kentucky, USA.

Saqib Jafarey, Department of Economics, City University, London, UK.

Geraint Johnes, Department of Economics, Lancaster University Management School, Lancaster, UK.

Jill Johnes, Department of Economics, Lancaster University Management School, Lancaster, UK.

Sajal Lahiri, Department of Economics, Southern Illinois University, USA.

Stephen Machin, Department of Economics, University College London and Centre for Economic Performance, London School of Economics, UK.

Michele C. McLennan, Department of Business and Economics, Ursinus College, Collegeville, USA.

Walter W. McMahon, Department of Economics, University of Illinois at Urbana-Champaign, USA.

David Mitch, Department of Economics, University of Maryland Baltimore County, USA.

Robin A. Naylor, Department of Economics, University of Warwick.

Anh Ngoc Nguyen, Department of Economics, Lancaster University Management School, Lancaster, UK.

Harry Anthony Patrinos, World Bank, Washington, DC, USA.

George Psacharopoulos, Hellenic Parliament, Athens, Greece.

Paulo Santiago, Directorate for Education, OECD, Paris, France.

John G. Sessions, Department of Economics and International Development, University of Bath, UK.

Jeremy Smith, Department of Economics, University of Warwick, UK.

Philip Stevens, National Institute of Economic and Social Research, London, UK.

Jim Taylor, Department of Economics, Lancaster University Management School, Lancaster, UK.

Martin Weale, National Institute of Economic and Social Research, London, UK.

Introduction

The modern analysis of the economics of education had its birth with Theodore Schultz's address to the American Economic Association in December 1960. That address introduced to a wide audience within the economics profession the notion that education can be regarded as an investment in human capital, an investment that is analogous to investments in physical capital. Individuals decide to invest in their own education, at the margin, just as firms decide to invest in new machinery; the investment in each case entails current costs, and yields future benefits; and an internal rate of return to the investment can in each case be calculated.

The study of the economics of education has expanded considerably in scope over the last four and a half decades – as is evidenced by the wide range of material in this volume. But the key insights of human capital theory remain central to any analysis of the demand for education, and it is therefore appropriate that this is where the volume should begin. Psacharopoulos and Patrinos outline the basics of the human capital model, emphasizing the role that education has to play in raising individuals' productivity. They also provide empirical estimates of the rate of return to education in a variety of countries. Estimates such as these have been particularly influential in shaping the educational policies of international organizations such as the World Bank, informing in particular the policy of loans to support education in developing countries and the goal of universal primary education.

Yet human capital is not the only game in town. Since the early 1970s, economists have also considered another family of models that aims to explain the relationship between education and earnings. This is the body of literature characterized by signalling and screening models. Such models emphasize the role played by educational credentials as indicators of individuals' innate ability or productivity. Firms that cannot or do not measure productivity directly can then reward productive individuals by using education as a signal of their likely productivity. In the more refined screening models, the allocation of tasks may be influenced by workers' credentials. By invoking the assumption that education is more costly for less able individuals, this broad class of models is able to explain how workers self-select into alternative education regimes. The general area of signalling and screening models is surveyed by Brown and Sessions.

Whatever the relative merits of the human capital and the signalling and screening models in the context of general education, one would expect vocational training programmes to contribute directly to productivity. There has emerged a substantial literature, surveyed by Dolton, on the evaluation of such programmes. Much of this literature is concerned with some severe statistical problems that attach to the evaluation process.

A key argument in favour of the human capital view of education is the evidence that has emerged in the last decade or so of the impact that education can have on economic growth. The rapid emergence of several South and East Asian economies, all of which have shared experience of rapidly expanding educational provision, has served to emphasize the key role that education can play in stimulating economic development. Stevens and Weale survey this literature in their chapter.

The growth of (some) developing countries may not have occurred without costs elsewhere, however. A number of authors have argued that the move towards globalization has allowed lower income countries to compete effectively for the production of tradeable goods by lower skill workers, and that this has served to widen the distribution of incomes in the developed world. An alternative argument, analysed in the chapter by Machin, is that technical change in the recent past has been biased in terms of its effects on workers with different skill levels. So, for instance, the development of information technology has allowed firms to switch into more capital-intensive forms of production, in which the new capital is a substitute for unskilled labour but a complement of skilled labour. This has generated shifts in the relative demand for labour of different skills, and has had a marked impact on both the returns to education and the income distribution in the West.

The first few chapters of the book therefore all concern, in one way or another, the return to education: its measurement at micro level, and its impact at macro level. Chapter 6, by McMahon, reminds us that there can be significant differences between the private returns to education and the social returns. Often forgotten in discussions of this distinction is the issue of externalities associated with education. McMahon presents a comprehensive assessment of such externalities and finds that the impact of education on society is pervasive.

The next two chapters, by Mitch and by Greenaway and Haynes, present an analysis of funding models for compulsory education and for higher education, respectively. In many countries there are debates about the appropriate mechanism for financing education, with an increased interest in voucher systems and in cost recovery. These two chapters together provide an insight into the variety of funding instruments that are available and that are in use in various countries around the globe. Clearly the role played by externalities, discussed in Chapter 6, is the key in understanding the choice of mechanism employed in each country.

Education presumably produces educated individuals who, if the human capital model has any empirical relevance at all, will have enhanced productivity. Yet the process by which education transforms (relatively) unproductive individuals into (relatively) productive ones is not one that is particularly well understood. Some gains have been made in recent years in understanding the educational production function, but a particularly controversial aspect of this literature has concerned the effect that class size has on pupil performance. Averett and McClennan discuss this literature in their chapter, and conclude that, while results have been ambiguous, the most sophisticated studies have found that smaller class sizes are associated with an improvement in pupil performance.

The next two chapters both build on the notion of educational production functions in order to examine the determinants of educational success. Bradley and Taylor examine this in the context of secondary education, while Naylor and Smith do so in the context of higher education. At any level, a concern in evaluating the performance of students is that the measure by which the evaluation takes place remains constant over time – that is, that standards are adhered to over time. This is an issue that is considered in detail in the chapter by Geraint Johnes.

The issue of standards also provides a reason to evaluate educational performance using means other than examination results. The transition into the labour market provides a natural alternative indicator of educational success, and this forms the topic of the chapter by Bradley and Nguyen. There are many pathways that individuals can take through education into work, including further education, higher education, apprenticeship schemes and so on. Individuals with different characteristics have different likelihoods of passing through any one of these pathways, and economists have had considerable success in recent years in modelling this transition.

The labour market for teachers, surveyed here by Santiago, is distinct from many occupation-specific labour markets, for a number of reasons. First, teacher training is a lengthy process, and so adjustments in the market take time. Secondly, many women are attracted into teaching by the coincidence of teachers' holidays and those of their children; the consequent concentration of women in the teaching profession, many of whom interrupt their careers for an unspecified period, has left the market with a large pool of latent supply. Thirdly, government often has an important part to play in both the demand and supply sides of the market. All these features make the market for educators substantially different from other labour markets, and require careful analysis.

The next chapter, by Cohn and Cooper, concerns the role of universities as multi-product firms. By definition, universities produce graduates in a variety of different fields and at a variety of different levels. They also, typically, produce new knowledge in the form of research. Drawing on work from the industrial organization literature, this chapter surveys the various attempts that have been made to estimate the cost function of such complex organizations, thereby yielding insights about the nature of scale and scope economies.

In estimating cost functions of this type, most recent studies have employed a form of frontier analysis, appropriate in this context because a theoretical cost function is by definition a frontier that describes how an efficient producer would produce each given vector of outputs. Frontier analysis and the evaluation of efficiency form the twin themes of the chapter by Jill Johnes. Two techniques have emerged from the literature that allow such analyses to be conducted: data envelopment analysis (DEA) and stochastic frontier analysis (SFA). Both are surveyed in some detail in this chapter.

The two chapters that finish the volume consider themes that have appeared earlier. The chapter by Jafarey and Lahiri develops themes that appear in the literature on human capital, specifically concerning the rate of return to human capital in developing countries. The authors focus specifically on the issue of child labour, and how policies can be developed to alleviate this. Hoyt develops some issues raised in the chapters on funding models in order to examine the local public finance aspects of education, focusing specifically on the complex effects that education can have on the housing market.

It is clear that, as it approaches its half-centenary, the economics of education has come a long way. In this volume, we have assembled chapters that say something about the state of the art. But this is a fast evolving subject of study, and it is clear that in a few years time we can expect much more to have been learned about subjects such as the relationship between education and growth, the impact on welfare of various funding models, and the educational production function.

In concluding this introduction, we would like to thank the team at Edward Elgar for their help in putting this volume together. Alexandra Minton, in particular, has been wonderful. We would also like to thank all the chapter authors for the way in which they have made easy our task as editors. We, the editors, were both introduced to the subject by one of these authors, Jim Taylor, and, as he approaches his retirement, we feel it appropriate to dedicate to him, with great thanks, our own input into this volume.

Geraint Johnes and Jill Johnes

1 Human capital and rates of return

George Psacharopoulos and
Harry Anthony Patrinos

1 Introduction

As with many other underpinnings in economics, the seeds of the theoretical link between education and productivity is in the writings of classical economists, but for reasons explained by Schultz (1971, p. 27), Adam Smith's insight was left dormant until the late 1950s, the time when the modern human capital school was born.

Among the most important historical landmarks in the field is Adam Smith's [1776] (1991) classic statement that 'a man educated at the expense of much labour and time to any of those employments which require extraordinary dexterity and skill, may be compared to one of those expensive machines. The work which he learns to perform, it must be expected, over and above the usual wages of common labour, will replace to him the whole expense of his education.' Alfred Marshall [1890] (1991) referred to industrial training as a national investment in his *Principles of Economics*. Soon after the Russian revolution a Soviet economist made estimates of the benefits to the nation from investment in universal primary and secondary education, based on his cost–benefit analysis of training in a Leningrad (St. Petersburg) factory (Strumilin, 1924). Walsh (1935) estimated the stock of human capital in the United States and the returns to formal schooling of college graduates. Friedman and Kuznets (1946) used the discounted value of future earnings to explain the incomes of doctors and dentists.

Such scattered work was formally modelled by the University of Chicago–Columbia University trio of Mincer (1958), Schultz (1960, 1961) and Becker (1975). Time and money spent on education builds human capital, hence one should be able to estimate the rate of return on such investment, in a way similar to investment in physical capital. In its short history, several economics of education textbooks have been written and one encyclopaedia volume (Blaug, 1970; Psacharopoulos, 1987; Cohn and Geske, 1990; Johnes, 1993). Mark Blaug's economics of education bibliography first appeared in 1966, with a second edition in 1970 and a third one in 1978 (Blaug, 1978). The reason Professor Blaug stopped producing the bibliography is that the field grew so much it was difficult to keep track of it.

1

Table 1.1   Pathways to measuring the returns to education

Nature of benefits	Data base	Empirical result	Methodology/approach
Market monetary	Micro data	Private returns	Full discounting
			Mincerian earnings function
		Narrow social returns	Full costing
National accounts monetary	Macro data	Contribution to growth	Within-country growth accounting
			Cross-country panel regression
Wide social	Micro/macro combination	Non-market benefits	Contingent valuation
		Externalities	New growth theory

The next section reviews the methodologies for estimating rates of return to education. This is followed by a presentation of the key findings in the literature, going back several decades and drawing on a number of comprehensive reviews. In addition to a discussion and presentation of the private rate of return to education, which is important for explaining private demand for education, the concept of social returns to education is scrutinized. Typical findings and patterns observed in the literature are shown in the following section. Next, a presentation of macroeconomic growth returns are presented. The non-market benefits and externalities typically associated with education are reviewed and the latest evidence is presented. The chapter closes with a discussion of the policy implications of empirical rates of return to education investments.

2   Methodology

Although similar to investments in physical capital, investment in human capital has its idiosyncrasies regarding the way costs and benefits are conceptualized and measured. In this section the road map shown in Table 1.1 is followed.

Two types of returns are usually estimated, each answering a different question: first, the *private* rate of return, that compares the costs and benefits of education as incurred and realized by the individual student who undertakes the investment; second, the *social* rate of return, that compares costs and benefits from the country as a whole or society's point of view. Private rates of return are used to explain the behaviour of individuals in seeking different levels and types of education, whereas social rates are used to formulate educational policies regarding the expansion, or contraction, of different levels and types of education.

There exists some confusion in the literature regarding the 'social' adjective attached to rates of return to investment in education. It has been the tradition in the mainstream economics of education literature to mean by a 'social' rate, a private rate adjusted for the full cost of schooling, rather than just what the individual pays for his or her education. However, in the economics literature at large, a 'social' rate should include externalities; that is, benefits beyond those captured by the individual investor.

Given this confusion, we will refer to the traditional social returns to education as 'narrow social', and to the returns that include externalities as 'wide social'. However it should be noted at the outset that the confusion between the two types of social returns was dictated by the circumstances, that is, the paucity of data suitable for the measurement of externalities.

The confusion is more than theoretical. By adding externalities to the narrow social returns, one can reach diametrically opposite policy conclusions. This is illustrated in Figure 1.1, where the privately optimum number of years of schooling S_p represents an overinvestment in schooling according to the narrow social returns (S_n equilibrium), but an underinvestment according to the wide social returns (S_w equilibrium).

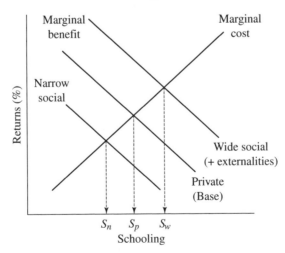

Figure 1.1   Private and social optimum levels of schooling

Private rate of return

The costs incurred by the individual are his/her forgone earnings while studying, plus any education fees or incidental expenses the individual incurs during schooling. Since education is mostly provided free by the state, in practice the only cost in a private rate of return calculation is the forgone earnings. The private benefits amount to what a more educated individual earns (after taxes), above a control group of individuals with less education. 'More' and 'less' in this case usually refers to adjacent levels of education, for example university graduates versus secondary school graduates (see Figure 4.2).

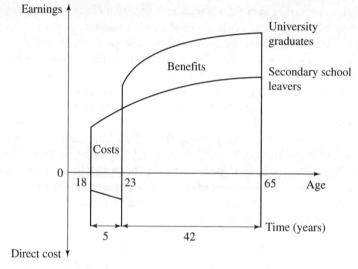

Figure 1.2   Stylized age–earnings profiles

The private rate of return to an investment in a given level of education in such a case can be estimated by finding the rate of discount (r) that equalizes the stream of discounted benefits to the stream of costs at a given point in time. In the case of university education lasting five years, for example, the formula is

$$\sum_{t=1}^{42} \frac{(W_u - W_s)_t}{(1 + r)^t} = \sum_{t=1}^{5} (W_s + C_u)_t (1 + r)^t,$$

where $(W_u - W_s)$ is the earnings differential between a university graduate (subscript u) and a secondary school graduate (subscript s, the control group). C_u represents the direct costs of university education (tuition, fees, books) and W_s denotes the student's forgone earnings or indirect costs.

A similar calculation can be made for the other levels of education. However, there is an important asymmetry between computing the returns to primary education and those to the other levels. Primary school children, mostly aged six to 12 years, do not forgo earnings during the entire length of their studies. On the assumption that children aged 11 and 12 help in agricultural labour, two or three years of forgone earnings while in primary schooling have been used in the empirical literature.

In addition, there may be no need to estimate a rate of return to justify investment in basic education: it is taken for granted that the literacy of the population is a goal that stands on its own merits for a variety of reasons other than economic considerations. Still private rates of return gauge private demand for education and are useful in determining incentives for enrolling at different levels of education, or for assessing the equity effect of scholarships. Furthermore, as one climbs the educational ladder and schooling becomes more specialized, it is imperative to estimate the costs and benefits of post-primary school investments, especially those in the vocational track of secondary education and higher education.

Narrow versus wide social rate of return
The main computational difference between private and social rates of return is that, for a social rate of return calculation, the costs include the state's or society at large's spending on education. Hence, in the above example, C_u would include the rental of buildings and professorial salaries. Gross earnings (that is, before taxes and other deductions) should be used in a social rate of return calculation, and such earnings should also include income in kind where this information is available.

A key assumption in a social rate of return calculation is that observed wages are a good proxy for the marginal product of labour, especially in a competitive economy using data from the private sector of the economy. Civil service pay scales are irrelevant for a social rate of return calculation as they are unlikely to represent marginal productivity. The pay of civil servants, however, should be used in calculating the private returns to education, as it reflects what people actually get, regardless of productivity.

The 'social' attribute of the estimated rate of return refers to the inclusion of the full resource cost of the investment (direct cost and forgone earnings). Ideally, the social benefits should include non-monetary or external effects of education: for example, lower fertility or lives saved because of improved sanitation conditions followed by a more educated woman who may never participate in the formal labour market. (See Chapter 6 in this volume.) Given the scant empirical evidence on the external effects of education, social rate of return estimates are usually based on directly observable monetary costs and benefits of education (but see Summers, 1992).

Since the costs are higher in a social rate of return calculation relative to the one from the private point of view, social returns are typically lower than a private rate of return. The difference between the private and the social rate of return reflects the degree of public subsidization of education.

The discounting of actual net age–earnings profiles is the most appropriate method of estimating the returns to education because it takes into account the most important part of the early earning history of the individual. However this method requires comprehensive data; one must have a sufficient number of observations in a given age-educational level cell for constructing 'well-behaved' age–earnings profiles (that is, not intersecting with each other).

The short-cut method   There is another method to arrive at approximate returns to education that is very easy to apply. Given the shape of the age–earnings profiles, one can approximate them as flat curves (see Figure 1.3). In such a case, the rate of return estimation is based on a simple formula:

$$private \ r = \frac{\bar{W}_u - \bar{W}_s}{5(\bar{W}_u)},$$

where $\bar{W}$ refers to the mean earnings of an individual with the subscripted educational level, and 5 is the length of the university cycle. The social rate of return in this case is simply given as

$$social \ r = \frac{\bar{W}_u - \bar{W}_s}{5(\bar{W}_s + \bar{C}_u)},$$

where C_u is the annual direct cost of university education.

Although the short-cut method is very easy to use, it is, by definition, inferior relative to any of the other methods described above. The weakness of the method lies in the abstraction that age–earnings profiles are concave, and that the discounting process (in estimating the true rate of return) is very sensitive to the values of the early working ages entering the calculation.

The reverse cost–benefit method   This is based on the short-cut rate of return formula and amounts to asking the question: given the cost of the investment, what level of annual benefits would produce a given rate of return (10 per cent, for instance) on the investment? This can be stated as annual benefit = 0.10 (education cost), or, in this case:

$$(\bar{W}_u - \bar{W}_s) = (0.1) \, [5(\bar{W}_s + \bar{C}_u)]$$

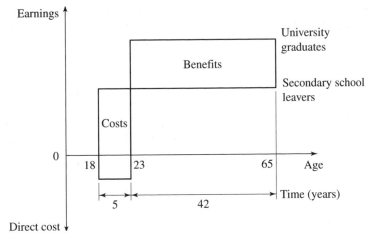

Figure 1.3   Flat age–earnings profiles

Although rough, this preliminary calculation can be made easily and can instigate further analyses on how to reduce the costs or increase the benefits to possibly justify the investment.

The earnings function method This method is also known as the 'Mincerian' method (see Mincer, 1974) and involves the fitting of a function of log-wages (*LnW*), using years of schooling (*S*), years of labour market experience (*EX*) and its square as independent variables (ibid.). Often weeks worked or hours worked are added as independent variables to this function as compensatory factors. The above is called a 'basic earnings function'. In this semi-log specification the coefficient on years of schooling can be interpreted as the average private rate of return to one additional year of schooling, regardless of the educational level this year of schooling refers to. The basic 'Mincerian' earnings function takes the form:

$$\ln W_i = \alpha + \beta S_i + \gamma_1 EX_i + \gamma_2 EX_i^2 + \varepsilon_i,$$

defined as (*Age − S − School starting age*). In this function, the β coefficient on years of schooling can be interpreted as the average rate of return to one additional year of schooling. Since $\beta = (\partial \ln W / \partial S)$, this is the relative increase in wages following an increase in *S*, or the rate of return to the marginal year of schooling. This method assumes that forgone earnings represent the only cost of education, and so measures only the private rate of return, and assumes further that individuals have an infinite time horizon.

In addition, this function does not distinguish between different levels of schooling. To solve this problem, the extended earnings function substitutes a series of 0–1 dummy variables for S, corresponding to discrete educational levels,

$$\ln W_i = \alpha + \beta_p D_p + \beta_p D_p + \beta_u D_u + \gamma_1 EX_i + \gamma_2 EX_i^2 + \varepsilon_i,$$

where D is the dummy variable for the subscripted level of schooling. To avoid matrix singularity, one of the mutually exclusive education categories should be omitted: for example, the dummy corresponding to those with no schooling.

The private rates of return between levels of education can then be calculated from the extended earnings function by the formulas,

$$r_p = \frac{\beta_p}{S_p},$$

$$r_s = \frac{\beta_s - \beta_p}{S_s - S_p},$$

$$r_u = \frac{\beta_u - \beta_s}{S_u - S_s},$$

where r_p is the rate of return to primary schooling, r_s is the rate of return to secondary and r_u is the rate of return to university.

This calculation resembles the short-cut method in that the rate of return is computed as a ratio of a constant annual benefits flow to the total education cost for attaining the next level of education.

The advantage of the Mincerian way of estimating the returns to education is that it can smooth out and handle low-count cells in an age–earnings profile matrix by level of education. The disadvantage, of course, is that it requires a large sample of individual observations, rather than pretabulated mean earnings by level of schooling. Although convenient because it requires fewer data, this method is slightly inferior to the full discounting method presented above as it in fact assumes flat age–earnings profiles for different levels of education (see Psacharopoulos and Layard, 1979).

Refinements and adjustments

Estimating the returns to investments in education, as for any other sector, involves an implicit projection of anticipated benefits over the lifetime of the investment. Since only the past earnings are observed or, most commonly, only a snapshot of the relative earnings of graduates of different levels of schooling is observed, adjustments have been used in the literature to provide a realistic projection of earnings of graduates. The most common adjustments refer to the anticipated real growth in earnings (g), mortality (m), unemployment (u), taxes (t) and innate ability (a). Thus, starting from the observed earnings of university graduates (W_u), their projected profile is adjusted as

$$\widehat{W}_u = W_u(1+g)(1-m)(1-u)(1-t).$$

The age–earning profile of the control group (W_s), say secondary school graduates, has to be adjusted in the same way, with growth, mortality, unemployment and tax rates specific to that group. In addition the resulting net benefit of higher education has been further adjusted to reflect differential ability (a) between the two groups of graduates:

$$\text{Net benefit of higher education} = (\widehat{W}_u - W_s)(1-\alpha).$$

Extensive empirical application of the adjustments described in these equations in the early literature from the 1960s on the economics of education led to the conclusion that the pluses and minuses essentially cancel out and one ends up with a net benefit almost equal to the unadjusted one. This is understood by the fact that the adjustments are dealing with differences in, for example, mortality rates or unemployment rates between the two groups of graduates, and this does not amount to much in practice.

Critique
Although the concept itself of the rate of return to investment in education is unassailable, empirical applications have been attacked in the literature on a number of grounds.

Ability   In the 1970s, the adjustment to the gross earnings differential that drew the most attention was that for differential ability between the two groups of graduates, often known as the 'filter' or 'screening' hypothesis (see Arrow, 1973). Researchers often attributed one-third of the private earnings to differential ability by multiplying the gross earnings differentials by a so-called 'alpha' (for ability) coefficient equal to 0·67 (see Blaug, 1970). But again extensive research, from the work of Griliches (1970) to that of natural experiments using identical twins who have been separated early in life (Ashenfelter and Krueger, 1994) has shown that the ability correction is not empirically validated; hence it is dropped in modern practice.

Perhaps the returns to education estimates that stem from the work of Ashenfelter and others using twins (Ashenfelter and Krueger, 1994;

Ashenfelter and Rouse, 1998; Miller *et al.*, 1995; Rouse, 1999; Behrman and Rosenzweig, 1999) and other natural experiments are the most reliable of all. According to this work, the overall private rate of return to investment in education in the United States is of the order of 10 per cent. This figure establishes a benchmark for what the social rate of return would be (a couple of percentage points lower, if not adjusted for externalities), or what the rate of return should be in a country with a lower per capita income than that of the United States (several percentage points higher, as based on the extrapolation of the not-so-comparable returns to education presented earlier).

Simultaneity   Instrumental variables (IV) estimates of the returns to schooling have been used to correct for the downward bias in ordinary least-squares (OLS) estimates caused by the simultaneity between schooling and earnings. Researchers have made imaginative uses of variables for instruments, the results showing a negative bias in OLS estimates. One example is the use of compulsory school attendance laws. Harmon and Walker (1995) use changes in the educational distribution of individuals caused by the raising of the minimum school-leaving age in the United Kingdom to provide instruments for schooling. This provides a good experiment because individuals who would otherwise have left school early stay on because of changes in the law. The findings show a large and negative bias in the least-squares estimate of the schooling-earnings relationship, providing further evidence of the downward bias in OLS estimates of the returns to schooling, as found in other studies (Angrist and Krueger, 1991).

These techniques have been criticized by some, especially if the source of the bias is due to differences in discount rates for educational investment since the use of instrumental variables may estimate the effect of the treatment on those individuals whose choices are affected by the instrument in question (Card, 1998). Card (2001) provides a very precise and rigorous review of the most important IV studies of the returns to schooling, and points to some potential problems. Overall, IV estimates of the return to schooling exceed the corresponding OLS estimates, often by 20 per cent or more. But the issue of the choice of instrument is important and the results need to be interpreted carefully. Even ideal IV estimates are imprecise and the empirical strategies are not based on true randomization, leading Card (2001) to conclude that no individual study is likely to be decisive in the debate over the magnitude of ability biases in OLS estimates of the returns to schooling.

Incidentally estimates of the returns to education based on analysis of twins' earnings – as well as estimates using IV measures (see, for example, Card,

2001) – come to an average rate of return that is very similar to the global average presented in a recent global compilation: 10 per cent (Psacharopoulos and Patrinos, 2004).

Family background   Casual empiricism may suggest that what appears to be a return to investment in education is in fact a rent derived from one's socioeconomic origins. At the theoretical level, this issue was addressed early on by Becker (1972), who noted that, if parents' education influences children's earnings, this is due to the fact that better off parents invest more in the education of their children. Thus the effect of family background is nothing other than an intergenerational effect of human capital.

At the empirical level, several studies have included measures of family background in the Mincerian earnings function, finding minimal effects on the returns to education. For example, Bedi (1997) finds in Honduras that the inclusion of parental education in the earnings function reduces the overall rate of return to investment in education from 12.1 to 11.3 per cent. Altonji and Dunn (1996), using sibling pairs from the United States Panel Study of Income Dynamics, find mixed evidence on whether parental education raises the return to education. Using a sample of Australian twins, Miller *et al.* (1995) find no evidence that the returns to education are over-estimated by the non-inclusion of family background factors.

Direct productivity   Perhaps the ultimate test for accepting that there are returns to education is to observe directly the productivity of workers with different levels of schooling. Beyond econometric shadow pricing, or observation shadow pricing, there is an immense line of work relating education to physical farm productivity. For example, in an early review of the literature, Jamison and Lau (1982) found that, on average, the difference between zero and four years of schooling among farmers results in a 10 per cent increment in production. Rosenzweig (1995) and Foster and Rosenzweig (1996) have shown that primary education has an impact on farmers adopting new high-yield varieties. In India, for example, high-yield variety use had an 18 per cent greater effect on the per area profitability for farmers with primary schooling, compared to farmers with no schooling (Rosenzweig, 1996).

School quality   A standard criticism of empirical estimates of the returns to education is that such returns refer to the quantity of schooling, saying nothing about school quality. Several studies have shown the importance of school quality in determining earnings (see, for example, Behrman and Birdsall, 1983; Salmon, 1985; Psacharopoulos and Velez, 1993; Bedi, 1997). This is not really a critique of the rate of return literature, rather it is pointing to an omission because of the difficulty of collecting information on school quality. Yet a counter-argument could be that rates of return to investment in education, as conventionally estimated, by definition refer to the average level of quality across all schools in the sample. So, if school quality is important in determining earnings, improving school quality must yield even higher returns to education.

Sample selectivity   Ideally a rate of return to investment in education should be based on a representative sample of the country's population. But in reality this is the exception rather than the rule. This is problematic when the estimated rates of return are based on a survey of firms (rather than households) because firm-based samples are highly selective. In order to control survey costs, such samples focus on large firms with many employees. Second, the questionnaire is typically filled in by the payroll department rather than by the individual employee, and this approach leads to the use of samples concentrated only in urban areas (as in Knight and Sabot, 1987).

Another problem occurs when rate of return estimates are based on samples that include civil servants. This is a problem because public sector wages typically do not reflect market wages. On average, the inclusion of civil service pay flattens the earnings differentials, giving lower returns among those working in the public sector (see Psacharopoulos, 1983). Of course, in many countries (although fewer now than in the past) the majority of university graduates end up in public sector employment. The concentration of graduates in public sector employment is identified as a problem in growth studies (see, for example, Pissarides, 2000). However civil service pay-based rate of return estimates are useful in private calculations regarding the incentives set by the state to invest in education – and opt for employment in the public sector.

Methodology   A less serious problem occurs when wage effects are confused with returns to education. Mincer (1974) has provided a great service and convenience in estimating returns to education by means of the semilog earnings function, first done in Becker and Chiswick (1966). However, for the sake of that convenience, many researchers use the raw coefficients of education in the extended (dummy-form) function to report returns to education, whereas these are wage effects.

Another methodological limitation, despite Becker's (1975) warning, is that many researchers feel obliged to throw in the regression whatever independent variables they seem to have in the data set, including occupation. In effect this procedure leads to stealing part of the effect of education on earnings that comes from occupational mobility.

3   The macro approach

The importance of education in the growth process re-emerged in the 1980s with the influential writings of Romer (1986, 1992) and Lucas (1988). Romer and Lucas start with a Solow-type (Solow, 1956, 1957) aggregate production function, augmented in two ways: first, beyond some measure of human capital that is actually used by different firms in the economy, total output also depends upon the average level of human capital. Second, human capital is endogenous, rather than exogenous, in the system; that is, human capital is produced by using resources. The dramatic theoretical implications of this formulation is that output is no longer constrained by the constant-returns-to-scale property of the Solow production function, and that 'knowledge' becomes a kind of public good that spills over the economy as an externality, allowing output to grow beyond the measurable inputs. The empirical implication of this formulation is that different countries need not converge to a common steady state path, as predicted by neo-classical economics. The level of per capita income between countries can diverge forever, rather than converge, as predicted by the earlier models. Another, equally important, implication of this model is that, by virtue of the average stock of human capital being a public good, there might be social underinvestment in human capital formation.

The returns to education using the macro approach are estimated by either (a) an aggregate production function explaining GDP of the type $Y = f(conventional\ inputs,\ an\ education\ measure)$, or (b) an aggregate 'macro-Mincerian' earnings function of the type $\ln Y = a + bS$, where the units of observation are individual countries, and Y and S are mean earnings and years of schooling within each country (Heckman and Klenow, 1998; Krueger and Lindahl, 2001).

Critique
Perhaps the weakest point in cross-country growth accounting is the measurement of the human capital input. Several efforts have been made to construct an international human capital input database, all of which have problems. The measurement of the education input leaves much to be desired, as rigorously documented by Behrman and Rosenzweig (1994). Such data have serious intertemporal and inter-country comparability problems, and there are data gaps often filled with constructed data based on interpolations and extrapolations.

There are two ways in which human capital is measured in growth accounting exercises: stock data, such as the educational level of the population or the labour force, and flow data, such as enrolments in year t by level of education. One way to create the stock is to start from school enrolments at different educational levels and years, thus building up the human capital stock by cumulating past enrolments, leading to graduates (Barro and Lee, 1993; Nehru *et al.*, 1995). The problem with this method is that past enrolments, because of the inefficiency of a school system, might not translate into the same human capital embodiment in different countries (for example, compare North America and Latin America, where grade repetition in the latter is excessive).

Another way is to start with labour force censuses, or special samples reporting the educational level of the workforce (Psacharopoulos and Arriagada, 1986, 1992). The problem with this method is that labour force censuses are very infrequent, typically taking place every decade. Also '1000 secondary graduates' in an Asian tiger must not be equivalent to the same number of graduates in an African country, because of quality differences in the educational systems of these countries.

There exist only two sources of original data on the basis of which the human capital stock can be estimated: stock data on the educational level of the population or the labour force as the latter is reported in country censuses of the population or special surveys; and, flow data on enrolments, as reported by UNESCO (2001) in its statistical yearbooks. These data are arrived at by UNESCO mailing a questionnaire to the ministries of education around the world. A major problem with these kinds of data is that, even if reported correctly or at all, they do not cover private schools.

If human capital has its measurement problems, the dependent variable used by most second-generation panel growth accountants is not as innocent as it appears. The state of the art is best summarized by quoting the author himself of the growth rates database. After enumerating the many quality problems of national accounts, especially in developing countries, Heston (1994, p. 51) notes: '[t]his leads me to conclude with plea to users of national accounts *especially in comparative work*, to explicitly question the reliability of data' (emphasis added).

Both stock and flow data are headcount measures, saying nothing about the quality of the education embodied in a given graduate. Being surprised that secondary school enrolment had a negative impact in their regressions, De Long and Summers (1992, pp. 116–17) observe that this strange result might be attributed to 'the large divergence between measured schooling and actual skills learned'.

Another reason that has been advanced to explain some of the strange results of growth accounting is that the more educated in developing countries are typically employed by the public sector. Hence their earnings potential cannot be fully released.

Cross-country regressions tacitly assume that all countries are on the same production frontier, yet this is hardly the case. The classic counterfactual is that of comparing Sri Lanka and other South Asian countries. Sri

Lanka has a highly educated labour force relative to its neighbours, yet its economic growth record has been dismal. The reason for such bad economic performance has not been the lack of education but rather the political environment that has dampened incentives and opportunities for human capital to release its productivity (Bruton, 1996; Lal and Myint, 1996).

Countries also differ in many other aspects than those measured by the physical and human capital stock; for example, there may be a different culture and discipline towards study and work. These omitted variables can lead to margins of error of hundreds of per cent in accounting for differences in the economic growth path between countries. Sometimes this issue is handled by 'eliminating the outliers' (Temple, 1999), but then it is hard to tell whether the outlier is so because of the quality of statistics or because of something else. After getting some very strange results from cross-country regressions, Temple and Voth (1998, p. 1359) note: 'Our own answer to this puzzle is that attempting to impose the framework of an aggregate production function is almost certainly the wrong approach for many developing countries.' One may add that trying to apply the *same* production function for *all* kinds of countries is the wrong approach, simply because countries differ in many respects other than those proxied in empirical applications of macro growth models.

Cross-country regressions treat the country as one unit of observation, yet, as any observant development economist knows, to treat Brazil or India as a single entity is absurd. For example, Rosenzweig (1996) reports that in Kerala, the most educated Indian state, the profit differential between schooled and unschooled farmers is 11.4 per cent, against 39.2 per cent in Punjab, a state with less schooling than Kerala. Such an apparent paradox is simply due to the fact that cultural and other non-measurable conditions are very different in Kerala relative to Punjab, an 'independent' variable that does not appear in cross-country regressions. But, of course, one would expect a higher wage gap in a state where educated labour is in such short supply and therefore paid a premium.

4 Typical findings

Given the several existing compilations, here we will be eclectic. Typical results from individual studies in several countries at different stages of development are presented. For the sake of completeness, supporting tables to the previous compilation that did not appear in print (Psacharopoulos, 1994) are presented in the annex.

The classic pattern of falling returns to education by level of economic development and level of education is maintained (see Table 1.2). Private returns are higher than 'social' returns where the latter is defined on the

Table 1.2   Returns to investment in education by level and per capita income (per cent)

Per capita income group	Social			Private		
	Primary	Secondary	Higher	Primary	Secondary	Higher
Low income ($755 or less)	21.3	15.7	11.2	25.8	19.9	26.0
Middle income (to $9265)	18.8	12.9	11.3	27.4	18.0	19.3
High income ($9266 or more)	13.4	10.3	9.5	25.6	12.2	12.4
World	18.9	13.1	10.8	26.6	17.0	19.0

Source: Psacharopoulos and Patrinos (2004).

basis of private benefits but total (private plus external) costs. This is because of the public subsidization of education and the fact that typical social rate of return estimates are not able to include social benefits. Nevertheless the degree of public subsidization increases with the level of education, which has regressive income distribution implications.

Overall, the average rate of return to another year of schooling exceeds the typical 10 per cent benchmark used in appraising projects. The highest returns are recorded for low and middle-income countries. Average returns to schooling are highest in Latin America and the Caribbean region and for the Sub-Saharan Africa region. Returns to schooling for Asia are at about the world average (see Table 1.3). The returns are lower in the high-income countries of the OECD. Interestingly, average returns to schooling are lowest for the non-OECD European, Middle East and North African group of countries.

Since 1990, average returns to schooling have declined by 0·6 percentage points (Psacharopoulos and Patrinos, 2004). At the same time, average schooling levels have increased. Therefore, and according to theory, everything else being the same, an increase in the supply of education has led to a slight decrease in the returns to schooling. There is sometimes great variability in returns to schooling over time. This can be as dramatic as in the case of Cyprus, where the overall private rate of return to another year of schooling declined from 11 per cent in 1984 to just over 5 per cent in 1994 (Psacharopoulos and Patrinos, 2004). However, in the Czech Republic, the overall rate of return to another year of schooling increased from 3 per cent in 1970, to 2·4 per cent for males and 4·2 per cent for females in 1984, to

*Table 1.3   Returns to investment in education by level and region
            (per cent)*

Region	Social			Private		
	Primary	Secondary	Higher	Primary	Secondary	Higher
Asia*	16.2	11.1	11.0	20.0	15.8	18.2
Europe/Middle East/North Africa*	15.6	9.7	9.9	13.8	13.6	18.8
Latin America/ Caribbean	17.4	12.9	12.3	26.6	17.0	19.5
OECD	8.5	9.4	8.5	13.4	11.3	11.6
Sub-Saharan Africa	25.4	18.4	11.3	37.6	24.6	27.8
World	18.9	13.1	10.8	26.6	17.0	19.0

Note: *non-OECD.

Source: Psacharopoulos and Patrinos (2004).

9 per cent overall in 1997 (Vecernik, 2001; Chase, 1998; Filer *et al.*, 1999). In the United States, the returns to schooling have increased significantly over time, despite a rapid increase in overall education levels, from 7·5 per cent in 1976 (Kling, 2001) to 10 per cent in 1995 (Psacharopoulos, 2000). Yet other countries, such as Norway, show no change over time in the returns to schooling (Barth and Roed, 1999). Table 1.4 shows some comparable returns over time in selected countries.

Overall, women receive higher returns to their schooling investments, but the returns to primary education are much higher for men (20 per cent) than for women (13 per cent). Women, however, experience higher returns to secondary education (18 versus 14 per cent) (Psacharopoulos and Patrinos, 2004). Table 1.5 shows some recent estimates of returns to schooling by level using the full discounting method. Note again that the social returns are always lower than the private returns, for the reasons enumerated above.

First, it should be noted that the private returns to primary education vary a lot within and between countries (for example, between 1.9 per cent in Turkey at the primary level in 1987 to 99.0 per cent in Botswana in 1983 (Psacharopoulos and Patrinos, 2004). This is sometimes due to the fact that some authors apply the arithmetic rate of return formula to that level of education, imputing six or nine years of forgone earnings to children in basic education. Of course this ignores the fact that, even in the presence

Table 1.4   Comparable returns over time to investment in education in selected countries (per cent)

Country	Austria	Bolivia	Finland	Netherlands
1980			9.1	
1981	11.6	12.2		
1982				7.0
1983	7.9			
1985	7.6			7.2
1986				5.2
1987	7.4		7.0	
1988		9.5		5.7
1989	7.6	7.1	8.2	7.3
1990		10.1		
1991	7.4	8.9	8.8	
1992		10.0		
1993	7.2	10.7	8.2	
1994				6.4

Note: No data available for 1984.

Sources: Austria: Fersterer and Winter-Ebmer (1999); Bolivia: World Bank (1996), Psacharopoulos and Mattson (1998); Patrinos (1995); Finland: Asplund (1999); Netherlands: Cohn and Addison (1998), Hartog *et al.* (1999).

of child labour, children aged six or seven do not have much in the way of forgone earnings. The averages for primary, secondary and higher are 26·6, 17·0 and 19·0 per cent, while the median is 19·5, 14·0 and 16·6 per cent. For rates of return in the 1990s alone, the private returns are 17·4, 12·0 and 16·8 per cent.

Another reason for the variability in scale is that most of these rates are based on earnings data that contain a large number of civil servants. It is well known that civil service pay scales are compressed, thus resulting in a lower rate of return relative to the one based on earnings differentials in the private sector (see Psacharopoulos and Williams, 1973). At the extreme, Tanzania's and Vietnam's low rates of return to primary education (of the order of 8–11 per cent) must be due to the egalitarian policies in these countries.

But when the appropriate forgone earnings have been assumed in the rate of return calculation, or focused in the private sector (as in Latin American countries), private rates of return to primary education are 24 per cent for the region and the private returns to higher education are 19 per cent. Private returns to investment in education by level estimated by the basic Mincerian earnings function are underestimates for several

Table 1.5   Returns to investment in education by level, full method (per cent)

Country	Year	Social			Private		
		Prim.	Sec.	Higher	Prim.	Sec.	Higher
Bolivia	1990	13	6	13	20	6	19
China	1993	14	13	11	18	13	15
El Salvador	1990	16	13	8	19	15	10
Ethiopia	1996	15	14	12	25	24	27
Greece	1993		7	6		8	8
Mexico	1992	12	15	11	19	20	16
Nepal	1999	16	8	9	17	9	12
New Zealand	1991		12	10		14	12
Paraguay	1990	20	13	11	24	15	14
Vietnam	1992	14	5	6	11	4	3

Source: See Psacharopoulos and Patrinos (2004).

reasons. First, by arithmetic necessity the Mincerian function assigns forgone earnings to students of all ages. This tacit assumption cannot be wholly true, even for low-income developing countries. Children do not work full time from age six. Second, given the fact that the Mincerian estimate is an aggregate average return and that there are diminishing returns on the investment, the higher the level of average education in a sample, the lower the aggregate return relative to the true return on primary education (if the latter could be measured separately). Third, there is the notion of the 'option value' of education. This is the fact that having completed one level of education allows one to proceed and benefit from the next level of education (Weisbrod, 1962). Such option value would enhance the returns to primary education, by whatever method the latter are being estimated.

Comparison with the returns to physical capital
The returns to investment in education, as estimated from cross-sectional data, are real, in the sense that they are net of inflation. So they have to be compared to some measure of the real returns to alternative forms of investment.

The IMF (1997) reports the nominal interest rate offered on a variety of bank deposits for a large number of countries, along with the inflation rate in each country. Subtraction of the latter from the former gave a set of real interest rates for 1993. In Table 1.6 these are compared to the latest year of the returns to education. In 12 out of the 15 pairs of returns in which this comparison was possible, the returns to investment in human capital exceed the alternative rate. The three exceptions refer to Latin American countries in a period of high inflation. Hence the comparison might not be as reliable, perhaps vindicating Mark Blaug's commandment, 'Thou shalt equalize rates of return in all directions' (Blaug *et al.*, 1969).

In an earlier work, McMahon (1991) reports that in the United States not only does the value of the stock of educational capital ($24 trillion) exceed that of physical capital ($18 trillion), but also the returns to investment in education exceed those of investment in housing: 12 per cent versus 4 per cent. In addition, Cohn and Hughes (1994) found that the social returns to investment in higher education in the United States between 1969 and 1985 have been consistently above the returns to investment in housing.

Bevc (1993) estimates that the rate of return to investment in education in former Yugoslavia in the 1980s has been of the order of 6.3 per cent, versus 3.7 per cent for physical capital. Her finding on the returns to education is a gross underestimate because earnings differentials have been arbitrarily discounted by an alpha coefficient equal to 0.66 to allow for unobserved ability.

On the basis of this information, and especially on the numbers cited for the United States and Canada, where the data on both kinds of returns are more reliable, one can reasonably conclude that the returns to investment

Table 1.6   Returns to investment in education and bank deposits (per cent)

Country	Investment in education	Real bank deposit rate
Bolivia	10.1	13.5
Canada	8.9	1.9
China	12.2	−4.6
Costa Rica	8.5	7.1
El Salvador	7.6	−3.2
Greece	7.6	−1.8
Guatemala	14.9	12.6
Honduras	9.3	0.9
Mexico	9.4	5.7
Nicaragua	12.1	−8.8
Paraguay	11.5	3.9
Spain	7.2	5.0
United States	10.0	0.2
Uruguay	9.7	−14.7
Venezuela	9.4	15.7

Source: Returns to investment in education, latest year, from Psacharopoulos and Patrinos (2003); returns to Bank deposits based on IMF (1997).

in education are likely to exceed those to alternative forms of investment. The gap between the two kinds of returns must be even greater in developing countries, given the relative scarcity of human capital.

Non-market benefits and externalities
Efforts to make estimates of externalities are numerous, but the estimates vary widely. The earnings of educated individuals do not reflect the external benefits that affect society as a whole but are not captured by the individual. Such benefits are known as 'externalities' or 'spillover' benefits, since they spill over to other members of the community. They are often hard to identify and even harder to measure. In the case of education, some have succeeded in identifying positive externalities but few have been able to quantify them (but see Weisbrod, 1964; Haveman and Wolfe, 1984, Chapter 6 by McMahon in this volume). If one could include externalities, then social rates of return might well be higher than private rates of return to education. A recent review finds that empirical evidence is scarce and inconclusive, providing some support for human capital externalities, but not very strong (Venniker, 2001). These studies estimate externalities in the form of individuals' human capital enhancing the productivity of other factors of production through channels that are not internalized by the individual (similar to Lucas's (1988) theory). As Venniker (2001) states, evidence is not unambiguous. In fact, some estimates give negative values, while others give very high estimates.

The benefits of education captured in the rate of return estimates reported above (private or narrow social) are market benefits. That is, they are based on the price more and less educated people command in the labour market. However there is another set of non-market benefits, stemming from a host of beneficial effects of education that are not traded in the market. Such non-market effects are often compounded with public or external effects, that is affecting not only the recipient of education but others as well. Table 1.7 provides a taxonomy in this respect.

One major and well-documented effect of education in the literature, is in reducing fertility. The mechanism by which this is achieved is that parental

Table 1.7   Classification of education benefits

Nature of benefits	Measured by	Availability of evidence
Market	Earnings differentials	Plenty
Non-market	Willingness to pay	Scant
External	Micro partial cross-effects Macro growth accounting	Rough

education enhances the adoption of contraceptive techniques, and most importantly that female education raises the opportunity cost of children (Becker and Lewis, 1973; Ben-Porath, 1973; Cochrane, 1979; Rosenzweig and Schultz, 1989; Barro, 1991). Education also reduces infant mortality. For example, a ten-percentage point increase in female primary education can be expected to decrease infant mortality by 4·1 deaths per thousand. Thus, in Pakistan, an extra year of schooling for an additional 1000 girls would prevent 60 infant deaths (UNICEF, 1999, p. 7). These are some of the most tangible effects of education, not captured in rate of return calculations.

Macro-level externalities   Azariadis and Drazen (1990) were the first to suggest in the modern/mathematical growth literature what educators (Anderson and Bowman, 1963) and economic historians (Easterlin, 1981) had been saying for a long time: that there might be a threshold in terms of human capital accumulation before a country can reap growth benefits. In their words, 'once ... the stock of knowledge surpass[es] certain critical values, aggregate production possibilities may expand especially rapidly' (Azariadis and Drazen, 1990, pp. 505–6). In a back of the envelope empirical testing of this theory, they found that the threshold might be early literacy.

As depicted in Figure 1.4, a country is trapped into a low-returns equilibrium (AA′) until the level of human capital accumulation rises, say, when the mean years of schooling of the population exceeds six years. Once the threshold is passed, the country rides on a higher returns-growth path (BB′).

Lau *et al.* (1996) using data from Brazil, found a threshold effect of education on output, namely an interval over which the effects are convex,

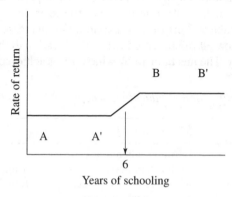

Figure 1.4   A critical level of human capital accumulation

between three and four years of average education. In other words, a country must have a critical mass of basic education before the returns to education manifest themselves, or there are increasing returns to the average level of education. This finding is consistent with Romer's (1986) hypothesis that there exist increasing returns to intangible capital.

Glaeser (1994) used the Mincerian earnings function in a country cross-section to decompose the effect of education on growth into (a) an effect of the changed returns to education over time, (b) an indirect effect of schooling's positive effect on schooling growth, and (c) a direct effect of education raising income, holding education growth constant. He found that the indirect, schooling-to-schooling effect had the greatest impact in the decomposition. This finding is in the spirit of Becker and Murphy (1992), suggesting that earlier human capital creates later human capital, and the new growth literature on increasing returns to scale. Several other studies have found that parental education is a strong determinant of children's school participation and eventual educational attainment (see, for example, Birdsall, 1985, on Brazil).

But this is practically all there is in terms of empirical evidence. As noted by Schultz (1994, p. 45): 'there is little concrete guidance in this literature on where precisely to look for this externality'. Mankiw (1995, pp. 301, 307) notes that 'for practical ... economists ... the payoff from endogenous growth theory is not clear ... [V]ariables such as knowledge are hard to bring to data ... There are two problems working in concert: the subtlety of the theories and the limitations of the data.'

5   Policy implications

Is there social underinvestment in human capital? The answer to this question is an unequivocal 'yes'. This position is not so much based on the results of cross-country growth accounting regressions, but on the most solid empirical evidence the economics of education has to offer as a benchmark: the private rate of return to investment in education in a competitive country setting. The private rate of return to an extra year of schooling in the United States is of the order of 10 per cent per year (in real terms). It is not a coincidence that returns three times as high have been reported for developing countries where human capital is scarcer. Subtracting the resource cost of schooling, one would be left with a narrow social rate of return that is a few percentage points lower relative to the private rate. Adding, even in a qualitative way, the many types of positive externalities reported above, one must end up with a very handsome wide social rate of return to investment in primary education in developing countries. To put it another way, one does not need to rely on the hard-to-digest macro evidence, putting it inside or outside the production function, dropping outliers or hair-splitting econometrics. One does not even have to rely on hard-to-measure externalities, the latter being just a bonus.

Estimates of the returns to schooling are a useful indicator of the productivity of education and incentive for individuals to invest in their own human capital. Public policy needs to heed this evidence in the design of policies and crafting of incentives that both promote investment and ensure that low-income families make those investments.

The results presented here lead to different policy frontiers by level of development. For many developed countries the priority clearly lies with advancing the level of education of the labour force as countries compete in the global knowledge economy. This leads to a discussion of the appropriate form of post-compulsory education (short versus long cycle) and the ensuing financing decisions. The importance of returns to education is seen in their adoption as a key indicator by the OECD (2001a) in their annual *Education at a Glance* series and other policy documents (OECD, 1997, 2001b). Increasingly governments and other agencies are funding studies of returns to education along with other research, to guide macro policy decisions about the organization and financing of education reforms.

For many developing countries, especially low-income countries that have yet to achieve universal primary education, the priority is clear, while at the same time innovative means of financing lifelong learning for those already in the labour force top the policy agenda. Literacy skills remain an important stepping stone to further learning opportunities. Innovative use of rate of return studies serves both to set overall policy guidelines and to evaluate specific programmes. Examples include the Indonesia school building programme (Duflo, 2001), which extended schooling opportunities significantly, and Ethiopia's major education sector investment programme (World Bank, 1998), which seeks to expand basic education opportunities and overhaul the education system.

6   Research frontier

The main research priorities in the economics of education include the following:

- *Returns to investment in education quality*. Most of the evidence presented above refers to a quantitative measure of education, mostly years of schooling. However one year of schooling in Northeast Brazil must represent a different level of human capital acquisition relative to a year of schooling in a Montessori school in Northern Italy. Thus one needs to link earnings to a measure of school quality, such as achievement (see, for example, Betts, 1999).

- *Returns to investment in training.* Although the economics of education started really as an inquiry into the costs and benefits of training, this has been set aside and researchers have concentrated on where the light is: that is, formal education, as the latter is easier to measure. But in order to study the returns to training, the challenge is to be able experimentally to assign trainee and non-trainee groups at random (see, for example, Heckman *et al.*, 1997). A useful application of random assignment, although used to evaluate a voucher programme, can be found in Angrist *et al.* (2002).
- *Externalities.* This is the latest research bay in the economics of education, but, for the reasons mentioned in the macro section above, the existing evidence is not persuasive. More is needed (see McMahon, 1999, and Chapter 6 in this volume).
- *Governance and accountability.* As economists turn their attention to outcomes, the question of appropriate forms of governance and systems of accountability takes centre stage. This is reflected in policy debates about standards and school choice (see, for example, Hoxby, 1996).

One major research gap is the marriage between the micro and the macro evidence on the returns to education. Whereas, in the micro case, as amply demonstrated above, it is established beyond any reasonable doubt that there are tangible and measurable returns to investment in education, such evidence is not as consistent and forthcoming in the macro literature (see, for example, Pritchett, 2001; and Psacharopoulos, 2000, and Krueger and Lindahl, 2001, for a different perspective).

Also more research on the social benefits of schooling is needed. For developing countries, there is a need for more evidence on the impact of education on earnings using quasi-experimental design. There are more opportunities today for this type of research. Moreover, this research needs to be used to create programmes that promote more investment and reform financing mechanisms.

References

Altonji, J.G. and T.A. Dunn (1996), 'The effects of family characteristics on the return to education', *Review of Economics and Statistics*, **78** (4), 692–704.

Anderson, C.A. and M.J. Bowman (1963), 'Concerning the role of education in development', in Clifford Geertz (ed.), *Old Societies and New States: The Quest for Modernity in Asia and Africa*, London: Collier Macmillan, pp. 247–79.

Angrist, J.D. and A.B. Krueger (1991), 'Does compulsory schooling attendance affect schooling and earnings?', *Quarterly Journal of Economics*, **106** (4), 979–1014.

Angrist, J., E. Bettinger, E. Bloom, E. King and M. Kremer (2002), 'Vouchers for private schooling in Colombia: evidence from a randomized natural experiment', *American Economic Review*, **92** (5), 1535–58.

Arends, M. (1992a), 'Female labor force participation and wages: a case study of Panama', in George Psacharopoulos and Zafiris Tzannatos (eds), *Women's Employment and Pay in Latin America: Country Case Studies*, Washington, DC: World Bank, pp. 349–72.

Arends, M. (1992b), 'Female labor force participation and earnings in Guatemala', in George Psacharopoulos and Zafiris Tzannatos (eds), *Women's Employment and Pay in Latin America: Country Case Studies*, Washington, DC: World Bank, pp. 273–98.

Arends, M. (1992c), 'Women's labor force participation and earnings: The Case of Uruguay', in George Psacharopoulos and Zafiris Tzannatos (eds), *Women's Employment and Pay in Latin America: Country Case Studies*, Washington, DC: World Bank, pp. 431–50.

Arrow, K.J. (1973), 'Higher education as a filter', *Journal of Public Economics*, **2** (3), 193–216.

Ashenfelter, O. and A.B. Krueger (1994), 'Estimates of the economic return to schooling from a new sample of twins', *American Economic Review*, **84** (5), 1157–73.

Ashenfelter, O. and C.E. Rouse (1998), 'Income, schooling, and ability: evidence from a new sample of twins', *Quarterly Journal of Economics*, **113** (1), 253–84.

Asplund, Rita (1999), 'Earnings and human capital: evidence for Finland', in Rita Asplund and P.T. Pereira (eds), *Returns to Human Capital in Europe*, Helsinki: ETLA (The Research Institute of the Finnish Economy), pp. 43–84.

Azariadis, C. and A. Drazen (1990), 'Threshold externalities in economic development', *Quarterly Journal of Economics*, **105** (2), 501–26.

Barro, R.J. (1991), 'Economic growth in a cross-section of countries', *Quarterly Journal of Economics*, **106** (2), 407–44.

Barro, R.J. and J.-W. Lee (1993), 'Losers and winners in economic growth', The World Bank, Annual Bank Conference on Development Economics, Washington, DC, 3–4 May.

Barth, E. and M. Roed (1999), 'The return to human capital in Norway', in Rita Asplund and P.T. Pereira (eds), *Returns to Human Capital in Europe*, Helsinki: ETLA (The Research Institute of the Finnish Economy), pp. 227–57.

Becker, Gary S. (1975), *Human Capital*, Chicago: University of Chicago Press.

Becker, G.S. (1972) 'Schooling and inequality from generation to generation: comment', *Journal of Political Economy*, **80** (3), S252–S55.

Becker, G.S. and B.R. Chiswick (1966), 'Education and the distribution of earnings', *American Economic Review*, **56** (2), 358–69.

Becker, G.S. and G.H. Lewis (1973), 'On the interaction between the quantity and quality of children', *Journal of Political Economy*, **81** (2, pt II), S279–88.

Becker, G.S. and K.M. Murphy (1992), 'The division of labor, coordination costs, and knowledge', *Quarterly Journal of Economics*, **107** (4), 1137–60.

Bedi, A. (1997), 'The importance of school quality as determinant of earnings in a developing country: evidence from Honduras', *International Journal of Educational Development*, 17 (4), 427–37.

Behrman, J.R. and N. Birdsall (1983), 'The quality of schooling: quantity alone is misleading', *American Economic Review*, **73** (5), 928–46.

Behrman, J.R. and M.R. Rosenzweig (1994), 'Caveat emptor: cross-country data on education and the labor force', *Journal of Development Economics*, **44** (1), 147–72.

Behrman, J.R. and M.R. Rosenzweig (1999), '"Ability" bias in schooling returns and twins: a test and new estimates', *Economics of Education Review*, **18** (2), 159–67.

Behrman, J.R., B.L. Wolfe and D.M. Blau (1985), 'Human capital and earnings distribution in a developing country: the case of prerevolutionary Nicaragua', *Economic Development and Cultural Change*, **34** (4), 1–29.

Bellew, R. and P. Moock (1990), 'Vocational and technical education in Peru', *Economics of Education Review*, **9** (4), 365–75.

Ben-Porath, Y. (1973), 'Economic analysis of fertility in Israel: point and counterpoint', *Journal of Political Economy*, **81**, 202–33.

Betts, J.R. (1999), 'Returns to quality of education', Economics of Education Series, Economics of Education Thematic Group, World Bank (www.worldbank.org/education/economicsed/research/econseries/betts_index.htm).

Bevc, M. (1989), 'Education as a factor of labour force quality and analysis of economic efficiency of investment in Yugoslavia by republics and autonomous provinces' (mimeo), Ljubljana.

Bevc, M. (1991), *Ekonomski pomen izobrazevanja* (The economic value of education), Radovljica, Slovenia: Didakta.

Bevc, M. (1993), 'Rates of return to investment in education in former Yugoslavia in the 1970s and 1980s, by region', *Economics of Education Review*, **12** (4), 325–43.

Birdsall, Nancy (1985), 'Public inputs and child schooling in Brazil', *Journal of Development Economics*, **18** (1), 67–86.

Blaug, Mark (1970), *Economics of Education*, London: Penguin.

Blaug, Mark (1978), *Economics of Education: A Selected Annotated Bibliography*, 3rd edn, Oxford: Pergamon Press.

Blaug, M., R. Layard and M. Woodhall (1969), *Graduate Unemployment in India*, London: Allen Lane, the Penguin Press.

Bonattour, Z.S. (1986), 'Economics of education: tackling the new policy issues', IREDU International Conference, Dijon, 23–25 June.

Bruton, H.J. (1996), *The Political Economy of Poverty, Equity and Growth: Sri Lanka and Malaysia*, Oxford: Oxford University Press.

Byron, R.P. and E.Q. Manaloto (1990), 'Returns to education in China', *Economic Development and Cultural Change*, **78** (4), 784–96.

Card, D. (1998), 'The causal effect of education on earnings', in Orley Ashenfelter and David Card (eds), *Handbook of Labor Economics*, vol. III, Amsterdam: North-Holland.

Card, D. (2001), 'Estimating the return to schooling: progress on some persistent econometric problems', *Econometrica*, **69** (5), 1127–60.

Chapman, B.J. and J.R. Harding (1985), 'Sex differences in earnings: an analysis of Malaysian wage data', *Journal of Development Studies*, 21 (3), 362–76.

Chase, R.S. (1998), 'Markets for communist human capital: returns to education in the Czech Republic and Slovakia', *Industrial and Labor Relations Review*, **51** (3), 401–23.

Cochrane, S. (1979), 'Fertility and education: what do we really know?', World Bank staff occasional paper no. 26.

Cohn, E. and J.T. Addison (1998), 'The economic returns to lifelong learning', *Education Economics*, **6** (3), 253–308.

Cohn, E. and T.G. Geske (1990), *Economics of Education*, 3rd edn, Oxford: Pergamon Press.

Cohn, E. and W.W. Hughes, Jr (1994), 'A benefit–cost analysis of investment in college education in the United States: 1969–1985', *Economics of Education Review*, **13** (2), 109–23.

Cohn E., B.F. Kiker and M.M. de Olivera (1987), 'Further evidence on the screening hypothesis', *Economics Letters*, **25** (3), 289–94.

Cox, Donald and George Psacharopoulos (1992), 'Female participation and earnings, Venezuela, 1987', in George Psacharopoulos and Zafiris Tzannatos (eds), *Women's Employment and Pay in Latin America: Country Case Studies*, Washington, DC: World Bank, pp. 451–62.

Dabos, M. and G. Psacharopoulos (1991), 'An analysis of the sources of earnings variation among Brazilian males', *Economics of Education Review*, **10** (4), 359–77.

Davis, D. (1977), 'Manpower planning, rate of return analysis, and the university medical schools: the case of Australia', *Higher Education*, **6**, 301–11.

DeLong, B. and L. Summers (1992), 'Equipment investment and economic growth', *Quarterly Journal of Economics*, **106** (2), 407–38.

Demetriades, E.L. and G. Psacharopoulos (1987), 'Educational expansion and the returns to education: evidence from Cyprus', *International Labour Review*, **126** (5), 597–602.

Dougherty, C.R.S. and E. Jimenez (1991), 'The specification of earnings functions: tests and implications', *Economics of Education Review*, **10** (2), 85–98.

Duflo, E. (2001), 'Schooling and labor market consequences of school construction in Indonesia: evidence from an unusual policy experiment', *American Economic Review*, **91** (4), 795–813.

Easterlin, R. (1981), 'Why isn't the whole world developed?', *Journal of Economic History*, **41** (1), 1–19.

Fersterer, J. and R. Winter-Ebmer (1999), 'Human capital and earnings in Austria', in Rita Asplund and P.T. Pereira (eds), *Returns to Human Capital in Europe*, Helsinki: ETLA (The Research Institute of the Finnish Economy), pp. 13–29.

Filer, R.K., S. Jurajda and J. Planovsky (1999), 'Education and wages in the Czech and Slovak Republics during transition', *Labour Economics*, **6** (4), 581–93.

Foster, A.D. and M.R. Rosenzweig (1996), 'Technical change and human capital returns and investments: evidence from the green revolution', *American Economic Review*, **86** (4), 931–53.

Friedman, Milton and Simon Kuznets (1946), *Income from Independent Professional Practice*, Cambridge, MA: NBER.

Gill, Indermit A. (1992a), 'Is there sex discrimination in Chile? Evidence from the CASEN survey', in George Psacharopoulos and Zafiris Tzannatos (eds), *Women's Employment and Pay in Latin America: Country Case Studies*, Washington, DC: World Bank, pp. 119–48.

Gill, Indermit A. (1992b), 'Is there sex discrimination in Peru? Evidence from the 1990 Lima living standards survey', in George Psacharopoulos and Zafiris Tzannatos (eds), *Women's Employment and Pay in Latin America: Country Case Studies*, Washington, DC: World Bank, pp. 97–430.

Gindling, T.H. (1991), 'Labor market segmentation and the determination of wages in the public, private-formal, and informal sectors in San Jose, Costa Rica', *Economic Development and Cultural Change*, **39** (3), 585–605.

Glaeser, E.L. (1994), 'Why does schooling generate economic growth?', *Economics Letters*, **44** (3), 333–7.

Glennerster H. and W. Low (1990), 'Education and the welfare state: does it add up?', *The State of Welfare*, Oxford: Clarendon Press.

Glewwe, P. (1991), 'Schooling, skills, and the returns to government investment in education', working paper no. 76, LSMS, The World Bank, Washington, DC.

Gomez-Castellano, L. and G. Psacharopoulos (1990), 'Earnings and education in Ecuador: evidence from the 1987 household survey', *Economics of Education Review*, **9** (3), 219–27.

Griliches, Z. (1970), 'Notes on the Role of Education in Production Functions and Growth Accounting', in W.L. Hansen (ed.), *Education, Income and Human Capital: Studies in Income and Wealth*, Vol. 35, New York: National Bureau of Economic Research.

Grootaert, C. (1990), 'Returns to formal and informal vocational education in Côte d'Ivoire: the role of the structure of the labor market', *Economics of Education Review*, **9** (4), 309–19.

Harmon, C. and I. Walker (1995), 'Estimates of the economic return to schooling for the United Kingdom', *American Economic Review*, **85** (5), 1278–86.

Hartog, J., J. Odink and J. Smits (1999), 'Private returns to education in the Netherlands', in Rita Asplund and P.T. Pereira (eds), *Returns to Human Capital in Europe*, Helsinki: ETLA (The Research Institute of the Finnish Economy), pp. 209–26.

Haveman, R.H. and B. Wolfe (1984), 'Schooling and economic well-being: the role of non-market effects', *Journal of Human Resources*, **19** (3), 128–40.

Heckman, J. and P. Klenow (1998), 'Human capital policy', in M. Boskin (ed.), *Capital Formation*, Stanford: Hoover Institution.

Heckman, J., H. Ichimura and P. Todd (1997), 'Matching as an econometric evaluation estimator: evidence from evaluating a job training programme', *Review of Economic Studies*, **64** (4), 605–54.

Heckman, J.J. and V.J. Hotz (1986), 'An investigation of the labor market earnings of Panamanian males: evaluating the sources of inequality', *Journal of Human Resources*, **21** (4), 507–42.

Heston, A. (1994), 'A brief review of some problems in using national accounts data in level of output comparisons and growth studies', *Journal of Development Economics*, **44** (1), 29–52.

Hill, M.A. (1983), 'Female labor force participation in developing and developed countries – consideration of the informal sector', *Review of Economics and Statistics*, **65**, 459–68.

Hinchliffe, K. (1990), 'The returns to vocational training in Botswana – research note', *Economics of Education Review*, **9** (4), 401–4.

Hossain, S. and G. Psacharopoulos (1994), 'The profitability of school investments in an educationally advanced developing country', *International Journal of Educational Development*, **14** (1), 35–42.

Hoxby, Carolyn M. (1996), 'The effects of private school vouchers on schools and students', in Helen E. Ladd (ed.), *Holding Schools Accountable*, Washington, DC: The Brookings Institution.

Indart, E.S. (1981), 'La rentabilidad de la educación en el Uruguay', mimeo, Universidad de la Republica, Uruguay.

International Monetary Fund (IMF) (1997), *International Financial Statistics*, Washington, DC: IMF.

Jakubson, George and George Psacharopoulos (1992), 'The effect of education on female labor force participation and earnings in Ecuador', in George Psacharopoulos and Zafiris Tzannatos (eds), *Women's Employment and Pay in Latin America: Country Case Studies*, Washington, DC: World Bank, pp. 255–72.

Jamison, Dean T. and Laurence Lau (1982), *Farmer Education and Farm Efficiency*, Baltimore: Johns Hopkins University Press.

Jamison, D.T. and J. van der Gaag (1987), 'Education and earnings in the People's Republic of China', *Economics of Education Review*, **6** (2), 161–6.

Jarousse, J.P. (1985), 'Une mesure de la rentabilité des diplômes entre 1969 et 1976', *Consommation*, **2**, 29–41.

Jarousse, J.P. and A. Mingat (1986), 'Le rôle des secteurs privé et public de l'emploi dans la structuration des salaires en France', Presentation at 1er Colloque International de la Revue, Lyon, 15–16 December.

Jarousse, J.P. and A. Mingat (1988), 'L'enseignement technique et professionnel: une évaluation par le marché', mimeo, IREDU, University of Dijon.

Johnes, Geraint (1993), *The Economics of Education*, London: Macmillan.

Khan, S.R. and M. Irfan (1985), 'Rates of return to education and the determinants of earnings in Pakistan', *Pakistan Development Review*, **24** (3 & 4), 671–83.

Khandker, Shahidur R. (1992), 'Women's labor market participation and male–female wage differences in Peru', in George Psacharopoulos and Zafiris Tzannatos (eds), *Women's Employment and Pay in Latin America: Country Case Studies*, Washington, DC: World Bank, pp. 373–96.

Kiker, B.F. and M.C. Santos (1991), 'Human capital and earnings in Portugal', *Economics of Education Review*, **10** (3), 187–203.

Kling, J. (2001), 'Interpreting instrumental variable estimates of the returns of schooling', *Journal of Business and Economic Statistics*, **19** (3), 358–64.

Knight, J.B. and R.H. Sabot (1987), 'The rate of return on educational expansion', *Economics of Education Review*, **6** (3), 255–62.

Komenan A.G. (1987), 'Education, expérience et salaires en Côte d'Ivoire: une analyse à partir de l'enquête de main d'œuvre de 1984', discussion paper no. 99, Education and Training Department, The World Bank, Washington, DC.

Krueger, A.B. and M. Lindahl (2001), 'Education for growth: why and for whom?', *Journal of Economic Literature*, **34** (4), 1101–36.

Kugler B. and G. Psacharopoulos (1989), 'Earnings and education in Argentina: an analysis of the 1985 Buenos Aires household survey', *Economics of Education Review*, **8** (4), 353–65.

Lal, Deepak and H.L. Myint (1996), *The Political Economy of Poverty, Equity and Growth: A Comparative Study*, Oxford: Clarendon Press.

Lambropoulos, H. and G. Psacharopoulos (1992), 'Educational expansion and earnings differentials in Greece', *Comparative Education Review*, **36** (1), 52–70.

Lau, Lawrence J., Dean T. Jamison, Shucheng Liu and Steven Rivlin (1996), 'Education and economic growth: some cross-sectional evidence', in Nancy Birdsall and Richard H. Sabot (eds), *Education in Brazil*, Washington, DC: Inter-American Development Bank/Baltimore: Johns Hopkins University Press, pp. 83–116.

Lorenz, W. and J. Wagner (1990), 'A note on returns to human capital in the eighties: evidence from twelve countries', working paper no. 54, The Luxembourg Income Study, University of Hanover.

Lucas, R.E. (1988), 'On the mechanics of economic development', *Journal of Monetary Economics*, **22** (1), 3–22.

Lucas, R.E.B. and O. Stark (1985), 'Motivations to remit: evidence from Botswana', *Journal of Political Economy*, **93** (5), 901–18.

Magnac, Thierry (1992), 'Female labor market participation and wages in Colombia', in George Psacharopoulos and Zafiris Tzannatos (eds), *Women's Employment and Pay in Latin America: Country Case Studies*, Washington, DC: World Bank, pp. 169–208.

Mankiw, N.G. (1995), 'The growth of nations', *Brookings Papers on Economic Activity* **1**, 275–326.

Marshall, Alfred ([1890] 1961), *The Principles of Economics*, London: Macmillan.

McGavin, P.A. (1991), 'Policy evaluation of investment in education: a Papua New Guinea study', *Economics of Education Review*, **10** (3), 213–26.

McMahon, W.W. (1991), 'Relative returns to human and physical capital in the U.S. and efficient investment strategies', *Economics of Education Review*, **10** (4), 283–96.

McMahon, W.W. (1999), *Education and Development: Measuring the Social Benefits*, Oxford/New York: Oxford University Press.

McMahon, W.W. and Boediono (1992), 'Universal basic education: an overall strategy of investment priorities for economic growth', *Economics of Education Review*, **11** (2), 137–51.

McMahon, W.W., J.H. Jung and Boediono (1992), 'Vocational and technical education in development: theoretical analysis of strategic effects on rates of return', *Economics of Education Review*, **11** (3), 181–94.

McNabb, R. and S. Richardson (1986), 'The relationship between earnings, education and experience: evidence for Australia', discussion paper no. 8605, Department of Economics, University College, Cardiff.

McNabb, R. and S. Richardson (1989), 'Earnings, education and experience: is Australia different?', *Australian Economic Papers*, **28**, 57–75.

Miller, P., C. Mulvey and N. Martin (1995), 'What do twins studies reveal about the economic returns to education? A comparison of Australian and U.S. findings', *American Economic Review*, **85** (3), 586–99.

Mincer, J. (1958), 'Investment in human capital and personal income distribution', *Journal of Political Economy*, **66**, 281–302

Mincer, Jacob (1974), *Schooling, Experience, and Earnings*, New York: National Bureau of Economic Research.

Mingat, A. and J.C. Eicher (1982), 'Higher education and employment markets in France', *Higher Education*, **11**, 211–20.

Mitch, D. (1984), 'Underinvestment in literacy? The potential contribution of government involvement in elementary education to economic growth in nineteenth-century England', *Journal of Economic History*, **44** (2), 557–66.

Moock, P. and R. Bellew (1988), 'Vocational and technical education in Peru', working paper no. 87, Policy, Planning and Research, The World Bank.

Nehru, V., E. Swanson and A. Dubey (1995), 'A new database on human capital stock in developing and industrial countries: sources, methodology and results', *Journal of Development Economics*, **46**, 379–401.

Ng, Chu Y. (1992), 'Female labor force participation and gender earnings differentials in Argentina', in George Psacharopoulos and Zafiris Tzannatos (eds), *Women's Employment and Pay in Latin America: Country Case Studies*, Washington, DC: World Bank, pp. 1–20.

Organisation for Economic Cooperation and Development (OECD) (1997), *Human Capital Investment: An International Comparison*, Paris: OECD.

Organisation for Economic Cooperation and Development (OECD) (2001a), *Education at a Glance: OECD Indicators 2001*, Paris: OECD.

Organisation for Economic Cooperation and Development (OECD) (2001b), *Education Policy Analysis 2001*, Paris: OECD.

Patrinos, H.A. (1995), 'Education and earnings differentials', mimeo, World Bank.

Paul, J.-J. (1990), 'Technical secondary education in Togo and Cameroon – research note', *Economics of Education Review*, **9** (4), 405–9.

Pissarides, C.A. (2000), 'Human capital and growth: a synthesis report', OECD Development Centre, technical papers no. 168.

Pritchett, L. (2001), 'Where has all the education gone?', *World Bank Economic Review*, **15** (3), 367–91.

Psacharopoulos, G. (1983), 'Education and private versus public sector pay', *Labour and Society*, **8** (2), 123–33.

Psacharopoulos, G. (1985), 'Returns to education: a further international update and implications', *Journal of Human Resources*, **20** (4), 583–97.

Psacharopoulos, George (ed.) (1987), *Economics of Education: Research and Studies*, Oxford: Pergamon Press.

Psacharopoulos, G. (1991), 'Educational investment priorities in Mexico', Latin American Technical Human Resources Division, The World Bank, Washington, DC.

Psacharopoulos, G. (1994), 'Returns to investment in education: a global update', *World Development*, **22** (9), 1325–43.

Psacharopoulos, G. (2000), 'The economic costs of child labour', *By the Sweat and Toil of Children*, Washington, DC: United States Department of Labor.

Psacharopoulos, G. and A. Alam (1991), 'Earnings and education in Venezuela: an update from the 1987 household survey', *Economics of Education Review*, **10** (1), 29–36.

Psacharopoulos, G. and A.M. Arriagada (1986), 'The educational composition of the labor force: an international comparison', *International Labour Review*, **125** (5), 561–74.

Psacharopoulos, G. and Arriagada, A.M. (1992), 'The educational composition of the labor force: an international update', *Journal of Educational Planning and Administration*, **6** (2), 141–59.

Psacharopoulos, G. and R. Layard (1979), 'Human capital and earnings: British evidence and critique', *Review of Economic Studies*, **46**, 485–503.

Psacharopoulos, G. and R. Mattson (1998), 'Estimating the returns to education: a sensitivity analysis of methods and sample size', *Journal of Educational Development and Administration*, **12** (3), 271–87.

Psacharopoulos, G. and H.A. Patrinos (2004), 'Returns to investment in education: a further update', *Education Economics*, **12** (2), (in press).

Psacharopoulos, G. and F. Steier (1988), 'Education and the labor market in Venezuela, 1975–1984', *Economics of Education Review*, **7** (3), 321–32.

Psacharopoulos, G. and E. Velez (1992), 'Schooling, ability and earnings in Colombia, 1988', *Economic Development and Cultural Change*, **40** (3), 629–43.

Psacharopoulos, G. and E. Velez (1993), 'Educational quality and labor market outcomes: evidence from Bogota, Colombia', *Sociology of Education*, **66**, 130–45.

Psacharopoulos, G and G. Williams (1973), 'Public sector earnings and educational planning', *International Labour Review*, **108** (1), July, 43–57.

Psacharopoulos, G. and Ying Chu Ng, (1994), 'Earnings and Education in Latin America', *Education Economics*, **2** (2) 187–207.

Psacharopoulos, G., A.M. Arriagada and E. Velez (1992), 'Earnings and education among self-employed males in Colombia', *Bulletin of Latin American Research*, **11** (1), 69–89.

Riveros, L.-A. (1990), 'The economic return to schooling in Chile: an analysis of its long-term fluctuations', *Economics of Education Review*, **9** (2), 111–21.

Romer, P. (1986), 'Increasing returns and long-run growth', *Journal of Political Economy*, **94**, 1002–37.

Romer, P. (1992), 'Two strategies for economic development: using ideas and producing ideas', *Proceedings of the World Bank Annual Conference on Development Economics*, Washington, DC: World Bank.

Rosenzweig, M.R. (1995), 'Why are there returns to schooling?', *American Economic Review*, **85** (2), 153–8.

Rosenzweig, M.R. (1996), 'When investing in education matters and when it does not', *Challenge*, March–April, 22–9.

Rosenzweig, M.R. and T.P. Schultz (1989), 'Schooling, information and non-market productivity: contraceptive use and its effectiveness', *International Economic Review*, **30** (2), 457–77.

Rouse, C.E. (1999), 'Further estimates of the economic return to schooling from a new sample of twins', *Economics of Education Review*, **18** (2), 149–57.
Ryoo, J-K. (1988), 'Changes in rates of return to education over time: the case study of Korea', PhD dissertation, Stanford University.
Sahn D.E. and H. Alderman (1988), 'The effects of human capital on wages, and the determinants of labor supply in a developing country', *Journal of Development Economics*, **29**, 157–83.
Salmon, L. (1985), 'Quality of education and economic growth', *Economics of Education Review*, **4**, 273–90.
Schultz, T.P. (1988), 'Education investment and returns', in Hollis Chenery and T.N. Srinivasan (eds), *Handbook in Development Economics*, vol. 1, Amsterdam: North-Holland, pp. 543–630.
Schultz, T.P. (1994), 'Human capital investment in women and men', occasional papers number 44, International Center for Economic Growth.
Schultz, T.W. (1960), 'Capital formation by education', *Journal of Political Economy*, **68**, 571–83.
Schultz, T.W. (1961), 'Investment in human capital', *American Economic Review*, **51**, 1–17.
Schultz, T.W. (1971), *Investment in Human Capital: The Role of Education and of Research*, New York: Free Press.
Scott, Katherine MacKinnon (1992a), 'Women in the labor force in Bolivia: participation and earnings', in George Psacharopoulos and Zafiris Tzannatos (eds), *Women's Employment and Pay in Latin America: Country Case Studies*, Washington, DC: World Bank, pp. 21–38.
Scott, Katherine MacKinnon (1992b), 'Female labor force participation and earnings: the case of Jamaica', in George Psacharopoulos and Zafiris Tzannatos (eds), *Women's Employment and Pay in Latin America: Country Case Studies*, Washington, DC: World Bank, pp. 323–38.
Shabbir, T. (1991), 'Sheepskin effects in the returns to education in a developing country', *Pakistan Development Review*, **30** (1), 1–19.
Shortlidge, R.L., Jr (1974), 'The labor market for agricultural graduates in India: a benefit–cost case study of G.B. Pant University of Agriculture and Technology', occasional paper no. 69, Department of Agricultural Economics, Cornell University.
Smith, A. ([1776] 1991), *The Wealth of Nations*, New York: Alfred A. Knopf.
Solow, R. (1956), 'A contribution to the theory of economic growth', *Quarterly Journal of Economics*, **70**, 65–94.
Solow, R. (1957), 'Technical change and the aggregate production function', *Review of Economics and Statistics*, **39**, 312–20.
Stager, D.A.A. (1989), *Focus on Fees: Alternative Policies for University Tuition Fees*, Toronto: Council of Ontario Universities.
Steele, Diane (1992), 'Women's participation decisions and earnings in Mexico', in George Psacharopoulos and Zafiris Tzannatos (eds), *Women's Employment and Pay in Latin America: Country Case Studies*, Washington, DC: World Bank, pp. 339–48.
Stelcner, Morton, J. Barry Smith, Jon A. Breslaw and George Monette (1992), 'Labor force behavior and earnings of Brazilian women and men', in George Psacharopoulos and Zafiris Tzannatos (eds), *Women's Employment and Pay in Latin America: Country Case Studies*, Washington, DC: World Bank, pp. 39–88.
Strumilin, S.G. (1924), 'Khoziaistvennoe znachenie narodnovo obrazovaniia' (Economic significance of national education), *Planovoe Khoziaistvo*, 9–10, translated and reprinted in English in UNESCO (1968), *Readings in the Economics of Education*, Paris: UNESCO, pp. 413–52.
Summers, L.H. (1992), 'Investing in all the people', Washington, DC, World Bank, Office of the Vice President, Policy Research working papers, report no. WPS 905.
Tan, J-P. and V. Paqueo (1989), 'The economic returns to education in the Philippines', *International Journal of Educational Development*, **9** (3), 243–50.
Tannen, M. (1991), 'Labor markets in northeast Brazil: does the dual market apply?', *Economic Development and Cultural Change*, **39** (3), 567–83.

Temple, J. and H.J. Voth (1998), 'Human capital, equipment investment, and industrialization', *European Economic Review*, **42** (7), 1343–62.

Thailand, Office of the Prime Minister (1989), 'Costs and contribution of higher education in Thailand', Educational Research Division, National Education Commission, Thailand.

Tilak, J.B.G. (1990), 'Education and earnings: gender differences in India', *International Journal of Development Planning Literature*, **5** (4), 131–9.

United Nations Educational, Scientific and Cultural Organisation (UNESCO) (2001), *Annual Statistical Yearbook*, Paris: UNESCO.

United Nations International Children's Fund (UNICEF) (1999), *The State of the World's Children 1999*, Oxford: Oxford University Press.

United States Agency for International Development (USAID) (1986), *Indonesia: Education and Human Resources Sector Review*, Washington, DC: USAID.

United States Agency for International Development (USAID) (1988), *Nepal: Education and Human Resources Sector Assessment*, Washington, DC: USAID.

Vaillancourt, F. (1992), 'Private and monetary returns to schooling in Canada', working paper no. 35, Economic Council of Canada, Ottawa.

Vaillancourt, F. and I. Henriques (1986), 'La rentabilité des études collégiales', *Recherches Sociographiques*, **27** (3), 481–93.

van der Gaag, J. and W. Vijverberg (1989), 'Wage determinants in Côte d'Ivoire: experience, credentials, and human capital', *Economic Development and Cultural Change*, **37** (2), 371–81.

Vecernik, J. (2001), 'Earnings disparities in the Czech Republic: evidence of the past decade and cross-national comparison', *Prague Economic Papers*, **3** (1), 201–21.

Velez, Eduardo and Carolyn Winter (1992), 'Women's labor force participation and earnings in Colombia', in George Psacharopoulos and Zafiris Tzannatos (eds), *Women's Employment and Pay in Latin America: Country Case Studies*, Washington, DC: World Bank, pp. 197–208.

Venniker, R. (2001), 'Social returns to education: a survey of recent literature on human capital externalities', CPB (Netherlands Bureau for Economic Policy Analysis), report 00/1.

Walsh, J.R. (1935), 'Capital concept applied to man', *Quarterly Journal of Economics*, **49** (2), 284–5.

Weisbrod, B. (1962), 'Education and investment in human capital', *Journal of Political Economy*, **70** (Supplement), 106–23.

Weisbrod, B.A. (1964), 'External benefits of education', Industrial Relations Section, Princeton University.

Wilson, R.A. (1985), 'A longer perspective on rates of return', *Scottish Journal of Political Economy*, **32** (2), 191–8.

Winter, Carolyn (1992), 'Female earnings, labor force participation and discrimination in Venezuela, 1989', in George Psacharopoulos and Zafiris Tzannatos (eds), *Women's Employment and Pay in Latin America: Country Case Studies*, Washington, DC: World Bank, pp. 463–76.

Winter, Carolyn and T.H. Gindling (1992), 'Women's labor force participation and earnings in Honduras', in George Psacharopoulos and Zafiris Tzannatos (eds), *Women's Employment and Pay in Latin America: Country Case Studies*, Washington, DC: World Bank, pp. 299–322.

World Bank (1991), 'Indonesia: strategy for a sustained reduction in poverty', a World Bank Country Study, World Bank, Washington, DC.

World Bank (1996), 'Bolivia: poverty, equity and income', report no. 15272–BO, World Bank, Washington, DC.

World Bank (1998), 'Ethiopia: Education Sector Development Program', report no. 17739-ET, World Bank, Washington, DC.

Yang, Hongyu (1992), 'Female labor force participation and earnings differentials in Costa Rica', in George Psacharopoulos and Zafiris Tzannatos (eds), *Women's Employment and Pay in Latin America: Country Case Studies*, Washington, DC: World Bank, pp. 209–22.

Bibliographical Note

There have been several compilations of the returns to education:

Psacharopoulos, G. (1972a), 'Rates of return on investment in education around the world', *Comparative Education Review*, **16** (1), 54–67.

Psacharopoulos, G. (1972b), 'The economic returns to higher education in twenty-five countries', *Higher Education*, **1** (2), 141–58.

Psacharopoulos, George (1973), *Returns to Education: An International Comparison*, Amsterdam: Elsevier; San Francisco: Jossey-Bass.

Psacharopoulos, G. (1981), 'Returns to education: an updated international comparison', *Comparative Education*, **17** (3), 321–41.

Psacharopoulos, G. (1982), 'The economics of higher education in developing countries', *Comparative Education Review*, **26** (2), 139–59.

Psacharopoulos, G. (1985), 'Returns to education: a further international update and implications', *Journal of Human Resources*, **20** (4), 583–604.

Psacharopoulos, G. (1989), 'Time trends of the returns to education: cross-national evidence', *Economics of Education Review*, **8** (3), 225–31.

Psacharopoulos, G. (1994), 'Returns to education: a global update', *World Development*, **22** (9), 1325–43.

Psacharopoulos, G. and H. Patrinos (2004), 'Returns to investment in education: a further update', *Education Economics*, **12** (2), (in press).

Each compilation builds upon the previous one, adding new sources. To minimize the number of references contained in each compilation, references to a previous update are not repeated. Thus, a source given as 'see Psacharopoulos (1985)' means that the exact reference on which the rate of return estimate was based can be found in Psacharopoulos (1985) – it does not mean that Psacharopoulos is necessarily the author of the estimate.

Appendix

Table 1A.1 Returns to education, by level of education and gender

Country	Year	Educational Level	Men	Women	Source (see References)
Argentina	1985	Overall	9.1	10.3	Kugler and Psacharopoulos (1989, p. 356)
Argentina	1989	Overall	10.7	11.2	Psacharopoulos and Ng (1994)
Austria	1981	Overall	10.3	13.5	See Psacharopoulos (1985)
Bolivia	1989	Overall	7.3	7.7	Psacharopoulos and Ng (1994)
Botswana	1975	Overall	16.4	18.2	See Psacharopoulos (1994)
Brazil	1980	Overall	14.7	15.6	Stelcner *et al.* (1992, Table 15)
Brazil	1989	Overall	15.4	14.2	Psacharopoulos and Ng (1994)
Chile	1987	Overall	13.7	12.6	Gill (1992a), Tables 6 and 7
Chile	1989	Overall	12.1	13.2	Psacharopoulos and Ng (1994)
China	1985	Overall	4.5	5.6	Jamison and van der Gaag (1987, p. 163)
Colombia	1973	Overall	18.1	20.8	Schultz (1988, p. 600)
Colombia	1973	Overall	18.1	20.8	See Psacharopoulos (1985)
Colombia	1973	Overall	10.3	20.1	See Psacharopoulos (1985)
Colombia	1988	Overall	11.1	9.7	Psacharopoulos and Velez (1992, Table 6)
Colombia	1989	Overall	14.5	12.9	Psacharopoulos and Ng (1994)
Costa Rica	1974	Overall	14.7	14.7	See Psacharopoulos (1985)
Costa Rica	1989	Overall	10.1	13.1	Yang (1992, Table 5)
Costa Rica	1989	Overall	10.5	13.5	Psacharopoulos and Ng (1994)
Cyprus	1984	Overall	8.9	12.7	Demetriades and Psacharopoulos (1987, p. 599)
Dominican Rep.	1989	Overall	7.8	12.0	Psacharopoulos and Ng (1994)
Ecuador	1987	Overall	11.4	10.7	Gomez-Castellano & Psacharopoulos (1990, p. 222)

Table 1A.1 (*continued*)

Country	Year	Educational Level	Men	Women	Source (see References)
Ecuador	1987	Overall	9.8	11.5	Psacharopoulos and Ng (1994)
El Salvador	1990	Overall	9.6	9.8	Psacharopoulos and Ng (1994)
Germany	1974	Overall	13.1	11.2	See Psacharopoulos (1985)
Germany	1977	Overall	13.6	11.7	See Psacharopoulos (1985)
Greece	1977	Overall	4.7	4.5	See Psacharopoulos (1985)
Guatemala	1989	Overall	14.2	16.3	Psacharopoulos and Ng (1994)
Honduras	1989	Overall	17.2	19.8	Psacharopoulos and Ng (1994)
India	1978	Overall	5.3	3.6	Tilak (1990, pp. 135–6)
Ivory Coast	1984	Overall	11.1	22.6	Komenan (1987, p. 39)
Jamaica	1989	Overall	12.3	21.5	Scott (1992b, Table 5)
Jamaica	1989	Overall	28.0	31.7	Psacharopoulos and Ng (1994)
Malaysia	1979	Overall	5.3	8.2	Chapman and Harding (1985, p. 366)
Mexico	1984	Overall	13.2	14.7	Steele (1992, Table 4)
Mexico	1984	Overall	14.1	15.0	Psacharopoulos and Ng (1994)
Nicaragua	1978	Overall	8.5	11.5	Behrman, Wolfe and Blau (1985, p. 13)
Panama	1989	Overall	9.7	11.9	Arends (1992a, Table 6)
Panama	1989	Overall	12.6	17.1	Psacharopoulos and Ng (1994)
Paraguay	1990	Overall	10.3	12.1	Psacharopoulos and Ng (1994)
Peru	1985	Overall	11.5	12.4	Khandker (1992, Table 6)
Peru	1990	Overall	8.5	6.5	Psacharopoulos and Ng (1994)
Philippines	1988	Overall	12.4	12.4	Hossain and Psacharopoulos (1994)
Portugal	1977	Overall	7.5	8.4	See Psacharopoulos (1985)
Portugal	1985	Overall	9.4	10.4	Kiker and Santos (1991, p. 192)

Country	Year	Level			Source
South Korea	1976	Overall	10.3	1.7	See Psacharopoulos (1985)
South Korea	1980	Overall	17.2	5.0	See Psacharopoulos (1985)
Sri Lanka	1981	Overall	6.9	7.9	See Psacharopoulos (1985)
Thailand	1972	Overall	9.1	13.0	See Psacharopoulos (1985)
Uruguay	1989	Overall	9.0	10.6	Psacharopoulos and Ng (1994)
Venezuela	1976	Overall	9.9	13.5	See Psacharopoulos (1985)
Venezuela	1987	Overall	10.0	13.1	Psacharopoulos and Alam (1991, p. 32)
Venezuela	1989	Overall	9.1	11.1	Winter (1992, Table 4)
Venezuela	1989	Overall	8.4	8.0	Psacharopoulos and Ng (1994)
Yugoslavia	1976	Overall	5.8	6.6	Bevc (1991, p. 204)
Yugoslavia	1986	Overall	4.9	4.8	Bevc (1991, p. 204)
Mean			11.1	12.4	
Great Britain	1841	Literacy	24.5	3.5	Mitch (1984, p. 563)
Great Britain	1871	Literacy	19.0	9.0	Mitch (1984, p. 563)
Indonesia	1982	Primary, Soc.	19.0	17.0	USAID (1988, Table 2.122)
Puerto Rico	1959	Primary	29.5	18.4	See Psacharopoulos (1985)
Taiwan	1982	Primary	8.4	16.1	See Psacharopoulos (1985)
Mean			20.1	12.8	
Canada	1980	Secondary	2.0	6.0	Vaillancourt and Henriques (1986, p. 49)
Canada	1985	Secondary	10.6	18.6	Vaillancourt (1992, Table 7)
France	1969	Secondary	13.9	15.4	See Psacharopoulos (1985)
France	1976	Secondary	14.8	16.2	See Psacharopoulos (1985)
Great Britain	1971	Secondary	10.0	8.0	See Psacharopoulos (1985)
Indonesia	1982	Secondary	23.0	11.0	USAID (1986, Table 2.122)
Indonesia	1986	Secondary	11.0	16.0	McMahon et al. (1992, Table 1)
Puerto Rico	1959	Secondary	27.3	40.8	See Psacharopoulos (1985)

Table 1A.1 *(continued)*

Country	Year	Educational Level	Men	Women	Source (see References)
South Korea	1971	Secondary	13.7	16.9	See Psacharopoulos (1985)
Sri Lanka	1981	Secondary	12.6	35.5	Sahn and Alderman (1988, p. 166)
Mean			13.9	18.4	
Australia	1976	University	21.1	21.2	See Psacharopoulos (1985)
Canada	1980	University, Priv.	5.5	10.5	Vaillancourt and Henriques (1986, p. 49)
Canada	1985	University	8.3	18.8	Vaillancourt (1992, Table 7)
France	1969	University	22.5	13.8	See Psacharopoulos (1985)
France	1976	University	20.0	12.7	See Psacharopoulos (1985)
France	1976	University	20.0	12.7	Jarousse (1985/6, p. 37)
Great Britain	1971	University	8.0	12.0	See Psacharopoulos (1985)
Indonesia	1982	University	10.0	9.0	USAID (1986, Table 2.122)
Indonesia	1986	Univ.,Soc.	9.0	10.0	World Bank (1991, p. 179)
Japan	1976	University	6.9	6.9	See Psacharopoulos (1985)
Japan	1980	University	5.7	5.8	See Psacharopoulos (1985)
Puerto Rico	1959	University	21.9	9.0	See Psacharopoulos (1985)
South Korea	1971	University	15.7	22.9	See Psacharopoulos (1985)
Mean			13.4	12.7	

Table 1A.2 The effect of selectivity correction on the returns to education, by gender

Country	Year	Male Uncorrected	Female Uncorrected	Female Corrected	Source (see References)
Argentina	1985	9.1	10.7	10.9	Ng (1992, Table 5)
Bolivia	1989	7.1	6.3	6.5	Scott (1992a, Table 6)
Chile	1987		12.6	11.9	Gill (1992a, Table 6)
Colombia	1980		15.7	17.4	Magnac (1992, Tables 11 & 12)
Colombia	1981	12.1	13.5	15.5	Magnac (1992, Tables 11 & 12)
Colombia	1982	12.6	13.2	15.2	Magnac (1992, Tables 11 & 12)
Colombia	1983	12.9	13.9	16.1	Magnac (1992, Tables 11 & 12)
Colombia	1984	13.2	14.4	16.9	Magnac (1992, Tables 11 & 12)
Colombia	1985	13.3	13.6	15.1	Magnac (1992, Tables 11 & 12)
Colombia	1988	12.0	11.2	9.9	Velez and Winter (1992, Table 5)
Costa Rica	1989	10.1	13.1	12.9	Yang (1992, Table 5)
Ecuador	1987	9.7	9.0	9.1	Jakubson and Psacharopoulos (1992, Table 4)
Guatemala	1989	14.3	16.4	14.6	Arends (1992b, Table 6)
Honduras	1989	14.1	13.2	11.5	Winter and Gindling (1992, Table 7)
Jamaica	1989	12.3	21.5	20.2	Scott (1992b, Table 5)
Mexico	1984	13.2	14.7	10.9	Steele (1992, Table 4)
Panama	1989	9.7	11.9	9.8	Arends (1992a, Table 6)
Peru	1985	11.5	12.4	13.1	Khandker (1992, Table 6)
Peru	1990	9.2	8.2	7.7	Gill (1992b, Tables 6 and 7)
Uruguay	1989	9.9	11.1	11.2	Arends (1992c, Table 5)
Venezuela	1987	10.6	12.2	11.3	Cox and Psacharopoulos (1992, Table 4)
Venezuela	1989	9.1	11.1	10.1	Winter (1992, Table 4)
Mean		11.3	12.7	12.6	

Table 1A.3 *Returns to secondary education, by curriculum type*

Country	Year	Academic/General		Technical/Vocational		Source (see References)
		Social	Private	Social	Private	
Argentina	1989		12.3		11.0	Psacharopoulos and Ng (1994)
Bolivia	1989		6.6		10.4	Psacharopoulos and Ng (1994)
Botswana	1986	35.0		25.0		Hinchliffe (1990, p. 403)
Brazil	1980		12.0		10.0	Dougherty and Jimenez (1991, p. 95)
Cameroon	1985			6.9	9.9	Paul (1990, p. 407)
Canada	1980	9.5		2.0		Vaillancourt and Henriques (1986, p. 491)
Chile	1989		9.4		13.1	Psacharopoulos and Ng (1994)
Colombia	1981	9.1		10.0		See Psacharopoulos (1985)
Costa Rica	1989		11.8		12.3	Psacharopoulos and Ng (1994)
Côte d'Ivoire	1985			3.9	15.8	Grootaert (1990, p. 319)
Cyprus	1975	10.5		7.4		See Psacharopoulos (1985)
Cyprus	1979	6.8		5.5		See Psacharopoulos (1985)
Dominican Rep.	1989		10.8		10.3	Psacharopoulos and Ng (1994)
France	1970	10.1		7.6		See Psacharopoulos (1985)
France	1977	8.1		5.4		Jarousse and Mingat (1988, p. 6)

Country	Year					Source
Honduras	1989		19.8		28.1	Psacharopoulos and Ng (1994)
Indonesia	1978	32.0		18.0		See Psacharopoulos (1985)
Indonesia	1982	23.0		19.0		USAID (1986, Table 2–122)
Indonesia	1986	19.0		6.0		World Bank (1991, p. 179)
Indonesia	1986	12.0		14.0		McMahon et al. (1992, pp. 21–2) senior
Indonesia	1986	11.0		9.0		McMahon et al. (1992, 21–2) junior
Liberia	1983	20.0		14.0		See Psacharopoulos (1985)
Mexico	1984		12.4		12.3	Psacharopoulos and Ng (1994)
Panama	1989		15.0		9.9	Psacharopoulos and Ng (1994)
Peru	1985		6.0		5.9	Bellew and Moock (1990, p. 372) private
Peru	1990		4.0		6.4	Psacharopoulos and Ng (1994)
Taiwan	1970	26.0		27.4		See Psacharopoulos (1985)
Tanzania	1982	6.3		3.7		See Psacharopoulos (1985)
Togo	1985			4.0	6.3	Paul (1990, p. 407)
Uruguay	1989		8.2		10.2	Psacharopoulos and Ng (1994)
Venezuela	1975	14.3		17.6		Psacharopoulos and Steier (1988, p. 330)
Venezuela	1984	10.5		12.0		Psacharopoulos and Steier (1988, p. 330)
Venezuela	1989		8.9		13.1	Psacharopoulos and Ng (1994)
Mean		15.5	10.6	11.7	10.5	

Table 1A.4 Returns to higher education, by subject

Country	Year	Subject	Social	Private	Source (see References)
Brazil	1962	Agriculture	5.2		See Psacharopoulos (1985)
Brazil	1980	Manag./Agric.		16.0	Dougherty and Jimenez (1991, p. 95)
Colombia	1976	Agronomy	16.4	22.3	See Psacharopoulos (1985)
Greece	1977	Agronomy	2.7	3.1	See Psacharopoulos (1985)
India	1971	Agriculture		16.2	Shortlidge (1974, p. 21)
Iran	1964	Agriculture	13.8	27.4	See Psacharopoulos (1985)
Malaysia	1968	Agriculture		9.8	See Psacharopoulos (1985)
Norway	1966	Agriculture	2.2		See Psacharopoulos (1985)
Philippines	1969	Agriculture	5.0	5.0	See Psacharopoulos (1985)
South Korea	1980	Agriculture		16.0	Ryoo (1988, p. 184)
Thailand	1987	Agriculture	8.2	19.0	Thailand (1989)
Mean			7.6	15.0	
Brazil	1980	Social Sciences		8.0	Dougherty and Jimenez (1991, p. 95)
Canada	1985	Arts	3.8	4.0	Stager (1989, p. 74)
Canada	1985	Social Sciences	8.8	10.8	Vaillancourt (1992, Table 10)
Canada	1985	Humanities	−0.1	0.7	Vaillancourt (1992, Table 10)
France	1976	Humanities		2.9	Jarousse (1985/6, p. 38)
Great Britain	1967	Social Sciences	13.0		See Psacharopoulos (1985)
Great Britain	1971	Social Sciences	11.0	48.0	See Psacharopoulos (1985)
Great Britain	1967	Arts	13.5		See Psacharopoulos (1985)
Great Britain	1971	Arts	7.0	26.0	See Psacharopoulos (1985)
India	1961	Humanities	12.7	14.3	See Psacharopoulos (1985)
Iran	1964	Humanities	15.3	20.0	See Psacharopoulos (1985)

Country	Year	Field			Source
Norway	1966	Arts	4.3	16.6	See Psacharopoulos (1985)
South Korea	1980	Social Sciences		15.9	Ryoo (1988, p. 184)
Thailand	1987	Humanities	11.2	8.0	Thailand (1989, pp. 6–35)
Venezuela	1984	Humanities			Psacharopoulos and Steier (1988, p. 330)
Mean			9.1	14.6	
Belgium	1967	Economics	9.5		See Psacharopoulos (1985)
Brazil	1962	Economics	16.1		See Psacharopoulos (1985)
Canada	1967	Economics	9.0	16.3	See Psacharopoulos (1985)
Canada	1985	Commerce	11.4	13.1	Stager (1989, p. 74)
Colombia	1976	Economics	26.2	32.7	See Psacharopoulos (1985)
Denmark	1964	Economics	9.0		See Psacharopoulos (1985)
Greece	1977	Economics and Pol.	4.4	5.4	See Psacharopoulos (1985)
Iran	1964	Economics	18.5	23.9	See Psacharopoulos (1985)
Norway	1966	Economics	8.9		See Psacharopoulos (1985)
Philippines	1969	Economics	10.5	14.0	See Psacharopoulos (1985)
South Korea	1980	Business		20.6	Ryoo (1988, p. 184)
Sweden	1967	Economics	9.0		See Psacharopoulos (1985)
Venezuela	1984	Economics		15.7	Psacharopoulos and Steier (1988, p. 330)
Mean			12.0	17.7	
Brazil	1962	Engineering	17.3		See Psacharopoulos (1985)
Canada	1985	Architecture	4.5	6.0	Stager (1989, p. 74)
Canada	1985	Engineering	11.7	23.0	Vaillancourt (1992, Table 10)
Canada	1967	Engineering	2.0	4.5	See Psacharopoulos (1985)
Canada	1985	Engineering	10.7	14.0	Stager (1989, p. 74)
Colombia	1976	Engineering	24.8	33.7	See Psacharopoulos (1985)
Denmark	1964	Engineering	8.0		See Psacharopoulos (1985)

43

Table 1A.4 *(continued)*

Country	Year	Subject	Social	Private	Source (see References)
France	1974	Engineering		17.5	Mingat and Eicher (1982, p. 214)
Great Britain	1967	Engineering	11.4	32.0	See Psacharopoulos (1985)
Great Britain	1971	Eng. and Technol.	6.0	12.2	See Psacharopoulos (1985)
Greece	1977	Engineering	8.2	21.2	See Psacharopoulos (1985)
India	1961	Engineering	16.6	30.7	See Psacharopoulos (1985)
Iran	1964	Engineering	18.2	13.4	See Psacharopoulos (1985)
Malaysia	1968	Engineering			See Psacharopoulos (1985)
Norway	1966	Engineering	8.7		See Psacharopoulos (1985)
Philippines	1969	Engineering	8.0	15.0	See Psacharopoulos (1985)
South Korea	1980	Engineering		20.0	Ryoo (1988, p. 184)
Sweden	1967	Engineering	7.5		See Psacharopoulos (1985)
Thailand	1987	Engineering	10.7	22.0	Thailand (1989, pp. 6–35)
Venezuela	1984	Engineering		20.3	Psacharopoulos and Steier (1988, p. 330)
Mean			10.9	19.0	
Belgium	1967	Law	6.0		See Psacharopoulos (1985)
Brazil	1962	Law	17.4		See Psacharopoulos (1985)
Canada	1985	Law	11.6	13.6	Stager (1989, p. 74)
Colombia	1976	Law	22.7	28.3	See Psacharopoulos (1985)
Denmark	1964	Law	10.0		See Psacharopoulos (1985)
France	1970	Law/Economics		16.7	See Psacharopoulos (1985)
France	1976	Law/Economics		14.3	Jarousse (1985/6, p. 38)
France	1974	MA. Law/Econ.		16.7	Mingat and Eicher (1982, p. 214)
Greece	1977	Law	12.0	13.8	See Psacharopoulos (1985)

Country	Year	Subject			Source
Norway	1966	Law	10.6		See Psacharopoulos (1985)
Philippines	1969	Law	15.0	18.0	See Psacharopoulos (1985)
Sweden	1967	Law	9.5		See Psacharopoulos (1985)
Thailand	1987	Law	12.2	15.4	Thailand (1989, pp. 6–35)
Venezuela	1984	Law		14.1	Psacharopoulos and Steier (1988), p. 330
Mean			12.7	16.8	
Australia	1973	Medicine		12.2	Davis (1977, p. 310)
Belgium	1967	Medicine	11.5		See Psacharopoulos (1985)
Brazil	1962	Medicine	11.9		See Psacharopoulos (1985)
Canada	1985	Medicine	17.2	21.6	Stager (1989, p. 74)
Canada	1985	Health Sciences	–0.7	9.2	Vaillancourt (1992, Table 10)
Colombia	1976	Medicine	23.7	35.6	See Psacharopoulos (1985)
Denmark	1964	Medicine	5.0		See Psacharopoulos (1985)
France	1974	Doct. Medicine		24.1	Mingat and Eicher (1982, p. 214)
France	1976	Medicine		12.6	Jarousse (1985/6), p. 38)
Malaysia	1968	Medicine		12.4	See Psacharopoulos (1985)
Norway	1966	Medicine	3.1		See Psacharopoulos (1985)
Sweden	1967	Medicine	13.0		See Psacharopoulos (1985)
Thailand	1987	Medicine	5.4	13.8	Thailand (1989, pp. 6–35)
Mean			10.0	17.7	
Great Britain	1957	Physics		20.0	Wilson (1985, p. 197)
Great Britain	1961	Physics		19.5	Wilson (1985, p. 197)
Great Britain	1965	Physics		18.5	Wilson (1985, p. 197)
Great Britain	1968	Physics		15.5	Wilson (1985, p. 197)
Great Britain	1977	Physics		10.0	Wilson (1985, p. 197)
Great Britain	1980	Physics		10.0	Wilson (1985, p. 197)

Table 1A.4 (*continued*)

Country	Year	Subject	Social	Private	Source (see References)
Greece	1977	Physics and Math.	1.8	2.1	See Psacharopoulos (1985)
Mean			1.8	13.7	
Belgium	1967	Sciences	8.0		See Psacharopoulos (1985)
Brazil	1980	Sciences		20.0	Dougherty and Jimenez (1991, p. 95)
France	1974	Sciences (M.A.)		12.3	Mingat and Eicher (1982, p. 214)
France	1970	Sciences		12.3	See Psacharopoulos (1985)
Great Britain	1967	Sciences	11.0		See Psacharopoulos (1985)
Great Britain	1971	Sciences	7.0	38.0	See Psacharopoulos (1985)
Norway	1966	Sciences	6.2		See Psacharopoulos (1985)
Thailand	1987	Sciences	9.5	19.5	Thailand (1989, pp. 6–35)
Venezuela	1984	Sciences		10.9	Psacharopoulos and Steier (1988, p. 330)
Mean			8.9	17.0	

Table 1A.5 Returns to education by economic sector

Country	Year	Private	Public	Source (see References)
Argentina	1985	9.6	7.0	Kugler and Psacharopoulos (1989, p. 356)
Argentina	1989	11.1	8.9	Psacharopoulos and Ng (1994)
Australia	1981	6.4	6.7	McNabb and Richardson (1986, Table 3)
Australia	1982	6.4	6.7	McNabb and Richardson (1989, p. 66)
Bolivia	1989	8.7	6.7	Psacharopoulos and Ng (1994)
Brazil	1970	19.3	14.9	See Psacharopoulos (1985)
Brazil	1989	15.0	11.4	Psacharopoulos and Ng (1994)
Chile	1989	11.4	11.2	Psacharopoulos and Ng (1994)
Colombia	1984	10.6	9.5	Psacharopoulos *et al.* (1992, Table 4)
Colombia	1988	11.0	11.3	Psacharopoulos and Velez (1992, Table 5)
Colombia	1975	14.6	13.4	See Psacharopoulos (1985)
Colombia	1978	11.7	12.9	See Psacharopoulos (1985)
Colombia	1989	13.7	11.9	Psacharopoulos and Ng (1994)
Costa Rica	1982	9.2	8.1	Gindling (1991, p. 597)
Costa Rica	1989	9.3	8.5	Psacharopoulos and Ng (1994)
Côte d'Ivoire	1984	10.8	11.2	Komenan (1987, p. 51)
Ecuador	1987	11.5	7.4	Gomez-Castellano and Psacharopoulos (1990, p. 222)
Ecuador	1987	11.3	7.1	Psacharopoulos and Ng (1994)
El Salvador	1990	9.4	6.2	Psacharopoulos and Ng (1994)
France	1977	11.5	7.9	Jarousse and Mingat (1986, p. 26)
Ghana	1989	7.1	7.4	Glewwe (1991, p. 13)
Greece	1975	4.8	6.4	Lambropoulos and Psacharopoulos (1992, Table 7)
Greece	1975	15.1	15.9	Lambropoulos and Psacharopoulos (1992, Table 5)
Greece	1977	7.0	6.2	See Psacharopoulos (1985)
Greece	1977	6.8	7.3	Lambropoulos and Psacharopoulos (1992, Table 7)

Table 1A.5   (*continued*)

Country	Year	Private	Public	Source (see References)
Greece	1981	13.7	10.7	Lambropoulos and Psacharopoulos (1992, Table 5)
Greece	1981	4.3	4.0	Lambropoulos and Psacharopoulos (1992, Table 7)
Greece	1985	10.2	7.4	Lambropoulos and Psacharopoulos (1992, Table 5)
Greece	1985	3.9	3.3	Lambropoulos and Psacharopoulos (1992, Table 7)
Guatemala	1977	12.7	10.6	See Psacharopoulos (1985)
Guatemala	1989	14.1	8.7	Psacharopoulos and Ng (1994)
Honduras	1989	17.4	12.3	Psacharopoulos and Ng (1994)
Jamaica	1989	24.9	16.0	Psacharopoulos and Ng (1994)
Japan	1970	19.3	6.5	See Psacharopoulos (1985)
Malaysia	1978	22.5	17.7	See Psacharopoulos (1985)
Mexico	1984	11.0	6.7	Psacharopoulos (1991, Table 5)
Mexico	1984	15.4	8.0	Psacharopoulos and Ng (1994)
Pakistan	1975	7.6	7.4	See Psacharopoulos (1985)
Panama	1989	12.2	11.0	Psacharopoulos and Ng (1994)
Paraguay	1990	11.9	8.3	Psacharopoulos and Ng (1994)
Peru	1990	9.0	9.0	Psacharopoulos and Ng (1994)
Philippines	1988	8.6	6.4	Hossain and Psacharopoulos (1994)
Portugal	1977	8.0	4.9	See Psacharopoulos (1985)
Portugal	1985	8.1	7.2	Kiker and Santos (1991, p. 192)
Tanzania	1980	14.2	10.7	See Psacharopoulos (1985)
United Kingdom	1975	8.7	6.3	See Psacharopoulos (1985)
United States	1978	9.4	9.2	Cohn *et al.* (1987, p. 292)
Uruguay	1989	10.5	5.7	Psacharopoulos and Ng (1994)
Venezuela	1984	11.1	10.6	See Psacharopoulos (1985)
Venezuela	1975	10.4	8.5	Psacharopoulos and Steier (1988, p. 327)
Venezuela	1984	9.8	9.7	Psacharopoulos and Steier (1988, p. 327)
Venezuela	1987	10.3	10.1	Psacharopoulos and Alam (1991, p. 31)
Venezuela	1989	9.7	6.6	Psacharopoulos and Ng (1994)
Mean		11.2	9.0	

Table 1A.6   Returns to education in self v. dependent employment

Country	Year	Self	Dependent	Source (see References)
Australia	1981	4.6	6.4	McNabb and Richardson (1986, p. 17)
Australia	1982	5.9	7.0	McNabb and Richardson (1989, p. 70)
Brazil	1980	13.8	14.7	Stelcner *et al.* (1992, Table 15)
Brazil	1980	18.3	15.7	Dabos and Psacharopoulos (1991, Table 12)
Colombia	1981	12.0	15.1	Magnac (1992, Table 13)
Colombia	1982	12.9	15.1	Magnac (1992, Table 13)
Colombia	1983	13.1	15.8	Magnac (1992, Table 13)
Colombia	1984	12.9	14.7	Magnac (1992, Table 13)
Colombia	1984	12.9	10.6	Psacharopoulos *et al.* (1992, Table 4)
Colombia	1985	11.0	15.6	Magnac (1992, Table 13)
Ecuador	1987	7.4		Gomez-Castellano and Psacharopoulos (1990, p. 222)
Peru	1990	9.5	9.1	Gill (1992b, Table 9)
United States	1978	9.0	8.6	Cohn *et al.* (1987, p. 292)
Venezuela	1987	7.7	10.0	Psacharopoulos and Alam (1991, pp. 31, 36)
Mean		10.8	12.2	

Table 1A.7 Returns to investment in education, by level over time: full method

Country	Year	Social			Private			Source (see References)
		Prim.	Sec.	Higher	Prim.	Sec.	Higher	
Australia	1969					14.0	13.9	See Psacharopoulos (1985)
Australia	1976					8.1	21.1	See Psacharopoulos (1985)
Brazil	1970					24.7	13.9	See Psacharopoulos (1985)
Brazil	1980					11.0	16.0	Dougherty and Jimenez (1991, p. 95)
Brazil	1989	35.6	5.1	21.4	36.6	5.1	28.2	Psacharopoulos and Ng (1994)
Canada	1960			14.9			17.4	Stager (1989, p. 74)
Canada	1985			12.1			14.0	Stager (1989, p. 74)
Chile	1960	17.2	10.6	11.6	33.1	12.5	6.8	Riveros (1990, p. 117)
Chile	1985	12.4	9.2	10.3	27.6	11.0	6.9	Riveros (1990, p. 117)
Chile	1989	8.1	11.1	14.0	9.7	12.9	20.7	Psacharopoulos and Ng (1994)
Cyprus	1975		10.5	9.7		11.6	8.6	See Psacharopoulos (1985)
Cyprus	1979		6.8	7.6		7.0	5.6	See Psacharopoulos (1985)
France	1962					11.5	9.3	See Psacharopoulos (1985)
France	1976					14.8	20.0	Jarousse (1985/6, p. 37)
Germany	1964						4.6	See Psacharopoulos (1985)
Germany	1978						10.5	See Psacharopoulos (1985)
Great Britain	1841	24.5						Mitch (1984, pp. 560, 563)
Great Britain	1871	19.0						Mitch (1984, pp. 560, 563)
Great Britain	1971			10.0				Glennerster and Low (1990, p. 67)
Great Britain	1971			7.0				See Psacharopoulos (1985)
Greece	1962		6.3	13.7		7.2	14.0	See Psacharopoulos (1985)
Greece	1977		5.5	4.5		6.0	5.5	See Psacharopoulos (1985)
India	1965	13.4	15.5	10.3	17.3	18.8	16.2	See Psacharopoulos (1985)

Country	Year							Source
India	1978	29.3	13.7	10.8	33.4	19.8	13.2	See Psacharopoulos (1985)
Indonesia	1978		16.2	14.8				See Psacharopoulos (1985)
Indonesia	1989		11.0	5.0				McMahon and Boediono (1992, Table 7)
Iran	1972	34.0	11.5	15.0				See Psacharopoulos (1985)
Iran	1976	15.2	17.6	13.6				See Psacharopoulos (1985)
Japan	1967						10.5	See Psacharopoulos (1985)
Japan	1980						8.3	See Psacharopoulos (1985)
Malawi	1978		15.1					See Psacharopoulos (1985)
Malawi	1982		15.2					See Psacharopoulos (1985)
Mexico	1963	25.0	17.0	23.0	32.0	23.0	29.0	See Psacharopoulos (1985)
Mexico	1984	19.0	9.6	12.9	21.6	15.1	21.7	Psacharopoulos and Ng (1994)
Pakistan	1975				20.0	11.0	27.0	See Psacharopoulos (1985)
Pakistan	1979				4.0	5.6	6.3	Khan and Irfan (1985, p. 675)
Papua N.G.	1979	19.9	13.9	1.0	29.4	17.6	11.4	McGavin (1991, p. 215)
Papua N.G.	1986	12.8	19.4	8.4	37.2	41.6	23.0	McGavin (1991, p. 215)
Peru	1972		19.8	16.3				See Psacharopoulos (1985)
Peru	1985		5.9	9.3				Moock and Bellew (1988, p. 29)
Peru	1990				13.2	6.3	39.7	Psacharopoulos and Ng (1994)
Philippines	1971	7.0	6.5	8.5	9.0	6.5	9.5	See Psacharopoulos (1985)
Philippines	1985	11.9	12.9	13.3	18.2	13.8	14.0	Tan and Paqueo (1989, p. 248)
Philippines	1988	13.3	8.9	10.5	18.3	10.5	11.6	Hossain and Psacharopoulos (1994)
South Korea	1967		9.0	5.0				See Psacharopoulos (1985)
South Korea	1986		8.8	15.5				Ryoo (1988, p. 158)
Taiwan	1970		26.5	15.0		17.6	18.4	See Psacharopoulos (1985)
Taiwan	1972		12.3	17.7		12.7	15.8	See Psacharopoulos (1985)
Tanzania	1980		11.0					Knight and Sabot (1987, p. 260)
Tanzania	1982		5.0					See Psacharopoulos (1985)
Thailand	1970			11.0			14.0	See Psacharopoulos (1985)

Table 1A.7 (*continued*)

Country	Year	Social			Private			Source (see References)
		Prim.	Sec.	Higher	Prim.	Sec.	Higher	
Thailand	1985			13.5			21.9	Thailand (1989, pp. 6–33)
Tunisia	1977					17.0	24.1	Bonattour (1986, p. 15)
Tunisia	1980					13.0	27.0	Bonattour (1986, p. 15)
Upper Volta	1970	25.9	60.6					See Psacharopoulos (1985)
Upper Volta	1982	20.1	14.9					See Psacharopoulos (1985)
United States	1939		18.2	10.7				See Psacharopoulos (1985)
United States	1987		10.0	12.0				McMahon (1991, Table 1)
Uruguay	1972		3.6			4.8	5.4	Indart (1981, p. 23)
Uruguay	1979		9.9			11.6	20.0	Indart (1981, p. 23)
Uruguay	1989	21.6	8.1	10.3	27.8	10.3	12.8	Psacharopoulos and Ng (1994)
Venezuela	1957	82.0	17.0	23.0		18.0	27.0	See Psacharopoulos (1985)
Venezuela	1989	23.4	10.2	6.2	36.3	14.6	11.0	Psacharopoulos and Ng (1994)
Yugoslavia	1969	9.3	15.4	2.8	7.6	15.3	2.6	See Psacharopoulos (1985)
Yugoslavia	1986	3.3	2.3	3.1	14.6	3.1	5.3	Bevc (1989, p. 6)

Table 1A.8   *Absolute change in the returns to investment in education, by level over time: full method (percentage)*

Country	Period (years)	Social Prim.	Social Sec.	Social Higher	Private Prim.	Private Sec.	Private Higher
Australia	7					−5.9	7.2
Brazil	19					−19.6	14.3
Canada	25			−2.8			−3.4
Chile	29	−9.1	0.5	2.4	−23.4	0.4	13.9
Cyprus	4		−3.7	−2.1		−4.6	−3.0
France	14					3.3	10.7
Germany	14						5.9
Great Britain	30	−5.5					
Greece	15		−0.8	−9.2		−1.2	−8.5
India	13	15.9	−1.8	0.5	16.1	1.0	−3.0
Indonesia	11		−5.2	−9.8			
Iran	4	−18.8	6.1	−1.4			
Japan	9						−5.5
Malawi	4		0.4			−18.5	
Mexico	21	6.0	−7.4	−10.1	−10.4	−7.9	−2.0
Pakistan	4				−16.0	−5.4	−9.3
Papua N.G.	7	−7.1	5.5	7.4	7.8	24.0	11.6
Peru	13		−13.9	−7.0			
Philippines	17	6.3	2.4	2.0	5.1	4.0	2.1
South Korea	19		−0.2	10.5			
Taiwan	2		−14.2	2.7		−4.9	−2.6
Tanzania	2		−6.0				
Thailand	15			2.5			7.9
Tunisia	3					−4.0	2.9
United States	48		−8.2	1.3			
Upper Volta	12	−5.8	−45.7				
Uruguay	17		4.5			5.5	7.4
Venezuela	32	−58.6	−6.8	−16.8		−3.4	−16.0
Yugoslavia	17	−6.0	−13.1	0.3	7.0	−12.2	2.7
Mean	15.0	−8.3	−5.7	−1.7	−2.0	−1.9	1.7

Source: Table 1A.7.

Table 1A.9   The coefficient on years of schooling: Mincerian rates of return (over time)

Country	Year	Mean years of schooling	Coefficient (per cent)	Source (see References)
Australia	1981		8.4	See Psacharopoulos (1985)
Australia	1987		5.4	Lorenz and Wagner (1990, pp. 13–14)
Botswana	1975		16.5	See Psacharopoulos (1994)
Botswana	1979		19.1	Lucas and Stark (1985, p. 917)
Brazil	1970		19.2	See Psacharopoulos (1985)
Brazil	1980		14.1	Tannen (1991, p. 572)
Brazil	1989	5.3	14.7	Psacharopoulos and Ng (1994)
Canada	1971		5.2	See Psacharopoulos (1985)
Canada	1981		5.2	Lorenz and Wagner (1990, pp. 13–14)
Chile	1960	7.6	11.2	Riveros (1990, p. 115)
Chile	1987	9.8	13.7	Gill (1992a, Table 7)
Chile	1989	8.5	12.0	Psacharopoulos and Ng (1994)
China	1985		5.0	Jamison and van der Gaag (1987, p. 163)
China	1986		3.7	Byron and Manalota (1990, p. 790)
Colombia	1965		17.3	See Psacharopoulos (1985)
Colombia	1988		10.5	Psacharopoulos and Velez (1993, Table 4)
Colombia	1989	8.2	14.0	Psacharopoulos and Ng (1994)
Costa Rica	1974		15.0	See Psacharopoulos (1985)
Costa Rica	1989		10.9	Psacharopoulos and Ng (1994)
Côte d'Ivoire	1984	6.9	11.3	Komenan (1987, p. 22)
Côte d'Ivoire	1986	4.5	20.1	van der Gaag and Vijverberg (1989, p. 374)
Cyprus	1975	6.9	12.5	See Psacharopoulos (1985)
Cyprus	1984		11.0	Demetriades and Psacharopoulos (1987, p. 599)

Country	Year			Source
El Salvador	1975		17.0	See Psacharopoulos (1985)
El Salvador	1977		7.7	See Psacharopoulos (1994)
El Salvador	1990	6.9	9.7	Psacharopoulos and Ng (1994)
France	1962		10.8	See Psacharopoulos (1985)
France	1977		10.0	Jarousse and Mingat (1986, p. 11)
Germany	1974		12.1	See Psacharopoulos (1985)
Germany	1987		4.9	Lorenz and Wagner (1990, pp. 13–14)
Greece	1960	3.1	9.2	Lambropoulos and Psacharopoulos (1992, Table 7)
Greece	1987	10.0	2.7	Lambropoulos and Psacharopoulos (1992, Table 7)
Guatemala	1975		10.8	See Psacharopoulos (1985)
Guatemala	1989	4.3	14.9	Psacharopoulos and Ng (1994)
Hong Kong	1976		6.3	See Psacharopoulos (1985)
Hong Kong	1981		6.1	See Psacharopoulos (1985)
Italy	1977	15.2	4.5	See Psacharopoulos (1994)
Italy	1987	10.7	2.3	Lorenz and Wagner (1990, pp. 13–14)
Japan	1970		7.3	See Psacharopoulos (1985)
Japan	1975		6.5	Hill (1983, p. 467)
Korea, South	1974		13.0	Ryoo (1988, p. 160)
Korea, South	1986		10.6	Ryoo (1988, p. 160)
Kuwait	1972	3.0	8.4	See Psacharopoulos (1994)
Kuwait	1983	8.9	4.5	See Psacharopoulos (1994)
Malaysia	1970		14.0	See Psacharopoulos (1985)
Malaysia	1979		9.4	Chapman and Harding (1985, p. 366)
Mexico	1963		15.0	See Psacharopoulos (1985)
Mexico	1984	6.6	14.1	Psacharopoulos and Ng (1994)
Pakistan	1975		7.4	See Psacharopoulos (1985)
Pakistan	1979		9.7	Shabbir (1991, p. 12)
Panama	1983	7.7	12.1	Heckman and Hotz (1986, p. 512)

Table 1A.9 (continued)

Country	Year	Mean years of schooling	Coefficient (per cent)	Source (see References)
Panama	1989	9.2	13.7	Psacharopoulos and Ng (1994)
Peru	1985	8.2	11.5	Khandker (1992, Table 6)
Peru	1990	10.1	8.1	Psacharopoulos and Ng (1994)
Philippines	1982		8.0	Tan and Paqueo (1989, pp. 246–7)
Philippines	1985		8.1	Tan and Paqueo (1989, pp. 246–7)
Philippines	1988	9.0	8.0	Hossain and Psacharopoulos (1994)
Portugal	1977		9.1	See Psacharopoulos (1985)
Portugal	1985		10.0	Kiker and Santos (1991, p. 192)
Tunisia	1977		12.3	Bonattour (1986, p. 15)
Tunisia	1980		8.0	Bonattour (1986, p. 15)
United Kingdom	1972		9.7	See Psacharopoulos (1985)
United Kingdom	1987		6.8	Lorenz and Wagner (1990, pp. 13–14)
United States	1959		10.7	See Psacharopoulos (1985)
United States	1987		9.8	Lorenz and Wagner (1990, pp. 13–14)
Venezuela	1975	4.6	13.7	Psacharopoulos and Steier (1988, p. 325)
Venezuela	1989	9.1	8.4	Psacharopoulos and Ng (1994)

Table 1A.10   *Absolute change in the coefficient on years of schooling: Mincerian rates of return (over time)*

Country	Period (years)	Mean years of schooling	Coefficient (per cent)
Australia	6		−3.0
Botswana	4		2.6
Brazil	19		−4.5
Canada	10		
Chile	29	0.9	0.8
China	1		−1.3
Colombia	24		−3.3
Costa Rica	15		−4.1
Côte d'Ivoire	2	2.4	8.8
Cyprus	9		−1.5
El Salvador	15		−7.3
France	15		−0.8
Germany	13		−7.2
Greece	27	6.9	−6.5
Guatemala	14		4.1
Hong Kong	5		−0.2
Italy	10	−4.5	−2.2
Japan	5		−0.8
Korea, South	12		−2.4
Kuwait	11	5.9	−3.9
Malaysia	9		−4.6
Mexico	21		−0.9
Pakistan	4		2.3
Panama	6	1.5	1.6
Peru	5	1.9	−3.4
Philippines	6		0.0
Portugal	8		0.9
Tunisia	3		−4.3
United Kingdom	15		−2.9
United States	28		−0.9
Venezuela	14	4.5	−5.3
Mean	11.8	2.4	−1.7

Source: Table 1A.9.

2 Signalling and screening
Sarah Brown and John G. Sessions

1 Introduction

The relationship between education and earnings has long intrigued economists and in recent years two contrasting views have emerged. The theory of human capital holds that education directly augments individual productivity and, therefore, earnings (Schultz, 1961; Mincer, 1974; Becker, 1975). By forgoing current earnings and acquiring, or more precisely, investing in, education, individuals can improve the quality of their labour services in such a way as to raise their future market value. Human capital, according to this view, is akin to physical capital, the acquisition of which entails a present cost but a future benefit. Thus education may be regarded as an investment good, and should be acquired until the point at which the marginal productivity gain equals the marginal opportunity cost.

There is, however, an alternative line of thought. The 'sorting' hypothesis attests that education also 'signals' or 'screens' intrinsic productivity (Spence, 1973; Arrow, 1973; Stiglitz, 1975).[1] Higher levels of education are associated with higher earnings, not because they raise productivity, but because they certify that the worker is a good bet for smart work. The intuition for this is straightforward. Educated workers are not a random sample. They tend, for example, to have lower propensities to quit or to be absent. They are also less likely to smoke, to drink or to use illicit drugs. Such attributes are attractive to firms, but are not readily observed at the time of hiring. It could be the case, then, that firms take into account this aspect of education when hiring workers, anticipating that graduates, for example, may be both more productive and less likely to absent. Following this line of thought, one might expect workers to anticipate the way firms hire when making their education decisions. For example, students may choose a particular course to 'signal' their desirable, but unobservable, attributes to potential employers. And firms, in turn, may insist on certain educational attainments when hiring to help them 'screen' potential applicants. By such signalling and screening, education is able to 'sort' workers according to their unobserved attributes.[2]

The debate over education and productivity is often presented as an 'either/or' question: education either raises productivity or it does not. Such views are stereotypical and even the most vociferous proponents of sorting would concede the productivity-augmenting power of education. Moreover, the observed correlation between education and earnings renders the debate largely redundant at an individual level. Regardless of whether schooling sorts or augments productivity, it certainly enhances lifetime earnings and, as such, represents a good investment for individual workers (Psacharopoulos, 1994). Whether or not schooling is a good investment for society is less clear. If its only purpose is to sort prospective workers then questions arise as to the appropriateness of investing in the expansion and/or qualitative upgrading of schooling: does it really need three years of undergraduate education to sort young adults effectively?[3] Such an issue is particularly pertinent in the present UK educational climate; the current expansion of student numbers is suggestive of productivity-augmenting sympathies, whilst the recent moves to student-centred funding would appear to indicate prima facie sorting leanings.[4]

The plan of this chapter is as follows: section 2 examines the background to sorting, focusing on the problems caused by asymmetric information; section 3 outlines the basic signalling model of education, while section 4 explores the ways in which firms may use education to sort potential applicants; section 5 reviews the empirical evidence regarding sorting and section 6 concludes.

2 Asymmetric information and the market for lemons

The need for sorting arises when information is asymmetric. Employers, for example, may be unable to observe an applicant's intrinsic productivity, and cannot rely on workers' pronouncements regarding their own attributes since all workers would claim to be highly able. More generally, the same problem can arise in any buyer–seller situation when goods can be differentiated in terms of quality and, without an effective sorting mechanism, the problems can be insurmountable.

If it is impossible to observe the quality of a particular good at the time of purchase, even if buyers do eventually learn of average quality, goods will be traded at a price reflecting this average. Moreover price will adjust until buyers' beliefs about this average quality are confirmed ex post. Such markets will tend to exhibit two undesirable characteristics: (a) sellers may attempt to lower cost by lowering quality; (b) if sellers cannot 'shave' quality, the sellers of high-quality products, with higher opportunity costs, may prefer to withdraw from the market. Average quality may thus fall below that in a world of complete information and adverse selection problems arise. This problem was highlighted by Akerlof (1970) who showed that the process would continue until only the lowest quality 'lemons' were traded on the market. Akerlof used the example of a second-hand car market and focused on a key information asymmetry: the owner of a used car is better informed about its quality than a potential buyer. Indeed the buyer may be unable to discern whether the car is a low-quality 'lemon' or a high-quality 'peach'.

If buyers are unable to observe the quality of a particular used car, then peaches and lemons will trade at a single price reflecting the average quality of cars on the market. The more lemons on the market, the lower the average quality and the lower the market price for all cars – good and bad. Faced with such a situation the owners of good cars may find it unattractive to sell their cars and may withdraw from the market. If there is a distribution of quality then we might envisage the owner of the highest-quality car withdrawing from the market, followed by the owner of the second-best car, and so on. It is feasible that the market may unravel completely, or that the market will move to an equilibrium in which only cars below a certain quality threshold are traded.

The key points of Akerlof's model can be ascertained in the following stylized example: Assume for simplicity a second-hand car market in which there are just two types of car, good quality cars (i.e. peaches) and bad quality cars (i.e. lemons). The reservations values to potential buyers and sellers are as follows:

Value to (£)	Peach (g)	Lemon (b)
Buyer	3000	2000
Seller	2500	1000

Assume also that it is known that there are three times as many bad cars as good cars on the market, (i.e. $N_b = 3N_g$), that each potential seller wants to sell one used car only, and each potential buyer wants to buy one used car only, and that all the bargaining power lies with sellers, so that at any trade it will be the buyers' reservation value that holds.

Symmetric information
Assume first that there is symmetric information amongst buyers and sellers. In this case the market should operate without problem. Firstly, if quality is known perfectly by both buyers and sellers then equilibrium will be characterized by the following prices:

$$p_g^* = £3000; \tag{2.1}$$

$$p_b^* = £2000.$$

That is, the market separates to allow trade of both good and bad cars at the buyers' reservation prices of £3000 and £2000 respectively. If quality is unknown by everybody then buyers and sellers will consider expected average quality in their calculation of 'bid' prices:

$$p^s = \left(\frac{1}{4}\right) p_g^s + \left(\frac{3}{4}\right) p_b^s = \left(\frac{1}{4}\right) \pounds 2500 + \left(\frac{3}{4}\right) \pounds 1000 = \pounds 1375, \qquad (2.2)$$

$$p^d = \left(\frac{1}{4}\right) p_g^d + \left(\frac{3}{4}\right) p_b^d = \left(\frac{1}{4}\right) \pounds 3000 + \left(\frac{3}{4}\right) \pounds 2000 = \pounds 2250. \qquad (2.3)$$

The offered 'supply' price, p^s, is thus a weighted average of the supply price for good (p_g^s) and bad (p_b^s) cars. Following our assumption that the buyers' reservation price holds, the market will clear at $p^* = \pounds 2250$. Problems arise, however, if only one side of the market is aware of the true quality of the cars.

Asymmetric information
It is reasonable to assume that sellers will have acquired some knowledge regarding the true quality of the car they are selling. Such information, however, is unlikely to be known by prospective buyers. Assume now that only sellers are able to observe quality. There will be no trade at all at any $p < \pounds 1000$, since at these prices even owners of 'lemons' are not prepared to sell. Owners of lemons would be willing to sell if $p \geq \pounds 1000$, but no 'peaches' will appear on the market until $p \geq \pounds 2500$. Therefore buyers will assume that any car offered for sale at a price $\pounds 1000 \leq p < \pounds 2500$ is a lemon, and so they will only be willing to pay a maximum of $p_b^d = \pounds 2000$. Such a price would be acceptable to sellers of lemons, and so lemons will trade for $p_b^* = \pounds 2000$. If $p \geq \pounds 2500$ then all sellers are willing to put their cars on the market and so there would be a 75 per cent chance of a car being a lemon and therefore buyers would be prepared to offer at most $p_d = \pounds 2250$, which would be unacceptable to sellers of peaches. Since buyers would be aware of this, they would (quickly) revise their offer down to $p_b^d = \pounds 2000$. Indeed there will be no demand at all at any $p \geq \pounds 2000$ because there will be no demand at any $p \geq \pounds 2250$, whilst at any $p \leq \pounds 2500$ demand only starts at $p \leq \pounds 2000$ since buyers assume that the car is a lemon. Such an equilibrium is obviously inefficient; further gains from trade are theoretically possible (i.e. between buyers and sellers of peaches). But such gains cannot be made because buyers do not know if they are getting a lemon.

The root of the market failure in Akerlof's model lies in the dual role being performed by the market price; it determines the average quality of cars offered for sale and then equilibrates this supply with market demand. We thus have one instrument aiming at two targets. Is there no way that such a failure can be salvaged? In terms of the second-hand car market, it would make sense for the owners of good cars to acquire independent, third party verification as to the quality of their car. Indeed this is what is actually offered in the second-hand car market by reputable organizations such as the Royal Automobile Club (RAC) and the Automobile Association (AA) in the UK, and the American Automobile Association (AAA) in the USA. Such organizations are effectively certifying quality, in much the same way, advocates of the sorting hypothesis would claim, as do universities.

3   Job market signalling

Extending the Akerlof model to the labour market, we can envisage two types of worker, 'good' and 'bad', where these are intrinsically productive qualities known only to the worker. If firms cannot spot the difference between good and bad workers, we might have an equilibrium in which only 'lemons' are traded: the competitive wage will necessarily reflect average quality and as such may fall below the reservation wages of the 'good' workers. We do not, however, see this occurring in real world labour markets: highly able individuals do work. The question is why, and there are perhaps two answers: first, buyers (i.e. firms) learn; second, firms and workers act to screen and signal particular productivities.

The first discussion of the role of information and search was initiated by Stigler (1962), who examined more closely the decision-making process of individuals as part of their job search under imperfect information. These and similar ideas were translated into a notion of signalling by Spence (1973), who concentrated on the job market and the role of signalling in transmitting the personal characteristics of an individual.

Essentially, the side to a transaction that has superior information will try to do something to indicate the quality of the good on offer, e.g. used car warranties. Such indicators will act as signals of quality. In terms of the labour market, it follows that 'good' workers might attempt to signal their quality to firms, hoping, by so doing, to increase their marginal products. This was the basis for the study by Spence (1973). If a seller of a high-quality product could find some activity that was less costly for him than the seller of a low-quality product, it might pay him to undertake (i.e. signal) the activity as an indication of high quality. Moreover, even if buyers (i.e. firms) were not aware of the underlying costs of the activity, they would quickly learn that the signal was associated with higher quality and therefore would be prepared to pay a premium price for it. And providing that the marginal cost of some activity was lower for sellers of high quality then an equilibrium would emerge in which quality would be perfectly inferred by buyers from the level of activity undertaken by sellers.

The basic idea
Assume a market situation in which signallers are relatively numerous and in the market sufficiently infrequently not to acquire reputations. Consider

further the hiring decision of the firm as a process of investment under uncertainty. The employer is unaware of the productive capability of the worker at the time of hiring. We thus have a situation of (a) *investment*, since it takes time for the firm to learn an individual's productive capability; and (b) *uncertainty*, since this capability is not known to the firm beforehand.

Now, although the firm cannot directly observe productivity, it can observe a plethora of personal data in the form of observable characteristics and attributes. That is: *signals*, observable characteristics attached to the individual and under the individual's control; and *indices*, observable, unalterable characteristics.

Some time after hiring, the firm will learn an individual's productive capabilities and, on the basis of previous experience in the market, will have conditional probability assessments over productive capacity given various combinations of signals and indices. At any point in time, when confronted by an individual applicant with certain observable characteristics, the firm's subjective 'lottery' with which it is confronted when making this investment decision is defined by these conditional probability distributions over productivity given the new data. Ignoring risk (i.e. assuming risk neutrality) the firm will have an expected marginal product for an individual for each configuration of signals and indices that it confronts. And, assuming a competitive atomistic market, these marginal products will be reflected in wages.

We can envisage the nature of the hiring process in terms of the feedback loop illustrated in Figure 2.1. An equilibrium occurs where any part of the loop repeats itself; for example, the employer's conditional probabilistic

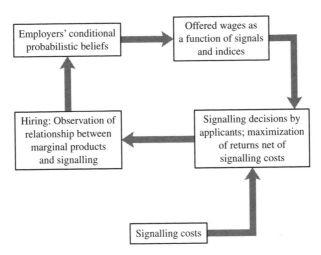

Figure 2.1

beliefs are not changed from one period to the next because they are not disconfirmed by the data.

Although individuals can do little about their indices, they can alter their signals, even if at some cost to themselves. Education is a classic example.

A formal model

Consider the following stylized model. There are two groups of individuals (Group I and Group II) with marginal products equal to 1 and 2, respectively. The population comprises a proportion q $(1-q)$ of Group I (II) individuals. Group II individuals are not only more productive than Group I individuals, but they can also acquire a particular signal, y, at a lower cost. Assume for simplicity that the cost to Group I (II) of acquiring y units of the signal is equal to y ($y/2$). In what follows we will interpret y in terms of education. Finally we assume that firms are competitive and pay workers a wage equal to their marginal product. The data of our model are summarized below.

Individual group	Marginal product	Proportion in population	Cost of acquiring education signal y
I	1	q	y
II	2	$1-q$	$y/2$

To locate an equilibrium we proceed by attempting to ascertain a set of self-confirming conditional probabilistic beliefs on the part of employers. Assume, for example, that an employer's beliefs are as follows.

$$If \; y<y^* \Rightarrow MP_L = 1 \; with \; probability \; 1$$
$$If \; y \geq y^* \Rightarrow MP_L = 2 \; with \; probability \; 1. \tag{2.4}$$

That is, if an individual has fewer than y^* units of education, he is a Group I individual, and he is a Group II individual otherwise. Such conditional beliefs imply the wage schedule set out in Figure 2.2.

Given the offered wage schedule, members of each group will select optimal levels of education. Consider a person who is considering acquiring $y<y^*$. It is apparent that such an individual will acquire $y=0$ because education is costly and, given the employer's beliefs, there are no benefits to increasing y until he reaches y^*. Conversely an individual who is considering acquiring $y \geq y^*$ will in fact acquire only $y=y^*$ since further increases in y would merely incur costs with no additional benefits. Thus individuals will only set either $y=0$ or $y=y^*$. An equilibrium will therefore require all Group I individuals setting $y=0$ and all Group II individuals setting $y=y^*$. The options available to each group are set out in Figure 2.3.

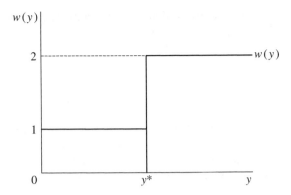

Figure 2.2

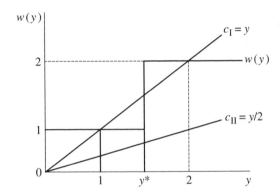

Figure 2.3

Each group sets y to maximize the difference between the offered wage and the costs of acquiring education, c_i, $i = I, II$. Given the level of y^* in the diagram and the assumption that $c_I = y > y/2 = c_{II}$, it is apparent that members of Group I will set $y = 0$ and members of Group II will set $y = y^*$. In this case the employer's beliefs are confirmed and we have a signalling equilibrium. More generally, a *separating* equilibrium will occur if:

$$1 > 2 - y^* \tag{2.5}$$

$$2 - \frac{y^*}{2} > 1 \tag{2.6}$$

Satisfaction of (2.5) will ensure that Group I individuals set $y^* = 0$, whilst satisfaction of (2.6) will ensure that Group II individuals set $y = y^*$. The two conditions can be combined to yield

$$1 < y^* < 2. \qquad (2.7)$$

Thus a separating equilibrium will occur if y^* lies between 1 and 2. It is apparent that there are an infinite number of possible equilibria. These are not, however, welfare equivalent. Increases in y^* (up to $y^* = 2$) hurt members of Group II, but leave members of Group I unaffected. This is illustrated in Figure 2.4, with the new critical level of education, y_a, set such that $y^* < y_a < 2$.

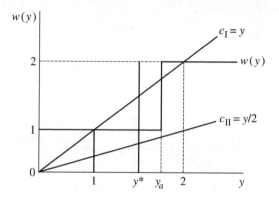

Figure 2.4

Note that, if the critical level of education is either greater than 2 or less than 1 so that (2.7) is not satisfied, separation breaks down and either no one ($y_b > 2$, Figure 2.5) or everyone ($y_c < 1$, Figure 2.6) acquires education. Given the firm's conditional probabilistic beliefs, neither of these would be an equilibrium.

Group I is worse off than it was with no signalling. Without signalling, employers would pay an average wage based on the unconditional expected marginal product which, providing $q < 1$, would be higher than the equilibrium Group I signalling wage:

$$\bar{w} = q1 + (1 - q)2 = 2 - q > 1. \qquad (2.8)$$

Group II *could* be worse off than it was without signalling if

$$2 - \frac{y^*}{2} < 2 - q \Rightarrow y^* > 2q. \qquad (2.9)$$

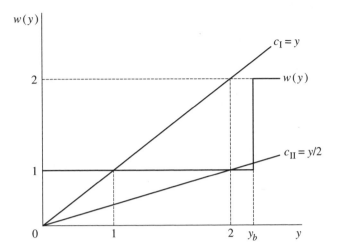

Figure 2.5

This will definitely be the case if $q \leq 0.5$ such that Group II comprises the majority of the population. In this case the non-signalling wage must be at least 1.5 whilst the signalling wage will be less than 1.5.

Other equilibria are possible. For example, assume that the employer's beliefs are as follows:

$$If \; y<y^* \Rightarrow MP_L=1 \; with \; probability \; q,$$
$$\Rightarrow MP_L=2 \; with \; probability \; 1-q, \qquad (2.10)$$
$$If \; y \geq y^* \Rightarrow MP_L=2 \; with \; probability \; 1.$$

Again the only levels of education will be $y=0$ or $y=y^*$. The firm's conditional probabilistic beliefs will be 'confirmed' if both groups set $y=0$. Thus, if the more able group, which finds the acquisition of education relatively less costly, sets $y=0$, so too will the less able group. Given the firm's beliefs, it will pay anyone with $y=0$ a wage equal to expected marginal product:

$$\bar{w}=q1+(1-q)2=2-q. \qquad (2.11)$$

We therefore require:

$$2-q>2-\frac{y^*}{2}\Rightarrow 4-2q>4-y^*\Rightarrow y^*>2q. \qquad (2.12)$$

This situation is illustrated in Figure 2.7. If the above condition is satisfied then neither group will acquire education and the firm's conditional

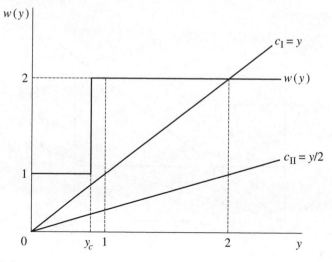

Figure 2.6

probabilistic beliefs will be confirmed (more accurately, not disconfirmed). A member of Group I would earn $2 - y^*$ from acquiring education, which, given (2.11) would be equal *at most* to $2 - 2q$, which is less than the non-education wage $\bar{w} = 2 - q$. A member of Group II would earn a maximum of $2 - y^*/2$, which, given (2.12) would imply a *maximum* possible wage of $2 - q$. Thus members of Group II would be, at best, if y^* is set at its lowest possible value, indifferent between acquiring and not acquiring education, and any increase in y^* will unequivocally deter members of Group II from acquiring education.

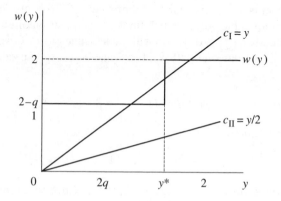

Figure 2.7

Notice the degenerative nature of this equilibrium. The firm's beliefs regarding $y \geq y^*$ are not disconfirmed because there are no data about such levels of y. Notice also that another pooling equilibrium in which all individuals acquire education is also possible. For this we simply require the firms' conditional probabilistic beliefs to be

$$If \; y < y^* \Rightarrow MP_L = 1 \; with \; probability \; 1,$$
$$If \; y \geq y^* \Rightarrow MP_L = 1 \; with \; probability \; q, \qquad (2.13)$$
$$\Rightarrow MP_L = 2 \; with \; probability \; 1 - q.$$

Again the only levels of education will be $y = 0$ or $y = y^*$. The firm's conditional probabilistic beliefs will be 'confirmed' if both groups set $y = y^*$. Thus, if the *less* able group, which finds the acquisition of education relatively more costly, sets $y = y^*$, so too will the more able group. Given the firm's beliefs, it will pay anyone with $y = 0$ a wage equal to 1, and anyone with $y = y^*$ a wage equal to $\bar{w} = 2 - q$. We therefore require:

$$(2 - q) - y^* > 1 \Rightarrow -y^* \geq -1 + q \Rightarrow y^* < 1 - q. \qquad (2.14)$$

If the above condition is satisfied then both groups will acquire education and the firm's conditional probabilistic beliefs will be confirmed. The *least* a member of Group I could earn from acquiring education is $(2 - q) - y^* \Rightarrow (2 - q) - (1 - q) = 1$, the same as the non-education wage. And any decline in y^* will unequivocally encourage members of Group I to acquire education. Unsurprisingly, Group II will also acquire education. The *least* they could earn from so doing is given by $(2 - q) - y^*/2 \Rightarrow (2 - q) - (1 - q)/2 = 1.5 - q/2 > 1.$[5]

The informational implication of indices
It is not just signals that can affect the nature of the equilibrium. Consider the informational implication of indices. Suppose the population comprises m males and $(1 - m)$ females. A proportion q of both males and females are low productivity:

Sex	Marginal product	Cost of acquiring education signal y	Proportion in group	Proportion in population
M	1	y	q	qm
M	2	$y/2$	$1 - q$	$(1 - q)m$
F	1	y	q	$q(1 - m)$
F	2	$y/2$	$1 - q$	$(1 - q)(1 - m)$

Assume that firms hold the following conditional probabilistic beliefs:

Males

$$If\ y<y^*_m \Rightarrow MP_L = 1\ with\ probability\ 1,$$
$$If\ y\geq y^*_m \Rightarrow MP_L = 2\ with\ probability\ 1. \tag{2.15}$$

Females

$$If\ y<y^*_f \Rightarrow MP_L = 1\ with\ probability\ 1,$$
$$If\ y\geq y^*_f \Rightarrow MP_L = 2\ with\ probability\ 1. \tag{2.16}$$

It is apparent that equilibrium conditions are given by

$$1<y^*_m<2,\ 1<y^*_f<2. \tag{2.17}$$

Thus it could be that $y^*_m \neq y^*_f$, even though males and females are identical and face the same opportunity sets. The signalling equilibrium for the two groups is completely independent: since both gender and education are observable, the employee can make his beliefs conditional on both. Indeed it could be the case that employers have the following conditional probabilistic beliefs:

Males

$$If\ y<y^*_m \Rightarrow MP_L = 1\ with\ probability\ 1,$$
$$If\ y\geq y^*_m \Rightarrow MP_L = 2\ with\ probability\ 1. \tag{2.18}$$

Females

$$If\ y<y^*_f \Rightarrow MP_L = 1\ with\ probability\ q,$$
$$\Rightarrow MP_L = 2\ with\ probability\ 1-q, \tag{2.19}$$
$$If\ y\geq y^*_f \Rightarrow MP_L = 2\ with\ probability\ 1.$$

In this case, providing $1<y^*_m<2$ and $y^*_f>2q$, some males would attend college and would enjoy utility $u_m(y^*_m)=2-y^*_m/2$, some males would not attend college and would enjoy utility $u_m(0)=1$. Females would not attend college and would earn $u_f(0)=2-q$. If $2-y^*_m/2>2-q \Leftrightarrow y^*_m<2q$ then male graduates are better off than females, even though females are better off than male non-graduates. In this case, it might be thought, somewhat incorrectly, that the lower pay of females is a reflection of their relatively lower education and productivity.

4 Employer screening

In the Spence signalling model, job applicants made the first move by choosing the level of education to signal optimally their intrinsic attributes. Employees then had to interpret that signal in order to make their wage offers, and they interpreted the signals according to their prior beliefs. Employers were essentially constrained in that they could not initiate a signal by, for example, requiring applicants to obtain a different level of signal from the level they had chosen. This generates rigidity in the model in that, from the employer's perspective, the applicant's signals were preset, the system yielding an equilibrium in which employers' beliefs about these preset signals turned out to be true.

We now turn the game around and investigate what happens when it is firms who make the first move, setting a particular signal (i.e. a level of education) they require from applicants. This was the situation investigated by Rothschild and Stiglitz (1976) – hereafter RS – who assumed that firms chose both the wage and the level of education, and that job applicants responded by self-selecting into their preferred contract. Such an approach allows employers considerable freedom as to the types of contract that appear on the market, and this can have profound implications for the nature of the equilibrium.

In what follows we illustrate a simplified RS screening game. We assume the order of moves in the 'game' is as follows. First, employers offer a menu of contracts for prospective job applicants. Each contract is defined by a wage–education pair; that is, each contract specifies a particular wage for a given level of education. The job applicant considers the menu of contracts on offer and chooses the one that maximizes their utility. We also assume that any screening equilibra will be characterized by the following conditions: (a) only contracts that at least break even will survive in equilibrium – loss-making contracts are withdrawn from the market; (b) there are no potentially profitable 'outside' contracts; that is, there are no contracts outside the market that would make expected positive profits if offered. If such contracts were feasible, we would expect employers within the market to introduce them. A convenient implication of these two conditions is that all contracts will just break even. Loss-making contracts are withdrawn, and those that make excess profits attract rival offers until expected profits are competed away.

In the signalling model, employers made expected normal profit. It is possible in that framework that there exist other contracts that would be profitable, but which never get introduced. Employers never get the chance to offer them because they respond passively to applicants' signals with wage offers. Under screening, employers are free to choose whatever wage–education combination they wish, in the form of an offered contract.

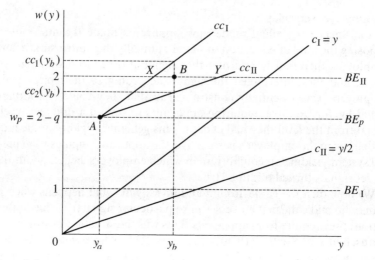

Figure 2.8

Competition amongst employers for job applicants then ensures that, if a contract is profitable, it is offered; if it loses money, it is not. Thus the assumption that no outside contracts make positive profits is a condition for equilibrium under screening, but not under signalling.

Figure 2.8 is adapted from Figure 2.3. We continue to assume that there are two types of workers as per the Spence signalling model with the costs of education acquisition as on page 64. What differs from Figure 2.3, however, is that the wage-offer schedule has been removed. Employers are now free to offer any contract they wish so that each point on the diagram can be envisaged as an employment contract specifying a particular wage–education pair (w, y). The horizontal 'break-even' lines denote all possible contracts that, if taken by a particular type of worker, would make exactly normal profit. For example, the line BE_I specifies all the possible 'break-even' contracts that could be offered to a Type I worker. All such contracts must pay the worker a wage equal to his marginal productivity of 1. The line is horizontal because education is assumed to have no intrinsic value and, therefore, has no implication for the profitability of the contract. Any point below (above) BE_I represents a profit (loss)-making contract for Type I workers. BE_{II} is defined analogously for Type II workers, and BE_p is the break-even line for pooled contracts: contracts offered along this line would make normal profits on average if all workers in the population took them. Recall that such pooled contracts would have to offer pay equal to average productivity:

$$w_p = q1 + (1 - q)2 = 2 - q. \tag{2.20}$$

RS investigated the nature of the equilibria that might occur in such a model and came to two important conclusions: first, no pooling equilibrium can exist; and second, any separating equilibrium that exists will be unique. We examine these points in turn.

No pooling equilibrium exists
Consider first the possibility of a pooling equilibrium. Any pooling contract must lie on the break-even line BE_p. Consider contract A in Figure 2.8 by way of example. The lines cc_I and cc_{II} are drawn parallel to the education acquisition lines c_I and c_{II} and represent the increase in costs to each worker type of acquiring more education relative to that already acquired at point A. Now consider any point, such as B, lying to the north-east of A within these two lines. Relative to A, the contract B offers a higher wage but demands more education. Would such a contract be attractive? The costs of acquiring the additional education are less than the increase in the wage for Type I workers. The increase in the wage is given by:

$$\Delta w = 2 - (2 - q) = q. \tag{2.21}$$

The increases in the costs to Type I and II workers of acquiring the additional education are:

$$\Delta c_I = cc_I(y_b) - (2 - q), \tag{2.22}$$

$$\Delta c_{II} = cc_{II}(y_b) - (2 - q). \tag{2.23}$$

The net benefit of moving to contract B for Type I and II workers is thus

$$\Delta w - \Delta c_I = 2 - cc_I(y_b) < 0, \tag{2.24}$$

$$\Delta w - \Delta c_{II} = 2 - cc_{II}(y_b) > 0. \tag{2.25}$$

We have a situation of 'cream-skimming': the more productive Type II workers would prefer contract B and the firm would be left with the less productive Type I workers. Can contracts A and B survive in equilibrium? Contract A would have to be withdrawn from the market, since it only attracts Type I workers but pays the pooled wage of $2 - q > 1$. Consider contract B. It is apparent that B is making normal profit: it is only offered to Type II workers, and it pays them their marginal product of 2. Indeed there are other cream-skimming contracts that would make super normal profits. Type II workers would weakly prefer any contract within the area AXY to contract A, and contracts in this area below BE_{II} would make supernormal profits for firms.

It is apparent that a similar argument could be constructed for any pooling contract. There will always be another contract that separates the high ability workers and makes at least normal profits. As RS concluded, there is no pooling equilibrium in a screening model.

If a separating equilibrium exists, it will be unique
Now consider the possibility of a separating equilibrium. Is it possible for a pair of contracts, such as A_I and A_{II} in Figure 2.9, to separate the two worker types? It is apparent that Type I (II) workers would prefer $A_I (A_{II})$. The net return to both types of worker from A_I is just 1. The net return from A_{II} to Types I and II is

$$u_{II}(A_{II}) = 2 - c_{II}(y_{II}) > 1 > 2 - c_I(y_{II}) = u_I(A_{II}), \qquad (2.26)$$

since $c_I(y_{II}) > 1 > c_{II}(y_{II})$. It is also apparent that both contracts yield normal profits. They cannot, however, be sustained in equilibrium because there are other potential contracts that would be profitable if offered. Consider, for example, contract β, which lies marginally below BE_{II}. Such a contract would be preferred by Type IIs to A_{II} since it offers virtually the

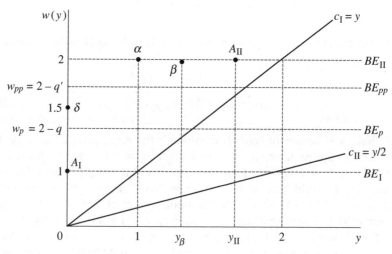

Figure 2.9

same wage ($w_\beta = 2 - \varepsilon$) but requires significantly less education. Type Is, however, would remain at A_I because the signalling costs of reaching β are still prohibitively high:

$$u_I(\beta) = 2 - [c_I(y_\beta) + \varepsilon] < 1 = u_I(A_I), \qquad (2.27)$$

since $c_I(y_\beta) > 1$. Thus β attracts only Type II workers and makes supernormal profits since $w_\beta = 2 - \varepsilon < 2$.

A similar argument could be made for any contract aimed at Type II workers and specifying $y > 1$. To survive in equilibrium, a contract aimed at Type II workers must lie on BE_{II}, but any contract specifying (marginally) lower wages and education would attract Type II (but not Type I) workers and would make supernormal profits. The only contract invulnerable to such cream skimming is $\alpha = (2,1)$. This contract specifies the lowest level of education that can be required of Type II workers without tempting Type I workers away from A_I.

The key question is whether the two contracts (A_I, α) yield a unique separating equilibrium. They certainly cannot be undermined by any other separating contracts. Any alternative separating contracts would make a loss because they would have to offer workers more than their marginal product: those aimed at Type II workers (i.e. alternatives to α) would have to offer $w > 2$, whilst those aimed at Type I workers only (i.e. alternatives to A_I) would have to offer $w > 1$.

Could (A_I, α) be undermined by a pooling contract? The net returns to Type I and II workers in the separating equilibrium (A_I, α) are

$$u_I(A_I) = 1, \qquad (2.28)$$

$$u_{II}(\alpha) = 2 - c_{II}(1) = 2 - 0.5 = 1.5. \qquad (2.29)$$

Thus both types would be tempted by a contract that offered $w \geq 1.5$. Just such a contract is depicted by δ in Figure 2.9, which offers $w_\delta \geq 1.5$ and requires no investment in signalling. Whether or not δ makes profits depends on the position of the BE_p line. If there are more Type I than Type II workers in the population then $q > 0.5$ and $w_p = 2 - q < 1.5$ and BE_p is below 1.5 as in Figure 2.8. In this case δ would make a loss; pooling would be unprofitable because there are too many low productivity workers in the population. Note, moreover, that if δ, which requires no education, is unprofitable, then so too would be any other pooling contract: any alternative pooling contract offering (as it must) $w \geq 1.5$ requiring $y > 0$ would have to compensate workers for the additional signalling costs by offering $w \geq w_\delta$

and so would earn even lower profits. Thus (A_f, α) cannot be undermined by the offer of a pooling contract if $q > 0.5$.

Assume now that the proportion of low productivity workers in the population is given by $q' < 0.5$ such that $w_{pp} = 2 - q' > 1.5$. With more high than low productivity workers in the population, the break-even line (BE_{pp}) lies above 1.5 and a contract such as δ is able to pool both types of workers profitably, thus undermining the separating equilibrium (A_f, α).

To summarize, if the relatively less productive workers predominate in the population $(q > 0.5)$ then the separating equilibrium (A_f, α) is unique and sustainable. If the more productive workers predominate, the separating equilibrium (A_f, α) will be undermined by a pooling contract. The latter possibility leads to an interesting conclusion. We have just shown that under certain conditions a separating equilibrium can be undermined by a pooling contract. But we have already seen that a pooling contract cannot survive in equilibrium since it too would be undermined by the introduction of a cream-skimming separating contract. We may thus have a situation of constant flux, with a separating equilibrium giving way to a pooling equilibrium, which is itself undermined by a separating equilibrium, and so on.[6]

5 Empirical evidence

Recent years have witnessed an ever-burgeoning mass of empirical work on the relevance of the sorting hypothesis. When interpreting these studies, it is important to remember the similarities between sorting and human capital models. In both approaches, profit-maximizing firms compete for utility-maximizing workers, and the discounted expected lifetime compensation of a worker with a given set of observed attributes is equal to the discounted expected lifetime productivity of a randomly selected worker with those attributes. And in both models individuals choose the quantity of education that equates the marginal returns and costs of schooling. The fundamental difference is that sorting models allow for unobservable attributes to be correlated with schooling.

Whether signalling or screening is a more accurate description of market sorting will depend on the nature of the market. In some markets it is reasonable to assume that the uninformed party makes the first move, and the informed one responds. In these situations, the 'screening' model would seem appropriate. In other markets it is more realistic to adopt the signalling model with the uninformed party responding to a move by the informed party. This is perhaps the case in the labour market, where it is more sensible to assume that job applicants first choose the level of the (education) signal, and then employers attempt to discern the applicant's productivity from that signal.

The possibility that education was primarily a way of signalling rather than augmenting productivity intrigued economists and led to a flurry of empirical research attempting to ascertain its true nature. The problem was how to discriminate between the human capital and signalling explanations, both of which implied that earnings increased with education. Most studies have focused on Mincerian earnings regressions, with the dependent variable being the logarithm of wages or earnings and the independent explanatory variables including a constant, observed demographic characteristics such as education measured in years of schooling, race, gender, and experience. The coefficient on the education term describes the percentage change in wages associated with each additional year of schooling and is generally interpreted as the private rate of return to schooling. Such an interpretation is reasonable providing there are no ability differences omitted from the wage equation that are observed by the firm. Whether the coefficient on education can be interpreted as an estimate of the productivity-enhancing effects of education is less clear. Such an interpretation would require wages to be proportionate to productivity and any unobservable attributes that affect productivity to be uncorrelated with schooling.

Early studies

Early studies concentrated on measuring the change in the coefficient on education in a wage equation when additional explanatory variables intended to capture ability differences are included. The usual finding was that the coefficient is not significantly affected and that unobserved ability differences do not have important effects on productivity. For example, in one of the earliest studies of this type, before the signalling hypothesis was explicitly formalized, Ashenfelter and Mooney (1968) found significant returns to years of education and ability, but also found that omitting the latter had little effect on the former.[7]

Such an interpretation is, however, incorrect. As Weiss (1995) argues, if firms are unable to observe the omitted variables then they will use education choices to draw inferences about an individual's ability. The coefficient on education should fully capture this inference process and will thus be unaffected by the inclusion of additional variables that are unobserved by the firm. Even if researchers are able to measure ability accurately through, perhaps, the results of accurate intelligence or personality tests, if the firm does not have access to that information then the sorting model predicts that including these variables in the wage equation will not affect the coefficient on schooling.

The first explicit test of signalling was undertaken by Taubman and Wales (1973) who investigated a sample of US Army Air Force volunteers who were given a number of tests measuring various types of ability in 1955 and 1969. By estimating a number of earnings equations for particular occupational categories, Taubman and Wales were able to predict what an individual with a given level of education, ability and demographic characteristics might have earned had he been employed in another occupation. They found that university, but not high school, graduates earned almost as much as they would have been predicted to earn in alternative occupations, whilst blue-collar workers earned significantly less than their predicted income in jobs that required higher levels of education. The authors concluded that educational credentials were thus significant barriers to entry, and that the returns to education might be reduced by as much as 50 per cent in some high-paying occupations in the absence of such screening.

Taubman and Wales also found large differences in earnings for a given level of education due to college *quality*. For example, dropouts from colleges ranked in the top fifth of colleges earned more than graduates of colleges ranked below the top fifth. Similarly, whilst a graduate from a low-quality university earned 53 per cent more than the average high school leaver, a graduate from a quality university earned 98 per cent more.

As was the case with Ashenfelter and Mooney, only mathematical aptitude was found to have any significant effect on earnings. Over time, the income of workers in the top fifth of the ability scale had risen at a faster rate than that of workers in the bottom fifth, and the earnings of workers in the middle of the scale were similar to the average high school graduate. Since the sample was drawn from the top half of the ability distribution, Taubman and Wales suggested that, for high school graduates and beyond, ability is a more important determinant of the range of income distribution than is education. They suggest that ability initially has little effect on wages, but that over time the effect grows, and at a faster rate for those with high ability.

Layard and Psacharopoulos (1974) – hereafter LP – criticized the ability proxies used by Taubman and Wales as being incapable of capturing all the crucial facets of ability, especially when it is assumed that firms are unable to obtain such information. They also suggested that the non-graduates who are hired for high-paying jobs are known by firms to differ in terms of non-recorded attributes (such as motivation, ambition, self-discipline) from those who are not hired. Warming to their theme, LP set out a defence of human capital theory by comparing the available empirical evidence against three predictions of the sorting hypothesis.

The first prediction considered by LP was that private returns were to certificates rather than years of education. If education is acting as a signal, certification from a course should convey more information to prospective employees about an applicant's ability than mere attendance. Wages should therefore increase faster with years of education if the year also has a cer-

Table 2.1   Completed and dropout rate of returns to education

Course	Dropout RR (%)	Completion RR %	Author
BA	15	11	Taubman and Wales (1973)
BA and MA	8	8	Taubman and Wales (1973)
High school	7	6	Rogers (1969)
BA	12	8	Rogers (1969)
High school	16.3	16.1	Hanoch (1967)
BA	7.1	9.6	Hanoch (1967)
High school	12.3	14.5	Hansen (1963)
BA	5.1	10.1	Hansen (1963)
BA	9.5	14.5	Becker (1975)

Source: Layard and Psacharopoulos (1974, p. 991).

tificate at the end of it. To test this prediction, LP compared dropout rates of return to those of course completion from a number of empirical studies (see Table 2.1) and found that in many cases (including Taubman and Wales) the rate of return for dropouts was not significantly below that for completers.

Layard and Psacharopoulos also claimed that Taubman and Wales's findings, that the effect of education on earnings rises both proportionately and absolutely with age, were evidence against sorting. The second prediction was that, holding ability constant, the effect of education on earnings would fall with worker experience as firms obtained better information about the worker's true productivity.

Finally the sorting hypothesis implies that education would not be demanded if cheaper alternative methods of sorting exist. According to LP, the sorting hypothesis implies that firms employ graduates at high wages because this is more profitable than employing non-graduates at a lower wage; firms believe that graduates are on average more able than non-graduates, and the cost of finding able non-graduates is at least as great as the wage differential between the able non-graduates and able graduates. LP argue that a private enterprise could set up an institution for the testing of non-graduates, and since no such institution has evolved this is evidence against the screening hypothesis.[8]

In the first major empirical attack on the sorting hypothesis, LP concluded that 'the theory of human capital is not after all in ruins' and that the sorting hypothesis plays an insignificant role in explaining the relationship between education and earnings.

In a defence of sorting, Riley (1979a) argued that LP's conclusions were rather suspect. Firstly, screening theorists had never suggested that firms look exclusively at certificates as a signal of ability, but rather at a vector of informational variables about workers, such as quality of schooling, grades obtained and field of study. Given the absence of these variables in some of the empirical work cited by LP, there is no reason why the rate of return should be lower for dropouts. Moreover no distinction is made between those dropouts who were forced out by the educational system, and those who were pulled out by attractive offers from firms. These latter individuals may be characterized by relatively high levels of ability and may therefore tend to increase the rate of return to dropouts.

Moreover, as we have seen, it is a necessary condition of any signalling equilibrium that a firm's conditional probabilistic beliefs are realized, and consequently one would not expect the returns to education to fall with work experience. Screening is presumably used to select able workers for jobs that require substantial on-the-job-training and, since both productivity and wages rise sharply in these jobs over time, the observed rise in the return to education is, according to Riley, hardly surprising.

Finally Riley argues that LP's critique is extreme in that they focus exclusively on 'strong' screening, where education is assumed only to signal innate productivity, and do not test the 'weak' version of the hypothesis where education both signals and enhances productivity. Since LP offer no analysis of the trade-off between the cost of sorting and productivity enhancement, their critique says nothing useful about the costs of educational screening when productivity is not immutable.

Sheepskin effects
LP's focus on the differential effects of certified and non-certified education initiated a long-running debate about the so-called 'sheepskin effects' of education.[9] Whether earnings relate to the time *spent* learning or to the credentials accumulated along the way has several important implications. There may be significant external costs associated with education if individuals ignore the effect of their investment decision on the market equilibrium. For example, additional education acquired by individuals of a given ability will raise the level of education required by the relatively more able to signal their superior talent. There may thus be a case for state intervention to *raise* the private cost of education (Riley, 1979a; Vella and Karmel, 1999).[10]

There is also the practical implication of what questions to include in labour force surveys. These usually ask about *either* years of schooling *or* highest qualifications. Indeed recent changes in the U.S. Current Population Survey reflect the belief that qualifications are the more important indicator of educational attainment, because of the effect of credentializing on labour market rewards (Kominski and Siegel, 1993).

Sheepskin effects may also be important even under weak screening. Graduates may be more efficient learners (Chiswick, 1973) and as a result may enjoy proportionately larger increases in their productivity than years of education alone would suggest. Alternatively, graduates may just have more perseverance, be better at following instruction or apply more effort. To the extent that these characteristics are valuable, owing, for example, to the likely impact of perseverance on absenteeism and quitting behaviour, firms may be willing to pay more for graduates (Weiss, 1995).

Sheepskin effects can be measured by introducing discontinuities in the years of education variable that correspond to the normal time required to complete a particular qualification. For example, if the ith and jth year of education are assumed to be synonymous with the receipt of A levels / high school diploma and bachelor's degree, respectively, an equation of the following form can be estimated:

$$\ln w = \mathbf{A}\mathbf{Z} + \mathrm{B}_1 D_i(s \geq i) + \mathrm{B}_2 D_j(s \geq j) + f(s) + \varepsilon, \qquad (2.30)$$

where w denotes the wage rate, s denotes years of education, and D_k is a dummy variable equalling one if $s \geq k$ where $k = (i, j)$. $\mathbf{Z}$ is a vector of control variables, and ε is the regression error. Most researchers model $f(s)$ as either a linear or cubic function of school years, or a linear spline with knot points corresponding to the A level/diploma and degree years.[11] An alternative is to use a string of dummy variables, one for each schooling year, thereby relaxing the assumption that education enters the wage equation linearly or piecewise linearly (Hungerford and Solon, 1987; Patrinos, 1996).

Positive estimates of B_1 and B_2 are interpreted as evidence of sheepskin effects associated with the receipt of an A level/high school diploma and a bachelor's degree. Their estimated values, $\hat{\mathrm{B}}_1$ and $\hat{\mathrm{B}}_2$, however, will be subject to measurement error if individuals take non-standard amounts of time to earn credentials. Moreover, using a battery of dummy variables for schooling years may also make the wrong comparison because the returns to a year that is usually associated with a credential are contrasted with the returns to other schooling years. A stronger test is to compare the earnings of those who have the credential and those who have not, conditional on the groups having the same number of years of schooling (Park, 1999). If information is available on both years of schooling and qualifications received, *direct* estimates of sheepskin effects can be estimated from an equation such as

$$\ln w = \mathbf{A}\mathbf{Z} + \sum_{m=1}^{M} \mathrm{B}_m D_m(s \geq m) + \sum_{n=1}^{N} \mathrm{B}_n D_n(s \geq n) + \varepsilon, \qquad (2.31)$$

where there are strings of dummy variables for both the vector of $m = 1, 2,$ ..., M qualifications and $n = 1, 2, ..., N$ years of education (Jaeger and Page, 1996). Equation (2.31) restricts the sheepskin effects associated with each qualification to be the same for all years of education received. For example, the gain in wages from having an A level compared to a GCSE is assumed to be the same regardless of whether one has 11, 12 or 13 years of education.

An even more general approach is to include separate dummies for the interaction terms for each year of education and each qualification (Jaeger and Page, 1996; Park, 1999):

$$\ln w = \mathbf{A}\mathbf{Z} + \sum_{m=1}^{M} \sum_{n=1}^{N} \mathbf{B}_{mn}[D_m(s \geq m) \cdot D_n(s \geq n)] + \varepsilon. \qquad (2.32)$$

For example $(\mathbf{B}_{Msc,18} - \mathbf{B}_{Bsc,18})$ measures the extra return to obtaining a master's degree, conditional on having 18 years of education, whilst $(\mathbf{B}_{Bsc,18} - \mathbf{B}_{Bsc,19})$ measures the extra return to obtaining an undergraduate degree after 18 rather than 19 years of study.

Several studies that infer sheepskin effects from the non-linear returns to years of education also examine the patterns across population subgroups. For example, Belman and Heywood (1991) find that women and minorities earn larger (smaller) sheepskin effects for university (high school) graduation than do white males. Signalling models that predict that minorities have smaller returns to low productivity signals but larger returns to high productivity signals are considered to be supported by this pattern (Golbe, 1985). It is not clear, however, whether these patterns across population subgroups hold up when sheepskin effects are measured directly using information on both years of education and qualifications received. Jaeger and Page (1996) and Gibson (2000), for example, find few statistically significant differences in sheepskin effects across gender and race groups and there is no consistent pattern to the differences that would lend support to the signalling model of Golbe (1985).

Another interesting pattern that has been found across population subgroups is that sheepskin effects appear to be significant for younger age cohorts but virtually non-existent for older workers (Belman and Heywood, 1997). Such a pattern would accord with predictions from a model where employers acquire additional information unorthogonal to the original educational signal about the actual productivity of their workers over time. To test their hypothesis that the returns to educational signals decline with experience, Belman and Heywood (1997) use data from the 1991 Current Pupulation Survey (CPS), split into five age cohorts. Because this CPS file has data on years of education but not on credentials, they use a linear spline with knot points at 8, 12 and 16 years of education to examine the pattern of (indirect) sheepskin effects across age cohorts.

Gibson (2003) replicates this test on New Zealand data and finds that, in direct contrast to the existing (indirect) evidence of declining sheepskin effects with age, for male workers the sheepskin effects for all qualifications except the post-school diploma are *larger* for the older cohorts, although the joint difference was not statistically significant. The results for females are even less supportive of the hypothesis, with significantly larger sheepskin effects found amongst the older workers for the university qualifications. Gibson concludes that his results are not necessarily inconsistent with the educational signalling hypothesis. As Riley (1979b) points out, a signalling equilibrium requires only that employers' conditional probabilistic beliefs are realized on average. Hence the wage increases for the workers who prove to be unexpectedly productive could offset the wage decreases for those workers who prove to be less productive than their credentials would have predicted. In other words, the effect of the signal on the level of wages is independent of labour market experience (Farber and Gibbons, 1996).

A related strand of research focuses on the information signalled by a divergence of actual years of education from 'efficient' years of education (Oosterbeek, 1992). For a given university course, 'efficient' years of study is the number of years nominally needed to obtain a degree. Human capital theory would suggest that extra time spent obtaining a degree should increase earnings since education augments productivity and the extra study time will lead to more thorough understanding of the course. Rushing through the degree, on the other hand, would result in less understanding and have a negative influence on earnings. In contrast, the signalling theory would predict that obtaining degrees in less (more) than the nominal time would signal above-average (below-average) productivity and positively (negatively) influence earnings.

Oosterbeek (1992) uses a sample of 1377 Dutch economists in 1987, and uses average test score in secondary education as an ability proxy. He finds that for a student of any ability a longer period of study increases earnings. The estimated coefficient represents a rate of return to one extra year of study of economics of approximately 8 per cent. This supports the human capital prediction that a student of any ability will find it profitable to spend longer than the nominal required time studying for their degree, and it therefore refutes the screening hypothesis that short study duration will enhance earnings.

This result appears to contradict the result of Layard and Psacharopoulos (1974) indicating that dropouts have a higher rate of return to their education than those who complete courses; both Oosterbeek and Layard and

Psacharopoulos claim to discredit the screening hypothesis, but with contrary results. However, the claim that a contradiction exists should be made with caution as we have seen that Oosterbeek was testing his own specific screening hypothesis based on efficient versus actual years of education rather than the more conventional 'sheepskin' hypothesis.

Oosterbeek and Groot (1994) develop this methodology further by decomposition of actual years of schooling into effective years, repeated years, skipped years, inefficient routing years and dropout years. Inefficient routing years are years spent on an educational path within the Dutch educational system which could have been avoided by correct routing; repeated years are years spent repeating classes; skipped years are years spent skipping classes; and dropout years are years spent in education without graduation from a course. This division of the 'schooling' variable is used to provide further evidence in the human capital versus screening debate.

The authors suggest that repeated years will have a negative effect on earnings in the screening model, since it is a 'bad' signal to employers, and a nonnegative effect in the human capital model. If the repeated year leads to increased understanding of a subject, there may be a small positive effect on earnings in the human capital framework. Indeed the two countries and samples in question are also different. The non-zero returns to dropping out in the USA may be to some extent a result of the credit system which operates in the US educational system.

Conversely skipped years will have a positive effect in the screening model and a non-positive effect in the human capital model. Inefficient routing years will have no effect on earnings in the screening model since they convey no useful information to employers, and in the human capital model they may have a positive effect if human capital is heterogeneous. The sheepskin argument of the screening models predicts that years of education without graduation from a course will have no effect on earnings, whereas the human capital model predicts a positive effect.

Oosterbeek and Groot use a detailed panel data set from surveys in 1952 and 1983 of Dutch workers. The authors find that skipped years have a significant negative effect on earnings, failing courses has a neutral effect, and dropout years have a significant positive effect on earnings. This result is analogous to that for dropouts in Layard and Psacharopoulos (1974). Overall, Oosterbeck and Groot's findings provide strong support for the human capital model and refute the screening hypothesis.[12]

'Screened' versus 'unscreened' sectors

A major implication of the sorting hypothesis is that workers acquire more education than they would do if firms could perfectly observe ability without reference to signals. Thus, for a given ability level, 'screened' workers should acquire more education than 'unscreened' workers. A number of papers have focused on this implication and attempted to investigate the sorting hypothesis by comparing the relationship between education and earnings across 'screened' and 'unscreened' groups.

The first study in this vein was Wolpin (1977) who attempted to isolate the signalling component of the rate of return to education by using self-employed people as a control 'unscreened' group, the argument being that such workers should acquire relatively less education as they have no need to signal productivity. Using the NBER-TH sample and a composite ability measure based on 17 ability tests for the US Army Air Force, Wolpin found no significant difference in the mean ability and education (measured in years) levels of the self-employed and paid employed (see Wolpin, 1977, p. 956). Assuming ability is controlled for successfully by the composite measure, and that the groups can proxy for screened and unscreened workers, Wolpin concludes that this result indicates 'only a minor screening function' for education.

However the result of similar mean education levels between the two groups is not particularly surprising because decisions about education come before the employment decision, and the choice of education does not rest entirely on employment aims. Wolpin's work does not allow for other non-monetary factors, such as social or family norms, that individuals may take into account when considering education. And, even from a purely monetary perspective, there are reasons why further education will be acquired even if an individual intends to be self-employed when leaving compulsory education. The individual cannot be sure that his plans will come to fruition and may require a certain level of education to hedge his risk in the labour market; and secondly, as Lazear (1977) suggests, certain professionals may acquire qualifications to signal the quality of their services to their potential client base.[13]

Self-selection may be another reason for the relatively low levels of education observed for the self-employed: individuals who have invested incorrectly in the educational signal act rationally in becoming self-employed to enhance income in a sector where education level is relatively less important in determining earnings. Grubb (1993) suggests that this may occur even when there is a higher risk involved in self-employment, because the highly educated may be more risk-averse and choose salaried positions despite the higher returns in self-employment.

Wolpin also found that education had a relatively larger impact on the earnings of the self-employed. This is because the two groups acquire a similar amount of education even though the self-employed in the NBER-TH sample appear to be more able. However earnings from self-employment will include some element of non-labour returns (such as profit or returns to capital), so the earnings differential between the self-employed and employees is biased upwards and this may invalidate this result. Indeed Riley (1979a) suggests that this result may in fact be consistent with the educational screening model.

Riley (1979a) presumes that screening will be more important in those sectors where productivity is relatively hard to measure. If different sectors are not segregated according to ability, a subset of types must be indifferent between working in the 'screened' and 'unscreened' sectors. But this will only be the case if, holding ability constant, jobs in the unscreened sector require less education and, holding education constant, wages in the unscreened sector are higher. Riley uses this argument to classify jobs as either low-education/above-average wages 'unscreened' or high-education/below-average wages 'screened'. He also raises the question as to how quickly firms identify true productivity. Where screening is important, one would expect the earnings function to explain wages very well early in the life cycle. Moreover, assuming that firms accumulate additional information about true productivity over the early years in the workforce, the explanatory power of education should decline. Thus the ratio of unexplained residuals for the 'screened' group to that for the 'unscreened' group should rise over time.

Riley tests these predictions on the Current Population Survey, 1971–1975 and obtains convincing evidence in support of sorting. He suggests that the weak screening hypothesis, where education signals and improves productivity, offers a more complete explanation of wage determination than human capital theory.

A number of studies have followed Wolpin (1977) and Riley's (1979a) approach. Those finding support for (at least) weak screening include Shah (1985) and Brown and Sessions (1998) for the UK, Brown and Sessions (1999) for Italy, Katz and Ziderman (1980) for Israel, Grubb (1993) for the USA and Heywood and Wei (2004) for Hong Kong. Less supportive evidence for the UK is put forward by Johnes (1998) and for the USA by Fredland and Little (1981), Cohn *et al.* (1987) and Tucker (1985).

P(sacharopoulos)-tests

A particular application of the 'screened versus unscreened' approach was adopted by Psacharopoulos (1979), who focused on the distinction between 'strong' and 'weak' screening. He argued that, under the former, wages would be set in excess of marginal productivity and would remain so even as tenure increases. Under the latter, however, wages would be revised downwards over time towards actual productivity. Psacharopoulos used data on approximately 5000 employed males from the 1975 UK General Household Survey to discriminate between the two types of screening by ascertaining whether firms remunerated in excess of marginal productivity only at the time of hiring, or continuously thereafter.

Psacharopoulos's methodology was to compare the rate of return to education across 'competitive' and 'non-competitive' sectors. These, he assumes, are characterized by different levels of screening: screening is more likely in the latter sector because wages here are more bureaucratic and linked to education, and thus can deviate from marginal products which are difficult to measure, particularly over time. Wages in the competitive sectors, on the other hand, will be largely determined by traditional market forces.[14]

Psacharopoulos classifies distributive trades as the competitive sector and public administration as the non-competitive sector, and finds that in both the ratio of mid-to-early career earnings increases with education. The differential in earnings growth, however, is more pronounced in the competitive sector, which would seem to contradict the strong screening hypothesis. Moreover estimated wage equations explain nearly twice the earnings determination in the competitive sector as compared to the non-competitive sector, whilst the returns to years of education are higher in the competitive than in the non-competitive sector. Psacharopoulos concludes that education must have an inherent productive value since it is valued more highly in the competitive than in the non-competitive sector and that, consequently, his findings refute the presence of strong screening.[15]

A number of authors have performed similar '*P*-tests' in their attempts to distinguish between strong and weak screening. Lee (1980) compares the rates of return to education in the private (competitive) and non-competitive (public) sectors of the Malaysian economy and finds that the coefficients on educational certificate dummies are generally significantly higher in the former than in the latter. Moreover his data suggest a significantly higher return to ability in the private sector which, even after on-the-job screening is accounted for, continues to place a higher value on education. Lee's finding that education has an inherent productive value is perhaps even more robust evidence against strong screening than Psacharopoulos (1979), since some potential omitted ability bias has been removed.

Other researchers who find evidence of weak, but not strong, screening from *P*-tests include Cohn *et al.* (1987), Ziderman (1992) and Lambropoulos (1992), who focus on US, Israeli, and Greek data, respectively. Tucker (1986) finds no evidence of even weak screening from US data.

All the *P*-test literature cited above presumes that the sectoral choice of employment is exogenous and thus makes no allowance for incidental sampling. Arabsheibani and Rees (1998) account for this deficit by estimating a two-stage Heckman model on UK General Household Survey data, 1985, thereby correcting any self-selection bias in the estimated returns to education. Their analysis finds no evidence of strong screening: the estimated rate of return to schooling in the private sector is actually significantly higher than that estimated for the public sector. Brown and Sessions (1998) apply a two-stage Heckman model to British Social Attitudes Survey data, 1985–1991, and similarly reject the presence of strong screening.

Wiles tests

Wiles (1974) argued that one could discern the presence of strong screening by considering the relationship to the return to education across occupations. If education acts purely to signal and/or screen intrinsic productivity, and if there is no subject-specific cost associated with its acquisition, any premium paid to workers employed in occupations directly related to their qualifications could be interpreted as evidence against strong screening. If, however, the qualification merits a premium irrespective of its relevance to a particular occupation, the strong screening hypothesis cannot be rejected. Given the detailed data sets necessary to apply the 'Wiles-test' it is not surprising to find that there appear to be only three articles which apply this methodology to data on university graduates.

Miller and Volker (1984) apply the test to the starting salaries of a sample of Australian university graduates in the fields of economics and sciences. They find that a premium is paid to graduates irrespective of the relevance of their qualification to their job and conclude that screening was 'alive and well in Australia' (Miller and Volker, 1984, p. 125). Dolton (1985) applies the test to 4000 UK first-degree graduates and finds evidence of weak, but not strong, screening. He stratifies his data according to the self-reported vocational relevance of the respondent's degree subject in their first job and finds no significant difference between the estimated earnings functions of 'relevant' and 'irrelevant' graduates. He rejects, however, the strong screening hypothesis, since certificates appear to enhance productivity, and concludes that 'there are reasonable grounds to support a compromise interpretation of the education–income association which gives credence to both human capital and screening theory but supports an extreme version of neither' (Dolton, 1985, p. 32).

Finally, Arabsheibani (1989) analyses the starting salaries of Egyptian university graduates separated by field of study. He finds that a premium is paid to graduates working in jobs where their education is relevant and thereby rejects the strong version screening hypothesis.

The hiring process

The paper by Albrecht (1981) is unique in that it tests the screening hypothesis by analysing the hiring process of the employer. Albrecht estimates a probit model in which job applicants are characterized by their education and the amount of information the hiring firm has about them. The firm is assumed to be unable to employ self-selection contracts and uses education to screen applicants. Moreover it is expected to give a positive weight to education in the hiring procedure and if part of this weight is due to an informational role then the weight should be expected to fall if alternative information is available. Albrecht therefore expects an interaction between education categories and a priori information, and a test of the hypothesis that a firm does not use education as a screen can be expressed as a test for zero interactive effects.

Albrecht's data are based on applicants for blue collar jobs at a Volvo car factory in June 1978. The critical split level between 'high' and 'low' education is assumed to be gymnasium graduation. There are three possible recruitment sources: recommendation by a Volvo employee, Swedish Labour Market Board referral or application from newspaper advertisements. The first source is assumed to be the high informational category, the second and third the low informational category.

Albrecht finds that completion of the gymnasium, Swedish or Finnish nationality and being male significantly raises the probability of being hired. Recommendation by a Volvo employee, age, and residence are insignificant determinants, as too are the education-information interaction effects. Albrecht concludes that Volvo's hiring decisions lend no support for the hypothesis that education is used for informational purposes in the hiring process.[16]

Natural experiments
Several writers have attempted to discriminate between sorting and human capital models by taking advantage of institutional and/or legislative changes to perform quasi-natural experiments. 'The basic idea underlying this new thrust of research is that instrumental features of the education system can be used to form credible instrumental variables for individual schooling outcomes that can cut through the Gordian Knot of endogenous schooling and unobserved ability' (Card, 2001, p. 1127). Lang and Kropp (1986), for example, focus on the effects of changes in mandated minimum education levels. They argue that, in a full information scenario, an increase in the school leaving age will only affect the education decision of those individuals who intended to leave school at the previous minimum leaving age, and will have no effect on those with education levels above the new minimum. Under an asymmetric information sorting scenario, however, the increase will raise the incentive for the relatively able types to acquire more education to signal that they are indeed more able. Thus the increase in the mandated level of education affects the whole of the distribution,

rather than just the bottom. Lang and Kropp test their hypothesis by examining the effects of changes in compulsory attendance laws in the USA and conclude that there is a significant 'ripple effect', as predicted by the screening model.

Chevalier *et al.* (2003) apply Lang and Kropp's (1986) test to UK data, focusing on the raising of the school leaving age (RoSLA) from 15 to 16 in England and Wales in 1973. Selecting only those cohorts that were born within the period 1953–63, the authors found that virtually all those who left school at age 15 prior to 1973 left at age 16 post-1973. There was, however, no effect on the 16-plus school leaving age distribution: the RoSLA simply shifted individuals from 15 to 16. Moreover earnings regressions showed that unqualified individuals earned significantly more in the post-RoSLA cohort, whilst there were no significant differences in the earnings of higher qualified individuals. The authors argue that the premium for unqualified individuals is consistent with a human capital story since they would have had an additional year of schooling as compared to otherwise similar individuals leaving school at 15 in the pre-RoSLA cohort.

Bedard (2001) adopts a similar approach. Her argument is that, under the educational sorting hypothesis, an environment in which some individuals are constrained from entering university will be characterized by increased pooling at the high school graduation level: potential high school dropouts and university enrollees choose the high school graduate designation in order to take advantage of high-ability individuals who are constrained from entering university. Human capital theory, in contrast, would predict higher university enrolment but identical high school dropout rates in regions with greater university access. Bedard's empirical analysis suggests that high school dropout rates are indeed higher where there is a university in close proximity, a result that is consistent with a signalling model and inconsistent with a pure human capital model.

Angrist and Krueger (1991) study the effect of birth date on returns to schooling, and find that individuals who are forced to continue in school because of the interaction between their date of birth and the school attendance law in their state enjoy the same rate of return to that education as do those who voluntarily continue their education. It might seem that this result supports a learning explanation for returns to schooling. However sorting also generates that result if employers are paying workers according to their observed characteristics and level of schooling, without adjusting for the effects of school attendance laws on individual education choices. The human capital model, on the other hand, can only generate that result if there are no aspects of individual productivity that are omitted from the wage equation and that are correlated with schooling. However post-secondary schooling is correlated with courses taken in high school, with grades on those courses, and with scores on both achievement and intelligence tests, so it seems unlikely that schooling would be uncorrelated with all other unobserved variables. In addition, in the absence of unobserved ability differences, it is difficult to explain the discontinuous changes in earnings associated with completion of high school and college.[17]

Studies that utilize changes in supply-side features of the educational system are not without their pitfalls. In a comprehensive review of the 'natural-experiment' literature, Card (2001) finds that the resulting estimates of the return to schooling typically exceed the corresponding ordinary least squares (OLS) estimates, often by 20 per cent or more. This would seem problematic given that it is generally assumed that OLS methods overestimate the true causal effect of schooling. Having considered a number of explanations for the discrepancy, Card (2001) concludes that there is an underlying heterogeneity in the returns to education, and that many of the natural-experiment studies recover returns to education for a subset of individuals with relatively high returns. Supply-side innovations generally affect the schooling choices of individuals who would otherwise have relatively low education. If this low education is a reflection of a relatively high marginal cost of schooling, rather than a relatively low marginal return to schooling, instrumental variable estimation based on school proximity and/or compulsory attendance will yield estimated returns to schooling above the average marginal return to schooling in the population, potentially even above the corresponding OLS estimates. Under this scenario both the OLS and instrumental variable estimates are likely to overestimate the average marginal return to education.

Twin studies

Perhaps the most pure natural experiment adopted in the literature has been the use of 'twin studies' which use the relationship between wages and education levels across identical twins to isolate the effect of education on earnings, holding ability differences constant. Consider for illustration the following education–earnings model. The wage of twin i in family j is assumed to be determined by

$$\log w_{ij} = \mathrm{B} S_{ij} + \Phi A_{ij} + \varepsilon_{ij}, \tag{2.33}$$

where $i = 1, 2, \ldots, I$ and $j = 1, 2, \ldots, J$. S_{ij} denotes the level of education or schooling and A_{ij} denotes the level of ability broadly defined (for example, intelligence, motivation, tenacity) and ε_{ij} is an independently and identically distributed error term. The problem in conventional (i.e. non-twin) studies is that that A_{ij} is typically poorly measured (if at all) so that estimates of (2.33) are prone to omitted variable bias. To be sure, the estimate of B in an equation such as (2.33) that excludes A_{ij} is given by

$$\hat{B}_{OLS} = B + \frac{\text{cov}(S_{ij}A_{ij})}{\text{var}(s_{ij})}. \qquad (2.34)$$

If, as would seem likely, schooling and ability are positively correlated then $\text{cov}(S_{ij}A_{ij}) > 0$ such that $\hat{B}_{OLS} > B$ and the effect of education on earnings is overestimated.[18] Assume now that 'ability' has a family-background (α_j) and genetic component (β_{ij}) such that

$$A_{ij} = \alpha_j + \beta_{ij} + \mu_{ij}, \qquad (2.35)$$

where μ_{ij} is an error term. We can rewrite (2.33) as

$$\log w_{ij} = BS_{ij} + \alpha_j' + \beta_{ij}' + v_{ij}, \qquad (2.36)$$

where $\alpha_j' = \Phi\alpha_j$, $\beta_{ij}' = \Phi\beta_{ij}$ and $v_{ij} = \Phi\mu_{ij} + \varepsilon_{ij}$. Consider now the wage equations for twins 1 and 2 in family j:

$$\log w_{1j} = BS_{1j} + \alpha_j' + \beta_{1j}' + v_{1j}, \qquad (2.37)$$
$$\log w_{2j} = BS_{2j} + \alpha_j' + \beta_{2j}' + v_{2j}.$$

The 'within-twin pair' estimator is thus

$$\log w_j = \log w_{1j} - \log w_{2j} = B(S_{1j} - S_{2j}) + (\beta_{1j}' - \beta_{2j}') + (v_{1j} - v_{2j}). \quad (2.38)$$

Equation (2.38) is attractive because it allows the family effect, α_j, to be differenced out. Moreover, if the twins are identical, $\beta_{1j}' = \beta_{2j}'$, so that the estimator reduces to

$$\log w_j = BS_j' + v_j', \qquad (2.39)$$

where $S_j' = S_{1j} - S_{2j}$ and $v_j' = v_{1j} - v_{2j}$. Thus within-twin estimation enables the returns to education to be measured controlling for that part of ability that arises from family and genetic endowments.[19]

There are two key problems with estimating an equation such as (2.39). First, it has been argued that some 10 per cent of the recorded variation in schooling is due to measurement error (Rouse, 1999). Differencing levels of schooling between twins will exacerbate this problem and render estimates of (2.39) prone to downward attenuation bias (Griliches, 1979; Ashenfelter and Krueger, 1994; Neumark, 1999).

The second issue is why identical twins should have different levels of schooling in the first place. Conventional OLS ability bias depends on the fraction of variance in schooling that is accounted for by variance in unobserved abilities that might also affect wages (Bound and Solon, 1999). Similarly, within-pair ability bias depends on the fraction of within-pair variance in schooling that is accounted for by the within-pair variance in unobserved abilities that also affect wages. This bias will be smaller if the endogenous variation is smaller within than between families. But there is no theoretical reason to assume that this is in fact the case. Indeed recent empirical evidence suggests that differences in schooling across twin pairs are due more to chance than to ability, being uncorrelated with birth order and a range of characteristics such as union status, self-employment, tenure and spouse's education. There are, however, significant correlations between average levels of family education and characteristics, and to the extent that these correlations capture differences in ability they indicate that any variation in ability is primarily between families, rather than between twins within a family (Ashenfelter and Rouse, 1998).

Weiss (1995) argues that a simple check of whether twin studies are confirming the predictions of sorting models is to analyse the wages of twins over time. The sorting model predicts that the return to schooling for all individuals should decline over time as firms acquire more information about their employees and thus are able to assign a greater weight to such information in their pay determination. Moreover the returns to schooling across twins, which are devoid of omitted variable bias, should decline more over time as compared to the return for the population. Weiss attempted to test this hypothesis on Ashenfelter and Krueger's (1994) data, but found the data were insufficient to measure it accurately. More recently, Miller *et al.* (2003) tested the hypothesis on Australian data and found that the return to education was lower amongst relatively older groups of identical twins, suggesting that the pure effect of education does decline with time in the labour market. Moreover the return to education amongst older groups of fraternal (non-identical) twins was typically higher than amongst groups of younger fraternal twins. Assuming that the returns to education for non-identical twins are biased by the omission of a measure of ability, the widening of the gap between the estimates for the two types of twins implies that the role of ability in the earnings determination process increases over time in the labour market, a result that is consistent with sorting models.

6 Final comments

Although models of sorting are increasingly popular amongst theorists and despite considerable empirical support, many labour and education economists remain distrustful of them. Why is this? One reason may be the common misinterpretation that sorting implies that education *only* signals productivity. But the pioneering theoretical work of Spence (1973), Arrow (1973) and Stiglitz (1975) only abstracted from an augmenting role for education to clarify their analysis. Indeed Arrow explicitly stated that he was merely applying Occam's Razor while, in his later work, Spence allowed for both a human capital and an informational role (see Spence, 2002). It could be argued that much of the empirical work in this area has tended to focus on too strong a hypothesis, and that in framing the debate in the context of human capital *versus* sorting, it has rather neglected the middle ground. It is certainly the case that research has tended to concentrate on the informational role of *years* of formal education. Such tests say little about the role of educational credentials as a signal of ability, and introspection would suggest that most personnel departments are perhaps more interested in certificates than in years of study.

Another disagreeable aspect of sorting models highlighted by sceptics is that they are Pareto-inefficient. As we saw in the simple Spence (1973) model, both types of workers could be made better off in the absence of signalling, and increases in the critical level of education hurt members of the high productivity group, but leave members of the low productivity group unaffected. It is unclear, however, whether there will be too much or too little education. Individuals may acquire more education than a job requires as a way of signalling potentially attractive attributes such as tenacity and self-discipline, or firms may demand more education than is requisite for a particular job as a way of discouraging potential absenters. In these cases the private rate of return to education will exceed the social rate of return.

Alternatively sorting may improve the match between workers and jobs, in which case the social rate of return from schooling may exceed the private rate of return (Stiglitz, 1975). Assume, for example, that individuals who find education more (less) costly to acquire have an absolute advantage in unskilled (skilled) jobs, and that employers are unable to observe the productivity of workers or to identify the different worker types. If those individuals who find education relatively less costly choose more education to separate themselves, average productivity and wages in the low-skill jobs rises, implying a social rate of return in excess of the private rate of return. Critics would argue that markets should emerge to remove these inefficiencies: for example using direct testing to reveal previously unobserved employee characteristics. That they have not, they conclude, is strong evidence against sorting.

There is undoubtedly an instinctive unease with anything that suggests the impact of education is overstated. But even the most virulent advocates of sorting would concede that education improves productivity in certain technical and managerial jobs. If such increases raise the demand for less-skilled labour, or if skilled and unskilled labour are complements, the coefficient on education in a wage regression might actually underestimate the impact of education on productivity. Moreover, if there is an element of job-matching with better educated workers having an absolute disadvantage in unskilled jobs, there will be additional downward biases in estimated returns to schooling. Such externalities could depress the private rate of return to education relative to the social rate, and may outweigh the sorting effects that cause private returns to overestimate social returns to schooling.

There is also an issue as to the general applicability of sorting. Evidence of screening has been found in Israel, Japan, Singapore and Australia, but not in Greece, Malaysia, the Netherlands, Sweden and Egypt. Mixed results have been found in the UK and the USA, while there is an almost complete absence of evidence in Western European countries such as France, Germany, Italy, Spain and Portugal. The extent to which education is used as a screen and/or signal must surely depend upon the nature of indigenous educational systems and labour markets. Some countries may have a policy of employing only university graduates as civil servants, others may have a system of 'closed shops' operating amongst professionals that specifies certain job-related qualifications. It is surely imprudent to generalize results across widely dissimilar countries.

As a final word, it is perhaps important to make the point that, whether education augments or sorts productivity, it is still one of the most valuable and 'human' activities in which individuals and societies can engage. Our desire to learn is hard-wired into our brains, and our thirst for knowledge is what separates us as a species. We do not need to justify the building of schools and universities because of their potential impact on economic growth. We should build them because they ameliorate our lives.

Notes

1. For excellent retrospectives of the sorting literature see Riley (2001) and Spence (2002).
2. In signalling models it is assumed that employees make the first move, choosing the level of education necessary to signal their inherent productivity to potential employers. Screening models, in contrast, assume that employers make the first move, setting a required level of education that discriminates between particular types of applicants. In what follows we use the term 'sorting' to describe both signalling and screening.
3. In terms of the original Spence (1973) analysis, there is no guarantee that a signalling equilibrium will be efficient (see Sicherman, 1991).
4. It could be argued that the debate is equally redundant at the social level. The fact that firms still pay higher wages to more educated workers means that either education raises productivity or it most efficiently signals desirable, but unobservable, individual characteristics (Lang, 1994).
5. Again notice the degenerative nature of this equilibrium. The firm's beliefs regarding $y < y^*$ are not disconfirmed because there are no data about such levels of y.

6. The possibility of a state of constant flux has encouraged economists to develop alternative equilibrium concepts. Riley (1979a) developed a 'reactive equilibrium' approach in which employers refrain from offering pooling contracts, such as δ in Figure 2.9, even when $q < 0.5$, because they realize that rival employers would offer separating contracts that would attract the best workers away from δ, leaving them with the least productive workers and, should they continue with δ, losses. Wilson (1977) made a similar criticism of the 'cream-skimming' contracts depicted in Figure 2.8. His 'anticipatory equilibrium' approach argued that a pooling contract such as A could survive in equilibrium because the emergence of a cream-skimming contract, such as B, which would initially attract only the more productive workers, would cause the pooling contract to make losses and be withdrawn from the market. With nowhere else to go, the least productive workers would be obliged to take B, rendering B loss-making since it offers a wage greater than average productivity of $2 - q$. Anticipating this, employers would not offer B and hence A survives as an equilibrium.

7. The robustness of the education coefficient to variations in ability has been taken to imply that unobserved ability differences do not have important effects on productivity. But it is usually assumed in signalling models that firms are unable to observe the attributes that affect worker productivity but which are omitted from a standard wage equation. Instead firms will attempt to use education signals as a way of inferring unobserved attributes. Such a process is fully captured by the coefficient on education and, importantly, would not be affected by the inclusion of additional unobservable explanatory variables. Irrespective of whether it is possible to record accurately attributes such as IQ, ambition or perseverance, if the firm does not have that information available then, according to the sorting model, including these variables in the wage equation will not affect the coefficient on schooling.

8. Such an argument is rather tenuous. As Stiglitz (1975) points out, there is an externality effect here and no single firm would be willing to embark on such a project given that other firms will poach high ability non-graduates. Thus the institution would have to be independent from any production process apart from the provision of information at a cost below the pay differential between graduates and non-graduates. As Wiles (1974) contends, although aptitude tests could be cheap for firms to use, educational screening occurs because the education system is subsidized, and it is therefore relatively cheaper for the firm to use education as a screening device.

9. The term originates from the tradition of presenting diplomas on parchments that are made from the skin of a sheep.

10. An implication of this argument is that the wage for a particular job depends upon a worker's relative educational attainment: an increase in the average level of schooling holding an individual worker's education constant should lead to a decline in that worker's remuneration. Johnes (1998), however, finds no evidence of such an effect from *International Social Survey Programme (ISSP)* data.

11. Hungerford and Solon (1987), for example, use the cubic and the linear spline; Belman and Heywood (1991, 1997) use the linear spline; Jaeger and Page (1996) use the linear spline; Park (1999) uses the simple linear function of school years.

12. Other studies in this vein include Sakamoto and Chen (1992) and Kroch and Sjoblom (1994). Sakamoto and Chen estimate logarithmic income functions for Japanese males with the human capital and sorting effects of education measured respectively by the number of years of education completed and the percentile ranking in distribution of years of education for the respondent's age cohort. They find that screening reduces the human capital effect of education by one-third. Kroch and Sjoblom (1994) extend Sakamoto and Chen's analysis to control for gender and find some support for the weak screening hypothesis for white females and non-white males but that overall the signalling role of education is small in comparison to its human capital role.

13. Tucker (1987) fails to find support for such 'consumer screening' amongst professional groups. However it is common practice to omit professional occupations to avoid possible biases due to consumer screening, when testing the screening hypothesis. Another explanation of high education amongst the self-employed is that they are screened by govern-

ment agencies or banks, so that not all those who wish to become self-employed can and those that do may be educationally screened to a certain extent by these institutions.

14. Ziderman (1990) criticizes the *P*-test methodology of analysing mid-to-early-career earnings ratios. The assumption is that screening implies irrational behaviour on the part of employers in paying wages to educated employees in excess of their productivity. But screening models generally presume profit-maximizing firms who pay wages equal to productivity. Ratio tests may therefore be unable to ascertain whether the high wages of educated workers reflect innate or augmented productivity.

15. Psacharopoulos concedes that no allowance is made for other factors that influence earnings, and that no ability measure is available in the data he uses. Such an omission may be inducing a potential source of bias with higher returns to higher levels of education simply reflecting efficient screening, in that those with higher ability have acquired higher levels of education compared to those with lower abilities.

16. It could be argued that, by using the hiring decision of the company as the dependent variable in his model, Albrecht has introduced a potential source of bias in his results. The decision to hire will also depend upon the interview performance of an applicant, a factor which is not controlled for. It may be the case that the number interviewed (i.e. who pass the educational filtering process) does not correspond to the number hired (i.e. who pass the second screening process). The omission of an interview performance variable may bias results away from the role of education as an information source since there is undoubtedly much alternative information to be gathered from an interview.

17. In a related literature, Card and Krueger (1992) and Weiss (1995) attempt to discriminate between sorting and human capital models by examining the relationship between class size, educational attainment and earnings. See Chapter 9 of the present volume for an extensive discussion.

18. Taubman (1976a, 1976b) found that not controlling for genetics and family background in earnings–education regressions may cause an overestimation of coefficients of up to two-thirds, since a significant proportion of the variance in earnings can be attributed to these factors. However Griliches (1977) and, more recently, Hogan and Rigobon (2002), conclude that the biases generated by omitted ability and negative measurement error tend to cancel each other out.

19. The presumption here, of course, is that ability is only affected by genetic endowment. This is open to question; see, for example, Griliches (1979), Bound and Solon (1999) and Neumark (1999).

References

Akerlof, G.A. (1970), 'The market for lemons: qualitative uncertainty and the market mechanism', *Quarterly Journal of Economics*, **84**, 488–500.

Albrecht, J.W. (1981), 'A procedure for testing the signalling hypothesis', *Journal of Public Economics*, **15**, 123–32.

Angrist, J. and A. Krueger (1991), 'Does compulsory school attendance affect schooling and earnings?', *Quarterly Journal of Economics*, **106**, 979–1014.

Arabsheibani, G. (1989), 'The Wiles Test revisited', *Economics Letters*, **29**, 361–4.

Arabsheibani, G. and H. Rees (1998), 'On the weak versus the strong version of the screening hypothesis', *Economics of Education Review*, **17** (2), 189–92.

Arrow, K. (1973), 'Higher education as a filter', *Journal of Public Economics*, **2** (3), 193–216.

Ashenfelter, O. and J.D. Mooney (1968), 'Graduate education, ability and earnings', *Review of Economics and Statistics*, **50**, 78–86.

Ashenfelter, O. and A. Krueger (1994), 'Estimating the returns to schooling using a new sample of twins', *American Economic Review*, **84**, 1157–73.

Ashenfelter, O. and C. Rouse (1998), 'Income, schooling and ability: Evidence from a new sample of identical twins', *Quarterly Journal of Economics*, 253–84.

Becker, G.S. (1975), *Human Capital*, Chicago: University of Chicago Press.

Bedard, K. (2001), 'Human capital versus signalling models: university access and high school dropouts', *Journal of Political Economy*, **109**, 749–75.

Belman, D. and J. Heywood (1991), 'Sheepskin effects in the returns to education: an examination', *Review of Economics and Statistics*, **73** (4), 720–24.

Belman, D. and J. Heywood (1997), 'Sheepskin effects by cohort: implications of job matching', *Oxford Economic Papers*, **49** (4), 623–37.

Bound, J. and G. Solon (1999), 'Double trouble: on the value of twins-based estimation of the return to schooling', *Economics of Education Review*, **18**, 169–82.

Brown, S. and J.G. Sessions (1998), 'Education, employment status and earnings? A comparative test of the strong screening hypothesis', *Scottish Journal of Political Economy*, **45** (5), 586–92.

Brown, S. and J.G. Sessions (1999), 'Education and employment status: a test of the strong screening hypothesis in Italy', *Economics of Education Review*, **18**, 397–404.

Card, D. (2001), 'Estimating the return to schooling: progress on some persistent econometric problems', *Econometrica*, **69** (5), 1127–60.

Card, D. and A. Krueger (1992), 'Does school quality matter? Returns to education and the characteristics of public schools in the United States', *Journal of Political Economy*, **100**, 1–40.

Chevalier, A., C. Harmon, I. Walker and Y. Zhu (2003), 'Does education raise productivity, or just reflect it?', mimeo.

Chiswick, B. (1973), 'Schooling, screening and income', in L. Solomon and P. Taubman (eds), *Does Schooling Matter?* New York: Academic Press.

Cohn, E., B. Kiker and M. Mendes De Oliveira (1987), 'Further evidence on the screening hypothesis', *Economics Letters*, **25** (2), 89–294.

Dolton, P.J. (1985), 'Signalling and screening in the graduate labour market', Hull Economic Research Paper no. 123.

Farber, H. and R. Gibbons (1996), 'Learning and wage dynamics', *Quarterly Journal of Economics*, **111** (4), 1007–47.

Fredland, J.E. and R.D. Little (1981), 'Self-employed workers: returns to education and training', *Economics of Education Review*, **1** (3), 315–37.

Gibson, J. (2000), 'Sheepskin effects and the returns to education in New Zealand: do they differ by ethnic groups?', *New Zealand Economic Papers*, **34** (2), 201–20.

Gibson, J. (2003), 'Time or paper? A direct test for sheepskin effects in the returns to education?', mimeo, University of Waikato.

Golbe, D. (1985), 'Imperfect signalling, affirmative action, and black–white wage differentials', *Southern Economic Journal*, **51** (4), 842–8.

Griliches, Z. (1977), 'Estimating the returns to schooling: some econometric problems', *Econometrica*, **45** (l), 1–22.

Griliches, Z. (1979), 'Sibling models and data in economics: beginnings of a survey', *Journal of Political Economy*, **87**, S37–S65.

Grubb, W.N. (1993), 'Further tests of screening on education and observed ability', *Economics of Education Review*, **12** (2), 125–36.

Hanoch, G. (1967), 'An economic analysis of earnings and schooling', *Journal of Human Resources*, **2**, 310–29.

Hansen, W.L. (1963), 'Total and private rates of return to investment in schooling', *Journal of Political Economy*, **71**, 128–40.

Heywood, J.S. and X. Wei (2004), 'Education and the signalling hypothesis: evidence from a highly competitive labour market', *Education Economics*, **12** (1), April (in press).

Hogan, V. and R. Rigobon (2002), 'Using heteroscedasticity to estimate the returns to education', NBER Working Paper 9145.

Hungerford, T. and G. Solon (1987), 'Sheepskin effects in the returns to education', *Review of Economics and Statistics*, **69** (1), 175–8.

Jaeger, D. and M. Page (1996), 'Degrees matter: new evidence on sheepskin effects in the returns to education', *Review of Economics and Statistics*, **78** (4), 733–9.

Johnes, G. (1998), 'Human capital versus sorting: new data and a new test', *Applied Economics Letters*, **5** (2), 85–8.

Katz, E. and A. Ziderman (1980), 'On education, screening and human capital', *Economics Letters*, **6**, 81–8.

Kominski, R. and P. Siegel (1993), 'Measuring education in the Current Population Survey', *Monthly Labour Review*, **116** (9), 34–8.

Kroch, E.A. and K. Sjoblom (1994), 'Schooling as human capital or a signal: some evidence', *The Journal of Human Resources*, **29** (1), 156–79.

Lambropoulos, H.S. (1992), 'Further evidence on the weak and the strong versions of the screening hypothesis in Greece', *Economics of Education Review*, **11** (1), 61–5.

Lang, K. (1994), 'Does the human capital / educational sorting debate matter for development policy?', *American Economic Review*, **84** (1), 353–8.

Lang, K. and D. Kropp (1986), 'Human capital versus sorting: the effects of compulsory attendance laws', *Quarterly Journal of Economics*, **101** (3), 609–24.

Layard, R. and G. Psacharopoulos (1974), 'The screening hypothesis and the returns to education', *Journal of Political Economy*, **82** (5), 985–98.

Lazear. E. (1977), 'Academic achievement and job performance: a note', *American Economic Review*, **67**, 252–4.

Lee, K.H. (1980), 'Screening, ability, and the productivity of education in Malaysia', *Economics Letters*, **5**, 189–93.

Miller, P.W. and P.A. Volker (1984), 'The screening hypothesis: an application of the Wiles Test', *Economic Inquiry*, **22**, 121–7.

Miller, P.W., C. Mulvey and N. Martin (2003), 'A test of the sorting model in Australia', mimeo, Business School, The University of Western Australia.

Mincer, J. (1974), *Schooling, Experience and Earnings*, New York: Columbia University Press.

Neumark, D. (1999), 'Biases in twin estimates of the return to schooling', *Economics of Education Review*, **18**, 143–8.

Oosterbeek, H. (1992), 'Study, duration and earnings – a test in relation to the human capital versus screening debate', *Economics Letters*, **40**, 223–8.

Oosterbeek, H. and W. Groot (1994), 'Earnings effects of different components of schooling: human capital versus screening', *Review of Economics and Statistics*, **76** (2), 317–21.

Park, J. (1999), 'Estimation of sheepskin effects using the old and new measures of educational attainment in the Current Population Survey', *Economics Letters*, **62** (3), 237–40.

Patrinos, H. (1996), 'Non-linearities in the returns to education: sheepskin effects or threshold levels of human capital?', *Applied Economics Letters*, **3** (3), 171–3.

Psacharopoulos, G. (1979), 'On the weak versus the strong version of the screening hypothesis', *Economics Letters*, **4**, 181–5.

Psacharopoulos, G. (1994), 'Returns to investment in education: a global update', *World Development*, **22** (9), 1325–43.

Riley, J. (1979a), 'Informational equilibria', *Econometrica*, **47**, 331–59.

Riley, J. (1979b), 'Testing the educational screening hypothesis', *Journal of Political Economy*, **87** (5), S227–S252.

Riley, J.G. (2001), 'Silver signals: twenty-five years of screening and signalling', *Journal of Economic Literature*, **34**, 432–78.

Rogers, D.C. (1969), 'Private rates of return to education in the United States: a case study', *Yale Economic Essays*, **9**, 89–134.

Rothschild, M. and J.E. Stiglitz (1976), 'Equilibrium in competitive insurance markets: an essay on the economics of imperfect information', *Quarterly Journal of Economics*, **90** (4), 629–49.

Rouse, C. (1999), 'Further estimates of the economic return to schooling from a new sample of twins', *Economics of Education Review*, **18**, 149–57.

Sakamoto, A. and M.D. Chen (1992), 'Effect of schooling on income in Japan', *Population Research and Policy Review*, **11** (3), 217–32.

Schultz, T. (1961), 'Investment in human capital', *American Economic Review*, **51**, 1–17.

Shah, A. (1985), 'Does education act as a screening device for certain British occupations?', *Oxford Economic Papers*, **37**, 118–24.

Sicherman, N. (1991), 'Over-education in the labour market', *Journal of Labor Economics*, **9** (2), 101–22.

Spence, M.A. (1973), 'Job market signalling', *Quarterly Journal of Economics*, **87**, 355–74.

Spence, M.A. (2002), 'Signalling in retrospect and the informational structure of markets', *American Economic Review*, **92** (3), 434–59.

Stigler, G.J. (1962), 'Information in the labour market', *Journal of Political Economy*, **70**, 94–105.

Stiglitz, J.E. (1975), 'The theory of "screening", education, and the distribution of income', *American Economic Review*, **65** (3), 283–300.

Taubman, P.J. (1976a), 'The determinants of earnings: genetics, family, and other environments: a study of white male twins', *American Economic Review*, **66** (5), 858–70.

Taubman, P.J. (1976b), 'Earnings, education, genetics and environment', *Journal of Human Resources*, **11** (4), 447–61.

Taubman, P.J. and T.J. Wales (1973), 'Higher education, mental ability and screening', *Journal of Political Economy*, **81**, 28–55.

Tucker I.B. (1985), 'Use of the decomposition technique to test the Educational Screening Hypothesis', *Economics of Education Review*, **4** (4), 321–6.

Tucker I.B. (1986), 'Evidence on the weak and the strong versions of the screening hypothesis in the United States', *Economics Letters*, **21**, 391–4.

Tucker, I.B. (1987), 'The impact of consumer credentialism on employee and entrepreneur returns to higher education', *Economics of Education Review*, **6** (1), 35–40.

Vella, F. and T. Karmel (1999), 'Evaluating the impact of educational expansion', *Australian Economic Papers*, **38** (3), 310–27.

Weiss, A. (1995), 'Human capital vs. signalling explanations of wages', *Journal of Economic Perspectives*, **9** (4), 133–54.

Wiles, P. (1974), 'The correlation between education and earnings: the external-test-not-content hypothesis (ETNC)', *Higher Education*, **3** (1), 43–58.

Wilson, C. (1977), 'A model of insurance markets with incomplete information', *Journal of Economic Theory*, **16**, 167–207.

Wolpin, K.I. (1977), 'Education and screening', *American Economic Review*, **67**, 949–58.

Ziderman, A. (1990), 'The role of educational certification in raising earnings: evidence from Israeli census data', *Economics of Education Review*, **9** (3), 265–71.

Ziderman, A. (1992), 'Evidence on screening: P-tests for Israel', *Economics of Education Review*, **11**, 67–9.

3 The economic assessment of training schemes

Peter J. Dolton

1 Introduction

Many countries[1] at one time or another have introduced large-scale state-run training schemes in an attempt to alleviate youth unemployment problems. This chapter provides an economic assessment of these training schemes. The focus will be primarily on recent non-experimental international empirical econometric evidence, although the literature relating to experimental investigations is set in context in section 2. The main question which merits careful attention is, to what extent has such expenditure and government intervention been justified? Therefore there is an important need to evaluate the effectiveness of these training programmes. To describe the basic issues, and introduce some notation in such an evaluation, a simple cost–benefit model is discussed in section 3.

The potential for evaluation of government-led training schemes has been enhanced in recent years with the collection of new cross-section and panel data relating to the labour market histories of young people. These data sets contain information about the jobs and training spells of the respondents, along with the unemployment experiences which may punctuate or even prevent the school-to-work transition. Details of participation in government-sponsored training schemes are known, permitting an evaluation of such schemes in helping the employment prospects of the individuals. However the availability of such detailed data presents us with a range of complex econometric modelling problems. The basic econometric framework for empirical questions is outlined in section 4 and elaborated in sections 5 and 6. Confounding factors are discussed in section 7 and an overview of the existing empirical work is later provided in sections 8 and 9.

The most well-known econometric problem with non-experimental data used to attempt to assess the potential earnings effects of training programmes is that of sample selection bias (Heckman, 1979). Such bias may be removed by the use experimental econometric methods (Fraker and Maynard, 1987; Lalonde, 1986). There are also other econometric problems with assessments of earnings effects including attrition bias in panel or longitudinal data (Hausman and Wise, 1979) as well as the standard array of endogeniety and specification issues. These problems are discussed in section 5. Research on the employment effects of training often involve duration data econometric methods. Of central importance in these data sets is the explanation of the probability of leaving unemployment or transiting to a job over time, conditional on training history. Many papers model this re-employment probability with the use of semi-parametric and non-parametric hazard function estimation. Care should be taken to allow for the censoring problems associated with those who have still not left unemployment at the time of the survey. Other technical econometric problems arise in an examination of data of this kind including unobserved heterogeneity, the inappropriate nature of parametric error assumptions in structural models, censoring and the presence of time-dependent covariates, to name but a few. The consequences of these econometric problems are discussed in more detail in section 6.

This chapter is a selective survey of the economic assessment of training schemes. As such it is distinct from other surveys which are general background overviews on the economics of training (Ziderman, 1978; Chapman, 1993), general assessments of active labour market policy (ALMP) (Riddell, 1991; Heckman *et al.*, 1999), experimental evaluations of training programmes (Burtless and Orr, 1986), the properties of estimates of earnings effects of training in non-experimental econometric studies (Heckman and Robb, 1985a, 1985b) and the effects of different kinds of job creation schemes and their relative merits, based on evidence in Sweden and the USA (Bjorklund *et al.*, 1991).[2] There has also been a thorough survey of the earnings effects of training by Barnow (1987),[3] but this concentrated only on evidence from the USA training programmes. This was updated in Haveman and Hollister (1991)[4] and then later by Lalonde (1995). The chapter is not a survey of the institutional arrangements for different training schemes which have been used, for example, in the UK over the last 30 years (see Metcalf, 1982; Finn, 1987; Chapman and Tooze, 1987; Sheldrake and Vickerstaff, 1987; Ainley and Corney, 1990; Shackleton, 1992; Aldcroft, 1992; Bradley, 1994), nor does it describe the changes in training and labour markets which have taken place in the UK in recent years (see HMSO, 1992; Evans, 1992; Dolton, 1993; King, 1995; Price, 2000; Ryan, 2002; Van Reenen, 2003 for summaries).[5] Also we do not consider, in detail, the large array of policies which have been implemented in the USA (see Hamermesh, 1971; Bloch, 1979; Johnson, 1979; Gay and Borus, 1980; Dickinson *et al.* 1986; Heckman *et al.*, 1987; Lalonde and Maynard, 1987; Bryant and Krupp, 1987; Hotz, 1992; Friedlander *et al.*, 1997; Greenberg, 1997). The most comprehensive review of the different policies is provided in Heckman *et al.* (1999). We do not attempt cross-country comparisons: there are relatively few such genuine comparisons of youth training, one exception being provided by Tan *et al.* (1991). Finally, although the chapter summarizes the main econometric challenges of the assessment of training programmes, our discussion is not exhaustive; the reader is referred to Heckman *et al.* (1999) and Blundell and Dias (2000) for this. In practice the majority of research papers in this area examine non-experimental outcomes at a specific point in time.

The emphasis of this chapter is to discuss the different possible approaches to the assessment of training schemes and consider the outcomes of such programmes over time and the wider policy context of the policy appraisal. This chapter puts into context the various types of econometric study which can be used for the evaluation of training schemes and the econometric modelling issues associated with most commonly available panel data. At the same time we briefly review the main empirical evidence relating to the adoption of countrywide, state-run training programmes, where appropriate, placing in context both cost–benefit studies, experimental and non-experimental research and empirical findings.

2 The assessment of training schemes: a background

The main prediction of human capital theory (Mincer, 1974; Becker, 1975) is that human capital investment will yield a return in the labour market. Therefore appropriate investment in training, whether on-the-job or off-the-job, will enhance productivity and hence earnings. However it was suggested long ago (see Pigou, 1912 and Hashimoto, 1981) that firms would underinvest in general training. Human capital theory also suggests that the firm will only have an incentive to finance firm-specific human capital acquisition since the reward to general human capital investment is hard for a firm to appropriate. These ideas led to the idea of a 'poaching externality' in which firms have an incentive to hire the trained workers from other firms. Since the development of human capital theory, there has been a slow growth in the economic theory of training,[6] most of it taking place in the last decade.

More importantly at the economy-wide level it has commonly been suggested (see Finegold and Soskice, 1988; Ritzen, 1991) that, if training is left exclusively to provision in the private sector by firms, those firms may underinvest in training relative to what is optimal for the economy.[7] A practical explanation offered for this market failure has been that firms would be unable to gain a return on this training if it were generally human capital-augmenting rather than firm-specific in nature. One radical solution to this market failure in training provided by the private sector is the introduction of a state-run training programme. The economic case for such programmes is difficult to assess. More specifically what does a training programme do for an individual and what might be the consequences for the economy and society? The answer to these questions is crucial to the assessment of training schemes. In this section we describe briefly some of the suggested effects of training on the individual, the firm and society.

The simplest assertion is that training increases the individual's human capital and enhances their employment probability. In this context it is not surprising that the predominant approach to the evaluation of training in the earliest studies (Borus, 1964, 1972; Thomas *et al.*, 1969; Ziderman, 1969, 1975a, 1975b; Oatey, 1970) was to perform a cost–benefit analysis based on aggregate data relating to mean post-training earnings of trainees and non-trainees and aggregate employment probabilities of the two groups. In essence the literature posed the most interesting question, namely, what is the overall economic case for training when all the costs and benefits of the scheme have been taken into account? The problem with this approach is that it relied on aggregate data which do not allow us to assess adequately the effect of training on an individual's earnings or employment effects, controlling for interpersonal differences. The cost–benefit approach also fails to control for the possibility that those who enter training may be much more highly motivated than those who do not and would anyway have secured a better wage and/or employment prospects. Fresh new insights into the assessment of training have been made possible with the advent of large-scale panel and cross-section individual data.

The second generation of studies attempted to use cross section data and concentrated on the rigorous evaluation of the earnings consequences of training. The earliest attempt (by Ashenfelter, 1978) was to adopt a human capital view that such training is an investment and its evaluation amounts to calculation of the rate of return on this investment. This led to a preoccupation with wage effects of trainees in jobs after their training courses. Later studies, for example Card and Sullivan (1988), Whitfield and Bourlakis (1990) and Main and Shelly (1990), have sought to focus instead on the proposition that such training enhances the probability of employment at some future date. Later work (Dolton *et al.*, 1994c) took the next logical step in evaluation by considering how long it takes to make the transition from school to work.

The problem of measuring the effects of training is complex. One may easily be able to consider employment and wage effects in the short run in the form of an increased probability of leaving the unemployment state and the earnings in work. However what could be much more important are the potential long-run effects of training. These long-run effects could be in the form of enhanced labour force participation over the whole work history and the long-run growth in earnings effects of the additional human capital. Another dimension of the value of training often overlooked is the possibility that training helps to alleviate 'underemployment' over the life cycle of the individual (see Hutt, 1939). That is to say, the individual who has acquired training may gain more suitable employment commensurate with their talent, ability and potential productivity, simply by having received training: the quality of the match (Jovanovic, 1979a; Barron *et al.*, 1989) of trained individuals is higher because more time has been spent in the transition process of pairing the individual employee with the right job and employer which may, in turn, mean that the individual's talents correspond more closely to their job requirements. There is very limited empirical evidence of the long-run effects of state training programmes. One paper by Dolton *et al.* (1999) suggests that the negative effects found by other authors could dissipate as little as seven years later in the labour market. Indeed there is some evidence of positive effects for women of state training programmes in the medium term.

Another view of government-led training schemes is that employers use them as a screening or signalling device to filter out the most promising trainees in order to decide which individuals to employ. Empirical evidence for this view has been provided by Sako and Dore (1986) and Begg *et al.* (1991) based on a survey of employers. They suggest that employers undervalue such schemes as human capital-augmenting mechanisms and stress their role as helping in the selection of the most able and promising employees. This is partially possible as the person can be relatively costlessly appraised while working 'on-the-job' which will invariably be a better predictor of future productivity as an employee. The value of training schemes as screens or filters for the labour market is difficult to assess.

One important negative component in the evaluation of training programmes is the scheme's 'displacement effects'. Such effects occur because the presence of schemes in which the government funds firm-based training will affect the incentives of the employers. Most notably the displacement effects can be divided into the 'deadweight loss' where employers substitute programme trainees for, say, apprentices that would otherwise have been taken on, so that in effect the firm's training bill is paid for by the government and there may be no net increase in training provision, and the 'substitution effect', where programme trainees are substituted for some other kind of workers (e.g. part-timers or older workers) and unemployment are created elsewhere. Deakin and Pratten (1987) attempted to investigate these effects by asking firms to identify whether Youth Training Scheme (YTS) placements were created by replacing jobs (either apprentices or other workers) or inducing new jobs. The answer was found to vary by firm size where the deadweight effect and the substitution effect were as large as 42 per cent and 20 per cent of jobs, respectively, for firms with under 100 employees, and 28 per cent and 4 per cent respectively for firms over 1000 employees. Further studies of the size of the displacement effects (reported in Jones, 1988) by various authors using different samples and different techniques have found the total displacement effect to be as small as 17 per cent of jobs. Hence the size of the total displacement effect (adding these estimates of the deadweight and substitution effects together) is very difficult to determine and could be anywhere between 17 per cent and 62 per cent of jobs, according to this evidence.

Not all of the externalities associated with training programmes are direct, in the form of displacement effects on jobs. Some of the negative externalities created by training programmes can be created indirectly. One such effect could be that the presence of many ex-programme trainees on the labour market could greatly increase the average length of queues for jobs for those individuals who have not been in receipt of this training. This could occur primarily because young workers are often cheaper to hire but also because their training has been undertaken recently and the attitude to employment and their work habits have not been interrupted by long spells of unemployment. This may severely affect older workers who have been made redundant.

One of the most widely held beliefs motivating the use of government-led training schemes is that they can be used as a countercyclical policy to ameliorate the worst effects of recession on youth unemployment.[8] Paradoxically it could be that the strongest positive effects of schemes are felt when the labour market is expanding rather than in a recession. This procyclical effect of training policies could be felt in both employment probabilities and earnings simply because outside a recession the chances of skilled and trained workers could be much higher than their unskilled counterparts. In contrast, in a recession very few new hires take place, and those that do are on depressed wages. Virtually no evidence exists of a cross cohort comparative nature in order to be able to assess these arguments.[9]

One additional perceived advantage of youth training schemes in times of high youth unemployment is that they may contribute to downward market pressure on the relative wages of young people. (See Junankar and Neale, 1987; Wells, 1987, for an examination of this issue.) Finn (1987) argues that this factor was heavily weighed by the Thatcher government who wished to see youth wages decline relative to adult earnings in order to stimulate growth and reduce unemployment.

A final effect or benefit of training schemes is that they may act as a powerful palliative to help the economy and society swallow the bitter pill of high youth unemployment; i.e. the existence of a state-run scheme can deflect criticism away from a government as they can defend the charge of not being sympathetic to the problem of youth unemployment by pointing to the large government expenditure which is being incurred in the programme. Such schemes may also alleviate social unrest and criminal activity which have other additional public costs.[10]

From the preceding discussion it should be evident that the economic assessment of training programmes is extremely complex. In order to attempt to clarify the main issues we will present the simplest form of notation to describe the main elements of any calculation on the assessment of training.

3 The basic cost–benefit model of training assessment

Cost–benefit analysis potentially provides a framework to judge the effectiveness of a training programme. Before the limitations of this analysis can be appreciated one must set out clearly what is involved. We introduce some concepts and simplifying notation which is also utilized in describing the econometric estimation problems.

The cost–benefit analysis of training programmes can be approached at four different levels: from the viewpoint of the individual recipient of training; from the position of the individual firm contemplating taking part in the training scheme; from the standpoint of the Treasury or Exchequer in the country; and finally from the perspective of society (or the government as the embodiment of society's preferences) as a whole.

Assuming all earnings and benefits to be expressed in real terms and all indexed by the rate of inflation, that the interest rate is zero[11] (hence there is no discounting) and that there is no access to capital markets, with each individual having perfect expectations about future employment probabilities (both with and without training) and future earnings (whether with or without training), let:

W_{it}^p = what the individual i would have earned at time t if he/she had been on the training programme p,

W_{it}^n = what the individual i would have earned at time t if he/she had not been on the training programme (n),

ρ_{it}^p = the probability that individual i attending the training programme (p) will be in a job at time t,

ρ_{it}^n = the probability that individual i who has not had training (n) will be in a job at time t,

B = unemployment benefit level (which we will assume to be constant in real terms over time),

C = cost of training to the firm (assumed constant for all individuals) which is borne by the government,

A = training allowance paid to the individual by the government while training.

The time periods $t \in T$ are divided for each person between the periods they are in employment $N \subset T$ or out of work $U \subset T$.

Assume all individuals can either enter the training programme (lasting one period) at period 0 after leaving school (incurring no disutility over and above the opportunity wage) or, if they have not found work, become unemployed; i.e. assume that there is a guaranteed training programme place for the unemployed. Assume all individuals live and work for T periods and then they die. In addition we ignore students who go on to higher education, and assume they incur no negative externalities as a result of the earlier members of their cohort.

The individual's private cost–benefit calculation
We may now write down the private calculation for the individual considering their decision of whether to enter a training programme or not. The reward to training for individual i is

$$R_i^p = \sum_{t=1}^{T} \rho_{it}^p W_{it}^p + \sum_{t=1}^{T} (1 - \rho_{it}^p)B + A. \tag{3.1}$$

The rewards for not entering the training programme for individual i are

$$R_i^n = \sum_{t=0}^{T} \rho_{it}^n W_{it}^n + \sum_{t=0}^{T} (1 - \rho_{it}^n)B. \tag{3.2}$$

Therefore the rational individual will decide to train if

$$R_i^p - R_i^n > 0. \tag{3.3}$$

Looking at these expressions it is fairly clear that, if the training allowance, A, is the same as the unemployment benefit level, B, and training increases W_{it}^p relative to W_{it}^n or makes $\rho_{it}^p > \rho_{it}^n$ for some large enough range of t, it clearly makes sense for the individual to participate in a training programme. However the reverse can also be seen to be true, namely that, if $A = B$ and $\rho_{it}^p \geq \rho_{it}^n$ or $W_{it}^p \leq W_{it}^n$ for some appreciable t, it could easily be the case that participation is not rational. Making the pessimistic assumption that there is no positive effect of training on wages or employment probabilities at all, simple algebra from (3.3) shows that to ensure participation in the scheme the government would have to take away (or reduce) the right of the unemployed to unemployment benefit if they refuse to take a place on the training programme. In view of these considerations the attention which has been focused in the empirical literature on the relative size of ρ_{it}^p and ρ_{it}^n, and W_{it}^p and W_{it}^n is not misplaced.

The individual firm's cost–benefit calculation
We now turn to the individual firm's decision whether or not to participate in a national training programme.[12] In the first instance we will assume that

the effect of the training programme is to act just like an employment subsidy.[13] Initially we therefore model none of the possible productivity-enhancing effects of training, nor do we allow firms to substitute between other types of employee recruitment and the use of programme trainees.

Assume that trade unions either do not exist or are powerless to affect materially whether a firm takes on trainees and makes other workers redundant. To make the model as simple as possible, assume that capital inputs to the production process are fixed and that all workers are perfect substitutes with individuals having different marginal products which the firm can observe perfectly. The firm faces a fixed price and fixed demand for its product.[14] These assumptions simply allow us to focus on the labour costs side of the firm's decision.

Although we assume the market for labour is purely competitive we also assume that each individual has a marginal product which is larger than their wage. We characterize the labour market with government training as one in which moving jobs is costly to the individual and there is an element of firm-specific human capital involved in firm-based training. This means that a trained worker will have a lower marginal product in any other firm they could move to compared to their own firm. These assumptions will ensure that firms can pay individuals a wage which is lower than their marginal product and still retain their services.

Let k denote firms and ki denote the i employees of the kth firm. In this model, then, it is appropriate for the firm to adopt the objective of minimizing the wage bill as this would be equivalent to maximizing profits (which in this case will simply be the sum of differences between the marginal product and the wage of the employees).

A non-participant firm at time t incurs the wage bill:

$$R_k^n = \sum_i W_{ki}^n. \tag{3.4}$$

A participant firm has three types of people to consider, those who are existing non-participant employees to be kept on, $i \in n$, new training programme employees, $i \in p$, and the displaced workers, $i \in j$. A participant firm's wage bill will be:

$$R_k^p = \sum_{i \in n} W_{ki}^n + \sum_{i \in p} (W_{ki}^p - C) - \sum_{i \in j} W_{ki}^n \tag{3.5}$$

where C is the per head government subsidy to employing a programme participant.

Therefore the kth firm will participate if

$$R_k^p - R_k^n < 0, \tag{3.6}$$

which will happen provided that the wage paid to the programme participants is lower than that which would have been paid to the displaced workers. This could easily be the case if there is greater potential for exploiting young workers or if the government subsidy, C, is large enough. Making the assumption that $W_{ki}^n = W_{ki}^p \ \forall i$, then using (3.6), simple algebra shows us that the firm will participate in the training programme if $C > 0$. Under these circumstances it is not surprising that employers would seek to become actively involved in the programme, if nothing else as a potential source of cheap labour.

We now proceed to elaborate this model by permitting training to have productivity-enhancing effects and also allowing firms to replace traditional 'firm-funded apprenticeships' (or junior employees) with programme trainees.[15] Consider that the surplus value that a firm (k) derives from employing an individual (i) at time t can be denoted by ω_{ki} which equals the ith person's difference between their marginal product and their wage at time t, working for firm k. Assume that there are two types of period $(t = 0,1)$, period 0 being the first opportunity to take programme trainees. Subsequent periods are all the same and denoted as type 1 periods. Assume that the firm ordinarily retires or loses j' workers each period and recruits y young people on apprenticeships or junior jobs. It also has the programme trainees, p in period 1 and has the opportunity to retain the services of the ex-programme trainees, p' in period 1. In this context the non-participant firm would have the following rewards (Π):

$$\Pi_k^n = \sum_{t=0,1} \sum_{i \in n} \omega_{ki}^n - \sum_{t=0,1} \sum_{i \in j'} \omega_{ki}^n + \sum_{t=0,1} \sum_{i \in y} \omega_{ki}^n \qquad (3.7)$$

The rewards to a participating firm are, in period 0,

$$\Pi_{k0}^p = \sum_{i \in n} \omega_{ki0}^n + \sum_{i \in p} (\omega_{ki0}^n + C) - \sum_{i \in j} \omega_{ki}^n - \sum_{i \in j'} \omega_{ki0}^n + \sum_{i \in y} \omega_{ki0}^n \qquad (3.8)$$

and the following rewards in each subsequent period:

$$\pi_{k1}^p = \sum_{i \in n} \omega_{ki1}^n + \sum_{i \in p} (\omega_{ki0}^p + C) - \sum_{i \in p'} \omega_{ki1}^{p'} - \sum_{i \in j'} \omega_{ki1}^n + \sum_{i \in y} \omega_{ki1}^n \qquad (3.9)$$

Let $\Pi_{k1}^p = T\pi_{k1}^p$ where T is the number of type 1 periods over which the firm takes decisions. Then the firm will participate if

$$\Pi_{k0}^p + \Pi_{k1}^p - \Pi_k^n > 0. \qquad (3.10)$$

Training may mean that the $\omega_{ki1}^{p'} > \omega_{kj}^p$, i.e. that the training programme enhances the marginal product of the individual in the next period.

However this does not necessarily mean that the individual on the programme will be kept on after the period in which they provide a per head subsidy of C. Indeed it will obviously only pay the firm to keep on an individual trainee *ceteris paribus* if

$$\omega_{ki1}^{p'} - \omega_{ki0}^{p} > C; \tag{3.11}$$

that is, the amount of the increase in productivity is sufficient to outweigh the subsidy C. If this is not true then, simplistically, the firm has an incentive simply to recruit a new batch of programme trainees each year, not retaining any of them as permanent employees. In reality it is of course possible that a person's marginal product could be enhanced more in subsequent years and therefore provide an incentive for retaining a programme trainee instead of recruiting a new person.

The ability of the firm to substitute programme trainee labour for traditional apprentices or junior people will therefore depend on the size of the subsidy vis-à-vis the productivity difference. A further institutional factor is that programme trainees have to have a minimum number of days' training off the job in a year. This may be substantially more than was offered to apprentices or junior employees. This then may prevent the substitution of programme trainees for traditional apprentices in certain contexts.

As represented here the firm's decision is simplistically portrayed. It may well be that a motivation for participation by the employer is provided by economizing on employer search costs or that programme trainees genuinely have a higher marginal product, especially later in their career, which can be exploited by the firm. However the picture is further complicated by the extent to which the training provided may be firm-specific rather than general and hence not transferable to another company. In this event the individual trainee or ex-trainee may be 'bid away' by the offer of a higher wage from another firm.

The Exchequer/Treasury cost–benefit calculation
It is possible to examine the effect of training programmes on the flow of government outgoings and receipts. Assume that m is the standard rate of income tax at which everyone is taxed on all of their income. Then the Exchequer calculation will be based on the balance of expenditure on the training programme with the public finance costs of unemployment and the receipts of tax payments from an individual who receives training will provide the Exchequer with

$$R_e^p = m \sum_{t=1}^{T} \rho_{it}^p W_{it}^p - \sum_{t=1}^{T} (1 - \rho_{it}^p) B - [A + C]. \tag{3.12}$$

Against the receipts from a person who does not receive training,

$$R_e^n = m\sum_{t=0}^{T} \rho_{it}^n W_{it}^n - \sum_{t=0}^{T}(1 - \rho_{it}^p)B. \tag{3.13}$$

Assume further that the training programmes have some displacement effects making some previously employed workers unemployed to make way for the trainees. Let us write the Exchequer effects of one of these displaced people j as

$$R_e^J = m\sum_{t=1}^{T} \rho_{it}^n W_{jt} - \sum_{t=1}^{T}(1 - \rho_{jt}^n)B. \tag{3.14}$$

Therefore the Exchequer would wish to maximize:

$$\sum_{i\in p} R_e^p + \sum_{i\in n} R_e^n + \sum_{j} R_e^J - S, \tag{3.15}$$

where S is the once and for all set-up costs of the training programme. (Assume that the unemployment benefits system already exists and involves no new set-up costs.)

Here again we can easily see that, provided $A + C + S$ is relatively small compared to B, this calculation is likely, on balance, to favour the adoption of a *training* programme if either $\rho_{it}^p \geq \rho_{it}^n$ or $W_{it}^p \geq W_{it}^n$ or both, for some appreciable t or i. That is, it is easily seen that, if a *government* training scheme genuinely raises employment probabilities and/or wage of its recipients, it is possible that the benefits of such a scheme may outweigh the costs, provided that the number of displaced workers is small relative to the trained group getting jobs. Hence again we emphasize the importance of wage and employment probability effects of training programmes.

Complicating factors in cost–benefit calculations
There are an enormous number of complicating factors associated with a rigorous cost–benefit analysis of training programmes. Firstly, we have made a large number of simplifying assumptions in setting out the above notation: one would immediately want to relax them in a more detailed model.

One of the most important assumptions to relax would be that of perfect expectations about ρ_{it}^p and ρ_{it}^n, and W_{it}^p and W_{it}^n, since we would like to be able to make policy assessments based on the expected values of uncertain future returns to training allowing for attitudes to risk. In addition one would wish to introduce discounting, although this should add no substantive conceptual problems. Another important restrictive assumption which we have made is that all labour is perfectly substitutable. In reality, any firm needs a variety of differently skilled individuals to operate. It may well be that the case for training individuals in areas of skill shortage is productive and rational.

Another difficulty associated with the framework described above is that we have only looked at a partial or static expression of the simplest model. Ideally one would like to incorporate the feedback effects of the instituting of training policies in a general equilibrium model of its effects. The first steps towards the specification of such a model are taken in Bjorklund *et al.* (1991).

A fourth significant weakness of the above analysis is that it assumes that the unemployed are homogeneous. Cockx (1991), in the context of an optimal control problem, has posed the question of what is the optimal mix of unemployment benefits and training over time given some fixed budget. The model suggests that it is rational for the government to set up training programmes for the long-term unemployed at the beginning of their spell of unemployment, mainly on the grounds that their cost to the state will be proportionately higher owing to their lower probability of getting a job and hence their longer-term higher cost to the state. Although the model of Cockx's paper has some logical omissions, the results do highlight the potential importance of distinguishing between the different types of unemployed. Indeed, taken to its logical conclusion, the Cockx result would imply a pruning of youth training programmes in favour of more training for the long-term unemployed.

The cost–benefit calculation for society/government
The cost–benefit calculation for the government is considerably more complex than the simple calculation described above for the Exchequer or Treasury. The setting up, or expansion, of a government training programme will impose certain opportunity costs on the economy, in the sense that the resources used to fund the programme will not be available to the economy for use in other ways.

The main reason for the complexity of the government's decision is that it must attempt to assess the overall contribution to the aggregate societal welfare function (SWF) of the various components of the Exchequer calculation in addition to the various factors we have described above:

$$SWF\left(\sum_{i\in p} R_e^p, \sum_{i\in n} R_e^n, \sum_j R_e^d, S, ID, \mathrm{AU}\right),\qquad(3.16)$$

where *ID* represents the aggregate indirect and general equilibrium effects of the training programmes and *AU* represents the aggregate additional societal consequences of the aggregate unemployment level in different regimes. The exact effect of adopting a training programme on welfare will depend on the distributional weights attached to each of the arguments of (3.16).

Conclusion

In the event that training had very little effect on either earnings or employment probabilities we have seen (a) from (3.3) that, provided unemployment benefits are not paid to those who refuse a programme placement, there is an incentive for individuals to participate in the training programme; (b) from (3.5), disregarding productivity and substitution effects of training, that firms may participate if there is a large enough subsidy, $C > 0$, for taking trainees; and (c) from (3.15) that the Exchequer should be willing to support the scheme if the costs of the programme are low relative to benefit levels.

Even though the government may be reluctant to increase spending it may still be introduced provided there is sufficient weight given to unemployment priorities in the SWF.

Naturally the simpler case is if the effect of the training programme is to enhance significantly the probability of employment and wages of the trainees. In this case the overall effect of the programme is beneficial to the Exchequer, the economy and society as a whole, each individual firm and each employee.

The decision of firms is made more complicated when we allow the firm to substitute programme trainee labour for traditional recruits and permit the possibility of training enhancing productivity. Nevertheless our basic framework, (3.7) to (3.10), suggests that it pays firms to use programme trainees as a yearly renewable source of cheap labour provided the subsidy for taking on such a trainee exceeds (a) the productivity enhancing effect of the training for extra trainees, and (b) the surplus associated with employing an ordinary young person (or continuing to employ an existing worker). To a large extent these issues are empirical problems and therefore the introduction of this simple notation to clarify these is justified.

4   The basic econometric framework and some data considerations

The basic econometric framework

Assume that all individuals are either a programme trainee, $i \in p$ or not, $i \in n$ in period $t = 0$. What determines an individual's participation will depend on many things, including educational attainment, ability and family background. Assume that a measurable, observable subset of these factors can be summarized by Z_i.

Assume further that all trained individuals look for a job in each time period following training $t = 1 \ldots T$. Meanwhile non-trained individuals look for a job all the time $t = 0, \ldots T$. Assume that for each specific time period the individual i either gets employment, $e_{ti} = 0$, or not, $e_{ti} = 1$, or receives training.

Assume that individuals stay in a job once obtained. Then let τ_i be the number of time periods that it takes an individual to transit to a job; that is,

$$\tau_i = \sum_{t=0}^{T} e_{ti}.$$

Assume that the factors which determine τ_i may, at least in part, be captured by a vector of regressors, Q. Once in a job, an individual i earns W_{it}, which may be stochastically conditioned on a set of exogenous regressors X_{it}. Unfortunately we cannot observe earnings (or transition times) for people in regimes that have not been chosen. This then prevents the full cost–benefit kind of calculations which were described in the previous section. In essence our econometric problem is to explain the joint distribution, $f(\tau_i, r_i, W_{it}, d_i)$ over the sample, conditional on Z_i, X_{it}, Q_{it} and a parameter vector θ which captures the parametric and/or economic modelling assumptions; that is,

$$f(\tau_i, r_i, W_{it}, d_i | Z_i, X_{it}, Q_{it}, \theta) \tag{3.17}$$

in such a way as to characterize the relevant parameters which may jointly determine the time taken to get a job, τ_i, the length of the time spent in training, r_i, subsequent earnings, W_{it}, and the training programme participation decision, d_i, conditional on the relevant sets of regressors, Z_i, X_{it} and Q_{it} and a parameter vector θ. We must also attempt to allow for the inadequacy of only observing W_{it} rather than the wage a person would get if they had been in the training regime, W_{it}^p, or not, W_{it}^n. Of course we never observe the counterfactual outcome of the earnings that a person would have earned in the regime that they did not choose. Much energy has been invested by econometricians in trying to recover the best estimate of this counterfactual outcome.

In practice the complexity of adequately modelling (3.17) is too difficult without simplifying identification assumptions. In practice, applied econometricians have been forced to have more modest modelling ambitions which allow them to focus on some limited subset of estimates of θ in (3.17) which are all, to a greater or lesser extent, inadequate approximations.

Sometimes this technical and complex estimation problem has been simplified by attempting to explain the limited marginal distribution,

$$f_2(W_{it} | X_{it}, d_i, \theta_w). \tag{3.18}$$

Such research, concerned only with the wage effects of training and ignoring the possibility of sample selection bias, were 'first generation' studies of training. We will examine the conclusions of this early work on training in the next section. Slightly more sophisticated econometric work has sought to model the joint distribution of wages, W_{it} and the participation in training programme decision, d_i:

$$f_3(W_{it}d_i|Z_i,X_{it},\theta_{w'}). \tag{3.19}$$

It is convenient to call the studies which attempt to model the selection into training as well as the effect of the training, 'second generation studies'.

Others have looked only at the probability, ρ_{it}, of individuals being in employment at some fixed point of time post training:

$$f_\rho(\rho_{it}|Q_{it},d_i,\theta_\rho).^{16} \tag{3.20}$$

Recent work is concerned with investigating the time taken until transit to a job:

$$f_\tau(\tau_i|Q_{it},d_i,\theta_\tau). \tag{3.21}$$

Such modelling will take the form of hazard function estimation.

The aim of any of the above approaches is to estimate the relevant subset of θ. We must, however, be careful not to confuse some element of θ, say θ_ρ, with others, such as θ_τ. They will be generated by completely separate partial reduced form econometric models which attempt only to approximate some fraction of the general problem in (3.17).

An alternative approach taken by some researchers has been to concern themselves with the process of transition from one labour market state to another (let ι be the states which could be unemployed (u), employed (n) and in a training programme (p)). In this case the modelling of the matrix of probabilities of the various transitions P_{u} given regressors X_{it} via Markov or semi-Markov methods is an insightful approach:

$$(P_u|X_{it}) \quad \iota = n, u, p. \tag{3.22}$$

This approach of (3.22) can be seen as a discrete version of the duration model of (3.21) generalized to the situation where we are concerned with more than one labour market state.

The framework of the stylized cost–benefit analysis and the ideal of the econometric analysis will invariably bear no relation to the reality facing the applied econometrician confronted with assessment of training schemes. A first step in an appreciation of these problems is to take note of what data one would ideally like for such study and what is typically available.

Some data considerations

To some extent the problem of assessing the effects of training schemes and appraising their effectiveness can be seen as a series of data problems. In theory a rigorous econometric assessment would require complete wage and duration work history information on large panel data over a lengthy period of time. In practice of course we very rarely, if ever, have access to this quality of data, and this has a considerable bearing on the nature of the econometric modelling difficulties associated with assessing training policies. The remainder of this section will briefly describe the features of the data which will cause specific problems.

First, ideally for the accurate assessment of the wage effect of training programmes one needs panel data with repeated measures of earnings at various points of time along with complete information regarding the potential correlates of this wage, i.e. occupation, sector, type of work, hours of work and educational qualifications, as well as changes in the circumstances of the individuals in the survey between the sweeps of the survey. Such information and changes in personal circumstances need to be dated; e.g. it may be important to know the timing of the acquisition of more educational qualifications.

Second, a rigorous assessment of employment effects of training requires the complete duration data on states and spells in different states of the labour market. Preferably these data should cover a fairly long period of the working lives of the respondents in order to permit econometric modelling.

Third, in addition to the above information, the panel data discussed would also need to be supplemented by detailed information on aggregate labour market conditions in order to control for the potential influences across time which may affect the prospects of the panel.

Fourth, the data would also have to be supplemented by local labour market information regarding regional and local labour market conditions which should be used to control for the different circumstances faced by respondents in different regions and localities.

Fifth, for a full assessment of the effects of training which may include a quantification of externalities and displacement effects it would be most useful to have information from each employer on how the job was created and filled and whether it involved any displacement of existing workers. It would also be very useful to have confirming data relating to the employers' wage, hours and contractual conditions of work and such quality data, are, in practice, not usually available.

Finally, the data would need to be supplemented by information describing the changing conditions in the labour market. Thus, as well as having aggregate labour market indicators, it is also important to have such data over time. This time series information is necessary to control for the ways in which the labour market conditions, as they change, affect separate cohorts differently.

5   Econometric modelling: non-experimental studies of earnings

One clear difficulty with the assessment of wage (or employment) effects of training programmes is that often participation on a training programme does not occur randomly in a sample. For example, it is quite possible that the individuals of lower ability, with fewer education qualifications, poorer family backgrounds, fewer contacts and lower self-confidence and motivation find getting a job most difficult and are hence more likely to enter a state-run training scheme.[17] Therefore a straight comparison of participants and non-participants of a training scheme could well be invalid. Indeed, to be more specific, if the stochastic error in an equation predicting participation is correlated with the error in the equation of interest (earnings or employment probability), the parameter estimates in this equation will be biased and inconsistent. There are various ways of dealing with this problem. The main alternatives which have been used in the literature are instrumental variable (IV) methods, control function or Heckman selection estimator, the fixed effects estimator, the difference-in-differences (D-in-D) estimator and the matching estimator. We will introduce only the central idea of each of these estimators. In practice the fixed effects and D-in-D estimators can only be used with panel data but the other methods, can (at least in theory) be used with a single cross-section data set. Details can be found in Blundell and Dias (2000) and Heckman *et al.* (1999).

The issue in the models then becomes the appropriate specification and identification of econometric models which have the selection procedure explained endogenously. The economic modelling framework is basically the same as the Roy (1951) model. In this model the criterion for choice between participating in a training programme and not participating comes down to an expected value calculation comparing the returns to the two regimes, akin to the model described in section 3 above. The empirical content of this model has been extended by Heckman and Honore (1990) who show how the assumption of log normality of wages is crucial for identification of their model. Such models are known to be very sensitive to specific forms of distribution assumption (see Heckman, 1990; Manski, 1988) and identification conditions (see Goldberger, 1983; Heckman and Robb, 1986). Effectively the identification problem can be resolved if there is at least one equation-specific regressor in each equation. Typically such models are estimated with several such exogenous variables in each equation. However a further problem in this class of models has been the sensitivity of parameter estimates to alternative overidentified model specifications.

Therefore what is required is more extensive use of Hausman (1978)-type specification tests or a more rigorous approach to specification testing based on conditional moment restrictions (see Pagan and Vella, 1989). The equation to explain observed earnings W_{it} may be written as a function of exogenous regressors X_{it} and a training indicator $d_i = 1$ if training is undertaken, 0 otherwise. (In reality the most common straightforward case considered is when we only have one post-training wage observation. In this situation we could omit the t subscript on all the following equations with no loss of generality.)[18]

$$W_{it} = X_{it}\beta + d_i\alpha + U_{it}, \tag{3.23}$$

where $t = 0, \dots T$, and where the training effect is assumed invariant across individuals and time,[19] and we assume $E(U_{it}|X_i) = 0 \; \forall i,t$. In the model selection bias is present if

$$E(U_{it}|d_i,X_i) \neq 0, \tag{3.24}$$

so

$$E(U_{it}|d_i,X_i) \neq X_{it}\beta + d_i\alpha, \tag{3.25}$$

in which case the ordinary least squares estimates of regressing W_{it} on X_{it} and d_i does not yield consistent estimates of α or β.

A stochastic relationship between d_i and U_{it} can arise for a variety of reasons, since participation in a training programme may be the result of a decision by the individuals eligible for the programme, by the programme administrators, or both. Let the index, D_i, which can be considered as the latent variable (propensity to participate in a training programme) be a function of both observables Z_i and unobservables V_i;

$$D_i = Z_i\gamma + V_i. \tag{3.26}$$

Then the ith individual's training status is given by $d_i = 1$ iff $D_i > 0$, $= 0$ otherwise, where V_i is assumed to be iid across persons.

Dependence between U_{it} and d_i can arise for one of two not necessarily mutually exclusive reasons: (a) dependence between Z_{it} and U_{it}, i.e. selection on observables, or (b) dependence between V_i and U_{it}, i.e. selection on unobservables. The appeal of experimental estimators can be seen in this context since it is essentially the case that truly random selection would break this link between Z_i and U_{it} and V_i and U_{it} and facilitate the consistent estimation of (3.23).

The IV estimator

The IV method needs at least one variable in Z_i which determines participation in training but does not influence the outcome of training. Specifically Z_i needs to be uncorrelated with U_{it}, given the exogenous regressors which determine training outcomes, and also not completely determined by X_{it}. If such a variable (or variables) can be found, this will provide the required randomness in the assignment rule to identify the impact of the training treatment of interest. The problem with the IV estimator of course is the difficulty of finding a variable which basically influences training participation but not training outcomes.

The control function or Heckman selection estimator

A commonly used method for obtaining consistent estimates of training effects is to consider the earnings determination at a single point in time, distinguishing between individuals who have been on training programmes, $i \in p$, and those who have not, $i \in n$, where the model is written in the form

$$W_p = X_p\beta_1 + U_p$$
$$W_n = X_n\beta_1 + U_n \qquad (3.27)$$
$$D_i = Z_i\gamma + V_i,$$

where U_p, U_n and V_i are independently normally distributed with zero mean and variance σ_1^2, σ_2^2 and σ_v^2, respectively, and $\sigma_{12} = \text{cov}(U_p, V_i)$ and $\sigma_{2v} = \text{cov}(U_n, V_i)$. In this model we can rewrite the conditional expectation of the wage equations for the two subpopulations to incorporate truncation corrections as additional regressors: $-\phi(\psi_i)/\Phi(\psi_i)$ and $-\phi(\psi_i)/[1 - \Phi(\psi_i)]$ in the participants and non-participants equations, respectively, where $\psi_i = Z_i\delta$ and ϕ and Φ are respectively the density and distribution functions of the standard normal distribution. The correction terms in these expressions can be estimated by probit participation equations at a first stage, to get an estimate of ψ_i. Then the wage equations can be estimated (consistently) at a second stage using ordinary least squares. The identification condition for this model derived by Manski (1988) shows that, if each wage equation is determined by at least one exogenous variable that does not appear in the other wage equation, a single cross-section data set would identify the joint distribution of wages. Further work on the model described in equations (3.27) has been generalized to allow for the distribution of the errors to remain unspecified. The non-parametric identification properties for such a model have been provided by Heckman (1990).

The fixed effects estimator
One way round the sample selection problem is provided for in situations in which the dependent variable of interest is observed at more than one point in time. In this case first differencing the dependent variable may purge the selectivity bias.[20] The fixed effect estimator method has been used by a number of papers which examine the effects of training.

Assume that the pre- and post-training set of U_{it} do not depend on d_i; hence

$$E(U_{it} - U_{it'}|d_i, X_i) = 0 \quad \forall t, t', \qquad t < p_t < t',$$

where $U_{it} = \phi_i + V_{it}$,

where ϕ_i is a zero mean, person-specific component, or fixed effect, and V_{it} is a zero mean random component independent of all other values of V_{it}, $(t \neq t')$ and ϕ_i, and p_t is the time period at which training took place.

For this model consistent estimates of the impact of training can be obtained by regressing the difference between W_{it} and $W_{it'}$, on d_i, and $X_{it} - X_{it'}$.

$$W_{it} - W_{it'} = \alpha_1 d_i + (X_{it} - X_{it'})\beta + (V_{it} - V_{it'}) \quad t < p_t < t'. \qquad (3.28)$$

Notice that in this formulation the effect of time-invariant regressors drops out. An important restriction on the suitability of the fixed effects model is that the resulting estimates are critically dependent on the assumption that the effect of the individual specific error term is constant over time.[21] This assumption may be inappropriate for applications which use data separated by a number of years, yet paradoxically we are most likely to be interested in the long-run effects of training since short-term effects on earnings could be negligible or even negative.

The difference-in-differences estimator
The D-in-D estimator measures the excess wage growth for the treated relative to the non-treated, i.e.

$$\hat{\alpha}_{DiD} = (\bar{W}_t^T - \bar{W}_{t'}^T) - (\bar{W}_t^C - \bar{W}_{t'}^C) \quad t < p_t < t', \qquad (3.29)$$

where $\bar{W}^T$ and $\bar{W}^C$ are respectively the mean outcomes for the treated and comparison groups. In contrast to other estimators, there is no need for data on regressors when using the D-in-D estimator. However strong restrictive assumptions are necessary on the error composition in the modelling of outcome effects – specifically we require the same assumptions as were used in the fixed effects estimator – namely that individual specific unobserved heterogeneity is constant across time and uncorrelated with other, time-dependent, sources of heterogeneity. In addition if there are time-specific sources of unobserved heterogeneity then this will complicate matters further and imply a more stringent set of criteria for the validity of the D-in-D estimator.[22] This criticism is particularly important if there are other macroeconomic changes taking place with respect to policy over the time periods for which the panel data are being observed.

A further worrying problem with a D-in-D estimator is that the period immediately prior to the training programme may be associated with a downward shift in earnings – called 'Ashenfelter's dip' in the literature – (see Heckman and Smith, 1999, for empirical evidence and consequences of this effect for evaluation). If this happens, depending on what causes this dip, it could complicate the estimation of the treatment effect.

The matching estimator
An alternative estimator which has been extensively used in the last ten years by applied econometricians is the matching estimator. This approach can be used with cross-section or panel data, but is more commonly used with the latter as it requires a lot of controlling data. It assumes that all the sources of the heterogeneity between the trained and the untrained people come through observable factors and that, once these have been conditioned for, it is valid to compare the treated (trained) and non-treated (untrained) group. The procedure is a simple non-parametric comparison of the treated outcome with the non-treated outcomes given that the groups used for this comparison have been matched up using a propensity score derived from the probability of receiving training.

Formally, consider the determination of wages for the treatment (T) and comparison (C) groups as

$$W^T = g(X) + U^T,$$
$$W^C = g(X) + U^C.$$

The goal of evaluation is to identify the impact of the treatment on the treated:

$$\alpha_T = E(W^T - W^C | X, d = 1).$$

The matching solution is to compare directly this outcome for the treated and those who look like the treated after they have been matched using a propensity score on the probability of participation. Such a comparison is valid if the conditional independence assumption holds:[23] if $W^C \perp d | X$; that is, that the wage outcomes of the non-trained are independent of participation status, once one controls for the observable variables, X. Hence the trick is to create a quasi-experimental comparison by creating an artificial control group who are identical given observables (i.e. in terms of propensity score) to the treated group. Then, under conditional independence, a comparison between these two groups is valid and identifies the effect of the treatment on the treated. In practice of course the assumption of participation status being completely determined by observables is very restrictive as it assumes that there is no role for unobserved heterogeneity in the comparisons.

Other selectivity issues
It is also worth remembering that the selection process into training schemes may not be a simple dichotomous one, i.e. it may not simply be the case that we can easily describe the process of selection into training schemes by a probit equation. Thus, rather than training scheme places being homogeneous, we could well find that there are clearly discernible categories of training regime. Dolton *et al.* (1994c) show that there is a clear statistical difference between the UK YTS trainees according to whether they are on formal apprenticeships as well or not. Such a diversity of training regimes may require a multinomial selection process in order to capture adequately the nature of the selection process into training. The sample selection bias problems associated with such multinomial selection can be handled by using the Lee (1983) corrections. Perhaps more worrying still is the underlying nature of the whole school-to-work transition process since clearly different categories of school leavers filter through different training, unemployment or higher education channels (of considerably different lengths) on their way into the world of work. The fact that this sorting process pushes individuals into these channels largely according to ability and educational achievement is actually endogenous to the whole process of the school-to-work transition process. Another example is the New Deal for Young People (NDYP) which has been in operation in the UK since 1998. In this programme the recipients have one of four options: further education, a placement in the voluntary sector or in the environmental task force or in work experience.[24]

Modelling such a process simultaneously with training participation may require a hierarchical selectivity process which acknowledges that programme trainees have inferior values of educational qualifications compared to those who take jobs, but are likely to have higher educational qualifications than those who do not enter jobs. Such factors may make the selection mechanism complex.

Training in many countries today is very different from the era when all training was in the form of traditional apprenticeships. A large proportion of programme trainees now have placements in white-collar occupations associated with the service sector. The kind of decision they face vis-à-vis training is now therefore partly endogenous to the kind of job they wish to do. The effect of ignoring the potential sample selection bias which may exist by excluding a consideration of the endogeneity of training and occupation choice is unclear. However such occupational differences may be an important component of the gender differences which have been found in the effects of training.[25]

Other econometric problems associated with modelling earnings effects of training
There are a large variety of other econometric problems which may affect the assessment of the earnings effects of training, depending on the kind of non-experimental data being used. An important problem encountered by many studies in the USA has been that typically the data set used oversamples those experiencing the treatment (training in this case). This *choice-based sampling* problem can cause bias and this then poses the problem of the best way to boost the sample of those who have not been on training as a control group.

An obvious problem with modelling earnings W_{it} which we described formally in section 4 was the endogeneity of τ_i and d_i. That is, so far we have assumed that training programme evaluation is simply a case of comparing earnings of ex-trainees with those who have received no training. What also needs to be taken into account for these two groups is the prospect of employment and how long it takes to secure. Since this probability is very likely to be affected by whether the individual undertook training and the wage on offer, they should really be modelled simultaneously.

A third problem concerns the fact that in modelling the training, decisions and school-to-work transition of young people we should also consider the female decision of whether to participate in the labour force. Typically any sample of young people from those actively engaged in the labour market will exclude women who have decided to be out of the labour force for family reasons. This raises another potential sample selection bias problem since those women who withdraw from training (or the school-to-work transition) may not be a random sample of all women. As a result we may get biased effects of training incidence and duration for women. This is particularly important in gender comparisons with men who typically do not face the same (family-induced) participation decisions.

A fourth area of difficulty with econometric modelling of wage effects concerns the problems generated by the frequent change of labour market state of the individuals in the sample and the possible effect of bias associated with attrition from the sample.[26] Since these issues are even more of a problem in handling duration data we will consider them in some detail in the next section.

6 Econometric modelling for non-experimental studies of the transition into employment

A prerequisite for econometric modelling is the formulation of an adequate economic theory. In the case of the evaluation of training it is debatable whether a satisfactory theory exists of what induces individuals to invest in training, what determines a firm's allocation of resources to training and what conditions a government's view regarding the provision of subsidy to either the individual or the firm, or both. Human capital models which distinguish between the acquisition of firm-specific or general human capital now seem too simplistic to capture the diversity of issues we have already reviewed.[27]

Setting aside the difficulties of specifying a theoretical model of training acquisition and timing and its role in the school-to-work transition process, the main problems associated with the econometric assessment of training programmes are those of identification and specification analysis. Such issues are difficult in the context of models which explicitly handle sample selection, attrition and duration data. The identification issue, in the context of sample selection, has been discussed by Heckman and Robb (1986) and, in the context of the competing risks model, has been analysed by Heckman and Honore (1989). A general framework for the specification analysis of models of this kind has been provided by Pagan and Vella (1989).

There are a large array of more specific potential econometric problems associated with the analysis of data collected for the purpose of the evaluation of training schemes. In this section the difficult and subtle nature of some of the econometric modelling problems is described. To aid the exposition we will refer to Figure 3.1, which schematically indicates various kinds of individual work history information, as it might have been collected by a sample survey. The description of the problems does not claim to be exhaustive, but rather is illustrative of the kind of difficulty which may be encountered.

To make the examples used in this section concrete we will assume that our survey consists of a sample of school leavers questioned at three points in time: six months after their official school leaving date and then at yearly intervals after that. Assume that the individuals are asked to record their labour market state at each month retrospectively back to the time of the previous questionnaire sweep. In addition, assume that the individuals are asked the dates at which key events occurred, like the start of a training programme or the start of a job. We also assume that information relating to earnings in jobs, benefits when out of work, type of job and occupation, educational qualifications and all relevant socioeconomic and demographic information is recorded.

The simplest transition model describes the duration of time, T, until a job is found. The *hazard function* $h(\tau)$ can be written as

$$h(\tau) = f(\tau)/[1 - F(\tau)], \tag{3.30}$$

where $f(\tau) = F'(\tau)$ is the duration density function and $[1 - F(\tau)]$ is the *survivor function* which, by integration, can be written

$$S(\tau) = 1 - F(\tau) = \exp \int_0^\tau -h(t)dt. \tag{3.31}$$

The incorporation of covariates, x, into this model which do not vary over time is relatively straightforward since the hazard function,

$$h(\tau,x)d\tau, \tag{3.32}$$

has a straightforward interpretation as the fraction of people who transit to a job in the short interval from τ to $d\tau$ in a large population of people who are homogeneous with respect to x. Difficulties arise, however when $\{x(\tau)\}$ varies stochastically over time.

One family of duration distributions which has proved particularly popular is the *proportional hazard* specification (see Cox and Oakes, 1984):

$$h(\tau,x) = \mu(x)\lambda(\tau), \tag{3.33}$$

where $x = X_i\beta + \alpha d_i$ and the X_i would capture the effect of the regressors and the d_i would indicate the active participation on a training programme.

By forming a partial likelihood function one can perform semiparametric estimation of the proportional hazard model, estimating a parametric specification of the time-invariant regressors in the term $\mu(x)$ without being committed to a parametric specification of the *baseline hazard* $\lambda(\tau)$. Estimation of this model would provide an estimate, α, of the importance of training to the conditional probability of employment at any particular time given that the individual had not been employed up to time t. We consider below some of the illustrative problems which we could have with such data which provide us with substantive econometric modelling problems.

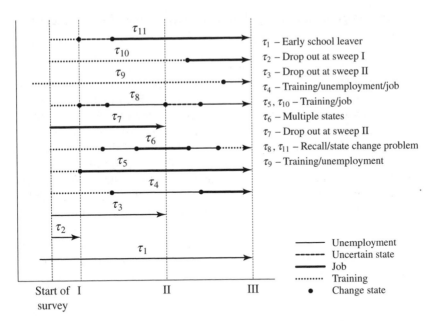

τ_1 – Early school leaver
τ_2 – Drop out at sweep I
τ_3 – Drop out at sweep II
τ_4 – Training/unemployment/job
τ_5, τ_{10} – Training/job
τ_6 – Multiple states
τ_7 – Drop out at sweep II
τ_8, τ_{11} – Recall/state change problem
τ_9 – Training/unemployment

——— Unemployment
------ Uncertain state
——— Job
·········· Training
• Change state

Start of I   II   III
survey

Figure 3.1

Right censoring
One of the most common features in panel data describing labour market histories is that many individuals in the sample will not have achieved any transition to a job by the date of the last sweep of the survey. In the context of Figure 3.1 observations τ_1, τ_8 and τ_9 are unemployed by the date of the sweep III in our example. The conceptual difficulty here is that there is some positive probability that these individuals will leave the unemployed state at some future date but we do not know when that will happen. The common solution to handling data with such right-censored observations is to include them all in a separate component of the likelihood function relating to uncompleted spells in the state in question.

The difficulty with this approach is that it potentially treats all censored observations the same when this may not be justified. Looking again at observations τ_1 and τ_9, we see that the individual with labour market history τ_1 has been continuously out of work ever since leaving school, whereas the individual with the history τ_9 has only recently left a training programme and therefore may not yet have had time to secure a good job. Fundamentally these observations are quite different and may not merit the same treatment in a likelihood function. Such questions raise the whole issue of how, econometrically, one should treat the time spent in

training programmes in any duration study of the effect of these programmes.

Controlling for unobserved heterogeneity in duration data

In duration data a central modelling issue which has received a great deal
of research attention in the last twenty years has been that of accounting
for unobserved heterogeneity. Often the price to be paid for being able to
model unobserved heterogeneity in a duration context has been the use of
a parametric distributional assumption on the form of the duration data in
order to allow a tractable model over the mixing distribution relating to
durations and unobserved heterogeneity. (See Lancaster, 1990.) Slowly,
applied econometric work has begun to implement the models suggested by
the theoretical work in this area. One advantage of the proportional hazard
framework is that it lends itself to the modelling of unobserved heterogeneity. This can be achieved by the appropriate choice of mixtures of probability distributions where a random time-invariant, person-specific, variable,
v enters the hazard function to capture this unobserved heterogeneity:

$$h(\tau, x, v). \tag{3.34}$$

Failure to account for unobserved heterogeneity can lead to the well known
problem of spurious duration dependence. The standard form used for this
hazard is the so-called 'mixed proportional hazard' model in which

$$h(\tau) = v.\exp(x\beta).\lambda(\tau), \tag{3.35}$$

where x is a vector which represents the observed variables, v is a random
variable which captures the unobserved variables and is usually taken as
orthogonal to x, and $\lambda(\tau)$ is the baseline hazard which captures the variation of the hazard with duration. In order to make this model operational
we must specify a distribution for v. This is used to form the likelihood
function appropriate to the sample.

The presence of individual specific time-varying covariates

One of the complexities introduced by the duration variables like the time
taken to obtain a job after completing a training programme is that the
circumstances of the individuals may change over the time involved. For
example, at the beginning of sweep I the individual may be unmarried but
at some time after that the individual gets married. Such a change is likely
to affect the individual's propensity and motivation to obtain a job with the
onset of other financial and personal responsibilities. Hence the fact that
the observation's marital state has changed, and also the timing of that

change, may be important factors in explaining their labour market transitions. Formally this complication means that the x regressors in (3.33) may have a subset of them which change over time, i.e. $\{x(t)\}$. Perhaps more important still than time-varying sociodemographic covariates is time-varying labour market information; such information, however, is very difficult to model econometrically. To understand these complexities, consider the handling of the variable associated with the timing and length of spells on the training programme. Clearly the timing of beginning a training programme can be treated as a time-varying covariate. The way in which such a variable may influence the likelihood of a successful transition to a job after a training programme is not clear a priori. The person who enters a training programme relatively quickly may be the lower-ability person who stands the smallest chance of getting a job without training. On the other hand the person who starts quickly may be the person who is most self-motivated and anxious about their labour market inactivity.

A second, more complex, issue is the correct way to handle the amount of time that an individual spends on the training programme. Little is known about the modelling of the impact of the duration of treatment effects. (See Abbring and Van den Berg, 2003; Eberwain *et al.*, 2002.) The very fact that time is spent on a training programme may limit the individual's capacity for job search and hence such time should effectively be extracted from any calculation of a 'transit to job' time. On the other hand the whole purpose of many training programmes is to provide the individual with some work experience and bridge the gap between school and the world of work. The effectiveness of this scheme is demonstrated by the high frequency with which a trainee is taken on by their placement employer. In this context it would be wrong to think of time on a training programme as time out of the labour market, not spent looking for a job; rather the actual time on the programme is also time spent looking for a job, and in some circumstances it may be qualitatively better 'job-search time' in the sense of having a potentially higher probability of ending in employment. Another factor is that any training placement can end at any time to allow an individual to take up a job, whether with the placement employer or not. In this sense the individual trainee can still be looking for a job. However, notwithstanding these facts, it could still be the case that the programme trainee on a good apprenticeship scheme, leading to a recognized qualification in a set period of time, is unlikely to be looking for a job with the intensity of an unemployed youth simply because they may be more secure in their perception of their future job prospects when they have completed their qualification. So far, models which handle single time-varying covariates are relatively straightforward (albeit computationally expensive) to estimate.

The estimation of models with more than one time-varying covariate are more difficult.

The modelling of competing risks

In modelling, for example, the duration of time until a spell of unemployment, we may often wish to consider the possibility that an individual will consider re-entry into a training programme or entry to higher education as an alternative to seeking a job, if a job proves very hard to get. The possibility that an individual may be 'at risk' of exit into more than one different labour market state may be modeled using the competing risks model (see Han and Hausman, 1990). The technicalities of estimating such a model are complex. Simplifying assumptions which make these technicalities much more tractable are those of independence or proportionality between the possible competing risks. Such an assumption in the context of labour market states would seem unreasonable. Narendranathan and Stewart (1991) propose a simple test. (See also Heckman and Honore, 1989.) A further difficulty associated with a competing risks model is that such a model may also need to incorporate time-varying covariates (see Sueyoshi, 1992).

Controlling for exogenous time-varying covariates

During the time that individual trainees are doing their training, various exogenous conditions which affect their personal circumstances may change. For example at certain key points in time their unemployment benefit entitlement may change. More specifically, in the UK, the Social Security Act of 1988 removed the general entitlement to income support (IS) of 16- and 17-year-olds (allowing only for IS to be awarded on a discretionary basis where 'severe hardship' might occur). This would mean that, as soon as the individual turned 18, their incentive to become, or remain, unemployed would change. Also, from 1986, any individual who had been unemployed for more than six months was called for a compulsory RESTART interview. This interview is primarily associated with helping the individual with job search methods and finding employment. However there is also an element of checking up on the labour market inactivity of the person and whether the unemployment experiences are genuinely involuntary.

Such discrete events constitute exogenous shocks to the position of the individual which may be reflected in their behaviour and decisions regarding training at particular points in time. Katz and Meyer (1990) have found evidence that the structure of unemployment compensation entitlements directly affect unemployment duration. Likewise Dolton and O'Neill (1996a and b, 2002) in a sequence of papers have found the importance of

RESTART is to induce people back to work after or around the time of the interview.

Modelling multiple spell duration data
Recent detailed labour market event history data are in the form of a diary of labour market states in each month over a given period of time. A commonly observed feature of such labour market panel data sets[28] which are collected over a period of years is the huge diversity of labour market histories which are experienced by the respondents. Such diversity results in their having a large number of separate spells of work and unemployment and possibly training. Such data are difficult to summarize, let alone use in structural econometric estimation. In the context of Figure 3.1, observation τ_6 has first a spell of training, then a spell out of work, followed by a job, followed by another spell out of work, followed by a second training spell. Such sequences of states are not uncommon, and indeed a large proportion of any labour market panel has much more complicated work histories than that of τ_6. There is also the added complexity, especially for women in the sample, of modelling their participation decision and possibly to choose the 'out of the labour force' state.

The econometric problems of modelling such multiple spell–multiple state data are considerable. The first theoretical steps have recently been taken to prepare for the analysis of such data (see Lancaster, 1990; Hui, 1991; Heckman and Singer, 1984a, 1984b) but little or no empirical work has successfully tackled the estimation difficulties involved. One way of considering multiple spell–multiple state data is to consider how transitions between labour market states occur, such as the transition between school and work. Advances in the modelling of non-Markov stochastic processes provide an opportunity for transition and mobility modelling (see Bartholemew, 1973). An alternative approach is to seek adequate summary measures of multiple spell unemployment experience, e.g. Shorrocks (1992), and use these as dependent variables.[29]

Modelling attrition from sweeps of a panel data set
Many data sets which have been used to model the effectiveness of training programmes have the characteristic of sample attrition between the original data collection and the follow-up survey(s). In the context of our example in Figure 3.1, observation τ_2 is seen at the initial sweep I, but is subsequently 'lost' to the survey in the sense that the person cannot be traced or they refuse to cooperate and provide their information. It is of course also likely that there is some initial non-response to the first survey at sweep I. Such initial sample attrition is not portrayed in Figure 3.1, but could be equally (or even more) important. Likewise observations τ_3 and τ_7 are seen

at sweep I and followed up at sweep II but are subsequently 'lost' thereafter for the same reasons. In principle, the simplest approach to modelling attrition could be to treat the state of attrition from the sample as another destination state in the relevant likelihood function.

However, the reason that such attrition is potentially so important is that it may not occur at random. (If it did there would be no potential biases to the estimation results.) For example, such non-randomness could be in the form of a higher response from whites and a higher likelihood of attrition from ethnic minorities. This could then bias our conclusions with respect to the importance of ethnicity as a qualitative factor in determining the probability of *training* programme participation or eventual unemployment. Hausman and Wise (1979) and Ridder (1990) have suggested methods for dealing with the biases which may be associated with such forms of selective data loss. However, so far, the available suggested corrections are for continuous dependent variables which are not in a duration form.

Alternative approaches to the handling of missing data (see Little and Rubin, 1987) which involve sample reweighting schemes to weight the observations which are used in the analysis 'as if' they came from the true population rather than the observed subsample, and multiple imputation schemes to replace missing data with imputed values need experimentation in the area of dealing with labour market panel data.

It is recognized in applied econometric work in this area that attrition between two sampling points may be endogenous. That is, the reasons which induced appearance at the original interview may also simultaneously affect appearance or non-appearance in the follow-up. If such an influence exists, the analysis of the relationship of the samples requires explicit treatment for this endogeniety. For example, it is possible that the likelihood of attrition may not be independent of the previous (or current) labour market state. For example, it might well be the case that the probability of attrition at sweep II is much higher for those individuals who are unemployed at that point in time. (This may be due to the greater difficulty in tracing a respondent who is more mobile in their attempt to find a job.) In terms of Figure 3.1 this means that amongst those who 'attrit' from the sample we may have a disproportionate fraction who are like observation τ_3 rather than observation τ_7. See Van den Berg *et al.* (1991)

Taking account of the decreasing reliability of duration and other data collected retrospectively
A common problem associated with panel data relates to the difficulty that the respondent may experience in recalling their work/unemployment history in earlier months. Most common is that, as the period of time for

which the respondent is asked to recall dates and labour market states lengthens, the accuracy of this information, on average, decreases.

In Figure 3.1 the individual with work history τ_8 could well not complete diary information relating to dates earlier than nine months prior to the date of the questionnaire sweep. This means there would then be 'gaps' in the data description of the sequence of labour market states and spells. There are only a limited number of ways of handling the problem. The most commonly adopted by economists is simply to delete the observation from the sample. The second approach is to attempt to infer what the missing data might be by imputing the most likely state from other questions and potentially trying to establish the 'most likely' state that the respondent was in during the time interval which is missing. If, for example, the person was in work at the end of sweep I and also in work at the first available recorded date in sweep II, it may be reasonable to assume that they were in work during the missing months. However such an assumption may not be fully justified. A final, much more complex route is to include the observation in the data for analysis using only the *information* which is reliable. (In the context of likelihood estimation this may mean having a likelihood equation which explicitly incorporated a separate component for such individuals.)

Sample selection effects
The sample selection problem discussed at length in section 5 in the modelling of earnings effects of training has a direct analogy in the modelling of transition time to work. The simplest stylized model of this sample selection is captured in the following model:[30]

$$h(\tau_i) = v_i.\exp(X_i\beta).\lambda(\tau_i)$$
$$D_i = Z_i\gamma + V_i. \tag{3.36}$$

In this case the sample selectivity can arise through the correlation of unobservables[31] where v_i is not independent of V_i. The technical difficulty of such a model arises in the multiple numerical integration associated with maximizing the relevant likelihood function which will be complex and depend on the joint form of the mixture distribution of v_i and τ_i and with the distributional assumption on V_i. As yet little is known about the identification of such a model and there has been no applied econometric work which attempts estimation.

7   Qualitative and institutional factors in assessment

In addition to the econometric and data complexities described in earlier sections of this paper, there are several qualitative and institutional factors which may be important in the assessment of training programmes. (For a more complete treatment of this topic, see Marsden and Ryan, 1990; Sako, 1991.)

Taking account of the heterogeniety of the possible final destination state
Most studies would simply presume that getting any job was sufficient as a final destination state. In reality there is great heterogeniety in the types of jobs which ex-trainees may take. Some of these jobs may be low-paid, short-term jobs with no further training and some may be jobs which are the first step towards a good career. Such 'proper jobs' are essentially the ones which count and it would be desirable for a thorough analysis to take account of the likelihood of getting these jobs rather than simply any job.

Are all training schemes the same?
In the same way as there are different types of jobs there is also great heterogeneity in the types of training that people may experience in different schemes and with different employers. Some schemes offer formal apprenticeships and formal qualifications; others, in contrast, offer little or no formal training and no certificated qualifications. For this reason we must try to distinguish between these types of training in our econometric assessment. However such distinctions are not straightforward to model econometrically.

The length of time spent on training
One important component which has largely been ignored in the empirical work to date is the differing lengths of time spent in training. Clearly a satisfactory model of the effects of training would take explicit account of the variable amount of time spent in training. Most studies, however, simply model whether training has taken place or not with a binary independent variable.

The variation of times spent in training is a characteristic not only of privately acquired training but also of that acquired on state schemes. A large proportion of trainees in the UK do not complete the YTS scheme. Is this important? Some will not complete their training scheme for the best of reasons, namely that they have found a suitable job. Others, in contrast, may leave the YTS scheme through disillusionment with the kind of training they are being offered or their prospects of future suitable employment. Hence the decision to remain in a training programme once entered or to leave is itself endogenous to the whole process of the school-to-work transition. One study by Jimenez and Kugler (1987) actually has the time spent on a training programme (treated as a qualitative variable) endogenous to the post-training earnings evaluation calculation. The authors reach the conclusion that such sample selection factors can be important in the assessment of earnings effects of training. They find substantial biases associated with ignoring the length of time spent on training.[32] Some of these distinctions are explored in Dolton *et al.* (1994c) and Mealli *et al.* (1996).

One reason why YTS trainees may leave a training scheme early is that there is a shortage of skilled, trained labour in a specific area and employers seek to 'poach' such skilled labour away from the employer who was responsible for their training. It is unclear to what extent such poaching takes place.

The process of entry onto training
Relatively little is known about the way people select themselves or are selected onto training schemes.[33] A more detailed knowledge of how this process works is important for a better understanding of the effects of training, since we would wish to have a clearer idea of the sample selection mechanism conditioning those who acquire training.

In the UK the YTS programme has to be open to anyone and therefore our interest would be in the factors which induce people to reject the scheme.[34] In the UK, the *Employment Gazette* (1986) suggests that around 6 per cent of young people, i.e. 20000–30000 school leavers, rejected the YTS scheme. They found that these people more frequently had a record of truancy at school, had fewer or no educational qualifications and were likely to be from a manual working background or a household dependent on state benefits. Many of those who reject YTS places cited poor rates of pay and the view that the work was 'slave labour' and 'not a proper job'. Those who reject the YTS scheme fall into two categories: those who retain some optimism and remain active in their job search and those who view YTS in a negative way and are more likely to remain economically inactive.

Those who leave the YTS scheme early to enter unemployment are very similar to those who reject the scheme without entry; i.e. they are much more likely to have a record of truancy at school, and are more commonly from manual backgrounds and households dependent on state benefits. Therefore the information we have about selection onto training programmes in the UK would lead us to suggest that the process is a very different one from that which might operate in other countries. For example, in Denmark (see Westergard-Neilsen, 1993) it is mainly the highly motivated workers who end up on training schemes.

8 Econometric modelling difficulties: experimental studies
As a result of the considerable difficulties associated with the sample selection problems described above it has been repeatedly suggested that controlled experiments should be used in the evaluation of training

programmes. This would work by assigning individuals to a training or non-training regime in an entirely random way. It is suggested that such an experimental setting with an appropriate control group is the only valid way of determining the effectiveness of a training programme free from sample selection biases. The problems associated with using experimental methods are described and largely dismissed in Burtless and Orr (1986). They examine the possibility that experimental studies may

- be more prone to non-response bias;
- result in less representative samples, since individuals have to agree to be part of the experiment;
- be prone to bias since the duration of experiments is usually limited to a specific period of time;
- be susceptible to Hawthorne effects which involve the possibility that an individual's behaviour actually changes simply because they know that the programme is part of an experiment. These effects then set apart the members of the training regime to a degree sufficient to make them a non-random subset of all the potential population. Hence we are back with a conventional, but less familiar, sample selection problem;
- provide the potential for 'queueing bias' associated with the problem that recipients of the training programme may 'jump' the queue for jobs and therefore impose an endogenous externality on those who were not on the training programme and are queueing for jobs.

Burtless and Orr (1986) quite rightly go on to explain that nearly all of these criticisms also apply to the more common non-experimental kind of study. They further discuss the ethical questions associated with administering an experimental study which involve the potential compensation of disappointed respondents who are not selected for the beneficial treatment (in this case the training programme) and the payment of fees to induce the cooperation of respondents in an experimental study. They provide a simple analysis for the cost–benefit appraisal of using experimental studies (since the experimental element of a sample design is not costless) and reach the conclusion that such studies are wholly worthwhile and may save a lot of money.

Lalonde (1986), Fraker and Maynard (1987) and Ham and Lalonde (1991) in influential research analysed data from a randomized experiment using non-experimental methods. They report an array of estimates of impacts of the same programme using different non-experimental methods. They conclude that there is no way of choosing among competing non-experimental estimators.

Heckman and Hotz (1989), using the same data as Lalonde and Fraker and Maynard, perform various model specifications tests. When such tests are performed, they eliminate all but the non-experimental models that reproduce the inference obtained by the experimental methods of Lalonde (1986) and Fraker and Maynard (1987). However it is true to say that each specification test proposed by Heckman and Hotz (1989) has its limitations. Changing the model specification from an overidentified to a just identified form can render the relevant specification test worthless. Unfortunately all non-experimental methods are based on some maintained, untestable assumptions. The superficial attraction of experimental methods is that they appear to require no assumptions. However Heckman (1992, 1993) shows that experimental methods do require fairly analogous assumptions. More specifically, he discusses at length the assumption, implicit in experimental methods, that randomization itself has no effect on the participation decisions or behaviour of the agents themselves. Alternatively experimental methods must assume that, if there is an effect of randomization on participation decisions, either (a) the effect of treatment is the same for all participants or (b) if agents differ in their response to treatments, their idiosyncratic responses to treatment do not influence their participation decisions. Another problem with experimental studies which Heckman discusses is that many evaluations require a multi-stage procedure: application, enrolment, assignment to treatment, review of performance and placement. In this context it is not clear at which stage randomization should occur; indeed it proves to be necessary at each stage of the multi-stage programmes. Not only is this impractical, but it could turn out to violate the randomization requirement if attrition from a multi-stage process takes place. This could turn out to be a real problem since, as Heckman (1992) documents, randomization experiments have often proved unpopular. A further technical difficulty which Heckman raises is that formally randomization may appear attractive when comparing first moments of distributions, but if one is concerned with median or higher moment evaluations then experimental methods may not be preferred. Heckman concludes that the assumptions necessary for experimental research are different, but not arguably better than the assumptions maintained in the non-experimental econometric studies.

The debate concerning the appropriateness of experimental versus non-experimental studies has continued, although there are signs that each side acknowledges the importance of the other's work and many of the leading researchers in the field are now advocating research which would use both experimental and non-experimental techniques. (See Burtless, 1993; Heckman, 1993.)

9   Econometric methods for assessment: a selective review of the literature
An overview of the empirical literature on training should distinguish
between the different econometric approaches to the task. The first
attempts to study the effects of training were in the context of cost–benefit
studies of the provision of state run training schemes. The second generation of studies attempted to use cross-section data and concentrated on the
rigorous evaluation of the earnings consequences of training. The earliest
research adopted a human capital view that such training is an investment
and its evaluation amounts to calculation of the rate of return on this
investment. This led to a preoccupation with wage effects of trainees in jobs
after their training courses. Later studies have sought to focus instead on
the proposition that such training enhances the probability of employment
at some future date or the way in which training may enhance career mobility. Recent work has taken the next logical step in evaluation by considering the effects of training on the duration of unemployment or how long it
takes to make the transition from school to work with and without training.

Cost–benefit studies
The earliest assessments of training used cost–benefit analysis to appraise
the impact of the training programme. The context of the first study by
Borus (1964) was in terms of assessing the costs and benefits of training
unemployed workers at government expense in an attempt to assess the
overall efficiency of this policy as an investment decision. Work by Thomas
et al. (1969) and Oatey (1970) made more explicit the nature of the
cost–benefit calculus associated with the firm's decision regarding the provision of training. Layard (1979) considered the costs and benefits of selective employment policies.

The simplest assertion is that training increases the individual's human
capital and enhances their employment probability. In this context it is not
surprising that the predominant approach to the evaluation of training in
the earliest studies (Borus, 1964, 1972; Thomas *et al.*, 1969; Ziderman,
1969, 1975a, 1975b; Oatey, 1970) was to perform a cost–benefit analysis
based on aggregate data relating to mean post-training earnings of trainees and non-trainees and aggregate employment probabilities of the two
groups. In essence the literature posed the most interesting question,
namely, what is the overall economic case for training when all the costs and
benefits of the scheme have been taken into account? The problem with this
approach is that it relied on aggregate data which do not allow us to assess
adequately the effect of training on an individual's earnings, or employment effects, controlling for interpersonal differences. Also the cost–benefit
approach does not control for the possibility that those who enter training

may be much more highly motivated than those who do not and would anyway have secured a better wage and/or employment prospects. Fresh new insights into the assessment of training have been made possible with the advent of large-scale panel or cross section individual data.

The study by Ziderman (1969) attempted to perform a cost–benefit analysis of adult retraining programmes. Using the best available aggregate data, Ziderman concludes that the short pay-back periods and the high rates of return provide strong prima facie evidence for the positive net benefits of government retraining centres from the viewpoint of the individual. Later studies by Ziderman reach similiar conclusions with respect to the introduction of manpower training schemes from the standpoint of the economy (Ziderman, 1975a) and from the perspective of setting up individual training centres in Scotland (Ziderman, 1975b). Cost–benefit analysis is less commonly used in more recent research, but Piggott and Chapman (1995), and Dolton and O'Neill (2002) provide modern examples of ALMP evaluations where it could be profitably applied and may yield favourable results.

The wage effect
The first attempt to assess the effect of training for the individual was developed from the tradition of human capital theory. In this context training is another form of human capital (Becker, 1975; Mincer, 1974) and hence costing training is seen as an investment which sought to measure the wage premium associated with training over and above the wages that would have been earned by those who had not been trained. In this sense they attempted to measure the effectiveness of the training programme if it resulted in the recipients as a whole earning more than those who had not received the training.

The first studies in this human capital tradition, such as Mincer (1962) found that the rate of return to selected individual investments in on-the-job training, such as apprenticeships and medical specializations, was not different from the rate of return on a college education and possibly in the range of 8–12 per cent. Such findings were to be confirmed many times in later studies of the rates of return to individual private investment in training. However the rates of return to government-sponsored training programmes (which began in the late 1960s and early 1970s in the USA) were quite a different matter.

Ashenfelter (1978) was one of the first of these studies to appreciate some of the subtleties involved in the assessment of the training programme. Using a fixed effects model suggested that there were significant forgone earnings associated with the participation in such schemes. In addition Ashenfelter tried to take the costs of the training into account in the

calculation of the net benefits of training, i.e. the earnings premium associated with the training minus the costs associated with the provision of the
training. He found that training does appear to have an effect of $150–500
per year for men (and more for women). However this effect seems to
decline in succeeding years and to be counterbalanced by a fall in income
immediately prior to programme entry.

The first study to model explicitly the selectivity bias problem in the
assessment of training effects on earnings was by Kiefer (1978). He was the
first to appreciate the theoretical importance of a randomized control
group in the experimental assessment of training. However, since this kind
of data was unavailable, he sought to use a carefully collected (but non-
random) control group to handle the problem of the bias generated by the
process of selection into training. He sought to model the effect of the
Manpower Development and Training Act (MDTA) of 1962 in the USA
by using data on federally sponsored training programmes. The sample,
collected in 1969, used matched samples on age, race and sex as a control
group. His estimated earnings equations (by race) show no significant
effects of the regressors associated with the length in weeks that the respondent has been in training. In addition the sample selection corrections were
also found to be insignificant. In a follow-up study Kiefer (1979a) used a
panel data model to incorporate time and individual effects, on data relating to the MDTA programme. Since the training status of (some) individuals in the sample changes during the sample period the pre- and
post-training and trainee/non-trainee contrasts in earnings can be made.
The model is used to avoid the potential cross-section bias, due to worker
heterogeneity, which arises when before and after information is not available. The estimation results revealed a small, 1.5 per cent, increase in wages
associated with training. The results of the paper show that the potential
bias in a cross section can be substantial.

The differences in the effects of training on earnings by sex and race were
further explored by Duncan and Hoffman (1979). They found that time
spent in on-the-job training increases earnings. This payoff was found to be
uniform for men and women and blacks and whites, and they found no evidence that minority workers received a lower rate of return on training than
white men. However they did find that there were large differences in the
amounts of training received by white men compared to other workers and
that these differential amounts of training account for almost 20 per cent
of the wage gap between white and black men and about 10 per cent of the
gap between white men and women. These results suggest that the nature
of the investment decision in training is very different by race and sex.

The problem associated with the non-random selection of trainees was
further investigated by Bassi (1983). Bassi attempted to use a US longitu-

dinal manpower survey with a fixed effects panel model to eliminate the bias associated with the non-random selection into training programmes. He found that such fixed effects estimates eliminated the selectivity bias and that, as a result, there were no appreciable earnings effects for men although there were such effects for women.

Ashenfelter and Card (1985) sought to use longitudinal data on the structure of earnings and a group comparison to estimate the effectiveness of training for participants in the US 1976 Comprehensive Employment and Training Act (CETA) programme. They suggest that the estimation results of these models are very sensitive to the specification of the econometric model and that participant earnings equations contain permanent, transitory and trend-like components of selection bias. They draw attention to the problems associated with checking the overidentifying conditions in these models. Notwithstanding these reservations, they conclude that training effects on earnings for men are very small (around $300 per annum), whereas the effect for women may be as large as $800–1500 per annum. Such effects were, however, subject to considerable variation under different equation specifications. The authors conclude with a plea for more experimental studies which would permit random assignment to the training group and the control group in order to be able to compare more rigorously effects of training programmes free from the econometric difficulties presented by the sample selection problem.

A more general assessment of the effect of training on earnings and earnings growth is provided by Lillard and Tan (1986), who use three different data sets from the Current Population Survey, the National Longitudinal Survey and the Employment Opportunities Pilot Projects Survey. They conclude that the effect of training on earnings and earnings growth vary by source and type. Company training is found to have the greatest effect on earnings, persisting over 13 years. The effects of other training sources are much smaller and persist for eight to ten years. When types of training are considered, managerial training increases earnings the most, but its effects are less enduring than the effects of semi-skilled manual training.

One of the first training studies using cross section data in Britain was that of Greenhalgh and Stewart (1987), who used the National Training Survey which contains records on 50 000 men and women. The focus of this work was the assessment of the effects of vocational training on wages and occupational status for men and women. They found that the returns to training for men and single women are predominantly from occupational advancement rather than increased earnings in the same job. They also found larger returns for both single and married women than for men.

Lynch (1992) uses the longitudinal data from the National Longitudinal

Survey of Youth (NLSY) cohort. The data contained over 3000 respondents between 14 and 21 years old, followed from 1983 to 1985. This study sought to distinguish between off-the-job and on-the-job training by assessing the return on company training, apprenticeships and training provided on business courses outside the firm. All three forms of training are associated with higher earnings when fixed effect or Heckman two-step estimators are used. However off-the-job training provided outside the firm is found to have the largest effect on earnings.

Main and Shelly (1990) in their examination of the possibility of a wage effect from YTS conclude that 'it is impossible to draw any statistically significant conclusions from these results'. They explicitly estimate a two-step Heckman model of wages using a probit equation to determine YTS participation. However their specification is puzzling as the only factor in the probit participation equation which is excluded from the wage equation is the father's occupation: it is questionable whether this should also be included in the wage equation, invalidating the identification condition. Also curious is the presence of a YTS completed dummy variable in the wage equation, as this is clearly related to YTS participation, as no non-particpant in YTS could have completed it; moreover they acknowledge in a footnote that this variable was imperfectly measured (i.e. they are unsure which individuals completed YTS). Dolton *et al.* (1994a) and Green *et al.* (1996) find no evidence of earnings effects of YTS participation.

An interesting contrast to the results of poor returns to training via state-run schemes in the UK like the YTS scheme is provided by an empirical study of a cohort of British individuals which relates to an earlier period when apprenticeships were the norm. The study by Baker (1992) shows how the return on both off-the-job training and apprenticeships is large. She accounts for the problem of sample selection and conditions on a rich array of sociodemographic and education variables. Another British study (Booth, 1991) also finds some tentative evidence for increased earnings as a result of training. Booth's study, using the British Social Attitudes Survey data, also reveals considerable gender differences in the provision of formal training.

Ackum (1991) used a survey in Sweden of 830 youths (16–24 years old) to evaluate the effects of public relief jobs and training on subsequent hourly earnings. Earnings equations are estimated using cross-section and panel data methods. The effect of labour market programmes was found to be negligible and this result was robust to the usual Heckman sample selection correction. Westergard-Neilsen (1993), using large-scale Danish panel data, sought to assess the effect of labour market training courses which are mainly intended to supply workers in employment with specific and general skills but are also open to the unemployed. The paper uses a fixed effect estimator and attempts to control for the effects of previous employment experience. The results show an overall 1 per cent increase in the post-training wage rate but the model does not recognize the endogeneity of previous employment experience.

Very few studies are in a position to evaluate the long term potential earnings premium associated with training.[35] A notable and interesting recent exception is Couch (1992) who reports results relating to training recipients up to eight years after their training. The study tracks earnings effects on the National Supported Work experiment (NSW) on the youth and Aid to Families with Dependent Children (AFDC) target groups. He finds that the NSW was found to have no discernible effect on earnings of the youth target group but the NSW's effect on the AFDC recipients ranged from \$375 to \$525 in 1978 dollars during the years 1982–86, which was more than enough to offset the costs of the training. If such results are representative of the comparative effects of training young people rather than older workers, they have dramatic implications for the provision of training subsidies, namely that they should be directed away from young school leavers towards older workers with family commitments. Clearly more empirical research is necessary relating to the long-term effects of training.

Raaum and Torp (2002) estimate the impact of a training programme on earnings in Norway using a panel of six years' worth of data. Unlike other non-experimental studies they examine the estimate of the training effect using a variety of different estimators, including the control model, the fixed effects and random growth model and the matching estimator. Their results are shown to be sensitive to the estimation procedure chosen. This study is valuable as it shows how the modelling of the effects of training on earnings can affect the conclusions. Specifically they find a positive effect for training on earnings in the linear control model but not in other models. They also show that the self-assignment into training is affected by unobservables and this raises important questions about the modelling of training treatment effects. Similar conclusions are reached by Regner (2002) using an administrative data set for Norway. Again specification tests reject the fixed effects and random growth models, and he finds both negative and positive effects of training on earnings.

The probability of employment at a specific date
The first study to model the post-training employment effect of training was also the paper by Kiefer (1978) (discussed in the previous section). He estimated a probit equation for the probability of being in employment eight months after the training programme.[36] His estimates indicate that the length of time spent in training (in weeks) does not significantly alter the probability of employment. An early study in the UK, by Main and Raffe

(1983), examined the determinants of employment and unemployment among Scottish school leavers.

Lillard and Tan (1986), using a large-scale comparative study with three different data sets from the Current Population Survey, the National Longitudinal Survey and the Employment Opportunities Pilot Projects Survey, conclude that, on average, training is associated with a subsequent decline in the likelihood of unemployment lasting approximately 12 years. Of all sources of training, they found that company training is the most enduring, while training taking place at educational institutions has an effect for only seven years. They also found that the type of training is important, in that technical and professional training had an effect which was of much longer duration than managerial training.

Main and Shelly (1990) consider a measure of the effectiveness of the YTS scheme by considering the ability of a school leaver to get a job, as a function of whether the respondent was on the YTS (as well as other exogenous factors). They argue that a basic function of YTS is to improve the attractiveness of the participant to potential employers, hence improving the individual's ranking in the queue for jobs. In the estimation results they find a significant YTS effect in the probit equation associated with being in a job three years after leaving school. Although the coefficient in question is relatively small it does nevertheless induce a 11–17 per cent rise in the probability of being employed according to whether or not the individual's background is 'advantaged' or 'disadvantaged'. Whilst Main and Shelly devote some effort to considering the sample selection problem relating to the wage effects of YTS, they ignore the possibility of a sample selection effect on their estimates of being in a job.

Main (1991), in a separate paper, reported the probit employment equations for the same data set only using information relating to their labour market state a further six months on, in October 1986. Here he found even larger employment effects of between 14 and 19 per cent when comparing the same advantaged and disadvanted groups by YTS status.

Breen (1991), using data from Ireland, also found mixed effects of the experience of having been on a government training scheme on the future probability of employment. He concludes that the training experience may not be unequivocally advantageous. More specifically his results suggest that having been on a training scheme increases the probability of obtaining a job immediately after finishing the training but that this effect becomes insignificant after a year. These results point to the need for econometric work which models the (post-training) conditional probability of being in work over time.

Whitfield and Bourlakis (1990) basically used the same kind of analysis as employed by Main and Shelly (1990), but applied it to the first Youth

Cohort Survey data. They found a small but significant effect of YTS participation which increased the YTS participant's probability of employment by 4 per cent over the base (or average) individual. Such an effect must be judged to be relatively small as in the same model the effect of being in a local area with a 27.7 per cent unemployment rate was −29 per cent, and being in an area with 4.5 per cent unemployment was 10 per cent over the base case. Whitfield and Bourlakis (1990) also ignore the potential sample selection effect of the endogeneity of entry into a YTS scheme. O'Higgins (1994), using a bivariate probit model to attempt to handle selectivity into training and the probability of getting a job jointly revises these positive estimated employment effects of YTS upwards to 4–10 per cent.[37] Dolton *et al.* (1994c), in an attempt to replicate the results of Main and Shelly (1990) and Whitfield and Bourlakis (1990), actually found negatively significant coefficients on a YTS dummy in the probability of being in employment three years after school for a later cohort. Zweimuller and Winter-Ebmer (1996) find negatively significant effects of training on the probability of subsequent unemployment using data from Austria.

D-in-D and matching methods have also been used by Blundell *et al.* (2000) to evelate the effect of the New Deal for Young People in the UK. Here they attempt to assess the effect of NDYP by comparing the outcomes of those receiving NDYP with a quasi-control who do not in the Non-Pathfinder areas. They find significant NDYP effects on the probability of being on Job Seekers Allowance six months to two years after the NDYP participation. Matching methods used by Eichler and Lechner (2002) find significant effects of the East German public employment programme on the probability of subsequent unemployment.

One completely different identification strategy which is employed in Dolton (2000) is to attempt to use local area data and their variation to attempt to identify the effects of a training programme in aggregate. In this case he uses unit of delivery data to examine the effects of NDYP over time by geographical location.

The stochastic process modelling approach
An important but seldom used empirical method for modelling the effect of training has been to use a stochastic process model to estimate transition intensities between different labour market states. Some of these studies, like Clark and Summers (1982), do not distinguish between the labour market state of 'not in the labour force' and in 'training' which make the analysis of training assessment problematic. However there have been several transition-based studies which explicitly treat training as a separate labour market state.

The earliest use of stochastic processes in the evaluation of training was by Smith (1971) who modelled the post-training labour market transitions of trainees between unemployment and employment in an attempt to evaluate the effects of training on the successful transition probabilities. The approach was also adopted by Ziderman and Driver (1973), who then used predicted transitional probabilities in their cost–benefit calculations of likely earnings of training programme participants. This then facilitated comparisons with average non-trainee earnings, in the absence of a control group. Kaitz (1979) addresses the problem of evaluating the effects of a public employment programme without a control group. He focuses on the effect of the programme on the labour force status of participants by modelling the change in that status over time using a stationary discrete time Markov chain. He solves the problem of the non-random selection of participants by assuming that the pre-treatment data have been generated by a backward Markov chain; that is, he conditions on the labour force state at the moment of entry into the programme. If the stochastic process is in equilibrium and if there is no treatment effect the backward and forward Markov chains have the same equilibrium distribution.

Ridder (1986) models labour market transitions using a non-stationary Markov chain. He uses a quasi-experimental design with a simple pre-treatment–post-treatment structure without an equivalent control group. He explicitly models labour market transitions assuming that the selection into the training programme is non-random with respect to the labour force state; i.e. the unemployed are more likely to enter a programme than the employed but selection to the programme is random with respect to other aspects of labour market history. The empirical results reported in this paper are based on data from the Netherlands, indicate that training programmes have a very restricted effect on the employment transition of the participants. The analysis is restrictive in the sense that the sample used relates to a single retrospective study. In addition there is also the possibility that unobserved heterogeneity causes a downward bias in the estimated treatment effects. However the author suggests how these difficulties may be overcome.

Olsen *et al.* (1986) also use a Markov transition model with exponential arrival rates for new job offers conditional on labour market state and a logit choice model. They test whether the restrictions implied by the choice framework hold and whether the rate of arrival of new information are the same regardless of the labour market state occupied by the chooser. In their data the labour market states are public sector employment, private sector employment or unemployment and the sample is generated from observations on a guaranteed jobs programme for young people. They conclude from their results that the actual specification of the labour market state choice process through time can make a difference in the estimates of the preference structure. Such results should lead us to question carefully the appropriate modelling of the choice of labour market state, given any kind of state training or job creation programme.

The employment effect conditional on previous labour market history
The approach adopted by Card and Sullivan (1988) was to compare the employment prospects of a control group with the trainees group conditioning on the complete (discrete) previous job (labour market) history. This approach has the advantage that it directly controls for the fact that the trainee parts of the sample have a different distribution over their previous labour market histories and therefore are a non-random subset of the whole population. Hence this approach aims to control for the sample selection problem directly by attempting to make the comparison of trainees with non-trainees conditional on labour market history.

As Card and Sullivan recognize, this approach may be a partial solution to the problem of sample selection but it still has some important limitations: (a) it is only possible to condition on a limited number of profiles (sequences of job states) since, even with large data sets, if we condition on such histories then the number of observations will become small within any particular cell (or sequence of states); (b) it assumes that the only factor which is generating the sample selection is the nature of past work histories; it may be the case that various other observable or unobservable factors play an important role in this selection process of entering training; (c) as Card and Sullivan concede, their method is not necessarily valid for certain specific kinds of profile.

The duration of unemployment until successful transition to a job
Various structural models of the transition process from school to work have used the search theory framework to estimate structural econometric models of the importance of the cost of search and the probability of receiving a wage offer (Wolpin, 1987) or the variable intensity of search (Jensen and Westergard-Neilsen, 1987) on the expected length of unemployment. However there have been relatively few attempts to incorporate the alternative of a training scheme into the set of possible labour market states or indeed to model the effect of a spell of training on the conditional probability of a successful transition to a job or even the duration of post-training unemployment time.[38]

One of the first studies to consider the duration of unemployment of participants in government training programmes was that by Keeley and Robins (1985). Using the Employment Opportunity Pilot Projects (EOPP) data (like Lillard and Tan, 1986) they focus on the question of whether job search requirements of the programme had a significant impact on the probability of employment. They found, using a simple log linear form on the hazard function, that the job search requirements of the programme had a positive impact.

Ham and Lalonde (1991) use data from a social experiment to estimate the impact of training on the duration of employment and unemployment spells for AFDC recipients of the National Supported Work demonstration (NSW). This employment programme was one of the first to employ an experimental design randomly to assign eligible welfare mothers to either a treatment group who receive training or a control group who do not. Their estimation results suggest that NSW improved the employment rates of its participants entirely through its effects on the duration of employment spells. The programme, however, appears to have had no positive effect on the likelihood that trainees would leave unemployment. However Ham and Lalonde's paper attempts to control for the sample selection problem that the controls are all in the midst of an unemployment spell when sampled.

Dolton *et al.* (1994c) attempt to model the time taken from leaving school (those entering higher education are omitted) to successful transit to a job. The time spent on YTS training is variously assumed, in separate estimations, to be time spent not looking for a job and time spent looking for a job. In addition the end state of a job was categorized as 'good' or 'bad' using dual labour market theory. The only positive employment effects on the hazard due to the YTS were for women in the transit time to a good job where the time spent on YTS is subtracted from the total transit time and regarded as time spent not looking for a job. The paper also attempts to control for the possible estimation biases induced by the sample selection problem, unobserved heterogeneity, attrition from the sample and the presence of time-dependent covariates to proxy for changing demand conditions. Unfortunately these econometric difficultes can only be handled one by one, but the results seem fairly robust.

Another paper which is concerned with modelling total transit time to a job is that of Beenstock (1992). He uses non-parametric estimation methods on Israeli National Insurance Institute data to model the hazard of entry into employment for trainees and nontrainees. Rather than use regressors he stratifies his model by type of individual. He finds that those who receive training enter jobs faster, but within the context of his data it is difficult to separate the effects of unemployment insurance entitlements on transit times from training effects. Beenstock suggests that such entitlements are, not suprisingly, a major influence on unemployment duration.

Gritz (1993) uses the Youth Cohort of the National Longitudinal Survey of Youth (NLSY) to investigate whether participation in training influences either the frequency or the duration of employment spells. The

NLSY provides information about individuals who have been trainees as well as those who have participated in training programmes. More specifically the NLSY contains information on participants in both private and government training. Labour market state is either in training (t), in employment (e) or out of the labour force (n), for each week in the sample period. Gritz uses these data to estimate continuous time models of the cause-specific hazards between each pair of possible labour market states. The estimation results indicate that participation in private training improves the prospects of women by increasing both the frequency and the duration of spells. The implications are less clear for men, in that participation in private programmes increases the length of both employment and non-employment episodes. Finally the estimation results indicate that participation in government-sponsored training programmes actually induces a deterioration in the labour market circumstances of individuals.

One of the important problems of the analysis by Gritz is that the time spent in training is not known for all the sample. This means that only a 0,1 indicator variable is used to assess whether training has taken place. Clearly this is unsatisfactory in an attempt to explain the role of training in employment frequency and duration. There are at least two important effects which will be overlooked by not modelling the time spent in training: the first is that, within a fixed sampling period, the more time an individual spends in training, the less time they will have left over to spend in employment; the second is that, if training is of a longer duration it is possible that the process of human capital skills acquisition may be more intensive, and this may, in turn, enhance productivity and potential employability. One common and disturbing characteristic of labour market panel data is that the reporting of changing a state between sweeps is much higher than it should be. That is, a disproportionate number of individuals report that they were, say, out of work at the end of sweep I, but then claim to be in work in the first month of sweep II. Some individuals may genuinely change their state and get a job at this point in time. However, if one graphs the distribution of durations, there is a 'spike' at eight and 20 months of those who leave unemployment, gaining a job. Undoubtedly many will start a job at this time but it is not clear how much of this 'change of state' is spurious, induced by the lack of memory of the individual attempting to recall their labour market state in sweep II for the first month after sweep 1. The same may happen in sweep III. Hence referring back to Figure 3.1 we are left with a disproportionate number of observations like τ_{11} or τ_8 in the data, indeed a number larger than one would expect.

Thierry and Sollogoub (1995) and Bonnal *et al.* (1997) study the effect of youth training in France on the subsequent employment and unemployment hazards. Thierry and Sollogoub find a negative effect on employment of training. In a more detailed study, Bonnal *et al.* (1997) confirm these findings of a negative effect on employment hazard and also find a positive effect on the unemployment hazard using the same data.

The effect of training on job mobility

Perhaps the earliest study of the effect of training on turnover is that of Pencavel (1972), who estimated a model of quits and wages for industry data (19 observations on manufacturing industries) and used schooling and the log of wages as proxies for firm-specific training. He claimed that his model showed the negative association of the acquisition of firm-specific human capital with turnover. However, since no training data are available, this 'result' stands or falls on the strength of education and log of wages as proxies for firm-specific training investment. The validity of this assumption remains unclear in the face of more research which has had direct data measures of training for individuals.

There is now a large literature on the relationship between training, the acquisition of firm-specific human capital and mobility.[39] Economic theory implies that, if firm-specific human capital is a significant determinant of an individual's wage, then, a priori, we should expect an inverse relationship between the level of investment and the likelihood of turnover. Many empirical papers follow the lead of Pencavel (1972) in attempting to proxy specific skills by the statistical significance of the 'return' to firm tenure. However length of firm tenure is a poor proxy for the level of investment in firm-specific capital, for two main reasons. Firstly, the employer/ employee sharing rule,[40] in terms of the costs and benefits of firm-specific capital, is unknown and, secondly, the positive correlation between earnings and tenure may reflect the match quality between employer and employee rather than the level of firm-specific investment. Recent papers by Topel (1991), Altonji and Shakotko (1987), and Abraham and Farber (1987) present evidence to suggest that the role of specific human capital has been overemphasized as a determinant of wages. The suggestion is that the coefficient on tenure in a log wage regression will generally be biased upwards owing to the matching process between workers and jobs and that, since theories of earnings growth and job mobility are observationally equivalent to Becker's original analysis, the theory is difficult to test.

An interesting departure from the literature is provided by Sicherman and Galor (1990). They found empirical support for the proposition that the returns to human capital investment may be indirect in the sense that the investment increases the probability of promotion or career advancement as well as (or even instead of) directly increasing the earnings within any given job. However the Sicherman and Galor paper does not have good data on different types of human capital acquisition and the model assumes that all human capital is acquired at the beginning of the individual's career. This is clearly an important restriction to any model of career mobility since a high proportion of job and occupation moves are made possible by investing in further specific training, or retraining.

Lynch (1992) uses the NLSY to examine the effect of on-the-job and off-the-job training on mobility. Using a Cox proportional hazard model she found that those young people who had some formal on-the-job training were much less likely to leave their employer, while those who participated in some form of off-the-job training were more likely to leave, suggesting that on-the-job training is more firm-specific human capital and off-the-job training more general human capital.

A paper by Dolton and Kidd (1998) empirically investigates the relationship between three different types of human capital acquisition (occupation-specific, firm-based and general academic qualifications) and job mobility. Employees are observed being able to remain in their present job (with or without promotion), leave for another job in the same occupation with a different firm or, more radically, change occupation. The data used are a one in six sample of 1980 UK graduates for whom labour market information is known over the first seven years of their careers. The estimation results suggest that individuals who obtain more firm-based capital (in the form of training days) are more likely to stay with the same firm or be promoted; and that those who acquire more occupation-specific human capital (relevant to their first chosen occupation) are likely to move jobs within the same occupation, or be promoted, but are less likely to change occupations. These are findings which accord with human capital investment theories.

10 Conclusion

The econometric assessment of the effects of training programmes is complex. The above discussion has highlighted the potential importance of attempting to derive reasonable estimates of the wage and probability of employment effects induced by training. However the practical estimation difficulties involved are considerable.

Bearing in mind the difficulties associated with the econometric analysis of the assessment of training, it is premature to attempt to reach definite conclusions on the basis of the available research. However there are certain empirical findings which seem to be relatively robust to studies across different countries as well as studies within the same country that use different data sets. Such findings also seem to stand up to different treatments of selectivity bias and therefore these findings merit a brief review:

1.   The empirical evidence which exists on different training programmes in different countries and over time is diverse and very heterogeneous.

2.   The main overall conclusion is that state training programmes do not significantly raise earnings or affect employment probabilities of the recipients in the short to medium term, but more research on the long-term effects of training is needed.

3.   Those employment and training programmes which do have an effect have their greatest impacts and largest social returns for those who have the least previous labour market experience. This includes women and the disadvantaged. Such a finding may prompt the conclusion that more training funds should be spent on women and older workers.

4.   There is some accumulated evidence that the rate of return to private vocational training is positive, especially in the case of off-the-job training, and firm-specific training lowers the leaving rate with general training inducing more turnover; however most of these effects are found outside state-run training schemes.

5.   The net redistributional effect of training programmes on earnings inequality is minimal. It is clear that, if the policy is aimed at significant income redistribution, it will be necessary to spend much more public money to secure a significant effect.

6.   Although much of the empirical evidence concerning mass state-run training schemes indicates that such programmes have very limited effects on earnings and employment probabilities,[41] there are clear technical evaluation problems which must be recognized. An important part of the assessment difficulties is that many of the recipients of this state training would otherwise be unemployed owing to aggregate economic conditions. It is not surprising that the most favourable results of these programmes are derived when the unemployed are accordingly used as the control group for comparisons.

7.   Some recent evidence from applied econometric work suggests that the estimates of training effects can be significantly affected by the estimation model used to derive their effects. This suggests that the alternative identification conditions used to obtain the estimates need to be carefully tested. In addition it means that any estimates of programme effects must be cautiously intrepreted as conditional on the identification assumption(s) used in their derivation.

Throughout this chapter the focus has been the assessment of the effects of the supply-side response to the introduction of a government training scheme. No mention has been made of the macroeconomic demand-side conditions which may impinge on the impact of a training programme. These aggregate macroeconomic conditions will dramatically affect the employment and earnings prospects of training recipients as they enter the labour market. Although a direct study of these effects is difficult, it may be possible to control partially for changes in aggregate market conditions by using cross-cohort studies, the aim of which might be to disaggregate the differences in the prospects of the cohorts into differences in the cohort characteristics and effects of different market conditions. This will be an important area for future research.

Acknowledgments

The author wishes to thank Jim Heckman and Gary Burtless for comments, Gerry Makepeace and John Treble for frequent discussions about training, Dan Seidmann, Tim Barmby, Colin Wren, the editors of this volume and participants at the Royal Statistical Society Seminar for comments on an earlier version of this chapter, and Tsung-Ping Chung for research assistance. Financial support for this work was provided by the ESRC grants R000233909, the EDWIN framework V project, and H519255006.

Notes

1. Some of the countries which have also introduced major youth training programmes are Australia, Austria, Belgium, Canada, Denmark, France, Germany, Ireland, Italy, Japan, Netherlands, Norway, Sweden, UK and USA.
2. There have also been some excellent symposia published over the years: Bloch (1979), the *Journal of Human Resources* in 1987 (see Moffitt, 1987), Stern and Ritzen (1991), Manski and Garfinkel (1992), the Ministry of Labour, Denmark (1993), Lynch (1994), McNabb and Whitfield (1994), the *Review of Economic Studies*, issue 4 of 1997, and *Labour Economics*, **9**(2) of 2002.
3. Barnow (1987) also provided a useful review of the (now difficult to obtain) consultancy reports by Westat, Mathematica and other companies which evaluated US training schemes.
4. Haveman and Hollister (1991) also provide a summary of the institutional details of the large array of different training and job creation schemes in the USA.
5. Evaluation of the retraining of adults and other kinds of training schemes are referred to, but not studied in depth, and the historical perspective of the different training schemes which have been used in the UK is not discussed. (See Metcalf (1982), Finn (1987), Sheldrake and Vickerstaff (1987), Chapman and Tooze (1987), and Greenhalgh and Mavrotas (1991b). Nor do we consider the individual's human capital investment decision, (see Greenhalgh and Mavrotas, 1991a) or explore the link between the adoption of new technology and training (see Greenhalgh and Mavrotas, 1991a). There is also a vast literature on the more general effects of training on the job: see Blundell *et al.* (1996) and Booth (1991), for example.
6. Many recent contributions to the theory of training now explain a variety of different aspects of the training process for firms. See Hashimoto (1981), Katz and Ziderman (1990), Stevens (1994a, 1994b, 1996), Acemoglou and Pischke (1999a, 1999b), and Malcolmson *et al.* (2003) for models of the provision of general or firm-specific training by firms under various market conditions. Stevens (1994c) and Acemoglou and Pischke (1998) provide theories of the supply of training by firms. A theoretical model of the relation between matching, job separations, job tenure and on-the-job specific training has been provided by Mortensen (1988). Gustman and Steinmeier (1988) develop a general equilibrium model of the youth labour market with heterogenous ability levels and consider alternative policies of a youth minimum wage, employment subsidies and training cost subsidies to employers. Johansson (1991) provides a conceptual framework

for cost–benefit rules for job training programmes. A survey of many of these contributions is available in Leuven (2001). Haveman and Hollister (1991) spell out the macroeconomic and exchange rate implications of training policy.

7.   See Ritzen (1991) and Stern and Ritzen (1991).

8.   Bassi and Ashenfelter (1986) point out that for the USA the timing of training expenditures as counter cyclical policy has been poor.

9.   Dolton *et al.* (1994a), using 1986 cohort data, report the identical equations to Whitfield and Bourlakis (1990), using 1984 cohort data, and very similar equations to Main and Shelly (1990), using a 1983 cohort, hence permitting some inter-cohort comparison. Dolton *et al.* (1994a) report negative employment probability effects of YTS, whereas the other studies found positive YTS effects on the probability of employment. Since unemployment was lower in 1983 and 1984 than in 1986 it is possible to conjecture that these results may indicate some procyclical effects of YTS.

10.   Finn (1987) suggests that a major reason for the Thatcher government's U-turn on the funding of YTS was the inner city riots in the summer of 1981.

11.   The logic can be extended to the case of a positive interest rate, but this complicates the notation unnecessarily.

12.   This section take the naïve view that the only costs and benefits associated with training in the firm relate to earnings and productivity. For a full discussion of the administrative costs of training and the detailed benefits, see Thomas *et al.* (1969) and Oatey (1970).

13.   Employment subsidies have been studied extensively and in a wide variety of ways. For the connection between training schemes and employment subsidies, see Metcalf (1982).

14.   These assumptions ensure that the firm cannot continue to expand indefinitely in the short run by capitalizing on the cheap labour which they can pay at a rate substantially below their marginal product.

15.   See Sako and Dore (1986) for evidence of how an employer may substitute between government training schemes and apprenticeships in the UK.

16.   Some studies have argued that r_i should be in (3.20) instead of d_i, but clearly r_i is endogenously defined in its own right.

17.   In some countries the training schemes do not operate like this and in contrast it is the highly motivated individuals who go on to the training programmes. This would give rise to a different form of selection bias.

18.   Further econometric problems can arise within this framework if we permit the possibility of some earnings being observed at certain points in time, but not others, and allow training to last different lengths of time, beginning at different points in time. We abstract from such complications at this juncture.

19.   See Blundell and Dias (2000) who discuss the case of estimation in the face of individually heterogeneous effects of training.

20.   Further methods for testing for selectivity in panel data models have been examined by Verbeek and Nijman (1992).

21.   Evidence of the importance and sensitivity of this assumption is demonstrated by the debate between Bloom (1984) and Bassi (1986) over Ashenfelter's (1978) results.

22.   See Blundell and Dias (2000), pp. 443–4 for details.

23.   See Rosenbaum and Rubin (1983) for details of the matching model and Heckman *et al.* (1997), and Dehejia and Wabba (1999) for examples of its application to training assessment.

24.   For further details see Dolton and Balfour (2001).

25.   See Duncan and Hoffman (1979), Barron *et al.* (1992) in the USA and Greenhalgh and Stewart (1987) and Green (1990) in the UK for evidence of the different treatment of the sexes with respect to training opportunities and the differential rate of return from training by gender.

26.   There are a large variety of other estimators which can be used for longitudinal and repeated cross-sections in an attempt to assess the effect of training on earnings. Heckman and Robb (1985b) have examined the robustness of such estimators to choice-based sampling and contamination bias. They conclude that the benefits of panel data can often be used to identify the same parameters as longitudinal data.

27. Theoretical economic models which give rise to econometrically testable models of training acquisition and earnings are rare. The example of Jovanovic (1979a) who uses a Brownian motion model (to an absorbing barrier) is an exception.
28. See Dolton *et al.* (1994c) for concrete descriptions of this complexity.
29. An additional problem we have not considered here is the extent to which the aggregation of the time units used to measure unemployment durations can affect the estimation results.
30. A version of this model is suggested by Hotchkiss (1993) and used in the training context by Dolton *et al.* (1994c).
31. It is arguable that sample selection which may occur through the effect of observables can be taken into account by including Z in X, since the hazard equation in (3.36) is a reduced form equation with Z and X exogenous.
32. It is interesting to note that one of the first studies of training by Kiefer (1978) used the amount of time spent on training as a regressor rather than a simple dummy regressor of being on the scheme or not.
33. See Bishop (1991) for an interesting exception.
34. In other countries the selection onto training schemes is voluntary from the unemployed, but there may be a selection process administered by government officials to get onto the programme. For example, in Norway (see Raaum and Torp, 1993) this makes modelling the effects of training very complex.
35. Lillard and Tan (1986) suggest, however, that training effects can only be identified between 8 and 13 years after training, as longer-term data on earnings may have their variance swamped by other factors.
36. Kiefer (1978) does not say how the dependent variable in his probit equation is defined, but it is most likely to be defined as this, given the description of his data.
37. O'Higgins (1994) does also find negative earnings effects of YTS of approximately 8 per cent.
38. Such a problem, with multiple destination states, could be modelled using the Burdett *et al.* (1984) approach.
39. See Parsons (1972), Mortensen (1978), Mincer and Jovanovic (1981), Mincer (1991), Hashimoto (1981, 1982), Brown (1989), Bartel (1991), Bartel and Borjas (1977).
40. See Hashimoto (1982) for a theoretical exposition of this.
41. Clark and Summers (1982, p. 229) suggest 'training and job matching programs offer little prospect for making a significant contribution to the solution of the youth unemployment problem . . . training programs cannot have the desired effects unless coupled with an expansion of the number of jobs'.

References

Abbring, J. and G. Van den Berg (2003), 'The non-parametric identification of treatment effects in duration models', *Econometrica*, **71**(5), 1491–1517.

Abraham, K. and H. Farber (1987), 'Job duration, seniority and earnings', *American Economic Review*, **77**, 278–97.

Acemoglu, D. and S. Pischke (1998), 'Why do firms train? Theory and evidence', *Quarterly Journal of Economics*, **113**(1), 79–119.

Acemoglu, D. and S. Pischke (1999a), 'Beyond Becker: training in imperfect labour markets', *Economic Journal*, **113**, F112–F142.

Acemoglu, D. and S. Pischke (1999b), 'The structure of wages and investment in general training', *Journal of Political Economy*, **107**(3), 539–72.

Ackum, S. (1991), 'Youth unemployment, labour market programs and subsequent earnings', *Scandinavian Journal of Economics*, **93**(4), 531–43.

Ainley, P. and M. Corney (1990), *Training for the Future: The Rise and Fall of the Manpower Services Commission*, London: Cassell.

Aldcroft, D.H. (1992), *Education, Training and Economic Performance 1944–1990*, Manchester: Manchester University Press.

Allen, H.L., B. McCormick and R.J. O'Brien (1991), 'Unemployment and the demand for retraining: an econometric analysis', *Economic Journal*, **101**, 190–201.

Altonji, J. and R. Shakotko (1987), 'Do wages rise with seniority?', *Review of Economic Studies*, **54**, 437–59.

Ashenfelter, O. (1978), 'Estimating the effect of training programs on earnings', *Review of Economics and Statistics*, **60**, 648–60.

Ashenfelter, O. and D. Card (1985), 'Using the longitudinal structure of earnings to estimate the effect of training programs', *Review of Economics and Statistics*, **67**, 648–60.

Baker, M. (1992), 'The effect of training on earnings: an analysis of the National Child Development Survey', mimeo, National Institute of Labour Studies, Flinders University.

Barnow, B. (1987), 'The impact of CETA programs on earnings: a review of the literature', *Journal of Human Resources*, **22**, 157–93.

Barron, J.M., D.A. Black and M.A. Loewenstein (1987), 'Employer size: the implications for search, training, capital investment, starting wages and wage growth', *Journal of Labour Economics*, **5**, 76–89.

Barron, J.M., D.A. Black and M.A. Loewenstein (1989), 'Job matching and on-the-job training', *Journal of Labour Economics*, **7**, 1–15.

Barron, J.M., D.A. Black and M.A. Loewenstein (1992), 'Gender differences in training, capital and wages', *Journal of Human Resources*, **28**(2), 343–64.

Bartel, A. (1991), 'On-the-job training and wage growth of professional employees', mimeo, Columbia University.

Bartel, A. and G. Borjas (1977), 'Specific training and its effects on the human capital investment profile', *Southern Economic Journal*, **44**, 333–41.

Bartholomew, D.J. (1973), '*Stochastic Models for Social Processes*', London: Wiley.

Bassi, L. (1983), 'The effect of CETA on the post-program earnings of participants', *The Journal of Human Resources*, **18**, 539–56.

Bassi, L. (1986), 'Estimating the effect of job training programs using longitudinal data: Ashenfelter's findings reconsidered: a comment', *Journal of Human Resources*, **22**, 300–303.

Bassi, L. and O. Ashenfelter (1986), 'The effect of direct job creation and training programs on low skilled workers', in S. Danziger and D. Weinberg (eds), *Fighting Poverty: What Works and What Doesn't*, Cambridge: Harvard University Press.

Becker, G. (1975), *Human Capital*, 2nd edn, New York: Columbia University Press.

Beenstock, M. (1992), 'Training and the time to find a job: some non-parametric results for Israel 1989–91', mimeo, Hebrew University of Jerusalem.

Begg, I.G., A.P. Blake and B.M. Deakin (1991), 'YTS and the labour market', *British Journal of Industrial Relations*, **29**(2), 223–36.

Bishop, J.H. (1991), 'On the job training of new hires', in D. Stern and J. Ritzen (eds), *Market Failure*.

Bjorklund, A., R. Haveman, R. Hollister and B. Holmlund (1991), *Labour market policy and unemployment insurance*, Oxford: Clarendon Press.

Bloch, F. (1979), *Research in Labor Economics: Evaluating Manpower Training Programs*, Greenwich, Conn: JAI Press.

Bloom, H. (1984), 'Estimating the effect of job training programs using longitudinal data: Ashenfelter's findings reconsidered', *Journal of Human Resources*, **19**(4), 544–56.

Blundell, R. and M. Dias (2000), 'Evaluation Methods for Non-Experimental Data', *Fiscal Studies*, **21**, 427–68.

Blundell, R., L. Dearden and C. Meghir (1996), *The Determinants of Work Related Training*, London: Institute of Fiscal Studies.

Blundell, R., C. Dias, C. Meghir and J. Van Reenen (2000), 'Evaluating the employment impact of mandatory job search assistance: the UK New Deal Gateway', mimeo, Institute of Fiscal Studies.

Bonnal, L., D. Fougère and A. Sernadon (1997), 'Evaluating the impact of French employment policies on individual labour market histories', *Review of Economic Studies*, **64**, 683–713.

Booth, A. (1991), 'Job related formal training: who receives it and what is it worth?', *Oxford Bulletin of Economics and Statistics*, **53**(3), 281–94.

Borus, M.E. (1964), 'A cost–benefit analysis of the economic effectiveness of retraining the unemployed', *Yale Economic Essays*, **14**(2), 371–429.

Borus, M.E. (ed.) (1972), *Evaluating the Impact of Manpower Programs*, Lexington, MA: Heath Lexington Books.

Bradley, S. (1994) 'The Youth Training Scheme: a critical review of the literature', *International Journal of Manpower*, **16**, 30–56.

Breen, R. (1991), 'Assessing the effectiveness of training and temporary employment schemes: some results from the youth labour market', *The Economic and Social Review*, **22**(3), 171–98.

Brown, J.N. (1989), 'Why do wages increase with tenure? On-the-job training and life-cycle wage growth observed within firms', *American Economic Review*, **79**(5), 971–91.

Bryant, E.C. and K. Rupp (1987), 'Evaluating the impact of CETA on participant earnings', *Evaluation Review*, **11**, 473–92.

Burdett, K., N.M. Kiefer, D. Mortensen and G.R. Neumann (1984), 'Earnings, unemployment, and the allocation of time over time', *Review of Economic Studies*, **51**, 559–78.

Burtless, G. (1993), 'The use of experimental and non-experimental designs in labor market program evaluation', paper presented at the Danish Presidency Conference, 'Measuring Labour Market Measures', Ministry of Labour, Copenhagen, Denmark.

Burtless, G. and L. Orr (1986), 'Are Classical Experiments Needed for Manpower Policy?', *Journal of Human Resources*, **21**, 606–39.

Card, D. and D. Sullivan (1988), 'Measuring the effect of subsidized training programs on movements in and out of employment', *Econometrica*, **56**(3), 497–530.

Chapman, P.G. (1993), *The Economics of Training*, Hemel Hempstead: Harvester Wheatsheaf.

Chapman, P.G. and M.J. Tooze (1987), *The Youth Training Scheme in the United Kingdom*, Aldershot: Avebury.

Clark, K. and L.H. Summers (1982), 'The dynamics of youth unemployment', in R.B. Freeman and D. Wise (eds), *The Youth Labor Market Problem: Its Nature, Causes and Consequences*, National Bureau of Economic Research, Chicago: University of Chicago Press.

Cockx, B. (1991), 'Unemployment benefits versus training', mimeo.

Couch, K.A. (1992), 'New evidence on the long-term effects of employment training programs', *Journal of Labor Economics*, **10**(4), 380–88.

Cox, D. and D. Oakes (1984), *Analysis of Survival Data*, London: Chapman Hall.

Deakin, B.M. and C.F. Pratten (1987), 'Economic Effects of YTS', *Employment Gazette*, **95**, 491–7.

Dehejia, R. and S. Wabba (1999), 'Causal effects in non-experimental studies: evaluating the evaluation of training programs', *Journal of American Statistical Association*, **94**, 1053–62.

Dickinson, K., T.R. Johnson and R. West (1986), 'An analysis of the impact of CETA programs on participants' earnings', *Journal of Human Resources*, **21**(1), 64–91.

Dolton, P.J. (1993), 'The economics of youth training in Britain', *Economic Journal*, **103**, 1261–78.

Dolton, P.J. (2000), 'Does the new deal match up?', mimeo, University of Newcastle-upon-Tyne.

Dolton, P.J. and Y. Balfour (2001), 'Youth unemployment, government training and the new deal in the UK', Appendix 8 in '*New Deal: An Evaluation*', House of Commons, Education and Employment Committee, 64–80, London: HMSO.

Dolton, P.J. and M. Kidd (1998), 'Job changes, occupational mobility and human capital acquisition: an empirical analysis', *Bulletin of Economic Research*, **50**(4), 265–95.

Dolton, P.J. and D. O'Neill (1996b), 'Unemployment duration and the restart effect: some experimental evidence', *Economic Journal*, **106**, 387–400.

Dolton, P.J and D. O'Neill (2002), 'The long-run effects of unemployment monitoring and work-search programs: experimental evidence from the UK', *Journal of Labor Economics*, **20**(2), 381–403.

Dolton, P.J., G.H. Makepeace and B. Gannon (1999), 'The earnings and employment effects of young people's vocational training in Britain', *The Manchester School*, **69**(4), 387–417.

Dolton, P.J., G. Makepeace and J.G. Treble (1994a), 'The wage effect of YTS : evidence from YCS', *Scottish Journal of Political Economy*, **41**(4), 444–53.

Dolton, P.J., G. Makepeace and J.G. Treble (1994c), 'The Youth Training Scheme and the school to work transition', *Oxford Economic Papers*, **46**(4), 629–57.

Duncan, G.J. and S. Hoffman (1979), 'On-the-job training and earnings differences by race and sex', *Review of Economics and Statistics*, **61**(4), 594–607.

Eberwain, C., J. Ham and R. Lalonde (2002), 'Alternative methods of estimating program effects in event history models', *Labour Economics*, **9**, 249–78.

Eichler, M. and M. Lechner (2002), 'An evaluation of public employment programmes in the East German state of Sachsen-Anhalt', *Labour Economics*, **9**(2), 143–86.

Employment Gazette (1986), 'Why some young people reject YTS', **94**(6), 271–3, HMSO.

Evans, B. (1992), *The Politics of the Training Market*, London: Routledge.

Finegold, D. and D. Soskice (1988), 'The failure of training in Britain; analysis and prescription', *Oxford Review of Economic Policy*, **4**(3), 21–53.

Finn, D. (1987), *Training without Jobs: New Deals and Broken Promises*, London: Macmillan.

Fraker, T. and R. Maynard (1987), 'Evaluating comparison groups designs with employment-related programs', *Journal of Human Resources*, **22**(2), 194–227.

Friedlander, D., D. Greenberg and P. Robins (1997), 'Evaluating government training programs for the economically disadvantaged', *Journal of Economic Literature*, **35**, 1809–55.

Gay, R.S. and M.E. Borus (1980), 'Validating performance indicators for employment and training programs', *Journal of Human Resources*, **15**(1), 29–48.

Goldberger, A. (1983), 'Abnormal selection bias', in S. Karlin, T. Amemiya and L. Goodman (eds), *Studies in Econometrics, Time Series and Multivariate Statistics*, Saint Louis, MO: Elsevier.

Green, F. (1990), 'Sex discrimination in job related training', *British Journal of Industrial Relations*, **29**, 295–304.

Green, F., M. Hoskins and S. Montgomery (1996), 'The effects of company training, further education and the youth training scheme on the earnings of young employees', *Oxford Bulletin of Economics and Statistics*, **58**, 469–88.

Greenberg, D. (1997), 'The leisure bias in cost–benefit of employment and training programs', *Journal of Human Resources*, **32**(2), 413–39.

Greenhalgh, C. and G. Mavrotas (1991a), 'Job training, new technology and labour turnover', University of Oxford, Institute of Economics and Statistics, Applied Economics Discussion Paper, no.121.

Greenhalgh, C. and G. Mavrotas (1991b), 'Workforce training in the Thatcher era – market forces and market failures', University of Oxford, Institute of Economics and Statistics, Applied Economics Discussion Paper, no. 120.

Greenhalgh, C. and M. Stewart (1987), 'The effects and determinants of training', *Oxford Bulletin of Economics and Statistics*, **49** (2).

Gritz, R.M. (1993), 'The impact of training on the frequency and duration of employment', *Journal of Econometrics*, **57**, 21–51.

Gustman, A.L. and T.L. Steinmeier (1988), 'A model for analyzing youth labor market policies', *Journal of Labor Economics*, **6**, 376–96.

Ham, J. and Lalonde, R. (1994), 'Estimating the effect on the incidence and duration of unemployment: evidence on disadvantaged women from experimental data', in McNabb and Whitfield.

Hamermesh, D. (1971), *Economic Aspects of Manpower Training Programs*, Lexington, MA: Lexington Books.

Han, A. and J. Hausman (1990) 'Flexible parametric estimation of duration and competing risk models', *Journal of Applied Econometrics*, **5**(1), 1–28.

Hashimoto, M. (1981), 'Firm specific human capital as a shared investment', *American Economic Review*, **71**(3), 475–82.

Hashimoto, M. (1982), 'Minimum wage effects on training costs on the job', *American Economic Review*, **72**, 1070–87.

Hausman, J. (1978), 'Specification tests in econometrics', *Econometrica*, **46**, 1251–71.

Hausman, J. and D. Wise (1979), 'Attrition bias in experimental and panel data: the Gary Income Maintenance Experiment', *Econometica*, **47**(2), 455–73.

Haveman, R. and R. Hollister (1991), 'Direct job creation: economic evaluation and lessons for the United States and Western Europe', in Bjorklund *et al.*

Heckman, J.J. (1979), 'Sample selection as a specification error', *Econometrica*, **47**, 153–62.

Heckman, J.J. (1990), 'Varieties of selection bias', *American Economic Review*, papers and proceedings, 313–18.

Heckman, J.J. (1992), 'Randomization and social policy evaluation', in C. Manski and I. Garfinkel (eds), *Evaluating Welfare and Training Programmes*, Cambridge, MA: Harvard University Press.

Heckman, J.J. (1993), 'Alternative approaches to the evaluation of social programs', Ministry of Labour, Denmark.

Heckman, J. and B. Honore (1989), 'The identifiability of the competing risks models', *Biometrika*, **76**, 325–30.

Heckman, J. and B. Honore (1990), 'The empirical content of the Roy model', *Econometrica*, **58**(5), 1121–49.

Heckman, J.J. and J.V. Hotz (1989), 'Choosing among alternative non-experimental methods for estimating the impact of social programs: the case of manpower training', *Journal of American Statistical Association*, **84**, 862–80.

Heckman, J.J. and R. Robb (1985a), 'Alternative methods for evaluating the impact of interventions', in J. Heckman and B. Singer, (eds), *Longitudinal Analysis of Labor Market Data*, New York: Cambridge University Press.

Heckman, J.J. and R. Robb (1985b), 'Alternative methods for evaluating the impact of interventions: an overview', *Journal of Econometrics*, **30**, 238–69.

Heckman, J.J. and R. Robb (1986), 'Alternative identifying assumptions in econometric models of selection bias', in D. Slottje (ed.), *Advances in Econometrics: Innovations in Quantitative Economics: Essays in honor of Robert Basmann*, Greenwich, Conn.: JAI Press, pp. 243–87.

Heckman, J.J. and B. Singer (1984a), 'Econometric analysis of longitudinal data', in Z. Griliches and M.D. Intriligator (eds), *Handbook of Econometrics*, Amsterdam: North Holland.

Heckman, J.J. and B. Singer (1984b), 'A method for minimizing the impact of distribution assumptions in econometric models for duration data', *Econometrica*, **52**(2), 271–320.

Heckman, J.J. and J. Smith (1999), 'The pre-programme dip and the determinants of participation in a social programme: implications for simple programme evaluation strategies', *Economic Journal*, **109**, 313–48.

Heckman, J.J., J.V. Hotz and M. Dabos (1987), 'Do we need experimental data to evaluate the impact of manpower training on earnings?', *Evaluation Review*, **11**, 395–427.

Heckman, J.J., H. Ichimura and P. Todd (1997), 'Matching as an econometric evaluation estimator: evidence from evaluating a job training programme', *Review of Economic Studies*, **64**(4), 605–54.

Heckman, J.J., R. Lalonde and J. Smith (1999), 'The economics and econometrics of active labor market programs', in O. Ashenfelter and D. Card (eds), *Handbook of Labor Economics*, Amsterdam: North Holland.

HMSO (1992), *Training Statistics*, London: HMSO.

Hotchkiss, J.L. (1993), 'The effect of transitional employment on the duration of search: A selectivity approach', mimeo, Georgia State University.

Hotz, J. (1992), 'Designing an evaluation of the Job Training Partnership Act', in C. Manski and I. Garfinkel (eds), *'Evaluating Welfare and Training Programmes*, Cambridge, MA: Harvard University Press.

Hui, W.T. (1991), 'Reservation wage analysis of unemployed youths in Australia', *Applied Economics*, **23**, 1341–50.

Hutt, W.H. (1939), *The Theory of Idle Resources: A Study in Definition*, London: Jonathan Cape.

Jensen, P. and N. Westergard-Neilson (1987), 'A search model applied to the transition from education to work', *Review of Economic Studies*, **54**, 461–72.

Jimenez, E. and B. Kugler (1987), 'The earnings impact of training duration in a developing country', *Journal of Human Resources*, **22**(2), 228–47.

Johansson, P-O. (1991), 'Cost–benefit rules for job-training programmes', in Bjorklund *et al.*

Johnson, G. (1979), 'The labor market displacement effect in the analysis of the net impact of manpower training programs', in F. Bloch (ed.), *Evaluating manpower training programs*, Greenwich, Conn.: JAI Press, pp. 227–54.

Jones, I. (1988), 'An evaluation of YTS', *Oxford Review of Economic Policy*, **4**(3), 54–71.

Jovanovic, B. (1979a), 'Job matching and the theory of turnover', *Journal of Political Economy*, **87**, 972–90.

Kaitz, H. (1979), 'Potential use of Markov processes to determine program impact', in Farrell Bloch (ed.), *Research in Labour Economics*, supplement 1, Greenwich, Conn.: JAI Press.

Katz, E. and A. Ziderman (1990), 'Investment in general training: the role of information and labour mobility', *Economic Journal*, **100**, 1147–59.

Katz, L. and B. Meyer (1990), 'The impact of potential duration of unemployment benefits on the duration of unemployment', *Journal of Public Economics*, **47**, 45–72.

Keeley, M.C. and P. Robins (1985), 'Government programs, job search requirements, and the duration of unemployment', *Journal of Labor Economics*, **3**, 337–62.

Kiefer, N. (1978), 'Federally subsidized occupational training and the employment and earnings of male trainees', *Journal of Econometrics*, **8**, 111–25.

Kiefer, N. (1979), 'Population heterogeneity and inference from panel data on the effects of vocational education', *Journal of Political Economy*, **87**(5), S213–S226.

King, D. (1995), *Actively Seeking Work? The Politics of Unemployment and Welfare Policy in the United States and Great Britain*, Chicago and London: University of Chicago Press.

Lalonde, R. (1986), 'Evaluating the econometric evaluations of training programs with experimental data', *American Economic Review*, **76**(4), 604–20.

Lalonde, R. (1995), 'The promise of public sponsored training programmes', *Journal of Economic Perspectives*, **9**, 149–68.

Lalonde, R. and R. Maynard (1987), 'How precise are evaluations of employment and training programs? Evidence from a field experiment', *Evaluation Review*, **11**, 428–51.

Lancaster, T. (1990), *The Econometric Analysis of Transition Data*, Cambridge: Cambridge University Press.

Layard, R. (1979), 'The costs and benefits of selective employment policies: the British case', *British Journal of Industrial Relations*, **17**.

Lee, L.F. (1983), 'Generalized econometric models with selectivity', *Econometrica*, **51**, 153–61.

Leuven, E. (2001), 'Studies in the economics of training', PhD, University of Amsterdam.

Lillard, D. and H. Tan (1986), 'Private sector training: who gets it and what are its effects?', *Rand Report*, R-331–DOL/RC.

Little, R. and D. Rubin (1987), *Statistical Analysis with Missing Data*, New York: Wiley.

Lynch, L. (1992), 'Private sector training and the earnings of young workers', *American Economic Review*, **82**, 299–312.

Lynch, L. (ed.) (1994), *International Comparisons of Private Sector Training*, NBER, Chicago: University of Chicago Press.

Main, B. and D. Raffe (1983), 'Determinants of employment and unemployment among school leavers: evidence from the 1979 survey of Scottish school leavers', *Scottish Journal of Political Economy*, **30**, 1–17.

Main, B.G.M. (1991), 'The effect of the Youth Training Scheme on employment probability', *Applied Economics*, **23**, 367–72.

Main, B.G.M. and M. Shelly (1990), 'The effectiveness of YTS as a manpower policy', *Economica*, **57**, 495–514.

Malcolmson, J., J. Maw and B. McCormick (2003), 'General training by firms, apprentice contracts and public policy', *European Economic Review*, **47**, 197–227.

Manski, C. (1988), 'Anatomy of the selection problem', *Journal of Human Resources*, **24**(3), 341–80.

Manski, C. and I. Garfinkel (eds) (1992), *Evaluating Welfare and Training Programs*, Cambridge, MA: Harvard University Press.

Marsden, D. and P. Ryan (1990), 'Institutional aspects of youth employment and training in Britain', *British Journal of Industrial Relations*, **28**, 351–69.

McNabb, R. and K. Whitfield (1994), *The Market for Training: International Perspectives on Theory, Methodology and Policy*, Aldershot: Avebury.

Mealli, F., S. Pudney and J. Thomas (1996), 'Training duration and post-training outcomes: a duration-limited competing risks model', *Economic Journal*, **106**, 422–33.

Metcalf, D. (1982), 'Alternatives to unemployment: special employment measures in Britain', Policy Studies Institute.

Mincer, J. (1962), 'On-the-job training: costs, returns and some implications', *Journal of Political Economy*, **70** (Supplement), 550–79.

Mincer, J. (1974), Schooling, Experience and Earnings, National Bureau of Economic Research, New York: Columbia University Press.

Mincer, J. (1991), 'Job training: costs, returns and wage profiles', in Stern and Ritzen.

Mincer, J. and B. Jovanovic (1981), 'Labour mobility and wages', in S. Rosen (ed.), *Studies in Labor Markets*, Chicago: University of Chicago Press.

Ministry of Labour, Denmark (1993), '*Measuring labour market measures*', Conference Proceedings, Kolding, Denmark.

Moffitt, R. (1987), 'Symposium on the econometric evaluation of manpower training programs: introduction', *Journal of Human Resources*, **22**(2), 149–56.

Mortensen, D. (1978), 'Specific capital and labour turnover', *The Bell Journal of Economics*, **9**, 572–86.

Mortensen, D. (1988), 'Wages, separations, and job tenure: on-the-job specific training or matching?', *Journal of Labour Economics*, **6**, 443–71.

Narendranathan, W. and M. Stewart (1991), 'Simple methods for testing the proportionality of cause-specific hazards in competing risk models', *Oxford Bulletin of Economics and Statistics*, **53**(3), 331–40.

Oatey, M. (1970), 'The economics of training with respect to the firm', *British Journal of Industrial Relations*, **8**, 1–21.

O'Higgins, N. (1994), 'YTS, employment and sample selection bias', *Oxford Economic Papers*, **46**, 605–28.

Olsen, R.J., A. Smith and G. Farkas (1986), 'Structural and reduced-form models of choice among alternatives in continuous time: youth employment under a guaranteed jobs program', *Econometrica*, **54**(2), 375–94.

Pagan, A. and F. Vella (1989), 'Diagnostic tests for models based on individual survey data: a survey', *Journal of Applied Econometrics*, **4**, S29–S59.

Parsons, D.O. (1972), 'Specific human capital: an application to quit rates and layoff rates', *Journal of Political Economy*, **80**, 1120–43.

Pencavel, J.H. (1972), 'Wages, specific training and labour turnover', *International Economic Review*, **13**, 53–64.

Piggott, J. and B. Chapman (1995), 'Costing the job compact', *Economic Record*, **71**, 313–28.

Pigou, A. (1912), *Wealth and Welfare*, London: Macmillan.

Price, D. (2000), *Office of Hope*, Policy Studies Institute, London: Central Press.

Raaum, O. and H. Torp (1993), 'Evaluations of labour market training programmes: some experiences with an experimental design', paper presented at the Danish Presidency Conference, 'Effects and Measuring of Effects of Labour Market Policy Initiatives', Kolding, April.

Raaum, O. and H. Torp (2002), 'Labour market training in Norway – effect on earnings', *Labour Economics*, **9**, 207–47.

Regner, A. (2002), 'A nonexperimental evaluation of training programs for the unemployed in Sweden', *Labour Economics*, **9**, 187–206.

Riddell, C. (1991), 'Evaluation of manpower and training programmes: the North American experience', *Evaluating Labour Market and Social Programmes: The Complex State of the Art*, Paris: OECD.

Ridder, G. (1986), 'Life-cycle patterns in labour market experience: a statistical analysis of labour histories of adult men', academisch proefschrift universiteit van amsterdam.

Ridder, G. (1990), 'Attrition in multi-wave panel data', in J. Hartog, G. Ridder and J. Theeuwes (eds.), *Panel Data and Labour Market Studies*, Amsterdam: North-Holland.

Ritzen, J.M. (1991), 'Market failure for general training and remedies', in Stern and Ritzen.

Rosenbaum, P. and D. Rubin (1983), 'The central role of the propensity score in observational studies for causal effects', *Biometrika*, **70**, 41–50.

Roy, A.D. (1951), 'Some thoughts on the distribution of income', *Oxford Economic Papers*, **3**, 135–46.

Ryan, P. (2002), 'The British "training market" issues and evidence', mimeo, University of Cambridge.

Sako, M. (1991), 'Institutional aspects of youth employment and training policy', *British Journal of Industrial Relations*, **29**, 485–90.

Sako, M. and R. Dore (1986), 'How the Youth Training Scheme helps employers', *Employment Gazette*, **94**, 195–204.

Shackleton, J.R. (1992), 'Training too much? A sceptical look at the economics of skill provision in the UK', IEA, Hobart paper 118.

Sheldrake, J. and S. Vickerstaff (1987), *The History of Industrial Training in Britain*, Aldershot: Avebury.

Shorrocks, T. (1992), 'Spell incidence, spell duration and the measurement of unemployment', mimeo, University of Essex.

Sicherman, N. and O. Galor (1990), 'A theory of career mobility', *Journal of Political Economy*, **98**, 169–92.

Smith, R.E. (1971), 'The opportunity cost of participating in a training program', *Journal of Human Resources*, Autumn.

Stern, D. and J.M. Ritzen (eds) (1991), *Market Failure in Training*, Berlin: Springer-Verlag.

Stevens, M. (1994a), 'Labour contracts and efficiency in on-the-job training', *Economic Journal*, **104**, 408–19.

Stevens, M. (1994b), 'A theoretical model of on-the-job training with imperfect competition', *Oxford Econoimic Papers*, **46**, 537–62.

Stevens, M. (1994c), 'An investment model for the supply of training by employers', *Economic Journal*, **104**, 556–70.

Stevens, M. (1996), 'Transferable skills and poaching externalities', in A. Booth and D. Snower (eds), *Acquiring Skills: Market Failures, their Symptoms and Policy Responses*, Cambridge: Cambridge University Press.

Sueyoshi, G.T. (1992), 'Semi-parametric proportional hazard estimation of competing risks models with time-varying covariates', *Journal of Econometrics*, **5**, 25–58.

Tan, H., B. Chapman, C. Peterson and A. Booth (1991), 'Youth training in the United States, Britain and Australia', *Rand-Report*, 4022–ED.

Thierry, P. and M. Sollogoub (1995), 'Les politiques françaises d'emploi en faveur des jeunes. Une évaluation économetrique', *Revue-Economique*, **46** (3), 549–59.

Thomas, B., J. Moxham and J.A.G. Jones (1969), 'A cost–benefit analysis of industrial training', *British Journal of Industrial Relations*, **7**, 231–64.

Topel, R. (1991), 'Specific capital, mobility and wages: wages rise with job seniority', *Journal of Political Economy*, **99**(l), 145–76.

Van den Berg, G., M. Lindeboom and G. Ridder (1991), 'Attrition in longitudinal panel data and the empirical analysis of dynamic labour market behaviour', mimeo.

Van Reenen, J. (2003), 'Active labour market policies and the British new deal for the young unemployed in context', National Bureau of Economic Research, working paper 9576.

Verbeek, M. and T. Nijman (1992), 'Testing for selectivity bias in panel data models', *International Economic Review*, **33**(3) 681–703.

Westergard-Neilsen, N. (1993), 'The effects of labour market training programs where initial conditions differ', paper presented at the Danish Presidency Conference, 'Effects and Measuring of Effects of Labour Market Policy Initiatives', Kolding, April.

Whitfield, K. and C. Bourlakis (1990), 'An empirical analysis of YTS, employment and earnings', *Journal of Economic Studies*, **18** (1), 42–56.

Wolpin, K. (1987), 'Estimating a structural model: the transition from school to work', *Econometrica*, **55**, 801–18.

Ziderman, A. (1969), 'Costs and benefits of adult training in Great Britain', *Economica*, **36**, 363–76.

Ziderman, A. (1975a), 'Costs and benefits of manpower training programmes in Great Britain', *British Journal of Industrial Relations*, **13**, 223–44.

Ziderman, A. (1975b), 'Cost–benefit analysis of government training centres in Scotland: a simulation approach', in M. Parkin and A.R. Nobay (eds), *Contemporary Issues in Economics*, Manchester: Manchester University Press.

Ziderman, A. (1978), *Manpower Training: Theory and Policy*, London: Macmillan.

Ziderman, A. and C. Driver (1973), 'A Markov chain model of the benefits of participating in government training schemes', *Manchester School*, 401–17.

Zweimuller, J. and R. Winter-Ebmer (1996), 'Manpower training programmes and employment stability', *Economica*, **63**, 113–30.

4   Education and economic growth
Philip Stevens and Martin Weale

1   Introduction

There are two very basic reasons for expecting to find some link between
education and economic growth. First of all at the most general level it is
intuitively plausible that living standards have risen so much over the last
millennium and in particular since 1800 because of education. Progress of
the sort enjoyed in Europe was not observed in the illiterate societies that
have gradually merged into the world economy over the last two hundred
years. To the most casual observer it must seem that there is a link between
scientific advance and the way in which education has facilitated the development of knowledge. Of course the Curies and the Newtons of this
world are few and far between. But people with only very limited education often find it difficult to function at all in advanced societies. Education
is needed for people to benefit from scientific advance as well as to contribute to it.

Secondly, at a more specific level, a wide range of econometric studies
indicates that the incomes individuals can command depend on their level
of education. If people with education earn more than those without,
should not the same be true of countries? If not the rate of change of
output per hour worked, at least the level of output per hour worked in a
country ought to depend on the educational attainment of the population.
If spending on education delivers returns of some sort, in much the same
way as spending on fixed capital, then it is sensible to talk of investing in
human capital, as the counterpart to investing in fixed capital. The process
of education can be analysed as an investment decision.

2   History

Some education has been available since ancient times. In England there is
a fairly large number of schools which can trace their origins back to the
days of Queen Elizabeth (although rather few much older than this).
Nevertheless, the expansion of education is largely something which has
happened in the last 200 years. In the United Kingdom elementary education did not become compulsory until 1870. Very limited free secondary
education was introduced in 1907 and it was not until 1944 that universal
free secondary education was introduced. Only a small minority benefited
from tertiary education until almost the end of the 20th century. Unlike the

case of primary and secondary education there is, however, a lively debate about what level of participation is desirable.

Easterlin (1981) points out that in 1850 very few people outside North-western Europe and North America had any formal education. Even in 1940 that was still true in Africa and in much of Asia and Latin America. The spread of formal school seems to have preceded the beginning of modern economic growth. It is also true that, in some countries, there have been sudden increases in schooling which are not followed by surges in economic development. Furthermore Easterlin suggests some evidence that the type of schooling is very important. Education in Spain was tightly controlled by the Church and focused on oral instruction in religion and a few manual skills. Illiteracy remained rife despite the level of school attendance. He argues that it was the combination of education and protestant Christianity which was responsible for the economic success of countries in North-western Europe and their offshoots, at a time when there was little economic development elsewhere. The link between secular education and the Reformation can be deduced from the observation above that few schools in the UK predate this.

Figure 4.1 shows the expansion of primary education measured as the enrolment rate per 10 000 population drawn from data provided by Easterlin. As an indicator of educational attainment this measure is obviously unsatisfactory, but historical data are limited. The lead of the North European countries is obvious, and they held this lead throughout the 19th century.

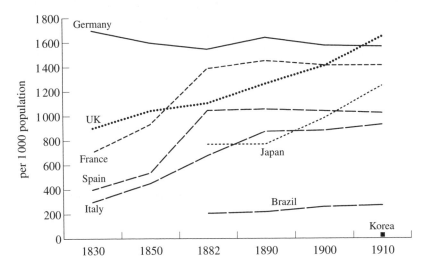

Figure 4.1   Primary school enrolment rates

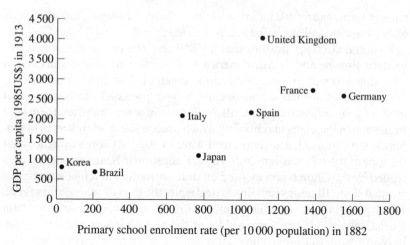

Figure 4.2   Education and GDP per capita

As to a link between education and economic performance, again over this historic period there are severe data limitations. However in Figure 4.2 we plot GDP per capita in 1913 from figures provided by Maddison (1991) against the primary school enrolment rates of 1882.[1] Whatever concerns one might have about drawing inferences from a plot of eight points, the picture is very clear, that high levels of GDP per capita are associated with high levels of primary school enrolment some 30 years earlier. The UK appears to be something of an outlier, with an income level higher than its school enrolment might lead one to expect. Since both levels of education and levels of GDP per capita in any particular year are closely related to those in earlier and later years, any conclusions drawn from the graph do not, of course, answer the question whether the high level of GDP in France, Germany and the UK is a consequence or a cause of the high level of education. The need to resolve this question of causation in a satisfactory manner has been one of the major problems faced by studies linking education and economic performance.

While any deductions from the graph can hardly be regarded as conclusive, it is nevertheless possible, by fitting a regression line, to analyse them in a manner which allows for some sort of comparability with later findings. The result of such an analysis yields the following result (with standard errors in parenthesis):

$$\ln GDP\ per\ capita = 0.35 \ln Enrolment\ Rate + 5.23 \qquad (4.1)$$
$$(0.12) \qquad\quad (0.77)$$
$$R^2 = 0.59$$

Thus this suggests that a 1 per cent increase in the enrolment rate raises GDP by 0.35 per cent. Or, to put it in perspective, suppose that an increase in the enrolment rate of 20 per cent raises the average number of years of education of the labour force from five to six. This is an increase of 0.18 log units which raises GDP by 6.5 per cent; the equation is logarithmic and only approximately linear in percentages. For a less well-educated population an increase from two to three years achieved by an increase in the enrolment rate of 50 per cent or 0.41 log units would raise GDP by 15.4 per cent. The equation has to be regarded very much as a reduced form. Countries with high GDP and high levels of education also have high capital stocks; thus this regression attributes to education effects which, in a fully specified model, would be attributed to the capital stock. Nevertheless we preserve the results for future reference.

3 Returns to education

Any analysis of the determination of economic growth has to have some connection with the microeconomic underpinning mentioned above. Because education delivers economic benefits to individuals, we should expect to see effects of education on groupings of individuals (nations). The effects of education on earnings are the subject of Chapter 1 of this volume. We therefore begin by providing only a brief survey of accounts of the effects of education on individuals.

A classic study was provided by Mincer (1974). He looked at individual earnings as a function of years of education and also other factors such as age and experience. He found that, for white males not working on farms, an extra year of education raised the earnings of an individual by about 7 per cent. However earnings appeared to be an increasing linear and decreasing quadratic function of years of work. When allowance was made for this, the return to a year's schooling increased to 10.1 per cent. The introduction of a quadratic effect in schooling and a cross-product term between education and experience suggested a more complicated pattern of returns but pointed to the early stages of education being more valuable than the later stages. The figure of 7 per cent or 10.1 per cent obviously overstates the return to society from investing in extra education for an individual. It ignores the cost of providing the education, the loss of earnings resulting from time spent being educated and the fact that the benefits of education may decay with age and certainly disappear once an individual retires from the labour force. Secondly, the analysis might be taken to infer that everyone is homogeneous. The benefits of extra education are obviously different for different individuals. People can be supposed to finish their education at the point at which the anticipated return of extra education to them is just balanced by the extra costs. Given this assumption the figure measures the average return per year of education up to the point at which the marginal return to education just equals the marginal benefit identified by the individual. With the reasonable assumption of declining marginal effects of education, it follows that this figure must be higher than the incremental benefit of an extra year's education.[2]

Psacharopoulos (1994) provides an international survey of rates of return to education. The figures cover 78 countries and show returns to primary education ranging from 42 per cent p.a. in Botswana to only 3.3 per cent p.a. in the former Yugoslavia and 2 per cent p.a. in Yemen. The largest return for secondary education was 47.6 per cent p.a. in Zimbabwe, falling to only 2.3 per cent in the former Yugoslavia. The range for tertiary education was somewhat narrower, between −4.3 per cent p.a. in Zimbabwe and 24 per cent p.a. in Yemen. It is not clear that much can be learned from these individual data, but aggregates, either by region or by income level, can average out some of the variability in the individual returns. Thus Psacharopoulos quotes the returns by income level shown in Table 4.1. The table shows that social returns decrease with the amount of education received by individuals and also that they decrease with the income of the country concerned (and thus, it may be assumed, with the abundance of educated labour).

Table 4.1   Rates of return to education

Income band income measured in 1985US$	Social Rate of Return (% p.a.)			
	Mean income	Primary	Secondary	Higher
Low income (< $610)	$299	23.4	15.2	10.6
Lower middle income ($610–$2449)	$1402	18.2	13.4	11.4
Upper middle income ($2500–$7619)	$4184	14.3	10.6	9.5
High income (> $7619)	$13100	n.a.	10.3	8.2
World	$2020	20.0	13.5	10.7

The Mincerian returns show a similar phenomenon (Table 4.2). This suggests that, if we are to look at the influence of education on economic growth through its effects on the education of individuals, we should look to one extra year's education to raise labour income by about 10 per cent, but by only about 6.5 per cent in advanced countries. In broad terms these figures are similar to the effects identified in section 2.

Table 4.2   Mincerian returns to education

Income band (1985 US$)	Mean income	Years' education	Mincerian return
Low income (<$610)	$299	6.4	11.2
Lower middle income ($610–$2449)	$1402	8.4	11.7
Upper middle income ($2500–$7619)	$4184	9.9	7.8
High income (>$7619)	$13100	10.9	6.6
World	$2020	8.7	10.1

4   Growth accounting: the basic framework

Perhaps the simplest framework in which to look at the effects of education on economic growth is offered by the growth accounting framework. The basic model is that output is a function of factor inputs, as described by Solow (1956). For ease of exposition it is assumed that there are two inputs, labour, L, and capital, K, with only one aggregate output, Y. The model extends happily to the case where there are multiple inputs and outputs provided the production function is homothetic. This has the implication that Divisia quantity indices of the inputs and outputs can be constructed, aggregating the inputs and outputs so as to reduce the problem to the structure shown below as explained by Samuelson and Swamy (1974). A represents 'total factor productivity'. As will become clear, the model is not closed because growth of A is assumed to be exogenous.

$$Y = AF(K,L).$$

Differentiating

$$\frac{\dot{Y}}{Y} = F_K \frac{K}{Y} \frac{\dot{K}}{K} + F_L \frac{L}{Y} \frac{\dot{L}}{L} + \frac{\dot{A}}{A}$$

If the factors of production are rewarded by their marginal products, then $F_K[K/Y]$ is the share of profits in the economy and $F_L[L/Y]$ is the share of labour. With a homothetic production function these shares sum to one, so that, if we denote $F_K[K/Y] = \alpha$ then $F_L[L/Y] = 1 - \alpha$ and

$$\frac{\dot{Y}}{Y} = \alpha \frac{\dot{K}}{K} + (1 - \alpha)\frac{\dot{L}}{L} + \frac{\dot{A}}{A}.$$

It should be noted that there is no requirement for α to be time-invariant. If the underlying production function is Cobb–Douglas, that is, however, the case.

Suppose there are different types of labour indexed by years of education, so that L_t is the input of labour with t years of education combined in some form to give an aggregate labour equivalent.

$$L = L(L_0, L_2, \ldots L_T).$$

Then we have

$$\frac{\dot{Y}}{Y} = F_K \frac{K}{Y} \frac{\dot{K}}{K} + F_L \sum \frac{\partial L}{\partial L_i} \frac{L_i}{Y} \frac{\dot{L}_i}{L_i} + \frac{\dot{A}}{A}. \qquad (4.2)$$

Here the marginal product of each type of labour is given as $[dF/dL]$ $[\partial L/\partial L_i] = w_i$ if each type of labour is paid its marginal product and the labour aggregator is also homothetic. This means that

$$\frac{\dot{Y}}{Y} = F_K \frac{K}{Y} \frac{\dot{K}}{K} + \sum w_i \frac{L_i}{Y} \frac{\dot{L}_i}{L_i} + \frac{\dot{A}}{A}.$$

It follows that the contribution of expansion of each type of labour is given as its rate of growth multiplied by the share of earnings of this type of labour in the total product.

The growth accounting framework can be used to indicate the implications of the figures of section 3 for economic growth. If a country increases the average number of years of education of its workforce by one, and one assumes that educated and uneducated labour are perfect substitutes for each other, so that it does not matter whether everybody's education has increased by the same amount, or whether some people have expanded their education by more, and others less, than one year, then the effective labour supply is increased by the same amount. The increase in output resulting from this is the increase in effective labour multiplied by the share of labour in the overall product. It is quite likely that countries with high levels of education will also have more capital per worker; indeed if the amount of capital per effective worker is the same before and after the increase in educational attainment, they will have to. As a result the overall percentage increase in output is likely to be the same as the increase in the effective labour force; using the Mincerian return for the world this is 10.1 per cent per extra year of education. But if the share of labour in the product is only 2/3 (for example, Mankiw *et al.*, 1992), one extra year's education contributes only 6.7 per cent to output growth and the remainder is due to the capital stock rising *pari passu*.

There are many practical examples of this calculation. For example, Matthews *et al.* (1982) imply that between 1856 and 1973 an improved level of education contributed 0.3 per cent p.a. to the growth of output in the UK (with overall growth of 1.9 per cent p.a.). Dougherty and Jorgenson (1997) provide the figures shown in Table 4.3 for the contribution of improved labour quality to labour input in the G7 countries. Using the growth accounting framework, their contribution to overall economic growth can be found by multiplying by the share of labour. The figures shown in Table 4.3 are calculated assuming a labour share of 2/3. It should be noted that labour quality is a wider variable than education; it reflects all factors leading to growth in the number of well paid relative to badly paid workers.

Table 4.3 *Growth of labour quality and its contribution to overall economic growth, 1960–89*

	Labour quality improvement	Contribution to growth	Growth of output per capita
Canada	0.74	0.50	2.93
France	0.73	0.49	3.04
Germany	0.41	0.28	2.91
Italy	0.19	0.12	3.74
Japan	1.16	0.79	5.39
United Kingdom	0.38	0.26	2.15
United States	0.59	0.40	2.07

A defect of the model, however, is the fact that growth in total factor productivity is exogenous. If the rate of growth of total factor productivity is itself dependent on the level or the rate of change of educational attainment, then growth accounting will understate the true contribution of education to economic growth.

5   Educated labour as a factor of production

There have been a number of studies comparing output per worker (or initially because of data constraints output per capita) in a number of different countries, based on variants of this approach. Perhaps the best known was by Mankiw *et al.* (1992). Instead of relying on the sort of growth accounting exercise described above, they assumed that there were two types of labour, educated and uneducated. The proportion of educated labour was indicated by the proportion of the labour force with secondary education. Thus, by contrast to the studies above, they assumed that the production function took the form

$$Y = K^{\alpha} H^{\beta} (AL)^{1-\alpha-\beta}, \tag{4.3}$$

where H is the stock of human capital.

To develop this further, we denote the fraction of income invested in physical capital by s_k and the fraction invested in human capital by s_h. L and A are assumed to grow at rates of n and g, respectively and these are assumed to be the same everywhere; δ is assumed to be the rate of depreciation of both physical and human capital. The rates of change of the stocks of physical and human capital per unit of effective labour are given by

$$\dot{k} = s_k y - (n + g + \delta)k$$
$$\dot{h} = s_h y - (n + g + \delta)h,$$

where $y = Y/AL$, $k = K/AL$ and $h = H/AL$ are quantities per effective unit of labour.

We can calculate from these expressions the steady-state values of k and h, using these to derive an expression in terms of the rate of saving and the rate of accumulation of human capital:

$$\ln\frac{Y}{L} = \ln A + gt + \frac{\alpha}{1 - \alpha - \beta}\ln(s_k) - \frac{\alpha + \beta}{1 - \alpha - \beta}\ln(n + g + \delta) \qquad (4.4)$$
$$+ \frac{\beta}{1 - \alpha - \beta}\ln(s_h).$$

Mankiw *et al.* explain differences in output per person in 98 countries which do not produce oil in 1985. They measure the rate of accumulation of human capital by the fraction of the working age population in secondary school. They find they can accept the restrictions that the coefficients on $\ln(s_k)$, $\ln(n + g + \delta)$ and $\ln(s_h)$ sum to zero[3] with a p-value of 0.41. The implied value of α is 0.31 and of $\beta = 0$ 28. They note that these figures are consistent with the idea that the proportion of income paid to capital is about 1/3 of the total and also that figures of the United States based on the relationship between the minimum wage and the average wage suggest that β is between 1/3 and 1/2. Thus, although these calculations are in many ways rough and ready, they give an answer which is plausible. The authors also present results showing that, if the human capital variable is omitted from the estimation (that is, $\beta = 0$), the estimate of α which emerges is 0.6. This is quite inconsistent with the observation that the share of output accruing to capital is 1/3. Although the sample is split between developing countries and the OECD countries the authors do not use any statistical test to explore whether they can accept the hypothesis that the coefficients are common to the OECD and the developing countries.

There are a number of reasons for being unhappy about this approach. First of all, the analysis assumes, *faute de mieux*, that the production function is Cobb–Doublas. In other words the elasticity of substitution between capital and each of the two types of labour is one, as is the elasticity of substitution between the two types of labour. Without information on wage rates it is not possible to test this. But *a priori* one might expect a higher elasticity of substitution between the two types of labour than between labour and capital. There could also be concerns about the use of 1985 data to infer steady state values and the assumption that the ratios of physical and, more particularly, human capital to effective labour have reached their steady states. The model has the same property as those discussed earlier; when the proportion of people with secondary education stops rising (as it eventually must), growth in output per capita can be generated only by rising capital intensity. The decline in the rate of return which follows from this will eventually mean that growth comes to a halt.

Nevertheless it is impossible to avoid the urge to make a comparison between the coefficients quoted by Mankiw *et al.* and those found in equation (4.1). If we assume that the enrolment data are proportional to saving in the form of human capital, then they play the role of s_h in equation (4.4). If saving in physical capital is uncorrelated with saving in human capital, then, with the values of α and β suggested by Mankiw *et al.*, in an equation explaining output levels by enrolment rates alone, we should anticipate a coefficient of 0.75. To the extent that s_h and s_k are positively correlated, we should expect a larger coefficient, with a maximum value being given by $(\alpha + \beta)/(1 - \alpha - \beta) = 1.5$. These figures are markedly higher than the value of 0.35 found in equation (4.1). It is nevertheless difficult to relate the two figures, or to derive a sensible estimate of the return to education from these estimates. The equation suggests here that a country with no secondary education will have zero output; equation (4.1) had the same implication about primary school education. Thus both equations are unlikely to be informative about the effects of expanding education (secondary in this case) from a very low base. While it made some sense to convert the primary school enrolment rates into years of education, even though schooling in backward countries is often interrupted, it is much harder to do this with secondary school enrolment figures because we do not know what primary school enrolment rates are linked with them. The simple assumption that everyone has primary school education before anyone embarks on secondary school education is plainly incorrect.

It is likely, nevertheless, that an increase in secondary school enrolment of 1 per cent has a smaller proportional effect on the average level of education of the labour force than does an increase in the primary school enrolment rate of the same proportion, making the gap between the figures presented here and that of equation (4.1) smaller. It is not obvious, however, how far this effect reduces the gap.

6   Education and endogenous growth

There are a number of ways in which the change in total factor productivity can be rendered endogenous. They tend to involve a departure from the production function above with its types of labour with different degrees of education. Instead Lucas (1988), for example, assumes that, in addition to the stock of physical capital, there is a metaphysical variable called human capital, h. A fraction u is devoted to production while the remainder is devoted to accumulation of human capital. The average level of human capital in the economy determines the level of total factor productivity. Lower-case variables are used to indicate *per capita* variables.

$$y = Ah_a^\gamma f(k, uh).$$

Here human capital plays two roles. First of all, if f has constant returns to scale, then, as human and physical capital increase in step, so does $f(k, uh)$. But if $\gamma > 0$ then there are overall increasing returns to scale. Output increases more than in proportion to increases in the supplies of factors of production. In particular increases in the stock of human capital should have a marked effect on the rate of growth of output.

The rate of growth of human capital is given as

$$\frac{h}{h} = \pi(1 - u).$$

These equations stand in sharp contrast to those provided by Mankiw *et al.* They assumed that the returns to the two factors of production, human capital and physical capital, were less than one. The implication was that, even if the stocks of human and physical capital rise without limit, overall output growth declines asymptotically to the rate set by the growth of the exogenous term, A. By contrast, in Lucas's model, output depends only on produced factors and, provided the stock of these increases, output can grow without limit. Note that, if the rate of accumulation of human capital were, instead, of the form

$$\frac{h}{h} = \pi(1 - u)h^{-\zeta},$$

then the accumulation of human capital would eventually decrease and if $\zeta > \gamma$ then output too would be bounded. The rate of growth can be increased by choosing to invest more labour in the expansion of human capital. However, if the whole of labour were invested in adding to human capital (expanding knowledge), no final output would actually be produced. The selected rate of accumulation of human capital will depend on the balance between current and future output.

In both this model and the previous one, an increase in educational attainment (assuming this is related to human capital) must lead to an increase in output. Lucas's model implies that human capital may increase even without any increase in educational attainment. Although the human capital of individuals may decay over time, there is a public body of knowledge, and accumulation of human capital can add to this. Thus, even when educational attainment has stopped increasing, human capital can continue to increase and thus continuing growth is possible. A similar model developed by Romer (1990) assumes that the growth of productivity depends on the existing stock of ideas and the number of people devoting their time to the accumulation of new ideas. In the model of section 5, by contrast, once the whole of the labour force had been educated to the maximum viable standard,[4] growth would be possible only through the accumulation of physical capital or from exogenous total factor productivity growth. Unless the elasticity of substitution between labour and capital is greater than one, without exogenous total factor productivity growth, expansion of output *per capita* would eventually come to an end. It is worthy of note that, in some advanced countries such as Germany, there is pressure to reduce the maximum duration of education. While this is perfectly consistent with continuing improvement in average educational standards for years to come, it does nevertheless suggest that the period in which the educational quality of the labour force has steadily increased is now drawing to a close. Thus the growth accounting model implies that we can now see a point at which human capital will cease to grow and therefore stop its contribution to economic growth.

7   The level and the growth rate

Within the empirical literature there is much, and in some sense unresolved, debate whether, after adjusting for other factors, a high level of education leads to a rapid growth rate, as Lucas's model suggests, or whether a high growth rate can be expected only if the stock of educated capital is expanded, rather as the augmented Solow model implies. The confusion has been augmented by the fact that some researchers instead claim to find that growth in output is unaffected by expansion of education although it is affected by the existing stock (Benhabib and Spiegel, 1994). It should be noted that this is implied by neither model but needs to be explained by the catch-up phenomenon – that countries are catching up with each other, but that differences in steady states will arise from differences in educational attainment. Put like this, the influence of education on the rate of growth can be regarded as describing a situation in which the steady state is defined by the Solow model. In such models with y output *per capita*, y_0 initial output *per capita*, i investment *per capita* and h measured by years of education, growth is given by

$$\Delta \ln y = \theta_0 + \theta_1 \ln y_0 + \theta_2 i/y + \theta_3 h. \tag{4.5}$$

The term in θ_1 indicates a catch-up effect and should be expected to be negative. Nevertheless the presence of the other terms means that output per person does not automatically catch up to some uniform value. Instead the value which is reached depends on the investment ratio and also on the educational standing of the country. The second term reflects the return to capital; θ_2 cannot be interpreted as a return to capital because the dependent variable is measured on a *per capita* basis.

Barro (1997), working with what is essentially equation (4.5), suggests that one extra year of education (for men) raises the growth rate by 1.2 per cent p.a. In fact he suggests a total impact of education on growth of even more than this, because in his framework countries with low incomes *per capita* tend to catch up with those with high incomes. The rate of catch-up depends positively on the number of years of education, reflecting the view that a high level of education makes it easier to absorb best-practice technology. The overall effect is described by Topel (1999) as a huge rate of return. Sianesi and van Reenen (2003) agree that the effect of such a change is implausibly large.

In fact, while there may be questions about the mechanisms, the rate of return implied by such an investment is perfectly reasonable. If a country decides to increase the level of education of its labour force by one year, the first impact is that the labour force falls because the youngest cohort starts work a year later than would otherwise be the case. The level of education of the labour force changes very slowly as the better educated young gradually displace the poorly educated old. Looking at an expansion of secondary/tertiary education from four to five years, we find that the rate of return to the extra education measured by balancing the output forgone in the early years against the extra output produced in the later years is 14 per cent p.a. This is indeed a high, but not implausibly high, rate of return. However, the equation developed by Barro (1997) does not have any explicit role for cooperating capital. The expansion of output resulting from extra education would certainly take place alongside an expansion of the capital stock and, in assessing the benefit of extra education, an adjustment must be made for this. If one assumes that 1/3 of the increase in output is due to accumulation of extra capital, then the rate of return of the investment in incremental education falls to 6.5 per cent p.a.

Topel develops this point, arguing that, if one year of education raises human capital by 13 per cent (rather than the 10.1 per cent identified in Table 4.2), and if countries tend to catch up with the technological leader at a rate of about 3 per cent p.a.,[5] the effects of one extra year of education should accrue only slowly; Topel argues that the impact of one extra year's education on growth will be given by 0.03×13 per cent $= 0.4$ per cent p.a. He argues that the figure of 1.2 per cent p.a. at three times this is 'vastly too big for the model they purport to estimate'; we have already noted that the rate of return implied by the model is inherently reasonable. This is not to say, of course, that Barro's figure is itself correct, but simply to point out that it is a mistake to dismiss it out of hand as implausible.

There is nevertheless an important methodological point. The model he estimates is a regression equation in which the change in output over ten or 20-year periods is a function of a number of variables including educational attainment but also including the initial level of output. Thus the effect of education on growth is conditional on the initial level of output and eventually an increase in education leads to higher output and not faster growth. This dampening effect has the consequence of reducing further the return to education below the figures described above.

Oulton (1997) looks at the role of human capital to explain growth in total factor productivity, thus removing the effects of possible interactions with the stock of physical capital. He finds that a 1 per cent increase in human capital per worker in 1965, measured using a 1996 version of Barro and Lee's (1993) data set, raises the rate of growth of total factor productivity by 0.0365 per cent. Or, to put it another way, an increase in years of education from five years to six years raises growth by 0.73 per cent p.a. The effect is therefore smaller than that identified by Barro; it is, however, calculated after taking account of the effects of any parallel increase in the capital stock and the difference is therefore less than might appear.

Benhabib and Spiegel (1994) work with a differenced version of equation (4.3) but also include lagged GDP per capita as an explanatory variable. They do not find any significant effect for human capital measured in the same way as Barro.[6] They then suggest an alternative model based on the work by Nelson and Phelps (1966). Suppose that, in the United States, where more or less everyone has secondary education, $Y_{US} = A_{US} L_{US}^{\alpha} K_{US}^{1-\alpha}$ and that in other countries $Y_{Other} = A_{Other} L_{Other}^{\alpha} K_{Other}^{1-\alpha}$. If in the other countries there are H_{Other} people with secondary education and $A_{Other} = A_{US} (H_{Other}/L_{Other})^{\gamma}$, then we find $Y_{Other} = A_{US} (H_{Other}/L_{Other})^{\gamma} L_{Other}^{\alpha} K_{Other}^{1-\alpha} = A_{US} H_{Other}^{\gamma} L_{Other}^{\alpha-\gamma} K_{Other}^{1-\alpha}$. The function of secondary education is, however, rather specific as compared to the general role ascribed to human capital. Given a technological frontier defined by the United States, absence of secondary education is a factor leading to production which is in some sense inefficient since the follower country does not utilize all of the available technology (Nelson and Phelps, 1966; Kneller and Stevens, 2002).

If, however, the level of human capital is a factor which influences the rate of adoption of American technology, it will influence the growth rate through its influence on the rate at which productivity catches up with levels in the United States.

$$\frac{\dot{A}_{Other}}{A_{Other}} = \phi \left(\frac{H_{Other}}{L_{Other}} \right) \frac{A_{US}}{A_{Other}}$$

and the rate of growth of log output (rather than productivity) will be given by the sum of the rate of growth of productivity and the rates of growth of the two inputs weighted by the coefficients on them in the production function. On this basis Benhabib and Spiegel (1994) estimate a regression equation in which growth in GDP is explained not by growth in the labour force and the capital stock but by the average level of education. Looking at 78 countries over the period 1965–85, they find evidence to support their view from a further regression which includes an interactive term in the product of human capital and the ratio of per capita GDP in the highest income country to that in the country in question. The effect identified is, nevertheless, very small, with an extra year's education raising output by only 0.35 per cent over 20 years, for a country whose initial per capita income level is half that of the highest income country. Thus they imply a rate of return which suggests that education is scarcely worth bothering with.

Krueger and Lindahl (2001) follow a different tack. In estimation, they split countries into three groups based on education levels. They find a statistically significant positive link between education and growth only for the countries with the lowest level of education. They then explore a quadratic relationship between economic growth and years of education. They find that, for low levels of education, education contributes positively to growth, while for high levels of education it depresses the rate of growth. The marginal effect of education on economic growth is positive for countries where the average worker spends less than 7.5 years in education. Above this, marginal education has a negative effect; the average level of education in the OECD is 8.4 years, so incremental education is expected to depress the growth rate in OECD countries. The authors point out that these findings are also consistent with results provided by Barro (1997).

Another approach is to estimate directly the effect of human capital on the distance of a follower country from the technical frontier in income and human capital levels (Kneller and Stevens, 2002). This overcomes, to some extent, the problems with measurement error that are exacerbated by first-differencing. Any change in variables negatively related to distance from the frontier will lead to higher growth. We consider this approach in more detail in section 11 below.

The evidence on whether the effect of human capital on economic growth is a level or a growth effect is inconclusive. It should, however, be noted that the fact remains that educated people are paid more than uneducated people. With the reasonable assumption that people's marginal product is measured by their wage rate, the most basic model (4.2) implies that an expansion of the number of educated people will lead to growth of output. This observation has such generality that it is difficult to come to any conclusion except that the absence of such an effect has to be regarded as a fundamental flaw of empirical work or, rather, a fundamental criticism of the way in which the empirical work is carried out. The point about the studies mentioned above is that the effects of growth of education were not statistically significantly different from zero. Just because the hypothesis that the effect of expansion of education is zero can be accepted statistically, this does not mean that it is a sensible restriction to impose. A more sensible restriction would be that the effect of education is that given by a coherent theoretical model. Greater emphasis should be put on the values taken by the other coefficients when a coherent restriction is imposed on the effect of growth of the educated labour force than when a zero coefficient is put on it.

8   What sort of education?

The study mentioned by Mankiw *et al.* (1992) defined the role of education by the proportion of the workforce with secondary education. This is obviously only one of a number of possible indicators and there have to be concerns that other equally plausible indicators might have delivered less satisfactory results. The role of different types of education is explored by Wolff and Gittleman (1993). They estimated regression equations which explained growth in output per capita on the basis of the share of GDP invested, the initial level of GDP per capita and groups of six possible indicators of educational standing denoted by $E_i (i = 1 \dots 6)$. These were enrolment rates in each of primary, secondary and tertiary education and attainment rates, that is, the fraction of the workforce with each of these types of education at a date close to the start date from which economic growth was measured.

Thus the equation was of the form

$$\Delta \ln y = \theta_0 + \theta_1 \ln y_0 + \theta_2 \, i/y + \sum_{i=1}^{k} \psi_i E_i. \tag{4.6}$$

Although the underlying model in principle should be used to explain growth in labour productivity, *faute de mieux*, in common with many other such studies growth in output per person is used instead, so no account is taken of the effects of variation in the ratio of hours worked to population in different countries. Wolff and Gittleman look at the world economy but also separate the industrial and upper middle income countries, as defined by the World Bank, from the lower middle income and poor countries. They find that, among the upper income group, where there is much more variation in tertiary education than in primary or secondary education, tertiary education is the only statistically significant variable. On the other hand, for the poor countries primary education is statistically significant while differences in tertiary education, which show rather little variation, are not. There has to be some concern that they consider enrolment in education at the start of the period a better indicator of subsequent economic growth than the educational attainment of the workforce.

9   Data concerns

The construction of the data sets needed for the range of empirical studies has been a substantial undertaking for the various researchers involved. There are obviously questions over the GDP figures used, and particularly so for relatively poor countries where non-market activity is likely to be more important than in advanced countries. However Krueger and Lindahl (2001) draw attention to the problems raised by the accuracy of the measures of education. They discuss two sources of data, those provided by Barro and Lee (1993) and by Kyriacou (1991). They find the correlation matrix between the two measures in 1965 and 1985, and the changes between them shown in Table 4.4.

This table shows that the individual measures are more closely correlated with themselves across time than they are with each other at the same time.

Table 4.4   Correlations between measures of schooling

	S_{65}^{BL}	S_{85}^{BL}	S_{65}^{K}	S_{65}^{K}	ΔS^{BL}	ΔS^{K}
S_{65}^{BL}	1					
S_{85}^{BL}	0.97	1				
S_{65}^{K}	0.91	0.92	1			
S_{85}^{K}	0.81	0.86	0.88	1		
ΔS^{BL}	0.23	0.46	0.36	0.51	1	
ΔS^{K}	−0.12	−0.03	−0.17	0.33	0.34	1

Note: The sample size is 68; *BL* indicates Barro–Lee data and *K* indicates Kyriacou data; the subscript indicates the year.

Other points worth noting are that the Barro–Lee data show the increment to education being positively correlated with the initial level, while Kyriacou's measure shows it negatively correlated with the initial level. Not surprisingly the effect of measurement errors is augmented when the connection between the changes in education using the two measures is studied: the correlation falls to a low level.

If measurement error is additive, that is, if the published data reflect the true data plus a measurement error which is uncorrelated with the true data, it follows that the less volatile series is the more reliable series, and also that a minimum variance estimate can be produced as a combination of the two based on the results of a regression of the one on the other (Smith *et al.*, 1998). Data on variances and covariances also provided by Krueger and Lindahl (2001) suggest that Kyriacou's figures ought to be preferred to those of Barro and Lee. But the change in education between 1965 and 1985 estimated by Kyriacou has a larger variance than that estimated by Barro and Lee, suggesting a more complex error pattern.

It is, of course, not possible to establish the variance of the measurement error simply from the existence of two different estimates of the same thing, both with measurement errors of unknown variance. And the general result that measurement error in a variable biases an estimate of a regression coefficient on it towards zero applies only to univariate regression. Nevertheless, given the obvious disparity between two measures of the change in years of education, it seems likely that there are substantial measurement errors present and, unless there are strong correlations between this variable and the others in a regression equation, it is likely that a regression coefficient on the change in education as measured by either of these variables will be depressed towards zero; the standard error associated with it will also be larger than would be observed were the variable measured precisely. Thus the failure to find a link between expansion of education and economic growth may easily be attributed to measurement error. Krueger and Lindahl argue that the effect of this is compounded when the change in the capital stock is included as an explanatory variable. Then the coefficient on the growth of capital is restricted to a value of 0.35 (approximating the share of capital internationally) and expansion of education appears to be an important factor behind economic growth. One extra year's education appears to raise GDP per capita by 8 per cent. This, bearing in mind that it is a partial effect, with the capital stock fixed, corresponds to an effect of education on labour income of about 12 per cent, and is therefore rather high. On the other hand the *t*-statistic of the estimate is less than two and, on that basis, it is clear that the estimate is consistent with a much lower (or much higher) true value.

10   Panel modelling

The models and analysis we have described so far tend to look at growth in a cross-section of countries and explain it in terms of initial levels of education, average saving during the period and, as we have discussed above, possibly growth in educational attainment during the period. The regressions have been either cross-section regressions, with growth rates in a number of countries explained by initial circumstances and sometimes capital accumulation during the period, or pooled regressions in which observations for the same country in different periods are combined in the same way as observations for different countries.

Islam (1995) sets out, for the first time, the problem of analysing growth rates as a panel regression problem in standard format. He finds that positive effects of human capital in cross-section regressions turn into negative, but insignificant, effects once panel methods are used. He hints, as Benhabib and Spiegel have suggested, that human capital may affect economic growth through its influence on the catch-up term. The catch-up is much more rapid than that identified by the earlier approaches.

Lee *et al.* (1997) argue that it is a mistake to take the standard Solow model as a reference point. This model has the implication that eventually all countries tend to the same growth rate; its extensions suggest that factors such as education influence the relative income levels of different countries but not their long-run growth rates of per capita income. Starting from a position in which different countries may have different rates of technical progress (represented by country-specific trends and period-by-period country specific shocks) and also different rates of labour force growth, they point out the usual model is a poor approximation to this. They reject the hypothesis of a common technological growth rate and also find a much faster rate of convergence. They do not explicitly look for effects of education but their results are nevertheless important in a discussion of the effects of education and growth because of the methodological issues they raise.

Two points should be made. First of all, if the degree of convergence forced on countries is weaker, because they are allowed different trend growth rates, it is not surprising that the rate at which they converge to their more individual growth paths is faster than if they are required all to converge to the same path. Secondly, since the only indicator variable they use is employment, it is not surprising that they find a degree of heterogeneity; other authors have reduced this by controlling for other effects. Over the time period analysed (1965–89) it must be difficult to distinguish the effects of different steady-state growth paths from the effects of slow convergence to a single growth rate. But, the smaller the number of control variables, the more likely it seems that statistically distinct growth paths will be found.

Recent work at the OECD has led to the construction of an annual data set of educational attainment for OECD countries to allow these issues to be addressed. The education data were combined with existing data on output, savings and labour input so as to make possible a pooled time-series/cross-section analysis. The starting point for the study by Bassanini *et al.* (2001) is equation (4.3), but with a more general expression to take account of factors other than physical and human capital and labour input.

With $Y = K^\alpha H^\beta (AL)^{1-\alpha-\beta}$ and $\alpha + \beta < 1$, they express labour productivity, A, as a function of institutional and other variables which may influence it, and also allow for the fact that labour productivity may grow over time. This general specification leads to steady-state output as a function of the steady-state savings rate, the level of human capital (measured in years of education) and the other influences on productivity. Since the world is not in a steady state, the equation has to be modified to include short-term dynamics to yield a function for the growth in output as a function of savings rates, the change to savings rates, the level and change to human capital and the levels and changes of the various other indicators of interest including inflation variability, government consumption and trade exposure. The analysis therefore addresses the question whether economic growth is influenced by the change in education as well as the level. Pooled mean group estimation (Pesaran *et al.*, 1999) is used to provide estimates of both short-run and long-run coefficients. Using this method, the short-run responses are allowed to vary country by country, while the hypothesis that the long-run responses are the same across all countries is imposed. The analysis suggests, depending on the precise form adopted, that one extra year of education for the workforce raises output by 4–7 per cent; the speed of convergence conditional on the stock of human capital remaining fixed is 12 per cent p.a. rather than the more usual figures of around 5 per cent p.a., but in keeping with the rate quoted by Lee *et al.* (1997); once again, this greater speed of convergence is probably a consequence of allowing greater country heterogeneity than was permitted by the earlier estimation methods. However, given the insignificant negative coefficients on the change to human capital, there is little point in assessing the effects of change in education on economic growth.

11 Education and inefficiency

The model put forward by Nelson and Phelps (1966) (see section 7) suggests that education, or rather the lack of it, is important as an explanation of why countries might fail to use the best-practice technology. The situation they describe is one where there is a single technological frontier on which efficient economies can perform. Those without adequate education are doomed to produce inefficiently, in the interior of the production possibility set rather than on its frontier. This framework is explored by Kneller and Stevens (2002) using stochastic frontier analysis.[7] The basic model stems from the production function given by equation (4.3) but with two stochastic terms introduced:

$$Y_{it} = f(K_{it}, L_{it}, H_{it}) \exp(-\eta_{it}) \exp(\varepsilon_{it}),$$

where Y_{it} is output of country, K_{it} is the capital stock, L_{it} is the labour input (adjusted for hours worked per week) and H_{it} is human capital; $\varepsilon \sim N(0, \sigma^2_\varepsilon)$ reflects the random disturbances which are needed to account for the fact that regression lines do not fit perfectly; η_{it} reflects economic inefficiency ($0 < \eta_{it} < 1$). A country which is fully efficient ($\eta_{it} = 1$) is able to produce on the frontier; otherwise it produces inefficiently with the degree of inefficiency measured by the size of η_{it}. The inefficiency effect is measured by a truncated normal distribution (Battese and Coelli, 1995) and the mean level of inefficiency is denoted by

$$\mu_{ijt} = \delta_0 + \sum_{k=1}^{\kappa} \delta_k z_{k,it}$$

where $z_{k,it}$ is a set of economic, geographic and social factors which influence technical efficiency.

The problem is that the η_{it} are not directly observed; one observes only $v_{it} = \eta_{it} + \varepsilon_{it}$. We can, however, define the efficiency predictor using the conditional expectation of $\exp(-\eta_{it})$ given the random variable ε_{it}:

$$E\varepsilon_{it} = E[\exp(-\eta_{it})|v_{it}]$$

$$= \left\{ \exp\left(-\theta_{it} + \frac{1}{2}\tilde{\sigma}^2\right) \right\} \times \left\{ \Phi\left(\frac{\theta_{it}}{\tilde{\sigma}} - \tilde{\sigma}\right) \Big/ \Phi\left(\frac{\theta_{it}}{\tilde{\sigma}}\right) \right\},$$

where $\Phi(.)$ denotes the distribution function of the standard normal variable,

$$\theta_{it} = (1-\gamma)\left\{\delta_0 + \sum_{k=1}^{\kappa} \delta_k Z_{k,it}\right\} - \gamma v_{it}, \quad \tilde{\sigma}^2 = \gamma(1-\gamma)\sigma^2, \text{ and } \gamma = \frac{\sigma^2}{\sigma^2_\varepsilon + \sigma^2}. \quad (4.7)$$

An operational predictor for the efficiency of country i at time t is found by replacing the unknown parameters in equation (4.7) with the maximum likelihood predictors. The log-likelihood function for this model is presented by Battese and Coelli (1993), as are its first derivatives. In this model the variance of the efficiency term, η_{it} relative to the variance of the overall error, v_{it}, measured by γ, tells us how far the overall variation in output, after adjusting for factor inputs, is due to inefficiency rather than pure stochastic variability. If $\gamma = 0$, then a standard non-frontier methodology is correct, while if $\gamma = 1$ then all of the variation has to be attributed to differing degrees of inefficiency. A statistically significant value of γ different from 0 indicates that the traditional regression approach is misspecified.

The production function is assumed to be determined by the factor inputs of labour, capital and human capital, as discussed above. Regional dummies are included to represent the idea that different technologies are appropriate to countries in different regions. Time dummies are also introduced to explain differences in productivity growth in 1974–87 relative to 1960–73.

Inefficiency is represented as a function of many of the variables which are often placed in straightforward regression equations. It depends on log human capital, openness (*swopen*, as measured by Sachs and Warner, 1995), whether countries are landlocked, their latitudes, inter-country risk, as assessed by Knack and Keefer (1995), the fraction of the population from ethnic minorities and the product of openness and log human capital. The results of the estimation are shown in Table 4.5.

Because the model is non-linear, there is no simple way of interpreting the coefficients on the efficiency terms. However, using the result obtained in Battese and Broca (1997), we can calculate the effect at mean level of efficiency. The effect is $\delta_k C_{it}$, where

$$
C_{it} = 1 - \frac{1}{\sigma} \left[\frac{\phi\left(\dfrac{\bar{\sigma}_{it}}{\sigma} - \sigma\right)}{\Phi\left(\dfrac{\bar{\theta}_{it}}{\sigma} - \sigma\right)} - \frac{\phi\left(\dfrac{\bar{\theta}_{it}}{\sigma}\right)}{\Phi\left(\dfrac{\bar{\theta}_{it}}{\sigma}\right)} \right].
$$

Thus, at mean values of θ, for a closed economy, an increase in years of education of 1 per cent reduces inefficiency by 0.02 per cent; but the same increase reduces inefficiency by 0.34 per cent in an open economy. An increase in education from seven to eight years is an increase of 14 per cent; thus this suggests an increase in output for an open economy of 5 per cent of GDP. This is coherent with the range of figures from microeconomic studies and thoroughly plausible. The determination of the frontier is less satisfactory. The effect of human capital is small but incorrectly signed, which may be due to the presence of h in the part of the model that explains efficiency. The coefficient on capital is considerably larger than is consistent with observed factor shares, while that on labour is correspondingly lower.

The overall conclusion one can draw from this study is that education does seem to be a factor accounting for inefficiency, or a failure to use the

Table 4.5   Parameters of the inefficiency model

	Coefficient	Standard error	t-ratio
Frontier			
Constant	1.673	0.106	15.745
k	0.776	0.007	112.461
l	0.226	0.007	30.592
h	−0.036	0.016	2.232
$t(60-73)$	−0.001	0.001	0.800
$t(74-87)$	−0.015	0.001	9.865
C_1	0.026	0.029	0.918
C_2	−0.132	0.024	5.423
C_3	−0.459	0.0319	14.374
C_4	−0.224	0.044	5.140
C_5	−0.167	0.027	6.200
Efficiency terms			
Constant	−0.011	0.169	0.065
h	−0.025	0.027	0.907
swopen	0.620	0.102	6.093
landlock	0.183	0.044	4.195
latitude	−0.007	0.001	4.773
tropical	0.169	0.067	2.522
ICRGE	−0.0536	0.012	4.633
eth. frac	0.006	0.001	6.209
swopen*h	−0.420	0.073	5.733
σ^2	0.170	0.019	8.838
γ	0.916	0.012	78.057
log likelihood function			59.900
LR test of the one-sided error			657.948

available technology to the best advantage, but, at the same time, only open economies can benefit from the effects of education in reducing inefficiency. That seems to be true even if education is also assumed to influence the position of the frontier.

12   Conclusions

It is difficult to be left completely satisfied by the wide range of studies looking at the effects of education on economic growth. Microeconomic analysis provides estimates of the effect of education on individual incomes, and researchers tend to feel most comfortable with those macroeconomic studies which provide estimates of rates of return similar to those found in microeconomic studies, in the range of 6–12 per cent p.a. Since results which suggested much higher or much lower returns would lack credibility, there has probably been an element of selection bias in the findings which are published. Thus the most that can be concluded from the various studies is that there has been no conclusive evidence suggesting that the returns to education are very different from this. There is, however, some evidence to support the view that education is needed as a means of allowing countries to make good use of available technology with the implication, observed in Mincerian returns, that returns to education diminish with levels of development.

Acknowledgment

Financial support from the Economic and Social Research Council is gratefully acknowledged.

Notes

1. The figure for Korea is in fact that of 1910.
2. There is a separate worry about measures of this sort. They measure the return to the individual, but is education a means of helping people to increase their earning because it helps them to stand out from the crowd? For more on the effects of signalling and screening, see Chapter 2 of this volume.
3. With n as the average rate of growth of the population aged 15–64 between 1960 and 1985 and $g + \delta$ set to 0.05.
4. Since people have finite working lives and each year of education deprives them of a year of work, then, even if increasing education always increases people's earning power once they are working, there is an upper limit to the duration of education which is economically viable.
5. Topel does not give any indication as to the basis for his assumption of a 3 per cent convergence rate.
6. There are a number of alternative explanations of their finding. Temple (1999) has shown that this result may be due to the presence of outliers. Another explanation, suggested by Temple (2001), is that the assumption that the productivity effect of an additional year of schooling is constant may be unduly restrictive. We deal with the third, measurement error, in section 9 below (Krueger and Lindhal, 2001).
7. For more on stochastic frontier analysis, see Chapter 16 of the present volume.

References

Barro, R. (1997), *Determinants of Economic Growth: a Cross-Country Study*, Cambridge, MA: MIT Press.
Barro, R. and J.-W. Lee (1993), 'International comparisons of educational attainment', *Journal of Monetary Economics*, **32**, 363–94.
Bassanini, A., S. Scarpetta and P. Hemmings (2001), 'Economic growth: the role of policies and institutions: Panel data evidence from OECD countries', OECD Economics Department Working Paper No. 283.
Battese, G. and S. Broca (1997), 'Functional forms of stochastic frontier production functions and models for technical inefficiency effects: a comparative study for wheat farmers in Pakistan', *Journal of Productivity Analysis*, **8**, 395–414.
Battese, G. and T. Coelli (1993), 'A stochastic frontier production function incorporating a model for technical inefficiency effects', Working Papers in Econometrics and Applied Statistics, no. 69, Department of Econometrics, University of New England.

Battese, G. and T. Coelli (1995), 'A model for technical efficiency effects in a stochastic frontier production function for panel data', *Empirical Economics*, **20**, 325–32.

Benhabib, J. and M. Spiegel (1994), 'The role of human capital in economic development: evidence from aggregate cross-country data', *Journal of Monetary Economics*, **43**, 143–74.

Dougherty, C. and D. Jorgenson (1997), 'There is no silver bullet: investment and growth in the G7', *National Institute Economic Review*, **162**, 57–74.

Easterlin, R. (1981), 'Why isn't the whole world developed?', *Journal of Economic History*, **41**, 1–19.

Islam, N. (1995), 'Growth empirics: a panel data approach', *Quarterly Journal of Economics*, **110**, 1127–70.

Knack, S. and P. Keefer (1995), 'Institutions and economic performance: cross-country tests using alternative institutional measures', *Economics and Politics*, **7**, 207–27.

Kneller, R. and P. Stevens (2002), 'The role of efficiency as an explanation of international income differences', National Institute Discussion Paper no. 206.

Krueger, A. and M. Lindahl (2001), 'Education for growth: why and for whom?', *Journal of Economic Literature*, **39**, 1101–36.

Kyriacou, G. (1991), 'Level and growth effects of human capital', C.V. Starr Center, New York University.

Lee, K., M. Pesaran and R. Smith (1997), 'Growth and convergence in a multi-country empirical stochastic Solow model', *Journal of Applied Econometrics*, **12**, 357–92.

Lucas, R. (1988), 'On the mechanics of economic development', *Journal of Monetary Economics*, **22**.

Maddison, A. (1991), *Dynamic Forces of Capitalist Development*, Oxford: Oxford University Press.

Mankiw, G., D. Romer and D. Weil (1992), 'A contribution to the empirics of economic growth', *Quarterly Journal of Economics*, **107**, 407–37.

Matthews, R., C. Feinstein and J. Odling-Smee (1982), *British Economic Growth: 1856–1873*, Oxford: Clarendon Press.

Mincer, J. (1974), *Schooling, Earnings and Experience*, New York: Columbia University Press.

Nelson, R. and E. Phelps (1966), 'Investment in humans, technical diffusion and economic growth', *American Economic Review*, **56**, 69–75.

Oulton, N. (1997), 'Total factor productivity growth and the role of externalities', *National Institute Economic Review*, **162**, 99–111.

Pesaran, M., Y. Shin and R. Smith (1999), 'Pooled mean group estimation of dynamic heterogeneous panels', *Journal of the American Statistical Association*, **94**, 621–34.

Psacharopoulos, G. (1994), 'Returns to education: a global update', *World Development*, **22**, 1325–43.

Romer, P. (1990), 'Endogenous technical change', *Journal of Political Economy*, **89**, S71–S102.

Sachs, J. and A. Warner (1995), 'Economic reform and the process of global integration', *Brookings Papers on Economic Activity*, **1**, 1–118.

Samuelson, P. and S. Swamy (1974), 'Invariant economic index numbers and canonical duality: survey and synthesis', *American Economic Review*, **64**, 566–93.

Sianesi, B. and J. van Reenen (2003), 'The returns to education', *Macroeconomics*, **17**, 157–200.

Smith, R., M. Weale and S. Satchell (1998), 'Measurement error with accounting constraints: point and interval estimation for latent data with an application to UK gross domestic product', *Review of Economic Studies*, **65**.

Solow, R. (1956), 'A contribution to the theory of economic growth', *Quarterly Journal of Economics*, **70**, 65–95.

Temple, J. (1999), 'A positive effect of human capital on growth', *Economics Letters*, **65**, 131–4.

Temple, J. (2001), 'Generalisations that aren't? Evidence on education and growth', *European Economic Review*, **45**, 905–18.

Topel, R. (1999), 'The labour market and economic growth', in O. Ashenfelter and D. Card (eds), *The Handbook of Labour Economics*, Amsterdam: North Holland.

Wolff, E. and M. Gittleman (1993), 'The role of education in productivity convergence: does higher education matter?', in A. Szimai, B. van Ark and D. Pilat (eds), *Explaining Economic Growth*, Amsterdam: Elsevier Science Publishers.

5 Skill-biased technical change and educational outcomes
Stephen Machin

1 Introduction

In recent years a great deal of attention has been placed on the skill-biased technical change hypothesis. The key premise of this hypothesis is that employers' demand for labour has shifted dramatically in favour of more skilled and educated workers, principally owing to the fact that they are better suited to working with the new kinds of technologies in modern workplaces. Consequently there have been considerable adjustments in the skill structures of the workforces of many countries as the labour market has altered to cope with these new demands for work and with the new work systems that now operate. This has resulted in a significant improvement in the labour market fortunes of more skilled and educated workers and a significant deterioration in labour market outcomes for the less skilled. In many countries more skilled and educated workers have increased, not only their relative employment, but also their relative wages, thereby increasing labour market inequality.

This chapter builds on, and in places reproduces, some of my earlier research on changes in relative labour demand and technology (some of which is cited in the references, especially Machin, 2002, 2003). It considers the skill-biased technical change hypothesis and its implications for economic outcomes. It explores the mechanisms that researchers have argued underpin the observed labour market shifts in favour of the more educated. The next section begins by presenting some descriptive material on temporal shifts in the skill/education structure of labour markets. Numbers are given for the UK and US labour markets, with a particular focus being placed upon shifts in the educational composition of the workforce, upon the wage payoffs received by educated workers as compared to their less educated counterparts and the implied shifts in labour demand associated with these changes. Section 3 then links the observed changes to measures of technological progress, revealing the skill-biased nature of labour demand across education groups. It also considers other explanations for relative demand having shifted in favour of the more skilled and educated, and some of the arguments proposed by those who are rather sceptical that skill-biased technical change matters. Section 4 concludes by summarizing and discussing the wider implications of the observed shifts.

2   Changes in the educational structure of labour markets

There have been dramatic changes in the education levels possessed by the workforce, and in the wage returns to those education levels, in the labour markets of advanced countries in the last quarter of a century. One striking feature has been the improving labour market position of more educated workers and the collapsing labour market for those with few or no educational qualifications. In most advanced countries the labour market position of more skilled and educated workers as compared to their less skilled counterparts has shifted in favour of the skilled in at least one dimension of relative wages, employment and unemployment. In some countries, most notably the USA and the UK, all of these labour market outcomes moved in favour of the more educated. These two countries also experienced big increases in wage inequality which, when put together with the employment shifts in favour of the skilled, resulted in large rises in overall labour market inequality.

Educational upgrading

The workforce is currently more educated in terms of formal educational attainment and qualifications than it was in the past. Indeed, the pace of change over recent decades has been very rapid. This is shown by the descriptive statistics given in Table 5.1. Column (1) of the table shows the percentage of workers who have a university degree (or higher qualification) for the labour markets of the UK (in Panel A) and the USA (in Panel B) at five-year intervals between 1980 and 2000.

The table reveals rapid increases in the employment shares of college graduates that have occurred in both countries. In the UK in 1980, 5 per cent of workers had a degree, but this rose sharply through the 1980s and 1990s to reach 17 per cent by the year 2000. In the USA there were many more graduates at the start of the 1980s, at around 19 per cent, but there were also rises over time as the graduate share reached over 27 per cent by 2000. In both countries, therefore, the relative supply of graduates increased very sharply between 1980 and 2000. If one considers hours shares of graduates rather than employment shares, reported in column (2) of Table 5.1, one sees a similar pattern with changes over time being of the same order of magnitude, but with a slightly bigger increase in the hours shares in both countries.

Rising wage returns to education

Simple models of supply and demand predict rising supply should dampen down wages. Hence it is natural to think that rising education supply reduces relative wages for the more educated. Column (3) of Table 5.1 considers changes through time in the relative wages of graduates as compared

Table 5.1   *Trends in graduate/non-graduate employment shares, hours shares and relative wages, UK and USA, 1980–2000*

	(1)	(2)	(3)
	A. UK Labour Force Survey/General Household Survey		
	Graduate share of employment (%)	Graduate share of hours (%)	Relative weekly wage (full-timers)
1980	5.0	5.1	1.48
1985	9.8	10.5	1.50
1990	10.2	11.0	1.60
1995	14.0	15.4	1.60
2000	17.2	18.8	1.64
1980–2000	12.2	13.7	0.12
1980–1990	5.2	5.9	0.08
1990–2000	7.0	7.8	0.04
	B. US Current Population Survey		
	Graduate share of employment (%)	Graduate share of hours (%)	Relative hourly wage (full-timers)
1980	19.3	20.4	1.36
1985	22.0	23.6	1.47
1990	23.8	25.6	1.55
1995	25.5	8.1	1.61
2000	27.5	29.5	1.66
1980–2000	8.2	9.1	0.30
1980–1990	4.5	5.2	0.19
1990–2000	3.7	3.9	0.11

Notes: Sample is all people age 18–64 in work and earning, except for relative wages which are defined for full-time workers. The relative wage ratios are derived from coefficient estimates on a graduate dummy variable in semi-log earnings equations controlling for age, age squared and gender (they are the exponent of the coefficient on the graduate dummy). The UK employment and hours shares are from the LFS. The relative wage gaps are from the GHS for 1980, 1985 and 1990 and the LFS in 1995 and 2000 (relative wages from regressions for the overlap year, 1995, were very similar in GHS and LFS). They are weekly wages due to changes to the hours question in the GHS in the 1980s that mean a consistent hourly wage cannot be defined through time. The CPS data are the Economic Policy Institute CPS ORG labour extracts data. I thank John Schmitt for making them available.

to non-graduates. It shows that in both countries, despite their increased numbers, the wages of graduates have not fallen relative to non-graduates. Hence the expected response to supply has not been observed.

The numbers given in column (3) of the table are the relative wages of graduates versus non-graduates for full-time workers (after standardizing for age and gender from a statistical regression). In both countries the relative wage for graduates rose between 1980 and 2000. The increase is very sharp in the USA, going from 1.36 to 1.66, whilst the UK increase is less marked, but shows a rise from 1.48 to 1.64.

There are some decade differences in the observed pace of change of relative wages. The relative wage gaps by education opened out by more in both countries in the 1980s. In the UK, 0.08 of the 0.12 change that occurred between 1980 and 2000 took place in the 1980s, and in the USA, 0.19 of the 0.30 change occurred between 1980 and 1990. It seems clear that from the 1980s onwards the educational wage structures of both countries widened, but at a faster rate in the 1980s than in the 1990s.[1]

Shifts in the relative demand and supply of educated workers
The numbers in Table 5.1 therefore demonstrate simultaneously rising relative wages and employment for the more educated. Hence it seems that increased education supply has not resulted in falling wage differentials between more and less educated people. A plausible, and attractive, way of thinking about why this might be is in terms of an economic model where the wages and employment of skilled and unskilled workers are the outcomes of a race between supply and demand (for example, Manning and Manacorda, 1998, adopt this approach[2]). In this context, to have generated simultaneously higher wages and employment for the skilled, relative demand must have increased by more than relative supply. Put alternatively, demand must have won the race between demand and supply so that employers are prepared to pay workers with appropriate skills and education more than less educated workers, despite there being many more of them supplying their labour.

One straightforward way to rationalize this is to think of the changes in the context of a simple relative demand and supply framework, as in Figure 5.1. The figure shows a labour market with two education types, high education (denoted by an H subscript) and low education (denoted by an L subscript). The initial equilibrium in the model is given by the intersection of the relative labour demand and supply curves given by D_0 and S_0 in the figure, with a relative wage of $(W_H/W_L)_0$ and relative employment of $(N_H/N_L)_0$.

In terms of the UK and US experience what seems to have happened is that the ratio of high to low education wages has gone up at the same time

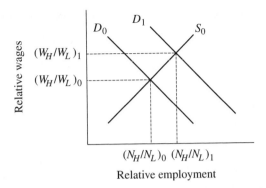

Figure 5.1   Shifts in skill demand in a simple relative demand–supply framework

as the ratio of high to low education employment. It becomes evident that, to get such an outcome, there has to have been an outward shift in the relative demand curve. Suppose the demand curve shifts out to D_1 (and hold supply fixed for expositional purposes). One then ends up with simultaneously higher relative wages and employment for the more educated at $(W_H/W_L)_1$ and $(N_H/N_L)_1$.

Changes in labour market inequality
It is evident that rising wage gaps between more and less educated workers have contributed to rising wage inequality. Some early work on rising wage inequality in the UK (Schmitt, 1995; Machin, 1996a) attributed a sizable gap of rising wage inequality in the 1980s to education. The same is true in some of the earlier US work (e.g. Juhn *et al.*, 1993). However considering more recent decade-on-decade changes yields even more insight.

Table 5.1 has already shown that wage gaps by education opened out by more in the USA and the UK in the 1980s. It is also the case that the 1980s appear to be the decade of faster overall wage inequality increases in both the UK and the USA. In the 1990s there seems to be less change in the wage structure. To reiterate this observation, Figure 5.2 shows the 90–10 hourly wage ratio for the UK and the USA from the mid-1970s onwards. The pattern shows the 1980s widening of the wage structure to be greater than was seen in previous periods, or has been seen since. This is also the time period when educational wage differentials increased most.

From what we know from elsewhere (e.g. Gosling *et al.*, 2000, for the UK, or Card and DiNardo, 2002, for the USA) the 1960s and 1970s saw small shifts in the inequality of wages. The 1975–80 changes in the figure bear this out. In fact the UK actually saw a compression that reduced wage

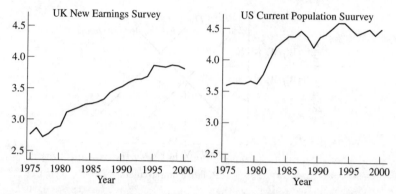

Figure 5.2   90–10 hourly wage ratios in the UK and USA, 1975–2000

inequality (related to the incomes policies introduced during that decade). From the 1980s onwards the wage structures of both countries widened, but at a faster rate in the 1980s than in the 1990s. There appear to be cross-country differences in the timing of when the 1990s slowdown began with the US 90–10 being flat for most of the decade, but the flattening out occurred in the UK from the mid-1990s. Nevertheless the timing of changes in educational wage differentials evolves very closely to the overall rise in wage inequality in both countries.

3   Changes in relative labour demand by education and technology

A lot of research attention has been motivated by the changes in labour market structure described in section 2. A by now large academic literature[3] has documented shifts in labour market inequality and in changing labour demand by skill and education. A considerable amount of research effort has been expended on testing hypotheses that specify particular factors as underpinning and driving the observed changes.

In this research great emphasis has been placed upon the role played by new technologies and how they have altered employers' demand for workers with different skills or education. It has been proposed that the kinds of new technologies diffusing into modern workplaces favour skilled and educated workers, so that they are biased towards such workers, and this skill-biased technology change (sbtc) has driven the observed changes.

One commonly cited recent example of this has been the computerization of work that seemed to occur at the same time as rising wage inequality and the increased relative demand for skills. Of course, one should exercise considerable caution in taking computerization as a classic, or an archetypical, example of sbtc. This can be highly misleading since technology–skill complementarity has been around for a long time. An interesting historical perspective is placed on this in Goldin and Katz (1998) who report evidence showing that industrial electrification at the start of the 20th century caused human capital–technology complementarity. Of course, other times in history have seen the opposite, with technology being substitutes with skilled labour and complements with unskilled labour (see, inter alia, Cain and Paterson, 1986).

Skill-biased technology change
The skill-biased technology change hypothesis is founded upon the notion that employers' demand for more skilled workers has been shaped by the kinds of new technologies that are permeating modern workplaces. The critical idea is that these new technologies lead to higher productivity, but that only some workers possess the necessary skills to use them. Consequently employers are prepared to increase the wages of the skilled workforce who are complements to the new technology. But at the same time less skilled workers do not possess enough skills to operate the new technologies and their wages are lowered or they lose their jobs. Relative wages and employment of the more skilled therefore rise.

There is a range of evidence that has been proposed to test this hypothesis. Some is rather indirect, and some relates the observed changes to direct measures of technology. We now consider these in turn.

Indirect evidence on sbtc
The sbtc hypothesis requires that technology introduction and diffusion drives shifts in skill demand. Because of this one should see variations in skill demand shifts occurring where employers have more to gain from new technology and consequently there should be systematic differences in the extent of relative demand shifts within particular workplaces, firms and industries (each of which is likely to differ in the extent of its use of new technologies).

A first indirect test of relevance to the sbtc argument therefore comes from a decomposition of aggregate changes in skill demand (usually measured by wage bill or employment shares of skilled workers), say ΔS, for j ($= 1, \ldots N$) industries as follows:

$$\Delta S = \sum_{j=1}^{N} \Delta S_j \bar{P}_j + \sum_{j=1}^{N} \Delta P_j \bar{S}_j.$$

The decomposition breaks the overall shift in skill demand into two components. The first is the within-industry component of skill upgrading (weighted by P, the relative size of industry j, and where a bar is a time mean). The second measures between-industry shifts, namely how much bigger or smaller an industry is becoming over time (weighted by the time averaged skill demand).

A number of studies have used this kind of decomposition and have systematically found that the bulk of the aggregate changes have occurred within, rather than between, industries or workplaces. These studies cover different countries, levels of aggregation, time period and skill measures. An example of this is given in Table 5.2 which, in the absence of international data over time on education shares, considers non-production employment measures as a skill proxy.[4] The table shows the bulk of industry shifts in non-production employment shares occurring within, rather than between, industries. That the bulk of the shifts are seen within industries (i.e. some industries have faster rates of skill upgrading than others) is essentially a prerequisite for skill-biased technological change even to be a starter as a possible explanation of the observed shifts in skill demand.

A second piece of indirect evidence on sbtc comes from considering

Table 5.2   Patterns of international skill upgrading in the 1970s and 1980s

Country	1970–80			1980–90			Note
	Change in % non-production (annualized)	% within	Change in wage ratio (%)	Change in % non-production (annualized)	% within	Change in wage ratio (%)	
USA	0.20	81	−2	0.30	73	7	
Norway	0.34	81	−3	–	–	–	1970,80,n/a
Luxembourg	0.57	90	6	0.30	144	12	
Sweden	0.26	70	3	0.12	60	−3	
Australia	0.40	89	−17	0.36	92	2	1970,80,87
Japan	–	–	–	0.06	123	3	n/a,81,90
Denmark	0.44	86	−11	0.41	87	7	1973,80,89
Finland	0.42	83	−11	0.64	79	−2	
W. Germany	0.48	93	5	–	–	–	1970,79,n/a
Austria	0.46	89	7	0.16	68	7	1970,81,90
UK	0.41	91	−3	0.29	93	14	
Belgium	0.45	74	6	0.16	96	−5	1973,80,85
Average	0.40	84.3	−1.8	0.28	91.5	4.2	

Notes: The per cent within column is based on comparing changes over time in the same 28 industries in each country (except for Belgium, 24, W. Germany, 22, Japan, 27, Luxembourg, 9 in 1970–80, 6 in 1980–90, and Norway, 26).

Source: Berman *et al.* (1998).

whether one can identify common patterns of cross-country change in industry skill upgrading. In particular, if one sees faster skill demand shifts occurring in the same sorts of industries in different countries one may view this as informing the sbtc hypothesis (to the extent that similar industries in different countries utilize similar technologies). Berman *et al.* (1998) looked at country-by-country pairwise correlations of industry skill demand shifts for the same industries in different countries (using data from the United Nations Industrial Statistics database for the countries in Table 5.2). They found that most industrial demand shifts covary positively across countries. In fact they report 31 out of 36 pairwise comparisons they calculate to be positive and a sizable number (13 of them) of the correlations are statistically significant. Bearing in mind the possible attenuation that looking at correlations of changes (rather than levels) may bring about, this suggests a tendency of similarly sized skill demand shifts to be clustered in the same sorts of industries across different countries. One can read this as indirect evidence that sbtc has been pervasive in changing labour market outcomes across the developed world.

A third piece of indirect evidence comes from extending the cross-country evidence to the developing world. In fact, when one does so, it is possible to find evidence of demand shifts in favour of the more skilled going on in much poorer countries. Some work has noted that one sees skill upgrading happening in the more technologically advanced industries of some developing countries (Feliciano, 2001; Hanson and Harrison, 1999; Robbins, 1995). This is entirely consistent with sbtc altering relative wage and employment outcomes globally.

Furthermore shifts in skill demand in the developing world appear to be correlated with the shifts seen in the developed world. Berman and Machin (2000, 2004) extend the analysis of Berman *et al.* (1998) to look at industry skill demand shifts in 28 high, middle and low-income countries.[5] They present evidence that patterns of industrial skill upgrading in some developing countries are similar in some respects to those seen in the higher income countries. They present pairwise correlation coefficients testing whether one sees common industry patterns and uncover patterns of similarity, certainly for the middle-income countries (the evidence is more mixed for the low-income countries).

More direct evidence on sbtc
The evidence of the previous subsection is in line with sbtc being important, but largely relies on empirical patterns that do not relate shifts in skill demand to observable technology indicators. Identification of the technology related characteristics of which industries have had faster rates of upgrading can be considered so as to shed more light on the sbtc hypothesis.

One (frequently used) way in which researchers have formally tested this is to estimate cost share equations that relate changes in the skilled wage bill/employment share in a given industry to observable measures of technology. A typical specification (Berman *et al.*, 1994; Machin and Van Reenen, 1998), measured for industry *j* in year *t*, is

$$\Delta(Skilled\ wage\ bill\ share)_{jt} = \alpha + \beta\Delta\log(Capital_{jt}) + \delta\Delta\log(Output_{jt})$$
$$+ \phi TECH_{jt} + \varepsilon_{jt},$$

where this cost share equation can be generated from a translog cost function with two labour inputs (skilled and unskilled) and assuming capital to be a quasi-fixed factor. The focus in these equations then becomes whether the coefficient ϕ on the technology indicator *TECH* is estimated to be positive.

Table 5.3 summarizes the US and UK estimates of ϕ. It is clear that, for a range of time periods, different levels of aggregation and technology measures, there exists a positive association between industry shifts in skilled wage bill or employment shares[6] and observable technology measures. Put differently, it appears to be the technologically more advanced industries where one has seen faster increases in the relative demand for skilled workers. This has been taken in some quarters as evidence in line with the hypothesis that skill-biased technology changes lie behind the demand shifts favouring relatively skilled workers.

A more controversial area of research in this field asserts that individuals receive a wage payoff for working with computers. If true, this would, of course, be very much in line with the sbtc hypothesis as it would imply computer users are rewarded for higher productivity linked to their use of computers. The most well known paper here is Krueger's (1993) study of US Current Population Survey data, where he augments standard human capital earnings functions with a computer usage dummy. Even after controlling for a range of human capital and job-related characteristics, he reports a sizable wage premium for computer users. In his most detailed specification, Krueger reports a 15 per cent wage premium in 1984 and this goes up, despite a coincident rise in the number of computer users, to 18 per cent by 1989.[7]

There are clearly some concerns with this, relating to possible reverse causation and omitted variable bias. Indeed DiNardo and Pischke (1997) adopt a similar approach replacing the computer use variable with a pencil use variable and uncover a wage premium linked to pencil use. This seems suggestive of the idea that the computer use variable may be proxying other unobserved characteristics of people not measured in the survey data (and

Table 5.3 *Regression Correlations of Skill Demand Changes and Technology Measures*

Study	Unit of analysis	Time period	Skill demand measure	Technology measure	Estimate of φ (standard error)	Controls
Autor et al. (1998)	140 US industries	1990–96	College wage bill share	Industry computer use (1984–93)	0.289 (0.081)	None
		1980–90			0.147 (0.046)	
		1970–80			0.127 (0.031)	
		1960–70			0.071 (0.025)	
	123 US industries	1960–90		Computer investment per FTE	0.130 (0.027)	Change in log(capital/labour), decade dummies
	450 US manufacturing industries	1959–89	Non-production wage bill share	Computer investment/ investment	0.027 (0.007)	Change in log(capital/ output), Change in log(output)
Berman et al. (1994)	143 US manufacturing industries	1979–87	Non-production wage bill share	Computer investment/ investment	0.028 (0.006)	Change in log(plant/ output), Change in log(equipment/output), Change in log(output)
				R&D / sales	0.097 (0.021)	

Table 5.3 (continued)

Study	Unit of analysis	Time period	Skill demand measure	Technology measure	Estimate of ϕ (standard error)	Controls
Machin (1996b)	16 UK manufacturing industries	1982–89	Non-production wage bill share	R&D/sales	0.065 (0.026)	Change in log(capital), Change in log(real sales), 1 digit industry dummies
	16 UK manufacturing industries	1980–85		Innovation count from 1970s	0.092 (0.053)	
	398 British workplaces	1984–90	Managers, senior technical and professional employment share	Micro computers introduced	0.044 (0.022)	Dummy for employment decline, 1 digit industry dummies
Machin and Van Reenen (1998)	15 UK manufacturing industries	1973–89	Non-production wage bill share	R&D/value added	0.026 (0.009)	Change in log(capital), Change in log(output), year dummies

therefore not controlled in the regression equation). Nonetheless the computer premia in Krueger's analysis are sizable and one would require a large unobserved heterogeneity (or endogeneity) bias to eliminate them. Thus they have also been cited in some quarters as evidence in line with the sbtc hypothesis.

A final more direct set of evidence comes again from the developing world. The studies by Berman and Machin (2000, 2004) correlate changes in skill demand in middle and low-income countries with industry technology measures from the advanced world.[8] Certainly in middle-income countries there is a significant positive link between faster industry skill upgrading and the advanced world industry technology measures. Thus, to the extent that new technologies are likely to diffuse across international borders in similar industries, one can think of this as being in line with technology altering the skill mix of wages and employment at a faster rate in favour of skilled workers in more technologically advanced industries in many countries in the world.

Some more recent evidence on relative demand shifts by education
The bulk of the research findings referred to thus far relate to the 1980s. One can, however, use the data described in Table 5.1, supplemented by other data sources, to investigate whether the technology shifts appear to operate in the 1990s as well. To do so the only data on technology that exist to carry out systematic cross-industry analysis through time are those measuring computer usage in the workplace. These do have limitations, but also have the advantage that they can be looked at for the labour markets of the UK and the USA, and that they are heavily correlated across countries. Indeed there is a very strong correspondence between industry computerization across the two countries. Figure 5.3 plots US and UK computer usage variables for the same industries in each country against each other. For the years with computer data available for both countries, there is a strong correlation between industrial computer usage (correlation coefficients equal 0.88 for 1997 and 0.86 for 1992/3).

Table 5.4 moves on to report correlations between changes over time in skilled wage bill shares and computer usage for US industries over time (reported as estimated coefficients from statistical regressions of changes in the graduate wage bill share on increases in computer usage, taken from Machin, 2002). They are reported in terms of changes between the years 1984, 1989, 1993 and 1997.[9]

Column (1) reports estimates from the overall period regression and shows a strong, statistically significant association between changes in graduate wage bill shares and increased computer usage. This very much confirms the picture from earlier research in this area: industries which

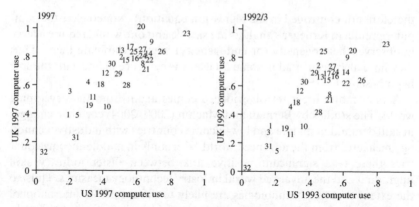

Notes: The industry codes are: 1 – Agriculture, Farming and Fisheries, 2 – Mining, Coal and Petroleum, 3 – Construction, 4 – Food, Drink and Tobacco, 5 – Textiles and Clothing, 6 – Paper and Pulp, 7 – Wood and Furniture, 8 – Printing and Publishing, 9 – Chemicals, 10 – Rubber and Plastics, 11 – Concrete, Glass and Stone, 12 – Metal Industries, 13 – Machinery, 14 – Electrical Goods, 15 – Transportation Equipment, 16 – Utilities and Sanitary, 17 – Wholesale Trade, 18 – Retail Trade, 19 – Rail and Bus Transport, 20 – Air Transportation, 21 – Other Transport, 22 – Postal Services and Telecommunications, 23 – Banking and Insurance, 24 – Real Estate, 25 – Business Services, 26 – Public Administration, 27 – Education, 28 – Health and Social Care, 29 – Membership Organizations, 30 – Entertainment Services, 31 – Personal Services, 32 – Private Households.

Source: UK, Skills Survey; USA Current Population Survey.

Figure 5.3   Cross-country correlations of industry computer usage, UK and USA, 1992/3 and 1997

Table 5.4   Industry-level regressions of changes in graduate wage bill shares on changes in computer usage in the USA, 1984–97

	Annualized change in graduate wage bill share			
	(1) 1984–97	(2) 1984–89	(3) 1989–93	(4) 1993–97
Changes in % using computer at work	.069 (.025)	.102 (.031)	.075 (.050)	.021 (.050)
Sample size	660	220	220	220

Notes:
1. Dependent variable is annualized change in graduate wage bill share.
2. All regressions weighted by average of industry wage bill across the relevant time periods.
3. Year dummies included in column (1).
4. Standard errors in parentheses.

introduced computers at a faster rate are those which saw more rapid labour demand shifts in favour of the skilled.

However, when one looks at the subperiod regressions, given in columns (2) to (4), the coefficient on computer usage falls over time and the relationship actually disappears by the time one reaches the final column specification looking at the 1993–7 sub-period. It appears that some technologically advanced industries have reached saturation point in terms of computer diffusion and as a result links between skill upgrading and increased computerization, at least measured in headcount terms, have gone away. Of course, this does not mean that skill-biased technology change no longer exerts an influence on the relative demand for skills, but it may cast some doubt on the suitability of simple headcount measures of computer use as picking up the labour market effects of technology change in the 1990s.

The UK situation in the 1990s is considered in Table 5.5, which reports a set of industry-level regressions of changes in graduate wage bill shares in the UK in the 1990s on changes in the percentage of people using a computer at work (in column (1)) and then on changes in the importance of computers (measured to varying degrees of how essential they are) amongst computer users in the remaining columns.

Table 5.5   Industry-level regressions of changes in graduate wage bill shares on changes in computer usage in the UK in the 1990s

	Annualized change in graduate wage bill share, 1994–7			
	(1)	(2)	(3)	(4)
Changes in % using computer at work	−0.045 (0.080)			
Changes in % using computer at work for whom fairly important, very important or essential		0.086 (0.057)		
Changes in % using computer at work for whom very important or essential			0.106 (0.068)	
Changes in % using computer at work for whom essential				0.138 (0.044)
Sample size	53	53	53	53

Notes:
1. Dependent variable is annualized change in graduate wage bill share.
2. All regressions weighted by average of industry wage bill across the relevant time periods.
3. Standard errors in parentheses.

The first column of the table shows no relation between 1990s skill upgrading and the increased use of computers in the 1990s. This mirrors the insignificant US finding over the same period and supports the notion that simple headcount computer usage measures may not be particularly good measures of technology change in the 1990s when computer use has reached such high levels in technologically advanced industries.

However, in the UK data, there is more detail on the computer use variable.[10] Once the basic variable is broken down by importance of the computer to the job one can recover evidence of industry skill upgrading associated with the increased importance of computers. As one moves across the table increasingly stringent measures of the importance of computers are considered. The strongest positive (and statistically significant) association is between changes in graduate wage bill shares and changes in the percentage using computers for whom the computer is essential to their job. It seems that relative demand is still shifting in favour of skilled workers in industries where computers are becoming more important, even in the 1990s.

So these findings seem to support the earlier literature on technology being important for shifts in labour demand by skill/education, but with one tweak, namely that headcount measures of computer usage may not be as good measures of technology change as they were in the 1980s work. It seems that, as computers have become a standard work aid, especially in technologically advanced industries, one requires more sophisticated measures (like the 'essential' measure in the UK data) to pick up correlations with relative demand shifts.[11]

What of other possible explanations?

Skill-biased technological change is not the only hypothesis that has been advanced to explain why relative labour demand has shifted so rapidly in favour of more skilled and educated workers. It is well known that there has been a vigorous – and often heated – debate on whether technology or trade matters most for rises in labour market inequality. The trade view is predicated on the notion that there has been a widespread opening up of markets to increased international competition and it is this, and not biased technical change, that has damaged the labour market prospects of low-skill workers. An alternative view is that the decline of labour market institutions, which traditionally propped up wages of less skilled people, explains the observed trends. Further alternative views tend to emphasize longer-term shifts in supply, or the endogenous nature of technological change and how it links with education supply. We now consider each of these in turn.

International trade   In its simplest form the trade argument goes as follows. Suppose there are two countries that, to start with, do not trade with each other. Both have skilled and unskilled workforces who respectively manufacture skill-intensive and unskill-intensive products. One country, the high-wage or developed country, has a comparative advantage in manufacturing skill-intensive products with skilled labour. The other country, the low-wage or developing country, has a comparative advantage in manufacturing low skill-intensive products with unskilled labour. Suppose these countries begin to trade with one another. Then (in the standard Heckscher–Ohlin model of international trade) the developed country will begin to import unskill-intensive products from the low-wage country, as they are cheaper to produce there. This will then lower the wages of unskilled workers in the developed country. It will also be likely to reduce the employment of less skilled workers. Consequently one sees the pattern of relative demand shifts that shift in favour of the more skilled, as discussed above, but here the relative wages and employment of skilled workers rise because of the opening up to trade with the developing country.

This argument has considerable intuitive appeal. However it has proved rather hard to back it up with empirical evidence, for several reasons:

- While rising very fast in recent years (from very low initial levels) trade flows with low-wage developing countries do not yet seem big enough to be able to explain the considerable changes in labour market inequality seen in a number of developed countries. Indeed, the bulk of trade is still between developed countries themselves.
- The industries that have seen the biggest increases in trade with the developing world do not actually appear to be the ones that have seen bigger labour market shifts in favour of more skilled workers (Machin and Van Reenen, 1998).
- One sees skill upgrading (higher relative wages and employment for more skilled groups of workers) going on in the developing world as well as in the developed world (Berman *et al.*, 1998; Berman and Machin, 2000, 2004). This runs counter to the Heckscher–Ohlin model which predicts that skill upgrading should increase in developed economies, but that the less skilled should do better in the developing world as demand for the products they manufacture rises.
- Skill upgrading appears to be happening in industries that do not trade across international borders (Desjonqueres *et al.*, 1999). Again, this runs counter to the Heckscher–Ohlin model. If one includes a traded sector and a non-traded sector in the model the prediction would be that the unskilled workers displaced from the traded sector by the opening up to trade should find jobs (or lower the wages of less skilled workers, or both) in the non-traded sector. In reality one

does not see this. In non-traded sectors (e.g. non-manufacturing industries like retail trade) one has also seen skill upgrading happening, and at similar rates to those in more traded sectors (like most manufacturing industries).

All this means that the literature has found it hard to present evidence in line with the notion that increased trade is the principal factor behind increased inequalities between the skilled and less skilled. Of course, this does not mean that trade will not necessarily have an impact on labour markets in future. It seems implausible to believe that globalization is unlikely to have serious ramifications for labour. Rather the bulk of the recent rises in labour market inequality and shifts in skill demand seen in the last couple of decades do not seem attributable to rising competition with low-wage countries.

Decline of labour market institutions   The other main explanation that has received attention, albeit less than technology or trade, is the decline of labour market institutions. The argument here is that the relative wages of less skilled workers are likely to have fallen because institutions that used to prop up wages of low-skill workers are less important in the new economy. The clearest example of this is trade unions, whose presence has sharply fallen in both the UK and the US labour markets relative to the past.[12] This explanation works well to explain patterns of change in relative wages, but it seems less clear how well it relates to labour demand patterns. One would normally think that, in the absence of any other changes, the reduced wages of the low skilled would make them more attractive to employers as they have become cheaper (i.e. because of the reduced role of unions). Thus the positive association between relative wages and employment seen in the data is somewhat hard to rationalize in this context.

Longer-term changes   A third possible explanation is a subtler and probably more significant one. Some commentators have appealed more to the longer term and argued that relative labour demand shifts in favour of the skilled have been happening for many years and it is longer-run supply changes that matter more. This argument rests on the notion that there has been a trend increase in demand for skills, and movements in relative wages around that trend shift are influenced by relative supply changes. For example, in the UK, education supply rose very fast in the 1970s, at a slower rate in the 1980s, and then likely speeded up again in the 1990s. The wage gap between educated and less educated workers fell in the 1970s, rose sharply in the 1980s and probably rose but at a much slower rate in the 1990s. This is entirely consistent with constant relative demand shifts and the wage gaps by education being shifted by longer-run, decade-length shifts in the relative supply of educated workers.

This argument clearly warrants attention, but there remain some difficulties associated with it. In particular, one feature of the recent changes is rising residual wage inequality. That is, wage inequality seems to rise within various groups (e.g. different age groups, or education groups, or industry etc) as well as between them. This seems difficult to square with the patterns of supply changes that one would think should influence between-group wage differentials. It does look as if the 1980s was the period of rapid wage inequality changes in the UK and the USA, but it is evident that one needs to delve deeper into wage and employment trends by skill at the micro level, and to develop plausible tests of whether demand shifts are indeed constant over time, and space to consider this in more detail.

The argument that labour demand has been shifting in favour of the skilled over the long term is also appealed to by those authors who argue that one actually needs an acceleration in skill bias to have occurred in the period when inequality rose most (in the UK and the USA, the 1980s). The evidence is somewhat unclear on this question, with some authors (e.g. Autor *et al.* 1998) arguing that one can find some (fairly weak) evidence of acceleration, but with others expressing some doubt. Again, this remains something of an unresolved issue, though not one which denies a role for sbtc, but one that doubts its plausibility as the main driving factor behind increasing labour market inequality.

Directed technical change and endogenous technology–skill complementarity
A final explanation emphasizes the endogenous nature of the complementarity between skills and technology. Machin and Manning (1997) and Acemoglu (1998, 2002a, 2002b) argue that increased supply can actually stimulate future demand. Thus, whilst the short-run impact of increased education or skill supply should be to damp down the relative wage of more skilled/educated workers, a longer-term mechanism can operate whereby the increased supply generates demand increases. In Machin and Manning (1997) the mechanism is that employers tend to adjust their hiring patterns to larger groups of workers, and in the Acemoglu work the increased supply induces skill-biased technology changes.[13] In both approaches one sees increased supply coupled with increased relative wages of skilled workers.

In these approaches, skill-biased technical change matters, but the driving force is the change in education supply. Thus the complementarity between education and technology arises endogenously. This, of course, matters for interpretation in that a larger market size of skilled workers results in biased technology change and in increased labour market inequality. But it is the source of the supply change that acts as the driving factor, rather than relative demand shifts or technology per se.

4　Conclusions

This chapter has considered education and skill-based shifts in the employment and wage structure of modern labour markets. There have been important changes in the way in which workers of different skills and education levels are rewarded in modern labour markets as compared to the past. Indeed, there is now a higher price to skills and higher qualifications than there used to be as employers increasingly are demanding more workers with the necessary skills and aptitudes to use the sorts of new technologies that have been diffusing into workplaces. Overall it seems rather hard to deny a role for technological change in explaining the relative demand shifts and movements in labour market inequality seen in the recent past. Therefore, whilst none of the evidence reported is wholly conclusive on the sbtc hypothesis, it does seem that technology matters for the education structure of employment and for educational wage differentials and their evolution through time. At the very least, even if one quibbles about relative magnitudes of explanatory power associated with different explanations, technology seems to be one of the key forces underpinning recent changes in labour market inequality.

There are many implications of the work discussed in this chapter. Some of the more important ones relate to the need to link the design of public policy to the observed trends in the skill structure of international labour markets. In particular, the worsening labour market position of less skilled workers stresses the need for government policy to devote resources to increased and improved industrial skill formation. Education and training policy should be formulated with this in mind so as to ensure that future generations of workers entering the labour market possess the skills needed to utilize present-day technologies in the workplace.

Notes

1.　If one looks at overall wage inequality, as measured by the ratio of the 90th to the 10th percentile of the wage distribution one sees the same. In the UK, the 90–10 ratio went from 2.90 in 1980 to 3.55 by 1990 and then to 3.86 by 2000. In the USA, the 90–10 ratio went from 3.63 (1980) to 4.39 (1990) to 4.53 (2000).
2.　Tinbergen (1975) characterizes movements in demand and supply as a race between the two by placing particular emphasis on technology and education in terms of a 'race between technological development and access to education' (quote reproduced from Goldin and Katz, 1998, footnote 1).
3.　See the review of Katz and Autor (1999) and the references contained therein.
4.　This is because the standard classification of skills in manufacturing surveys is into production and non-production categories. Production workers are involved in assembly and production of goods, up to the rank of working foreman. Non-production workers are all other workers. The latter are universally more highly paid. Berman et al. (1998)

report that non-production workers have higher education and work in higher paying occupations.

5. The high income-countries are the 12 in Table 5.2; the middle-income countries are Colombia, Cyprus, Czechoslovakia, Greece, Guatemala, Hungary, Ireland, Malta, Portugal, South Korea, Spain and Turkey; the low income countries are Bangladesh, Egypt, Ethiopia, India, Nigeria and Tanzania. The sample of countries considered is entirely driven by data availability on industry skill demand shifts over time from the United Nations Industrial Statistics database.

6. Results often prove similar with wage bill or employment shares as the dependent variable but (as noted in Goldin and Katz, 1998) the wage bill shares seem theoretically more appropriate in that they embody hours and labour quality differences.

7. These are calculated as [exp(0.140) − 1]X100 and [exp(0.162)-1]X100 where 0.140 and 0.162 are the coefficients on the computer use dummy in a semi-log wage equation controlling for education, experience, race, part-time job status, living a metropolitan area, gender, veteran status, whether married, whether a union member and broad occupation. Computer usage rises from 25 to 37 per cent between 1984 and 1989.

8. Specifically they consider US computer usage and OECD R&D intensity matched up by industry to the industries of developing countries.

9. These are years in the 1980s and 1990s in which the US Current Population Survey had an occasional supplement on computer usage.

10. I am very grateful to Francis Green for providing me with the UK computer data. See Green *et al.* (2004) for more detail on these data.

11. See also Autor *et al.*'s (2003) detailed discussion on the skill content of technical change: they convincingly argue that empirical work on sbtc increasingly requires more refined data to measure the nature of skill bias and its impact on outcomes.

12. Union density, the percentage of the workforce that are trade union members, was 29 per cent in the UK in 2001 as compared to around 58 per cent when it reached its height 22 years earlier, in 1979. In the USA, union density was 14 per cent in 2001 as compared to 24 per cent in 1979.

13. Acemoglu (1998, 2002b) refers to this as directed technical change. See also Shi (2002).

References

Acemoglu, Daron (1998), 'Why do new technologies complement skills? Directed technical change and wage inequality', *Quarterly Journal of Economics*, **113**, 1055–89.

Acemoglu, Daron (2002a), 'Technical change, inequality and the labor market', *Journal of Economic Literature*, **40**, 7–73.

Acemoglu, Daron (2002b), 'Directed technical change', *Review of Economic Studies*, **69**, 781–809.

Autor, David, Lawrence F. Katz and Alan Krueger (1998), 'Computing inequality: have computers changed the labor market?', *Quarterly Journal of Economics*, **113**, 1169–214.

Autor, David, Frank Levy and Richard Murnane (2003), 'The skill content of recent technological change: an empirical exploration', *Quarterly Journal of Economics*, **118**, 1279–334.

Berman, Eli and Stephen Machin (2000), 'Skill-biased technology transfer around the world', *Oxford Review of Economic Policy*, **16**(3), 12–22.

Berman, Eli and Stephen Machin (2004), 'Globalization, skill-biased technological change and labour demand', in Marco Vivarelli (ed.), *Understanding Globalization, Employment and Poverty Reduction*, (forthcoming).

Berman, Eli, John Bound and Zvi Griliches (1994), 'Changes in the demand for skilled labor within U.S. manufacturing industries: evidence from the Annual Survey of Manufacturing', *Quarterly Journal of Economics*, **109**, 367–98.

Berman, Eli, John Bound and Stephen Machin (1998), 'Implications of skill-biased technological change: international evidence', *Quarterly Journal of Economics*, **113**, 1245–80.

Cain, Louis and Donald Paterson (1986), 'Biased technical change, scale and factor substitution in American industry, 1850–1919', *Journal of Economic History*, **46**, 153–64.

Card, David and John DiNardo (2002), 'Skill biased technological change and rising wage inequality: some problems and puzzles', *Journal of Labor Economics*, **20**, 733–83.

Desjonqueres, Thibaut, Stephen Machin and John Van Reenen (1999), 'Another nail in the coffin? Or can the trade based explanation of changing skill structures be resurrected?', *Scandinavian Journal of Economics*, **101**, 533–54.

DiNardo, John and Steve Pischke (1997), 'The returns to computer use revisited: have pencils changed the wage structure too?', *Quarterly Journal of Economics*, **112**, 291–303.

Feliciano, Zadia (2001), 'Workers and trade liberalization: the impact of trade reforms in Mexico on wages and employment', *Industrial and Labor Relations Review*, **55**, 95–115.

Goldin, Claudia and Lawrence Katz (1998), 'The origins of capital–skill complementarity', *Quarterly Journal of Economics*, **113**, 693–732.

Gosling, Amanda, Stephen Machin and Costas Meghir (2000), 'The changing distribution of male wages, 1966–92', *Review of Economic Studies*, **67**, 635–66,

Green, Francis, Alan Felstead and Duncan Gallie (2004), 'Computers and the changing skill-intensity of jobs', *Applied Economics*, forthcoming.

Hanson, Gordon H. and Ann Harrison (1999), 'Trade, technology, and wage inequality in Mexico', *Industrial and Labor Relations Review*, **52**, 271–88.

Juhn, Chinhui, Kevin Murphy and Brooks Pierce (1993), 'Wage inequality and the rise in returns to skill', *Journal of Political Economy*, **101**, 401–42.

Katz, Lawrence and David Autor (1999), 'Changes in the wage structure and earnings inequality', in Orley Ashenfelter and David Card (eds), *Handbook of Labor Economics*, Amsterdam: North-Holland.

Krueger, Alan (1993), 'How computers have changed the wage structure: evidence from micro-data, 1984–1989', *Quarterly Journal of Economics*, **108**, 33–60.

Machin, Stephen (1996a), 'Wage inequality in the UK', *Oxford Review of Economic Policy*, **12**, 47–64.

Machin, Stephen (1996b), 'Changes in the relative demand for skills in the UK labour market', in Alison Booth and Dennis Snower (eds), *Acquiring Skills: Market Failures, Their Symptoms and Policy Responses*, Cambridge: Cambridge University Press.

Machin, Stephen (2002), 'The changing nature of labour demand in the new economy and skill-biased technology change', end of project report paper for Leverhulme Trust project 'The Labour Market Consequences of Technological and Structural Change', *Oxford Bulletin of Economics and Statistics*, **63**, 753–66.

Machin, Stephen (2003), 'Skill-biased technical change in the new economy', in Derek Jones (ed.), *New Economy Handbook*, Amsterdam: Elsevier Academic Press.

Machin, Stephen and Alan Manning (1997), 'Can supply create its own demand? Implications for rising skill differentials', *European Economic Review (Conference Volume)*, **41**, 507–16

Machin, Stephen and John Van Reenen (1998), 'Technology and changes in skill structure: evidence from seven OECD countries', *Quarterly Journal of Economics*, **113**, 1215–44.

Manning, Alan and Marco Manacorda (1998), 'Just can't get enough: more on skill-biassed change and labour market performance', Center for Labour Economics Working Paper 7, Berkeley.

Robbins, Donald (1995), 'Trade, trade liberalization and inequality in Latin America and East Asia – Synthesis of seven country studies', mimeo, Harvard.

Schmitt, John (1995), 'The changing structure of male earnings in Britain, 1974–88', in Richard Freeman and Lawrence Katz (eds), *Differences and Changes in Wage Structures*, Chicago: University of Chicago Press.

Shi, Shouyong (2002), 'A directed search model of inequality with heterogeneous skills and skill-biased technology', *Review of Economic Studies*, **69**, 467–91.

Tinbergen, Jan (1975), *Income Differences: Recent Research*, Amsterdam: North-Holland Press.

6 The social and external benefits of education

Walter W. McMahon

Education externalities are social or public benefits from the education of each individual that benefit others in the society in both current and future generations. They are over and above the private benefits that the individual decision maker takes into account in making his or her private decision to invest in education. They include education's impacts on economic development goals that are part of the quality of life but that also benefit future generations.

Standard estimates of social rates of return include only a portion of the total social effects of education. They are limited to the market (or monetary) returns and do not include the non-market private or the non-market externality benefits of education. The purely private non-market benefits are taken into account by individuals when they make their decisions about how far to go in school. But the externality benefits, both market and non-market, are taken for granted and do not affect private decisions. The size of these externalities which include education's impacts on development goals are the main rationale on efficiency grounds for government support of education Based on the analysis of all of the returns to schooling including externalities in relation to all investment costs, if there is under- or overinvestment, the result is not efficient and an optimal rate of economic development is not achieved. Better estimates of education externalities and impacts on development goals are therefore very important to obtain.

There have been prior surveys of the research relevant to education externalities. These include Haveman and Wolfe (1984), McMahon (1987, 1998a), Wolfe (1994, pp. 2208–12), Venniker (2001) and Wolfe and Haveman (2001). There is also a survey of externalities in general by Benhabib and Jovanovic (1991). None of these seeks to appraise the total value of education externalities. The work by Wolfe and Haveman focuses primarily on non-market *private* returns; it includes some intra-family externalities but it does not consider education's impacts on development goals. The latter, in Romer's (1990) terms, are 'non-rivalrous goods' or in public finance are 'public goods' generated by education.

Section I defines the theoretical basis for the identification and estimation of education externalities. This includes distinguishing market from non-market impacts, as well as a static shorter-term view from a dynamic longer-term view of the neoclassical model. The latter, which includes a broader theory of endogenous development, has important implications for identifying externalities and for resolving the measurement issues surrounding what is to be measured.

Section II presents a taxonomy of education's public good externalities and reviews estimates in the literature of the overall size and value of these externalities. It indicates how these are affected by choice of the narrower static view versus dynamic view of the neoclassical growth model. It also considers how these are affected by various measurement issues, including the way in which variables are measured and the types of data used. It does not, however, survey the wider scope of all of the microeconomic research on the specific market returns to education since this is a vast subject. Also surveys such as those done by Card (1999) and by Krueger and Lindahl (2001) are readily available and need not be repeated here.

Section III considers estimates of the non-market impacts of education on specific development goals. These are pure externalities, just as are the indirect effects from education through these development outcomes as they feed back and affect both the monetary returns from education and pure economic growth. Section IV offers approximations of total social rates of return that these estimates of education externalities imply.

Section V identifies the separate *private* non-monetary returns in order to distinguish them from the public good development outcomes. They are not education externalities, but placing an estimated value on them is a necessary step to estimating the indirect effects of education which are externalities. Section VI considers the implications for investment criteria, while section VII summarizes the conclusions, qualifications and the needs for further research.

I   The theoretical basis for identifying and estimating externalities

The market outcomes of education in the Lucas (1988) production function are shown in eq. (6.1) below. They consist of the direct effects from the use of human capital in production during work hours, $\mu_1 h$, and the externality benefits, h_a^γ, the latter defined by Lucas as the average education level in the community. Factors of production within the firm including physical capital, K, are shown within square brackets. The education externalities coming from outside the firm that benefit productivity are outside the brackets:

$$Y = A \left[(\mu_1 h\, N)^{1-\alpha}\, K^\alpha \right] h_a^\gamma \qquad (6.1)$$

Here

Y = output, usually measured in the aggregate as GDP,
μ_1 = the fraction of time the typical worker devotes to production,
$\mu_1 h$ = human capital inputs within the firm. This is the average education
or skill level, h, times the fraction of time devoted to production, μ_1,
N = the number of persons employed,
K = physical capital,
h_a = the average level of education in the community, and
A = the level of technology.

A growth equation relating changes, or growth of GDP over time, to flows of investment is implied by this Lucas function. This is made apparent by taking the logs, totally differentiating with respect to time, and dividing through by real output. This is then converted to per capita terms by subtracting the rate of growth in the number of persons from both sides. It shows that the rate of growth of per capita GDP depends primarily on growth of human capital per capita as a percentage of GDP, and on investment in physical capital per capita as a percentage of GDP. The dependence on the growth of raw unimproved labour, N, is small (since N has been subtracted from both sides), although difference in the proportion of the population gainfully employed can contribute something. But basically positive economic growth depends on total physical and human capital deepening.

Romer's (1990) model is similar in its dependence on human capital. However, in his model, h_A, the *stock* of human capital employed in the R&D sector, increases technological progress through greater innovation, ($d \log A/dt = ch_A$). The stock of human capital not employed in the R&D sector also aids production directly, as in Lucas. So the Romer formulation implies that the levels of GDP per capita are related to the levels, or stock, of human capital as usually measured by average educational attainment using the Barro and Lee (1993) data. It is this *stock* of human capital that facilitates innovations. Romer's emphasis on human capital used in R&D to stimulate innovations is relevant in those OECD countries that hold technological leadership (as shown by Griliches, 2000), but probably less so in the other 130 or so developing countries in the world that are less able to afford all of the failed experiments. There the emphasis by Lucas (1988) on the average level of education available to facilitate dissemination is very likely to be much more relevant. It is apparent that most technology and knowledge necessary to effective civic institutions does not disseminate or get put to use in the poor countries, especially in rural areas where most of the people live and where illiteracy is widespread, even after hundreds of years. There is little capacity to gain access to this knowledge, much less use it productively. When most adults have not completed primary school, the Internet, libraries, printed media, modern physical capital and effective governmental institutions all appear to be out of reach for most in the population (World Bank, 2003, UNESCO data via USAID, 2003).

The externality effects from human capital, h_a in the Lucas (1988) model, can be analysed into education's impacts on more specific development goals, which in turn affect economic growth and future development. This implies a broader model of endogenous development (McMahon 2002a, 2002b). These include the following:

$H(Y,h_a)$ = health effects of education as it reduces infant mortality, increases longevity, and improves child, spousal, and public health,

$F(Y,h_a)$ = fertility effects as female education lowers fertility rates,

$N(Y,h_a)$ = net population growth rate effects, derived by combining the two above,

$D(Y,h_a)$ = democratization and human rights, as education improves civic institutions,

$S(Y,h_a)$ = political stability, aided by democratization and education,

$C(Y,h_a)$ = crime rate reduction and lower incarceration costs, with white-collar crime a negative externality,

$P(Y,h_a)$ = poverty reduction and reduced inequality, via wider distribution of education,

$E(Y,h_a)$ = environmental influences, all of which are indirect, and

$A(Y,h_a)$ = education's contribution to R&D, and to diffusion of new technology.

Education externalities operating through these development goals affect GDP per capita, as well as earnings, to a limited extent in the short run but much more substantially as time passes. They are summed up as the 'market return' externality outcomes in Figure 6.1 below, and are feedbacks affecting market outcomes from the non-market externalities listed in Table 6.1. Research on these total market externality impacts will be surveyed in Table 6.2 and discussed there. The portion of the externalities that have an impact on market outcomes is illustrated by area B-1 in Figure 6.1 below. A small fraction of direct market benefits in area A-1 of Figure 6.1 may also be externalities, such as intra-firm externalities that arise through communication with co-workers within firms, but it is the 'indirect effects' of education operating through intervening variables that are pure externalities as shown in Figure 6.1 that are more easily measured. They are community effects taken for granted by the individual doing the investing:

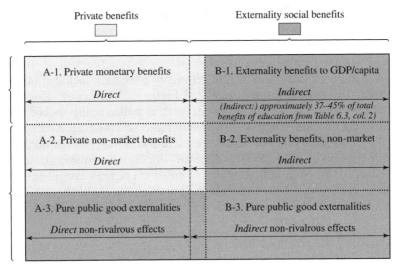

Figure 6.1   Total net benefits of education

their level cannot be affected by the individual. To some extent their level is also determined by investments in education by prior generations.

The non-market effects of education are illustrated in the two bottom rows of Figure 6.1. They arise as individuals use their human capital during time not spent in the labour market in household production, either at home or in the community, of final outcomes. The household production function is shown in eq. (6.2). Z, total final satisfactions, are produced by time not spent in the labour force, $\mu_2 hN$, made more valuable by education, in combination with market goods, Y, and with education externalities, h_a^ϕ. The latter are again analysed into education's impacts on specific development goals, as was done for impacts on market outcomes:

$$Z = B \, [(\mu_2 hN)^{1-\beta} \, Y^\beta] \, h_a^\phi. \tag{6.2}$$

Here

Z = final satisfactions, or Becker (1965) commodities,

μ_2 = the proportion of time used in household production. The remainder $(1-\mu_1-\mu_2)$ is used in the production of human capital,

$\mu_2 h$ = human capital used during leisure time within the household or the community,

h_a = the average level of education in the community, an external effect on household production, and

B = the technology level as it relates to non-market activities, assumed constant.

Other variables are as previously defined.

A portion of these non-market returns to education included in Z are private, such as own health (area A-2 of Figure 6.1), but a portion are pure public goods, or 'non-rivalrous goods' such as public health, public television or the benefits of democracy, human rights and political stability (area A-3). These are goods to which the exclusion principle does not apply. Consumption by one individual generally does not diminish consumption by others. Using only indirect effects to measure externalities will omit A-3, the direct effects of these non-rivalrous public goods. But if the static interpretation of the neoclassical model is used (that focuses on direct short-term impacts and controls for indirect effects), these direct effects can be assumed to be relatively small.

For empirical estimation, eq. (6.2) implies that there should be a control for per capita income, Y, to avoid double counting the market returns to education contained in Y. The non-market returns, direct and indirect, are therefore over and above the market returns to education.

Finally there must be an equation in this simple three equation endogenous development model that determines and makes endogenous investment in education. The production of human capital formation is also endogenous within the Lucas (1988) model. To complete the model:

$$\partial h/\partial t = G\,(1-\mu_1-\mu_2)\,h \tag{6.3}$$

$\partial h/\partial t$ = investment in human capital formation through education,
              G = government investment in education,
$(1-\mu_1-\mu_2)$ = fraction of private time invested in education. This will be a function of G, since G affects the price, and
h = the individual's (or family's) human capital, which is also a proxy for income.

This function is linear in h, with G a constant, similar to Uzawa (1965). So there are no diminishing returns to the stock of human capital, h. As Lucas (1988, p.19) emphasizes, human capital accumulation is a social activity involving extension of further education to additional groups of people. In eq. (6.3) a given *percentage* increase in the stock, h, in successive population cohorts requires the same effort, which, as he says, has no counterpart in the production of physical capital. This linearity feature is a sufficient basis for sustained per capita growth from endogenous human capital accumulation alone. But education externalities also lay the foundation for sustained per capita growth in a dynamic interpretation of the neoclassical model.

Note also that, if G increases, as a result larger government investment in education, human capital formation increases. This induces more private saving and investment by families in the form of forgone earnings, or forgone consumption by parents as children remain in school longer. If this is carried too far, at, say, the primary level, eventually the social rate of return will fall as universal education at that level reaches saturation in the population. But the long-term experience is that the rates of returns at successively higher levels then rise, reflecting relative scarcities in the labour force. This third equation, expressing increased investment in education as average education levels and per capita income rise, then completes a logical system, and will be part of the measurement issues and empirical estimates to be discussed.

II Estimates of market-based education externalities

What follows first presents a taxonomy in Table 6.1 identifying the source of education externalities more specifically. It then surveys the literature that attempts to estimate their total collective economic value. The latter is tantamount to considering the net impact of the average level of education in the community represented by the externality terms, h_a, in the Lucas (1988) production function, eq. (6.1), and in the household production function, eq. (6.2).

Which effects are pure education externalities?

It is useful to identify education impacts on development goals more specifically, since they are pure externalities. An individual cannot affect their community-wide average. This is not only because his or her investment in education is very small in relation to the entire community, which is the usual rationale for perfect competition; it is also because these education impacts operate very slowly and are long delayed, most primarily affecting future generations.

But the increments to each aspect of community development can also contribute to earnings and GDP per capita, an indirect effect of education through development goals to growth that are a better way to measure externalities. For example, immigrants to the United States from Haiti or Mexico, or to Britain from southeastern Europe and South Asia, know that they can earn more after arriving. This is partly because of the spillover benefits from democracy, the rule of law, and dissemination of new technology that are functions of education in prior generations. These externality effects of education disappear when they are not identified as externalities and statistical devices are used to eliminate them.

Table 6.1   Identification of education public good externalities

---

I. Externality feedbacks on per capita growth: Table 6.3 (and B-1 Fig.1)
    1.1 Higher investment rates in physical capital as education improves stability
    1.2 Higher investment in education as education induces income growth
    1.3 Non-market and new technology effects on growth
    1.4 Education's contribution to R&D and to innovation (e.g. Romer, 1990)
    1.5 Slower population growth, an indirect effect from private benefits via
         fertility

II. Education's non-market effects on development: Table 6.3 (A-3 + B-3)
    Population and health effects (controlling for Y, or income)
     1. Better public health
     2. Lower net population growth rates
    Strengthening civic institutions and the rule of law (controlling for Y)
     3. Democratization: authoritarian regimes depend on illiteracy; also greater
        volunteering and financial giving strengthen civic institutions
     4. Human rights: a function of democratization and of education
     5. Political stability: aided by better civic institutions (democratization)
    Lower crime rates (controlling for Y)
     6.1 Lower homicide rates, lower property crime rates
     6.2 Less policing, incarceration, fewer court system and private security costs
    Indirect environmental effects (controlling for Y)
     7. Less deforestation (for cooking, less dependence on timber exports)
     8. Less water pollution as education slows population growth
     9. More air pollution (a negative externality of education-induced growth)
    Reduction of poverty and inequality (controlling for Y)
    10. Urban and rural poverty reduction, via smaller families, farm technology
    11. Reduction of inequality, only with wider dissemination of education
         (indirect effects only, via greater stability and less crime)
    Geographic spillovers
    12. Less migration to urban ghettoes: more assimilation in provinces
    13. More emigration of workers after college (a negative externality)

Empirical estimates of education externalities on GDP per capita
The empirical research measuring education's net externality effects operating through these development outcomes *on market-based income per capita or earnings* is summarized in Table 6.2. As has been noted, technology, A, is constant in the Lucas (1988) model where its role in growth is replaced by the average level of education in the community, h_a^γ in eq. (6.1), which can be regarded as the means of disseminating technology, without

which it is not effective. In Romer's (1990) model, technology or the stock of knowledge is a non-rival input and is not constant but is dependent on the amount of human capital employed in research as well as in production directly, all of which again depends on prior education. 'Technology' is a term that for long years has been used by economists, not always admitting that it is a black box. Gradually, though, this research is being dissected and made more specific.

The effects of technology   As Topel (1999) points out, narrowly interpreted, the neoclassical model implies that current investment in education leads to a one-time surge in output as new human capital is applied in production. This narrow interpretation is also a static interpretation since it implies controlling for technology and includes only 'direct effects' that exclude indirect effects that operate through intervening variables and through lags that feed back and affect outcomes in the future. These direct effects of own education are what are normally measured in the private returns estimated using a Mincer earnings function when the community feedback effects are not separately analysed. They are what is measured also in a growth equation that controls for female fertility rates and/or for life expectancy. Regressions that use such controls as those for political stability, regional dummies or time dummies without analysing the extent to which these in turn depend on prior education and without generating lagged effects over time produce a similar result. The narrower static interpretation can be quite useful for some purposes, but it minimizes or eliminates most education externalities as they are defined here since most operate through intervening variables as indirect effects and through delayed feedbacks. From one point of view these education externalities are largely eliminated by the time dummies in Topel's (1999) regressions which therefore lead to his interpretation of that specification as a means of implementing the static view.

Although the narrower static interpretation is legitimate, it does have implications not only for the specification of the equations estimated but also for type of data used. Choice of this interpretation appears to be the main basis for disagreement among economists about the size and even the very existence of education externalities. Neoclassical models also can be legitimately interpreted to include dynamic feedback effects and indirect effects operating through technology. Not only do Romer (1990) and Lucas (1988) do this, but this interpretation has also been chosen by Nelson and Phelps (1966), Griliches (2000), Topel (1999, p.2953) and McMahon (2002a, 2002b).

The empirical effect of using the narrower static interpretation is shown by comparing the results of studies in sections I and IV of Table 6.2, which use a dynamic interpretation, with those in section II and III, which largely use the narrower static view. In section I, when the effects from the dissemination of technology are not eliminated by use of time dummies or other means, Topel (1999) estimates the social rate of return to be 23 per cent and Heckman and Klenow (1997) estimate it to be 30 per cent from cross-country data. This somewhat overestimates the social rates of return because there are no controls for variables other than education which also affect growth. In Section IV McMahon (2002a, chs 3 and 4) controls for the rate of investment in physical capital and for the initial level of GDP per capita and gets lower social rates of return and lower externality components for example. Initial GDP per capita removes some externalities, but then these are regenerated as simulations of the dynamic model over 40 years to pick up the cumulative externality effects.

Topel (1999) and Heckman and Klenow (1997) estimate externalities by first estimating the social rate of return to schooling from cross-country GDP per capita regressions (the 23–30 per cent) and then subtracting the private return to schooling based on individual earnings data and Mincer regressions. To get some idea as to how externalities may vary by region, I have subtracted the most recent average private rates of return by region, based on micro earnings data using the Mincer method of 7–9 per cent as given by Psacharopoulos and Patrinos (2002) from Topel's (1999) world-wide 23 per cent social rate of return estimate. The result is an estimate of pure externalities at 15.7 per cent in Africa, 14.8 per cent in Latin America, 14.2 per cent in Asia and 14 per cent in OECD countries, as shown in section I. Across regions the externality component averages 14.67 per cent, or 63 per cent of the social rate of return. The larger externalities occur in the poorest and most unstable nations. Although this overestimates the size of the education externality component because of the lack of all controls, this same pattern reappears in section IV, where other controls were used and the estimates were based on dynamic simulations over time.

Using a narrower static interpretation of the neoclassical model that controls for differences in technology in section II of Table 6.2, these externalities largely disappear. Heckman and Klenow's (1997) 30 per cent becomes only 10.6 per cent after they control for technology differences by using life expectancy, which they treat as a proxy for medical technologies and hence, presumably, for all technologies. After the average worldwide private rate of return of 8.3 per cent is subtracted, this leaves only 2.3 per cent for externalities. Topel's (1999) estimate of a 23 per cent social rate of return becomes 6.2 per cent when they control for technology by using time dummies. When this is followed by subtracting the 8.3 per cent private return to education, it wipes out externalities altogether.

Benhabib and Spiegel (1994) and Pritchett (1997) also can be interpreted as using a static interpretation since they remove most human capital effects on per capita income or growth by using controls for political instability and inequality and also in other ways. As indicated in Table 6.2, section II they wind up with no externalities. As in Topel (1999) and Heckman and Klenow (1997) they use the average years of schooling as a measure of past investment in human capital and, in sharp contrast to the individual-level data on education attainment and income, they find little or no human capital effects. This is clearly a function of these controls, but it also is likely to be that, for the individual, educational attainment reflects the change in each individual's education and the embodiment of new technology that comes with the additional investment. In contrast, for the society, to the extent that investment in education is replacement investment, replacing those who die or retire, which is most of it, average educational attainment does not change. The change in education is called for by differentiation with respect to time of the Lucas (1988) model, and, as pointed out by Krueger and Lindahl (2001, p. 1130), the change in education is positively associated with growth after measurement error in education is accounted for. Furthermore using average educational attainment data from Barro and Lee (1993), for example, can be interpreted as what is implied by the static view of the neoclassical model since it eliminates the effect of technology embodied by replacement investment, and hence probably the main means for dissemination and use of technology and new knowledge. When embodiment of technology is included by using gross enrolment rates as the measure of investment in education, this adds considerably to the significance and robustness of education's power in explaining economic growth (see McMahon, 1998b, pp. 164–5, 2002a, pp. 56–7, 61–3).

Gross enrolment rates do overstate actual attendance, and do tend also to be overestimated as countries report them to UNESCO. But this overstatement which is likely to be largest in the poorer countries is similar to overstatement as individuals report their own educational attainment to survey researchers. The measurement error in the education variable that results is well known to offset approximately the effects of unmeasured ability and family factors when estimating the true returns to education. This offset will also occur in the international data. Although it is not exact, it will be in the same direction and is likely to be of roughly the same order of magnitude. The quality of the data when it comes to any measure of education inputs is not perfect, whether average educational attainment or gross enrolment rates are used. Other measures such as spending on education as a percentage of GDP, net enrolment rates and literacy rates also have flaws. But some are worse than others. It is postulated that leaving out replacement investment in either physical or human capital investment rates leaves out a lot.

Table 6.2   Education externalities as a portion of the monetary returns to education

Externality component of social rate of return	Basis for estimate	Source
I. Market-measured social returns; dynamic interpretation of the neoclassical model		
AFRICA: 23% – 7.3% = 15.7%	Schooling coefficient from cross-country	Topel (1999) (23%) minus pvt
LAC: 23% – 8.2% = 14.8%	GDP/Cap Mincer regressions, less private	rates of return by region from
ASIA: 23% – 8.8% = 14.2%	returns from individual wage-based Mincer	Psacharopoulos and Patrinos (2002).
OECD: 23% – 9.0% = 14.0%	regressions	Heckman and Klenow (1997) get (30%)
II. Static interpretation after removing education's role in disseminating technology		
8.4% – 8.3% ≅ 0%	Cross-country coefficient as above, with controls for differences in technology	Average of Heckman and Klenow (1996: 10.6%) and Topel (1999:6.2%), less average pvt rate of 8.3%
0%	Human capital measure used is av. ed. attainment which excludes technology effects	Benhabib and Spiegel (1994) Prichett (1997) (Note that Benhabib and Spiegel, 1994 stress
0%	of replacement investment. Also 1 yr of schooling raises the stock of HC more in LDCs. Controls for political instability and inequality remove other education externalities	effects of education in raising physical capital investment, an externality also not included in column 1)

III. Intra-country externalities only (inter-country differences ignored)

Primary	17%	Differences among cities; wage is higher if average education level is higher by 0.03av. ed./0.048 indiv. ed.	Rauch (1993, pp. 389, 399): 68% of the market rate
Secondary	11%		
Higher	12%	Exponents based on US data, 1909–57	Lucas (1988): 60% of the mkt. rate
US higher ed. only:	11.0%	Earnings differences among cities	Moretti (2002, p. 24) (i.e. 25–14%)
	0%	Poor proxies for av. schooling, IV instruments remove most externalities	Acemoglu and Angrist (2000). Inter-state data.
	7%	Increase in total factor productivity, 163 US cities '70–90. Regional dummies remove most externality effects.	Ciccone and Peri (2002, p. 38). 7% = 0.085 (Δ average schooling)

IV. Education's market-measured externalities via indirect effects

AFRICA average: (45% of market return)	17%	Indirect effects are externalities that feed back on GDP. Cross-country data are used to estimate net education effects on democratization, civic institutions, political stability and physical capital investment. Lower pop. growth and higher economic growth also raise per capita investment in education.	McMahon (2002a, p. 236); Appiah and McMahon (2002, p. 55)
LAC (Brazil): (41% of market return)	6%		McMahon (2002a, p. 232)
ASIA (India): (39% of market return)	5%		McMahon (2002a, p. 234)
OECD: (US): (37% of market return)	4%		McMahon (2002a, p. 240)

223

Another possible factor contributing to the insignificance of Benhabib and Spiegel's (1994) and Pritchett's (1997) results leading to underestimation of the contribution of education is that their measure of average educational attainment does not reflect the quality of education. Quality is well known to contribute to earnings in both advanced and developing countries (e.g. Behrman *et al.*, 2002). As an example of leaving out indirect effects of education, Benhabib and Spiegel (1994) stress the effects of human capital in raising the rate of investment in physical capital, but do so almost as an aside, as do Barro and Sala-I-Martin (1995, pp. 433, 451–2). They do not include this externality under the broader interpretation in their estimate of 0 per cent externalities shown in Table 6.2.

Inter-country versus intra-country externalities   A number of empirical studies of externalities cited in section III, Table 6.2 are limited to differences among states (or provinces) within the same country, e.g., see Acemoglu and Angrist (2000). This choice of data base appears to average out larger variation and result in smaller estimates of externalities than those showing up in differences among cities as found by Rauch (1993) and Moretti (2002), shown in section III. It clearly omits other kinds of externalities that show up in inter-country differences such as those studied by Barro (1991, 1997) and McMahon (2002a). In particular, citizens of the same nation enjoy a relatively similar degree of political stability, similar civic institutions and a similar rule of law. These all potentially reflect education externalities conducive to growth and development. Wider variation in inter-country data in political stability and civic institutions is not independent of the level of education and helps to explain differences in growth and development. This is ruled out if these variables are excluded by choice of a relatively homogeneous data base. Acemoglu and Angrist (2000) nevertheless find a 7 per cent private return to schooling, slightly lower than what most researchers estimate but in a roughly similar range, and they find education externalities based on OLS of 7.3 per cent which are smaller than Topel (1999) and Heckman and Klenow (1997) and somewhat larger than McMahon (2002a).

It is only when they introduce the instrumental variables of changes in compulsory attendance laws and in child labour laws by states that the education externalities largely disappear. This is a clever procedure for trying to get around the possible migration of more 'able' individuals to the states that have higher average education levels. But the validity of the results depends on the quality of the instruments. Questions have been raised, by Rouse (2001), among others, about the use of these instruments. She notes that these laws are negatively correlated with college attendance rates, for example, so that the laws also are related to less externalities from college attendance, a point taken up by Blanchard and by Mankiw in the discussion of Rouse (2001, p. 73).

But the most important critique of Acemoglu and Angrist (2000) by Rouse (2001, p. 71) and Bils (2001, p. 65) is that it captures a relatively narrow form of externality. It addresses secondary education externalities only, leaving out externalities generated by primary education, community colleges and higher education in general. It also leaves out 'the effects on tax revenues, government transfers, and criminal activity' (Rouse, 2001, p. 71), along with 'schooling benefiting a future spouse', voting behaviour and 'lower crime from keeping young men in a monitored setting' (Bils, 2001, p. 65). It is these and other externalities largely left out by Acemoglu and Angrist (2000) that are the focus of this chapter. Beyond this they capture largely the narrowly defined shorter run static effects (Venniker, 2001), so they leave out dynamic effects such as those from new technology embodied in replacement human capital investment and from the intergenerational transmission of education benefits to grandchildren.

Turning to differences among cities or SMSAs (Standard Metropolitan Statistical Areas, which include nearby areas) also addressed in section III of Table 6.2, the Ciccone and Peri (2002) study based on US cities uses regional dummies as 'controls'. These can be expected to remove many externality effects using the broader dynamic interpretation of the neoclassical model. The authors' estimate of 7 per cent externalities is below that obtained by Rauch (1993), probably because of this procedure. It is also slightly below Moretti's (2002) 11 per cent, although the latter relates only to higher education. Rauch (1993) estimates education externalities overall to be 68 per cent of the market rate and Lucas (1988) estimates them to be 60 per cent of the market rate. Multiplying the mean of these by the private rates of return at each education level given by Psacharopoulos and Patrinos (2002) gives an estimate of education externalities in the USA equivalent to 17 per cent at the primary level, 11 per cent at the secondary level and 12 per cent at the higher education level, as shown in section III of Table 6.2. This is interesting since they are so close that Rauch (1993) and Moretti (2002), who both focus on differences in human capital across cities, estimate higher education externalities to be 12 per cent and 11 per cent.

The estimates of the externality component as a proportion of the market returns to education obtained by simulation methods are shown in section IV of Table 6.2, from McMahon (2002): 45 per cent for Africa on average, 41 per cent for Brazil as an example for Latin America, 39 per cent for India as an example from Asia, and 37 per cent for the USA, an OECD member nation. These are lower than the aforementioned 68 per cent obtained by Rauch (1993), 60 per cent by Lucas (1988) and 63 per cent based on Heckman and Klenow (1997) and Topel (1999).

Externalities as indirect effects and endogenous feedbacks The previous paragraph begins to consider another way to estimate externalities using a dynamic interpretation of the neoclassical model. It is to identify and estimate separately education's net marginal product in generating each of the various externality outcomes from investment in education in the community. These marginal products are the direct effects in Figure 6.1, Area A-3. These direct effects feed back, affecting per capita income and earnings in the next period, as well as the levels of the other non-market indices of development such as improvement of civic institutions and political stability, thereby laying the foundation for future growth. As the difference equation model simulates these impacts over time, feeding the lags in each period as it iterates forward, the time path generated by the simulations illustrates how it builds the foundations for future growth in more specific terms. The more immediate direct initial impacts (as in the narrower static interpretation of the neoclassical model) can easily be seen to be only a small fraction of the total cumulative impacts over time. The simulations of the model are run by McMahon (2002a) for only 40 years, although the total cumulative impacts of the simulations as time approaches infinity are likely to be larger.

The externality effects from a change in education on GDP per capita are based on the indirect effects, the latter obtained by subtracting the direct effects from the total effects from an identical change in education in each of 78 countries separately. The direct effects are estimated by a separate simulation with the indirect effects of education that operate through other variables suppressed. When indirect effects (externalities) are expressed as a proportion of the total education effects on GDP per capita (i.e., as a fraction of the market social rate of return), these indirect externality effects are higher in the poorer countries of Africa (45 per cent and up) than in the middle-income Latin American and Asian countries (39–41 per cent), which in turn are higher than in the high-income OECD nations (37 per cent) as shown in section IV of Table 6.2. If these proportions are multiplied by the average market-based social rates of return given by Psacharopoulos and Patrinos (2002) for Africa, Asia and Latin America, and by McMahon (2002a) for the USA, the result is a pure externality return on the form of market outcomes of 17 per cent in Africa, 6 per cent in Brazil (as an example from Latin America), 5 per cent in India (as the example from Asia) and 4 per cent in the USA. These are somewhat lower than the 14–15.7 per cent based on Heckman and Klenow (1997) and Topel (1999) in section I of Table 6.2, the estimates that are the most comparable.

Conclusions regarding total education externalities
It is concluded that choosing the narrower static interpretation of the neoclassical model where the specifications tend to focus on direct effects, and

especially focusing on regressing levels rather than changes, externalities are often found to be negligible, or even zero. However, choosing a dynamic interpretation that allows for indirect effects that set the stage for future growth, the evidence for substantial externalities is strong. The static interpretation implies a regression equation that uses controls that remove the net contribution of past investment in education to state variables such as the level of technology, civic institutions, political instability, inequality and regional dummies. Under these static conditions, when accompanied by lack of any dynamic simulations that allow for the build-up over time, the evidence for externalities is inconclusive, as has been noted by Venniker (2001). When this is accompanied by other choices, such as measurement of human capital inputs by using stocks as given by average level of educational attainment, this excludes replacement investment and thereby the dynamics of new technologies that are embodied by over 90 per cent of the total gross investment in education. This has elements akin to the static interpretation.

Krueger and Lindhal (2001) have argued that the relationship between the *initial level of human capital stock* and growth may not be linear, in which case the effect of education on growth cannot necessarily be demonstrated. It is a good point, but it does not apply to all of the studies reviewed here. When, for example, the growth equation uses *investment* in education (a flow, not a stock) and separates this into primary, secondary and higher education levels, while also using gross investment lagged 10 to 20 years rather than average educational attainment, the marginal product of education can vary in the estimates by education level. Extensive new evidence is offered by Keller (2003). When accompanied by simulations that channel most new investment first to the basic education levels until universal education is attained, the relative returns to investment at those levels will fall, relative to the higher education levels. For these reasons, the problem Krueger and Lindahl (2001) cite with respect to linearity as regards the initial human capital stock is not relevant to these specifications. It should also be noted that there is little variation in the social rate of return *within* Asian, European and Latin American regions at each education level (Psacharopoulos and Patrinos, 2002; Table 6.2). So if separate primary, secondary and higher education investment rates are used, and the growth equation is estimated using panel data specific to each region, or for developed and less developed countries in separate groups, as by Keller (2003), the problem with non-linearities is minimized.

Overall it can also be tentatively concluded that inter-state variation within the USA excludes important externalities since some important nationwide community effects do not vary within countries. Overall it can also be tentatively concluded that choosing static or shorter run interpretations of the neoclassical model minimizes most externalities. A dynamic interpretation that allows for impacts from technology and education's impacts on other community effects over longer periods of time leads to larger education externalities. Using such a dynamic interpretation, both inter-city and cross-country data that allow for wider variation and yet control for impacts of factors other than education find substantial and robust evidence of education externalities. However overall it can also be tentatively concluded that, if empirical estimates do not control for factors other than education affecting development, the estimates overstate education externalities.

Overall it can also be concluded, on the basis of dynamic simulations, as in McMahon (2002a) or Topel's (1999) experiments with short and long time periods, that the size of education impacts and externalities both depend on the length of the period over which the impacts are estimated.

Finally very tentative educated guesses as to the total value of education externalities are summarized in Table 6.3. They are best expressed as a percentage of the total market plus non-market returns to education. This can be done, and explained, using Figure 6.1 by first expressing total market externalities as a percentage of the market returns to education, as discussed above and shown in Table 6.2. Then, if externalities as a percentage of the non-market private returns based on eq. (6.2) are roughly similar, which would seem to be a reasonable assumption, and if non-overlapping private non-market returns are about 80 per cent of the market returns to education (as developed later, in Table 6.6) then this gives an estimate of the

Table 6.3   *Education externalities as a percentage of total returns to education*

| Region | Value of development outcomes as a percentage of total returns to education* | |
	Upper bound computed from Heckman & Klenow (1997) and Topel (1999) (1)	Lower bound McMahon (2002a), and Appiah and McMahon (2002) (2)
Africa	68	45
Latin America	64	41
Asia	62	39
OECD	61	37

Note: * These are *not* rates of return.

Source: Table 6.2 and explanation in the text.

total value of all education externalities or social benefits realized by individuals. Expressed in terms of the areas shown in Figure 6.1, this is all indirect effect externalities represented by areas B-1 + B-2 + B-3 expressed as a percentage of total market and non-market returns to education on which a value can be placed (i.e. areas A-1 + A-2, plus B-1 + B-2 + B-3). The direct effects on development outcomes can be and are measured and quantified as discussed here and shown in area A-3, but presumably they only have value to the extent to which they affect individual private utilities. This perhaps reflects more of an English philosophical view of the state as composed of individuals engaged in John Locke's social contract than a Continental philosophical view of the state as a separate organic entity.

The total value of externalities is likely to be less than the 61–8 per cent of the value of market plus non-market private outcomes implied by a dynamic interpretation of Topel's (1999) and Heckman and Klenow's (1997) models in column 1 of Table 6.3 (i.e., 61–8 per cent of 1.8 times the value of market outcomes). This is because there is a lack of all controls in these initial specifications in their papers for impacts by factors other than education on development outcomes. (Their controls using proxies for technology in later specifications in contrast go too far, for the reasons discussed, and wipe out all externalities.) But as a more realistic lower bound the value of externalities is likely to be larger than the 37–45 per cent of total education outcomes found by McMahon (2002a) and Appiah and McMahon (2002) as shown in column 2. This is because these estimates do not take differences in education quality fully into account, because the direct value to individuals of the social development outcomes is still not fully included (Figure 6.1, area A-3), and because the externalities generated by investment in R&D that are both due to and disseminated by higher education are not fully included. This omission of higher education externalities causes externalities as a percentage of the returns to education to appear to be larger in the poorer countries and regions. This pattern is unlikely to be sustained if investment in R&D and higher education in the leading countries is given explicit attention in the regressions.

Finally this particular numerical valuation should be interpreted as no more than an educated guess because the simulations were run for only 40 years, a period within which they do not fully converge. Running the simulations for longer periods leads to an even larger build-up of externality impacts. This effect is also implied by Topel's (1999) experiments using longer periods, as well as by most theoretical solutions dealing with longer run steady states. It is not this particular numerical estimate of externalities that will be carried forward into the final conclusions, but instead the conclusion that the size and value of education externalities depend on the time period chosen over which education's 'community effects' are allowed to cumulate.

III   Empirical estimates of specific non-market externality effects

Estimates of the *net* impacts of education on specific types of non-market externalities are summarized in Table 6.4. They are generated as individuals use their human capital during non-labour market hours in the community. They again represent the net impacts after 40 years, impacts that follow an increase of 2 per cent of income per capita invested in education. About half of this additional investment is in the form of earnings forgone by parents as their children stay in school longer. There are lags of 10, 15 or sometimes 20 years after this increase in investment because it takes time for these students to graduate, and still more time before they have an impact on their communities, and hence before the effects are detectable empirically.

The methods need to be briefly explained. First, education's *net* marginal product as it relates to each outcome is estimated (i.e., the direct effects, area A-3 in Figure 6.1) normally based on cross-country data for 78 countries worldwide. This first step is interpreted as estimating the direct effects because in each case there is a control for per capita income to remove the indirect effects of education as well as controls for all other variables that logically can be expected to influence that outcome and that are statistically significant. The logic of the theory such as that summarized in eqs (6.2) and (6.3) above and spelled out more fully below informed these specifications. So, although simplifications are necessary, the specifications are not merely ad hoc. Surveys of the literature on each development outcome to see what others have found to be empirically significant were also conducted (with abbreviated summaries below). The economic theory, and the theory in other fields such as political science in cases where this is relevant, often suggests variables that have a logical connection to the outcome but that are not found to be empirically significant. Most of these cannot be discussed here because of space, but see McMahon (2002a). When all is said and done, there always remains an unexplained residual, so results can be improved by future researchers. Problems with simultaneous bias due to endogeneity are reduced by the lags which make each equation recursive, but probably not entirely eliminated. Endogeneity is also addressed by testing for simultaneous bias in the parameters using two-stage least squares estimating methods wherever simultaneity appeared to be a problem, as in for example the growth and investment equations (see McMahon, 1998b, 2002). There probably is some bias due to simultaneity that remains, but steps were taken seeking to minimize it. There are also measurement errors and other offsetting biases in the direction of underestimating education's true effects.

Table 6.4 Estimates of non-market education externalities, simulations of outcomes over 40 years, static plus delayed effects

Type of outcome affected by education (1)	Percentage change in outcome of education after 40 years* (2)	Basis for estimate (after a $13.80 increase in per capita investment in Africa) (3)	Source (4)
1. Better public health	Positive, but public v. private health effect unknown	Microregressions only, AIDS educ. potential ↓ fertility but↑ health	Grossman & Kaestner (1997)
2. Lower pop. growth	0% in Africa,↓ elsewhere		
3. Democratization	36% ↑ in democracy (i.e. Freedom House Index up 2.9 (from 3.7) to 6.6) Includes 2.3% for more volunteering: 2% of mkt rate Includes more fin.gifts: 12% give over 3% of their income	Note: this investment of $13.80 per capita raises gross enrolment rate by about 20 percentage points Volunteering and financial giving are at each income level	Democratization: Appiah and McMahon (2002, pp. 50–51, 65–7), data from *Freedom House* (1999, p. 536); volunteering and financial giving: NCES (1995, 1998)
4. Human rights	4% ↑ in human rights, on Freedom House Index		
5. Political stability	3.1% ↑ in political stability, Internat. Country Risk Guide		Appiah & McMahon (2002, p.51)

Table 6.4 *(continued)*

Type of outcome affected by education (1)	Percentage change in outcome of education after 40 years* (2)	Basis for estimate (after a $13.80 increase in per capita investment in Africa) (3)	Source (4)
6. Lower crime rates	2% ↓ in homicide rate 1.2% ↑ in property crime Plus 2% rate of return due to lower incarceration costs	*Secondary* enrolment reduces property crime by 9% if income controlled for	Appiah and McMahon (2002, pp. 51–2) Lochner (1999)
7. Deforestation	0.3% ↓ in annual forest (and wildlife) destruction rate	All occur from combined indirect effects of slower population growth, less poverty, more democracy and faster economic growth.	Appiah & McMahon (2002, pp. 41, 52) McMahon (2002a, pp. 216, 234–5)
8. Water pollution (for India, better data)	13% ↓ in water pollution		
9. Air pollution	14% ↑, growth increases it		
10. Poverty reduction	18% ↓ in poverty	If primary and junior secondary education is extended to rural villages	A.&M. (2002, p. 51)
11. Inequality reduced	8% ↓ in inequality (in GINI)	Only if access widened	A.&M. (2002, p. 51)
12. } Geographic 13. } spillovers	Positive as HC is gained, negative where HC leaves	Jr. Sec helps provinces, higher ed. ↑ emigration	
14. Informal knowledge dissemination	Overlaps 1–13 above, unknown net effects	Technologies raise non-market productivity too	e.g. Moretti (2002)
15. More schooling	20% ↑ in enrolment rates	From 2% ↑ in investment	McMahon (2002a, p. 164)

Note: * Column 2 estimates calculated from Appiah and McMahon (2002, pp. 50–52) as the total increment by 2040 (col. 4, op. cit.) following a policy change in 2000 divided by the initial level in 2000 (given in col 1, op.cit); alternative specifications are shown in McMahon (2002a, chs 2–13).

Cross-country data are chosen because they allow for wider variation in many outcomes such as differences in political stability permitting not only the effects of education on these to be observed but also more stable statistical estimates of the coefficients than when the data are too homogeneous. This is also Barro's (2001) opinion. Second, a difference equation for each outcome results in a difference equation system that can then be used for simulations of all of the outcomes. A time path is generated for each as the lags are fed, so new community effect levels in each period lay the foundation for continuing growth, with net impacts of education that cumulate over time. Lest it be complained that 40 years is too farsighted, let it be stressed that the purpose is not forecasting but instead to isolate the net effects of one particular education policy change under predefined conditions. Most steady-state theoretical solutions run out to where time approaches infinity. The choice of 40 years is also primarily to see if the processes begin to converge, and a shorter period can be chosen to look at the net impacts if desired. The initial conditions, or starting point, for the simulations for each country are the actual initial values of all of the endogenous variables inherited from the past for that country. Each new generation inherits an improved platform from which to start, not only in per capita income but also in the non-market aspects of development.

Public health externalities
Grossman and Kaestner's (1997) survey identifies not just own health but also some externality-type public health effects. No simulations of impacts are possible for this outcome. However education reduces the spread of infectious diseases to others and thereby improves public health. Education is also necessary to improving medical technologies through continuing R&D.

Lower population growth rates
Since better health increases population growth rates and falling fertility rates reduce them, there are structural equations addressing the determinants of each that underlie determination of net population growth. The equations are for infant mortality, which depends on female education lagged 20 years (and other controls), and for life expectancy, which depends on a combination of infant mortality, education lagged 20 years and GNP per capita (and on other controls). Together these generate 'better health' and increase net population growth, but population growth is reduced by lower fertility rates. This also depends on female education lagged 20 years, as well as other controls. A definitional identity relates this offsetting of more education on better health and on falling fertility rates to determine net population growth. In Africa, female basic education first increases net

population growth as its effects on better health dominate. But then, as female education reaches about 9th grade (age approximately 13 or 14 years old) on average in the population, the effects on reducing fertility rates begin to dominate, and population growth stabilizes. In the simulations for Africa, increasing investment in education takes about 40 years before the improvements in health begin to be offset by falling fertility, which is shown as a 0 per cent net effect on population growth rates in row 2 of Table 6.4. This slowdown of net population growth is a social benefit because it is accompanied by better health but also because it reduces poverty within each family. Slower population growth also has spinoff benefits through less pressure on the environment and other effects that will be seen below.

In the low middle and middle-income countries of East Asia and Latin America, most females have reached 9th grade, so the effects of female education in lowering fertility rates dominate education's effects in improving health, and population growth rates are falling (e.g., McMahon 2002a, 188, 194, 200, 203). The major problem with high population growth rates is in the very poorest countries where a high percentage of females have not completed junior secondary education. There the effects of education on better health cause net population growth rates to continue to rise, as in India, Bangladesh, Pakistan, Nepal, Bolivia and most of Sub-Saharan Africa. Unfortunately it is necessary to use a longer planning horizon in these poorest countries because of the huge deficits in female education levels there.

Democratization and development of civic institutions
'Democratization' is used here as shorthand to reflect the building of civic institutions, development of the rule of law, protection of the role of opposition parties and candidates in the electoral process, lack of domination by the military, and the other items in the Freedom House (1999) index. These all require a literate population since authoritarian dictatorial regimes find a more hospitable climate where poverty and illiteracy are widespread.

This rationale for the role of both education and higher per capita income as determinants of democratization is drawn primarily from political science. It is that rising per capita income, associated with a growing middle class, gives rise to demands for participation in the political process that increasingly cannot be ignored by authoritarian regimes (Diamond, 1992; Huber *et al.*, 1993). To be employed productively, a widespread middle class requires a literate population, and probably at least some secondary education.

Empirically, essentially all countries in the world with per capita incomes below about $600 are authoritarian. The one exception is India. There a very influential individual, Pandit Nehru, believed deeply in democracy. There was also a heritage of English laws, the rule of law, trained civil servants and viable parliamentary institutions. It is unfortunate that he did not have an equal commitment to basic education as a source of economic growth and development (McMahon, 2002a, pp. 193–9). Perhaps largely as a result, primary education there until very recently was viewed only as a family welfare benefit in government budgets. Its contribution to slowing population growth rates and to per capita economic growth remained largely unrecognized. It is not surprising that population growth rates remained high, and that real per capita income 50 years after independence was no higher than at the time of independence. Female illiteracy in rural areas and net population growth rates are still high. There have been some improvements in very recent years with shifts of education investment from higher education to basic education and with better per capita growth. But, with respect to democracy, Pakistan is more typical of the worldwide pattern. There a civil war resulting in the separation of Pakistan from India was led by Muslims who did not share Nehru's beliefs in democracy. This resulted in a military dictatorship that persists, along with extensive illiteracy of females in the rural areas as in India.

The determinants of democratization in cross-country data that are significant by standard t-tests are found to be investment in secondary education (as measured by secondary gross enrolment rates lagged 15 years), per capita income growth (lagged five years) and military expenditure as a percentage of government budgets (also lagged five years). The latter has a negative relation to democratization. Additional potential explanatory variables, such as urbanization or newspaper/TV access, are not significant. However Clague *et al.* (1996) tried a dummy variable for British heritage and found it to be significant. The dummy variable for Islam religion remains negative but is insignificant when the other variables mentioned are included. The adjusted R^2 is 0.49, which is not high, but also not too bad for cross-section data. An unexplained variation remains, however. Alternative specifications containing secondary educational attainment instead of enrolment rates with lower t statistics and a lower adjusted R^2 are shown and discussed in McMahon (2002a, pp. 98–101).

With respect to military expenditure as a percentage of the government's budget, it is possible that there is some reverse causal flow, with democracies spending less on the military and more on education because they are democracies. But although some two-way causation is likely, some regimes hang on longer with large military expenditure, as did the former Soviet Union, and regimes in North Korea and Myanmar. This is consistent with the lagged effect from military expenditure on democratization in this equation. Also the eventual changeover to fragile democracies from military dictatorships in Latin America has been remarkable in the last 40 years.

With respect to the potential significance of a two-way causal flow from democratization to economic growth and to investment in education, the preponderance of the political science literature reviewed by Diamond (1992) suggests that the main direction of causation is from rising per capita income and increasing education to democratization. It is noteworthy that all 28 current OECD members have relatively high education levels and also are democratic by Freedom House's (1999) measure. Huber *et al.* (1993) further document this process. Barro (1997, 2001) and Clague *et al.* (1996) also find that, when literacy is included as a determinant of democratization, its *t*-statistic is very high. The net effect on democratization of increased investment in education alone is estimated to be a 36 per cent increase in democratization after 40 years, as indicated in Table 6.4, based on Appiah and McMahon (2002, p. 41).

There are three other aspects of the influence of education on the development of civic institutions on which there is empirical evidence. They are the effects of education on civic knowledge and attitudes, the extent to which those with more education at each income level contribute more volunteer time, and the extent to which they voluntarily contribute more financial resources to civic organizations. With respect to the civic returns to education, Dee (2003) finds large and significant effects on subsequent voter participation and support for free speech, as well as the quality of civic knowledge as measured by the frequency of newspaper readership. With respect to the number of hours volunteered for community service, a Gallup survey in the United States reveals that, within each income group, 22 percent of those with some post-secondary education give generously of their time to community service activities. This is nearly twice as often as the 12 per cent of those with a high school education (NCES, 1995, p. 98) who give generously. Hodgkinson and Weitzman (1988) found a similar pattern in an earlier nationwide survey. With respect to financial giving to eleemosynary institutions, the evidence is that the college educated give 3 per cent or more of their income to charity about twice as often as high school graduates. This is true in lower income groups where 24.7 per cent of the college educated give generously as compared to 12.5 per cent of the high school graduates. It is also true in higher income groups where 19.1 per cent with college versus 7.5 per cent with high school educations give generously.

This benefits others and there is a social benefit externality even though the giver also gains some private satisfaction (see areas B-1 and B-2 in Figure 6.1). It contributes to the strengthening of eleemosynary institutions, many of which are civic institutions fundamental to effective democracy. If such surveys were conducted in developing countries with controls for per capita income (there are none to the author's knowledge), it seems reasonable to expect that similar patterns would be found. Nevertheless, ex ante, most students do not weigh the possibilities for community service very highly when making college investment decisions, as revealed in a national survey of prospective students in the United States (McMahon, 1984). That is, they may see some private returns (areas A-1 and A-2) but take the externalities for granted. When public leadership is well educated and committed to public service, there can be external social benefits for many generations to come (Bowen, 1977; Thomas Jefferson, 1787, in his *Notes on the State of Virginia* recommending a basic law for universal education in W. Peden (ed.) 1955, p. 148).

With respect to the *indirect* effects of education on growth through democratization (part of the possible two-way causal flow), the preponderance of the evidence in the cross-country data is that democracy does not contribute to growth directly (Barro, 1991, 1997; McMahon, 2002a). Instead it contributes to political stability and this in turn to investment in physical capital and growth (McMahon, 2002a, Appiah and McMahon, 2002, p. 41, Barro and Sala-I-Martin 1995, p. 451). However whether democracy contributes to growth directly or not is much debated (e.g., De Haan and Siermann, 1995). Oliva and Rivera-Batiz (2002) find positive direct effects from democracy but still stronger indirect effects as it encourages foreign direct investment (FDI). The latter finding is generally consistent with the relationship postulated here. Democratization may also contribute to growth indirectly through encouraging more schooling and hence influencing the next round of growth.

Human rights
Human rights include freedom of the press, radio and TV, freedom of assembly, an independent judiciary, no imprisonment for political crimes, gender equity, avoidance of use of torture and absence of serious corruption. They are therefore defined here as they normally are by political scientists in the West and by Freedom House (1999), although the UN Declaration of Human Rights and eastern political scientists tend to define them more broadly to include education and health, which we analyse separately here. The rationale for the determinants of human rights is similar to that for democratization discussed above. Empirically human rights do improve significantly with democratization after controlling for per capita income. Military expenditure as a percentage of the government's budget has a significant negative relationship to human rights (McMahon, 2002a, ch.7). As with democracy, human rights can be regarded as a public good, the enjoyment of which is essentially free to all, although there are of course serious questions about the effective access of the poor to equal treatment within the court system. Education's marginal contribution therefore is largely an externality.

In the simulations, human rights increase by 4 per cent in Africa after 40 years from where they are currently. The measure of human rights is the Freedom House index, and this improvement follows the same two percentage point increase in education investment rates (Appiah and McMahon, 2002, p. 51).

Political stability
Political stability is measured by the International Country Risk Guide (1995). The theory generating the hypotheses tested concerning the determinants of political stability again draws from political science. As with democratization and human rights, rising income and higher levels of education contributing to a larger middle class are conducive to greater democratic participation, democratization and hence greater political stability. Empirically the OECD nations on average have higher per capita income, widespread education and democracy are also highly stable, and the lower middle-income countries are in a zone of transition.

The theoretical relation of military expenditure to political stability again is more problematical. Authoritarian regimes and stability can be supported by large military expenditures in the short run at least, as suggested earlier, but this may be less sustainable in the long run. In fact in the longer run, excessively high military expenditure may be destabilizing and conducive to coups d'états. Empirically the positive determinants of political stability significant at or close to the 0.05 level are per capita economic growth (lagged five years), secondary education enrolments (lagged 20 years) and democratization. Military expenditure (lagged five years) has a significant negative relationship. Although political stability is correlated with democratization, there are instances of governments that are authoritarian and also politically stable (China, Singapore, Saudi Arabia). But stability did not persist in Latin American countries that delayed democratization, nor did it in Europe earlier (e.g. with the French revolution).

Political stability increases by 3 per cent on average in Africa, as shown in Table 6.4, or by 7 per cent in the very poorest countries. This is as shown by simulations over 40 years following an increase of two percentage points in the rate of investment in primary and secondary education (Appiah and McMahon, 2002, p. 51). This includes the indirect effects from investment in education through increases in per capita income and through improvement of democratization. As indicated above, although neither Barro (1997), Barro and Sala-I-Martin (1995, p. 426), nor McMahon (2002a) find that democratization contributes directly to growth, McMahon (2002a) and now Oliva and Rivera-Batiz (2002) find that it contributes to political stability, and all find that political stability in turn contributes to growth.

Lower crime rates

In an interesting survey of the crime literature, Witte (1997) finds that the average educational attainment of individuals already prone to crime has no relation to their criminal activity. But this survey also indicates that the presence of large numbers of unsupervised teenagers on the streets is very significantly related to crime rates. New work has also been done on this by Lochner and Moretti (2003).

Consistent with this, in cross-country data higher secondary gross enrolment rates are found to be significantly related to lower homicide rates (5 percent lower in spite of growth). Property crime rates are 1.2 per cent higher after 40 years, the latter effect due largely to economic growth, (McMahon 2002a, ch.10; Appiah and McMahon, 2002). If income growth is controlled for, increased secondary enrolments (that keep young boys off the streets) are associated with lower property crime. This direct effect from education which is also probably partly from better peer group relationships is strengthened by the indirect effects of education, as it lowers crime through lower urban poverty and less inequality. The latter effects appear strongest in the property crime equation. The unemployment rate lagged two years also has a significant effect on homicide rates both worldwide and in US data after controlling for per capita income. But as property crime rates rise with per capita income, this is a negative externality. It includes white-collar crime and, with rising income, this offsets some of the benefit from more education.

Beyond this, better education reduces the costs of building prisons, of incarceration and of costs to victims. This is estimated by Lochner (1999) to be 20 per cent of the private monetary return, a 2 per cent add-on externality shown in Table 6.4. Early work by Spiegleman (1968) and Ehrlich (1975) should also be noted. Research on productivity in US schools that limits school productivity to increases in academic test scores (e.g., Hanushek, 1994, 1997), although useful for some purposes, overlooks an important externality as higher secondary enrolment rates lower murder and property crime rates.

Deforestation

The logic behind education's *indirect* effects on the environment is that forests are cleared for agriculture as population grows (e.g. in Brazil), and for heating and cooking where poverty rates are high (e.g. in Nepal, or historically in Britain). Forests are also cut for raw material exports which are higher relative to manufacturing exports where human capital is low (raw material exports of timber, such as in Indonesia and Thailand). Deforestation in turn is the source of most destruction of wildlife mammals. These problems increase at a rapid pace.

Empirically the indirect effects of education on reduction of population growth rates and on poverty are considered above and later. The effects of higher population growth in reducing the rate of reforestation (i.e., increasing deforestation) is highly significant in cross-country data. But the direct effects of education above and beyond this are not significant (McMahon, 2002a, p. 129). This same combination of effects shows up in data for Latin American countries alone (ibid., p. 130). However the reader must consider the possibility of spurious correlation.

A two percentage point increase in investment in education generates only a 0.3 per cent net reduction in the rate at which these forests are destroyed in Africa, largely through slower population growth, as shown in Table 6.4 (from Appiah and McMahon, 2002, pp. 52, 68). The destruction of forests also continues in some OECD countries. But in simulations for these countries, the indirect effects as increased investment in education further slows population growth are associated with slower rates of forest destruction there (McMahon, 2002a, pp. 159–62).

Water and air pollution
The effects of more education on water and air pollution are also almost entirely indirect. In the case of water pollution, education again first reduces poverty and population growth rates. Then these two effects, after controlling for per capita income, are robust in their association with less water pollution (McMahon, 2002a, p. 134, models 1 to 6).

Together these indirect effects generated by the same increase in education as before in the simulations lead to about a 13 per cent reduction in the amount of water pollution (Appiah and McMahon, 2002, p. 41). The empirical estimates of water pollution effects are only for India, where the water pollution data are better than in Africa, but perhaps they are somewhat representative. With respect to air pollution, in Africa the same education policy change leads, through combined indirect effects on population growth, democratization and economic growth, to about a 14 per cent increase in air pollution. Although the latter is a negative externality, it should also be stressed that these same indirect effects of education on air pollution controlling for growth are associated with reduced air pollution. The issue of global warming needs to be addressed differently since some countries contribute more in absolute terms than others to this problem. But the tentatively adverse effects of growth on global warming, and the tentatively desirable effects of poverty reduction, slower population growth and democratization may be suggestive of some directions for further research.

Poverty reduction
There are significant effects in cross-country data between extending secondary education to more of the population, especially in poor rural areas, and reduction of rural poverty. Economic growth and secondary education are both significant in reducing absolute poverty in cross-country data, by 18 per cent over 40 years in Africa, for example, as shown in Table 6.4 (McMahon 2002a, ch. 8; Appiah and McMahon, 2002, p. 41). Garfinkel and Haveman (1977, p. 53) find a strong negative relation between the education of the head of the household and poverty status, with its associated welfare and medical costs.

Inequality
The main rationale is that the income distribution effects of education depend primarily on who gets the education. Economic growth and increasing education per se do not necessarily reduce inequality. This is illustrated in Brazil's record, with high inequality accompanying rapid growth in per capita income at the top of the inverted U of the Kuznets curve (see Harbison and Hanushek, 1992, pp. 192–9). But with controls for the way the education itself is distributed, Psacharopoulos (1977) and Ehrlich (1975) also found a strong relation between inequalities in schooling and the relative number at the poverty end of the income distribution. Reflecting this difference in the distribution of education, in East Asia, where many countries, starting with Japan and including South Korea, Taiwan, Hong Kong, Singapore and Malaysia, extended basic and then secondary education widely in the 1950s and 1960s, this was followed not just by fast per capita growth but also by falling inequality (McMahon, 2002a, ch. 8; World Bank, 1993). The recent financial crisis interrupted this long-term trend of fast growth and falling inequality. But now growth has resumed in most East Asian countries. Employing the model, simulations tracing the impact of a further 2 per cent increase in investment in education reduce inequality by an additional 8 per cent. This effect on the GINI coefficient measure of inequality is shown in Table 6.4. This same kind of effect of more education on the reduction of inequality in subsequent years is found by Sylwester (2002, p. 43) to be 'robust to the inclusion of various control variables'.

Geographic spillovers: rural migration to urban ghettoes and emigration of college graduates
The net costs and benefits to cities of the internal migration from poor rural areas where education has been inadequate to urban slums has not been estimated precisely, but some effects are rather obvious. Observe, for example, migration from rural Pakistan to the slums of Karachi, rural

migration into slums in Cairo, Buenos Aires and Rio de Janeiro, and migration from rural Mississippi to the black ghettoes of Chicago. These are partly the result of technological displacements and the hope of better economic conditions in urban areas. Some of these immigrants move into productive employments, but some do not. The costs to the urban education, criminal justice and welfare systems are partly a result of deficiencies in the education systems in the rural areas from which the migrants come. They are negative geographic externalities within nations that often are not addressed by national education policies.

Internationally there is also a brain drain from developing countries. There are gains to the receiving country and loss to the country from which the immigrants come that depend on immigration policies. But they also depend on education policies in low-income countries where the higher education system has been disproportionately subsidized or expanded. For example, in Pakistan, India and Sub-Saharan Africa, where too few in the labour force have basic education, the job opportunities for college graduates are more limited. These emigrants have incurred education costs that are not recouped, so the social rates of return can be negative. Empirically the size of these geographic externalities is not known. But they differ among countries and in some cases are partially offsetting. Beyond calling attention to their existence, no attempt is made here to estimate their size.

Knowledge creation and dissemination

It is suggested here that 'technical change' which is often cited by economists as a key factor in the economic growth process really reflects the impacts of new knowledge and its diffusion through education in all fields as it contributes to the more specific 13 or so development outcomes discussed above. They replace undefined time dummies frequently introduced as an unexplained control for 'technology' in economists' models. They do include the contributions of education to innovative capacities in all fields stressed by Romer (1990), Eliasson *et al.* (1990) and earlier by Schumpeter, but they do not include explicit investment in R&D as a percentage of GDP, which facilitates innovation in the nations leading in new technologies. This can raise the rates of return to higher education in these leading countries, so it is explicitly recognized here.

More schooling

Schooling is also endogenous in the basic theoretical model in this paper (via eq. (6.3) in section I). It is a function of G, government investment (the 2 per cent of GDP increase in investment in education per capita), as well as of the amount of human capital brought forward from the past (which essentially determines family income). These and the other regressors determining gross enrolment rates at each level are shown in detail in McMahon (2002a, p. 164), with R^2 0.66 to 0.99. Then, treating the percentage of GDP invested in education as a variable increased by government investment policies, the simulations show that this additional investment, combined with its endogenous feedback effects, results in an approximately 20 percentage point increase in both primary and secondary education enrolments. Primary gross enrolment rates are capped at 112 per cent, so when universal primary education is achieved, the funds are channelled more heavily to secondary and higher levels.

IV Social rates of return

As these impacts of education on development goals combine, and operate endogenously over time to lay improved foundations for continuing growth, it is possible to use the result to get some idea of a more comprehensive and new social rate of return to investment in education that includes the value of non-market indirect effects. Unlike private rates of return, the social rates of return reflect the full investment costs. These are not just those to the individual and his or her family, including their forgone earnings costs, but also those to the society in the form of institutional costs and grants. They also reflect all benefits, not just the monetary benefits to the individual but also, as estimated with the assumptions indicated above, the market and non-market education externalities benefiting current and future generations that individuals take for granted.

Column 1 in Table 6.5 shows conventional monetary social rates of return. These are as calculated by the full method given by Psacharopoulos and Patrinos (2002) who distil the results of 50–60 refereed articles. These conventional social rates do not include the non-monetary returns shown in columns 2 and 3. They are best interpreted, however, as including the effects on money earnings from education externalities generated by others and by past generations (i.e. area B-1 in Figure 6.1). Column 2 gives new estimates of non-monetary rates of return based on the non-market returns enjoyed by individuals over and above market returns (i.e. areas A-2 and B-2 in Figure 6.1). These are based primarily on valuations by Haveman and Wolfe (1984), Wolfe and Haveman (2001) and Grossman and Kaestner (1997) that are shown in Table 6.6, plus necessary adjustments for consistency that will be discussed there.

Column 3 estimates non-market public good externalities limited to the indirect effects as a percentage of the total returns to education identified by McMahon (2002a) that were given in Table 6.4, column 2 and illustrated as area B-3 in Figure 6.1. These percentages are lower than those calculated on the basis of Heckman and Klenow (1997) and Topel (1999) using a dynamic interpretation of the neoclassical model. So, from this point of

Table 6.5   Estimates of total social rates of return including non-market education externalities

Region of the world	Components of total social rates of return to investment in education (investments increasing access and/or improving quality)[1]			
	Conventional monetary social rates of return[2] Fig. 6.1: A1 + B1	Non-market private returns 80 per cent of col. 1,[3] from Table 6.6 Fig. 6.1: A2 + B2	Non-market education externalities[4] (indirect effects) Fig. 6.1: B-3	Total social rates of return (includes non-monetary)[5] (cols 1+2+3)
	(1)	(2)	(3)	(4)
Africa				
Primary	25.4	20.3	9.1	54.8
Secondary	18.4	14.7	6.6	39.7
Higher	11.3	9.0	4.0	24.3
Latin America				
Primary	17.4	13.9	5.7	37.0
Secondary	12.9	10.3	4.2	27.4
Higher	12.3	9.8	4.0	26.1
Asia				
Primary	16.2	13.0	5.0	34.2
Secondary	11.1	8.9	3.5	23.5
Higher	11.0	8.8	3.4	23.2
OECD				
Primary	8.5	6.8	2.5	17.8
Secondary	9.4	7.5	2.8	19.7
Higher	8.5	6.8	2.5	17.8

Notes:
1. Behrman *et al.* (2002) find positive and roughly equal returns to quantity and quality.
2. From Psacharopoulos and Patrinos (2002).
3. Valuations by Haveman and Wolfe (1984) and Wolfe and Haveman (2001) as shown in Table 6.6, followed by deleting external benefits outside the family from their lists.
4. Estimated value of public goods externalities is based on the assumption that the public good non-market indirect effects (area B-3 in Figure 6.1) are approximately the same percentage of private non-market returns as the indirect effects are of market returns.
5. A simple sum of cols 1–3 is legitimate because the investment cost base for each of these rates of return is the same.

view, they could be regarded as conservative. There is a piece missing in the puzzle, the public good externality *direct* effects (area A-3 in Figure 6.1). These are assumed to be small, based on the earlier discussion of the negligible effects found from use of the static interpretation of short-run effects in the neoclassical model. But this may help to define an important problem that needs to be addressed by future research.

The total social rates of return in column 4 are the sum of these, the monetary and non-monetary returns realized by individuals and the benefits to society (and future generations) realized from progress in achieving social development goals. Standard social rates of return are much criticized for the omission of these direct effects.

The total social rates of return in column 4 are higher than the conventional monetary rates because they include non-monetary improvements in the quality of life now and in the future generated by the use of human capital at home and in the community. They seem reasonable at most education levels and in most regions, but extraordinarily high at the primary level in Africa and Latin America and the Caribbean. The high rates of return to basic education in the poor countries reflect higher standard monetary rates of return there, but also larger social benefits from improvements in health, democratization and political stability revealed by the simulations. These areas have the highest illiteracy rates and highest primary education deficits. This pattern is consistent with Colclough (1980), who also finds high returns at the primary level in Africa.

V Non-market private returns to education

A brief digression from the focus on externalities is necessary to identify and explain the basis for the valuation of non-market *private* returns to education. This is to distinguish them as not overlapping with the social development goal externalities. It is also necessary to support the basis for the valuations of non-market returns to individuals that appear in Table 6.5, column 2.

Private non-market outcomes of education are taken here to be those that benefit not only the individual but also his or her family. The reason for including intra-family externalities as private benefits enjoyed by the family is that, for education investment decisions throughout basic education and undergraduate higher education, the primary decision-making unit that finances the student and absorbs most of the forgone earnings costs is the family. This is therefore relevant when it comes to financing policies, and who should pay, which is a primary reason for estimating education externalities. It is also because the indirect effects include effects from the education of prior generations (e.g. Wolfe's child education and child health) that feed back and are a part of the non-market benefits of education realized by individuals (i.e. area B-2 in Figure 6.1).

To avoid overlap, first, between market returns to education and the non-market returns listed in column 1 of Table 6.6 below, only those studies are considered that control for per capita income. This eliminates double counting of the market returns to education. To avoid overlap, second, the impacts of more education on achieving higher labour force participation rates, lower unemployment rates and more part-time employment after retirement are not included since these are included by most methods of estimation in the monetary returns. To avoid overlap, third, between non-market *private* benefits (in Table 6.6) and non-market benefits to social development goals, the list of private benefits in Table 6.6 and the list of development goals in Table 6.4 were compared and duplication eliminated. The result of the latter is that the costs of crime and the value of volunteer hours contributed to the community are removed from the Haveman and Wolfe (1984), Wolfe and Zuvekas (1997), and Wolfe and Haveman (2001) valuation totals. Few significant overlaps remain, although the benefits from lower fertility rates are hard to split between private benefits to the family and spillover social benefits.

The 12 main types of non-market private returns in Table 6.6 do not include the benefits and costs of shifts in personal tastes attributable to more education, such as those from enjoyment of stock car racing and bull-fights to enjoyment of symphony concerts and public television. This is because, although these taste shifts can be quantified, they merely displace other tastes and partially cancel out, and because their valuation across individuals involves interpersonal comparison of utilities that economists reject. The costs (and sometimes benefits) of divorce and benefits of remarriage are also excluded for the same reason, although the education of females appears to increase both.

The empirical basis in the research on each type of non-market private return is surveyed elsewhere and is readily available, so it will not be repeated here. See Michael (1982), Haveman and Wolfe (1984), McMahon (1998a), Wolfe and Zuvekas (1997), Grossman and Kaestner (1997), and Wolfe and Haveman (2001). Wolfe's co-authored articles all explain the methods of valuation. The citations in Table 6.6 are limited to those that seek to place a value on these private non-market outcomes.

The estimated value of non-market outcomes from additional education is very substantial. Based on Wolfe and Haveman's (2001) and Haveman and Wolfe's (1984) methods which use the cost of producing the same outcomes by alternative means using market-produced inputs (e.g. better health produced by purchased health care inputs), I estimate the total value of the *private* non-market benefits of education to be roughly 80 per cent of the value of the market outcomes when the benefits to society external to the family are excluded. Not only is this large, but the value of the additional education in improving own health, longevity, child health and infant mortality, and the spouse's health alone is estimated at a sizable 40 per cent of the value of the market returns to the additional education by

Table 6.6 *Estimates in the literature of the value of non-market private returns*

Private non-market effect of further education (1)	Value as a percentage of market returns (2)	Size or value of impacts from one additional year of education (3)	Source of estimate or of coefficients (4)
1. Better individual & family health	40	132 studies surveyed	Grossman & Kaestner (1997)
2. Own health & longevity		0.07 (sec. enrolment)	Appiah & McMahon (2002, p. 41)
3. Child health, less infant mortality		0.03 (female sec. enrol.)	Appiah & McMahon (2002, p. 41)
4. Better spousal health		Wife's educ. better male health	Grossman (1975)
5. Cognitive development of children	11.2	Mean of 4 studies cited: value of parents' ed. input	Wolfe & Haveman (2001, p. 244)
6. Fertility, family size & poverty reduction (private benefits only)	6	Mean, 3 studies reviewed $-0.2(\Delta GER1) - 0.49(\Delta GER2)$	Wolfe & Haveman (2001, p. 240), McMahon (1998a, 2002a)
7. Consumption efficiency	1.3	$290 in family income	Wolfe & Haveman (2001, p. 244)
8. Higher return on financial assets	2	Higher return on equities than on savings accounts	Solomon (1975)
9. Reduced obsolescence of human capital via new leisure-time learning	5	The N-M parallel of educ. effect via uses of R&D	Nelson & Phelps (1966), Griliches (2000)
10. Non-market job satisfactions	4	Better working conditions	Duncan (1976)
11. Greater amenities in urban life	2	Lower salaries accepted where crime rate is low	Chambers (1996: 25)

Table 6.6 (continued)

Private non-market effect of further education (1)	Value as a percentage of market returns (2)	Size or value of impacts from one additional year of education (3)	Source of estimate or of coefficients (4)
12. Pure consumption effects (while in school, or learning)	9	Enjoyment of high school and college yrs over work	Lazear (1977), Pascarella & Terenzini (2002, ch. 12)
Total value of pvt. non-market returns as a percentage of market returns	80.5		Wolfe & Haveman's (2001, p. 245) 100% less Lochner's (1999) 20% for reduced crime costs and 0.5% for more volunteer hours, moved to social benefit externalities later below

Notes: To convert to per centages of market returns to education as shown in column 2, Wolfe and Haveman's (2001, p. 245) valuations in rows 5–7 of non-market returns to education which are sometimes shown by them in absolute dollar amounts are re-expressed as a percentage of average earnings in the USA. This results in a conservative estimate of these non-market returns since it implicitly assumes that the returns to raw unimproved labour in the USA is zero. Average earnings are taken to be $22 055 in 1996 US dollars as used in their computations. The percentages in rows 6–12 are less precise estimates since they are based on the underlying education coefficients reflecting the marginal product of education in producing the outcome in question relative to the per capita income coefficient (i.e. the alternative means) for producing that outcome. Studies included are those that address the valuation of outcomes.

Grossman and Kaestner (1997) as well as by Wolfe and Haveman (2001) as shown in Table 6.6. Their first approximation estimates of education's contributions to the cognitive development of children are 11.2 per cent, and to lower fertility and family size with consequent effects reducing family poverty are 6 per cent, of the market returns. A crude estimate of the value of reduced obsolescence of human capital is 5 per cent (probably underestimated) and to non-market job, environmental and consumption amenities 4 per cent, 2 per cent and 9 per cent of market earnings, respectively. Together these nearly double the monetary rates of return conventionally estimated. More precisely they increase the monetary rate by 80 per cent. If these private benefits were more clearly identified and understood, they would contribute a powerful incentive for additional private investment in human capital by families and individuals.

These estimates of non-market returns must be qualified in various ways. First, again, they are not offered as precise values but instead as first approximations in an effort to estimate a total social rate of return. If research by others will focus on this objective, the precision undoubtedly can be increased. These valuations of private returns to the family make possible the new estimates of total externalities and total social rates of return in Tables 6.4 and 6.5.

A second qualification is that some studies find smaller non-market effects and some find larger effects. The studies that find smaller effects usually do so by including control variables beyond the key ones. Most are implicitly using the static interpretation of the neoclassical model that rules out most indirect effects. Nevertheless, although Table 6.6 may go modest steps beyond Wolfe and Haveman's (2001) work, it is based heavily on their estimates.

The third qualification is that, although the non-market private returns to additional education appear to be substantial, it is doubtful that families and prospective students are aware in specific terms of what they are or of their value. That is, although families and students do value better health, greater longevity, better child education, better child health, non-market job satisfactions and other amenities, it is unlikely that they are aware of the extent to which these are specifically connected to their further education. Furthermore many of these are benefits to them from education in prior generations that they take for granted (area B-2 in Figure 6.1). Another way to put this is that they are likely to be myopic in not valuing very highly the expected contributions of their education to the health and education of children and grandchildren not yet born. This means that they will discount these future non-market returns heavily, and will underinvest.

To get some idea of what the size of this discount is likely to be, a recent survey of college freshmen reports that 73 per cent said making more money or getting a better job were the most important reasons for attending college (see Flacks and Thomas, 1997). This suggests that only 27 per cent estimated the non-market private and social returns to be at least equally important. If the value of these non-market returns is approximately 80 per cent of the value of the market returns, they are not equally important. But there is some indication in the surveys that their value is being underestimated. Consistent with this, when specific non-market returns including better education and health of future children, stimulation of lifelong learning later in life, and finding a spouse with college-developed values were tested in a nationwide sample of 1863 entering freshmen, McMahon (1984, p. 87–8) found each of these (except the last) to be of very limited significance relative to expected money earnings. Although non-market returns may be poorly understood, taken for granted and discounted by prospective students, this is not a basis for discounting them when seeking optimum social efficiency.

VI   Investment criteria

Investment in education is a shared enterprise that includes private investment by families and students. Families normally bear over 50 per cent of the total investment costs since forgone earnings must be included as part of the investment. An objective of estimating education externalities is to get some idea of how these costs should be shared between private support by families and employers and public support by government and by donors if efficiency is to be achieved, since private decision makers take these external benefits for granted, and they will not be provided without external intervention to correct this source of market failure.

There can of course also be government failure, with inefficiency and corruption. Public education is not perfectly efficient, but a major source of government failure in the developing world is government officials who divert resources to their own ends. They also operate tax systems that are ineffective and fail to collect taxes due. These contribute to underinvestment in basic education, a type of government failure that is particularly relevant in the poor countries.

Using total social rates of return as efficiency criteria
Where the total *social rates of return* to education investments are high in relation to the average total return on alternative investments, usually taken to be about 10 per cent in real terms, there is underinvestment in education. Governments and donors need to invest more, which induces additional private investment by families and employers as higher enrolment rates incur forgone earnings and as the quality of education improves. Where total social rates of return are below this 10 per cent that taxpayers could

earn on average if resources were retained and invested privately, investment in education needs to be decreased if an efficient optimal growth and development path is to be attained. This assumes that governments and donors respond to the appropriate economic criteria, including social rates of return properly estimated to include the non-market values of education. This they do not always do.

Private and public shares in financing   Before considering private versus public shares in financing, different sources of market failure and of government failure need to be addressed by different kinds of policies, not all of which are considered here.

- *Poor information.* The main remedy for this is efforts to improve the information available to students. This should help to reduce 'discounting' as well as inaccurate information. However some of the non-market returns realized by individuals may be indirect effects that are long delayed from prior generations and are taken for granted.
- *Imperfect capital markets* for the financing of human capital investments. Students' lack of collateral that can be repossessed means that banks usually will not lend without loan guarantees. The lack of access to employer training programmes may also limit private investment, even though private rates of return to individuals may be high. Relevant policies where this is the problem include guaranteed student loan programmes at post-secondary levels, and perhaps even employer tax write-offs for training unskilled workers who lack basic education.
- *Weak private sector training capacities.* Where little or no private capacity exists, programmes to develop these are needed. Where employer skill bases are more adequate, employer-sponsored training is known to be more effective (Kim, 1987; Bishop, 1994).
- *Government failure.* Inefficiency in public education or in tax systems requires sustained efforts to reduce this inefficiency. Social rates of return do take inefficiency into account, however, since they reflect the full actual institutional costs, whatever the level of inefficiency, and the actual quality, however poor it is. Reduced inefficiency will increase returns and lower costs, raising rates of return. The objective always needs to be the provision of higher quality education at lower cost to the extent this is reasonable and possible. If government failure is due to corruption that diverts resources to the personal ends of a ruling elite, the underinvestment will be reflected in high social rates of return. Sustained investment in basic education may be needed to overturn this corruption.

- *Equity considerations* are not included in this analysis. They are relevant to financing methods, and often are a separate justification (beyond efficiency) for investment in some types of education. The impacts of the distribution of education on inequality, however, have indirect effects on some development outcomes that are included.

Turning to the implications of the size of education externalities for the size of the public or donor's share in the financing of education, Table 6.3 offers evidence suggesting that externalities as a percentage of total returns to education average a little over 40 per cent. Estimates there suggest that they are about 45 per cent in Africa, 41 per cent in Latin America and the Caribbean, 39 per cent in Asia and 37 per cent in OECD nations, based on McMahon (2002a). Heckman and Klenow's (1997) and Topel's (1999) estimates computed using a dynamic interpretation of their models are 68 per cent to 61 per cent by region. But these are judged by the present author to be overestimates of education externalities because of the lack of controls for factors other than education affecting development outcomes.

The 40 per cent figure is not far from the current public share of total investment in basic education in these regions. The fees at the primary and secondary levels in public schools, especially in developing countries, mean that individuals and families are covering more than 50 per cent of the investment costs even at those levels. In Indonesia, for example, a recent survey reveals that, in the public primary schools, there are six types of fees, accounting for 34 per cent of the non-salary budgets at the school level (McMahon *et al.*, 2002a, p. 61). Fees at the junior and senior secondary levels include supplements to teachers' salaries and tend to be even higher. In OECD nations, especially considering that a fraction of the pupils are in private and parochial schools, the public and private shares are not drastically different.

With respect to higher education, where forgone earnings costs are higher, in the United States undergraduate students typically pay about 30–33 per cent of the direct institutional costs in tuition in most four-year public universities. This means that students and their families are covering privately about 74 per cent of the total investment costs, and governments and/or other donors about 26 per cent. These percentages are based on annual forgone earnings costs averaging about $18170 for males and females, and institutional costs averaging about $10558 in the year 2000 (McMahon, 2003, cost appendix for ch. 2). At private universities both the institutional costs and the percentage of total costs covered by tuition are somewhat higher, so the percentage covered by state scholarships and by private endowments is typically less than 26 per cent. However in South Asia, Africa and some other countries, tuition and fees are low, means tests are not used effectively and, as a result, there is far less resource recovery and a larger government share in higher education financing.

The high total social rates of return to education in Table 6.5 suggests that rates of investment in education need to be increased in many countries if something closer to optimum efficiency in the rates of economic development is to be achieved. But this does *not* mean that government's share of the total investment costs need necessarily increase. If education externalities are a little over 40 per cent of the total returns to education, a 40 per cent government share of the total investment cost is appropriate on efficiency grounds (equity to the side). Governments can potentially raise their investment in education as a percentage of GDP, which induces additional private investment of forgone earnings, and also through higher tuition revenue as enrolments (and quality) increase. This increase in private investment seems likely to be roughly proportionate to the public increase over longer periods of time. For example, consider estimates of human capital investment equations like eq. (6.3), and the effects of increased public investment in expansion of community colleges in the USA since 1960 which induced private parental participation in financing via forgone earnings as well as public grants supporting tuition at private institutions. In this case the public/private shares in financing education remain approximately the same.

VII Conclusions

Most prior research on education externalities has focused on the effects on market earnings or on GDP per capita. A taxonomy of the marginal products of education influencing specific economic development outcomes offered here suggests that this is only part of the story. A dynamic interpretation of the neoclassical model that incorporates them in the development process suggests that the non-monetary returns to education are considerable. Many are indirect, and long delayed. Most are education externality benefits taken for granted by individuals.

Based on the narrower static interpretation, a number of the approaches surveyed find limited and inconclusive evidence of externalities. They also sometimes find limited evidence for the significance of education's impacts on money earnings and on per capita economic growth. It is concluded that, if the narrower static interpretation is chosen, this rules out most indirect and delayed effects. This affects the specifications of the regression equations to be estimated in such a way that the impacts are smaller and the evidence for externalities is inconclusive. If a dynamic view of the neoclassical model is taken, and indirect effects operating through other variables are traced, each year's investment in human capital affects the initial conditions for the next period. This cumulatively sets the stage for future growth and development. If this view is taken, it can be concluded that the evidence for education externalities is substantial and robust.

The value of the externality component is estimated to be something less than 61–68 per cent of the total returns to education calculated as an upper bound, based on Topel (1999) and Heckman and Klenow (1997) using their dynamic interpretation. (These percentages should not be mistaken for rates of return.) Their dynamic specification does not remove the effects of technology either by use of time dummies or by use of life expectancy as a proxy for medical technologies. It overestimates education's impacts, however, because of the lack of any controls for factors other than education that have an impact on development outcomes. The externality component can also be estimated to be somewhat greater than 37 per cent to 45 per cent of the total returns to education. This is by means of dynamic simulations of short-term impacts over a 40-year period based on McMahon (2002a) and Appiah and McMahon (2002). (These percentages are not rates of return either). It is judged to be a lower bound because the value of direct impacts of education on development goals are not included, because differences in the quality of education are not fully taken into account, because the complementarity of R&D specifically with higher education in the leading countries is not fully included, and because the simulations were run for 40 years rather than for the longer time period that is implicit in some of Topel's (1999) and Heckman and Klenow's (1997) cross-country estimates.

This 37–45 per cent educated guess of the total value of education externalities as a percentage of the total returns to education results after employment of 54 control variables controlling for most significant impacts on development outcomes by factors other than education. Some of these control variables are endogenous. But all education impacts and many of the control variables operate with lagged effects, which makes most of the relations recursive from a statistical point of view. For this particular estimate, education outcomes, for example, were always dependent on education investments within each country 10 to 20 years earlier. Beyond this, additional efforts were made to control for simultaneous bias by estimating some of the sets of equations by two-stage least squares where this seemed to be a problem. But it must stand as a qualification that, although there were vigorous searches for unmeasured effects and efforts to deal with endogeneity, the possibility of some remaining unmeasured effects and some remaining simultaneous bias still exists. Unexplained variation remains to be addressed by continuing research. Although this estimate of externalities is smaller than many in the literature, it must be considered that there are sources of bias offsetting those from endogeneity and from unmeasured effects discussed above that operate in the other direction.

Based on the above analysis, preliminary estimates of total social rates of return that include non-market returns and externalities are computed. Most are significantly higher than a benchmark return of, say, 10 per cent in real terms available on average for private investment alternatives in bonds or physical capital. These imply that there is underinvestment in education, both by governments and by private households and firms. But this does not mean that the gap should be closed by public investment alone, any more than by private investment by households and firms. However, as the government increases its investment first, private investment by households and firms follow, since as enrolments increase private investment of forgone earnings occurs and, as on-the-job and off-the-job training is offered by firms, both employees and educational institutions frequently also lend support. The 40/60 ratio of public to private investment need not change significantly.

More research is needed in estimating the impacts of education on development outcomes, as well as both theoretical and empirical work on placing an economic value on the direct effects of education on development outcomes. For the latter, perhaps an expanded theoretical solution for endogenous development offers promise. It is clearly concluded that further research on these education externalities is most needed using a dynamic interpretation of the neoclassical model. The narrower static interpretation appears to reveal less, often ignoring indirect effects, and not tracing education impacts over long enough time periods. With a dynamic interpretation, unexplained time dummies that are frequently used to represent 'technology' can be replaced by a better analysis of the process by which technology and new knowledge in all fields is disseminated through education and made effective.

But, apart from presenting a further developed conceptual framework, the main conclusion of this chapter at an empirical level may be unsettling to some. It is that the empirical size and value of education externalities is no fixed number. Instead it depends heavily on the length of the period over which simulations are allowed to run or that education impacts are studied. It is by this dynamic process with long delays that education continually affects development outcomes, repeatedly setting a new stage in each successive period and thereby providing for continuing future growth and development.

Acknowledgments
The author would like to thank Harry Patrinos, George Psacharopoulos and Geraint and Jill Johnes for their comments, as well as the World Bank for their permission to adapt two tables from the author's World Bank paper on 'Lifelong Learning' and for their earlier support of that project. The author is alone responsible for all conclusions and any errors.

References

Acemoglu, Daron and J. Angrist (2000), 'How large are human capital externalities? Evidence from compulsory schooling laws', in B. Bernake and K. Rogoff (eds), *NBER Macroeconomics Annual 2000*, Cambridge, MA: MIT Press, pp. 9–59.

Appiah, Elizabeth and Walter W. McMahon (2002), 'The social outcomes of education and feedbacks on growth in Africa', *Journal of Development Studies*, 38 (4), 27–68.

Barro, Robert (1997), *The Determinants of Economic Growth; A Cross Country Empirical Study*, Cambridge, MA: MIT Press.

Barro, Robert (2001), 'Education and economic growth', in John Helliwell (ed.), *The Contribution of Human Capital and Social Capital to Sustained Economic Growth and Well Being*, Ottawa and Paris: Government of Canada and OECD, pp. 13–41.

Barro, Robert and Jong-Wha Lee (1993), 'International comparisons of educational attainment', *Journal of Monetary Economics*, 32, 363–94.

Barro, Robert J. (1991), 'Economic growth in a cross section of countries', *Quarterly Journal of Economics*, 106 (2), 407–44.

Barro, Robert J. and Xavier Sala-I-Martin (1995), *Economic Growth*, New York: McGraw-Hill.

Becker, Gary S. (1965), 'A theory of the allocation of time', *Economic Journal*, 75 (299), 493–517; reprinted in G. Becker (ed.), *The Economic Approach to Human Behavior*, Chicago: University of Chicago Press, pp. 89–130.

Behrman, Jere, David Ross and Richard Sabot (2002), 'Improving the quality vs increasing the quantity of schooling', Penn Institute for Economic Research Working Paper 02–022, Dept of Economics, University of Pennsylvania, Philadelphia, available at http:.ssrn.com/ abstract id-322200.

Benhabib, J. and M.M. Spiegel (1994), 'The role of human capital in economic development; evidence from cross country data', *Journal of Monetary Economics*, 34, 143–73.

Benhabib, Jess and Boyan Jovanovic (1991), 'Externalities and growth accounting', *American Economic Review*, 81 (1), 82–113.

Bils, Mark (2001), 'Comment' (on Acemoglu and Angrist), in *NBER Macroeconomics Annual 2000*, New York: National Bureau of Economic Research, pp. 59–68.

Bishop, John (1994), 'The incidence and payoff to employer training', Working Paper 94–17, Center for Advanced Human Resource Studies, Cornell University, Ithaca, NY.

Bowen, H.R. (1977), *Investment in Learning: The Individual and Social Value of American Higher Education*, San Francisco: Jossey-Bass.

Card, David (1999), 'The causal effect of schooling on earnings', in Orley Ashenfelter and David Card (eds), *Handbook of Labor Economics*, Amsterdam: North-Holland.

Chambers, Jay (1996), 'Public school teacher cost differences across the United States; introduction to a teacher cost index (TCI)' in Wm. J. Fowler (ed.), *Developments in School Finance 1995*, NCES 96–344r, Washington, DC: US Dept. of Education, pp. 21–32.

Ciccone, Antonio and G. Peri (2002), 'Identifying human capital externalities: theory with application to US Cities', IZA Discussion Paper no. 488, Institute for the Study of Labor, Bonn, Germany.

Clague, Christopher, Suzanne Gleason and Stephen Krack (1996), 'Determinants of lasting democracy in poor countries', mimeo, Department of Economics, University of California, San Diego: November.

Colclough, Chris (1980), 'Primary education and economic development: a review of the evidence', World Bank Staff Working Paper no. 399, The World Bank, Washington, DC.

Dee, Thomas (2003), 'Are there civic returns to education?', NBER working paper, Economics Department, Swarthmore College and National Bureau of Economic Research (August), Cambridge, MA.

De Haan, Jakob and C.L.J. Siermann (1995), 'New evidence on the relationship between democracy and economics growth', *Public Choice*, 86, 175–98.

Diamond, Larry (1992), 'Economic development and democracy', *American Behavioral Scientist*, 35, 450–99.

Duncan, G.J. (1976), 'Earnings functions and non-pecuniary benefits', *Journal of Human Resources*, 11, 462–83.

Ehrlich, I. (1975), 'On the relation between education and crime', in F.T. Juster (ed.), *Education, Income, and Human Behavior*, New York: McGraw-Hill.

Eliasson, Gunnar, S. Folster, T. Lindberg, T. Pousette and E. Taymaz (1990), *The Knowledge Based Information Economy*, The Industrial Institute for Economic and Social Research, Stockholm: Almqvist and Wikell International.

Flacks, R. and S. Thomas (1997), 'College students in the nineties: report on a project in progress', paper presented at the ASHE Conference in Albuquerque, NM, The Association for The Study of Higher Education, Washington, DC.

Freedom House (1999), *Freedom in the World 1995–6*, Lanham, MD and London: National Book Network.

Garfinkel, I. and R.H. Haveman (1977), *Earnings Capacity, Poverty, and Inequality*, New York: Academic Press.

Griliches, Z. (2000), *Education, R&D, and Productivity, a Retrospective*, Cambridge, MA: Harvard University Press.

Grossman, M. (1975), 'The correlation between health and schooling', in N. Terleckyj (ed.), *Household Production and Consumption*, New York: Columbia University Press for the NBER, pp. 147–211.

Grossman, Michael and Robert Kaestner (1997), 'Effects of education on health', in J. Behrman and N. Stacey (eds), *The Social Benefits of Education*, Ann Arbor: University of Michigan Press.

Hanushek, Eric (ed.) (1994), *Making Schools Work: Improving Performance and Controlling Costs*, Washington, DC: The Brookings Institution.

Hanushek, Eric (1997), 'The productivity collapse in schools', in W.J. Fowler (ed.), *Developments in School Finance, 1996*, National Center for Education Statistics, Washington, DC: U.S. Department of Education.

Harbison, R.W. and E.A. Hanushek (1992), *Educational Performance of the Poor; Lessons from Northeast Brazil*, New York: Oxford University Press.

Haveman, Robert and Barbara Wolfe (1984), 'Schooling and economic well being: the role of non-market effects', *The Journal of Human Resources*, **19** (3), 377–407.

Heckman, James and P. Klenow (1997), 'Human capital policy', Working Paper, Economics Department, University of Chicago.

Hodgkinson, V. and M. Weitzman (1988), *Giving and Volunteering in the United States: Findings from a National Survey, 1988 Edition*, Washington, DC: Independent Sector.

Huber, Evelyne, D. Rueschemeyer and J.D. Stephens (1993), 'The impact of economic development on democracy', *Journal of Economic Perspectives*, **7** (3), 71–85.

International Country Risk Guide (1995), *A Business Guide to Political Risk for International Decisions*, 2nd edn, New York: Political Risk Services.

Keller, Katrina R. (2003), 'Investment in education levels and the effects on growth', working paper, Department of Economics, Susquehanna University, Selingsgove, PA.

Kim, S. (1987), *In-Service Training as an Instrument for the Development of Human Resources in Korea*, Paris: OECD Development Center.

Krueger, Alan B. and M. Lindahl (2001), 'Education for growth. Why and for whom?', *Journal of Economic Literature*, **39** (4), 1101–36.

Lazear, E.P. (1977), 'Education: consumption or production?', *Journal of Political Economics*, **85**, 569–97.

Lochner, L. (1999), 'Education, work and crime: theory and evidence', mimeo, University of Rochester.

Lochner, Lance and E. Moretti (2003), 'The effect of education on crime: evidence from prison inmates, arrests, and self-reports', resubmitted to *American Economic Review* (also NBER Working Paper 8605, 2002.)

Lucas, Robert E. (1988), 'On the mechanics of economic development', *Journal of Monetary Economics* **22** (1), July, 3–42.

McMahon, W.W. (1984), 'Why families invest in education', in S. Sudman and M. Spaeth (eds), *The Collection and Analysis of Economic and Consumer Data; Essays in Honor of Robert Ferber*, Urbana, IL: University of Illinois Press.

McMahon, Walter W. (1987), 'Externalities in education', in George Psacharopoulos (ed.), *Economics of Education; Research and Studies*, Oxford and New York: Pergamon Press.

McMahon, Walter W. (1998a), 'Conceptual framework for the analysis of the social benefits of lifelong learning', *Education Economics*, **6** (3), 309–46.

McMahon, Walter W. (1998b), 'Education and growth in East Asia', *Economics of Education Review*, **17** (2), 159–72.

McMahon, Walter W. (2001), 'The impact of human capital on non-market outcomes and feedbacks on economic development', in John F. Helliwell (ed.), *The Contribution of Human and Social Capital to Sustained Economic Growth and Well Being*, Hull, Quebec: Government of Canada, and Paris: OECD.

McMahon, Walter W. (2002a), *Education and Development: Measuring The Social Benefits*, Oxford and New York: Oxford University Press.

McMahon, Walter W. (2002b), 'Endogenous growth or endogenous development?', working paper, Department of Economics, University of Illinois.

McMahon, Walter W. (2003). *Market, Non-Market and Social Benefits of Higher Education and Research* (book manuscript in process).

McMahon, Walter W., with N. Suwaryani, Boediono, and E. Appiah (2002), *Improving Education Finance in Indonesia*, UNICEF and UNESCO, and Institute for Research and Development, MONE, Government of Indonesia.

Michael, Robert T. (1982), 'Measuring non-monetary benefits of education: a survey', in Walter W. McMahon and Terry G. Geske (eds), *Financing Education: Overcoming Inefficiency and Inequity*, Urbana, Chicago and London: University of Illinois Press.

Moretti, Enrico (2002), 'Estimating the social return to higher education: evidence from longitudinal and repeated cross-section data', Working Paper 9108, August 2002, National Bureau of Economic Research, Cambridge, MA.

NCES (1995), *The Condition of Education 1995*, National Center for Education Statistics, Washington, DC: U.S. Department of Education.

NCES (1998), *The Condition of Education 1998*, National Center for Education Statistics, Washington, DC: U.S. Department of Education.

Nelson, R. and E. Phelps (1966), 'Investment in humans, technological diffusion, and economic growth', *American Economic Review*, **56**, 69–75.

Oliva, Maria-Angels and Luis A. Rivera-Batiz (2002), 'Political institutions, capital flows, and developing country growth: an empirical investigation', *Review of Development Economics*, **6**, 248–62.

Pascarella, Ernest T. and P.T. Terenzini (2002), *How College Affects Students*, San Francisco, CA: Jossey-Bass.

Peden, W. (1955), *Thomas Jefferson's Notes on the State of Virginia*, Chapel Hill: University of North Carolina Press.

Pritchett, L. (1997), 'Where has all the education gone?', Policy Research Working Paper, World Bank, Washington, DC.

Psacharopoulos, George (1977), 'Unequal access to education and income distribution', *De Economist*, **125**, 383–92.

Psacharopoulos, George and Harry A. Patrinos (2002), 'Returns to investment in education: a further update', World Bank Policy Research Working Paper 2881, Washington, DC.

Rauch, J. (1993), 'Productivity gains from geographic concentration of human capital, Evidence from the Cities', *Journal of Urban Economics*, **34**, 384–400.

Romer, Paul (1990), 'Endogenous technical change', *Journal of Political Economy*, **98** (5), S71–S98.

Rouse, Cecilia (2001), 'Comment' (on Acemoglu and Angrist), *NBER Macroeconomics Annual 2000*, New York: National Bureau of Economic Research, pp. 68–74.

Solomon, L.C. (1975), 'The relation between schooling and savings behavior', in F.T. Juster (ed.), *Education, Income and Human Behavior*, New York: McGraw-Hill.

Spiegleman, R.G. (1968), 'A benefit/cost model to evaluate educational programs', *Socio-Economics Planning Science*, **1**, 443–60.

Sylwester, Kevin (2002), 'Can education expenditures reduce income inequality?', *Economics of Education Review*, **21** (1), February, 43–52.

Topel, Robert (1999), 'Labor markets and economic growth', in O. Ashenfelter and D. Card (eds), *Handbook of Labor Economics*, vol.3C, Amsterdam: Elsevier, pp. 2942–84.

USAID (2003), 'UNESCO indicators', available on www.USAID/GED Online.

Uzawa, Hirofumi (1965), 'Optimal technical change in an aggregative model of economic growth', *International Economic Review*, **6** (January), 18–31.

Venniker, R. (2001), 'Social returns to education: a survey of recent literature on human capital externalities', CPB (Netherlands Bureau for Economic Policy Analysis), Report 00/1 (http://www.cpb.nl/eng/cpbreport/2000 1/s 3 4.pdf).

Witte, Ann Dryden (1997), 'Social benefits of education: crime', in J. Behrman and N. Stacey (eds), *The Social Benefits of Education*, Ann Arbor: University of Michigan Press.

Wolfe, Barbara L. (1994), 'External benefits of education', *International Encyclopedia of Education*, 2nd edn, Oxford: Pergamon, pp. 2208–12.

Wolfe, Barbara and R. Haveman (2001), 'Accounting for the social and non-market benefits of education', in John Helliwell (ed.), *The Contribution of Human and Social Capital to Sustained Economic Growth and Well Being*, Paris: OECD.

Wolfe, Barbara L. and Samuel Zuvekas (1997), 'Non-market outcomes of schooling', in *Recent Advances in Measuring the Social and Individual Benefits of Education*, a special issue of *International Journal of Education Research*, **27** (7), 74–94.

World Bank (1993), 'The East Asian miracle: economic growth and public policy', Policy Research Report, Policy Research Department, The World Bank (July).

World Bank (2003), 'World development indicators', WDI Online.

7 School finance
David Mitch

School finance deals with the issues that have arisen as societies throughout the world have developed ways of funding schools. These issues are shaped by the fact that provision of schooling has generally not been left solely to market responses to profit incentives. Intervention in the market for schooling has been justified on the grounds of externalities attributable to education, on the grounds of capital market imperfections and on the grounds of the impact of education on equality of opportunity. Consequently a variety of state, religious and other non-profit institutions have developed throughout the world to fund, provide and manage schools. Thus, in 1999, for some ten developing countries, the public share of expenditure on education at all levels came to 72 per cent and for OECD countries in the same year averaged 88 per cent. In 2000, for both OECD and these same ten developing countries, over three-quarters of students at the primary and secondary levels were enrolled in publicly managed schools (OECD, 2002).

The imperative to develop means of funding schools becomes of further moment when one realizes that current levels of educational funding are quite sizeable relative to national income throughout the world. For OECD and developing countries alike, expenditure on primary and secondary schooling in recent years has averaged 3 to 4 per cent of GDP. It should be noted that such high levels are a phenomenon of the 20th century. In the 19th century, expenditure on education relative to national income was well below 2 per cent and, by some estimates, well below 1 per cent (West, 1975; Lindert, 2004). And around this 3 to 4 per cent average, variations between the developing countries in the World Education Indicators survey were substantial, ranging in 1999 from 2.1 per cent for Uruguay to 7.5 per cent for Jamaica (the 0.8 per cent share reported for Indonesia appears to be due to underreporting; see OECD, 2002, p. 183, n. 8). For OECD countries, the range has been considerably narrower, ranging in 1999 from 2.6 per cent for Greece to 4.4 per cent for France, Sweden and Switzerland (OECD, 2002).

A basic accounting framework that provides perspective on gauging influences on national expenditure requirements on schooling is to decompose the influences on expenditure on education per capita into (a) the percentage of the population of school age and more specifically at various levels of schooling, (b) the percentage of the relevant population age group that is actually enrolled in the appropriate level of schooling, and (c) expenditure per student at each level of schooling relative to national income per capita (OECD, 1976, pp. 14–18). It should be emphasized that this decomposition is simply an accounting identity and leaves for further consideration the behavioural determinants of each of the three components involved. This simple decomposition implies that expenditure on education relative to national income can vary because of (a) changes and differences in the size of the school age population relative to the total population – what could be labelled a demographic factor; (b) changes in enrolment rates per age group at each level of education, and (c) changes in relative expenditure per student.

Another compositional change associated with these three factors concerns the distribution of activity across primary, secondary and tertiary levels of education. Over time, educational attainment tends to rise as larger percentages of the population move on from primary schooling to secondary schooling and in turn to tertiary schooling. In addition to increasing the proportion of the population in school, such rising educational attainment will increase aggregate expenditures given that expenditures per student tend to be considerably greater at higher than lower levels of schooling. In recent decades, as more countries have approached universal enrolments during the primary age range, this has implied a tendency for convergence in educational expenditures per capita. Countries experiencing a demographic transition and falling birth rates have experienced a decline in relative size of the school age population, while countries still experiencing rapid population growth have experienced a rise with ensuing demands on increasing schooling expenditures given enrolment rates and expenditures per student. The latter two variables are of course not given but subject to policy considerations pertinent to the planning of educational finance. Indeed, given limited resources, societies generally face tradeoffs between extending access to educational systems by endeavouring to expand enrolment rates at various levels and enhancing the quality of education for those in the system by raising expenditure per student.

As with health care, there are issues as to what limits there may be in how far both access to schooling and quality of schooling can and should expand. For example, in the 17 developing economies covered by the World Education Indicators survey (hereafter WEI), in the year 2000, the mean (unweighted by population) expected years of schooling for a five-year-old was 13.0 years, while the mean life expectancy at birth for 13 of these countries in 1999 with figures available was 66.8 years, implying that almost 20 per cent of one's life on average in these countries would be devoted to school.[1] For 27 OECD countries in 2000, the unweighted mean for this same school expectancy for a five-year-old was 16.8 years while, for a broad sample of developed countries, average life expectancy in 1999 at birth was

78.[2] This implies that 21 per cent of one's life on average in these countries would be spent in school. And school attendance has typically extended recently further into the adolescent years with a resultant rise in forgone earnings and opportunity cost compared with attendance at younger ages. For OECD countries in 1999 on average, 76.9 per cent of the population aged 15 to 19 was enrolled in school, while for WEI countries the average was 51.7 per cent (OECD, 2001, p. 134). This entails not only a substantial opportunity cost for students but also a substantial resource cost to maintain instruction for such a large section of the population over extended periods of time.

Table 7.1 compares the expenditure components of primary and secondary schooling expenditure relative to GDP for the mean of the developing countries in the WEI survey with the mean of OECD countries as well as the high and low expenditure countries within each group, namely Jamaica, Uruguay, France and Greece. These comparisons reveal that the approximately similar levels of schooling expenditure per GDP for the WEI and OECD means reflect that the higher enrolment rates and expenditure per student levels for the OECD countries were offset by the higher percentage of population of school age in the WEI countries. However the high expenditure on education relative to GDP for Jamaica reflected the quite high level of expenditures per student rather than an unusually high proportion of population of school age, while the low level in Uruguay reflected to a large extent the low level of expenditure per student. As Table 7.1 indicates, all three factors made some contribution in particular cases to variation in expenditure per student.

Two underlying issues have shaped discussions of educational finance. The first concerns the role of public and private elements in education. While public and non-profit funding of schooling has become dominant in most countries, funding of schools has always had and continues to have some element of user payments, even if in a very restricted exclusive sector. This can be seen as reflecting both the desire to incorporate incentive effects of responding to users and equity considerations that those benefiting from education should make some contribution to its funding. Related to this is the point of cost recovery from users simply as a way of relieving the financial burden on the state. Also related to this is the role of government versus non-governmental non-profit organizations in providing and funding schools. This discussion often takes the form of the role of public versus private provision of education. Control over the source of funding leads on further to what is sometimes called the role of demand-side financing or alternatively the role of choice and vouchers in influencing school funding, i.e. what role parental and local community choosers should have in influencing the funding of schools.

Table 7.1 Accounting for international variation in school expenditures relative to GDP

Region or country	Expend. non-tertiary as % 1999 GDP	Primary Component				Secondary Component			
		Pop. aged 5 to 14 (%)	Pop. aged 5 to 14 in school (%)	Primary expend. per pupil/ GDP per capita	Total primary component	Pop. aged 15 to 19 (%)	Pop. aged 15 to 19 in school (%)	Secondary expend. per pupil/ GDP per capita	Total secondary component
WEI mean	3.8	21	88.9	14	2.6	10	54.7	21	1.15
OECD mean	3.6	13	97.9	19	2.4	7	77.3	25	1.35
Jamaica (high WEI)	7.5	20	88.6	21	3.7	10	39.6	30	1.2
Uruguay (low WEI)	2.1	16	97.8	11	1.7	8	60.7	14	0.7
France (high OECD)	4.4	13	99.8	18	2.3	7	86.4	31	1.9
Greece (low OECD)	2.6	10	99.8	14	1.4	7	87.4	18	1.1

Source: OECD (2002).

A second issue concerns the degree of centralization versus decentralization in both funding and provision of schooling. On the one hand, a school is inherently local since it must be located near residences of children and their parents to be used effectively. And actors at the local level are likely to face far stronger incentives to operate schools efficiently than more remote, centralized actors. On the other hand, centrally determined standards of optimal social investments in schooling are frequently invoked to justify public rather than private funding of schools, centralized sources of funding are commonly used to fund public schools, and often centralized sources of funding are required to redistribute resources to educationally relatively deprived localities.

While the remainder of this survey will focus on these two issues, it should be noted that the finance of schools is inevitably intertwined with the economics and politics of schooling generally, ranging from educational outcomes achieved by schools to political support for funding schools.

I   Private versus public provision of education

Explanations of the dominance of the public provision of education
The dominance of the public sector in school funding and provision would seem to require some sort of explanation. Moreover, it is important to understand this dominance in order to understand the forces behind the relatively large public expenditures on schooling that characterize most countries in recent decades. The mean (unweighted) public share in overall expenditure for OECD countries on primary, secondary and post-secondary non-tertiary education in 1999 was 92.1 per cent. And of the 25 OECD countries, 17 had public shares of educational expenditure above 90 per cent with only Germany below 80 per cent at a figure of 75.6 per cent reflecting private industry financing of post-secondary apprenticeships (OECD, 2002). For the 12 developing countries in the WEI survey, considerably more variation was evident around the considerably lower mean public share of 78.3 per cent (see Table 7.2). As James (1993) documents, the private share is typically considerably higher at the secondary than at the primary level.

At least in principle, schooling can be supplied in response to normal market mechanisms. While normative and positive explanations can overlap, what is required here is a positive explanation of the dominance of public activity in the funding and provision of schooling. That is, the point of this analysis is to explain why this has occurred rather than provide justifications for whether this ought to have occurred. In explaining the public presence in schooling markets, funding should be distinguished from provision/management of schooling. Although most publicly funded schools

Table 7.2 *Relative percentages of public and private expenditure on primary, secondary and post-secondary non-tertiary education, 1999*

Country	Public sources	Private sources
Argentina	88.6	11.4
Chile	69.2	30.8
China	55.8	44.2
India	95.3	4.7
Indonesia	76.6	23.4
Jamaica	61.8	38.2
Jordan	98.4	1.6
Paraguay	59.5	40.5
Peru	76.8	23.2
Philippines	66.8	33.2
Thailand	97.8	2.2
Uruguay	93.6	6.4
WEI mean	78.3	21.7

Source: OECD (2002).

are also publicly managed, in some countries there are substantial proportions of the schooling sector in the category of government-dependent private, defined as having over 50 per cent of core funding coming from government agencies. Responsibility for school provision can be contracted out and subsidized at public expense. It is also important to use some care in defining the terms 'public' and 'private'. In the literature surveyed here, the term 'public' generally refers to the activity of government, whether local, national or provincial. The term 'private' includes both for-profit enterprises and non-profit enterprises run either by religiously affiliated organizations or by philanthropic organizations.

In trying to account for the large public presence in schooling markets, one can employ the common distinction between public interest motives and special interest motives entailing some sort of resource transfer.

One class of public interest explanations focuses on market failure. One source of market failure is the presence of externalities or, in other words, spillover effects associated with schooling that students and their parents do not take account of in schooling decisions. One such spillover is that a certain minimum standard of educational attainment facilitates citizenship. Another is that raising educational attainment lowers the probability of crime. It has also been suggested that schooling promotes cultural homogeneity, which in turn promotes social stability. As Friedman (1955,

1962) points out, these considerations do not have to entail public funding of schools. Parents could simply be required to provide some minimal standard of schooling for their children. However, limitations on ability of many parents to pay for schooling and the unwillingness of societies to break up families in such situations suggest the appropriateness of government finance. A further related consideration is that in some instances there may be parental nonfeasance in providing for their children; in order to protect children from irresponsible decisions by their parents some minimal level of schooling should be funded by the government.

Another commonly mentioned source of market failure stems from imperfect capital markets that limit the ability to borrow in order to invest in human capital of individuals or families with limited wealth or assets to put up as collateral. Without government funding, it is argued, underinvestment in human capital relative to other forms of assets will occur. Soares (2003) develops an overlapping generations model with complementarities between physical capital and skills in production with the implication that savers will support a publicly financed schooling system to increase their return on capital. Gradstein (2000) presents a model in which uniform public schooling enables a government to commit itself in advance to restraints on future income redistribution. By encouraging the accumulation of human capital and economic growth, this commitment may be politically preferred. Another class of public interest explanations focuses on the enhancement in equality of opportunity associated with public support of schooling, with equality of opportunity promoting the social cohesiveness of the society and the cultivation of talent from humble origins.

While the redistributive effects of public support for education can be viewed as socially desirable, they can also be seen as serving particular interest groups in the society. Thus one general class of special interest explanations focuses on the political coalitions that would form in support of public schooling owing to the ability to gain from the resource transfers involved. This approach attempts to specify the basis for some coalition to form that would be able to derive benefits from publicly funded schooling in excess of their tax payments. Stigler (1970) proposed Director's law as the basis of such a coalition. Director's law states that government redistributive activity tends to occur towards the middle classes from the rich and poor groups in a society. The concept underlying Director's law as applied to schooling is that groups in the middle of the income distribution will tend to benefit and use public schooling disproportionately relative to their tax payments in comparison with either poor or richer elements; and the middle of the income distribution can form a large enough coalition with adjacent elements to form a majority. At certain times the majority coalition can entail more links with the rich and at other times with the poor. The director's law principle has since been refined as applied to public schooling, first by Barzel (1973) and more recently in further detail by Epple and Romano (1996) (also see Fernandez and Rogerson, 1995) who propose a middle versus ends political tension. The argument of Barzel and then Epple and Romano is that the middle of the income distribution values expenditure levels on public schooling more highly than poorer elements who put relatively less value on schooling, while the wealthiest elements would prefer a level of schooling greater than that which is politically feasible to support and hence would opt for higher quality private schooling rather than public schooling. With the highest income elements thus out of the majority coalition, the median voter influencing education decisions would have an income lower than the median income in the society.

Putting such coalition formation in long-term historical perspective, some economic historians have argued that great imbalances in power and wealth distributions in societies militate against forming effective political coalitions supporting mass schooling. They suggest that the extent of the franchise can be used as a measure of whether there is sufficient equality of power in societies to generate political support for mass schooling (Lindert, 2004; Mariscal and Sokoloff, 2000).

Another special interest explanation focuses on the government itself as the interest benefiting from schooling by the opportunity to convey ideology supportive of the government regime in a given society (Lott, 1990). Further special interest approaches highlight the interests that teachers' unions and educational establishment bureaucrats have in maintaining the public schooling sector as a monopoly.

These explanations only account for the public *funding* of schools. This still leaves open why, in so many countries, such a large proportion of schools are established and *operated* by governments. Explanations of public provision and management of schools include both efficiency and special interest considerations. Friedman (1955, 1962) has acknowledged that there may be natural monopoly arguments for public provision in cases of low population density which would not otherwise support more than one school. He also acknowledges that public operation can help ensure cultural homogeneity in what is taught in a situation of religious diversity. Another class of explanations briefly acknowledged by Friedman (ibid.) and developed in more detail by Brown (1992) is that public operation of schools is required to deal with problems of monitoring school activities and transactions costs involved in contracting out the provision of schooling. Brown argues that, owing to the inherent incompleteness of contracts involving provision of educational services, for-profit provision would be subject to opportunism. Non-profit provision and in particular provision by religiously affiliated organizations can provide a signal to both parents and funding governments that opportunism is less likely. However, direct and continuous government operation provides the best way to handle the monitoring costs and potential for opportunism associated with schooling. Historically concerns have been raised that privately provided schools whether for-profit or non-profit have tended to use unqualified teachers and an inadequate curriculum.

It has been noted that private, philanthropically provided education tends to involve elements of complementarity between various types of education. In particular, religiously affiliated schools seek both to propagate religious doctrines and to convey more secular instruction. It has been suggested that governments are willing to subsidize private education via religiously managed schools, and parents to contract with such schools because of greater trust or confidence that they will not indulge in opportunism compared with for-profit schools.

One set of special interest arguments for schooling having been publicly provided is to maintain a monopoly with restricted entry to create rents for members of teachers' unions and others in the public educational establishment. Another approach put forward by Lott (1990) is that publicly operated schools provide the most effective ways for government regimes to promulgate ideological indoctrination in their populations supportive of those regimes. According to Lott's view, by restricting entry into schooling markets, regimes can generate rents for teachers which in turn will make them willing to indoctrinate students with beliefs supportive of those regimes. In contrast with the Lindert (2004) and Mariscal and Sokoloff (2000) view that democracy and egalitarianism promote public schooling, Lott (1987, 1990) argues that totalitarian regimes are more likely to provide more resources in support of public schooling; he explicitly forecast that the demise of totalitarian regimes in Eastern Europe would lead to a marked decline in support for education. In the event, analyses of schooling trends in Central Europe in the 1990s showing considerable expansion (Fiszbein, 2000; Koucky, 1996) would seem to undermine Lott's thesis.

Resolving the actual importance of these various arguments for the presence of the government in the provision of schooling requires several types of evidence. One important source of evidence would be the magnitude of the actual externalities/spillovers associated with schooling. Chapter 6 in this volume (by McMahon) takes up the issue of schooling externalities. Here it can be suggested that the presence of compulsory schooling legislation and associated efforts to extend education to the groups who are the most reluctant to obtain it would seem to indicate the presence of such spillovers as opposed to a purely redistributive motive. However other political economy factors such as teacher union interests could be adduced to explain such efforts. The extent of redistributive motives surely varies from situation to situation. And it would seem likely that both public and special interest considerations are involved. However it is unlikely that continuing political support for public school funding would occur at the level that is seen worldwide without some sort of redistributive element involved. One particular piece of empirical evidence that has been cited is that childless families appear less supportive of tax increases to fund public schools than families with children (Barzel, 1973, p. 176).

Picking up this theme, a number of recent studies have considered whether areas with higher shares of the elderly in their populations tend to have lower support for public education. Using state-level evidence, Poterba (1997) finds that states with relatively high proportions of their populations over the age of 65, other factors held constant, tend to have relatively low levels of spending per child on primary and secondary schooling. However Ladd and Murray (2001) and Harris *et al.* (2001) find that this depressing effect of the elderly share on school spending either disappears or weakens considerably when more disaggregated county and district-level data are analysed. Ladd and Murray (2001) argue that any effect of the elderly on education spending takes place indirectly through a tendency to live in counties with low proportions of children and hence raise the tax price of schooling in other counties. Harris *et al.* (2001) argue that the elderly tend to be more resistant to state-level spending on schooling than local level schooling since only the latter is capitalized into housing prices. In a more international context, Zhang *et al.* (2003) construct an overlapping generations model to show the conflicting effects of rising longevity on median voter support for public education. At initially high levels of mortality, improvements in longevity most strongly affect child survival, which increases support for public education; but as the probability of survival at older ages comes to dominate consumption demands at these ages, political support for public schooling falls.

Empirical evidence on the determinants of public versus private funding
The primary focus of this section will be on international studies. Studies of regional variation in the private–public share within a given country will be considered more fully in sections below considering the interaction between public and private sectors.

One set of variables that has drawn particular attention in international studies of public support for education consists of measures of where countries stand on a democratic–totalitarian continuum. Lott (1990) finds for some 98 countries in 1975 a substantial positive impact of a measure of political totalitarianism on educational spending. However James (1993), using the same totalitarianism variable for 1975 but with a sample of 50 countries and with different dependent variables distinguishing primary from secondary schooling, finds a negative coefficient on totalitarianism measures. This would seem to reflect conflicting possible ways in which more totalitarian regimes could have an impact on educational spending. On the one hand, according to Lott, more dictatorial governments may want to use education spending to indoctrinate support for their regimes. On the other hand, as James indicates, more dictatorial governments may not require such spending on indoctrination to remain in power, instead preferring to minimize educational expenditure on their populations.

A second strand in this literature concerns the impact of income on public relative to private expenditures and enrolment. Lott (1990) finds a significant and positive effect of income on public education spending across countries. Fernandez and Rogerson (2001) find the same result in their longitudinal analysis of US states with an implied unitary income elasticity. James (1993) uses as her starting point the commonly observed phenomenon that the private share of both educational spending and enrolments tends to be higher in countries ranked at lower levels of economic development. Fuller analysis indicates that these differences by level of economic development relate to secondary, not primary, education. Ultimately it is the political coalition factors that seem to explain her results. Her differentiated demand measures as reflected in religious diversity measures explain much of the variation across countries in the private enrolment percentage at the secondary level. Downes (1996) provides a similar interpretation as to the influence of income on mid-19th-century California enrolment rates. His main measure of diversity is more indirect, however: population size per district, the idea being that a larger population size per unit area would translate into a more heterogeneous population. Downes notes that directly ascertaining the impact of heterogeneity as such from cross-section evidence is problematic since population characteristics associated with some in more heterogeneous relative to homogeneous areas may be the true causal factors at work rather than heterogeneity. And, as James herself acknowledges, measures of heterogeneity in demand for education in cross-country measures are inevitably quite broad-brush. More refined national case studies are required to disentangle more fully the impact of population heterogeneity on demands for private schooling. Nevertheless James's evidence provides grounds for thinking this an important factor.

While basic versions of James's (1993) model indicate that private enrolments fall with income per capita and measures of development stage, once political coalition variables, as measured by demographic share of school-age children, interact with the secondary level, the development stage variables diminish considerably in importance. She interprets this as reflecting that, at the secondary level, the broad segment of the income distribution does not want to pay taxes to support additional schooling for their children, especially in situations of large family size. And those in the upper end of the income distribution, while demanding schooling for their own children, are unwilling to foot the bill for those much lower down on the income distribution. However they would do so for primary education insofar as they perceived this as a larger source of externalities. With political support present for only relatively restricted public provision of secondary schooling in countries with relatively large population shares of school age, the private sector in James's scenario expands to fill the gap in such cases. Thus, James's findings underscore the importance of understanding the political interest groups and political coalitions at work supporting public provision of schooling.

Interactions between public and private sector
An important consideration in decisions to expand the size of public commitments to education is what impact this will have on private educational activity. It should be noted that the longer-term trends involved can change in nature. Historically public schooling can be seen as developing to fill in for inadequacies in private provision. Thus one concern is the extent to which expanding public activity will displace private activity. Indeed historically there has been concern to minimize such displacement in order to minimize the additional public resources required to expand schooling. However James (1993) has also described situations in which the private sector has developed in response to expanding demand in order to fill in the gaps in public provision. In whatever direction the trends have gone, some estimates have been attempted of the extent to which an expanding public sector displaces private provision. Insofar as public schooling can be provided at a cheaper private price than private provision and insofar as public provision eases schooling needs, one would expect displacement of private schooling activity.

A further point that has arisen in the literature is whether, in addition to leading to some redundancy by displacing useful private activity, increased public schooling support leads to perverse negative effects by inducing substitution due to lower public fees from higher quality private schools to lower quality public schools. This possibility was proposed by Peltzman (1973). West (1975) offered the case of Victorian England as an example of this perverse displacement where expenditure per student was used as the quality measure. More recently this idea has been revived with Toma's (1996) comparison of public and private schooling outcomes across five case studies. For this result to hold it must be the case that the relevant private sector is indeed of higher quality than the comparable public sector.

On the basis of international cross-country comparisons, James (1993) suggests sizeable tradeoffs between the sizes of private and public sector schooling. Goldhaber's (1999) study across districts within New York also finds displacement but of considerably smaller magnitude than suggested by James's international study. Goldhaber points to ambiguities in the interaction between private and public schooling activity and finds evidence of simultaneous determination. He distinguishes between switching endogeneity, in which the decisive voter on public schooling expenditures switches between public and private sectors within a given district, and Tiebout endogeneity, which involves movement of families between communities in accord with their preferences for government provision of schooling. In contrast with James's (1993) cross-section study, Goldhaber's data set is a pooled cross-section time series and his results point to the importance of fixed effects in allowing for Tiebout sorting. A further recent application of the pooled cross-section time series approach for developing countries is the Jimenez and Sawada (2001) study of districts in the Philippines. It finds an elasticity of substitution between public spending and private enrolment roughly comparable to James and somewhat greater than Goldhaber. The possibility of simultaneous determination of private and public schooling shares points to the value of a natural experiment. Downes and Greenstein (1996, 2002) find such a case for California with its restrictions on public spending in recent decades and consider determinants of private entry given public schooling expenditure. They find that private entrants are more likely to enter in districts with low public expenditure per pupil. A similar finding is suggested by Martinez-Vazquez and Seaman (1985) who report that, in US school districts with more competition between public schools, private school enrolments are lower, which they interpret as suggesting that the competition was efficiency enhancing.

Demand-side considerations
The analysis of public–private displacement presumes that policies to promote the expansion of public schooling make no allowance for private sector responses. In fact there are a variety of ways in which public provision has made allowance for this.

One long-standing approach to the problem is to offer public subsidies on a matching basis to private schools. It should be noted that this entails public financing but not provision or administration. The argument in favour of this is that not only does it avoid displacement of scarce private resources but it rewards further effort in school provision and would seem to channel resources to the place where the most initiative and effort will be employed with them. However the counter to this is that the most initially disadvantaged areas become relatively even more so under a matching programme.

Once it is granted that some government funding should occur, the issue remains of how far that should go. It is common to argue in favour of user fees simply so that families using schools do not completely take them for granted, in other words so that those actually receiving schooling demonstrate some minimal commitment to it. However, as increasingly societies have aimed at making access to primary and then secondary schooling universal, fees are commonly waived so as not to constitute an impediment to access.

As efforts have been made to increase access and as simultaneously demands for education have risen, the resources required to expand public education on a matching basis have also risen. This has led to efforts to stem such a rise. One approach developed in Victorian England to deal with this secular rise in educational spending was the so-called 'payment by results' system, according to which central government payments per pupil were contingent on student examination results (Hurt, 1971; Morris, 1977). While this system has often been interpreted as an attempt to spur efficiency through rewarding good performance, in fact it appears to have developed more as a way of stemming the rising tide of educational expenditure.

There has been increasing interest recently in educational accountability schemes by which resources allocated to schools would be related in some fashion to student outcomes. There is considerable variety in the nature of such schemes and how much is at stake in them. In some cases the aim is one of providing incentives for effective teaching, going back to Adam Smith's (1776) principle that the exertion made in any profession depends upon the incentives provided for it. This leads to so-called 'high-stakes' testing in which allocations of money to schools and to teachers for salaries depend on student examination outcomes and in which schools with consistently poor examination results face reorganization and even possible closure. School average results on standardized tests can also be made public as a way of providing information on school effectiveness to parents in choosing between schools. Two general criticisms have been raised to this approach. First, it cultivates teaching to the exam or, more generally, given the difficulty of measuring educational outcomes, it leads to distorted measures of educational outcomes with corresponding distorted efforts and allocation of resources. Figlio and Getzler (2002) report evidence that schools from six Florida districts reclassified low performing students as disabled at significantly higher rates than previously, following the introduction of high-stakes testing. They suggest that schools did this in order to alter the composition of students taking accountability tests.

Second, it tends to worsen the situation of poorly performing schools when in fact it could well be in society's best interest to devote more resources to such schools to improve their performance. Insofar as schools with students prone to poor performance are likely to fare badly on school accountability measures some allowance should be made for this. Value-added approaches have been suggested for this purpose (Ladd, 2001). Further issues concern what level of accountability is most appropriate, whether teacher, school, or school district. Figlio (2001) notes inconsistencies between whether schools are evaluated by value-added measures which assess contributions to individual student performance and measures which focus on average scores or percentage of students reaching some adequacy level. He also reports that school rankings can bounce around considerably from year to year, depending on which accountability measures are used. He suggests that it can be demoralizing to teachers and school principals to think that their performance will be graded randomly. No consensus is evident on whether accountability policies enhance school performance. Figlio and Lucas (2004), however, report empirical results indicating that teachers that impose higher grading standards improve subsequent student performance. In fact much would seem to depend on the details of their implementation. It would seem that both equity and dealing with externalities of schooling would entail some allocation of support for schools serving low-performing students. An additional concern about accountability policies is raised by Figlio and Page (2003) in their study of the Florida plan, according to which students in schools judged failing by test results are offered vouchers for use at other schools. This concern is that such accountability policies substitute the judgment of the state in the form of examination outcomes for that of individual parents as to school effectiveness. The authors point out an inconsistency inherent in giving additional schooling choices to parents whose children are in schools that are deemed to be failing when in some sense the parents have initially chosen such schools.

So-called 'demand-side financing' has been proposed with an aim of promoting more efficiency through greater responsiveness to parental and student choosers (Patrinos and Ariasingam, 1997). In conjunction with this approach increased attention has been given in recent decades to choice and voucher plans as ways of implementing this demand-side approach, with Friedman (1955, 1962) as one of the earliest and most influential advocates. A key issue that has emerged in this literature regards the impact of competition, whether from private schools or other public schools, on public school efficiency (Hoxby, 2000; Bradley *et al.*, 2001). A basic principle of voucher advocates is that competition should promote efficiency. In order to retain students, a school should have to maximize educational quality for a given expenditure of resources and minimize costs for a given level of educational quality if students can readily switch to other schools that may offer higher quality or lower costs. As Hoxby (2003b) points out, private schools clearly face the incentive to maximize quality for a given expenditure because their revenues depend directly on fees or vouchers. It is less evident that public schools face such incentives, since their revenues are usually tax or bond-financed. Insofar as a publicly financed voucher for use at a private school comes from the same pool of revenues that could be used to fund public schools, public schools have incentives to minimize the flow of students to private schools.

However a key issue in this regard concerns the presence of economies of scale with respect to the number of students in the public system subject to competition from voucher-financed private schools. With constant returns to scale and/or with public schools facing expected enrolments well above the cost-minimizing level, the diversion of students from a public school to private competitors would not directly provide incentives for the public school to improve efficiency and raise quality relative to its current practice. And as Hoxby (2003b) points out, a voucher that is small relative to per pupil spending would actually imply that the public school could benefit from having students diverted to private schools by having larger revenues available per student through this diversion. Furthermore, as argued in Hoxby (2000), with inter-district competition between public school districts, Tiebout sorting through the housing market implies efficient provision of school services by public schools. For a survey of the interactions between schooling and housing markets, see Chapter 18 of the present volume. Hoxby (2000) also finds that increasing Tiebout choice improves school productivity even controlling for household sorting, suggesting that the impact of choice is on efficiency.

However a central concern raised by critics of voucher systems remains, namely that the diversion of students and correspondingly funding from poorly performing public to private schools will put such public schools in a weaker position to improve and indeed through 'cream skimming' leave them with students even more costly to educate effectively and with weakened political support for their funding. Hoxby (2003b) addresses this concern by assessing the impact on school productivity (allowing for reduced expenditures) and achievement of schools subject to increased competition from vouchers or charter schools in Milwaukee, Michigan and Arizona. She finds evidence in all three cases that the public schools subject to such increased competition actually improved their performance in the face of increased competition from private and charter schools. Moreover, in the case of the Milwaukee experiment, the schools most subject to competition were those with relatively poor and presumably more difficult to educate students. She suggests that these productivity and achievement gains may be sufficient to offset for a given student within a few years the peer effects of any cream skimming associated with increased choice.

However, given the limited scale of the three programmes under evaluation and their limited period of operation, considerable uncertainty remains about the impact on initially poorly performing schools of widespread introduction of vouchers and choice.

The impact of school choice and vouchers may be limited if the marginal chooser in public schools is lowered in degree of responsiveness through displacement of the most responsive choosers to private schools (Hirschman, 1970; Rangazas, 1997). There has also been widespread concern that choice and voucher plans result in sorting behaviour which shift higher ability students into private schools, leaving public schools with students of lower capabilities than before the introduction of voucher plans. Studies of the national level choice and voucher plans implemented in the last two decades in Chile and New Zealand do indicate substantial cream-skimming by private schools of higher ability students (Winkler and Rounds, 1996; Gauri, 1998; Fiske and Ladd, 2000). However Hoxby (2003b) warns that the student sorting processes at work would appear to be quite complex and that increased cream-skimming is only one of a number of possible outcomes in response to increased choice and vouchers. She argues that, with the decentralized system at work in the United States and in the presence of Tiebout sorting, the general equilibrium effects of increased choice are difficult to predict and depend on the details of how such plans are constructed. In general, the introduction of choice plans in the USA has been on too restricted a basis to assess their impact.

A number of recent simulation studies have demonstrated the complexity of forces at work on student sorting when choice is introduced. In one influential example, Epple and Romano (1998) construct a model in which peer group effects are central to educational attainment. They consider a private schooling sector in which private schools use student ability to attract student clientele. On the one hand, higher income parents are willing to pay more to put their children in schools with higher ability peers. On the other hand, high ability students with low income parents can get tuition breaks from private schools desiring to enhance their ability levels. This results in private schools being able to price discriminate according to both income and ability. In this model, public school finance is unaffected while public school size is.

An important consideration in properly examining the impact of choice, vouchers and other demand-side proposals is to allow for the decentralization inherent in many national school systems.

II   Centralization versus decentralization of educational finance

There is considerable international variation in the extent to which sources of funding and administrative control of schools come from local, regional or national levels of government. At one extreme, schools in colonial North America and the USA in the 18th, 19th and 20th centuries were funded and administered by local communities, though with limited degrees of state supervision. Local school districts formed and relied on property taxes as their primary source of funding. At the other extreme, various other former colonies in Latin America, Africa and the Middle East, most typically with Spain and France as former rulers, have generally been very centralized in their provision and funding of schooling and this has been attributed to the colonial heritages of the respective countries.

In fact, from both directions, there has been a trend towards what has been termed 'federalism' or in other words mixed central and local sources of funding and provision, though with considerable complexity and variation as to the nature of this mixture. Indeed the literature on fiscal federalism provides a useful general framework for considering the specific situation with regard to school finance.

Quantifying the extent of centralized versus local sources or control over funding for schools internationally is problematic owing to lack of

Table 7.3   International variation in central government as source of total educational expenditures in 1973

Country	Percentage of total educational revenues from central government, circa 1973
United States	4
Federal Republic of Germany	1
Switzerland	9
Canada	7
Norway	44
Sweden	57
United Kingdom	65
Denmark	67
Austria	65
Netherlands	73
Belgium	74
Luxembourg	75
Italy	77
France	90
Spain	67
Ireland	94

Source: David R. Cameron and Richard I. Hofferbert, 'The impact of federalism on educational spending: patterns within and across nations', paper delivered at the 9th World Congress of the International Political Science Association, 1973.

Table 7.4   Level of government where key educational expenditure decisions are made: number of OECD and WEI countries in which decisions are made at a given level

Level of government where decision is made	Allocation of resources for teaching staff	Allocation for other current expenditures	Allocation for capital expenditure
Central			
Full	7	6	5
With consultation	2	1	4
Total central	9	7	9
Intermediate			
Full	4	4	3
With consultation	7	8	9
Total intermediate	11	12	12
Local			
Full	2	5	5
With consultation	6	4	4
Total local	8	9	9
School			
Full		1	
With consultation			
Total school		1	
Overall total	28	29	30

Source: OECD (1998).

comparable statistics over various levels of government expenditure. Table 7.3 provides one of the few estimates that has been compiled of the role of centralized funding sources for a number of countries from 1973. Table 7.4 provides another set of indicators for a more recent time period from an OECD survey of locus of governmental decision-making authority for some 30 OECD and WEI countries for 1998. Table 7.4 shows the importance of centralized decision making and that local decision making over these resource allocation decisions pertained in only a minority of cases.

In general developing countries tend to be far more centralized in their provision of schooling than more developed ones (Tan and Mingat, 1992; Winkler, 1999).

Fiscal federalism in education finance
Both funding and administration of schooling commonly involve multiple levels of government throughout the world. Even the case of the USA,

commonly depicted as highly decentralized, still entails substantial state-level transfers to local governments. Recently around half of local expenditures on schooling came from state-level sources in the USA. Elsewhere in the world, government expenditures tend to be much more centralized. However, in recent decades, there seems to have been increasing movement towards more decentralization, especially of administrative functions.

This phenomenon of multiple levels of government in educational finance can be seen as an example of what has been termed 'fiscal federalism' more generally. In the case of education funding this typically entails transfers from a more centralized level of government to a more localized one. One can see at work here what Oates (1999, p. 1122) has termed the basic principle of decentralization, 'the presumption that the provision of public services should be located at the lowest level of government encompassing, in a spatial sense, the relevant benefits and costs'. The basic motivation is that local provision allows variation in response to variation in local benefits and costs. The formulation can be traced back to Mill (1860) in which he noted that local officials had more familiarity with local circumstances and thus were in a better position to administer local public goods. Among other things, leaving administration to be decentralized at the local level avoids the administrative costs entailed in centralized administration. It has also been suggested that the pluralism and heterogeneity associated with decentralization fosters innovation and flexibility of response to diverse circumstances (Winkler, 1999, p. 54). Another attraction of decentralization is that it can be used by central governments to shift the financial burden of schooling to the local level (ibid.).

Despite this argument in favour of decentralized provision of public goods, centralized funding can be rationalized generically on grounds of correcting for regional variations in wealth and income levels and hence ability to fund, and on grounds of superior centralized knowledge of appropriate standards of provision, a point emphasized by Mill. It has also been suggested that local elites may be more subject to special interest influences than national ones (Winkler, 1999, p. 54). In the case of schooling, the case for centralized involvement is further enhanced with labour mobility because then the externalities involved in schooling are no longer localized. For a more generally sceptical view of the advantages of decentralization for developing countries, see Prud'homme (1995). Johnes (1995) employs state level data on costs per pupil and an index of central state control over education to estimate empirically an optimal, cost-minimizing level devolution of decision-making authority and school autonomy.

It should be noted here that centralization in the case of schooling typically involves not only funding but other dimensions such as standards in various features of schooling including curriculum and teacher qualifications as well as other aspects of administration (Winkler, 1989, 1993, 1999; Bray, 1996; Fiske, 1996; Hanson, 1995). Costrell (1997) considers in this regard a theoretical model of the extent to which centralized standards raise welfare compared with decentralized ones. He finds in his simulations that substantial inter-district migration, in other words the presence of non-local externalities, is required for centralization of standards to raise welfare and that in general some allowance for districts preferring higher standards to be able to deploy them raises welfare overall.

Most modelling has been done of the responses of local governments to centralized funding. There has been limited work done on the determination of centralized provision to local levels. In the absence of a general model of joint determination of local and centralized provision of schooling, one can draw on the literature on fiscal federalism more generally to note tendencies for a balance between local and centralized provision.

In surveying the international situation with respect to fiscal federalism and school finance, one can usefully view trends as proceeding in two directions. The USA, as already mentioned, is notable for the extent to which its school finance decisions have been decentralized, with the authority residing primarily in local districts. However, in recent decades, there has been an increasing move towards centralized control in one form or another over these decentralized arrangements. In much of the rest of the world, school finance decisions have been highly centralized, with authority often placed with national-level agencies. However, in recent decades, there has been an increasing move in many countries towards decentralization of school finance decisions. The following discussion will turn first to the US situation, considering the tendencies for increasing centralized control over a largely decentralized system. Then our attention will turn to international trends elsewhere towards decentralization.

Fiscal federalism in the US decentralized system
Historically, in the USA schools developed locally. In funding local schools, local property taxes have commonly been used. It has been argued that basing school funding on local property taxes assures local autonomy in the administration of schools. Unlike sales taxes or income taxes, the object of taxation, real estate property, is not mobile in response to rising tax rates. The property itself provides security for payment of the tax obligation. The yield on the property tax is less subject to fluctuation than the yield on sales or income taxes, assuring stability in maintaining school services. The property tax rate can be varied with much lower adjustments in accounting arrangements than local businesses would have to make in adjusting sales or payroll tax rates. Perhaps above all, since the property tax is highly

visible, it provides a clear indication of the tax price of providing school services, thus placing the consumer, in Tiebout's words, in the position of 'walking to the community where the prices (taxes) of community services are set' (cited in Oates, 1991, p. 410). Property taxes have been criticized as regressive and implying unequal provision of school services insofar as the property tax base can vary widely across localities. However, as Oates (1991) points out, if property taxes are considered relative to permanent rather than transitory income they seem far less regressive. Moreover the property tax base is itself endogenous, reflecting Tiebout sorting, and this is also reflected in housing price capitalization with high taxes tending to lower housing prices controlling for school quality (see Chapter 18 of the present volume).

Early on in the USA it became evident that education was of more than local concern. This can be seen as inherently tied to the positive externalities associated with education along with labour mobility. A further consideration is on equity grounds. Furthermore even local governments could not act without some central state authorization of their taxation sources. State governments have to authorize property as taxable for various purposes before local governments can proceed. In the case of Britain, in the 19th century this was a continuing source of tension. In the case of the USA, individual state governments increasingly found themselves called on to equalize differences among local districts in ability to fund schooling (see Evans *et al.*, 1997).

By the early 1920s in the USA, states were increasingly trying to provide compensating payments to localities whose funding resources were more limited. Various funding formulas developed. Indeed one of the staples of the US educational finance literature has been the various formulas for revenue transfers and accomplishing equalization.

In considering intergovernmental funding transfers from a more centralized to a more localized level for schooling, it is useful to distinguish various motives for such transfers. From a public choice perspective, such transfers can be regarded as providing a way for certain interest groups from various localities to redistribute resources to themselves from interest groups more concentrated in other localities. A model along these lines has been developed recently by De Bartolome (1997), who argues that states experiencing relatively large increases in income inequality were more likely to increase aid to local school districts. An alternative set of perspectives emphasizes public interest motives. One tradition based on Musgrave and Musgrave (1973) is to view schooling as a merit good for which governing centralized elites have a socially superior view of appropriate levels than either children and parents themselves or, following Mill (1860), local elites. Thus centralized funding would correct for underinvestment by myopic parents and local elites. Another related but distinct tradition views schooling as a matter of categorical equity (Feldstein, 1975). According to this view, activities such as schooling or medical care are fundamental and society as a whole has an interest either in avoiding large differences across individuals in levels of consumption of each or at least in any differences not being strongly related to ability to pay (ibid., p. 76). These differences in motivation for centralized to local funding transfers would seem to account for whether the transfers aim, as a public choice perspective would suggest, to be primarily redistributive without intent to equalize, or to be stimulative but possibly leading to increases in inequality as a merit good perspective might imply, or to be equalizing as a categorical equity perspective would suggest.

One can distinguish a number of types of central to local government grants according to the way they interact with local educational circumstances and funding (Hoxby, 2001). Categorical grants are based, not on local property values, but on population characteristics of a school district such as poverty rates or household income. Their aim is to provide funds to districts with populations that may be particularly difficult to educate. Categorical flat grants give a flat per pupil grant in a given district that depends on population characteristics of that district.

Matching categorical grants set a matching ratio with local district spending that depends on population characteristics of the given district. Equalizing grants aim to compensate for variations across districts in the property tax base. A third type could be termed incentive-based, in that the amount of the grant depends in some way on local schooling activity as opposed to local funding ability. This would include grants that are on a per student basis. It would also include grants that are geared to student educational outcomes. A fourth type of centralized funding that would affect local educational expenditures is revenue-sharing grants in which central governments share tax revenue with local governments; sometimes these are justified on the basis of economies of scale and efficiencies in centralized tax collection. By raising local government revenues generally, they could raise expenditures on education in particular.

A large literature has developed around equalizing grants. Hoxby (2001) provides a valuable overview of this literature. Following Downes and Pogue (1994), one can distinguish two basic types of equalizing grants from central to local authorities, foundational grants and power-equalizing grants (also see Hoxby, 2001). Foundational grants set a foundation level of spending per student or what could be regarded as an adequacy level of spending per student. They also set a common foundation tax rate (in the US case, this would be on property) across districts. The foundational grant then provides aid from central funds to a given district equal to the difference between the foundation level of aid per student and the tax revenue generated on the per student tax base value (again in the USA on property) of the district. Without recapture, if the tax revenue generated in the district would exceed the foundational level, the grant from central sources would be set equal to zero:

$Ai = F -$ tax rate* Bi if tax revenue per student i is less than foundation level,

$Ai = 0$ if tax revenue per student i is greater than or equal to the foundation level,

where i indexes school districts, $Ai =$ foundation aid to district i, F is the foundation level of funding and Bi is the tax base in district i.

If all districts spend the foundation level and per student cost does not vary across districts then educational opportunities in terms of expenditure per student and school tax burdens are location-neutral. As Downes and Pogue (1994) emphasize, the first condition will only be realized if districts are constrained from spending either more or less than the foundational level.

The aim of power-equalizing grants is to guarantee that all districts can raise at least as much revenue as some reference district. Power-equalization grants are sometimes termed 'guaranteed tax base' or 'guaranteed yield' programmes.

With power equalization:

$Ai = Ti*$ (reference per student tax base $-$ per student tax base i) if per student tax base is less than the reference per student tax base,

$Ai = 0$ if per student tax base is greater than or equal to the reference per student tax base,

where Ti is the tax rate in district i.

Locational neutrality will occur under power equalization either with recapture from districts whose tax base exceeds the reference tax base or if the reference tax base is that of the district with the highest per student tax base. Additional requirements, however, are that each district chooses to spend the same amount per student and that the per student cost of educational services is the same in each district. Feldstein (1975) has emphasized that these latter requirements are unlikely to hold generally.

In considering the impact of intergovernmental grants, further consideration should be given to the way local governments respond to receipt of such grants. As already noted, equalization formulas such as power equalization have been criticized for not taking due account of such responses.

Tsang and Levin (1983) distinguish three possible ways local districts can respond to receipt of grants for schooling from centralized sources. First, the district can use the grant to increase expenditure on schooling, presumably the purpose of the grant. This Tsang and Levin term a 'stimulative' outcome. Indeed with matching it is possible that expenditure on schooling could be increased beyond the amount of the central grant. Second, the district can respond to the central grant by reducing funding from local sources for schooling and reallocating those funds to other public spending uses. Finally, the central funds for schooling can be used to lower local tax support in general. In these last two cases, the central source of funding is substituting for local funds. In considering the last two possibilities, one issue that has arisen in the literature is whether a grant directed at schooling has a stronger impact on resultant district school expenditures than a general unrestricted revenue grant. Insofar as the basic grant has an impact on resultant spending by raising resources available to the district given possibilities of substituting local funds to other uses, it is unclear whether a grant earmarked for schools should have a stronger effect on school expenditures than an unrestricted grant. In fact a variety of studies have found that earmarked grants have a stronger effect than unrestricted grants, the so-called 'fly-paper' effect; funds tend to stick to the use for which they were earmarked (see Hines and Thaler, 1995, for a survey of this literature).

In an alternative taxonomy of local districts' response to categorical and equalization grants, Hoxby (2001) distinguishes between equalizing that results in levelling down, in which on average districts lower their level of expenditure per student, and equalizing that results in levelling up, in which on average districts raise their level of expenditure per student. Her analysis indicates that state schemes that level up provide incentives for states to undertake more modest equalizing than schemes that level down. She suggests this is because it is inexpensive to states to prohibit high spending by districts while considerable state tax revenue would have to be diverted to induce districts that would prefer to spend little on education to spend at high levels. She finds that equalization schemes may actually lower levels of spending in some initially most disadvantaged districts through levelling down effects. She argues in favour of categorical grants as a way of avoiding these unintended consequences.

In contrast, Fernandez and Richardson (2003b) find in their simulation results of the political economy of various school finance systems that equalization schemes increase levels of education spending. They also prove in their political economy model that power equalizing with recapture would win in majority voting contests over the other school finance schemes they consider. As Hoxby (2001, p. 1199) notes, the Fernandez and

Richardson approach assumes that local school revenues come from local taxes on income even though property is more commonly used as the tax base and local property taxes have different implications for households' location and voting decisions than local income taxes.

Tsang and Levin's survey of empirical studies of intergovernmental grants on education spending finds that unrestricted state grants for education or foundation equalization grants increase local expenditure on schools on less than a one-for-one basis. They suggest an approximate average for these studies that every additional dollar of state grants for education increases local spending on schooling by 50 cents, with a range from 16 cents to $1.07. In states employing matching grants which can be viewed as lowering the local price of spending on schooling, they find wide ranges in estimated price elasticities from close to 1 to close to zero.

In the case of the USA, a landmark event with regard to equalization was the Serrano decision of 1971 which ruled that states have certain minimal legal obligations to equalize educational expenditures across districts. Evans *et al.* (1997) provide evidence that court decisions had stronger impacts on equalization than legislative incentives in equalization formulas. However Hoxby (2001, pp. 1210–13) argues that the dummy variable approach that Evans *et al.* (1997) employ does not adequately capture the impact of equalization schemes on the tax incentives voters face to support schooling.

Subsequent to the Serrano decision, a number of states established property tax limitations on local government spending. Fischel (1989) has argued that in the case of California these limits were a rational response to earlier Serrano equalization mandates. These mandates substantially limited the ability of wealthier districts to spend more than average on schooling and this in turn undermined political support for the property tax in such districts. Since voters in a given district could no longer use property taxes to improve schools in that district, they were in favour of constraining public officials' access to the tax.

A literature has developed examining whether property tax limits actually impeded the effectiveness of schooling. According to the Leviathan model of public spending proposed by Niskanen (1971), government bureaucrats seek to maximize the growth of spending on their respective agencies. Applying this model to public spending on schooling implies that the expansion of such spending is driven by budget-maximizing bureaucrats. A limit on such spending could reduce rents to school administrators and teachers' unions and other sources of waste and inefficiency without lowering productive educational spending and conceivably without lowering educational performance. In favour of this view is McGuire's (1999) observation that most districts given a choice chose not to override the tax limits, suggesting this reflected local voters' preferences for limiting government. However Downes and Figlio (1999) point out that budget-maximizing bureaucrats could respond to the tax limits by preserving administrative budgets while cutting expenditures on teachers and for other real instructional purposes. Indeed they survey evidence suggesting a decline in educational performance over time that can be attributed to the tax limits. And Figlio (1997) finds that, in areas passing these limits, administrative budgets were not cut, while starting teacher salaries were. Indeed Figlio and Rueben (2001) note that in some regions it was starting salaries of teachers that were cut rather than those of teachers with more seniority, consistent with teacher union influence, resulting in a subsequent decline in qualifications of teachers.

One subtheme in this literature concerns the impact of tax limits and equalization on Tiebout sorting processes. This issue has been taken up more fully in conjunction with modelling the presence of vouchers as well. Fernandez and Rogerson (1996) have modelled the way in which policies that increase intra-district heterogeneity can make all parties better off through raising overall educational expenditures and lowering tax rates. They are particularly concerned with correcting for the presence of imperfect capital markets in schooling investments. In a number of papers, they have taken into account the dynamic effects of changes in income distribution implied by correcting for imperfections in the human capital market. Fernandez and Rogerson (1997) provide simulation results indicating aggregate welfare increases of around 10 per cent in switching from a pure local system of educational finance to a pure centralized state system in which all students receive equal levels of expenditure. This result is due to the concavity of the production of future income with respect to per student spending. Fernandez and Rogerson (2003a) consider the impact of voucher plans on changing educational and income distributions through simulations. In particular they distinguish between lump sum, means-tested and means-equalizing voucher plans according to the relation vouchers bear to parental income. When they allow for the level of each type of voucher to be endogenously determined through majority voting, they find considerable differences between the types of vouchers in the level that will be set by the political process. They find that the means-equalizing voucher leads to the largest reduction in education inequality while the means-tested voucher leads to relatively little increase in education spending for the poorest groups in society.

International decentralization

If, with the USA, the trend in school finance in recent decades has been to more centralized control, from local to state governments, internationally the trend has been towards decentralization. This is difficult to measure empirically, in part because decentralization entails political and administrative dimensions as well as economic and funding dimensions and in part because of the difficulty of constructing comparable measures across countries of sources of financing from various levels of government. The literature on educational decentralization as an international phenomenon has tended to focus more on its political dimensions than its economic dimensions and has tended to be more normative, considering the pros and cons, than explanatory or analytical (Bray, 1996; Winkler, 1989, 1993, 1999; Fiske, 1996; Hanson, 1995). There has been virtually no attempt systematically to examine the international determinants of decentralization or of variation in its extent.

One can draw on the general fiscal federalism literature for the stylized fact that provision of government services tends to get more decentralized with economic development, though subject to important caveats of interpretation regarding direction of causation and universality (Oates, 1999). In early stages of the development of schooling in a country, centralized funding can be seen as responding both to regional special interests to redistribute central funding in their favour and to efforts to compensate for lack of ability to fund minimum standards in some regions. As development proceeds and schooling proceeds, the cost of centralized funding presumably increases, as does the desire of central authorities to shift funding responsibilities to the local level.

Winkler (1999) distinguishes between educational decentralization to lower levels of government and decentralization directly to schools. He sees educational decentralization to lower levels of government as shaped by the same forces motivating government decentralization more generally in developing countries. One of the aims of decentralization to lower levels of government is to give those in local communities greater voice in running their affairs, thus making local government more responsive to local concerns. In addition, government decentralization can be seen as promoting technical efficiency by facilitating (a) greater responsiveness to local variations in prices and input availability, (b) monitoring and accountability of local schools through superior information of local officials about local conditions compared with central officials, and (c) innovation due to the diversity of sources of authority and possible initiatives. Winkler sees decentralization of authority to individual schools as motivated by initially poor school performance with decentralization enhancing accountability and the incentives that local school leaders and teachers face to improve performance. Behrman and King (2001) argue that school decentralization in developing countries can influence the reliability of information about the costs and returns of schooling to households. They argue that household responses to changes in information associated with decentralization may reduce efficiency in some respects while increasing it in others, leaving the net result dependent on context and details of implementation.

However trends towards decentralization in a number of countries have been restrained by the tendency of inequality in educational provision across regions within a given country to rise with decentralization. China (see Tsang, 1996) has moved since 1980 to decentralization of funding for its educational system. However primary school funding was already initially decentralized at the local level, so actual decentralization primarily pertained to secondary education. While this has permitted increased mobilization of non-government sources of funding, it has failed to address the large dispersion across regions of China of resources available to support primary, let alone secondary, education. While China has been able to increase spending on basic education from 2 to 3 per cent of GDP between 1980 and 1990, this spending is still considerably below world averages. It would appear that some sort of centralized intergovernmental transfers will be required to bring all regions up to the desired average. Thus the Chinese case underscores the limits of decentralization. Stewart's (2000) study of decentralization of educational finance in Russia since 1989 also finds a widening in regional disparities. While her findings are not uniform, she also finds some evidence that areas initially relatively well-provided tended to increase their advantage relative to poorly provided areas over this period.

In considering general trends towards decentralization, the complexity of dimensions involved should be kept in mind. Frequently decentralization has entailed increasing delegation of various forms of decision making while control of funding has remain centralized. A problem faced in Russia and much of Eastern Europe in this regard is that no local fiscal source has emerged as a source of funds independent of centrally administered grants (Stewart, 2000; Fiszbein, 2000; Koucky, 1996; Cerych, 1997).

One economic issue that has emerged in the literature on developing countries is whether increasing the local share relative to central funding of schools increases their efficiency as measured by lowering costs after controlling for enrolments and student achievement. Jimenez and Paqueo (1996) in their study of Philippine primary schooling distinguish between technical and incentive effects as to why increasing the local share would lower schooling costs, other things being equal. The technical effect is that local control permits more responsiveness in adjusting the mix of schooling inputs used in response to local cost conditions. The incentive effect is that local schooling managers are more likely to be effectively monitored by local providers of funding than by more distant centralized sources of funding. Hence, as the local share of funding increases, local schooling managers can be expected to face stronger incentives to pursue efficient, cost-reducing practices. In their empirical work on a sample of Philippine schools from the early 1980s, the authors find that increasing the local share in school funding does substantially lower schooling costs, controlling for enrolment and student achievement measures.

James *et al.* (1996) provide further support for Jimenez and Paqueo's finding that increasing local funding shares lowers schooling costs in their analysis of an Indonesian data set. However they extend Jimenez and Paqueo's study in a number of dimensions. First, they consider possible simultaneity between the share of local funding and costs per student, for example the possibility that areas that face higher schooling costs per student might receive more funding support from central sources. However the instrumental variable specifications of their estimates do not change the basic finding that local funding lowers costs. Second, they find that the impact of local funding is non-linear, with the impact diminishing as local funding share increases. Related to this point they find that the impact of local share is stronger for public than for private schools. They also find that private schools have lower schooling costs per student. Finally, they analyse the determinants of cross-sectional variation in local funding share. They find that urban areas, higher income areas, private schools and areas with relatively high proportions of population of school age tend to have higher local shares of school funding. These latter cross-sectional findings could possibly be interpreted as supporting a view that, with economic development over time, decentralization of school funding will tend to occur.

A further point that arises in the Jimenez and Paqueo and James *et al.* studies concerns the role of private share and in particular of charging tuition or user fees. In addition to helping provide funding to extend the availability of schooling, their studies raise the issue of whether relying on student fees as one source of income enhances efficiency by enhancing responsiveness of schools to children and parents. These considerations have to be traded off against the restriction of access implied by fees.

Two studies by World Bank economists, Jimenez and Sawada (1999) and King and Ozler (2000), examined whether public schools run by local communities in El Salvador and in Nicaragua had higher student achievement than more centrally run public schools. The Jimenez and Sawada study of El Salvador concluded that more decentralized schools did achieve better educational outcomes through increased accountability to the local community. However Glewwe (2002) notes problems with the selection correction techniques employed in these studies and calls in general for the use of random assignment studies to assess the impact of privatization and decentralization of schools in developing countries.

Chile and New Zealand provide examples of decentralization to the level of the school. The case of Chile illustrates Steuerle's (2000) observation that a voucher can be viewed as the ultimate in decentralization. In 1980, Chile introduced a national system of government-funded grant per student that would go to either municipal or private schools, depending on which a given student chose. The result was an expansion in government-subsidized private schooling. The clientele for these private schools seems to have come disproportionately from parents of higher socioeconomic status as measured by income and educational levels, supporting the criticism that voucher plans foster stratification by socioeconomic background (Winkler and Rounds, 1996; Parry, 1997; Gauri, 1998). And Gauri (1998) argues that, once allowance is made for variation in quality within the categories of public and private schools, the degree of stratification evident appears to be even wider. However there is also evidence that competition from private schools did raise public school performance after controlling for student background (Parry, 1997). The policy of centralized per pupil grants in the case of Chile has maintained the financial standing of public municipal schools and has avoided the degree of inequality in expenditure per student across the nation observed, for example, in the USA either between or within states. However the centralized grants have not always been maintained in real value and some inequality has emerged, given the possibility of supplements from local sources (Winkler and Rounds, 1996; Gauri, 1998).

In the case of New Zealand, reforms in 1989 introduced per pupil grants to schools from the central government along with block grants to schools for teacher salaries effectively decentralizing educational decision making. With parents free to send their children to the school of their choice within this system, competition was introduced into the system. Assessments in 1999, some ten years after the initial reform, did suggest increased perception of competition between schools, with 30 per cent of principals reporting the perception that their school competed with others (Wylie, 1999). However increasing numbers of principals reported that they found centralized government funding inadequate, and that there has been increased reliance on local sources of funding, but increased difficulty in finding such sources of funding. Counter to the intent of decentralization, parental involvement in schools has been reported to have declined. Fiske and Ladd (2000) find in their analysis that New Zealand's reforms led to increasing concentration of minority and disadvantaged students in schools least able to compete for other students. They also find that loss of students to competitors in such schools did not improve their efficiency and that they lacked the ability to recruit higher quality teachers more likely to be able to cope with the challenges of teaching more disadvantaged students. The government's remedy for such schools of attempting to improve management performance did not appear to address underlying issues of improving teaching effectiveness and retaining more able and more teachable students.

The shift in opposite directions in the USA, on the one hand, from extreme decentralization and in many developing countries, on the other hand, from centralization towards a mix of centralized and decentralized elements would seem to suggest the value of retaining both elements in balance. Doing so in practice has entailed considerable policy challenges in both situations, as the review above would suggest.

Allocation among levels of education

Allocations of expenditure between primary, secondary and tertiary levels can be viewed in an accounting sense as due to the relative size of the demographic age groups from which students at each level would be drawn, the percentage of each age group attending various levels of schooling and the average expenditure per student at each level. Of course, the latter two factors are in some measure matters of choice. It seems to be accepted that provision of universal access to primary education is a basic desideratum. Access to secondary education and, *a fortiori*, tertiary education is a matter that varies with economic development. However, even at the primary level, there is no commonly accepted funding formula to guarantee that local providers of schooling will have the resources required to provide universal access.

One point of controversy has been whether developing countries overinvest in tertiary education relative to lower levels, in part because controlling elites favour such allocations. Mingat and Tan (1985, 1986) find considerable inequity in developing countries in the distribution of public educational resources. They find for developing countries as a group that 71 per cent of a given cohort, those with primary or no schooling, were allocated only 22.1 per cent of the public schooling resources for that cohort while the 6.4 per cent obtaining higher education received 38.6 per cent of the cohort's resources. Rate of return estimates by level of education indicate considerably higher rates of return to primary and secondary education than tertiary, also suggesting overinvestment at the higher level. However there is controversy as to whether these estimates fully capture the relative social returns involved (Birdsall, 1996; Psacharopoulos, 1996). Further analysis of the political economy and public choice factors contributing to this allocation across levels of schooling promises to provide further insight into this issue.

III Concluding summary

The field of school finance started out largely as a subfield of state and local public finance. However, in recent decades, as concerns about education and schools have become central matters for public policy, the issues involved have become considerably broader. Issues of political economy and public choice and intergovernmental federalism, as well as parents and children as central players in the process of schooling, have all come to figure prominently in analyses of school finance.

This broadening of issues has been evident in the empirical models of the determinants of public school expenditure that have been developed over the last three decades. In the early 1970s, the main framework was that of a basic supply and demand model involving income and demographic variables on the demand side and teacher salary, pupil–teacher ratios and scale on the supply side, with taxes incorporated as an accounting identity, as in McMahon (1970). By the early 1980s, public choice considerations figured far more prominently, with the inclusion of median voter models of tax determination along with allowance for Tiebout sorting (Rubinfield, 1987; Megdal, 1984; Bergstrom *et al.*, 1982). More recently empirical models of public school expenditure have made increasingly sophisticated allowance for sorting and for more complex tax policies with simultaneous interaction between various levels of government (Goldhaber, 1999; James, 1993; James *et al.*, 1996; Hoxby, 2003a).

There is now a quite extensive and rich empirical literature on the determinants of public expenditure on schooling for the USA. International studies are much less developed. An important issue in developing an agenda of international school funding research concerns the role of further cross-country studies versus extending the range of studies within countries. There is surely scope for both types of studies. Further studies at lower levels of aggregation will be central for providing insights into the underlying determinants at work. An important gap in the economics of education literature concerns school finance issues in developed countries outside the USA. However more cross-countries studies along the lines of James (1993) are critical for seeing the forest from the trees.

Acknowledgments

I would like to thank, without implicating, Douglas Lamdin and Peter Lindert for helpful comments on this chapter.

Notes

1. The expected years of schooling estimate comes from OECD (2002, p. 192). Life expectancy figures were averaged for males and females and come from *The Economist* (2001).
2. Source for schooling expectancy is OECD (2002, p. 192). Source for life expectancy is Maddison (2001, p. 31).

References

Barzel, Yoram (1973), 'Private schools and public finance', *Journal of Political Economy*, **81**, 174–86.

Behrman, Jere and Elizabeth M. King (2001), 'Household schooling behaviors and decentralization', *Economics of Education Review*, **20**, 321–41.

Bergstrom, Theodore C., Daniel L. Rubinfield and Perry Shapiro (1982) 'Micro-based estimates of demand functions for local school expenditures', *Econometrica*, **50**, 1183–205.

Birdsall, Nancy (1996), 'Public spending on higher education in developing countries: too much or too little?', *Economics of Education Review*, **15**, 407–19.

Bradley, Steven, Geraint Johnes and Jim Millington (2001), 'The effect of competition on the efficiency of secondary schools in England', *European Journal of Operational Research*, **135**, 545–68.

Bray, Mark (1996), *Decentralization of Education: Community Financing*, Washington, DC: World Bank.

Brown, Byron (1992), 'Why governments run schools', *Economics of Education Review*, **11**, 287–300.

Cameron, David R. and Richard I. Hofferbert (1973), 'The impact of federalism on educational spending: patterns within and across nations', ERIC No. 087655.

Cerych, Ladislav (1997), 'Educational reforms in Central and Eastern Europe: processes and outcomes', *European Journal of Education*, **32**, 75–96.

Costrell, Robert M. (1997), 'Can centralized educational standards raise welfare?', *Journal of Public Economics*, **65**, 271–93.

De Bartolome, Charles A.M. (1997), 'What determines state aid in school districts? A positive model of foundation aid as redistribution', *Journal of Policy Analysis and Management*, **16**, 32–47.

Downes, Thomas A. (1996), 'Do differences in heterogeneity and intergovernmental competition help explain variation in the private school share? Evidence from early California statehood', *Public Finance Quarterly*, **24**, 291–318.

Downes, Thomas A. and David N. Figlio (1999), 'Economic inequality and the provision of schooling', *Federal Reserve Bank of New York Policy Review*, **5**, 99–110.

Downes, Thomas A. and Shane M. Greenstein (1996), 'Understanding the supply decisions of nonprofits: modelling the location of private schools', *Rand Journal of Economics*, **27**, 365–90.

Downes, Thomas A. and Shane M. Greenstein (2002), 'Entry into the schooling market: how is the behavior of private suppliers influenced by public sector decisions?', *Bulletin of Economic Research*, **54**, 341–71.

Downes, Thomas A. and Thomas F. Pogue (1994), 'Accounting for fiscal capacity and need in the design of school aid formulas', in John E. Anderson (ed.), *Fiscal Equalization for State and Local Government Finance*, Westport, Connecticut and London: Praeger, pp. 55–83.

The Economist (2001), *Pocket World in Figures*, London: The Economist Newspaper Ltd.

Epple, Dennis and Richard E. Romano (1996), 'Ends against the middle: determining public service provision when there are private alternatives', *Journal of Public Economics*, **62**, 297–325.

Epple, Dennis and Richard E. Romano (1998), 'Competition between private and public schools, vouchers and peer-group effects', *The American Economic Review*, **88**, 33–62.

Evans, William N., Sheila E. Murray and Robert M. Schwab (1997), 'Schoolhouses, courthouses, and statehouses after Serrano', *Journal of Policy Analysis and Management*, **16**, 10–31.

Feldstein, Martin S. (1975), 'Wealth neutrality and local choice in public education', *The American Economic Review*, **65**, 75–89.

Fernandez, Raquel and Richard Rogerson (1995), 'On the political economy of education subsidies', *Review of Economic Studies*, **62**, 249–62.

Fernandez, Raquel and Richard Rogerson (1996), 'Income distribution, communities, and the quality of public education', *Quarterly Journal of Economics*, **111**, 135–64.

Fernandez, Raquel and Richard Rogerson (1997), 'Education finance reform: a dynamic perspective', *Journal of Policy Analysis and Management*, **16**, 67–84.

Fernandez, Raquel and Richard Rogerson (2001), 'The determinants of public education expenditures: longer-run evidence from the states', *Journal of Education Finance*, **27**, 567–83.

Fernandez, Raquel and Richard Rogerson (2003a), 'School vouchers as a redistributive device: an analysis of three alternative systems', in Caroline M. Hoxby (ed.), *The Economics of School Choice*, Chicago and London: University of Chicago Press, pp. 195–225.

Fernandez, Raquel and Richard Rogerson (2003b), 'Equity and resources: an analysis of education finance systems', *Journal of Political Economy*, **111**, 858–97.

Figlio, David N. (1997), 'Did the "tax revolt" reduce school performance?', *Journal of Public Economics*, **65**, 245–69.

Figlio, David N. (2001), 'What might school accountability do?', *NBER Reporter*.

Figlio, David N. and Lawrence S. Getzler (2002), 'Accountability, ability and disability: gaming the system', NBER Working Paper 9307.

Figlio, David N. and Maurice Lucas (2004), 'Do high grading standards affect student performance?', *Journal of Public Economics*, forthcoming.

Figlio, David N. and Marianne E. Page (2003), 'Can school choice and school accountability successfully coexist?', in Caroline M. Hoxby (ed.), *The Economics of School Choice*, Chicago and London: University of Chicago Press, pp. 49–66.

Figlio, David N. and Kim S. Rueben (2001), 'Tax limits and the qualifications of new teachers', *Journal of Public Economics*, **80**, 49–71.

Fischel, William A. (1989), 'Did Serrano cause proposition 13?', *National Tax Journal*, **42**, 465–73.

Fiske, Edward B. (1996), *Decentralization of Education. Politics and Consensus*, Washington, DC: The World Bank.

Fiske, Edward B. and Helen F. Ladd (2000), *When Schools Compete. A Cautionary Tale*, Washington, DC: Brookings Institution Press.

Fiszbein, Ariel (ed.) (2000), *Decentralizing Education in Transition Societies. Case Studies from Central and Eastern Europe*, Washington, DC: The World Bank.

Friedman, Milton (1955) 'The role of government in education', in Robert A. Solo (ed.), *Economics and the Public Interest*, New Brunswick, NJ: Rutgers University Press, pp. 123–44.

Friedman, Milton (1962), 'The role of government in education', in *Capitalism and Freedom*, Chicago and London: University of Chicago Press, pp. 85–107.

Gauri, Varun (1998), *School Choice in Chile. Two Decades of Educational Reform*, Pittsburgh, PA: University of Pittsburgh Press.

Glewwe, Paul (2002), 'Schools and skills in developing countries: education policies and socioeconomic outcomes', *Journal of Economic Literature*, **40**, 436–82.

Goldhaber, Dan (1999), 'An endogenous model of public school expenditures and private school enrollment' *Journal of Urban Economics*, **46**, 106–28.

Gradstein, Mark (2000), 'An economic rationale for public education: the value of commitment', *Journal of Monetary Economics*, **45**, 463–74.

Hanson, E. Mark (1995), 'Democratization and decentralization in Colombian education', *Comparative Education Review*, **39**, 101–19.

Harris, Amy, William Evans and Robert Schwab (2001), 'Education spending in an aging America', *Journal of Public Economics*, **81**, 449–72.

Hines, James and Richard Thaler (1995), 'The flypaper effect', *Journal of Economic Perspectives*, **9**, 217–26.

Hirschman, Albert O. (1970), *Exit, Voice, and Loyalty. Responses to Decline in Firms, Organizations, and States*, Cambridge, MA: Harvard University Press.

Hoxby, Caroline M. (2000), 'Does competition among public schools benefit students and taxpayers?', *The American Economic Review*, **90**, 1209–38.

Hoxby, Caroline M. (2001), 'All school finance equalizations are not created equal', *Quarterly Journal of Economics*, **106**, 1189–231.

Hoxby, Caroline M. (ed.) (2003a), *The Economics of School Choice*, Chicago and London: The University of Chicago Press.

Hoxby, Caroline M. (2003b), 'School Choice and Productivity. Could School Choice Be a Tide that Lifts All Boats?' in Caroline M. Hoxby (ed.) *The Economics of School Choice*, Chicago and London: University of Chicago Press, pp. 287–341.

Hurt, John S. (1971), *Education in Evolution. Church, State, Society and Popular Education 1800–1970*, London: Rupert Hart-Davis.

James, Estelle (1993), 'Why do different countries choose a different public–private mix of educational services?', *The Journal of Human Resources*, **28**, 571–92.

James, Estelle, Elizabeth M. King and Ace Suryadi (1996), 'Finance, management, and costs of public and private schools in Indonesia', *Economics of Education Review*, **15**, 387–98.

Jimenez, Emmanuel and Vicente Paqueo (1996), 'Do local contributions affect the efficiency of public primary schools?', *Economics of Education Review*, **15**, 377–86.

Jimenez, Emmanuel and Yasuyuki Sawada (1999), 'Do community-managed schools work? An evaluation of El Salvador's EDUCO program', *World Bank Economic Review*, **13**, 415–41.

Jimenez, Emmanuel and Yasuyuki Sawada (2001), 'Public for private: the relationship between public and private school enrollment in the Philippines', *Economics of Education Review*, **20**, 389–99.

Johnes, Geraint (1995), 'School management: how much local autonomy should there be?', *Educational Management and Administration*, **23**, 162–67.

King, Elizabeth and Berk Ozler (2000), 'What's decentralization got to do with learning? Endogenous school quality and school performance in Nicaragua', Development Research Group, World Bank.

Koucky, Jan (1996), 'Educational reforms in changing societies: Central Europe in the period of transition', *European Journal of Education*, **31**, 7–24.

Ladd, Helen F. (2001), 'School-based educational accountability systems: the promise and the pitfalls', *National Tax Journal*, **54**, 385–400.

Ladd, Helen F. and Sheila E. Murray (2001) 'Intergenerational conflict reconsidered: county demographic structure and the demand for public education', *Economics of Education Review*, **20**, 343–57.

Lindert, Peter H. (2004), *Growing Public: Social Spending and Economic Growth since the Eighteenth Century*, Cambridge: Cambridge University Press.

Lott, John R. Jr (1987), 'Why is education publicly provided?', *The Cato Journal*, **7**, 475–501.

Lott, John R. Jr (1990), 'An explanation for public provision of schooling: the importance of indoctrination', *The Journal of Law & Economics*, **33**, 199–232.

Maddison, Angus (2001), *The World Economy. A Millennial Perspective*, Paris: OECD Press.

Mariscal, Elisa and Kenneth Sokoloff (2000), 'Schooling, suffrage, and the persistence of inequality in the Americas, 1800–1945', in Stephen Haber (ed.), *Political Institutions and Economic Growth in Latin America. Essays in Policy, History, and Political Economy*, Stanford, CA: Hoover Institution Press, pp. 159–217.

Martinez-Vazquez, Jorge and Bruce Seaman (1985), 'Private schooling and the Tiebout hypothesis', *Public Finance Quarterly*, **13**, 293–318.

McGuire, Therese (1999), 'Proposition 13 and its offspring: for good or evil?', *National Tax Journal*, **52**, 129–38.

McMahon, Walter W. (1970), 'An economic analysis of major determinants of expenditures on public education', *The Review of Economics and Statistics*, **52**, 242–52.

Megdal, Sharon Bernstein (1984), 'A model of local demand for education', *Journal of Urban Economics*, **16**, 13–30.

Mill, John Stuart (1860), *Considerations on Representative Government*, reprinted (1958), Indianapolis, IN and New York: Library of Liberal Arts.

Mingat, Alain and Jee-Peng Tan (1985), 'On equity in education again: an international comparison', *Journal of Human Resources*, **20**, 298–308.

Mingat, Alain and Jee-Peng Tan (1986), 'Who profits from the public funding of education: A comparison of world regions', *Comparative Education Review*, **30**, 260–70.

Morris, Norman (1977), 'Public expenditure on education in the 1860s', *Oxford Review of Education*, **3**, 3–21.

Musgrave, Richard A. and Peggy B. Musgrave (1973), *Public Finance in Theory and Practice*, 2nd edn, New York: McGraw-Hill.

Niskanen, William (1971), *Bureaucracy and Representative Government*, Chicago: Aldine-Atherton.

Oates, Wallace E. (1991), 'The theory and rationale of local property taxation', in Therese J. McGuire and Dana Wolfe Naimark (eds), *State and Local Finance for the 1990s: A Case*

Study of Arizona, Tempe, AZ: School of Public Affairs, Arizona State University, pp. 407–24.

Oates, Wallace E. (1999), 'An essay on fiscal federalism', *Journal of Economic Literature*, **37**, 1120–49.

OECD (1976), *Public Expenditure on Education*, OECD Studies in Resource Allocation, no. 2.

OECD (1998), *Education at a Glance: OECD Indicators 1998*, Paris: OECD Publications.

OECD (2001), *Education at a Glance: OECD Indicators 2001*, Paris: OECD Publications.

OECD (2002), *Financing Education – Investments and Returns. Analysis of the World Education Indicators 2002 Edition*, Paris: OECD Publications.

Parry, Taryn Rounds (1997), 'Theory meets reality in the education voucher debate: some evidence from Chile', *Education Economics*, **5**, 307–32.

Patrinos, Harry Anthony and David Lakshmanan Ariasingam (1997), *Decentralization of Education. Demand-Side Financing*, Washington, DC: The World Bank.

Peltzman, Sam (1973), 'The effect of government subsidies-in-kind on private expenditures: the case of higher education', *The Journal of Political Economy*, **81**, 1–27.

Poterba, James (1997) 'Demographic structure and the political economy of public education', *Journal of Policy Analysis and Management*, **16**, 48–66.

Prud'homme, Remy (1995), 'The dangers of decentralization', *The World Bank Research Observer*, **10**, 201–20.

Psacharopoulos, George (1996), 'Public spending on higher education in developing countries: too much rather than too little', *Economics of Education Review*, **15**, 421–20.

Rangazas, Peter (1997), 'Competition and private school vouchers', *Education Economics*, **5**, 245–63.

Rubinfield, Daniel L. (1987), 'The economics of the local public sector', in A.J. Auerbach and M. Feldstein (eds), *Handbook of Public Economics*, vol.II, Amsterdam: Elsevier Science Publishers, pp. 571–645.

Smith, Adam (1776), *An Inquiry into the Nature and Causes of the Wealth of Nations*, reprinted in W.B. Todd (ed.) (1976), *Glasgow Edition of the Works and Correspondence of Adam Smith*, vol.1, Oxford: Oxford University Press.

Soares, Jorge (2003), 'Self-interest and public funding of education', *Journal of Public Economics*, **87**, 703–27.

Steuerle, C. Eugene (2000), 'Common issues for voucher programs', in C. Eugene Steuerle, Van Doorn Ooms, George Peterson and Robert D. Reischauer (eds), *Vouchers and the Provision of Public Services*, Washington, DC: Brookings Institution Press, pp. 3–39.

Stewart, Kitty (2000), *Fiscal Federalism in Russia. Intergovernmental Transfers and the Financing of Education*, Cheltenham, UK and Northampton, MA, USA: Edward Elgar.

Stigler, George J. (1970), 'Director's law of public income redistribution', *Journal of Law & Economics*, **13**, 1–10.

Tan, Jee-Peng and Alain Mingat (1992), *Education in Asia. A Comparative Study of Cost and Financing*, Washington, DC: The World Bank.

Toma, Eugenia Froedge (1996), 'Public funding and private schooling across countries', *Journal of Law & Economics*, **39**, 121–48.

Tsang, Mun C. (1996), 'Financial reform of basic education in China', *Economics of Education Review*, **15**(4), 423–44.

Tsang, Mun and Henry M. Levin (1983), 'The impact of intergovernmental grants on educational expenditure', *Review of Educational Research*, **53**, 329–67.

West, E.G. (1975), 'Educational slowdown and public intervention in 19th-century England: a study in the economics of bureaucracy', *Explorations in Economic History*, **12**, 61–87.

Winkler, Donald R. (1989), *Decentralization in Education: An Economic Perspective*, Washington, DC: The World Bank.

Winkler, Donald R. (1993), 'Fiscal decentralization and accountability in education: experiences in four countries', in Jane Hannaway and Martin Carnoy (eds), *Decentralization and School Improvement. Can We Fulfill the Promise?*, San Francisco: Jossey-Bass, pp. 102–34.

Winkler, Donald R. (1999), 'Empowering municipalities or schools? The decentralization of education', in Shahid Javed Burki, Guillermo E. Perry and William R. Dillinger (eds), *Beyond the Center: Decentralizing the State*, Washington, DC: The World Bank, pp. 53–98.

Winkler, Donald R. and Taryn Rounds (1996), 'Municipal and private sector response to decentralization and school choice', *Economics of Education Review*, **15**, 365–76.

Wylie, Cathy (1999), *Ten Years On: How Schools View Educational Reform*, Wellington: New Zealand Council for Educational Research.

Zhang, Jie, Junsen Zhang and Ronald Lee (2003), 'Rising longevity, education, savings, and growth', *Journal of Development Economics*, **70**, 83–101.

8 Funding higher education
David Greenaway and Michelle Haynes

1 Introduction

Over the last 20 years of the 20th century there was a remarkable increase in participation in higher education in a number of OECD and non-OECD countries (for details, see OECD, 2002). In the case of the former, this was partly demand-driven, with key factors being increased female participation and increasing private rates of return to a first degree. In some countries, it was also supply-driven, with policy initiatives to increase the number of universities and increase publicly funded places to support development of the 'knowledge-based economy'.

One of the key debates triggered by increased participation is how to pay for it.[1] Governments have become less capable of financing higher education expansion owing to increased competition for public funds. This has triggered two questions: should the beneficiaries of higher education make a larger contribution to the costs of provision and, if the answer to this question is 'yes', how and when should they make that contribution?

In section 2 we review the broad patterns in participation and higher education funding across OECD countries. Any argument that beneficiaries should make a greater contribution to tuition costs relies on a demonstration that they would be better off than otherwise as a result of having experienced higher education. There is extensive evidence on this topic which we review briefly in section 3. Section 4 assesses a range of funding options for higher education. Section 5 examines some of the recent innovations by OECD countries to diversify the funding base. This has largely involved the introduction of fee contributions from beneficiaries, accompanied by a greater availability of income-contingent loans. Finally, section 6 concludes.

2 Context

International comparisons of students in higher education

Participation in higher education   If current entry rates across the OECD extend into the future, almost one in two of today's young people will enter higher education at some time in their life. Table 8.1 compares entry rates across countries. For tertiary type A programmes,[2] Finland is the highest OECD country at over 70 per cent. Hungary, Iceland, New Zealand and

Table 8.1   Net entry rates for tertiary-level education (2000)

OECD countries	Type B	Type A
Australia	–	59
Austria	–	33
Belgium	34	36
Czech Republic	9	25
Denmark	35	29
Finland	a	71
France	21	37
Germany[1]	13	30
Hungary	2	65
Iceland	10	66
Ireland	26	31
Italy	1	43
Japan[2]	32	39
Korea[2]	50	45
Mexico	1	26
Netherlands	1	51
New Zealand	37	70
Norway	7	59
Poland[2]	1	62
Slovak Republic[1]	3	37
Spain	15	48
Sweden	7	67
Switzerland	14	29
Turkey	9	21
UK	28	46
US	14	43
Country mean	15	45

Notes: Sum of net entry rates for single ages where net entry refers to rate of first-time tertiary entry at all ages. First-time entry rates for each level of education cannot be added together to obtain tertiary-level entrance rates because of the possible double counting of entrants (persons who enter non-university tertiary programmes may also enter university-level programmes later in their lives).
'a' indicates country value is not applicable.
[1] Entry rate for type B programmes calculated as gross entry rate.
[2] Entry rate for type A and B programmes calculated as gross entry rate.

Source: OECD (2002).

Sweden all exceed 60 per cent, above the overall average (45 per cent). Turkey and the Czech Republic have noticeably lower participation rates at 21 and 25 per cent, respectively. For some, such as Belgium and Denmark, wide access to tertiary type B education counterbalances low entry rates to

Table 8.2   Index of change in enrolment in tertiary education (2000)

| | Change in Enrolment (1995=100) | | |
| | | attributable to | |
OECD countries	Total tertiary enrolment	change in population	change in enrolment rates
Australia	108	102	106
Austria	109	69	144
Belgium	111	94	117
Canada	101	–	–
Czech Republic	150	102	147
Denmark	115	95	121
Finland	116	100	116
France	98	91	107
Germany	95	89	107
Greece	143	96	151
Hungary	180	110	164
Iceland	133	101	131
Ireland	125	109	116
Italy	103	–	–
Korea	148	87	161
Mexico	128	106	121
Norway	105	94	112
Poland	208	119	173
Portugal	124	98	127
Spain	120	93	129
Sweden	122	95	129
Turkey	86	110	79
UK	112	97	115
Country mean	124	98	127

Source: OECD (2002).

type A. However, for other countries, most noticeably Korea, New Zealand and the UK, entry rates at type A and type B programmes are among the highest in the OECD.

As Table 8.2 shows, participation in tertiary education increased in almost all OECD countries in the late 1990s. The Czech Republic, together with Greece, Hungary and Korea, experienced increases of over 40 per cent and, in Poland, the number of tertiary students enrolled more than doubled. It is clear from Table 8.2 that increases in enrolment are mainly attributable to higher participation rates rather than an increase in population at the relevant ages. In France and Germany, the number of student enrolments fell, reflecting a fall in the student-age population, even though enrolment levels as a proportion of the population rose. In contrast, Turkey also experienced a fall in participation despite an increase in population at the relevant ages.

Gender balance   As Table 8.3 shows, entry rates for women for type A and B programmes are higher than for men for the majority of OECD countries. For type A, Finland, Iceland, New Zealand and Sweden all exceed 80 per cent, against an OECD average of 48 per cent. An important element in the growth in higher education has been increased female participation.

Mode of enrolment   For the OECD, on average, 15 per cent of type A and 21 per cent of type B students are part-time (Table 8.4). There is wide variation across countries, with the highest levels (over 40 per cent) for type B programmes in Hungary, Poland and the US. For countries with data available the importance of part-time study is even more important at the type A level. In Australia, Switzerland, the US and UK more than 55 per cent of students at this level are part-time.

Age Mix   Traditionally entry into higher education has occurred immediately after completion of upper secondary education. In some OECD countries this is still the case (see Table 8.5). For example, in France and Ireland, more than 80 per cent of all first-time entrants are 20 years or younger. In others, the transition to university is often delayed. In Denmark, Iceland and Sweden, for example, more than 50 per cent of students enter for the first time after 22 and less than 20 per cent are younger than 20.

Completion rates   Table 8.6 reports on completion rates. The proportion of entrants who successfully complete a tertiary type A programme varies widely across OECD countries: from over 80 per cent in Ireland, Japan, Turkey and the UK to 60 per cent or less in Austria, Belgium, France and Sweden, down to 42 per cent in Italy. Across the OECD, about a third of all entrants for a Type A programme leave university education without graduating. The figure is slightly lower for type B programmes.

International comparisons of funding
The proportion of national financial resources allocated to education is one of the key choices made by each OECD country. Table 8.7 shows the share of national income or GDP that is spent on tertiary education in 1995 and

Table 8.3   Net entry rates for tertiary-level education, by gender (2000)[1]

OECD countries	Type B		Type A	
	Men	Women	Men	Women
Australia	–	–	52	66
Austria	–	–	30	37
Belgium	28	39	36	36
Czech Republic	6	12	26	24
Denmark	26	45	27	32
Finland	a	a	62	81
France	22	21	30	44
Germany[2]	9	18	30	30
Hungary	1	2	60	70
Iceland	11	9	48	84
Ireland	23	28	29	34
Italy	1	1	38	49
Japan[3]	22	43	47	30
Korea[3]	51	49	48	41
Mexico	1	1	27	26
Netherlands	1	2	48	54
New Zealand	31	42	57	84
Norway	9	6	45	74
Slovak Republic[2]	1	5	38	36
Spain	15	16	42	54
Sweden	7	6	54	81
Switzerland	15	13	32	26
Turkey	11	8	26	17
UK	24	32	42	49
US	12	15	37	49
Country mean	14	17	40	48

Notes:
[1]   See notes to Table 8.1.
[2]   Entry rate for type B programmes calculated as gross entry rate.
[3]   Entry rate for type A and B programmes calculated as gross entry rate.

Source: OECD (2002).

1999. Canada, Korea and the US contribute over 2 per cent of their national income to funding tertiary education. By comparison, the Czech Republic, Italy and the Slovak Republic contribute less than 1 per cent. Despite the huge increases in participation, only a minority of OECD countries increased their share of GDP spent on tertiary education between 1995 and 1999.

Table 8.4 Distribution of students by mode of enrolment in tertiary education (2000)

| OECD countries | Mode of enrolment | | | |
| | Type B | | Type A | |
	Full-time	Part-time	Full-time	Part-time
Australia	32.3	67.7	62.1	37.9
Austria	66.1	33.9	100.0	a
Belgium	74.4	25.6	94.9	5.1
Canada	85.2	14.8	68.2	31.8
Czech Republic	100.0	n	92.4	7.6
Denmark	100.0	a	100.0	a
Finland	100.0	a	100.0	a
France	100.0	a	100.0	a
Germany	84.9	15.1	100.0	a
Greece	100.0	a	100.0	a
Hungary	87.7	12.3	58.0	42.0
Iceland	71.2	28.8	80.9	19.1
Ireland	60.7	39.3	86.8	13.2
Italy	100.0	a	100.0	a
Japan	96.7	3.3	90.6	9.4
Korea	100.0	a	100.0	a
Luxembourg	99.3	0.7	100.0	a
Mexico	100.0	a	100.0	a
Netherlands	69.3	30.7	82.6	17.4
New Zealand	45.0	55.0	69.7	30.3
Norway	87.2	12.8	72.8	27.2
Poland	78.0	22.0	53.9	46.1
Slovak Republic	64.8	35.2	71.9	28.1
Spain	99.6	0.4	91.5	8.5
Sweden	93.0	7.0	54.0	46.0
Switzerland	32.9	67.1	94.5	5.5
Turkey	100.0	a	100.0	a
UK	30.5	69.5	76.0	24.0
US	44.2	55.8	64.7	35.3
Country mean	79.4	20.6	85.0	15.0

Notes: 'a' indicates country value is not applicable; 'n' indicates the country value is negligible.

Source: OECD (2002).

Table 8.5   Age distribution of type A tertiary level new entrants (2000)

OECD countries	Age at		
	20th percentile[1]	50th percentile[1]	80th percentile[1]
Australia	18.4	19.9	27.4
Austria	19.1	20.5	23.6
Belgium	18.3	18.9	22.7
Czech Republic	18.7	19.7	21.8
Denmark	20.8	22.4	27.9
Finland	19.9	21.6	26.9
France	18.3	18.9	20.2
Germany	20.1	21.4	24.3
Hungary	19.2	21.0	26.5
Iceland	20.9	22.7	28.5
Ireland	18.3	19.0	19.9
Mexico	18.3	19.5	25.7
Netherlands	18.5	19.8	22.8
New Zealand	18.9	22.7	<40
Norway	20.1	21.6	29.6
Slovak Republic	18.6	19.5	21.3
Spain	18.4	19.2	22.1
Sweden	20.2	22.7	32.1
Switzerland	20.3	21.8	26.3
Turkey	18.3	19.6	23.2
United Kingdom	18.4	19.4	25.4
United States	18.4	19.4	26.8

Notes: [1]20/50/80 per cent of new entrants are below this age.

Source: OECD (2002).

Where does the financing of higher education come from? Table 8.7 also shows higher education expenditure from public and private sources as a percentage of GDP. The issue of cost-sharing between the participants in higher education and society as a whole is one that is under current discussion in many OECD countries.[3] The distribution of public and private funding and how these figures have evolved since 1995 is reported in Table 8.8. Whilst public expenditure provides a substantial part of higher education funding (the OECD average is 79 per cent), private funding is playing an increasingly important role. In a number of OECD countries, private expenditure on tertiary education grew by more than 30 per cent between 1995 and 1999. In most countries, however, this growth in private spending was not associated with a reduction in the overall level of public spending

Table 8.6   Completion rates in tertiary education (2000)

OECD countries	Type A	Type B
Australia	69	—
Austria	59	—
Belgium	60	88
Czech Republic	61	77
Denmark	69	84
Finland	75	–
France	59	72
Germany	70	75
Iceland	73	55
Ireland	85	50
Italy	42	51
Japan	94	86
Korea	79	74
Mexico	69	81
Netherlands	69	58
Poland	—	84
Spain	77	74
Sweden	48	85
Turkey	88	77
United Kingdom	83	—
United States	66	62
Country mean	70	73

Source: OECD (2002).

on tertiary education. The highest proportions of public funding are in Belgium, Greece and Austria. The US, Japan and Korea contribute the largest proportion of private funding to tertiary education.

Considering Table 8.8 with Table 8.7 shows that some of the countries with the highest total spending relative to GDP, such as Canada, Korea and the US, muster these resources with substantial help from private sources. Conversely, in countries with relatively low overall spending, such as the Czech Republic, Italy and the Slovak Republic, private individuals tend to contribute relatively little.

Table 8.9 (which adjusts for purchasing power parities) compares higher education expenditure across OECD countries per full-time equivalent (FTE) student. Mean expenditure per student in the OECD was $9210 in 1999. The US has the highest expenditure per student ($19 220), whilst the lowest spenders were Greece, Mexico, Poland, Portugal and Turkey (all less

Table 8.7 *Tertiary education expenditure as a percentage of GDP (1995, 1999)*

OECD countries	1999			1995
	Public	Private	Total	Total
Australia	0.8	0.7	1.5	1.7
Austria[1]	1.4	n	1.5	1.5
Belgium	1.3	–	–	–
Canada[2]	1.6	1.0	2.5	2.2
Czech Republic	0.8	0.1	0.9	1.0
Denmark[1]	1.5	n	1.6	1.6
Finland	1.8	n	1.8	1.9
France	1.0	0.1	1.1	1.1
Germany	1.0	0.1	1.1	1.1
Greece[1]	1.0	n	1.0	0.7
Hungary	0.8	0.2	1.1	1.0
Ireland[3]	1.1	0.3	1.4	1.3
Italy	0.7	0.1	0.8	0.8
Japan[4]	0.5	0.6	1.0	1.0
Korea	0.5	1.9	2.4	–
Mexico	0.8	0.3	1.1	1.1
Netherlands	1.0	0.3	1.3	1.2
New Zealand	0.9	–	–	1.1
Norway	1.4	0.1	1.5	1.7
Poland	0.8	0.2	1.0	–
Portugal[1]	1.0	0.1	1.1	0.9
Slovak Republic[1,3]	0.8	0.1	0.8	–
Spain	0.9	0.3	1.1	1.0
Sweden[3]	1.5	0.2	1.7	1.6
Switzerland	1.2	n	1.2	–
Turkey[1]	1.0	n	1.0	0.7
United Kingdom	0.8	0.3	1.1	1.2
United States[2]	1.1	1.2	2.3	–
Country mean	1.0	0.3	1.3	1.2

Notes: 'n' indicates the country value is negligible.
[1] Public subsidies to households not included in public expenditure, but in private expenditure.
[2] Post-secondary non-tertiary included in tertiary education.
[3] Direct expenditure on tertiary-level educational institutions from international sources exceeds 1.5 per cent of all public expenditure.
[4] Post-secondary non-tertiary included in both upper secondary and tertiary education.

Source: OECD (2002).

Table 8.8   Public and private funding of tertiary education in the OECD (1995, 1999)

OECD countries	1999		1995	
	Public sources	Private sources[1]	Public sources	Private sources[1]
Australia	52.4	47.6	64.2	35.8
Austria	98.7	1.3	97.6	2.4
Belgium	100.0	n	–	–
Canada[2]	59.3	40.7	59.1	40.9
Czech Republic	84.7	15.3	71.0	29.0
Denmark[2]	97.7	2.3	–	–
Finland	97.4	2.6	–	–
France	85.7	14.3	84.3	15.7
Germany	91.5	8.5	92.7	7.3
Greece	99.9	0.1	–	–
Hungary	76.6	23.4	80.3	19.7
Ireland	73.4	26.6	69.7	30.3
Italy	80.3	19.7	82.8	17.2
Japan[3]	44.5	55.5	42.8	57.2
Korea	20.7	79.3	–	–
Mexico	71.8	28.2	77.4	22.6
Netherlands	77.6	22.4	88.3	11.7
Norway	94.4	5.6	93.6	6.4
Poland[4]	82.8	17.2	–	–
Portugal	92.9	7.1	96.5	3.5
Slovak Republic	91.9	8.1	–	–
Spain	74.2	25.8	74.4	25.6
Sweden	88.4	11.6	93.6	6.4
Switzerland	96.7	3.3	–	–
Turkey	95.3	4.7	96.6	3.4
United Kingdom	63.2	36.8	63.9	36.1
United States[2]	46.9	53.1	–	–
Country mean	79.2	20.8	–	–

Notes: 'n' indicates country value is negligible.
[1] Including subsidies attributable to payments to educational institutions received from public sources.
[2] Post-secondary non-tertiary included in tertiary education or missing.
[3] Post-secondary non-tertiary included in both upper secondary and tertiary education.
[4] Public institutions only.

Source: OECD (2002).

Table 8.9   Expenditure per student (US dollars) (1999)

OECD countries	Tertiary education
Australia	11725
Austria	12070
Belgium	9724
Canada	15211
Czech Republic	5688
Denmark	10657
Finland	8114
France	7867
Germany	10393
Greece[1]	4260
Hungary[1]	5861
Ireland	9673
Italy[1]	7552
Japan	10278
Korea	5356
Mexico	4789
Netherlands[2]	12285
Norway[1]	12096
Poland[1]	3912
Portugal	4802
Slovak Republic	5325
Spain	5707
Sweden	14222
Switzerland[1]	17997
Turkey[1]	4328
United Kingdom	9554
United States[3]	19220
Country mean	9210

Notes: Converted to US dollars using purchasing power parities; based on full-time equivalents.
[1] Public institutions only.
[2] Public and government-dependent private institutions only.
[3] Public and independent private institutions only.

Source: OECD (2002).

than $5000). Although the US has the highest expenditure per student, its level of public funding is relatively small, in fact the third lowest, at 47 per cent. In the majority of OECD countries tertiary expenditure per student has declined, mainly owing to the rapid increase in the number of students participating in higher education.

Table 8.10 *Public expenditure on education as a percentage of total public expenditure (1999)*

OECD countries	Primary, secondary and post-secondary non-tertiary education	Tertiary education
Australia	11.0	3.4
Austria	8.0	3.2
Belgium	6.9	3.0
Czech Republic	6.6	1.9
Denmark	8.7	4.3
Finland	7.6	4.2
France	8.0	2.0
Germany	6.2	2.3
Greece	4.5	2.0
Hungary	8.0	2.6
Ireland	9.4	3.6
Italy	6.6	1.7
Japan[1]	7.1	1.2
Korea	13.7	2.4
Mexico	16.0	4.3
Netherlands	6.8	2.9
Norway	9.0	4.2
Poland	8.3	1.9
Portugal	9.7	2.4
Slovak Republic	9.6	2.5
Spain	8.2	2.3
Sweden	8.9	3.7
Switzerland	11.0	3.4
United Kingdom	8.1	2.6
Country mean	8.7	2.8

Note:
[1]Excluding public subsidies to the private sector. Post-secondary non-tertiary included in both upper secondary and tertiary education.

Source: OECD (2002).

Table 8.10 compares public expenditure on education as a percentage of total public expenditure and indicates the value of education relative to the value of other public investments such as health care, social support, defence and security. Denmark, Finland, Mexico and Norway contribute over 4 per cent of total public expenditure to higher education. Tertiary education is given the lowest priority in the Czech Republic, Italy, Japan and Poland.

Conclusions
International comparisons of participation and funding are illuminating. All OECD countries experienced a more rapid growth of enrolments than public funding in higher education. As a result, all of them have experienced a rapid decline in expenditure per student. Given recent trends in the public funding of higher education, there is little prospect that the taxpayer will provide the additional resources necessary to bring higher education funding to a level necessary to sustain the quality of higher education across OECD countries.

3   Who should pay for higher education?
If the prospect of taxpayers providing additional resources for higher education is limited, then where should additional investment be drawn from? In this section we briefly examine the private and social benefits to higher education. We conclude that a greater financial contribution should come from beneficiaries.

Private benefits
The simplest measure of the private benefits to tertiary education is the higher salaries graduates receive compared with non-graduates.[4] Across OECD countries, earnings of tertiary graduates in the age group 30–44 years are significantly higher than those of non-graduates. The figure is between 60 and 90 per cent in the Czech Republic, Hungary, Portugal, the UK (51 per cent for males and 83 per cent for females) and the US. However women still earn less than men with similar levels of educational attainment. The additional income earned by a graduate (over a non-graduate with two 'A' levels) over a working life has been estimated at £400 000 in the UK.[5]

In addition to higher pay, graduates benefit from higher labour force participation. Labour force participation rates for 25–64-year-olds in tertiary type A programmes are much higher compared to those without upper secondary qualifications. The OECD mean is 93 per cent for males and 83 per cent for females. While there is a gender gap, it is only half as big for tertiary-level graduates as for those with lower qualifications. Across the OECD, tertiary-level graduates in the age group 25–64 years also have markedly lower unemployment rates (2.8 per cent for males and 3.5 per cent for females) than those without upper secondary qualifications (8.9 per cent for males and 9.4 per cent for females). They are also less likely to be among the long-term unemployed (see Blondal, Field and Giroard, 2002). These are useful summary statistics, but the more usual means of summarizing the returns to higher education (HE) is via rate of return analysis.

Table 8.11 *Private internal rates of return to tertiary education (1999–2000)[1]*

OECD countries	Males	Females
Canada	8.1	9.4
Denmark	13.9	10.1
France	12.2	11.7
Germany	9.0	8.3
Italy[2]	6.5	m
Japan	7.5	6.7
Netherlands[3]	12.0	12.3
Sweden[4]	11.4	10.8
United Kingdom	17.3	15.2
United States	14.9	14.7
Country mean[5]	11.8	11.3

Notes: 'm' indicates not available.
[1] The rate of return to tertiary education is calculated by comparing the benefits and costs with those of upper secondary education.
[2] Data for males derive from 1998 post-tax earnings data.
[3] Year of reference 1997.
[4] In tertiary education, the theoretical length of standard tertiary courses is used in the calculations rather than the average theoretical length of different programmes for men and women. For women, earnings differentials between upper and lower secondary levels are not large enough to permit a positive rate of return calculation.
[5] Data for men exclude Italy; data for women in upper secondary education exclude Sweden and the United Kingdom.

Source: OECD (2002).

Private rates of return to higher education[6]

There is an extensive empirical literature on the returns to higher education.[7] The consensus is that higher education provides measurable returns for individuals that are well in excess of the potential rate of return on investing in the costs of undertaking a university course.

Table 8.11 compares private rates of return to tertiary education for a number of OECD countries. In all countries, the private return exceeds the relevant real interest rate, and often significantly. At the lower end of the scale, for ten countries for which comparable data are available, it stands for men at around 7 per cent in Italy and Japan, rising to between 10 per cent and 15 per cent in Denmark, France, the Netherlands, Sweden and the US, and to 17 per cent in the UK

Social and cultural benefits
There is a widespread presumption that higher education generates non-pecuniary spillovers. For instance, graduates tend to be more active agents of national and international tolerance and social inclusion, more active citizens in participating in voluntary organizations, and they may give more to the democratic process.[8] Bynner and Egerton's (2000) findings point to a clear link between higher education and participation in community affairs, democratic processes, egalitarian attitudes, parenting and voluntary work. Moreover they report that these links hold even after one adjusts for other potential causal factors such as family background. Such social and cultural benefits are fundamentally important and no doubt promote social cohesion. Insofar as they do, they will have knock-on effects on direct economic benefits, for example reduced public expenditure on criminal justice and social security. Some attempts have been made to quantify these effects. For example, Lochner and Moretti (2001) calculate the social savings from crime reduction associated with high school completion. Their estimates suggest that a 1 per cent reduction in male high school drop-out rates would save as much as $1·4bn or about $2100 per additional male high school graduate. Kenkel (1991) estimates the effects of health knowledge and schooling on health behaviour. The positive effects of schooling on good health remain after differences in health knowledge are controlled for. McMahon estimates that the average US college graduate gains a lifetime equivalent of $488000 in health-related benefits above those with only a high school diploma. (A comprehensive review of the wider benefits of education can be found in Carr-Hill, 2001; OECD, 2001.)

Social rates of return to higher education[9]
The social rates of return to higher education are typically lower than the returns to individuals since they also include the additional costs borne by society. Table 8.12 reports the social rates of return across OECD countries. These range from between 4 and 14 per cent for females and 6 and 15 per cent for males. As is the case for private returns, the UK has the highest observed values among the countries for which comparable data are available. These returns are still well above the relevant real interest rates.

Education and growth
There is a considerable amount of cross-country evidence internationally which points to a positive association between investment in education and economic growth (see, for example, Barro and Sala-I-Martin, 1995; Barro, 1991; Bassanini and Scarpenta, 2001 and Chapter 4 in the present volume (Stevens and Weale)). In many OECD countries, the impact of increases in educational attainment on economic growth is stronger than other factors

Table 8.12   Social rates of return to tertiary education (1999–2000)[1]

OECD countries	Males	Females
Canada	6.8	7.9
Denmark	6.3	4.2
France	13.2	13.1
Germany	6.5	6.9
Italy[2]	7.0	m
Japan	6.7	5.7
Netherlands	10.0	6.3
Sweden	7.5	5.7
United Kingdom	15.2	13.6
United States	13.7	12.3

Notes: 'm' indicates not available.
[1] The rate of return to tertiary education is calculated by comparing the benefits and costs with those of upper secondary education.
[2] In Italy, the sample size of earnings for women was not large enough to allow for the calculation of rates of return.

Source: OECD (2002).

commonly associated with growth, such as trade exposure, variability of inflation or the investment share (OECD, 2002). Moreover higher education seems to be the most relevant education variable in more developed countries. Key findings from the literature are, first, countries with higher average years of education tend on average to grow faster; second, OECD countries which expanded their higher education sector more rapidly from the 1960s experienced faster growth; third, education is more important via its effects on productivity than directly as a factor input; fourth, there is some evidence that education positively affects physical investment in the economy, which in turn further increases growth rates. Conservative estimates suggest that the wider effects of education on economic growth could add at least 2 per cent to the typical social rates of return presented in the previous section. However the estimates from the literature are subject to wide margins of uncertainty and there is also a potential problem of reverse causality (Gemmell, 1997).

Conclusions

The fact that social returns are relatively high and externalities present underpins the case for continued taxpayer investment in higher education. However the excess of private over social rates of return confirms that most benefits from higher education are probably captured by individuals who do not pay as much as they should for their higher education. Moreover, given the socioeconomic mix of students in universities, it also means that the subsidies being transferred are likely to be regressive. Both justify a shift towards a more equitable financial partnership with a greater financial commitment coming from beneficiaries.

4   Alternative funding options

Across the world there is a robust debate about the funding of higher education and this has resulted in systemic reform in a number of countries, including Australia, New Zealand, South Africa and the UK (for details, see Chapman and Greenaway, 2004). In this chapter we will not review the full range of options but instead confine ourselves to a narrow range of possibilities that have figured prominently in recent discussions. These are enhanced taxpayer funding through grant allocations, the introduction of a graduate tax, issuing vouchers and higher contributions from beneficiaries via deregulation of fees. If the last of these were progressed it would need to be accompanied by an efficient income-contingent loan system, the principles of which we also discuss.

Increased taxpayer contributions via enhanced grant allocations

One obvious option is to fund higher education entirely from public expenditure. Given the record on public funding in many OECD countries, it is unlikely that significant additional resources can realistically be expected from this source. In addition, it could be argued that even if it *could* happen, it *should not* happen because, on average, public funding redistributes resources from low-income taxpayers to (future) high-income taxpayers and is therefore regressive. At the other extreme one could privatize the whole HE sector. Without a complete overhaul of student support arrangements this too would be unlikely to deliver an equitable solution. The social and private benefits to HE discussed in section 3 support the case for a continued mix of private and public funding but with a shift to the latter. We focus on three of the possibilities mentioned above, and illustrate how in the UK context each is consistent with evolution of the present system.

Introduction of a graduate tax

A graduate tax, by definition, is a tax supplement which applies only to graduates rather than being a levy on all taxpayers. Thus it is an obvious device for securing additional funding from the primary beneficiaries of HE, which is an obvious attraction. Moreover, because the revenue is generated from future earnings, payment is deferred and HE continues to be free at the point of consumption. This too is an attractive feature. Finally, since in principle the collection mechanism is straightforward, administration costs could be very low, which is another attraction.[10]

Although it would seem to be relatively straightforward to introduce a graduate tax, there are cogent arguments against it. One problem is that it is unlikely to deliver significant additional resources rapidly.[11] Second, it is not conducive to a more flexible and competitive system and in itself is unlikely to do anything about social exclusion. A third unattractive feature is that the amount graduates pay is invariant to differences in costs between degrees. Fourth, from a purely national perspective, potential leakage of revenue is considerable.[12] Finally, and most crucially, in some countries there is no reliance on hypothecated taxes. If a graduate tax is not hypothecated then collections become part of government's general revenue and any expansion in resources again becomes subject to a political process. There is no reason to suppose that the existence of a graduate tax would make higher education a higher priority in the competition for taxpayers' funds. It is perhaps not surprising that there is no fully fledged graduate tax in operation in the OECD.[13]

Education vouchers

The potential for using vouchers, or learning entitlements, in the education market place has been debated for a long time, though largely in the context of primary and secondary rather than tertiary education.[14] The basic idea is straightforward: those who have satisfied the relevant entry requirements receive a voucher to a given value to use at a university of their choice. The voucher's value could be geared to the cost of the course, could be geared to the student's family circumstances or could vary with the type of course, for example to stimulate participation in shortage subjects.

Vouchers are therefore potentially a flexible instrument for distributing public monies. In themselves, however, they do not alter the overall level of funding going into higher education, only the way it is distributed. In effect, one is disbursing public funds via the individual rather than, as at present, via institutions. Students would be empowered to a greater extent than at present and universities would have to compete more directly to attract the best students. Moreover the scheme also offers the potential for earmarking public funds more effectively than now with, for example, the value of a voucher varying on a means-tested basis. The only way in which vouchers could bring in additional resources is if students were able to top up their value, which they would need to do were vouchers used as a device for distributing public subventions to students in an environment where universities were permitted to set differential fees,

Deregulation of fees

In some OECD countries contributions from fees are well embedded. This is most obviously so in the US, where the private sector is well established and full-cost fees are very common. In most of the OECD, however, reliance on fees is limited and higher education remains free at the point of consumption.

The case for giving universities greater freedom in setting tuition fees and actually retaining fee income has been hotly debated in recent years as public funding has been compressed. The case for doing so rests upon several arguments. First, the evidence on earnings profiles and rates of return reported above strongly suggests that students should make a greater contribution than at present, since private rates of return typically exceed social rates of return. Second, in most countries, different universities have different cost structures, fashioned by subject mix, the balance of activities between teaching, research and technology transfer, whether their focus is regional or international, and their wage structures. Moreover, in countries like the UK where there has been a rapid increase in participation, the variation in costs is much greater than 40 years ago. There are more – and more different – universities, and the range of subjects is greater. Third, the present arrangements mean that the contribution students make is unrelated to the costs of teaching, the quality of infrastructure or the expected rate of return on their degree. Finally, as can be seen from the US context, deregulation of fees usually brings with it greater market discipline and less need for costly regulation.

Income-contingent loans
The potential yield from differential fees is considerable, as US experience suggests. But what about the impact of higher fees on demand, especially from entrants from low-income backgrounds? In fact, the most widely cited argument against differential fees is that they would have an adverse effect on access. It can be argued however that, if combined with better funded scholarships and a well thought out income contingent loan scheme, they would be at worst neutral and could even have a positive impact on widening participation. Take, first of all, the role of loans. In a series of articles, Barr (1997) and Barr and Crawford (1998) have set out the ingredients of, and mechanics for, a loan scheme which could generate additional resources, improve access and avoid the revenue leakages identified by Albrecht and Ziderman (1993). Their scheme is designed with three purposes in mind: first, for those who wish to avoid up-front payments, they ensure that education can remain free at the point of consumption; second, all loans should be fully income-contingent, rather than mortgage-based; third, to the maximum extent possible, they should derive from non-public sources. The first two ensure that the scheme helps access since up-front charges are avoided and repayments are a smaller proportion of start-up income; the latter that additional non-taxpayer funds are drawn into the system.

So is it possible to get the benefits of income contingency and additional private funding? It is possible to use the services of the national tax collection agency (in the case of the UK, the Inland Revenue) as a collection mechanism yet securitize student debt by selling it to the private sector.[15] Collection via the central tax agency makes the debt more attractive to the private sector. This attractiveness would be further enhanced if graduates paid a positive real interest rate on loans, broadly equal to the government's borrowing rate. If loans were securitized, the potential for an immediate and substantial injection of private funds is considerable.

On equity and efficiency grounds, the case for income-contingent loans covering fees as well as maintenance, collected through the Inland Revenue and fully securitized, is compelling. The only real barrier to implementation is the nuances of public sector accounting. If repayments are collected via the tax collection agency, it can be argued that insufficient risk is transferred to the private sector when the loan book is securitized and therefore all lending to students has to count against the current public sector cash requirements. This could indeed be an impediment to bringing in additional private resources rapidly. Barr (1997), however, offers a range of practical solutions to this problem involving some combination of revising public sector accounting arrangements and/or further privatizing the organization and finance of student loans.

Fees, loans and widening participation
The final issue we consider is access. As we noted earlier, it has been argued that, if differential fees increase the price of HE, then one can expect demand to contract and this contraction will affect differentially students from low-income backgrounds. We have argued that increasing the availability of income-contingent loans provides a partial solution to this problem by effectively ensuring that HE remains free at the point of consumption. (Scholarships and fee remission effectively do the same thing, though probably less efficiently.) Recent evidence from Australia confirms that the combination of fees and loans has not damaged access. In a recent evaluation of experience with HECS, drawing upon a range of cohort studies, Chapman and Ryan (2001) conclude that participation in HE has continued to increase despite the introduction of HECS and that they have not resulted in a decrease in participation of students from low-income families. Blondal *et al.* (2002) echo this and reach the same conclusion with regard to experience in New Zealand.

It should be noted, however, that reducing social exclusion in university participation requires policies that are much better directed than 'free' tuition while at university. Powerful evidence on this point has recently been produced by Cameron and Heckman (2001) in a detailed analysis of educational attainment and college participation in the US. They conclude that 'the importance of short-term credit constraints is greatly exaggerated' and argue that policies aimed at long-term improvements in family environment will be much more successful than short-run policies aimed at tuition reduction.

5 Recent developments[16]

In response to the 'financial crisis' confronted by many higher education systems, a number of countries have initiated major higher education reforms. Perhaps the most profound reform programmes were launched in Australia, New Zealand, South Africa and the UK. These countries had an important common characteristic underlying their changed financing policy approach. This was that they instituted higher education charges on students in place of arrangements in which higher education had previously been free at the point of consumption for participants and adopted income-contingent loans. They also had common goals to promote greater diversity and specialization among tertiary institutions and to make more efficient use of all available financing.

Two major justifications were used for the introduction of student charges. One is that higher education was in need of expansion in an environment in which governments were not prepared to finance this growth without contributions from beneficiaries. This is explicit in statements made in Australia,[17] New Zealand[18] and the UK,[19] and is implied for South Africa in Ishengoma (2002) and Jackson (2002). Secondly, it was considered that a higher education system financed entirely from the public purse can be seen to be a regressive use of taxpayers' resources. Both rationales are consistent with the basis of the conceptual discussion offered in sections 3 and 4.

The experiences of the four countries are now explored.

Australia

In 1989, Australia instituted the world's first broadly based income-contingent charging system for higher education, known as the Higher Education Contribution Scheme. When HECS was introduced, higher education was essentially free of charge, and this had been the case since 1973.[20] HECS seeks to recover a part of tuition costs, and is not concerned with student income support.[21] In 1989, HECS was characterized by the following:

- a charge of $A1800 (in 1989 terms) pro-rated by course load, but with no variation by discipline;
- on enrolment students could choose to incur the debt, to be repaid through the tax system depending on personal income; or

- students could avoid the debt by paying up-front, which was associated with a discount of 15 per cent (later increased to 25 per cent);
- those students choosing to pay later faced no repayment obligation unless their personal taxable income exceeded the average income of Australians working for pay (about $A30 000 per annum, in 1989 terms);
- at the first income threshold of repayment a former student's obligation was 2 per cent of income, with repayments increasing in percentage terms above the threshold; and
- HECS could be paid up-front with a discount, but there was no additional interest rate, although the debt and the repayment thresholds were (and remain) indexed to the CPI.

While its essence remains, the HECS arrangements changed significantly in 1997, in three respects: all the charges increased significantly, by about 40 per cent on average; differential charges were introduced according to course, with the new charges essentially reflecting cost differences; the income thresholds for repayment were reduced significantly.[22]

While many other countries introduced income-contingent loans (ICLs) after the beginning of the 1990s, the Australian system remains the most studied. Several broad conclusions can be drawn from research completed thus far. First, HECS has turned out to be very inexpensive in administrative terms (Chapman and Ryan, 2002). That is, while around $A800mn (at current prices) is currently collected per annum, it costs less than 3 per cent of this to administer the programme. This low cost is traceable to the fact that students' debts, and their collection, were fairly straightforward given the mechanisms of the Australian Taxation Office – a point emphasized in ensuing discussion of other countries' administrative arrangements.

Second, HECS has delivered considerable revenue, of the order of $A6bn in current dollars over the 13 years since its introduction. It is projected that the system will provide around $A1.2bn per year in current dollars by 2005, which will be about 20 per cent or more of annual recurrent costs.

A third factor is that there have apparently been no consequences for the accessibility to higher education for students from relatively disadvantaged backgrounds. Broadly speaking, the socioeconomic make-up of the higher education student body was about the same in the late 1990s as it was before HECS was introduced.[23] Finally, higher education enrolments in Australia have increased considerably, by around 50 per cent, since the introduction of HECS. This has happened for two reasons: there were no obvious overall deterrent effects from the new system and, in response to the expectation of high future revenue, governments substantially increased higher education expenditure, particularly in the early periods after the institution of HECS.

Overall HECS is seen to have been a successful policy innovation, as reflected in policy and public debate. Even so, Barr (2001) offers some criticisms, nevertheless supporting the arrangements generally. He suggests that the weaknesses are the absence of a real interest rate on the debt and that the centralized nature of funding limits the prospects for HECS having any implications for allocative efficiency. Overall, however, in collection terms, the scheme has served as a template for several other countries with respect to the adoption of ICLs.

New Zealand

The second country to adopt a broadly based ICL was New Zealand, in 1991. The New Zealand system shares several features of HECS, specifically:

- loan repayments depend on an individual's income, and are collected through a tax system which made this simple in operational terms;
- there is a first income threshold of repayment, after which there is a progressive percentage rate of collection.

However, the New Zealand arrangements differed importantly from those introduced in Australia. In particular:

- the loans are designed to cover both university fees and some living expenses, although there is also a system of means-tested grants for students from poor backgrounds;
- initially the loans carried a market rate of interest;
- universities are free to set their own fees (although it is notable that the resulting charge regimes did not differ much between institutions).

In other words, the New Zealand system was designed to be more consistent with free market principles. For example, there is a potential for resource allocation efficiencies through the freedom of institutions to choose fee levels. Further, having a market rate of interest on the debt arguably reflects the true opportunity cost of loans (Barr, 2001). However, in response to public disquiet over the interest rate regime, the government changed the scheme significantly in early 2000. The changes introduced a zero nominal interest rate for the period a student was enrolled, and variations to the real rate of interest depending on graduates' employment circumstances. These complications have apparently added to the administration costs of the scheme, with some commentators estimating that it now costs three times as much to run the New Zealand system compared to HECS.[24]

Unlike HECS, the New Zealand system seems to be fairly controversial. It is currently under further review and additional changes are likely to be made in the next short period. Much of this controversy is apparently about the interest rate regimes chosen on the debt.[25] Even so, in administrative terms, the New Zealand ICL has apparently worked well. The use of the tax system as the collection agency has proved to be an effective mechanism, as is clearly the case with respect to HECS.

South Africa

The South African government introduced an ICL in 1991, known as the National Student Financial Aid Scheme. NSFAS was motivated essentially by a concern that without assistance the marked racial skewing of the higher education system away from non-white students would remain (Jackson, 2002). While bursaries could have been used instead of an ICL, it was considered that the costs involved 'would not be financially sustainable' (ibid., p. 83). The scheme initially provided resources to about 7500 students, but by 2002 this number had risen to over 100 000, or more than 20 per cent of South Africa's higher education students.

Resources are distributed via universities, with preference going to prospective students who are both poor and academically able. Collection takes the form of former students repaying directly to NSFAS when their income reaches R26 000 per annum, at a rate of 3 per cent of income, and this proportion rises to a maximum of 8 per cent of income per year when income exceeds R59 000. In this sense the collection parameters are similar to HECS in that they are progressive, but there are two major differences between the South African approach and those used in both Australia and New Zealand.

The first difference concerns the first rate of repayment, which at about $A5000 is very much lower than the thresholds used in other countries' ICLs. Second, in the first instance the student repays directly to the lending institution. That is, the taxation system is not the first port of call, but is instead a last resort. Employers are required to be involved only when a student is apparently not maintaining expected debt repayments. It is unclear how much this adds to administrative costs, but it would seem to be the case that collection would cost more with such an approach.

United Kingdom

Higher education financing policy over the last 15 years or so in the UK has been characterized by considerable instability. Until very recently there were no tuition charges: such charges have now been introduced with the adoption of (a highly modified) version of HECS. As well, there have been notable changes over time in the value and institutional nature of student income support. In the 1980s, grants covering living costs were offered on the basis of parental income, but the real value of this support eroded significantly and Barr (2001) argues that 'by the late 1980s [it] was no longer adequate fully to support a student's living costs'.

In 1990, a student loan scheme was introduced, but collection was not based on a former student's income. In fact it resembled a mortgage repayment scheme. The loans were designed to replace half of the maintenance support previously covered by the grant. In effect, however, their impact on public finances was likely to be greater than this, given that they attracted a zero real rate of interest. Barr (2001, p. 202) notes critically that 'It would have been cheaper to give the money away', given the subsidized interest rate, high administrative costs and non-negligible default.

In 1995 the then Conservative government set up a wide-ranging review of higher education funding, due to report after the election of 1997. Chaired by Sir Ron Dearing, its Report[26] recommended strongly the adoption of a scheme based on HECS. It had the following features:

- a uniform charge of about 25 per cent of average course costs;
- the charge to take the form of a debt, with loan recovery to be contingent on income and collected through the tax system;
- the debt to be adjusted over time, but with less than the market rate of interest charged on loans; and
- revenue from the scheme to flow to the Internal Revenue.

The Labour government, elected in 1997, adopted a heavily modified version of the Dearing Committee's recommendation. A modest contribution to tuition of £1000 per annum (indexed to the rate of inflation) was introduced, but liability for this was means-tested.[27] One very important change that was introduced but not widely noted, however, was the switch in the maintenance loan from a mortgage repayment scheme to one in which repayments depend on future income; this is then the UK's first experience with an ICL.

The Dearing recommendations were seen as not going far enough by many and, following several years of debate and a number of Reports and enquiries, a further Review of Higher Education was published in January 2003. The major changes proposed in this Review were (a) the introduction of some price discretion for universities, but with a cap of £3000 per full-time student year; and (b) the introduction of tuition fees for all students, but with the poorest being provided with subsidies.

The critical point for our purposes is that these higher loans will continue to be repayable on an income-contingent basis and the collection mechanism, through the tax system and depending on a student's future income, remains unchanged. As with the Australian and New Zealand schemes, the UK ICL policy is likely to be relatively inexpensive to administer, which is directly traceable to the fact that income tax arrangements in these countries facilitate the operation of ICLs.

Common factors in OECD adoption of ICLs

There are several factors shared by these four countries which help in understanding their adoption of ICL schemes within a similar time frame. Two critical aspects relate to shared institutional background.

The first is that Australia, South Africa, New Zealand and the UK all have in place taxation systems that could be used to collect efficiently student charges on the basis of future incomes. The data noted above with respect to administration costs of ICLs in Australia illustrate how cost-effective such approaches can be. This is a critical administrative issue, and is fundamental to the prospects of the adoption of ICLs in other countries. It is interesting that in the South African case the authorities chose to use the tax system as a back-up rather than the port of first call for loan collection, but it still remains the case that the tax system is available for collection.

Second, in all four countries there is a similar higher education system, essentially inherited from the UK. An important characteristic is that the vast majority of universities are public sector institutions. This has meant that the recovery of a loan designed to pay a charge is uncomplicated if the collection authority is also part of the public sector, that is the Internal Revenue service or equivalent. Indeed, in the Australian and UK cases, the revenue from ICLs was centralized and accrued to the Treasury without reference to, and with no implications for, the direct financing of universities. This has meant that the more complicated problems associated with delivery of a direct revenue base to specific universities have been avoided.[28]

It is also worth stressing that in all of these countries there was a clear recognition that the time for 'free' higher education was over. The expansion of the number of university places, or improvements in the quality of the service, were seen to be desirable, and none of the governments was prepared to finance the required outlays from additional taxation or reduced public services elsewhere. This can be traceable to a worldwide move towards more parsimonious government, an increased demand for higher education and the recognition that university education financed without direct contributions from the private beneficiaries is in essence regressive and inequitable.

It is possible that the apparent successful implementation of the Australian ICL helped motivate administrative change in these directions in some of the other countries. New Zealand policy advisers were aware of developments in Australia, and there is little doubt that direct contact between analysts from Australia and the UK influenced the nature and form of debate in the latter country. Perhaps the policy point is, as Boulding once observed: 'If it exists, then it is possible.'

The non-emergence of ICLs outside the OECD
While there have been significant reforms in the direction of adopting ICLs in the above countries, this has not so far been a shared experience in developing countries. This is the case even though there has been a significant amount of attention with respect to ICL reforms from the World Bank, the UK Department for International Development and other international aid agencies.

There have been many missions to developing countries exploring higher education financing reform, with a particular focus on the possibility of introducing ICLs. Specifically, these have been to Indonesia (1995 and 1998), Papua New Guinea (1996), Namibia (1996), Malaysia (1999), Ethiopia (2000), Rwanda (2001) and the Philippines (2002 and 2003).[29] The major problem seems to be that of implementation and administration.

Chapman and Nicholls (2003) argue that the essential point is that developing countries, with some notable exceptions, typically do not enjoy the soundly based, efficient and comprehensive income tax arrangements that characterize the four countries examined earlier. Most often, alternative parallel systems of collection, such as universal social security systems, are also not to be found. These countries are often beset by problems of corruption in public administration, and their informal economies are comparatively large. There is intense competition between various priorities for public finance and, owing in part to weaknesses in the taxation system, there is little revenue for propitious public administration.

Where government-subsidized student loan schemes, of any description, exist or have been tried, failures and extremely high default rates have induced scepticism about the potential for success of any future programmes in this area. The legislative frameworks surrounding the financial sector are often weak, archaic and/or undeveloped, with the practical effect that there is little legal recourse where borrowers default on loans of any kind. Furthermore, in some countries, a culture has developed among students and former students that relates specifically to student loans: namely, an atmosphere of disregard for the integrity of student loans as legitimate policies.

Chapman and Nicholls argue that the minimum conditions to implement a successful system are the following:

- a reliable, preferably universal, system of unique identifiers;
- an efficient way of determining with accuracy, over time, the actual incomes of former students;
- accurate record-keeping of the accruing liabilities of students (while studying); and
- a collection mechanism with a sound and, if possible, computerized record-keeping system.

In the absence of the above, it is difficult to see how an effective ICL can be made operational. While the case for financing reforms in these countries seems as strong as it was in Australia, New Zealand, South Africa and the UK, at least at the moment progress seems stalled in a way that can be traced to institutional barriers.

6 Conclusions

The financing of higher education has been in recent years an area of considerable public debate and some interesting policy innovation. The debate has been triggered largely by growing funding constraints in many OECD countries where tertiary education had hitherto been publically funded and provided. Many governments have made increased participation a major plank of policy and in some cases the resultant increases have been dramatic. Inevitably, however, this has squeezed public funding per student to levels which have been deemed unsustainable, triggering a search for alternative or complementary sources of funding.

In this chapter we began by documenting trends in HE participation and funding across the OECD, paying particular attention to growing funding constraints. We then went on to ask who should pay and what the balance of responsibility should be between public and private sources. We argued that the evidence on private and social rates of return provides a strong case for beneficiaries making a greater contribution than at present in many countries. We then turned our attention to alternative sources of funding, concluding that greater reliance on deferred fees repaid through an income-contingent loan system was potentially the most effective and efficient mechanism available. Finally we looked at policy innovation in four OECD countries which have moved in this direction.

Issues around the funding of HE in general and the appropriate balance as between public and private sources are likely to continue to be a source of discussion and debate, not only in the major OECD countries but also in the transition countries, and in developing countries, and the policy option of funding via deferred payments is likely to become more common.

Notes

1. Until recently, this debate has been conducted at a very applied level. An interesting recent theoretical contribution is that of De Fraja (2002).
2. Tertiary type A programmes are designed to provide sufficient qualifications for entry to advanced research programmes and professions with high skill requirements. Type A programmes have a minimum duration of three years' full-time equivalent. These programmes are not offered exclusively at universities. Tertiary type B programmes focus on practical, technical or occupational skills for direct entry in the labour market. They have a minimum duration of two years' full-time equivalent at the tertiary level. See OECD (2002) for more details.
3. Indeed the World Bank has long advocated the advantages of financial diversification. We shall examine this issue in more detail in later sections.
4. Although not all of the differences in pay between graduates and non-graduates may be caused by differences in education. This will be discussed later.
5. See, for example, Greenaway and Haynes (2000), Skidelsky (2000) and the UK's Department for Education and Skills (2003). As Skidelsky (2000) pointed out, to realize a comparable return one would have to invest £100 000 in government bonds.
6. To calculate the private rate of return to higher education, we compare costs, measured as earnings forgone plus any education-related expenses the student has to pay, with private benefits. These are the increase in the expected income of a graduate over and above a non-graduate over the individual's working life. The private rate of return is the discount rate that equates these two streams. There is a significant literature on both the technical aspects of calculation and rate of return estimates themselves. We will not focus on the former beyond discussing how much of the return can reliably be ascribed to higher education. Instead we focus on recent estimates, which are most relevant for future policy.
7. See Chapter 1 in the present volume (Psacharopoulos and Patrinos).
8. For a comprehensive review of the externalities to education see Chapter 6 in the present volume (McMahon).
9. These are calculated in a similar way to private rates but with the addition of costs and benefits borne by the rest of society (particularly the taxpayer). The social rate of return is the discount rate that equates social costs (measured as the value of output forgone, plus teaching costs) to social benefits (measured as higher earnings and higher tax revenues after graduation).
10. For a more detailed discussion of the graduate tax see, for example, Glennerster *et al.* (1968), Glennerster (1997), Barr (1989).
11. In the UK for instance, it has been estimated that every 1 per cent of graduate tax, with a participation rate of 40 per cent, could yield close to £4bn, but it would take 43 years to reach steady state (CVCP, 1993).
12. For example, EU nationals who pay the same (heavily subsidized) fee as British students are outwith the jurisdiction of the Inland Revenue if they return home after graduation.
13. The Australian Higher Education Contribution Scheme (HECS) arrangements are often referred to as a graduate tax: they are not. Although repayments are made through the income tax system, this is simply to minimize collection costs. Graduates repay what they borrowed on an income-contingent basis. See Chapman (1997).
14. See, for example, Friedman (1962), Peacock and Wiseman (1965), West (1965).
15. This principle has already been accepted in the UK since two tranches of debt under the old mortgage scheme have been sold by the Students Loan Company (SLC). The first was £1bn to Greenwich NatWest in 1998, the second £1.3bn to Deutsche Bank/Nationwide in 1999. The exact details of the transactions have not been made public but it is believed that the debt was sold for around 50 per cent of its face value. Estimates suggest that the missing 50 per cent breaks down into about 15 per cent because of low income, early death and so on and 35 per cent due to the interest subsidy. As it happens, these costs are consistent with the estimates of Barr and Falkingham (1993).
16. This section draws heavily on Chapman and Greenaway (2004).

17. See Wran Committee Report (1988).
18. See New Zealand Government (1988).
19. See the Dearing Committee Report (1997).
20. For a brief history of Australian higher education financing, see the Wran Committee Report (1988).
21. In the main, income support takes the form of means-tested grants.
22. Chapman and Salvage (2001) argue that the last of these changes was the most likely policy variation to affect access.
23. See Chapman and Ryan (2002).
24. Private conversation with Australian tax authorities who have explored the comparative costs of the two policies.
25. See Warner (1999).
26. See Dolton *et al.* (1997) for a summary of the economic issues, and Dearing (1997) for the full Report.
27. This decision would seem to reflect a concern by the government that relatively disadvantaged students would be more likely than others to find a loan a deterrent to higher education participation, a view at variance with the evidence from the Australian experience.
28. As Chapman (1997), Barr (2001) and others note, this characteristic of ICLs has the important cost of not delivering any resource allocation benefits from price competition.
29. For description and analyses of these experiences, see Chapman and Nicholls (2003).

References

Albrecht, D. and A. Ziderman (1993), 'Student loans: an effective instrument for cost recovery in higher education?', *World Bank Research Observer*, **8**, 71–90.

Barr, N. (1989), *Student Loans: The Next Steps*, London: Freedom Press.

Barr, N. (1997), 'Student loans: towards a new public/private mix', *Public Money and Management*, **17**, 31–40.

Barr, N. (2001), *The Welfare State as Piggy Bank*, Oxford: Oxford University Press.

Barr, N. and I. Crawford (1998), 'Funding higher education in an age of expansion', *Education Economics*, **6**, 45–70.

Barr, N. and J. Falkingham (1993), 'Paying for Learning', Welfare State Programme, Discussion Paper WSP/94, London School of Economics.

Barro, R.J. (1991), 'Economic growth in a cross-section of countries', *Quarterly Journal of Economics*, **106**, 407–44.

Barro, R.J. and Sala-I-Martin (1995), *Economic Growth*, New York: McGraw-Hill.

Bassanini, S. and S. Scarpenta (2001), 'Does human capital matter for growth in OECD countries? Evidence from pooled mean-group estimates', OECD Economics Department Working Papers, no. 282, Paris.

Blondal, S., S. Field and N. Giroard (2002), 'Investment in human capital through upper second and tertiary education', *OECD Economic Studies*, **34**, 41–89.

Bynner, J. and M. Egerton (2000), 'The social benefits of higher education: insights using longitudinal data', Centre for Longitudinal Studies, Institute of Education, London.

Cameron, S. and J. Heckman (2001), 'The dynamics of educational attainment for black, hispanic and white males', *Journal of Political Economy*, **109**, 455–99.

Carr-Hill, R. (2001), *Wider Benefits of Learning: A Review of the Literature and Models*, London: Institute of Education.

Chapman, B. (1997), 'Conceptual issues and the Australian experience with income contingent charging for higher education', *Economic Journal*, **107**, 1178–93.

Chapman, B. and D. Greenaway (2004), 'Learning to live with loans? Policy transfer and the funding of higher education', *The World Economy* (forthcoming).

Chapman, B. and J. Nicholls (2003), 'Income contingent loans for higher education: implementation issues for developing countries', The World Bank, Washington.

Chapman, B. and C. Ryan (2001), 'Income contingent financing of student charges for higher education: assessing the Australian innovation', discussion paper no. 449, Centre for Economic Policy Research, Australian National University.

Chapman, B. and C. Ryan (2002), 'Income contingent financing of student higher education charges: assessing the Australian innovation', *The Welsh Journal of Education*, **11**, 64–81.

Chapman, B. and C. Ryan (2003), 'The access implications of income contingent charges for higher education: lessons from Australia', mimeo, Centre for Economic Policy Research, Australian National University, Canberra.

Chapman, B. and T. Salvage (2001), 'The Australian government's new approach to post-graduate charges', *Agenda*, **8**, 1–18.

CVCP (1993), *Review of Options for the Additional Funding of Higher Education*, London: CVCP.

De Fraja, G. (2002), 'The design of optimal education policies', *Review of Economic Studies*, **69**, 437–66.

Dearing, Sir Ron (chairman) (1997), *Higher Education in a Learning Society*, London: UK government.

Department for Education and Skills (2003), *The Future of Higher Education*, London: HMSO.

Dolton, P., D. Greenaway and A. Vignoles (1997), 'Whither higher education? An economic perspective for the Dearing committee of enquiry', *Economic Journal*, **107**, 710–26.

Friedman, M. (1962), *Capitalism and Freedom*, Chicago: University of Chicago Press.

Gemmell, N. (1997), 'Externalities to higher education: a review of the new growth literature', Report 8, National Committee of Inquiry into Higher Education.

Glennerster, H. (1997), *Paying for Welfare: Towards 2000*, Hemel Hempstead: Prentice-Hall.

Glennerster, H., G. Wilson and S. Merrett (1968), 'A graduate tax', *Higher Education*, **1**(1), 26–38.

Greenaway, D. and M. Haynes (2000), 'Funding universities for national and international competitiveness', School of Economics Policy Report, University of Nottingham (www.nottingham.ac.uk/economics/funding/funding.pdf).

Ishengoma, Johnson M. (2002), 'Financing higher education in post-apartheid South Africa: trends, developments, and challenges ahead', The International Comparative Higher Education Finance and Accessibility Project, The State University of New York at Buffalo, NY.

Jackson, R. (2002), 'The South African student assistance scheme', *The Welsh Journal of Education*, **12** (1), 63–79.

Kenkel, D. (1991), 'Health behaviour, health knowledge and schooling', *Journal of Political Economy*, **99**, 287–305.

Lochner, L. and E. Moretti (2001), 'The effect of education on crime: evidence from prison inmates, arrests and self-reports', NBER Working Paper 8605.

New Zealand Government (1988), 'Student Loan Scheme Paper B: Longer Term Initiatives', p. 2 (5 August), released under the Official Information Act 1982.

OECD (2001), *The Well Being of Nations*, Paris: OECD.

OECD (2002), *Education at a Glance*, Paris: Organisation for Economic Co-operation and Development.

Peacock, A. and J. Wiseman (1965), *Education for Democrats*, London: Institute of Economic Affairs.

Report of the Committee on Financing Higher Education (the Wran Report) (1988), Canberra: Australian Government Printing Service.

Schultz, T.W. (1975), 'The value of the ability to deal with disequilibria', *Journal of Economic Literature*, September, 827–43.

Skidelsky, R. (2000), *Hansard*, 14 June, pp. 1685–7.

Warner, A. (1999), 'Student Loans in New Zealand', Master of Commerce thesis, University of Auckland.

West, E. (1965), *Education and the State*, London: Institute of Economic Affairs.

Woodhall, M. (1995), 'Student loans', in M. Carnoy (ed.), *International Encyclopaedia of the Economics of Education*, Oxford and Tarrytown, NY: Pergamon.

9 Exploring the effect of class size on student achievement: what have we learned over the past two decades?

Susan L. Averett and Michele C. McLennan

Introduction

Parents and educators almost universally identify small classes as a desirable attribute of successful school systems and class size reduction initiatives have been implemented widely.[1] Despite this and decades of study, researchers remain divided on whether smaller classes actually have positive effects on student outcomes and/or whether the magnitude of the effect justifies the high cost of implementing class size reductions. In fact, a larger debate focuses on whether increasing resources to schools in any way improves student outcomes. This discussion is being carried out throughout the world, with somewhat different frameworks between developed and developing countries. In developed countries, where access to primary and secondary education is essentially universal but the quality of education is varied, researchers are concerned with identifying specific treatments to improve student outcomes, such as reducing class size, increasing teacher salaries or expanding teacher education. Developing countries are often still dealing with the tradeoff between increasing access to education and improving the quality of existing education. Improving quality in this context can mean providing textbooks and adequate facilities, more fundamental needs than are the focus in the developed world.

In this chapter we will consider the value of class size reductions in both contexts with a focus on the developed world. We focus our review on those studies that have examined the relationship between class size and student achievement where achievement is measured by test scores. There is also an extensive body of work relating class size to other outcomes such as future wages, retention and graduation rates.[2] There is an enormous body of research on this issue and so we focus our attention on research primarily conducted over the last two decades.

In 1966, the Coleman report concluded that social and family background conditions, not the quality of school inputs, largely determined a student's academic success. This finding has had a critical effect on education policy, suggesting that additional spending on schools will not improve student outcomes. We will trace the research spurred by this report in the past few decades, some of which agrees with the Coleman conclusion and some of which strongly refutes it. In this chapter we first present some basic education and economic statistics to highlight the differences across countries and time. Next we provide an explanation of the education production function and how economists and educators often model it. Finally we turn to the available empirical evidence grouped by type of study, with some concluding comments on policy implications of class size reduction initiatives.

Class size and student achievement across countries
Table 9.1 provides data on expenditures per pupil, pupil–teacher ratios, class sizes, standardized test scores, GDP per capita and enrolment rates for 27 countries. Data on the pupil–teacher ratio are more readily available than class size so it is often the variable that is referenced; however pupil–teacher ratios and class size are not completely interchangeable. The use of specialist teachers in subjects such as music, art and physical education, the differences between numbers of classes taken by students and numbers taught by teachers, as well as the assignment of teachers to small special education classes mean that the pupil–teacher ratios are generally lower than the actual class size (Akerhielm, 1995; Boozer and Rouse, 1995).

The achievement data are from the Third International Mathematics and Science Study (TIMSS), which provides a cross-section look at achievement in 40 countries around the world.[3] Data on expenditures per pupil, GDP per capita and enrolment rates are provided to highlight other relevant differences across countries.

The pattern is clear: countries with larger class sizes score higher on these achievement tests. In fact, some of the countries with the largest class sizes have the highest scores (Korea and Japan, for example).[4] However, because educational systems around the world vary dramatically, comparisons of this sort must be done carefully. Countries such as the United States and, to a lesser extent, Canada and Australia, have very decentralized educational systems; while other countries, such as Singapore, Hong Kong and South Korea have very centralized educational systems. School finance, curriculum and class size are all determined at the national level in these countries. The European countries tend to fall somewhere in between, with some having nationally set curriculums (France) while Germany entrusts curricular decisions to each of its 16 states. Some countries have national tests while others such as the USA do not. For all of these reasons, we should make cross-country comparisons cautiously.

Statistics on class size and achievement in the USA
Throughout the 20th century, pupil–teacher ratios in the USA fell dramatically, while expenditures per pupil increased. The pupil–teacher ratio stood

Table 9.1

Country	Expenditures per pupil, 1998		Pupil–teacher ratio, 1999		Class size	TIMSS 8th grade, 1999		GDP per cap., 2001	Enrolment rates, 1999	
	Primary	Secondary	Primary	Secondary		Maths	Science		Age 5 to 14	Age 15 to 19
Australia	$3981	$5830	17.30	12.68	27	525	540	$23200	97.7	80.3
Belgium (Fl.)	3799	6238	13.90	8.80	20	558	535	25300	98.8	90.6
Canada	NA	NA	18.70	19.30	28	531	533	24800	96.6	75.3
Chile	1500	1713	33.40	29.10	NA	392	420	10100	91.3	65.2
Czech Republic	1645	3182	23.40	12.37	26	520	539	12900	99.3	74.8
Finland	4641	5111	17.40	13.50	NA	520	535	22900	91.2	84.5
Hong Kong	NA	NA	22.00	18.00	41	582	530	25400	99.9	71.0
Hungary	2028	2140	10.90	10.60	NA	NA	NA	NA	99.8	78.1
Indonesia	116	497	23.10	18.70	NA	403	435	2900	76.0	37.0
Israel	4135	5115	17.40	11.30	NA	466	468	18900	97.1	61.4
Italy	5653	6458	11.30	10.30	NA	479	493	22100	99.2	70.7
Japan	5075	5890	21.20	15.40	36	579	550	24900	101.2	NA
Korea	2838	3544	32.00	22.20	51	587	549	16100	91.8	81.2
Malaysia	919	1469	21.60	19.30	NA	519	492	10300	96.6	44.4
Netherlands	3795	5304	16.60	17.70	NA	540	545	24400	99.4	87.7

331

Table 9.1 (continued)

Country	Expenditures per pupil, 1998		Pupil–teacher ratio, 1999		Class size	TIMSS 8th grade, 1999		GDP per cap., 2001	Enrolment rates, 1999	
	Primary	Secondary	Primary	Secondary		Maths	Science		Age 5 to 14	Age 15 to 19
New Zealand	NA	NA	20.50	16.00	NA	491	510	17700	98.8	72.5
Philippines	689	726	34.40	32.90	NA	345	345	3800	84.8	61.9
Romania	NA	NA	NA	NA	27	472	472	5900	93.2	75.9
Russia	NA	NA	17.60	11.50	NA	526	529	7700	79.1	32.0
Singapore	NA	NA	NA	NA	32	604	568	26500	NA	NA
Slovenia	NA	NA	NA	NA	24	530	533	12000	93.9	89.5
South Africa	NA	NA	NA	NA	NA	275	243	8500	95.2	NA
Thailand	1048	1177	20.70	22.70	NA	467	482	6700	98.7	57.5
Tunisia	891	1633	23.90	23.80	NA	448	430	6500	86.4	51.8
Turkey	NA	NA	30.00	16.10	NA	429	433	6800	76.9	30.5
UK	3329	5230	22.50	14.70	NA	496	538	22800	99.0	72.5
USA	6043	7764	16.30	15.63	26	502	515	36200	100.7	78.1

Notes:

Expenditures per pupil from www1.oecd.org/els/education/ei/eag Table B1.1.

Pupil–teacher ratios from www1.oecd.org/els/education/ei/eag Table D5.1.

Class size from Woessmann and West (2002).

TIMSS results from http://nces.ed.gov/timss/results.asp.

GDP per capita from www.worldfactsandfigures.com/gdp_country_asc.php.

Enrolment rates from www1.oecd.org/els/education/ei/eag Table C1.2 except for Romania, Slovenia and South Africa. These are from www.worldbank.org/data/dataquery.html.

Hong Kong pupil–teacher ratios and enrolment rates from www.info.gov.hk/yearbook/2000/eng/09/c09–06.htm.

at 27:1 in 1955, but had fallen to 17.4:1 in 1995. Over this same time period, expenditures per pupil increased from $1697 to $6300 in 1995/ real dollars. Thus we can clearly see that resources devoted to education in the USA have dramatically increased over time.[5]

Measures of student achievement do not exhibit such a consistent pattern. The longest time series data available on student achievement is the SAT score (Scholastic Aptitude Test), taken by students who are seeking entrance to college. During the 1960s and 1970s there was a notable decline in average SAT scores, but the interpretation of this as reflecting an actual decline in achievement is problematic. Since, over the course of the 20th century, more students of lower ability have increasingly had access to a college education, this fall in SAT scores may result from increased participation in the test, not lower achievement in a stable set of students.[6]

Another, perhaps more reliable, measure of student achievement is the scores from the National Assessment of Educational Progress (NAEP), also known as 'the Nation's Report Card'.[7] NAEP is a nationally representative series of tests, initially conducted in 1969, in reading, mathematics, science, writing, US history, civics, geography and the arts. Examinations are periodically administered to fourth, eighth and twelfth graders (ages 10 years, 13–14 years and 17–18 years respectively). In reading and mathematics, between 1971 and 1996, the scores have remained relatively flat, while they have declined slightly in science and writing. However blacks and Hispanics have seen remarkable increases in their scores over this same time period (Rouse, 2000).

In summary, while class sizes have fallen dramatically in the USA, achievement has not simultaneously increased across all demographic groups. This is only a simple correlation and we need to consider other factors that have also been changing over this time period before we can conclude that class size reductions have not helped. For example, child poverty rates have increased, as has the number of children raised in single parent families: both of these social factors are linked to lower achievement. In addition, the percentage of mothers with young children working outside the home has increased dramatically, perhaps indicating a reduction in social capital invested in children. At the same time, family sizes have fallen and parental education has risen, factors we would expect to lead to an increase in student achievement (Hanushek, 1996; Krueger, 2003; Grissmer *et al.*, 1994). Sophisticated measurement techniques are needed to isolate the effect of class size on student outcomes given this plethora of changes, with both positive and negative influences on student test scores.

Modelling class size and student achievement empirically
The typical approach taken towards modelling the effect of class size on student achievement is to estimate an education production function. The

standard education production function posits that student achievement outcomes (such as test scores or educational attainment) depend on individual characteristics (such as innate ability), family background (such as parents' education and income) and classroom features (such as class size or teacher's experience), as well as neighbourhood, school and district effects (such as the percentage of the school that is low-income and the expenditures per pupil). The function is specified as: $A_i = f\{X_i, F_i, Z_{c,n,s,d}\}$, where A is a measure of student achievement, X represents individual characteristics, F family background variables and Z features of the class, neighbourhood, school or district. In addition to the inputs mentioned here, researchers often include a lagged value of A as a way to control for individual ability (Goldhaber and Brewer, 1997; Hedges *et al.*, 1994).

Correa (1993) presents a theoretical model of the effect of class size on student outcomes based on the time allocation of rational teachers. He hypothesizes that teachers are constrained to divide their time between activities that affect the entire class (e.g. preparation), those that affect individual students (e.g. answering questions) and those outside teaching. A teacher's utility function includes the average performance of the class as well as the time in non-educational activity. The average performance of the class is increased by time spent by the teacher on educational activities; however the average is increased more by those activities which affect the whole group. For this reason, teachers will focus on the overall performance of the class and this is more likely to harm individual students as class size increases.

Lazear (2001) provides another theoretical model suggesting that class size is important in the education production function because of its effects on classroom atmosphere and is likely to be more effective for improving outcomes for disadvantaged students. A number of theoretical explanations for including class size in the function come to mind: improved classroom management, differences in teaching techniques and positive peer effects. Small classes may ease classroom management chores. Teachers may know their students better and meet parents/guardians more frequently. Teachers may control the classroom better and spend less time on discipline and transitions. Students may be 'on task' more consistently.

In addition, teachers may be more effective in small classes. In small classes, the curriculum may take on more variety, breadth, depth or richness because teachers have more time to focus on planning. With smaller classes teachers are able to individualize instruction according to the students' needs, using a variety of approaches, and allowing teachers to provide students with opportunities to reveal their abilities and understanding. Teachers can offer more frequent critique and feedback to each student. While some studies show that activities are more varied and innovative in small classes, a number of studies suggest that teachers do not change their methods according to the size of the class (Shapson *et al.*, 1980).

Small classes may result in positive peer effects. Research indicates that student relationships are improved in smaller classes. Teacher and student morale is reported to be higher. Students in small classes may identify more with the schooling process. This may be particularly helpful to minority or low-income students at risk of being detached from the education system (Blatchford and Mortimore, 1994; Cooper, 1989; Finn *et al.*, 1990; Finn, 1998).

Estimating the education production function

Researchers typically estimate the effect of class size by employing analysis of variance (ANOVA) or ordinary least squares regression (OLS). The objectives are to determine whether reductions in class size *cause* student achievement to increase and, if so, the magnitude of the effect. When test scores are the outcome, researchers usually calculate the effect size as the difference in mean test scores between small and other class sizes divided by the standard deviation of the test score. The standard deviation can be measured across individual students or across classes. These effect sizes are relative to the difference in class sizes being studied.

Technical issues

In the case of OLS analysis, a typical education production function is estimated as

$$A_i = \alpha_0 + \alpha_1 X_i + \alpha_2 F_i + \alpha_3 Z_{c,n,s,d} + \alpha_4 CS_i + \varepsilon_i,$$

where A_i is a measure of student achievement, X_i is a vector of individual student attributes, F_i is a vector of family background variables, Z is a vector of class, school, neighbourhood and district characteristics, CS_i is class size and ε is a random error term. Lagged values[8] of A are often included in X to control for individual student ability. Interpreting the coefficient α_4 as an estimate of the causal effect of class size on the outcome is problematic. The problems lie in the areas of measurement, data availability and causation identification.

Measurement and data availability

While we are interested in the effect that being taught in a smaller group has on students' test scores, we do not always have adequate data to identify a student's actual class size. Often we only come across data for the pupil–teacher ratio which, as we have discussed above, can vary significantly from class size. In addition, while we want the information to reflect an individual student's situation, the class size and teacher characteristics data are often compiled and available only at the school, district or even state level rather than the classroom level. So we often use aggregate averages, which may suffer from aggregation bias, rather than actual measures. By aggregating data to the level of the state or district, omitted variables which operate at that level (i.e. state-specific determinants of performance such as state political variables) can bias estimates of class size effect upward (Hanushek *et al.*, 1996). Grogger (1996) also finds that aggregating measures of schooling inputs by state yields much higher estimates of the effect of school expenditure on earnings than aggregating measures of inputs by school district, and that, when district-level measures are used, estimates of the effect of schooling inputs are positive but extremely small.

Many potentially important predictors of student achievement are often not observable to the researcher. These include the innate ability and motivation of both students and teachers. In addition, a rich set of family, neighbourhood, school and district background variables are required to control for effects not directly attributable to class size, but which are not always available. Another drawback is the cross-sectional nature of many of the data sets which does not allow the researcher to control for fixed or non-contemporaneous effects of students, schools, districts or states.

Causation

Assuming that test scores are a direct effect of observed class size ignores the process of selection into different class sizes. For a number of reasons, different class sizes may result from a non-random sorting of students into smaller classes both between and within schools. Parents view small class sizes as a desirable aspect of their children's education; therefore families with greater resources may seek out small classes either by enrolling their children in private schools or by purchasing homes in school districts with smaller than average class sizes (referred to as Tiebout sorting). If these same parents are also those who make other unobserved human capital investments in their children, such as private tutoring or time spent reading, students' test scores may be higher than average because their parents invest significant human and social capital in them, rather than because of the small size of their class. A spurious negative correlation between class size and test scores would result.

On the other hand, good schools may attract more students, resulting in larger class sizes. This would lead to a positive correlation between class size and outcomes which is also spurious. These examples highlight between-school sorting.

Sorting may also take place within a given school. School administrators may sort students according to needs. If principals place low achieving students in smaller classes to provide remediation, we would observe a positive correlation between class size and student outcomes. On the other hand, if advanced classes, for which only high achieving students are eligible, tend to be smaller, there will be a negative relationship between class size and outcomes. For all of these cases, an OLS analysis of the relationship between class size and student outcomes would misrepresent the true causal relationship. Since class size is correlated with unobserved ability or social capital investments, the coefficient on class size will be biased.

Correcting the selection bias

The ideal way to ascertain the true, *ceteris paribus*, causal effects of class size on achievement is to design a random experiment. Figure 9.1 illustrates the basic idea. A sample of subjects is chosen and then is randomly assigned to one of two groups: an experimental or treatment group that is placed in the smaller class and a control group that is in the larger class. Many medical experiments are 'double blind', implying that neither the participants nor the researchers know which group is which. Of course, in education, it is impossible not to reveal to the participants whether or not they are receiving the treatment.

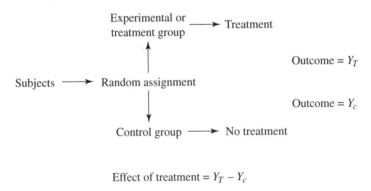

Figure 9.1

The outcome would be the test score, administered at the end of the school year. The treatment is considered effective if the difference in outcomes between the two groups is statistically significant and relevant in terms of magnitude.

With a true random assignment experiment, there is no need to control for pre-existing differences across individuals that may affect the outcome. The researchers do not need to worry about these other factors because the random assignment guarantees that these variables are unrelated to (uncorrelated with) the differences in the outcome between the two groups.

Some researchers criticize these experiments, arguing that selection bias still exists because the programmes are never implemented entirely randomly. In addition, 'Hawthorne' or 'Henry' effects may occur which suggest that, because the subjects are aware that they are involved in a study, which could have an impact on policies that concern them, they will behave in a way to influence the study results. The Hawthorne effect occurs if teachers/administrators/parents or students associated with small classes put forth more effort to show the positive effect. The Henry effect would occur if teachers or others assigned to other class types put forth more effort than normal as if in competition with those receiving the treatment.

In response to this criticism, researchers have also taken advantage of differences that arise in class sizes from sources other than selection or random assignment, such as population fluctuation or mandatory caps on class size. These differences are arguably not related to the selection issues we discuss above and provide a valid source of exogenous variation in class size.[9]

Todd and Wolpin (2003) point out that random experiments that do not control for background variables are designed to answer the policy question of 'what would be the total effect of an exogenous change in class size on achievement, not holding other inputs constant?' (p. F8) which is different from the education production function parameter estimate which attempts to identify the effect of class size, holding all other inputs constant. They believe that differences in results of experimental and observational studies can be explained as responding to two different questions.

Another strategy taken by researchers to mitigate the selection effect is to analyse the value added of small classes.[10] Students' initial academic position is measured and it is the difference between this and a subsequent measure that is evaluated.[11] If students with low ability are sorted into small classes, researchers control for that effect by looking at the change in test scores rather than the absolute level of test scores. While this effect does reduce the selection problem it does not eliminate it if the initial achievement measure also reflects the rate of advancement (Krueger, 1999).

The instrumental variables technique is another means of correcting for the endogeneity of class size. The non-random allocation of students both between and within schools is likely to produce a correlation between class size and the error term, ε, in the education production function, resulting in a biased estimate of the parameter on class size. Researchers attempt to identify proxies for class size, which are not correlated with the residuals of a test score regression, but are important predictors of class size. In this way, we solve the problem of endogenous class size. We will review both longitudinal and cross-sectional studies that utilize this approach. A significant problem here is identifying powerful instruments that are not also an issue in terms of selection. For instance, average expenditures per pupil at a school is a good predictor of class size; however it is also likely that parents with greater resources have selected schools with higher expenditures, making this a poor instrument.

Meta-analysis

Because a large number of studies on class size across various populations have been conducted with no clear agreement on the question of whether and by how much class size affects student outcomes, researchers have also conducted meta-analyses. They evaluate a group of studies together to determine if the weight of the studies supports or refutes the conclusion that small class size is beneficial. 'Meta-analysis involves synthesis of the results of a series of research studies by combining quantitative indices of effect magnitude from each study' (Hedges and Stock, 1983). We summarize conclusions of a number of these analyses.

Results of empirical studies

Here we discuss the results of the recent research that has been conducted on class size, organized around type of study methodology.

OLS and ANOVA studies

Early research on class size and student achievement tended to estimate linear regression or ANOVA models without any regard for or discussion of the non-random assignment to class size that occurs both within and between schools. We do not discuss that research here because it is well known and documented that such an approach often leads to a spurious positive correlation between class size and achievement, implying that attending larger classes increases student achievement. However, many current researchers provide an estimate of the OLS coefficient on class size in the education production function as a starting point or benchmark. Generally, these researchers include a wide array of covariates to capture some of the nonrandom sorting.

For example, using US cross-sectional data (National Education Longitudinal Study, described below), Akerhielm (1995) and Goldhaber and Brewer (1997) both find a positive and significant effect of class size on student test scores. Interestingly, Argys and Rees (1995), who also use the NELS, find a negative but statistically insignificant effect of class size on test scores. All three sets of these researchers include extensive controls, though not the same set.

Angrist and Lavy (1999) also find a positive relationship between class sizes and test scores for Israeli data in OLS estimates when no other controls are included. Blatchford and Mortimore (1994) list a number of ANOVA studies using British data that find similar results. Reviewing simple international relationships between class size and student achievement, Hanushek (1998) notes that class size is not significant in explaining student performance. Woessmann and West (2002) and Pong and Pallas (2001) use data from the TIMSS and find positive and often significant class size effects in several different countries using OLS.

Time series evidence at first glance also suggests that class size reductions in the USA over the last three decades have not led to improvements in student performance (Hanushek, 1998). Hanushek and Luque (2003) find that correlations between class size and student test scores across countries over time are also positive.

A number of researchers have investigated the question of whether these positive correlations are spurious because of the non-random sorting of students that occurs both within and between schools. In the USA, Title 1 (also known as Chapter 1) funds are routinely used to reduce class size for students requiring remedial help. Cooper (1989) finds that the percentage of remedial instruction delivered in groups of five or fewer pupils ranges from 37 per cent to 100 per cent across districts he studies. Akerhielm (1995) notes that in the USA students in need of remedial attention are often placed in smaller classes. These effects would lead to a spurious positive impact of class size on student achievement. On the other hand, Kremer (1995) argues that property values in the USA are higher in areas with low class size, indicating that parents are willing to pay for this element of education.

Angrist and Lavy (1999) note that rural schools in Israel, which tend to be small because of population distribution, also tend to be less able schools. Looking at a variety of countries, Hanushek and Luque (2003) find evidence of a compensatory model, suggesting that students with low achievement are placed in smaller classes. On the basis of this and other research, it is generally acknowledged that sorting into class sizes does occur and should be accounted for in an investigation of effects of class size on achievement.

Random experiments

As we noted earlier, the ideal way to avoid the problem of selection into different size classes, and to some extent omitted variables, has been to arrange for the random assignment of teachers and students to classes of varying sizes and to track the performance of these students. There are a small number of these experiments which have been implemented on a significant scale and these have primarily been in the USA. The most well documented experiment is the Tennessee Student Teacher Achievement Ratio

(STAR) project. Indiana, New York, Nevada and North Carolina are other states where such projects have been implemented. Internationally the Toronto Board of Education (Canada) conducted a similar study in the early 1970s (Shapson *et al.*, 1980).

Design of STAR

The US Tennessee STAR program,[12] which ran from 1986 to 1989, was described by Fredrick Mosteller (1995, p. 113) as 'one of the most important educational investigations ever carried out and illustrates the kind and magnitude of research needed in the field of education to strengthen schools'. Children entering kindergarten in a variety of schools across districts in Tennessee were randomly assigned to different class sizes. Students continued in a small class (15–17 students), a regular class (22–25 students) or a class with an aide (22–25 students) through third grade (8–9 year olds), then returned to regular classes in fourth grade (9–10 year olds). About 6400 students participated in the first year and data on approximately 11 600 students were accumulated over the four years. The effects of these different class sizes on a variety of outcomes have been studied as the students have progressed through their academic careers.

Only certified teachers were included and they were assigned randomly to different class sizes. The schools were not, however, chosen randomly. Schools participated in the programme voluntarily and were required to have sufficient students to enrol at least one of each type of class in each grade. A total of 79 elementary schools from 42 school districts participated, representing a wide range of demographics (wealthy and poor districts; minority and white students; urban, rural and suburban settings).[13] However the participating schools had a higher percentage of minority students, lower test scores and higher expenditures per pupil than the average schools in Tennessee.

Data were collected on student performance on norm and criterion-referenced achievement tests. From kindergarten to third grade (approximately 5–9 years old), students completed the Stanford Achievement Test, a nationally normed achievement test in mathematics and reading (referred to here as SAT-1 to distinguish it from the Scholastic Aptitude Test), the Basic Skills First (BSF) test designed to cover the state curriculum, and they completed questionnaires on self-concept and motivation. In follow-up studies in grades 4 to 8, students completed the Comprehensive Test of Basic Skills (CTBS).

Results of STAR

The principal investigators of Project STAR have published a number of reports on the study, primarily using ANOVA to obtain results. The reviews of grades kindergarten to 3 include these findings (Word *et al.*, 1990; Finn *et al.*, 1990; Nye *et al.*, 2000, 2001): at each grade level, small class students had significantly higher scores on standardized tests for both mathematics and reading than their peers in regular or regular plus aide classes; the small class effects were significant for girls and boys, those of high and low socio-economic status (SES), minority and white students, as well as urban, inner city, suburban and rural schools, and only in the first grade sample was any positive effect of adding an aide detected. In first grade reading, minority students received a differentially positive effect of small classes over their white peers. Small class advantages are noticeably greater in inner city and suburban schools than elsewhere.

These researchers find not only a significant relationship but also an educationally relevant effect size. Table 9.2 displays, for various populations, the effect sizes for reading and mathematics, which are the portion of a standard deviation change that occurs when class size is reduced from about 25 to 15 (roughly 30 per cent). For instance, on average a kindergarten student in a small class performed one-fifth of a standard deviation better on the reading test than his or her large class peers. The standard deviation across students (not classes) is used here. The size of the effect drops after grade 1 but does not disappear.

Table 9.2

	Kindergarten	Grade 1	Grade 2	Grade 3
Reading				
All	0.21	0.34	0.26	0.24
High SES	0.19	0.32	0.20	0.21
Low SES	0.23	0.35	0.33	0.25
Bottom 1/5	–	0.26	0.12	0.12
Maths				
All	0.17	0.33	0.23	0.21
High SES	0.20	0.34	0.21	0.20
Low SES	0.14	0.30	0.22	0.18
Bottom 1/5	–	0.09	0.25	0.23

While Finn and Achilles (1990) find a differential effect for minorities, low income and low achieving students, Nye *et al.* (2002) do not find this effect for low achievers. (They do not evaluate minorities separately.)

The principal investigators for STAR and the Lasting Benefits Study (LBS) have also found continuing positive effects of small classes in the primary grades as students progress through their education (Nye and

Hedges, 2001). Effect sizes for grades 4 to 7 are included in Table 9.3 (Finn, 1998; Mosteller, 1995).[14]

Some of these researchers find a significant effect of small class in eighth grade but not in ninth (Pate-Bain *et al.*, 1997). Two potential explanations are that the test instrument was changed between eighth and ninth grades (aged 9–14 years) and students who scored well on the standardized test in eighth grade were not required to take the test in ninth. Data suggest that a higher percentage of small class students were exempted from the test. Some additional results are that small class students were less likely to have been retained in a grade up to grade nine, were more likely to be taking foreign language and/or advanced classes (suggesting they are more likely to be preparing for college) and experienced fewer suspensions and discipline problems (ibid.). In one county for which data are available, small class students received significantly higher grades in English, mathematics and science, but not in social studies or foreign language. Those from small classes are also less likely to have dropped out of high school (19 per cent for small, 23 per cent for regular and 26 per cent for regular plus aide) and more likely to graduate on schedule (Pate-Bain *et al.*, 1999).

Table 9.3

	Grade 4	Grade 5	Grade 6	Grade 7
Effect size on composite test scores	0.11 to 0.16	0.17 to 0.34	0.14 to 0.26	0.08 to 0.16

Economists have utilized multiple regression analysis with STAR and LBS data to determine the effects of small classes on student performance. These and the ANOVA studies can be compared because both sets of researchers check for significance and calculate an effect size based on standard deviations.

Krueger (1999) uses the composite mathematics and reading SAT-1 test scores as his dependent variable and finds significant positive effects of small classes for kindergarten to third grade. He finds no strong consistent effect of adding an aide to the classroom. He controls for available family background and school characteristics. His effect estimates for small class attendance are 0.20 σ for kindergarten, 0.28 σ for first grade, 0.22 σ for second grade and 0.19 σ for third grade. These effects are somewhat smaller than those found by the principal investigators but they are not calculated separately for reading and mathematics.

In Krueger's study, with data pooled across grades, the increase in scores for small classes persists. Initially the effect is larger for boys, but their cumulative effect is smaller. Black students and those receiving a free lunch have both a larger initial effect and a larger cumulative effect. Inner city students have a more beneficial effect in the first year and a sharper gain.

Krueger and Whitmore (2001) investigate the effect of being in a small class in the primary grades on middle school and college preparation using STAR and LBS data. They find that formerly small class students, both black and white, are more likely to take college entrance exams and that the effect is larger for blacks. This results in a decrease in the gap between the percentages of black and white students taking the exams. Some 43.7 per cent of students from small classes took a college entrance examination, while only 40 per cent of students from regular and regular plus aide classes did so. For blacks, 31.7 per cent took college entrance exams if they experienced regular classes, while 40.2 per cent of those from small classes did. These differences are statistically significant at 5 per cent. After correcting for selection (because of differential retention discussed below), Krueger and Whitmore find that those from small classes have higher college entrance examination scores. For the whole sample the difference is 0.13 standard deviations, for blacks the effect size ranges from 0.20 to 0.26 of a standard deviation.

Problems with STAR
While these results point to significant, positive and lasting effects on students' academic achievement of being in small classes in the primary grades, the STAR study has been criticized on a number of dimensions. Even if the design of the experiment is appropriate to control for selection, there have been issues with implementation.

Random procedures for assignment were mandated but no pre-test was administered so we are unable to assess whether in actuality there are any pre-existing differences in cognitive ability between class types. We also have no data to support the assertion that teachers were randomly assigned. However these criticisms are minor if we accept that the project was implemented in good faith. In addition, since the STAR project is not a double blind experiment, some have speculated that there may be a Hawthorne or Henry effect which biases the results (Hoxby, 2000).

The project was designed to start with kindergarten, but, because kindergarten was not mandatory in Tennessee, a high number of students entered the programme in first grade. These students were randomly assigned across class types but no data on prior treatment were gathered. In other words, we are unsure which of these students had been in private kindergartens the previous year and which had simply skipped this year of schooling.

Not surprisingly, some parents complained about their children's assignments if they were placed in regular classes. The first year of data found no significant difference in performance for students in regular classes or regular plus aide classes; therefore children who had been in regular or regular plus aide classes were randomly reassigned across these two types of classes as they entered first grade. Small class students were not reassigned and other students were not systematically reassigned to small classes.[15] However Krueger (1999) estimates that 10 per cent of students were reassigned between small and regular classes because of behavioural problems or parents' requests. In any case, the reassignment of students complicates the analysis because these students are less likely to remain with the same cohort of peers, which might also have an effect on academic achievement. The issue is also complicated if the effect of small classes is cumulative.

Students remained in the project if and only if they continued with their cohort through school and had observable test scores. Any students who moved to a non-participating school, were retained in a grade, advanced a grade or did not have valid test scores were dropped from the study.[16] Only 48 per cent of students who started the programme in kindergarten remained in the database in third grade (Hanushek, 1999). A substantive issue is whether the attrition in the study was different for students who started in small as opposed to regular classes.

Researchers have argued that it is important to control for school fixed effects because, while students were randomly assigned within schools, schools themselves did not enter the programme randomly. Schools participated voluntarily but had to have enough entering kindergarten students and classroom space to fill at least one class of each type. While 100 schools expressed interest, only 79 were ultimately included in the study. Some 33 per cent of the participating schools' populations was black, while the average across the state was 23 per cent. These schools also had higher than average expenditures per pupil and teacher salaries and slightly lower standardized test scores for second grade mathematics and reading (Hanushek, 1999; Finn and Achilles, 1990).

While acknowledging these potential biases in the data, researchers have tried to estimate whether the results are still valid. Krueger (1999) argues that initial assignments are random because race, gender and socioeconomic status do not explain the assignment to small classes. In addition he claims that reassignments are not a significant problem because only 0.3 per cent of those in the experiment in third grade were not enrolled in a class type to which they were initially assigned. He then investigates whether the reassignments invalidate the results by conducting two stage least squares (2SLS) with initial rather than realized class assignment as the instrument for actual class type. He continues to obtain positive and significant effects of reducing class size. The effect occurs in the first year in a small class, regardless of when a student entered the project.

Several other studies also demonstrate that attrition is different between the small and regular classes. Pate-Bain *et al.* (1997) find that students in small classes are less likely to be retained in a grade up to grade nine, suggesting that low ability students are more likely to remain in the sample if in small classes than otherwise. However, if you calculate the kindergarten effect size for students in the sample in third grade, you find that it is double the kindergarten effect size for the original sample of kindergarteners, suggesting that high achieving students in small classes are more likely to stay in the sample (Hanushek, 1999). Despite this, Krueger (1999) argues that non-random attrition does not significantly affect results. He imputes test scores for students who have dropped from the sample in order to include them and does not find qualitatively different results.

Overall the STAR project data strongly support the hypothesis that students in classes of 15 or fewer students perform better over a long period than those in classes of 22 or more. Not all random experiments have produced such clear evidence in support of reducing class sizes to improve student achievement. We will look at three others, which have mixed results; however, because of the superior design of STAR it is given more weight by researchers.

Other random experiments

Other random experiments were conducted in Toronto, Canada in the early 1970s, in Indiana, USA in 1984 as a prelude to STAR, and in North Carolina, USA in 1991, partly in response to STAR.[17] All three experiments were implemented in the elementary grades, although Toronto's study of fourth and fifth graders used older subjects than the other two or STAR. A variety of class sizes were compared. In Toronto, students and teachers were randomly assigned to classes of 16, 23, 30 and 37. In Indiana, the experiment, known as Prime Time, reduced class size to an average of 18 students, or to 24 students with an instructional assistant, in grades 1 to 3. In North Carolina, students in grades 1 to 3 were evaluated in classes of 15 and 25. The North Carolina study was not a within-school design: four schools were selected to have small classes and seven schools with regular class sizes were matched with these four on the basis of racial composition, socioeconomic background and test scores in the previous year. Only the North Carolina study provides consistent evidence in favour of small classes. Achilles *et al.* (1995), in reviewing the North Carolina initiative, report that students in reduced classes in first and second grade outperform others in reading and mathematics. The effect size estimate, calculated for class standard deviations, is 0.45 σ for mathematics and 0.56 σ for reading after second grade. The class size reductions are similar to those for STAR. In the Toronto study, researchers find no significant differences in achievement for art, composition, vocabulary, reading or mathematics problem solving, although students in small classes did perform better on mathematics concepts (Shapson *et al.*, 1980). In Prime Time, the results for academic achievement are mixed: in some cases, small classes improved performance but in others they did not. Significant problems with study design suggest that these results should be interpreted cautiously (Finn, 1998).

Studies with non-experimental data

Researchers with non-experimental data use a number of approaches to control for the endogeneity and omitted variable problems in estimating the effect of class size on performance. Recall that endogeneity arises both within schools, since students of differing abilities may be sorted into different class sizes, and between schools, since parents may choose schools on the basis of their average class sizes. Approaches to handle this include evaluating 'natural experiments', controlling for a wide array of background variables and employing instrumental variables or fixed effects techniques or some combination of these methods. The results of these studies are often contradictory, highlighting the difficulty in correctly specifying the educational production function with non-random data.

Hoxby (2000), Angrist and Lavy (1997) and Case and Deaton (1999) all take advantage of variation in class size due to exogenous circumstances in various settings to test for the effect of class size on educational outcomes. Hoxby examines the effects of class size on achievement employing a natural experiment combined with the instrumental variables technique. Her outcome measures are the scores on fourth and sixth grade standardized tests in mathematics, reading and writing administered at the beginning of the school year. She uses variation in class size across cohorts resulting from either natural variation in population or mandatory maximums to identify instruments for class size. Using approximately 24 years of enrolment data from the state of Connecticut, USA, she estimates the expected trend in enrolment and identifies a random error, which is correlated with actual enrolment but not with the error associated with the deterministic component of enrolment. This error arises essentially from biology and not from unobservable family or location characteristics that are potentially associated with schooling achievement. Hoxby uses this error as her first instrument for class size. She compares cohorts within schools, which mitigates the school fixed effect, and between-school sorting problems. She estimates the effect of this class size variable on student achievement in the second stage controlling for location, school and cohort characteristics as well as changes in number of classes. Her results suggest, 'The effect of reducing class size is rather precisely estimated to be close to zero' (Hoxby, 2000, p. 1273).

Hoxby also estimates the relationship with another instrument, generated when school districts have a cap on the maximum number of students in a class. This causes a discontinuity in the relationship between enrolment and class size at multiples of the maximum number. For instance, if the maximum class size is 25 and enrolment is 75, then three classes of 25 would result. If, however, enrolment were 80, there would be four classes of only 20 students each. Hoxby identifies instances where crossing over one of these multiples triggers a change in the number of classes in a grade in a school and therefore a difference in class size between cohorts just one grade apart. She then looks at the difference of average achievement across these classes and determines whether differences in class size can explain it.

Hoxby estimates the effect of class size with this second identification strategy using all the instances of changes in number of classes and then with just those changes that occur within a few students of the mandated cap. While she finds a significant effect of reducing classes on mathematics scores in fourth grade, this effect disappears once she refines her sample to relevant discontinuities. Her hypothesis is that the significance is generated by the changes in number of classes related to unobserved factors correlated to student achievement. Hoxby suggests that her results differ from STAR's because in that project teachers, aware of their participation in a study, may have taken advantage of small classes to improve student outcomes more than would occur with random fluctuation. In addition, Hoxby's participants are not in the very early grades, where STAR suggests the most important effect occurs.

Angrist and Lavy (1997) use a similar technique to Hoxby's second identification strategy with Israeli data. Maimonides' Rule specifies that up to 40 students may be taught the Torah in one class. Israeli schools have essentially adopted this rule for all subjects and have an implicit cap on class size of 40. These researchers use the instrumental variables technique to identify the effect of class size on achievement.

Angrist and Lavy use a standard national test for reading and mathematics instituted in 1991 in Israel as their dependent variable. Fourth and fifth graders were tested in the first year. In 1992, third grade students were added.[18] The authors find a significant negative effect of large classes on fifth grade reading and mathematics scores. Scores for fourth graders in small classes were significantly larger in reading but not in mathematics. The size of the effect was smaller for fourth than for fifth graders. Angrist and Lavy detect no significant effect of class size on the scores of third graders. They note that this may be because remedial help was provided to low performing schools between 1991 and 1992 or because class size effects are cumulative.

These researchers calculate the effect size in terms of the class standard deviation and find it to be 0.36 σ for fifth graders and 0.17 σ for fourth graders for class size changes comparable to STAR. When STAR results are calculated with class level standard deviations, the effect size ranges from 0.32 σ to 0.66 σ.

Using data from the end of the apartheid era in South Africa, Case and Deaton (1999) estimate the effect of pupil–teacher ratios on educational attainment, enrolment and test scores. They study the effects on black and white students separately. Data on black students are particularly relevant. Pupil–teacher ratios in black schools varied widely, from 20 to 80 to one. However the problem of selection bias is minimized because of the way education was provided. White administrators made decisions on school funding centrally. Residential location was severely restricted for blacks. While household expenditures and education of the head of household have large, significant effects on children's educational outcomes, these characteristics have no effect on pupil–teacher ratios. Black parents had little control over school quality for their children.

Case and Deaton find that pupil–teacher ratios affect test scores directly and by increasing educational attainment for black students. While the effect of pupil–teacher ratios is insignificant (and positive) for whites, for blacks higher pupil–teacher ratios significantly affect mathematics scores negatively. The effect on literacy scores is also negative but not significant. The authors caution that these results for pupil–teacher ratios really represent an overall level of school resources, since they did not control for other measures of school quality, such as the presence of a library, which are highly correlated with pupil–teacher ratios.

Many researchers have made extensive use of the US National Education Longitudinal Study (NELS)[19] to examine the effect of class size on achievement. The NELS is a particularly rich, nationally representative sample of students, first surveyed and tested as eighth graders in 1988. A subset of these respondents was interviewed again in 1990, 1992, 1994 and 2000. In two of these years they were also retested. Not only students, but also parents, teachers and school administrators, were interviewed. Students reported on a range of topics, including school, work and home experiences; educational resources and support; the role in education of their parents and peers; neighbourhood characteristics; educational and occupational aspirations; and other student perceptions. An advantage of this data set is the ability to use actual class size rather than pupil–teacher ratios. A drawback is the middle school age of the students since some research indicates that effects of small class sizes are most effective in the early grades.

Goldhaber and Brewer (1997) use the NELS to investigate the effects of schooling inputs (including class size) on student achievement. They

motivate their research by noting that the inconsistent findings from previous research that estimated educational production functions suffered from
omitted variable bias, in that crude measures of teacher quality and schooling inputs were often used. Leaving out key measures of teacher quality
and schooling meant that parameter estimates for included variables were
often biased. They note that there are two possible solutions, fixed effects
and random effects estimation, although neither is perfect. The random
effects estimator relies on the assumption that the random effect, which
may reflect heterogeneity across schools or teachers, is uncorrelated with
included variables (family background, individual characteristics, school
and teacher characteristics), while the fixed effect estimator will not allow
you to recover estimates of the effect of fixed school variables (often of
primary interest) if you differentiate across schools.

Goldhaber and Brewer use data from three years of the NELS (1988,
1990 and 1992) with test scores measured in the eighth and tenth grades.[20]
They use a rich set of controls for teacher ability, including teacher's education and certification, as well as a set of variables that control for teacher
behaviours. They also make use of a rich set of individual-level controls,
including a previous test score to control for student ability.

As we noted earlier, they document a positive and statistically significant
effect of class size on tenth grade scores using OLS. This effect remains even
after controlling for a broad array of family background and school characteristics, again indicating the endogeneity of class size. They then estimate both school fixed effects and teacher fixed effects models. The school
fixed effects models control for the notion that better schools might also be
those that have small classes. If there is something systematic and unobservable about these better schools, the fixed effects estimator will account
for the unobservable factor or factors. The teacher fixed effects models
control for unobserved differences in teacher quality. However neither of
these methods controls for the non-random sorting into smaller classes that
occurs within schools. Nor do they control for the fact that highly educated
and motivated parents may find the best schools for their children and that
is often reflective of smaller classes. Thus it is no surprise that, in their fixed
and random effects specifications, the effect of class size remains positive
and significant: they have not captured the *ceteris paribus* effect of class size
on achievement. They do find that there does not appear to be any bias
from failing to control for teacher or school unobservables.

Akerhielm (1995) uses data from the 1988 NELS with test results for
eighth graders in mathematics, science, English and history to estimate the
educational production function. She is primarily concerned with the endogeneity that arises if schools assign less able students to smaller classes. Her
OLS results confirm her hypothesis that there is non-random sorting by

ability into smaller classes because she finds that students in smaller classes have lower test scores, all else equal. Her solution is to use two stage least squares (2SLS) and instrument class size.

Akerhielm uses two instruments for actual class size: the average class size for a given subject in the student's school and the eighth grade enrolment in the school. She argues that the average class size variable is exogenous because it is an aggregate, so within-school non-random allocation of students is no longer an issue. The total enrolment of eighth graders in a school is also argued to be exogenous to an individual student in part because larger schools are more likely to allocate their students in a non-random way because they have the resources to do so. Her 2SLS results indicate that, once the endogeneity of class size is taken into account, the effect of class size on student achievement changes from positive to negative for all outcomes and in two cases (science and history) the results are statistically significant, indicating that there are returns to investing in smaller classes for some students. She finds the effect is larger for non-white students and splines show that the effect of class size is not independent of the level of class size and that there are non-linearities in the effects of class size. Her results indicate that studies which find no effect may not be looking at a range of change that matters. Decreasing class size from 25 to 15 in history and science would improve students' scores by 0.7 and 0.8 of a point, respectively.

However, as in all cases where instrumental variables are used, the validity of the findings depends on the strength of the instruments. In particular, Akerhielm's findings depend on the assumption that school size does not affect achievement. In other words, smaller schools do not have an advantage in educating students. Some have questioned her instruments because of this assumption (Pong and Pallas, 2001). The performance of her instruments is mixed. She finds that eighth grade enrolment is not significant but the average class size variables are very statistically significant. She does not report joint significance of her instruments; however, with the strong performance of the average class size variable, it is likely that they are jointly significant. She does not perform other standard tests of her instruments such as an overidentification restrictions test to ascertain whether or not the instruments can legitimately be excluded from the second stage. However, a Hausman specification test indicates that the OLS and 2SLS results are statistically different and that class size is not exogenous. Also she does not have a prior test score to control for individual ability, although she does control for family background. Finally, although her IV approach does control for within-school sorting, it does not control for between-school sorting, although this too is somewhat controlled for by including family background characteristics in the model.

In addition, while she controls for teacher quality using years of teaching experience, she does not use other measures of teacher quality available in NELS in her model. This is problematic if teachers are systematically assigned to either large or small classes depending upon their own abilities. Principals may use high-quality teachers in large classes to accommodate the size or they may assign the best teachers to remedial or advanced classes with fewer students. In either scenario, it is possible that the coefficient on class size is biased by this omission. For example, Goldhaber and Brewer (1997) note that conclusions about whether or not teachers matter for student performance are sensitive to the teacher quality controls included in the model.

Boozer and Rouse (1995) use data from the NELS to examine whether or not differences in school quality can help explain the black/white wage gap. They note that, on the surface, using pupil–teacher ratios, the schools that blacks and whites attend appear to be similar in quality. However, as we know, pupil–teacher ratios are a problematic proxy for class size. When they examine actual class size Boozer and Rouse find that blacks attend schools with larger class sizes. Furthermore, OLS regressions reveal a positive and significant effect of class size on test scores for tenth and twelfth graders.

They then re-estimate the educational production function and instrument class size with a measure of state special education policy. They justify this instrument choice by noting that special education has become increasingly important in US school systems. Special needs classes are roughly half the size of regular classes. Actual class size will be correlated with the state regulations to the extent that schools base the entire structure of their class sizes on such state policy. Their instruments are jointly significant, suggesting that they are good predictors of class size, although the authors note that their results are only suggestive since their instruments did not pass a test of overidentification. The instrumental variable estimates indicate that the effect of class size is generally negative and significant, indicating both that students are not randomly assigned to classes and that students in larger classes perform less well on standardized tests. They also run a first differenced version of the educational production function, which will control for any time-invariant individual level heterogeneity. Such estimates do not, however, control for within-school sorting or between-school sorting. In fact, they note that these results are very similar to the OLS results.

For Britain, a particularly rich source of data is the National Child Development Study (NCDS), a longitudinal study of students born in March 1958. Originally conceived as a perinatal mortality study, the first wave of data, collected shortly after the subjects' birth, contains detailed medical and socioeconomic histories of their families. Further data were collected when the subjects were seven, 11, 16, 23, 33 and 42 years of age. The studies between ages seven and 16 contain information on educational attainment, schooling, health and family circumstances, including socioeconomic status and parental attitudes about education. An actual class size measure is available. One drawback is that, unlike the NELS, little information is available about teacher quality.

Iacovou (2001) reports that evidence from NCDS suggests that less able students are assigned to smaller classes, so there is an endogeneity problem with using class size itself. She creates an interactive variable of school type multiplied by school size to use as an instrumental variable class size.

In Britain there are two types of schools for young students, infant schools and combined schools. Infant schools include only children aged five to seven, while combined schools have age ranges from five to 11. Iacovou finds a significant difference in class sizes for infant and combined schools at age seven but not at age 11. Combined schools have significantly smaller class sizes at these young ages. Thus she argues, 'Although it is quite likely that both the size and type of school are related to student outcomes, the interaction between these two variables may be used as an exogenous instrument for class size' (Iacovou, 2001, p. 17). She argues that this interaction is a valid instrument as long as it is related to class size but not to student achievement. The latter will be true if being in a large school (or a small school) has the same effect on performance regardless of whether the school is an infant or a combined school and the effect of being in an infant or a combined school does not vary according to whether the school is large or small.

Iacovou finds that, for reading scores, class size is not significant in OLS but it is significant in instrumental variables equations. This is true under a number of specifications. The results are large: scores increase by 0.288 standard deviations for a reduction in class size of eight pupils, but not out of line with those found by other researchers. However no relationship between class size and mathematics scores emerges under either OLS or instrumental variables specifications. Perhaps it is harder to explain mathematics attainment than reading or perhaps the mathematics test was a poor one to measure attainment. Interestingly all groups got the same benefit of smaller class sizes for reading and all got no help in mathematics. This contradicts much of the US evidence that disadvantaged children are helped more by small classes. For the whole sample there is no evidence that the test score advantages persist to age 11; however there is persistence for girls (both reading and mathematics) and children from larger families (mathematics).

One shortcoming of Iacovou's analysis is that she drops observations in very small (<20) or very large (>45) classes. If the presence of a class size effect is only seen in very small classes (such as was suggested by Glass and Smith, 1979), then this effect will not show up in her sample. In her data, the average class size is slightly above 35. Since the NCDS data do not contain measures of teacher quality, Iacovou faces the same problem of bias that Akerhielm encounters, omitted variable bias to her class size coefficients. In addition Iacovou, like Akerhielm, focuses on within-school sorting but does not address between-school sorting or individual ability except by controlling for family background.

Others have also used the NCDS data to examine the class size and achievement link. Feinstein and Symons (1999) estimate a value added model for reading and mathematics attainment at age 16, controlling for reading and mathematics attainment at age 11. They note that, since a test score inevitably contains measurement error, some instrumentation is required. Like Iacovou, they are concerned about the endogeneity of class size: they too note that in Britain it is apparent from the NCDS data that the brightest students are placed in the largest classes and that inner-urban schools tend to have lower pupil–teacher ratios. They also use an instrumental variables approach but their instruments are local education authority variables, which Iacovou argues are likely correlated with achievement. Perhaps this is why, in contrast to Iacovou, they find no effect of class size on student achievement.

The international database of the Third International Mathematics and Science Study (TIMSS) is a rich source of international data. The TIMSS database provides data on representative samples of students in three distinct populations: nine-year-olds, 13-year-olds and those enrolled in their final year of secondary school from about 40 countries. Students completed standardized tests in mathematics and science. In addition extensive background information was gathered through student, teacher and school principal questionnaires. Each country was to gather information for a sample of at least 150 schools. While not all countries met this goal, some, such as Canada, gathered data from over twice as many schools.

Pong and Pallas (2001) use the TIMSS data, from a select group of countries (USA, Canada, Australia, France, Germany, Hong Kong, Iceland, Korea and Singapore) to study the effects of class size. They run hierarchical linear models (HLM)[21] separately by country. HLM models are able to account for the fact that observations are not independent if they are nested within families, classrooms, schools or districts.

In their models that only control for student-level variables and do not account for the non-random sorting of students into classes, there is a significant, positive effect of class size for Australia, Hong Kong, Korea, Singapore and France. In the other countries, the effect of class size is either positive and insignificant or negative and insignificant. However the authors acknowledge that these results are most likely spurious. To deal with this, they control for various factors correlated with class size directly in the educational production function. In particular they control for students' socioeconomic status and teachers' evaluations of classroom ability to control for individual ability. (They do not use a previous test score as a control for ability.) Furthermore there is evidence that whether or not a student is in a large class depends on the size of the school, so they control for the size of the school. [22] When they enter these variables into their HLM model, they find that class size is not linearly associated with mathematics achievement in any of the countries they study.

However they also allow the effect of class size to be non-linear, using three groups: the quintile of classrooms that has the fewest number of students, the next 60 per cent and the quintile of classrooms with the greatest number of students. When they enter class size non-linearly, they find no significant effects, with the following exceptions. First, in Hong Kong and Singapore the best performing students are in the largest classes. These are both highly centralized educational systems, which Pong and Pallas theorize may explain the positive effect of larger classes on achievement. Second, by way of contrast, in the USA, the most decentralized educational system, they find that those in the very smallest classes actually perform the best. These non-linear effects for Hong Kong and the USA disappear when they add controls for curriculum and instruction but they emphasize that these curricular controls are very crude.

A more recent study that makes use of the TIMSS data is that of Woessmann and West (2002), who use data from 18 educational systems around the world. As reported earlier, they too find that, when OLS is applied, class size is often positive and statistically significant. They posit a unique identification strategy to deal with both within-school and between-school sorting issues. The authors adopt what they call a 'quasi-experimental' approach where they use instrumental variables estimates to restrict the analysis to using only that portion of variation in class size that is truly exogenous to student achievement. They remove that portion that is due to the non-random sorting.

Although the TIMSS data have information on some 40 countries, only 18 of them had rich enough data for Woessmann and West to be able to apply them to this analysis. Their analysis requires test scores for a student at two different times and information on two different classes from each school. They eliminate between-school sorting (Tiebout sorting) by controlling for school fixed effects with a dummy variable for each school. However there may still be within-school sorting going on as long as schools have more than one class per grade. School fixed effects will not eliminate this type of non-random sorting. The authors eliminate within school-sorting by replacing actual class sizes with the average class size in the relevant grade at each respective school. They argue that the remaining variation, which is variation in class size between classes at different grades of a school, and presumably reflects natural fluctuations in student enrolment, is random. It is this random variation that identifies the causal effect of class size on student performance. Thus their paper improves upon the work of Akerhielm and of Goldfarber and Brewer by essentially combining both of their strategies. Their instrument for class size is one of the instruments that Akerhielm used, namely the average class size at the respective grade level of the school. They argue that this variable is highly correlated with actual class size: given school staffing rigidities, schools usually do not have the flexibility to allocate class size resources across grades in response to differences in the performance level of adjacent classes. They also argue that it is uncorrelated with the error term; that is, that it is not likely it affects achievement in any other way than through its effect on their actual class size.

The authors' estimation results indicate that there is no clear pattern of whether or when class size affects achievement. For most countries they find no significant effect of class size on mathematics or science test scores. They find significant benefits to smaller classes for mathematics in France and Iceland and for science in Greece and Spain. Portuguese data suggest a positive relationship between class size and mathematics scores. Greece and Iceland benefit from small classes but are not particularly effective systems; their students do not perform well overall on these tests and their low teacher salaries may be an indicator that their teachers are of lower ability than those in other countries. One hypothesis is that low-quality teachers only perform well in a small class environment and are not able to perform as well in a larger class environment. Furthermore the authors find no clear relationship between GDP and class size effects, ruling out the possibility that class size effects are a resource issue. They conclude, 'Smaller classes have an observable beneficial effect on student achievement only in countries where the average capability of the teaching force appears to be low' (p. 29).

A number of studies have found that there may be differences in the way class size affects students according to characteristics of the students themselves. Some researchers, including Levin (2001) and Eide and Showalter (1998), have addressed this issue by evaluating subsamples of the population, based on level of achievement. Levin (2001) uses data from the Dutch PRIMA study, a longitudinal survey containing information on Dutch pupils who were enrolled in grades 2, 4, 6 and 8 in the 1994/5 school year. Levin uses the data for children in grades 4, 6 and 8, as the class information in grade 2 is unreliable. This survey is very rich, like the NELS and the NCDS, and has many variables measured at the pupil, class and school levels. It includes teacher experience and total enrolment of the school, among other class and school-level controls. The author also has a measure of actual class size but, like others, recognizes the endogeneity problem generated by running OLS regressions of achievement on test scores. Thus an instrumental variables approach is used.

The approach is similar to that used by Angrist and Lavy (1999). The Dutch Ministry of Education links total school enrolment (weighted by socioeconomic status of the student body) to the number of teachers for which a school receives funding. Thus Levin knows for each school exactly how many teachers the ministry has authorized and uses this to construct the predicted average class size, calculated as total school enrolment divided by the predicted number of allocated teachers, using the ministerial rules. Class size is found to be positively and significantly related to eighth grade mathematics and language scores.

However Levin notes that this result applies to the *average* student. In order to discern whether the effect of class size varies by the ability of the student, Levin runs quantile 2SLS regression models by examining students at the 10th, 25th, 50th, 75th and 90th quantiles of achievement. Levin finds that, other than eighth graders at the 50th percentile, where there is a positive and significant effect of class size on mathematics and language, there is absolutely no evidence that class size affects achievement. The advantage of the quantile regression procedure is that it allows the researcher to examine whether or not class size matters at different points in the achievement distribution. Thus the quantile regressions answer the question about who really benefits from a class size reduction.

Eide and Showalter (1998) also evaluate by quantiles when examining the effect of school quality (including class size) on achievement. They use US data from the 'High School and Beyond' survey, which is a survey of students who were sophomores in public high schools in 1980 and who finished their secondary education at that same school. This study examines students at the 5th, 25th, 50th, 75th and 95th achievement quantiles. Their measure of class size is the pupil–teacher ratio, which, as discussed earlier, is not the ideal measure. Furthermore the focus of their paper is not on class size per se, so they do not control the endogeneity of class size. They do have a wide array of family background controls as well as class, school and district-level control variables. OLS results reveal no effect of class size on achievement and the quantile regression results concur with this.

Finally, Behrman *et al.* (2002) collect detailed data on education variables in rural Pakistan to measure the effect of pupil–teacher ratios on students' test scores. This data set is unique in that data on the ability of students and teachers, family background variables, schooling characteristics and local wages are available. The researchers find that lowering pupil–teacher ratios by 10 per cent raises the predicted reading score by 2 per cent and the predicted mathematics score by 1 per cent. They conclude that, while it is still important to increase access to primary schools in developing countries, improving the quality of primary schools may be a better investment than increasing access to middle school edcuation.

Meta-analyses

We look at a number of meta-analyses chronologically, beginning with the seminal work of Glass and Smith (1979). These authors try to identify any significant effect of class size on student achievement by jointly analysing individual studies performed from 1902 to 1979. Their improvement over previous summaries was an extensive literature review (including not only published studies but also dissertations) and the use of quantitative along with qualitative methods.

Their final analysis includes approximately 80 studies, about 45 per cent of which were released between 1910 and 1929, and another 45 per cent after 1950. The studies covered a wide range of subjects, including tennis (a frequent criticism is the inclusion of several non-academic subjects). Roughly half of the studies used data on elementary school children and the other half on secondary school children. There were a few studies on college age individuals. In 15.2 per cent of the studies, assignments to class sizes were random, but fully half of the studies had no selection controls. Glass and Smith construct the effect size of small classes as the difference in the means of the scores for students in small and large classes divided by the standard deviation for the class. They then estimated the fit of the following model:

$$\Delta_{S-L} = \beta_0 + \beta_1 S + \beta_2 S^2 + \beta_3 (L - S) + \varepsilon$$

where $\Delta_{S-L} = \overline{(X_S - X_L / \sigma)}$, Xs are the mean test scores, S is the size of the small class and L is the size of the large class. The results are consistent: as the number of students in a small class increases, the advantage declines, but at a decreasing rate, and, as the difference in class size increases, so does the small class advantage.

While the overall effect size is one-tenth of a standard deviation, the measured effect sizes for a variety of class sizes are shown in Table 9.4. For instance, if we compare classes of 10 and 40 students, the students in the smaller class would score 0.268σ higher on average than the students in the larger class. The authors conclude that class size differences at the low end of the scale are important, while those at the high end are not. Essentially classes above 30 are all similar. Several other findings are significant. In contrast to recent studies, Glass and Smith find a greater effect at the secondary than at the elementary school level. Research conducted before 1940 shows no significant relationship between class size and student achievement, while those studies dated after 1940 find a strong relationship. Studies that employ random assignment of students are much more likely to find a significant relationship than those which do not control for assignment. The authors argue that the studies with random assignment are superior to others.

Table 9.4

Small class size	Large class size	Effect size
1	40	0.565
10	40	0.268
20	40	0.051
30	40	−0.048
1	25	0.552
5	25	0.409
10	25	0.256
15	25	0.133
20	25	0.039

Glass and Smith conclude that 'there is little doubt that, other things equal, more is learned in smaller classes'. However their conclusion was not universally accepted. In 1980, the Educational Research Service (ERS) released a critique of this meta-analysis. While the ERS do find that small classes could increase student achievement in the early primary grades, classes must be very small to do so. They find no significant differences in classes ranging from 25 to 34 students. Students of lower ability or from socially or economically disadvantaged backgrounds appear to be helped more than other students (Cooper, 1989).

Hedges and Stock (1983) undertook to re-evaluate the sample of studies used by Glass and Smith, but applied what they argue are more optimal techniques. Their primary criticisms are that Glass and Smith used a biased estimate of the effect size and employed OLS. In the case of studies with small sample sizes, the positive effect of treatment had been overstated. The use of OLS gives equal weight to 'good' and 'poor' estimates. Hedges and Stock (1983, p. 68)[23] conclude that the overall results found by Glass and Smith hold, but the magnitude of the effect is somewhat smaller than predicted.

Robert Slavin (1989) disagrees, stating, 'Not until class size approaches one is there evidence of meaningful effects.' Slavin's primary complaint is that Glass and Smith include a wide range of studies, many of which are irrelevant to the actual policy question of whether reducing class size is an effective means of improving student performance. Focusing on a subset of the Glass and Smith studies which employ randomized assignment or initial controls for student quality, Slavin finds extremely small effects of class size on achievement. The same holds when he reduces the sample to those studies dealing with elementary schools. He concludes that the class size effects are consistent but small in kindergarten to third grade, slight in fourth to eighth and non-existent in ninth to twelfth grade. Multi-year studies find no cumulative effect. Slavin argues that more dramatic effects are realized with one-to-one tutoring of low-performing students.

Hanushek (1986, 1989, 1995, 1997, 1998, 2003) has conducted extensive meta-analyses on the issue of the relationship between class size (and other resources) and student achievement. He includes studies conducted between the early 1960s and 1994. His inclusion criteria are that a study must be published in a book or journal, include some measure of family background and provide information about the statistical significance of the estimates. The 1997 and 1998 meta-analyses include 90 publications and 377 studies, defined as any separate estimate of the education production function. Of these, 277 included an estimate of the teacher–pupil ratio. Hanushek's technique is primarily one of 'vote counting'. Table 9.5 displays the percentage of studies that find either positive or negative relationships and whether they are significant.

He argues that no significant relationship emerges from these data between teacher–pupil ratio and student outcomes. Even when elementary

Table 9.5

Teacher–pupil ratio	Number of estimates	Statistically Significant		Statistically Insignificant		
		Positive (%)	Negative (%)	Positive (%)	Negative (%)	Unknown sign (%)
All schools	277	15	13	27	25	20
Elementary schools	136	13	20	25	20	23
Secondary schools	141	17	7	28	31	17
All schools–value added	78	12	8	21	26	35
Studies of developing countries	30	27	27	NA	NA	47

schools are evaluated separately, to address whether younger students receive the gain, he finds no consistent effect. Hanushek argues that studies based on a value-added measure of student performance are preferable because they partially control for endogeneity. The value-added subset in this table suggests no relationship emerges from an analysis of these studies. Finally his analysis of studies involving developing countries shows that almost half of the studies find no significant effect and the studies that are significant are divided equally between positive and negative findings. He concludes that the weight of the evidence shows no consistent positive effect of reducing class size on student outcomes.

Several researchers have criticized Hanushek's analyses and conclusions. Hedges *et al.* (1994)[24] argue that Hanushek's 'vote counting' technique is inappropriate. These authors employ combined significance tests to see whether or not we can reject the null hypotheses of no positive and/or no negative relationship between class size and student outcomes. They use combined estimation methods to evaluate the magnitude of the effect. Hedges *et al.* use the same evidence as Hanushek except where there was not enough information (for instance, if the study concluded there was an insignificant effect but did not report the sign). The authors conducted their analysis on the whole sample of studies, on a subset of studies they deemed 'independent' (by grouping estimates that are possibly correlated together), on a sample which excludes the top and bottom 10 per cent, and finally on a sample excluding the single most influential study.

Their results are that a significant number of studies show positive achievement gains for small classes, regardless of the sample. A significant number of negative results arise from the whole sample, but not other samples. Combined estimates effects are decidedly mixed, revealing a pattern of both positive and negative effects. The authors hypothesize that this may be because fewer data are available to evaluate the estimates than to evaluate the significance. They find stronger evidence in support of the positive effect of schooling resources other than pupil–teacher ratio, such as per pupil expenditures and teacher experience, on student achievement.

These authors and Krueger (2003) also argue that the data set compiled by Hanushek is itself problematic. A number of studies did not include sufficient information on insignificant results to be included. Studies from the early 1960s may no longer be relevant to education policy today. Some of the studies, particularly older ones, include very weak measures of family background. Most of the studies are cross-sectional and therefore it is difficult to control for school fixed effects. Hanushek has suggested that there may be publication bias in favour of finding a strong relationship; however, Hedges *et al.* (1994) argue that it is unclear in which direction the publication bias is pointing.

Krueger (2003) complains that Hanushek includes all of the estimates in a publication, which gives undue weight to studies that calculate multiple estimates, perhaps with subsamples, which are less valuable. In addition he implies there may be some favouritism in terms of studies included; and, in some cases, the studies incorporate class size only as a control, and it is not the focus of the study. When Krueger re-analyses the data by reassigning the weights of the estimates he obtains the results shown in Table 9.6.

Table 9.6

Results	Hanushek's weights	Studies equally weighted	Studies weighted by journal impact factor	Regression adjusted weights
Positive and significant	14.8%	25.5%	34.5%	33.5%
Positive and insignificant	26.7%	27.1%	21.2%	27.3%
Negative and significant	13.4%	10.3%	6.9%	8.0%
Negative and insignificant	25.3%	23.1%	25.4%	21.5%
Unknown sign and insignificant	19.9%	14.0%	12.0%	9.6%
Ratio of positive to negative	1.07	1.57	1.72	2.06
P-value	0.500	0.059	0.034	0.009

Only in the first column does the p-value suggest that there is not a relationship. Krueger's results suggest that class size reductions can have a significant effect on student outcomes. He goes on to calculate an internal rate of return to investing in class size reductions and finds a 6 per cent return on reductions of seven students. He uses future wage increases to evaluate benefits.

Policy implications and conclusions

In this chapter we have surveyed the immense literature on class size and student achievement as measured by test scores. Our goal has been to review the empirical work as well as the underlying theory and methodological issues that arise when one tries to get at the causal impact of class size on student test achievement. We have not discussed other potential benefits arising from reduced classes, such as increased future wages or improved student and teacher morale, in detail.

There is no definitive answer to the questions of whether and by how much reducing class size increases student performance. However, when examining those studies that carefully control for the endogeneity of class size brought on by the non-random sorting that takes place both between schools and within schools, the weight of the evidence indicates to us that smaller classes do result in higher student achievement for some students and some classes. Despite this, it is unclear whether the cost of implementing class size reductions is justified by the benefits or whether there are other uses of resources that may be more effective in improving student outcomes.

Widescale implementation of class size reductions also raises other issues. While small-scale experiments may not have a significant effect on the demand for resources (and therefore the price of these resources), this may not be true on a larger scale. The increased demand for teachers could result in deterioration of average teacher quality, offsetting any small class gains, and an increase in average teacher salaries, imposing even more cost on school districts. In addition classrooms and facilities may be scarce, compelling districts to utilize less desirable locations for teaching or to construct new ones. The class size reduction initiative implemented in the state of California in 1996 has resulted in significant teacher shortages and some districts, particularly poor ones, have been forced to hire teachers with lower credentials, suggesting that these concerns are legitimate, at least in the short-term, before teacher education policies can compensate (Bohrnstedt and Stecher, 2002; Brewer *et al.*, 1999). Policy makers need to incorporate these limitations, as well as the potential benefits, of small classes not revealed through student test scores into their decision-making processes.

Notes

1. For example, in the USA by 1998, at least 19 states had initiated some sort of class size reduction measure. See ECS (1998). However the cost of such measures is high and a recent article in the *Los Angeles Times* reported that many states are backing away from such measures (Hayasaki, 2002).
2. See for instance Card and Krueger (1992) and Betts (1995).
3. We discuss the TIMSS in more detail later in the chapter.
4. A simple OLS regression (not shown here) of test score on class size yields a positive and statistically significant coefficient for both mathematics and science scores.
5. Picus (1999) and Hanushek (1998) present and discuss the time series evidence on achievement in the USA in more detail. Specifics are also available at http://nces.ed.gov/pubs98/yi/yi30.pdf.
6. For more discussion, see Hedges and Greenwald (1996).
7. See http://nces.ed.gov/nationsreportcard/about/.
8. Alternatively some researchers model the change in test scores rather than the level of test score. See Todd and Wolpin (2003) for a discussion of the problems with these approaches.
9. If studies look at students across districts, some with and some without class size caps, selection is still an issue.
10. Todd and Wolpin (2003) discuss the differences between adding a lagged value of a test score as an independent variable and using the difference of the two scores as the dependent variable. Assumptions needed to make either approach valid are detailed.
11. In some cases only a previous test measure and not the difference is available.

12. Project STAR was conducted by a consortium of people from the Tennessee State Department of Education, STAR staff, four universities, representatives from the State Board of Education and the State Superintendents' Association, as well as several outside consultants. Further data collection and research has been funded by the state and by outside groups including the National Education Association and the American Federation of Teachers. The Lasting Benefits Study (LBS) has been conducted by the Center of Excellence for Research in Basic Skills at Tennessee State University.
13. An inner city school in these data is defined as a metropolitan school with at least 50 per cent of its student population eligible for subsidized lunch. Suburban schools are the remaining schools in the metropolitan area. Urban schools are in a district in a town of more than 2500 students. All other schools are considered rural. Approximately 22.7 per cent of the sample is in inner city schools, 12.2 per cent in urban, 18.5 per cent in suburban and 46.5 per cent in rural (Finn and Achilles, 1990).
14. The fact that these effect sizes change as the distance from the treatment changes implies that using a lagged test score as an independent variable or a differenced test score as the dependent variable may not be accurate since this assumes either the same effect over time or an effect that declines by the same amount for each time period. See Todd and Wolpin (2003).
15. After this year, project administrators were convinced that these reassignments could have a negative impact on the project design and it was not undertaken in future years.
16. Between 3 per cent and 12 per cent of students did not complete the test in any given year.
17. Robert Slavin (1989) lists a number of earlier experimental studies, which we do not discuss here.
18. The test was discontinued after 1992, possibly because of the poor effects on student achievement.
19. For more information, see http://nces.ed.gov/surveys/nels88/.
20. The authors control for unobserved ability, in part, by including the eighth grade test score as a control measure.
21. The HLM technique essentially performs regressions on a set of submodels grouped by the level of observation. This avoids the problem of interdependence across the observations of students in the same class or school. See Bryk and Raudenbush (1992) for details.
22. Akerhielm (1995) used school size as an instrument for class size but Pong and Pallas (2001) argue against that variable as an instrument, citing evidence that school size has been found to have a direct impact on student achievement, invalidating the assumption necessary for school size to be an appropriate instrument for class size.
23. A detailed technical discussion is included in their article.
24. See also Greenwald *et al.* (1996).

References

Achilles, C.M., P. Harman and P. Egelson (1995), 'Using research results on class size to improve pupil achievement outcomes', *Research in the Schools*, **2** (2), 23–30.
Akerhielm, Karen (1995), 'Does class size matter?', Economics of Education Review, **14** (3), 229–41.
Angrist, Joshua D. and Victor Lavy (1999), 'Using Maimondides' rule to estimate the effect of class size on scholastic achievement', *Quarterly Journal of Economics*, 533–75.
Argys, Laura M. and Daniel I. Rees (1995), 'Unionization and school productivity: a reexamination', *Research in Labor Economics*, **14**, 49–68.
Behrman, Jere, David Ross and Richard Sabot (2002), 'Improving the quality versus increasing the quantity of schooling: evidence in rural Pakistan', mimeo.
Betts, Julian R. (1995), 'Does school quality matter? Evidence from the national longitudinal survey of youth', *The Review of Economics and Statistics*, **77** (2), 231–50.
Blatchford, Peter and Peter Mortimore (1994), 'The issue of class size for young children in schools: what can we learn from the research?', Oxford Review of Education, **20** (4).

Bohrnstedt, George and Brian Stecher (2002), 'What we have learned from class size reductions in California', California Department of Education, Sacramento, CA.

Boozer, Michael and Cecilia Rouse (1995), 'Intraschool variation in class size: patterns and implications', NBER Working Paper 5144.

Brewer, Dominic, Cathy Krop, Brian Gill and Robert Reichardt (1999), 'Estimating the cost of national class size reductions under different policy alternatives', *Educational Evaluation and Policy Analysis*, **21** (2), 179–92.

Bryk, Anthony S. and Stephen W. Raudenbush (1992), *Hierarchical Linear Models: Applications and Data Analysis Methods*, Newbury Park, CA: Sage Publications.

Card, David and Alan B. Krueger (1992), 'Does school quality matter? Returns to education and the characteristics of public schools in the United States', *The Journal of Political Economy*, **100** (1), 1–40.

Case, Anne and Angus Deaton (1999), 'School inputs and educational outcomes in South Africa', *Quarterly Journal of Economics*, **114** (3), 1047–84.

Coleman, James S. (1966), *Equality of Educational Opportunity*, Washington, DC: U.S. Government Printing Office.

Cooper, H.M. (1989), 'Does reducing student to instructor ratios affect achievement?', Educational Psychologist, **24**, 79–98.

Correa, Hector (1993), 'An economic analysis of class size and achievement in education', *Education Economics*, **1** (2), 129–35.

ECS (1998), 'Class size reduction measures', Education Commission of the States, Information Clearinghouse.

Eide, E. and M. Showalter (1998), 'The effect of school quality on student performance: a quantile regression approach', *Economics Letters*, **58**, 345–50.

Feinstein L. and J. Symons (1999), 'Attainment in secondary school', *Oxford Economic Papers*, **51**, 300–321.

Finn, J. (1998), 'Class size and students at risk: what is known? What is next?', Department of Education, Washington, DC.

Finn, Jeremy D. and Charles M. Achilles (1990), 'Answers and questions about class size: a statewide experiment', *American Educational Research Journal*, **27** (3), 557–77.

Finn, Jeremy D., Charles M. Achilles, Helen Pate-Bain, John Folger, John M. Johnston, M. Lintz and Elizabeth R. Word, (1990), 'Three years in a small class', *Teaching and Teacher Education*, **6** (2),127–36.

Glass, Gene V. and Mary Lee Smith (1979), 'Meta-analysis of research on class size and achievement', *Educational Evaluation and Policy Analysis*, **1** (1), 2–16.

Goldhaber, D.D. and D.J. Brewer (1997), 'Why don't schools and teachers seem to matter? Assessing the impact of unobservables on educational productivity', *Journal of Human Resources*, **32**, 505–23.

Greenwald, Rob, Larry V. Hedges and Richard D. Laine (1996), 'The effect of school resources on student achievement', *Review of Educational Research*, **66** (3), 361–96.

Grissmer, David W., Sheila Nataraj Kirby, Mark Berends and Stephanie Williamson (1994), 'Student achievement and the changing American family: an executive summary', RAND/MR-535–LE.

Grogger, Jeffrey T. (1996), 'Does school quality explain the recent black/white wage trend?', *Journal of Labor Economics*, **14** (2), 231–53.

Hanushek, Eric A. (1986), 'The economics of schooling: production and efficiency in public schools', *Journal of Economic Literature*, **24** (3), 1141–77.

Hanushek, Eric A. (1989), 'The impact of differential expenditures on school performance', *Educational Researcher*, **18** (4), 45–51.

Hanushek, Eric A. (1995), 'Interpreting recent research on schooling in developing countries', *The World Bank Research Observer*, **10** (2), 227–46.

Hanushek, Eric A. (1996), 'The economics of schooling: production and efficiency in public schools', *Journal of Economic Literature*, **24** (3), 1141–77.

Hanushek, Eric A. (1997), 'Assessing the effects of school resources on student performance: an update', *Educational Evaluation and Policy Analysis*, **19** (2), 141–64.

Hanushek, Eric A. (1998), 'The evidence on class size', W. Allen Wallis Institute of Political Economy Working Paper, University of Rochester.

Hanushek, Eric A. (1999), 'Some findings from an independent investigation of the Tennessee STAR experiment and from other investigations of class size effects', mimeo, Stanford University.

Hanushek, Eric A. (2003), 'The failure of input-based schooling policies', *Economic Journal*, **113**, F64–F98.

Hanushek, Eric A. and Javier A. Luque (2003), 'Efficiency and equity in schools around the world', *Economics of Education Review*, **20** (4).

Hanushek, Eric A., Steven G. Rivkin and Lori L. Taylor (1996), 'Aggregation and the estimated effects of school resources', *The Review of Economics and Statistics*, **78** (4), 611–27.

Hayasaki, Erika (2002), 'Class-size reduction initiatives faltering', *The Los Angeles Times*, 18 May.

Hedges, Larry and R. Greenwald (1996), 'Have times changed? The relation between school resources and student performances', in Gary Burtless (ed.), *Does Money Matter?*, Washington, DC: The Brookings Institution, pp. 74–92.

Hedges, Larry, Richard Laine and Rob Greenwald (1994), 'Does money matter? A meta-analysis of studies of the effects of differential school inputs on student outcomes', *Educational Researcher*, **23** (3), 5–14.

Hedges, Larry V. and William Stock (1983), 'The effects of class size: an examination of rival hypotheses', *American Educational Research Journal*, **20** (1), 63–85.

Hoxby, Caroline M. (2000), 'The effects of class size and composition on student achievement: new evidence from natural population variation', *Quarterly Journal of Economics*, 1239–85.

Iacovou, Maria (2001), 'Class size in the early years: is smaller really better?', mimeo, Institute for Social and Economic Research.

Kremer, Michael (1995), 'Research on schooling: what we know and what we don't. A comment on Hanushek', *The World Bank Research Observer*, **10** (2), 247–54.

Krueger, Alan B. (1999), 'Experimental estimates of education production functions', *Quarterly Journal of Economics*, **114** (2), 497–532.

Krueger, Alan B. (2003), 'Economic considerations and class size', *The Economic Journal*, **113** (485), F34–F63.

Krueger, Alan B. and Diane M. Whitmore (2001), 'The effect of attending a small class in the early grades on college-test taking and middle school test results: evidence from project STAR', *The Economic Journal*, **111** (468), 1–28.

Lazear, Edward (2001), 'Educational Production', *Quarterly Journal of Economics*, **116** (30), 777–803.

Levin, Jesse (2001), 'For whom the reductions count: a quantile regression analysis of class size and peer effects on scholastic achievement', *Empirical Economics*, **26** (1), 221–46.

Mosteller, Frederick (1995), 'The Tennessee study of class size in the early school grades', *The Future of Children*, **5** (2), 113–27.

Nye, Barbara and Larry Hedges (2001), 'Are effects of small classes cumulative? Evidence from a Tennessee experiment', *The Journal of Educational Research*, **94** (6), 336.

Nye, Barbara, Larry V. Hedges and Spyros Konstantopoulos (2000), 'The effect of small classes on academic achievement: the results of the Tennessee class size experiment', *American Educational Research Journal*, **37** (1), 123–52.

Nye, Barbara, Larry V. Hedges and Spyros Konstantopoulos (2001), 'The long term effects of small classes in early grades: lasting benefits in mathematics achievement in grade 9', *The Journal of Experimental Education*, **69** (3), 245.

Nye, Barbara, Larry V. Hedges and Spyros Konstantopoulos (2002), 'Do low achieving students benefit more from small classes? Evidence from the Tennessee class size experiment', *Educational Evaluation and Policy Analysis*, **24** (3), 201–21.

Pate-Bain, Helen, Dewayne Fulton and Jayne Boyd-Zaharias (1999), 'Effects of class size reduction in the early grades (K–3) on high school performance', http://www.nea.org/issues/classsize/bain.html.

Pate-Bain, Helen, Jayne Boyd-Zaharias, Van A. Cain, Elizabeth Word and M. Edward Binkley (1997), 'The student/teacher achievement ratio (STAR) project follow up studies 1996–1997', HEROS, Inc.

Picus, Lawrence O. (1999), 'Class size reduction: effects and relative costs', Technical Report for the Joint Legislative Audit and Review Committee, Washington State Legislature.

Pong, Suet-ling and Aaron Pallas (2001), 'Class size and eighth grade math achievement in the U.S. and abroad', *Educational Evaluation and Policy Analysis*, **23** (3), 251–73.

Rouse, Cecilia Elena (2000), 'School reform in the 21st century: a look at the effect of class size and school vouchers on the academic achievement of minority students', Industrial Relations Section Working Paper 440, Princeton University.

Shapson, Stan M., Edgar N. Wright, Gary Eason and John Fitzgerald (1980), 'An experimental study of the effects of class size', *American Educational Research Journal*, **17** (2), 141–52.

Slavin, R. (1989), 'Class size and student achievement: small effects of small classes', *Educational Psychologist*, **24**, 99–110.

Todd, Petra and Kenneth Wolpin (2003), 'On the specification and estimation of the production function for cognitive achievement', *The Economic Journal*, **113** (485), F3–F33.

Woessmann, Ludger and Martin West (2002), 'Class size effects in school systems around the world: evidence from between-grade variation in TIMSS', Working paper presented at NBER Education Meeting.

Word, Elizabeth, John Johnston, Helen Pate-Bain, B. DeWayne Fulton, Jayne Boyd-Zaharias, Charles M. Achilles, Martha Nannette Lintz, John Folger and Carolyn Breda (1990), 'The state of Tennessee's student/teacher achievement ratio project final summary report 1985–1990', Tennessee State Department of Education.

10 The economics of secondary schooling
Steve Bradley and Jim Taylor

I Introduction

> The expense of the institutions for education and religious instruction, is like-wise, no doubt, beneficial to the whole society, and may, therefore, without injus-tice, be defrayed by the general contribution of the whole society. This expense, however, might perhaps with equal propriety, and with some advantage, be defrayed altogether by those who receive the immediate benefit of such educa-tion and instruction, or by the voluntary contribution of those who think they have occasion for either one or the other. (Adam Smith, *Wealth of Nations*, Book 5, Chapter 1, p. 298)

> As we have seen, both the imposition of a minimum required level of schooling and the financing of this schooling by the state can be justified by the 'neigh-bourhood effects' of schooling. A third step, namely the actual administration of educational institutions by the government, the 'nationalisation', as it were, of the bulk of the 'education industry' is much more difficult to justify on these, or, as far as I can see, any other, grounds. (Milton Friedman, *Capitalism and Freedom*, p. 89)

The debate about the most appropriate method of providing mass educa-tion has a very long history, though the intensity of this debate has fluctu-ated according to the ability of the state to provide 'quality' education at any particular time or in any particular place. The critique of state-pro-vided education is often based on the observation of large numbers of young people with no, or low, qualifications, associated problems of illiter-acy and innumeracy, truancy and dropping out of secondary school, which is often linked to juvenile crime, and 'too small' a proportion of young people proceeding to post-compulsory education. Nevertheless, in spite of the warnings delivered by Smith in the 18th century, and the recent inter-ventions by Friedman and other right-wing academics, the trend until very recently has been towards increasing government intervention in education by the state. In fact, it was only after the election of 'New Right' govern-ments in the USA, the UK and elsewhere in the late 1970s and early 1980s that serious and substantial reforms of state provision of education began.

As Tooley (1996) notes, governments intervene in education by regulat-ing its content (e.g. with respect to the curriculum and testing), its demand (i.e. through laws regarding compulsory attendance) and through deter-mining the level of funding and provision. State provision relates to both building schools and employing teachers, whereas funding can be either direct (e.g. 'free' schooling) or indirect (e.g. education vouchers). Since these types of intervention are independent and separable, Tooley argues that 'Without government intervention in any of these areas (except general regulation to provide the legal framework for contracts and the rule of law), there would be a pure "market" in education. Lying between this extreme and the other of detailed state regulation, provision and finance, is an (infinite) variety of possibilities, all of which embody some features of markets and aspects of state control' (ibid., p. 14) If a government gives up control in any of the areas of regulation, funding and provision, there can be said to be a move towards a market in education.

At the heart of the debate about state provision of education is the efficiency–equity trade-off. Proponents of centralized educational provision argue that a market-based system will lead to an increase in socioeconomic segregation and greater income inequality (Ball, 1990; Levin, 1991a, 1991b). It is also claimed that the wider social benefits generated by education, the so-called 'neighbourhood effects', can only be internalized through centralized provision. These wider social benefits include the promotion of citizenship, a deeper sense of community, support for democracy and knowledge spillovers. Gradstein and Justman (2000) discuss these social benefits in some detail and also present a theoretical model showing that public education increases social cohesion.[1] In contrast, those who propose a greater role for markets in education, such as the voucher system in the USA or the quasi-market in the UK, argue that inequality of educational opportunity exists even under a centralized system of education provision (Chubb and Moe, 1988; Smith and Tomlinson, 1989). Furthermore, state provision of education will lead to a reduction in allocative and productive efficiency. Hoxby (1994, 1996, 1999) therefore argues that a market-based system will increase efficiency and improve equity because it is more likely to lead to optimal decision making by households in their investment in their children's education.[2]

Several recent studies have investigated international differences in educational attainment to ascertain the impact of different types of school systems (see Hanushek and Luque, 2001). Woessmann (2000), for example, argues that international disparities in student performance result primarily from institutional differences in education systems rather than differences in the resources allocated to schools. However there is still a dearth of empirical evidence on the effects of alternative ways of organizing and providing education. This problem is compounded by the lack of agreement about the determinants of educational outcomes. A vast literature exists which suggests that educational outcomes may be determined by a variety of personal, family, peer group and school-related factors. Coleman

(1966) and Hanushek (1986, 1992) conclude that school-related factors, or 'school quality', provide little or no explanation for individual differences in educational attainment. Although the jury is still out about the impact of school quality on educational attainment, it is important to bear in mind the complexity of the educational production function (Hanushek, 2003, 2004; Krueger, 2000, 2003).

The rest of this chapter is structured as follows. In section II we briefly discuss the educational reforms that have been implemented in several countries in an effort to increase the role of the market in the provision of education. A more extensive description of the educational reforms in the UK, which led to the creation of the so-called 'quasi-market' in secondary education, is provided, since this forms a basis for our own empirical work reported in this chapter. Section III reviews the literature on the economics of school choice. Studies of school choice analyse the impact of introducing parental choice of education on educational outcomes, including voucher systems and charter schools in the USA and the quasi-market in the UK. It is expected that the introduction of school choice will improve educational outcomes by increasing competition between schools for pupils. However, in recognition of the complexity of educational production, section III also reviews the evidence relating to the effect of school quality, school size, family background and personal characteristics on educational outcomes. This is followed in section IV by a discussion of recent trends in school performance and in the social segregation of pupils between schools in England. Section V provides an empirical analysis of the determinants of educational outcomes, such as exam scores, value added and truancy, focusing on the impact of competition between schools, but also recognizing the importance of other factors such as type of school, school inputs and the family background of pupils. Section VI presents the results of a statistical analysis of the effect of introducing market forces into secondary education on exam performance and on the polarization of pupils between schools. Section VII concludes.

II Educational reform

Markets in education: a comparative view
In the last two decades several countries have implemented wide-ranging reform programmes in an attempt to improve the performance of their education systems. Different approaches have been adopted around the world, but all have the common features of attempting to increase school choice and hence stimulate competition between schools so that educational outcomes can be improved. New Zealand and the UK have adopted reforms that have much in common. In the latter case, these reforms have

led to the introduction of a quasi-market in education. In New Zealand, radical reforms were introduced in 1989 under a plan known as 'Tomorrow's Schools'. This involved the decentralization of decision making from the central government to locally elected boards of trustees, new systems of financing, the abolition of neighbourhood enrolment zones and an increase in parental choice of school. As a result, schools found themselves in competition for pupils.[3] In Chile, reforms were introduced in the 1980s that led to decentralization of educational decision making to the municipal level and to the privatization of schools through the provision of a public voucher payments system (McKeekin, 2003). These voucher payments were based on average student attendance per month and were paid to both private and public schools. Standardized tests were also introduced and schools received monetary prizes based on their achievement in these tests, the level of parental involvement in the school and 'equity considerations'.

Education voucher systems have been introduced in a number of other countries, including Sweden, New Zealand, the Czech Republic and the USA. Education vouchers have a long history, though modern versions stem from Friedman (1962). Levin (1992) discusses some of the early voucher programmes and notes that their usefulness as a means of improving educational standards was stimulated by the work of Chubb and Moe in 1988. Several versions of the voucher system have been tried in the USA, notably in Cleveland, Dayton, Florida, Milwaukee, New York and Washington DC. A range of voucher systems exists, from those offering universal provision of vouchers to 'selective' or means-tested vouchers. Some schemes also allocate vouchers randomly for experimental purposes. The privately funded voucher schemes in Dayton, New York and Washington DC are aimed at students from low-income families who attend a public school and provide 'partial' vouchers which the family can then supplement from their own resources.

Alongside these voucher experiments, the US government has recently (in 2002) introduced 'No Child Left Behind' legislation. This requires all US states to introduce accountability systems based on achievement tests and to provide incentives for schools to improve their performance (McKeekin, 2003). This appears to be a move in the direction of the UK quasi-market approach, and has led to concern about whether school choice and accountability can successfully coexist (Figlio and Page, 2001). Other methods of increasing choice and competition used in the USA include the introduction of charter schools financed by the state and run privately, magnet schools and within-district choice systems. The US approach to the introduction of markets in education is therefore extremely diverse compared to the more coherent approach that has evolved in the UK.

Educational reform in the UK

Following the Education Reform Act (1988), successive UK governments have introduced a series of reforms which have led to the creation of a market in education. Le Grand (1991) terms it a 'quasi-market' and Glennester (1991) explains why it is not a full market solution. In essence, the bureaucratic and centralized model of educational finance, which rested heavily on the Local Education Authority, has been replaced by a more decentralized approach where parents have greater control over the choice of school for their child and schools have more power over budgets, staffing and resource allocation. Recently schools have also been allowed to acquire 'specialist' status, which has led to more diverse educational provision. The major feature of this quasi-market is that schools compete for pupils. It was expected that successful schools would thrive and grow, while unsuccessful schools would decline, and perhaps even close unless they improved their performance and became more attractive to their potential customers. Bradley *et al.* (2000) provide evidence that the quasi-market is working in the way expected.[4]

There are several important characteristics of the quasi-market. First, parents are free to choose their child's school, subject to the school's physical capacity and conditional on the child meeting other selection criteria such as those imposed by denominational schools. Second, schools are now allowed to compete for pupils and the incentive is that funding is directly related to age-weighted pupil numbers. Third, control over financial resources has been devolved from the local education authority to the schools themselves, through the Local Management of Schools initiative, which means that school managers can determine the allocation of resources within their school. Fourth, until the election of the Labour government in 1997, schools were encouraged to opt out of local authority control by becoming grant-maintained, and their funding was obtained directly from the Department for Education and Employment (now the Department for Education and Skills). Regulation of the system was maintained through the introduction of a national curriculum and the adoption of an inspection system, the latter being undertaken by the Office for Standards in Education (OFSTED). However the introduction of city technology colleges and the more recent establishment of specialist schools since 1998, based upon specific subject areas such the arts, languages, technology and sport, have permitted schools to bend the national curriculum towards their subject specialism. To help parents to make informed choices, and to improve information flows between rival schools, the government publishes annually School Performance Tables, which contain information about each school's exam performance over a four-year period, its current truancy rate and total enrolment.

Greater parental choice was expected to result in an increase in *allocative* efficiency since parents would be able to send their child to the 'right' school. Moreover allowing schools to determine their own allocation of pupil-led funding between school inputs was expected to result in greater *productive* efficiency. Hence efficiency and educational outcomes were expected to improve as a consequence of fundamental changes on both the demand side and the supply side of the 'education market'. The potentially important effect on the socioeconomic segregation of pupils, and hence the issue of equality of educational opportunity, was largely ignored, although Education Action Zones have been created where additional resources are directed at the worst performing schools. Nevertheless it is well known that parents with a good education themselves are more likely to be successful in getting their child into a school with a 'good' exam performance. To the extent that schools that perform well can 'cream skim' the market, which is likely when a school faces an excess demand for places, the outcome will be a greater concentration of those pupils with the best chance of success ending up in the 'best' schools.[5] The reverse will happen in those schools with a 'poor' exam performance, and consequently the operation of the quasi-market could lead to a more socially segregated school system. We return to these issues in sections IV and V below.

III   A review of the literature

In this section, we review the research on the so-called 'education production function', which focuses on the determinants of test and exam performance. Most of the previous research in this area is based on the USA, with very little evidence for the UK (Vignoles *et al.*, 2000). We also briefly discuss the results of voucher experiments, and then provide a more extensive review of the literature on the effects of competition on the performance of schools. In recognition of the complexity of educational production, this section discusses the impact of school, personal, family and peer group factors on educational attainment.

The effect of school quality and type of school

The school itself is expected to affect educational outcomes. Previous research can be grouped into one of two alternative lines of enquiry: first, the relative merits of private versus public schooling; and second, the impact of what may be termed 'school quality' as indicated by class size (see Chapter 9 above) and expenditure per pupil. We discuss each in turn.

In the USA, several studies have investigated the impact of Catholic school attendance on educational outcomes, since Catholic schools make up the largest share of private schools. When compared with public schools, Catholic schools are regarded as having a better school ethos, better discipline, greater focus on a core curriculum, less bureaucracy and are more focused on advanced academic courses (Sander, 2000, p. 260). Substantial controversy surrounds the effects of Catholic schooling on educational outcomes, however, because of the non-random assignment of pupils to schools. Consequently previous research has generally proved inconclusive. For instance, a number of studies show that attending a Catholic school has several advantages. It improves exam performance (Neal, 1997), increases the high school graduation rate (Sander and Krautmann, 1995; Evans and Schwab, 1995), lowers the dropout rate (Nguyen *et al.*, 2001) and increases the incidence of college education (Evans and Schwab, 1995; Nguyen and Taylor, 2003). In contrast, several other studies show that Catholic schooling has no effect (Figlio and Stone, 1999; Goldhaber, 1996) or at best an inconsistent effect, on exam performance (Altonji *et al.*, 2002). One of the main obstacles to progress in this area of research is finding a suitable instrument, which is correlated with choice of Catholic school but is not correlated with educational outcomes. Nguyen *et al.* (2003) sidestep this problem by using matching methods and show that attendance at a Catholic school improves test scores in maths, but only for boys.

For the UK, attendance at a selective (grammar) school is associated with a 'good' exam performance, whereas the opposite is the case for attendance at a secondary modern school (Bradley and Taylor, 2002). This is because selective schools can cream skim the education market, leaving secondary modern schools with less academically able pupils. Attendance at a voluntary aided (primarily denominational) school also has a modest effect in raising a pupil's exam performance compared to schools under local authority control. A critical question that has still not been satisfactorily addressed is whether those pupils attending either a selective or a voluntary aided school would perform as well if they attended a comprehensive school. A limitation of previous research on the impact of UK schools on educational outcomes is that researchers have typically ignored the endogeneity of school choice.[6]

Evidence of the impact of school quality, such as class size, teacher quality and expenditure per pupil, on educational outcomes is scarce (Hanushek, 1986; Hanushek *et al.*, 1996; Hanushek and Luque, 2001; Haveman and Wolfe, 1995; see also Chapter 9 above). In more recent work on educational attainment in the USA, Hoxby (1998) finds that class size has no effect on attainment even after allowing for the endogeneity of class size. Similarly Hanushek (1998) concludes that evidence to support the claim that smaller classes raise educational attainment is very weak. (See, however, the exchange between Krueger and Hanushek in the 'class size policy debate' in Rothstein, 2000, and more recently in Hanushek, 2003 and Krueger, 2003.)

Evidence from UK studies is more encouraging. Bradley *et al.* (2000) find a significant negative relationship between the change in the pupil–teacher ratio (a proxy for class size) and the change in exam performance at school level; and Dolton and Vignoles (1996) and Bradley and Taylor (2004) find a significant negative effect at the individual level. With respect to expenditure on schools, Card and Payne (2002) investigate the effect of school finance reform in the USA on test scores. They show that an equalization of education spending led to a narrowing of test scores between children of highly educated and children of poorly educated parents by about 5 per cent.

Some studies also examine the effect of school inputs, or resources, on the subsequent earnings of pupils, reflecting the lasting impact of schooling in raising an individual's productivity. Betts (1995) and Grogger (1996) show that the effect of school expenditure and class size on subsequent earnings is small, implying inefficiency in the use of resources in the public school system, whereas Card and Krueger (1992, 1996) show that higher education expenditure is positively related to labour market outcomes. Currie and Thomas (1999) also show that there are substantial returns to cognitive achievement.

The effect of school size

If school choice is increased, either through a voucher system or through the creation of a quasi-market, one would expect 'good' schools to grow in size and small schools to wither. It is therefore important to know what the relationship is between school size, measured by the number of pupils enrolled, and educational outcomes.

There are several reasons why school size might affect a pupil's exam performance (Bradley and Taylor, 1998). Firstly, small schools may offer a less diverse range of courses than large schools because small schools are less able to employ subject specialists. Consequently, pupils in small schools may be less able to 'match' their talents with particular subjects in which they could expect to perform well. Evidence for the USA shows that larger schools offer more comprehensive curricula, though for any given school size the diversity of subjects offered varies considerably (Haller *et al.*, 1990). Secondly, teachers in small schools may have to be 'generalists', teaching a range of subjects across the curriculum, whereas teachers in large schools are more likely to concentrate on their own specialist subject. Thirdly, there is greater opportunity to group pupils of similar ability in large schools, creating more homogeneous classes, thereby making the class easier to teach. Fourthly, teachers in small schools may have to undertake more administrative tasks compared to teachers in large schools, which may divert their attention from teaching per se, thereby reducing their effectiveness. Fifthly, because they have more resources, larger schools can invest more in libraries, computers and other equipment, which serves to enhance the educational experience of their pupils. As a result of these five factors, educational performance should be positively related to school size.

However schools, like firms, can become too big, at which point diseconomies of scale occur and educational performance declines. Diseconomies of scale can arise in several ways. First, there is likely to be less interaction between pupils and teachers outside the classroom simply because there are too many pupils and this could harm the learning process. Second, large schools may be more difficult to manage, giving rise to disciplinary problems (Haller, 1992). Third, there may be problems of low teacher morale and motivation, arising in part from disciplinary problems. Finally, if some schools flourish and grow in size, whereas others wither and close, the creation of larger schools actually serves to erode competition for pupils and reduce the incentive for a school to perform well. School closures, however, are a very rare event.

As with the effect of other measures of school quality on educational outcomes, the empirical evidence on the relationship between school size and academic performance is mixed. Luyten (1994) estimates its effect for the USA, Sweden and the Netherlands, and finds that school size is not significantly related to achievement in mathematics and science. In contrast, Heck and Mayer (1993) find that school size is negatively related to a number of outcomes, including maths score, reading score and attendance. Deller and Rudnicki (1993) and Fowler and Walberg (1991) also find evidence of an inverse relationship between school size and school outcomes. Sander (1993), on the other hand, finds strong evidence of a positive relationship in his study of schools in Chicago, but Lamdin (1995) finds no evidence of any relationship for schools in Baltimore. Bonesrønning and Rattsø (1994) investigate the efficiency of 34 Norwegian high schools, using Data Envelopment Analysis, where the outputs refer to the number of high school graduates produced and the quality of those outputs, as measured by average value added. They find that school size and efficiency are positively correlated. For the UK, Bradley and Taylor (1998) show that there is a statistically significant non-linear relationship between school size and exam performance, represented by an inverted U. The school size that maximizes the exam performance of schools is estimated to be about 1200 for 11–16 schools and 1500 for 11–18 schools.

The effect of personal characteristics, family background and peer group
The most important personal characteristics with respect to educational outcomes are a pupil's health, gender, ethnicity and innate ability. Dolton

et al. (1999), for instance, find that Asian youths in the UK do better than white youths in exams at 16, but that white youths do better than black youths. Bell (1997) examines the educational attainment of immigrants to the UK and shows that they typically have 1.1 years more schooling compared to the native born population. More recently, Bradley and Taylor (2004) find that all ethnic minority groups except for Afro-Caribbeans perform better in national exams than whites (after controlling for family background and schooling).

Dolton *et al.* (1999) also investigate the gender gap in exam performance and show that girls have a higher probability of success in GCSE exams than boys. Moreover the gender gap has grown wider since the mid-1980s. They argue that this may be because girls are more 'tuned in' to education than boys, or because they are more forward-looking in terms of their view of what they have to achieve at school in order to improve their prospects in the job market.

Although inherent ability is likely to have a substantial effect on exam performance, lack of appropriate data prevents direct tests of this hypothesis. The best available evidence appears to be the close link between test scores at an early age and subsequent exam results (Feinstein, 1999; Robertson and Symons, 2003). Early test scores and the socioeconomic status of parents, however, may interact in a complex way, the upshot being that early test scores may not be an efficient proxy for innate ability (Currie and Thomas, 1999). Moreover measures of prior ability are likely to be correlated with other variables that are included in models of subsequent educational attainment, such as their parents' socioeconomic status.

Since the publication of the Coleman Report (1966), many studies have shown that family background is of considerable importance as a determinant of exam performance (Hanushek, 1986; Loeb and Bound, 1996). Recent studies using British data investigate the effect of several family-related factors, including parents' education, parents' occupation, household income, family structure and parental involvement in their child's education (Emrisch and Francesconi, 1997; Feinstein and Symons, 1999; Bradley and Taylor, 2004). All these factors are highly positively correlated with educational attainment. Several recent studies have attempted to disentangle the nurture (i.e. family) effect from the nature (i.e. genetic) effect. Plug and Vijverberg (2001) use data for a sample of families comparing the attainment of biological and adopted children, and estimate that only 65 per cent of parental ability is genetically transmitted. Sacerdote (2000) also finds that the impact of parents on adopted children is large, especially with respect to college attendance and future wages. Furthermore the impact of parental background on test scores does not diminish through time, suggesting that the nurture effect is long-lasting.

A child's peer group has also been found to be an important factor in determining exam performance, because of the transmission of academic values within the group (Robertson and Symons, 2003). Feinstein and Symons (1999) quantify this effect and find that a child's peer group raises educational attainment by around 8 per cent. Streaming pupils by academic ability also improves performance, especially for those pupils in the top ability stream. In contrast, Betts and Shkolnik (2000) find that grouping (streaming) students on the basis of ability has little effect on average maths achievement growth. This may arise because schools that stream also allocate resources (i.e. teachers of similar education and experience) between classes in a similar way to those schools that do not explicitly stream. In a recent study, Fertig (2003) has investigated the impact of peer group heterogeneity on individual academic attainment, and shows that the more heterogeneous this is the lower attainment will be.[7]

Voucher experiments
Lankford and Wyckoff (1992) provide one of the first empirical tests of education voucher programmes in their analysis of private (Catholic) versus public school choice in New York. They show that parental choice of school is affected by various measures of school quality, pupil characteristics and tuition fees. They use the estimates from their models to simulate the effect of a voucher (i.e. zero tuition fees at Catholic schools) on the change in enrolments from public to private schools. The results suggest that enrolments in Catholic schools would double, but this would have a small effect on the racial and social composition of both public and private schools. Consequently there would be almost no deterioration in the resource base and the 'quality' of the peer group in public schools, which is a cause for concern amongst critics of education vouchers.

Estimating the impact of school choice is difficult because of the non-random assignment of pupils from different family backgrounds and with different prior ability to secondary schools. To overcome this problem, a series of experiments have been conducted in which pupils from poorer backgrounds attending public schools are randomly given an education voucher that enables them to purchase private schooling. Witte (2000) evaluates the first of these programmes in Milwaukee, whereas Peterson *et al.* (2001) estimate the effects on students and their families of the offer of a voucher that enables switching from public to private education. Vouchers were allocated via a lottery. Base line data on test scores and family background were collected prior to the switch from public to private school, and then follow-up information on test scores was collected up to two years later. A control group was randomly selected from those parents and children who did not win the lottery. Their results suggest that the offer of a voucher had no significant effect except for African Americans. A greater improvement in test scores was observed for maths than for reading after one year, whereas the positive gain in test scores after two years was large for both subjects. The upward trend in the improvement in test scores is revealing since it suggests that switching schools for African Americans has a cumulative effect. Chubb and Loveless (2002) and Howell and Peterson (2002) provide evidence from other evaluations of voucher programmes.

The effect of competition between schools and school districts
Where data on randomized trials are not available, researchers have focused on the effect of competition from 'rival' schools and districts on educational outcomes. In the USA, the focus is on the district, whereas in the UK the emphasis is on the school. Moreover, in the UK, there have also been attempts to measure the impact of the 'quality' of the performance of rival schools, rather than focus simply on the number of rivals.

Only a handful of US papers consider the effect of competition on test scores and other educational outcomes (Borland and Howsen, 1992, 1993; Blair and Staley, 1995; Hoxby, 1994, 1996; Marlow, 1997, 2000; Zanzig, 1997).[8] Borland and Howsen (1992) analyse school performance in Kentucky, and find weak evidence that exam grades are positively related to the degree of competition in the same county. In a subsequent paper, Borland and Howsen (1993) address the closely related issue of whether the effect of competition becomes insignificant above some threshold level. Their empirical work suggests such a cut-off may indeed arise, and at a surprisingly high level of market concentration. They obtain a Herfindahl index of 0.5, which implies that test scores can be raised in circumstances where there is little schooling choice.[9]

Blair and Staley (1995) look for evidence of spillover effects with respect to competition from neighbouring districts, reflected by the average test score of contiguous school districts. Using data for 266 school districts in Ohio, they show that test performance is raised in school districts bounded by high-performing 'competing' districts. Hoxby (1996) shows that greater school choice in metropolitan areas, reflected by exogenous variation in the concentration of school districts (i.e. the share of enrolments), raises average student performance. Marlow (1997) in a cross-state study finds that the number of school districts increases performance in average SAT scores and eighth grade maths (13–14 year olds), and reduces high school dropout rates. In a study of school performance in California, Zanzig (1997) finds similar results using the number of school districts per county and the Herfindahl index as measures of competition. According to this study, only three to five school districts are required to create a competitive education market. Marlow (2000) also analyses spending and test performance disparities across Californian counties and finds a negative relationship between test performance and the degree of monopoly power.

From a UK perspective, it is inappropriate to define a market in education as a school district, since pupils can cross education district boundaries to attend a school of their choice. Competition for pupils in the UK therefore occurs between schools rather than between education districts. A different approach to assessing the impact of competition between schools on educational outcomes is therefore necessary for the UK. Until quite recently, however, the effect of competition between schools on exam performance had largely been ignored. Most of the early research, based on case studies, was undertaken by educationalists (Woods, 1996; Levacic and Hardman, 1998).

Several recent studies have examined the impact of competition between schools using multivariate analysis (Bradley *et al.*, 2000, 2001; Bradley and Taylor, 2002; Millington and Bradley, 1998). These studies use the number of pupils obtaining five or more GCSEs at grades A* to C as the measure of school performance. Their data refer to over 3000 publicly funded secondary schools in England observed annually between 1992 and 2000. Bradley *et al.* (2000) and Bradley and Taylor (2002) focus on the impact of the quality of rival schools' output (i.e. exam performance) on a school's own exam performance. It is expected that, the better the exam performance of rival schools, the more likely it is that a school will attempt to improve its own performance to encourage a high demand for places and to ensure that it maintains its market share (see pages 372–3). They show that an improvement of three percentage points in the exam performance of a school's competitors is followed by an improvement of one percentage point in the school's own exam performance. Thus competition between schools does appear to improve the exam performance of pupils. However it is also worth noting that the most substantial determinant of a school's exam performance is family background, as indicated by the proportion of pupils eligible for free school meals.

Millington and Bradley (1998) and Bradley *et al.* (2001) adopt a different approach. The former study explicitly models spatial competition between schools by constructing a set of overlapping education markets, which enables them to examine whether the effect of competition decays with distance. The effect of competition between schools is then reflected by the number of non-selective schools in each spatially delimited education market, and also by the number of selective schools. The former measures are expected to be positive, but may fall as the effect of more distant rivals is considered, whereas the latter are expected to be negative because of cream skimming effects. A school's exam performance is found to be positively related to the intensity of local competition.

The technical efficiency of all secondary schools in England is estimated by Bradley *et al.* (2001), who use Data Envelopment Analysis. This non-parametric technique has the advantage that a school is allowed to produce multiple outputs, in this case exam results and the inverse of the truancy rate. Having obtained the efficiency scores for each school, regression methods are used to estimate the determinants of school efficiency over time. Schools with more rivals are estimated to be more efficient and the strength of this effect increased during the 1990s as the quasi-market in secondary education evolved. Furthermore the degree of competition is found to be an important determinant of the *change* in technical efficiency over time, and there is evidence that less efficient schools had improved by more than the most efficient schools over the study period.

In summary, for both the USA and the UK, there is evidence that greater competition between schools and between school districts leads to better educational outcomes, as measured by exam results.

Polarization
We have referred in several places to the idea that schools can cream skim the market. We have also suggested that one of the downsides of introducing market forces into education is that they may exacerbate inequalities of educational opportunity. There has been very little empirical work on this issue, although some recent exceptions are Bradley *et al.* (2000) and Bradley and Taylor (2002). They investigate whether greater competition for pupils between schools in the UK has had any adverse effects on the way in which pupils from different socioeconomic backgrounds are distributed between schools. Their results indicate that schools with 'good' exam results, relative to other schools in the same education market, have experienced a reduction in the proportion of pupils coming from low-income families. Conversely schools with a comparatively 'poor' exam performance have experienced an increase in the proportion of pupils coming from low-income families. However their evidence suggests that this 'polarization' has not occurred to any great extent.

IV The performance of secondary schools in England
We now turn to an empirical investigation of the determinants of secondary school performance, which updates and extends some of our earlier work.

Measuring school performance
The performance of schools can be measured in different ways. The indicator most commonly employed for secondary schools in England is the exam results obtained by each school's pupils in national examinations at the end of

compulsory education. More recently, the results of tests taken at various stages in a pupil's progression through the educational system have been used to calculate the value added by each school to its annual intake of pupils. Specifically, all pupils are tested at four key stages (KS). The KS1 and KS2 tests are taken in Years 2 and 6, respectively, in primary school. These are followed by further tests in Year 9 (KS3) and then by the battery of exams (known as the GCSE and GNVQ exams)[10] taken at the end of compulsory education in Year 11, when pupils reach the age of 16 (KS4). The availability of test and exam results at four key stages means that performance can be assessed not only in terms of the *level* of performance but also by the *change* (or value added) in the level of attainment between each key stage.

It is worth noting at the outset that the exam score achieved by a school at any of the four key stages is simply an indicator of the performance of the pupils themselves. It is essentially an indicator of the knowledge and academic skills acquired by each school's pupils at each point in time. This will include the impact of personal factors such as ability and effort, family background and peer group as well as the impact of the school. The exam performance of secondary schools at KS4 (GCSE/GNVQ), for example, is highly correlated with the KS3 results taken three years earlier in Year 9 ($r = 0.94$). It is therefore necessary to control for initial attainment if exam performance is to be measured. This is the purpose of the value added measure, which attempts to quantify the amount of knowledge acquired by pupils during a specific period of time.

Several indicators of exam performance at school level are now published annually in the School Performance Tables for all publicly funded secondary schools in England. These include the following:

- the exam score of pupils in the KS3 tests;
- the percentage of pupils in the final year of compulsory education who obtained five or more A* to C grades in the KS4 exams (GCSE/GNVQ);
- the average exam score of pupils in the GCSE/GNVQ exams (calculated from the best eight grades obtained by each pupil);
- the value added score between KS2 and KS3;
- the value added score between KS3 and KS4.

The truancy rate[11] is also included in the School Performance Tables since truancy is regarded as harmful, not only for the truants themselves, but also because of the link between truancy, crime and other social problems. It is consequently important to discover why the truancy rate differs between schools so that appropriate policies can be devised for reducing it, particularly in those schools in which it is persistently high. Truancy is only a small part, however, of the overall pupil absence from school. The rate of authorized absence is 7.8 per cent, compared to an unauthorized absence rate of only 1.2 per cent. There may be considerable overlap in practice, however, between authorized and unauthorized absence and, since absence from school for any reason is detrimental to educational attainment, it will be useful to investigate the determinants of the overall absence rate rather than focusing exclusively on truancy.

Differences in performance between secondary schools in England
Exam results vary tremendously between schools. Much of this variation can be explained by differences in the characteristics of the pupils themselves, such as their educational attainment on entry into a school, and by their family background. Figure 10.1, for example, clearly demonstrates the high negative correlation between exam performance and the proportion of pupils from low-income families, proxied by eligibility for free school meals. As was suggested in section III, schools themselves can be expected to exert some influence on the exam performance of their pupils in addition to the effect of personal and family-related factors. It is therefore instructive to see how exam performance varies between different types of school.

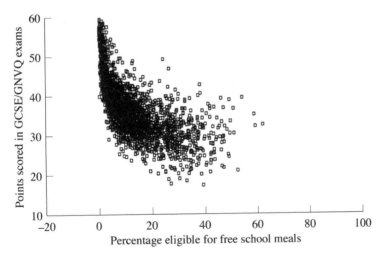

Figure 10.1   Exam score versus percentage eligible for free meals, 2002

Schools can be classified according to a range of characteristics, such as their governance, their admissions policy, the gender of their pupil intake, whether they specialize in specific areas of the curriculum, their size (in terms of pupil numbers) and the eligibility of their pupils for free school meals. As can be seen from Table 10.1, exam scores are higher (on average)

Table 10.1   Measures of performance: secondary schools in England, 2002

School characteristic	Number of schools	Score in GCSE/ GNVQ exams	Value added KS3 to KS4	Truancy (%)	Overall absence (%)
School governance					
Community school	1984	32.6	98.4	1.4	9.5
Voluntary aided/controlled	606	37.6	99.2	0.8	8.1
Foundation schools	493	37.9	98.9	0.8	8.1
City Technology College	15	43.4	101.0	0.4	7.0
Admissions policy					
Comprehensive	2755	33.7	98.7	1.2	9.2
Secondary modern	179	30.2	97.8	1.1	9.4
Selective	164	52.6	99.4	0.2	5.1
School gender					
Mixed	2686	33.5	98.5	1.2	9.2
Boys only	185	39.0	98.2	1.1	8.2
Girls only	227	42.1	101.1	0.8	7.9
Age range					
11–16	1294	32.1	98.6	1.3	9.6
11–18	1804	36.2	98.8	1.1	8.7
School specialism					
Languages	156	39.8	99.6	0.8	7.8
Maths, science, etc.	57	39.7	99.8	0.6	7.6
Technology	435	35.8	99.3	1.0	8.5
Arts	172	34.8	99.2	1.3	8.9
Sport	158	33.2	98.5	1.2	9.4
Non-specialist	2120	33.7	98.4	1.3	9.3
School size					
Under 600 pupils	306	30.2	98.2	1.5	10.3
600–799 pupils	590	33.0	98.3	1.3	9.5
800–999 pupils	725	34.8	98.6	1.2	9.1
1000–1199 pupils	653	35.5	98.9	1.1	8.8
1200 pupils and over	824	36.0	99.0	1.0	8.5
Eligibility for free school meals (quintiles)					
Under 5.8%	619	43.7	99.6	0.5	6.7
5.8% to 10.1%	620	37.1	99.1	0.7	7.9
10.2% to 16.5%	620	33.8	98.3	1.0	8.9
16.6% to 28.3%	620	30.7	97.8	1.4	9.9
Above 28.3%	619	27.0	98.5	2.2	11.5
All schools	3098	34.5	98.7	1.2	9.1

Notes:
1. The characteristics of schools refer to their status in 2002. Community schools were previously county schools; foundation schools were previously grant-maintained schools.
2. Schools have been able to apply for special status (for funding purposes) since 1997.
3. Not all secondary schools could be included since information for each school in 2002 had to be matched with information for the same school in 1992 and this was not possible for all schools. There are 3202 and 3098 schools in the original 1992 and 2002 data sets, respectively.
4. % truancy = per cent half-days lost owing to unauthorized absence; % sickness = % half days lost owing to authorized absence.

Sources: School Performance Tables, 1992 and 2002; Schools' Census (Form 7), 1992 and 2002.

for voluntary aided and foundation (formerly grant-maintained) schools than for community (formerly county) schools. Schools selecting their pupils on academic ability have far higher exam success rates than comprehensives; single sex schools achieve far higher grades than mixed schools; and schools specializing in languages, maths/science and technology have a higher success rate than non-specialist schools. There is also some indication that small schools (especially those with fewer than 600 pupils) achieve poorer exam results than larger schools.

As far as changes in exam results over the longer term are concerned, Figure 10.2 shows that the success rate increased steadily and substantially during 1992–2002. In 1992, the proportion of pupils obtaining five or more A* to C grades in GCSE/GNVQ exams was 36 per cent. This increased to 50 per cent by 2002.[12] Although all types of school experienced a substantial improve-

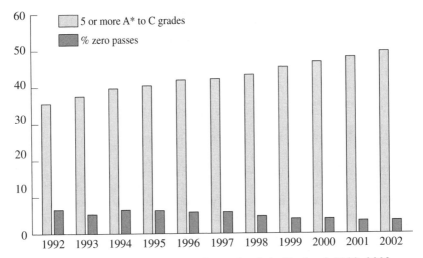

Figure 10.2 Exam results in secondary schools in England, 1992–2002

ment in exam results, Table 10.2 indicates that some types of school experienced a greater improvement in exam results than did others. Community schools, for example, improved their exam results by less than foundation schools, and the initial gap between girls-only schools and mixed schools widened still further during 1992–2002. Schools specializing in technology also improved their exam results relative to other schools; small schools had a smaller improvement in exam results than large schools. Finally, although schools with a high proportion of pupils on free school meals improved their exam results substantially, the improvement was less than for schools with a low proportion of pupils on free school meals. This suggests some widening of the gap in exam results between schools with pupils from high-income families compared to schools with pupils from low-income families.

The truancy rate and the overall absence rate exhibit a very similar pattern across schools (see Table 10.1). They are higher in community schools than in voluntary assisted schools, lower in schools specializing in languages, maths and science and lower in larger schools. The most striking differences, however, occur between schools with a low proportion and schools with a high proportion of pupils on free school meals. Schools in the top quintile of pupils on free school meals have a truancy rate that is four times as high as schools in the bottom quintile (2.2 per cent compared to 0.5 per cent) and the overall absence rate is nearly twice as high (11.5 per cent compared to 6.7 per cent). The link between truancy, eligibility for free school meals and educational outcomes is indicated in Table 10.3, which shows that the proportion of pupils on free school meals rises dramatically as the truancy rate increases above 1 per cent. Although fewer than 50 schools had a truancy rate exceeding 5 per cent, the proportion eligible for free school meals rises to 40 per cent for this group of schools compared to the mean of 16 per cent. Table 10.3 also shows that exam performance dips sharply as the truancy rate increases above 1 per cent. Further investigation reveals a remarkably high (negative) correlation between the overall absence rate and attainment in the GCSE/GNVQ exams as indicated by average exam score in each school (see Figure 10.3).

V   Estimating the determinants of school performance

The education production function
The partial approach to investigating differences in performance between schools provided above is at best suggestive. Although it is clear that strong statistical relationships exist between exam results and specific school characteristics, a multivariate approach is needed if the influence of individual factors is to be estimated. It is therefore necessary to specify an appropriate model for estimating the determinants of school performance.

Table 10.2 Changes in exam performance and eligibility for free school meals: secondary schools in England, 1992–2002

School characteristic	Number of schools (2002)	% pupils with 5 or more A* to C grades (1992)	% pupils with 5 or more A* to C grades (2002)	Change in % pupils with 5 or more A* to C grades (1992–2002)	% pupils eligible for free school meals (2002)
School governance					
Community school	1984	32.9	44.9	12.0	18.2
Voluntary aided/controlled	606	43.3	58.3	15.0	13.5
Foundation schools	493	43.3	59.1	15.8	10.1
City Technology College	15	–	82.9	–	13.1
Admissions policy					
Comprehensive	2755	34.5	47.9	13.4	16.9
Secondary modern	179	19.9	37.6	17.7	14.0
Selective	164	90.7	97.5	6.8	2.2
School gender					
Mixed	2686	34.2	47.5	13.2	16.1
Boys only	185	50.1	62.9	12.8	13.9
Girls only	227	53.4	68.7	15.3	16.1
Age range					
11–16	1294	30.5	43.4	12.9	20.8
11–18	1804	41.0	54.6	13.6	12.6

Table 10.2 (continued)

School characteristic	Number of schools (2002)	% pupils with 5 or more A* to C grades (1992)	% pupils with 5 or more A* to C grades (2002)	Change in % pupils with 5 or more A* to C grades (1992–2002)	% pupils eligible for free school meals (2002)
School specialism					
Languages	156	49.5	63.9	14.4	10.4
Maths, science, etc.	57	47.3	64.5	17.2	10.7
Technology	435	37.0	54.1	17.1	14.1
Arts	172	36.3	51.0	14.7	16.7
Sport	158	33.2	46.6	13.4	19.4
Non-specialist	2120	35.5	47.8	12.3	16.8
School size					
Under 600 pupils	415	25.8	35.2	9.4	24.0
600–799 pupils	628	33.6	43.8	10.2	20.0
800–999 pupils	744	37.9	48.6	10.7	17.7
1000–1199 pupils	612	39.1	50.7	11.6	15.4
1200 pupils and over	731	39.5	51.6	12.1	13.8
Eligibility for free school meals					
Under 5.8%	619	60.8	74.9	14.1	–
5.8% to 10.1%	619	41.5	57.1	15.6	–
10.2% to 16.5%	620	34.5	47.9	13.4	–
16.6% to 28.3%	620	26.9	39.3	12.4	–
Above 28.3%	620	18.5	30.4	11.9	–
All schools	3098	36.6	49.9	13.3	16.0

Notes:

1. Exam performance is measured in this table as the proportion of year 11 pupils obtaining A* to C grades in the GCSE/GNVQ national examinations.
2. The characteristics of schools refer to their status in 2002. Community schools were previously county schools; foundation schools were previously grant-maintained schools.
3. Voluntary assisted/controlled schools are primarily those with a religious affiliation.
4. Secondary modern schools exist primarily in areas where there are selective schools, which select pupils according to their academic ability.
5. Schools have been able to apply for specialist status (for funding purposes) since 1997.
6. Not all secondary schools could be included since information for each school in 2002 had to be matched with information for the same school in 1992 and this was not possible for all schools. There are 3202 and 3098 schools in the original 1992 and 2002 data sets, respectively.

Sources: School Performance Tables, 1992 and 2002; Schools' Census (Form 7), 1992 and 2002.

Table 10.3   Truancy, eligibility for free school meals and exam results:
secondary schools in England, 2002

| | Truancy rate (% unauthorized absence in 2002) | | | |
	0–1	1–2	2–5	Over 5
Number of schools	1796	636	442	49
% pupils eligible for free school meals	12.0	20.0	28.3	39.6
Proportion of pupils with no GCSE passes	2.9	5.0	7.1	13.0
Proportion of pupils with 5 or more A*–C grades	55.4	40.7	31.9	18.7

Source: Schools' Census (Form 7) and School Performance Tables.

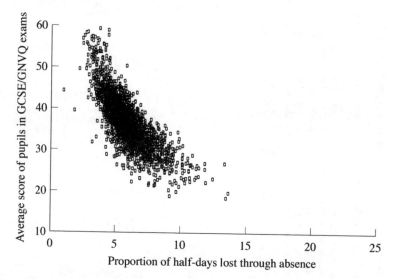

Figure 10.3   Exam score versus overall absence rate, 2002

Following the existing literature and the seminal work of Hanushek (1979), we treat schools as production units. They employ inputs such as teachers and support staff, purchase books and other materials, maintain their buildings and invest in new capital stock in order to produce an output loosely referred to as education. Implicit in this approach to explaining educational attainment is the assumption that the primary objective of schools is to maximize the academic achievement of pupils, subject to the resources available. This is usually taken to mean that schools aim to maximize the proportion of pupils obtaining 'good' exam results, though it could easily be extended to other objectives such as minimizing truancy, again subject to resource constraints.

The educational attainment achieved by a school's pupils, however, is not entirely within the control of the school itself. A number of factors external to the school may be expected to exert an impact on the educational attainment level achieved by its pupils. As shown in section III, these include the personal characteristics of the pupils (such as gender, ethnicity, innate ability, motivation and attitude to schooling), peer group effects and the family background of pupils.

The exam performance of a school's pupils has also been shown to depend on the extent to which schools compete for pupils in their local education market. It was argued earlier (in section II) that a school operating in a competitive environment will respond positively to the performance of its immediate competitors in the local market for pupils. An improvement in the exam performance of a school's competitors, for example, will be an incentive for it to follow suit in order not to lose market share. The magnitude of the local competition facing a school will depend on the number of schools in the same locality and on the quality of education offered by these schools. It is likely to be the case, for example, that the competition for pupils will be more intense in highly urbanized (metropolitan) areas than in less densely populated areas because of the greater choice of school.

The educational attainment level of a school's pupils is therefore likely to be determined by several factors in addition to the contribution of the school itself. We suggest the following general functional relationship:

$$A = f(A^*, PUPILS, FAMILY, PEERS, SCHOOL, COMPETITION)$$

$$(10.1)$$

where A is the educational attainment of a school's pupils at the end of the period of schooling. The explanatory variables include prior attainment (A^*), the personal characteristics of pupils (*PUPILS*), family background (*FAMILY*), peer group effects (*PEER*), school inputs (*SCHOOL*) and a measure of the degree of competition for pupils in the school's catchment area (*COMPETITION*). All variables other than initial attainment are assumed to have a cumulative effect on the acquisition of educational attainment during the period of schooling. Initial attainment is itself determined by family background, peer group effects and schooling in the preceding period, and omission of a measure of prior attainment is likely to increase the significance of the other explanatory variables.[13] An alternative formulation of the relationship between inputs and output is to use the change in educational attainment (or value added) as the output measure:

$$A - A^* = g(PUPILS, FAMILY, PEERS, SCHOOL, COMPETITION)$$

$$(10.2)$$

Finally, the inclusion of the truancy rate in the School Performance Tables implies that schools are expected to devise policies for keeping this to a minimum. The fact that some schools have a particularly high truancy rate suggests that it may be useful to investigate the factors that determine differences in the truancy rate between schools. In particular we need to discover the predominant determinants of truanting if appropriate action is to be taken to eradicate it. Since truancy can be treated as negative attainment (in so far as truanting is a rejection of the formal education process), the factors affecting educational attainment will also affect truancy, but in the opposite direction. In addition, truancy may have a geographical dimension (*LOCALITY*) in so far as some localities may be more prone to truancy than others owing to specific local factors, such as a tradition of truanting in the most deprived neighbourhoods. The district levels of the truancy rate and the proportion eligible for free school meals, for example, are significantly positively correlated ($r = 0.56$ in 2002). We therefore postulate the following general model of truancy:

$$TRUANCY = h(PUPILS, FAMILY, PEERS, SCHOOL, LOCALITY)$$

$$(10.3)$$

Since the performance of a school's pupils depends crucially on the attendance rate of its pupils, we also investigate total absence from school in addition to truancy. Indeed it is possible that the distinction between authorized and unauthorized absence is not as clear as the terms imply. We therefore investigate the determinants of the overall absence rate as well as the truancy rate *per se*.

Estimation of the determinants of exam results

The statistical analysis of the exam performance reported here is based on data obtained from two sources: the annual Schools' Census and the School Performance Tables. The Schools' Census provides information on variables such as type of school governance, admissions policy, support staff, the pupil–teacher ratio, pupils with special needs, pupils eligible for free school meals and pupils taking A-level courses. The School Performance Tables provide information about exam results and truancy rates, as described above.

Two measures of exam performance are regressed on a range of variables that reflect the potential influence on exam performance of the broad range of factors specified in equations (10.1) and (10.2). The two dependent variables are (a) the school's average score in the KS4 exams and (b) the value added between KS3 and KS4. Equations are estimated both with and without initial attainment, estimated by KS3 test scores,[14] in order to examine the effect of including this variable on the estimated coefficients of the other explanatory variables. The other variables included in the regressions are given in Appendix 2, along with some descriptive statistics. Table 10.4 shows the results.

As expected, the inclusion of initial attainment in the KS4 regression has the effect of reducing the estimated coefficients on many of the other explanatory variables. The same set of variables, however, maintain their statistical significance even though their estimated impact on the KS4 score is reduced. As noted previously, the reason for the smaller estimated impact of some of the variables (such as family background) is that initial attainment is itself likely to be influenced by the same variables. We focus here on the main findings from this regression analysis.

Competition for pupils   One of the primary results of interest is that a school's own exam performance is related to the performance of all other schools in the same district, which is consistent with the view that school performance is responsive to competition between schools. The coefficient on the exam performance of other schools in the same district, for example, indicates that a one-point increase in the value-added score of other schools is associated with an increase in a school's own value-added score by nearly 0.3.

School choice   Not surprisingly the selection of pupils according to ability has substantial effects on exam score. Although the estimated impact is substantially smaller when initial attainment is taken into account, it is still substantial and highly significant. Selective schools, for example, have a higher exam score than comprehensive schools (the base group) even allowing for the initial attainment of pupils; and girls-only schools also have a positive effect on exam score, whereas boys-only schools have a negative effect compared to mixed schools (after controlling for initial attainment and other explanatory variables). The estimated effect of selecting pupils by ability is surprisingly reversed in the value-added equation, in which selective schools are now estimated to have a negative effect on value added compared to mixed gender/comprehensive schools. This may be a consequence of the way in which value added is measured since selective schools admit pupils with high academic ability who then achieve high scores at KS4. Why boys-only schools perform worse than girls-only schools and mixed gender schools in both their exam score and value added is a puzzle, but the result is consistent with the view that the gender gap in

Table 10.4 Estimated regression equations, exam results 2002

Explanatory variables	Dependent variable		
	Key Stage 4 score (x=34.5 s=7.5)		Value added: KS3 to KS4 (x=98.7 s=2.6)
Constant	43.533 (1.286)	−14.357 (1.670)	76.545 (3.665)
Initial attainment (KS3 score)		1.525*** (0.035)	
Competition			
Exam score of other schools in district (lagged)	0.096*** (0.015)	0.070*** (0.012)	0.271*** (0.036)
School governance and selection policy			
Voluntary aided/controlled	1.761*** (0.171)	0.504*** (0.127)	0.168 (0.106)
Foundation schools	0.559** (0.176)	0.330 (0.135)	0.167 (0.112)
Secondary modern	−2.830*** (0.279)	−0.895*** (0.241)	−0.344 (0.203)
Selective	9.030*** (0.365)	0.241 (0.320)	−1.195*** (0.233)
Boys only	−0.056 (0.324)	−0.917*** (0.232)	−0.982*** (0.220)
Girls only	3.412*** (0.260)	1.757*** (0.202)	1.592*** (0.169)
School specialism			
Arts	0.631* (0.252)	0.644*** (0.180)	0.365* (0.160)
Languages	1.392***	1.006***	0.460*

	(1)	(2)	(3)
	(0.263)	(0.212)	(0.184)
Sport	-0.093	0.392	0.131
	(0.285)	(0.223)	(0.181)
Technology	0.704***	0.581***	0.635***
	(0.170)	(0.132)	(0.113)
Other (maths, science, business)	1.590***	0.672*	0.644*
	(0.365)	(0.291)	(0.260)
School characteristics			
School has A-level pupils	-1.436***	-0.688***	-0.519***
	(0.149)	(0.120)	(0.096)
Part-time/full-time teachers	3.831***	0.905*	1.484***
	(0.499)	(0.394)	(0.337)
Pupil–teacher ratio	-0.269***	-0.106**	-0.139***
	(0.050)	(0.039)	(0.033)
Pupils/100	0.569***	0.170*	0.143*
	(0.093)	(0.078)	(0.067)
Pupils/100-squared	-0.017***	-0.005	-0.005
	(0.004)	(0.003)	(0.003)
Pupil characteristics and family background			
Proportion of pupils with special needs	-10.460***	-2.753***	-1.118*
	(0.879)	(0.687)	(0.571)
% authorized absence from school	-1.058***	-0.504***	-0.433***
	(0.049)	(0.038)	(0.030)
Proportion of pupils eligible for free meals	-21.108***	-5.584***	-1.138
	(1.033)	(0.845)	(0.597)
Proportion of ethnic minority pupils	3.143***	3.730***	3.317***
	(0.429)	(0.336)	(0.321)
R-squared	0.78	0.87	0.34
n	2964	2945	2982

Notes: ( ) = robust standard errors; x = mean, s = standard deviation; * = significant at 0.05, ** = significant at 0.01, *** = significant at 0.000. The base group includes community schools, comprehensive schools, mixed gender schools and schools with no specialism.

educational attainment is not explained by the coeducation of boys and girls.

A further aspect of school selection (by pupils and by schools) is the rapid expansion in the number of schools specializing in particular subject areas, an option introduced in 1998. By 2003, over 45 per cent of secondary schools had a subject specialism. The results in Table 10.4 indicate that schools specializing in maths/science, technology and languages perform substantially better than non-specialist schools, in terms of both exam performance and value added.

School inputs   Both exam performance and value added are positively related to the part-time/full-time teacher ratio. Schools able to draw on part-time staff may therefore be able to respond more quickly and more flexibly to staff input needs, though there may well be other explanations for this result, such as differences in management practices between schools in the employment of teaching staff. A further explanation is that the productivity of part-time teachers may be higher since they are less likely to be overburdened with administrative duties and their effectiveness may be greater since they are teaching for fewer hours.

More easily explained is the significant negative relationship between exam performance and the pupil–teacher ratio. A similar result is found for the pupil–teacher ratio in the value-added equation. It must be cautioned, however, that, although the estimated coefficient is statistically significant, its magnitude indicates that a reduction in the pupil–teacher ratio would have only a small impact on exam performance and value added (Hanushek, 1998).

The estimated impact of school size on exam performance discovered in earlier work (Bradley and Taylor, 1998) is also found here, but only when initial attainment is excluded from the estimated equation. Exam performance therefore ceases to be related to school size when the initial level of attainment of pupils is taken into account. There is also no evidence that school size affects value added. On the other hand, the estimated coefficient on the variable identifying schools with post-16 pupils indicates a negative effect on both exam score and value added. This suggests that schools with a sixth form may put less emphasis on achieving high scores at KS4 compared to schools which do not teach beyond KS4.

Pupil characteristics and family background   As in previous research, pupil characteristics and family background are found to dominate the explanation of exam results. The proportion of pupils on free school meals and the proportion of pupils missing school through authorized absence are both strongly negatively related to exam performance. Exam performance declines rapidly as these two variables increase. Similar results are obtained for the proportion of pupils with special educational needs. Opposite results are obtained for the ethnicity variable, which indicates that school exam performance improves as the proportion of pupils from an ethnic minority increases. Ethnicity and authorized absence are also highly statistically significant in the value-added equations. Both variables have a strong impact on value added, indicating that schools with a high proportion of ethnic minority pupils and a low proportion of pupils absent from school are likely to obtain significantly higher value added scores.

Estimation of the determinants of truancy and absence from school
Differences between schools in the truancy rate can only be partially explained by the variables included in the regression model shown in Table 10.5. The two main explanatory variables are the truancy rate of other schools in the same district and family background (as indicated by the proportion of pupils on free school meals). A one-point increase in the truancy rate in other schools, for example, is associated with a 0.5 point increase in a school's own truancy rate. Similarly an increase in the proportion of pupils eligible for free school meals is associated with a significant increase in a school's truancy rate. Both variables therefore have a potentially large impact on truancy.

There is some evidence that truancy rates are likely to be lower in voluntary aided schools and in schools specializing in technology and maths/science. Truancy is also significantly lower in girls-only schools compared to boys-only schools and mixed schools. In addition a high pupil–teacher ratio is associated with a higher truancy rate and the proportion of pupils in the sixth form is also positively related to truancy. This latter result is probably explained by the fact that truancy is higher amongst older pupils.

The results for the overall absence rate are very similar to those for truancy, but the estimated impact of individual variables is greater and more variables are statistically significant in the overall absence equation. Overall absence from school, for example, is significantly lower in selective schools and also in larger schools, whereas these two variables are insignificant in the truancy equation. The main point to note, however, is that broadly the same variables 'explain' both truancy and overall absence.

VI The efficiency and equity effects of the quasi-market on secondary education

The impact of market forces on school exam performance
We turn now to the fundamental issue raised at the beginning of this chapter. To what extent has the introduction of market forces into secon-

Table 10.5   Absence from school, 2002

Explanatory variables	Dependent variable	
	Truancy rate (%) ($x=1.19$ $s=1.24$)	Overall absence rate (%) ($x=9.06$ $s=2.54$)
Constant	−1.050	3.673
	(0.346)	(0.547)
Truancy rate in other schools in district	0.462***	
	(0.039)	
Absence rate in other schools in district		0.300***
		(0.031)
School governance and selection policy		
Voluntary aided / controlled	−0.304***	−0.709***
	(0.048)	(0.091)
Foundation schools	−0.152***	−0.214**
	(0.044)	(0.081)
Secondary modern	0.089	0.311*
	(0.085)	(0.155)
Selective	−0.090	−1.510***
	(0.080)	(0.208)
Boys only	0.078	−0.254
	(0.101)	(0.169)
Girls only	−0.308***	−0.401**
	(0.069)	(0.139)
School specialism		
Arts	−0.013	−0.190
	(0.089)	(0.142)
Languages	−0.146*	−0.426**
	(0.067)	(0.145)
Sport	−0.069	0.042
	(0.083)	(0.141)
Technology	−0.176***	−0.418***
	(0.050)	(0.087)
Other (maths, science, business)	−0.267**	−0.519**
	(0.095)	(0.172)
School characteristics		
School has A-level pupils	0.243***	0.655***
	(0.049)	(0.078)
Part-time/full-time teachers	−0.143	0.104***
	(0.147)	(0.027)
Pupil/ teacher ratio	0.063***	−0.597*
	(0.018)	(0.266)

Table 10.5   (continued)

	Dependent variable	
Explanatory variables	Truancy rate (%) ($x=1.19$ $s=1.24$)	Overall absence rate (%) ($x=9.06$ $s=2.54$)
Pupils/ 100	−0.043 (0.032)	−0.198*** (0.054)
Pupils/ 100-squared	0.002 (0.001)	0.007** (0.002)
Pupil characteristics and family background		
Proportion of pupils with special needs	1.753*** (0.316)	4.470*** (0.493)
Proportion of pupils eligible for free meals	3.984*** (0.306)	11.353*** (0.538)
Proportion of pupils from ethnic minority	−0.829*** (0.146)	−3.783*** (0.246)
R-squared	0.34	0.53
n	2859	2859

Notes: ( ) = robust standard errors; x = mean, s = standard deviation; * = significant at 0.05, ** = significant at 0.01, *** = significant at 0.000. The base group includes community schools, comprehensive schools, mixed gender schools and schools with no specialism.

dary education affected the performance (i.e. efficiency) of schools and have there been any detrimental equity effects? To answer this question it is more appropriate to look at changes over time.

The statistical analysis reported in the previous section suggests that many factors interact in a complex way to determine a school's exam performance. Several of these factors, however, are fixed over time and others are unobservable in available data. We overcome some of these drawbacks here by estimating a first difference model of exam performance over the period 1992–2002, which represents the first ten years of the operation of a quasi-market in secondary education in England. Since the model is estimated in first differences, with a one-year lag on the explanatory variables to reduce the problem of endogeneity, all fixed effects (such as school selection policy) are excluded from the model. This approach also has the advantage of removing the effect of school-level unobserved heterogeneity.

The impact of competition for pupils on a school's exam performance is estimated through the inclusion of the (lagged) exam performance of all other schools in the same district ($\Delta EXAMD$).[15] A positive coefficient is expected on this variable.

The change in the 'quality' of pupils is captured by three variables. These are, first, the change in the proportion of pupils with special educational needs (ΔSEN); second, the change in the proportion of pupils eligible for free school meals ($\Delta ELIG$); and third, the change in the proportion of pupils staying on at school (after the end of compulsory education at 16) to take more advanced courses ($\Delta ALEVEL$). The first two variables are expected to be negatively related to the change in a school's exam performance. A positive coefficient is expected on $\Delta ALEVEL$.

Changes in school inputs are represented by two variables. First, the change in the pupil–teacher ratio ($\Delta PUP/TEACHER$) is included to capture the effect of teaching resources available to the school and is expected to have a negative effect on a school's exam performance. Second, since previous work indicates that larger schools perform better in exams than smaller schools, the change in the number of pupils on the school roll (ΔPUP) is included as an explanatory variable. ΔPUP is expected to be positively related to the change in exam performance. The model to be estimated is as follows:

$$\Delta EXAM_t = f(EXAM^*, \Delta EXAMD_{t-1}, \Delta ELIG_{t-1}, \Delta SEN_{t-1}, \Delta ALEVEL_{t-1},$$
$$\Delta PUP_{t-1}, \Delta PUP/TEACHER_{t-1}) \qquad (10.4)$$

where

$\Delta EXAM_t$	= change in the school's exam performance (1993–2002),
$EXAM^*$	= initial school exam performance (1993),
$\Delta EXAMD_{t-1}$	= change in exam performance of other schools in same district (1992–2001),
$\Delta ELIG_{t-1}$	= change in proportion of pupils eligible for free school meals (1992–2001),
ΔSEN_{t-1}	= change in proportion of pupils with special educational needs (1992–2001),
$\Delta ALEVEL_{t-1}$	= change in proportion of pupils taking A-level courses (1992–2001),
$\Delta PUP/TEACHER_{t-1}$	= change in pupils per full-time equivalent (FTE) teacher (1992–2001),
ΔPUP_{t-1}	= change in number of pupils on school roll (1992–2001).

Results   Although the results of the regression analysis shown in Table 10.6 indicate that only a small proportion of the variation in the change in exam results is explained by the model, there is nevertheless firm support for the view that competition between schools has led to an improvement in exam performance. The equation for *all districts* indicates that a 1-point improvement in the exam performance of other schools in the same district is associated with an improvement of 0.26 of a point for the individual school. The estimated effect is much greater, however, for schools located in metropolitan areas than for schools located in non-metropolitan areas. This suggests that the impact of competition has been considerably greater for metropolitan schools, which is consistent with the hypothesis that the quasi-market is likely to be more effective in areas where there is greater school choice.

A school's exam performance has responded to a number of other factors in addition to the effects of the increase in competition for pupils. An increase in the proportion of pupils eligible for free school meals is associated with a statistically significant decrease in the proportion of pupils obtaining 5 or more A* to C grades. Other variables significantly related to exam performance are the proportion of special needs pupils, the pupil–teacher ratio and the proportion of pupils on A-level courses. In all cases, the results are similar to those obtained in the 'levels' regressions reported in Table 10.4.

Finally, the change in enrolment has the expected positive relationship with exam results, which again is consistent with the estimated regression equations in Table 10.4. The estimated coefficient implies an elasticity of 0.20. Expressed in terms of numbers of pupils, this suggests that an increase of 100 pupils is associated with an increase in exam performance of 1 percentage point, which can be compared to the average annual increase of 1.3 percentage points for all schools during 1992–2002. This estimate is consistent with earlier work (Bradley and Taylor, 1998; Bradley *et al.*, 2000).

The estimated effect of market forces on the social segregation of pupils between schools

It was argued earlier that the establishment of a quasi-market in secondary education may have led to an increase in the social segregation of pupils between schools. The impact of the educational reforms on the social segregation of pupils is likely to have taken some time to occur, however, and may not have been felt for several years. Our strategy for investigating the impact of the reforms on the social segregation of pupils between schools is therefore to examine the effect of market forces on *changes* in the social composition of schools during 1993–2002 (see Table 10.7). One approach is to use the proportion eligible for free school meals as an indicator of the social composition of schools. This is appropriate since eligibility for free school meals is 'means tested' and is determined by household income,

Table 10.6 Change in exam performance, 1993–2002

Explanatory variables	Δ exam performance 1993–2002		
	All districts	Metropolitan county	Non-metropolitan county
Constant	0.127	0.121	0.126
	(0.008)	(0.015)	(0.009)
Initial exam performance (1993)	−0.152***	−0.156***	−0.151***
	(0.010)	(0.018)	(0.012)
Competitiveness			
Δ exam performance of other schools in district, 1992–2001	0.261***	0.410***	0.181***
	(0.041)	(0.084)	(0.046)
Pupil effects			
Δ proportion of pupils eligible for free school meals, 1992–2001	−0.322***	−0.275***	−0.402***
	(0.041)	(0.052)	(0.066)
Δ proportion of pupils with special needs, 1992–2001	−0.382***	−0.676**	−0.234
	(0.119)	(0.242)	(0.135)
School effects			
Δ proportion of pupils on A-level courses, 1992–2001	0.253***	0.410***	0.151**
	(0.049)	(0.085)	(0.056)
Δ pupil/teacher ratio, 1992–2001	−0.004**	−0.007***	0.000
	(0.001)	(0.002)	(0.002)
Δ school enrolment (in thousands), 1992–2001	0.010***	0.007***	0.012***
	(0.001)	(0.002)	(0.001)
R-squared	0.15	0.17	0.15
N	2891	1030	1864

Notes: Exam performance = proportion of pupils in year 11 obtaining 5 or more GCSEs at grades A* to C; ( ) = robust standard errors; * = significant at 0.05, ** = significant at 0.01, *** = significant at 0.000.

which is, in turn, highly correlated with the socioeconomic status of parents.

The impact of the increase in competition on the social segregation of pupils between schools is estimated through the inclusion of changes in the exam performance of the school itself, together with changes in the exam performance of other schools in the same district. If the forces of competition are working, schools with a 'good' exam performance will experience an increase in demand for places, particularly from parents who are keen to get their children into a 'good' school. Schools with a 'poor' exam performance will be left with pupils whose parents are less interested in their children going to a 'good' school. In addition, some parents will be more able than others to transport their children to school and will therefore have greater choice of school. A negative sign is therefore expected on the school's own exam performance (lagged one period) and a positive sign is expected on the (lagged) exam performance of other schools in the same district.

Several variables are also included to reflect the academic ability of each school's pupils. These include the change in the proportion of pupils taking A-level courses ($\Delta ALEVEL$), the change in the proportion of special needs pupils (ΔSEN) and the change in the school roll ($\Delta ENROL$). It is also necessary to control for the effect of changes in the economic circumstances of families. Schools in districts experiencing large increases in unemployment, for example, can be expected to experience corresponding increases in pupils eligible for free school meals ($\Delta ELIGD$). A further control that needs to be included is the initial *level* of eligibility in order to allow for convergence effects. The model is specified as follows:

$$\Delta ELIG_t = f(ELIG^*, \Delta ELIGD_t, \Delta EXAM_{t-1}, \Delta EXAMD_{t-1}, \Delta SEN_{t-1}, \\ \Delta ALEVEL_{t-1}, \Delta ENROL_{t-1}) \qquad (10.5)$$

where

$\Delta ELIG_t$ = change in proportion of pupils eligible for free school meals (1993–2002),

$ELIG^*$ = initial proportion of pupils eligible for free school meals (1993),

$\Delta ELIGD_t$ = change in proportion of pupils eligible for free school meals in other schools in the same district (1993–2002).

The other variables in the model are as specified for equation (10.4).

Results   The result of greatest interest here is that the quasi-market has contributed to the increase in the social segregation of pupils between schools. Both the exam performance of each school and the exam performance of other schools in the same district have had the expected impact on the proportion of pupils eligible for free school meals. Although the estimated effects are small in magnitude, they are nevertheless highly statistically significant and are a clear sign that schools with 'good' exam results (compared to other schools in the same district) have experienced a reduction in the proportion of pupils coming from poor families. Conversely schools with a 'poor' exam performance compared to other competitor schools have experienced an increase in the proportion of pupils coming from poor families.

There is also some evidence that the social segregation of schools has responded more vigorously to the introduction of a quasi-market in metropolitan than in non-metropolitan areas. This result is consistent with the view that the impact of market forces is likely to be more powerful in metropolitan areas than in non-metropolitan areas because of greater choice of school.

Two further variables are significantly correlated to the change in the proportion of pupils eligible for free school meals. First, the positive relationship observed for the change in the proportion eligible for free school meals in other schools in the same district indicates the existence of district level factors that affect all schools simultaneously. Second, schools that expand more quickly have a smaller increase in the proportion eligible for free school meals. Rapidly expanding schools are therefore less likely to increase their intake of pupils from poor families. This could indicate that expanding schools are more 'popular' and are consequently more able to select pupils from higher-income families in order to increase their likelihood of achieving 'good' exam results.

VII   Conclusion

In this chapter we have reviewed the literature on the economics of secondary schooling and investigated the determinants of school outcomes for the secondary education sector in England over the period 1992–2002. This time-period is of particular interest in so far as major reforms were implemented that led to the creation of a quasi-market in the education sector. The purpose and consequences of these reforms are discussed in the context of the large and growing literature on the education production function. We review experiments with vouchers, competition between schools, and the effect of the schools themselves on educational outcomes, compared to the influence of family background and personal characteristics.

One of the primary questions addressed in this chapter is whether these reforms had beneficial effects on the secondary education sector. We investigate this question by extending previous statistical analyses of the effect

Table 10.7 Change in the proportion of pupils eligible for free school meals, 1993–2002

Δ proportion eligible for free school meals 1993–2002			
Explanatory variables	All districts	Metropolitan county	Non-metropolitan county
Constant	0.016	0.021	0.021
	(0.003)	(0.008)	(0.004)
Initial proportion of pupils eligible for free meals (1993)	−0.073***	−0.104***	−0.104***
	(0.012)	(0.017)	(0.016)
Δ proportion eligible for free meals in other schools in district (1992–2001)	0.872***	0.838***	0.806***
	(0.042)	(0.060)	(0.050)
Competitiveness			
Δ exam performance of school, 1992–2001	−0.093***	−0.122***	−0.078***
	(0.011)	(0.023)	(0.010)
Δ exam performance of other schools in district, 1992–2001	0.114***	0.194***	0.064***
	(0.019)	(0.050)	(0.017)
School effects			
Δ proportion of pupils with special needs, 1992–2001	0.367***	0.764***	0.213**
	(0.067)	(0.140)	(0.073)
Δ proportion of pupils on A-level courses, 1992–2001	−0.072***	−0.119**	−0.040*
	(0.019)	(0.040)	(0.017)
Δ school enrolment (in thousands), 1992–2001	−0.043***	−0.056***	−0.046***
	(0.006)	(0.011)	(0.006)
R-squared	0.31	0.34	0.31
n	2891	1030	1864

Notes: Exam performance = proportion of pupils in year 11 obtaining 5 or more GCSEs at grades A* to C; ( ) = robust standard errors; * = significant at 0.05, ** = significant at 0.01, *** = significant at 0.000.

of the reforms on several measures of school performance. Thus we estimate the determinants of exam scores, value added, truancy and the overall pupil absence rate as indicators of school outputs.

Our principal conclusions from the empirical analysis are as follows.

1. There has been a substantial improvement in school exam results since the early 1990s. The proportion of pupils obtaining five or more A*–C grades in GCSE exams increased from 37 per cent to 50 per cent between 1992 and 2002. This is a phenomenal increase over a ten-year period.

2. Our statistical analysis confirms the findings of earlier studies that family background has a predominating effect on a school's exam performance. Family background does not have the same impact, however, on a school's value added score. The proportion of pupils on free school meals, for example, is a highly significant determinant of a school's exam performance but plays no part in explaining differences between schools in the value added score.

3. The only family background factor that is strongly related to both exam performance and value added is the proportion of pupils from an ethnic minority background. The greater the proportion of ethnic minority pupils, the higher the exam score and the value added score.

4. When initial attainment is included in the exam score equation, the estimated effect of individual variables falls considerably. Indeed, when initial attainment is included in the exam score equation, the results obtained for individual variables are very similar to those obtained in the value added equation. The significance of many of the same variables in the exam score and value added equations indicates that a school's basic characteristics play a vital role in explaining its performance, whether this is measured by exam scores or by the value added measure.

5. The increased competition for pupils has had a significant positive effect on exam performance. The most convincing results are those obtained for the change in exam performance during 1992–2002. An increase of 10 percentage points in the proportion of pupils obtaining 'good' exam results in competitor schools, for example, is associated with an increase of 2.6 percentage points for the individual school. The impact is estimated to rise to over 4 percentage points, however, in metropolitan areas where competition between schools is likely to be more intense because of greater school choice.

6. A new finding in the present study is that specialization in particular subjects (such as languages, maths, science and technology) is asso-

ciated with significantly higher exam scores. This result, it should be noted, is obtained after controlling for a wide range of other potential explanatory variables including initial attainment.

7. A similar set of factors explains differences between schools in the truancy rate and the overall absence rate. Family background plays the predominant role, especially the proportion of pupils on free school meals. Schools with a high proportion of ethnic minority pupils also have significantly lower truancy and absence rates.

8. There is some evidence of an increase in the polarization of pupils between schools, but this does not appear to have happened to any significant extent. Schools that have improved their exam performance relative to their competitors, for example, have simultaneously decreased the proportion of pupils on free school meals. The main variable affecting the change in a school's proportion of pupils on free school meals, however, is the change occurring in this variable in the local district in which a school is situated.

In summary, we find that the introduction of market forces into secondary education since the early 1990s has had a beneficial effect in raising educational performance. Moreover there is little evidence that this improvement in performance has been achieved at the cost of any significant increase in the polarization of pupils between schools.

Acknowledgments

The authors are grateful to the Department for Education and Skills for making data from the Schools' Census and the School Performance Tables available to us. They are also grateful to Jill Johnes and Geraint Johnes for helpful comments. The authors accept full responsibility for all errors and omissions.

Notes

1. This could be regarded as a disadvantage of state education insofar as 'A general State education is a mere contrivance for moulding people to be exactly like one another . . . it establishes a despotism over the mind, leading by natural tendency to one over the body' (Mill, 1859, p. 175, 1972 edn, cited in Tooley, 1996).
2. See Adnett and Davies (2000) for a fuller discussion of the arguments for and against markets in education.
3. The reforms to secondary schooling in New Zealand are evaluated by Fiske and Ladd (2000) and Lauder and Hughes (1999).
4. Another line of enquiry has investigated whether parents are, in fact, sensitive to differences in school performance as reflected by house prices. This research focuses on elementary or primary school choice. For the USA, Black (1999) uses house prices to infer the value parents place on school quality, the latter being proxied by test scores. This relationship is strong, since a 5 per cent increase in test scores leads to a 2.1 per cent rise in house prices. Similar results are obtained by Cheshire and Sheppard (2002), who estimate a house price differential of 19 per cent between a location in the vicinity of the 'worst' secondary school and the location of the 'best' secondary school (after control-

ling for other factors such as employment deprivation). See also Gibbons and Machin (2001) who investigate the relationship between property prices and primary school attainment.

5. Comprehensive schools are constrained by regulations that allow only a limited proportion of pupils to be selected by ability. This constraint does not apply in areas that have selective education (i.e. grammar schools).

6. Bradley and Taylor (2004) are an exception; however school choice in this context refers to whether a pupil attends a 'good' school or not, defined according to school exam performance.

7. Gibbons (2002) investigates the additional effect of an individual's neighbourhood on academic attainment and finds that there is an effect, albeit a small one.

8. Other theoretical papers that use simulation methods to demonstrate the effect of different systems of education finance on efficiency and equity include Bearse *et al.* (2000), Fernandez and Rogerson (1999), Hoxby (1999) and Nechyba (2000).

9. The Herfindahl index is a measure of the degree of competition in a market. A value of 0 indicates perfect competition whereas a value of 1 would reflect monopoly.

10. GCSE is the General Certificate of Secondary Education and GNVQ is the General National Vocational Qualification, both of which cover a number of different subjects.

11. The truancy rate is the proportion of half-days lost owing to unauthorized absence.

12. It could be argued that trends in exam results over time may not reflect true changes in performance owing to changes in assessment methods and standards. The five-yearly review of exam outcomes for a range of GCSE subjects by the Qualifications and Curriculum Authority concluded that standards had been maintained during 1995–9. See *Five-yearly Review of Standards Reports: Summary*, Qualifications and Curriculum Authority, 2001.

13. Feinstein and Symons (1999), for instance, find that family background variables have little explanatory power in regressions which have attainment at 16 as the dependent variable when test score at 11 is included as a regressor.

14. The KS3 score was not available to the authors but was calculated by subtracting the KS4 score from the value added between KS3 and KS4. See Appendix 1.

15. Inclusion of the number of schools in the same catchment area was found to have little effect on the estimated equations and this was therefore excluded from the regression model.

References

Adnett, N. and P. Davies (2000), *Markets in Schooling*, London: Routledge.

Altonji, J.G., E.E. Todd and C.R. Taber (2002), 'An evaluation of instrumental variable strategies for estimating the effects of Catholic schools', NBER Working Paper no. 9358.

Ball, S.J. (1990), *Markets, Morality and Equality in Education*, Hillgate Group Paper 5, London: The Tufnell Press.

Bearse, P., G. Glomm and B. Ravikumar (2000), 'On the political economy of means-tested education vouchers', *European Economic Review*, **44**, 904–15.

Bell, B.D. (1997), 'The performance of immigrants in the United Kingdom: evidence from the GHS', *Economic Journal*, **107**, 333–44.

Betts, J.R. (1995), 'Does school quality matter? Evidence from the national longitudinal survey of youth', *Review of Economics and Statistics*, **77**, 231–50.

Betts, J.R. and J.L. Shkolnik (2000), 'The effects of ability grouping on student achievement and resource allocation in secondary schools', *Economics of Education Review*, **19**, 1–15.

Black, S.E. (1999), 'Do better schools matter? Parental valuation of elementary education', *Quarterly Journal of Economics*, **114**, 578–99.

Blair, J.P. and S. Staley (1995), 'Quality competition and public schools; further evidence', *Economics of Education Review*, **14**, 193–208.

Bonesrønning, H. and J. Rattsø (1994), 'Efficiency variation among the Norwegian high schools: consequences of equalisation policy', *Economics of Education Review*, **13**, 289–304.

Borland, M.V. and R.M. Howsen (1992), 'Student academic achievement and the degree of market concentration in education', *Economics of Education Review*, **11**, 31–9.

Borland, M.V. and R.M. Howsen (1993), 'On the determination of the critical level of market concentration in education', *Economics of Education Review*, **12**, 165–9.

Bradley, S. and J. Taylor (1998), 'The effect of school size on exam performance in secondary schools', *Oxford Bulletin of Economics and Statistics*, **60**(3), 291–324.

Bradley, S. and J. Taylor (2002), 'The effect of the quasi-market on the efficiency–equity trade-off in the secondary school sector', *Bulletin of Economic Research*, **54**, 295–314.

Bradley, S. and J. Taylor (2004), 'Ethnicity, educational attainment and the transition from school', *Manchester School*, forthcoming.

Bradley, S., G. Johnes and J. Millington (2001), 'The effect of competition on the efficiency of secondary schools in England', *European Journal of Operational Research*, **135**, 545–68.

Bradley, S., R. Crouchley, J. Millington and J. Taylor (2000), 'Testing for quasi-market forces in secondary education', *Oxford Bulletin of Economics and Statistics*, **62**, 357–90.

Card, D. and A.B. Krueger (1992), 'Does school quality matter? Returns to education and the characteristics of public schools in the United States', *Journal of Political Economy*, **100**, 1–40.

Card, D. and A.B. Krueger (1996), 'Labour market effects of schooling quality: Theory and evidence', in G. Burtless (ed.), *Does Money Matter? The Effect of School Resources on Student Achievement and Adult Success*, Washington, DC: Brookings.

Card, D. and A.A. Payne (2002), 'School finance reform, the distribution of school spending, and the distribution of student test scores', *Journal of Public Economics*, **83**, 49–82.

Cheshire, P. and S. Sheppard (2002), 'Capitalising the value of free schools: the impact of supply constraints and uncertainty', Department of Geography and Environment, London School of Economics.

Chubb, J.E. and T. Loveless (2002), *Bridging the Achievement Gap*, Washington, DC: Brookings.

Chubb, J.E. and T.M. Moe (1988), 'Politics, markets and the organisation of schools', *American Political Science Review*, **82**, 1065–87.

Coleman, J.S. (1966), *Equality of Educational Opportunity*, Washington, DC: US GPO.

Currie, J. and D. Thomas (1999), 'Early test scores, socio-economic status, school quality and future outcomes', mimeo, Department of Economics, UCLA.

Deller, S.C. and E. Rudnicki (1993), 'Production efficiency in elementary education – the case of Maine public schools', *Economics of Education Review*, **10**, 45–57.

Dolton, P. and A. Vignoles (1996), 'The impact of school quality on labour market success in the United Kingdom', mimeo, Department of Economics, University of Newcastle upon Tyne.

Dolton, P., G. Makepeace, S. Hutton and R. Audas (1999), 'Making the grade: education, the labour market and young people', Work and Opportunity Series no. 15, Joseph Rowntree Foundation, York.

Emrisch, J. and M. Francesconi (1997), 'Family matters', Working Papers of the ESRC Centre on Micro-social Change, paper no. 97-1, University of Essex.

Evans, W. and R. Schwab (1995), 'Finishing high school and starting college: Do Catholic schools make a difference?', *Quarterly Journal of Economics*, **110**, 941–74.

Feinstein, L. (1999), 'The relative economic importance of academic, psychological and behavioural attributes developed in childhood', Employment and Education Economics Group Conference, Swansea.

Feinstein, L. and J. Symons (1999), 'Attainment in secondary schools', *Oxford Economic Papers*, **51**, 300–321.

Fernandez, R. and R. Rogerson (1999), 'Equity and resources: an analysis of education finance systems', NBER working paper 7111, Cambridge, MA.

Fertig, M. (2003), 'Educational production, endogenous peer group formation and class composition: Evidence from the PLSA 2000 Study', Discussion paper 714, Institute for the Study of Labor (IZA), Bonn.

Figlio, D.N. and M.E. Page (2001), 'Can school choice and accountability successfully coexist?', mimeo, University of Florida.

Figlio, D. and J. Stone (1999), 'School choice and student performance: are private schools really better?', *Research in Labor Economics*, **18**, 115–40.

Fiske, E.B. and H.B. Ladd (2000), *When Schools Compete: A Cautionary Tale*, Washington, DC: Brookings.

Fowler, W.J. and H.J. Walberg (1991), 'School size, characteristics and outcomes', *Educational Evaluation and Policy Analysis*, **13**, 189–202.

Friedman, M. (1962), *Capitalism and Freedom*, Chicago: University of Chicago Press.

Gibbons, S. (2002), 'Neighbourhood effects on educational achievement: evidence from the Census and National Child Development Study', discussion paper no. 018, Centre for Economics of Education, LSE.

Gibbons, S. and S. Machin (2001), 'Valuing primary schools', discussion paper no. 015, Centre for Economics of Education, LSE.

Glennester, H. (1991), 'Quasi-markets for education?', *Economic Journal*, **101**, 1268–76.

Goldhaber, D. (1996), 'Public and private high schools: is school choice an answer to the productivity problem?', *Economics of Education Review*, **15**, 93–109.

Gradstein, M. and M. Justman (2000), 'Human capital, social capital and public schooling', *European Economic Review*, **44**, 879–90.

Grogger, J. (1996), 'School expenditures and post-schooling earnings: evidence from high school and beyond', *Review of Economics and Statistics*, **78**, 628–37.

Haller, E.J. (1992), 'High school size and student indiscipline: another aspect of the school consolidation issue?', *Educational Evaluation and Policy Analysis*, **14**, 145–56.

Haller, E.J., D.H. Monk, A. Spotted Bear, J. Griffiths and P. Moss (1990), 'School size and program comprehensiveness: evidence from high school and beyond', *Educational Evaluation and Policy Analysis*, **12**, 109–20.

Hanushek, A.E. (1979), 'Conceptual and empirical issues in the estimation of educational production functions', *Journal of Human Resources*, **14**, 351–88.

Hanushek, E.A. (1986), 'The economics of schooling: production and efficiency in public schools', *Journal of Economic Literature*, **24**, 1141–77.

Hanushek, E.A. (1992), 'The trade-off between child quantity and quality', *Journal of Political Economy*, **100**, 84–117.

Hanushek, E.A. (1998), 'The evidence on class size', occasional paper 98-1, University of Rochester, NY.

Hanushek, E.A. (2003), 'The failure of input-based schooling policies', *Economic Journal*, **113**, F64–F98.

Hanushek, E.A. (2004), 'What if there are no best practices?', *Scottish Journal of Political Economy*, forthcoming.

Hanushek, E.A. and J.A. Luque (2001), 'Efficiency and equity in schools around the world', Department of Economics, Rochester University.

Hanushek, E.A., S.G. Rivkin and L.L. Taylor (1996), 'Aggregation and the estimated effects of school resources', *Review of Economics and Statistics*, **78**, 611–27.

Haveman, R. and B. Wolfe (1995), 'The determinants of children's attainments: a review of methods and findings', *Journal of Economic Literature*, **33**, 1829–78.

Heck, R.H. and R.A. Mayer (1993), 'School characteristics, school academic indicators and student outcomes: implications for policies to improve schools', *Journal of Education Policy*, **8**, 143–54.

Howell, W.G. and P.E. Peterson (2002), *The Education Gap: Vouchers and Urban Schools*, Washington, DC: Brookings.

Hoxby, C.M. (1994), 'How school choice affects the achievement of public school students', in P. Hill (ed.), *Choice with Equity*, Stanford: Hoover Institution Press.

Hoxby, C.M. (1996), 'Are efficiency and equity in school finance substitutes or complements?', *Journal of Economic Perspectives*, **10**, 51–72.

Hoxby, C.M. (1998), 'The effects of class size and composition on student achievement: new evidence from natural population variation', NBER, working paper 6869, Cambridge, MA.

Hoxby, C.M. (1999), 'The productivity of schools and other local public good producers', NBER working paper 6911, Cambridge, MA.

Krueger, A.B. (2000), 'Understanding the magnitude and effect of class size on student achievement', in R. Rothstein (ed.), *The Class Size Policy Debate*, Working Paper 121, Economic Policy Institute, Washington.

Krueger, A.B. (2003), 'Economic considerations and class size', *Economic Journal*, **113**, F34–F63.

Lamdin, D.J. (1995), 'Testing for the effect of school size on student achievement within a school district', *Education Economics*, **3**, 33–47.

Lankford, H. and J. Wyckoff (1992), 'Primary and secondary school choice among public and religious alternatives', *Economics of Education Review*, **11**, 317–37.

Lauder, H. and D. Hughes (1999), *Trading in Futures: Why Markets in Education Don't Work*, Buckingham: Open University Press.

Le Grand, J. (1991), 'Quasi-markets and social policy', *Economic Journal*, **101**, 1256–67.

Levacic, R. and J. Hardman (1998), 'Competing for resources: the impact of social disadvantage and other factors on English secondary schools' financial performance', *Oxford Review of Education*, **24**, 303–28.

Levin, H.M. (1991a), 'The economics of educational choice', *Economics of Education Review*, **10**, 137–58.

Levin, H.M. (1991b), 'Views on the economics of educational choice: a reply to West', *Economics of Education Review*, **10**, 171–5.

Levin, H.M. (1992), 'Market approaches to education: vouchers and school choice', *Economics of Education Review*, **11**, 279–85.

Loeb, S. and J. Bound (1996), 'The effect of measured school inputs on academic achievement: evidence from the 1920s, 1930s and 1940s birth cohorts', *Review of Economics and Statistics*, **78**, 653–63.

Luyten, H. (1994), 'School size effects on achievement in secondary education: evidence from the Netherlands, Sweden and the USA', *School Effectiveness and School Improvement*, **5**, 75–99.

McKeekin, R.W. (2003), *Incentives to Improve Education: A New Perspective*, Cheltenham: UK and Northampton, MA, USA, Edward Elgar.

Marlow, M.L. (1997), 'Public education supply and student performance', *Applied Economics*, **29**, 617–26.

Marlow, M.L. (2000), 'Spending, school structure, and public education quality: evidence from California', *Economics of Education Review*, **19**, 89–106.

Millington, J. and S. Bradley (1998), 'The effect of spatial competition on secondary school exam performance', discussion paper, Department of Economics, Lancaster University.

Neal, D. (1997), 'The effects of Catholic secondary schooling on educational achievement', *Journal of Labour Economics*, **15**, 98–123.

Nechyba, T.J. (2000), 'Mobility, targeting and private-school vouchers', *American Economic Review*, **90**, 130–46.

Nguyen, A. and J. Taylor (2003), 'Post high school choice: new evidence from a multinomial logit model', *Journal of Population Economics*, **16**, 287–306.

Nguyen, A., J. Taylor and S. Bradley (2001), 'High school dropouts: a longitudinal analysis', Department of Economics, Lancaster University.

Nguyen, A., J. Taylor and S. Bradley (2003), 'The effect of Catholic schooling on educational and labour market outcomes: further evidence from NELS', mimeo, Department of Economics, Lancaster University.

Peterson, P.E., W.G. Howell, P.J. Wolf and D.E. Campbell (2001), 'School vouchers: results from randomised experiments', paper presented at the NBER Conference on School Choice.

Plug, E. and W. Vijverberg (2001), 'Schooling, family background, and adoption: is it nature or is it nurture?', discussion paper no. 247, IZA, Bonn.

Robertson, D. and J. Symons (2003), 'Do peer groups matter? Peer group versus schooling effects on academic attainment', *Economica*, **70**, 31–54.

Rothstein, R. (2000), 'The class size debate', working paper no. 121, Economic Policy Institute, Washington.

Sacerdote, B. (2000), 'The nature and nuture of economic outcomes', NBER working paper 7949.

Sander, W. (1993), 'Expenditure and student achievement in Illinois: new evidence', *Journal of Human Resources*, **52**, 403–16.

Sander W. (2000), 'Parochial schools and student achievement: findings for older adults', *Education Economics*, **8**, 259–68.

Sander, W. and A. Krautmann (1995), 'Catholic schools, dropout rates and educational attainment', *Economic Inquiry*, **33**, 217–33.

Smith, Adam (1776), *An Inquiry into the Nature and Causes of the Wealth of Nations*, reprinted in Everyman's Library (1910), London: Dent Publishers.

Smith, D.J. and S. Tomlinson (1989), *The School Effect: A Study of Multi-Racial Comprehensives*, London: Policy Studies Institute.

Tooley, J. (1996), *Education Without the State*, Institute of Economic Affairs, London: IEA.

Vignoles, A., R. Levacic, S. Machin, D. Reynolds and J. Walker (2000), *The Relationship between Resource Allocation and Pupil Attainment: a Review*, DfEE Research Report 228.

Witte, J.F. (2000), *The Market Approach to Education: An Analysis of America's First Voucher Program*, Princeton: Princeton University Press.

Woods, P. (1996), 'Choice, class and effectiveness', *School Effectiveness and School Improvement*, **7**, 324–41.

Woessmann, L. (2002), *Schooling and the Quality of Human Capital*, Berlin: Springer-Verlag.

Zanzig, B.R. (1997), 'Measuring the impact of competition in local government education markets on the cognitive achievement of students', *Economics of Education Review*, **16**, 431–41.

Appendix 1   Calculation of the KS3 score

The value added between KS3 and KS4 is the difference between a pupil's actual points score at KS4 and the score that a pupil was expected to attain at KS4 given the KS3 score. For the school as a whole, the value added (V) is computed as follows:

$$V_j = 100 + \frac{1}{n} \sum_i^n (s_{ij} - s_{ij}^*)$$

where:

s = actual score,
s^* = expected score,
i = ith pupil,
j = jth school,
n = number of pupils for whom scores at KS3 and KS4 were available.

The expected score (s^*) is calculated by comparing the pupil's KS4 score with the median KS4 of those pupils who had the same prior attainment at KS3. Each pupil's expected KS4 score is therefore based on a conversion of the KS3 score into an equivalent KS4 score for all pupils for which both scores are available. Hence KS3 = KS4 – V + 100.

Source: Department for Education and Skills, *Value Added*, Technical Annex, 2002.

Appendix 2   Descriptive statistics of variables used in regressions

Variables used in regressions	Mean	Standard deviation
Community school	0.64	–
Voluntary aided	0.16	–
Voluntary controlled	0.03	–
Foundation schools	0.16	–
Comprehensive	0.89	–
Secondary modern	0.06	–
Selective	0.05	–
Mixed gender	0.87	–
Boys-only school	0.06	–
Girls-only school	0.07	–
School with no subject specialism	0.68	–
School specialism: arts	0.06	–
School specialism: languages	0.05	–
School specialism: sport	0.05	–
School specialism: technology	0.14	–
School specialism: maths, science, eng, business	0.02	–
Key Stage 3 score	33.79	3.61
Key Stage 4 score (GCSE/GNVQ)	34.47	7.52
% pupils with 5 + A* to C grades (GCSE/GNVQ)	49.95	20.30
Value added Key Stage 2 to Key Stage 3	99.82	1.50
Value added Key Stage 3 to Key Stage 4	98.67	2.58
% pupils with unauthorized absence	1.19	1.24
% pupils with authorized absence	7.75	1.92
Key Stage 3 score for district (excluding school)	33.93	1.85
GCSE/GNVQ score in district (excluding school)	50.69	9.31
Sixth form pupils/total pupils	0.09	0.09
Part-time/full-time teachers	0.18	0.14
Pupil/teacher ratio	16.85	1.62
Proportion of pupils eligible for free school meals	0.16	0.14
Proportion of pupils with special needs	0.20	0.10
Proportion of pupils from ethnic minority	0.12	0.21
Total pupils on school roll (all ages)	1004	337

Note: All variables refer to 2002 data.

Sources: Schools' Census (Form 7) and School Performance Tables.

11 Determinants of educational success in higher education

Robin A. Naylor and Jeremy Smith

1 Introduction

The issue of what characteristics are associated with a student's level of academic attainment at university is a very topical one. This is particularly true of the United Kingdom, which will provide the focus for much of our discussion in this chapter. The reasons for the current high level of interest are many and varied. First, for example, there is a concern with differences in educational attainment by gender. It is well known that, in both primary and secondary education, girls are performing significantly, and often increasingly, better than boys in many countries. Perhaps surprisingly, there is growing evidence, as we summarize later in this chapter, that this is also true of degree-level tertiary education. Exploring the possible reasons for this is an important project.

Second, as in many countries, UK government policies over the charging of fees to home-based university students have undergone radical changes over the last two decades, as has the system of funding and supporting students' maintenance costs while at university. In the UK, policy over both fees and funding continues to be the source of discussion and debate. An important element in this debate concerns the extent to which a student's capacity to study is compromised by the need to engage in labour market activity to support himself or herself financially. Such a risk is likely to vary with the student's social class background. Additionally there are sociological and sociopsychological reasons for expecting student performance to vary across socioeconomic groups.

Third, the majority of UK students (and the overwhelming majority of English students) attending university in the UK study A-levels prior to entering higher education. Offers of places at university are typically made conditional on students' A-level attainment (including both choice of subject and level of attainment). In this context, it is interesting to analyse the extent to which performance at A-level and at university are correlated with each other. This is especially valuable at a time, as at present, when there is policy discussion over reform of the A-level system.

Fourth, there has been considerable debate in the UK about the extent to which access to higher education is fair and equal. In the context of a

415

much-cited case in 2000 concerning a very highly qualified state-educated applicant rejected by the University of Oxford, the Chancellor of the Exchequer expressed concern about possible elitism in the admissions policies of a particular UK university. The crucial context for the case is the fact that the percentage of independent school-educated students at some of the UK's top universities is higher than 50 per cent, despite the fact that only a small minority (approximately 7 per cent) of pupils attend independent schools in the UK. In the light of this issue, and in the context of the more general and important literature on the effects of schools on later performance, it is interesting to examine whether there is any association between degree performance of students and the type of their pre-university schooling.

Fifth, as in a number of countries, the government in the UK is promoting greater participation in higher education as an engine both of economic growth and of social justice. Policies have been implemented to expand university enrolment and to widen participation. In a little over two decades, the participation rate of 18–21-year-olds in university in the UK rose from about 10 per cent to over 30 per cent and the government has recently announced a target of 50 per cent of 18–30-year-olds. The objective of widening participation stems from the fact that students from outside professional or related social class groups are disproportionately underrepresented in higher education. There is also variation in the participation rate by age, ethnicity and disability status. Policies of lifelong learning have also aimed at generating greater incentives for more mature students to take up higher education places. These policies suggest that an interesting question concerns the extent to which the higher education performance of students is sensitive to characteristics such as social class background, age, ethnicity, disability status and prior qualifications. Furthermore, decisions to enrol in higher education by individuals from various groups are themselves likely to be influenced by the perception that individuals have about their prospects at university.

Sixth, performance indicators (PIs) of public services have become increasingly prevalent in many countries. In part, PIs are substitutes for price signals in services delivered through public sector quasi-markets. Government-produced league tables of performance in primary and secondary schools are well established in the UK. To these was added a set of PIs for higher education institutions (HEIs) from December 1999. PIs for HEIs in the UK cover criteria such as access, progression, research, teaching and graduate employment. PIs are designed in part to furnish potential university applicants with better quality information. In the present chapter, we address the issue of the determinants of student progression and draw conclusions regarding university performance indicators based on progression rates.

Seventh, there is strong evidence that post-university labour market prospects themselves depend on university performance. For example, Naylor *et al.* (2002a, 2002b) have shown that there is a premium of 10 per cent–15 per cent associated with the award of a first class degree compared to a third class. Evidence on the sensitivity of graduate labour market outcomes to the graduate's university performance renders an analysis of the latter of further significance (see also Smith *et al.*, 2000).

Finally, most of what we have described above is framed in terms of an analysis of the degree class obtained by students. In the current chapter, we primarily review work of two distinct kinds. First, we focus on analyses of degree outcomes distinguishing between different classes of degree. Essentially, the possible outcomes are first, upper second, lower second and third class honours, non-honours degrees and non-qualification. One form of non-qualification is non-progression through the different stages of the degree. In a second focus of this chapter, we review work on the factors associated with non-progression. This is particularly important in the light of both discussion about the possible adverse effects on progression associated with increasing the fees and costs of study and the increasing importance attached to PIs on progression.

The work reviewed in this chapter is typically based on data sets which contain information on university students but which do not contain complementary data on non-students. This means that there is no control group and hence the analyses described are to be interpreted as conditional on university entrance. It is our view that the analysis of university participation, selection and admission is relatively underdeveloped and should be the focus of further analysis.

The rest of this chapter is organized as follows. In section 2, we review the existing literature on determinants of student performance at university. In section 3, we focus specifically on an appraisal of the literature on the issue of dropping out of higher education. In section 4, we present the results of new work in which we update the evidence on UK university degree performance with an analysis of data for more recent cohorts of university leavers than have been considered in previous work. Section 5 closes the chapter with conclusions and further remarks.

2   Determinants of degree outcome

In this section of the chapter, we focus primarily on the analysis of higher education performance based on full cohorts of UK university students. This focus stems from the fact that full-cohort data for UK universities have become available recently and there has been a consequent research interest in this area. We also refer to evidence for other countries. Later in this chapter, we present results from new work we have conducted for the UK, but first we begin this section by reviewing results from earlier work.

Analysis based on student-level data: sub-samples of students and aggregated data

Prior to the availability to researchers of administrative data on full cohorts of UK university students, analysis of degree class outcomes was based either on aggregated university-level data or on individual-level data for subgroups of students at particular institutions or studying for particular degree subjects. Work tended to focus on differences by personal character- istics, institution, course and prior qualifications.

Personal characteristics   There is a long tradition in the UK of analyses of the determinants of degree class. Many studies have focused on differences in degree performance by age and gender, though typically they have not controlled for a wide range of personal or other characteristics. In this tra- dition, Hoskins *et al.* (1997), with data for Plymouth University for the period 1991–5, found a significant gender influence, with females perform- ing better than males. Rudd (1984) used aggregated data by university for 1967, 1978 and 1979 and found no gender differences in average perfor- mance, but greater variation in performance for males. Chapman (1996a) obtained data for university departments of geography, and found strong gender differences for first class degrees. Chapman (1996b) used individual- level data for eight subject areas over a 21-year period, but presented results at an aggregated departmental level. McCrum (1994) found that, on average, men performed better than women at Oxbridge for the period 1987–91. This result, differing as it does from findings for other UK univer- sities, is also the focus of analysis by Mellanby *et al.* (2000). Using univer- sity-level data, Johnes and Taylor (1990) found that the ratio of male to female graduates was unrelated to degree outcomes.

In the context of government policies to widen access to universities and to encourage 'lifelong learning', a key concern for educationalists in recent years has been the effect of age on higher educational attainment. However there seems to be no general consensus on age effects. Different studies have produced different results depending on the data set used. Bee and Dolton (1985), using aggregated university-level data, find age to be the only sig- nificant personal characteristic affecting degree class and pass rate averages across universities: the effect is negative. Hoskins *et al.* (1997), on the other hand, find that the level of performance increases with age.

For the USA, Borg and Stranahan (2002a, 2002b) have addressed the question of whether race, gender and personality type are important influ- ences on student performance in Economics courses. Borg and Stranahan

(2002a) analyse the performance in a Principles of Macroeconomics course of a sample of 119 students at the University of North Florida. They focus on interactions between the student's personality type and race and gender. They find that race and gender combine with temperament 'to form more subtle, interactive effects on a student's probability of success in economics' (ibid., p. 597). Borg and Stranahan (2002b) show that similar results hold for performance at upper level as well as at principles level.

Differences across university and course　In the UK, Bee and Dolton (1985) reported large and persistent differences across universities in the proportion of students obtaining first and upper second class honours degrees. The same was true for the proportions passing their degrees successfully. Chapman (1996a) found very different patterns of degree results across university geography departments, especially when disaggregated by gender. For the study of economics, Nevin (1972), using aggregate student returns, found that degrees awarded in Economics tended to be skewed towards lower seconds and thirds, even relative to other social sciences. In general, Nevin found variation between universities exceeded that between subject groups. Hoskins *et al.* (1997) found that faculty of study had a significant effect on degree class: in particular, there was a significant positive effect associated with the technology and arts faculties. Johnes and Taylor (1990) found that a very high proportion of the (considerable) differences in degree results across institutions could be explained by a parsimonious set of control variables for university characteristics.

Previous education　The impact of school quality on pupil/student performance has attracted growing interest, not least in the UK with the production of school performance measures and the associated debate on value-added and socioeconomic context. In the USA, there is mixed evidence regarding the effects of school quality on pupil performance (see, for example, Eide and Showalter, 1998, and Chapter 9 in the present volume). With respect to the student's own pre-university academic performance, a number of studies have focused on the correlation between A-level scores and degree performance. Sear (1983), found a correlation coefficient of about 0.3 between A-level grades and degree classification, using grouped data. In similar analyses, Bourner and Hamed (1987) reported an average correlation of 0.2 with variation across disciplines, whilst Peers and Johnston (1994) found a correlation of 0.28 across all universities (including both pre- and post-1992 universities), with a greater correlation for the older universities. Chapman (1996b) calculates the correlation coefficient between mean A-level scores and the proportion of students obtaining good degrees for a subset of UK university departments. He finds large differences in the correlation coefficient by subject area (for example, he calculates 0.47 for biology and 0.23 for politics). He also finds that the relationship is very stable over time for most of the individual departments. Johnes and Taylor (1990) found that the mean A-level score of entrants explained a large proportion of the cross-university differences in degree performance.

Other factors   An interesting question concerns the extent to which study habits affect student performance in higher education. Does it help or hinder to have a significant involvement in extracurricular activities? To what extent does attendance and participation in lectures and seminars have an impact on degree performance? We regard this work as important but largely beyond the scope of the current chapter. We refer the reader to Brauer *et al.* (1994), Devadoss and Foltz (1996) and Romer (1993). A particular question which has aroused significant interest recently concerns peer effects on educational attainment. Sacerdote (2000), for example, analyses peer effects on student academic effort (and on other aspects of student behaviour) for students in the classes of 1997 and 1998 at Dartmouth College. Sacerdote reports that study effort is significantly influenced by peer effects operating through room-mate behaviour. Crucially the analysis is able to overcome well-known problems in the identification of peer effects (see, for example, Manski, 1993) through the fact that freshmen at Dartmouth are randomly assigned to rooms and dorms.

Analysis based on data from general cohort studies
Blundell *et al.* (1997) conducted an ordered probit analysis of education attainment on a sample of individuals from the National Child Development Study (NCDS) and ran separate regressions for men and women. One interesting difference across the equations was that school type has a statistically significant effect on higher education attainment only for women (in a separate analysis of A-level attainment, Blundell *et al.* (1997, 2000) find that school type has a positive significant effect for both sexes). Dearden *et al.* (1998), also using NCDS data, report that inputs such as pupil-teacher ratio, LEA funding per pupil and teacher salaries do not have significant effects on educational attainment (as measured by whether the individual obtains a degree or not). They find that school type, however, is significant, as is attendance at a single-sex school for females. Blundell *et al.* (1997) find that family background characteristics such as parental occupation and education are significant determinants of A-level attainment and are (at least jointly) significant for higher educational attainment. They also find that demographic variables are jointly significant for men's higher educational attainment. These variables include proportions of households in the

local authority with head of household unemployed, with head of house-hold in top social class, together with measures of home ownership/tenancy.

Analysis based on student-level data for full cohorts of students in HE
UK universities maintain administrative records on each student entering their institution. These records contain the following kinds of information on each student:

1. personal characteristics (such as age, gender, nationality and, for more recent – that is, post-1994 – cohorts, ethnicity and disability status);
2. prior qualifications, including subjects taken and grades achieved at, for example, A-level;
3. previous (UK) school (identifying the individual school itself);
4. country/county of prior residence;
5. parental occupation (at the three-digit SOC code level);
6. course studied (at the detailed four-digit Universities and Colleges Admissions Service (UCAS) code level);
7. course characteristics (full-time/part-time, official length, actual duration, if sandwich course, if year abroad and so on);
8. other study-related characteristics (including fees status, accommo-dation type);
9. reason for and timing of leaving university (including information on whether the student had succeeded academically or left for some other reason, such as non-completion of studies);
10. qualification outcome, including information on both the level of qualification, if any, and any degree class awarded.

To these sets of information can be matched various sets of complemen-tary data. For example, given that the student's pre-university school is identified, information on school characteristics, such as school league table performance measures, school census data and teacher/pupil ratios, can be merged into the data set. School fees data can also be merged for the case of independent schools, along with other information on independent schools, such as boarding arrangements. Similarly the school postcode can be used to match with indicators of the economic and sociodemographic features of the school neighbourhood through, for example, census infor-mation and local labour market data. Additionally information on paren-tal occupation can be recoded into a social class background indicator.

Clearly administrative data on entire cohorts of UK university students represent a valuable resource. The data from all universities (and, since

1994, all higher education institutions) are collected together into a central depository. Before 1972, this was the University Grants Committee (UGC). From 1972 to 1994, the organization responsible for holding and managing the data was the Universities Statistical Record (USR). Similar records for polytechnic and further education institutions were held by the Further Education Statistical Record (FESR). Since 1994, the central source for the individual and institution-level statistics for all higher education institutions (HEIs) has been the Higher Education Statistics Agency (HESA). Typically there is and has been only limited access to student records data for independent researchers. It is notable, for example, that as recently as 1990 the seminal analysis published in Johnes and Taylor (1990) was based on student records aggregated to the university level. However a window allowing unlimited access to the full records for the cohorts leaving university between the academic years 1971/2 and 1992/3 opened when HESA replaced USR as the central source in 1994. At that point the USR records became available and have been used subsequently for the purposes of various analyses of student behaviour and outcomes.

It is our belief that the USR/HESA data sets are unique in an international sense, providing an invaluable resource with which researchers are able to address issues relating to HE student outcomes on the basis of rich and highly detailed information for complete student cohorts. We are not aware of the existence of equivalent data for other countries. It is for this reason that much of the focus of this chapter concentrates on the evidence founded on USR/HESA data for the UK.

In the subsequent sections of the chapter, we proceed to review much of this work. We also review work which is based on more recent access to some of the HESA records. First, we make some preliminary remarks describing some of the key contextual and institutional features regarding university admission in the UK.

The admissions process in UK universities
All admissions to UK universities for full-time undergraduate courses are through a central organization which processes applications. This organization is the Universities and Colleges Admissions Service (UCAS). Currently an applicant is permitted to apply through UCAS for a maximum of six distinct university courses. In each annual round, the closing date for applications is in mid-December (or mid-October in the case of Oxbridge candidates) of the calendar year prior to university entry. It follows that applicants intending to proceed from school to higher education within the same year – that is, without any 'gap year' interval – will submit their application form *prior to* the completion of their school studies and hence without knowledge of their final school grades (that is,

at A-level, in the majority of cases).

This makes the application choices of students complex and uncertain. Furthermore university replies to applicants are also made prior to applicants taking their final school examinations. In such cases, the university reply can either be a rejection of the application or an offer of a place. Such an offer would be made conditional on the applicant achieving certain minimum grades. Some institutions also interview candidates. Finally applicants must respond to offers before they have taken their final school examinations. Each applicant can accept a maximum of two offers: one being a 'firm' acceptance and the other being an 'insurance' acceptance. If, when the applicant's grades are subsequently published, the grades satisfy the conditions of the conditional offer, then both the university making the offer and the applicant firmly accepting the offer are committed to respecting the offer/acceptance contract. If the applicant's grades do not meet the conditions of the firmly-accepted offer, then he or she is guaranteed a place on the university course for which an offer was accepted by the applicant on an 'insurance-accept' basis, *provided that* the grades meet the conditions of that offer. Any student whose grades fall below the standard required by both the firm and insurance accepted conditional offers is able to enter into a 'clearing' process in which unplaced applicants match themselves with unfilled university places (if applicants' grades fall below the offer required, they might nonetheless be accepted by one or other of their firm or insurance-accepted universities if the university has unfilled places). The clearing process is also administered by the central admissions organization.

Some students take a gap year prior to entering higher education. These students can choose between applying during their final school year, as described above, for a *deferred* university place and applying in the subsequent admissions round once they have received their final school grades. In this latter case, both the applicant and the institution to which the application has been made have full information about grades achieved. The university response to an application is then either to reject or to make an unconditional offer. The student made one or more unconditional offers can firmly accept only one.

University departmental admissions tutors determine admissions policies for their courses in order to achieve various objectives and to satisfy particular constraints. Most crucially, they aim to recruit the ablest applicants while equating the number of entrants to a target entry population. Many pieces of information contained in the application form might be taken into account, including a personal statement, a school reference, grades already attained and predicted grades, in making an offer and setting a conditional grade requirement. The distribution of the grades offered to applicants for a particular university course will be set so that the predicted number accepting and making the conditions of the offer will equal the number of places available. *Ceteris paribus*, the higher the typical offer the smaller will be the number of successful applicants.[1] Thus the typical offer acts as a rationing device. If demand for a particular university course grows over time, there will be a tendency for the required grades to grow too. This is also likely to lead to a better qualified and higher ability entry cohort for the degree course, other things being equal. Universities have a further motivation for setting a high offer: the average pre-university grade attainment of its students is likely to be taken as an indicator of university quality. Against this, there is the risk that high offers will preclude entry from potential students with high ability but relatively poor pre-university schooling opportunities. This issue is very relevant for recent debates on access to UK higher education and will be discussed further in the contexts of results we review in subsequent sections of the chapter.

Whilst pre-university qualifications such as A-levels are based largely on public examinations which are nationally set and assessed, higher education qualifications are awarded by individual institutions which set and mark their own examinations and coursework. Thus, while, say, a grade B in Mathematics A-level indicates the same level of attainment for any individual regardless of where they have studied, a particular degree classification, such as an upper second class honours degree, in any given subject, does not necessarily indicate the same level of attainment for students at different universities or on different courses. There is an external examination process by which subject-specific examination boards awarding degrees contain academics from outside institutions. However this system does not impose strict conformity across universities. There are, for example, no nationally agreed benchmarks on criteria which should be attained for the award of each particular degree class.

Also, by way of institutional background, it is important to note that in 1992 there was a major structural change in the higher education sector in the UK. The long-standing binary divide between the university sector and the rest of the higher education sector (comprising the polytechnics, for example) was abolished. At a stroke, this expanded greatly the nominal university sector. This has rendered comparisons of trends and behaviour either side of 1992 difficult. In section 4 of this chapter, where we present some new results for 1998 graduates, we focus on only those institutions which had pre-1992 university status. In this way we attempt to make approximately like-for-like comparisons.

Methodology for the analysis of degree performance
The standard analysis of degree performance and its determinants involves an ordered probit approach. The dependent variable is the individual

student's degree classification, Y_i, which is a discrete ordered dependent variable categorized into one of, typically, five response codes: first class honours degree, upper second class honours degree, lower second class honours degree, third class honours degree, and other. The latter category then consists of unclassified honours degree, pass degree, aegrotat degree, other degree level qualification and failure to obtain a qualification. Clearly alternative categorizations are possible. An alternative approach would involve a sequential structure in which one first models the probability of obtaining a qualification (as opposed to, say, dropping out or failing) and then the probability of the degree class awarded, conditional on qualification.[2]

The assumption underlying the ordered probit model is that there is a latent unobservable continuous variable, Y_i^*, which measures a student's academic performance at university and which is a function of a vector of observable characteristics, X_i:

$$Y_i^* = \alpha + \beta X_i + u_i.$$

Although Y_i^* is not observed, Y_i, which is essentially a censored form of the latent variable Y_i^*, is observed, and takes the values

$$
\begin{aligned}
Y_i &= 0 \text{ if } Y_i^* \leq \mu_1, \\
Y_i &= 1 \text{ if } \mu_1 < Y_i^* \leq \mu_2, \\
Y_i &= 2 \text{ if } \mu_2 < Y_i^* \leq \mu_3, \\
Y_i &= 3 \text{ if } \mu_3 < Y_i^* \leq \mu_4, \\
Y_i &= 4 \text{ if } \mu_4 > Y_i^*,
\end{aligned}
$$

where the μ_i, $(i = 1, \ldots, 4)$, are the unknown threshold parameters dividing the discrete degree classes. The imposed assumption adopted in work to date is that these threshold values are common across courses and institutions. An interesting issue for further work would be to test the extent to which this is supported by the data. Under the assumption that u_i is normally distributed, the respective probabilities are given by

$$
\begin{aligned}
P(Y_i = 0) &= F(\mu_1 - \beta'X), \\
P(Y_i = 1) &= F(\mu_2 - \beta'X) - F(\mu_1 - \beta'X), \\
P(Y_i = 2) &= F(\mu_3 - \beta'X) - F(\mu_2 - \beta'X), \\
P(Y_i = 3) &= F(\mu_4 - \beta'X) - F(\mu_3 - \beta'X), \\
P(Y_i = 4) &= 1 - F(\mu_4 - \beta'X),
\end{aligned}
$$

where $F(z)$ is the cumulative distribution function of a standard normal. It is then straightforward to estimate the parameters in an ordered probit model. Essentially this is the approach adopted in the papers reviewed below.

Results based on USR data for full university leaving cohorts prior to 1994
In this section of the chapter, we review a selection of results from a series of recent papers which have exploited USR data comprising individual student records for full UK university leaving cohorts.

First, we present and discuss summary and descriptive statistics based on these USR data. In particular, we describe the composition of UK university student populations by characteristics such as school and social class background, gender, prior qualifications, age and degree subject. We focus on background characteristics as these are relevant to the recent policy focus on the issues of access and widening participation in UK higher education.

Summary statistics

School background   We start by discussing at some length the composition of the student body in terms of prior schooling. This is chiefly because issues of access have been so central to much recent discussion and current debate within the sector.

Much has been made of the fact that, among universities in the UK, one finds a number of cases in which 50 per cent or more of students come from the independent school sector. It has been argued that this is very unrepresentative of the school population. Indeed, compared to a figure of 7 per cent for the proportion of all school pupils in the independent sector, 50 per cent looks very disproportionate. But is 7 per cent the right point of comparison? Universities can pick only from those staying on into the sixth form. Thus a more appropriate benchmark figure would be the percentage of sixth form students who had attended an independent school. This figure is about 20 per cent.[3] Yet even this figure of 20 per cent is probably not the right one with which to compare the 50 per cent figure. This is because admission selectors in the top universities are typically looking for students with very high levels of achievement at A-level. So a more appropriate comparison might be the proportion of students with, say, AAB or AAA at A-level.

In this subsection on school background, we use data collected from four entrant cohorts of students for the years 1989, 1990, 1991 and 1992, and limit the analysis to full-time, non-overseas students (who were less than 24 years old on entry) starting at an English university. We limit attention to these students in order to be able to make an appropriate match between each student and the school they attended prior to entering university.

Our analysis suggests that over the four-year period from 1989 to 1992, about 36 per cent of those with at least AAB had attended an independent school before university. In order to produce the 36 per cent figure for the benchmark against which to judge the extent of overrepresentation of independent-educated students at certain UK universities (or university types) we have looked at the composition of the student body by school type and by the student's performance in their A-level examinations prior to university, and upon which entry into university is conditional. Students traditionally have taken three A-levels, which are graded as A down to E, below which is a fail grade. A UCAS points system then ascribes 10 points for an A grade down to 2 points to an E grade and so across three A-levels students are scored out of 30 points. Table 11.1 reports the proportion of students at university from the independent school and non-independent school sectors with good A-level grades. These students predominantly sat their A-levels around ten years ago; owing to the increase in A-level offers at almost all universities over this period, we actually present figures for a variety of A-level scores, and not simply for 30 points.

Table 11.1 A-level scores by school sector and sex, 1989–92 entrants

A-level points	Females		Males	
	Independent	Non-indep.	Independent	Non-indep.
30	0.405	0.595	0.407	0.593
28+	0.358	0.642	0.373	0.627
26+	0.342	0.658	0.360	0.640
24+	0.326	0.674	0.351	0.649
22+	0.314	0.686	0.345	0.655
20+	0.300	0.700	0.336	0.664

The proportion of students from an independent school with 28 points or more in their best three A-levels (reported in Table 11.1) are similar to figures reported by the Department for Education and Skills (DfES) for students with 30 points from independent schools in 1997–8. One might conclude that, against this benchmark of 36 per cent, the figure of 50 per cent for the percentage of students at top universities who had been to an independent school still seems disproportionately high.[4] The results we report below suggest that achieved grade scores of less than AAB for applicants from less privileged school backgrounds are likely to underpredict the true potential of these applicants. If one takes this into account, a fairer benchmark for comparison is likely to be less than 36 per cent.

We now exploit the richness of the USR data to analyse how the proportion of students from independent schools varies across universities. We find that around 30 per cent of all English university entrants came from the independent school sector.[5] This figure is remarkably constant over the entire period for which we have examined USR data (that is, 1982–1992). Figures 11.1a and 11.1b show the proportion of males and females coming from the independent school sector for each university, respectively. We distinguish between four groups of universities based on Figures 11.1a and 11.1b: Group 1 universities have more than 40 per cent of their students from the independent school sector,[6] Group 2 have between 30 and 40 per cent, Group 3 have between 20 and 30 per cent and Group 4 have less than 20 per cent.

Table 11.2 gives basic summary statistics for these four groups of universities for males and females separately.

Each of these four university groups comprises at least six universities, with more than 18000 students within each group. For males, the average number of students coming from any independent school is quite large for Group 1 at 49.1 per cent. For females, it is 46.8 per cent.

These aggregate statistics show a high concentration of students from the independent school sector in some universities. However, given the richness of the USR data, we are able to extend the analysis beyond the extent of overrepresentation of students from the independent sector as a whole. We are able to compute concentration ratios for each university, by which we measure the proportion of a university's students who attended particular independent schools. This is because, using school-level data from the DfES performance indicators from 1992, the school register and other sources, we are able to match the previous school for the cohort of students

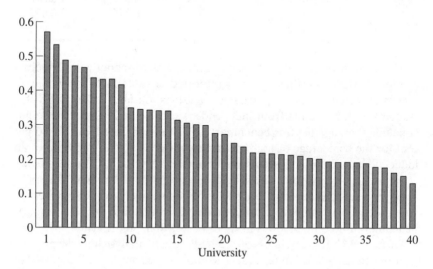

Figure 11.1a   English universities' student intake from independent schools, males (1989–92 entrants)

in the USR database with their school details, including the name of the independent school attended.

For each individual university we now define the university's own 10, 20 and 30 most-represented independent schools, ranked by the total number of students these schools send to that university. The analysis is done separately for males and females. We construct concentration ratios for each university, as the proportion of the universities' students coming from its leading independent schools. For all universities in England, the leading 30 English independent schools account for 9.4 per cent and 7.3 per cent of all students at university for males and females, respectively. For the 20 (10) leading schools the corresponding numbers are 6.8 per cent (4.0 per cent) and 5.4 per cent (3.1 per cent) for males and females, respectively. However, there is substantial variation around this average figure for individual universities. In Figures 11.2a and 11.2b, we show the variation in the concentration ratios across the aggregated four groups of universities for males and females, respectively. From Figures 11.2a and 11.2b it is clear that the concentration ratio is greater amongst males than females. In addition, the figures show that, for Group 1, the leading 30 (20) [10] schools account for 19.1 per cent (14.6 per cent) [9.0 per cent] of all male students at these universities. That is, about one in five of the 32011 male students at the nine universities in Group 1 come from just 30 independent schools. The corresponding figures for females are 14.9 per cent (11.4 per cent) [6.9 per cent].

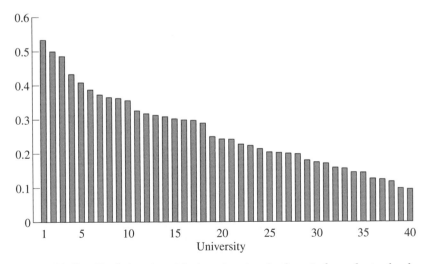

Figure 11.1b   *English universities' student intake from independent schools, females (1989–92 entrants)*

Table 11.2 Summary statistics for the four university groups, 1989–92 entrants

	Males					Females				
	All	1	2	3	4	All	1	2	3	4
No. universities	40	9	10	13	8	40	6	11	11	12
No. students	124045	32011	35822	37727	18485	94737	18776	29482	21795	24684
No. independent	38692	15710	11385	8415	3182	27436	8791	9596	5177	3872
% independent	31.2	49.1	31.8	22.3	17.2	29.0	46.8	32.5	23.8	15.7

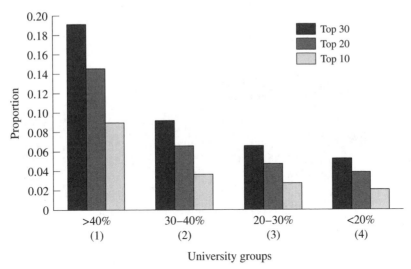

Figure 11.2a Proportion of students within the four groups from leading schools (males)

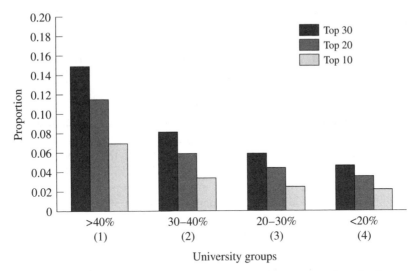

Figure 11.2b Proportion of students within the four groups from leading schools (females)

Social class background The proportion of UK university students from Social Class I was about 16 per cent in 1993 (compared to 4 per cent for Great Britain as a whole). This is a significantly higher proportion than that

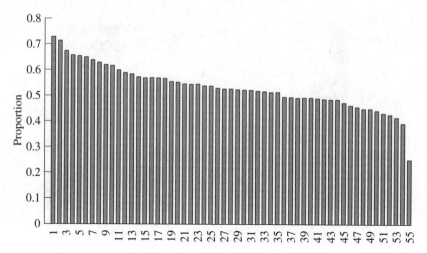

*Figure 11.3   Proportion of students from SC I or SC II, by all UK
universities (1993 leavers)*

for the population as a whole. A further 37 per cent of students were from
Social Class II. Figure 11.3 shows how the total proportion of students
from either Social Class I or II varies across universities. Given this variation and an expectation that degree performance is likely to vary by social
class background, one would expect degree performance to vary across
institutions.

Gender and age   Between 1982 and 1992, there was a substantial increase
in the number of students going to a UK university. Over the same period,
the proportion of female students rose dramatically, suggesting that a disproportionate amount of the expansion originated in the relative growth of
female participation in higher education in the UK. Figure 11.4 shows that
the total number of UK university entrants rose from less than 70 000 in
1982 to about 105 000 in 1992, an increase of about 50 per cent. The proportion of these students who are male fell from almost 60 per cent to less
than 53 per cent over this period, as shown in Figure 11.5. At the same time,
there was a tendency for a higher proportion of more mature students to
participate in higher education. Figure 11.6 shows that the proportion aged
under 19 on entry to university fell from almost 60 per cent to about 52 per
cent in the period. There was, however, very little change in the proportion
studying full-time.

Prior qualifications   Around three-quarters of UK university students
took A-level qualifications prior to university, with a slight decline during

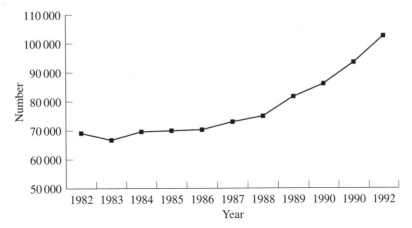

Figure 11.4   Number of undergraduate students entering any UK university, 1982–92

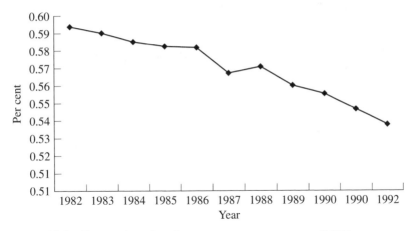

Figure 11.5   Proportion of males amongst new entrants, all UK universities, 1982–92

the 1982–92 period, as shown in Figure 11.7. In contrast, there was a growth in the proportion of students who already had a degree-level qualification. Of those taking A-levels, there was a change over time in the proportions of A-level subjects offered by entrants, as seen in Figure 11.8. Subjects in decline included mathematics, German and general studies, with small increases across a range of other subjects. There was a marked tendency for the average A-level points to rise over the period, especially for female entrants, as shown in Figure 11.9. This is particularly surprising in the context of the pattern of growth in student numbers, referred to above. The picture is not inconsistent with grade inflation in A-level scores over the period. As we can see from Figure 11.10, among students who had taken A-levels, there was a tendency for the proportion of students with maximum scores to increase (from 9 per cent with 30 A-level points in 1982 to 12 per cent in 1992). Figure 11.11 shows that there is a far from uniform distribution of entrants with high scores (28 points or more) at A-level (and similarly for Scottish Highers) across institutions.

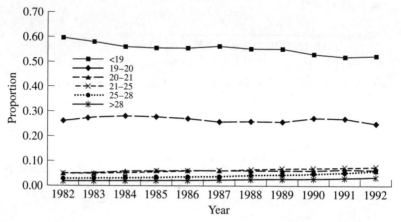

Figure 11.6   New entrants, by age category, for all UK universities, 1982–92

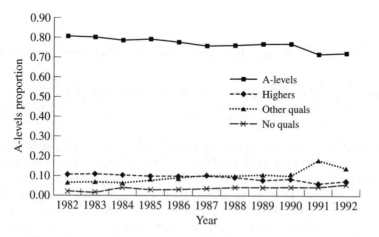

Figure 11.7   New entrants, by prior academic qualifications, for all UK universities, 1982–92

Degree subjects   Figure 11.12 shows the changing pattern of registrations by degree subject over the 1982–92 period. There is notable stability over time, with a small number of individual cases exhibiting significant change. For example, the largest course (by number of registered students) is engineering, which shows a decline over time.

Degree classification: patterns and trends   Figure 11.13 shows the breakdown of degree class by gender over time during the 1982–1992 period. We

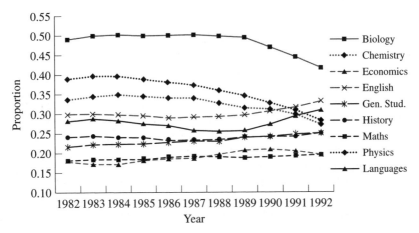

Figure 11.8   *New entrants' A-level subjects for all UK universities, 1982–92*

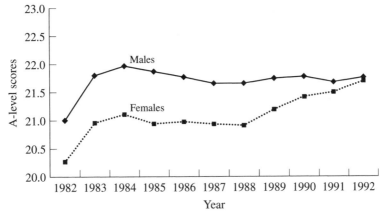

Figure 11.9   *New entrants' average A-level score (out of 30) for all UK universities, 1982–92*

can see that the proportion of students with first class degrees was never more than 10 per cent. This percentage has risen over time and remains typically greater for males than for females. The biggest change, however, was around the upper/lower second class border, with a movement towards more upper second class degrees. The proportion of students with upper seconds is much greater for females than for males. Figure 11.14 shows that the proportion of students with at least an upper second class degree varies substantially across universities.

Empirical results

Prior qualifications   Smith and Naylor (2001a) and McNabb *et al.* (2002) have examined the effects of A-level points scored on the individual's degree performance. In an ordered probit model of the kind described above, both papers find that there is a significant statistical relationship between A-level score and the probability of doing well at university. Smith and Naylor (2001a), for example, estimated that an extra grade in each A-level subject taken (for example, BBB rather than CCC) is associated with an approximate 10 percentage point greater probability of obtaining a 'good' degree (that is, an upper second or first class honours degree). Smith and Naylor (2001a) also report that there are significant and sizeable premia – in terms of a greater probability of obtaining a good degree – associated with having studied mathematics before going to university.

Previous schooling   Both Smith and Naylor (2001a) and McNabb *et al.* (2002) have examined the relationship between the type of school attended prior to university and subsequent degree class attainment. Both papers report that students educated in private or independent schools perform less well at university than do otherwise observationally equivalent students educated in state-sector 'LEA' (local education authority) schools. Smith and Naylor (2001a) estimate that a student from an independent school is about 9 percentage points less likely to obtain a good degree than is a student from an LEA school, *ceteris paribus*. McNabb *et al.* (2002, p. 491) conclude, 'This lends support to the idea that students from private schools have an advantage over those from state schools in gaining admission to university because they are able to achieve higher average A-level grades for a given level of student quality. It also suggests that consideration should be given to this when formulating university admissions policy, and it lends some support, at least, for policies aimed at widening access to university.' Indeed, one could argue that the empirical results imply that policies to widen participation can be justified not just on grounds of social justice and equity, but also on efficiency criteria: if a university wants to

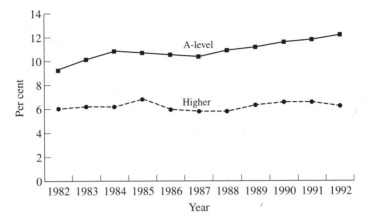

Figure 11.10   Proportion of new entrants with top A-level/Higher score for all UK universities, 1982–92

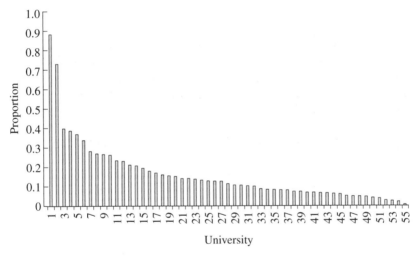

Figure 11.11   Students with at least 28 (14) A-level (Higher) points at all UK universities (1993 leavers)

recruit the most able students, it might be advised to give lower offers to applicants from particular educational backgrounds. Recently in the UK, individual universities implementing such admissions strategies have been criticized for alleged discriminatory practices. By way of defence, they have been able to cite the empirical evidence reported in Smith and Naylor (2001a) and McNabb *et al.* (2002). The magnitude of the effects reported

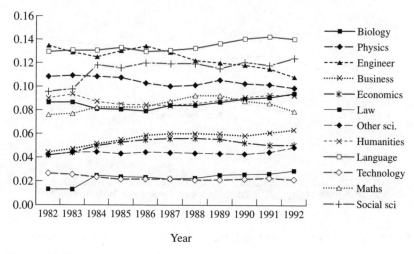

*Figure 11.12   New entrants' course of study at all UK universities,
1982–92*

in Smith and Naylor (2001a) implies that, to equalize the probabilities of a good degree across applicants from LEA and independent schools, applicants from the latter will need to achieve approximately one grade higher in each of the three A-level subjects, other things being equal.

In addition to the effects of the *type* of previous schooling on degree performance, Smith and Naylor (2001a) examine the associations between degree attainment and other characteristics of the previous school attended. This is possible because knowledge of the identity of the school attended enables DfES school 'league table' information to be matched to the USR dataset. Amongst other results, they report that there is a positive association between the student's university performance and the performance of the previously attended school against official criteria (such as the average A-level points attainment of pupils at the school). In the light of the school type association, this is a particularly interesting result as one might have expected the opposite. Instead it seems as though attendance at, say, a well-performing LEA school enables a pupil to do better both at A-level and at university. This contrasts with the received interpretation of the independent school effect by which the educational boost appears to be a short-term one only.

Betts and Morrell (1999) analyse the determinants of the undergraduate grade point average for more than 5000 students at the University of California, San Diego. They find that graduates of different high schools obtain significantly different scores, *ceteris paribus*. They suggest that, in

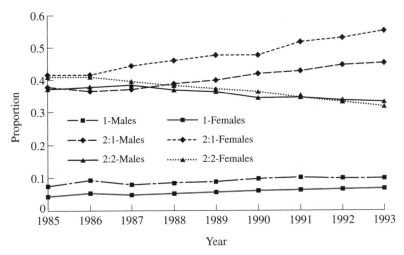

Figure 11.13   Degree classification of students at all UK universities (1985–93 leavers)

part, the school effects reflect neighbourhood characteristics such as poverty levels and local education levels in the adult population.

Personal characteristics   Given the finding that a relatively privileged schooling prior to university seems to have the short-term effect of raising A-level performance, it might be hypothesized that the same would be true of a relatively privileged family background. In other words, one might expect that a student from a Social Class I family class background with, say, 3 grade Bs at A-level, would, other things constant, possess less ability than a student with the same grades but from, say, Social Class IV. It is well known that local neighbourhood social class composition has a strong influence on school performance, for example (see Gibson and Asthana, 1998). One would then expect a better performance at university from the student from the Social Class IV background, *ceteris paribus*. The empirical finding, however, is not consistent with this hypothesis. It emerges instead that, for both men and women, there is a very well-determined and monotonically positive effect defined over Social Classes I to V: academic performance at university is better the more 'advantaged' is the student's home background, as Smith and Naylor (2001a) report. We note, however, that there is evidence from Smith and Naylor (2001b) that the effects of social class background might be influencing degree performance through their effects on the probability of failure through non-completion.

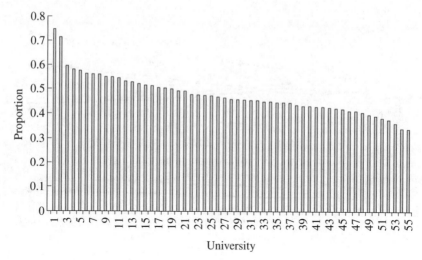

Figure 11.14   Students with a 'good' degree at all UK universities (1993 leavers)

Smith and Naylor (2001a) find that degree performance is monotonically increasing in age for female students. For men, degree performance reaches its peak prior to the age of 34: this is consistent with the finding of McNabb *et al.* (2002). Smith and Naylor (2001a) show that full-time students do better than part-time and that overseas students do less well than home students, on average.

The main focus of the paper by McNabb *et al.* (2002) is on differences in degree performance by gender. Like Smith and Naylor (2001a), they find that, *ceteris paribus*, females are more likely to be awarded a good degree than are male students. Thus, on average, there is evidence that at university – just as at earlier stages of the education process – females outperform males. They also find, however, that female students are less likely to graduate with a first class degree than are men. Both McNabb *et al.* (2002) and Smith and Naylor (2001a) compute an Oaxaca decomposition of the gender differences and find that nearly all of the differences are explained by differences in estimated coefficients rather than by differences in characteristics. McNabb *et al.* (2002) conclude that a possible explanation for the observed gender differences in degree performance is the existence of gender differences in unobserved characteristics such as psychological attitudes to performance and risk-taking behaviour in studying and in examinations.

Course and institutional effects   Both McNabb *et al.* (2002) and Smith and Naylor (2001a) show that, *ceteris paribus*, there are significant differences in the probability of a good degree outcome according to both subject studied and characteristics of the institution attended. For example, Smith and Naylor (2001a) estimate that the probability of a good degree tends to be higher in biological science, literary and classical studies and lower in mathematics, computing and languages. They also report that degree performance was found to be positively associated with the average level of staff salaries and with the level of academic expenditure per student. McNabb *et al.* (2002) report evidence of a positive association between degree performance and both research income and measures of teaching quality.

Bratti (2002) examines differences in degree performance across UK universities by specifying and estimating a subject-specific educational production function (for life sciences) and finds that there are significant differences across universities after the inclusion of a wide range of controls. He also reports that a large part of the university marginal effects cannot be explained by the typical set of institutional characteristics. Finally, Bratti finds significant differences between an unadjusted ranking of universities (ranked by the proportion of good degrees) and an adjusted ranking based on the *ceteris paribus* estimated marginal effects.

Further analysis   A number of the findings reported above have stimulated further analysis. In this section, we review some of this work, beginning with the independent school effect. Earlier we described the principal hypothesis proposed in the literature to explain the finding that, *ceteris paribus*, attendance at an independent school is associated with an inferior performance at university. The hypothesis was based on the idea that independent schools exert a short-term boost on A-level performance, with LEA-educated pupils catching up at university. The A-level boost implies that the LEA-educated student who manages to achieve the same A-level grades as his/her independent-educated counterpart is of greater underlying ability and this explains the better university performance of the LEA-educated, *ceteris paribus*. We can identify two further principal hypotheses to explain the estimated effect associated with school type. The three hypotheses are not mutually exclusive.

The second hypothesis is that the environment and methods of study characterizing LEA schools equip their pupils with skills which enable them to perform better at university, on average, than independent school pupils, even though the latter are better equipped to perform at A-level.

A third hypothesis is that students who had attended an independent school prior to university might perform less well than others as a result of investing less effort in their university studies. For example, it might be that, on average, they calculate that their post-university prospects, judging by the

school they went to, their A-level score and the university attended, are sufficiently good without the need to distinguish themselves further with a good
class of degree. In other words, independent-educated students might make
a rational utility-maximizing decision to expend less effort at university if
they perceive that the marginal return to a degree class is low. In contrast,
an LEA-educated student might perceive that there is a higher marginal
return to a good performance at university. A difference in the expected
returns to degree performance might also originate in differences in connect-
edness to career openings and career networks during and after university.

Naylor and Smith (2002) attempt to shed light on these various hypotheses. They find considerable and significant variation in degree performance across students from different independent schools, *ceteris paribus*.
They find that degree performance is negatively correlated with the magnitude of private school fees. This could be consistent with the third hypothesis above, with students from more expensive (and hence more famous)
independent schools facing a lower marginal return to a good performance
at university. However Naylor *et al.* (2002a) find that, although post-
university occupational earnings are greatest for students from the most
expensive independent schools, the marginal returns to degree class are
constant over school background. Naylor and Smith (2002) conclude that
the evidence is most consistent with the first hypothesis, with the A-level
boost being greatest in the more expensive – and hence better-resourced –
independent schools. It is worth noting that Wright (1999) examines the
relationship between earnings and private schooling and reports no significant difference in the rate of return to education across state and privately
educated pupils.

In terms of the robustness of the effect of independent school over time,
Naylor and Smith (2004), analysing data for economics students, show that
the negative effect associated with having previously attended an independent school is consistent across the 1984–5 to 1992–3 cohorts.

We turn now to robustness of results. Smith and Naylor (2001a) conduct
the ordered probit analysis of degree performance both on all students and,
additionally, separately on particular subsamples of students, such as by
degree subject, by university type, by academic background and by various
personal characteristics. They also compare these results with those generated by models with the inclusion of equivalent interaction terms. They find
that, with very few exceptions, the sign and significance of the estimated
effects are robust across the separate population subsamples. Two exceptions are prominent. First, the superior performance of females (in terms
of the probability of obtaining a good degree) holds across all subgroups
with the exception of students at Oxbridge, where males perform better
than females, on average. Second, the negative marginal effect associated

with having attended an independent school before going to university is particularly large for the subsample of students studying at Oxbridge. This could indicate that Oxbridge colleges are more discriminating over ability when recruiting students from the state sector than they are when recruiting from the private school sector.

Finally we consider relative and absolute levels of prior qualifications. Naylor and Smith (2004) focus on the issue of the impact on an individual's degree performance of pre-university educational attainment, distinguishing between an absolute measure of achievement and also the students' relative performance – or rank – within their own university year cohort. The analysis is conducted for students of economics. This relative performance analysis has received more attention in the context of the dropout/completion issue discussed in the next section of this chapter. Full details of the method are left to that section. Naylor and Smith (2004) report that both absolute and relative performance in prior qualifications are important in determining success in an economics degree. They find that an extra A-level grade increases the probability of a good degree by around two percentage points, although this effect is non-linear, with a greater marginal effect for students with top marks in their A-levels. They also find that, for a given A-level score, being in the top-ranked group of students in a university subject is associated with a greater probability of obtaining a good degree. Finally we note that Naylor and Smith also report that having an A-level in economics does not affect the probability of doing well at degree level, but that having studied mathematics at A-level is associated with a markedly greater probability of being awarded a good degree.

3 Dropping out of higher education

The previous section of the paper focused largely on the factors associated with whether a UK university student would obtain a good degree or not. The ordered probit analysis typically has a number of categories, however, one of which is failure to obtain a degree. One reason for failure is non-completion, or university withdrawal (or 'dropping out'). In 1999, the UK government introduced an annually published performance indicator (PI) for all higher education institutions (HEIs) based on the proportion of students dropping out of their studies. The analysis of dropping out behaviour is consequently of significant policy interest and relevance. Much recent analysis (see, for example, Smith and Naylor, 2001b; Arulampalam *et al.*, 2003, 2004a, 2004b; Johnes and McNabb, 2004) has preferred a more specific focus on completion versus dropout behaviour rather than an approach based on an ordered probit model of the kind described earlier in this chapter. In this section, we review some of the key findings of the recent literature.

Until recently, the analysis of dropping out of university in the UK was of relatively little interest, at least from a policy perspective. In large part, this was because the dropout rate was remarkably low by international standards: at about 8 per cent in the pre-1992 universities. Recently, however, with the expansion in the higher education sector in the UK, the dropout rate has approximately doubled and, as noted above, in the context of a demand for quasi-market performance indicators, calculation of dropout rates has become central to educational policy concerns.

Traditionally the issue of dropout behaviour has received more attention in the USA. Reviewing the US literature, Kalsner (1992) emphasizes that decisions to withdraw are typically based on personal, social and financial considerations, with only a small minority of departures resulting from academic dismissal. One of the most influential theoretical explanations of student attrition is the path analysis model of Tinto (1975, 1988). This model suggests that the student's social and academic integration into the educational institution is the major determinant of completion, and identifies a number of key influences on integration. These include the student's family background, personal characteristics, previous schooling, prior academic performance and interactions between students and with faculty. Family background is likely to influence not only the financial capacity of the student to complete their studies, but also the student's preparedness for college and, related to this, their post-college occupational aspirations. Card and Lemieux (2000) analyse trends and behaviour in both college entry rates and in education completion in the USA. They find that tuition costs and local unemployment rates both influence schooling decisions and that schooling attainment is greater for individuals in smaller cohorts.

Smith and Naylor (2001b) is the first analysis of the probability of dropping out for individual UK university students based on data for full entry cohorts. The data set used by Smith and Naylor is based on the anonymized individual Universities Student Records (USR) for the full populations of undergraduate students leaving the traditional 'pre-1992' universities in one of the years 1990, 1991, 1992 or 1993. The data contain information on approximately 400000 students: about 100000 per cohort. From information on each of these 'leaving cohorts', a data set is generated comprising all those students who entered university at the start of the academic year 1989–90 to study for a full-time three or four-year undergraduate degree and who either completed their degree course (successfully or unsuccessfully) at the end of three or four years, or left university prior to completion. For the purposes of estimating the individual's dropout probability, the constructed entry cohort is used, instead of the leaving cohort, in order to standardize for time-varying influences. The final sample consists of 33851 female and 42407 male students who entered university in Autumn 1989. The non-completion rate was 10.3 per cent for male and 7.1 per cent for female students with considerable variation in the raw dropout rate across universities, ranging from about 1 per cent to 23 per cent for males and from 2 per cent to 19 per cent for females. Based on this population, Smith and Naylor (2001b) conducted a gender-specific binomial probit regression analysis of the probability that an individual withdraws from university.[7] They report probit estimates of the probability of dropping out, with controls for educational background, personal characteristics, degree subject and related attributes, characteristics of the university department, unemployment in the county of prior residence and university attended.

With respect to educational background, Smith and Naylor (2001b) report that the student's A-level points have statistically significant effects on both the male and female dropout probabilities. For males, a point on the A-level average (equivalent to one extra A-level grade for a student with two A-levels) reduces the dropout probability by about 1.4 percentage points, *ceteris paribus*. For females, the marginal effect, although statistically significant, is smaller. The analysis also attempts to take account of the effects of academic preparedness in the sense of the closeness of the match between the subject studied at university and the prior subjects studied at A-level. The results suggest that the subject match is important only for science and social science-based subjects. Like Johnes (1997), Smith and Naylor (2001b) report significant differences in dropout behaviour by degree subject studied. Johnes (1997) also reports significant differences across subjects in the effects of other determinants of dropping out.

For both men and women, the results show that the dropout probability largely increases with age. This may indicate that older students integrate less well into the social environment of UK universities. Alternatively, there may be differences in outside opportunities and responsibilities. Male students from Social Class I are less likely to drop out, *ceteris paribus*. Parents of students from SC I backgrounds are most likely to have studied at university and this may increase the preparedness and motivation of such students to complete their degree studies. Alternatively it might indicate an income effect on the capacity of students to complete their studies.

Consistent with the hypotheses of Tinto and others on the importance of social integration at university, Smith and Naylor (2001b) find that students who live at the parental address are around 2–2.5 percentage points more likely to drop out, and students who live off campus are around 5 percentage points more likely to drop out than are students who live on campus. In order to examine other aspects of social integration, Smith and Naylor (2001b) included the percentage of male students in the university department, but found that gender mix had no significant effects, for either males or females. Additionally they interacted the dummy variable indicating whether the individual student had previously attended an independent school with a variable measuring the proportion of students in the university department who had previously attended such a school. Similarly they also included equivalent interaction terms for students from lower social class backgrounds, for mature students, for overseas students and for fee-paying students. The interaction term for the proportion of students from independent schools was significant, indicating that, for a student who had come from the independent school sector, the probability of dropping out of university is lower the greater the proportion of similarly educated students in the department. The only other significant interaction term was that for female overseas students, with an estimated negative effect implying a positive externality working for this subgroup.

Smith and Naylor (2001b) also examined whether student dropout behaviour is influenced by labour market conditions and, in particular, by unemployment in the county of prior residence. There might be various, potentially offsetting, mechanisms operating to generate an effect of local unemployment on the dropout rate. On the one hand, higher local unemployment reduces the opportunity cost of remaining at university. On the other hand, students may base their expectations of post-university employment probabilities on the unemployment rate observed in their pre-university local labour market. In this case, a high rate of unemployment would lead to a higher withdrawal probability: this effect is likely to be particularly strong for individuals who expect their post-university employment to be in their previous local rather than in the national labour market. Thus, Smith and Naylor (2001b) examine whether any positive relationship between the unemployment rate and the withdrawal probability is stronger for individuals with poorer post-university prospects and for students with limited access to capital markets for funding their studies. They find that the county-level unemployment rate has a well-determined positive effect on the individual drop-out probability, and that, for males, there is a positive and significant interaction between social class background and local unemployment, indicating that students from lower social class backgrounds are more sensitive to local labour market conditions.

University performance indicators on non-progression

As we have noted, the UK government publishes annual performance indicators of university dropout rates. The UK government's Funding Council has stated that, 'If all students qualified within the expected time, then the institution would be 100 per cent efficient' (HEFCE Press Release, 3 December 1999). We note, however, that although there are clearly costs associated with university withdrawal, it is unlikely that the optimal withdrawal rate is zero. As Johnes and Taylor (1989) argued, non-completion does not mean that a student has received no benefit from his or her studies. Indeed, in an uncertain world, a successful matching between degree courses and students is likely to require that some withdrawal is desirable on efficiency grounds.

From the estimated university marginal effects derived in their models of the student dropout probability, Smith and Naylor (2001b) derived *adjusted* rankings of university performance and compared these with the raw or unadjusted rankings. The comparison is shown in Figure 11.15. Each point in the figure represents an institution and the coordinates represent the adjusted and unadjusted rankings. Ranked number 1 on the horizontal axis is the university with the lowest unadjusted dropout probability and, on the vertical axis, is the university with the lowest marginal effect estimated from the probit model of the individual's dropout probability. It is clear from the figure that the ranking of universities on the basis of the adjusted effects is very different from that based on the unadjusted data.

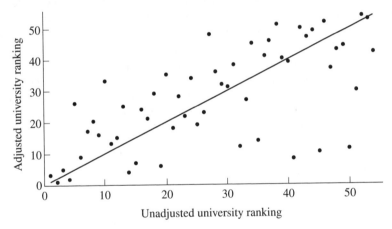

Figure 11.15   Comparison of adjusted and unadjusted university rankings (males)

Following the analysis of Goldstein and Spiegelhalter (1996), Smith and Naylor (2001b) examine the statistical reliability of a league table based on the adjusted ranking. Figure 11.16 presents the 95 per cent confidence intervals for the adjusted university marginal effects on the male dropout probabilities, ordered by their marginal effect. A line is drawn through the point estimate for the median university. This line cuts the majority of the confidence intervals, indicating that one can have little confidence in the rank position of most of the universities relative to the median.

Students who drop out of university are likely to do so for diverse reasons. In particular, some may quit for 'negative' reasons related to disutility associated with their university studies while others may quit for 'positive' reasons related to alternative opportunities. Although all students leaving UK universities are asked to complete a First Destination Survey (FDS) indicating their labour market status in the year following their university departure, very few university dropouts respond to the survey: just 0.3 per cent of dropouts in our sample. Thus the data do not provide information for inferring motives for university withdrawal.

There is, however, direct information in the data regarding the student's reason for leaving, as reported by the university. The university records the withdrawing student as having left either because of academic failure or for 'other reasons'. There are a number of reasons to be cautious about the officially recorded reason for leaving. For example, there are likely to be cases in which apparent academic failure does not capture the real reason for withdrawal. Conversely students who are coded as withdrawing for 'other reasons' may have calculated that they are going to fail and hence leave prior to sitting examinations. Nonetheless one can use the information on reason for withdrawal to distinguish between (i) completion (ii) academic failure and (iii) 'voluntary' withdrawal, and hence estimate a multinomial model rather than the simpler binomial model of Smith and Naylor (2001b). Similarly the data enable one to distinguish between those leaving university altogether and those transferring between courses. Three papers which exploit these additional pieces of information are Johnes and McNabb (2004) and Arulampalam *et al.* (2004a, 2004b).

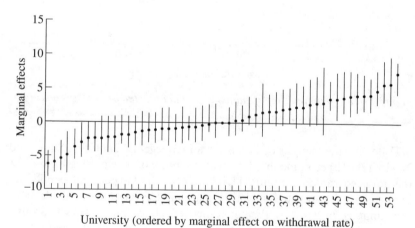

Figure 11.16　95 per cent confidence intervals for university marginal effects on withdrawal (males)

Johnes and McNabb (2004) base their analysis on 1993 leavers and find that the probabilities of both 'voluntary' and 'involuntary' non-completion are negatively related to prior educational attainment. They focus on peer group effects on the non-completion probabilities and consider the A-level score of each student relative both to the mean A-level score of students on the same course and to the university mean. Johnes and McNabb (2004) find that the dropout probability is higher for students with a high relative score. This is consistent with the hypothesis that the more able are transferring to find a more challenging course elsewhere.

Arulampalam *et al.* (2003) also focus on the effects of the relative A-level scores of students. They hypothesize that weaker students (in terms of levels of achievement in prior qualifications) within a university course may be more likely to drop out if they use knowledge of their relatively poor prior performance to form an expectation that they will not do well on their course. If this is true, then average and stronger students will be less likely to drop out. Furthermore Arulampalam *et al.* (2003) hypothesize that the greater is the variation in prior qualifications within a university course, the more likely it is that students will feel dissatisfied and hence the more likely it is that they will drop out. To assess these hypotheses, Arulampalam *et al.* assign each student to one of five rank groups within the university course, where the ranking is based on the levels of attainment in prior qualifications. In the probit regression analysis, dummy variables are included for these groups, along with the coefficient of variation in prior attainment. The results indicate that, for male students, there is a monotonic relationship between prior qualification rank and the probability of dropping out, with the weaker students being more likely to drop out. For females, the relationship is non-monotonic. The weakest students are the most likely to drop out, but the strongest students are also more likely to drop out than are the students whose rank is close to the mean. This suggests that the behaviour of these strong female students is consistent with the conjecture of Johnes and McNabb (2004) who hypothesized that relatively strong students would have an incentive to quit their studies in order to improve their curriculum vitae by transferring to courses attended by students with higher average prior scores.

Recall that, in the UK system, as we described in an earlier section of this chapter, university application and conditional acceptance decisions by students are made, typically, prior to their being informed about their scores in pre-university qualifications. Given this uncertainty, students can find themselves poorly matched with the university which they are contracted to enter and hence dropping out can be a consequence of an attempt to make a better match. This result is also consistent with the findings of Light and Strayer (2000) for college completion probabilities in the

USA. The authors conclude that students have a higher probability of graduating if their observed skill level is a close match with the quality level of their college.

The models we have described so far have all adopted an approach in which there is a single point in time, during a student's degree course registration, at which the student is defined either to have dropped out of his or her studies or not. In contrast, Arulampalam *et al.* (2004a) apply a hazard model which identifies more than one point in time at which a student might drop out. In theory, the hazard model could analyse the probability of dropping out, say, in each university term, conditional on not having dropped out in a previous term. However data limitations and the fact that the dropout rate is anyway low imply that the number of time points at which to model the hazard must be restricted. Arulampalam *et al.* (2004a) examine the dropout probability of medical students within a hazard framework. The case of medical student progression is an important one in the current context of government policy to expand the number of trained medical students in the UK. Arulampalam *et al.* (2004a) also adopt both single and competing risks frameworks. Among other results, they find that academic preparedness, both in the sense of levels of attainment prior to university and in the choice of, say, A-level subjects, is the major influence on medical student withdrawal. A further innovation in that paper is that it explicitly adopts a multi-level model. This is common in the analysis of data on school pupil outcomes, for example, but is an approach which has not previously been adopted in the analysis of USR data on UK university students.

4   Evidence for more recent cohorts: HESA data

Much of this chapter has surveyed work on USR data for entire cohorts of UK university students leaving (a pre-1992) university in 1993 or earlier. Data of similar richness and quality for more recent cohorts is not readily available. However, we have been able to gain access to administrative records, held by HESA, for the entire population of 1998 leavers in order to conduct an ordered probit analysis of the degree performance of these students. In this section of the chapter, we present our preliminary findings. We note that, compared to the USR data, the HESA data we are using do not contain the same detail of information on students' prior qualifications. For example, we know only the students' A-level points out of the maximum score of 30: we do not know which subjects the students took (nor, therefore, do we know the individual subject scores). Nor do the HESA data provide accurate information on previous school characteristics. On the other hand, the HESA data do provide information on ethnicity and disability, information not previously available.

Summary statistics for the 1998 cohort
Figures 11.17 and 11.18 show the degree class breakdown for male and female students, respectively, leaving a UK higher education institution in 1998. We can see that, as for the earlier USR cohorts, a higher proportion of females are awarded good degrees than is the case for males. However, as also for earlier cohorts, a higher proportion of males obtain first class degrees. We also notice that, in the pre-1992 universities, the proportions of good and of first class degrees awarded in 1998 exceed those for the earlier cohorts, with almost 10 per cent (9 per cent) of male (female) students obtaining a first. Higher proportions of firsts and good degrees are awarded at pre-1992 universities.

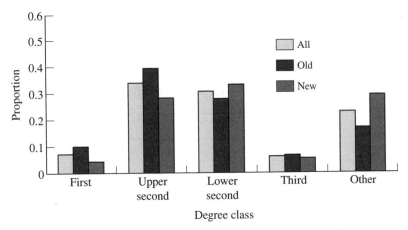

Figure 11.17   Degree class breakdown for 1998 leavers (males)

Table 11.3 shows summary statistics for particular variables to be used in the ordered probit analysis of degree class. The table presents information for males and females separately and for both 'All' higher education institutions and, separately, for pre-1992 universities. As we have noted, unlike the USR data, the HESA data provide information on both ethnicity and disability and the breakdowns by these characteristics are shown in the table.

From Table 11.3, we see that half of all male students leaving a higher education institution in 1998 had attended a pre-1992 university. Slightly less than half of female students had done so. A little over three-quarters of students leaving all HEIs had reported themselves to be of a white ethnic origin. The corresponding fraction for pre-1992 universities was a little over four-fifths. Close to 90 per cent reported no disability, with a tendency for a lower fraction with a disability at pre-1992 than at other universities.

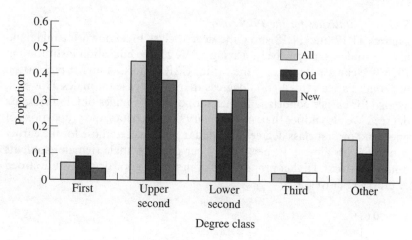

Figure 11.18   Degree class breakdown for 1998 leavers (females)

Table 11.3   Summary statistics for HESA 1998 leavers

	Males		Females	
	All	Pre-1992	All	Pre-1992
University type				
Old (pre-1992) universities	0.499	1.000	0.477	1.000
New (post-1992) universities	0.501	0.000	0.523	0.000
Ethnic origin				
White	0.769	0.803	0.785	0.826
Black Caribbean	0.029	0.012	0.035	0.014
Indian	0.063	0.043	0.053	0.035
Chinese	0.020	0.021	0.018	0.016
Other	0.015	0.013	0.016	0.013
Not known	0.104	0.109	0.093	0.095
Disability				
No disability	0.891	0.869	0.893	0.869
Dyslexia	0.012	0.012	0.008	0.007
Blind/partially sighted	0.002	0.002	0.001	0.001
Deaf/hearing impaired	0.002	0.002	0.002	0.002
Wheelchair user	0.001	0.001	0.001	0.001
Personal care support	0.001	0.001	0.001	0.001
An unseen disability	0.021	0.023	0.025	0.026
Multiple disabilities	0.002	0.001	0.001	0.001
Other	0.004	0.003	0.004	0.003
Not known	0.063	0.086	0.063	0.089

Table 11.3 (*continued*)

	Males		Females	
	All	Pre-1992	All	Pre-1992
Social class				
SC I	0.096	0.137	0.093	0.135
SC II	0.236	0.297	0.254	0.318
SC IIIM	0.068	0.079	0.076	0.084
SC IIINM	0.100	0.103	0.099	0.100
SC IV	0.044	0.043	0.043	0.040
SC V	0.011	0.010	0.010	0.009
Armed Forces	0.006	0.007	0.005	0.006
Missing	0.434	0.319	0.414	0.304
Retired	0.001	0.001	0.001	0.001
Unemployed	0.005	0.004	0.005	0.004
Age group				
<24	0.742	0.833	0.754	0.837
24–6	0.105	0.068	0.077	0.050
27–30	0.061	0.038	0.051	0.034
31+	0.093	0.061	0.118	0.079
Prior qualifications				
HNC, HND	0.069	0.025	0.044	0.013
A-level	0.630	0.786	0.662	0.798
Scottish Highers	0.002	0.002	0.002	0.002
ONC, OND	0.058	0.022	0.039	0.013
Not known	0.091	0.086	0.085	0.082
Other	0.150	0.080	0.168	0.091
Degree class				
Other	0.230	0.167	0.158	0.108
Third	0.056	0.062	0.029	0.026
Lower second	0.306	0.279	0.302	0.255
Upper second	0.339	0.396	0.448	0.526
First	0.069	0.096	0.063	0.085
n	90 812	45 334	91 476	43 596

Similarly the social class background measure is more skewed towards upper social classes at the pre-1992 universities. This is not surprising. It is likely that A-level performance, which forms the basis for admission to university, is correlated with social class background. Pre-1992 students also tend to be from the younger age groups.

From Table 11.3, we can see that there is a higher proportion of students with pre-qualifications other than A-levels compared to previous cohorts of students leaving pre-1992 universities. There are also higher proportions of students who are mature, part-time and taking sandwich courses.

We have conducted the gender-specific degree class analysis for (i) all degree-level students in UK higher education institutions, (ii) degree-level students in 'old' (pre-1992) universities and (iii) degree-level students in HEIs other than the 'old' universities. Table 11.4 presents selected results from the gender-specific ordered probit analysis of degree class for the 1998 cohort leaving a pre-1992 university. These results are the ones most comparable with those based on USR data for earlier cohorts.

From Table 11.4 we can see that the estimated coefficients on the dummy variables for a non-white ethnic origin are all negative and are strongly significant in all cases except that for female Chinese students. The implied marginal effects associated with obtaining a 'good' degree are very large. In the case of Indian students, for example, the implication is that there is an approximately 10 per cent lower probability of getting a good degree than in the case of a student of white ethnic origin, *ceteris paribus*. A number of reported disabilities also have significant negative effects on degree performance. For example, dyslexia is associated with a 6 per cent (7 per cent) lower probability of a good degree in the case of male (female) students. There are also some significant effects associated with social class background. Students from Social Class I have an approximately 2 per cent higher probability of a good degree than do students from Social Class II, *ceteris paribus*.

From Table 11.4 we can also see that more mature (male and female) students have a much higher probability of being awarded a good degree, while the pattern of effects associated with prior qualifications other than A-levels is more mixed and there are few well-determined coefficients. The results suggest that male students who took HNCs or HNDs prior to university have a higher probability of a good degree than an otherwise comparable A-level student. Of students who had taken A-levels prior to university, degree performance is significantly related to A-level score, non-linearly. For example, each extra grade at A-level raises the probability of a good degree by approximately 2.5 percentage points. For students with the maximum A-level score of 30 points, rather than 28 points, there is a marginal increase of 17 (14) percentage points in the probability of a good degree.

The table shows that there is considerable variation in degree performance across subjects, *ceteris paribus*. Compared to the default case of a degree in business, the probability of a good degree is significantly lower in physics, agriculture, mathematics, engineering, architecture, economics and politics. In no subject is the probability of a good degree significantly higher for both men and women than in the case of business.

Table 11.4 Ordered probit results for students in pre-1992 universities

	Males			Females		
	Coeff.	p-value	ME[1]	Coeff.	p-value	ME
Ethnic origin (base = white)						
Black Caribbean	−0.418	0.000	−20.84	−0.370	0.000	−19.26
Indian	−0.166	0.000	−10.06	−0.239	0.000	−9.29
Chinese	−0.161	0.000	−8.50	−0.076	0.058	−6.28
Other	−0.217	0.000	−10.24	−0.123	0.008	−8.99
Disability (base = no disability)						
Dyslexia	−0.198	0.000	−6.27	−0.178	0.003	−7.11
Blind/partially sighted	−0.080	0.539	−2.61	0.068	0.663	−0.15
Deaf/hearing impaired	0.067	0.561	2.70	0.018	0.882	−2.18
Wheelchair user	−0.303	0.078	−3.03	−0.269	0.095	−6.91
Personal care support	−0.631	0.006	−20.16	−0.436	0.012	−17.91
An unseen disability	−0.041	0.230	−0.29	−0.042	0.209	−2.94
Multiple disabilities	−0.384	0.007	−8.04	−0.374	0.010	−14.37
Other	−0.187	0.022	−6.46	−0.166	0.099	−9.81
Social class (base = SC II)						
SC I	0.065	0.000	1.54	0.061	0.000	1.93
SC IIIM	0.024	0.223	0.02	0.007	0.713	0.05
SC IIINM	−0.008	0.669	−0.17	−0.066	0.001	−1.48
SC IV	−0.012	0.650	−0.48	−0.057	0.043	−2.29
SC V	−0.037	0.490	−0.71	−0.078	0.181	−3.84
Unemployed	−0.255	0.002	−15.00	−0.277	0.000	−12.31

Table 11.4 (continued)

	Males			Females		
	Coeff.	p-value	ME[1]	Coeff.	p-value	ME
Age group (base = <24)						
24-6	0.054	0.019	6.86	0.025	0.372	7.07
27-30	0.418	0.000	19.22	0.309	0.000	16.08
31+	0.429	0.000	20.99	0.301	0.000	17.68
Prior qualifications[2]						
HNC, HND	0.258	0.000	2.56	0.072	0.336	−4.05
Highers	0.142	0.336	−0.36	−0.128	0.311	−5.62
ONC, OND	0.024	0.710	0.37	−0.072	0.330	−3.30
Other	0.103	0.078	0.00	0.154	0.014	0.00
A-level performance						
Score	−0.003	0.563		0.002	0.811	
Score-squared[3]	0.001	0.000	2.50	0.001	0.000	2.64
Top score[4]	0.348	0.000	17.36	0.354	0.000	14.14
Course of study (base = business)						
Medical related	0.046	0.191	2.72	−0.031	0.337	1.22
Biological science	−0.057	0.038	−1.29	0.016	0.602	0.41
Agriculture and related	−0.303	0.000	−7.13	−0.483	0.000	−12.50
Physical science	−0.246	0.000	−5.30	−0.146	0.000	−3.22
Mathematical science	−0.223	0.000	−6.46	−0.240	0.000	−6.49
Engineering	−0.352	0.000	−7.63	−0.428	0.000	−10.61
Technology	−0.364	0.000	−5.49	0.021	0.841	4.68
Architecture and building	−0.412	0.000	−5.26	−0.463	0.000	−10.16
Social science	−0.065	0.030	−0.71	−0.113	0.000	−4.03

Economics	−0.118	0.000	−0.38	−0.236	0.000	−5.12
Law	0.080	0.019	3.94	−0.022	0.614	0.43
Politics	−0.112	0.000	−0.25	−0.206	0.000	−5.01
Mass communications	0.076	0.218	6.41	−0.095	0.149	2.19
Languages (Modern European)	0.105	0.001	6.10	−0.033	0.278	−0.36
Languages (Other)	−0.057	0.155	−0.13	−0.135	0.000	−3.89
Humanities	0.020	0.474	3.00	−0.039	0.224	−0.27
Creative art	0.195	0.000	10.49	0.010	0.784	5.11
Education	−0.008	0.878	−5.19	0.146	0.006	−0.11
Other	−0.136	0.000	−4.13	−0.132	0.000	−5.93
Sandwich course	0.246	0.000	6.33	0.208	0.000	6.51
Accommodation (base = university)						
Parental/guardian home	−0.193	0.000	−10.35	−0.216	0.000	−11.53
Own home	−0.125	0.000	−4.12	−0.110	0.000	−5.48
Other	0.019	0.400	1.52	0.036	0.132	1.82

Notes:
1. ME is the marginal effect on the probability of a 'good' degree.
2. Prior qualification MEs are calculated relative to an A-level student with 12 points.
3. The marginal effect is calculated for an extra 2 points (1-grade), given 18 points.
4. Top score is a binary indicator for those students with 30 points. The marginal effect is calculated as an increase from 28 points to 30 points (and includes the effect of score and score-squared).

457

Finally, we note that, as we found with USR data for earlier cohorts, the probability of a good degree is highest for students who live in university accommodation. We believe this to be consistent with the analysis of Tinto (1975, 1988) which stresses the impact of social integration on student success at university.

5 Conclusions

Recent analysis on the determinants of degree success in the UK has been able to use administrative records on individual students for entire cohorts of students and has generated a large number of new and important results, many of which have direct implications for public policy in the area of higher education. This chapter has summarized much of this recent work.

On the question of degree class outcomes in the UK, we have seen that there are many robust and significant influences on student performance. Here we highlight four distinct sets of factors. First, the level of performance in prior qualifications has a major effect. Second, and more surprisingly, so do the characteristics of previous schooling. For example, we have seen that students who previously attended an independent school do much worse at university than otherwise observationally equivalent students previously educated in the state (LEA) sector. This result has significant policy implications in terms of the admissions, access and participation agenda. Third, family background has an influence on degree performance. This could be a result of cultural or aspirational transmission within the family. Alternatively it could be that students from less affluent backgrounds have to supplement their income with part-time labour market employment. The work surveyed in this chapter is not able to address this hypothesis directly. But the issue is an important one in the context of the debate about the appropriate level of fees and costs for students. Fourth, there are significant differences in performance by gender, just as is the case in primary and secondary education. The studies reviewed here have been able to shed little light on why this occurs in higher education. The issue needs further work, based, perhaps, on more detailed information regarding methods of assessment and teaching delivery.

With regard to student withdrawal probabilities, we conclude from the work surveyed in this chapter that academic preparedness for the university course is the major influence. This captures various elements including (i) the absolute level of performance in pre-university study, (ii) the relative performance (or quality of skills match) of the student to that of other students on the course and (iii) the match in the subjects studied before and at university. Another important set of factors concerns the extent of social integration at university. Finally we have found that, although there are differences across institutions in the withdrawal probabilities of students, these differences are correlated with various compositional differences across universities. Hence what we have termed *adjusted* and *unadjusted* rankings of universities are very different from each other. Furthermore many of the differences between universities are not statistically significant. These results suggest one should be both careful in the construction and cautious in the interpretation of league table exercises ranking higher education institutions on the basis of student withdrawal.

We have also presented in this chapter the results of a preliminary analysis of HESA data for 1998 university leavers. We have shown that there are significant *ceteris paribus* differences in degree performance associated with factors such as ethnicity, disability, age, gender, social class background, degree subject, accommodation type and pre-university educational attainment.

There is much more work to be done on the issue of student performance, of course. For example, much of the work we have surveyed in this chapter has been based on data sets containing rich information on university students, but with no complementary information on any control group of 'non-students'. Hence results are to be interpreted as conditional on participation in higher education. An issue which is important concerns the analysis of the decision to participate in higher education – and, indeed, in post-compulsory education generally. From a policy point of view, for example, a crucial question concerns the extent to which raising the private cost of education deters university entrance. The work described in this chapter on university withdrawal can be developed further to examine differences over time in withdrawal as private costs of education have risen. But a more important question concerns participation itself.

Acknowledgments

We are grateful to Wiji Arulampalam and Mark Stewart for helpful comments. We also acknowledge support from HESA in the provision of data. We bear full responsibility for all analysis and interpretation of results.

Notes

1. Although, especially in a dynamic setting, there might be a tendency for the number of applicants (and firmly-accepted offers) to increase as the offer increases. This might occur, for example, if the offer acts as a signal of institution quality.
2. A 'good' degree is typically defined as an upper second or first class honours degree.
3. Authors' own calculations based on data from DfES (2003) and Independent Schools Information Service ISCIS (2003).
4. Clearly we only observe students at the university and not students applying to the university, it could of course be the case that there is a substantial larger proportion of students from the independent sector applying to these leading institutions, relative to students from the state sector.
5. We take students aged 21 years old or younger.

6. For female students each university in Group 1 has more than 39 per cent independent school students.
7. Johnes (1990), for example, finds significant gender differences in the determinants of student non- completion.

References

Arulampalam, W., R.A. Naylor and J. Smith (2003), 'Effects of in-class variation and student rank on the probability of wthdrawal: cross-section and time-series analysis for UK university students', forthcoming, *Economics of Education Review.*
Arulampalam, W., R.A. Naylor and J. Smith (2004a), 'A hazard model of the probability of medical school dropout in the United Kingdom', *Journal of the Royal Statistical Society (Series A)*, **167**, 157–78.
Arulampalam, W., R.A. Naylor and J. Smith (2004b), 'Factors affecting the probability of first-year medical student dropout in the UK: a logistic analysis for the intake cohorts of 1980–1992', *Medical Education*, **38**, 492–503.
Bee, M. and P. Dolton. (1985), 'Degree class and pass rates: an inter-university comparison', *Higher Education Review*, **17**, 45–52.
Betts, J.R. and D. Morell (1999), 'The determinants of undergraduate grade point average: the relative importance of family background, high school resources, and peer group effects', *Journal of Human Resources*, **34**, 268–93.
Blundell, R., L. Dearden, A. Goodman and H. Reed (1997), *Higher Education, Employment and Earnings in Britain*, London: Institute for Fiscal Studies.
Blundell, R., L. Dearden, A. Goodman and H. Reed (2000), 'The returns to higher education in Britain: evidence from a British cohort', *Economic Journal*, **110**, F82–F99.
Borg, M.O. and H. Stranahan (2002a), 'The effect of gender and race on student performance in principles of economics: the importance of personality type', *Applied Economics*, **34**, 589–98.
Borg, M.O. and H. Stranahan (2002b), 'Personality type and student performance in upper-level economics courses: the importance of race and gender', *Journal of Economic Education*, **33** (Winter), 3–14.
Bourner, T. and M. Hamed (1987), *Entry Qualifications and Degree Performance*, London: Council for National Academic Awards.
Bratti, M. (2002), 'Does the choice of university matter? A study of the difference across UK universities in life science students' degree performance', *Economics of Education Review*, **21**, 431–43.
Brauer, J., K. Stephenson and W.A. Powell (1994), 'Should class attendance be mandatory?', *Journal of Economic Perspectives* (correspondence), **8**, 205–15.
Card, D. and T. Lemieux (2000), 'Dropout and enrolment trends in the post-war period: what went wrong in the 1970s?', NBER Working Paper 7658.
Chapman, K. (1996a), 'An analysis of degree results in geography by gender', *Assessment and Evaluation in Higher Education*, **21**, 293–311.
Chapman, K. (1996b), 'Entry qualifications, degree results and value-added in UK universities', *Oxford Review of Education*, **22**, 251–62.
Dearden, L., J. Ferri and C. Meghir (2002), 'The effect of school quality on educational attainment and wages', *Review of Economics and Statistics*, **84**, 1–20.
Devadoss, S. and J. Foltz (1996), 'Evaluation of factors influencing student class attendance and performance', *American Journal of Agricultural Economics*, **78**, 499–507.
Eide, E. and M. Showalter (1998), 'The effect of school quality on student performance: a quantile regression approach', *Economics Letters*, **58**, 345–50.
Gibson, A. and S. Asthana (1998), 'Schools, pupils and exam results: contextualising school "performance"', *British Educational Research Journal*, **24**, 269–82.
Goldstein, H. and D. Spiegelhalter (1996), 'League tables and their limitations: statistical issues in comparisons of institutional performance', *Journal of the Royal Statistical Society (Series A)*, **159**, 385–443.

Hoskins, S.L., S.E. Newstead and I. Dennis (1997), 'Degree performance as a function of age, gender, prior qualifications and discipline studied', *Assessment and Evaluation in Higher Education*, **22**, 317–28.

Johnes, G. and R. McNabb (2004), 'Never give up on the good times: student attrition in the UK', *Oxford Bulletin of Economics and Statistics*, **66**, 23–47.

Johnes, J. (1997), 'Inter-university variations in undergraduate non-completion rates: a statistical analysis by subject of study', *Journal of Applied Statistics*, **24**, 343–61.

Johnes, J. and J. Taylor (1989), 'Undergraduate non-completion rates: differences between UK universities', *Higher Education*, **18**, 209–25.

Johnes, J. and J. Taylor (1990), *Performance Indicators in Higher Education*, Oxford: SRHE/ OUP.

Kalsner, L. (1992), 'Issues in college student retention', *The Higher Education Extension Service Review*, **3**, 73–81.

Light, A. and W. Strayer (2000), 'Determinants of college completion: school quality or student ability', *Journal of Human Resources*, **35**, 299–332.

McCrum, N.G. (1994), 'The academic gender at Oxford and Cambridge', *Oxford Review of Education*, **20**, 5–26.

McNabb, R., P. Sarmistha and P. Sloane (2002), 'Gender differences in student attainment: the case of university students in the UK', *Economica*, **69**, 481–503.

Manski, C. (1993), 'Identification of endogenous social effects: the reflection problem', *Review of Economic Studies*, **60**, 531–42.

Mellanby, J., M. Martin and J. O'Doherty (2000), 'The "gender gap" in final examination results at Oxford University', *British Journal of Psychology*, **91**, 377–90.

Naylor, R.A. and J. Smith (2002), 'Schooling effects on subsequent university performance: evidence for the UK university population', University of Warwick working paper, no. 657.

Naylor, R.A. and J. Smith (2004), 'Degree performance of Economics students in UK universities: absolute and relative performance in prior qualifications', *Scottish Journal of Political Economy*, forthcoming.

Naylor, R.A., J. Smith and A. McKnight (2002a), 'Why is there a graduate earnings premium for students from Independent schools?', *Bulletin of Economic Research*, **54**, 315–39.

Naylor, R.A., J. Smith and A. McKnight (2002b), 'Sheer class? The impact of degree class on graduate labour market outcomes', University of Warwick working paper, no. 659.

Nevin, E. (1972), 'How not to get a First', *Economic Journal*, **82**, 658–73.

Peers, I. and M. Johnston (1994), 'Influence of learning context on the relationship between A-level attainment and final degree performance', *British Journal of Educational Psychology*, **64**, 1–18.

Romer, D. (1993), 'Do students go to class? Should they?', *Journal of Economic Perspectives*, **7**, 167–74.

Rudd, E. (1984), 'A comparison between the results achieved by women and men studying for first degrees in British universities', *Studies in Higher Education*, **9**, 47–57.

Sacerdote, B. (2000), 'Peer effects with random assignment: results for Dartmouth roommates', NBER working paper 7469, Cambridge, MA.

Sear, K. (1983), 'The correlation between A-level grades and degree results in England and Wales', *Higher Education*, **12**, 609–19.

Smith, J. and R.A. Naylor (2001a), 'Determinants of individual degree performance: evidence for the 1993 UK university graduate population from the USR', *Oxford Bulletin of Economics and Statistics*, **63**, 29–60.

Smith, J. and R.A. Naylor (2001b), 'Dropping out of university: a statistical analysis of the probability of withdrawal for UK university students', *Journal of the Royal Statistical Society (Series A)*, **164**, 389–405.

Smith, J., A. McKnight and R.A. Naylor (2000), 'Graduate employability: policy and performance in Higher Education in the UK', *Economic Journal*, **110**, F382–F411.

Tinto, V. (1975), 'Dropout from higher education: a theoretical synthesis of recent research', *Review of Educational Research*, **45**, 89–125.

Tinto, V. (1988), 'Stages of student departure: reflections on the longitudinal character of student leaving', *Journal of Higher Education*, **59**, 438–55.

Wright, R.E. (1999), 'The rate of return to private schooling', IZA discussion paper, no. 92.

12 Standards and grade inflation
Geraint Johnes

1 Introduction

The human capital and the sorting models have very different implications for the role played by assessment in education. In the human capital model, education is a productivity enhancer (see Chapter 1 of this book). At the level of the individual, any use of assessment to evaluate the extent of learning is of little direct interest, since productivity gains are measured by subsequent remuneration in the labour market. Given the stock of human capital, the success or failure of an individual (say through luck) in gaining a credential is irrelevant to her future earnings. Education matters for productivity, but performance in assessment is incidental.

In the case of the signalling and screening models of the kind discussed in Chapter 2 of this volume, however, summative assessment is the key; success in such assessment is an individual's ticket to remunerative employment. This is because, in these models, it is the individual's rank in a cohort of workers, rather than any absolute measure of productivity, that determines earnings. And rank can only be determined through the competition with other labour market entrants that is provided by the system of summative assessment.

While assessment is not important at the level of the individual in the human capital model, there is a case for assessment in order to evaluate the performance of the educational system. Assuming constant standards, changes in the average performance of students in assessed work can be used as a barometer of success or failure of the educational system; barometer readings have clear policy implications. If average grades are falling, then the prospects for the future prosperity of the economy are compromised, and the authorities may want to take remedial action. If, on the other hand, average grades are increasing, then something is clearly going right. Aggregate assessment results can therefore serve as a policy guide. But, as noted above, this assumes the constancy of standards.

If standards are not constant, there are implications within both the human capital and the sorting models. Suppose standards are falling; this is the case that is often referred to as 'grade inflation'. Consider first the human capital model. With falling standards, we can no longer easily use aggregate assessment results as a measure of the performance of the education system, since these results conflate the effects of changing performance with those of changing standards of assessment. Summative assessment therefore loses its value as a measure of systemic performance.

Consider next the signalling and screening models. The impact of grade inflation is a little less clear in this case. If the grade inflation takes place in such a way as to preserve the rank order of students, then it is not damaging: assessment retains its power to distinguish and identify students with different levels of innate ability. If, however, the grade inflation is more extreme, it might result in a bunching of students in the higher grades. In this case, some of our ability to distinguish between students with different productivity levels is lost. In this case, too, summative assessment loses value.

There has been concern in many countries about the possible existence of grade inflation. This arises both from the fact that the ability of assessment to serve as a measure of national educational standards is compromised (the human capital issue) and from the fact that the ability of assessment to discriminate between workers of different productivity levels is compromised (the sorting issue). The concern has arisen because much evidence suggests that grades have been increasing over the years. In contexts where policy is such that the allocation of resources to education depends on measured performance (as in the United States, where many states provide financial incentives for schools and teachers to boost test scores, or in the United Kingdom, where schools are set targets which, if not met, can trigger an adverse policy reaction) the integrity of the grading system is clearly important for other reasons.

But it should be borne in mind that evidence that grades are rising, on its own, is not sufficient to demonstrate grade inflation, since there are many other reasons why grades might have been rising, at least from a human capital perspective. For example, as society becomes richer, the importance attached to education by students might be increasing; an increasingly competitive labour market likewise might lead students towards greater diligence; educational reforms might have been working. And, of course, since grade inflation might be occurring, it is not clear either that we can use assessment results as an indication that any of these other factors are at work. Many studies of grade inflation do not take into full account the implications of this conundrum, though some recent studies do.

The remainder of this chapter is structured as follows. First we consider the nature of academic standards as a public good. Secondly, we investigate the role played by standards and target-setting in modern educational systems. This leads us to consider, thirdly, theories that highlight the incentives that academic institutions have to compromise these standards. Fourthly, we shall examine the empirical evidence on grade inflation. This evidence comes from a variety of countries. Finally, some policy options are considered.

2   Academic standards as a public good

When grading students' work, academics are applying a set of laws, rules, standards or norms which map work possessing particular characteristics onto a particular grade. The laws, rules, standards or norms may usefully be regarded as public goods (Marks, 2002). If a norm is defined, then its 'consumption' is non-excludable and non-rival. Everybody knows what the standard is (so nobody is excluded from this knowledge) and that the same standard applies to everybody (so the application of the norm to one person does not deny anyone else the capacity to be judged according to the same norm).

A characteristic of public goods is that stakeholders have an incentive to free-ride; that is, in the knowledge that the good is both non-rival and non-excludable, they seek to rely on others to 'pay' for the good. Everyone wants the benefit, but no-one wants to bear the cost. To bring this a little closer to the context of laws and rules, everyone wants everyone else to drive safely, but few people mind if they themselves break the speed limit. And to bring the argument closer still to the case of norms and standards in education, everybody wants to work in an institution that has high standards, but everyone might also have an incentive to cheat on those same standards: plagiarism amongst students is one example. Another might be the tendency for university faculty to tilt their time allocation towards research and away from teaching. In a nutshell, the private and public interest diverge, and we have a case of market failure.

The respects in which norms within education have this public good characteristic are numerous. As an example, admission standards to selective schools and to institutions of higher education represent a type of norm. When students apply to a given school, they are making a decision that is analogous to the local public goods choice made by players in a Tiebout (1956) world. They face a menu of locales (or institutions) in which they could study, and *ceteris paribus* they choose the one that suits them best, the one whose norms they can most readily accept. Thus able students will tend to choose to enrol on the most challenging programmes, since they can expect to complete successfully while adding to their human capital stock and/or acquiring an effective signal of their worth in the labour market. Likewise less able students will choose programmes which they can expect to pass, though the human capital and signalling effects of these programmes may be more modest.

Marks (2002) identifies several ways in which free-riding may occur that serves to compromise the standards or norms associated with an educational institution. Students may wish to be associated with those norms – for instance they might wish to receive a degree from a prestigious institution – but they might nonetheless seek to free-ride on those same norms.

For instance they might attend few classes, or read too little, or cheat when doing assessed work, or otherwise behave inappropriately, while expecting their peers to conduct themselves in a manner that upholds the institution's norms, the norms with which they themselves aspire to be linked. Meanwhile faculty might also have an interest in free-riding. Student feedback might be positive if classes take the form of 'edutainment'; to an extent this might be a good thing, but beyond that extent it might compromise a standard in the delivery of learning. Indeed the pressure on faculty that has been imposed by the introduction of student feedback mechanisms has often been cited as a major determinant of grade inflation (Trout, 1997; Ridley *et al.*, 2003).

An aspect of free-riding that might give rise to particular concern is the grading process. The use of summative assessment is widespread, partly because it provides an incentive to students to learn, and partly because, according to the signalling and screening model, it serves as an indicator to stakeholders (such as employers) about the measure of human capital that is embodied in the student. Students would like to achieve as high a grade as possible, given their input of work. Meanwhile, faculty might also face an incentive to award high grades, partly as a result of pressure from students and partly also because grades may be used as a measure of the quality of learning in a class. These incentives can lead individual faculty to seek to free-ride on the grading norms that they hope their peers will support. While all faculty might share a belief that the standard has to be upheld in order to preserve an institution's reputation and in order to ensure that future intakes of students will be of high quality, the incentive for each grader covertly to exempt herself from the norm, thereby compromising the standard, is ever-present. This is one route whereby grade inflation can occur – we shall discuss others in the sequel.

Other aspects of standards and norms as public goods in education include pressures to increase class sizes for economic reasons, the temptation to divert expenditures on academic resources such as libraries or information technology in the direction of increased slack in administration, and the integrity and ethicality of research. In all cases, players may have incentives to behave in a manner that challenges the standards that they would like their peers within the same organization to espouse.

Having established that standards in educational institutions are rendered fragile by their public good characteristics, an obvious question arises as to how this situation can be remedied. A number of solutions suggest themselves. First, free-riding is most easily prevented when players are organized into small groups. It is difficult for students to free-ride in small tutorials, but easier in large lectures, simply because the probability of detection is that much greater when the group is small. Likewise faculty who compromise grading standards are more likely to be detected if they are working in smaller groups. Of course, running small classes is costly. Similarly organizing faculty into small departmental groups is expensive in terms of the time required to administer each group. So a balance has to be struck between the marginal benefits and marginal costs of operating at different scales. Secondly, free-riding occurs because players face incentives to exempt themselves from the norm; if incentives can be changed, then the problem of free-riding can be removed. In effect, the compromising of standards is a principal–agent problem. To take an example, faculty are likely to free-ride in the awarding of grades to their students if faculty are judged by their students' grades; but if grades are replaced by, say, graduate employability as a measure of teaching success, the behaviour of faculty is likely to be tilted in a direction that does not compromise standards. So the behaviour of the various stakeholders in educational institutions can be very sensitive to the choice of incentive mechanism. This whole issue of incentives in education is an underresearched area, though more recent literature has provided some examples of the potential of work in this area (Ferris, 1992; Johnes, 1999).

3   Target setting

So incentives are important. This being the case, in recent years many countries have adopted education policies that are grounded in the setting of targets. The incentives that are then offered to stakeholders in order to ensure that the targets are met become crucial in determining the ability of the educational system to maintain its standards or norms. In this section, we shall briefly discuss the target-setting policies pursued in four countries: the USA, Canada, the UK and Australia.

In the USA, almost all states are currently engaged in some sort of standards-based reform at secondary education level (Wycoff and Naples, 2000). Typically this has involved the introduction of state-wide targets that are aligned with students' performance in high school exit examinations, the coverage of these examinations being defined by published standards or norms. Incentives are provided both for students and for schools to meet targets. These incentives are often aimed at ensuring that the performance of individuals or schools in examinations are associated with 'high stakes'. So, in the case of students, graduation from high school might not be permitted if a student fails to meet target performance. In the case of schools, meanwhile, incentives take a variety of forms: some are linked directly to financial reward, but equally incentives might involve a reduced bureaucratic commitment, or simply good publicity. The drive for standards-based reform has involved states in a multiplicity of expenditures including investment in technology and other learning materials, staff development, the reduction of class sizes and performance-related pay. Bishop (1997) provides some evidence in support of the positive effects that target setting and standards can have on educational performance in the USA.

Just as educational policy is devolved to state level in the USA, in Canada such policies are made at province level. One of the provinces at the forefront of target setting initiatives has been Alberta, which in 1994 introduced a new accountability framework. In this province, schools and school authorities are required to set quantitative targets for pupil performance in their education plans. Progress at achieving the goals thus set is typically measured by reference to performance in provincial examinations which provide a standard. Schools must publish the targets, and subsequently must publish also quantitative data on their students' achievements, so that the public can compare the latter with the former.

In Australia, the National Goals for Schooling were published in 1999 (the so-called Adelaide Declaration which is available at http://www. curriculum.edu.au/mceetya/nationalgoals/index.htm). This document sets a variety of goals, and much effort since its publication has been directed at ensuring that measurable and timed targets are set that link into these goals. Six areas have been prioritized: literacy, numeracy, student participation and attainment, vocational education and training, science, and information and communications technology. Benchmarks and timetables for the achievement of goals in these spheres have been defined. Academic testing of students for the measurement of performance takes place at state level using defined standards. Schools report their achievements in the key areas to parents who are then able to compare the school's performance against the national benchmark. Some states have experimented with the publication of league tables of school performance. There are, however, no plans in Australia for attaching high stakes to the realization of targets, either at school or at pupil level.

Targets are also set by primary and secondary schools in the UK. By law these targets are set by the school itself in consultation with the Local Education Authority (LEA). But the LEA has an obligation to ensure that schools within its jurisdiction on average meet national performance targets and, although it cannot impose targets on schools, it does have the upper hand in determining the targets which are formally set by the school for itself. The targets refer to national scholastic aptitude tests in the primary sector, and at the secondary level include performance in the main national school leaving subject-specific examinations: the General Certificate of Secondary Education (GCSE), which students typically undertake at 16 years of age, and the Advanced Level (now the AS and A2 level qualifications) typically gained at age 18. During the regular school inspections process conducted for the government's Office for Standards in

Education (OFSTED), inspectors are required to comment on 'the school's progress towards its targets, including comment on whether the targets are sufficiently challenging' (*OFSTED Inspectors' Handbook*, available at http://www.ofsted.gov.uk). The consequent favourable or adverse publicity that success or failure in meeting targets can generate should encourage schools to rise to the challenge. This provides quite a sharp incentive in the UK, where parents have wide discretion over which school their children should attend, and where the allocation of funds to schools depends largely on the number of pupils they can attract. Beyond that, however, no system of financial incentives has been introduced explicitly to reward schools that meet their targets or to penalize those that do not.[1] At teacher level, it is possible for teachers to receive a financial award if they exceed a 'performance threshold', though the introduction of performance-related pay has met with vehement union opposition.

The countries whose systems of target setting are described above are illustrative of the international trend towards identifying and aiming at challenging educational standards. Indeed Goldstein (2004) has written about the 'globalization' of target setting, referring to the worldwide educational goals set by the United Nations Educational, Scientific and Cultural Organization (UNESCO) for the first 15 years of the new millennium. Goldstein emphasizes the danger that, by setting targets for measurable variables such as test performance, the achievement of unmeasurable but desirable objectives that the measurables themselves are supposed to proxy (such as learning) may be jeopardized. Thus targets for test performance might encourage teachers to teach to the test, thereby narrowing the curriculum. Likewise teachers might increasingly devote one-on-one time to marginal students who can, with effort, be tutored to pass the test, while ignoring the needs both of potential high-flyers and of no-hopers.

The incentives that schools have to meet the targets that they themselves have set clearly vary considerably from jurisdiction to jurisdiction. In some American states, schools face high stakes, with funding being positively related to performance. In the UK, too, schools have much to gain from meeting their targets – or at least they have much to lose from not meeting them. In Canada and Australia, it remains to be seen whether the lack of incentives that bite will limit the effectiveness of the target-setting regimes.

A further issue which is of concern in this context is the accuracy of test scores as a measure of school performance. For many schools, the size of cohort being tested in any one year is small, thus leading to imprecision; the existence within the cohort of tiny numbers of students at either end of the ability distribution can severely distort the quality of the mean test score as a measure of school performance. Moreover, because of averaging effects, the variation between schools in the average test performance achieved by pupils is small. In other words there is not much to distinguish good schools from bad schools and, this being the case, random blips in the performance of one or two individuals can have a substantial effect on a small school's position in the league tables. This being so, it is crucial that school performance is measured using more than a single year's worth of data. Indeed Kane and Staiger (2002a, 2002b) have found that about three-quarters or more of the variance across schools in the change in test scores is due to purely transitory effects. In other words most of the variation in this measure across schools is due to noise rather than to signal. This emphasizes the need to use data for more than one year in the evaluation of school performance.

It is a straightforward matter to consider the information on target setting in this section alongside the discussion of free-riding in the last section, and to conclude that there are now many incentives for stakeholders in the education system to seek covertly to exempt themselves from norms that they might wish to see others uphold. In the remainder of this chapter we proceed to discuss one of these norms, that concerning grading, in greater detail.

4 Grade inflation: conceptual issues and some evidence

One rationale for the existence of grade inflation has been alluded to earlier, namely the tendency for stakeholders in education to free-ride on the commitment to adhere to standards. In this section, a number of alternative theories will be discussed at some length.

An early contribution to this literature is that of McKenzie and Tullock (1981), who note that the demand for and supply of higher education places both fluctuate over time. Demand and supply in this market depend not only on the explicit monetary price of a university education (tuition fees) and on opportunity costs (forgone income) but also on other hedonic factors. For instance, the demand for places at a university might depend on the quality of accommodation, the employability of graduates, the rigour of the education and the toughness of grading practices. McKenzie and Tullock argue that there was an excess demand for places at universities in the USA during the post-Sputnik era. Universities responded to this excess demand by increasing their tuition fees. This led, by the early 1970s, to a surplus of places available, since universities tended to overshoot the equilibrium.

Now universities that set their tuition fees at a level above the equilibrium may face difficulty in adjusting back to a steady state. This is so for a number of reasons. First, they are typically not-for-profit organizations, and their costs rise in tandem with their revenues; since many employees are on long-term contracts, it is not easy to cut costs and so it is not easy to make decisions that would reduce revenues. The decision to raise tuition fees may therefore be largely irreversible. Moreover cutting tuition fees might send the market an adverse signal. So, for several reasons, a cut in the monetary price of studying at a given university might not be a feasible option. This means that the university must try to increase demand by making its product more attractive to students than it has previously been; that is, it must reduce the hedonic price. One way in which this can be done is to become increasingly lenient in grading.[2]

Freeman (1999) has extended the McKenzie and Tullock argument by investigating the differentials in grading standards that appear to exist between subject areas. Assuming tuition fees per hour of learning to be constant across subject areas, and assuming all other things including grading practices to be equal, students in fields where graduates face a relatively buoyant labour market are offered a better deal than students in other subject areas. In the latter case, there may therefore emerge a surplus of places at university, and so the hedonic price may be reduced by way of grading leniency.

This extension of the basic model allows Freeman to test the market hypothesis of grade inflation, simply by comparing grades awarded with labour market performance of graduates across different disciplines. To be more specific, he uses data, aggregated to subject level, from the 1996 American National Center for Education Statistics survey of 1992–3 bachelor's degree graduates in order to estimate the relationship between the mean subject-specific grade point average and a vector of explanatory variables. The latter include, crucially, subject-specific values for the first two moments of earnings one year after graduation; the regression also controls for mean quality and age of the student intake, gender and ethnicity indicators, other risk factors and the proportion of students attending a private sector institution. The results indicate that there is a significantly negative relationship between mean earnings after graduation and the mean grade point average. This would appear to support the hypothesis that grade point averages are inflated in disciplines where labour market prospects are relatively poor.

Dickson (1984) has also provided a test of the market model of grade inflation by comparing grade inflation across disciplines, and has found that departments with lower student:faculty ratios tend to award higher grades. He attributes this to faculty being insecure about their jobs; they will therefore be permissive in their grading practice in order to encourage more students to enrol. An alternative, and arguably more plausible, interpretation of the result is that small class size allows learning to take place more effectively. This interpretation is given greater force when set alongside our earlier observation that free-riding is less likely to be observed when groups are small.

Similar analyses of subject differentials have been conducted by Sabot and Wakeman-Linn (1991) and by Anglin and Meng (2000). The evidence in these papers, which draw on data from both the USA and Canada, suggests that rising grades have been particularly pronounced in English and music, but that grades are relatively low and have altered relatively little in mathematics, chemistry and economics. This pattern of results lends further support to the view that grade inflation is more likely in subjects where the labour market for graduates is relatively thin.

The contribution of Sabot and Wakeman-Linn is particularly interesting because it establishes that student enrolment on a course is positively influenced by the grades that are typically awarded on that course. Using a probit analysis of course choice, they found that a male minor student who took Economics 101 was (after controlling for various student characteristics) 18 per cent less likely to take a further course in economics if his grade for Economics 101 was a B rather than an A; and 28 per cent less likely to do so if his grade was a C rather than an A. Similar results are reported also for English, where the percentage reductions in the probability of taking further English courses are 14 per cent and 20 per cent, respectively.

The rationalization of grade inflation that underpins all of the studies referred to above relies on a phenomenon that is often observed in game theory, where the behaviours of a number of economic agents are strategically linked (Correa, 2001). One view is this: students perceive that greater leniency raises their own grade (and, under signalling or screening, it raises also their labour market prospects), but they do not perceive that others' grades will rise too, thereby reducing the potential value of their own qualification in the labour market. This is clearly related to the idea of money illusion (we could call it 'grade illusion'), a phenomenon that likewise has been rationalized by appeal to strategic complementarity of the type found in games (Haltiwanger and Waldman, 1989; for experimental evidence, see Fehr and Tyran, 2001). Another view is that students, each fearing that leniency will be applied to other students, all pressurize faculty to award them higher grades so that they do not get left behind. This links to the literature on herding (King, 1995) and similarly connects with game-theoretic models.

To tease out the connection between grade inflation and game theory a little more clearly, consider the following extremely simple model. There exist two students, both of whom believe that their labour market prospects depend on their rank order in grading. Hence the utility of the ith student is given by $U_i = x_i - x_j, j \neq i$, where x_i is the ith student's grade. The mark awarded to the ith student depends in part on some absolute standard of the work produced, x_{0i}. But it also depends on whether students exert pressure on the marker to become more lenient. We may measure this pressure using a binary variable δ attached to each student. Let the mark awarded to the ith student then be measured as $x_i = x_{0i} + \delta_i + \sigma\delta_j, j \neq i, 0 < \sigma < 1$. The Nash equilibrium is easily seen to be one in which each student sets $\delta = 1$. In other words, the nature of the game encourages the stakeholders to behave in a manner that encourages grade inflation, even though both players may recognize that the outcome when $\delta_i = 1$ $\forall i$ is no better than that which obtains when $\delta_i = 0$ $\forall i$.

Further conceptual analyses of grade inflation suggest that the increased tendency to award high grades might be a 'one-shot' phenomenon. Elton (1998) has argued that changes in assessment methodologies have resulted in an improvement in grades. These changes include the move toward continuous assessment of student work, and more recently toward peer evaluation and self-evaluation. Bracey (1994) has argued that the introduction of word processors has facilitated an improvement in the content (as well as the presentation) of coursework. Many of the changes listed above are themselves the consequence of developments in teaching and learning styles, accompanying the shift toward student-centred learning.

It should not go unnoted at this stage that another possibility is that the improvement in grade averages in higher education is not a symptom of grade inflation at all, but rather reflects an improved quality of intake (perhaps caused by teaching reforms affecting primary or secondary education) or a genuine improvement in the pedagogical technology or efficiency of higher education institutions themselves. Such possibilities will be considered further in the sequel.

That said, there is, as an empirical phenomenon, evidence to suggest that grade inflation has occurred in many countries. In the USA, the issue has gained considerable prominence owing to reports of grade inflation at Ivy League universities. In particular, Harvard University has received much adverse publicity, following revelations by the *Boston Globe* and the determination of new president Larry Summers to reinforce academic standards.[3] But the evidence suggests that Harvard is far from being unique in this respect.

Kolevzon (1981) and Compton and Metheny (2000) are amongst many authors who have conducted statistical investigations finding evidence of grade inflation in the USA. From 1960 to 1975, Trow (1977) found that the percentage of students receiving B+ grade averages or better at American universities doubled, from 18 to 36 per cent. Similar findings are reported by Kolevzon (1981) for this period. More recently, Compton and Metheny (2000) have found that this trend continued through the 1990s, albeit at a slower pace, in some subject areas but not in others. And Eiszler (2002) finds that the proportion of students expecting A or A− grades increased by some 10 percentage points over the 1990s. Kuh and Hu (1999), however, find that the increase in grades from the mid-1980s to mid-1990s is concentrated in the more prestigious research institutions and liberal arts colleges, suggesting that competitive forces in this part of the sector were particularly strong over this period.

In the UK, grade inflation has been of considerable concern at all levels of education, and raises an annual furore in the media. Tymms and Fitz-Gibbon (2001) survey a large body of literature on standards in primary and secondary schools. At primary school level, the official Key Stage 2 tests conducted since 1995 indicate a very dramatic improvement in pupil performance. Evidence from other sources[4] suggests that a more modest improvement did indeed occur over this period, and that this improvement followed a period of declining performance during the early 1990s.

Tymms and Fitz-Gibbon also examine data on standards at secondary level, and find some evidence of grade inflation in the national A-level examinations taken at age 18. Students scoring a given grade on the International Test for Developed Abilities (ITDA) tended to score higher grades in the mathematics A-level in 1994 than was the case in 1988; there is some evidence to suggest that this trend has continued into the late 1990s.

There has been concern in Britain also over the possible occurrence of grade inflation at higher education level. Johnes and McNabb (2002) report evidence to suggest that standards fell during the mid-1980s, but not since.

There is further evidence of grade inflation taking place at various levels of education in several other countries, including Australia (Marginson, 1995), India (Altbach, 1993) and France (Chauvel, 1999). Elsewhere the literature seems to be sparse. This might indicate that the perception that standards have declined is a local one, but equally it might reflect different systems of higher education in different countries. In systems where the norm is for students to graduate without a grade being awarded, evidence of a decline in standards might be hard to come by.

Having established that there is at least prima facie evidence of grade inflation in a number of countries, the next question to ask is: does it matter? There are several reasons why it might. In the presence of grade inflation, it becomes difficult for the authorities to disentangle the effects of changes in the efficiency of educational institutions from changes in the standards that they use to grade students' work. Consequently the authorities might make false inferences from the data, and may make misguided policy.

But suppose we know the extent of grade inflation. Does grade inflation matter then? Clearly, if the grade inflation entails a bunching of marks into a small number of grades at the top end, information about the relative merits of different students can be lost. This is a concern that has been voiced recently in the UK by the Institute of Directors (2001). In the USA, meanwhile, commentators have been expressing concern about this for several decades. Grieves (1982), for instance, remarks that grade inflation has 'obliterated virtually all informational content of grades'.[5] However Millman *et al.* (1983) have strongly contested this view, arguing that the grade point average system used in the USA continues to discriminate effectively between stronger and weaker students; this is particularly so where 'plus' or 'minus' qualifiers are attached to grades (for instance, A−, B+).

A further reason why grade inflation matters has been highlighted by Figlio and Lucas (2000).[6] Building on theoretical work by Becker and Rosen (1992), Costrell (1993, 1994) and Betts (1998), they argue that the maintenance of the integrity of grades is essential in order to provide an incentive for students to work hard and perform well.[7]

To discuss this in more detail, let us consider the salient features of Costrell's theoretical model. Consider a typical student, i, whose utility, U_i, is a function of leisure, L_i, and future remuneration, w_i. The student's school performance is given by y_i, which is characterized by a production function that is decreasing and concave and has leisure as the only argument. If there were perfect information, then the relationship between leisure and earnings would therefore look like the nonlinear relationship ABC in Figure 12.1. It is nonlinear because, when a large amount of leisure is being consumed, sacrificing a little leisure in order to acquire schooling can increase future remuneration greatly, while the marginal return to schooling declines as the amount of leisure consumed falls. Superimposing onto this diagram I_0, the highest attainable indifference curve of the student which is defined by utility level $\overline{U}_i$, we see that utility is maximized at point B. Note that educational standards play no role in this model because, in setting wages, firms measure students' human capital perfectly without appeal to examinations graded by standard.

In reality, however, the student's prospective employers do not have perfect information. Typically they might know only whether the student passes or fails a given programme of study. This means that the student gains from sacrificing leisure only at the margin between passing and failing a course. In this instance, where information is limited, the constraint that the student faces becomes $CDEF$. Students may either do no work (that is, consume the maximum possible amount of leisure) and then subsequently enjoy remuneration of w_0, or they may sacrifice $C - L_1$ hours of leisure in order to secure a qualification.

Now suppose that the potential future earnings of students follow a given distribution with supports w_0 and w_{max}. Students will then sort themselves into two groups. A proportion $F(w^*)$ will choose not to exert any effort at all in their studies and will earn w_0. The second group, comprising a proportion $1 - F(w^*)$ of all students, will exert the effort needed to pass successfully through their programme of study. If the standard that is

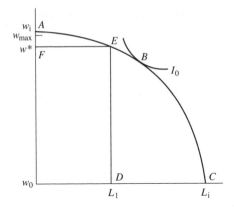

Figure 12.1   Endogenous standard setting in Costrell's model

required to pass is raised, then the kink in the discontinuous constraint of Figure 12.1 shifts to the left, and fewer students will pass.

Suppose now that the standard is determined by a centralized regulator whose objective function is the sum of all students' future incomes.[8] Hence the regulator seeks to maximize $V = [1 - F(w^*)]w^* + F(w^*)w_0$. Differentiating this with respect to the choice of standard, w^*, yields the first order condition $[1 - F(w^*)] - (w^* - w_0)f(w^*) = 0$. Solving this for w^* allows the optimal standard to be defined.

The first order condition contains two components: the first is the marginal social benefit of a rise in the toughness of the standard. This is the increased productivity of graduates who were encouraged to acquire more human capital during their studies in order to pass their course. The second term is the marginal social cost of the rising standard, namely the cost that represents students who no longer choose to exert effort and so fail the programme.

The first of these two components – the gain in societal human capital stock that is due to the raising of the standard – is the focus of attention for Figlio and Lucas (2000) in their empirical work. They use a panel data set of pupils who take the Iowa tests of basic mathematics and reading, and regress, at pupil level, the change in test scores from one year to the next against a vector of independent variables which includes a measure of the grading standards adopted by the pupils' teachers.[9] Toughness of standards is shown positively to improve test scores in both mathematics and reading; it is also shown to reduce disciplinary problems, though the statistical significance of some of the results reported is marginal.

The second term in Costrell's first order condition suggests that a rise in standards should raise the dropout rate from educational programmes. This is tested empirically by Lillard and DeCicca (2001) using data on American high school dropouts. Using a panel of data on states over years during the 1980s and early 1990s, these authors find that high school attrition rates tend to be higher in states that have high course graduation requirements. This result is confirmed when data disaggregated to the level of the individual pupil are used. Lillard and DeCicca estimate that a one standard deviation increase in course graduation requirements would cause an increase of between 3.0 and 7.4 per cent in the number of high school dropouts.

5   Further evidence on grade inflation

A difficulty with many of the studies of grade inflation reported above is that they fail fully to get to grips with the problems that are associated with identifying grade inflation in practice. Hence evidence that grades have risen over time is taken as evidence that standards must have fallen. But in fact there are several reasons why grades may have risen, and grade inflation is only one of them.

First, a rise in grades may be due to an improvement in the quality of the student intake. Students may be better prepared for higher levels of education than in the past, for a number of reasons. School reforms may have been successful, occupational shifts in the labour market may have created a culture in which parents more strongly emphasize the importance of education, or technological change in the classroom may have had beneficial pedagogical effects. Moreover the quality of student intake may improve if there is an enhancement of students' assiduousness. This may happen if the economic returns to successful completion of an educational programme increase.[10] Clearly the quality of the student intake needs to be controlled for in any analysis of changing grades over time.[11]

Secondly, students of a given quality may be working with better resources now than in the past. In addition to current expenditure, educational institutions spend vast sums of money on capital expenditure, including investments in library facilities, information technology and other learning resources. It would be surprising, and indeed damning, if these investments did not yield a return in terms of the educational achievements of students. The improvement over time in educational infrastructure also, therefore, needs to be controlled for in analysing changing grades.

A more subtle aspect of technology concerns the improvements over time in pedagogical methods. In US universities one of the engines driving these improvements has been the introduction of student evaluations of faculty. In the UK, the main engine has been the bureaucratic quality assurance process epitomized by the Quality Assurance Agency (QAA). Again it would be damning (both on the universities and on the agency) if the burden imposed on institutions by the QAA had not resulted in any improvement in the prospects of students. So allowance has to be made in the model for this type of technological improvement too. Inescapably this is difficult to measure.

A related point is that educational institutions may be more efficient now than in the past at converting inputs into outputs. In other words, institutions may now be operating closer to a given production frontier than they were able to do in the previous years. Even in an industry such as education, which is atypical in the sense that most units of production operate as not-for-profits, one might reasonably expect managerial inefficiencies to erode over time owing to competitive pressures.

Finally, grade inflation may indeed have occurred. Of course the possible presence of grade inflation makes it very difficult to identify whether efficiency gains have indeed been realized, just as the possible existence of efficiency gains makes it difficult for us to measure grade inflation. So, faced with the task of measuring grade inflation (as opposed to simply finding evidence consistent with its existence), we face something of a dilemma.

Recent advances, using the methods of frontier analysis, have allowed us to make some progress toward finding a solution. Frontier analysis has been extensively applied in the education sector, and is discussed at length in Chapter 16 of this book.[12] The standard stochastic frontier model, applied to a panel of universities over time, is

$$Y_{it} = f(X_{it}) - \varepsilon_{it},$$

where Y_{it} denotes the output of the ith university in the tth time period, X_{it} is a vector of university and time-specific variables, and ε_{it} is a residual which (dropping the subscripts for convenience) is defined as

$$\varepsilon = v + u \quad \text{and} \quad v \sim N[0, \sigma_v^2].$$

The second component of the residual, u, follows a non-normal distribution, and is assumed to provide a measure of efficiency; a common assumption is that u is a truncated normal.

This method is used by Johnes and McNabb (2002) in order to examine the determinants of students' measured performance over time in English and Welsh universities. The dependent variable is the proportion of graduating students who receive first class or upper second class honours degrees, and explanatory variables include measures of gender and nationality mix, parental background and residence, that are known from previous work to be determinants of degree performance (Johnes and Taylor, 1990). The quality of student intake is measured by the mean A-level score of entrants to each university. In addition, a full set of time dummies is included in the equation. On the assumption that the one-sided residual will capture changes in universities' efficiency over time, these dummy variables should provide a measure of pure grade inflation, that is, a measure of grade inflation that is not confounded by changes over time in the efficiency of institutions.[13]

The results are reported for two separate time frames, namely 1973–93 and 1995–2000. Over the latter period, the authors find no evidence of significant grade inflation, but the earlier period is more interesting. The full set of results for this period is reported in Table 12.1.[14] Many of the results are unsurprising. Hence universities with a high preponderance of students with parents working in managerial and professional occupations and students who have attended an independent school tend to have a relatively good record of passing students with good degrees.[15] Universities with a high proportion of male students, and those with a high proportion of students who live at their parental home,[16] tend to have relatively few students graduating with good degrees. As might be expected, the quality of student intake exerts a positive and highly significant influence on the proportion of degrees awarded in the top two classes. If the mean A-level score were to increase by the equivalent of one letter grade in each of three subjects studied, then the proportion of firsts and upper seconds awarded by a university would rise by four percentage points.

Of greater interest in the present context, however, is the pattern of coefficients observed on the time series dummy variables. With 1973 as the omitted year, the time dummies remain insignificant until 1984. By 1988, the proportion of degrees that were awarded in the top two honours classes had risen by about 14 percentage points. From this date onwards, the coefficient on the time dummies remained roughly constant. Since efficiency changes are being accounted for in the modelling of the residual, positive coefficients on the time dummies cannot be reflecting improvements in efficiency. The results therefore suggest that substantial grade inflation occurred in English and Welsh universities over a five-year period during the mid-1980s, but has not occurred since.[17]

It is interesting also to plot over time the evolution of the one-sided residual, averaged across all universities; that is, to see how inefficiency has changed over the years. This is done in Figure 12.2. It is readily observed from this figure that there was a downward trend, albeit only a slight one, in inefficiency over the period from 1973 to 1999. In 2000, inefficiency seems to have increased, but it is too early yet to judge whether this represents a reversal of the trend or rather a blip.

6   Conclusion

There has been considerable concern in recent years about the hypothesized existence of grade inflation. This concern has cut across national boundaries. Certainly there are reasons to suppose that standards in education will

Table 12.1   Stochastic frontier estimates, 1973–93

Variable	Coefficient
constant	0.4477 (9.20)
% parental background: professional and managerial	0.031 (1.27)
% independent school	0.239 (9.53)
% UK domicile	−0.10 (2.09)
% live at parental home	−0.02 (0.80)
% male	−0.147 (6.6)
mean A-level score	0.007 (8.01)
Time dummies	
1974	0.0008 (0.05)
1975	0.018 (1.21)
1976	0.0107 (0.69)
1977	0.0065 (0.44)
1978	0.0043 (0.28)
1979	0.0023 (0.16)
1980	−0.0094 (0.56)
1981	−0.0141 (0.83)
1982	0.0034 (0.20)
1983	0.0136 (0.85)
1984	0.0433 (3.0)
1985	0.039 (2.54)
1986	0.065 (4.14)
1987	0.066 (4.10)
1988	0.137 (7.81)
1989	0.091 (5.83)
1990	0.121 (7.97)
1991	0.120 (7.89)
1992	0.131 (7.86)
1993	0.142 (8.20)
σ_u/σ_v	1.33 (9.57)
$\sqrt{(\sigma^2_v + \sigma^2_u)}$	0.0892
log likelihood	1277.676
number of observations	1008

tend to erode over time, since many stakeholders face incentives to free-ride on their peers' willingness to uphold the accepted norms. This suggests that it is inevitable that standards will need to be redefined periodically. But the empirical measurement of grade inflation is fraught with difficulty, not least because changing standards and variations over time in efficiency are mutually confounding.

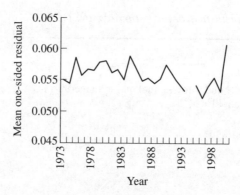

Figure 12.2   Estimated mean university inefficiencies

In any event, there is much popular confusion about whether grade inflation should be regarded as a 'Bad Thing'. If, as a consequence of grade inflation, grades are 'squashed' at the top end and therefore lose informational content, employers, as stakeholders in the educational process, may feel that they have lost out. But this can only be the case to the extent that the signalling and screening models hold good. If job allocation and remuneration is determined by human capital, and if employers can quickly ascertain workers' productivity, the costs borne by employers will be limited. On the other hand, if grade inflation masks a deterioration in the true performance of an educational system, then, by obfuscation, it might contribute to poor policy making. But in this case it is the worsening performance of the system, not the grade inflation per se, that is causing harm.

Nevertheless we should be aware that there may be perverse incentives lurking within educational institutions that contribute to a decline in standards over time, and that these diminutions in standards may not always be easily perceived. Where such a decline in standards has an adverse impact on the nation's stock of human capital, this can result in inferior prospects for future growth and development of the economy. If for this reason alone, it is therefore desirable that we should be able to disentangle true improvements in educational efficiency from those that are merely illusory.

Notes

1. Though the ultimate sanction for an adverse OFSTED report which is not followed by satisfactory progress is closure of the school.
2. As perceived by prospective students, but not by other stakeholders such as employers.
3. *Business Week*, 18 February, 2002.
4. Davies and Brember (1997) provide a particularly interesting analysis in that they use common test materials across all years of their study.
5. Murnane and Levy (1998) have more recently voiced similar concerns.
6. Similar work has also been conducted by Betts and Grogger (2000).

7. A further and more recent contribution to this theoretical body of literature is De Fraja and Landeras (2002). In their model, schools invest in resources and exert teaching effort in response to incentives, while students exert effort in learning. The relationship between the student and the school takes the form of a game, and it is possible that increasing the incentives for schools to improve their provision has perverse effects, since students might respond by reducing their own effort.

8. This could be a weighted sum, with less weight being attached to those endowed with higher ability, so that the regulator is in effect an egalitarian. Under such conditions, the analysis is slightly altered, and it is easy to show that the regulator would choose a lower standard than in the case where all students' incomes are weighted equally.

9. In fact, three measures of the toughness of each teacher's grading standards are used. All three use data on the scores obtained by students in the Florida Comprehensive Assessment Test (FCAT), a high-stakes test administered to standards set at state level. The first measure is the mean difference, across pupils and years, between the FCAT score and letter grade scores awarded by the teacher. The second is the coefficient on a teacher fixed effect term in a regression of FCAT scores against letter grades awarded by teachers. The third is the average FCAT score achieved by all students of a given teacher who were awarded a grade of B. In all cases, the higher the measure, the tougher are the grading standards adopted by the teacher.

10. This is tested for by Johnes and McNabb (2002), but they do not find any significant effect.

11. The analysis assumes no grade inflation at lower levels of education.

12. Methods similar to those described here have also been used in the health sector. See, for example, Ferrari (2003).

13. As noted earlier, this assumes no grade inflation at earlier levels of education. If grade inflation has affected the integrity of A-level scores, then the absence of significant time dummies shows only that there has been no decline in the *value added* by higher education.

14. The data refer to traditional (pre-1992) universities in England and Wales. Scotland has an education system that is distinct from that of the other countries in Great Britain. At university level this is witnessed by the fact that graduation with honours at bachelor degree level typically requires four years' study in Scotland but only three in the rest of Great Britain; also Scottish universities commonly award ordinary degrees (without honours), while this is rare in England and Wales. More recently the funding mechanisms for universities in Scotland have also been distinct. So, for all of these reasons, Scotland is omitted from the study.

15. This finding on the independent school effect curiously contrasts with the finding of Smith and Naylor (2001), who use the same dataset, but who conduct their analysis at a disaggregated level. The difference in findings is likely due to aggregation bias, though more detailed study of this apparent paradox is needed.

16. This result contrasts with the finding of Smith and Naylor (2001), but is in concordance with that of Johnes and Taylor (1990).

17. Since the specification of the model includes the quality of the intake, as measured by A-level scores, as an explanatory variable, the findings on grade inflation assume that there has been no grade inflation at A-level. As we have already seen, this is a questionable assumption. So, strictly speaking, it can only be claimed that there has been no grade inflation at university level since 1988 *over and above* grade inflation that might have happened at A-level. An alternative interpretation of the rising values of estimated coefficients on time dummies for the mid-1980s is that teaching technology may have improved; this is certainly possible, with developments in information technology, but in the absence of further evidence it is not an interpretation that I endorse.

References

Altbach, Philip G. (1993), 'The dilemma of change in Indian higher education', *Higher Education*, **26**, 3–20.

Anglin, Paul M. and Ronald Meng (2000), 'Evidence on grades and grade inflation at Ontario's universities', *Canadian Public Policy*, **26**, 361–8.

Becker, William E. and Sherwin Rosen (1992), 'The learning effect of assessment and evaluation in high school', *Economics of Education Review*, **11**, 107–18.

Betts, Julian (1998), 'The impact of educational standards on the level and distribution of earnings', *American Economic Review*, **88**, 266–75.

Betts, Julian and Jeff Grogger (2000), 'The impact of grading standards on student achievement, educational attainment and entry level earnings', NBER working paper 7875.

Bishop, John H. (1997), 'The effect of national standards and curriculum-based exams on achievement', *American Economic Review, Papers and Proceedings*, **87**, 260–64.

Bracey, Gerald W. (1994), 'Grade inflation', *Phi Delta Kappan*, **76**, 328–31.

Chauvel, Louis (1999), 'Cohort changes in education, social stratification and mobility, the case of France, 1964–1995', mimeo, Fondation Nationale des Sciences Politiques.

Compton, David M. and Brenda Metheny (2000), 'An assessment of grade inflation in higher education', *Perceptual and Motor Skills*, **90**, 527–36.

Correa, Hector (2001), 'A game theoretic analysis of faculty competition and academic standards', *Higher Education Policy*, **14**, 175–82.

Costrell, Robert M. (1993), 'An economic analysis of college admission standards', *Education Economics*, **1**, 227–41.

Costrell, Robert M. (1994), 'A simple model of educational standards', *American Economic Review*, **84**, 956–71.

Davies, Julie and Ivy Brember (1997), 'Monitoring reading standards in Year 6: a seven year cross-sectional study', *British Educational Research Journal*, **23**, 615–22.

De Fraja, Gianni and Pedro Landeras (2002), 'Could do better: the effectiveness of incentives and competition in schools', paper presented at the European Economic Association Conference.

Dickson, Vaughan A. (1984), 'An economic model of faculty grading practices', *Journal of Economic Education*, **15**, 197–203.

Eiszler, Charles F. (2002), 'College students' evaluations of teaching and grade inflation', *Research in Higher Education*, **43**, 483–501.

Elton, Lewis (1998), 'Are UK degree standards going up, down, or sideways?', *Studies in Higher Education*, **23**, 35–42.

Fehr, Ernst and Jean-Robert Tyran (2001), 'Does money illusion matter?', *American Economic Review*, **91**, 1239–62.

Ferrari, Alessandra (2003), 'The measurement of hospital efficiency: a stochastic distance function approach', paper presented at the Royal Statistical Society Conference, 14 January.

Ferris, James M. (1992), 'School-based decision making: a principal–agent perspective', *Educational Evaluation and Policy Analysis*, **14**, 333–46.

Figlio, David N. and Maurice E. Lucas (2000), 'Do grading standards affect student performance?', NBER working paper 7985.

Freeman, Donald G. (1999), 'Grade divergence as a market outcome', *Journal of Economic Education*, **30**, 344–51.

Goldstein, Harvey (2004), 'Education for all: the globalisation of learning targets', *Comparative Education*, forthcoming.

Grieves, Robin (1982), 'A policy proposal regarding grade inflation', *Educational Research Quarterly*, **7**, 2–4.

Haltiwanger, John and Michael Waldman (1989), 'Limited rationality and strategic complements: the implications for macroeconomics', *Quarterly Journal of Economics*, **104**, 463–83.

Institute of Directors (2001), Press release, 22 August.

Johnes, Geraint (1999), 'The management of universities', *Scottish Journal of Political Economy*, **46**, 505–22.

Johnes, Geraint and Robert McNabb (2002), 'Academic standards in UK universities: more for less or less for more?', paper presented at the Royal Economic Society Conference, 27 March.

Johnes, Jill and Jim Taylor (1990), *Performance Indicators in Higher Education*, Buckingham: Open University Press.

Kane, Thomas J. and Douglas O. Staiger (2002a), 'The promise and pitfalls of using imprecise school accountability measures', *Journal of Economic Perspectives*, **16**(4), 91–114.

Kane, Thomas J. and Douglas O. Staiger (2002b), 'Volatility in school test scores: implications for test-based accountancy systems', in Dian Ravitch (ed.), *Brookings Papers of Education Policy*, Washington: Brookings, pp. 235–83.

King, Stephen P. (1995), 'Search with free-riders', *Journal of Economic Behavior and Organization*, **26**, 253–71.

Kolevzon, Michael S. (1981), 'Grade inflation in higher education: a comparative study', *Research in Higher Education*, **15**, 195–212.

Kuh, George D. and Shouping P. Hu (1999), 'Unraveling the complexity of the increase in college grades from the mid-1980s to the mid-1990s', *Educational Evaluation and Policy Analysis*, **21**, 297–320.

Lillard, Dean R. and Philip P. DeCicca (2001), 'Higher standards, more dropouts? Evidence within and across time', *Economics of Education Review*, **20**, 459–74.

Marginson, Simon W. (1995), 'The decline in the standing of educational credentials in Australia', *Australian Journal of Education*, **39**, 67–76.

Marks, Denton (2002), 'Academic standards as public goods and varieties of free-rider behaviour', *Education Economics*, **10**(2), 145–63.

McKenzie, Richard B. and Gordon Tullock (1981), *The New World of Economics*, Homewood: Irwin.

Millman, Jason, Simeon P. Slovacek, Edward Kulick and Karen J. Mitchell (1983), 'Does grade inflation affect the reliability of grades?', *Research in Higher Education*, **19**, 423–9.

Murnane, Richard and Frank Levy (1998), 'Standards, information and the demand for student achievement', *Federal Reserve Bank of New York Policy Review*, 117–24.

Ridley, Dennis R., Michael B. Quanty and Mark Sciabica (2003), 'Grading standards and course challenge: an analytical–empirical approach', mimeo, Virginia Wesleyan College.

Sabot, Richard and John Wakeman-Linn (1991), 'Grade inflation and course choice', *Journal of Economic Perspectives*, **5**(1), 159–70.

Smith, Jeremy and Robin A. Naylor (2001), 'Determinants of degree performance', *Oxford Bulletin of Economics and Statistics*, **63**, 29–60.

Tiebout, Charles M. (1956), 'A pure theory of local expenditures', *Journal of Political Economy*, **64**, 416–24.

Trout, Paul A. (1997), 'What the numbers mean: providing a context for numerical student evaluations of courses', *Change*, **29**, 24–30.

Trow, Martin (1977), *Aspects of American Higher Education, 1969–75*, Berkeley: Carnegie Council on Policy Studies in Higher Education.

Tymms, Peter and Carol Fitz-Gibbon (2001), 'Standards, achievement and educational performance: a cause for celebration?', in Robert Phillips and John Furlong (eds), *Education, Reform and the State: 25 Years of Politics, Policy and Practice*, London: RoutledgeFalmer, pp. 156–73.

Wycoff, James H. and Michelle Naples (2000), 'Educational finance to support high learning standards: a synthesis', *Economics of Education Review*, **19**, 305–18.

13 The school-to-work transition
Steve Bradley and Anh Ngoc Nguyen

I Introduction

If the early part of an individual's working life had no negative immediate or long-term consequences, the school-to-work transition would be of little importance.[1] Unfortunately this is not the case. The early part of an individual's career is the optimal time to invest in education and training. In fact, in many countries institutional arrangements are such that entry to vocational training programmes, such as apprenticeships, is restricted to 'young' people. Training leads to the acquisition of skills and hence entry to skilled occupations. Similarly those young people who leave school at the minimum age and who do not take up training opportunities are likely to cut themselves off from higher education opportunities which lead to professional and managerial occupations. The consequence is that these young people are likely to enter unskilled 'dead-end' occupations in the secondary labour market (Doeringer and Piore, 1971). A lack of training and entry to unskilled occupations is likely to reduce lifetime earnings and increase the risk of experiencing periodic spells of unemployment.[2] Indeed it is argued that unemployment has a 'scarring effect' and serves to reduce the probability of employment and future earnings and increase the risk of future unemployment (Arulampalam, 2001).

A recent study by Omori (1997) reports clear evidence of lagged duration dependence of unemployment for US youths. After controlling for unobserved heterogeneity, he finds that 'a one-month increase in the duration of past non-employment lengthens the expected duration of future non-employment by 0.39 months on average' (p. 396). In addition, he finds evidence of negative duration dependence, which he argues is consistent with stigma and human capital decay.[3] Mroz and Savage (1999) also find a small positive effect of prior unemployment on the duration of the current unemployment spell as evidence of lagged duration dependence.

As far as occurrence dependence is concerned, Narendranathan and Elias (1993) report that 'the odds of becoming unemployed are 2.3 times higher for youths who were unemployed last year than for youths who were not unemployed' (p. 183). Arulampalam et al. (2000) find that unemployment tends to bring future unemployment, whereas Burgess et al. (1999) find that early-career unemployment has some effect on later unemployment, but this effect varies for high and low-skill individuals. Arranz and

Muro (2001) investigate state dependency of unemployment for young workers in Spain and find that past unemployment experience causes longer future unemployment spells.

Longer-term state dependency is also investigated. Gregg (2000) reports strong evidence of state dependency induced by early unemployment using data for the UK. The effects of youth unemployment persist well into the future, at least until age 33. An additional two months of youth unemployment is found to lead to an extra month of unemployment by age 33. In a study of the effects that early career experiences have on later outcomes for France, Germany and the United States, Margolis *et al.* (1999) report that a lower employment probability is associated with a longer time to first job.

In terms of earnings effects, Kletzer and Fairlie (1999), using data for the USA, estimate that for young unemployed workers the costs of job loss in terms of annual earnings are 8.4 per cent and 13.0 per cent lower, relative to the expected level, for boys and girls, respectively.[4] Mroz and Savage (1999) report a long-term scar of youth unemployment on future earnings. In particular, they report a negative effect of prior unemployment on earnings which is both large and persistent. For example, a six-month unemployment spell occurring as long as four years ago is found to reduce wages by 2.3 percentage points. This leads them to conclude that 'the magnitude and duration of the unemployment effect are simply too great to consider unemployment as a mere blemish' (p. 33).[5] Gray (2000) examines the effect of unemployment on the earnings of young Australians and reports negative effects of early unemployment on both hourly earnings and weekly earnings. The length of time spent in unemployment also affects future earnings.

In addition to imposing permanent scars on future employability and future earnings, unemployment can also leave scars on the individuals' general well-being, which may also hamper future employment prospects. Korpi (1997, p. 127) argues that these scars may 'lead to discouragement, inability to acquire new skills, or unsatisfactory performance at job interviews, all translating into a low job offer probability'.[6] Evidence of scars that unemployment imposes on subjective well-being can be found in Clark and Oswald (1994), Korpi (1997) for Sweden and Clark *et al.* (2001) for Germany. Clark and Oswald (1994), using data for Britain, report a lower mental well-being for those unemployed than for those employed. Moreover high and persistent levels of youth unemployment carry significant economic and social risks such as drug abuse, crime, vandalism and social unrest (Blanchflower, 1999).

A bad start in one's working life, or an unsuccessful transition from school, can therefore be expected to have dire short-term and long-term consequences. Furthermore, if too few young people choose to continue their education or train, there may be long-term macroeconomic consequences, such as the emergence of a 'skills gap' (Prais, 1995), with a resultant negative effect on labour productivity and economic growth.

In view of the importance of the school-to-work transition, this chapter seeks to review the international literature on this topic to identify common themes, while remaining sensitive to variations in the institutional context in each country. In particular we review time series, cross-sectional and longitudinal studies and evaluate each type of study. We then estimate a set of pooled time series and cross-sectional models of the school-to-work transition for England using a unique data set, which combines information on individual and family with that on their school background and local labour market. A key finding from the literature is that a young person's exam performance at school is the most important determinant of the school-to-work transition. However, unlike most of the previous literature in this area, we allow for the endogeneity of exam performance at school in our models of the school-to-work transition. We also investigate the importance of several interaction effects between covariates to see if we can identify important 'causal' transmission mechanisms (Lenton, 2003).

The remainder of the chapter is structured as follows. In section II we briefly describe the human capital model, which has provided the traditional framework within which to examine the school-to-work transition. Section III reviews the extensive literature in this area, focusing on US and UK studies, and distinguishes between time series, cross-sectional and longitudinal approaches. We also identify the factors that affect the school-to-work transition in this section. In section IV we turn to the data that we use to estimate a set of multinomial models of the school-to-work transition for England for the period 1992–8. Section V presents the results of our analysis, which is followed by our conclusions.

II   Theoretical background

Human capital theory is the most widely adopted framework for investigating the school-to-work transition. This is because the transition from school is often conceptualized as an investment decision to be made by young people, although there clearly is an element of consumption in the decision to go to college. We concentrate here only on the investment aspect of the decision. Accordingly young people are assumed to choose from two alternatives: to continue to invest in more education or training beyond the current level of education or to stop investing in formal schooling and enter the labour market. Under the human capital investment model developed by Becker (1964, 1993), young people will choose to attend college only if the present value of the expected benefits exceeds the present value of the expected costs associated with this choice. There are costs associated with college enrolment, such as tuition fees, books and accommodation, forgone earnings and non-monetary costs. These costs are offset by expected benefits, including higher expected earnings, more secure and pleasant jobs, lower expected unemployment rates and also non-monetary benefits.

Human capital theory highlights the importance of an individual's ability and family background in the decision to invest in more education or training (Becker, 1993). Young people with higher ability will have a greater demand for more education since they are more able to reap the benefit from investment in post-secondary education. The marginal benefit obtained from investment in education is higher for those with a higher level of ability, thus requiring more investment to equate marginal benefit with marginal cost. Human capital theory also suggests that, in the presence of constraints in the capital market, family background plays an important role in the decision to invest in more education and training. This is because individuals from wealthier families have a lower marginal cost of investment.

III A review of the literature

There is an extensive literature on the factors influencing the school-to-work transition. This literature consists mainly of studies for the USA and the UK, although recently empirical work has been undertaken for other countries (see Merz and Schimmelpfenning, 1999; Riphahn, 1999 for Germany; Soro-Bonmati, 2000, for Italy). Our focus is on the US and the UK literature. This literature is essentially concerned with the human capital investment decision, but there are differences of focus. In the UK, the typical choices facing young people at age 16 are whether they stay on for further education (for academic or vocational courses), enter the labour market and become employed or unemployed, or choose a government-funded youth training programme (such as Youth Training). In contrast, in the USA, young people at age 18 choose between going to college (two years versus four years; public versus private) and entering the labour market to become employed or unemployed.

Aggregate studies

Different approaches have been adopted in empirical research. One approach employed in the earlier literature uses aggregate data to model the college enrolment decision and the staying-on decision in the USA and the UK, respectively. In the USA, the proportion of the eligible population enrolling in a post-secondary institution is regressed on explanatory variables. In the UK, the dependent variable is the proportion of school leavers who stay on for further education.

For the purpose of this chapter, only a very brief account of these earlier studies is given because this literature has been reviewed extensively else-where (Jackson and Weatherby, 1975; Leslie and Brinkman, 1987; Becker, 1990). While there is only time series analysis in the UK literature, the US literature includes both time series and aggregate cross-sectional studies. The typical explanatory variables employed in the regression include measures of tuition fees at the institution attended, the cost of attending substitute institutions, labour market conditions, the proximity of substitute institutions, financial aid at the institution and socioeconomic variables. The issue that is most often investigated by these studies is the variation in demand for higher education or college enrolment. Therefore researchers have attempted to estimate the income and cost effects on college attendance. The income effect is a measure of the way changes in family income affect college attendance. The cost effect is a measure of the way changes in college costs (such as tuition fees, transport costs) influence college attendance. However there is no consensus on the appropriate measure of income and the specification of the cost variable varies across institutions according to whether the institution is public or private. These differences led Becker (1990) to conclude that the estimates of these two variables are 'sensitive to the definition of other variables included as regressors and the type of data base employed' and are dependent on 'the functional form specification and the estimation techniques employed' (ibid., p. 163).

The UK literature is mostly concerned with the post-compulsory education choice of young people at the age of 16, using time series analysis. The dependent variable in these studies is therefore the proportion of school leavers who stay on for further education.[7] An exception is Pissarides (1982) who investigates the determinants of the proportion of 18-year-olds entering university. As compared with the US literature, the UK studies use more consistent data and more advanced econometric techniques. Pissarides (1981), analysing the time series data for staying on for the period 1955–78, concludes that variations in the proportion of young people proceeding to further education were the result of movements of relative earnings between manual workers and highly qualified workers, coupled with changes in household permanent income. Whitfield and Wilson (1991) argue that Pissarides' model (1981) lacks robustness when applied to more recent data. They then apply vector auto-regression techniques for a longer period, from 1956/7 to 1985/6. In their study they identify the unemployment rate, the rate of return to education, the social class structure and the proportion of school leavers in youth training schemes as the main determinants of the long-run staying on decision. McVicar and Rice (2001) extend the work of Pissarides (1981) and Whitfield and Wilson (1991) by applying cointegration analysis to an extended period from 1955 to 1994. They find that increases in the participation rate are due to improvements in the level of exam attainment at school and the expansion of the higher education sector. Other important factors are labour demand fluctuations and changes in unemployment. McIntosh (2001) presents similar findings for Germany, the Netherlands, Sweden and England.

Cross-sectional discrete choice studies
A major limitation of the studies discussed in the previous section is that they do not model individual-level data, which is actually the level at which the school-to-work transition decision is made. Cross-sectional discrete choice studies have the advantage that they model the school-to-work transition using individual-level data. Researchers have tended to adopt increasingly sophisticated econometric techniques. For instance, some studies adopt the binary choice logit or probit model, whereas others use ordered or multinomial logit models. Fundamentally the specification of the econometric model depends on the conceptualization of the choice set available to young people.

Early research in particular conceptualized the choice set as a binary choice problem in which, for instance, high school graduates are assumed to have two alternatives: college attendance or labour market entry. In the UK context, young people reaching the end of compulsory schooling either stay on or enter the labour market. This is perhaps the most common specification. Earlier studies include Christensen *et al.* (1975), Willis and Rosen (1979), Borus and Carpenter (1984) and Micklewright (1988). More recent literature includes Kane (1994), Evans and Schwab (1995), Ganderton and Santos (1995), McElroy (1996) and Ellwood and Kane (2000). Even with this simple binary choice model the definition of the dependent variable varies between studies. For example, in the US literature the dependent variable has been defined as 'years of completed schooling greater than 12' (Averett and Burton, 1996), or as 'attending four-year college' (Evans and Schwab, 1995; McElroy, 1996; Ellwood and Kane, 2000) or simply as 'attending college' in other studies. The definition of the dependent variable in the UK literature is more consistent and is defined as the decision to stay on or proceed to further education, typically made at age 16. This simple dichotomy has been criticized as inadequate to capture the complexity of the school-to-work transition (Andrews and Bradley, 1997). More recently researchers have moved away from specifying the binary choice model toward either ordinal or multinomial models.

Multinomial logit models have been used to model the transition from school. Examples for the USA are studies by Corman (1982), Rouse (1994) and Hilmer (2001). For the UK, typical studies include Andrews and Bradley (1997), Armstrong (1999), Bradley and Taylor (2002) and Rice (2000). The definition of the choice set that students face when graduating from high school is more consistent. The differences remain mainly because of institutional differences between countries. In the US literature, the common choice set that students are facing is often specified as consisting of (i) two-year college, (ii) four-year college, and (iii) no college – labour market entry. This specification helps overcome the arbitrary definition of college enrolment evidenced in the review of the literature that uses the binary choice model. Still this specification has several drawbacks. First, the choice set of college alternatives is still highly aggregated, consisting of only two choices. This specification might cause loss of valuable information when a more disaggregated specification is more appropriate. Secondly, it treats different labour market states (employed versus non-employed/searching for a job) as the only non-schooling alternative to college enrolment choices. It is reasonable to suspect that splitting up the 'labour market' alternative into employed and non-employed is more appropriate. Nguyen and Taylor (2003) have shown that a more disaggregated specification is appropriate.

The ordered probit model has also been specified to model the decision to attend college. Hilmer (1998) has suggested that the student's decision to attend college follows a natural ordering that depends on his or her college graduation probability. In particular he suggests that students with a high probability will attend a four-year college, those with a mid-range probability will attend a two-year college and those with a low probability will attend neither. This led him to employ the ordered probit model for the decision to attend college. Although the ordering of four-year/two-year/non-attendance seems appealing, Hilmer (2001) admitted that this ordering may not be appropriate, particularly when one is considering the choices between public and private four-year college. The ordered probit/logit model might not be appropriate, however; if there is no clear ordering, the multinomial logit model is the preferred specification. For the UK, Dustmann *et al.* (1996, 1998) estimated an ordered probit model which specifies the following ordinal outcomes: join the labour market full-time, enrol in a training scheme or continue in full-time education.

The impact of covariates   In addition to the role of the earnings differential, human capital theory also suggests other important factors that might influence the transition from school. The following sections contain a brief discussion of the factors found important in the literature. Owing to the difficulty caused by the huge differences between countries in the model specifications and definitions of variables employed in these studies, it is easier to discuss the empirical findings reported in the literature by grouping the factors into (i) personal characteristics, (ii) family background, (iii) school-related variables; and (iv) labour market conditions.

The first personal characteristic is *ability/academic attainment*. Measured ability has been incorporated into empirical work. Human capital theory suggests that an individual's ability may play an important role in the decision to invest in post-school education. More able students will be more likely to make further investment in post-secondary education, other things equal, because their expected returns from college should be higher and they are more able to reap the benefits.

Empirical studies invariably report that ability is a powerful predictor of college-going behaviour or the decision to stay on (for example, Christensen *et al.*, 1975; Borus and Carpenter, 1984; Micklewright, 1988; Ganderton and Santos, 1995; Rouse, 1994; Averett and Burton, 1996; Hilmer, 1998, 2001; Rice, 2000). Measures of ability reported in the literature are high school achievement, that is test score, grade and class rank, but the most often used is test score. Various test scores have been included in empirical work as a measure of ability.

There is a potential problem of endogeneity associated with the inclusion of prior attainment in models of the school-to-work transition. For example, young people who have a very clear plan to attend college have a strong motivation to perform well in these tests and exams. Students' decisions about working to achieve high test or exam scores in compulsory schooling are therefore influenced by their ambition to proceed to post-compulsory education. On the other hand, students who have decided to end their education after compulsory schooling will be less motivated to perform well in these tests or exams. As a result of this selection process, the test score used in empirical work might well be endogenous. Very few studies have attempted to deal with this problem appropriately. Some authors acknowledge this problem (McVicar, 1999a), while others exclude the measure of ability from their model. For example, Evans and Schwab (1995) report that they had to exclude this measure because of potential endogeneity. Exceptions are the studies by Behrman *et al.* (1992) and Bradley and Taylor (2002), both of which use the instrumentation technique to overcome the endogeneity problem.[8]

Relatively few studies examine *gender differences*, particularly for the USA. However girls usually have a higher probability of enrolling in college (Borus and Carpenter, 1984; Kane, 1994). Rouse (1994) reports that girls have a higher probability of enrolling in both two-year college and four-year college. There is some evidence pointing to the opposite, with boys found to be more likely to enrol in college (Hilmer, 2001).

Several studies address the difference between boys and girls by estimating separate models for each gender (for example, Andrews and Bradley, 1997) because of differences in preferences. The most able girls have a strong preference for non-vocational continuing education. Rice (1999) estimates separate models for boys and girls and reports evidence of gender differences for the least able group, with girls being twice as likely as boys to continue in full-time education, whereas the gender differences become negligible for the most able group. In a subsequent study, Rice (2000) reports that the gender gap with respect to participation in further education tends to widen as the level of ability, reflected by performance in GCSE exams, declines.[9]

Averett and Burton (1996) estimate separate probit models for boys and girls to examine gender differences using data from the National Longitudinal Survey of Youth. They report a number of gender differences with respect to family background factors and the college wage premium; that is, the earnings differential between those with a high school diploma and those with a college education. Boys are found to be responsive to the college wage premium, whereas the effect on girls is not significant.

Ethnicity is a third personal characteristic of importance, with a growing body of research on differences between ethnic groups in the school-to-work transition. A common perception, which may arise from an analysis of simple descriptive statistics, is that young people from ethnic minority groups are less likely to choose the post-compulsory education route than whites. This may be because they are from a poor socioeconomic background and their parents' educational attainment is relatively low. Multivariate analyses demonstrate that this perception is incorrect, since young people from ethnic minority backgrounds are more likely to make their transition to post-compulsory education. In the USA, Evans and Schwab (1995), Averett and Burton (1996) and Ellwood and Kane (2000) report that black and Hispanic high school graduates are more likely to attend college, *ceteris paribus*. DesJardin *et al.* (1999) also report that blacks and Asians are more likely to attend college, whereas Hispanics are not significantly different from whites. Ganderton and Santos (1995) estimate probit models for separate ethnic groups, including white, black and Hispanic. In general, they find that more able high school graduates are more likely to attend college regardless of ethnic group.

Evidence from multinomial choice models is less clear-cut. Nevertheless there is evidence of young people from minority ethnic groups taking a more academic route, that is, four-year college. Hilmer (2001), Rouse (1994) and Nguyen and Taylor (2003) report that black students are more likely to enrol in college than white students, but tend towards four-year college. For other ethnic groups, Rouse does not find any evidence of ethnic differences. Ordovensky (1995) shows that both blacks and Hispanics are more likely than whites to enrol in four-year college and in an academic programme in two-year college, but are not different from whites in enrolling for a vocational programme in two-year college or a vocational trade school.

Evidence of ethnic differences can also be found in the UK literature.

Leslie and Drinkwater (1999), Rice (2000) and Bradley and Taylor (2002) explicitly examine the effect of ethnicity on the school-to-work transition. A general finding is that students from ethnic minority backgrounds are more likely to make the transition into further education. Leslie and Drinkwater (1999) pay particular attention to the situation of ethnic minority groups and find evidence of a separate ethnicity effect influencing the decision to stay on for further education. In particular the higher probability of ethnic minorities participating in further education is related to the higher expected future benefits and fewer current opportunities. Rice (2000) investigates racial differences in the participation rate in further education, training and the labour market. She finds that differences vary across the spectrum of academic attainment as measured by GCSE attainment. One of the problems with this study is that the labour market entry outcome is treated as homogeneous, in so far as it combines the employed with the unemployed. Bradley and Taylor (2002) extend this approach and identify five outcomes: academic further education, vocational further education, employment, training and unemployment. Ethnic minority students are more likely to participate in further education than their white counterparts.

One reason advanced in the literature for the higher probability of participation in post-compulsory education is racial discrimination in the labour market (Rice, 1999, 2000; Leslie and Drinkwater, 1999). If a person believes that he is going to face discrimination in the labour market, we expect that person to make further investment in education. This is because of (i) the lower opportunity costs of further education (that is, forgone earnings would be small if the probability of being unemployed is high); or (ii) the higher return to additional qualifications than that to similarly qualified individuals from the majority group. This helps to compensate for the disadvantages resulting from labour market discrimination.

As regards *family background*, several measures have been used in the literature: parental education, family income, parental occupation, family size and family structure. The more education a parent has received, the greater will be their encouragement with respect to their child's investment in education. In addition, parental education is likely to be an indicator of the amount of intellectual heredity that children receive (Haveman and Wolfe, 1995).

In both the college enrolment model and staying-on models, parental education is found to be one of the most powerful factors. The more education parents have acquired, the more likely are their children to make the transition to college in the USA or stay on to further education in the UK. A variety of measures of parental education have been used in the literature. Some researchers use 'years of schooling' (Willis and

Rosen, 1979; Averett and Burton, 1996; McElroy, 1996) while others use various dummy variables to capture this effect (Christensen *et al.*, 1975; Kane, 1994; Rouse, 1994; Ellwood and Kane, 2000; Evans and Schwab, 1995). Using an ordered probit model, Hilmer (1998) finds that the level of parental education has a positive effect on the probability of going to college. In multinomial choice models, Rouse (1994) and Ordovensky (1995) also report a significant and positive effect of parents' education on the probability of enrolling in college.

Family/parental income has long been believed to be an important factor determining the school-to-work transition because it is the primary determinant of resources available to finance education. High parental income should therefore be positively related to post-secondary education. Measures of family income have been found to be an important factor in many empirical studies. Earlier evidence includes Christensen *et al.* (1975), Corman (1982) and Micklewright *et al.* (1990). More recent evidence includes Kane (1994), Rouse (1994), Evans and Schwab (1995), DesJardin *et al.* (1999), Ellwood and Kane (2000) and Hilmer (1998, 2001). It is noted here that the definition of income varies across studies. Ellwood and Kane (2000) measure income in quartiles. DesJardin *et al.* (1999) use dummy variables to control for income. Others use continuous measures of income. Recently Cameron and Heckman (1998) have criticized these approaches in so far as the decision to enrol in college depends on a family's 'permanent income' rather than 'temporary income'. An important issue that is closely related to that of family income is the question of the effects of financial aid and tuition on the college enrolment of high school graduates. Several studies have found a positive effect of financial aid on the college enrolment rates.[10]

Parental occupation is another measure of family background that is often found to be an important determinant of the school-to-work transition. From the perspective of investment in human capital, parents who have acquired high occupational status will be more likely to encourage their children to follow educational routes and, more importantly, have more resources available to support their children's education. Parental occupation has been included in empirical work for both the USA and the UK, and is generally found to be important. Although the definition of parental occupation varies between studies, in general young people whose parents are professionals or managers are more likely to choose post-compulsory education rather than labour market entry. In empirical studies, occupations of both parents are often included (for example, Averett and Burton, 1996; Ordovensky, 1995; Rice, 1999; Bradley and Taylor, 2002).

Parental employment is often used as a measure of family resources in empirical work. Within the context of binary choice models, evidence of the effect of parental employment on the staying on decision has been reported in several studies. Leslie and Drinkwater (1999) and Gregg (2000) report a positive effect of parental employment on the staying on decision. Rice (1999) obtains this result for mother's employment for boys. In the US literature, Kane (1994) controls for the potential effects of parents' employment but fails to obtain a statistically significant result. It is noted here that the failure to obtain a significant result for parents' employment may be due to other measures having already captured the effects of family resources.

In multinomial choice models, there is some evidence of the effect of parents' employment status. Armstrong (1999) reports that young people whose mothers are employed full-time are more likely to stay on, but this variable has little effect on other outcomes. More striking is that father's employment status has no effect whatsoever on the choice made by students. Bradley and Taylor (2002) find only weak evidence of the importance of parents' employment status. For example, they report that students whose parents are both workless are more likely to be unemployed. Rice (2000) failed to obtain any effect of parents' employment. This might be explained by the fact that her models control extensively for family resources, namely parents' occupation, number of siblings and the type of housing.

Family size, as measured by the number of siblings, is often included as an explanatory variable in models of college attendance. The importance of this variable derives from a belief that there is a tradeoff between child quality and quantity. Families are seen as solving a constrained maximization problem. A family's utility is maximized with respect to the quantity and quality of children as well as other goods. The constraints are budget and time. The tradeoff exists since parents' resources and time are limited and must be spread more thinly with more children (Becker and Tomes, 1976, 1979; Hanushek, 1992). The theory implies that, the larger the number of siblings in the family, the less likely high school graduates are able to make the transition to college. Despite its supposed importance, only a few studies have examined its effect.

For the USA, several studies find the number of siblings to be an important factor in explaining the college attendance decision. For example, Rouse (1994), Ganderton and Santos (1995), Averett and Burton (1996) and DesJardin *et al.* (1999) report that the presence of siblings in the family reduces the probability of enrolling in college. However Willis and Rosen (1979) fail to find such evidence. For the UK, several empirical studies report the negative effect of family size on college attendance (Micklewright, 1989; Micklewright *et al.*, 1990; Dustmann *et al.*, 1998; Armstrong, 1999).

Family structure has received little attention in the literature. The study by Evans and Schwab (1995) is among one of the very few studies that allow for the effects of family structure on the transition decision. They report that non-intact families have a negative effect on the probability of attending college. Ellwood and Kane (2000) estimate a binary probit model explaining the decision to attend college. They find a positive effect of family structure on the decision to attend college, but fail to find such evidence when they define the dependent variable as the decision to enrol in four-year college. Bradley and Taylor (2002) report some evidence of the disadvantages associated with being in a single-parent family. They report a higher probability of being unemployed if boys live in a single-parent family and a lower probability of being employed or in a youth training scheme for both boys and girls. Their results also indicate that students from a single-parent family are no less likely than those from a two-parent family to make the transition into academic and vocational further education.

School-related variables are a further factor. Do schools matter with respect to the school-to-work transition? Surprisingly, the literature is very thin on this question, with only a few studies attempting to control for school effects. In the US literature, studies examine the effect of a public school versus a private school and in particular the effect of a Catholic school. This is because the private school sector is made up largely of Catholic schools (Neal, 1997). Catholic schools in the USA are believed to provide a better service to students. Students graduating from Catholic schools are believed to be better prepared academically and more likely to go to college (Evans and Schwab, 1995; Ganderton and Santos, 1995; Ellwood and Kane, 2000). Evans and Schwab (1995) examine the effects of attending Catholic school on the probability of attending four-year college using data from *High School and Beyond*. They define college students as those attending four-year college, but not those attending two-year college. Because of the possible endogeneity of attending a Catholic school, they estimate a bivariate probit model as well as a single equation probit model and find that students enrolled in Catholic schools have a significantly higher probability of attending college and that no evidence of selection bias is found in the single equation probit model.

Evidence of the effects of school type can also be found in the UK literature, where comparisons are often drawn between grammar, private (both selective) and comprehensive schools (Micklewright, 1989; Andrews and Bradley, 1997; Dustmann et al., 1998; McVicar, 1999a; Rice, 1999, 2000; Bradley and Taylor, 2002). The general finding is that students from selective schools are more likely to make the transition to further education than students from comprehensive schools.

Other aspects of high schools have also been included in the model as control variables. School size is found to have had an impact on the school-to-work transition (Borus and Carpenter, 1984; DesJardin *et al.*, 1999). There is some evidence that the pupil/teacher ratio has a negative effect on post-school outcomes (Borus and Carpenter, 1984) for the USA, but Dustmann *et al.* (1998) fail to obtain such evidence for the UK. McVicar (1999b) even finds the unexpected result that a higher pupil/teacher ratio improves the chance of staying on. A school's exam performance, which could be taken as a measure of school quality, is found to be an important factor in the UK context. It increases the chance of students staying on rather than opting for other choices (Andrews and Bradley, 1997; Armstrong, 1999; Bradley and Taylor, 2002).

Finally we consider the effect of *local labour market conditions*. Local labour market conditions, in particular the local unemployment rate, have been postulated to affect the choices made by young people about to leave school. There are two contrasting arguments. One is the human investment decision and the other is the discouraged worker effect. On the one hand, the unemployment rate in the local area where the young person lives could be expected to affect the opportunity cost of attending college. A higher unemployment rate would lower the opportunity cost of further education if that rate meant that the individual has a greater probability of being unemployed. On the other hand, a higher local unemployment rate might indicate that the family is less likely to have resources to support college education for their children. Higher unemployment rates also mean that it is difficult for youths to find employment while in college, forcing youths to enter the labour market.

In the UK literature it seems that there is consistent evidence with respect to the effect of local unemployment rates on the school-to-work transition. Rice (1987, 1999, 2000), Andrews and Bradley (1997) and Bradley and Taylor (2002) find that higher unemployment rates encourage greater participation in further education. However, the picture is less clear in US literature. In part, this is because there are only a small number of studies that attempt to control for this variable, owing to a lack of data. A higher unemployment rate is reported by Averett and Burton (1996) to encourage college enrolment, whereas Hilmer (2001) reports that the local unemployment rate has no effect on college enrolment for either two-year and four-year college but has a positive effect on non-college choice.

Longitudinal studies: the time to first job
The focus of the time to first job literature is on unemployment duration and the re-employment hazard.[11] The question addressed in the literature is how successfully the individuals enter the labour market, and how the

probabilities of exiting to first job change over time (duration dependence). The main advantage of explicitly modelling the time to first job is that it shows how the employment probability of school leavers varies over time: whether it is constant, increasing or decreasing. This can be seen through the shape of the baseline hazard, which is drawn for the 'base group'. The shape of the baseline hazard can be determined parametrically, in which case its shape is determined by the parameters of an underlying statistical distribution, or non-parametrically, where the shape is determined by the data.

The shape of the baseline hazard   Evidence of negative duration dependence is reported in Franz *et al.* (2000), Nielsen *et al.* (2001) and Chuang (1999). Franz *et al.* (2000) estimate a non-parametric baseline hazard model for the time to first job of German youths. Their estimation results show that the hazard rate of employment after the first three months is about 11 percentage points, but then drops to 5 percentage points for the next three months and to 4 percentage points thereafter. Nielsen *et al.* (2001), investigating the transition from school to work for second-generation immigrants in Denmark, report evidence of negative duration dependence for youths. They find that the hazard rate is very high during the first month after leaving school, after which it tends to become constant until 12 months after leaving school, and declines thereafter.

While Franz *et al.* (2000) and Nielsen *et al.* (2001) estimate a flexible non-parametric baseline hazard, they fail to control for unobserved heterogeneity. It is well known that failure to control for unobserved heterogeneity may bias the results, and the evidence of negative duration dependence reported in these studies may well be spurious. In contrast to other studies mentioned above, Andrews *et al.* (2002), model the school-to-work transition of school leavers in a competing risks framework and control for unobserved heterogeneity with three alternative distributions, parametrically (Gaussian and Gamma) and non-parametrically (Heckman and Singer). After controlling for unobserved heterogeneity the evidence of negative duration dependence seems to disappear. However, in common with other studies, Andrews *et al.* (2002) find that the hazards of exit to jobs are very high in the first few weeks in the labour market and then fall dramatically to a much lower level.

Elsewhere the literature concentrates on the effects of vocational training and apprenticeships on the transition to first job (Franz *et al.*, 2000; Bonnal *et al.*, 2000; Genda and Kurosawa, 2000). Bonnal *et al.* (2000), for example, compare the effect of apprenticeships with the effect of the traditional vocational schooling programmes in France on the hazard of exiting to first job. They find that having an apprenticeship has a distinct advantage over the traditional vocational schooling programme. Genda and Kurosawa (2000) estimate Cox proportional hazards models using data for Japan and find that school leavers enrolled in special high school vocational programmes have a significantly shorter time to become full-time workers.

The impact of covariates   The impact of covariates on the re-employment probability is very similar to those reported for the cross-section studies discussed above. Academic attainment has the strongest effect and increases the re-employment probability. Gender and ethnic differences have also been found (Eyland and Johnson, 1989; Chuang, 1999; Franz *et al.*, 2000; Lassibille *et al.*, 2001; Dolton *et al.*, 1994; Bonnal *et al.*, 2000; Andrews *et al.*, 2001). While Eyland and Johnson (1989) report that girls take longer to find their first job than boys in Australia, the opposite result is found for Denmark by Bratberg and Nilsen (2000). Using Spanish data, Lassibille *et al.* (2001) report that 'girls are less likely to find their first job in less than 10 months compared with boys' as evidence of 'discrimination against women at a very early stage of their working life' (p. 142). Genda and Kurosawa (2000) also report a lower hazard rate for girls, thus supporting the finding by Lassibille *et al.* (2001). But this finding is reversed for Taiwan, where boys have a lower hazard rate than girls (Chuang, 1999). Franz *et al.* (2000) report no difference in the hazard rate of exiting to a job for boys and girls in Germany. Andrews *et al.* (2002) report that most girls are found to exit to jobs that match their occupational preferences and no girls end up in a mismatching Youth Training programme. A majority of boys are found to exit to mismatching jobs and a mismatching scheme.

Ethnic differences in the transition to first job of school leavers have also been investigated in both structural models and reduced-form models. Wolpin (1992) estimates a structural model for the transition from school to full-time employment for black and white high school graduates using data for the USA. He reports that blacks have a higher probability of receiving job offers but face a lower wage return to experience and a less diverse wage offer distribution. In a later study, Eckstein and Wolpin (1995) report that blacks have a longer unemployment duration and lower accepted mean wage. However they conclude that 'differences in unemployment durations by race [...] are primarily due to differential rates at which job offers are accepted rather than to differential job offer probabilities, which are found to be close to one' (Eckstein and Wolpin, 1995, p. 285). Bowlus *et al.* (2001) conclude that 'the longer unemployment duration for Blacks stems from their lower arrival rate of job offers while unemployed' (p. 334).

In the UK literature, both Dolton *et al.* (1994) and Upward (1999) find that ethnic minorities do not have lower rates of exit to the first job.

In contrast, a competing risks model employed by Andrews *et al.* (2002) reveals interesting findings of ethnicity differences with respect to both unemployment duration and matching in the labour market. Non-white boys and girls are found to leave unemployment more quickly than their white counterparts. They are also found to prefer a job to a training scheme even though the job does not match their occupational preferences. Andrews *et al.* conclude that this is evidence of discrimination in the labour market against ethnic minorities. Further evidence of discrimination against ethnic minorities can also be found in Andrews *et al.* (2001) where 'job seekers from a minority ethnic background have a lower probability of a match, particularly in terms of application to YTS vacancies' (p. 353).

Several family background factors have been found to influence the re-employment hazard and equivalently the duration of job search of school leavers. Franz *et al.* (2000) report that the occupational status of the head of the household is a decisive determinant of the duration of non-employment of youths. They argue that their results support the notion that 'qualified staff receive an extra premium by having their children favoured in the recruitment process' (p. 407). Andrews *et al.* (2001) report similar results indicating that youths whose parents are in professional and non-manual occupation groups have a higher employment probability and shorter non-employment duration. However this is not always supported by findings from other studies. Dolton *et al.* (1994), for example, find that girls with parents in higher occupation groups have higher hazard rates, but this result does not apply to boys and disappears when the whole sample is used. Lassibille *et al.* (2001), on the other hand, find that social class background proxied by father's occupation does not have any effect on the probability of getting a job.

Eyland and Johnson (1989) show that young people who have at least one parent with post-secondary education have a shorter time to first job. The result that higher parental educational levels lead to higher children's employment probability is also reported in Main (1985). But Main and Raffe (1983) find a negative effect of parental education on employment probability. This corroborates the findings of Nielsen *et al.* (2001) that 'the education of the parents seems to exert a "perverse" effect on the probability of entering the first job after leaving the educational system' (p. 21). In particular a higher level of education of parents seems to 'prolong the non-employment spell'. Betts *et al.* (2000) also report a negative effect of mother's years of education on the hazard of exit to first job for Canadian university graduates. In this connection, Chuang (1999) finds that parental education does not have any effect on the hazard of exiting to first job. This 'perverse' effect can be reconciled by the fact that parental education levels may correlate with family income. Children from higher-income families may have more resources to search longer for a better matching job since they are more likely to reject 'low-quality' job offers. Alternatively, they may simply have a higher reservation wage.

Another aspect of family background is the number of siblings, which has been found to have a negative effect on the hazard of exiting to first job (Dolton *et al.*, 1994) and to be associated with a longer search period for the first job (Bratberg and Nilsen, 2000).

Various other factors that reflect aggregate employment opportunities (or aggregate labour market conditions) have also been controlled for in several empirical studies. However there is little consensus with respect to the specification of these factors. They include urbanicity (Lassibille *et al.*, 2001), conditions in the local labour market (Dolton *et al.*, 1994; Bratberg and Nilsen, 2000; and Andrews *et al.*, 2002), geographical areas (Betts *et al.*, 2000; Nielsen *et al.*, 2001) and the business cycle (Andrews *et al.*, 2002).

IV   The school-to-work transition in the 1990s

In this section we estimate several cross-sectional models of the school-to-work transition for England for the period 1992–8. These are in keeping with the literature discussed above (pages 489–97), except that we try to control for the endogeneity of school choice and exam performance. These issues are discussed in more detail below, but first we describe a unique database that has been constructed for our analysis, which combines data from several sources.

The Youth Cohort survey

We use individual-level data from the Youth Cohort Studies (YCS) for 1992, 1994, 1996 and 1998, which correspond to YCS6–YCS9. Respondents completed the YCS questionnaires in the year following the end of their compulsory education at school. This is combined with data for each young person's school obtained from the annual Schools' Census and the annual School Performance Tables. District-level unemployment rates were obtained from the National Online Manpower Information Service, and county-level earnings data were derived from the New Earnings Survey. The use of district level (rather than travel-to-work area) unemployment rates can be justified on the grounds that young people are less geographically mobile than their adult counterparts. Table 13A.1 in the Appendix shows the means for each covariate.

The effect of personal characteristics is captured by gender and ethnic background. Following Bradley and Taylor (2002), ethnicity is split into white, Afro-Caribbean, Bangladeshi/Pakistani, Indian and Chinese/other. Several variables capture the effect of family background, such as whether a young person comes from a single-parent family, where we distinguish between having a father only and mother only, the number of siblings and parental occupation.[12] The impact of family income and the quality of the neighbourhood is indicated by the family's accommodation (public/private rented or owner-occupied) and by whether or not the young person's parents are both in work or both workless.

Rather than include numerous measures of school quality, we adopt a more parsimonious approach by including the proportion of pupils achieving five or more GCSEs grades A*–C. This can be regarded as an 'index' of school quality. Several other school-level variables are used as instruments to predict the exam score of each school (see below and note 8). The literature review suggested that school-to-work transition depends on conditions in the local labour market, therefore we include the local unemployment rate, measured at the district level, and the youth wage relative to the adult wage. The relative wage is chosen because it is a general measure of forgone earnings that is likely to have an impact on all post-school outcomes.

Finally the exam performance of the young person is included in our models. This refers to attainment in up to ten GCSE exams, which is classified into one of six mutually exclusive categories, ranging from no exams to ten GCSE A*–Cs. Rather than include the actual value of this variable, we include the predicted value in light of the potential endogeneity bias referred to above.

Econometric framework
Young people approaching the end of their compulsory schooling face a wide range of choices, or options. We identify $J + 1 = 5$ choices. These are as follows: to continue in education either for an academic course, such as A-levels ($y = 0$) or a vocational course ($y = 1$); to enter a publicly funded training programme ($y = 2$); to enter permanent employment ($y = 3$); or to become unemployed or economically inactive ($y = 4$). These five categories make up the dependent variable, that is, $y = j; j = 0,....,J$. We estimate multinomial logit regressions and denote P_{ij} as Prob($Y_i = j$), the probability that the ith young person chooses the jth option, which can be written as

$$\log(P_{ij}/P_{io}) = x_i(\beta_j - \beta_0), \tag{13.1}$$

where i refers to N individuals and j to the $0,...,J$ choices.

In view of the results surveyed in the literature review, separate models are estimated for boys and girls. Only the estimated marginal effects, which are evaluated at the means of the independent variables, are reported here.

Endogeneity and identification

Several sources of endogeneity could be present in our analysis. First, we have already discussed the possibility that educational attainment may be endogenous in models of the school-to-work transition. To deal with this problem educational attainment is instrumented, and identification is achieved by including variables such as the pupil/teacher ratio, school type and school size (see Bradley and Taylor, 2002, for more details). Second, the pupil/teacher ratio variable itself could also be endogenous in our exam attainment model if parents with greater resources send their child to a school with a 'good' exam performance. The effect of this is to raise the pupil/teacher ratio in 'good' schools. The instruments used to identify the pupil/teacher ratio are random demographic change in the relevant age cohort, teacher shortages and the pupil/teacher ratio in each school's local education authority area (LEA), a policy variable. Third, parents who intend to encourage their child to proceed to further and higher education will choose a school of high quality for their child. This will induce an upward bias on the school quality variable, hence this variable is also instrumented using a large number of school level variables. (See Bradley and Taylor (2002) for additional details.)

V   Results

In this section we discuss the estimates from the multinomial logit models of the school-to-work transition. Unlike the previous literature, we also explore whether there are interaction effects between covariates and then estimate predicted probabilities to illustrate the quantitative impact of personal, family and other characteristics on the school-to-work transition. Tables 13.1 and 13.2 report the main results.

Determinants of the school-to-work transition

Educational attainment and the quality of schooling   In previous work, two of the most highly significant influences on the school-to-work transition were found to be the young person's 'predicted' exam performance and the performance of their school, measured by its exam results (Bradley and Taylor, 2002). A key difference between this analysis and our previous work is that we predict exam performance based on an ordered logit model of exam attainment categorized into one of six mutually exclusive categories. Previously we simply predicted whether a young person obtained five or more GCSE grades A*–C or not. The treatment of the school's exam performance is the same as before.

The main difference between our earlier work and the present analysis is that the quantitative importance of a young person's predicted exam per-

Table 13.1   *The determinants of the school-to-work transition (girls)*

	Unemployed			Vocational further educatic		
	Marginal effect	s.e.	p-value	Marginal effect	s.e.	p-valu
Predicted exam performance	−0.014	0.008	0.057	−0.038	0.019	0.044
Cohort 7	−0.002	0.004	0.668	−0.060	0.009	0.000
Cohort 8	0.016	0.005	0.001	0.039	0.012	0.001
Cohort 9	0.004	0.005	0.415	0.089	0.011	0.000
Father only	0.001	0.009	0.868	0.011	0.021	0.610
Mother only	−0.004	0.004	0.398	−0.003	0.011	0.760
Father – professional	−0.024	0.011	0.029	−0.063	0.025	0.011
Father – manager	−0.015	0.007	0.031	−0.012	0.015	0.412
Father – associate professional	−0.012	0.009	0.213	−0.031	0.020	0.126
Father – skilled non-manual	−0.011	0.008	0.207	−0.027	0.018	0.148
Father – skilled manual	0.003	0.003	0.290	0.016	0.007	0.027
Mother – professional	−0.002	0.012	0.874	−0.083	0.026	0.002
Mother – manager	−0.011	0.007	0.115	−0.003	0.014	0.839
Mother – associate professional	−0.014	0.008	0.074	−0.036	0.017	0.036
Mother – skilled non-manual	−0.012	0.006	0.060	−0.007	0.014	0.633
Mother – skilled manual	−0.010	0.008	0.244	−0.006	0.020	0.752
Indian	−0.026	0.011	0.015	0.019	0.019	0.298
Afro-Caribbean	−0.015	0.010	0.127	0.073	0.024	0.003
Bangladeshi/Pakistani	−0.006	0.008	0.463	0.014	0.021	0.501
Chinese/other ethnic	−0.015	0.013	0.254	−0.024	0.028	0.391
Social housing	0.035	0.008	0.000	0.011	0.019	0.568
Other housing	0.047	0.007	0.000	−0.009	0.019	0.640
Both parents work	0.000	0.003	0.976	−0.006	0.007	0.411
Both parents unemployed	0.007	0.005	0.157	−0.010	0.012	0.429
Local unemployment rate	−0.025	0.036	0.488	−0.330	0.086	0.000
Log(relative wage)	−0.012	0.026	0.662	−0.131	0.062	0.034
Index of school quality	−0.066	0.021	0.002	−0.159	0.054	0.003
One sibling	−0.026	0.003	0.000	0.019	0.008	0.023
Two siblings	−0.022	0.004	0.000	0.023	0.009	0.012
Three siblings	−0.025	0.005	0.000	0.002	0.013	0.889
Four siblings	−0.013	0.007	0.053	0.034	0.017	0.045
Constant	−0.025	0.012	0.042	0.059	0.028	0.036

Number of observations
Log likelihood
Pseudo R2

Youth Training			Employment			Academic further education		
Marginal effect	s.e.	p-value	Marginal effect	s.e.	p-value	Marginal effect	s.e.	p-value
−0.033	0.009	0.000	−0.019	0.010	0.051	0.104	0.022	0.000
−0.010	0.004	0.019	−0.006	0.005	0.232	0.077	0.011	0.000
−0.007	0.006	0.251	−0.006	0.007	0.387	−0.042	0.015	0.004
0.006	0.005	0.267	0.018	0.006	0.003	−0.117	0.014	0.000
−0.010	0.011	0.330	0.012	0.011	0.274	−0.014	0.026	0.588
−0.009	0.006	0.108	−0.008	0.006	0.179	0.024	0.013	0.059
−0.020	0.013	0.126	−0.043	0.014	0.002	0.150	0.028	0.000
−0.010	0.008	0.173	−0.012	0.008	0.143	0.050	0.018	0.006
−0.017	0.011	0.116	−0.018	0.011	0.116	0.077	0.023	0.001
−0.011	0.009	0.215	−0.010	0.010	0.343	0.058	0.021	0.006
0.004	0.003	0.236	0.000	0.004	0.998	−0.023	0.009	0.010
−0.056	0.016	0.000	−0.079	0.016	0.000	0.221	0.031	0.000
−0.013	0.007	0.079	−0.008	0.007	0.255	0.035	0.016	0.028
−0.014	0.009	0.120	−0.042	0.010	0.000	0.104	0.020	0.000
−0.006	0.007	0.417	−0.029	0.007	0.000	0.052	0.016	0.001
0.018	0.008	0.025	0.015	0.009	0.093	−0.017	0.023	0.476
−0.063	0.013	0.000	−0.140	0.020	0.000	0.210	0.024	0.000
−0.076	0.017	0.000	−0.109	0.023	0.000	0.127	0.034	0.000
−0.080	0.013	0.000	−0.099	0.018	0.000	0.171	0.029	0.000
−0.057	0.018	0.001	−0.097	0.022	0.000	0.193	0.034	0.000
−0.004	0.008	0.674	0.035	0.010	0.000	−0.078	0.023	0.001
−0.015	0.009	0.096	0.033	0.010	0.001	−0.056	0.023	0.014
0.001	0.004	0.795	0.022	0.004	0.000	−0.017	0.009	0.051
−0.008	0.006	0.161	−0.013	0.007	0.074	0.024	0.015	0.113
0.115	0.039	0.003	−0.219	0.049	0.000	0.459	0.109	0.000
0.191	0.032	0.000	0.032	0.034	0.356	−0.079	0.075	0.290
−0.077	0.023	0.001	−0.089	0.027	0.001	0.391	0.065	0.000
−0.005	0.004	0.246	−0.019	0.004	0.000	0.031	0.010	0.002
−0.007	0.004	0.117	−0.019	0.005	0.000	0.025	0.011	0.017
−0.005	0.006	0.457	−0.017	0.007	0.017	0.044	0.016	0.004
−0.003	0.008	0.756	−0.012	0.010	0.214	−0.006	0.021	0.757
0.041	0.013	0.002	0.016	0.016	0.308	−0.091	0.035	0.009
	26898							
	−31111							
	0.0915							

formance is much lower. There are also differences between boys and girls in terms of the size of the marginal effects. For instance, a higher predicted exam score means that it is more likely both boys and girls will proceed to 'Academic' further education; however note that the marginal effect for boys (0.181) is almost twice that for girls (0.104). For both boys and girls, the marginal effects on 'Unemployment' and 'Employment' are small and negative, whereas those for 'Vocational' further education and 'Youth Training' are still negative but much larger. Added together they suggest that more able young people have a strong preference against the so-called 'vocational route' to occupations.

To capture the effect of school quality on the school-to-work transition we have included the predicted exam performance of the school attended. The important finding is that our index of school quality has a much larger effect, especially for girls, on the options chosen post-school than a young person's own exam performance. This suggests that school choice is important. Young people who attend a school of 'high' quality are far more likely to proceed to 'Academic' further education. Boys from high-quality schools are far less likely to enter the labour market and get a job or become unemployed whereas, interestingly, for girls, not only are they less likely to enter the labour market, they least prefer the 'Vocational' further education route.

In sum, the school attended by a young person provides an additional, and substantial, effect on the school-to-work transition. School quality does indeed matter in this context.

Personal characteristics   Non-white youths are far less likely to enter the labour market and more likely to proceed to further education than white youths. There are, however, interesting variations between ethnic groups and between boys and girls. For boys of all ethnic groups the negative marginal effects for the 'Employment' and 'Youth Training' outcomes are counterbalanced by positive marginal effects for the 'Academic' and 'Vocational' further education. In the case of girls, the comparison is between the two labour market options and academic further education. However the ranking of ethnic groups with respect to the academic further education option is exactly the same for boys and girls, and the magnitude of the marginal effect is almost identical. Indian youths are ranked highest, whereas Afro-Caribbeans are ranked lowest. Afro-Caribbean boys, and to a lesser extent Bangladeshi/Pakistani boys, are almost equally likely to choose vocational courses in further education, which could reflect their lower prior educational attainment or the fact that they have different occupational preferences compared to other ethnic groups. The avoidance of labour market discrimination is another plausible explanation.

Family background The occupational status of a young person's parents has been found to be a powerful and significant determinant of the school-to-work transition. This is also the case here, although mainly with respect to girls. The higher the occupational status of the father, the more likely it is that the daughter will proceed to 'Academic' further education. Compare, for instance, the marginal effect for 'Father – professional' (0.150) with that for 'Father – skilled manual' (−0.023). Furthermore, for girls, there are also differences between the impact of mother's occupation and a father's occupation. Having a professional mother has a more powerful effect on the probability of staying on for academic courses (marginal effect = 0.221) than having a professional father (0.150). A similar pattern occurs for boys, although the results are less clear-cut.

The type of accommodation a young person lives in may be regarded as a proxy for family wealth. However it may also give some idea of the quality of the neighbourhood. Social or council housing is normally located on estates, which comprise a large share of the poor and deprived families. Amenities and schooling are also typically of lower quality. It is therefore likely that young people who live in social housing will have a different school-to-work transition than their counterparts who live in owner-occupied housing. What we find is that young people from social housing are more likely to enter the labour market and are equally likely to get a job or become unemployed. Girls are much less likely to stay on for academic further education, which is an important finding in view of the UK government's current policy of widening participation in higher education amongst young people from the working class.

For girls there are some interesting sibling effects. Girls with more siblings tend to proceed to further education, vocational and academic, and are less likely to enter the labour market and become unemployed. One possible explanation for this is that any financial constraint on investments in continued education are reduced by having older brothers and sisters who may be working and therefore contributing to the family budget.

Local labour market The higher the local unemployment rate the more likely it is that young people will proceed to academic further education. This effect is very large and highly significant for both boys and girls. As expected, both boys and girls are less likely to leave school and enter employment when the local labour market is slack; however, rather than become unemployed, they enter government-funded Youth Training programmes. Youth Training programmes are fixed-term training programmes for 16- and 17-year-old youths that also absorb any temporary excess supply of youth labour. The effect is larger for boys than for girls, which is seen by comparing the marginal effects on 'Youth Training' (0.230 and 0.115, respectively). Some young

Table 13.2   The determinants of the school-to-work transition (boys)

	Unemployed			Vocational further educatio		
	Marginal effect	s.e.	p-value	Marginal effect	s.e.	p-valu
Predicted exam performance	−0.024	0.008	0.003	−0.068	0.016	0.000
Cohort 7	−0.010	0.004	0.015	−0.011	0.009	0.237
Cohort 8	0.018	0.004	0.000	0.076	0.011	0.000
Cohort 9	0.000	0.005	0.913	0.105	0.009	0.000
Father only	0.009	0.008	0.271	0.014	0.021	0.488
Mother only	0.014	0.004	0.002	0.015	0.012	0.201
Father – professional	−0.019	0.012	0.122	0.021	0.023	0.365
Father – manager	−0.013	0.007	0.071	0.031	0.014	0.025
Father – associate professional	−0.018	0.010	0.060	0.021	0.018	0.265
Father – skilled non-manual	−0.023	0.009	0.009	0.022	0.016	0.164
Father – skilled manual	−0.004	0.003	0.239	0.004	0.008	0.623
Mother – professional	0.012	0.012	0.286	0.001	0.023	0.963
Mother – manager	0.006	0.007	0.341	0.012	0.014	0.420
Mother – associate professional	−0.007	0.007	0.327	0.008	0.015	0.564
Mother – skilled non-manual	−0.014	0.006	0.023	0.022	0.012	0.070
Mother – skilled manual	−0.007	0.008	0.396	−0.005	0.021	0.809
Indian	−0.016	0.011	0.141	0.125	0.021	0.000
Afro-Caribbean	−0.035	0.014	0.010	0.110	0.025	0.000
Bangladeshi/Pakistani	−0.007	0.008	0.428	0.139	0.020	0.000
Chinese/other ethnic	−0.020	0.013	0.123	0.090	0.026	0.001
Social housing	0.022	0.007	0.002	−0.024	0.015	0.104
Other housing	0.018	0.007	0.013	−0.012	0.018	0.492
Both parents work	−0.003	0.003	0.397	0.002	0.007	0.777
Both parents unemployed	0.000	0.005	0.951	0.008	0.012	0.500
Local unemployment rate	−0.090	0.039	0.021	−0.141	0.093	0.128
Log(relative wage)	0.011	0.020	0.584	−0.236	0.049	0.000
Index of school quality	−0.069	0.021	0.001	0.000	0.052	0.994
One sibling	−0.010	0.004	0.005	0.007	0.008	0.428
Two siblings	−0.005	0.004	0.220	−0.011	0.009	0.236
Three siblings	−0.006	0.005	0.261	−0.020	0.013	0.128
Four siblings	0.000	0.007	0.973	−0.045	0.017	0.009
Constant	−0.009	0.011	0.386	−0.077	0.029	0.009

Number of observations
Log likelihood
Pseudo R2

Youth Training			Employment			Academic further education		
Marginal effect	s.e.	p-value	Marginal effect	s.e.	p-value	Marginal effect	s.e.	p-value
−0.062	0.013	0.000	−0.027	0.011	0.018	0.181	0.022	0.000
−0.009	0.006	0.112	−0.016	0.006	0.011	0.046	0.012	0.000
0.019	0.008	0.012	−0.030	0.007	0.000	−0.083	0.014	0.000
0.034	0.007	0.000	−0.009	0.007	0.161	−0.130	0.013	0.000
−0.033	0.014	0.019	0.007	0.014	0.619	0.003	0.026	0.908
−0.026	0.008	0.001	−0.016	0.009	0.068	0.013	0.015	0.386
0.000	0.019	0.998	−0.082	0.018	0.000	0.080	0.030	0.008
0.001	0.010	0.928	−0.032	0.010	0.001	0.014	0.018	0.444
−0.005	0.014	0.703	−0.037	0.014	0.008	0.040	0.023	0.090
0.001	0.011	0.954	−0.023	0.012	0.044	0.024	0.020	0.236
0.014	0.005	0.004	0.010	0.005	0.051	−0.024	0.010	0.018
−0.027	0.020	0.175	−0.083	0.019	0.000	0.096	0.030	0.001
0.012	0.010	0.224	−0.022	0.010	0.032	−0.008	0.018	0.665
−0.007	0.011	0.513	−0.047	0.011	0.000	0.053	0.019	0.005
0.005	0.009	0.582	−0.023	0.009	0.008	0.010	0.016	0.509
0.023	0.011	0.038	−0.018	0.015	0.216	0.008	0.025	0.757
−0.121	0.022	0.000	−0.240	0.031	0.000	0.253	0.030	0.000
−0.102	0.025	0.000	−0.086	0.026	0.001	0.113	0.038	0.003
−0.168	0.022	0.000	−0.129	0.021	0.000	0.164	0.031	0.000
−0.094	0.029	0.001	−0.159	0.033	0.000	0.183	0.039	0.000
−0.010	0.011	0.357	0.027	0.011	0.011	−0.015	0.021	0.480
−0.002	0.012	0.876	0.052	0.011	0.000	−0.056	0.023	0.015
−0.008	0.005	0.074	0.031	0.005	0.000	−0.022	0.009	0.014
−0.015	0.007	0.050	−0.019	0.009	0.034	0.026	0.016	0.101
0.230	0.056	0.000	−0.441	0.067	0.000	0.442	0.120	0.000
0.268	0.029	0.000	−0.024	0.033	0.452	−0.018	0.061	0.767
−0.048	0.032	0.136	−0.134	0.034	0.000	0.251	0.072	0.000
0.011	0.005	0.047	−0.007	0.006	0.229	0.000	0.011	0.968
0.007	0.006	0.217	−0.007	0.006	0.265	0.016	0.012	0.178
0.008	0.008	0.361	−0.003	0.009	0.739	0.022	0.016	0.177
0.009	0.011	0.428	0.006	0.013	0.612	0.030	0.023	0.186
−0.001	0.017	0.934	0.065	0.019	0.001	0.023	0.039	0.555
	22662							
	−27921							
	0.0906							

Table 13.3   Interaction effects (girls)

Panel A	Unemployed			Vocational		
	Marginal effects	Std err	P value	Marginal effects	Std err	P valu
Predicted exam performance* local unemployment rate	0.037	0.031	1.17	0.115	0.075	0.126
Predicted exam performance* school quality	0.007	0.008	0.384	−0.056	0.015	0.000
Predicted exam performance* social housing	0.009	0.004	0.034	0.023	0.012	0.054
Social housing* school quality	0.053	0.019	0.006	0.029	0.056	0.608

Panel B	Unemployed			Vocational		
	Marginal effects	Std err	P value	Marginal effects	Std err	P value
Predicted exam performance* local unemployment rate	0.034	0.033	0.300	0.068	0.080	0.396
Predicted exam performance* school quality	0.023	0.008	0.004	−0.070	0.019	0.000
Predicted exam performance* social housing	0.004	0.006	0.501	0.028	0.015	0.067
Social housing* school quality	0.070	0.026	0.006	−0.197	0.078	0.012

people in depressed labour markets may therefore have been 'pushed' into the Youth Training programme because of a lack of jobs. However other young people were 'pulled' into participating in the programme because of the quality of the training and the prospect of higher earnings. Evidence for the latter effect is provided by the positive and significant effect of the relative wage variable on the 'Youth Training' outcome.

Interaction effects   Tables 13.3 and 13.4 report the effect of various interaction terms that have been included alongside the main effects reported in Tables 13.1 and 13.2. We have chosen interaction terms for variables that had a large or statistically significant effect in the main model.

Tables 13.3a and 13.4a report the marginal effects when each interaction term is included in our model of the school-to-work transition separately. These results suggest that boys and girls who have higher predicted exam attainment who live in labour markets with higher unemployment rates are less likely to proceed to academic further education. Rather they are more likely to enter the labour market and enter employment or Youth Training

Training			Employment			Academic		
Marginal effects	Std err	P value	Marginal effects	Std err	P value	Marginal effects	Std err	P value
0.105	0.033	0.002	0.164	0.044	0.000	−0.422	0.095	0.000
−0.037	0.010	0.000	−0.008	0.010	0.442	0.094	0.022	0.000
0.014	0.006	0.013	0.020	0.006	0.003	−0.067	0.016	0.000
0.036	0.023	0.133	0.110	0.029	0.000	−0.229	0.074	0.000

Training			Employment			Academic		
Marginal effects	Std err	P value	Marginal effects	Std err	P value	Marginal effects	Std err	P value
0.066	0.037	0.073	0.147	0.047	0.002	−0.315	0.098	0.001
−0.042	0.013	0.002	0.020	0.011	0.083	0.068	0.025	0.006
0.012	0.007	0.097	0.007	0.009	0.413	−0.051	0.019	0.007
−0.069	0.033	0.036	0.097	0.040	0.015	0.099	0.094	0.292

programmes. Thus, if more able young people enter depressed labour markets, they are more likely to be at the front of the 'job queue', as one would expect.

Earlier it was argued that school quality mattered for post-school destinations. We explore this effect further by including an interaction term between the young person's exam performance and the exam performance of their school. More able young people who attend higher quality schools are more likely to proceed to academic further education. The magnitude of the effects are 13 percentage points and 9 percentage points for boys and girls, respectively. It is worth noting that the main effects on the two exam variables are similar in magnitude to those in Tables 13.1 and 13.2 when we include their interaction effect. Thus being an academically able student in a good school has an additional bonus in terms of post-school destinations.

Finally, we explore the joint impact of social housing and a young person's exam performance, and social housing and our measure of school quality. Attending a high-quality school does not appear to have a favourable effect for young people from council estates in so far as they are much

Table 13.4   Interaction effect (boys)

Panel A	Unemployed			Vocational		
	Marginal effects	Std err	P value	Marginal effects	Std err	P value
Predicted exam performance* local unemployment rate	0.022	0.039	0.556	0.034	0.078	0.658
Predicted exam performance* school quality	0.015	0.011	0.197	−0.057	0.018	0.002
Predicted exam performance* social housing	0.006	0.006	0.285	0.022	0.013	0.108
Social housing* school quality	0.050	0.022	0.020	0.079	0.061	0.197

Panel B	Unemployed			Vocational		
	Marginal effects	Std err	P value	Marginal effects	Std err	P value
Predicted exam performance* local unemployment rate	0.034	0.042	0.422	−0.033	0.086	0.705
Predicted exam performance* school quality	0.036	0.011	0.001	−0.071	0.022	0.001
Predicted exam performance* social housing	0.001	0.008	0.861	0.013	0.017	0.441
Social housing* school quality	0.085	0.030	0.004	−0.064	0.080	0.423

less likely to proceed to academic further education. They are more likely to enter the labour market and, especially in the case of boys, enter employment or Youth Training, or they become unemployed. Interestingly the marginal effect for the interaction term between social housing and school quality on the 'Unemployment' outcome is larger than the main effect for social housing. For girls, a similar pattern of effects is observed with respect to the interaction term between the young person's exam performance and social housing, although they are smaller in magnitude.

Tables 13.3b and 13.4b report the marginal effects when all of the interaction effects are included in the main models reported in Tables 13.1 and 13.2. The picture is broadly similar to that described above, although the magnitude and statistical significance of some of the effects does fall.

VI   Conclusion

In this chapter we have reviewed the extensive literature on the school-to-work transition, focusing on studies of the UK and the USA. We have also

Training			Employment			Academic		
Marginal effects	Std err	P value	Marginal effects	Std err	P value	Marginal effects	Std err	P value
0.198	0.052	0.000	0.255	0.066	0.000	−0.510	0.103	0.000
−0.060	0.017	0.001	−0.030	0.015	0.040	0.132	0.028	0.000
0.019	0.008	0.026	0.023	0.009	0.022	−0.071	0.019	0.000
0.163	0.032	0.000	0.120	0.039	0.003	−0.412	0.084	0.000
Training			Employment			Academic		
Marginal effects	Std err	P value	Marginal effects	Std err	P value	Marginal effects	Std err	P value
0.118	0.059	0.046	0.224	0.071	0.002	−0.343	0.112	0.002
−0.033	0.023	0.144	−0.005	0.017	0.742	0.074	0.030	0.015
−0.010	0.012	0.388	0.008	0.013	0.570	−0.012	0.024	0.623
0.120	0.052	0.021	0.055	0.056	0.329	−0.196	0.109	0.071

undertaken an analysis of the determinants of the school-to-work transition for England for the 1990s. Our main conclusions are as follows.

1. A bad start to a young person's working life has immediate and long-lasting economic, personal and social costs.
2. There has been a shift away from aggregate time series and cross-sectional studies of the school-to-work transition towards discrete choice modelling. With respect to the latter, researchers have typically moved away from a simple binary classification of the choices facing young people about to leave compulsory schooling to a multinomial characterization. This is far more realistic because it reflects the complexity of the school-to-work transition process facing young people in the UK and the USA.
3. In recent years increased attention has focused on the length of time it takes for young people to move from school to their first job. The move towards a competing risks framework is a potentially more fruitful development than a single risk framework.

4. A wide range of personal, family, school and local labour market factors have been found to be associated with the school-to-work transition and the time to first job. One of the most powerful effects arises from prior ability, or more specifically a young person's exam performance during compulsory schooling.

5. We have modelled the school-to-work transition using a unique data set that combines personal, family, school and local labour market variables suggested by the existing literature. Unlike most of the previous literature we allow the exam performance of the young person and 'school quality' to be endogenous.

6. Compared to our own earlier work using the same data set, we find that predicted exam performance has a less powerful effect on the school-to-work transition, because in this analysis the full range of exam performance is predicted.

7. We also find that a young person's school background, as reflected by our measure of school quality, has a much larger effect, especially for girls, on the school-to-work transition. In particular young people who attend a school of 'high' quality are far more likely to proceed to 'Academic' further education.

8. In keeping with the existing literature, we find that non-white youths are more likely to proceed to further education, although there are differences between ethnic groups and between boys and girls.

9. A higher local unemployment rate encourages young people to proceed to 'Academic' further education and, for those young people who enter the labour market, the Youth Training programme acts as an alternative to unemployment.

Acknowledgments

Bradley thanks the Nuffield Foundation (grant EDU/00328/G) for financial support, and Nguyen thanks the ESRC for financial support.

Notes

1. The school-to-work transition is described in various ways in the literature: 'transition from school', 'first destination from school', 'college choice' and 'staying-on'. Essentially all of these descriptions refer to the choice made by individuals at a critical transitional stage in their lives, that is, at the end of their compulsory schooling in the UK or when to graduate in the USA. We refer to this decision throughout this chapter as the school-to-work transition.

2. For instance, in the USA college graduates with a bachelor's degree earn substantially more than those with only high school education. In 1997, annual earnings for those with a bachelor's degree were US$42 000 and US$26 000 for males and females, respectively, as compared with US$25 000 for male high school graduates and US$13 000 for female high school graduates (Bureau of the Census, 1997).

3. Earlier studies find no effect of the duration of past non-employment on the duration of current non-employment (Heckman and Borjas, 1980) or on the re-employment hazard (Lynch, 1989). Omori (1997) notes that these studies are flawed in so far as they adopt

restrictive parametric assumptions, have limited sample size, fail to deal with censored observations and use inconsistent maximum likelihood estimation.

4. Recent studies report that, after displacement, earnings remain from 10 to 18 per cent below expected levels (Jacobson *et al.*, 1993). Stevens (1997) reports that earnings remain 9 per cent below the expected level six years after initial displacement.

5. Neumark (1998) find a positive effect of early labour market stability on adult wages.

6. Korpi (1997) notes that a negative effect of unemployment on well-being may be the link between previous unemployment and future unemployment if such a link exists.

7. Further education typically occurs between the ages of 16 and 18, when young people choose either academic courses (A and AS levels) as a preparation for university entrance, or vocational courses, which have more immediate value in the labour market.

8. Estimated test scores are used instead of the actual measured test score. The instruments used to predict the test score variable include measures of school background, such as the pupil/teacher ratio, the gender composition of the school and the admissions policy of the school.

9. The General Certificate of Secondary Education (GCSE) is taken in up to 10 subjects at the end of compulsory schooling. The gender gap varies between ethnic groups.

10. Cameron and Heckman (2000) show that short-run liquidity constraints at the college-going ages are much less important than long-run family background factors in promoting college attendance.

11. The re-employment hazard refers to the instantaneous probability of leaving unemployment for employment at time *t*, conditional on having been unemployed to time *t*. Alternatively, a hazard can be thought of as an exit rate at time *t*.

12. Bradley and Taylor (2004) discuss the classification of occupation chosen.

References

Andrews, M. and S. Bradley (1997), 'Modelling the transition from school and the demand for training in the United Kingdom', *Economica*, **64**, 387–413.

Andrews, M., S. Bradley and D. Stott (2002), 'The School-to-Work transition, skill preferences and matching', *Economic Journal*, **112**, C201–C219.

Andrews, M., S. Bradley and R. Upward (2001), 'Estimating the probability of a match using micro-economic data for the youth labour market', *Labour Economics*, **8**, 335–57.

Armstrong, D. (1999), 'School performance and staying on: a microanalysis for Northern Ireland', *The Manchester School*, **67**, 203–30.

Arranz, J. and J. Muro (2001), 'New evidence in state dependence on unemployment histories', Universidad de Alcala, Spain.

Arulampalam, W. (2001), 'Is unemployment really scarring? Effects of unemployment experiences on wages', *Economic Journal*, **111**, 585–606.

Arulampalam, W., A. Booth and M. Taylor (2000), 'Unemployment persistence', *Oxford Economic Papers*, **52**, 24–50.

Averett, S. and M. Burton (1996), 'College attendance and College wage premium: differences by gender', *Economics of Education Review*, **15**, 37–49.

Becker, G. (1964), *Human Capital: A Theoretical and Empirical Analysis, with Special Reference to Education*, New York: Columbia University Press.

Becker, G. (1993), *Human Capital: A Theoretical and Empirical Analysis, with Special Reference to Education*, Chicago: University of Chicago Press.

Becker, G. and N. Tomes (1976), 'Child endowments and the quantity and quality of children', *Journal of Political Economy*, **84**, S143–S162.

Becker, G. and N. Tomes (1979), 'An equilibrium theory of the distribution of income and intergenerational mobility', *Journal of Political Economy*, **87**, 1153–89.

Becker, W. (1990), 'The demand for higher education', in S. Hoenack and E. Collins (eds), *The Economics of American University*, Albany: State University of New York Press.

Behrman, J., L. Kletzer, M. McPherson and M. Schapiro (1992), 'The college investment decision: direct and indirect effects of family background on choice of postsecondary enrollment and quality', Economics Department, University of Pennsylvania.

Betts, J., C. Ferrall and R. Finnie (2000), 'The transition to work for Canadian university graduates: time to first job, 1982–1990', research paper no. 141, Business and Labour Market Analysis, Statistics Canada.

Blanchflower, D. (1999), 'What can be done to reduce the high levels of youth joblessness in the world?', working paper 99-8, Dartmouth College University.

Bonnal, L., S. Mendes and C. Sofer (2000), 'Access to the first job: a comparison between apprenticeship and vocational school in France', University of Orleans.

Borus, M. and S. Carpenter (1984), 'Factors associated with college attendance of high school seniors', *Economics of Education Review*, **3**, 169–76.

Bowlus, A., N. Kiefer and G. Neumann (2001), 'Equilibrium search models and the transition from school to work', *International Economic Review*, **42**, 317–43.

Bradley, S. and J. Taylor (2004), 'Ethnicity, educational attainment and the transition from school', *The Manchester School*, forthcoming.

Bratberg, E. and O. Nilsen (2000), 'Transition from school to work and the early labour market experience', *Oxford Bulletin of Economics and Statistics*, **62**, 909–29.

Bureau of the Census (1997), *Money Income in the United States 1997*, Current Population Reports, US Department of Commerce.

Burgess, S., C. Propper, H. Rees and A. Shearer (1999), 'The class of 81: The effects of early-career unemployment on subsequent unemployment experiences', Economics Department, University of Bristol,

Cameron, S. and J. Heckman (1998), 'Life cycle schooling and dynamic selection bias: models and evidence for five cohorts of American males', *Journal of Political Economy*, **106**, 262–333.

Cameron, S. and J. Heckman (2000), 'The dynamics of educational attainment for black, Hispanic, and white males', Economics Department, Columbia University.

Christensen, S., J. Melder and B. Weisbrod (1975), 'Factors affecting college attendance', *Human Resources*, **10**, 174–88.

Chuang, H. (1999), 'Estimating the determinants of the unemployment duration for college graduates in Taiwan', *Applied Economics Letters*, **6**, 677–81.

Clark, A. and A. Oswald (1994), 'Unhappiness and unemployment', *Economic Journal*, **104**, 648–59.

Clark, A., Y. Georgellis and P. Sanfey (2001), 'Scarring: The psychological impact of past unemployment', *Economica*, **68**, 221–41.

Corman, H. (1982), 'Postsecondary education enrollment responses by recent high school graduates and older adults', *Human Resources*, **17**, 247–67.

DesJardin, S., H. Dundar and D. Hendel (1999), 'Modelling the college application decision process in a Land-Grant university', *Economics of Education Review*, **18**, 117–32.

Doeringer, P.B. and M.J. Piore (1971), *Internal Labour Markets and Manpower Analysis*, Lexington, MA: D.C. Heath.

Dolton, P., G. Makepeace and G. Treble (1994), 'The youth training scheme and the school-to-work transition', *Oxford Economic Papers*, **46**, 629–57.

Dustmann, C., N. Rajah and A. van Soest (1996), 'Part-time work, school success, and school leaving', Department of Economics, University College, London.

Dustmann, C., N. Rajah and A. van Soest (1998), 'School quality, exam performance and career choice', discussion paper no. 120, Center for Economic Research, Tilburg.

Eckstein, Z. and K. Wolpin (1995), 'Duration to first job and the return to schooling: estimates from a search-matching model', *Review of Economics Studies*, **62**, 263–86.

Ellwood, D. and T. Kane (2000), 'Who is getting a college education? Family background and the growing gaps in enrollment', in S. Danziger and J. Waldfogel (eds), *Securing the Future: Investing in Children from Birth to College*, New York: Russell Sage Foundation.

Evans, W. and R. Schwab (1995), 'Finishing high school and starting college: do Catholic schools make a difference?', *Quarterly Journal of Economics*, **110**, 941–74.

Eyland, A. and W. Johnson (1989), 'The transition from full-time study to work', *Australian Journal of Statistics*, **31A**, 213–25.

Franz, W., J. Inkmann, W. Pohlmeier and V. Zimmermann (2000), 'Young and out in Germany: on youths' chances of labor market entrance in Germany', in D. Blanchflower and R. Freeman (eds), *Youth Employment and Joblessness in Advanced Countries*, Chicago: University of Chicago Press.

Ganderton, P. and R. Santos (1995), 'Hispanic college attendance and completion: evidence from the High School and Beyond Surveys', *Economics of Education Review*, **14**, 35–46.

Genda, Y. and M. Kurosawa (2000), 'Transition from school to work in Japan', paper presented at NBER Conference on Unemployment.

Gray, M. (2000), 'The effects of unemployment on the earnings of young Australians', discussion paper no. 419, Centre for Economic Policy Research, Australian National University.

Gregg, P. (2000), 'The impact of youth unemployment on adult unemployment in the NCDS', working paper no. 1018, Economics Department, Bristol University.

Hanushek, E. (1992), 'The trade-off between child quantity and quality', *Journal of Political Economy*, **100**, 84–117.

Haveman, R. and B. Wolfe (1995), 'The determinants of children's attainments: a review of methods and findings', *Journal of Economic Literature*, **33**, 1829–78.

Heckman, J. and G. Borjas (1980), 'Does unemployment cause future unemployment? Definitions, questions and answers from a continuous time model of heterogeneity and state dependence', *Economica*, **47**, 247–83.

Hilmer, M. (1998), 'Post-secondary fees and the decision to attend a university or a community college', *Journal of Public Economics*, **67**, 329–48.

Hilmer, M. (2001), 'A comparison of alternative specifications of the college attendance equation with an extension to two-stage selectivity-correction models', *Economics of Education Review*, **20**, 263–78.

Jackson, G. and B. Weatherby (1975), 'Individual demand for higher education: a review and analysis of recent empirical studies', *Journal of Higher Education*, **46**, 623–52.

Jacobson, L., R. LaLonde and D. Sullivan (1993), 'Earning losses of displaced workers', *American Economic Review*, September, 685–709.

Kane, T. (1994), 'College entry by Blacks since 1970: the role of college costs, family background, and the returns to education', *Journal of Political Economy*, **102**, 878–911.

Kletzer, L. and R. Fairlie (1999), 'The long-term costs of job displacement among young workers', Economics Department, University of California, Santa Cruz.

Korpi, T. (1997), 'Is utility related to employment status? Employment, unemployment, labor market policies and subjective well-being among Swedish youth', *Labour Economics*, **4**, 125–47.

Lassibille, G., L. Gomez, I. Ramos and O. Sanchez (2001), 'Youth transition from school to work in Spain', *Economics of Education Review*, **20**, 139–49.

Lenton, P. (2003), 'The school-to-work transition in England and Wales: evidence from a pooled cross-sectional analysis', working paper, Economics Department, Lancaster University.

Leslie, D. and S. Drinkwater (1999), 'Staying on in full-time education: reasons for higher participation rates among ethnic minority males and females', *Economica*, **66**, 63–77.

Leslie, L. and P. Brinkman (1987), 'Student price response in higher education', *Journal of Higher Education*, **58**, 181–204.

Lynch, L. (1989), 'The youth labor market in the eighties: determinants of re-employment probabilities for young men and women', *Review of Economics and Statistics*, **71**, 37–45.

Main, B. (1985), 'School-leaver unemployment and the youth opportunities programme in Scotland', *Oxford Economic Papers*, **37**, 426–47.

Main, B. and D. Raffe (1983), 'Determinants of employment and unemployment among school leavers: evidence from the 1979 survey of Scottish school leavers', *Scottish Journal of Political Economy*, **30**, 1–17.

Margolis, D., E. Plug, V. Simonnet and L. Vilhuber (1999), 'The role of early career experiences in determining later career success: an international comparison', TEAM-Université de Paris 1 Panthéon-Sorbonne.

McElroy, S. (1996), 'Early childbearing, high school completion, and college enrolment: evidence from 1980 high school sophomores', *Economics of Education Review*, **15**, 303–24.

McIntosh, S. (2001), 'The demand for post-compulsory education in four European countries', *Education Economics*, **9**, 69–90.

McVicar, D. (1999a), 'Selective secondary education and staying-on', working paper no. 41, Northern Ireland Economics Research Centre.

McVicar, D. (1999b), 'School quality and staying-on: resources, peer groups or ethos?', working paper no. 45, Northern Ireland Economics Research Centre.

McVicar, D. and P. Rice (2001), 'Participation in further education in England and Wales: an analysis of post-war trend', *Oxford Economics Papers*, **53**, 47–66.

Merz, M. and A. Schimmelpfenning (1999), 'Career choices of German high school graduates: evidence from the German socio-economic panel', working paper no. 99/11, European University Institute.

Micklewright, J. (1988), 'Choice at sixteen', *Economica*, **56**, 25–39.

Micklewright, J., M. Pearson and S. Smith (1990), 'Unemployment and early school leaving', *Economic Journal*, **100**, 163–9.

Mroz, T. and T. Savage (1999), 'The long-term effects of youth unemployment', unpublished paper, Department of Economics, University of North Carolina.

Narendranathan, W. and P. Elias (1993), 'Influences of past history on the incidence of youth unemployment: empirical findings for the UK', *Oxford Bulletin of Economics and Statistics*, **55**, 161–85.

Neal, D. (1997), 'The effects of Catholic secondary schooling on educational achievement', *Journal of Labor Economics*, **15** , 98–123.

Neumark, D. (1998), 'Youth labor market in the US: shopping around vs. staying put', working paper no. 6581, NBER.

Nguyen, A. and J. Taylor (2003), 'Post- high school choices: new evidence from a multinomial logit model', *Journal of Population Economics*, **16**, 287–306.

Nielsen H., M. Rosholm, N. Smith and L. Husted (2001), 'Intergenerational transmissions and the school-to-work transition of 2nd generation immigrants', discussion paper no. 296, IZA, Germany.

Omori, Y. (1997), 'The stigma effects of nonemployment', *Economic Inquiry*, **35**, 394–416.

Ordovensky, F. (1995), 'Effects of institutional attributes on enrolment choice: implications for postsecondary vocational education', *Economics of Education Review*, **14**, 335–50.

Pissarides, C. (1981), 'Staying on at school in England and Wales', *Economica*, **48**, 345–63.

Pissarides, C. (1982), 'From school to university: the demand for post-compulsory education in Britain', *Economic Journal*, **92**, 654–67.

Prais, S.J. (1995), *Productivity, Education and Training: An International Perspective*, Cambridge: Cambridge University Press.

Rice, P. (1987), 'The demand for post-compulsory education in the UK and the effects of educational maintenance allowances', *Economica*, **54**, 465–75.

Rice, P. (1999), 'The impact of local labour markets on investment in further education; evidence from England and Wales youth cohort studies', *Journal of Population Economics*, **12**, 287–312.

Rice, P. (2000), 'Participation in further education and training: how much do gender and race matter?', Department of Economics, University of Southampton.

Riphahn, T. (1999), 'Residential location and youth unemployment: the economic geography of school-to-work transitions', working paper no. 99, IZA, Germany.

Rouse, C. (1994), 'What to do after high school: the two-year versus four-year college enrollment decision', in R.G. Ehrenberg (ed.), *Choices and Consequences: Contemporary Policy Issues in Education*, Ithaca, NY: ILR Press.

Soro-Bonmati, A. (2000), 'Labour market transitions of youth in Germany and Italy', *International Journal of Manpower*, **21**, 206–26.

Stevens, H. (1997), 'Persistent effects of job displacement: the importance of multiple job losses', *Journal of Labor Economics*, **15**, 165–88.

Upward, R (1999), 'Evaluating outcomes from the Youth Training Schemes using matched firm-trainee data', School of Economics, University of Nottingham.

Whitfield, K. and R. Wilson (1991), 'Staying on in full-time education: the educational participation rate of 16-year-olds', *Economica*, **58**, 391–404.

Willis, R. and S. Rosen (1979), 'Education and self-selection', *Journal of Political Economy*, **87**(5), S7–S36.

Wolpin, K. (1992), 'The determinants of Black–White differences in early employment careers: search, layoffs, quits, and endogenous wage growth', *Journal of Political Economy*, **100**, 535–60.

Appendix A

Table 13A.1   Descriptive statistics

The dependent variable Post-school outcome	Boys	Girls	Total
Unemployed/inactive	1973	2480	4453
Academic further education	15322	18828	34150
Vocational further education	6315	8452	14767
Youth Training	3246	2763	6009
Employed	3785	3252	7037
Total	30641	35775	66416

Summary statistics for the covariates

	Girls		Boys	
	Mean	Standard deviation	Mean	Standard deviation
Predicted exam performance	1.040	1.087	1.030	1.051
Cohort 7	0.257	0.437	0.252	0.434
Cohort 8	0.222	0.416	0.219	0.413
Cohort 9	0.212	0.409	0.218	0.413
Father only	0.017	0.129	0.020	0.140
Mother only	0.076	0.266	0.069	0.254
Father – professional	0.101	0.301	0.109	0.312
Father – manager	0.178	0.383	0.181	0.385
Father – associate professional	0.061	0.240	0.060	0.237
Father – skilled non-manual	0.049	0.216	0.050	0.218
Father – skilled manual	0.226	0.418	0.213	0.410
Mother – professional	0.082	0.274	0.085	0.278
Mother – manager	0.063	0.243	0.061	0.239
Mother – associate professional	0.078	0.268	0.081	0.272
Mother – skilled non-manual	0.198	0.399	0.193	0.395
Mother – skilled manual	0.023	0.149	0.023	0.149
Indian	0.028	0.166	0.030	0.170
Afro-Caribbean	0.013	0.113	0.011	0.102
Bangladeshi/Pakistani	0.026	0.159	0.026	0.160
Chinese/other ethnic	0.017	0.129	0.017	0.128
Social housing	0.137	0.344	0.122	0.328
Other housing	0.042	0.201	0.034	0.180
Both parents work	0.507	0.500	0.506	0.500
Both parents unemployed	0.098	0.297	0.095	0.294
Local unemployment rate	0.097	0.041	0.096	0.040
Log (relative wage)	0.286	0.048	0.190	0.067

Summary statistics for the covariates (*continued*)

	Girls		Boys	
	Mean	Standard deviation	Mean	Standard deviation
School quality	0.455	0.169	0.442	0.156
One sibling	0.482	0.500	0.483	0.500
Two siblings	0.218	0.413	0.220	0.414
Three siblings	0.070	0.255	0.072	0.259
Four siblings	0.045	0.208	0.041	0.199
Number of observations	26898		22662	

14 The labour market for teachers
Paulo Santiago

Introduction and conceptual framework

The fact of, or potential for, shortfalls in the quality of the teaching work-force is a major consideration in any nation's aspirations to attain, or maintain, an educational system of high quality. Teachers constitute the core of the educational system and their importance in student performance has been widely confirmed by many credible research studies.[1] Thus the development of policies which potentially lead to the improvement of the quality of teachers and reduce the disparities in their distribution across schools is a central concern for governments.

In this context, a good understanding of the functioning of the teacher labour market is imperative for teacher policy development. Key aspects include the responsiveness of teachers to incentives, the tradeoffs governments face in defining the number of teachers needed, and the role of the mechanisms which match teachers to schools.

The labour market concept is used by economists to describe and explain the processes which match individuals to specific jobs in society. The analysis focuses on the determinants of labour demand and supply, and the role of the market structure which shapes the mechanisms through which demand and supply interact. The aspiration is to explain the outcomes observed, such as levels of employment and unemployment, compensation levels (for example, wages) or equity issues such as gender wage differentiation.[2]

The functioning of the teacher labour market determines, for a given school system, the number and characteristics of teachers, their distribution across schools, and the prevailing employment conditions, including the wage structure. Teacher labour market analysis typically studies the determinants of the number of teachers needed, the factors which influence individuals' willingness to prepare for a teaching job, enter the teaching profession and remain in or return to teaching throughout their working lives, and the role of labour market institutions such as collective bargaining, recruitment and selection processes and contractual elements in the matching between potential teachers and educational authorities.

The size of the teacher labour market is considerable in all countries. Across OECD countries, on average, considering primary and secondary education only, it corresponded to 2.6 per cent of the total labour force in 1999 (see Table 14.1 for the country-level detail). In addition, the expenditure

Table 14.1   Teachers as a percentage of total labour force and compensation of teachers as a percentage of current expenditure in pre-tertiary education

	Classroom teachers in primary and secondary education as a percentage of total labour force, based on head counts (1999)	Compensation of teachers and all school staff as a percentage of current expenditure on educational institutions from public and private sources, for primary, secondary and non-tertiary education (2000)	
		Compensation of teachers	Compensation of all staff
Australia[1]	2.3	56.1	72.2
Austria	2.6	69.7	78.2
Belgium (Flemish Community)	3.6	68.1	81.8
Canada[a]	1.7	61.3	76.4
Czech Republic	2.1	46.5	62.9
Denmark	2.8	52.3	78.4
Finland[2]	2.4	56.3	68.4
France	2.7	m	78.8
Germany	1.9	m	85.7
Greece[b]	m	m	91.0
Hungary[b]	3.6	m	74.9
Iceland	3.3	m	m
Ireland[b]	2.8	76.3	81.9
Italy[3,b]	2.9	66.9	82.5
Japan	1.5	m	88.1
Korea	1.4	75.0	83.5
Luxembourg	2.9	m	m
Mexico[b]	2.5	80.6	95.0
Netherlands	2.8	m	76.7
New Zealand	2.6	m	m
Norway	3.7	m	81.7
Poland[b]	m	m	77.0
Portugal	m	m	94.3
Slovak Republic	m	58.1	76.1
Spain	2.7	76.4	85.9
Sweden	2.8	46.3	61.6
Switzerland[b]	2.3	71.9	84.7
Turkey[b]	2.0	m	93.4
United Kingdom	2.4	53.1	73.6

Table 14.1   (continued)

	Classroom teachers in primary and secondary education as a percentage of total labour force, based on head counts (1999)	Compensation of teachers and all school staff as a percentage of current expenditure on educational institutions from public and private sources, for primary, secondary and non-tertiary education (2000)	
		Compensation of teachers	Compensation of all staff
United States[a,b]	2.2	55.9	82.1
Country mean	2.6	63.0	80.3

Notes: Notes indicated by numbers refer to data on first column while notes indicated by lower-case letters refer to data on the second and third columns; m = data not available.
1.   The number of teachers is expressed in full-time equivalents.
2.   The data include teachers only in educational institutions in the regular education system and exclude sports institutes, music and folk schools and military vocational institutes.
3.   Slightly underestimated because teachers working in programmes such as regional vocational education are not included.
a.   Post-secondary non-tertiary education not included.
b.   Public institutions only.

Sources: Data on first column: OECD (2001, Table D2.4); data on second and third columns: OECD (2003a, Table B6.3).

on the compensation of teachers is typically very high relative to total current expenditure in non-tertiary educational institutions: 63 per cent for the OECD countries, on average, in 2000 (Table 14.1).

The teacher labour market is also distinct in several ways. It is well known that the teacher labour market is not perfectly competitive. The market *hidden hand* does not ensure that the compensation structure (such as wages), employment levels and skills distribution of the teaching workforce adjust rapidly in order to achieve an equilibrium in which the employers and the teachers are compensated for the value of their marginal utility and productivity. What particular features of the teacher labour market explain this? The following have a marked influence: (i) the dominant position of the government in the education sector as a provider and regulator; (ii) the segmented and stratified nature of the market; (iii) the characteristics of the established labour market institutions, such as collective bargaining, reward mechanisms or public servant status of teachers; (iv) the features of the procedures for recruitment, selection and dismissal; (v) the presence of market imperfections such as imperfect/asymmetric information, uncertainty and risk, and transaction costs; and (vi) the contextual structure of incentives that participants in the teacher labour market face arising from the organization of the school system.

First, the dominant role of the government at different levels considerably reduces market competition. The demand for teachers is dominated by the public sector in most countries as the government is a near-monopolistic supplier of schooling and a near-monopsonistic buyer of teachers' services. The government decides on the size of the public expenditure on education and compels school attendance. It should be noted, however, that both the existence of different levels of government and the presence of school management as an additional decision maker reduce the impact of such a dominant role. In addition, the government plays an important role on the supply side as it is involved in the supply of qualified teachers: it is generally a near monopolistic supplier of teacher education programmes and it establishes the requirements to certify teachers. Moreover the government also regulates the functioning of the teacher labour market by establishing bargaining laws, reward mechanisms or recruitment and selection processes. It also runs the public educational system and therefore defines aspects such as school financing, school choice or areas of responsibility of schools which greatly affect the functioning of the teacher labour market.

Second, the highly segmented nature of the teacher labour market relative to other economic sectors considerably reduces the scope for a completely open market. Segmentation by economic sector occurs when workers within a given sector develop qualitatively different skills, keeping them from moving easily from one sector to the other, a phenomenon entrenched in education. In teaching, in particular, mechanisms have been created to grant access to the profession only to a restricted number of individuals shown to hold the required skills: certification and licensure of teachers. In addition, teachers need to go through a specific extended period of preparation needed to secure the necessary certification. A related facet which strengthens the sector segmentation is that teaching is more a career type of occupation (rather than just a job) as moving up the scale of skill, prestige and compensation is encouraged within the profession itself. Another important attribute is that the labour market for teachers is highly stratified fundamentally according to the level of education, type of programme, subject matter, type of provider (public or private) and geographical location. Hence teaching services are not a homogeneous good which is typical of perfectly competitive markets.

Third, teacher labour market institutions also have a marked role. The level of centralization of bargaining is among the most influential. Salaries (or, more broadly, compensation packages) and/or levels of employment are typically determined through a political process of collective bargaining involving various levels of government and teacher unions, which reduces the flexibility of the labour market: characteristics of individual teachers are not reflected in negotiated compensation packages, or entry from outside the profession is restricted. In addition teachers are often selected and recruited by levels of administration (for example school management or local education authorities) which do not define the reward structure.

Certain characteristics of the available bargaining instruments also influence labour market outcomes. For instance, compensation packages (including wages) are tied to specific positions and not to the market value of the service provided by individual teachers. Rewards are not generally negotiated individually and the level of the compensation often depends on factors other than productivity, such as qualifications or seniority. Also, to a large extent, reward mechanisms ignore the stratified nature of the market; for example, they do not depend on the subject matter.

Contractual elements are a further influential dimension. The type of appointment (such as fixed-term versus indefinite), the institution of a probationary period or the existence of mechanisms for dismissal have a considerable influence over the rate at which the teacher labour market is able to adjust to mismatches between schools and teachers. For instance, the risks associated with making a selection error are decreased if the employer has the ability to make use of probationary periods to dismiss an underperforming teacher. In practice, in many countries, teachers are typically able to obtain, at some stage of their career, a permanent public servant status, making the termination of contracts virtually impossible. This critically limits the ability of educational authorities to make efficiency adjustments in the teaching workforce, but provides teachers with extensive job security.

Fourth, another powerful influence on the efficiency of the teacher labour market is the organization of the recruitment and selection of teachers. The process leading to the hiring of skilled teachers is complex and relatively expensive. Employers and employees are faced with substantial labour market *transaction costs* associated with the acquisition and interpretation of information influencing decisions. In the teacher labour market, given its size and degree of specialization, these costs are substantial. This often leads employers to use inexpensive and easily measured qualification criteria (such as certification status, years of experience, university attended) as opposed to a broader assessment of candidates (for example personal interviews, specific work assignments, demonstration class) raising questions about the efficiency of the selection. In addition the often limited participation of schools in the selection of their teachers considerably limits the *organizational fit* of the teacher.

Fifth, efficiency in the teacher labour market is affected by information gaps. Employers do not have perfect information on candidates for teaching positions and the candidates do not have precise information on the schools to which they apply. In the same way, individuals looking for a teaching position are often not aware of the overall range of opportunities presented to them, such as in areas remote from their area of residence.

Finally, what incentives do employers in the labour market have to make the choice that is most appropriate to achieve the objectives of the school system? This greatly depends on the incentive structure shaped by the organization of the school system. For example, it is clear that principals in schools subject to evaluation and accountability procedures are considerably more pressured to make an appropriate selection of teachers than a group of individuals at the central level of educational administration. Similarly, if schools are financed through the parents (rather than directly by the government) and if free school choice is established, strong incentives exist for schools to select teachers with the quality that attracts students.

To study and understand the factors involved in the functioning of the teacher labour market, it is first necessary to have a conceptual framework for distinguishing among, defining and relating, the various aspects involved. This chapter develops such a conceptual framework. A second purpose, following the identification of the main policy issues, is to provide an account of current empirical evidence on issues relevant to the functioning of the teacher labour market. The emphasis is on the impact of policy tools available to policy makers on the outcomes of the teacher labour market.

The proposed conceptual framework is shown in Figure 14.1. This framework identifies four interrelated main areas, each of which is treated separately in the next sections of the chapter. First, the demand for teachers deals with the aspects that determine the number and skills of teachers needed for educational systems to respond to the education needs of the school-age population. The first section provides an account of these aspects and explains the tradeoffs educational authorities face when defining the number of teachers needed.

Second, the supply of teachers deals with the factors that define the number of potential individuals willing to teach in the current school system as well as the distribution of their skills. The second section brings together the two main dimensions of the supply of teachers. It starts by identifying the main factors that shape the attractiveness of the profession and provides a detailed description of the empirical evidence on the impact of a number of factors on the supply decisions of potential teachers. It then turns to the analysis of the role of teacher education programmes and certification policies in defining the distribution of skills of teaching workforces.

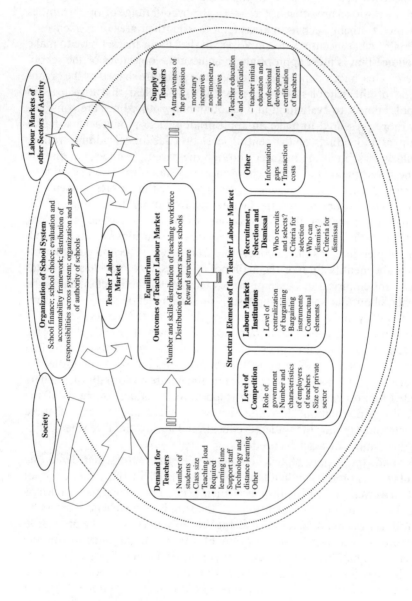

Figure 14.1 Framework of the teacher labour market

A third central area is made up of the structural elements which shape the mechanisms through which demand and supply interact. Their role on teacher labour market outcomes is explored in the third section with particular focus on the organization of the school system, labour market institutions, recruitment and selection procedures, market segmentation and information gaps.

The outcomes of the teacher labour market are treated in the fourth section. A basic model of demand and supply is proposed to explain how supply, demand and structural elements come together into a given market equilibrium. The section then turns to the traditional approaches used to characterize equilibrium, with a particular emphasis on the concept of shortage of teachers. Finally, the conclusions provided in the fifth section offer some policy directions and identify research gaps.

Demand for teachers
This section focuses on the demand for teachers defined as the number of individuals with given qualifications the school system needs to hire in order to respond to the education needs of the school-age population. It has two main objectives. First, it provides an account of the range of factors which determines the demand for teachers with pre-specified skills. This examination permits the identification of the main policy tools available to educational authorities in the management of teacher demand. Second, it explains the typical tradeoffs governments face as a result of budgetary restrictions.

Determinants of demand for teachers
The demand for teachers with pre-specified skills depends on a limited number of factors, some of which are politically manipulable. The main factors are the size of the school-age population, average class size, teaching load of teachers, required learning time for students, use of teaching assistants and other support staff, use of technology and distance learning, enrolment and in-grade retention rates, starting and ending age of compulsory education, policies pertaining to curriculum, students' preferences over elective courses and over educational programmes and, in the specific case of teachers in public schools, parents' preferences between private and public schools.

In a simplified way, ignoring the fact that differences are observed at subject, educational programme, grade and geographical levels, the demand for teachers can be expressed in the following way:

$$D^T = \frac{S}{C} \cdot \frac{L^S}{L^T},$$ (14.1)

where D^T, S, C, L^S, L^T denote demand for teachers, aggregate student population, average class size, average number of required learning hours for students and average teaching load of teachers, respectively.

Aggregate student population is determined by the age structure of the school-age population, enrolment and in-grade retention rates, and starting and ending age of compulsory education. The size of the school-age population is a dominant factor largely outside the control of the government. Successions of baby booms and baby busts hit school systems, entailing substantial fluctuations in the number of students.[3] Enrolment rates, in particular for non-compulsory schooling, are another important factor and depend greatly on local educational returns to schooling as dictated by local labour market conditions. In turn, in-grade retention rates depend on established academic standards that define requirements for graduation and passing from one grade level to the next. The remaining key element defining the number of enrolled students, starting and ending ages of compulsory education, is still subject to changes in many countries, namely for pre-primary education.

The other major determinants of demand for teachers are the average class size, the average teaching load of teachers and the average number of required learning hours for students. The relationship between these factors defines the student–teacher ratio (r_T^S),[4]

$$r_T^S = \frac{S}{T} = C \cdot \frac{L^T}{L^S},$$ (14.2)

where T denotes the total number of teachers in equilibrium and the remaining elements of the equation are defined as before.

Typically adjustments are made to these factors to smooth the effects of rapid enrolment changes, to accommodate established staffing patterns and budgets, and to take into account existing contractual agreements with teachers, in the case of enrolment declines.

A small adjustment either in average class sizes or the average number of classes assigned to teachers (ratio between teachers' teaching load and number of required learning hours) can cause a significant change in the demand for teachers. It should also be noted that teaching load refers to in-class contact time with students, a given fraction of the total workload of teachers. The former is affected by other elements such as the use of teaching assistants and other support staff in schools and the use of technology or distance learning.

The description so far has considered the number of teachers in the aggregate. However, as the market is stratified and decisions are often made at the local level, it is important to specify demand in greater detail, that is by subject matter, grade level, educational programme, region of the country or preparation for serving the special needs of students (for example, students with limited proficiency in the country's language).

Policies pertaining to curriculum are the dominant influence in defining the skills of teachers needed. The definition of the curriculum has a direct impact on the relative demand for teachers in specific subject fields. For example, a changing balance of the secondary school curriculum towards technology and computing leads to an increased need for teachers of these subjects. Similarly an introduction of foreign languages in primary schools leads the system to seek primary teachers with good foreign language skills. In addition, graduation requirements or even entrance requirements of colleges and universities define whether more course work is to be developed in given areas such as science or mathematics.

Another influence on the type of teachers needed arises from the flexible part of students' curriculum. Students' preferences over elective courses and the choice of students over educational programmes (for example general versus vocational programmes) define such influence. Finally, in determining the demand for public school teachers, the key factors are parents' preferences between public and private education, greatly influenced by their relative price and quality, the availability of free school choice, and the existence of subsidies for private school attendance.

Policy tools, budgetary restrictions and tradeoffs
As illustrated in the previous subsection, educational authorities draw on several policy tools to influence the number of teachers needed. Typically class size, teaching loads, required quantity of instruction for students, or the number and role of teaching assistants and other support staff, are the main tools used. However the overall budget planned for teacher salaries together with existing salary scales imposes restrictions on the number of teachers that can be hired by the school system. The budgetary restriction that educational authorities face when hiring teachers can be expressed as

$$\overline{E} = T \cdot w, \tag{14.3}$$

where $\overline{E}$, T and w denote total budget for teacher salaries, total number of teachers and average salary of teachers, respectively.

Therefore the number of teachers that can be hired is entirely defined by the average salary of teachers and a given overall budget for teacher salaries. It turns out that this number might be incompatible with that implied by set desirable targets for the student–teacher ratio as expressed in (14.2).[5] An additional factor is that the different instruments (budget for teacher salaries, average salary, class sizes and teaching loads) are often determined separately by different levels of the educational administration.

Defining the number of teachers in the school system entails some stark tradeoffs in teacher policy. Among the most important and avidly debated is the tradeoff between the average size of classes and the average salary of teachers, assuming a given expenditure in salaries. On the one hand, reduced class sizes potentially improve in-class interaction[6] and teachers' working conditions,[7] but require a larger number of teachers to whom lower individual salaries have to be offered. On the other hand, larger class sizes give room for funding higher teacher salaries, potentially attracting better individuals to schools,[8] but at the cost of weakening the quality of classroom interaction. The tradeoff is often expressed in short as 'more teachers or better teachers?'

Policy makers are often confronted with the need to assess the optimal levels for class size and teacher salaries which maximize the learning of the students. This problem, which results from the tradeoff between class size and teacher salaries, can be illustrated using the model proposed by Stoddard (2003).[9] In this model, the educational authority is assumed to maximize the average learning of students, a basic version of the education production function (f):

$$L = f(q, r_S^T, x). \tag{14.4}$$

The average learning of students, L, depends on the average quality of teachers, q, the teacher–student ratio, r_S^T and other factors, x, such as average student characteristics including socioeconomic background, peer effects, organization of schools or quality of school facilities. Note that $r_S^T = 1/r_T^S$, r_T^S being defined in (14.2). In addition teaching load and the required learning time for students are fixed, making the choice of class size and student–teacher ratio equivalent.

The educational authority also faces a budget constraint. For simplification, it is assumed that expenditures per student, e, correspond to teacher salaries per student:

$$e = r_S^T \cdot w \tag{14.5}$$

The salary determination equation completes the model. It is assumed that higher-quality teachers have better non-teaching job opportunities than lower-quality teachers, and therefore educational areas that offer higher salaries have applicants of higher average quality. This is expressed as follows:

$$w = w_a + p \cdot q. \tag{14.6}$$

This equation can be thought of as a hedonic relationship relating the quality of teachers to their salaries.[10] The constant term in this equation, w_a, can be interpreted as the median alternative salary in the educational area for median quality workers (when teacher quality is indexed at zero for median quality workers). The slope term, p, reflects the return to skill, or skill price, in the area. Given differences in costs and circumstances across areas, these parameters will vary across labour market areas.

Equation (14.5) can then be rewritten as

$$e = r_S^T \cdot (w_a + p \cdot q). \qquad (14.7)$$

The educational authority's problem is then to maximize the average learning of students, given the level of expenditures per student. Demands from the student learning maximization problem for the teacher–student ratio and teacher quality are then functions of prices and expenditures:

$$q = Q(p, w_a, e, x), \quad r_S^T = R(p, w_a, e, x). \qquad (14.8)$$

Figure 14.2 presents this problem in graphic form: $f(q, r_S^T, x) = \overline{L}$ represents combinations of r_S^T and q leading to the same average learning of students, $\overline{L}$, while the two other curves depict the budget constraint for two different values of the skill price, $p^0 > p^1$. The problem faced by the educational authority is analogous to a traditional utility maximization problem with a nonlinear constraint. The slope of the budget constraint is $-e \cdot p/(w_a + p \cdot q)^2$, less steep as q increases and dependent on p.

Provided that the level curves of the average student learning function are more convex than the budget constraint, a solution to the maximization problem exists. The solution is where the ratio of the marginal product of teacher quality to the marginal product of smaller classes is equal to the

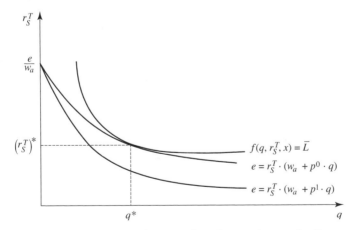

Figure 14.2   The teacher–student ratio/teacher quality tradeoff

ratio of their marginal prices as expressed by the first-order conditions of the problem:

$$\frac{f_q}{f_r} = \frac{p \cdot r_S^T}{w_a + p \cdot q}, \tag{14.9}$$

where $p \cdot r_S^T$ is the marginal price of teacher quality and $w_a + p \cdot q$ is the marginal price of the teacher–student ratio. Graphically the solution of the maximization problem is the pair $(q^*, (r_S^T)^*)$.

Stoddard uses this model to estimate the demands empirically in (14.8). The initial motivation of the paper is to explain why, in the United States since 1970, the number of teachers per student rose while teacher quality apparently declined. The paper examines the role of the price of skill for women in explaining the divergent trends in the number and quality of teachers in a context of major expansion in education expenditures. The model described above shows that a rise in the skill price may induce schools to substitute away from teacher quality towards smaller classes. If the substitution effect is large enough, schools hire more low-quality teachers instead of a few high-quality teachers.

Estimation of the effect of the rise in education expenditures indicates that, had all else remained the same, they would have led to both larger teacher–student ratio and better teacher quality. However, trends in the labour market for women mitigated the impact of these increased expenditures; both alternative wages and the price of skill rose. The results show that the effect of expenditures was significantly positive and large, resulting in larger teacher–student ratios. In contrast, both the skill price and the alternative wage acted to reduce teacher quality, counterbalancing the effect of increased demand for expenditures and leading to a decline in teacher quality.

Another paper, by Jepsen and Rivkin (2002), investigates the tradeoff between smaller classes and teacher quality by looking at the effects of the recent California class size reduction programme. The results show that, all else equal, smaller classes raise third-grade mathematics and reading achievement, particularly for lower-income students. However the expansion of the teaching force required to staff the additional classrooms appears to have led to deterioration in average teacher quality in schools serving a predominantly black student body. This deterioration partially or, in some cases, fully offset the benefits of smaller classes, demonstrating the importance of considering all implications of any policy change.

Supply of teachers

This section concentrates on the supply of teachers defined as the number of individuals (i) who acquired skills necessary to qualify as a teacher, and

(ii) who are willing to provide teaching services given a specific set of incentives. In view of that, this section has two main purposes. First, it identifies the main factors that shape the attractiveness of the profession as depicted in the academic and policy literatures. It is known that the number of teachers in a given field willing to work in a given location depends on a number of incentives, including the availability of teaching positions, salaries, opportunity cost salaries, working conditions or the status of the profession. Second, it analyses the role of teacher education programmes and certification policies in defining the skills distribution of the teaching workforce. Before pursuing such investigation, the main sources of the supply of teachers are outlined and the set of decisions bringing individuals into the classrooms is described.

Sources of supply and set of relevant decisions
The supply of public school teachers in a given year is defined, in the aggregate, as the number of eligible individuals available from all sources willing to supply their services under prevailing conditions. The most important element of teacher supply for a given year is the retention of people returning from the previous year. The other main element corresponds to new entrants. Continuing teachers typically have the option of remaining in the same position from one year to the next. Nonetheless many choose to apply for teaching positions in other schools within the same region, in other subject matter fields, or in a different region. Thus the flows of practising teachers within the public education system constitute a major source of teachers hired into, or reassigned to, open teaching positions.

A large number of new individuals are also hired by the public system each year. Such entering teachers are drawn from four sources. The largest corresponds to the so-called 'reserve pool'. This group is composed of experienced former teachers and past graduates of teacher preparation programmes who did not enter teaching when they graduated but could be attracted to teaching careers with the right incentives. The second source consists of recent graduates of teacher preparation programmes. A third group consists of individuals who obtain alternative or emergency certification. These are university graduates who have not completed a teacher preparation programme and who have not previously taught. They are sometimes referred to as entrants via alternative routes. In most regions virtually any university graduate, with or without certification or experience, can be counted in the potential supply of new entrants. Certification is obtained on the basis of intensive training or apprentice teaching programmes, and hiring is carried out on an emergency certification basis. Finally, the last source of new entrants in public school systems are teachers employed in private schools who might wish to migrate to the public system.

The supply behaviour of teachers involves a series of decisions: whether to train to become a teacher, whether to become a teacher, whether to switch teaching location, how long to stay in teaching and whether to return to teaching after a career interruption. These decisions are affected by a common set of factors but to different extents. For instance, the decision of whether or not to enrol in teacher training is likely to be particularly sensitive to the existing supply of teacher education programmes or the provision of specific incentives such as scholarships. In turn, the decision on whether or not to become a teacher is likely to be particularly responsive to relative salaries of teachers and opportunities outside teaching. Similarly factors such as relative working conditions (for example safety and composition of student body) are likely to be predominant in the decision on where to teach. These influences are analyzed in the next sub-section.

What shapes the attractiveness of the profession?
This subsection summarizes what is known in the empirical literature about the role that particular incentives play in the decisions that lead an individual to embrace a teaching career. The empirical literature identifies the following set of factors as being the most relevant:

- relative salaries and alternative opportunities,
- career structure,
- merit-based incentives,
- working conditions,
- teacher professionalism and the status of the profession,
- school leadership,
- personal circumstances,
- teacher education and certification.

In what follows, the role of these factors in the supply decisions of teachers is described. Results are presented with the following facts in mind: first, responsiveness to incentives depends on personal characteristics of individuals (for example, gender, academic ability, subject area); second, responsiveness to a specific type of incentive varies depending on which decision is being made.

Relative salaries and alternative opportunities[11]   Many policy makers advocate substantial salary increases as a means of attracting and retaining talented teachers and of encouraging harder work by current teachers. Salary policies are also often cited as important for offsetting changes in demands in competing occupations and for dealing with unattractive working conditions in particular sets of schools. Such proposals are premised on the belief that raising salaries will make teaching more attractive relative to other occupations and help alleviate current or potential shortages. As could be expected, the empirical evidence strongly suggests that relative salaries have a strong impact on the decisions leading an individual to teach.

A series of influential studies employing data from Michigan and North Carolina (Murnane and Olsen, 1989, 1990) have demonstrated that teacher salaries are an important determinant of the time that teachers stay in teaching. In these studies, the authors analyse the impact of salaries and opportunity costs on how long teachers stay in teaching. The results indicate that teachers who are paid more stay longer in teaching, and that teachers with higher opportunity costs, as measured by test scores or degree subject, stay in teaching for less time than other teachers.

Using more refined estimation techniques and more detailed measures for opportunity costs, Dolton and van der Klaauw (1999) reach similar conclusions. The authors examine what influences a teacher's propensity to leave teaching for a different career or for a non-labour market alternative. Their study distinguishes between the different destinations (non-teaching job versus non-employment) and reasons for leaving the job or occupation (voluntary exits for career reason, exits caused by a contract ending, or because of family reasons). However their analysis suffers from a major limitation: non-pecuniary characteristics of activities were not considered. The data set corresponds to a large sample of individuals who graduated from universities in the United Kingdom in 1980. An unusual feature of these data is that observations on earnings are available for the individuals in the sample at several points in their career. The results of the research point to the importance of salaries and relative forgone earnings in turnover decisions. Higher opportunity salaries increase the tendency among teachers to switch careers and leave the profession voluntarily. Conversely the intensity of leaving teaching for the non-employment state and the propensity to quit teaching either involuntarily or for family reasons are solely influenced by teacher salaries, not by salaries in the outside option.

In the same context of teaching duration, Stinebrickner (1999a) confirms the importance of relative salaries. He proposes a structural dynamic model, which includes information on some non-pecuniary aspects of teaching. In this way, he is able to analyse the effects of policies that change the career wage structure of a person and he can examine the potential effectiveness of improving the non-pecuniary aspects of teaching (for example, by decreasing the pupil–teacher ratio in schools) relative to the commonly proposed wage increases. Quite appropriately, he points out the fact that ignoring school characteristics may lead to incorrect conclusions about the effects of wages if wages are correlated with omitted non-pecuniary school characteristics. The model is estimated using the National Longitudinal Study of the

Class of 1972 (NLS-72) carried out in the United States. The results suggest that educational policies which address teaching wages may be more effective than educational policies which concentrate on the non-pecuniary aspects of the teaching profession (at least in terms of the pupil–teacher ratio). These results are consistent with the non-structural findings of Stinebrickner (1998, 1999b) which used these data and found wages to be a more significant predictor of teaching spell duration than the student–teacher ratio. Similar analyses by the same author (Stinebrickner, 2001a, 2001b) provide similar results. This set of studies suffers from two main limitations: the results relate to an old 1972 cohort, and non-pecuniary characteristics of teaching are limited to pupil–teacher ratios and ability level of students.

Focusing on the decision to become a teacher, Dolton (1990) investigates the relevance of relative earnings and personal non-pecuniary factors. He models the decision to enter the teaching profession using a large cross-section data set on UK graduates. The results suggest that relative earnings in teaching and non-teaching occupations and the corresponding growth in earnings in the two choices have a marked effect on graduates' choices. In particular, the lower are relative wages or wage growth in teaching, the less likely is a graduate to choose that career. A similar analysis was conducted by Wolter and Denzler (2003) to assess the wage elasticity of teacher supply in Switzerland, using data on university graduates for the period 1981–99. They find that teacher supply is responsive to salary levels but to a lesser extent than in other countries, a result explained by the relatively high salaries of teachers in Switzerland.

According to studies conducted by Hanushek and Pace (1994, 1995), relative earnings seem to be less relevant when the decision is whether to enter teacher training or not. They analyse the choice of preparing for a teaching career in university. They use the High School and Beyond longitudinal data set following American high school seniors from 1980 to 1986. The results for the effects of teacher salaries do not indicate that they have a particularly powerful influence on student choices. Even though relative earnings of teachers compared to all college graduates vary considerably across the United States, they do not have a large or statistically significant impact on student preparation for teaching.

The influence of salaries on the decision of whether or not to switch teaching locations has been studied by Hanushek et al. (1999). This paper relies upon a panel data of the UTD Texas School Project to investigate how shifts in salary schedules affect the composition of teachers within a district. Among other things, they study the relationship among mobility, school district pay and other characteristics by investigating the determinants of transitions both between and out of Texas public schools. The pattern of teacher transitions provides strong evidence that teachers prefer particular student characteristics and somewhat weaker evidence that salaries affect transitions. In fact the evidence strongly suggests that teachers prefer certain types of students over others. Except for Black teachers, the typical Texas teacher appears to favour higher achieving, non-minority students. Net salaries adjusted for compensating differentials also appear to influence mobility and exiting, but to a lesser extent than characteristics of students. Similar results are provided by a more recent paper, (Hanushek *et al.*, 2001).

There is also evidence on the decision of whether to return to teaching after a career interruption. According to Murnane (1996), in the United States, approximately one in four teachers who leave the classroom returns within five years. Beaudin (1993) finds that the teachers most likely to return are those with subject area specialities that provide limited opportunities for better paying employment outside of public schools, those who have more than two years of experience coupled with a master's degree and those who interrupted their careers at an older rather than a younger age. This pattern supports the hypothesis that decisions to return to teaching are sensitive to opportunity costs.

Another interesting aspect is that higher salaries might raise student achievement by raising the effort of current teachers. As Hanushek *et al.* (1999) state, this would be particularly the case if salary negotiations explicitly linked higher salaries with an expansion of responsibilities. Teachers may simply work harder in order to raise the likelihood of retaining their now more desirable job. In particular one would expect untenured teachers to have the strongest response in terms of effort.

Responsiveness to relative earnings greatly depends on personal characteristics. For instance, incentives have different effects for teachers with different teaching experiences. In fact, attrition rates seem to follow a U-shaped distribution (see Grissmer and Kirby, 1987). Young, inexperienced teachers tend to have high attrition rates. Then the probability that a teacher will leave the profession declines with experience, before it begins to climb again as teachers approach retirement age. This pattern has been recently confirmed by Stinebrickner (1999b). According to his results, the early years are very important in determining whether a teacher has a long career in the field. The teacher's probability of leaving teaching increases in the initial four years of the teaching career, but then begins to decrease dramatically. These results suggest that policies aimed at reducing teacher attrition should focus on the early years of teachers' careers.

It has also been suggested that the responsiveness depends on the academic ability of individuals. Stinebrickner (2001a) shows that individuals with higher academic ability, as measured by scores on the SAT (Scholastic Aptitude Test) exam, teach for a smaller proportion of years than other teachers. His results support the notion that lower teaching participation rates for academically gifted teachers stem in part from the ability of these teachers to obtain wage premiums in the non-teaching sector but not in the teaching sector. According to the analysis carried out in this research project, from the standpoint of improving the ability composition of the teaching workforce, policies which reduce the rigidity of the teaching wage structure by allowing wage increases to be correlated with the opportunity costs of teachers are likely to be more promising than traditional, uniform wage increases. The same type of conclusions were reached by Murnane and Olsen (1990).

Some studies also show that high school teachers tend to stay in teaching for a shorter duration than primary school teachers do (Murnane and Olsen, 1989, 1990; Murnane *et al.*, 1989). Furthermore career paths of secondary school teachers also differ, depending on subject specialities. Murnane *et al.* (1988), using a sample of North Carolina teachers who began their careers in the late 1970s, show that chemistry and physics teachers tended to leave teaching sooner than did secondary school teachers with other subject specialities. In addition, they were also more unlikely to come back to teaching once they had left the system.

· Another important aspect is that women and men respond differently to incentives. Many studies have pointed to the fact that women leave the profession for different reasons. In particular, Murnane *et al.* (1988) suggest that young women are typically the teachers with the shortest spells. Finally Dolton and van der Klaauw (1999) have identified the following effects: women from higher social classes and privileged schools are more likely to leave the workforce; those with an education degree are less likely to quit teaching and to leave for a non-teaching job; those with professional postgraduate degrees are more likely to leave teaching, irrespective of destination or reason; those who initially entered the profession reluctantly are more likely to exit involuntarily or for family reasons and to exit to the non-employment state.

The impact of the availability of alternative opportunities to teaching is well documented as a result of the expansion in employment opportunities for women during the second half of the twentieth century. Analysing the case of the United States for the period 1957–92, Corcoran *et al.* (2002) examine how the propensity for talented women to enter teaching has changed over time. They find that, while the quality of the average new female teacher has fallen only slightly over this period, the likelihood that a female from the top of her high school class will eventually enter teaching has fallen dramatically from 1964 to 1992: from almost 20 per cent to under 4 per cent. According to the authors, the explanation lies in the fact that employment opportunities for talented women outside teaching have soared. These results are confirmed by Bacolod (2002), Stoddard (2003) and Temin (2002).

Given that teacher supply is sensitive to opportunities outside teaching, it is predictable that it will suffer the influence of the economic cycle.

Recently Dolton *et al.* (2003) examined how the economic cycle affects the market for teachers. The evidence suggests that wages in teaching relative to those in alternative professions have a significant impact on the likelihood of graduates choosing to teach and that the impact depends upon the market situation at the time.

Career structure Most teachers in most countries work in schools that employ uniform salary scales. Under such salary structures, all teachers with the same credentials and experience receive the same salary, irrespective of subject speciality or perceived performance.

In this context it has been difficult to conduct research on the way teachers respond to career opportunities provided by specific career structures. A single study, Brewer (1996), provides some evidence on this issue. Brewer tests the hypothesis that later career opportunities affect decisions about leaving by examining the relationship between teaching and school administration. Emphasizing the fact that, in most cases, it is not clear what are the later opportunities for individual teachers, the author intends to provide some evidence on the effect of promotion prospects and rewards on the decisions of teachers to leave. In particular, Brewer is interested in the responsiveness of teachers to later career opportunities in school administration. He tests the proposition that school administration affects teacher behaviour, using a sample of newly hired New York teachers from 1978 to 1988.

The results suggest that male teachers are somewhat sensitive to expected administrative rewards. Higher district salaries for new administrators in positions that teachers usually fill decrease the likelihood that a teacher will leave their district. Conversely, if salaries for new administrators rise in the surrounding districts in the county, teachers are more likely to leave their districts. There is less robust evidence that more new openings in administration in a district decrease teachers' propensity to leave. Finally there is no evidence that female teachers respond to administrative variables, consistent with fewer opportunities and lower monetary rewards for women in school administration.

Merit-based incentives Many policy makers argue that improving the quality of education offered by public schools requires a change from uniform salary schedules to a compensation scheme that bases a teacher's salary on performance as measured either by gains in student test scores or by supervisors' evaluations of the teacher's actions in the classroom. Such performance-based compensation plans are typically called 'merit pay'.

In the United States, most attempts to implement merit pay for public school teachers over the last 75 years have failed. In the face of opposition from teachers and teacher unions, school systems that have introduced merit pay have generally backed away after a few years. According to Ballou (2001), 'We've tried it and it doesn't work' summarizes the prevailing view of merit pay among educators. Murnane (1996) reinforces this view by noting that the results of extensive research lead to the conclusion that merit pay based on supervisors' performance evaluations simply does not work. He notes that, in the vast majority of cases where school districts have adopted merit pay plans for teachers, they have dropped them within five years. He points out that there is no example of a troubled district that has successfully used merit pay to improve its performance.

In a highly influential paper, Murnane and Cohen (1986) argue that teaching is not an activity that satisfies the conditions under which performance-based pay is an efficient method of compensating workers. As a consequence the authors claim that merit pay does not provide a solution to the problem of motivating teachers. Murnane and Cohen base their conclusion on the following ideas. First, teachers' output is hard to observe. It is a joint product in which the several contributions can be difficult to isolate. In addition, some results of the educational process are difficult to measure. Compensation algorithms that reward only those dimensions of performance for which each teacher's contribution can be measured could create perverse incentives (for example, teaching to the test), inducing teachers not to engage in teamwork. Secondly, administrators are often unable to explain why one teacher is more effective than another. As a result, they cannot detail the basis for merit awards to those denied them or indicate what steps the latter can take to succeed next time. Finally, competition for merit awards can result in opportunistic and non-cooperative behaviour among teachers.

In a more recent paper, Ballou (2001) reopens the issue by comparing the use of merit pay in public and private schools. Ballou argues that, given the general absence of strong competitive pressures in public education, school administrators may lack the incentives to undertake unpopular reforms. According to the author, public school administrators, particularly in unionized systems, lack many of the powers and prerogatives enjoyed by managers in business, a circumstance that can make it difficult to implement personnel policies that create resentments among staff.

He then suggests comparing public elementary and secondary schools to their counterparts in the private sector. As private schools operate in a competitive business environment, the notion that merit pay has failed because it is inherently ill-suited to teaching, and not because of weak management, can therefore be tested by comparing the use of performance-based pay in public and private schools.

The author concludes that teacher unions have played a key role in obstructing the spread of incentive pay plans in the public sector. In those districts where teachers do not have union representation in collective bargaining, the incidence of merit pay is nearly as great as it is among the non-sectarian private schools. In the same way, the size of merit awards also exhibits an inverse relationship to the degree of union influence: indeed there is no detectable impact on recipients' salaries in districts where teacher unions engage in collective bargaining.

Working conditions Satisfaction in the workplace is naturally associated with working conditions. In the particular case of teachers, working conditions are more often associated with factors such as the following:

- class size, number of classes taught, teaching load;
- percentage of class time spent in areas outside of a teacher's certification area;
- flexibility to take temporary leave;
- composition of the student body, composition of the faculty;
- percentage of time spent in out-of-classroom activities;
- safety;
- quality of facilities;
- quality of instructional materials;
- opportunities for participation in professional development activities.

Little research has been devoted to the role of working conditions in the supply decisions of teachers. One of the few studies devoted to it is Mont and Rees (1996). The authors examine the effect of class load characteristics and other factors on teacher turnover. Unlike previous studies, factors such as class size, number of classes taught and percentage of class time spent in areas outside of a teacher's certification area are included, along with salary, personal characteristics and district characteristics in a model to simulate the effects of changing classroom characteristics on high school teacher turnover. The paper uses data from the New York State Education Department's Personnel Master File for the years 1979 to 1989.

The issue is relevant, as a solution for reducing the effects of teacher shortages is to raise teaching loads. In this context, it is important to investigate whether teachers respond to larger or more frequent classes by quitting, in which case such policy could simply be increasing demand for new teachers.

The results indicate that class load characteristics are important correlates of job turnover. Average class size was found to be positively associated with the job abandonment of high school teachers, although this effect begins to occur at roughly the mean average class size in the sample. Similarly teaching outside one's area of certification was also associated with higher job abandonment rates. It is reasonable to conclude, therefore, that efforts to reduce education costs by increasing class size and asking teachers to teach outside their areas of certification may be undermined by increased teacher turnover. However the Mont and Rees study concluded that, controlling for average class size, the number of classes taught seems to have no effect on teachers' rates of leaving the profession.

More recently, in the context of American schools, Stinebrickner (1999a) concludes that the pupil–teacher ratio plays a significant role in whether the individual considers a school to be desirable even if to a lesser extent than wages. He also concludes that the ability level of students does not have much of an effect on the way the teacher views the school. As pointed out earlier, Hanushek *et al.* (1999, 2001), when focusing on the reasons why teachers switch teaching locations, identify the characteristics of the student body (income, race and achievement) as extremely relevant.

Work by Vandenberghe (2000) provides evidence concerning the behaviour of beginner teachers in the French-speaking Community of Belgium. The study focuses on the factors influencing the decision of beginning teachers on whether or not to stay in the profession. He concludes that non-monetary working conditions, namely the access to a full-time permanent teaching job, are more influential than salary levels.

Another aspect deemed relevant in the teaching profession is its 'flexibility' dimension. This aspect is particularly important for women who are predominant in the profession. Flyer and Rosen (1997) investigate whether teaching provides more flexible movements between the market and home sector relative to other occupations and if this 'flexibility' option is valued. This issue becomes more important as greater market opportunities for women raise the supply price of teaching. Their model is applied to National Longitudinal Survey of Youth (NLSY, 1979–91) female college graduates to determine whether transitions between the home and the market sector are less costly for female teachers than for other female graduates. The empirical findings are affirmative. Teachers do not suffer wage penalties for time spent out of the labour market, while other college graduates take wage reductions of roughly 9 per cent for each year spent out of the market sector. Most importantly, such 'flexibility' of the teaching profession is shown to be an important attraction to women.

The influence of other factors such as safety, quality of facilities and instructional materials, or possibility of participating in professional development activities, has received little attention in empirical research.

Teacher professionalism and the status of the profession   Many policy makers advocate that teachers should have professional autonomy and responsibility similar to that typically accorded to members of other professions. They argue that conferring professional autonomy on teachers will enhance the attractiveness of the profession as a career choice and will improve the quality of the classroom teaching practice. Typically, the 'professionalization' of teaching would involve policies such as the following:

- decentralization of authority over major aspects of school operations placing teachers in key decision-making roles as council members;
- well-defined certification standards giving control to a professional teaching body over the number and origin of undergraduate degrees granted in education each year;
- in-service training;
- peer instruction and evaluation;
- rewards for teachers who earn additional credentials or who are more productive;
- career ladders.

Almost no research has been done on what would be the impact of implementing policies leading to a higher degree of professionalism on teacher supply. On the one hand, some teachers might find these policies difficult and time-consuming. They require special training for decision making and management and, in addition, require released time from instruction. On the other hand, many teachers might want teaching to become more professional, in the sense of becoming filled with high productivity individuals who receive rewards closely linked to their performance.

In two of the few studies addressing this aspect, Ingersoll (2001a, 2001b) investigates the effects of organizational conditions of the schools on teacher turnover. He uses data from the Schools and Staffing Survey from the US Department of Education. He finds that, in particular, low salaries, inadequate support from the school administration, student discipline problems and limited faculty input into school decision making all contribute to higher rates of turnover, after controlling for the characteristics of both teachers and schools. In more recent work, Ingersoll (2003) draws on the same surveys as well as wide-ranging interviews with high school teachers and administrators to analyse further the organization of teachers' work in schools and how it affects their effectiveness and degree of satisfaction.

Two other aspects of initiatives seeking to promote the professionalism of teachers stand out. First, the notion of accountability acquires new importance: teachers would be given more responsibility for their own practices. In addition, this trend would require teachers to engage in research activities seeking to examine their own practices, test new ideas and improve their practices on the basis of these examinations.

School leadership   A particularly important influence in empowering and motivating teachers is that of school management and leadership. In a recent paper Mulford (2003) reviews the literature addressing the impact of school leaders on the work and motivation of teachers. He concludes that the main channels through which school leaders can strengthen the recruitment, development and retention of teachers are to value and support teachers; provide professional autonomy to teachers and a sense of ownership and purpose to their work; introduce distributive leadership and a sense of collegiality which could bring a sense of collective teacher efficacy; and help buffer teachers against excesses of the external pressures. The author argues that school principals should focus on sustaining school improvement by developing teacher school capability and foster decentralization within schools on educational matters in addition to administrative matters.

Personal circumstances   Research by Stinebrickner (1999c) brings attention to an important phenomenon. Using data from the US National Longitudinal Survey of 1972, his analysis finds that, contrary to the common notion that teaching exits are primarily the result of teachers leaving for attractive non-teaching job alternatives, approximately 60 per cent of all exiting teachers leave the workforce altogether.

He finds that important reasons for leaving the workforce altogether are changes in marital status or changes which occur in the size of families. This aspect is likely to be important because a large percentage of starting teachers are both young and female. Results obtained by Stinebrickner (2001b) reinforce the idea that children play an important role in the decision to leave the workforce. If the decision to remain in teaching implies that daycare must be paid for, the birth of a child lowers the effective wage in the person's teaching job. This suggests that childcare subsidies may represent a cost-effective way to increase teacher labour supply. Similar results are obtained in Stinebrickner (1999b, 2001a).

Teacher education and certification   The structure of teacher education and the requirements to obtain a teaching licence have an important impact on the decision about whether to become a teacher or not. In a series of studies, Hanushek and Pace (1994, 1995) analyse the decision of college students on whether to complete a teacher education programme. They use the longitudinal data from the High School and Beyond survey that follows, in the United States, high school seniors from 1980 to 1986.

The authors conclude that university students are less likely to complete education majors in states that require candidates for teaching licences to complete a relatively larger number of education-related courses. This requirement raises the cost of obtaining an education degree, especially for college students who either plan to teach for a few years before moving to another occupation or want to obtain a teaching licence as 'insurance' in case opportunities in other fields prove unattractive.

Similarly the authors conclude that requiring applicants for teaching licences to score above a pre-specified cut-off on a standardized test (National Teacher's Examination) reduces the number of college students who train to become teachers and the number of college graduates who obtain teaching licences. Hence barriers that states set up for certification indeed inhibit supply.

Another relevant aspect is how the existence of 'emergency certification' mechanisms affects the decisions of individuals to become a teacher. No empirical studies provide evidence on this issue.

Other A few other aspects less explored in the research literature are also likely to have an impact on the attractiveness of the profession. Fringe benefits for teachers, job security in those systems where teachers benefit from tenure and public servant status, the social status or *prestige* of teaching,[12] and geographic location are certainly influential, but the evidence on their impact is scarce. Mitchell *et al.* (1999) explore the potential effects of these factors. They also point out that an important characteristic of the teaching workforce is the possession of a core set of altruistic beliefs and attitudes that, to some extent, shape their motivation around a vocation.

The role of teacher education and certification policies[13]
The supply of teachers depends not only on the willingness of individuals to provide teaching services but also on their ability to acquire the skills necessary to qualify as teachers. Therefore teacher education programmes and certification policies play a key role in defining the skills distribution of the supply of teachers. This subsection focuses on this role by reviewing the literature which relates the relevant measurable teacher characteristics to student achievement.[14]

Teacher initial education: subject-matter knowledge The analysis concentrates on the impact of subject-matter knowledge and pedagogical preparation. To date, researchers conducting studies have relied on proxies for subject-matter knowledge, such as degree field, coursework on subject matter, or tested ability on subject matter. The research that does exist is limited and, in some cases, the results are contradictory. The conclusions do not provide evidence supporting a strong link between university study of subject-matter area and teacher effectiveness. A survey of studies by Hanushek (1997, 2002, 2003) indicates that only 9 per cent of the estimates for the effect of teacher education on student performance are both positive and statistically significant, considerably lower than similar percentages for other resources: 29 for teacher experience, 14 for teacher–pupil ratio or 27 for expenditure per pupil.

Several studies show a positive relationship between teachers' subject-matter preparation and both higher student achievement and higher teacher performance on evaluations, particularly in mathematics, science and reading (Darling-Hammond, 1999a, 1999b; Goldhaber and Brewer, 2000; Guyton and Farokhi, 1987; Monk, 1994). Another study, Monk and King (1994), finds both positive and negative, generally insignificant effects of teachers' subject-matter preparation on student achievement. Similarly, Ferguson and Womack (1993) find that teachers' scores on national teacher examinations and grade point averages in the major accounts for only small proportions of the variance in teaching performance of prospective secondary teachers. In turn, Goldhaber and Brewer (2000) find a positive relationship between teachers' degrees in mathematics and their students' test scores but do not find this relationship in science. Using the same data set, Rowan *et al.* (1997) find a positive relationship between student achievement in mathematics and teachers' majors in mathematics, but the effect size is quite small. In the same way, Monk (1994) finds no effect of having a full mathematics major even if having course work in mathematics matters. In the same study, while the author identifies a significant positive relationship between teachers' course work in the physical sciences and student achievement, he does not identify the same effect for course work in life sciences.

It may be that these results are mixed because subject-matter knowledge is a positive influence up to some level of basic competence in the subject but is less important thereafter. This interpretation is supported by the study by Monk (1994). Using data on 2829 students from the Longitudinal Study of American Youth, Monk finds that teachers' content preparation, as measured by course work in the subject field, is positively related to student achievement in mathematics and science, but that the relationship is curvilinear, with diminishing returns to student achievement of teachers' subject-matter courses above a threshold level.

Another important issue is the assessment of the importance of the value added by teacher education course work or, more specifically, 'pedagogical preparation'. 'Pedagogical preparation' refers to the various courses that teachers take in such areas as instructional methods, learning theories, foundations of education and classroom management. Studies have found a somewhat stronger and more consistently positive influence of education course work on teachers' effectiveness. However research on pedagogical preparation has remained at a high level of aggregation, giving little detail about possible differences across grade level or subject area. Ashton and Crocker (1987) find significant positive relationships between education course work and teacher performance in four of seven studies they review. Likewise Evertson *et al.* (1985) report a consistent positive effect of teachers' formal education training on supervisory ratings and student learning, with 11 of 13 studies showing greater effectiveness for fully prepared and certified versus uncertified or provisionally certified teachers. With respect to subject matter course work, five of eight studies they review find no relationship, and the other three find small associations.

A very debated policy is the requirement of holding a graduate degree in education. In the United States, several states require that teachers earn a master's degree within a specific period of time after initial hiring. Policy makers raise many doubts about the efficacy of such policy. The fact is that the preponderance of evidence is that teachers with master's degrees are no more effective than teachers who do not hold these degrees. A summary of the evidence can be found in Hanushek (1986). More recently, Rivkin *et al.* (2001) find no evidence that having a master's degree improves teacher skills. As they emphasize, the results raise serious doubts about policies that require or strongly encourage graduate education for teachers. An additional consequence of such policy, as pointed out by Murnane (1996), is the fact that such requirement raises the cost of choosing teaching as a career and may have the effect of dissuading potentially effective teachers from entering the profession.

Teacher certification　Certification or licensing status is a measure of teacher qualifications that combines aspects of knowledge about subject-matter and about teaching and learning. Its meaning varies because of differences in licensing requirements, but a standard certificate generally means that a teacher has been prepared in an accredited teacher education programme and/or has completed either a major or a minor in the field(s) to be taught with a minimum of education credits. In addition obtaining a licence might also depend on passing a national teacher examination and/or having a short teaching experience. More recently, as a way of reducing shortages in critical areas and attracting non-traditional entrants, authorities allow the hiring of teachers who have not met their licensing standards. Some allow the hiring of teachers with no licence. Others issue emergency, temporary or provisional licences. And others again provide alternative routes for certification. Most of these are master's degrees programmes which offer an education degree and are often aimed at mid-career entrants who already have a bachelor's degree. In other cases, candidates complete a short summer course of study and assume full teaching responsibilities, with or without completing additional course work.

The research available points to the fact that, generally, a certification status tends to be associated with higher teacher effectiveness. Hawk *et al.* (1985) find that the students of certified mathematics teachers score higher on standardized mathematics tests than those of uncertified teachers. Similarly, using data from Texas, Fuller (1999) finds that students in districts with greater proportions of licensed teachers were significantly more likely to pass the Texas state achievement tests, after controlling for student socioeconomic status, school wealth and teacher experience. Teacher licensing was found to be especially influential on the test performance of elementary students. Along the same lines, in a recent school-level analysis of mathematics test performance in California high schools, Felter (1999) finds a negative relationship between average student scores and the percentage of teachers on emergency certificates.

In another study, Darling-Hammond (1999a, 1999b) finds a positive relationship between a state's percentage of fully certified teachers and student achievement in mathematics and reading. The same study finds a negative relationship between student achievement and three indicators of a state's less-than-fully-certified teachers: percentage of all less-than-fully-certified teachers; percentage of new entrants to teaching who were uncertified; and percentage of newly hired uncertified teachers. In turn, Goldhaber and Brewer (2000) find evidence that students of teachers who hold standard certification in mathematics achieve higher levels in mathematics than students whose teachers are uncertified. However the same authors find no difference in the achievement of students who had teachers with certification versus those with temporary emergency credentials. This conclusion is strongly challenged in a response by Darling-Hammond *et al.* (2001) in which they criticize the methodological grounding for the findings.

The question of whether alternative licensing programmes have a negative impact on teacher effectiveness is more controversial. Research indicates that alternative route programmes have been successful in recruiting a more diverse pool of teachers. However the research shows that alternative routes have a mixed record in attracting the 'best and brightest', very often the main objective for the existence of alternative routes. Feistritzer and Chester (2000) provide a good summary of the evidence.

Professional development   Continuing professional development refers to specific episodes of on-the-job or in-service training. More recently it has received more attention from researchers and is seen potentially as a crucial factor in teacher effectiveness.[15] Currently little evidence about the effects of continuing professional development on pupil attainment is available. The problem is that we still know very little about the nature and extent of professional development as an activity. The impression is that the activity is very diverse and the outcomes are very dependent on the particular circumstances in which it is undertaken.

Some studies have found that higher levels of student achievement are associated with mathematics teachers' opportunities to participate in sustained professional development focused on content-specific pedagogy linked to the new curriculum they are learning to teach. One such study is Cohen and Hill (1997). The authors base their results on analyses of a survey that they administered to a random sample of California elementary teachers and on achievement scores for the students of these teachers. They report that, when teachers had extensive opportunities to learn in what they called 'student curriculum workshops' in elementary mathematics, their practices more closely resembled those envisioned by the new curriculum framework and their students' achievement on mathematics assessments was significantly higher. Studies with similar results are Wiley and Yoon (1995) and Brown *et al.* (1995).

More recently, Wenglinsky (2000) links student results from the 1996 eighth-grade National Assessment of Educational Progress tests, in the United States, to teacher education levels, years of experience, classroom practices and professional development. This study finds that some kinds of professional development for teachers made a big difference. In mathematics, students whose teachers received professional development in working with special populations (such as culturally diverse students, limited English proficient students, and students with special needs) outperformed their peers, as did students whose teachers received in-service education in higher-order thinking skills. In science, students whose teachers received on-the-job education in laboratory skills also outperformed their peers.

Perhaps the most detailed and methodologically sophisticated study on the effects of a specific professional development programme is the one by Angrist and Lavy (2001). The authors present an evaluation of teacher training in Jerusalem elementary schools with the purpose of estimating the causal effect of a specific programme on pupils' test scores. The training programme was designed to improve the teaching of language skills and mathematics. In an attempt to overcome the methodological difficulties inherent in an evaluation study of this type, the authors explore the fact that in 1995 a handful of public schools in Jerusalem received a special infusion of funds that were primarily earmarked for teachers' on-the-job training. According to the authors, this programme presents an unusual research opportunity because, even though the intervention was not allocated using experimental random assignment, the Jerusalem intervention can be studied with the aid of a matched group of students from schools not subject to the intervention. Considerable information is available on the students enrolled at the affected schools both before and after the intervention began. Similar information is also available for a group of comparison schools in adjacent neighbourhoods and elsewhere in the city, so these schools can play the role of a control group.

The results suggest that the training received by teachers in the non-religious branch of the Jerusalem school system led to an improvement in their pupils' test scores. The estimates for religious schools are not clearcut but, according to the authors, this may be because the training programme in religious schools started later and was implemented on a smaller scale. In an attempt to assess the economic value of the training programme, the authors of the study compare the treatment effect and costs of training to the effect, size and costs of alternative school improvement strategies involving reductions in class size and lengthening the school day. Their analysis suggests that teacher training may provide a less expensive strategy for raising test scores than reducing class size or adding school hours.

However professional development programmes can take many forms and can be applied to very different contexts. Their impact naturally depends on their specificity. But it seems clear that some forms of on-the-job training can be very effective. In this way, researchers are appropriately moving from the question 'should we support in-service professional development?' to the question 'what kinds of in-service training should be supported?' Recently Rice (2003) shed further light on the incidence and impact of various types of professional development on teachers.

Structural elements shaping the labour market for teachers

This section explores the role of particular factors in framing the structure of the teacher labour market and therefore defining the mechanisms through which teachers are matched to schools. A number of elements such as the structure of the school system (for example school choice, school autonomy in teacher recruitment, the management of schools, the evaluation and accountability framework), teacher labour market institutions (collective bargaining, bargaining instruments, contractual elements), recruitment and selection procedures, segmentation of market and information gaps, constrain the interaction between supply of and demand for teachers. The analysis reviews the empirical literature on the impact of these elements on the efficacy of the schools–teachers matching by looking at their effects on the resulting distribution of teacher skills, level of rewards for teachers and teacher effectiveness in schools.

Organization of the school system

The labour market for teachers is a provider of inputs for the market for schooling. As a result anything that fundamentally characterizes the organization of the school system can affect the way the labour market for teachers operates. In fact the structure of the market for schooling defines basic constraints and incentives that schools, education administrators, teachers, parents and students face with potential significant effects on the way participants in the teacher labour market interact. This subsection reviews some of these potential effects.

Level of competition in the school system, school choice and local autonomy in hiring teachers   In most countries, governments not only provide a majority of the funding but also typically operate the schools. This greatly reduces market competition in the school system. However certain mechanisms of school choice for parents, coupled with some local autonomy in the management of schools, bring in some basis for competition.

Assuming that schools or local education administrations have some discretion in the selection of their teachers, the following approaches to school choice have implications for the incentives faced by the participants in the teacher labour market:

- open enrolment within the regular public system allowing parents to send their children to public schools[16] outside their area of residence;
- publicly subsidized private schools or vouchers: the government either funds directly private schools, ensuring free or reduced tuition for all students, or provides each parental household with a voucher for each school-aged child, which would be redeemable at a public or private school of the parent's choice.

If the above options are not available, choice of schools is limited to choice of residential location (parents *choose* schools by choosing where they live) and non-subsidized private schools. In either case, public schools are also subject to some competition pressures.

Hanushek and Rivkin (2003) use variation in the most common form of public school choice in the United States (parents choosing among schools by selecting their area of residence) to examine the effect of public school competition on teacher quality. They argue that better job performance might lead school superintendents to improve their ability to move to another district, principals to enlarge the scope of their autonomy or improve their ability to remain in a school, and teachers to benefit from better working conditions as a result of the higher quality of their colleagues. The evidence suggests that more competition tends to increase teacher quality, particularly for schools serving predominantly lower-income students.

In the same way, using exogenous variation in the availability and costs of private school alternatives to public schools, Hoxby (1994) examines the effects of inter-school competition on public schools. She finds that greater private school competitiveness significantly raises the quality of public schools, as measured by the educational attainment, wages and high school graduation rates of public school students. In addition she finds some evidence that public schools react to greater competitiveness of private schools by paying higher teacher salaries.

More recently, Hoxby (2000) focuses on the way choice affects teachers. She investigates whether schools that face stronger choice-based incentives have greater demand for certain teacher characteristics and (if so) which teacher characteristics. The author uses data on traditional forms of choice (parents choosing a school by choosing a residence, choice of private schools) and a new survey of charter school teachers in the United States. The paper's empirical strategy is based on a simple economic argument: if schools that face stronger choice-based incentives have greater demand for a certain teacher characteristic, the wage they pay for that characteristic should be greater and the amount of that characteristic they hire should be greater. The test for whether a characteristic is demanded more by choice-driven schools is whether the characteristic is paid a higher wage and in greater abundance in them.

The evidence presented in Hoxby's paper suggests that school choice could change the teaching profession by raising the demand for teachers with high-quality college education, with subject area (especially maths and science) skills, who make extra effort and are independent, and by lowering the demand for certification. In summary, the evidence suggests that school choice would create a more high-powered incentive environment within the teaching profession, in the sense that teachers would be required to have higher levels of human capital and effort in return for higher marginal wages for such characteristics. Hence, according to Hoxby, under increased school choice, less able or less motivated incumbent teachers might find themselves earning smaller salary increases than some of their peers. Such teachers might be more likely to leave the teaching profession early. This would reverse the current pattern, in which able teachers are more likely to exit early.

Another important aspect of the consequences of the progressive introduction of market mechanisms is whether productivity is increased and, that being the case, whether it is related to an improvement of the quality of teachers drawn into the profession. Recent work by Hoxby (2003) addresses this issue. She first emphasizes the importance of the productivity issue as the school choice impact on productivity potentially determines whether choice will benefit all children as opposed to specific subsets of children. The author presents evidence on three recent choice reforms: vouchers in Milwaukee, charter schools in Michigan and charter schools in Arizona. In each case she finds that regular public schools boosted their productivity when exposed to competition. Most importantly she notes that one of the channels through which productivity increases is a different reward system that draws better individuals into teaching.

Along the same lines, Rapp (2000) investigates whether school choice enhances the work effort of teachers. His paper tests whether choice influences the behaviour of public school teachers, arguably the link between policy and outcome. Using data from the US Department of Education School and Staff Survey, he finds mixed results. He is unable to establish universal influence of school-system competitiveness on teacher effort. Neither 'open enrolment' school-choice policies nor the traditional private school option and residential location option have a statistically significant effect on the amount of time teachers spend on their jobs outside class time. However, where intra-district choice plans are in place and are widely utilized, teachers spend far more time on their jobs.

Who is the employer and who selects the teachers are aspects particularly relevant for competition in the school system to have an impact on the quality of the teachers recruited. This is pointed out by Merrifield (1999) who tests, for the particular case of the state of Texas, the hypothesis that teachers' salaries are affected by the competitiveness of their regional labour market. He explains that the very unusual feature of Texas that teachers' salaries are not determined by collective bargaining between district officials and teacher unions makes it especially well-suited to the task of disentangling monopsony effects from other labour forces. The results suggest that teachers are paid less in less competitive markets. He emphasizes two important points. First, the problem of lack of competition is aggravated by the fact that most teachers cannot easily change careers, since the skills of most teachers are often worth little in non-teaching jobs. Second, the employers of teachers being school districts and not individual schools, the consequences of the lack of competition are exacerbated. The important point is that reduced salary competition has significant policy implications, as the attractiveness of the profession depends greatly on salary levels.

Making schools the employers might have a great impact on the level of competition in the markets for teachers. This is the issue explored by Vedder and Hall (2000), who argue that competition in the market for educational services also introduces labour market competition. They hypothesize that, with the introduction of viable private school alternatives, there should be greater salary competition between educational providers in order to lure better teachers, leading to higher salaries in public schools. Using detailed data on over 600 Ohio school districts, the authors find that increased private school competition does indeed lead to higher salaries for public school teachers.

Another way to gain insight into the effects of stronger market forces on the way schools hire teachers is by comparing public and regular private schools. After all, private schools are routinely subject to market forces and have an incentive to employ teachers who attract tuition-paying students. Ballou (1996) and Ballou and Podgursky (1997, 1998) provide a comprehensive comparison of public and private school teachers. They find that private schools value teacher aptitude more in hiring decisions than public schools do. They also find that teacher pay is less compressed and more closely related to aptitude and scarce skills (such as maths and science skills) in private schools than in public schools. Ballou's conclusion is that public schools face little competition for students, and so do not invest sufficient effort in finding the best applicants for teaching jobs.

It is also important to note that the issue of school choice is interdependent of that of school finance. For instance, school financing can be based on direct funding from the government on a per student basis or established through tuition fees collected from parents benefiting from a large-scale voucher system. In the latter case, the fact that the money follows the student is likely to confine schools' behaviour: as seen before, better individuals might be drawn into teaching (Hoxby, 2003). Another example in which school choice and school finance intersect is when choice is limited to the area of residence and sources of revenue for school funding are to some extent based on property taxes. As pointed out by Boyd *et al.* (2003), this form of financing is likely to lead to serious inequities in the distribution of quality teachers: differences in the ability to raise revenue for schools are typically reflected in the level of teacher salaries and other working conditions, crucial elements in attracting teachers. Their results indeed show striking differences in the qualifications of teachers across school districts.

Organization of schools   Cohen *et al.* (2000) note that researchers report that schools and teachers with the same resources do different things, with different results for students' learning. They indicate that resource use is influenced by the management of certain key problems of instruction, including coordination, incentives to use resources and management of instructional environments. Along the same lines, Hanushek (1998) emphasizes that the current organization of schools might explain why resources seem to matter less than expected: 'The existing work does not suggest that resources never matter. Nor does it suggest that resources could not matter. It only indicates that the current organisation and incentives of schools do little to ensure that any added resources will be used effectively.' As a result, school management is likely to have a considerable impact on the efficacy of the school teaching body. In particular the internal organization of schools defines the effectiveness of the within-school matching of teachers to tasks, namely to the specific classes to be taught. In this context Ingersoll (2001b, 2002) shows that the problem of 'out-of-field' teaching (teachers being assigned subjects for which they are not certified), acute in many school districts in the United States, is due to a great extent to a number of aspects of the administration and organization of schools. In recent work Darling-Hammond and Snyder (2003) also conclude that changes in the organization of schools that allocate greater resources to teaching, teacher learning and time for students and teachers to build stronger relationships and participate more in in-depth work appear to create new potential for student learning gains. Research on the role of the organization of schools in the effectiveness of school teaching bodies, however, has been quite limited.

Evaluation and accountability   Granting more autonomy and responsibility to schools over a broader range of areas is increasingly common in many countries. In particular increased authority of schools over matters such as the recruitment and selection of teachers or the setting of the incentive structure for teachers (for example definition of wages) is likely to have a great effect on the efficiency of the matching between schools and teachers. However, as generally agreed, it is important that greater autonomy goes along with appropriate accountability mechanisms. In fact, if public school principals have the ability to set salaries for individual teachers, they may abuse such discretion. Preferential treatment or specific discriminations may well influence pay setting in such a system. In this context, accountability systems which tie rewards for schools to objective measures of school performance could generate incentives for principals to hire the best teachers as well as incentives for teachers to teach well. However, as pointed out in the literature, straightforward incentive systems based on objective standards are often problematic because objective performance measures are difficult to establish and can generate perverse incentives (Koretz, 2002; Eberts *et al.*, 2002).

A recent trend is to move from evaluation of teachers at the individual level to the evaluation of schools as a whole, possibly linked to rewards for the entire teaching body as a result of good performance. It would be interesting to assess what type of incentives such arrangements generate for recruitment practices and teachers' collective efficacy in schools. Evidence on this issue is scarce.[17] Similarly, little is known on how teacher evaluation schemes affect the matching between schools and teachers; schools with well established teacher evaluation systems might end up with a mix of teacher characteristics different from that of schools where evaluation of schools is not carried out.

Labour market institutions

Level of centralisation of bargaining and the role of unions   Given that, in the market for teachers, unions traditionally play a very relevant role, this subsection concentrates on their impact. Most research on this role addresses the issue of whether or not unions affect the productivity of public schools. In this context, Hoxby (1996) examines how teachers' unions affect the educational production function.

In her work, Hoxby considers that unions might affect the production of education at least through three channels. First, unions are expected to change – probably increase – the overall budget that funds school inputs. Second, unions are expected to reallocate any given budget among alternative inputs. This reallocation will generally be efficiency-enhancing if the union's different objective reflects superior information, but efficiency-reducing if the union is rent seeking. Finally, because teachers interact with inputs to produce education, unions may affect the productivity of each input. For instance, if the union conveys superior information and class size reflects teachers' preferences as a result, teachers may plan on smaller class size and make better use of it. In contrast, if the union performs a rent-seeking role and protects incumbent teachers from outside teachers competing for better-paid jobs, a teacher salary increase may be less productive in a unionized school than in a non-unionized school.

Using panel data on US school districts and state laws that facilitate teachers' unionization, Hoxby finds that teachers' unions are primarily rent-seeking. More specifically she finds that teachers' unions raise per-pupil spending, raise the share of spending devoted to inputs that have potential benefits for teachers, and lower student achievement by decreasing the productivity of these inputs. In addition, she makes clear that the potential effects of unions on schools are expected to be magnified when the market for schooling is imperfectly competitive. This is because rents will be available for rent-seeking unions and less information will be conveyed by the market in the absence of active choice among schools by parents and teachers.

This study is part of a literature on teachers' unions that has produced mixed results. In fact the negative impact of unions on schools' productivity found by Hoxby (1996) has not gathered consensus. For instance, Eberts and Stone (1987) use the Sustaining Effects Survey and the High School and Beyond survey in the United States to find that union districts are 7 per cent more productive for average students. For students who are significantly above or below average, however, non-union districts are more productive by about the same margin, apparently because teacher unions reduce the use of specialized instructional techniques. The authors argue that the result is consistent with the view that unions tend to standardize the workplace. Along the same lines, Argys and Reese (1995) reach similar conclusions. In another study (Kurth, 1987), the results suggest that the growth in teachers' unions during 1972–83 was the most significant factor in the decline of student performance, as measured by SAT scores. Kleiner and Petree (1988), using state aggregate data from 1972 to 1982, find more generous resources and higher student performance in states where a greater share of teachers is unionized. In the same way, the work of Register and Grimes (1991) indicates that students in a unionized environment score higher on their college entrance exams than their counterparts from a non-union environment. More recently, Steelman *et al.* (2000) find a statistically significant and positive relationship between state teacher unionization rates and state standardized student test scores. This decidedly mixed set of findings is due at least in part to differences in union measures employed, choices of dependent variables studied, units of analysis used, difference in demographic variables for which they control, and other methodological issues.

Other aspects of the influence of unions on public schools have been studied. According to other studies, teacher unions increase salaries (Ballou and Podgursky, 2002; Baugh and Stone, 1982; Dolton and Robson, 1996; Bee and Dolton, 1995) and costs (Eberts and Stone, 1986), alter the allocation of resources and the time teachers spend in the classroom (Eberts, 1984) and influence district educational policies (Goldschmidt and Stuart, 1986; Woodbury, 1985).

Certain schools systems such as those in Sweden[18] are getting away from heavily union-influenced systems and have introduced individually negotiated components to teacher contracts. Little is known about the impact of such initiatives but it is predictable that the functioning of the labour market for teachers is extensively affected.

Bargaining instruments   Reward packages for teachers are traditionally made of salaries, leave benefits and future pension benefits. Few countries have introduced instruments such as signing bonuses, housing subsidies, provision of childcare or opportunities for continuing professional development activities as a result of good performance. In turn, the level of teachers' compensation is typically associated with qualifications, level of education taught and years of experience, and only in a few systems does it depend on variables such as performance, level of professional development activities, responsibility/complexity of tasks or whether the school is located in a difficult/isolated area.

Therefore the *average* school system is still characterized by little flexibility regarding the instruments used to define the incentive structure that teachers face. Teachers are generally paid the same, irrespective, for example, of level of shortages in subject/level, level of difficulty of the area where school is located, or responsibility/complexity of tasks. The stratified nature of the labour market for teachers is not acknowledged by the existing incentive structure. This results, for instance, in the absence of strategies for developing selective approaches to address specific problems (such as shortages in specific subjects) or for promoting mobility of teachers within a given country.

The impact of the above-mentioned instruments (differentiated pay, performance-based rewards and so on) on the individual behaviour of teachers has been widely explored by researchers (see pages 536–47) but their effect both on the ability of the labour market for teachers to adjust to imbalances and on the efficiency of the matching of teachers to schools has not been addressed in the empirical literature.

Contractual elements, mechanisms for dismissal and retirement-related policies   The degree of flexibility of the teacher labour market depends on further regulatory dimensions. Contractual elements such as the type of appointment (for example fixed-term versus indefinite), whether teachers benefit from the status of public servants or not, the existence of a probationary period, the existence of mechanisms to dismiss underperforming teachers, or retirement-related policies allowing teachers to work beyond retirement age have a great influence on the ability of the labour market for teachers to adjust to mismatches between teachers and schools. Regrettably the existing empirical research tells us little about how such contractual elements affect either the effectiveness of the schools–teachers matching or the flexibility of the teacher labour market to operate adjustments.

Recruitment and selection procedures
A key dimension that shapes the quality of the teaching workforce is the way school systems select and recruit teachers. Recruitment and selection practices are essential mechanisms through which incentives are potentially tied to the quality of the teaching workforce. For instance, if hiring practices are inefficient in linking teacher compensation to teacher quality (by not leading to the selection of the best candidates from a given pool of applicants) increases in salaries will not lead to improvements in the quality of the teaching workforce.

A rather surprising empirical finding in the literature is that there is little evidence supporting a strong positive impact of salaries on the overall quality of teaching workforces (Ballou and Podgursky, 1997; Hanushek *et al.*, 1999).[19] Recruitment and selection procedures have been among the most prominent elements to explain this finding.

Many authors have pointed out the fact that public schools do not exhibit a marked preference for teachers whose academic backgrounds signal strong cognitive ability and command of subject-matter. One such study (Ballou, 1996), reports the results of an investigation of the education and recruitment of prospective teachers, drawing on a series of large, nationally representative surveys of new college graduates in the United

States. According to the author, these data enable him to separate the influence of academic ability on the self-selection of teacher trainees from its role in hiring decisions. The results show that college quality has virtually no influence on the likelihood that a candidate will receive an offer of full-time employment in a public school. Moreover a degree in education carries more weight than a subject-area major. The author then argues that the fact that turnover is higher among teachers with stronger academic backgrounds does not justify giving preference to weaker students in recruitment. Ballou asserts that the evidence strongly suggests that public school officials undervalue cognitive skills and subject-matter knowledge when screening new applicants and that hiring decisions are suboptimal as a result. Ballou and Podgursky (1997, 1998) provide additional evidence that school administrators do not hire the best teaching candidates, thereby weakening the link between quality and pay.

There are various reasons why many schools do not value academic talent, according to Ballou (1996). Explanations include patronage, the weight attached to skills other than teaching ability, such as coaching skill, and the possibility that academically strong candidates lack thorough teacher preparation. In addition administrators' lack of interest in strong candidates may reflect the weakness of competitive pressures in public education. In fact hiring practices differ substantially in the private sector (Ballou and Podgursky, 1998). A policy implication is that some sort of reform, focusing on administrators' decision making, may be required.

The substantial costs associated with the acquisition and interpretation of information influencing decisions limit the efficiency of the selection. A more direct interaction through personal interviews, work assignments discussed with applicants, acquaintance with schools by candidates and teaching demonstrations are costly approaches but are likely to have a substantial impact on which candidates are selected and how fully committed they become to the mission and the work requirements of the jobs they eventually accept (Murnane *et al.*, 1991).

An important issue is the extent to which schools have a say in selecting their teachers, likely to have a considerable impact on the *organizational fit* of the teacher. It would seem that those who are closest to the reality of schools potentially make the best-informed decisions and seek those characteristics of teachers which best fit the identity of schools. Nonetheless, in many countries, school participation in teacher selection remains limited, on the grounds of the complexity involved, the potential resulting inequitable distribution of teachers and the possibility of favouritism in teacher selection by schools. The latter aspect can be addressed by introducing accountability policies forcing the schools to become more responsive to local needs through the inclusion of parents and community members on decision-making committees, while the inequity dimension can be tackled by providing additional resources to those schools located in low-income areas.

A final relevant aspect in systems where the recruitment of teachers is undertaken at the central level is that of the deployment of teachers. Criteria for assigning teachers to schools are critical to ensure that all students are provided with quality teachers. In particular, assignment practices should ideally ensure that less privileged school areas are staffed with quality teachers.

Segmentation and information gaps

The labour market for teachers is particularly segmented as entry is restricted to the individuals in possession of the skills granting them teacher certification. Workers with experience in other economic sectors but with no prior teaching experience and no initial training as teachers can obtain a job as a teacher only in exceptional cases. Recently, as a result of teacher shortages, some countries have introduced alternative certification programmes, opening entry into the teaching profession to individuals with no regular certification. The impact of such policies in the functioning of the teacher labour market is potentially considerable given that the interaction with other labour markets is likely to intensify. Research has concentrated on the relative effectiveness of teachers recruited through alternative certification (see page 549). The effects on the functioning of the teacher labour market as a result of the potential greater competitive pressures, for example on salary levels, relative demand by schools for individuals with experience outside education and number of individuals pursuing the traditional teacher education pipeline, have received little attention, certainly as a result of the limited scope of current alternative certification programmes.

Another interesting phenomenon, in particular in English-speaking countries such as Australia, New Zealand, the UK, the USA and Canada, has been the recent internationalization of some teacher labour markets. These countries have developed specific policies to attract foreign teachers (for example immigration waivers and recognition of credentials and teaching experience in country of origin) but their effect has received little attention thus far.

Information gaps impose further constraints in the functioning of the teacher labour market. For instance, individuals looking for a teaching position are often not aware of the overall range of opportunities presented to them, especially when recruitment systems are highly decentralized. Also schools often need to replace some teachers temporarily, making the need to identify available candidates promptly particularly acute. Schools are often faced with circumstances such as a pregnancy, sick leaves or absences as a result of professional development activities. In this context governments need to develop mechanisms which reduce the information gaps between the agents involved in the teacher labour market, making the matching more timely and efficient. Examples of existing mechanisms are the *supply pool* in the UK and the *replacement pool* in the Flemish Community of Belgium. Another approach is the admittance to the market of intermediaries such as the teacher private employment agencies currently in place in the UK.[20]

Equilibrium analysis

This section brings demand, supply and structural elements together and characterizes equilibrium in the teacher labour market. First, it describes a basic model of demand and supply that has been used as a useful tool to understand the interaction between the multiple factors involved. It then moves on to the issue of teacher shortages, explaining their implications, our ability to measure them and summarizing what is known about their severity. The last subsection draws attention to educational equity concerns by analysing the distribution of teacher resources across schools.

A basic model of demand and supply

It is useful to bring demand and supply together in a model where equilibrium can be depicted. A diagram makes clear the interrelationship between the main factors described in the previous sections and the effect of a change on any of these factors can be worked through with typical comparative static techniques. The model described below was originally proposed by Zabalza *et al.* (1979) and further developed by Dolton (1996).

In Figure 14.3, the average teacher wage, w, and the number of teachers, T, are plotted on the vertical and horizontal axes, respectively. D^T represents the demand for teachers as described in equation (14.1). It essentially reflects, for a given student population, the desirable targets of educational authorities regarding class size, teaching loads and required learning time for students. $\bar{E}$ represents the constraint on the market imposed by the level of total government expenditure on teachers – the budget constraint introduced on page 531. Finally, S represents the aggregate supply of qualified teachers. It reflects the supply behaviour of teachers and therefore depends on factors such as relative salaries and working conditions. Aggregate supply is an increasing function of the average teacher wage, assuming that the non-teacher wage is fixed.

Figure 14.3 depicts equilibrium in the teacher labour market and illustrates the potential incompatibility between desirable targets for the student–teacher ratio and budget constraints. The planned number of teachers compatible with given targets for the student–teacher ratio is given

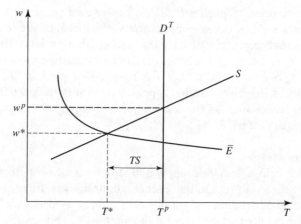

Figure 14.3   Supply and demand for teachers

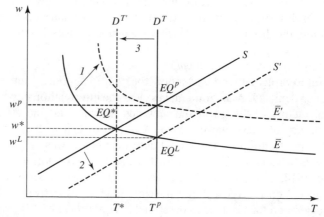

Figure 14.4   Facing a teacher shortage

by T^p, requiring a minimum salary of w^p to attract enough individuals. However the budget constraint $\bar{E}$ is only consistent with a supply level at T^*, a teacher shortage of $TS = T^p - T^*$ resulting.

Figure 14.4 portrays the potential responses of governments to overcome the existing teacher shortage.[21] A first solution is simply to increase the budget devoted to teacher salaries, shifting out the budget constraint curve from $\bar{E}$ to $\bar{E}'$. This permits the government to raise the average teacher salary to w^p and therefore move equilibrium from EQ^* to EQ^p. A second solution is to relax entry requirements in the profession and hire less-qualified individuals. This is reflected in the new equilibrium EQ^L which results from an interaction between demand, budget constraint and the aggregate supply curve of less-qualified individuals, S'. The position of S' relative to S mirrors the lower reservation wage of individuals with lower credentials. Finally, the demand side of the market provides a third option: the government can reduce the number of teachers needed by increasing class size or the teaching load, causing the demand curve to shift in and establish a new equilibrium at EQ^*.

This model is naturally a simple device, used to understand the functioning of the teacher labour market, and hides realities such as the stratification of the market or the heterogeneity of teacher qualifications. Also, since it is a static model, it cannot picture the influence of the structural elements described on pages 552–63.

Characterizing a shortage of teachers[22]

What do teacher shortages translate into? It is important to recognize that shortages are more of a quality than a quantity issue. The implications of teacher shortages for the quality of the educational system can be understood by looking at the way educational systems respond to a situation in which demand exceeds the available supply of teachers. In the short run the typical strategies used are as follows. The first is to relax qualification requirements during hiring (supply side). If a qualified applicant is not available to fill an open teaching position, a less qualified applicant will typically be hired. Many teachers are hired on emergency certificates ('out-of-licence' teaching) while others are experienced teachers with poor performance records. Another solution consists of requiring teachers to teach outside their areas of certification ('out-of-field' teaching). A third strategy is to raise teaching loads (demand side). The demand for teachers can be reduced and brought into line with available supply by increasing the workloads of employed teachers. This can be achieved both by increasing class sizes and by increasing the average number of classes assigned to teachers.

Hence, in the short term, school systems adjust to excess demand situations either by relaxing qualification requirements or by increasing teachers' workloads. Most importantly, in either case, quality suffers. Alternatively, in situations where demand exceeds supply, it might be expected that a significant proportion of teaching positions will remain unfilled, yet that is rarely the case. Hiring practices ensure that teachers are present to staff almost all classrooms. In this way, the immediate effect of a shortage is more likely to be a lower quality of teachers and teaching than a dramatic tale of classrooms full of uninstructed pupils. In fact there may be no observed quantity imbalance but instead a change in the quality characteristics of the teaching workforce.[23]

In the long run, systems have a wide range of strategies for enhancing the supply of teachers. The most common is to raise salaries substantially so as to make the profession more competitive with other occupations. Additional strategies are available to educational authorities, namely working conditions, the status of the profession, the career ladder or signing bonuses.

Approaches to assessing teacher shortages   As described in the previous subsection, a teacher shortage is more likely to indicate an inadequate distribution of teacher quality than to mean that there are insufficient numbers of teachers to staff courses. In addition a teacher shortage is a relative concept and depends on the country-specific quality standards defining a 'qualified' teacher. Thus the meaning of a shortage is not necessarily the same across countries. It is, then, not surprising that there is no clear, universally agreed measure of what actually constitutes a shortage in relation to a given number of teaching posts and given a set of requirements necessary to be considered a 'qualified' teacher.

Teacher shortages can be captured through two dimensions of the outcome of recruitment processes.[24] The first is vacancy rates: the simplest measure is the number of unfilled vacancies for teachers. Despite its appeal, such a measure is likely not to be reliable. Very few vacancies cannot be filled in some way (teachers with emergency certification, temporary staff). As seen before, schools tend to relax teaching requirements and hire less-qualified teachers if they have trouble filling a position. Second, it is possible that some schools might not create vacancies for staff if they are convinced that a particular post will not be filled by a teacher with the appropriate skills and abilities. However, even if a low proportion of unfilled vacancies does not necessarily mean the absence of shortages, a high level of unfilled vacancies provides strong evidence of their presence. What is of greater interest is the number of 'difficult to fill' vacancies, those which have been 'unfilled' for a significant period of time, or the proportion of positions filled by teachers with 'emergency certification'. Hence the set of strategies schools use when they have difficulties filling in positions could provide valuable information.

The second dimension is hidden shortages. These are said to exist when teaching is carried out by someone who is not qualified to teach the subject. It is often referred to as 'out-of-field' teaching and is usually measured as the proportion of teachers teaching a subject in which they are not qualified. Nevertheless this measure also suffers from certain limitations as 'out-of-field' teaching might result not only from shortages but also from the way schools are managed. In fact many principals find that assigning teachers to teach out of their fields is often more convenient, less expensive or less time-consuming than the alternatives (Ingersoll, 1999).

The measures above reveal, in a somewhat imperfect way, the extent to which school systems face problems in recruiting teachers. This problem is closely related to that of retention, as the demand for new teachers depends crucially on how many teachers leave the profession in a given year. It is thus extremely relevant also to look at measures providing information about flows out of the teaching profession. Such information potentially provides valuable insights for explaining shortages. Such information could include turnover or attrition rates, characteristics of leavers, or reasons for leaving the teaching profession.

Another aspect is that problems of shortages are uneven. In some regions, subject areas, educational or grade levels shortages can be particularly acute. For example, shortages tend to be more intense in certain subjects such as science and mathematics, in teaching fields such as special education, and in rural areas.

Information regarding the qualifications of the current stock of teachers also provides valuable insights regarding its adequacy. Useful information includes the percentage of teachers holding a degree in education, the distribution by highest degree earned, certification status, years of experience and levels of participation in professional development activities. Although such characteristics are only indirect and imperfect measures of the quality of teachers, most analysts agree that they provide useful information on the overall quality of teaching workforces.

Other valuable information is that provided by the age distribution of the current teaching workforce. It provides a basis for assessing how acute retirement-related supply shortages can be. Finally evidence on factors related to the attractiveness of the profession, such as relative salaries, fringe benefits and working conditions of teachers, can prove useful in explaining the development of shortages. Finally, as an insufficient number of teachers is defined relative to given needs, it is also important to look at the pressures on the demand side, in particular at expected changes in the size of the school-age population.

Evidence on teacher shortages　The analysis in OECD (2002) uses available data in OECD countries to review evidence in regard to actual or looming shortfalls in teacher supply. The situation is particularly well-documented in a set of countries that are particularly active in developing statistics on teachers. The limited but suggestive data available provide indications that some countries, such as the Netherlands and the UK, are currently experiencing difficulties in recruiting and retaining qualified teachers. Typically, in such countries (i) the proportion of unfilled vacancies is sizeable; (ii) attrition and turnover rates have increased in recent years; (iii) the proportion of 'out-of-field' teaching assignments is high in some key subject areas; (iv) the age profile of teachers is skewed towards the upper end of the age range; and (v) school principals report that a teacher shortage/inadequacy is hindering student learning. But, within the OECD area, this situation cannot be generalized. Other countries, such as France, Japan and Korea, still seem to have relatively large pools of qualified individuals from which to recruit. These countries may still consider teacher quality to be an issue, but not because of shortages of qualified staff.

A recent survey by the OECD (International Survey of Upper Secondary Schools) provides new international evidence on the current balance between supply of and demand for teachers in upper secondary schools of 15 OECD countries. School principals were asked about vacancies and modes of covering vacancies in their schools. The results, published in OECD (2003, 2004), show that there are large differences among systems in the extent of teacher shortfalls. The percentage of full-time teachers who are not fully qualified is on average 14.3 per cent in the countries surveyed, but with large disparities among countries: in Sweden, Norway and Mexico, about a quarter of the teaching workforce is not qualified, while in Korea and Ireland there are virtually no teachers without the required qualifications. School principals also provided their perceptions regarding the difficulty of hiring qualified teachers in various study areas. The area in which difficulties are greatest is computer sciences/information technology, with 49 per cent of upper secondary students attending schools where the principal reported that hiring fully qualified teachers is difficult. Other problem subject areas are mathematics (33 per cent), technology (33 per cent), foreign languages (32 per cent) and sciences (30 per cent).

Distribution of teachers and educational equity
Another fundamental dimension is the equilibrium distribution of teacher resources across schools. Ensuring that all students are provided with quality teachers is a policy issue of the highest importance in the educational agenda of governments.

The connection between the distribution of teachers across schools and educational equity is particularly well documented in the United States. Lankford *et al.* (2002) use data on New York State teachers to determine the extent and type of variation of the attributes of teachers across schools. Their results show striking differences in the qualifications of teachers across schools. Low-income, low-achieving and non-white students, particularly those in urban areas, find themselves in classes with many of the least skilled teachers. In addition the authors conclude that salary variation rarely compensates for the apparent difficulties of teaching in urban settings and, in some cases, contributes to the disparities.

These results are confirmed by Murphy *et al.* (2003), who attempt to estimate the size and nature of the teacher shortage of the late 1990s by using data from the 1999–2000 School and Staffing Survey conducted by the US Department of Education. They find that the shortage problem was distributed unevenly: urban schools and those with relatively high populations of minority and low-income students were more severely affected by the teacher shortfall. Similar findings are provided by Iatarola and Stiefel (2003) in their analysis of intra-district equity of public education resources in New York City. The work of Ingersoll (2002) corroborates these findings by showing that the number of teachers with no regular certification, less experience, fewer qualifications, and without a major or a minor in the area taught is highest in high poverty, high minority urban schools in the United States. These findings suggest that inequity in the distribution of teacher resources is a serious problem that policy makers should keep in mind when they design policies to improve teacher recruitment and retention.

In recent work, Boyd *et al.* (2003) explore the features of US teacher labour markets that more markedly affect the distribution of teachers. They argue that teacher labour markets are characterized by several institutions that enhance the likelihood of an inequitable distribution of qualified teachers. Three aspects of such institutions are referred to as having a particular negative effect. First, the use of the existing single salary schedule makes it very difficult to raise salaries to attract more qualified teachers to hard-to-staff schools without also raising salaries in other schools in the district. Second, the post-and-fill, seniority-based recruiting method employed in many districts leads teachers in hard-to-staff schools to transfer easily to other schools within the district after gaining some experience, taking their on-the-job training with them. Third, reliance on local property wealth for funding is likely to encourage substantial differences in ability to pay for education across school districts.

Another important aspect is the matching between the demographic composition of the student body and that of the teaching workforce. This issue is explored by Mitchell *et al.* (1999) for the case of the United States. They survey the ethnic composition and changing demography of the general population, the students attending public schools and the teaching staff in public schools. They conclude that there is a striking imbalance between the cultural diversity of public school students and the predominant number of white teachers who serve them.

Conclusions
Teachers form the core of the school system and their quality is a key determinant of student learning. Improving the performance and efficiency

of education systems depends, in large measure, on improving the quality of teachers. Teachers also constitute the largest single share of expenditure on schools and their labour market is of significant magnitude in every country.

This chapter develops a conceptual framework for understanding the functioning of the teacher labour market and summarizes what is known about its components, the main factors involved, their interrelationship and the way they frame the behaviour of the main agents involved. The analysis focuses on the determinants of the demand for teachers, the factors influencing the supply of teachers and the role of the institutional structure of the labour market in defining the interaction between demand and supply.

Evidence on the career decisions of teachers shows that they do respond to incentives. Salaries and alternative opportunities strongly influence who goes into teaching, who stays in teaching, teaching location and who returns to teaching after a career interruption. Other factors, such as working conditions, teacher education and certification procedures and school leadership also play a very relevant role according to current research. In addition other evidence shows that responsiveness to incentives greatly depends on personal characteristics. The teacher's probability of leaving the profession is higher in the first few years of the career. More academically able teachers and those working in subject areas which provide more opportunities outside education are more likely to leave the profession and less likely to come back once they leave. Another important aspect is that women and men respond differently to incentives.

Other aspects of the supply behaviour of teachers are less explored. A relatively neglected area of study has been the examination of career opportunities and the promotion process in the teaching profession, at a time when policy makers are considering getting away from seniority-based salary schedules. A related aspect is that empirical research says little about the difficulty of implementing performance-based compensation systems. This might be linked to the fact that there has been surprisingly little focus on the specificity of teaching as a profession, namely its intrinsic aspects which are likely to be central in attracting many individuals. Another often debated issue is that of the professionalism of teachers, which relates to their degree of intervention, core tasks and roles in schools. Despite the importance of these aspects, current research says little about ways in which job characteristics affect teachers' job satisfaction. This results from a concentration of studies on the decision of whether or not to provide teaching services at the cost of neglecting the study of what motivates and drives the effort of teachers while in the profession.

A major area for improvement is the development of good measures of the several aspects involved in the teaching profession. A particularly remarkable fact is that the currently available measures for teacher quality are unsatisfactory. Even if a number of studies have clearly shown the key role of teachers, there is very little agreement on how to characterize a 'quality teacher': characteristics such as subject-matter knowledge, qualifications, certification status or teaching experience explain less of the variation in teacher quality than expected. The explanation might be that other characteristics that are more challenging to measure, for example the ability to convey ideas in clear and convincing ways or to work effectively with colleagues and the school community, might have greater explanatory power. This measurement problem has created difficulties for researchers in explaining outcomes in the teacher labour market. Similarly researchers have often found it difficult to use measures which describe the environment in which teachers work or the process which leads to the hiring of teachers.

It is also clear that researchers have devoted relatively little attention to the elements that structure the teacher labour market, such as contractual mechanisms, level of competition or recruitment practices. A limited number of studies relates these elements to the efficacy of the market in terms of the matching between schools and teachers. The existing studies concentrate on the role of unions and the level of competition in the market for educational services. The literature also points to the key role recruitment and selection practices play in ensuring the existence of a positive effect of teacher compensation on teacher quality. However important research gaps exist. Examples of questions still to be addressed in the literature are the following. What are the effects of making schools the direct recruiters and/or employers of teachers? What is the role of school organization in ensuring an appropriate match between a given teacher and the tasks he or she is assigned? Do job security, a public servant status or the existence of a probationary period shape the ability of teaching workforces to adapt? What are the effects of opening the profession to individuals with experience outside education by creating alternative pathways into teaching? Another aspect is that researchers rarely develop empirical models that account for the institutional structure of teacher labour markets. For instance, the impact of salaries on the supply behaviour of teachers is likely to depend on the level of competition in the teacher labour market or on whether the monetary rewards are a result of an evaluation scheme put into action.

Perhaps the most remarkable aspect has been the inability of research to assess the relative impact of different alternative uses for the same resources. As put by Hanushek (2002), 'most attention has focussed on whether or not a particular input has a positive and statistically significant effect on achievement. But knowing that something might be expected to improve student performance is insufficient to make it the object of public policy. One would clearly want to know whether there were alternative uses of funds that produced higher achievement.' For instance, this is critical in the analysis of the tradeoff between class size and teacher salaries. The appropriate balance between 'better teachers or more teachers' depends on the relative gains in student learning resulting from a financially equivalent investment in either higher salaries or reduced class sizes. Another example is the career structure of teachers and whether, for instance, we want to raise the salaries of beginning teachers at the cost of lowering those of more experienced teachers (see Ballou and Podgursky, 2002). It happens that research still tells us little on the relative advantages of alternative policies and a series of empirical difficulties still need to be overcome before such a point is reached. But policy makers are certainly anxious for research to deliver such results.

Acknowledgments

I am particularly grateful to Phillip McKenzie for his critical advice, valuable ideas and permanent encouragement. The work presented in this chapter has also greatly benefited from my interaction with my colleagues at OECD, policy makers in numerous countries and the general forum generated by OECD Project *Attracting, Developing and Retaining Effective Teachers*. The opinions expressed in this paper are the sole responsibility of the author and do not necessarily reflect those of the OECD or of the governments of its member countries.

Notes

1. In recent work, Rivkin *et al.* (2001) conclude that teacher quality is the most important within-school factor explaining student performance. They attribute at least 7 per cent of the total variance in test-score gains to differences in teachers and they argue this is a lower bound. For further evidence on the importance of teacher quality, see Hanushek (2002, 2003), Santiago (2002) and Vignoles *et al.* (2000).
2. For a detailed overview of the economic theory of labour markets, see Benjamin *et al.* (2002).
3. Denton *et al.* (1994) link the market for teachers to the time path of fertility in the general population.
4. Note that student–teacher ratios and class size are not equivalent. At the country level, two countries can have the same teacher–student ratios but very different class sizes because of variations in teaching loads, teaching assignments, the number of classes per student, and other factors. At the school level, the two indicators might differ for a variety of reasons, including the provision of specialized instruction (as with special education), the use of teachers in supervisory and administrative roles, and the contractual classroom obligations of teachers.
5. A basic model of demand and supply where these relationships are introduced appears on p. 563.
6. Chapter 9 sheds light on the class size debate.
7. See pp. 536–47 for a discussion.
8. See pp. 560–62 for a discussion.
9. A limitation of the model is that the effect of class size on the working conditions of teachers is ignored.
10. Note that this relationship makes the choice of quality of teachers and teacher salaries equivalent.
11. A perspective on the role of teacher pay in the labour market for teachers at the international level (The Netherlands, Germany, France, Sweden, England, Australia, New Zealand and the United States) is provided by Waterreus (2001, 2003).

12. Ingersoll (2001c) explores the status of teaching as a profession.
13. This subsection is partly based on Wilson, Floden, and Ferrini-Mundi (2001) and Darling-Hammond (1999b). Other recent summaries of the literature include Allen (2003) and Darling-Hammond and Youngs (2002).
14. The impact of teacher education programmes and certification policies on the supply behaviour of individuals was treated in the previous subsection.
15. A detail account of professional development practices in several countries is provided in OECD (1998).
16. These might include public schools with special management arrangements outside the context of the education bureaucracy's rules. For instance, in the United States, charter schools receive funding based on enrolment, and the school's charter specifies the results for which it will be held accountable. If the school fails to deliver on these results, it receives no more public money.
17. Work conducted by Milanowski (2000) does not provide clear results on the effects of school-based performance award programmes on teacher motivation.
18. See Ministry of Education and Science, Sweden (2003).
19. See Santiago (2002) for a detailed discussion.
20. The role of such agencies is explored in Morrison (1999).
21. This example is provided in Wolter and Denzler (2003).
22. This subsection is based on OECD (2002).
23. A recent survey of upper-secondary schools in 15 countries by the OECD confirms that, as a method to respond to unfilled vacancies, cancelling planned courses comes last in a set of four revealed strategies. The methods used more often, in decreasing order of importance, are to hire a teacher with less than a full qualification, add courses to other teachers' normal teaching hours, and expand the size of some of the classes (OECD, 2003, 2004).
24. See Wilson and Pearson (1993).

References

Allen, Michael (2003), 'Eight questions on teacher preparation: what does the research say?', ECS Teaching Quality Research Reports, Education Commission of the States, Denver.
Angrist, Joshua and Victor Lavy (2001), 'Does teacher training affect pupil learning? Evidence from matched comparisons in Jerusalem public schools', *Journal of Labor Economics*, April, **19**(2), 343–69.
Argys, L.M. and D.I. Reese (1995), 'Unionization and school productivity: a reexamination', *Research in Labor Economics*, **14**, 49–68.
Ashton, P. and L. Crocker (1987), 'Systematic study of planned variations: the essential focus of teacher education reform', *Journal of Teacher Education*, May–June, 2–8.
Bacolod, Marigee P. (2002), 'Do alternative opportunities matter? The role of female labor markets in the decline of teacher supply and teacher quality, 1940–1990', economics working paper no. 02-03-02, Department of Economics, University of California, Irvine.
Ballou, Dale (1996), 'Do public schools hire the best applicants?', *Quarterly Journal of Economics*, **111**(1), 97–134.
Ballou, Dale (2001), 'Pay for performance in public and private schools', *Economics of Education Review*, February, **20**(1), 51–61.
Ballou, Dale and Michael Podgursky (1997), *Teacher Pay and Teacher Quality*, Kalamazoo, MI: W.E. UpJohn Institute for Employment Research.
Ballou, Dale and Michael Podgursky (1998), 'Teacher recruitment and retention in public and private schools', *Journal of Policy Analysis and Management*, **17**(3), 393–417.
Ballou, Dale and Michael Podgursky (2002), 'Returns to seniority among public school teachers', *Journal of Human Resources*, **37**(4), 892–912.
Baugh, William H. and Joe A. Stone (1982), 'Teachers, unions and wages in the 1970s: unionism now pays', *Industrial and Labor Relations Review*, **35**(3), 368–76.
Beaudin, B.Q. (1993), 'Teachers who interrupt their careers: characteristics of those who return to the classroom', *Educational Evaluation and Policy Analysis*, **15**(1), 51–64.

Bee, M. and P. Dolton (1995), 'The remuneration of school teachers: time series and cross section evidence', *Manchester School*, **63**, 11–22.

Benjamin, Dwayne, Morley Gunderson and Craig Riddell (2002), *Labour Market Economics*, 5th edn, Toronto: McGraw-Hill Ryerson.

Boyd, Don, Hamilton Lankford, Susanna Loeb and Jim Wyckoff (2003), 'Understanding teacher labor markets: implications for educational equity', in Margaret L. Plecki and David H. Monk (eds), *School Finance and Teacher Quality: Exploring the Connections*, 2003 Yearbook of the American Education Finance Association, Larchmont, New York: Eye on Education.

Brewer, D. (1996), 'Career paths and quit decisions: evidence from teaching', *Journal of Labor Economics*, **14** (April), 313–39.

Brown, C.A., M.S. Smith and M.K. Stein (1995), 'Linking teacher support to enhanced classroom instruction', paper presented at the annual meeting of the American Educational Research Association, New York.

Cohen, D.K. and H. Hill (1997), 'Instructional policy and classroom performance: the mathematics reform in California', paper presented at the annual meeting of the American Educational Research Association, Chicago, IL.

Cohen, David K., Stephen W. Raudenbush and Deborah L. Ball (2000), 'Resources, instruction, and research', research report, December, Center for the Study of Teaching and Policy, University of Washington.

Corcoran, Sean P., William N. Evans and Robert S. Schwab (2002), 'Changing labor market opportunities for women and the quality of teachers 1957–1992', working paper no. 9180, National Bureau of Economic Research, Cambridge, MA.

Darling-Hammond, Linda (1999a), 'Teacher quality and student achievement: a review of state policy evidence', research report, Center for the Study of Teaching and Policy, University of Washington.

Darling-Hammond, Linda (1999b), 'State teaching policies and student achievement', Teaching Quality Policy Brief, Center for the Study of Teaching and Policy, University of Washington.

Darling-Hammond, Linda and Jon Snyder (2003), 'Organizing schools for student and teacher learning: an examination of resource allocation choices in reforming schools', in Margaret L. Plecki and David H. Monk (eds), *School Finance and Teacher Quality: Exploring the Connections*, 2003 Yearbook of the American Education Finance Association, Larchmont, New York: Eye on Education.

Darling-Hammond, Linda and Peter Youngs (2002), 'Defining "highly qualified teachers": what does "scientifically-based research" actually tell us?', *Educational Researcher*, December, **31**(9), 13–25.

Darling-Hammond, Linda, Barnett Berry and Amy Thorenson (2001), 'Does teacher certification matter? Evaluating the evidence', *Educational Evaluation and Policy Analysis*, **23**(1).

Denton, Frank T., Christine H. Feaver and Byron G. Spencer (1994), 'Teachers and the birth rate: the demographic dynamics of a service population', *Journal of Population Economics*, **7**(3), 307–29.

Dolton, Peter J. (1990), 'The economics of UK teacher supply: the graduate's decision', *The Economic Journal*, **100**, 91–104.

Dolton, Peter J. (1996), 'Modelling the labour market for teachers: some lessons from the UK', *Education Economics*, **4**(2), 187–205.

Dolton, P. and M. Robson (1996), 'Trade union concentration and the determination of wages: the case of teachers in England and Wales', *British Journal of Industrial Relations*, **34**(4), 539–56.

Dolton, Peter J. and Wilbert van der Klaauw (1999), 'The turnover of teachers: a competing risks explanation', *The Review of Economics and Statistics*, August, **81**(3), 543–52.

Dolton, Peter J., Andrew Tremayne and Tsung-Ping Chung (2003), 'The economic cycle and teacher supply', paper commissioned for the 'Attracting, Developing and Retaining Effective Teachers' Activity, Directorate for Education, OECD, Paris.

Eberts, Randall W. (1984), 'Union effects on teacher productivity', *Industrial and Labor Relations Review*, **37**(3), 346–8.

Eberts, Randall W. and Joe A. Stone (1986), 'Teacher unions and the cost of public education', *Economic Inquiry*, October, **24**, 631–43.

Eberts, Randall W. and Joe A. Stone (1987), 'Teacher unions and the productivity of public schools', *Industrial and Labor Relations Review*, April, **40**(3), 354–63.

Eberts, Randall, Kevin Hollenbeck and Joe Stone (2002), 'Teacher performance incentives and student outcomes', *Journal of Human Resources*, **37**(4), 913–27.

Evertson, C., W. Hawley and M. Zlotnik (1985), 'Making a difference in educational quality through teacher education', *Journal of Teacher Education*, **36**(3), 2–12.

Feistritzer, C. Emily and David Chester (2000), *Alternative Teacher Certification: A State-by-State Analysis*, Washington, DC: National Center for Education Information.

Felter, M. (1999), 'High school staff characteristics and mathematics test results', *Education Policy Analysis Archives*, **7**(9).

Ferguson, P. and S.T. Womack (1993), 'The impact of subject matter and education coursework on teaching performance', *Journal of Teacher Education*, **44**, 155–63.

Flyer, Frederick and Sherwin Rosen (1997), 'The new economics of teachers and education', *Journal of Labor Economics*, **15**(1), part 2, S104–S139.

Fuller, E.J. (1999), 'Does Teacher Certification Matter? A Comparison of TAAS Performance in 1997 Between Schools with Low and High Percentages of Certified Teachers', University of Texas at Austin, Charles A. Dana Center, Austin, Texas.

Goldhaber, D.D. and D.J. Brewer (2000), 'Does teacher certification matter? High school teacher certification status and student achievement', *Educational Evaluation and Policy Analysis*, **22**(2), 129–45.

Goldschmidt, Steven M. and Leland E. Stuart (1986), 'The extent and impact of educational policy bargaining', *Industrial and Labor Relations Review*, **39**(3), 350–60.

Grissmer, D.W. and S.N. Kirby (1987), *Teacher Attrition: the Uphill Climb to Staff the Nation's Schools*, Santa Monica, CA: The Rand Corporation.

Guyton, E. and E. Farokhi (1987), 'Relationships among academic performance, basic skills, subject matter knowledge, and teaching skills of teacher education graduates', *Journal of Teacher Education*, **38**, 37–42.

Hanushek, Eric A. (1986), 'The economics of schooling: production and efficiency in public schools', *Journal of Economic Literature*, **24** (September), 1141–77.

Hanushek, Eric A. (1997), 'Assessing the effects of school resources on student performance: an update', *Educational Evaluation and Policy Analysis*, **19**(2), 141–64.

Hanushek, Eric A. (1998), 'Conclusions and controversies about the effectiveness of school resources', *Federal Reserve Bureau of New York Economic Policy Review*, March, **4**(1), 11–28.

Hanushek, Eric A. (2002), 'Publicly provided education', in A.J. Auerbach and M. Feldstein (eds), *Handbook of Public Economics*, vol. 4, Amsterdam: Elsevier Science B.V.

Hanushek, Eric A. (2003), 'The failure of input-based schooling policies', *The Economic Journal*, February, **113**, F64–F98.

Hanushek, Eric A. and Richard R. Pace (1994), 'Understanding entry into the teaching profession', in R.G. Enhrenberg (ed.), *Choices and Consequences: Contemporary Policy Issues in Education*, Ithaca: ILR Press.

Hanushek, Eric A. and Richard R. Pace (1995), 'Who chooses to teach (and why)?', *Economics of Education Review*, **14**(2), 101–17.

Hanushek, Eric A. and Steven G. Rivkin (2003), 'Does public school competition affect teacher quality?', in C.M. Hoxby (ed.), *The Economics of School Choice*, Chicago: University of Chicago Press.

Hanushek, Eric A., John F. Kain and Steven G. Rivkin (1999), 'Do higher salaries buy better teachers?', working paper no. 7082, National Bureau of Economic Research, Cambridge, MA.

Hanushek, Eric A., John F. Kain and Steven G. Rivkin (2001), 'Why public schools lose teachers', working paper no. 8599, National Bureau of Economic Research, Cambridge, MA.

Hawk, P.P., C.R. Coble and M. Swanson (1985), 'Certification: it does matter', *Journal of Teacher Education*, **36**(3), 13–15.

Hoxby, Caroline M. (1994), 'Do private schools provide competition for public schools?', working paper 4978, National Bureau of Economic Research, Cambridge, MA.

Hoxby, Caroline M. (1996), 'How teachers' unions affect education production', *Quarterly Journal of Economics*, **111**(3).

Hoxby, Caroline M. (2000), 'Would school choice change the teaching profession?', working paper 7866, August, National Bureau of Economic Research, Cambridge, MA.

Hoxby, Caroline M. (2003), 'School choice and school productivity (or, could school choice be a tide that lifts all boats?)', in C.M. Hoxby (ed.), *The Economics of School Choice*, Chicago: University of Chicago Press.

Iatarola, P. and L. Stiefel (2003), 'Intradistrict equity of public education resources and performance', *Economics of Education Review*, **22**(1), 69–78.

Ingersoll, Richard M. (1999), 'The problem of underqualified teachers in American secondary schools', *Educational Researcher*, March, **28**(2), 26–37.

Ingersoll, Richard M. (2001a), 'A different approach to solving the teacher shortage problem', policy brief, January, Center for the Study of Teaching and Policy, University of Washington.

Ingersoll, Richard M. (2001b), 'Teacher turnover, teacher shortages, and the organization of schools', research report, January, Center for the Study of Teaching and Policy, University of Washington.

Ingersoll, Richard M. (2001c), 'The status of teaching as a profession', in Jeanne H. Ballantine and Joan Z. Spade (eds), *Schools and Society: A Sociological Approach to Education*, Belmont: Wadsworth.

Ingersoll, Richard M. (2002), 'Out-of-field teaching, educational inequality, and the organization of schools: an exploratory analysis', research report, Center for the Study of Teaching and Policy, University of Washington.

Ingersoll, Richard M. (2003), *Who controls teachers' work? Power and accountability in America's schools*, Cambridge, MA: Harvard University Press.

Jepsen, Christopher and Steven Rivkin (2002), 'What is the trade-off between smaller classes and teacher quality?', working paper 9205, National Bureau of Economic Research, Cambridge, MA.

Kleiner, M. and D. Petree (1988), 'Unionism and licensing of public school teachers: impact on wages and educational output', in R. Freeman and C. Ichiowski (eds), *When Public Sector Workers Unionize*, Chicago: University of Chicago Press, pp. 305–19.

Koretz, Daniel (2002), 'Limitations in the use of achievement tests as measures of educators' productivity', *Journal of Human Resources*, **37**(4), 752–77.

Kurth, M. (1987), 'Teachers' unions and excellence in education: an analysis of the decline in SAT scores', *Journal of Labor Research*, **8**, 351–87.

Lankford, Hamilton, Susanna Loeb and James Wyckoff (2002), 'Teacher sorting and the plight of urban schools: a descriptive analysis', *Educational Evaluation and Policy Analysis*, **24**(1), 37–62.

Merrifield, John (1999), 'Monopsony power in the market for teachers: why teachers should support market-based education reform', *Journal of Labor Research*, Summer, **20**(3), 377–90.

Milanowski, Anthony (2000), 'School-based performance award programs and teacher motivation', *Journal of Education Finance*, **25** (Spring), 517–44.

Ministry of Education and Science, Sweden (2003), Country background report prepared for the 'Attracting, Developing and Retaining Effective Teachers' Activity, Directorate for Education, OECD, Paris.

Mitchell, Douglas E., Linda D. Scott and Duane Covrig (1999), 'Cultural diversity and the teacher labour market: a literature review', research paper, California Educational Research Cooperative, University of California, Riverside.

Monk, D.H. (1994), 'Subject area preparation of secondary mathematics and science teachers and student achievement', *Economics of Education Review*, **13**, 125–45.

Monk, D.H. and J. King (1994), 'Multi-level teacher resource effects on pupil performance in secondary mathematics and science', in R.G. Ehrenberg (ed.), *Contemporary Policy Issues: Choices and Consequences in Education*, Ithaca: ILR Press, pp. 29–58.

Mont, D. and D. Rees (1996), 'The influence of classroom characteristics on high school teacher turnover', *Economic Inquiry*, January, **34**, 152–67.

Morrison, Marlene (1999), 'Temps in teaching: the role of private employment agencies in a changing labour market for teachers', *Journal of Education Policy*, **14**(2), 167–84.

Mulford, Bill (2003), 'School leaders: changing roles and impact on teacher and school effectiveness', paper commissioned for the 'Attracting, Developing and Retaining Effective Teachers' Activity, Directorate for Education, OECD, Paris.

Murnane, Richard J. (1996), 'Staffing the nation's schools with skilled teachers', in E. Hanushek and D. Jorgenson (eds), *Improving America's Schools: The Role of Incentives*, National Research Council, Washington, DC: National Academy Press.

Murnane, Richard J. and D.K. Cohen (1986), 'Merit pay and the evaluation problem: why most merit pay plans fail and a few survive', *Harvard Educational Review*, **56**(1), 379–88.

Murnane, Richard J. and Randall J. Olsen (1989), 'The effects of salaries and opportunity costs on duration in teaching: evidence from Michigan', *The Review of Economics and Statistics*, May, **71**, 347–52.

Murnane, Richard J. and Randall J. Olsen (1990), 'The effects of salaries and opportunity costs on duration in teaching: evidence from North Carolina', *Journal of Human Resources*, Winter, **25**(1), 106–24.

Murnane, Richard J., Judith D. Singer and John B. Willet (1988), 'The career paths of teachers: implications for teacher supply and methodological lessons for research', *Educational Researcher*, August–September, 22–30.

Murnane, Richard J., Judith D. Singer and John B. Willet (1989), 'The influences of salaries and opportunity costs on teachers' career choices: evidence from North Carolina', *Harvard Education Review*, **59**(3), 325–46.

Murnane, Richard J., Judith D. Singer, John B. Willet, J.J. Kemple and Randall J. Olsen (1991), *Who Will Teach? Policies that Matter*, Cambridge, MA: Harvard University Press.

Murphy, P., M. DeArmond and K. Guin (2003), 'A national crisis or localized problems? Getting perspective on the scope and scale of the teacher shortage', *Education Policy Analysis Archives*, **11**(23).

OECD (1998), *Staying Ahead: In-service Training and Teacher Professional Development*, Paris: CERI.

OECD (2001), *Education at a Glance 2001: OECD Indicators, Paris: CERI*.

OECD (2002), 'The teaching workforce: concerns and policy challenges', chapter 3 in *Education Policy Analysis 2002*, Paris.

OECD (2003), *Education at a Glance 2003: OECD Indicators*, Paris.

OECD (2004), *Completing the Foundation for Lifelong Learning: An OECD Survey of Upper Secondary Schools*, Paris.

Rapp, Geoffrey C. (2000), 'Agency and choice in education: does school choice enhance the work effort of teachers?', *Education Economics*, **8**(1), 37–63.

Register, Charles A. and Paul W. Grimes (1991), 'Collective bargaining, teachers, and student achievement', *Journal of Labor Research*, **12**(2), 99–109.

Rice, Jennifer (2003), 'The incidence and impact of teacher professional development: implications for education productivity', in Margaret L. Plecki and David H. Monk (eds), *School Finance and Teacher Quality: Exploring the Connections*, 2003 Yearbook of the American Education Finance Association, Larchmont, New York: Eye on Education.

Rivkin, Steven G., Eric A. Hanushek and John F. Kain (2001), 'Teachers, schools, and academic achievement', working paper 6691 (revised), National Bureau of Economic Research, Cambridge, MA.

Rowan, B., F.S. Chiang and R.J. Miller (1997), 'Using research on employees' performance to study the effects of teachers on students' achievement', *Sociology of Education*, **70**, 256–84.

Santiago, Paulo (2002), 'Teacher demand and supply: improving teaching quality and addressing teacher shortages', OECD education working paper no. 1, OECD, Paris.

Steelman, Lala C., Brian Powell and Robert M. Carini (2000), 'Do teacher unions hinder educational performance? Lessons learned from state SAT and ACT scores', *Harvard Educational Review*, Winter, **70**(4).

Stinebrickner, Todd R. (1998), 'An empirical investigation of teacher attrition', *Economics of Education Review*, **17**(2), 127–36.

Stinebrickner, Todd R. (1999a), 'Using latent variables in dynamic, discrete choice models: the effect of school characteristics on teacher decisions', *Research in Labor Economics*, **18**, 141–76.

Stinebrickner, Todd R. (1999b), 'Estimation of a duration model in the presence of missing data', *The Review of Economics and Statistics*, August, **81**(3), 529–42.

Stinebrickner, Todd R. (1999c), 'The reasons that elementary and high school teachers leave teaching: an analysis of occupational change and departure from the labor force', research report, University of Western Ontario.

Stinebrickner, Todd R. (2001a), 'A dynamic model of teacher labor supply', *Journal of Labor Economics*, January, **19**(1), 196–230.

Stinebrickner, Todd R. (2001b), 'Compensation policies and teacher decisions', *International Economic Review*, **42**(3), 751–80.

Stoddard, Christiana (2003), 'Why has the number of teachers per student risen while teacher quality has declined? The role of changes in the labor market for women', *Journal of Urban Economics*, **53**(3), 458–81.

Temin, Peter (2002), 'Teacher quality and the future of America', working paper no. 8898, National Bureau of Economic Research, Cambridge, MA.

Vandenberghe, V. (2000), 'Leaving teaching in the French-speaking Community of Belgium: a duration analysis', *Education Economics*, **8**(3), 221–39.

Vedder, Richard and Joshua Hall (2000), 'Private school competition and public school teacher salaries', *Journal of Labor Research*, Winter, **21**(1), 161–8.

Vignoles, Anna, Rosalind Levacic, James Walker, Stephen Machin and David Reynolds (2000), 'The relationship between resource allocation and pupil attainment: a review', report 228, Centre for the Economics of Education, London School of Economics and Political Science.

Waterreus, J.M. (2001), *Incentives in Secondary Education: an International Comparison*, Amsterdam: Max Goote Kenniscentrum voor Beroepsonderwijs en Volwasseneneducatie.

Waterreus, J.M. (2003), 'Lessons in teacher pay: studies on incentives and the labor market for teachers', doctoral dissertation, University of Amsterdam.

Wenglinsky, Harold (2000), *How Teaching Matters: Bringing the Classroom Back Into Discussions of Teacher Quality*, Policy Information Center Report, October, Educational Testing Service.

Wiley, D. and B. Yoon (1995), 'Teacher reports of opportunity to learn: analyses of the 1993 California learning assessment system', *Educational Evaluation and Policy Analysis*, **17**(3), 355–70.

Wilson, Andrew and Richard Pearson (1993), 'The problem of teacher shortages', *Education Economics*, **1**(1), 69–75.

Wilson, Suzanne M., Robert E. Floden and Joan Ferrini-Mundy (2001), 'Teacher preparation research: current knowledge, gaps, and recommendations', research report, February, Center for the Study of Teaching and Policy, University of Washington.

Wolter, Stefan C. and Stefan Denzler (2003), 'Wage elasticity of the teacher supply in Switzerland', discussion paper no. 733, Institute for the Study of Labor, Bonn.

Woodbury, Stephen (1985), 'The scope of bargaining and bargaining outcomes in public schools', *Industrial and Labor Relations Review*, **38**(2), 195–210.

Zabalza, A., P. Turnbull and G. Williams (1979), *The Economics of Teacher Supply*, Cambridge: Cambridge University Press.

15 Multi-product cost functions for universities: economies of scale and scope
Elchanan Cohn and Samuel T. Cooper

Introduction

> The structure of knowledge began to change radically in the late nineteenth and early twentieth centuries. Although these changes did not originate in universities and colleges, they were to affect them greatly. . . . In higher education, a different set of wide-ranging changes transformed what was taught, who taught it, and how it was taught. They created a new relationship between research and teaching and affected both the scale and scope of higher education. . . .
> Most of these changes also served to increase economies to scale and to raise the number of faculty members and students that were required to remain viable. . . . In 1897, the median private institution [in the USA] had only 130 students; the median public-sector institution, at 240 students, was not much larger. . . . As we approached the turn of the twenty-first century, the median number of students per institution was about 1600 in the private sector and almost 8200 in the public sector. (Goldin and Katz, 2001, pp. 8–9)

Universities and colleges, wherever they are located, must be considered multi-product enterprises. As Goldin and Katz (2001) point out, 'the typical American university as it emerged at the beginning of the twentieth century was a veritable department store of higher education services' (p. 9). Among the outputs produced in the typical institution of higher education (IHE) are knowledge creation (research) and knowledge dissemination (teaching). Public service is another output. The 'public service function in American higher education is . . . an active, usually nonformal, functional activity based on the scholarship of the university and directed to widely dispersed and varied audiences beyond the campus' (McDowell, 2001, p. 20). Social critique is another output, related to the other outputs (Aitkin, 2001). Additional outputs produced by colleges and universities include theatre, art, athletics, music and other forms of entertainment and enjoyment, but these latter outputs have not yet been incorporated into educational cost analysis. The outputs normally included in IHE cost functions are discussed below.

Teaching
Knowledge dissemination, or teaching, can occur at varying levels of sophistication. The teaching output is often decomposed into undergraduate

instruction and postgraduate instruction (masters or doctoral studies). Furthermore teaching can occur within the boundaries of an increasing number of disciplines. These disciplinary divisions can range from the fine arts to social sciences to the biological and physical sciences – as well as new hybrid disciplines. While teaching technology (that is, pedagogy) has evolved rather slowly, the technology of producing history majors differs from that of producing a bioengineer. Similarly, while instruction in philosophy or classical studies typically occurs in a lecture hall or a library, instruction in physical science and engineering typically combines lectures with experimental laboratories. Some of the studies reviewed below examine the effects of these technological differences on the cost structure of multi-product educational processes.

Research

Knowledge creation, or research, can either be applied or basic, both of vital importance to societal advancement. As McDowell (2001) states, 'new knowledge is the main business of the contemporary land-grant university' (pp. 28–9).[1] And, as Ward (2002) states, 'Good universities must be research led. Research is expensive in terms of resources, and demanding of faculty . . . It requires them to stay on top of their field and students support this with their contribution. A lot of what we learn through the research report process is relevant in our teaching.' With particular respect to basic research, Enz (2002) writes, 'we consider it valuable to learn the basic principles underlying a phenomenon without the necessity of developing an immediate application for those principles' (p. 3). Thus research production within the university setting has both direct and spillover effects on society. Ward (2002) also infers that there may well be complementarities between the production of research and that of teaching. The issue of complementarity is specifically addressed in a number of studies reviewed later in this chapter (for example, Hashimoto and Cohn, 1997; Koshal and Koshal, 1999; Koshal et al., 2001).

Public service

Public service represents a flow of productive resources and activities between the university and the public at large. The goal of this flow is to improve the understanding of social and technical issues, so that society is more prepared to resolve the dilemmas it faces. Unfortunately universities have come under increasing criticism for their failure to produce adequate, relevant and functional public service. According to Wagner (1993), the successful production of public service has become increasingly challenging owing to the evolution that has occurred both within the academy itself and in the public it serves. Wagner suggests that internal change in the structure of the university, current social and technical change, and an increasingly diverse and complex public being served by the academy are among the challenges that are present in successful production of public service. The controversy surrounding public service is not a new one. Lucas (1996), citing Hutchins (1936), states, 'As for the university's service function, Hutchins's settled conclusion was that society would be better advised to look elsewhere or to devise new institutions for the purpose' (pp. 81–2). This aside, numerous writers now view public service as being an element of a social and political contract between the university or college and the public (for example, Wagner, 1993; McDowell, 2001). Consequently, successful production of public service activities is likely to be important to administrators as they seek continued public funding for their programmes.

As stated above, Wagner (1993) suggests that there has been an evolution of the internal structure and mission of universities and colleges. An example of this is the expansion of enrolment opportunities to a larger and more diverse student population. Historically access to teaching, and to some extent research and public service, has been limited to the upper echelons of society. In other words, colleges and universities have been elite clubs that produced (or helped maintain) a social aristocracy. Recent developments, however, have seen the global democratization of higher education. This democratization, in reality, represents a form of product differentiation within the historical context of university production processes. For example, in the United States, the Morrill Land-Grant Act of 1862 'represented a uniquely American approach to democracy – providing for the "vulgarization" of higher education to the "industrial classes" of society' (McDowell, 2001, p. 3). In Australia, there was a similar expansion in enrolments. Just prior to World War II, there were 14 000 university or college students enrolled in higher education programmes; by 1954, the number had increased to 30 000, ten years later there were 80 000, and by 1974 there were 120 000 university students in addition to 100 000 in advanced education (Aitkin, 2001). African universities are no different: 'Each year the number of students increases, and universities are forced to increase their enrolments. For example, according to the AAU, the University of Yaoundé, Cameroon, which opened in 1960 with 5000 students, by 1992 had 45 000 students with facilities planned for 50 000' (Morna, 1995). The state of Texas (USA) 'is aiming to enrol an additional 500 000 college students by 2015' (Gose, 2002, p. A.20).

Given this democratization of higher education, and the resultant growth in teaching production, there is an obvious need for administrators to be concerned with economies of scale and scope. As a result, there has developed a body of literature that examines the multi-product IHE by exploring the cost structure of universities and colleges. Inherent in this analysis is an indirect study of the production functions generating the multiple outputs produced within the university. There are a plethora of assumptions that must be made in conducting this analysis. Many assumptions are related to the definition of output measures, quality of outputs, teaching technology and, in some cases, factor prices. The studies employ a set of analytical tools that are designed to provide objective measures of the cost and production environment present within higher education.

The remainder of this chapter includes sections that provide some international, US and South Carolina data on costs of IHEs, the theoretical nature of the cost and production functions in higher education, data analysis techniques and a detailed review of recent literature related to multi-product educational production. The chapter will conclude with a brief discussion of technological changes occurring as a result of the Internet, and a summary of the state of multiproduct educational research.

Costs of higher education
How much does it cost to provide education to a student enrolled in an IHE? How much is invested each year in higher education? Some preliminary answers to these questions are provided in this section.

Country-level data
Table 15.1 provides data on expenditure per student in tertiary studies for 16 OECD and seven other countries in 1998. The USA spends the most ($19 802) and Uruguay (not in the table) the least ($2081), with mean spending at $9063. Expenditures are higher in IHEs of 'type A and advanced research programmes', which includes universities, than 'type B', which includes non-university tertiary education.

Expenditures per student in all IHEs relative to GDP per capita range from 24% in Uruguay to 401% in Zimbabwe, with the OECD country mean at 44% (OECD, 2001, Table B1.2). United Nations data on public spending on education relative to GNP are shown in Table 15.2 for selected countries. Column 1 provides data on public educational expenditures at all levels as a percentage of GNP, where countries are arrayed according to the UN's Human Development Index (where Norway is first and Sierra Leone is last). The country with the highest percentage is the Republic of Moldova, at 10.6%, and the lowest is Nigeria, at 0.7%, and the mean for the selected countries in Table 15.2 is 5.1%. Column 2 shows expenditure on higher education as a percentage of expenditure on all levels of education, ranging from 4.7% in Luxembourg to 37.1% in Hong Kong. The mean for the selected countries in Table 15.2 is 20.6%. In Column 3 we present expenditure on tertiary public education as a percentage of GNP, which (for the group of countries selected for our analysis) ranges from 0.3% in Korea to more than 2.4% in Canada, with a mean value of 1.1%. Thus, for the

Table 15.1 *Expenditure per student (1998) in US dollars converted using PPPs on public and private institutions, based on full-time equivalents: selected OECD and other countries*

	All	Tertiary type B	Tertiary type A and advanced research programmes
OECD countries			
Australia	11539	8341	12279
Canada	14579	13795	14899
Czech Republic	5584	3191	6326
Finland	7327	5776	7582
France	7226	7636	7113
Germany	9481	5422	10139
Greece[1]	4157	3232	4521
Italy[2]	6295	6283	6295
Japan	9871	7270	10374
Korea	6356	4185	7820
Mexico	3800	NA	3800
Netherlands	10757	7592	10796
Spain	5038	4767	5056
Switzerland[2]	16563	10273	17310
United Kingdom[1]	9699	NA	NA
United States	19802	NA	NA
OECD country mean	9063	–	–
OECD total	11720	–	–
Other countries			
Chile	5897	3121	6565
Israel	10765	8413	11400
Peru	2085	1033	3035
Thailand	6360	4971	6951
Tunisia[2,3]	5136	5753	NA
Uruguay[2]	2081	NA	NA
Zimbabwe	10670	5355	13521

Notes:
NA = not available.
1. Public and government-dependent private institutions only.
2. Public institutions only.
3. Year of reference 1999.

Source: *Education at a Glance: OECD Indicators*, Paris: OECD, 2001.

Table 15.2　Public spending on education, 1995–7, selected countries

Country	Expenditure as % of GNP (all levels) (1)	Expenditure on IHEs as % of all levels (2)	Expenditure on IHEs as % of GNP [(1)*(2)]/100 (3)
Norway	7.7	27.9	2.15
Canada	6.9	35.3	2.44
Australia	5.5	30.5	1.68
United States	5.4	25.2	1.36
Netherlands	5.1	29.3	1.49
Japan	3.6	12.1	0.44
France	6.0	17.9	1.07
United Kingdom	5.3	23.7	1.26
Israel	7.6	18.2	1.38
Korea	3.7	8.0	0.30
Argentina	3.5	19.5	0.68
Poland	7.5	11.1	0.83
Mexico	4.9	17.2	0.84
Russian Federation	3.5	19.3	0.68
Lebanon	2.5	16.2	0.41
China	2.3	15.6	0.36
South Africa	7.6	14.3	1.09
Egypt	4.8	33.3	1.60
India	3.2	13.7	0.44
Congo	6.1	28.0	1.71
Ethiopia	4.0	15.9	0.64

Source:　United Nations Development Program, *Human Development Report*, 2002 data base (URL: http://www.undp.org/hdr 2002/indicator/index_indicators.html).

21 countries shown here, on average, more than 1% of GNP is devoted annually to spending on public higher education.

United States

Table 15.3 provides data on general and educational expenditures by US IHEs per full-time equivalent student in 1995–6. Expenditures per pupil range from $9438 in Arizona to $26 911 in the District of Columbia. They are even higher at US military service academies ($65 775 per student) and self-standing medical schools (for example, in 1999–2000, costs per pupil of educational and general operations at the Medical University of South Carolina were $148 273: SC Commission on Higher Education, 2002). The average cost per student in the USA was $14 096 in 1995–6. Costs in the

Table 15.3   Per pupil expenditures for IHEs in the United States, 1995–6, by control, selected states

State	Public ($)	Private ($)	All ($)
Arizona	10694	2444	9438
California	11265	18812	12726
District of Columbia	32798	26583	26911
Florida	9892	13143	10629
Illinois	10805	22297	14254
Massachusetts	12151	28785	22474
Michigan	13772	11840	13427
Minnesota	13775	13419	13679
New Hampshire	12030	20349	15847
New Jersey	13471	20646	15008
New York	13071	23930	18099
Ohio	12460	15752	13336
Pennsylvania	13613	21713	17240
Rhode Island	12041	19768	16257
South Carolina	12342	11762	12235
Texas	12008	17483	12830
Utah	12571	9686	11731
Vermont	18362	19152	18729
Virginia	10855	14169	11526
Washington	11733	13062	11932
United States (average)	12209	19503	14096

Source: Calculated from the *Digest of Education Statistics*, 2001 edn, Washington: National Center for Education Statistics, US Department of Education, 2002, Tables 202 and 354.

private sector exceeded those in the public sector, on average, by 38%. Although, in some states (for example, Arizona, Hawaii, Idaho, and New Mexico), per student costs in the public sector exceeded those in the private sector one cannot judge the costliness of each sector without controlling for the type of education provided by each sector.

The average size of American IHEs (full-time equivalent students per institution) in 1999–2000 was 2538 (see Table 15.4). The average size of public IHEs was more than four times the average size of private IHEs. Also IHEs' average size varies greatly among the states, ranging from 1188 in Vermont to 5019 in Utah.[2]

South Carolina
We have extensive data on public IHEs in South Carolina, derived from the *Statistical Abstract* of the SC Commission of Higher Education (2002).

Table 15.4   Average size of IHEs in the United States, by control, 1999–2000, selected states (FTE students/number of IHEs)

State	All	Public	Private
Alaska	2019	3447	238
California	3080	7276	905
Colorado	2418	5266	684
District of Columbia	3455	1553	3709
Florida	2703	8789	804
Illinois	2772	5852	1244
Massachusetts	2737	3920	2311
Michigan	3524	7107	1061
Minnesota	1827	2899	913
New Hampshire	1944	2923	1394
New Jersey	4009	5537	1991
New Mexico	1692	2496	415
New York	2468	4840	1574
Ohio	2359	4967	964
Pennsylvania	1802	3906	1083
Rhode Island	4314	8494	3060
South Carolina	2194	3362	865
Texas	3426	5368	1125
Utah	5019	8536	2507
Vermont	1188	2651	727
Virginia	2746	5390	937
Washington	2929	4372	1020
United States (average)	2538	4635	1105

Source: Calculated from the *Digest of Education Statistics*, 2001 edn, Washington: National Center for Education Statistics, US Department of Education, 2002, Tables 202 and 245.

Table 15.5 shows FTE enrolments and total education and general expenditures per FTE student for all public IHEs in South Carolina, for 1999–2000. As noted earlier, the Medical University of South Carolina (MUSC) is very costly, followed by the two doctoral-granting IHEs in the state (USC–Columbia and Clemson). On the whole, the two-year technical colleges are the least costly, with the exception of Williamsburg Tech, with an FTE of only 309 students.

Theoretical considerations related to multi-product enterprises

The cost function
By its very definition, the cost function represents a frontier relationship.

Table 15.5   *Education and general expenditures on public IHEs in South
Carolina, 1999–2000*

	FTE Enrolment	Expenditure per FTE Enrolment
Doctoral granting IHEs		
Clemson	14953	$23443
USC – Columbia	18448	23788
Medical University of SC	2264	148273
Four-year IHEs		
Citadel	3098	13663
Coastal Carolina	4280	10530
College of Charleston	9363	9385
Francis Marion	2494	13384
Lander	2141	11181
SC State	3622	18188
USC – Aiken	2369	11872
USC – Spartanburg	3146	10177
Winthrop	4552	12296
Two-Year IHEs		
USC – Beaufort	591	9867
USC – Lancaster	527	11409
USC – Salkehatchie	426	11851
USC – Sumter	708	10938
USC – Union	162	12903
Selected technical colleges		
Greenville Tech	6068	9230
Midlands Tech	5934	8673
Spartanburg Tech	2180	9053
Trident Tech	6161	7995
Williamsburg Tech	309	17312
York Tech	2173	10084

Source: *Statistical Abstract 2002*, Columbia, SC; SC Commission on Higher Education,
2002.

As such, the theoretical concept has embedded within it a basic assumption, agent optimization. Optimization, however, may differ within the public and not-for-profit sectors when compared to the for-profit sector. In higher education there is some debate as to the appropriateness of the cost minimization assumption (for example, Brinkman, 1990; Ehrenberg, 2000). Ehrenberg (2000) states that university 'administrators are like cookie monsters searching for cookies. They seek out all the resources that they can get their hands on and then devour them' (p. 11). Current developments in the field of higher education, however, suggest that there is an increasing number of for-profit institutions being founded, and an increase in the number of for-profit divisions within traditionally not-for-profit institutions (Borrego, 2001). In addition recent budgetary concerns for public institutions also suggest that university administrators are likely becoming increasingly aware of cost management. Thus environmental forces appear to be such that administrators are increasingly encouraged to optimize the efficiency of resource usage, and thus minimize the costs related to educational production. As a result, the agent optimization assumptions from classical microeconomics are probably reasonably realistic in their application to higher education.

Any discussion related to costs should specify carefully the particular cost concept being considered. As Cohn and Geske (2004) point out, economic costs are generally more inclusive than accounting costs. An important factor differentiating economic costs from accounting costs is the concept of opportunity costs. Opportunity costs represent the value of a forgone opportunity when some other choice is made. Within economic analysis, it is generally assumed that agents will consider this more inclusive nature of costs (that is, accounting costs plus opportunity costs) as they pursue functional optimization.

According to Varian (1984), 'the cost function summarizes all economically relevant information about the technology of the firm' (p. 37). In fact there are several key concepts that are useful in any analysis of a firm's (or school's) cost structure. In particular, economies of scale and scope can reveal considerable information concerning the management of costs within an organization. These concepts expose how costs vary as the levels of outputs vary, or as the firm increases the number of outputs generated within its production process.

Furthermore temporal considerations must be included in any analysis of the production and cost environment. Primarily economists divide costs into either the short-run or the long-run periods. When analysing the production/cost structure of an organization, the short run typically refers to a period of time during which at least one input is fixed. In higher education, for example, the short run may represent the time during which it is not possible to construct a new laboratory or build a new lecture hall. It should be noted that at any particular point in time an organization is operating in the short run. Likewise the long run represents a time of sufficient length that all inputs are variable. Thus the short run is an operational concept, while the long run is a planning concept.

With respect to the analysis of costs, the short run versus long run distinction reveals itself in the fixed costs component of the cost function.

Short-run cost functions contain a fixed cost element, while in the long run there are no fixed costs (that is, all inputs are variable). Thus, in the long run, lecture halls can be built, new distance learning technology installed and additional dormitories can be built to house an expanded enrolment.

A single-output cost function

Based upon this more inclusive cost concept, the cost function defines the minimum cost locus for producing a given level of output, dependent upon the inputs to the production process, input prices and the underlying nature of the production function. Naturally the cost minimization criterion assumes that inputs are, to some extent, substitutes in the production process. Traditionally cost functions have related a single output to the minimum cost of producing the output such that

$$C(y) = f(y; p_i, x_i) \tag{15.1}$$

where $C(y)$ represents the total cost of producing y units of output; p_i represents the price of input i; x_i represents input i, and f represents the functional relationship relating costs to the level of output. The function f is defined by the underlying production technology that is responsible for the rate that inputs are converted into outputs. In fact, the total cost function is the dual of the production function (Henderson and Quandt, 1980).

Economies of scale   Economies of scale exist when there are decreasing long-run average costs. In the context of higher education, economies of scale suggest that the university, or an individual department, experiences lower per unit costs, and diseconomies of scale suggest that the university, or an individual department, experiences higher per unit costs, by increasing its output of a particular product. Economies of scale can result from specialization, bulk purchasing and other factors contributing to increasing returns to scale. For a single-output cost function, one method of estimating economies of scale is to examine the ratio between marginal and average costs. In this context, marginal costs (MC) and average costs (AC) are defined as $MC = dC(y)/dy$ and $AC = C(y)/y$.

If $MC/AC < 1$, then economies of scale are said to exist (Brinkman, 1990), in which case an institution is operating to the left of the minimum point of its average cost curve. Average costs could be reduced by expanding output up to the point where $MC = AC$. Diseconomies of scale can also exist, when $MC/AC > 1$, in which case an institution is operating to the right of the minimum point of its average cost curve. Average costs could be reduced by reducing output up to the point where $MC = AC$.

Example A cursory examination of Table 15.5 suggests that costs per pupil, within each category of institutions in South Carolina, declines when FTE rises. A simple regression model, patterned on equation (15.1) using data for all 32 public IHEs in the state, was developed to test for the existence of economies of scale.[3] The results are shown in the following equation:

$$PPEXP = 12\ 021\ -0.95*FTE + 0.00004*FTE^2 + 138\ 191*MEDICAL$$
$$\quad (13.09)\ (-2.42)\qquad (1.24)\qquad\qquad (64.81)$$
$$\quad + 16\ 324*DOCTORAL + 3194*FOURYR - 182*TWOYR$$
$$\quad\quad (3.17)\qquad\qquad\qquad (3.46)\qquad\qquad (-0.15)$$
$$\quad (N = 32,\ \text{adjusted } R^2 = 0.99,\ F = 721),$$

where *PPEXP* is expenditures per pupil, *FTE* is full-time equivalent enrolment, FTE^2 is the square of *FTE*, *MEDICAL*, *DOCTORAL*, *FOURYR* and *TWOYR* are fixed effects for the IHE types (the technical schools are in the intercept) and the numbers in parentheses are the *t*-ratios of the respective estimated coefficients. All coefficients, except for those of FTE^2 and *TWOYR*, are statistically significant at the 5% level or better. The results show economies of scale up to FTE enrolment of approximately 12000, suggesting that only the two doctoral-granting institutions are sufficiently large to take advantage of economies of scale.

Multiple-output cost functions
The simple case shown above is, in all likelihood, not representative of the production and cost of higher education. Higher education is more appropriately modelled as a multi-product enterprise.[4] As discussed earlier, obvious outputs from the higher education system include undergraduate teaching, graduate teaching, research and public service. As a result, most recent research has used a multi-product model to study the cost structure of higher education. Such a model may be represented by

$$C(\mathbf{y}) = f(\mathbf{y}; \mathbf{p}_i, \mathbf{x}_i). \tag{15.2}$$

In this case, **y** represents a vector of outputs, **p** the input price vector and **x** the vector of inputs used in the process of producing the **y** outputs. Again, *f* represents the underlying technological relationship within the production process.

Multiple-product cost functions are modelled on the seminal work of Baumol *et al.* (1982) and Mayo (1984). Three primary functional forms have been described in the literature to estimate such cost functions: qua-

dratic, translog and constant elasticity of substitution (CES). As Baumol
et al. point out, pure theory does not provide the foundation upon which
one might decide which functional form is superior. Operationally,
however, there are important differences among the methods. For example,
in some cases the translog method does not permit any of the variables to
take the value of zero.[5] Although the Box–Cox method may be used in such
a situation, the Box–Cox transformations may make the analysis unnecessarily complicated. Furthermore, in some cases, it is possible that convergence will not be obtained in the process of estimating a maximum
likelihood function. Because zeros are present in many data sets, it is not
surprising that most authors have selected to employ the quadratic form
used by Mayo (1984) and Cohn *et al.* (1989), that is, the flexible fixed cost
quadratic cost function.

A flexible fixed cost quadratic function (FFCQ) has the following general
form:

$$C = a_0 + \sum_i a_i F_i + \sum_i b_i Y_i + (1/2) \sum_i \sum_j c_{ij} Y_i Y_j + v, \qquad (15.3)$$

where a_0, the a_i, the b_i and the c_{ij} coefficients are real numbers, v is an error
term, Y_i is the ith output (out of n outputs), and the F_i are dummy variables
such that $F_i = 1$ when output i is positive and $F_i = 0$ otherwise.

The corresponding translog function takes the following form:

$$\log C = a_0 + \sum_i b_i \log(Y_i) + \sum_{i \leq j} c_{ij} \log(Y_i) \log Y_j + v. \qquad (15.4)$$

As deGroot *et al.* (1991) point out, dummy variables can be added to the
equation to account for a variety of factors not included in the basic model.

Finally, the CES function takes the following general form:

$$C = a_0 + \left[\sum_i b_i Y_{ij}^{\delta} \right]^{\rho} + v, \qquad (15.5)$$

where δ and ρ are parameters to be estimated by a nonlinear least squares
method.

Economies of scale   There is no simple analogy to the average cost function in a multi-product environment. But one can estimate ray economies
of scale and product-specific economies of scale. Baumol *et al.* (1982) relate
ray economies of scale in a multi-product firm to economies of scale in a
single-output firm. Ray economies of scale assume that the composition of
output remains constant, while its scale is allowed to expand.

Assume that there are three outputs, i, j and k. Estimating equations

(15.3, 15.4 or 15.5) permits an analysis of economies of both scale and scope. Following Baumol *et al.* (1982), we first define the average incremental cost of the product Y_i as

$$AIC_i = \frac{C(Y_i, Y_j, Y_k) - C(0, Y_j, Y_k)}{Y_i}, \tag{15.6}$$

where $C(Y_i, Y_j, Y_k)$ represents the total costs of producing Y_i units of product i, Y_j units of product j, and Y_k units of product k, and where $C(0, Y_j, Y_k)$ is total cost when the *i*th output is zero. The average incremental costs for products j and k are estimated in an analogous manner. Ray (overall) economies of scale may exist when the quantities of the products are increased proportionally. Ray economies of scale are defined by

$$S_R = \frac{C(Y_i, Y_j, Y_k)}{Y_i MC_i + Y_j MC_j + Y_k MC_k}, \tag{15.7}$$

where $MC_i = \partial C / \partial Y_i$ is the marginal cost of producing product i. Ray economies of scale are said to exist if $S_R > 1$, and ray diseconomies of scale are said to exist if $S_R < 1$.

It is possible that a multi-product enterprise will expand output non-proportionally, in which case ray economies of scale are not applicable. In such an environment, estimation of product-specific economies of scale will allow the analysts to gain a better understanding of the organization's cost structure. 'The magnitude of the multiproduct firm's operations may change through variation in the output of one product, holding the quantities of other products constant. Therefore, the product-specific expansion in a product set becomes an important feature of multiproduct cost concepts' (Dundar and Lewis, 1995, p. 122). To estimate product-specific scale economies, we compute

$$S_i = \frac{AIC_i}{MC_i}. \tag{15.8}$$

When $S_i > 1$, economies of scale are said to exist for the product i, and when $S_i < 1$, diseconomies of scale are said to exist for the product i.

Economies of scope   Global economies of scope are said to exist when the total cost of producing multiple outputs in conjunction with each other is less than the total cost of producing each output separately. In other words, if a university department produces three outputs, namely undergraduate courses, graduate course and research, economies of scope suggest that the total cost will be less than if three departments are established to produce each output separately.

Following Dundar and Lewis (1995), economies of scope are divided into the cases of global and product-specific economies of scope. The degree of global economies of scope in the production of all products is computed from

$$SG_G = \frac{C(Y_i,0,0) + C(0,Y_j,0) + C(0,0,Y_k) - C(Y_i,Y_j,Y_k)}{C(Y_i,Y_j,Y_k)}. \qquad (15.9)$$

Global economies of scope are said to exist if $SC_G > 0$, and global diseconomies of scope are said to exist if $SC_G < 0$. More generally, according to Dundar and Lewis (1995), *global* economies of scope exist when

$$C(y) \leq C(y_{N-t}) + C(y_t), \qquad (15.10)$$

where $C(y_t)$ is the cost of producing an output bundle t and $C(y_{N-t})$ is the cost of producing all other outputs other than the ones in bundle t. In contrast, *product-specific* economies of scope exist when

$$SC_i = [C(y_i) + C(y_{N-i}) - C(y)] / C(y) \geq 0, \qquad (15.11)$$

where $C(y_{N-i})$ represents the costs of producing all outputs jointly except the ith one. If $SC_i \geq 0$, there are complementarities from producing output i in conjunction with the other outputs. Another (equivalent) way to view product-specific economies of scope is by computing

$$SC_i = \frac{C(Y_i,0,0) + C(0,Y_j,Y_k) - C(Y_i,Y_j,Y_k)}{C(Y_i,Y_j,Y_k)}. \qquad (15.12)$$

Again, product-specific economies of scope associated with product i are said to exist if $SC_i \geq 0$.

Waldman and Jensen (1998) suggest several potential factors that create economies of scope. A primary factor is the sharing of a single input in a production process. For example, in higher education, a fixed support staff may help faculty with producing undergraduate and graduate education. Likewise lecture halls may go unused in the afternoons by undergraduate classes and are thus available for graduate classes. According to Waldman and Jensen, 'If demand for a single product is not great enough to exhaust the economies of scale, the firm may look for other products that can utilize the same fixed factor of production' (p. 108). In the multi-product environment, estimation of global and product-specific economies of scope is useful, the better to understand the relationship between the cost structure and expansion of a given output.

Assumptions concerning the cost function
As is the case with any economic analysis, application of theoretical concepts requires that certain basic assumptions be made. Following the work of Getz *et al.* (1991), certain assumptions are often made when estimating multi-product cost functions for higher education.

Homogeneous outputs   This assumption implies that all institutions have similar objectives and produce the same quality of output. According to Getz *et al.*, this assumption may be reasonably accurate for some categories of institutions, but not for all institutions across categories. For example, they suggest that the homogeneity assumption is workable when considering two-year colleges. In their opinion, these institutions produce a similar output of annual undergraduate enrolments. Large research universities, however, may not produce outputs that are considered homogenous; this is especially true where some institutions have on-campus medical schools and others do not.

Non-profit status   Historically nearly all colleges and universities have operated as non-profit enterprises. This brings into question the typical assumption of profit maximization or cost minimization. Recent developments related to legislated accountability of resource usage by public institutions has, in all likelihood, encouraged educational administrators to behave as cost minimizers. Private institutions also are being forced to manage their affairs optimally owing to increased competition for student enrolments by both non-profit and for-profit colleges and universities.

Technology   '[S]tatistical cost studies of higher education scale economies implicitly assume that the technology and factor prices faced by each institution in the sample were similar when each selected its production methods' (Getz *et al.*, 1991, p. 204). In other words, if institutions adopted different technologies based on the time when they began producing educational outputs, statistical analysis might be unable to distinguish between scale economies and a shift in the long-run cost curves. Given that technological change in educational production has been rather stagnant, at least until recently, this assumption should not hinder estimation of scale economies in higher education.

Public ownership   Many institutions of higher education are publicly owned and financed. This institutional arrangement provides incentives that encourage all revenues to be spent out of fear of losing unspent funds.

Long-run equilibrium   The use of cross-sectional data to estimate the long-run scale effects assumes that each institution is operating at an output level associated with the minimum long-run average cost. To the extent that a college or university is temporarily experiencing above or below-normal enrolments, the cross-sectional data are not representative of long-run equilibrium (ibid., pp. 203–5).

While failure to satisfy the above assumptions would throw doubt on the validity of statistical results of multi-product cost studies, there have been considerable advances in the techniques employed in this type of research. The studies that are reviewed later in this chapter will reveal an evolutionary path in which many of the criticisms pointed out above have been directly addressed. These statistical advances, along with the changed 'market structure' of higher education, allow for greater confidence in the research results.

Empirical considerations

Theoretical considerations generally provide guidance for data analysis. In cost analysis, however, the transition from theory to statistical analysis is complicated. In part, the difficulties associated with cost analysis derive from the fact that cost functions are dependent on the underlying production function. It is also the case that rather simple production functions can give rise to complex cost functions. With respect to educational production, the process is further complicated by the lack of understanding of the processes of educational production.

In addition, the variables to be included in an educational cost function are difficult to measure. Educational output is especially troublesome to quantify. It is generally assumed that universities produce increases in human capital through the generation and transmission of general and specific knowledge. Attempts to measure the contribution of instruction to the increase in knowledge among students have been proxied by numerous quantifiable variables. One approach is to use a standardized test to measure value added to the student's knowledge base. This approach, however, is not generally available at the university level owing to the absence of standardized tests capable of determining knowledge gain across disciplines (for example, art, biology, sociology, philosophy) (Nelson and Hevert, 1992).

In the absence of such standardized exams, other proxy measures are generally used to quantify educational output. Frequently analysts use some measures of enrolments at the university or department. Numerous variations on enrolments have been used in cost modelling. These include student head count for the entire university, full-time equivalent student enrolment and credit hours taught within individual university departments.

Further if it is accepted that teaching different levels of students represents multiple outputs, a multi-product cost function may include more than one measure of student enrolment, for example lower-level undergraduates, upper-level undergraduates and postgraduate enrolments. Such distinctions among levels of student enrolments are common in recent studies.

Perhaps even more perplexing is the measurement of the research output. Analysts have accounted for research output either by including in the cost function the inputs into the research process (assuming that the research input is correlated to the research output), or by offering a more explicit measure of the research output. A typical proxy of research input is the amount of funds spent on research or the hours that faculty devote to the research activity (Lloyd *et al.*, 1993). Numerous studies have used the input measures in the estimation of multi-product cost functions in higher education (for example, Verry and Layard, 1975; Cohn *et al.*, 1989; Nelson and Hevert, 1992; Johnes, 1997). Other studies, however, have attempted to construct an output index for university research activities (for example, deGroot *et al.*, 1991; Lewis and Dundar, 1995; Dundar and Lewis, 1995). Usually the research output index will include some measure of the number of articles, books, conference papers, presentations, works of art or similar productive outputs generated by a particular department or university.

Most analysts also recognize public service as an important output from the higher education production process. It is difficult, however, to obtain reliable data for public service activities. As a result, most analysts omit public service from their cost functions. Because input prices can alter the output mix, it is appropriate to include some input prices in the cost function. Since IHEs are a labour-intensive enterprise, faculty salaries are probably the most important input price. Several studies have incorporated faculty salaries into their multiple-output cost functions (for example, Cohn *et al.*, 1989). Ideally separate factor wages for undergraduates, graduates and research facilities would be appropriate, if a bidirectional relation between mean faculty compensation and output mix might arise. When input prices are entered into the FFCQ function in the same manner as outputs, the linear homogeneity property of the cost function with respect to factor prices may be sacrificed. When only one input price is included, however, the issue is moot (Friedlaender *et al.*, 1983).

Review of empirical studies

Prior to the mid-1980s, most empirical research into the cost structure of higher education used rather simple methods of estimating marginal and average costs (*MC* and *AC*). As discussed above, the ratio *MC*/*AC* was then calculated to determine the existence of economies of scale. In addition, statistical modelling prior to the mid-1980s generally took the form of a single-output regression analysis (Brinkman, 1989). The review that follows is temporally structured, with earlier studies being reviewed first. This will allow the reader to gain an understanding of the evolutionary advances in multi-product cost modelling (for example, use of more advanced statistical or programming techniques, and the inclusion of quality and structural variables in the analysis).

The best known early cost study to consider multiple outputs is Verry and Layard (1975). Verry and Layard employ cross-sectional data from all universities in the United Kingdom (with the exceptions of Cambridge and Oxford) for the 1968/9 period. Of particular interest is the fact that the authors perform an analysis such that marginal cost is estimated for a variety of disciplines. This analysis is expanded to survey the results on disciplinary costs with respect specifically to undergraduate versus postgraduate educational production. The Verry and Layard study suggests that marginal costs are higher for postgraduate students than for undergraduate students. They also find that marginal cost increases progressively through the following programmes: arts, social sciences, mathematics, physical science, biological science and engineering (ranked from lowest to highest cost). This, in the words of Verry and Layard, is due to the increase in 'hardware intensity' necessary to produce instruction in these disciplines.

Although it does not cover Verry and Layard's study, Brinkman (1990) provides a detailed survey of higher education cost functions. In this article, Brinkman not only reviews the basic theoretical considerations related to cost functions, but also discusses how basic production and cost theory from microeconomics imperfectly fits the analysis of higher education. Additionally Brinkman discusses the evolution of cost studies, beginning with Stevens and Elliot's (1925) analysis of unit costs in higher education, and reviews more than 40 studies, the most recent being Cohn *et al.* (1989). Since the purpose of this study is to review multiple-output cost studies, we confine the analysis to recent studies not covered in Brinkman, with the exception of Cohn *et al.*

To the best of our knowledge, the first multi-product cost analysis in education was Jimenez (1986), reporting on Paraguayan and Bolivian primary and secondary schools. Cohn *et al.* (1989), however, was the first study to apply a multi-product cost function to higher education. In their analysis, Cohn *et al.* use full-time equivalent undergraduate enrolment, full-time equivalent graduate enrolment and the dollar value of grants for research received by an IHE as measures of educational outputs. Their sample consists of 1195 public institutions and 692 private institutions in the United States, for the academic year 1981–2. Using an FFCQ cost function, they find that the parameter estimates differ significantly between the public and private institutions, suggesting that the underlying cost structures are different between the two types of institutions. Furthermore their findings suggest that there are ray economies of scale for private institutions up to 600% of mean output, while public institutions exhaust ray economies around mean output. Product-specific scale economies for undergraduate enrolments are not found in the private institutions, and in the public institutions are found only at very low enrolment levels. For graduate enrolments, Cohn *et al.* found that product-specific scale economies exist even at high enrolment levels in the public institutions, but not at all in the private setting. Also they found evidence that product-specific economies exist for research in the public sector up to 200% of mean output, and then reappear at 500% of mean output. They observed economies of scope for all output levels in both sectors, with the exception of output levels below 150% of the output means for the public sector.

The evidence suggests that research and teaching are complements in production (ibid., p. 288). To illustrate the practical application of the results, they show that, when all outputs are at 300% of their respective means, the cost of production at public speciality IHEs is 8.4% higher than at IHEs that provide multiple outputs. The comparable figure for private IHEs is 33.2%. Moreover Cohn *et al.* compare results from the multiple-output cost equations to analogous results from a single-output equation in which the output is the sum of undergraduate and graduate enrolments. In the single-output model, both sectors experience scale economies, with minimum costs occurring at the public sector when enrolment is 2110 and in the private sector when enrolment is 5120. These results are fundamentally different from those obtained from the multi-output case, strongly suggesting that multiple-output cost functions should be employed whenever possible.

In an analysis of 147 doctorate-granting IHEs in the USA, deGroot *et al.* (1991), employing 1983 data, seek to gain an understanding of how sensitive parameter estimates are to changes in output measures. Of particular interest is how an explicit measure of research output (that is, number of publications) affects estimation of the cost function compared to the input-related variable of the dollar value of research grants used by Cohn *et al.* (1989). Also deGroot *et al.* include information on programme quality and state regulations in their estimated cost functions. Their basic model employs a translog specification that includes undergraduate instruction, graduate instruction and research production as the output measures of doctorate-granting institutions.

Two dummy variables that indicate whether the university contains a medical school and whether there is private ownership of the institution are also included in the deGroot *et al.* study. General findings indicate economies of scale at the mean output, economies of scope between undergraduate and graduate instruction, and that private versus public ownership does not play a significant role in the institutions' cost structure. This latter finding is somewhat different from that of Cohn *et al.* (1989) in which there did appear to be a difference between private and public control. This difference in findings between the two studies may be due to the fact that Cohn *et al.* used a larger and more heterogeneous data set. Unlike Cohn *et al.*, deGroot *et al.* do not find evidence of economies of scope between graduate teaching and research (this also differs from Cohn *et al.*, where research and teaching were found to be complements in production). Another novel aspect of the deGroot *et al.* study is the sensitivity analysis that they conduct. Five different models are estimated. In each case, the major conclusions of the study are validated.

If expansion of output, especially instructional output, is achieved by expanding average class size, educational quality may suffer. The benefits from the existence of economies of scale and scope in IHEs, as shown above, might be misleading. One study that specifically examines the effect of class size on economies of scale is Nelson and Hevert (1992). Using data from 1979–83 for 31 academic departments at the University of Delaware, Nelson and Hevert estimate a translog cost function to examine the effect of class size on costs. They find that economies of scale exist only when class size is allowed to increase. They conclude that failure to include class size as an argument in the cost function results in specification bias, and thus an overestimate of scale economies. Unfortunately their work does not reveal if there are negative quality effects that result from increasing class size. Also holding class size constant may not be sensible, because an important advantage of large-size IHEs is that you have enough students to use classroom space, graduate students and instructors' talents more efficiently precisely by increasing class size, without reducing instructional quality. Finally Nelson and Hevert's sample is from a single institution, from which it is inappropriate to generalize to the USA or other countries.

Lloyd *et al.* (1993) look at the way in which amalgamation of universities and colleges affects the market structure and relative costs of producing multiple outputs in Australia. In 1989, the Australian government created a unified national university system. This unification resulted from the government's desire to eliminate the high unit costs associated with small institutions, and also to ensure that all institutions have a broad educational profile. As a result, the minimum size of institutions under the unified system was set at 5000–8000 students (p. 1082). The authors recognize that Australian universities produce both teaching and research outputs. They point out that there is no standardized method of measuring research in Australia, and as a result focus primarily on teaching production. Given that teaching outputs are not homogenous (that is, they range from undergraduate to PhD and vary with respect to teaching technology), Lloyd *et al.* define ten separate teaching outputs produced by the universities.

Using an FFCQ cost function for 69 Australian IHEs in 1988, Lloyd *et al.* estimate cost functions in an effort to approximate economies of scale and scope under the unified system. The amalgamation of colleges and universities may result in both types of economies. As a result, the following metric was developed to provide an estimate of cost savings:

$$S_m = [C(y) - \sum C(\mathbf{y}^\mathrm{j})] / \sum C(\mathbf{y}^\mathrm{j}), \quad y = \sum_j \mathbf{y}^\mathrm{j}. \qquad (15.13)$$

In equation (15.13), $\mathbf{y}^\mathrm{j}$ represents a vector of outputs produced by the *j*th college or university prior to amalgamation, $C(y^j)$ is the costs of producing the multiple outputs in the *j*th institution and $C(y)$ is the cost of producing the vector $\mathbf{y}$ in the amalgamated institution. Thus S_m provides a measure of costs savings (or dissavings) after merger of two or more Australian institutions: 'It combines the effects of economies of both scale and scope' (Lloyd *et al.*, 1993, p. 1085). Findings suggest that all amalgamations considered resulted in cost savings. In general the economies of amalgamation were small for the smallest institutions relative to the savings for larger institutions. Finally Lloyd *et al.* provide a decomposition of S_m in an effort to discern the individual effects of economies of scale versus economies of scope. The findings suggest that economies of scale are much more important than economies of scope as a general rule: 'For amalgamations involving a large or extra large university (with another university or college) diseconomies of scope always occur' (ibid., p. 1087).

Lewis and Dundar (1995) recognize the importance of controlling for quality in their analysis of higher education costs in Turkey. Data were collected from all of Turkey's 28 universities, which include 186 college faculties in 1991–2. Four outputs are measured: undergraduate enrolment, masters enrolment, doctoral enrolment and research productivity (measured by number of publications). Although they faced considerable data limitations, Lewis and Dundar collected entrance examination scores to proxy institutional quality. It is assumed that higher entrance scores represent a higher quality of student input into the educational production process, and that these better students apply to the universities that are perceived to be superior. Lewis and Dundar cite work by Gedikogulu (1985) indicating that, 'when Turkish universities had the option to make decisions about their numbers of students admitted during the 1970s, they decided to reduce the number of students due to concerns about declining quality' (Lewis and Dundar, 1995, p. 144).

Unfortunately the collection of entrance examination scores proved so problematic that they were omitted from the estimated model. Employing an FFCQ cost function, Lewis and Dundar find that average incremental and marginal costs tend to be higher for graduate students and research, and lower for undergraduate instruction. The findings also suggest that, of the three disciplinary areas reviewed (social sciences, engineering and health sciences), social sciences have the lowest cost of production and health sciences have the highest. The authors find that there are economies of scope associated with the multi-product production of instruction and research across the three disciplinary fields analysed in this study. Surprisingly, however, there appears to be little cost complementarity between undergraduate and graduate education in Turkey (ibid., pp. 153–4).

Dundar and Lewis (1995) explore the multi-product production process in American research universities. Data for 119 departments in 18 public research universities in the USA, for the academic year 1985–6, are employed. All but one of the 18 universities were among the top 30 public research universities in the nation. As with other studies, Dundar and Lewis focus on the outputs of teaching and research. Specifically the outputs used in the study include undergraduate student credit hours, master student credit hours, doctoral student credit hours and the number of publications. In an effort to produce greater detail in their analysis, the authors estimate a series of FFCQ cost functions that include departmental dummy variables and a proxy for quality. Similar to Lewis and Dundar (1995), the departmental variables identify social sciences, physical sciences and engineering sciences departments. The quality proxy is a reputational rating of the departments. The general findings suggest that economies of scale do exist across departments in the production of graduate and undergraduate teaching, as well as research. Dundar and Lewis do not find, however, a significant relationship between programme quality and departmental costs: 'The insignificance of output quality effects on costs . . . likely result from the relatively homogenous nature of [the] subsample of public research universities' (Dundar and Lewis, 1995, p. 127).

Other interesting findings from Dundar and Lewis (1995) include evidence that product-specific economies of scope exist for all three academic department types. Additionally they simulate various production levels that range from 10% to 400% of mean output for the production processes reviewed. With respect to ray economies of scale, the authors find that such economies are present at output levels below the mean, but that ray diseconomies appear around 300% of mean output. In the social sciences, product-specific economies exist at all levels of output examined. In the physical sciences, however, the production of doctoral teaching suffers from product-specific diseconomies of scale if output exceeds 200% of mean production. Product-specific economies of scale exist for all other outputs produced in the departmental environment. In engineering departments, the authors find that product-specific economies of scale exist at all output levels examined for only masters-level teaching and research. Diseconomies are present in undergraduate teaching in engineering at lower levels of output, and economies appear once output has reached 200% of mean (ibid., pp. 138–41). Similar to Cohn *et al.* (1989), Dundar and Lewis find that, in general, there are cost complementarities when joint production of teaching and research occurs.

Similar to Verry and Layard (1975), Johnes (1997) explores the cost structure and industrial organization of multi-product British IHEs. The sample includes 99 British and Northern Irish universities for the academic year 1994–5. The outputs considered are undergraduate student load in the arts and in the sciences, graduate student load and the value of research grants. Johnes uses a CES cost function for this analysis. Universities are categorized into three classes, based upon metrics representing the relative importance of the four outputs produced across the 99 universities. He finds product-specific economies of scale for all outputs except for science undergraduates in all university types. Ray economies of scale are found for two university classes, but not in universities where only 25% of students study art (Johnes, 1997, p. 731). Unlike what Cohn *et al.* (1989) and Dundar and Lewis (1995) find for IHEs in the USA, Johnes (1997) finds, that in the British system, 'Economies of scope are exhausted in all types of institutions considered . . . providing little evidence to support the commonly held belief that synergies are endemic in the higher education system' (ibid., p. 731).

Johnes also performs a tabu search in an effort to determine the most efficient industrial structure for British higher education production.[6] The tabu analysis reported in the 1997 article suggests that the number of universities currently producing educational outputs in the UK is close to optimal. However there does appear to be room for reallocation of activities and resources within the system to maximize efficiency. First, given the teaching outputs of the universities currently operating, a concentration of research activities to approximately 40 institutions provides a cost savings of 7.5%. When the tabu analysis allows for a change in the number of IHEs, Johnes finds that there is the potential for up to 39% cost savings by reallocating production activities and reducing the number of IHEs from 99 to 96. In addition there would be a greater concentration of production within the 96 institutions. Accordingly the optimal outcome of the tabu would have each institution producing only two or three of the four outputs defined in the analysis (ibid., pp. 732–3).

In a subsequent reanalysis, Johnes (1998) points out that the solution reported above 'is a local, but not the global optimum' (p. 1275). His revised findings 'alter [the] earlier conclusions that costs would rise, *ceteris paribus*, if research were to be concentrated in fewer than 40 institutions. They also suggest that the scope for mergers is greater than [his] earlier results implied. However, the main thrust of the paper – that cost savings would result from a more concentrated allocation than exists at present, especially of research and postgraduate tuition – remains unaffected' (ibid.).

In a multi-product cost study of Japanese private universities, Hashimoto and Cohn (1997) estimate an FFCQ function for 94 institutions for 1991. They focus on three specific outputs: number of undergraduate students, graduate students and research grant funding. Among the findings are that marginal costs for graduate students greatly exceed those of undergraduates. Following the recommendation of Jimenez (1986), Hashimoto and Cohn include faculty salaries to proxy factor prices related to educational production. When faculty salaries are included in the model, the parameter estimates suggest that graduate teaching and research, as well as undergraduate teaching and research, are complements in the production process (although the parameters are not statistically significant at the usual levels). In addition the research indicates that there are product-specific economies of scale for undergraduate and graduate students in small universities, although the study does not suggest that these economies exist at or above mean output (Hashimoto and Cohn, 1997, p. 112). The authors also find evidence that there are global and specific economies of scope for the range of data examined in their study. In fact, 'when all outputs are 300% of their respective means, the cost of production at private Japanese universities who specialize in only one output . . . is 23.3% higher than that for a university producing all three outputs' (ibid., p. 113). They find that the marginal cost of graduate enrolment is *50 times as large* as the marginal cost of undergraduate enrolment.

In a detailed analysis of comprehensive universities in the USA, Koshal and Koshal (1999) model the effect of output quality, public versus private ownership, faculty salaries and class size in their analysis. In addition the authors specifically test their results for the existence of heteroscedasticity. The study uses data for 1990–91 for 158 private and 171 public comprehensive universities. Koshal and Koshal specify the number of full-time equivalent (FTE) undergraduate students, the number of FTE graduate students and the dollar value of research activities as the three outputs produced by the universities. Estimation of the multiple-output FFCQ models yields a plethora of interesting results. However, for the equation that contains both public and private IHEs, Ramsey's RESET test suggests that the results are inefficient because of heteroscedasticity. The authors then estimate separate models for private and public institutions, and find that the equations are homoscedastic. As a result, the private–public comparison becomes the focus of the study.

One of the findings is that the marginal costs (MC) for graduate FTEs is greater than the MC of undergraduate FTEs for private institutions, regardless of output level. Public universities, on the other hand, experience higher MC for graduate FTEs only at or beyond the mean value of output. The study also suggests that the MC is greater for private institutions for both teaching outputs when compared to the public institutions. In fact the MC of graduate FTEs for private universities is double that of the public universities. Both types of institutions experience increasing MC for research as output expands (Koshal and Koshal, 1999, pp. 272–4). The authors also calculate the cross-marginal cost (CMC) at the mean value of outputs.[7] The CMCs suggest an insignificant cost complementarity between graduate FTEs and research output at private institutions. For public institutions, the CMCs suggest substitutability between both undergraduate FTEs and research and graduate FTEs and research (ibid., p. 274). In addition, ray economies of scale are found to exist for comprehensive universities. Private institutions appear to experience product-specific economies of scale for research, while public institutions exhibit constant product-specific returns to scale for research. Private universities also experience global economies of scope at all output levels except at 300% of mean production (ibid., p. 276).

In a study similar to their 1999 work, Koshal and Koshal, with Gupta (2001) explore the multi-product nature of bible colleges. Using data for 184 bible colleges located in the USA, for 1994–5, multi-product FFCQ functions are estimated in an effort to gain an understanding of efficient production in these speciality colleges. Unlike Koshal and Koshal (1999), the bible college study does not contain a measure of academic quality. Undergraduate and graduate FTEs are the two outputs modelled in the study. The estimation of a simple model suggests, as do most studies, that economies of scale exist for the production of both undergraduate and graduate teaching. Koshal *et al.* then expand the model by introducing variables that control for faculty salary, class size, dummies for the three largest religious schools and a set of interaction terms. Before inclusion of these variables, the results of the study were statistically inefficient owing to heteroscedasticity. The introduction of these variables, however, resulted in statistically efficient parameter estimates. The findings suggest that the MC of undergraduate teaching is less than that of graduate teaching and that MC for undergraduate FTE declines as output increases. MC for graduate teaching, on the other hand, increases as teaching output increases. In general economies of scale exist for bible colleges, although product–specific economies exist only at and beyond the mean output. In addition global economies of scope exist for all output levels examined in the study.

The final study to be reviewed here is by Izadi *et al.* (2002). The authors estimate a frontier CES multi-product cost function for 99 British universities, 1994–5 (the same data as in Johnes 1997, described above). While estimation of frontier functions has been attempted before (for example, Cooper and Cohn, 1997; Worthington, 2001), the authors argue that they are the first to estimate a frontier non-linear multi-product cost function. The authors estimate the cost function with and without the frontier procedure and derive estimates of average incremental costs, ray and product-specific economies of scale and global economies of scope. They also estimate the degree of technical inefficiency for each IHE in the sample. Universities are divided into three classes, as in Johnes (1997).

Izadi *et al.* (2002) conclude that the frontier method 'provides a better model of the data than does the non-linear maximum likelihood approach' (p. 67). Average incremental costs 'are broadly in line with earlier estimates' (ibid.). Concerning economies of scale, the authors find nearly constant costs for undergraduates, very strong economies of scale for postgraduates and considerable economies of scale for research (though far less so than for postgraduates). The coefficient of ray economies of scale is very close to unity for all university types. Since the coefficient of economies of scope is negative for all university types, the authors conclude that economies of scope are absent.

The most efficient (or least inefficient) British university is Oxford, followed by Sheffield, Cambridge and De Montfort. The least efficient universities are Lampeter, Guildhall, Anglia Polytechnic University and (interestingly) London Business School. The London School of Economics, one of the least efficient IHEs, is ranked 87.

Some extensions

Quality of output
One issue that has not received sufficient attention is output quality. This is particularly relevant for teaching outputs, but is also relevant for research output when research funds or sum of publications (without regard to quality) are employed as proxies. Although Koshal and Koshal (1995) employ a single-output production function, which, as we have explained,

can provide incorrect results, they specifically explore the issue of quality and economies of scale in higher education. This study examines 204 PhD-granting institutions in the USA for the academic year 1990–91. The 204 institutions are subdivided into four categories, as defined by the Carnegie Foundation, reflecting the institutions' focus on research activities. Group I institutions are committed to graduate education, place significant focus on research and grant 50 or more PhDs annually. Group IV institutions, at the other end of the scale, focus less on research and grant 20 or more PhD degrees in one field or 10 PhD degrees in three or more fields. Group II and III institutions fall between these two extremes (ibid., p. 774).

Koshal and Koshal include average SAT scores for entering freshmen and a quality index based on *US News and World Report*'s academic rankings as their proxies for institutional quality. An interesting finding is that the estimated minimum efficient scale is 11 758 for Group IV institutions and 30 957 for Group I institutions. In addition, a one-unit increase in SAT scores for entering freshmen costs US$52.89 for Group I and US$5.17 for Group IV institutions. Furthermore an increase in the student/faculty ratio by one unit decreases average total costs by US$929.32 for Group I institutions and US$1 425.58 for Group IV institutions (ibid., p. 777). Thus Koshal and Koshal's findings suggest that the efficient size of the four categories of institutions varies directly with the measures of academic quality: 'The lower the overall quality, *ceteris paribus*, the lower will be the size of the minimum efficient scale (*FTE*)' (ibid., p. 778).

Market structure
Getz *et al.* (1991) and Lloyd *et al.* (1993) include in their studies components that allow for an increased understanding of the evolving market structure of multiproduct IHEs. Getz *et al.* discuss and study the basic assumptions of the theory of cost functions, and build into their study an analysis of the effects created by disequilibrium. Disequilibrium is likely to exist if the IHEs are experiencing either significant increases or decreases in enrolments. Such increases or decreases in enrolment, according to Getz *et al.*, will move the institution out of long-run equilibrium and to a higher point on the multi-product cost function. Using data for the periods 1978–9 and 1987–8 for 2045 colleges and universities, they find that average annual growth rates ranged from −18.5% to +19.5%. The median growth rate for enrolment was +0.8% (ibid., p. 205). They divide the 2045 institutions into three groups that are defined as decreasing enrolment (enrolment growth is less than zero), stable enrolment (zero to 1.8%) and rapidly increasing enrolment (greater than 1.8%). The study limits the analysis to the stable enrolment institutions to help ensure that the parameter estimates are less likely to be biased by those colleges and universities that are operating in

'disequilibrium'. The study found that there was no relationship between average expenditures and enrolments for Liberal Arts I colleges that are experiencing stable enrolment. In other words, 'using only those Liberal Arts I colleges with stable enrolments yields a horizontal average cost curve' (ibid., p. 208).

Data envelopment analysis (DEA)

In addition to examining economies of scale and scope, a number of studies have looked at other elements of the efficiency of IHEs. DEA is one technique that has been used in recent years. A recent example of DEA, concerning Australian universities, is Abbott and Doucouliagos (2003). The authors estimate frontier production functions to determine the level of technical and scale efficiencies for individual institutions. This study, as with other recent studies of Australian higher education (for example, Lloyd *et al.*, 1993), was motivated by an interest in the recent merger activity among colleges and universities set forth by the Australian federal government. Abbott and Doucouliagos use DEA to estimate the level of technical efficiency based on 1995 data among the 36 universities that exist after the government-directed amalgamation. As in previous study, the outputs include teaching and research. The findings suggest that all Australian universities are performing well. Abbott and Doucouliagos are careful to point out that the relatively high efficiency levels found among the 36 institutions do not suggest that there is no room for improvement. Since DEA compares individual institutions to the best practices as defined within the data set, there may be room for improvement for the group of institutions when taken together. To the extent that there are efficiency differentials, the traditional universities tend to have the higher rankings. The authors also point out that the findings of high efficiency among Australian universities do not indicate that they are comparably efficient to universities in other countries.

Changes in technology

While distance education is not new to higher education, it is obvious that changes in electronic- and communication-related technologies are having an impact on educational production. Over the past quarter-century, distance education has taken the form of video instruction, satellite broadcasts and faculty teaching courses at remote sites. The Internet, however, is revolutionizing the methods of distance education. Most IHEs have been exploring how to deliver instruction via the Internet. Internet instruction represents yet another form of product differentiation in the output mix produced by the multi-product university or college.

As has been suggested above, instructional technology has tended to evolve rather slowly. However the Internet does represent a technological change in instructional delivery methods. According to Yablon and Katz (2001), 'the Internet provides the potential to deliver efficiently and on a mass scale individualized, highly engaging learning and instructional content to almost any desktop and makes information available to the teacher and student anytime day or night. Thus, the very essence of the Internet is the efficiency effectiveness, and its facilitating qualities that promise a long-awaited educational breakthrough at all educational levels' (p. 18). Regardless of Yablon and Katz's comment, the question of instructional effectiveness for Internet-delivered courses is one that needs to be explored. Research is now being conducted to help determine the effectiveness of this new technology in instructional production. Two studies (Yablon and Katz, 2001; Crawford, 2001) are discussed below.

Yablon and Katz (2001) explore whether a group of students taking an introductory statistics course by Internet instruction perform as well as students taking the same course in a traditional lecture environment. An experimental group of 186 students enrolled in the Internet course are compared to 63 students taking the course in the traditional format (the control group). Interestingly nearly 90% of the students in this study are female. This may result from the fact that the course was taught in the School of Education at Bar-Ilan University. Yablon and Katz (2001) administered a 15-item questionnaire both before and after the course. The results suggest that, compared to the control group, the experimental group experienced lower attitudinal and satisfaction levels towards online learning both before and after taking the course. It is interesting that students in the experimental group display a more favourable attitude and higher level of satisfaction at the end of the course than at the beginning. The research also reveals that students taking statistics via the Internet attained a level of achievement similar to or surpassing that in the traditional format.

In a similar study, Crawford (2001) looks at a fluid mechanical engineering laboratory in which some students obtain laboratory instructions online and others receive the instructions by lecture. Crawford gathered data both by administering a survey to measure eight outcome categories and by personally observing behavioural reactions of students in the laboratory environment. A total of 85 students completed the survey instrument. The survey indicated that the Internet sessions benefited students who were late or absent and provided more background and theory than the lecture-led sessions. Student responses to the survey suggest that the additional theory was not necessarily helpful in completing the laboratory assignments. In addition the students did experience difficulty with the Internet sound quality and the Internet instruction took more time than the corresponding lecture. Crawford concludes that the Internet should be considered only as a teaching aid, not as a substitute for the teacher.

Both Yablon and Katz (2001) and Crawford (2001) find that Internet instruction reduces the number of faculty needed to serve a given student load. Therefore there may be cost savings associated with the use of Internet technologies in higher education production. Differences in the quality of education are still being studied, and no firm conclusion can yet be drawn on the effectiveness of this teaching methodology. Nonetheless it appears that the use of the Internet will continue to expand in higher education. With this expansion, learning resources will continue to become increasingly available and flexible. Thus the Internet is expanding the product mix of the typical university and college.

Concluding comments

The studies reviewed above suggest that there are some common findings related to multi-product educational processes. In general economies of scale and scope exist for most institutions of higher education. Other findings suggest that, in general, MC tends to be greater for graduate studies than for undergraduate studies. There also appear to be numerous complementarities in the multi-product production processes of IHEs.

It is important, however, to include measures of output quality so that scale or scope economies are not overstated. Unfortunately, as is evidenced by the exclusion of output quality variables in most studies, data limitations might result in biased parameter estimates. Even when an attempt is made to control for quality differences among IHEs, researchers have to rely on imperfect proxies. Likewise, to the extent that universities produce public service, the present studies must be viewed with caution. Not a single study includes public service production as an output in the estimation of the multi-product cost functions. Lack of easily accessible data on public service output is a major cause of the omission. Furthermore studies omit other outputs, such as distance education. Also, as Getz *et al.* (1991) point out, studies generally assume that IHEs operate in an equilibrium. If that is not the case, some adjustments should be made. It was also noted earlier that alternative specifications of the cost function are possible. It is likely that different results emerge when alternative functions are employed, but which specification is most appropriate is difficult to determine a priori. Finally existing studies may have neglected to account for a variety of statistical problems, such as heteroscedasticity. Researchers contemplating further work in this area should consider the various shortcomings of existing studies and offer improvements in methodology, data collection and statistical analysis.

The above caveats notwithstanding, we have observed that many IHEs appear to be smaller and more specialized than what might be efficient. But is it necessarily true that public policy should be directed to consolidate institutions into larger, multi-product entities? One could argue that the answer is not necessarily in the affirmative. One reason is that consolidation of IHEs is likely to reduce access to higher education. A common policy in the USA is to provide ready access to higher education. For example, South Carolina established its network of technical colleges around the state so that most citizens would live within commuting distance of an IHE. Even though the technical colleges in South Carolina are relatively small and specialized, the loss in economies of scale and scope was considered worthwhile to achieve greater access. Multi-product cost studies are still valuable, because they indicate the extent of cost saving that is forgone, and serve to improve decisions concerning the establishment of new IHEs or the continued public financial support of existing ones.

Furthermore it should be recognized that smallness might produce important benefits. By limiting enrolments, students are able to study in a more friendly and familiar setting. Students and faculty are more likely to know one another, creating positive interactions that might provide important benefits, at least to some students. The late T.W. Schultz was a strong advocate of small schools. Growing up in rural Nebraska, Schultz attended a one-room school, where one teacher taught all subjects to students from first to twelfth grade. The one-on-one student–teacher approach might, indeed, produce superior results. Again, if smallness is advocated, the policy makers must be aware of the costs that it entails. Rational policy requires the balancing of costs and benefits of social programmes and endeavours.

Notes

1. Land grant universities were created by the donation of federal lands to the states, as specified in the Morrill Act (1862). The act granted to each state 30 000 acres for each congressional seat held, the proceeds of which were to be used to support a state college. For more information, see Cohn and Leslie (1980).
2. Note that our data differ from those of Goldin and Katz (2001) described earlier. The apparent reasons for the difference are that we use FTE (full-time equivalent) enrolments rather than headcount enrolment, and that we provide *mean* values, in contrast to Goldin and Katz, who provide *median* values.
3. There are two main differences between the cost equation used for the SC data and equation (15.1). First, instead of a *total* cost function we estimated an *average* cost function. Second, we did not include any input quantities or prices, other than the proxies for IHE type. Whether one should estimate an average or a total cost function has been a subject of some debate.
4. As Cohn *et al.* (1989) demonstrate, a model based on a single-output cost equation yields results that may be fundamentally different from those obtained through the multiple-output cost approach.
5. This is not true in the case of the hybrid translog method proposed by Baumol *et al.* (1982).
6. As Johnes (1997) points out in the appendix to his paper, 'the problems concern the assignment of a given vector of global outputs across a (fixed or variable) number of producers. Any rearrangement of the outputs across producers . . . might be expected

either to increase or decrease global costs'. Tabu search makes it possible to select a subset of all possible allocations (p. 737).

7. The cross-marginal cost for product i and j is given by:

$$C_{ij} = \frac{\partial^2 C}{\partial Y_i \partial Y_j}.$$

If the sign of C_{ij} is negative, cost complementarity is implied; that is, there are positive effects of joint production between products i and j. If it is positive, the products are cost substitutes.

References

Abbott M. and C. Doucouliagos (2003), 'The efficiency of Australian universities: a data envelopment analysis', *Economics of Education Review*, **22** (1), 89–97.

Aitkin, Don (2001), 'Higher education: a short history of change', *Australian Academic & Research Libraries*, **32** (2), April, S31.

Baumol, W.J., J.C. Panzar and R.D. Willig (1982), *Contestable Markets and the Theory of Industry Structure*, New York: Harcourt Brace Jovanovich.

Borrego, Anne Marie (2001), 'Study tracks growth of for-profit colleges', *The Chronicle of Higher Education*, 10 August.

Brinkman, Paul T. (1989), 'Instructional costs per student credit hour: differences by level of instruction', *Journal of Educational Finance*, **15** (Summer), 34–52.

Brinkman, Paul T. (1990), 'Higher education cost functions', in Stephen A. Hoenack and Eileen L. Collins (eds), *The Economics of American Universities*, Albany, NY: State University of New York Press, pp. 107–28.

Cohn, Elchanan and Terry G. Geske (2004), *The Economics of Education*, 3rd edn, Cincinnati: South Western.

Cohn, Elchanan and Larry L. Leslie (1980), 'The development and finance of higher education in perspective', in Howard P. Tuckman and Edward Whalen (eds), *Subsidies to Higher Education: The Issues*, New York: Praeger Publishers, pp. 11–32.

Cohn, Elchanan, S.L.W. Rhine and M.C. Santos (1989), 'Institutions of higher education as multi-product firms: economies of scale and scope', *Review of Economics and Statistics*, **71**, 284–90.

Cooper, Samuel T. and Elchanan Cohn (1997), 'Estimation of a frontier production function for the South Carolina education process', *Economics of Education Review*, **16** (3), 323–7.

Crawford, Garry (2001), 'A case evaluation in Internet assisted laboratory teaching', *Academic Exchange Quarterly*, **5** (Winter), 168–74.

deGroot, Hans, Walter W. McMahon and J. Fredericks Volkwein (1991), 'The cost structure of American research universities', *The Review of Economics and Statistics*, **73** (3), 424–31.

Dundar, Halil and Darrell R. Lewis (1995), 'Departmental productivity in American universities: economies of scale and scope', *Economics of Education Review*, **14** (2), 119–44.

Ehrenberg, Ronald G. (2000), *Tuition Rising: Why College Costs So Much*, Cambridge, MA: Harvard University Press.

Enz, Cathy A. (2002), 'The nature of university research', *Cornell Hotel & Restaurant Administration Quarterly*, **43** (1), 3.

Friedlaender, Ann, Clifford Winston and Kung Wang (1983), 'Costs, technology, and productivity in the US automobile industry', *Bell Journal of Economics*, **14** (Spring), 1–20.

Gedikoglu, T. (1985), 'The development of Turkish higher education in the republic period, 1923–1985', unpublished doctoral dissertation, University of Pittsburgh.

Getz, Malcolm, John J. Siegfried and Hao Zhang (1991), 'Estimating economies of scale in higher education', *Economics Letters*, **37**, 203–8.

Goldin, Claudia and Lawrence F. Katz (2001), 'The shaping of higher education in the United States and New England', *Boston Federal Reserve Regional Review*, **Q4**, 5–11.

Gose, Ben (2002), 'The fall of the flagships: do the best state universities need to privatize to thrive?', *The Chronicle of Higher Education*, **48** (43), A19–A21.

Hashimoto, Keiji and Elchanan Cohn (1997), 'Economies of scale and scope in Japanese private universities', *Education Economics*, **5** (2), 107–15.
Henderson, James M. and Richard E. Quandt (1980), *Microeconomic Theory: A Mathematical Approach*, New York: McGraw-Hill.
Hutchins, Robert Maynard (1936), *The Higher Learning in America*, New Haven, CT: Yale University Press.
Izadi, Hooshang, Geraint Johnes, Reza Oskrochi and Robert Crouchley (2002), 'Stochastic frontier estimation of a CES cost function: the case of higher education in Britain', *Economics of Education Review*, **21** (1), 63–71.
Jimenez, Emmanuel (1986), 'The structure of educational costs: multiproduct cost functions for primary and secondary schools in Latin America', *Economics of Education Review*, **5** (1), 25–39.
Johnes, Geraint (1997), 'Costs and industrial structure in contemporary British higher education', *The Economic Journal*, **107**, 727–37.
Johnes, Geraint (1998), 'Corrigendum', *The Economic Journal*, **108**, 1275.
Koshal, Rajindar K. and Manjulika Koshal (1995), 'Quality and economies of scale in higher education', *Applied Economics*, **27**, 773–8.
Koshal, Rajindar K. and Manjulika Koshal (1999), 'Economies of scale and scope in higher education: a case of comprehensive universities', *Economics of Education Review*, **18**, 269–77.
Koshal, Rajindar K., Manjulika Koshal and Ashok Gupta (2001), 'Multi-product total cost function for higher education: a case of bible colleges', *Economics of Education Review*, **20**, 297–303.
Lewis, Darrell R. and Halil Dundar (1995), 'Economies of scale and scope in Turkish universities', *Education Economics*, **2**, 133–57.
Lloyd, P.J., M.H. Morgan and R.A. Williams (1993), 'Amalgamations of universities: are there economies of scale or scope?', *Applied Economics*, **25**, 1081–92.
Lucas, Christopher J. (1996), *Crisis in the Academy: Rethinking Higher Education in America*, New York: St Martin's.
Mayo, John W. (1984), 'Multiproduct monopoly, regulation, and firm costs', *Southern Economic Journal*, **51**, 208–18.
McDowell, George R. (2001), *Land-grant Universities and Extension into the 21st Century: Renegotiating or Abandoning a Social Contract*, Ames: Iowa State University Press.
Morna, Colleen Lowe (1995), 'The plight of the universities', *Africa Report*, **40** (2), 30–33.
Nelson, Randy and Kathleen T. Hevert (1992), 'Effects of class size on economies of scale and marginal costs in higher education', *Applied Economics*, **24** (5), 473–82.
OECD (2001), *Education at a Glance: OECD Indicators*, Paris.
SC Commission on Higher Education (2002), *Statistical Abstract 2002*, Columbia, SC.
Stevens, E.B. and E.C. Elliot (1925), 'Unit costs of higher education', *The Educational Finance Inquiry*, 13, New York: Macmillan.
Varian, Hal R. (1984), *Microeconomic Analysis*, 2nd edn, New York: W.W. Norton & Company.
Verry, D.W. and P.R.G. Layard (1975), 'Cost functions for university teaching and research', *The Economic Journal*, **85** (337), 55–74.
Wagner, Jon (1993), 'Social contracts and university public service; the case of agriculture and schooling', *Journal of Higher Education*, **64** (6), 696–729.
Waldman, Don E. and Elizabeth J. Jensen (1998), *Industrial Organization: Theory and Practice*, Reading, MA: Addison-Wesley.
Ward, Mike (2002), 'Good universities must be research-driven', *Africa News Service*, 25 June, p. 1008176u5202.
Worthington, Andrew C. (2001), 'An empirical survey of frontier efficiency measurement techniques in education', *Education Economics*, **9** (3), 245–68.
Yablon, Yaacov B. and Yaacov J. Katz (2001), 'Statistics through the medium of Internet: what students think and achieve', *Academic Exchange Quarterly*, **5** (4), 17–22.

16 Efficiency measurement
Jill Johnes

1 Introduction

The measurement of how well institutions of education perform has been the subject of increased attention in recent years. Variables purporting to measure various aspects of the performance of schools and universities are published regularly in many countries at both local and national level. Such indicators often take the form of ratios which represent efficiency in producing outputs (for example, the ratio of pupils in a given year obtaining a minimum level of achievement to total pupils in the year) or efficiency in using resources (for example, cost per student). From this point it is a simple step to produce 'league tables' of school and university performance which aim to inform consumer choice and resource allocation.

The dangers of using these so-called 'indicators of performance' are, by now, well known. First, the institutions of interest (schools or universities, for example) operate under different conditions and in different environments which are not adequately accounted for by simple ratios. Secondly, institutions of education produce an array of outputs from a range of inputs. A ratio of one output to one input, for example, cannot capture the complete performance of an organization across the breadth of its activities and it is, at best, only a partial indicator.

As a consequence, a number of techniques have been developed and applied in the context of education in an effort to measure the true efficiency of organizations. Statistical techniques have progressed from ordinary least squares (OLS) regression to stochastic frontier analysis, while simple ratios of one output to one input have been replaced by composite ratios of efficiency derived from linear programming (LP) methods. The aim of this chapter is therefore, first, to identify and present the most common methods of efficiency measurement in the context of education and, second, to review the empirical studies of efficiency measurement at all levels of education provision in order to assess the usefulness of these methods to consumers, managers and policy makers.

The chapter is in six sections of which this is the first. Section 2 presents some definitions of efficiency derived from production theory. Sections 3 and 4 describe techniques for measuring efficiency, while section 5 identifies the drawbacks and uses of applying these methods in the context of education. Conclusions are drawn in section 6.

2   Definitions of efficiency

A useful starting point in any discussion of efficiency measurement is Farrell (1957), who defines three types of efficiency which will be considered below. Consider a firm which uses inputs x_1 and x_2 to produce a given level of output y in quantities denoted by the point P in Figure 16.1. In the context of education, the firm could be a school producing the output of qualified leavers (y) from inputs of staff (x_1) and pupils (x_2). The curve SS' represents the isoquant joining all combinations of x_1 and x_2 from which an efficient firm might choose to produce the given level of output, and there are, at this stage, constant returns to scale (CRS). The technical efficiency (TE) of the firm producing at point P is defined as the proportion of inputs used by the firm which is *actually necessary* to produce the output observed at point P, and can be written as:

$$TE = \frac{OQ}{OP}.$$

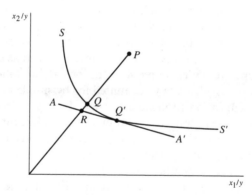

Figure 16.1   Measuring technical efficiency in an input–oriented framework

The quantity $1 - TE$ is therefore a measure of technical inefficiency, and is actually the proportion by which the firm's inputs could be reduced (while holding the input ratio constant) without reducing the level of output currently produced at point P (Worthington, 2001). A further measure of efficiency can be defined by introducing the input prices into the diagram by means of the line AA' which represents the price ratio of the two inputs.[1] The point Q' represents both technical and allocative (or price) efficiency, and therefore incorporates the idea that inputs are used in the optimal (that is, cost minimizing) proportions given the prices of inputs. Since the costs of production at Q' are also represented by point R further along the line AA', the measure of the allocative efficiency (AE) of the firm is defined as:

$$AE = \frac{OR}{OQ}.$$

The points Q and Q' are both technically efficient, but the costs of production at Q' are the fraction OR/OQ of the costs at Q. Thus the reduction in costs of production (given input prices) which could be achieved by using the cost-efficient input proportions is represented by the distance RQ.

Finally the overall (or total economic) efficiency (OE) of the firm is defined as

$$OE = \frac{OR}{OP}$$

and this is also the product of technical and allocative efficiency. The quantity $1 - OE$ is therefore a measure of inefficiency, and the distance RP represents reduction in costs of production which could be achieved by the firm switching its production point from P to the cost-minimizing point Q'.

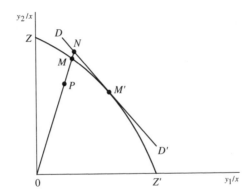

Figure 16.2   Measuring technical efficiency in an output-oriented framework

The approach adopted by Farrell (1957) is input-oriented since it seeks to answer the question: by how much can the firm reduce inputs proportionally without changing the quantity of output produced? One could equally well take an output-oriented approach, thereby seeking an answer to the question: for a given set of inputs, by how much could the firm's outputs be proportionally increased? The output-oriented approach to efficiency measurement is illustrated in Figure 16.2. In this case, the firm produces two outputs, y_1 and y_2, from a given level of input, x. Thus the firm might be a university producing the outputs of teaching (y_1) and research (y_2) from one input, namely staff time (x). The firm faces the production possibility curve ZZ' and so technical efficiency, which is the ratio of observed output to maximum possible output, is

$$TE = \frac{OP}{OM}.$$

In this case $1 - TE$, which is a measure of inefficiency, measures the proportion by which the firm's outputs could be increased (while holding the output ratio constant) without increasing the level of input used at the observed production point P.

Allocative efficiency is identified by the introduction of an isorevenue line, DD'.[2] The point M' is both technically and allocatively efficient. Since M' has the same revenue as the point N along the line DD', allocative efficiency can be measured by

$$AE = \frac{OM}{ON}.$$

The points M and M' are both technically efficient, but the revenue from production at N is the fraction OM/ON of the revenue at M', and the increase in revenue which the firm could achieve by producing the correct (revenue maximizing) output proportion is the distance MN.

Overall efficiency is therefore

$$OE = \frac{OP}{ON},$$

and is the product of technical and allocative efficiency. Thus $1 - OE$ is a measure of inefficiency, and the distance PN is the amount by which the firm could increase its revenue by moving from the observed production point at P to the revenue-maximizing point at M'.

In the case of constant returns to scale, the technical efficiency measures obtained under input orientation and output orientation are identical. But they differ in general when variable returns to scale (VRS) exist.

The measures of efficiency identified with the aid of Figures 16.1 and 16.2 fail to incorporate any idea of social preferences. In order to define a measure of social efficiency (SE) the social welfare function between two outputs needs to be added to Figure 16.2. This is done in Figure 16.3, where the curve JJ' denotes the social preferences between the two outputs. The ideal point of production from a social welfare viewpoint is located at point L'. However the utility derived from the combination of outputs at L' is equivalent to the utility derived from the bundle of goods at point L, and so a measure of social efficiency for the firm located at point P, which is defined as the ratio of observed output to the level of output desired by society, is

$$SE = \frac{OP}{OL}.$$

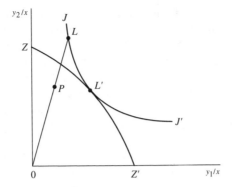

Figure 16.3 Measuring social efficiency in an output-oriented framework

Note that, by this definition, it is possible to be socially efficient while being allocatively inefficient; it is also possible to be allocatively efficient while being socially inefficient.

All the definitions of efficiency considered so far have been based on the assumption of constant returns to scale. This is restrictive since a firm may experience inefficiency from being the wrong size. Any inefficiencies emanating from being the wrong scale would, with the measures defined so far, be attributed to technical inefficiency. In Figure 16.4, a firm which produces one output, y, from one input, x, produces at point P and faces a production frontier given by OT. For comparison, the CRS production frontier is also on the diagram and is represented by the straight line OT'.

Consider, first of all, the CRS situation. In an input-oriented framework (where output is fixed and input can vary), technical efficiency of the firm is measured using the horizontal distance of the production point from the

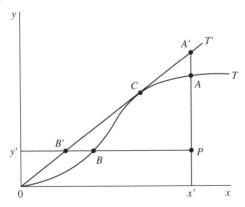

Figure 16.4 Measuring scale efficiency

frontier. Thus technical efficiency is measured by the ratio $TE^I_{CRS} = y'B'/y'P$. In an output-oriented framework, on the other hand (where input is fixed and output can vary), technical efficiency is measured using the vertical distance of the production point from the frontier. So technical efficiency in this case is given by the ratio $TE^O_{CRS} = x'P/x'A'$. These measures can be compared with those derived using the VRS production frontier. Using an input-oriented framework, technical efficiency is measured by the ratio $TE^I_{VRS} = y'B/y'P$, whereas an output-oriented framework gives a measure of technical efficiency $TE^O_{VRS} = x'P/x'A$.

Two points immediately become obvious. First, under VRS, the value of technical efficiency varies depending upon whether an input- or an output-oriented framework is used. The two measures are only equal under CRS. Secondly, for a given orientation, the measured technical efficiency of this inefficient firm is higher when a VRS rather than a CRS production frontier is used, and this is true irrespective of orientation, and for all possible production points inside or on the VRS production frontier, with the exception of point C (where the two measures will be identical). Thus the CRS measure attributes to technical inefficiency what is, in fact, inefficiency caused by being an unfavourable size (the distance $B'B$ in the input-oriented measure and the distance AA' in the output-oriented measure for the firm at point P). Furthermore it can be shown that, for the firm at point P,

$$TE^I_{CRS} = \frac{y'B'}{y'P} = \frac{y'B}{y'P} \cdot \frac{y'B'}{y'B},$$

where the first component $y'B/y'P = TE^I_{VRS}$; that is the input-oriented measure of technical efficiency under VRS, and the second component is the input-oriented CRS efficiency measure of a hypothetical firm located at point B. It is therefore the measure of inefficiency due to the divergence between the actual scale of operation at B and the most productive scale, and can be used to reflect scale efficiency. Thus, in an input-oriented framework, overall technical efficiency of the firm located at point P is given by the ratio $y'B'/y'P$, and this can be divided into a measure of pure technical efficiency, $y'B/y'P$, and a measure of scale efficiency, $y'B'/y'B$. Similarly, using an output-oriented framework,

$$TE^O_{CRS} = \frac{x'P}{x'A'} = \frac{x'A}{x'A'} \cdot \frac{x'P}{x'A},$$

and so overall technical efficiency is given by the ratio $x'P/x'A'$, which can be divided into a measure of pure technical efficiency, $x'P/x'A$, and a measure of scale efficiency, $x'A/x'A'$.

Throughout this section we have been examining possible measures of the efficiency of a firm in a specific time period, so differences between firms in the level of output produced are considered to be a consequence of differences in efficiency. No consideration has been given to the role of production technology in performance. In order to do this, let us now consider firm P which produces two outputs, y_1 and y_2, from a given level of input x, over two time periods: a base period, q, and an end period, t. In Figure 16.5, PPC^q and PPC^t refer to the production possibility curves for firm P's industry in the two time periods respectively. Clearly, improvements in production technology have occurred (since PPC^t is outside PPC^q) in a non-neutral way (since the shift in production possibility curves is skewed rather than parallel). Firm P's actual production position has changed from P_q to P_t over the two periods. The fact that neither point lies on its associated production possibility curve indicates that the firm is technically inefficient in both time periods.

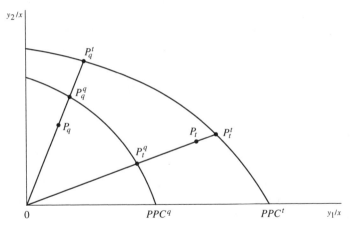

Figure 16.5 Measuring change in efficiency over time: output-oriented framework

Let us consider first of all the production points of the different time periods separately. The technical efficiency of the firm (using Farrell's output-oriented definition of section 2) in time period q (TE_q) and time period t (TE_t) is, respectively $TE_q = OP_q/OP_q^q$ and $TE_t = OP_t/OP_t^t$. Let us define the output distance function for period q (denoted by $D_O^q(x_q,y_{1q},y_{2q})$, where the subscript q on the input and outputs denotes the quantities used in time period q, as the inverse of the maximum amount by which output could be increased (given the level of inputs remains constant) while still remaining within the feasible production possibility set. This is just the value measured by TE_q and so $TE_q = D_O^q(x_q,y_{1q},y_{2q})$. Similarly it is the case that $TE_t = D_O^t(x_t, y_{1t}, y_{2t})$ where $D_O^t(x_t, y_{1t}, y_{2t})$ denotes the output distance function for period t and the subscript t on the input and outputs denotes the quantities used in time period t.

An examination of the way the productivity of the firm has changed over the two time periods can be approached in two ways: the two production points can be compared by using the technology in period q as the reference technology, or by using the technology in period t as the reference technology. Using the first method, the technical efficiency of the firm at point P_t is measured by comparing actual output at time t relative to the maximum that could be achieved *given period q's technology* (that is, OP_t/OP_t^q which can be denoted by $D_O^q(x_t, y_{1t}, y_{2t})$), and this is compared to the technical efficiency of the firm at point P_q measured by comparing actual output at time q relative to the maximum that could be achieved, also given period q's technology (that is, OP_q/OP_q^q which can be denoted by $D_O^q(x_q, y_{1q}, y_{2q})$). A measure of the growth in productivity between the two periods using the technology of period q as the reference technology is known as the Malmquist (Malmquist, 1953) output-oriented productivity index defined relative to the initial period's technology (M_O^q) and is given as

$$M_O^q = \frac{D_O^q(x_t, y_{1t}, y_{2t})}{D_O^q(x_q, y_{1q}, y_{2q})} = \frac{OP_t/OP_t^q}{OP_q/OP_q^q}. \tag{16.1}$$

Using the second method, the technical efficiency of the firm at point P_t is measured by comparing the output at time t relative to the maximum that could be achieved given time t's technology (that is, OP_t/OP_t^t, which can be denoted by $D_O^t(x_t, y_{1t}, y_{2t})$), and this is compared to the technical efficiency of the firm at point P_q measured by comparing the output at time q relative to the maximum that could be achieved also *given period t's technology* (that is OP_q/OP_q^t, which can be denoted by $D_O^t(x_q, y_{1q}, y_{2q})$). The measure of the growth in productivity between the two periods using the technology of period t as the reference technology is known as the Malmquist output-oriented productivity index defined relative to the final period's technology (M_O^t) and is given by

$$M_O^t = \frac{D_O^t(x_t, y_{1t}, y_{2t})}{D_O^t(x_q, y_{1q}, y_{2q})} = \frac{OP_t/OP_t^t}{OP_q/OP_q^t}. \tag{16.2}$$

We therefore have two measures of the change in productivity over the two periods (*n* measures in the *n* period case) and it is unclear which measure is the appropriate one to use, since the choice of base technology would be arbitrary. This problem is overcome by using the Malmquist output-oriented productivity change index (M_O) which is defined as the geometric mean of M_O^q and M_O^t (Färe *et al.*, 1994):

$$M_O = \left[M_O^q \cdot M_O^t \right]^{\frac{1}{2}} = \left[\frac{D_O^q(x_t, y_{1t}, y_{2t})}{D_O^q(x_q, y_{1q}, y_{2q})} \cdot \frac{D_O^t(x_t, y_{1t}, y_{2t})}{D_O^t(x_q, y_{1q}, y_{2q})} \right]^{\frac{1}{2}}$$

$$= \left[\frac{OP_t/OP_t^q}{OP_q/OP_q^q} \cdot \frac{OP_t/OP_t^t}{OP_q/OP_q^t} \right]^{\frac{1}{2}}. \tag{16.3}$$

The index can be rewritten as

$$M_O = \frac{D_O^t(x_t, y_{1t}, y_{2t})}{D_O^q(x_q, y_{1q}, y_{2q})} \left[\frac{D_O^q(x_t, y_{1t}, y_{2t})}{D_O^t(x_t, y_{1t}, y_{2t})} \cdot \frac{D_O^q(x_q, y_{1q}, y_{2q})}{D_O^t(x_q, y_{1q}, y_{2q})} \right]^{\frac{1}{2}}$$

$$= \frac{OP_t/OP_t^t}{OP_q/OP_q^q} \left[\frac{OP_t/OP_t^q}{OP_t/OP_t^t} \cdot \frac{OP_q/OP_q^q}{OP_q/OP_q^t} \right]^{\frac{1}{2}}. \tag{16.4}$$

The first component of equation (16.4) is the ratio of technical efficiency in time period t (the final period) to technical efficiency in time period q (the initial period) and therefore measures the change in technical efficiency between the two periods. The ratio equals 1 if there is no change in technical efficiency over the two periods, and is greater than 1 (less than 1) if technical efficiency has improved (declined) over the two periods.

The second component measures the change in production technology (that is, shifts in the frontier) between the two periods q and t. It is the geometric mean of the change in technology between the two periods evaluated at x_t and x_q, respectively. This component has the value 1 when there is no change in production technology, and is greater than 1 (less than 1) if change in production technology has had a positive (negative) effect.

The Malmquist productivity index can also be defined in an input-oriented framework. First we must define the input distance function which is the maximum amount by which all inputs could be reduced (given the level of outputs remains constant) while still remaining in the feasible input set. In Figure 16.6, the firm now uses two inputs x_1 and x_2 to produce output y, and I_q and I_t refer to the isoquants in period q and t, respectively. Improvements in production technology have occurred, since I_t is inside I_q. The observed production points for the firm in time periods q and t are P_q and P_t, respectively, neither of which is technically efficient since each lies beyond its own isoquant. The value of the input distance function for the firm in time period q is $D_I^q(x_{1q}, x_{2q}, y_q) = OP_q/OP_q^q$. This is the reciprocal of the Farrell input-oriented measure of technical efficiency for firm P at time q. Similarly the distance function for firm P in time period t is $D_I^t(x_{1t}, x_{2t}, y_t) = OP_t/OP_t^t$.

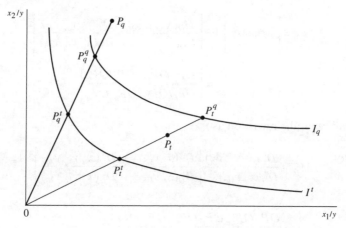

Figure 16.6   Measuring change in efficiency over time: input-oriented framework

As with the output-oriented approach, the measurement of how productivity has changed over two time periods can be approached in two ways: the two production points can be compared using period q technology, or they can be compared using period t technology. Using the first method, the technical inefficiency of the firm at point P_t is measured by comparing the actual input at time t relative to the minimum required *given period q's technology* (that is, OP_t/OP_t^q, which can be denoted by $D_I^q(x_{1t},x_{2t},y_t)$). This is compared to the technical inefficiency of the firm at point P_q measured by comparing the actual input at time q relative to the minimum required, also given period q's technology (that is, $OP_q/OP_q^q = D_I^q(x_{1q},x_{2q},y_q)$). A measure of the change in productivity between the two periods given the technology of period q as the reference technology is known as the Malmquist input-oriented productivity index defined relative to the initial period's technology (M_I^q) and is given as

$$M_I^q = \frac{D_I^q(x_{1t},x_{2t},y_t)}{D_I^q(x_{1q},x_{2q},y_q)} = \frac{OP_t/OP_t^q}{OP_q/OP_q^q}. \tag{16.5}$$

Using the second method, the technical inefficiency of the firm at point P_t is measured by comparing the actual input at time t relative to the minimum input required given the technology of period t (that is, $OP_t/OP_t^t = D_I^t(x_{1t},x_{2t},y_t)$). This is compared with the technical inefficiency of the firm at point P_q measured by comparing the actual input at time q relative to the minimum input required given period t's technology (that is,

OP_q/OP_q^t, which can be denoted by $D_I^t(x_{1q},x_{2q},y_q)$). The Malmquist input-oriented productivity index defined relative to the final period's technology (M_I^t) is given as

$$M_I^t = \frac{D_I^t(x_{1t},x_{2t},y_t)}{D_I^q(x_{1q},x_{2q},y_q)} = \frac{OP_t/OP_t^t}{OP_q/OP_q^t}. \qquad (16.6)$$

The problem of the arbitrary choice of which technology to use as the base technology when comparing productivity change over two periods is again overcome by defining the Malmquist input-oriented productivity change index (denoted by M_I) as the geometric mean of M_I^q and M_I^t:

$$M_I = \left[M_I^q \cdot M_I^t \right]^{\frac{1}{2}} = \left[\frac{D_I^q(x_{1t},x_{2t},y_t)}{D_I^q(x_{1q},x_{2q},y_q)} \cdot \frac{D_I^t(x_{1t},x_{2t},y_t)}{D_I^t(x_{1q},x_{2q},y_q)} \right]^{\frac{1}{2}}$$

$$= \left[\frac{OP_t/OP_t^q}{OP_q/OP_q^q} \cdot \frac{OP_t/OP_t^t}{OP_q/OP_q^t} \right]^{\frac{1}{2}}. \qquad (16.7)$$

This can be rewritten as

$$M_I = \frac{D_I^t(x_{1t},x_{2t},y_t)}{D_I^q(x_{1q},x_{2q},y_q)} \left[\frac{D_I^q(x_{1t},x_{2t},y_t)}{D_I^t(x_{1t},x_{2t},y_t)} \cdot \frac{D_I^q(x_{1q},x_{2q},y_q)}{D_I^t(x_{1q},x_{2q},y_q)} \right]^{\frac{1}{2}}$$

$$= \frac{OP_t/OP_t^t}{OP_q/OP_q^q} \left[\frac{OP_t/OP_t^q}{OP_t/OP_t^t} \cdot \frac{OP_q/OP_q^q}{OP_q/OP_q^t} \right]^{\frac{1}{2}}. \qquad (16.8)$$

The components of this index can be interpreted in the opposite way from components of the output-oriented productivity index of equation (16.4). Specifically $D_I^t(x_{1t},x_{2t},y_t)/D_I^q(x_{1q},x_{2q},y_q)$ represents the change in technical efficiency between periods t and q and equals 1 if there has been no change, and is less than 1 (greater than 1) if there has been an improvement (decline) in technical efficiency. The second component,

$$\left[\frac{D_I^q(x_{1t},x_{2t},y_t)}{D_I^t(x_{1t},x_{2t},y_t)} \cdot \frac{D_I^q(x_{1q},x_{2q},y_q)}{D_I^t(x_{1q},x_{2q},y_q)} \right]^{\frac{1}{2}},$$

measures the change in production technology between periods t and q and equals 1 if there has been no change, and is less than 1 (greater than 1) if the effects of production technology have been positive (negative).

This section has established basic concepts of efficiency which might be of interest in the context of measuring performance in education. In practice the data available to analysts for estimating production functions in the context of education are at the aggregate production unit level (for example, the school, university, local education authority or school district) or they are disaggregated to the level of the pupil or student. The methods which might be appropriate for measuring the types of efficiency considered in this section in each of these cases (that is, aggregated or disaggregated data) are therefore considered separately in the next two sections.

3 Techniques for measuring efficiency: level of analysis is the production unit

There are two basic approaches to the measurement of efficiency: the statistical (or econometric) approach and the non-statistical (or programming approach). The distinction between the two approaches derives from the underlying assumptions. First, the statistical approach assumes that the efficiencies (the difference between the firm's observed output and the output which could be achieved if it were producing on the production frontier) follow a specific distribution (Førsund *et al.*, 1980). The statistical approach is often (but not always) parametric, which means that a particular functional form for the production function is also assumed, for example the Cobb–Douglas (Sengupta, 1999). Statistical, parametric methods therefore use a simple mathematical form to represent production technology, and hence provide estimates of the parameters of the frontier, the significance of which can be tested using standard errors (Schmidt, 1985–6). However any misspecification errors (either of the production function or of the inefficiency distribution) are incorporated in the efficiency measure (Lovell, 1993). Furthermore the statistical, parametric approach is not easily applied in a situation where there are multiple inputs *and* multiple outputs.

The non-statistical approach makes no assumptions regarding the distribution of inefficiencies. In addition it is often (but not always) non-parametric, which means that the input and output data are used to compute, using linear programming methods, a convex hull to represent the efficiency frontier (Sengupta, 1999). The non-statistical, non-parametric approach avoids the problems of misspecification (of both the production function and the distribution of efficiencies), since no distributions are specified. Furthermore programming methods can easily be used in a production situation where there are both multiple inputs and multiple outputs. A disadvantage of the non-statistical, non-parametric approach is that it provides no estimates or significance tests of parameters (Geva-May, 2001). Another is that the convex hull is defined by using information on only a small number of observations in the sample.

The final distinction between alternative methods is that they can be either stochastic or deterministic (Schmidt, 1985–6; Lovell, 1993). The stochastic approach is based on the premise that deviations from the production function are a consequence not just of inefficiency, but also of measurement errors, random shocks and statistical noise (Lovell, 1993; Ondrich and Ruggiero, 2001). The objective of stochastic models is therefore to separate the residual into two components: one the result of inefficiency and one random. In practice this involves assuming a specific distribution for each error component. Stochastic methods therefore have the advantage that efficiency measures do not incorporate random shocks or measurement errors, but they may be affected by misspecification errors. Deterministic methods, in contrast, assume that any deviation in observed output from the production frontier is solely a consequence of inefficiency (Lovell, 1993; Ondrich and Ruggiero, 2001). While there can be no misspecification errors in deterministic methods (since there is no specification to misspecify), the disadvantage is that any errors in measurement or stochastic errors are incorporated into the measurement of efficiency.

In summary, a method for measuring efficiency can be statistical or non-statistical, parametric or non-parametric, deterministic or stochastic. Of the eight possible permutations of these characteristics, the most common methods fall into one of three of these categories: statistical parametric methods (deterministic or stochastic) and deterministic non-statistical non-parametric methods. The remainder of this section will present and discuss some of the most common methods, including more recent developments, in the context of efficiency measurement in education.

Statistical parametric methods

Deviations from the frontier are deterministic Suppose that producer *i* converts *m* inputs (*x*) into output (*y*), and the process is represented by equation (16.9):

$$y_i = f(x_{i1}, \ldots, x_{im}) e^{-u_i}.$$ (16.9)

Under the assumption of Cobb–Douglas technology, this can be written as

$$\ln(y_i) = \ln[f(x_{i1}, \ldots, x_{im})] - u_i = \alpha_0 + \sum_{j=1}^{m} \alpha_j \ln x_{ij} - u_i.$$ (16.10)

Note that the residuals are $-u_i$, where $u_i \geq 0$ and represents the efficiency of producer *i*.

Technical efficiency of producer *i*, as defined in the output-oriented representation in Figure 16.2, is the ratio of the actual output of producer *i* to the maximum possible output which it could achieve as represented by the production frontier. Thus, from equation (16.9), technical efficiency is

$$TE_i = \frac{y_i}{f(x_{i1},\ldots,x_{im})} = e^{-u_i}.$$ (16.11)

Under the assumption that the residuals are deterministic, there are various possible ways of estimating the production frontier in equation (16.9) and hence estimating technical efficiency. First, a distribution for the production function is assumed (such as Cobb–Douglas as in the above example) and the parameters are estimated using OLS. The intercept is then shifted up until all residuals (denoted here by $-u_i$) are non-positive (ensuring that the u_i are non-negative) and at least one is zero.[3] This approach is referred to here as corrected OLS (COLS). It should be stressed that no distribution is specified for the residual term, and the entire deviation from the frontier for a particular producer is attributed to inefficiency.

The alternative approaches assume a distribution for the u_i. This is commonly a half-normal distribution, although an exponential distribution might alternatively be used (Lovell, 1993). Thus the parameters of equation (16.9) are estimated using OLS and an additional parameter, namely the mean of the u_i, is also estimated and used to shift upwards the OLS intercept. This approach is referred to variously as (rather confusingly) COLS (Førsund *et al.*, 1980) or modified OLS (MOLS) (Lovell, 1993). In addition to the disadvantage of deterministic residuals, MOLS has the disadvantage that the production function is not necessarily shifted far enough to ensure that all observations lie on or below the frontier, and so some residuals may have the wrong sign (Førsund *et al.*, 1980; Lovell, 1993).

Maximum likelihood estimation (MLE) can be used as an alternative to least squares to estimate simultaneously the assumed distribution of the u_i *and* the parameters of equation (16.9) (a functional form for the production function also having been assumed). The MLE production function consequently envelops all observations, but the estimated parameters differ from those derived using least squares (since the relationship between inputs and outputs is non-linear) and therefore allows efficient observations (that is, those lying on the frontier) to differ in terms of technology compared to observations lying inside the frontier (Lovell, 1993).

All these methods suffer from the disadvantages of statistical parametric deterministic models. In addition, it should be stressed that COLS and MOLS methods produce an identical ranking of producers to OLS. Finally the methods are unsuitable, as presented here, for application where there are multiple outputs as well as multiple inputs.[4] A comparison of these three deterministic methods can be found in Lovell (1993) and is illustrated for the single output single input case in Figure 16.7.

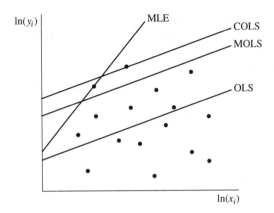

Figure 16.7   Comparing different frontiers

Deviations from the frontier are stochastic   In order to allow for stochastic residuals, equation (16.9) is modified as follows:

$$y_i = f(x_{i1},\dots,x_{im})e^{\varepsilon_i}, \tag{16.12}$$

where $\varepsilon_i = v_i - u_i$ and so equation (16.10) becomes

$$\ln(y_i) = \ln[f(x_{i1},\dots,x_{im})] + \varepsilon_i = \alpha_0 + \sum_{j=1}^{m}\alpha_j\ln x_{ij} + \varepsilon_i, \tag{16.13}$$

where $v_i \sim N(0,\sigma_v^2)$, u_i and v_i are statistically independent and $u_i \geq 0$ (Aigner *et al.*, 1977). The residuals are therefore split into two components. One is normal and is attributed to measurement error and random fluctuations (v_i), while the second component is one-sided (typically exponential or half-normal) and is attributed to technical inefficiency (u_i). The parameters of the function can be estimated using MOLS (Førsund *et al.*, 1980; Lovell, 1993) or MLE methods. This is the technique known as stochastic frontier analysis.

In the case where u_i is half-normal, for example, the log likelihood function is given by

$$\ln L = -n\ln\sigma - \frac{n}{2}\ln\frac{2}{\pi} - \frac{1}{2}\sum_i\frac{\varepsilon_i^2}{\sigma^2} + \sum_i\ln\Phi\left(\frac{-\varepsilon_i\lambda}{\sigma}\right), \tag{16.14}$$

where $\sigma^2 = \sigma_u^2 + \sigma_v^2$, $\lambda = \sigma_u/\sigma_v$ and Φ is the cumulative distribution function of the standard normal distribution.

It is then possible to estimate the errors, ε_i, as the difference between the observed output and estimated output. On the assumption that

$u_i \sim |N(0,\sigma_u^2)|$, the mean overall technical inefficiency is $\sigma_u \sqrt{(2/\pi)}$ and can be evaluated using the estimate of σ_u. Stochastic frontier analysis also allows information to be gained about the technical efficiency of each production unit using a technique pioneered by Jondrow *et al.* (1982). In the normal plus half-normal residual specification, the unit-specific estimates are obtained as follows.[5]

Note that ε_i is readily estimated $\forall i$, and so the task is to divide this estimate of ε_i (denoted by $\hat{\varepsilon}_{i}$), *for each i*, into its $\hat{u}_i$ and $\hat{v}_i$ components.[6] It can be shown that the conditional distribution of u_i given ε_i is $N(\mu_{*i},\sigma_*^2)$ truncated at 0, where $\mu_{*i} = \varepsilon_i\sigma_u^2/\sigma^2$ and $\sigma_*^2 = \sigma_u^2\sigma_v^2/\sigma^2$. A point estimate of u_i is then given by the mean of this conditional distribution,

$$E(u_i|\varepsilon_i) = \frac{\sigma_u\sigma_v}{\sigma}\left[\frac{\phi(\varepsilon_i\lambda/\sigma)}{1 - \Phi(\varepsilon_i\lambda/\sigma)} - \frac{\varepsilon_i\lambda}{\sigma}\right], \tag{16.15}$$

where ϕ is the standard normal distribution. Since μ_{*i} and σ_*^2 are unknown, employment of this procedure necessitates use of their estimated values; the sampling error due to this approximation vanishes asymptotically, and so it can be ignored for large enough samples.

Stochastic frontier analysis is appealing owing to its statistical nature and to its grounding in economic theory. Some critics have, however, suspected that the confidence intervals which attach to the inefficiency estimates might be too wide for the method to gain credibility in practice; the analyst is asking a lot of the method to discriminate accurately between the two components of the residual. Obviously this is an empirical issue. Moreover the imposition of a particular distributional form (be it half-normal or exponential) on that component of the residual which is deemed attributable to technical inefficiency remains an assumption which has no grounding in theory; there is no reason to prefer any one distribution to another, and any misspecification errors are incorporated into the measure of efficiency. Indeed, in the case in which efficiency of organizations (which comprise many individuals of varying efficiency) is being evaluated, by the central limit theorem we might expect the distribution of organizations' efficiencies to be normal. Stochastic frontier analysis cannot, however, be used to evaluate efficiency when the u_i are normally distributed because the u_i in this case would become indistinguishable from the v_i.

Deterministic non-statistical non-parametric methods
We now turn to examine deterministic non-statistical non-parametric methods. The most commonly used method in this category for measuring technical efficiency is known as data envelopment analysis (DEA). The basic ideas of DEA are considered below.

DEA with constant returns to scale The purpose of DEA, developed by Charnes *et al.* (1978) following work by Dantzig (1951) and Farrell (1957), is to estimate a production possibility frontier and hence to assess the technical efficiency of each firm, or decision making unit (DMU), relative to the frontier. In its simplest form, DEA assumes constant returns to scale (CRS).

Consider, first, a simple example of five universities (A, B, C, D, E) producing two outputs, y_1 (the number of graduates achieving 'good' degrees) and y_2 (the number of graduates going into employment) from one input, x (the number of students enrolled at the university). The ratio of output y_1 to input can be plotted against the ratio of output y_2 to input, as in Figure 16.8, where the piecewise linear boundary which joins up universities A, B, C and D can be considered the efficiency frontier, since no unit on the frontier can produce more of *both* outputs (for a given input) than any other unit on the frontier, and so all universities on the frontier are technically efficient. University E, however, lies inside the frontier. Moreover the ray from the origin drawn through DMU E and extended through to the frontier which it meets at point E' indicates that a DMU which was a combination of DMUs B and C could produce more of both outputs (given the input) than DMU E. In fact, university E's outputs could be proportionally increased (*without increasing input*) by the amount $1 - OE/OE'$, while OE/OE' would represent the level of efficiency of DMU E *relative to the others in the sample*, a measure consistent with Farrell's output-oriented definition of technical efficiency. An alternative approach, whereby the ratio of input to each output is plotted, would provide a piecewise linear boundary estimating the frontier SS' illustrated in Figure 16.1, and an input-oriented measure of technical efficiency could then be estimated. Under conditions of CRS, the input- and output-oriented measures of technical efficiency derived from DEA are identical.

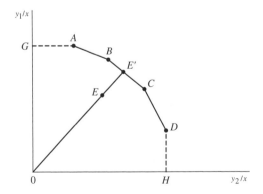

Figure 16.8   Diagrammatic representation of DEA

In practice DMUs may produce many outputs from multiple inputs, and so programming techniques are used to identify the piecewise linear frontier joining up all efficient DMUs which provide an estimate of the frontier SS' in Figure 16.1 (if an input-oriented approach is taken) or of DD' in Figure 16.2 (if an output-oriented approach is taken). The technical efficiency of DMU k is defined as the ratio of the weighted sum of outputs to the weighted sum of inputs (Charnes *et al.*, 1978):

$$TE_k = \frac{\sum\limits_{r=1}^{s} u_r y_{rk}}{\sum\limits_{i=1}^{m} v_i x_{ik}}, \tag{16.16}$$

where there are s outputs and m inputs; y_{rk} is the amount of output r produced by DMU k; x_{ik} is the amount of input i used by DMU k; u_r is the weight applied to output r; and v_i is the weight applied to input i. TE_k therefore corresponds to the measure of technical efficiency defined in section 2, but it should be noted that this measure of technical efficiency is *relative* to all other DMUs in the data set.

DMU k maximizes its efficiency score subject to certain constraints: (i) that the weights are universal: that is, the weights used by DMU k when applied to each DMU in the data set cannot produce an efficiency score exceeding unity; (ii) the weights on the outputs and the weights on the inputs are strictly positive.[7] For each of the n DMUs in the data set, therefore, the following linear programming problem must be solved:

maximize $$\frac{\sum\limits_{r=1}^{s} u_r y_{rk}}{\sum\limits_{i=1}^{m} v_i x_{ik}} \tag{16.17}$$

subject to $$\frac{\sum\limits_{r=1}^{s} u_r y_{rj}}{\sum\limits_{i=1}^{m} v_i x_{ij}} \leq 1 \qquad j = 1,\dots,n \tag{16.18}$$

$$u_r, v_i > 0 \quad \forall r = 1,\dots,s; i = 1,\dots,m.$$

This fractional or ratio linear programming problem can be transformed either by maximizing the weighted sum of outputs and holding inputs constant (an output-oriented approach) or by minimizing the weighted sum of inputs and holding outputs constant (an input-oriented approach). Primal[8] equations for each approach are given below:

Output-oriented primal (CRS)

Minimize $\displaystyle\sum_{i=1}^{m} v_i x_{ik}$ (16.19a)

Subject to

$$\sum_{i=1}^{m} v_i x_{ij} - \sum_{r=1}^{s} u_r y_{rj} \geq 0 \quad j=1,\dots,n$$

$$\sum_{r=1}^{s} u_r y_{rk} = 1 \quad\quad (16.20a)$$

$$u_r, v_i > 0 \quad \forall r = 1,\dots,s; i = 1,\dots,m$$

Input-oriented primal (CRS)

Maximize $\displaystyle\sum_{r=1}^{s} u_r y_{rk}$ (16.19b)

Subject to

$$\sum_{i=1}^{m} v_i x_{ij} - \sum_{r=1}^{s} u_r y_{rj} \geq 0 \quad j=1,\dots,n$$

$$\sum_{i=1}^{m} v_i x_{ik} = 1 \quad\quad (16.20b)$$

$$u_r, v_i > 0 \quad \forall r = 1,\dots,s; i = 1,\dots,m$$

In practice it is often the dual (the equations for each approach are given below) which is used in computation since it is more tractable than the primal, with only $s + m$ constraints rather than the $n + 1$ constraints of the primal.

Output-oriented dual (CRS)

Maximize ϕ_k (16.21a)

Subject to

$$\phi_k y_{rk} - \sum_{j=1}^{n} \lambda_j y_{rj} \leq 0 \quad r = 1,\dots,s$$

$$x_{ik} - \sum_{j=1}^{n} \lambda_j x_{ij} \geq 0 \quad i = 1,\dots,m$$

$$\lambda_j \geq 0 \;\; \forall j = 1,\dots,n \quad (16.22a)$$

Input-oriented dual (CRS)

Minimize θ_k (16.21b)

Subject to

$$y_{rk} - \sum_{j=1}^{n} \lambda_j y_{rj} \leq 0 \quad r = 1,\dots,s$$

$$\theta_k x_{ik} - \sum_{j=1}^{n} \lambda_j x_{ij} \geq 0 \quad i = 1,\dots,m$$

$$\lambda_j \geq 0 \;\; \forall j = 1,\dots,n \quad (16.22b)$$

We have, in the preceding exposition, ignored the role of slacks in measuring efficiency. The problem of slacks arises because of the sections of the efficiency boundary which run parallel to the vertical and horizontal axes (*DH* and *GA* in Figure 16.8). Suppose an additional DMU, F, was included in the data set, and its position on Figure 16.8 was on the line segment *DH*. It would lie on the boundary and would therefore have an efficiency score of 1, yet there would exist another DMU in the data set, namely DMU D, which is producing the same level of output y_2 and *more* of output y_1 relative to the same quantity of input. DMU F could therefore increase its efficiency in terms of one of the outputs, and so there is said to be output slack. It is also possible for input slack to exist where it is possible to decrease the quantity of at least one of the inputs without altering the level of output(s) produced. The above equations can therefore be rewritten with output and input slacks (represented by s_r and s_i, respectively):

Output-oriented dual with slacks (CRS)

Maximize $$\phi_k + \varepsilon \sum_{r=1}^{s} s_r + \varepsilon \sum_{i=1}^{m} s_i \tag{16.23a}$$

Subject to

$$\phi_k y_{rk} - \sum_{j=1}^{n} \lambda_j y_{rj} + s_r = 0 \quad r = 1,\dots, s$$

$$x_{ik} - \sum_{j=1}^{n} \lambda_j x_{ij} - s_i = 0 \quad i = 1,\dots, m$$

$$\lambda_j, s_r, s_i \geq 0 \quad \forall j = 1,\dots, n; r = 1,\dots, s; i = 1,\dots, m \tag{16.24a}$$

Input-oriented dual with slacks (CRS)

Minimize $$\theta_k - \varepsilon \sum_{r=1}^{s} s_r - \varepsilon \sum_{i=1}^{m} s_i \tag{16.23b}$$

Subject to

$$y_{rk} - \sum_{j=1}^{n} \lambda_j y_{rj} + s_r = 0 \quad r = 1,\dots, s$$

$$\theta_k x_{ik} - \sum_{j=1}^{n} \lambda_j x_{ij} - s_i = 0 \quad i = 1,\dots, m$$

$$\lambda_j, s_r, s_i \geq 0 \quad \forall j = 1,\dots, n; r = 1,\dots, s; i = 1,\dots, m \tag{16.24b}$$

Thus DMU k is efficient if the efficiency score $TE_k = (1/\phi_k) = 1$ (equivalently, $TE_k = \theta_k = 1$), *and* the slacks $s_r, s_i = 0, \forall r = 1,\dots, s$ and $i = 1,\dots, m$.

DEA with variable returns to scale   The CRS assumption can be relaxed and the DEA model can be easily modified to incorporate variable returns to scale (VRS) (Banker *et al.*, 1984). The assumption of VRS as opposed to CRS affects the values of the efficiency scores of the DMUs, as is illustrated in Figure 16.9. The CRS efficiency frontier (the dashed line) and the VRS efficiency frontier (the solid line *BACD*) are drawn for a situation where there is only one input and one output. Consider DMU E, for example, which has an efficiency score equal to the ratio OE/OE' under VRS which is higher than OE/OE'',[9] its efficiency score under CRS.

It should be noted that the *set* of DMUs identified as inefficient under VRS will be the same whether an input- or output-oriented approach is taken. The value of the efficiency score of an inefficient DMU, however, will vary with the choice of approach (either input- or output-oriented) as illustrated in Figure 16.4. This is in contrast to the CRS situation where choice of orientation does not affect the efficiency score of inefficient DMUs.

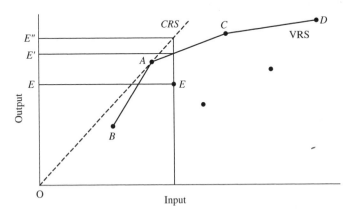

Figure 16.9   DEA frontiers: constant v. variable returns to scale

Under VRS the following linear programming problem must be solved for each of the n DMUs:

Output-oriented primal (VRS)

Minimize

$$\sum_{i=1}^{m} v_i x_{ik} - c_k \qquad (16.25a)$$

Subject to

$$\sum_{i=1}^{m} v_i x_{ij} - \sum_{r=1}^{s} u_r y_{rj} - c_k \geq 0 \quad j = 1,\dots, n$$

$$\sum_{r=1}^{s} u_r y_{rk} = 1$$

$$u_r, v_i > 0 \quad \forall r = 1,\dots, s; \ i = 1,\dots, m \qquad (16.26a)$$

Input-oriented primal (VRS)

Maximize

$$\sum_{r=1}^{s} u_r y_{rk} + c_k \qquad (16.25b)$$

Subject to

$$\sum_{i=1}^{m} v_i x_{ij} - \sum_{r=1}^{s} u_r y_{rj} - c_k \geq 0 \quad j = 1, \ldots, n$$

$$\sum_{i=1}^{m} v_i x_{ik} = 1$$

$$u_r, v_i > 0 \quad \forall r = 1, \ldots, s; \, i = 1, \ldots, m \qquad (16.26b)$$

where c_k is a measure of returns to scale for DMU k, and the dual linear programming equations are as follows.

Output-oriented dual (VRS)   *Input-oriented dual (VRS)*

Maximize ϕ_k (16.27a)   Minimize θ_k (16.27b)

Subject to   Subject to

$$\phi_k y_{rk} - \sum_{j=1}^{n} \lambda_j y_{rj} \leq 0 \quad r = 1, \ldots, s \qquad\qquad y_{rk} - \sum_{j=1}^{n} \lambda_j y_{rj} \leq 0 \quad r = 1, \ldots, s$$

$$x_{ik} - \sum_{j=1}^{n} \lambda_j x_{ij} \geq 0 \quad i = 1, \ldots, m \qquad\qquad \theta_k x_{ik} - \sum_{j=1}^{n} \lambda_j x_{ij} \geq 0 \quad i = 1, \ldots, m$$

$$\sum_{j=1}^{n} \lambda_j = 1 \qquad\qquad\qquad\qquad\qquad \sum_{j=1}^{n} \lambda_j = 1$$

$$\lambda_j \geq 0 \quad \forall j = 1, \ldots, n \quad (16.28a) \qquad \lambda_j \geq 0 \quad \forall j = 1, \ldots, n \qquad (16.28b)$$

Slacks can be incorporated into the equations as follows:

Output-oriented dual (VRS)

Maximize $\displaystyle \phi_k + \varepsilon \sum_{r=1}^{s} s_r + \varepsilon \sum_{i=1}^{m} s_i$ (16.29a)

Subject to

$$\phi_k y_{rk} - \sum_{j=1}^{n} \lambda_j y_{rj} + s_r = 0 \quad r = 1, \ldots, s$$

$$x_{ik} - \sum_{j=1}^{n} \lambda_j x_{ij} - s_i = 0 \quad i = 1, \ldots, m$$

$$\sum_{j=1}^{n} \lambda_j = 1$$

$$\lambda_j, s_r, s_i \geq 0 \quad \forall j = 1, \ldots, n; r = 1, \ldots, s; i = 1, \ldots, m \qquad (16.30a)$$

Input-oriented dual (VRS)

Minimize $\displaystyle \theta_k - \varepsilon \sum_{r=1}^{s} s_r - \varepsilon \sum_{i=1}^{m} s_i$ (16.29b)

Subject to

$$y_{rk} - \sum_{j=1}^{n} \lambda_j y_{rj} + s_r = 0 \quad r = 1,\dots, s$$

$$\theta_k x_{ik} - \sum_{j=1}^{n} \lambda_j x_{ij} - s_i = 0 \quad i = 1,\dots, m$$

$$\sum_{j=1}^{n} \lambda_j = 1$$

$$\lambda_j, s_r, s_i \geq 0 \quad \forall j = 1,\dots, n; r = 1,\dots, s; i = 1,\dots, m \qquad (16.30b)$$

Overall technical efficiency of DMU k is measured by $TE_k = 1/\phi_k$ (in the output-oriented framework) or $TE_k = \theta_k$ (in the input-oriented framework) and scale efficiency can be identified by calculating the following ratio for DMU k:

$$SCE_k = \frac{TE_{k,CRS}}{TE_{k,VRS}}. \qquad (16.31)$$

Furthermore it can be established whether a DMU is operating at increasing or decreasing returns to scale by running the non-increasing returns to scale (NIRS) model,[10] in addition to the CRS and VRS, and comparing the results of each (Coelli *et al.*, 1998).

DEA and allocative efficiency   All discussions of DEA so far have focused on measuring technical efficiency. DEA can, however, provide measures of overall and hence allocative efficiency for each DMU, as defined in section 2. In order to achieve this, knowledge of all input prices (w_i) *or* all output prices (p_r) is required. For schools and institutions of higher education such information is rarely available (any observed prices are likely to be regulated rather than market prices) and so the methodology for deriving allocative efficiency is presented only briefly.

Allocative efficiency is related to overall efficiency and technical efficiency as follows:

$$AE_k = \frac{OE_k}{TE_k} \qquad (16.32)$$

and can be found by means of either an input-oriented (cost-minimization) or an output-oriented (revenue maximization) approach (see section 2). In the case of revenue maximization, the first step is to compute measures of technical efficiency (TE_k) using an output-oriented approach (CRS or VRS as appropriate). The second step is to solve a revenue-maximization DEA, the equations for which are given below for a VRS scenario (see equations (16.33a) and (16.34a)).

Output-oriented (VRS)

Maximize
$$\sum_{r=1}^{s} p_{rk} y_{rk}^{*} \qquad (16.33a)$$

Subject to

$$y_{rk}^{*} - \sum_{j=1}^{n} \lambda_{j} y_{rj} \leq 0 \quad r = 1,\dots, s$$

$$x_{ik} - \sum_{j=1}^{n} \lambda_{j} x_{ij} \geq 0 \quad i = 1,\dots, m$$

$$\sum_{j=1}^{n} \lambda_{j} = 1$$

$$\lambda_{j} \geq 0 \quad \forall j = 1,\dots, n \qquad (16.34a)$$

where p_{rk} is the price of output r ($r = 1,\dots, s$) for DMU k, y_{rk}^{*} is calculated from the linear programming problem and is the revenue-maximizing quantity of output r ($r = 1,\dots, s$) for DMU k, given its input levels x_{ik} and output prices p_{rk}.

Input-oriented (VRS)

Minimize
$$\sum_{i=1}^{m} w_{ik} x_{ik}^{*} \qquad (16.33b)$$

Subject to

$$y_{rk} - \sum_{j=1}^{n} \lambda_{j} y_{rj} \leq 0 \quad r = 1,\dots, s$$

$$x_{ik}^{*} - \sum_{j=1}^{n} \lambda_{j} x_{ij} \geq 0 \quad i = 1,\dots, m$$

$$\sum_{j=1}^{n} \lambda_{j} = 1$$

$$\lambda_{j} \geq 0 \quad \forall j = 1,\dots, n \qquad (16.34b)$$

where w_{ik} is the price of input i ($i = 1,\dots, m$) for DMU k, x_{ik}^{*} is calculated from the linear programming problem and is the cost-minimizing quantity of input i ($i = 1,\dots, m$) for DMU k, given its output levels y_{rk} and input prices w_{ik}.

Overall efficiency for DMU k, as defined in section 2, is then computed from the following:

$$OE_k = \frac{\sum_{r=1}^{s} p_{rk} y_{rk}}{\sum_{r=1}^{s} p_{rk} y_{rk}^*} \tag{16.35}$$

and allocative efficiency can be found using the relationship in equation (16.32).

In the case of cost minimization, the first step is to compute measures of technical efficiency (TE) using an input-oriented approach (CRS or VRS as appropriate). The second step is to solve a cost minimization DEA, the equations for which are given above for a VRS scenario (see equations (16.33b) and (16.34b)). Overall efficiency for DMU k, as defined in section 2, is then computed from the following:

$$OE_k = \frac{\sum_{i=1}^{m} w_{ik} x_{ik}^*}{\sum_{i=1}^{m} w_{ik} x_{ik}} \tag{16.36}$$

and allocative efficiency can again be found using the relationship in equation (16.32).

DEA and preferences   Various attempts to incorporate information regarding prior preferences into DEA have been made. The simplest method is to place restrictions on the weights assigned to the various inputs and outputs. Thus, for example, in setting output targets (for given inputs), it might be wished that one of the outputs should be given pre-emptive priority. In effect, this amounts to holding inputs and some (but not all) outputs constant in the target-setting procedure (see, for example, Thanassoulis and Dunstan, 1994). Such a procedure goes some way towards parameterizing the production function.

Most recently, Halme *et al.* (1999) have adapted DEA to incorporate the preferences of the 'decision maker' (DM). The procedure is illustrated in an output-oriented perspective in Figure 16.10, with five DMUs producing two outputs from a single input. The first stage is to perform a standard DEA in order to identify the piecewise linear frontier (*ABCD* in Figure 16.10). Thus the DMU located at *P* has technical efficiency measured by the ratio $TE = OP/OP_1$. The next step is to identify the DM's most preferred combination of inputs and outputs known as the most preferred solution (MPS) which lies on the efficiency frontier. Halme *et al.* use a multi-objective linear programming search procedure to locate the MPS, but it is possible to use alternative search procedures.

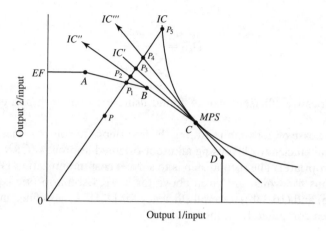

Figure 16.10　Measuring value efficiency

The final step is to provide a measure of efficiency which incorporates the DM's preferences, termed by Halme *et al.* (1999) 'value efficiency' (VE). It is assumed that the MPS also lies on the (unknown) indifference curve reflecting all points of equivalent utility to the DM (denoted by *IC* in Figure 16.10). The true value of efficiency which incorporates the DM's preferences is therefore given by the ratio $VE = OP/OP_5$, but, since the indifference curve is unobserved, this ratio cannot be evaluated. It is further assumed that all points on the indifference curve lie above a line which is tangent to the efficiency frontier at the MPS (the line of tangency is denoted by *IC′* in Figure 16.10). This line of tangency could be used to provide an estimate of value efficiency, namely OP/OP_3 (Korhonen *et al.*, 2001). In practice this first best estimate of value efficiency cannot be computed and one must instead use the line *IC″* in Figure 16.10 to calculate a second best estimate given by the ratio $VE^* = OP/OP_2$, which gives an upwardly biased estimate of value efficiency.[11] The evaluation of VE^* for all DMUs in the set involves the solution of a set of LP equations similar to those solved for a standard DEA (see Korhonen *et al.*, 2001).

DEA, technical efficiency and production technology changes　Section 2 described how the Malmquist productivity index (input-oriented or output-oriented) could be used to separate productivity changes over time into the component due to changes in technical efficiency and the component caused by changes in production technology. DEA can be easily adapted to compute the required Malmquist productivity index. For example, closer examination of the Malmquist output-oriented[12] productivity index (see equation (16.37) below) reveals that just four output distance functions need to be evaluated.

$$M_O(x_t, y_t, x_q, y_q) = \frac{D_O^t(x_t, y_t)}{D_O^q(x_q, y_q)} \left[\frac{D_O^q(x_t, y_t)}{D_O^t(x_t, y_t)} \cdot \frac{D_O^q(x_q, y_q)}{D_O^t(x_q, y_q)} \right]^{\frac{1}{2}}, \quad (16.37)$$

where x_q and x_t are the vector of inputs used at time q and t respectively, and y_q and y_t are the vector of outputs produced at time q and t, respectively. $D_O^q(x_q, y_q)$ and $D_O^t(x_t, y_t)$ are found by solving standard DEAs in a CRS output-oriented framework using the data for each time period separately. Specifically:

Evaluating $D_O^t(x_t, y_t)$

$$\frac{1}{D_O^t(x_t, y_t)} = \text{Maximize } \phi_k \quad (16.38a)$$

Subject to

$$\phi_k y_{rkt} - \sum_{j=1}^{n} \lambda_j y_{rjt} \leq 0 \quad r = 1, \dots, s$$

$$x_{ikt} - \sum_{j=1}^{n} \lambda_j x_{ijt} \geq 0 \quad i = 1, \dots, m$$

$$\lambda_j \geq 0 \quad \forall j = 1, \dots, n \quad (16.39a)$$

Evaluating $D_O^q(x_q, y_q)$

$$\frac{1}{D_O^q(x_q, y_q)} = \text{Maximize } \phi_k \quad (16.38b)$$

Subject to

$$\phi_k y_{rkq} - \sum_{j=1}^{n} \lambda_j y_{rjq} \leq 0 \quad r = 1, \dots, s$$

$$x_{ikq} - \sum_{j=1}^{n} \lambda_j x_{ijq} \geq 0 \quad i = 1, \dots, m$$

$$\lambda_j \geq 0 \quad \forall j = 1, \dots, n \quad (16.39b)$$

where subscripts q and t refer to time periods q and t, respectively. The final two output distance functions which need to be evaluated are found by solving the following two sets of LPs:

Evaluating $D_O^t(x_q, y_q)$

$$\frac{1}{D_O^t(x_q, y_q)} = \text{Max } \phi_k \quad (16.40a)$$

Subject to

$$\phi_k y_{rkq} - \sum_{j=1}^{n} \lambda_j y_{rjt} \leq 0 \quad r = 1, \dots, s$$

$$x_{ikq} - \sum_{j=1}^{n} \lambda_j x_{ijt} \geq 0 \quad i = 1, \dots, m$$

$$\lambda_j \geq 0 \quad \forall j = 1, \dots, n \quad (16.41a)$$

Evaluating $D_O^q(x_t, y_t)$

$$\frac{1}{D_O^q(x_t, y_t)} = \text{Max } \phi_k \quad (16.40b)$$

Subject to

$$\phi_k y_{rkt} - \sum_{j=1}^{n} \lambda_j y_{rjq} \leq 0 \quad r = 1, \dots, s$$

$$x_{ikt} - \sum_{j=1}^{n} \lambda_j x_{ijq} \geq 0 \quad i = 1, \dots, m$$

$$\lambda_j \geq 0 \quad \forall j = 1, \dots, n \quad (16.41b)$$

It should be noted that the φs and λs will not necessarily take the same values in each set of equations. In addition, the value of the optimand in the final two LPs may not be greater than or equal to one as in a standard output-oriented DEA. In the case of these two LPs, the production point of one period is being compared to the frontier for a different period (and hence different production technology) and therefore may lie outside the feasible production set for that period. This is particularly likely when the production point for the final time period (t in this case) is compared to the frontier for the initial period (q in this case).

Bootstrapping   One of the main reservations regarding DEA is its inability to provide traditional methods of statistical inference. However bootstrapping procedures have been developed to overcome this criticism by providing estimated confidence intervals for the efficiencies derived from DEA. One such method (Simar and Wilson, 1998, 1999) works as follows. Denote the vector of s outputs used by DMU j ($j=1,...,n$) by y_j and the vector of m inputs used by DMU j by x_j.

Step 1 involves estimating the efficiency scores for the data set and reflecting the data. DEA is applied to the given data on inputs and outputs to obtain an estimate of efficiency for each DMU in the set, and this is denoted by $\hat{D}(x_j,y_j)$. These estimates must be reflected around unity, and this is done by computing $2-\hat{D}(x_j,y_j)$ for each $\hat{D}(x_j,y_j)$, $j=1,...,n$, providing $2n$ observations in total (that is, n observations of $\hat{D}(x_j,y_j)$ and n observations of $2-\hat{D}(x_j,y_j)$).

Step 2 involves deriving bootstrap values. This step actually involves a number of procedures. First, a bandwidth h must be set for use in the drawing of the bootstrap values. This value can be set arbitrarily, such as $h=0.05$ (with subsequent small changes to assess the effect of the size of h on the estimated confidence intervals), or various alternative methods can be used for setting the value of h; these are discussed and illustrated in Simar and Wilson (1998). Secondly, it is necessary to draw n independently and identically distributed observations (denoted by $\varepsilon_j j = 1,...,n$) from the probability density function used as the kernel distribution (for example, uniform or standard normal distribution). Thirdly, draw n values (denoted by $d_j j=1,...,n$) independently and uniformly from the set of $2n$ reflected distance function estimates. From these, calculate the mean,

$$\bar{d} = \sum_{j=1}^{n} d_j \big/ n \qquad (16.42)$$

then compute the value

$$d_j^* = \bar{d} + \sqrt{(1 + h^2/s^2)} \, (d_j + h\varepsilon_j - \bar{d}), \qquad (16.43)$$

where s^2 is the sample variance of $v_j = d_j + h\varepsilon_j$. Finally calculate the bootstrap values (D_j^*) as

$$D_j^* = \begin{cases} d_j^* & \text{if } d_j^* \leq 1 \\ 2 - d_j^* & \text{otherwise} \end{cases}. \tag{16.44}$$

Step 3 involves defining the pseudo-data and obtaining the bootstrap estimates of the efficiencies. Having obtained the bootstrap data, the next step is to define a pseudo-data set with input and output vectors (denoted by x_j^*, y_j^*) given by

$$y_j^* = D_j^* y_j / \hat{D}(x_j, y_j), \tag{16.45}$$
$$x_j^* = x_j. \tag{16.46}$$

A number, say B, of bootstrap estimates of the efficiency score for each DMU j ($j = 1, \dots, n$) are obtained by applying DEA to the pseudo-data B times. These bootstrap estimates can be denoted for DMU k by $\{\hat{D}_b^*(x_k, y_k)\}_{b=1}^B$.

In step 4, estimated confidence intervals for the efficiency scores are computed. The $100(1 - \alpha)\%$ confidence interval for the true efficiency for DMU k can be calculated by finding the values b_α, a_α such that:

$$Pr(-b_\alpha \leq \hat{D}(x_k, y_k) - D(x_k, y_k) \leq -a_\alpha) = 1 - \alpha. \tag{16.47}$$

The values b_α, a_α are not known but can be estimated from the bootstrap estimates $\{\hat{D}_b^*(x_k, y_k)\}_{b=1}^B$ by sorting the values $\hat{D}_b^*(x_k, y_k) - \hat{D}(x_k, y_k)$ in increasing order and deleting $(100\alpha/2)\%$ of the observations at each end of this list. Thus estimates of $-b_\alpha$ and $-a_\alpha$ (denoted by $-\hat{b}_\alpha$ and $-\hat{a}_\alpha$) are the endpoints of the remaining array of values such that $\hat{a}_\alpha \leq \hat{b}_\alpha$. The bootstrap approximation of equation (16.47) is therefore

$$Pr(-\hat{b}_\alpha \leq \hat{D}(x_k, y_k) - D(x_k, y_k) \leq -\hat{a}_\alpha) \approx 1 - \alpha, \tag{16.48}$$

and so the estimated $100(1 - \alpha)\%$ confidence interval for the efficiency score of DMU k is found by evaluating:

$$[\hat{D}(x_k, y_k) + \hat{a}_\alpha, \hat{D}(x_k, y_k) + \hat{b}_\alpha]. \tag{16.49}$$

Further information provided by DEA   It is worth pausing at this stage to consider the specific advantages and disadvantages of DEA compared to statistical parametric methods in the context of education. In the sections above we have seen that a standard DEA can produce information about the efficiency (technical and scale) of all decision-making units in the sample. In addition, adaptations of the technique can provide further measures of allocative or even value efficiency. But DEA offers more than simply an evaluation of efficiency. By solving a DEA problem, we acquire a wealth of managerial information which, advocates of the method argue, can be used in the drive to enhance efficiency. This information forms the substance of the present subsection.

First, results from the DEA can be used to identify, for each technically inefficient producer, a set of efficient producers which it should seek to emulate. The latter producers are collectively known as the peer group or the efficient reference set of the inefficient decision-making unit. The efficient reference set associated with an inefficient producer does not necessarily include all producers lying on the frontier; rather it comprises those producers which dominate the inefficient decision-making unit.[13] In the simple example illustrated in Figure 16.8, the inefficient DMU E could become efficient by moving to point E' on the frontier, a point which is a combination of the output and input levels of DMUs B and C. These DMUs therefore form DMU E's efficient reference set. An inefficient decision-making unit is likely to find useful the identification of its peer group, because it can then see which producers it should imitate in order to become efficient.

Secondly, the efficiency frontier can be used to set targets for inefficient decision-making units (Färe *et al.*, 1989; Pedraja-Chaparro *et al.*, 1999). These targets could lie anywhere along the efficiency frontier. Often it is useful to set an output target which reflects the output which would be needed to bring the producer up to the technical efficiency frontier if inputs remained unchanged (point E' in Figure 16.8 would reflect the output targets which DMU E should aim to achieve in order to become efficient). Alternatively an input target could be imposed under the assumption that output remains unchanged. Any mix of these approaches is possible. The targets thus set are attainable and realistic in the sense that they merely reflect current best practice. The aim of such targets is to demonstrate to inefficient producers exactly what other (best practice) producers could achieve. The targets could be set by the inefficient decision-making units themselves, or could be imposed by some umbrella organization.

Thirdly, the ease with which DEA accommodates multiple outputs *and* multiple inputs (Banker *et al.*, 1984, 1989; Färe *et al.*, 1989; McCarty and Yaisawarng, 1993; Pedraja-Chaparro *et al.*, 1999; Mante, 2001) is a considerable advantage in the context of education where it is generally agreed that a variety of outputs is produced from numerous inputs. Consider, for example, the higher education sector where universities produce both teaching and research. These in turn are measured by, for example, the degree results and labour market success of graduates (teaching) and the books, journal articles and conference papers produced (research). These outputs are produced from a number of inputs including, for example, students (for which measures of both quantity and quality need to be included), staff and raw materials.[14]

Fourthly, the non-parametric nature of the method allows each DMU to select its own weights on inputs and outputs, rather than requiring a judgment on their relative importance (Pedraja-Chaparro *et al.*, 1999). In a not-for-profit sector such as education this is ideal since there are no prices with which to measure the relative importance of the outputs and the inputs. Such flexibility therefore allows DMUs to differ in terms of circumstances and to have different objectives (Pedraja-Chaparro *et al.*, 1999).

Finally, all variants of DEA have in common the feature that they measure efficiency against the benchmark of current best practice. There is no absolute standard of efficiency in these models (nor could there be). This approach has the advantage that it is known that current best practice is attainable. The drawbacks of the technique, however, must not be forgotten. Perhaps the biggest shortcoming of DEA is its non-stochastic characteristic. Thus the existence of omitted variables, errors of measurement of the inputs and outputs and any other statistical noise will contaminate the efficiency scores. In the context of education, specification and measurement of input and output variables is particularly difficult (see section 5 for a further discussion on this topic) and errors in the efficiency scores caused by omitted variables, use of a sample smaller than the population, the presence of outliers and measurement errors are highly likely, although the extent of the problems is unknown. The development of stochastic DEA (Lovell, 1993) and introduction of other adaptations of DEA designed to reduce the problems of measurement errors in the input and output variables (Thanassoulis, 1999) are therefore welcome advances in the technique.

Many of the remaining problems of DEA arise from attributes which have been considered to be advantageous. Although DEA can accommodate numerous inputs and outputs, the specification of these (particularly the number of each) can affect the efficiency levels of the DMUs estimated by DEA (Pedraja-Chaparro *et al.*, 1999). Moreover, since DEA is non-statistical and non-parametric, there are no familiar parametric tests with which to check the validity of the model. Thus it is wise to consider the results from a number of possible specifications in order to assess the sensitivity of results to specification changes.

Second, including large numbers of outputs or inputs can lead to multicollinearity, the effect of which on the DEA results is a relatively underresearched problem. This is discussed further in section 5. Third, the assumption of VRS where there are, in fact, no returns to scale effects, can distort the efficiencies. As can be seen from Figure 16.9, the VRS frontier envelops the data more closely than the CRS frontier. As a consequence, if a VRS model is applied when the true model is CRS, the efficiencies for the DMUs at the extremes (that is, the smallest and largest) will be overestimated (Dyson *et al.*, 2001).

4   Techniques for measuring efficiency: level of analysis is the individual

Various criticisms have been made of methods for measuring the performance of production units which aggregate individual data to the level of the production unit itself. Woodhouse and Goldstein (1988) make a number of arguments against the use of residuals from regression-based models, applied to aggregate level data, as measures of the efficiency of production units such as schools, LEAs or universities. Many of these criticisms can be levelled against any of the statistical models of efficiency measurement.

First of all, it is argued that the use of data measured at the level of the production unit does not allow for variation of within-unit relationships. For example, in an analysis of universities, output might be measured by average degree result and input by average entry score. A university-level analysis imposes the same relationship between entry score and degree result for each university. Yet it might be the case that university X performs better in terms of degree results than university Y for students with low entry scores, but the opposite is the case for students with high intake scores (see Figure 16.11). Ideally, therefore, if the within-university relationship between degree result and entry score is known, it should be taken into account when measuring the performance of universities. Aggregate studies, it is argued, preclude this possibility.[15]

Second, the residuals of regression based models can vary substantially depending on the predictors included in the model. The variation in residuals can cause unit rankings to vary across various possible statistical models. Furthermore it can be difficult to choose between models which appear to fit the data equally well because aggregate-level studies inevitably can be based on small samples.

Measuring the efficiency of production units using aggregate-level DEA is also open to serious objections (Woodhouse and Goldstein, 1988). The efficiency score of a DMU is computed as the ratio of the weighted outputs to weighted inputs. In a simple one output (y), one input (x) case (for example, y = average degree results and x = average entry score), DMU k's efficiency is measured as a simple ratio of output to input: $\theta_k = y_k/x_k$. However there is clearly a relationship between degree results and entry scores and, supposing the relationship takes the form $y_k = a + bx_k$, DMU k's efficiency is represented by $\theta_k = a/x_k + b$, and is therefore inversely propor-

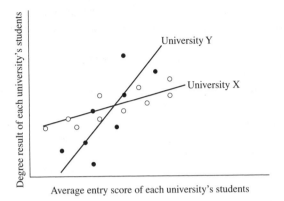

Figure 16.11   *Differential effectiveness of two universities in producing degree results*

tional to the input measure. This argument can be extended to the situation with multiple inputs and multiple outputs (ibid.). Thus aggregate-level DEA also fails to measure performance adequately.

This section therefore looks at some methods for measuring the performance of a production unit using data from the individuals which comprise that unit.

Statistical parametric methods

A number of commonly used statistical techniques can be applied to individual school pupils and university students in order to derive measures of the efficiency of the institution attended. The specific technique used depends on the nature of the dependent variable. Thus OLS regression is appropriate if the dependent variable is continuous (for example, the earnings of graduates in the labour market), whereas logit or probit models are appropriate for limited dependent variables (for example, whether or not a student completed his degree) and ordered logit or probit models can be used when the dependent variable is both limited and ordered (for example, the degree result of a graduate, or the examination result of a school pupil). Details of the ordered probit model can be found in Chapter 12.

However statistical models which use individual-level data to look at the relationship between educational outcomes and educational inputs, but which make no allowance for the effects of the educational institution attended, may be considered unsatisfactory for two reasons. First, significance tests are often biased and overoptimistic. Second, if institutional effects are ignored, the model fails to offer insights into the influence of the institution attended on the education process (Goldstein, 1997); that is, such models indicate nothing about the performance or efficiency of institutions. Multi-level models, however, explicitly incorporate institutional effects into the relationship between individuals' outcomes and the inputs.

Multi-level modelling assumes that the data to be analysed are hierarchical; for example, pupils are nested within schools, students are nested within universities. Both of these are examples of data with two levels, the students (pupils) are level 1 and the universities (schools) are level 2. Additional levels could be added; for example, pupils are nested within schools which in turn are nested within local education authorities. Only a brief overview of multi-level modelling with specific reference to its application in efficiency measurement will be presented here, and the interested reader is referred to Aitkin and Longford (1986) and Goldstein (1995) for additional details and extensions.

Consider first a simple model in the context of higher education. Let y_{ij} denote the degree result of the ith student in the jth university; then the following model,

$$y_{ij} = b_j + e_{ij} = b_0 + u_j + e_{ij}, \tag{16.50}$$

indicates that an individual's degree performance can be divided into a university-specific contribution (β_j) and a deviation (e_{ij}) from his university's contribution. The university-specific contribution (β_j) is further broken down into a mean value across all universities (β_0) and a deviation from the mean (u_j). These u_j are often referred to as 'effects' (here they are university effects) and will be discussed in more detail below.

A number of points need to be noted. First, the universities are assumed to be a random sample from the population of universities. The u_j, which are therefore distributed among universities, are normally distributed with mean zero and variance σ_u^2. The student residuals (e_{ij}) are also normally distributed with mean zero and variance σ_e^2. Dedicated software is available to estimate the unknown parameters, $\beta_0, \sigma_u^2, \sigma_e^2$, following which estimation of the u_j (denoted by $\hat{u}_j$) can be accomplished from the following equation:

$$\hat{u}_j = \frac{n_j \sigma_u^2}{n_j \sigma_u^2 + \sigma_e^2} \cdot \frac{\sum_i (y_{ij} - \hat{y}_{ij})}{n_j}, \tag{16.51}$$

where n_j = the number of students at university j. Each university's estimated effect $\hat{u}_j$ has a sampling error, hence confidence intervals can also be computed. It is the estimates and confidence intervals of the university effects which, it is suggested, might be used to indicate a university's performance. The convention is to rank the institutions according to value of

$\hat{u}_j$ from lowest to highest and plot these with associated upper and lower bound from a specified confidence interval. It is argued that, if these intervals overlap, there is no significant difference between institutions in terms of performance.

The simple model can be adapted to incorporate predictors of the dependent variable. For example, the best predictor of the degree performance of a student is likely to be his entry qualification score (x_{ij}). The model therefore becomes

$$y_{ij} = b_0 + b_1 x_{ij} + u_j + e_{ij}. \tag{16.52}$$

In this model, the slope of the relationship between y_{ij} and x_{ij} remains constant, while the intercept varies between universities. Thus β_0 and β_1 are fixed quantities and u_j and e_{ij} are the random part of the model. The addition of the explanatory or input variable leads to the interpretation of the estimated residuals $\hat{u}_j$ from this model as indicators of a university's effectiveness in terms of 'value added'. Clearly any number of explanatory variables could be added to this model.

Finally we consider a model which allows the slope of the relationship between y_{ij} and x_{ij} to vary between universities as well as the intercept. This is written as

$$y_{ij} = b_0 + b_{1j} x_{ij} + u_j + e_{ij}, \tag{16.53a}$$

$$\beta_{1j} = \beta_1 + v_j. \tag{16.53b}$$

Thus the overall mean slope for the population of universities is β_1, and each university can deviate from this by v_j. The terms u_j and v_j follow a multivariate normal distribution (here it is bivariate normal because there are just two random variables at level 2) with mean equal to zero. The variance of u_j measures the variation across the universities' lines in their intercepts and is denoted by $\text{var}(u_j) = \sigma_u^2$; the variance of v_j measures the variation across the universities' lines in their slopes and is denoted by $\text{var}(v_j) = \sigma_v^2$; and the covariance between u_j and v_j measures the covariance between the university-level intercept and slope and is denoted by $\text{cov}(u_j, v_j) = \sigma_{u,v}$. Students' degree results vary from their summary line by the amount e_{ij}. In this model, β_0 and β_1 are fixed quantities and v_j, u_j and e_{ij} are random coefficients.

The problem with multi-level models is that, in order to model the complexities of the educational production process, they must themselves become complex and as a consequence can become difficult for any but the expert to understand and interpret. Moreover more advanced variants of multi-level modelling (for instance those involving limited dependent variables) can be computationally intractable.

Non-statistical non-parametric methods

An alternative to these statistical methods exists in the form of DEA where the DMU, rather than being a school, university, department or district, is, in fact, the individual pupil or student (Thanassoulis, 1999; Portela and Thanassoulis, 2001; Thanassoulis and Portela, 2002). For example, consider a student at an institution of higher education whose output is his degree result and his input his entry qualification. Each student's efficiency score is then obtained from applying DEA to all students in the higher education sector, but this efficiency score would incorporate a component which was a consequence of the student's own efforts and a component which was a consequence of the efficiency of teaching at the university attended by the student. In order to assess the efficiency of the institutions of higher education, it would therefore be necessary, as a first step, to decompose the students' efficiency scores into these two components using a method pioneered by Portela and Thanassoulis (2001) and Thanassoulis and Portela (2002). Consider a hypothetical data set of students from two universities, each producing graduates with degrees, the quality of which is measured by degree results, using initial student quality, measured by entry qualification. The output and input data can be plotted for all students (see Figure 16.12).

The boundary *EFCD* envelops all students and can be termed the student-within-all-institutions efficiency boundary, students lying on segments *EF* and *CD* being on the boundary but not efficient (because of slacks). Thus, using the traditional (output-oriented) DEA definition of efficiency, student *F*, who lies on the student-within-all-institutions efficiency frontier, has an efficiency score of 1, whereas student *Y*, who lies inside the student-within-all-institutions efficiency frontier, has an overall efficiency level of OY/OY'', which is less than 1. In other words, OY/OY'' represents the proportion of degree achievement obtained by student *Y* relative to the best achievement obtained by students from all universities, *and* given student *Y*'s initial qualifications.

This student-within-all-institutions efficiency score, however, ignores the effect that the university has on the student's level of achievement. Students from university *T*, for example, have their own efficiency boundary (termed the student-within-own-institution efficiency boundary), defined by *ABCD*. Similarly the student-within-own-institution efficiency boundary for university *S* is *EFGH*. Thus student *Y* (from university *T*) has a student-within-own-institution efficiency score of OY/OY', which represents the proportion of degree achievement obtained by student *Y* relative to the best achievement obtained by students from university *T* only *and* given student *Y*'s initial qualifications. The distance $Y'Y''$ gives a measure of the impact of student *Y*'s university on his degree result. The institution-within-

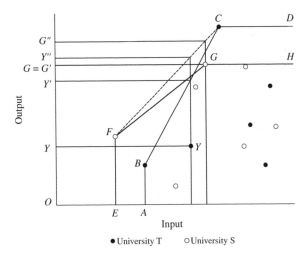

Figure 16.12   Decomposing efficiencies using DEA

institutions efficiency score, specific to student Y, is defined as the ratio OY'/OY'', and varies with the level of input.

In summary, student Y has a student-within-all-institutions efficiency of OY/OY'', of which OY/OY' is due to the student's own efforts, and OY'/OY'' is due to the efficiency of the university attended by student Y. This can be contrasted with student G from university S who has a student-within-own-institution efficiency score of 1 (this student is achieving the best degree that he can relative to students within the same university and given his entry qualification), but an institution-within-all-institutions efficiency score of $OG'/OG'' = OG/OG''$ (that is, less than 1) because of the university's inefficiency.

The efficiency of each institution can then be examined by comparing the array of institution-within-institutions efficiency scores of each institution's own students. This component is a measure of the efficiency of the institution itself, and is not contaminated by the effects of students' own efforts. However a comparison of all three components can offer useful insights, particularly to decision makers within each institution, into how greater efficiency can be achieved (Portela and Thanassoulis, 2001; Thanassoulis and Portela, 2002).

5   Empirical studies

A detailed survey of all the empirical applications of the methods described in the preceding sections in the context of education and higher education is beyond the scope of this section. As a consequence, references are made to a limited number of studies in order to highlight some of the problems and uses of the techniques of efficiency measurement in the education context. A summary of the findings of a more complete list of empirical studies can be found in the appendix.

The unit of analysis
Efficiency studies have been performed using a variety of units of analysis. Within the school sector, the unit of analysis has been the pupil, the school, the school district and the local education authority (Goldstein and Thomas, 1996; Bradley *et al.*, 2001; Engert, 1996; Mayston and Jesson, 1988). In higher education, studies have attempted to evaluate performance using the individual students, the same department or cost centre across different universities, different departments within one university, and the universities themselves as the units of analysis (Johnes, 1996, 2003; Beasley, 1995; Friedman and Sinuany-Stern, 1997). Individual-level studies provide large quantities of information, but the results may be complex and difficult to interpret. Aggregate level studies, on the other hand, are often straightforward to interpret but this is achieved at the cost of loss of information in the aggregation process. Perhaps the pertinent question is whether the analyses performed on different levels of data provide different measures of efficiency.

Supporters and practitioners of the multi-level modelling approach argue that application of this technique to individual-level data is the only method which can capture adequately the complex effects of individual institutions on student outcomes (Aitkin and Longford, 1986). The school effects derived using multi-level modelling have been shown to provide different rankings of schools compared to rankings based on raw output variables (Sammons *et al.*, 1993). Similar results are derived from probit models applied to university students and graduates (Bratti, 2002; Naylor *et al.*, 2000; Smith and Naylor, 2001a; Smith *et al.*, 2000). No study, however, has yet compared the rankings of institutions based on multi-level model effects, the marginal effects from a probit model or rankings derived from aggregated data.

The application of DEA to individuals rather than institutions is a relatively recent innovation. Despite the suggestion that the application of DEA to individual pupils in schools could be useful in terms of improving the efficiency of teachers by providing information on which pupils use resources inefficiently (Bessent *et al.*, 1982), most of the studies in the field of education having been carried out using department, institution or administrative area-level data. This is, no doubt, a consequence of the vast computing resources required to perform individual-level DEAs: the number of observations determines both the number and complexity of linear programmes which need to be solved. To date, individual-level DEAs have varied in size from over 2500 individuals (Johnes, 2003) to over 6500 individuals (Portela and Thanassoulis, 2001). Preliminary evidence suggests that rankings of universities derived from individual-level DEAs differ from rankings derived from DEAs applied to the same data aggregated to university level (Johnes, 2003). Clearly further investigations are required and, if the result is confirmed, this may have an effect on the way in which DEA is applied to evaluate efficiency in education in the future.

A question which is perhaps more relevant in the context of higher education than schools is whether data should be aggregated across subjects. There is clear evidence that the determinants of research output, degree results and non-completion rates vary by department or subject (Johnes *et al.*, 1993; Smith and Naylor, 2001a, 2001b). This suggests that studies of efficiency in universities should at least be disaggregated by subject, and calls into question the validity of comparing different departments within one university.

At school level, there is limited evidence that the role of pupils' background factors and their initial attainment is greater in accounting for the variation in reading than in mathematics, and that school effects are greater in mathematics than in reading (Sammons *et al.*, 1993). Moreover the correlation of rankings of schools based on the school effects of two models, one derived from reading outcomes and one derived from mathematics outcomes, is not particularly high (ibid.). This may therefore suggest that, even at school level, care should be taken to investigate differences between subjects when evaluating the performance of institutions.

The outputs
As with the level at which an analysis of efficiency is performed, the specification of outputs is also influenced by data considerations. Ideally measures of all outputs should be included. The problem (apart from data constraints) is that it is not actually clear what are the outputs of the education process. Teaching output can be broken down into a number of components, all of which can be considered outputs of the education process. These include student achievement, increased productivity in the labour force, and present and future consumption benefits.

Student achievement can often be well approximated since testing is performed at many levels of education and data are therefore often available for a variety of test and examination results. The raw number of students graduating or achieving a particular grade is a common measure of student achievement in aggregate school analyses (Bessent and Bessent, 1980; Kirjavainen and Loikkanen, 1998) and aggregate university studies (Athanassopoulos and Shale, 1997; El-Mahgary and Lahdelma, 1995;

Engert, 1996; Madden *et al.*, 1997). Such measures, however, do not adequately take account of the quality of achievement and so mean institution examination scores and percentage success rates are often preferred in aggregate analyses, while examination points scored are obvious measures of output in individual-level studies (see, for example, Chalos and Cherian, 1995; Bradley *et al.*, 2001; Johnes and Taylor, 1990, for applications at the aggregate level in elementary schools, secondary schools and universities, respectively; see Goldstein and Spiegelhalter, 1996, and Smith and Naylor, 2001b, for examples in individual-level studies in secondary and higher education, respectively).

There has been concern at the use of examination data to reflect teaching output, since examinations do not test all the skills which might be considered desirable outcomes of education (Bifulco and Bretschneider, 2001) and academic achievement is only one outcome of the teaching process (Bessent *et al.*, 1982). Measures of the efficiency with which institutions enhance students' productivity in the labour market would reflect an additional output of teaching, but data on labour market success are not always available. The First Destinations Survey of university graduates in the UK which reports on graduates' destinations six months after graduation has permitted the construction of output measures which reflect labour market success in studies of university efficiency in the UK (Johnes and Taylor, 1989b; 1990; Johnes, 1996; Bratti *et al.*, 2003; Smith *et al.*, 2000). Additional databases have also allowed the construction of output measures based on graduates' earnings (Naylor *et al.*, 2000, 2002; Belfield and Fielding, 2001).

In the process of teaching, institutions of education also produce individuals who fail to attain a qualification. Wastage due to failure of examinations, truancy (at school level) or dropping out (at upper secondary, further and higher education levels) is a by-product of the teaching process and its incidence is often concealed if numbers of successful or enrolling students, or labour market successes of graduates, are used to reflect teaching output. Thus non-completion rates (or retention rates) or attendance rates have been included to reflect this aspect of teaching output in school and higher education studies (Bradley *et al.*, 2001; Harrison and Rouse, 2002; Ruggiero, 1996; Johnes and Taylor, 1989a; Johnes, 1996; Mante, 2001; Ramanathan, 2001).

Data constraints on the availability of adequate measures of achievement, labour market success and non-completion rates have made the use of input data to reflect output levels an attractive alternative option. Given that the aim of efficiency studies is to establish the relationship between inputs and outputs in order to calculate a measure of performance, however, there is a surprisingly large number of cases where teaching output is proxied by teaching inputs such as student numbers or enrolments

(Abbott and Doucouliagos, 2003; Ahn and Seiford, 1993; Avkiran, 2001; Beasley, 1990, 1995; Tomkins and Green, 1988) and number of credit hours (Ahn *et al.*, 1989; Friedman and Sinuany-Stern, 1997).

Measures of the consumption benefits of education (present or future) or of the other externalities from the teaching process (such as the instillation of desirable work habits, the benefits to firms of sorting, selecting and screening, and occupational guidance to students) are difficult to construct. No studies to date have satisfactorily incorporated measures of such outputs.

In institutions of higher learning, research and teaching are equally important outputs, and so an analysis of the efficiency of universities would not be complete without an examination of performance in producing research output. As with teaching output, input measures such as research income or expenditure have been popular proxies for research output (Beasley, 1990, 1995; Friedman and Sinuany-Stern, 1997; Johnes and Johnes, 1993; Tomkins and Green, 1988; Hashimoto and Cohn, 1997). More satisfactory measures of research output which incorporate both quantity and quality include ratings derived from peer reviews, data for which are now available for Australian and UK universities (Abbott and Doucouliagos, 2003; Avkiran, 2001; Sarrico and Dyson, 2000; Tomkins and Green, 1988; Johnes and Taylor, 1990, 1992; Johnes, 1996; Johnes *et al.*, 1993). In the absence of peer review data, publications counts offer an alternative measure of research productivity (Johnes and Johnes, 1992, 1993; Madden *et al.*, 1997; Tomkins and Green, 1988) or, in order to account for quality as well as quantity of research, publications counts in 'core' journals (Johnes and Johnes, 1992, 1993; Madden *et al.*, 1997).

Problems arising from the specification of the outputs frequently occur in efficiency studies. It is generally accepted that multiple outputs are produced from an array of inputs into the education process. Yet there is no one consistent method for measuring efficiency in the presence of both multiple inputs and multiple outputs. DEA is an attractive option as it easily handles multiple variables on both the input and output sides. However little is known about how the DEA efficiencies are affected (if at all) by the presence of multicollinearity amongst the outputs or by the nature of the production of the outputs (that is, joint, simultaneous or separate).

Statistical techniques, on the other hand, are traditionally applied with one dependent variable and an array of explanatory variables. Thus statistical techniques can easily handle situations where there is one input and multiple outputs, or one output and multiple inputs, but have not satisfactorily been used in the education context in situations of both multiple outputs and multiple inputs.[16] The most common approach when estimating efficiency using statistical methods in the context of multiple inputs and outputs is to estimate a separate equation for each output (Gray *et al.*, 1984; Johnes and Taylor, 1990; Yang *et al.*, 1999; Johnes, 1996; Sammons *et al.*, 1993; Goldstein, 1997; Goldstein *et al.*, 1993). An alternative is to compute a composite measure of output and to use this as the dependent variable (Sengupta and Sfeir, 1986; Bates, 1997). These approaches give rise to a number of problems.

First, if the outputs are joint products, the efficiencies may not be adequately estimated by a separate equation for each output, the problem with which is that no allowance is made for any possible tradeoff between different educational outputs from reallocating inputs. Thus an institution might be judged inefficient on the basis of one outcome, and changes to inputs suggested to improve performance. However separate estimation provides no information on how a change in inputs designed to improve one output will affect (either positively or negatively) any of the other outputs of the production process (Mayston and Jesson, 1988). Chizmar and Zak (1983) conclude that modelling multiple outputs as joint products is superior empirically and theoretically to modelling them using separate equations. Secondly, there are problems of interpretation if the result is an array of efficiency measures. Techniques such as principal components may offer insights in such a situation (Johnes, 1996).

The inputs
Labour and human capital inputs into the education production process are often measured by student and staff numbers, such data being readily available at both school, administrative area and higher education levels (for example, Ahn and Seiford, 1993; Athanassopoulos and Shale, 1997; Chalos, 1997; Barrow, 1991; Avkiran, 2001; Grosskopf and Moutray, 2001). More refined measures of labour input have been used, such as the time spent by students on homework and number of classes taken (Lovell *et al.*, 1994), but such data are rarely available. An alternative to including data on both students and staff numbers is to combine these into one composite measure, namely the student–staff ratio (Bradley *et al.*, 2001; Belfield and Fielding, 2001; Johnes and Taylor, 1990; Mancebon and Mar Molinero, 2000; Mante and O'Brien, 2002).

Attempts to capture the quality of staff input are frequently made by including staff salaries or variables reflecting the academic qualifications, age or experience of the staff (for example, Sengupta and Sfeir, 1986; Ahn and Seiford, 1993; Chalos, 1997; Friedman and Sinuany-Stern, 1997; Ruggiero, 1996, 2000; Bradley *et al.*, 2001; Soteriou *et al.*, 1998). Student quality is reflected by mean achievement scores of the student population on entry or proportion of the entry population achieving a given qualification in aggregate-level studies of efficiency (Athanassopoulos and

Shale, 1997; Bessent and Bessent, 1980; Chalos, 1997; Johnes and Taylor, 1990; Johnes, 1996; Barrow, 1991; Thanassoulis and Dunstan, 1994) and by mean entry qualification score in individual level studies (for example, Johnes, 2003; Portela and Thanassoulis, 2001; Aitkin and Longford, 1986; Yang *et al.*, 1999; Bratti *et al.*, 2003; Smith and Naylor, 2001b). Measures of student entry achievement and student numbers are often included together to incorporate the effects of both student quality and the size of the institution on the outputs produced (Athanassopoulos and Shale, 1997).

The frequent publication of financial data for educational establishments provides scope for the construction of input variables which measure the physical capital input into the education production process. Expenditures on various inputs (such as library or computing facilities), income derived for specific purposes, the value of assets and level of investment are used in numerous studies to incorporate measures of physical capital (for example, Harrison and Rouse, 2002; Abbott and Doucouliagos, 2003; Mante, 2001; Mayston and Jesson, 1988). When available, the numbers of books or computers have been used as alternatives to financial data (Lovell *et al.*, 1994; Ruggiero, 1996, 2000).

In addition to these labour and capital inputs, the socioeconomic background, race and gender of individuals, as well as parental occupation and income, are all important inputs into the education production process, and variables which purport to reflect such characteristics are frequently included at all levels of analysis (Bessent and Bessent, 1980; Johnes and Taylor, 1990, provide examples at aggregate school and university levels; Goldstein, 1997, and Bratti *et al.*, 2003, are studies of individuals in schools and universities, respectively). The institutions themselves will also have characteristics such as curriculum, extracurricular provision, location, administrative and selection polices, and teaching practices which should be and are considered as inputs (Lovell *et al.*, 1994; Goldstein *et al.*, 1993; Goldstein and Thomas, 1996; Yang *et al.*, 2002; Johnes and Taylor, 1990; Johnes, 1996; Barrow, 1991).

Several problems immediately arise from attempting to incorporate so many input and output measures into studies of the efficiency of institutions of education. First, with such a vast array of potential input measures, all of them apparently important a priori, there is likely to be multicollinearity. This is known to be a problem when using statistical techniques, and there is some evidence that it causes problems in non-parametric techniques such as DEA, and that the effect differs with different sample sizes and dimension (Pedraja-Chaparro *et al.*, 1999).

A consequence of the difficulties in measuring some of the inputs is that some important input variables may be omitted. Since, in the context of education, the inputs included are likely to be correlated with the omitted input(s), the omission of the variable(s) will cause biased results in statistical studies (Bifulco and Bretschneider, 2001). Omission of important input variables is likely also to affect efficiency scores in a DEA.

Following on from this is the problem of which input variables to include when constructing measures of efficiency. With a statistical technique, the convention is to use only those input variables which are statistically significant (although this might be difficult to determine in the presence of multicollinearity). In the case of DEA, statistical tests of significance are not available. Including all possible variables as inputs (whether significant or not) would be an appropriate approach only if the results of DEA were unaffected by the number of input variables included. Yet this is not the case (see, for example, Athanassopoulos and Shale, 1997), and potential problems caused by multicollinearity make this strategy even less appealing. One suggestion is to choose variables on the basis of peer judgment and prior statistical analysis: Chalos and Cherian (1995) suggest a number of criteria which should be met for an input to be included in a DEA.

First, there should be previous empirical evidence to support the inclusion of a variable. Second, a board of 'experts' should consider the inputs to be important. Third, a statistical analysis should find a significant relationship between the inputs and specified outputs. Finally, the inputs should have neither missing nor zero values. An alternative and more easily implementable approach (Mancebon and Bandrés, 1999; Mancebon and Mar Molinero, 2000) involves adopting a strategy from which a test statistic is derived, analogous to an F test on a subset of variables in multiple regression. First, all the possible inputs and outputs to be included in the DEA should be specified. Then one variable (either an input or an output) is chosen, and the DEA efficiencies are estimated both with the variable (the total model) and without the variable (the reduced model). The third step is to calculate the ratio (denoted by ρ) of reduced model efficiencies to total model efficiencies for all DMUs. Finally, if ρ differs significantly from 1 in a large number of DMUs, the variable should be included in the DEA. Mancebon and Mar Molinero adopt the decision rule that, if less than 15% of the DMUs have a value of $\rho \leq 0.9$, then the variable can be dropped from the DEA.

Further concerns regarding the choice of inputs arise from the distinction between inputs which can be controlled by institutions and those which cannot, such as environmental factors. There are two contrasting approaches to the problem. The first approach is to include all inputs, whether controllable or not, in the efficiency analysis (Cubbin and Tzanidakis, 1998; Grosskopf, 1996). The problem with the first approach is that adequate allowance may not be made for institutions facing a harsh environment, and they therefore may be judged inefficient when in fact their performance is a consequence of their environment. Thus inefficiency may be overestimated in models where all inputs are included at the start.[17] The second approach is to adopt a two-stage procedure whereby the efficiency scores for a set of institutions are derived using an appropriate technique (see section 4), and then these efficiencies are analysed at a second stage in relation to the non-controllable inputs using an appropriate statistical technique.[18]

Many studies of efficiency adopt the second approach (Bratti, 2002; Bradley *et al.*, 2001; Duncombe *et al.*, 1997; Kirjavainen and Loikkanen, 1998; Lovell *et al.*, 1994; Mancebon and Mar Moliero, 2000; McCarty and Yaisawarng, 1993; Ramanathan, 2001; Ray, 1991; Grosskopf and Moutray, 2001), yet there are a number of caveats which should be remembered regarding the two-stage procedure. First, this method requires a specification of a functional form of the relationship between the non-controllable inputs and the production function (Ruggiero, 1996). Thus misspecification errors may be introduced at the second stage.

Secondly, the efficiency scores vary from 0 to 1 and so either they should be appropriately transformed or an appropriate limited dependent variable technique such as Tobit analysis should be used at the second stage (Lovell, 1993).

Thirdly, it can be difficult to distinguish between the inputs which should be included at the first stage and those which should be included in the second stage. Lovell (1993) suggests that it should be strictly those variables over which the institution has no control which are included in the second stage. However the definition of a non-controllable variable can vary according to the context of analysis, and the decision regarding which variables are reserved for the second stage must therefore be taken in that context.

Finally the decision over whether to use a one-stage or two-stage procedure depends on the assumptions regarding the precise relationship the non-controllable inputs have with the production process and with efficiency. A two-stage procedure assumes that the second stage (usually non-controllable) input variables affect the *efficiency* with which the outputs are produced from the inputs. In contrast, the one-stage procedure assumes that all the inputs, including the non-controllable inputs, affect the *process of production* of the outputs from the inputs (ibid.). Analysts should therefore be aware of the distinction and should, ideally, choose the technique which matches their assumptions. In reality, it is often practical considerations which determine which approach to use. For example, when there is multicollinearity between the controllable and non-controllable inputs, a one-stage procedure is more appropriate if the first-stage technique is statistical (ibid.).

There are few comparisons of the results derived from one-stage and two-stage procedures. An exception is a study by McCarty and Yaisawarng (1993), who adopt a two-stage approach, using a Tobit model in the second stage to link the DEA efficiencies to variables beyond the control of the DMU. They compute a new set of efficiencies from this second stage, and find that the efficiencies generated from the two-stage approach differ little from the results of a one-stage DEA which includes the non-controllable as well as controllable factors as inputs.

Occasionally measuring the effect of an environmental variable, such as location of institution or the effect of a policy change, on efficiency is the specific aim of an analysis. If statistical techniques are employed, appropriate dummy variables can be included to assess the effect. If DEA is the technique of choice, it is not so clear how the strength of the effect may be examined. A method, adopted by Soteriou *et al.* (1998), to assess the effect of a school's location (urban or rural) on its performance is to run, first of all, separate DEAs on the divided sample (divided on the basis of school location). Secondly, the inputs of all inefficient DMUs are adjusted to what they would be if they were on their location-specific frontier, while those of efficient DMUs are left unchanged. DEA is then applied to the pooled set of modified data. Finally the efficiencies from this DEA are compared for each group and the possible existence of significant differences is assessed using Mann–Whitney non-parametric tests. Using this approach, Soteriou *et al.* (1998) find no significant differences in efficiency by location of school. A similar approach is adopted to assess the influence of a programme introduced into schools to improve teaching effectiveness (Diamond and Medewitz, 1990).

There are clearly considerable problems in terms of the specification of inputs and outputs in the context of education. The next section examines the evidence from empirical analyses concerning the effect on the measurement of efficiency of model specification and the choice of technique of analysis.

Reliability of the results of efficiency analyses
The success of efficiency analyses in producing reliable and consistent rankings of institutions, which are not sensitive to the specification of inputs and outputs, the number of observations included, the assumption of returns to scale, or the technique used to produce the efficiency score, is of particular importance and has been the subject of investigation. Several results have emerged.

Individual-level studies using statistical techniques (such as multi-level or probit models) consistently find that the majority of institutions cannot be separated on the basis of efficiency. In studies based on school pupils, the confidence intervals for the school effects are very wide, and so very few schools can be separated in terms of their performance (Goldstein *et al.*, 1993; Goldstein and Spiegelhalter, 1996; Goldstein and Thomas, 1996) and there is only a significant difference between the best and worst performers. In studies of non-completion amongst university students, the university effects are significantly different from the median for only the six lowest and the 12 top placed universities (Smith and Naylor, 2001a). A similar result is obtained when labour market variables are the output measures in the computation of university effects (Smith *et al.*, 2000). The conclusion from these results is that league tables based on effects which cannot discriminate amongst most of the institutions would therefore not be appropriate (Yang *et al.*, 1999).

A substantial amount of research has been undertaken with regard to the effect of the specification of inputs and outputs on efficiency scores, much of it in the context of DEA rather than statistical techniques, where the significance of a set of inputs or outputs can be tested. In the context of higher education, the conclusions range from rankings being reasonably stable regardless of input and/or output specification (Tomkins and Green, 1988; Abbot and Doucouliagos, 2003; Johnes, 2003) to results being sensitive to specification (Ahn and Seiford, 1993; Johnes and Johnes, 1992). In a study of the research efficiency of UK university departments of economics, the results of 192 possible specifications are compared, and cluster analysis reveals there to be just two distinct groups of results (Johnes and Johnes, 1993). The main distinctive feature appears to be the inclusion of per capita research grants as an input in one cluster, and its exclusion from the models in the second cluster.

In an analysis of the performance of Training and Enterprise Councils (TECs) in the UK, the addition of more variables is found to increase the number of TECs found to be efficient (Cubbin and Zamani, 1996), although the results are found not to be sensitive to the orientation (input or output) of the DEA.

In the context of secondary schooling, results are similarly mixed (Färe *et al.*, 1989; Harrison and Rouse, 2002; Smith and Mayston, 1987; Kirjavainen and Loikkanen, 1998; Mante, 2001; Engert, 1996). In an analysis of secondary schools in Finland, a particularly interesting finding emerges, namely that the secondary schools at the top and the bottom (in terms of efficiency score) are less affected by the change in model specification than those in the middle (Kirjavainen and Loikannen, 1998). This is perhaps unsurprising given the results of individual-level analyses which fail to distinguish, in terms of performance, between middle-ranked institutions.

The mixed nature of these results regarding model specification may, to some extent, be a consequence of whether the purpose of a study is to measure the same type of efficiency with each model (for example, Johnes (2003) examines the efficiency of university economics departments at producing 'good' degrees using different specifications of inputs and outputs), or whether efficiency at achieving a different objective is being measured by each specification (for example, the two models specified by Athanassopoulos and Shale measure cost efficiency and outcome efficiency, respectively). Lovell *et al.* (1994) examine the efficiency of schools at achieving short-, medium- and long-term objectives. The efficiency scores derived from the model of short-term objectives are significantly different from those derived from models of medium- and long-term objectives, respectively. Moreover the determinants of each of the three sets of efficiency scores also vary. Similarly differences in efficiency scores arise when looking at different types of efficiency. Results of measuring technical efficiency and value efficiency reveal that fewer DMUs are efficient in terms of the latter than of the former (Korhonen *et al.*, 2001).

Evidence from statistical studies also supports the hypothesis that efficiency scores differ when derived from evaluating the efficiency of institutions at achieving different objectives. In a study of four different measures of university performance using data on, respectively, graduate destinations in the labour market, degree results, non-completion rates (note that the negative of non-completion is used to construct this indicator to allow a consistent interpretation across performance indicators) and research rating, rank correlation coefficients vary from −0.40 to 0.13,[19] thereby exhibiting considerable inconsistency in terms of performance across the four sets of efficiency scores (Johnes, 1996). Similarly, in an analysis based on individual school children, efficiency scores derived from, respectively, reading test results and mathematics test results are correlated ($r = 0.62$) but not particularly highly (Sammons *et al.*, 1993). In addition, in a stochastic frontier analysis of the efficiency of public schools in New York, mean efficiency is shown to vary according to definition of output (five possible measures of output are defined and mean efficiency varies from 0.55 to 0.91), and there is some variation in the input variables found to be significant in each model (Kang and Greene, 2002).

There is less evidence concerning the effect of the omission of institutions on the stability of the estimated production function, and hence the efficiency measures. Smith and Mayston (1987) find, not surprisingly, that the sensitivity of the results to the omission of a DMU depends on whether or not the omitted DMU is an outlier, in which case the results are affected substantially. One method of assessing the influence of observations is to use a jackknifing procedure whereby, for a given DEA model, one DMU is omitted at a time and the mean efficiency scores from these $(n-1)$ runs compared with those derived from a DEA on all n observations. In the contexts of Missouri school districts and Finnish high schools, the results of the jackknifing approach indicate that efficiencies are stable (Färe *et al.*, 1989; Bonesrønning and Rattsø, 1994).

Evidence of the effect on efficiency measurement of returns to scale is limited. In the context of DEA, Cubbin and Zamani (1996) find that the number of efficient DMUs increases (as would be expected) with the assumption of VRS rather than CRS. Ahn and Seiford (1993) find that their results are insensitive to the assumption of returns to scale, as indeed they are to whether an additive or multiplicative model is used. Athanassopoulos and Shale (1997) find that the effect of assumptions regarding returns to scale differs according to model: the results of a DEA measuring cost efficiency vary according to whether a CRS or VRS model is used; in contrast, there is little effect of choice of returns to scale on the results of a DEA of outcome efficiency.

There is a considerable body of evidence concerning the effects of the choice of technique of analysis on efficiency scores and rankings of institutions, most of the studies focusing on comparisons between DEA and statistical techniques (both deterministic and stochastic). Banker *et al.* (1993) use simulated data to compare COLS (with deterministic errors) and DEA, and find that the performance of one compared to the other depends largely on the true distribution of inefficiencies and sample size, although DEA appears to outperform COLS for the smallest sample size examined ($n = 25$). However, in a situation of high measurement errors, neither technique performs particularly well. This result is confirmed by Bifulco and Bretschneider (2001) also using simulated data. They show that, for data sets which are complex and contain both endogeneity and measurement errors (characteristics likely to be exhibited in education data sets), neither COLS nor DEA can place more than 31% of (simulated) schools in their true performance quintile.

A number of empirical studies have compared the results of using OLS (with deterministic errors) and DEA. The context of economics teaching in schools in the USA provides the evidence of the strongest correlation between efficiency scores derived from three OLS specifications and DEA efficiency scores (r ranges from 0.712 to 0.822) (Diamond and Medewitz, 1990). Bates (1993) finds that patterns of efficiency derived from OLS and DEA in LEAs in the UK are particularly similar at the top and bottom of the efficiency rankings. However another study of LEAs in the UK finds rather low correlation (r varies from 0.32 to 0.53) between the efficiency scores from two OLS specifications and those derived from DEA. Further evidence that choice of technique (OLS or DEA) affects efficiency ranking is provided in the context of TECs (Cubbin and Zamani, 1996).

DEA has also been compared to stochastic frontier efficiencies. Gong and Sickles (1992), using simulated data, find that the greater the misspecification of functional form in the stochastic frontier model, and the higher the correlation between inefficiency and the explanatory variables, the greater is the appeal of DEA relative to stochastic frontier estimation methods. Empirical studies provide mixed evidence on the consistency of the efficiencies estimated from each method, ranging from little correlation in the context of TECs in the UK (Cubbin and Zamani, 1996) and UK universities (Johnes, 1998a), to reasonably high correlation in the context of LEAs in the UK (Bates, 1997). When Tobit analysis is used to relate the DEA efficiencies to uncontrollable inputs at the second stage, the ranking of school districts based on the Tobit residuals is similar to those derived from a stochastic frontier analysis with half-normal error term (Chakraborty *et al.*, 2001).

More recently, individual-level DEA has been compared with multi-level modelling. Preliminary examination of the results reveals a strong correlation between the pupil-within-school efficiencies estimated using, respectively, individual-level DEA and multi-level modelling, although the actual value of efficiency differs (Thanassoulis *et al.*, 2003). A similar strong correlation is found for pupil-within-all-schools efficiencies estimated by each method. There is, however, a need to assess the relationship between the institution efficiencies derived using multi-level modelling and individual-level DEA.

Comparisons of statistical techniques have produced similarly mixed results. When different functional forms estimated using OLS are compared, similarities are much greater in the study of economics classes in the USA (r varies from 0.831 to 0.956) than in the context of LEAs in the UK (r varies from 0.21 to 0.60). However OLS and stochastic frontier methods appear to provide similar efficiency rankings in the context of LEAs (Barrow, 1991) and TECs (Cubbin and Zamani, 1996), although the former study finds (as would be expected) that the actual inefficiency scores are considerably higher when estimated using COLS rather than in the stochastic model.

6   Conclusion

The measurement of efficiency in education has progressed considerably since the days when institutions might be ranked on the basis of their level of production of one output. It is now accepted that institutions of education produce an array of outputs using a variety of inputs, and that any ranking of institutions purporting to reflect efficiency must take this into account.

It is clear from the survey of the literature presented in this chapter, however, that anyone interested in measuring the efficiency of institutions of education is faced with an array of techniques of analysis and methods of approach. Furthermore the production environment in education differs from that of more traditional industries and this causes problems when undertaking an analysis of efficiency. A review of the empirical applications of methods of efficiency measurement in the context of education indicates, moreover, that the outcomes from efficiency studies in terms of the rankings of institutions under investigation can vary according to the choice of technique (for example, parametric or non-parametric); the specification and measurement of the inputs and outputs (and the treatment of inputs which are not under the control of the institutions under examination); the level of data used (for example, individual, subject or institution); and the assumptions of the model applied (for example, the functional form of the production function or whether there are variable as opposed to constant returns to scale). It is important to remember this when analysing the results of any study of efficiency.

The strength of studies of efficiency is therefore not so much the 'league tables' which can be compiled from such studies, but more the rich source of information which emerges. Such information depends on the technique used. A statistical technique may indicate the significant determinants of educational outcomes; a non-parametric technique can provide information on realistic targets for an inefficient institution, as well as information on a set of similar (in terms of input and output mix) but better-performing institutions whose practices the inefficient organization can realistically try to emulate.

Techniques of efficiency measurement continue to be developed and extended, and this ensures the need for continued empirical research into their application in the context of education.

Notes

1. We assume that input prices are given, that is, the firm is not a monopsonist.
2. We assume that output prices are given, that is, the firm has no monopoly power.
3. In fact, early studies in education did not adjust the residuals, using instead the estimates of the 'average' production function and the related unadjusted residuals to measure performance (see, for example, Johnes, 1996; Gray *et al.* 1984).
4. See Lovell (1993) for a discussion of how to adapt the methods for a multiple input, multiple output scenario.
5. Jondrow *et al.* (1982) provide a derivation also for the normal–exponential case.
6. The former is simply a measure of technical inefficiency (represented by u_i in equation (16.13)) and can be used to find the technical efficiency of each producer by substituting it into equation (16.12).
7. The need for strictly positive weights (as opposed to non-negative weights) was introduced by Charnes *et al.* (1979) in which they corrected their earlier model (Charnes *et al.*, 1978), which required that weights be only non-negative. Strict positivity of weights ensures that a DMU classed as efficient (i.e. with an efficiency score of 1) does not have any slack on its inputs or outputs.
8. The primal terminology is consistent with Charnes *et al.* (1978). But note that output maximization from given inputs (i.e. an output-oriented approach) is achieved through a primal which minimizes the objective function (Norman and Stoker, 1991).

9. Note that the efficiency scores are derived using the vertical distance from the frontier and hence indicate an output-oriented framework. The efficiency scores could equally well be derived using the horizontal distance from the frontier and would indicate an input-oriented approach.

10. This is as the VRS except that the equality constraint $\Sigma_{j=1}^{n}\lambda_{j} = 1$ is replaced by the inequality $\Sigma_{j=1}^{n}\lambda_{j} \leq 1$.

11. Alternatively, a line IC''' extended from DC would intersect the ray OP at P_4 (say) and $VE^{**} = OP/OP_4$ would give a more conservative (but equally valid) measure.

12. Note that only the methodology for calculating the Malmquist output-oriented productivity index is shown here. Input-oriented DEA can be adapted to find the value of the Malmquist input-oriented productivity index.

13. That is, some linear combination of their input and output vectors is more technically efficient than that of the inefficient producer.

14. The possible inputs and outputs of education will be considered at length in section 5.

15. In fact, Thanassoulis (1996) develops a methodology based on DEA for setting appropriate targets for differentially effective schools and to identify suitable role model schools which a differentially effective school can emulate.

16. The stochastic frontier estimation method can, however, be adapted to handle multiple outputs as well as multiple inputs. See Sickles *et al.* (1998) for an application to the airline industry.

17. This problem is addressed by Ruggiero (1996) who develops an approach, in the context of DEA, so that each DMU has in its reference set only those DMUs which face at least as harsh an environment as itself.

18. The equations for the two stages (i.e. the first stage estimation of efficiency and the second stage estimation of the determinants of efficiency) can be estimated either separately or simultaneously. Examples of the former approach are referred to in the text. The latter approach is a recent development and involves employing a method developed by Battese and Coelli (1995) whereby maximum likelihood methods are used to estimate simultaneously the first stage efficiencies by SFA *and* the second stage equation in which the first stage efficiencies are related to variables which might explain the inter-institution variation. An example of an application of this method in the context of costs in UK higher education is Stevens (2001).

19. In fact, the performance indicator based on graduate success in the labour market is negatively related to all of the other three performance indicators, with r ranging from -0.07 to -0.40. The remaining performance indicators are positively correlated with each other.

References

Abbott, M. and C. Doucouliagos (2003), 'The efficiency of Australian universities: a data envelopment analysis', *Economics of Education Review*, **22**(1), 89–97.

Ahn, T. and L.M. Seiford (1993), 'Sensitivity of data envelopment analysis to models and variable sets in a hypothesis test setting: the efficiency of university operations', in Y. Ijiri (ed.), *Creative and Innovative Approaches to the Science of Management*, Westport, CT: Quorum Books, pp. 191–208.

Ahn, T., V. Arnold, A. Charnes and W.W. Cooper (1989), 'DEA and ratio efficiency analyses for public institutions of higher learning in Texas', *Research in Governmental and Nonprofit Accounting*, **5**, 165–85.

Aigner, D.J., C.A.K. Lovell and P. Schmidt (1977), 'Formulation and estimation of stochastic frontier production function models', *Journal of Econometrics*, **6**(1), 21–37.

Aitkin, M. and N. Longford (1986), 'Statistical modelling in school effectiveness studies', *Journal of the Royal Statistical Society, Series A*, **149**, 1–43.

Arcelus, F.J. and D.F. Coleman (1997), 'An efficiency review of university departments', *International Journal of Systems Science*, **28**(7), 721–9.

Athanassopoulos, A.D. and E. Shale (1997), 'Assessing the comparative efficiency of higher education institutions in the UK by means of data envelopment analysis', *Education Economics*, **5**(2), 117–34.

Avkiran, N.K. (2001), 'Investigating technical and scale efficiencies of Australian universities through data envelopment analysis', *Socio-Economic Planning Sciences*, **35**(1), 57–80.

Banker, R.D., A. Charnes and W.W. Cooper (1984), 'Some models for estimating technical and scale inefficiencies in data envelopment analysis', *Management Science*, **30**(9), 1078–92.

Banker, R.D., V.M. Gadh and W.L. Gorr (1993), 'A Monte Carlo comparison of two production frontier estimation techniques: corrected ordinary least squares and data envelopment analysis', *European Journal of Operational Research*, **67**, 332–43.

Banker, R.D., A. Charnes, W.W. Cooper, J. Swarts and D. Thomas (1989), 'An introduction to data envelopment analysis with some of its models and their uses', *Research in Governmental and Nonprofit Accounting*, **5**, 125–63.

Barrow, M. (1991), 'Measuring the Local Education Authority performance: a frontier approach', *Economics of Education Review*, **10**(1), 19–27.

Bates, J.M. (1993), 'The efficiency of Local Education Authorities', *Oxford Review of Education*, **19**(3), 277–89.

Bates, J.M. (1997), 'Measuring predetermined socio-economic "inputs" when assessing the efficiency of educational outputs', *Applied Economics*, **29**(1), 85–93.

Battese, G.E. and T.J. Coelli (1995), 'A model for technical inefficiency effects in a stochastic frontier production function for panel data', *Empirical Economics*, **20**, 325–32.

Beasley, J.E. (1990), 'Comparing university departments', *Omega*, **18**, 171–83.

Beasley, J.E. (1995), 'Determining the teaching and research efficiencies', *Journal of the Operational Research Society*, **46**(4), 441–52.

Belfield, C.R. and A. Fielding (2001), 'Measuring the relationship between resources and outcomes in higher education in the UK', *Economics of Education Review*, **20**, 589–602.

Bessent, A.M. and E.W. Bessent (1980), 'Determining the comparative efficiency of schools through data envelopment analysis', *Educational Administration Quarterly*, **16**(2), 57–75.

Bessent, A.M., E.W. Bessent, E.W. Kennington and B. Reagan (1982), 'An application of mathematical programming to assess the productivity in the Houston independent school district', *Management Science*, **28**, 1355–67.

Bifulco, R. and S. Bretschneider (2001), 'Estimating school efficiency: a comparison of methods using simulated data', *Economics of Education Review*, **20**, 417–29.

Bonesrønning, H. and J. Rattsø (1994), 'Efficiency variation among the Norwegian high schools: consequences of equalization policy', *Economics of Education Review*, **13**(4), 289–304.

Bradley, S., G. Johnes and J. Millington (2001), 'The effect of competition on the efficiency of secondary schools in England', *European Journal of Operational Research*, **135**, 545–68.

Bratti, M. (2002), 'Does the choice of university matter? A study of the differences across UK universities in life sciences students' degree performance', *Economics of Education Review*, **21**, 431–43.

Bratti, M., A. McKnight, R. Naylor and J. Smith (2003), 'Higher education outcomes, graduate employment and university performance indicators', Department of Economics, University of Warwick.

Breu, T.M. and R.L. Raab (1994), 'Efficiency and perceived quality of the nation's "Top 25" national universities and national liberal arts colleges: an application of data envelopment analysis to higher education', *Socio-Economic Planning Sciences*, **28**(1), 33–45.

Chakraborty, K., B. Biswas and W.C. Lewis (2001), 'Measurement of technical efficiency in public education: a stochastic and nonstochastic production frontier approach', *Southern Economics Journal*, **67**(4), 889–905.

Chalos, P. (1997), 'An examination of budgetary inefficiency in education using data envelopment analysis', *Financial Accountability and Management*, **13**(1), 55–69.

Chalos, P. and J. Cherian (1995), 'An application of data envelopment analysis to public sector performance measurement and accountability', *Journal of Accounting and Public Policy*, **14**, 143–60.

Charnes, A., W.W. Cooper, and E. Rhodes (1978), 'Measuring the efficiency of DMUs', *European Journal of Operational Research*, **2**, 429–44.

Charnes, A., W.W. Cooper and E. Rhodes (1979), 'Measuring the efficiency of decision making units: a short communication', *European Journal of Operational Research*, **3**(4), 339.

Chizmar, J.F. and T.A. Zak (1983), 'Modeling multiple outputs in educational production functions', *American Economic Review, Papers and Proceedings*, **73**(2), 18–22.

Coelli, T., D.S.P. Rao and G.E. Battese (1998), *An Introduction to Efficiency and Productivity Analysis*, Norwell, MA: Kluwer Academic.

Cubbin, J. and G. Tzanidakis (1998), 'Regression versus data envelopment analysis for efficiency measurement: an application to the England and Wales regulated water industry', *Utilities Policy*, **7**, 75–85.

Cubbin, J. and H. Zamani (1996), 'A comparison of performance indicators for Training and Enterprise Councils in the UK', *Annals of Public Choice and Cooperative Economics*, **67**(4), 603–32.

Dantzig, G.B. (1951), 'Maximization of a linear function of variables subject to linear inequalities', in T.C. Koopmans (ed.), *Activity Analysis of Production and Allocation*, New York: Wiley.

Deller, S.C. and E. Rudnicki (1993), 'Production efficiency in elementary education: the case of Maine public schools', *Economics of Education Review*, **12**(1), 45–57.

Diamond, A. and J.N. Medewitz (1990), 'Use of data envelopment analysis in an evaluation of the efficiency of the DEEP program for economic education', *Journal of Economic Education*, **21**, 337–54.

Duncombe, W., J. Miner and J. Ruggiero (1997), 'Empirical evaluation and bureaucratic models of inefficiency', *Public Choice*, **93**, 1–18.

Dyson, R.G., R. Allen, A.S. Camanho, V.V. Podinovski, C.S. Sarrico and E.A. Shale (2001), 'Pitfalls and protocols in data envelopment analysis', *European Journal of Operational Research*, **132**(2), 245–59.

El-Mahgary, S. and R. Lahdelma (1995), 'Data envelopment analysis: visualizing the results', *European Journal of Operational Research*, **85**, 700–710.

Engert, F. (1996), 'The reporting of school district efficiency: the adequacy of ratio measures', *Public Budgeting and Financial Management*, **8**(2), 247–71.

Färe, R., S. Grosskopf and C.A.K. Lovell (1988), 'An indirect efficiency approach to the evaluation of producer performance', *Journal of Public Economics*, **37**(1), 71–89.

Färe, R., S. Grosskopf, M. Norris and Z. Zhang (1994), 'Productivity growth, technical progress and efficiency change in industrialized countries', *American Economic Review*, **84**(1), 66–83.

Färe, R., S. Grosskopf and W.L. Weber (1989), 'Measuring school district performance', *Public Finance Quarterly*, **17**(4), 409–28.

Farrell, M. (1957), 'The measurement of productive efficiency', *Journal of the Royal Statistical Society, Series A*, **120**, 253–81.

Førsund, F.R., C.A.K. Lovell and P. Schmidt (1980), 'A survey of frontier production functions and of their relationship to efficiency measurement', *Journal of Econometrics*, **13**, 5–25.

Friedman, L. and Z. Sinuany-Stern (1997), 'Scaling units via the canonical correlation analysis in the data envelopment analysis context', *European Journal of Operational Research*, **100**, 629–37.

Ganley, J.A. and J.S. Cubbin (1992), *Public Sector Efficiency Measurement: Applications of Data Envelopment Analysis*, Amsterdam: North-Holland.

Geva-May, I. (2001), 'Higher education and attainment of policy goals: interpretations for efficiency indicators in Israel', *Higher Education*, **42**(3), 265–305.

Goldstein, H. (1995), *Multilevel Statistical Models*, London: Wiley and Sons.

Goldstein, H. (1997), 'Methods in school effectiveness research', *School Effectiveness and School Improvement*, **8**(4), 369–95.

Goldstein, H. and P. Sammons (1997), 'The influence of secondary and junior schools on sixteen year examination performance: a cross-classified multilevel analysis', *School Effectiveness and School Improvement*, **8**(2), 219–30.

Goldstein, H. and D.J. Spiegelhalter (1996), 'League tables and their limitations: statistical issues in comparisons of institutional performance', *Journal of the Royal Statistical Society, Series A*, **159**(3), 385–443.

Goldstein, H. and S. Thomas (1996), 'Using examination results as indicators of school and college performance', *Journal of the Royal Statistical Society, Series A*, **159**(1), 149–63.

Goldstein, H., J. Rabash, M. Yang, G. Woodhouse, H. Pan, D. Nuttall and S. Thomas (1993), 'A multilevel analysis of school examination results', *Oxford Review of Education*, **19**(4), 425–33.

Gong, B.-H. and R.C. Sickles (1992), 'Finite sample evidence on the performance of stochastic frontiers and data envelopment analysis using panel data', *Journal of Econometrics*, **51**, 259–84.

Gray, J., D. Jesson and B. Jones (1984), 'Predicting differences in examination results: does school organisation matter?', *Oxford Review of Education*, **10**, 45–68.

Grosskopf, S. (1996), 'Statistical inference and nonparametric efficiency: a selective survey', *Journal of Productivity Analysis*, **7**, 161–76.

Grosskopf, S. and C. Moutray (2001), 'Evaluating performance in Chicago public high schools in the wake of decentralization', *Economics of Education Review*, **20**, 1–14.

Häkkinen, I., T. Kirjavainen and R. Uusitalo (2003), 'School resources and student achievement revisited: new evidence from panel data', *Economics of Education Review*, **22**(3), 329–35.

Haksever, C. and Y. Muragishi (1998), 'Measuring value in MBA programmes', *Education Economics*, **6**(1), 11–25.

Halme, M., T. Joro, P. Korhonen, S. Salo and J. Wallenius (1999), 'A value efficiency approach to incorporating preference information in data envelopment analysis', *Management Science*, **45**, 103–15.

Harrison, J. and P. Rouse (2002), 'Measuring the performance of Auckland secondary schools: a pilot study using data envelopment analysis', Department of Accounting and Finance, The University of Auckland.

Hashimoto, K. and E. Cohn (1997), 'Economies of scale and scope in Japanese private universities', *Education Economics*, **5**(2), 107–15.

Izadi, H., G. Johnes, R. Oskrochi and R. Crouchley (2002), 'Stochastic frontier estimation of a CES cost function: the case of higher education in Britain', *Economics of Education Review*, **21**, 63–71.

Jesson, D., D. Mayston and P. Smith (1987), 'Performance assessment in the education sector: educational and economic perspectives', *Oxford Review of Education*, **13**, 249–67.

Johnes, G. (1996), 'Multi-product cost functions and the funding of tuition in UK universities', *Applied Economics Letters*, **3**(9), 557–61.

Johnes, G. (1997), 'Costs and industrial structure in contemporary British higher education', *Economic Journal*, **107**, 727–37.

Johnes, G. (1998a), 'The costs of multiproduct organizations and the heuristic evaluation of industrial structure', *Socio-Economic Planning Sciences*, **32**(3), 199–209.

Johnes, G. (1998b), 'Corrigendum: costs and industrial structure in contemporary British higher education', *Economic Journal*, **108**, 1275.

Johnes, G. (1999), 'The management of universities: Scottish Economic Society/Royal Bank of Scotland Annual Lecture', *Scottish Journal of Political Economy*, **46**, 505–22.

Johnes, G. and J. Johnes (1992), 'Apples and oranges: the aggregation problem in publications analysis', *Scientometrics*, **25**(2), 353–65.

Johnes, G. and J. Johnes (1993), 'Measuring the research performance of UK economics departments: an application of data envelopment analysis', *Oxford Economic Papers*, **45**, 332–47.

Johnes, J. (1990), 'Unit costs: some explanations of the differences between UK universities', *Applied Economics*, **22**, 853–62.

Johnes, J. (1996), 'Performance assessment in higher education in Britain', *European Journal of Operational Research*, **89**, 18–33.

Johnes, J. (2003), 'Measuring teaching efficiency in higher education: an application of data envelopment analysis to graduates from UK universities 1993', discussion paper EC7/03, Department of Economics, Lancaster University.

Johnes, J. and J. Taylor (1987), 'Degree quality: an investigation into differences between universities', *Higher Education*, **16**, 581–602.

Johnes, J. and J. Taylor (1989a), 'Undergraduate non-completion rates: differences between UK universities', *Higher Education*, **18**, 209–25.

Johnes, J. and J. Taylor (1989b), 'The first destination of new graduates: comparisons between universities', *Applied Economics*, **21**(3), 357–74.

Johnes, J. and J. Taylor (1990), *Performance Indicators in Higher Education: UK Universities*, Milton Keynes: Open University Press and The Society for Research into Higher Education.

Johnes, J. and J. Taylor (1992), 'The 1989 research selectivity exercise: a statistical analysis of differences in research rating between universities at the cost centre level', *Higher Education Quarterly*, **46**(1), 67–87.

Johnes, J., J. Taylor and B. Francis (1993), 'The research performance of UK universities: a statistical analysis of the results of the 1989 research selectivity exercise', *Journal of the Royal Statistical Society, Series A*, **156**(2), 271–86.

Jondrow, J., C.A.K. Lovell, I.S. Materou and P. Schmidt (1982), 'On the estimation of technical inefficiency in the stochastic frontier production function model', *Journal of Econometrics*, **19**, 233–8.

Jones, J.T. and R.W. Zimmer (2001), 'Examining the impact of capital on academic achievement', *Economics of Education Review*, **20**, 577–88.

Kang, B.-G. and K.V. Greene (2002), 'The effects of monitoring and competition on public education outputs: a stochastic frontier approach', *Public Finance Review*, **30**(1), 3–26.

Kirjavainen, T. and H.A. Loikkanen (1998), 'Efficiency differences of Finnish senior secondary schools: an application of data envelopment analysis and Tobit analysis', *Economics of Education Review*, **17**(4), 377–94.

Korhonen, P., R. Tainio and J. Wallenius (2001), 'Value efficiency analysis of academic research', *European Journal of Operational Research*, **130**, 121–32.

Lovell, C.A.K. (1993), 'Production frontiers and productive efficiency', in H.O. Fried, C.A.K. Lovell and S.S. Schmidt (eds), *The Measurement of Productive Efficiency*, Oxford: Oxford University Press, pp. 3–67.

Lovell, C.A.K., L.C. Walters and L.L. Wood (1994), 'Stratified models of education production using modified data envelopment analysis and regression analysis', in A. Charnes, W.W. Cooper, A.Y. Lewin and L.M. Seiford (eds), *Data Envelopment Analysis: Theory, Methodology and Applications*, Dordrecht: Kluwer Academic.

Madden, G., S. Savage and S. Kemp (1997), 'Measuring public sector efficiency: a study of economics departments at Australian Universities', *Education Economics*, 153–67.

Malmquist, S. (1953), 'Index numbers and indifference surfaces', *Trabajos de Estatistica*, **4**, 209–42.

Mancebon, M.J. and E. Bandrés (1999), 'Efficiency evaluation in secondary schools: the key role of model specification and of *ex post* analysis of results', *Education Economics*, **7**(2), 131–52.

Mancebon, M.J. and C. Mar Molinero (2000), 'Performance in primary schools', *Journal of the Operational Research Society*, **51**(7), 843–54.

Mante, B. (2001), 'Measuring the performance of state secondary schools in Victoria: an application of data envelopment analysis', *Education Research and Perspectives*, **28**(1), 105–32.

Mante, B. and G. O'Brien (2002), 'Efficiency measurement of Australian public sector organisations: the case of state secondary schools in Victoria', *Journal of Educational Administration*, **40**(3), 274–96.

Mayston, D. and D. Jesson (1988), 'Developing models of educational accountability', *Oxford Review of Education*, **14**, 321–39.

McCarty, T.A. and S. Yaisawarng (1993), 'Technical efficiency in New Jersey school districts', in H.O. Fried, C.A.K. Lovell and S.S. Schmidt (eds), *The Measurement of Productive Efficiency*, Oxford: Open University Press, pp. 271–87.

Montmarquette, C., S. Mahseredjian and R. Houle (2001), 'The determinants of university dropouts: a bivariate probability model with sample selection', *Economics of Education Review*, **20**(5), 475–84.

Naylor, R., J. Smith and A. McKnight (2000), 'Occupational earnings of graduates: evidence for the 1993 UK university population', Department of Economics, University of Warwick.

Naylor, R., J. Smith and A. McKnight (2002), 'Why is there a graduate earnings premium for students from independent schools?', *Bulletin of Economic Research*, **54**(4), 315–40.

Norman, M. and B. Stoker (1991), *Data Envelopment Analysis: The Assessment of Performance*, Chichester: Wiley.

Ondrich, J. and J. Ruggiero (2001), 'Efficiency measurement in the stochastic frontier model', *European Journal of Operational Research*, **129**, 434–42.

Pedraja-Chaparro, F., J. Salinas-Jimenez and P. Smith (1999), 'On the quality of the data envelopment analysis model', *Journal of the Operational Research Society*, **50**, 636–44.

Peraita, C. and M. Sanchez (1998), 'The effect of family background on children's level of schooling and attainment in Spain', *Applied Economics*, **30**, 1327–34.

Portela, M.C.A.S. and E. Thanassoulis (2001), 'Decomposing school and school-type efficiency', *European Journal of Operational Research*, **132**(2), 357–73.

Ramanathan, R. (2001), 'A data envelopment analysis of comparative performance of schools in the Netherlands', *Opsearch*, **38**(2), 160–82.

Ray, S.C. (1991), 'Resource use efficiency in public schools: a study of Connecticut data', *Management Science*, **37**, 1620–28.

Ruggiero, J. (1996), 'On the measurement of technical efficiency in the public sector', *European Journal of Operational Research*, **90**, 553–65.

Ruggiero, J. (2000), 'Nonparametric estimation of returns to scale in the public sector with an application to the provision of educational services', *Journal of the Operational Research Society*, **51**, 906–12.

Ruggiero, J. and D.F. Vitaliano (1999), 'Assessing the efficiency of public schools using DEA and frontier regression', *Contemporary Economic Policy*, **17**(3), 321–31.

Sammons, P., D. Nuttall and D. Cuttance (1993), 'Differential school effectiveness: results from a reanalysis of the Inner London Education Authority's junior school project data', *British Educational Research Journal*, **19**, 381–405.

Sarrico, C.S. and R.G. Dyson (2000), 'Using data envelopment analysis for planning in UK universities – an institutional perspective', *Journal of the Operational Research Society*, **51**, 789–800.

Sarrico, C.S., S.M. Hogan, R.G. Dyson and A.D. Athanassopoulos (1997), 'Data envelopment analysis and university selection', *Journal of the Operational Research Society*, **48**, 1163–77.

Schmidt, P. (1985–6), 'Frontier production functions', *Econometric Reviews*, **4**(2), 289–328.

Sengupta, J.K. (1987), 'Production frontier estimation to measure efficiency: a critical evaluation in light of data envelopment analysis', *Managerial and Decision Economics*, **8**, 93–9.

Sengupta, J.K. (1990), 'Tests of efficiency in DEA', *Computers Operations Research*, **17**(2), 123–32.

Sengupta, J.K. (1999), 'The measurement of dynamic productive efficiency', *Bulletin of Economic Research*, **51**(2), 111–24.

Sengupta, J.K. and R.E. Sfeir (1986), 'Production frontier estimates of scale in public schools in California', *Economics of Education Review*, **5**(3), 297–307.

Sengupta, J.K. and R.E. Sfeir (1988), 'Efficiency measurement by data envelopment analysis with econometric applications', *Applied Economics*, **20**, 285–93.

Sickles, R.C., D.H. Good and L. Getachew (1998), 'Specification of distance functions using semi- and non-parametric methods with an application to the dynamic performance of Eastern and Western European air carriers', discussion paper, Rice University.

Simar, L. and P.W. Wilson (1998), 'Sensitivity analysis of efficiency scores: how to bootstrap in nonparametric frontier models', *Management Science*, **44**(1), 49–61.

Simar, L. and P.W. Wilson (1999), 'Performance of the bootstrap for DEA estimators and iterating the principle', discussion paper, Université Catholique de Louvain.

Smith, J. and R. Naylor (2001a), 'Dropping out of university: a statistical analysis of the probability of withdrawal for UK university students', *Journal of the Royal Statistical Society, Series A*, **164**(2), 389–405.

Smith, J. and R. Naylor (2001b), 'Determinants of degree performance in UK universities: a statistical analysis of the 1993 student cohort', *Oxford Bulletin of Economics and Statistics*, **63**, 29–60.

Smith, J., A. McKnight and R. Naylor (2000), 'Graduate employability: policy and performance in higher education in the UK', *Economic Journal*, **110**, F382–F411.

Smith, P. and D. Mayston (1987), 'Measuring efficiency in the public sector', *Omega*, **15**, 181–9.

Soteriou, A., E. Karahanna, C. Papanastasiou and M.S. Diakourakis (1998), 'Using data envelopment analysis to evaluate the efficiency of secondary schools: the case of Cyprus', *International Journal of Educational Management*, **12**(2), 65–73.

Stevens, P.A. (2001), 'The determinants of economic efficiency in English and Welsh universities', discussion paper no. 185, National Institute of Economic and Social Research, London.

Thanassoulis, E. (1996), 'Altering the bias in differential school effectiveness using data envelopment analysis', *Journal of the Operational Research Society*, **47**, 882–94.

Thanassoulis, E. (1999), 'Setting achievement targets for school children', *Education Economics*, **7**(2), 101–19.

Thanassoulis, E. and P. Dunstan (1994), 'Guiding schools to improved performance using data envelopment analysis: an illustration with data from a local education authority', *Journal of the Operational Research Society*, **45**(11), 1247–62.

Thanassoulis, E. and M.C.A.S. Portela (2002), 'School outcomes: sharing the responsibility between pupil and school', *Education Economics*, **10**(2), 183–207.

Thanassoulis, E., G. Simpson, G. Battisti and A. Charlesworth-May (2003), 'DEA and multi-level modelling as alternative methods for assessing pupil and school performance', Discussion Paper, Aston Business School.

Tomkins, C. and R. Green (1988), 'An experiment in the use of DEA for evaluating the efficiency of UK university departments of accounting', *Financial Accountability and Management*, **4**(2), 147–64.

Woodhouse, G. and H. Goldstein (1988), 'Educational performance indicators and LEA league tables', *Oxford Review of Education*, **14**, 301–19.

Worthington, A. (2001), 'An empirical survey of frontier efficiency measurement techniques in education', *Education Economics*, **9**(3), 245–68.

Yang, M. and G. Woodhouse (2001), 'Progress from GCSE to A and AS level: institutional differences and gender differences, and trends over time', *British Educational Research Journal*, **27**(3), 24–46.

Yang, M., H. Goldstein, W. Browne and G. Woodhouse (2002), 'Multivariate multilevel analyses of examination results', *Journal of the Royal Statistical Society, Series A*, **165**(1), 137–53.

Yang, M., H. Goldstein, T. Rath and N. Hill (1999), 'The use of assessment data for school improvement purposes', *Oxford Review of Education*, **25**(4), 469–83.

Appendix: table of empirical studies

I Aggregate-level models

a DEA (and related non-parametric methods)

Author(s)	Units analysed	Country	Outputs	Inputs	Comments
Abbott & Doucouliagos, 2003	38 universities	Australia	Model 1 research quantum number of full-time equivalent students Model 2 medical research income non-medical research income number of full-time equivalent students Model 3 research quantum number of full-time equivalent students	Model 1 total number of full-time equivalent academic staff total number of full-time equivalent non-academic staff expenditure on all inputs except labour value of non-current assets Model 2 total number of full-time equivalent academic staff total number of full-time equivalent non-academic staff expenditure on all inputs except labour Model 3 total number of full-time equivalent academic and non-academic staff expenditure on all inputs except labour	Results of various DEAs are compared. The final model is performed on a split sample, the criterion for the split being the ranking (high or low) from the initial DEAs

a DEA (and related non-parametric methods) *(continued)*

Author(s)	Units analysed	Country	Outputs	Inputs	Comments
Ahn *et al.*, 1989	33 institutions of higher learning	USA	number of undergraduate enrolments number of graduate enrolments total semester credit hours generated amount of federal government and private research funds	total faculty salaries state funds appropriated for research expenditures for administrative and academic support total investment in physical plants	A comparison of the DEA results with cost per student data reveals the need to take account of the multiple output–multiple input structure
Ahn & Seiford, 1993	153 institutions of higher learning	USA	Model 1 undergraduate FTEs graduate FTEs Model 2 total FTEs Model 3 undergraduate degrees graduate degrees grants	Model 1 faculty salaries physical investment overhead expenses Model 2 faculty salaries physical investment overhead expenses Model 3 faculty salaries physical investment overhead expenses	Various models and subsets are used and the results are compared. In particular, separate DEAs are applied to 49 private and 104 public institutions. The conclusions as to which type of institutions are more efficient depend on what variables are used as outputs. While conclusions were sensitive to inputs and

672

Author	Sample	Country			Notes
Arcelus & Coleman, 1997	academic units in one university	Canada	average enrolment per class average number of classes taught FTE undergraduates (UGs) FTE postgraduates (PGs) no. UGs receiving a degree no. PGs receiving a degree Model 4 total degrees grants	FTE teachers FTE support staff operating expenses library expenses Model 4 faculty salaries physical investment overhead expenses total enrolment undergraduate FTEs graduate FTEs	outputs, they were not sensitive to type of DEA model, i.e. VRS, CRS, additive or multiplicative

a DEA (and related non-parametric methods) *(continued)*

Author(s)	Units analysed	Country	Outputs	Inputs	Comments
Athanassopoulos & Shale, 1997	45 universities	UK	Model 1 number of successful leavers number of higher degrees awarded weighted research rating Model 2 number of successful leavers number of higher degrees awarded weighted research rating	Model 1 general academic expenditure research income Model 2 number of FTE undergraduates number of FTE postgraduates number of FTE academic staff mean A-level entry score over the last 3 years research income expenditure on library and computing services	DEA is applied to whole sample and subsets based on subject orientation (i.e. science, science and balanced orientation). Additional DEAs are performed using value judgments to restrict input and output weights

Avkiran, 2001	36 universities	Australia	Model 1 undergraduate enrolments postgraduate enrolments research quantum Model 2 student retention rate (%) student progress rate (%) graduate full-time employment (%) Model 3 overseas fee-paying enrolments non-overseas fee-paying postgraduate enrolments	Model 1 FTE academic staff FTE non-academic staff Model 2 FTE academic staff FTE non-academic staff Model 3 FTE academic staff FTE non-academic staff	Provides a set of recommendations for researchers wishing to apply DEA
Beasley, 1990	52 chemistry and physics university departments	UK	number of undergraduates number of taught postgraduates number of research postgraduates research income if a department is rated outstanding at research if a department is rated above average at research if a department is rated average at research if a department is rated below average at research	general expenditure equipment expenditure research income	

a DEA (and related non-parametric methods) (continued)

Author(s)	Units analysed	Country	Outputs	Inputs	Comments
Beasley, 1995	52 chemistry and physics university departments	UK	number of undergraduates number of taught postgraduates number of research postgraduates research income if a department is rated outstanding at research if a department is rated above average at research if a department is rated average at research if a department is rated below average at research	general expenditure equipment expenditure research income	A method is developed to calculate efficiencies in teaching and research separately. Value judgments are used to provide constraints on the weights
Bessent & Bessent, 1980	55 schools in an urban school district	USA	median percentile reading achievement test score in 1977 median percentile mathematics achievement test score in 1977	median percentile reading achievement test score in 1976 median percentile mathematics achievement test score in 1976 % Anglo-American pupils % pupils not from low-income families	

% in average daily attendance

mobility index

number of professional staff
   per 100 pupils

total per pupil expenditure
   for instruction

job satisfaction

social interaction between
   teachers

teachers motivated by
   principal's personal
example of work orientation

principal's friendliness and
   cooperation with teachers

a DEA (and related non-parametric methods) (*continued*)

Author(s)	Units analysed	Country	Outputs	Inputs	Comments
Bessent *et al.*, 1982	167 elementary schools	USA	mean composite Iowa Test of Basic Skills (ITBS) score at grade 3 mean ITBS score at grade 6	mean ITBS score at grade 2 mean ITBS score at grade 5 % non-minority enrolment % pupils paying full lunch price % attendance number of professionals per 100 pupils local and state expenditures per pupil federal money allocated per pupil number of special programmes in school % teachers with masters degrees % teachers with more than 3 years' experience % teaching days that assigned teachers were present	The study identifies the problem of obtaining appropriate measures of inputs and outputs not necessarily related to test results. A suggestion is made for DEA to be applied to individual pupils to identify which pupils are using resources efficiently. It is suggested that this information would improve teachers' efficiency in terms of planning a good learning environment for pupils

Study	Sample	Country	Outputs	Inputs	Notes
Bonesrønning & Rattsø, 1994	34 high schools	Norway	Model 1 number of students Model 2 number of graduates average value added Model 3 number of graduates × average value added	All models teacher manyears	Jackknifing is used to check the sensitivity of the results to outliers. A fourth model applies DEA to samples split by size of DMU, and some differences emerge
Bradley *et al.*, 2001	all secondary schools	England	proportion of 5+ GCSE grades A*–C attendance rate	proportion of pupils ineligible for school meals proportion of qualified teachers	Tobit analysis is used at the second stage to examine the determinants of the efficiencies for a given year. The main findings are that the degree of competition, spending on teachers, spending on books, being a girls-only school are all found positively to affect efficiency; the pupil–teacher ratio has a negative effect on efficiency

a DEA (and related non-parametric methods) (*continued*)

Author(s)	Units analysed	Country	Outputs	Inputs	Comments
Breu & Raab, 1994	25 universities	USA	graduation rate freshman retention rate	average SAT score % faculty with doctorates faculty student ratio educational and general expenditure per student tuition charges per student	
Chalos & Cherian, 1995	207 elementary school districts	USA	Math Illinois Goal Assessment Program score for year 6 Math Illinois Goal Assessment Program score for year 8 Verbal Illinois Goal Assessment Program score for year 6 Verbal Illinois Goal Assessment Program score for year 8	operating expenditures per pupil pupil attendance rate % teachers with masters degrees % non-low income % non-minority	The DEA efficiencies are examined in the context of district revenue sources

Study	Sample	Country	Outputs	Inputs	Comments
Chalos, 1997	207 elementary school districts	USA	Math Illinois Goal Assessment Program score for year 6; Math Illinois Goal Assessment Program score for year 8; Verbal Illinois Goal Assessment Program score for year 6; Verbal Illinois Goal Assessment Program score for year 8	operating expenditures per pupil; ratio of administrative to instructional expenditures; ratio of local to total revenue; % non-minority; % non-low income; pupil attendance rate; % teachers with masters degree; student enrolment; level 6 verbal score; level 8 verbal score; level 6 math score; level 8 math score	The DEA efficiencies are examined in the context of budgetary characteristics of the districts. Efficient school districts have, on average, compared to inefficient districts, smaller operating budgets, lower ratios of administrative expenses to operating budgets and proportionately lower local to state sources of financing
Coelli *et al.*, 1998	36 universities	Australia	total number of students (FTEs); total number of staff (FTEs)	expenditure on administrative staff; other administrative costs	The purpose of the study is to evaluate the efficiency of the administration sector of universities

a   DEA (and related non-parametric methods)   (continued)

Author(s)	Units analysed	Country	Outputs	Inputs	Comments
Duncombe et al., 1997	585 school districts	USA	operating expenditure per pupil	average test score in reading average test score in mathematics average test score in social studies inverse of the dropout rate environment index teacher salary index % children in poverty % households with school-age children % adults with college education % single-parent households % children at risk % students with limited English	DEA is used to assess cost efficiency. In a second stage, Tobit analysis is applied to explain the inefficiencies in the context of competition, government size, characteristics of the population and fiscal circumstances
El-Mahgary & Lahdelma, 1995	20 universities	Finland	annual number of first degrees granted annual number of advanced degrees granted inverse of the median of the number of years	total expenditure for educational puposes inverse of the acceptance rate of its applicants	Some basic approaches for visualizing the results of a DEA are presented and examined

needed to complete the degree
number of students who complete their studies

Engert, 1996	214 school districts	USA	Model A	Model A	The DEA efficiencies are
			number of students	total expenditures	compared with crude
			achieving at a basic	dropouts	ratios. The overall
			level of competency		agreement between the
			number of high school		DEA efficiencies and
			graduates who received		the ratios was
			the regents' diploma		not particularly high
			the number of 1989–90		
			high school graduates		
			entering a post-secondary		
			institution in fall 1990		
			Model B	Model B	
			number of students	administration expenditures	
			achieving at a basic	instruction expenditures	
			level of competency	operations expenditures	
			number of high school	transportation expenditures	
			graduates who received	other expenditures	
			the regents' diploma	dropouts	
			the number of 1989–90		
			high school graduates		
			entering a post-secondary		
			institution in fall 1990		

a DEA (and related non-parametric methods) (*continued*)

Author(s)	Units analysed	Country	Outputs	Inputs	Comments
Engert, 1996 (*continued*)					
			Model C number of students achieving at a basic level of competency number of high school graduates who received the regents' diploma the number of 1989–90 high schoolgraduates entering a post-secondary institution in fall 1990	Model C administration expenditures instruction expenditures operations expenditures transportation expenditures other expenditures dropouts majority students	
Färe *et al.*, 1988	40 public schools	USA	number of 8th grade students passing reading test number of 8th grade students passing mathematics test number of 8th grade students passing government and economics test	number of 8th grade teachers (variable) number of 8th grade students (fixed)	The study uses Shepherd's indirect production function to calculate cost indirect technical efficiency, and allows inputs to be either variable or fixed

	Sample	Country	Inputs	Outputs	Comments
Färe, Grosskopf & Lovell, 1988	40 public school districts	USA	number of teachers number of students	number of students passing the 8th grade reading test number of students passing the 8th grade mathematics test number of students passing the 8th grade government and economics test	An indirect production function approach is used to derive budget-constrained, output-based efficiency measures. Note that the inputs are split according to whether they are variable (number of teachers) or given (number of students)
Friedman & Sinuany-Stern, 1997	21 departments within one university (Ben-Gurion)	Israel	Model 1 operational expenditure faculty salaries Model 2 operational expenditure faculty salaries	Model 1 grant money number of publications number of graduate students number of credit hours given in the departments Model 2 grant money number of publications number of credit hours given in the departments	Canonical correlation analysis is used in conjunction with DEA, and determines the outputs to be included in the second DEA model. Correlation between the rankings of units from DEA and from canonical correlation analysis are high and significant

a DEA (and related non-parametric methods) (continued)

Author(s)	Units analysed	Country	Outputs	Inputs	Comments
Ganley & Cubbin, (1992)	96 LEAs	UK	% achieving 5 or more O levels/CSEs % achieving 6 or more O levels/CSEs 100 minus the % achieving no grades O levels/CSEs	secondary school teaching expenditure per pupil % with head of household non-manual 100 minus the % in household lacking 1 or more standard amenities 100 minus the % born outside UK, Ireland, USA, Old Commonwealth persons per hectare	
Grosskopf & Moutray, 2001	high schools	USA	attendance rate high school graduate rate value added in American Collegiate Test (ACT) score (English) value added in ACT score (mathematics)	number of teachers average teacher salary number of administrators average administrator salary fixed factors based on ACT score in, respectively, mathematics and English	Changes in performance in high schools between 1989 and 1994 are assessed following a policy change. Malmquist productivity indices are developed and separated into indices of technological change and efficiency change, respectively. There appears to be little change. A second

Reference	Sample	Country	Outputs	Inputs	Comments
					stage regression analysis of the three indices suggests that schools with increasing per pupil expenditures had lower productivity
Haksever & Muragishi, 1998	40 MBA programmes	USA	average starting salary % students who have a job by graduation index of quality of MBA programme	average graduate management administration test score on entry tuition costs index of publications by academic staff % students with working experience	Various additional inputs are considered and the number reduced to the 4 listed here using statistical methods. A variety of DEA runs are performed (44 in all) to check the sensitivity of results
Harrison & Rouse, 2002	69 Auckland secondary schools	New Zealand	Model 1 total headcount roll at 1/7/94	Model 1 total government funding of teacher salaries for each school total government funding for school operations (excluding teacher salaries) the latest valuation of each school's land and buildings	OLS regression of the DEA efficiencies on the socioeconomic decile for the areas from which each school draws its students indicates a significant relationship

a DEA (and related non-parametric methods) *(continued)*

Author(s)	Units analysed	Country	Outputs	Inputs	Comments
Harrison & Rouse, 2002 *(continued)*					
			Model 2 % of School Certificate (SC) papers grade A or B (1994) number of SC candidates in 1994 divided by the number of form 3 students at the school in 1992 expressed as % % University Bursary/ Entrance or Scholarship papers sat in 1994 graded either S, A or B % school leavers who left with a Form 7 qualification 100 minus the % school leavers who left with no formal qualification	Model 2 total government funding of teacher salaries per student for each school total government funding for school operations per student (excluding teacher salaries) the latest valuation of each school's land and buildings per student	
Jesson *et al.*, 1987	96 LEAs	England	% getting 5 or more graded O level passes (or CSE grade 1) % getting 3 or more	% children in LEAs catchment whose head is non-manual % children not from one-	The study establishes a framework of analysis but the authors point out limitations on the

Study	Country	Sample	Outputs	Inputs	Comments
			graded O level passes (or CSE grade 1)	parent families % children (or head of family) born outside UK, Ireland, USA, Old Commonwealth secondary school expenditure per pupil	adequacy of the data
Johnes & Johnes, 1992	UK	36 university departments of economics	Model 1 papers in academic journals papers and letters in the core journals of economics	Model 1 person-months of teaching and research staff employed in 1983–8	The analysis illustrates that DEA results can be sensitive to the specification of input and/or output variables
			Model 2 papers in academic journals papers and letters in the core journals of economics	Model 2 person-months of teaching and research staff employed in 1983–8 per capita value of external research grants received during 1983–8	
			Model 3 papers in academic journals papers and letters in the core journals of economics	Model 3 person-months of research only *and* teaching and research staff employed in 1983–8	

a   DEA (and related non-parametric methods)   (*continued*)

Author(s)	Units analysed	Country	Outputs	Inputs	Comments
Johnes & Johnes, 1993	36 university departments of economics	UK	Model 1 papers in academic journals contributions to edited works papers or communications in core journals of economics Model 2 authored books papers or communications in core journals of economics Model 3 papers in academic journals letters in academic journals contributions to edited works papers or communications in core journals of economics research grants	Model 1 person-months of teaching and research staff person months of teaching and research only staff Model 2 papers in academic journals contributions to edited works papers or communications in core journals of economics per capita research grants Model 3 papers in academic journals contributions to edited works papers or communications in core journals of economics	Some 192 DEA runs are performed and the results of these are separated into 2 distinct groups using cluster analysis. Using per capita research grants as an input is the feature which distinguishes between the 2 clusters. The efficiencies of various DEA runs are also tested against a normal distribution using a Jarque-Bera test

| Kirjavainen & Loikkanen, 1998 | 291 senior secondary schools | Finland | Model 1
number of students who passed their grade
number of graduates

Model 2
as Model 1

Model 3
as Model 1 plus
score in compulsory subjects in matriculation examination
score in additional subjects in matriculation examination

Model 4
as Model 3 | Model 1
teaching hours per week
non-teaching hours per week

Model 2
as Model 1 plus
admission level

Model 3
as Model 2 plus
experience of teachers
education of teachers

Model 4
as Model 3 plus
educational level of students' parents | In a second stage, the DEA inefficiency scores are related to a number of explanatory variables using Tobit analysis. The significance of the explanatory variables depends on the DEA model used to provide the dependent variable |

a DEA (and related non-parametric methods) *(continued)*

Author(s)	Units analysed	Country	Outputs	Inputs	Comments
Korhonen *et al.*, 2001	18 research units in a school of economics	Finland	quality of research indicator research activity indicator impact of research indicator activity in educating doctoral students indicator	estimated monthly cost of producing research	The results of the value efficiency analysis are compared with the results of DEA. Fewer DMUs are efficient in the former analysis compared with the latter
Lovell *et al.*, 1994	530 to 585 schools	USA	Model 1 average number of math classes taken × enrolment average number of science classes taken × enrolment average number of vocational education classes taken × enrolment average number of foreign language classes taken × enrolment extra-curricular activity index × enrolment school course offering index total instruction hours received by typical	Model 1 total number of staff (all types) number of volumes in school library physical facilities index	The DEA technique is modified by deleting the DMU being evaluated from its own reference set, thereby producing efficiency scores which range from 0 to ∞. The three models represent performance at achieving short-, intermediate- and long-term objectives, respectively. The schools appear to be more successful at the

692

last two than the first. The distribution of efficiency scores obtained from this modified DEA is then explained at a second stage using OLS regression. The variables included at this second stage vary according to model used to derive the DEA scores (i.e. 1, 2 or 3). A small but significant part of the variation in efficiency scores is explained by a number of variables in each of the three cases

Model 2
average number of math classes taken
average number of science classes taken
average number of vocational education classes taken
average number of foreign language classes taken
extracurricular activity index
total instruction hours received by typical student in a year
average time spent by students on homework

Model 3
as Model 2

student in a year × enrolment

Model 2
standardized test score
ratio of follow-up test score to base year test composite score
average teacher's assessment of % students who will likely proceed to college

Model 3
average post-secondary grades
average 1983 income
average 1985 income
average highest educational level attained

a DEA (and related non-parametric methods) *(continued)*

Author(s)	Units analysed	Country	Outputs	Inputs	Comments
Madden *et al.*, 1997	24 university departments of economics	Australia	number of graduating undergraduate students number of graduating postgraduate students papers in core journals papers in other journals number of books contributions to edited books occasional, discussion, conference papers	number of teaching and research staff	The study looks at performance before and after new funding arrangements were introduced
Mancebon & Bandrés, 1999	35 secondary schools	Spain	% pupils who pass the university entrance exam ratio of average mark to the standard deviation of the entrance exam in sciences ratio of average mark to the standard deviation of the entrance exam in arts	operating expenses (excluding personnel costs) number of teachers per pupil socioeconomic factor human capital factor	The final two inputs are reflected using the first two principal components of 12 variables reflecting academic quality and socioeconomic level. The study applies a method for testing pairs of nested DEA models

Study	Sample	Country	Outputs	Inputs	Notes
Mancebon & Mar Molinero, 2000	176 primary schools	UK	Model 1 % pupils achieving level 4 or more in English SAT at key stage 2 Model 2 % pupils achieving level 4 or more in English SAT at key stage 2 % pupils achieving level 4 or more in science SAT at key stage 2	All models teacher–pupil ratios % pupils ineligible for school meals	Various additional variables are tried and a method is applied to determine which variables to include or exclude. At a second stage, a small number of variables are found to be significantly related to the efficiencies including religious orientation of the school and parental support
Mante & O'Brien, 2002	26 or 27 state secondary schools	Australia	Models 1 & 2 proportion of students with tertiary entrance rank scores of 50 and above year 12 apparent retention rate	Model 1 staff–pupil ratio adjusted special learning needs index Model 2 expenditure per pupil	A comparison of the two models suggests that socioeconomic status of students is an important characteristic affecting a school's ability to transform inputs into outputs
Mante, 2001	57 state secondary schools	Australia	Models 1 & 2 proportion of students with tertiary entrance rank scores of 50 and above year 12 apparent retention rate	Model 1 staff–pupil ratio adjusted special learning needs index Model 2 expenditure per pupil	

a DEA (and related non-parametric methods) *(continued)*

Author(s)	Units analysed	Country	Outputs	Inputs	Comments
McCarty & Yaisawarng, 1993	27 school districts	USA	Model 1 % students who pass the high school proficiency tests in mathematics % students who pass the high school proficiency tests in reading % students who pass the high school proficiency tests in writing Model 2 % students who pass the high school proficiency tests in mathematics % students who pass the high school proficiency tests in reading % students who pass the high school proficiency tests in writing	Model 1 number of staff per pupil ratio proportion of total staff who have an MA or PhD expenditure per pupil (excluding salaries) Model 2 number of staff per pupil ratio proportion of total staff who have an MA or PhD expenditure per pupil (excluding salaries) index of students' socio-economic status	Tobit analysis is used at the second stage to relate Model 1's efficiency scores to the uncontrollable input i.e. students' socio-economic status. Residuals from this Tobit analysis are used to rank DMUs. The rankings based on these residuals are more closely related to the DEA efficiencies of Model 2 (where students' socio-economic status is included in the DEA) than to the DEA efficiencies of Model 1

| Ramanathan, 2001 | 46 schools | Netherlands | % pupils successfully proceeding without delay from the start of the 3rd school year until the final diploma at the end of the 6th year
% pupils successfully examined in more than the prescribed minimum of 7 subjects
the average grade obtained by pupils in subjects which were centrally examined | constant value dummy for all schools (to reflect cost per pupil being the same across all schools) | The effect of non-discretionary input variables is considered at a second stage which uses regression techniques. The DEA efficiencies are significantly positively influenced by size of school, type of school being grammar, and religious orientation of school being Roman Catholic/Protestant Christian. Location in The Hague has no significant effect |

a DEA (and related non-parametric methods) (*continued*)

Author(s)	Units analysed	Country	Outputs	Inputs	Comments
Ray, 1991	122 districts operating high schools	USA	average mathematics score at 9th grade average language arts score at 9th grade average writing score at 9th grade average reading score at 9th grade	FTE classroom teachers per pupil FTE support staff per pupil FTE administrative staff per pupil	The sensitivity of the DEA efficiencies is tested by excluding specific variables and the efficiencies are found to be reliable. Regression analysis (with a one-sided error term) is used at the 2nd stage to relate the DEA efficiencies to socio-economic factors. College education of adults in the district population, % students from ethnic minorities and % children from single parent families significantly explain nearly two-thirds of the variation in efficiencies

| Ruggiero, 1996 | 556 school districts | USA | reading score
math score
social studies score
drop out rate | teacher salary expenditures
pupil personnel instruc-
tional expenditures
books per pupil
microcomputers per pupil
% adults with college
  education
all other instructional
  expenditures | DEA is modified to make
allowance for
differences between
DMUs in terms of the
environmental factors
faced. The advantage
is that the DMUs in an
inefficient DMU's
reference set are
constrained to face
a similar environment
to the inefficient
DMU |
| Ruggiero, 2000 | 556 school districts | USA | reading score
math score
social studies score
drop out rate | teacher salary expenditures
pupil personnel instruc-
tional expenditures
books per pupil
microcomputers per pupil
% adults with college
  education | DEA is modified to make
allowance for
differences between
DMUs in terms of the
environmental factors
faced. The advantage
is that the DMUs in an
inefficient DMU's
reference set are
constrained to face a
similar environment to
the inefficient DMU |

a DEA (and related non-parametric methods) *(continued)*

Author(s)	Units analysed	Country	Outputs	Inputs	Comments
Sarrico & Dyson, 2000	university departments	UK	teaching rating research rating library spending accommodation score (representing % students in university-maintained accommodation) proportion of home students going into employment or further study cheapness of living (derived from average student debt)	entry requirements	Various aspects of performance are considered, which are of interest to different groups, eg. prospective students, university managers and the government. DEA results are compared with other measures reflecting different aspects of performance. Graphical presentation of the various measures can aid interpretation
Sarrico et al., 1997	university departments	UK	customized for university applicants	customized for university applicants	The study focuses on the applicant's interest in university performance, and DEA models are tailor-made, based on the attributes which an applicant considers important in order to rank universities. Weights are used to reflect importance of specific characteristics

Sengupta, 1990	public elementary schools	USA	standardized test scores in reading standardized test scores in writing standardized test scores in spelling standardized test scores in mathematics	average instructional expenditure proportion of minority enrolment average class size parental socioeconomic background	The analysis is performed in the context of illustrating the use of canonical correlation theory in developing a set of statistical tests for DEA models
Smith & Mayston, 1987	96 LEAs	England	% leavers getting 1 or more A level pass % leavers getting 5 or more graded O level passes (or CSE grade 1) % leavers getting 6 or more graded O level passes (or CSE grade 1) % leavers getting 1 or more graded O level passes (or CSE grade 1)	% pupils from households whose head is in a high socioeconomic group % children not living in poor housing % pupils from households with a single parent expenditure per pupil	The study examines the sensitivity of results to the omission of specific outputs or inputs or extreme DMUs. Questions are raised regarding criteria for which inputs/outputs to include and how to assess the sensitivity of results

a   DEA (and related non-parametric methods) (*continued*)

Author(s)	Units analysed	Country	Outputs	Inputs	Comments
Soteriou *et al.*, 1998	55 secondary schools	Cyprus	All models international mathematics score	Model 1 age of teacher education level of teacher parents' education level socioeconomic status Model 2 as model 1 plus school size Model 3 as model 2 plus number of books in students' homes	A method is applied to investigate whether there are differences between urban and rural schools. None is found
Thanassoulis & Dunstan, 1994	secondary schools	UK	average GCSE score per pupil % pupils not unemployed after GCSE	mean verbal reasoning score per pupil on entry % not receiving school meals	A method is developed for computing targets and identifying peers for inefficient DMUs which reflect various preferences regarding the relative desirability of different outcomes

Thannassoulis, 1996	14 schools	UK	average GCSE score per pupil % pupils placed after GCSE	mean verbal reasoning score per pupil on entry % not receiving school meals	This paper addresses the problem that schools are differentially effective, i.e. they may be more (or less) effective in converting specific groups (such as high ability or high socioeconomic pupils) into outputs. A method is developed which sets targets and identifies peer groups for DMUs which are differentially effective
Tomkins & Green, 1988	20 university departments of accounting	UK	Model 1 undergraduates research postgraduates taught postgraduates total income Model 2 as Model 1 plus publications Model 3 as Model 2	Model 1 full time staff numbers Model 2 as Model 2 Model 3 as Model 2 plus non-staff expenditure	DEA shows some stability in ranking over the various specifications

a DEA (and related non-parametric methods) (*continued*)

Author(s)	Units analysed	Country	Outputs	Inputs	Comments
Tomkins & Green, 1988 (*continued*)					
			Model 4 as Model 2	Model 4 academic salaries non-staff expenditure	
			Model 5 undergraduates research postgraduates taught postgraduates publications research council income other research income other income	Model 5 academic salaries non-staff expenditure	
			Model 6 as Model 5	Model 6 expenditure	

b Statistical techniques (excluding stochastic frontier analysis)

Author(s)	Units analysed	Country	Outputs	Inputs	Comments
Gray et al., 1984	96 LEAs	England	% leavers obtaining 5 or more graded passes at O level/CSE grade 1 % leavers obtaining 1 or more graded passes at O level/CSE grade 1	% children in low socioeconomic households % children in high socioeconomic households % children non-white or born abroad % children living in one-parent families whether an LEA was fully comprehensive or not	The main purpose of the study is to establish whether LEA performance, in terms of examination results, differs according to whether or not LEAs are fully comprehensive. Regression methods are used to relate each output measure, separately, to the input measures. Once other factors are taken into account, whether or not an LEA is fully comprehensive is not a significant determinant

b Statistical techniques (excluding stochastic frontier analysis) (*continued*)

Author(s)	Units analysed	Country	Outputs	Inputs	Comments
Johnes & Taylor, 1987	45 universities	UK	degree results	entry score % graduates living at home library expenditure degree subject type of university location of university size student–staff ratio ratio of males to females	Regression analysis demonstrates that 90% of the inter-university variation in degree results can be explained by a small number of variables. The validity of using the regression residual to represent performance is questioned
Johnes & Taylor, 1989a	37–45 universities	UK	non-completion rate	entry score type of degree subject living accommodation location of university (other variables including gender, school type and student–staff ratio found insignificant)	A substantial amount of inter-university variation in non-completion rates can be explained (using OLS) by a small number of determinants, suggesting that unadjusted non-completion rates are unsatisfactory performance indicators

Study	Sample	Country	Variables	Comments
Johnes & Taylor, 1989b	45 universities	UK	**Model 1** variable based on graduate entering permanent employment (adjusted for subject mix) **Model 2** variable based on graduate entering further education and training (adjusted for subject mix) **Both models** entry score degree result % graduates attending grammar or independent school age of university location of university regional unemployment rate employer visits to university	A substantial amount of inter-university variation in graduates entering employment or further education and training is explained (using OLS) by subject mix and additional university characteristics. This calls into question whether measures of performance based on these data are of use
Johnes & Taylor, 1990	45 universities	UK	**Model 1** unit costs **Model 2** non-completion rates **Model 1** subject mix % undergraduates student–staff ratio **Model 2** entry score type of degree subject living accommodation location of university student–staff ratio	Regression techniques are used for all analyses. The relationship between raw output values and performance indicators derived from OLS residual is weak. Simultaneous evaluation of performance across all 5 models is difficult as performance varies according to output variable used

b Statistical techniques (excluding stochastic frontier analysis) *(continued)*

Author(s)	Units analysed	Country	Outputs	Inputs	Comments
Johnes & Taylor, 1990 *(continued)*					
			Model 3 degree results	Model 3 entry score % students living at home library expenditure type of university location of university	

			Model 4
			first destination of
			graduates
				Model 4
				entry score
				% graduates from grammar
				  or independent
				  school
				careers visits to university
				regional unemployment
				  rate
				age of university
				type of university
				location of university	

			Model 5 research rating	Model 5 % total staff who are research only	

Study	Sample	Country	Dependent variable	Independent variables	Results
Johnes & Taylor, 1992	cost centres within universities	UK	research rating	student–staff ratio; research expenditure per member of staff; type of university; location of university	OLS techniques indicate that size and research rating of the rest of the university are the significant and consistent determinants of a cost centre's research rating
Johnes, 1990	45 universities	UK	ratio of general expenditure on academic departments to FTE students (i.e. unit cost)	size; research rating of rest of university; research expenditure per member of staff; student–staff ratio; type of university; location of university; subject mix; % undergraduates; % graduates obtaining an honours degree; % postgraduates who are taught; student–staff ratio; % FT academic staff who are professors; % FT academic staff who are 55 or over; % income from research contracts; size	OLS regression methods demonstrate that subject mix accounts for two-thirds of the inter-university variation in unit costs. The student–staff ratio and student composition are also significant determinants of unit costs

b Statistical techniques (excluding stochastic frontier analysis) (continued)

Author(s)	Units analysed	Country	Outputs	Inputs	Comments
Johnes, 1996	45 universities	UK	Model 1 first destination of graduates	Model 1 entry score careers visits to university type of university location of university	Regression residuals are used to construct 4 measures of performance. These measures give inconsistent pictures of university efficiency (rank correlation coefficients range from −0.40 to 0.13) and are relatively uncorrelated with raw output variables (r ranges from 0.35 to 0.47). Attention is drawn to the random nature of regression residuals, which is undesirable in the context of measuring performance. Principal components are used to reduce the dimensionality of the
			Model 2 degree results	Model 2 entry score library expenditure type of university location of university	
			Model 3 non-completion rate	Model 3 entry score subject of degree location of university	
			Model 4 research rating	Model 4 % total staff who are research only student–staff ratio type of university location of university	

| Johnes, Taylor & Francis, 1993 | cost centres within universities | UK | research rating | student–staff ratio
research expenditure per member of staff
size of cost centre
size of university
research rating of rest of university
location of university
type of university | efficiency measures and offer insights into the priorities and aims of individual universities

A cumulative logit model is used to analyse determinants of research rating by cost centre. Size of cost centre and research rating in the rest of the university are the most consistent determinants of research rating. Type of university and research expenditure per member of staff are also significant |

b Statistical techniques (excluding stochastic frontier analysis) *(continued)*

Author(s)	Units analysed	Country	Outputs	Inputs	Comments
Jones & Zimmer, 2001	more than 500 school districts	USA	Michigan's Education Assessment Program (MEAP) district mean score for each of four tests (maths, 2 reading, science) at each of three grades	previous academic level (using MEAP test results) racial composition college education of adults income level unemployment rate current operating expenditure of school % students classed as SEN (special educational needs) location school district per student debt level	Weighted two-stage least squares is used to examine the effect on achievement of capital stock, which is found to be significant
Sengupta & Sfeir, 1986	elementary school districts	USA	Model 1 average of test scores in reading, mathematics, writing and spelling Model 2 test score in reading	All models total average expenditure per average daily attendance (ADA) × ADA average teacher salary average class size proportion of minority	A translog production function is estimated in each case using regression methods and LP methods

Model 3
test score in
   mathematics

Model 4
test score in writing

Model 5
test score in spelling

c Stochastic frontier analysis

Author(s)	Units analysed	Country	Outputs	Inputs	Comments
Deller & Rudnicki, 1993	elementary schools	USA	3-year cumulative average test score	school size % parents with college degree per capita income in school district local unemployment rate teaching expenditure per pupil administrative expenditure per pupil operations expenditure per pupil bussing expenditure per pupil	The study finds that peer influences and family background may be more important determinants of output than school inputs, and therefore questions whether increased financial resources will cause increased efficiency

c Stochastic frontier analysis (*continued*)

Author(s)	Units analysed	Country	Outputs	Inputs	Comments
Hashimoto & Cohn, 1997	94 private universities	Japan	number of undergraduates number of graduates research grants dummy variable for if number of graduates > 0 dummy variable for if research grants > 0 plus some interaction and quadratic terms	total cost	A flexible fixed-cost quadratic function is used to estimate a multiple output cost function. Evidence is found of ray economies of scale, and global and product-specific economies of scope
Izadi *et al.*, 2002	99 universities	UK	undergraduate student load in arts undergraduate student load in science postgraduate student load value of research grants and contracts received	total expenditure	Inefficiencies are broken down by university using the method developed by Jondrow *et al.* (1982). Only modest inefficiencies are found to exist
Johnes, 1997	99 universities	UK	UG load in science UG load in arts PG load all subjects value research grants	total costs	Further information is provided in Johnes (1998b)

| Kang & Greene, 2002 | 788 school districts | USA | average % students passing 3 mathematics and 4 science regent examinations
% graduate candidates receiving a regent diploma
% graduates going to a 4-year college
% graduates going to a 2- or 4-year college
dropout rate | efficiency units of teachers per student (incorporates quality based on salary)
ratio of paraprofessional staff to students
efficiency units of professional staff per student (incorporates quality based on salary)
number of library books per student
number of instructional rooms per student
number of computers per student
total number of students in a school district
% Indian, black & Hispanic students
median household income in school district
% people with at least bachelors' degrees in school district
% housing owners in school district | A stochastic frontier production function is estimated for each output separately. There is some variation in the effect of input variables on the different outputs which leads to some ambiguous policy implications |

c Stochastic frontier analysis (continued)

Author(s)	Units analysed	Country	Outputs	Inputs	Comments
Kang & Greene, 2002 (continued)				ratio of county population to area of county % Catholic population in county of school % households with school children in school district	
Stevens, 2001	higher education institutions	England & Wales	number of UG arts number of UG science number of PGs total research funding average A level score number of firsts or upper seconds	total expenditure average staff costs staff characteristics student characteristics	SFA is used to derived efficiencies where total expenditure is the dependent variable and all other input and output variables are independent variables. The determinants of efficiencies are investigated simultaneously using the method described by Coelli *et al.* (1998)

II Individual-level analyses

a DEA

Author(s)	Units analysed	Country	Outputs	Inputs	Comments
Johnes, 2003	2568 individual graduates from university departments of economics	UK	Model 1 degree value	Model 1 entry score	This study calculates a measure of efficiency derived for each department based on a DEA of individual graduates. Various specifications of inputs and outputs are used. These results are then compared with the results of DEAs of the same data at department level. A comparison of results shows that individual-level DEAs produce rankings of departments which differ from those derived from department-level DEAs
			Model 2 degree value	Model 2 entry score gender marital status nationality	
			Model 3 degree value	Model 3 entry score gender marital status nationality type of degree (i.e. part-time) living at home type of previous school attended (i.e. not independent)	

a DEA (*continued*)

Author(s)	Units analysed	Country	Outputs	Inputs	Comments
Johnes, 2003 (*continued*)					
			Model 4 degree score	Model 4 as Model 1	
			Model 5 degree score	Model 5 as Model 2	
			Model 6 degree score	Model 6 as Model 3	
Portela & Thanassoulis, 2001	6700 pupils from secondary schools	England	Total A and AS points A and AS points per attempt	Total GCSE points GCSE points per attempt	The study examines data at three levels, i.e. pupils within schools within type of school. For each pupil it is possible to see whether improvement can be achieved through an improvement in the pupil's own efforts or from improvement in the performance of the school

| Thanassoulis & Portela, 2002 | 6700 pupils from secondary schools | England | Total A and AS points A and AS points per attempt | Total GCSE points GCSE points per attempt | The study examines the data at two levels, i.e. pupils within schools. It concludes that both pupils and schools can contribute to improvements in pupil attainment, but the larger component can come from the pupils' own efforts |

b Statistical methods: single-level modelling

Author(s)	Units analysed	Country	Outputs	Inputs	Comments
Bratti *et al.*, 2003	68 767 male & 77 263 female graduates from universities who responded to the First Destinations Survey (FDS)	UK	in employment or further study 6 months after graduation	previous academic achievement age social class region of residence disability ethnic background degree course type of study accommodation type degree class genders analysed separately	The possibility of bias from using the FDS to construct performance indicators is investigated. Use of this database ignores leavers without qualifications and those who have not responded. As a consequence of non-random differential response rates, measures of institutional performance and hence university rankings are sensitive to whether effects are measured conditionally or unconditionally. Concern is raised that performance indicators constructed in this

paper are adjusted for a large number of control variables, most of which can be influenced by the institutions themselves

Bratti, 2002	7997 life science university leavers	UK	degree classification	gender marital status age accommodation type university effects previous academic achievement subject of previous qualifications type of previous school quality of previous school social class residence prior to university	Rankings of universities which are unadjusted for input variables differ from those created here, which account for the quality and background of student intake. The rankings can vary according to the definition of value added used. In a second stage, the university effects are regressed on a number of variables reflecting institution characteristics, and expenditure on residences is found to be significantly related

b Statistical methods: single-level modelling *(continued)*

Author(s)	Units analysed	Country	Outputs	Inputs	Comments
Häkkinen *et al.*, 2003	20 505 students at senior secondary schools	Finland	matriculation examination score	mother's education father's education teaching expenditure per student gender whether student works during senior secondary school number of students in school comprehensive school Grade Point Average (GPA)	Fixed-effect panel data models are estimated specifically to assess the effects of changes in resources on student performance. The effects of resource changes on student performance are found to be not significant, while previous education attainment and parents' education are the strongest explanatory variables
Montmarquette *et al.*, 2001	3418 students at one university	Canada	dropout or not	gender age academic performance at college GPA after first year type of college attended full-time or part-time character of programme mother tongue of student	

| Naylor et al., 2000 | 44 814 graduates from universities in employment 6 months after graduation | UK | a graduate's occupational earnings | region of origin
size of programme
previous academic achievement
age
marital status
fee-paying status
parental occupation
type of school attended
quality of previous school
degree subject
degree result
genders analysed separately | The rankings of universities based on raw graduate earnings and those based on graduate earnings adjusted for significant determinants are compared. The correlation is 0.55, and the standard deviation falls from 26.5 to 16.95 after adjustment |

b Statistical methods: single-level modelling (*continued*)

Author(s)	Units analysed	Country	Outputs	Inputs	Comments
Naylor *et al.*, 2002	51167 graduates from universities	UK	earnings	academic qualifications at university academic qualifications at school age marital status social class type of school attended degree subject academic expenditure of university total expenditure of university staff wages staff–student ratio proportion of male students proportion of students from independent school proportion of students with good degrees proportion of staff who are professors proportion of staff who	The study investigates the specific effect of having attended an independent school on graduate earnings. Earnings for a graduate who attended an independent school are found to be 3% to 3.5% greater than the earnings of a graduate who attended an LEA school (*ceteris paribus*)

Study	Sample	Country	Dependent variable	Independent variables	Comments
				are sen. lecturers proportion of staff who are aged under 35 genders analysed separately	
Peraita & Sanchez, 1998	2852 male and 2665 female school pupils	Spain	level of school attainment	socioeconomic status parental income siblings city size	An ordered logit model is used
Smith & Naylor, 2001a	33 851 female & 42 407 male students entering university in autumn 1989	UK	dropout from university or not	academic achievement prior to university preparedness for university subject gender orientation of school attended size of school attended age marital status parental occupation nationality type of accommodation degree subject local unemployment rate genders analysed separately	The correlation between rankings of universities based on the university effects adjusted for the determinants of wastage and rankings based on unadjusted effects is 0.66 for males. Once significant determinants of wastage are accounted for, we can have little confidence in the rank position of most universities. Only the 6 lowest and the 12 top universities perform significantly differently from the median

b Statistical methods: single-level modelling *(continued)*

Author(s)	Units analysed	Country	Outputs	Inputs	Comments
Smith & Naylor, 2001b	94 485 university leavers	UK	degree classification	degree subject fee-paying status type of accommodation age marital status parental occupation previous academic achievement genders analysed separately	
Smith *et al.*, 2000	33 171 male & 28 847 female graduates from universities	UK	Model 1 unemployed or inactive rather than employed or in further study 6 months after graduation Model 2 in employment rather than in further study	Model 1 previous academic achievement age marital status social class degree subject degree class genders analysed separately Model 2 as above	Adjusted and unadjusted rankings of universities are compared using various models. When model 1 is used to derive confidence intervals for the adjusted marginal effects for males, there is no distinction between the majority of universities: only 5 universities perform significantly

			6 months after graduation Model 3 in a graduate occupation 6 months after graduation	Model 3 as above	better than the mean, and 12 significantly worse than the mean

c Statistical methods: multi-level modelling

Author(s)	Units analysed	Country	Outputs	Inputs	Comments
Aitkin & Longford, 1986	907 pupils from secondary schools in one LEA	UK	total O level/CSE score	verbal reasoning quotient gender	This study examines the need to model the multi-level structure of the data and compares the method with alternative approaches which ignore the multi-level structures
Goldstein *et al.*, 1993	5748 pupils in secondary schools	UK	total GCSE score (subsequently uses, respectively, mathematics GCSE score, English GCSE score)	standardized London reading test score verbal reasoning category gender school gender school religious domination	The confidence intervals for the school effects are wide, so that few schools can actually be separated in terms of their performance. The study therefore argues that no rank ordering based on the effects should be produced

c Statistical methods: multi-level modelling (*continued*)

Author(s)	Units analysed	Country	Outputs	Inputs	Comments
Goldstein & Spiegelhalter, 1996	21 654 pupils from secondary schools	UK	total A/AS-level score	total GCSE score	There is considerable overlap of the confidence intervals for the school effects: around two-thirds of all possible comparisons between institutions do not allow separation
Goldstein & Thomas, 1996	pupils in secondary schools	UK	total A/AS-level score	basic model: total GCSE score gender additional variables: number of GCSEs age type of school various interactions between the above	Institutions cannot be separated on the basis of the confidence intervals for the school effects
Goldstein & Sammons, 1997	758 pupils	UK	total GCSE score	gender eligible for free school meals verbal reasoning score London reading test score additionally: 8-year English score 8-year mathematics score	Junior school effects on the pupil affect performance, not just at junior school but also in the secondary school

Reference	Sample	Country	Output variable	Predictor variables	Comments
Goldstein, 1997	728 pupils in junior schools	UK	mathematics test score at age 11	mathematics test score at age 8 socioeconomic status gender	
	5562 pupils in secondary schools	UK	total GCSE score	reading test score at age 11 gender school gender	
Sammons et al., 1993	1115 pupils in junior schools	UK	Edinburgh Reading Test score at year 5	Edinburgh Reading Test score at year 3 gender father's occupation incomplete fluency in English eligible for free school meals ethnic background age at test in year 5	Background factors and initial attainment account for more variation in reading than in mathematics. School differences may be greater in mathematics. The school effects from the two analyses are positively but not perfectly correlated ($r = 0.62$). The school effects from each model give different school rankings from the raw output variables
	1240 pupils in junior schools	UK	Basic mathematics test score at year 5	Basic mathematics test score at year 3 gender age at test in year 5 ethnic background father's occupation incomplete fluency in English eligible for free school meals	

c Statistical methods: multi-level modelling *(continued)*

Author(s)	Units analysed	Country	Outputs	Inputs	Comments
Yang *et al.*, 1999	6400 pupils in primary schools >4300 pupils in junior schools	UK	Key stage 1 outcomes (considered separately): reading test score writing test score mathematics test score	English baseline score mathematics baseline score science baseline score school mean English interactions of the above various additional variables, including: gender special educational needs (SEN) pupil LEA nursery education age eligible for free school meals number of absences number of terms in school number of terms in other schools % entitled to free school meals vertical grouping % on SEN register % changes schools type of schools number of unemployed adults in class	The need for reliable data is highlighted. In particular, the reliability of baseline measures is questioned. This could affect the estimates of residuals. The ranking of schools by raw output data is shown to be different from the ranking by school effects. It is suggested that the effects would not be suitable for the construction of league tables

Key stage 2 outcomes
(considered separately)
reading test score
writing test score
mathematics test score
science test score

Key stage 1 reading
test score
Key stage 1 writing
test score
Key stage 1 mathematics
test score
school means of above
various additional
variables, including:
gender
eligible for free school
meals
SEN
number of absences
number of terms in school
age
number of teachers in class
% entitled to free school
meals
% absences
type of school

c Statistical methods: multi-level modelling (*continued*)

Author(s)	Units analysed	Country	Outputs	Inputs	Comments
Yang & Woodhouse, 2001	696 660 pupils	UK	total A/AS level score	performance at GCSE gender age establishment type region time various interactions establishment mean GCSE score establishment mean number of GCSEs taken establishment standard deviation of GCSE mean score	4 levels of analysis considered: pupils within year cohort within establishment within LEA. Establishment effects vary from year to year: there is only a slight correlation of effects two or more years apart. There is little remaining variation between LEAs
Yang *et al.*, 2002	52 587 pupils	UK	A level mathematics score AS level mathematics score	GCSE performance gender age institution type examination board various interactions	Choice of subject is shown to be strongly associated with performance

III Comparisons of techniques

Author(s)	Units analysed	Country	Outputs	Inputs	Comments
Barrow, 1991	57 LEAs	England	real average cost per pupil in secondary schools in each LEA	number of pupils proportion of pupils receiving free school meals proportion of pupils attaining 5 or more graded passes at O level proportion of pupils from low socioeconomic households proportion of pupils with additional educational needs change in school roll over previous 2 years location in metropolitan area	A deterministic model (COLS) and stochastic model (stochastic frontier methods) are estimated for 5 years of data and compared. For a single year, deterministic and stochastic models provide very similar rankings of LEAs. Rankings change from one year to another. Inefficiency is estimated at a much higher level (11–20%) in the deterministic model than in the stochastic model (4–7%)

III *Comparisons of techniques*   *(continued)*

Author(s)	Units analysed	Country	Outputs	Inputs	Comments
Bates, 1993	96 LEAs	UK	Model 1 proportion of pupils obtaining 5 or more passes at O level/CSE proportion of pupils obtaining 1 or more passes at A level Model 2 as model 1	Model 1 teaching expenditure per pupil non-teaching expenditure per pupil Model 2 as model 1 plus proportion of pupils in high socioeconomic group	Statistical analysis of input and output variables offers valuable insights relevant to a DEA. When the DEA results of model 2 are compared with OLS efficiencies (i.e. 2 equations estimated, one for each output, using the inputs of model 2 as explanatory variables) the results are similar. The top 7 LEAs in the OLS all have an efficiency of 1 in the DEA; the 26 worst LEAs in DEA all have negative residuals in the OLS

Bates, 1997	LEAs	UK	A level results O level results (combined into composite measure for statistical analysis)	teaching expenditure per pupil non-teaching expenditure per pupil proportion of pupils in high socioeconomic group % pupils from unemployed household % pupils from two-parent family	DEA and stochastic frontier analysis are compared. Measurements of efficiency vary according to the assumptions of the models, but there is a high degree of correlation in the relative measures of efficiency between the two methods
Belfield & Fielding, 2001	3019 female & 2721 male graduates	UK	graduate's earnings 6 years after graduation	student–staff ratio subject-adjusted expenditure age characteristics of the job characteristics of the firm qualifications prior to university degree qualification subject of degree genders analysed separately	Multi-level models and OLS regression are compared and both find that earnings are positively related to resources and negatively related to the student–staff ratio

III Comparisons of techniques (continued)

Author(s)	Units analysed	Country	Outputs	Inputs	Comments
Chakraborty et al., 2001	40 school districts	USA	standardized test score for 11th-grade students	controllable inputs: student–teacher ratio % students having an advanced degree % teachers with >15 years' experience uncontrollable inputs: % population with high school education % students receiving subsidized lunch net assessed real property value per student	Stochastic frontier analysis (SFA) and 2-stage DEA are separately applied. The SFA efficiency measures are insensitive to choice of distribution of the one-sided error term. The Tobit residuals from the 2nd-stage DEA give similar rankings to the half-normal efficiency measures from the SFA

| Cubbin & Zamani, 1996 | Training and Enterprise Councils (TECs) | UK | number of trainees leaving the scheme output points per leaver | cost additional variables (explanatory variables in statistical analysis, inputs in DEA): local unemployment rate median duration of unemployment % change in service industry employment previous academic achievement % with SEN socioeconomic status regional dummy | OLS, deterministic and stochastic frontiers are fitted with the input as the dependent variable, and the efficiencies and rankings derived. Various DEA models are applied and compared. It is found that orientation (i.e. output maximization v. input minimization) makes no difference to the results. VRS raises the number of efficient DMUs relative to CRS, as does the addition of more and more variables. Correlation coefficients comparing raw, DEA, regression and stochastic frontier data vary from 0.28 to 0.89, stochastic frontier and regression being the most closely related |

III Comparisons of techniques (continued)

Author(s)	Units analysed	Country	Outputs	Inputs	Comments
Diamond & Medewitz, 1990	46 classes	USA	class average of number of questions answered correctly on the Test of Economic Literacy (TEL)	verbal mathematics SAT score % mothers who are college graduates % students who are white % students who are male % students who had previously studied economics	The efficiencies from 3 regression specifications (where residuals are used to reflect efficiency) are compared with DEA. The correlations between the 4 sets of efficiencies vary from 0.712 to 0.956. Generally the correlation between the DEA and regression efficiencies is lower than the correlation between the 3 sets of regression efficiencies. DEA is used to investigate whether there are substantial (positive) differences in efficiency caused by a programme aimed at improving teaching in economics. The results are mixed

| Johnes, 1998a | universities | UK | number of arts undergraduates
number of science undergraduates
number of arts postgraduates
number of science postgraduates
arts research (value of research grants received)
science research (value of research grants received) | total costs | The efficiencies derived from DEA and stochastic frontier analysis are compared and found to have low rank correlation ($r_s = 0.133$). An heuristic method is used to find the optimal (cost-minimizing) industry structure for UK higher education. A system of heterogeneous firms and greater concentration in the provision of science tuition is suggested by the results |
| Johnes, 1999 | 99 universities | UK | UG load in science
UG load in arts
PG load in all subjects
Value of research grants | total costs | The efficiencies derived from DEA and stochastic frontier analysis are compared and the resulting rank correlation is -0.56 |

III *Comparisons of techniques* *(continued)*

Author(s)	Units analysed	Country	Outputs	Inputs	Comments
Mayston & Jesson, 1988	96 LEAs	England	% leavers getting 5 or more graded O level passes (or CSE grade 1) % leavers getting 6 or more graded O level passes (or CSE grade 1) % leavers getting 1 or more graded O level passes (or CSE grade 1)	% pupils from households whose head is in a high socioeconomic group % pupils from households with a single parent % pupils from households whose head is unemployed expenditure per pupil	Regression techniques (linear and Cobb–Douglas) are compared with DEA in terms of measuring the performance of LEAs. Regression is applied to each output separately and resulting residuals are not highly correlated (*r* varies from 0.21 to 0.60). When all outputs and inputs are included in a DEA, the resulting efficiencies are not highly (rank) correlated with the regression residuals from the three separate models (*r* varies from 0.32 to 0.53). Thus choice of technique makes a difference to assessment of LEAs

| Ruggiero & Vitaliano, 1999 | 520 school districts | USA | standardized reading test score standardized mathematics test score standardized social studies test score dropout rate graduation rate | operating expenditure per pupil teachers' salary index % single-parent female-headed households official poverty rate % households with school-age children | DEA is applied to all outputs and one input, namely operating expenditure. A second-stage Tobit relates the DEA efficiencies to the remaining input variables to produce a ranking of institutions. SFA relates operating expenditure to all outputs and the remaining inputs to produce a ranking of institutions. The rank correlation between the efficiencies derived from the 2 methods is 0.86 |
| Sengupta, 1987 | school districts | USA | average of students' test scores in: reading mathematics writing spelling | average instructional expenditure proportion of minority students index of quality of school district | The methods of frontier production function estimation and DEA are compared and it is shown that the methods may not always provide the same information. However, under certain conditions, identical efficiency rankings can occur |

III Comparisons of techniques (continued)

Author(s)	Units analysed	Country	Outputs	Inputs	Comments
Sengupta & Sfeir, 1988	25 public elementary schools	USA	achievement scores of 6th grade pupils	average teacher salary proportion of Anglo-American students in class average class size parental socioeconomic background	The analysis is performed to compare the sensitivity of the methods of DEA and OLS
Thanassoulis *et al.*, 2003	3017 girls in 21 girls' schools and 2677 boys in 22 boys' schools	UK	mean score per GCSE attempt total GCSE score	key stage 3 English score key stage 3 mathematics score key stage 3 science score proportion of pupils not eligible for free school meals	Efficiencies from multi-level modelling and individual-level DEA are compared. The single output of mean score per GCSE attempts is used in the multi-level modelling framework. Pupil-within-school efficiencies derived from the two methods are highly correlated, as are the pupil-within-all-schools efficiencies

17 Education, child labour and development
Saqib Jafarey and Sajal Lahiri

1 Introduction

The link between education and economic growth has been explored else-where in this volume.[1] Economic growth is arguably the main ingredient of economic development, but it is by no means the only one. In the developing world, economic growth is accompanied by a whole host of social, political and institutional changes. In addition to being a vital engine of economic growth, education also plays a key role in these other aspects of the development process.

One of the immediately obvious roles that education plays in a developing country is that, along with health care, nutrition, shelter and legal protection, it forms part of the nexus of factors that promote the welfare of children. Education is not only a form of investment towards gainful employment later on in life, it is also believed to help a child evolve into a responsible, rational and socially well adjusted adult. Because of this, the right to a decent education has come to be recognized by the international community as a basic human right of each child.[2]

Unfortunately, however, a large number of children are compelled to spend their formative years working to support themselves and their families rather than enrolling in full-time education. Work and study are not mutually exclusive activities, in that many children undertake both to some extent. They are also not collectively exhaustive since a third manner in which children might spend their time is leisure. Nonetheless the evidence suggests that engaging in child labour does interfere with full-time and uninterrupted school attendance. Children who work are both less likely to attend school full-time and more likely to drop out or intermit their studies (see, for example, Drèze and Gandhi-Kingdon, 2001; Maitra and Ray, 2002).

While some of the children who work are employed as apprentices and learn skills for use in later life, this is not true for most of the work done by children. In addition many children who work are exposed to dangerous conditions which pose a threat to their health and emotional development. For these reasons, international organizations such as the International Labour Organisation (ILO) and UNICEF are actively pursuing the elimination of most forms of child labour. Needless to say, increasing access to and enrolment in full-time education is an important part of this drive.

In recent years, economists have used economic theory and econometric techniques to study the causes of child labour[3] and to analyse various policies which have been proposed or are already being implemented to reduce child labour and increase educational enrolment.[4] In this chapter, we shall present a summary of these contributions and suggest ways in which economists might contribute to this debate in the future. But, before doing so, we shall offer a brief survey of the nature and magnitude of the child labour problem at present.

2   The extent of the problem

According to the ILO, the definition of child labourer covers all children of less than 12 years of age who are engaged in any sort of economic activity, whether paid or unpaid, part- or full-time, legal or illegal, formal or informal. It excludes children of 12–14 years of age who engage in permitted light work for only a few hours a week and also those in the 15–17 age group who are economically active in permitted activities on a full-time basis.[5] But it includes all children regardless of age group who are engaged in work deemed either 'hazardous' or one of the 'unconditional worst forms of child labour': slavery, trafficking, prostitution, warfare and other illicit activities.[6] Together the latter two categories are defined as the 'worst forms of child labour'.

All activities that come under the definition of child labour are marked for eventual elimination by the ILO, under a programme known as the International Programme for the Elimination of Child Labour (IPEC), but, at the current juncture, the priority is eliminating the worst forms.

The ILO has recently published estimates which show that, in 2000, there were approximately 245 million child labourers, or 16 per cent of the under-18 age group, globally. Of these, 186 million belonged to the 5–14 age group, while 59 million were 15–17-year-olds engaged in hazardous work. Of the 186 million 5–14-year-olds engaged in child labour, an astonishing 111 million were engaged in hazardous labour. This represented 9 per cent of all children in that age group. Another 8 million children were engaged in the unconditional worst forms of child labour. Further details are presented in Table 17.1.

Regional breakdowns are available only for the broader category of 'economically active children' rather than for those specifically classified as child labourers. Table 17.2 lists these. It is clear that, in sheer numbers, the Asian continent dominates, but in terms of child labour participation rates, the problem is most severe in sub-Saharan Africa.

Some additional stylized facts will help place the problem of child labour and its relationship with child schooling in sharper perspective. First, broadly speaking, there appears to be a steady downward trend in child labour and a steady upward trend in school enrolment figures across the

Table 17.1   Numbers and percentages of children working in 2000

	5–14 years		5–17 years		Total	
	No. ($\times 10^6$)	As % of age group	No. ($\times 10^6$)	As % of age group	No. ($\times 10^6$)	As % of age group
Economically active	210.8	18	140.9	42	351.7	23
of which, child labour	186.3	16	59.2	18	245.5	16
of which, worst forms	N/A	N/A	N/A	N/A	178.9	11.5
of which, hazardous work	111.3	9	59.2	18	170.5	11
unconditional worst forms	N/A	N/A	N/A	N/A	8.4	0.5

Note: N/A = not available.

Source: *A Future without Child Labour*, International Labour Organisation, May 2002.

Table 17.2   Estimates of 5–14-year-olds working in 2000, by region

Region	Economically active children (millions)	As percentage of economically active children	As percentage of children in region
Developed economies	2.5	1	2
Transition economies	2.4	1	4
Asia and the Pacific	127.3	60	19
Latin America and Caribbean	17.4	8	16
Sub-Saharan Africa	48	23	29
Middle East and North Africa	13.4	6	15
Total	211	99*	16*

Note: *The numbers do not sum to 100 because of rounding.

Source: *A Future without Child Labour*, International Labour Organisation, May 2002.

developing world. Needless to say, neither of these trends is uniform across different countries or even continents, but, on the whole, they give grounds for cautious optimism.

Second, offsetting the good news somewhat is the realization that the nature of work performed by child labourers is possibly worse than was previously thought. More than two-thirds of all child labourers are engaged in the so-called 'worst forms' of child labour. Getting these children out of work and into school is an immediate priority.

Third, there are substantial gender differences on both sides of the labour–schooling dichotomy. Boys are more likely than girls to be engaged in child labour, particularly in its hazardous forms, but they also are more likely to be enrolled in school. This constitutes an important stylized fact which international agencies and non-governmental organizations (NGOs) are increasingly engaging with.

Finally, it has to be acknowledged that some types of child work do lead to skill acquisition and work experience, while the kind of schooling available to many children in developing countries is often dubious in this respect. The problem is that skill acquisition and learning are not easily separated from the undesirable aspects of child labour: exploitation by unscrupulous employers, dangerous work conditions, long working hours and so on. For this reason, international agencies are aiming to eliminate most forms of work carried out by children under 15 years of age. The question is how to design policies which do not end up hurting the very children who have to be helped. This is where economic theory is of help.

3   Theories of child labour

Most economic theories of child labour focus on the choice between work and education during a child's formative years. This choice is assumed to be made by a rational and benevolent parent, acting in response to the conditions facing the household. Several factors are suggested as influencing this decision: (i) a low level of income and asset ownership by the parent, (ii) low pecuniary returns to schooling, (iii) lack of credit, (iv) imperfections and coordination failures in labour markets for adults.

The role of credit markets
The following is a simple model which studies the role of three of the factors listed above, namely credit opportunities, parental incomes and pecuniary returns to schooling. It is based on Ranjan (2001) and Jafarey and Lahiri (2002).

Consider a household with one parent and N children. The household lasts two periods, $t = 1$ and $t = 2$. At $t = 1$, the parent decides what fraction, $e\,(0 \leq e \leq 1)$, of her children to send to school. The remainder, $1 - e$, are sent to labour. Each child sent to work earns a wage, w^c, at $t=1$ and grows up to be an unskilled labourer, earning a wage, w^u, at $t=2$. Each child sent to school earns nothing at $t=1$ but grows up to be a skilled worker and earns a wage w^s at $t=2$. The only cost of sending a child to school is the forgone child wage; adding explicit schooling costs does not contribute further insight. The parent's own income is w^p during $t=1$ and it is assumed that the parent does not work at $t=2$.

Welfare is described by a household utility function:

$$U = u(c_1) + \beta u(c_2),$$

where c_1 and c_2 represent total household consumption at $t=1$ and $t=2$, respectively; u are additively separable sub-utility functions and β represents the subjective discount factor between the two periods. It is assumed that each subutility function is increasing and concave and that $0 \leq \beta \leq 1$. Note that household utility depends only on aggregate consumption and not on its distribution across different members. This reflects (somewhat extremely but with no loss of generality) altruism within the household.

Perfect credit markets The question arises as to whether the household can borrow and/or save in order to smooth its income stream between the two periods. First consider the case in which the household can borrow or save as much as it wants at a given interest rate, r. Its budget constraint in each period can be formally written as:

$$c_1 = w^p + (1-e)Nw^c + b;$$
$$c_2 = eNw^s + (1-e)Nw^u - (1+r)b,$$

where b represents borrowing, which may be either positive or negative (in which case the household acts as a saver). Plugging the two constraints into the utility function leads to the following objective function:

$$U = u[w^p + (1-e)Nw^c + b] + \beta u[eNw^s + (1-e)Nw^u - (1+r)b],$$

which is maximized by choosing b and e. The first-order conditions are:

$$b: \frac{u_1}{\beta u_2} = 1 + r \tag{17.1}$$

$$e: +\beta u_2 (w^s - w^u) \begin{Bmatrix} > \\ = \\ < \end{Bmatrix} u_1 w^c \Rightarrow e \begin{Bmatrix} = 1 \\ \in (0,1) \\ = 0 \end{Bmatrix}, \tag{17.2}$$

where u_i is the marginal utility of consumption in period i.

The first-order condition describing borrowing/saving is known as an Euler condition. It states that b is set to equate the marginal rate of substitution between first- and second-period consumption $(u_1/\beta u_2)$ to the relative price of first-period consumption $(1 + r)$.

The first-order condition describing the labour/education decision reflects the constraint that e must lie between zero and unity. Educating an extra child leads to a loss of income of w^c units at $t = 1$ and to a *change* in income of $w^s - w^u$ units at $t = 2$; these lead to a marginal utility loss of $u_1 w^c$ and a marginal utility *change* of $\beta u_2(w^s - w^u)$ in the two periods, respectively. Obviously, for schooling to make any sense whatsoever, it must be the case that $w^s - w^u > 0$; that is, the child must receive a *premium* in later life from having gone to school. Assuming this to be the case, the second term in (17.2) captures a marginal utility gain.

If the marginal utility gain at $t = 2$ exceeds the marginal utility loss at $t = 1$ for all values of e, then e is chosen to equal unity (there is no child labour), if the reverse is true at all values of e, it is chosen to equal zero (there is no schooling), but if there is some *interior* value of e for which the marginal gain and loss become equal, then e is set equal to that interior value; some children are educated and some are sent to work.

Equation (17.2) can be rewritten after rearranging the terms and substituting from equation (17.1):

$$\frac{w^s - w^u}{1 + r} - w^c \begin{Bmatrix} > \\ = \\ < \end{Bmatrix} 0 \Rightarrow e \begin{Bmatrix} = 1 \\ \in (0,1) \\ = 0 \end{Bmatrix}, \tag{17.3}$$

which simply states that e is chosen to be unity if the present value of the wage premium earned by an educated child at $t = 2$ exceeds the opportunity cost of sending the child to school instead of to work at $t = 1$. If the reverse is true, e equals zero.

While a positive educational premium is clearly necessary for sending any child to school, it is not sufficient. What is necessary and sufficient is for the *present value* of the educational wage premium to exceed the opportunity cost, that is, the lost wages of child labour. This amounts to the condition that schooling raises the *net* present value of household income when aggregated over the two periods. The three factors that determine this are the educational wage premium, the market interest rate and the wage from child labour. A high wage premium, a low interest rate and a low wage for child labour all raise the net present value of returns to schooling.

Note that the direction of the inequality in (17.3) is independent of the household's own choice of e, which does not affect any of the terms in (17.3). Thus, depending on which way the inequality goes, the choice will be either $e = 1$ or $e = 0 - e$ will be interior only in the 'knife-edge' case where the condition is satisfied as an equality. The reason that the terms in equation (17.3) do not depend on e is that, while e affects the *stream* of income between the two periods, this effect can, under perfect credit markets, be offset by the parent saving less or borrowing more. This point will be analysed in detail in the following sub-section.

Note also that, with a perfect credit market, the parent's own income does not affect e, although it does influence the parental choice of saving or borrowing in the first period. If it is profitable (in net present value terms) to send a child to school, the parent will borrow more or save less and send the child to school even if her own first-period income is very low.

To summarize the implications of the model studied above, if credit markets were perfect, child labour would exist if and only if the net present value of returns to schooling was negative. But where child labour did exist, its incidence would be massive. Allowing for differences in child wages, educational wage premia and interest rates across countries and across different regions of the same country, we would expect either high concentrations of child labour or none at all. The distribution of wealth and income across heads of households would not play any role in determining the incidence of child labour in a given region.

Imperfect credit markets   We now consider a case in which the household cannot borrow on a perfect credit market. In fact we shall go so far as to assume that there is no credit market. The more realistic case of imperfect credit markets with limited borrowing opportunities is qualitatively similar to the case studied below. As for the possibility of a household wanting to use the credit market to save, we discount that on the grounds that households which send children to labour are not likely to be net savers, at least when their children are young. At any rate, the child labour decisions of a household that has access to and wishes to save on a deposit market depend only on the pecuniary returns to schooling, just like those for households which face a perfect credit market.

With no credit market, b is exogenously set at zero in the household's budget constraint, so the optimization involves choosing e to maximize

$$U = u(w^p + (1 - e)Nw^c) + \beta u(eNw^s + (1 - e)Nw^u),$$

which yields the same first-order condition as described above in (17.2). The difference is that now the choice of e affects the household's marginal rate of substitution between the two periods: the latter can no longer be equated to the market interest rate by an unrestricted choice of borrowing or saving. Rather, since e affects the stream of income between the two periods, it affects how much the household consumes each period. This in turn affects the marginal rate of substitution between consumption in the two periods. Rewriting the first-order condition as

$$\frac{w^s - w^u}{w^c} \begin{Bmatrix} > \\ = \\ < \end{Bmatrix} \frac{u_1}{\beta u_2} \Rightarrow e \begin{Bmatrix} = 1 \\ \in (0,1) \\ = 0 \end{Bmatrix}, \tag{17.4}$$

it is now possible for there to be a value of e such that the condition holds exactly as an equality.[7]

Assuming imperfect credit markets, we now have a model in which child labour and child schooling coexist within a household and also within regions which might face common labour market and schooling conditions. It is also easy to show that parental income will now affect the choice of e. To see this, assume that (17.4) is initially satisfied as an equality and assume that there is an increase in w^p. This will make consumption at $t = 1$ rise while consumption at $t = 2$ will be unaffected. Thus the marginal utility of consumption at $t = 1$ will fall relative to that at $t = 2$. This makes the right-hand side of (17.4) fall, so that, to restore equality with the left-hand side, e would have to rise. Thus parents with higher income (or wealth) will send more children to school.[8]

One peculiarity of the model studied so far is that the parents are assumed to be subjectively neutral on the issue of labour versus schooling; child labour decisions are based entirely on pecuniary factors. In the next subsection we shall amend the household's welfare function by assuming that parents have an innate preference for sending their children to school rather than subjecting them to labour.

Subjective preference for education   We now assume an additional component in the household utility function, which captures the utility that parents get from sending their children to school. The utility function is now written as

$$U = u(c_1) + \beta u(c_2) + g(Ne),$$

where g is an increasing and concave function. This term captures the assumption that parents get additional utility from having more of their children educated. This could reflect either a positive preference for educating children or an aversion to having a child work. There is considerable anecdotal and survey evidence to suggest that both interpretations are valid.[9] It also strengthens the assumptions of parental altruism that most economists prefer to work with, in the spirit of not 'blaming the victim'.

The household's problem is analogous to the one studied on pages 747–9. It chooses b and e in order to maximize

$$U = u(c_1) + \beta u(c_2) + g(Ne)$$

subject to

$$c_1 = w^p + (1-e)Nw^c + b;$$
$$c_2 = eNw^s + (1-e)Nw^u - (1+r)b.$$

The first-order conditions are

$$\frac{u_1}{\beta u_2} = 1 + r \qquad (17.5)$$

$$\beta u_2 (w^s - w^u) + Ng'(Ne) \begin{Bmatrix} > \\ = \\ < \end{Bmatrix} u_1 w^c \Rightarrow e \begin{Bmatrix} = 1 \\ \in (0,1) \\ = 0 \end{Bmatrix}, \qquad (17.6)$$

where $g'(\cdot)$ denotes the marginal utility of educating an extra child. Note that the first-order condition for b is unaffected by the inclusion of $g(\cdot)$ in the utility function, but the first-order condition for e now has an extra positive term. For any set of values of w^c, w^s and w^p and a given choice of e, it becomes more likely that the first-order condition will be positive rather than negative. This reflects the 'tilt' towards education in parental preference.

Further, combining the two equations,

$$\frac{w^s - w^u}{1+r} - w^c + \frac{g'(Ne)}{u_1} \begin{Bmatrix} > \\ = \\ < \end{Bmatrix} 0 \Rightarrow e \begin{Bmatrix} = 1 \\ \in (0,1) \\ = 0 \end{Bmatrix}, \qquad (17.7)$$

so that, even when r is exogenous in a perfect credit market, it is possible to have an interior value of e. It is important to spell out when this happens: it happens when the first two terms in equation (17.7) are jointly negative. This in turn implies that the discounted pecuniary returns to education are negative, because either the educational wage premium is very low or the interest rate is very high, or the forgone wage of child labour is very high. Without a subjective parental preference for education, e would equal to zero; but, with it, e can still be positive, as the household equates the subjective marginal utility of education to its marginal cost, that is the discounted net income loss from educating an extra child. In this case, the driving motive for education is not that it makes the household better off, but that parents derive subjective benefits from educating their children.

Since a situation in which the discounted pecuniary returns to education are negative might sound implausible to economists, it is worthwhile to defend its relevance to the problem at hand. Note that about 70 per cent of the world's child labour takes place in rural areas of developing countries where either schools are thin on the ground or, where they exist, the quality of facilities, curriculum and teaching staff is low. This is itself a point of policy relevance which we shall address later on. But first let us analyse the results of a survey, published in 1999, which found that educational wage premia in India were so modest as to suggest strongly that the *discounted* net returns to education could indeed be negative.

The survey found that children who have completed primary school in India earn educational wage premia of between 20 and 100 per cent (see the Probe Team, 1999, p. 21). Assuming that primary education takes five years to complete, that child labour earns the unskilled wage and that the skilled wage is earned indefinitely after leaving primary school, it is easy to show that positive discounted returns to primary education require that

$$r \leq \left(\frac{w^s}{w^u}\right)^{1/5} - 1.$$

Thus, if $w^s/w^u = 1.2$, an interest rate of 3.7 per cent or less is needed to make primary education profitable. Even if $w^s/w^u = 2$, the interest rate would have to be less than 14.9 per cent.[10] In reality, of course, households do not face perfectly elastic funds at *any* interest rate. But assuming that they had unlimited access to funds, the interest rates they do face range from 16 per cent to over 200 per cent (see Basu, 1997, p. 267). Thus, on the basis of the Probe Team's findings, one could argue that negative discounted returns might have existed in the areas covered by the survey.[11]

There is also complementary evidence to support the scenario sketched out above. For example, the Probe Team (1999) survey also found that a large number of poor households cited non-economic motives as important in their decision to send children to school. This supports the existence of a subjective bias in favour of education. Similarly, surveys in Pakistan indicate high levels of dropout and absenteeism among primary school children of working class background, with one of the major factors cited as a reason for this being that education is considered somewhat of a luxury with a low prospect of improving a child's earning capacity in the future, while child labour is seen as a valuable source not just of current income but also of survival skills (see PILER, 1998). This again suggests that formal education is desired for its own sake, while purely pecuniary calculations by households tend to make them favour child labour.

Because condition (17.7) allows for interior choices of *e* to exist under a variety of scenarios concerning the credit market, the model it is based on becomes quite useful for carrying out comparative static exercises. For example, in this model, parental income will also affect educational outcomes positively under any credit market scenario. This is because higher income will induce a greater subjective 'demand' for education. But comparative static exercises are particularly useful for policy analysis. We turn to policy issues next.

Policy implications   One of the most obvious questions to ask is how does varying access to credit markets by poor household affect child labour? In Jafarey and Lahiri (2002), the above question is studied in the context of a model which is very similar to the one used in this subsection. They consider three discrete scenarios: (i) perfect access at the household level to a world credit market, with an exogenous interest rate, r_w; (ii) each household faces a binding borrowing constraint, $\bar{b}$, which could be zero or positive; (iii) a domestic credit market in which two classes of households exist, poor ones who act as borrowers and richer ones who act as lenders.[12]

For the third case, which represents an intermediate situation as far as access to credit by poor households is concerned, let the saving behaviour of rich households be captured by a function $S(r)$ which is assumed to be upward sloping.[13] To save on notation, we shall describe the general equilibrium for this case, and only qualitatively discuss the modifications that would have to be made to this model in the other two cases.

The first-order conditions, equations (17.5) and (17.6), implicitly define b and e as functions of r, assuming of course that (17.6) holds as an equality.[14] Assuming that there are M poor households, each identical to the other, r itself can be determined from the market-clearing equation:

$$Mb = S(r). \tag{17.8}$$

In the case of perfect access to the world credit market, equation (17.8) would be replaced by $r = r_w$, where r_w is exogenous. In the case of a binding borrowing constraint, equation (17.8) would be replaced by $b = \bar{b}$. In each case, there would be three equations and three unknowns, b, e and r.

Figure 17.1 illustrates the solution to the above model and also compares outcomes from the three credit scenarios under plausible restrictions. The first panel represents borrowing as a function of r along with the supply curve of loans; the second panel represents the relationship between e and r; the third panel represents the relationship between b and e; the fourth panel simply translates values of b from the third panel back to the first panel.[15] All of these can be derived by totally differentiating the systems of equations, but it is more instructive to consider a heuristic explanation.

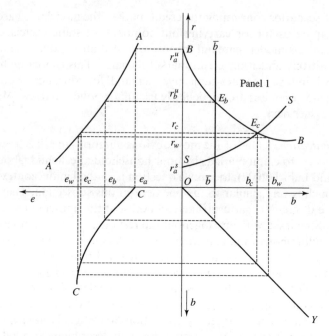

Figure 17.1   The equilibria

The relationship between b and r is downward sloping for reasons of the conventional income and substitution effects: an increase in r makes present consumption more expensive and also lowers overall income for a household that borrows. Both effects tend to discourage first-period consumption and to lower the demand for borrowing. In addition, in this model, as we argue next, an increase in r lowers e and raises first-period income at the expense of the second period. This further lowers desired borrowing. So the demand for borrowing is more elastic than it would be in a model without child labour.

The relation between e and r is also downward sloping. An increase in r lowers the present value of the educational wage premium enjoyed at $t = 2$, so this tilts incentives towards less education. Furthermore, for a borrowing household, an increase in r leads to a negative income effect and this lowers the subjective demand for education (associated with $g(Ne)$). Note that e and b are positively related, since a fall in r makes both go up. Indeed, the third panel simply portrays the derived relationship between these two variables by combining their resulting values at different levels of r.

Note several features of the first panel. First, the supply of loans is drawn with a lower intercept than the demand for loans. This reflects the fundamental assumption that, in the absence of a domestic credit market, rich households would have lower marginal rates of intertemporal substitution. This is what drives the outcome that rich households act as lenders in the presence of such a market. Second, the world interest rate lies strictly below the domestic equilibrium interest rate. This suggests that, if the economy had in place a domestic credit market which then opened up to external flows of credit, it would act as a net borrower from the world (although some rich households might be net savers). This too appears a reasonable assumption to make for a developing economy. Third, the implicit interest rate which results from a binding borrowing constraint is higher than the interest rate in either scenario with a credit market present. This reflects an assumption that, in the absence of a properly functioning credit market, a poor household will have access to strictly less credit than in the presence of a market. In other words, borrowing constraints will 'bind' relative to what could be achieved in a free market equilibrium.

As Figure 17.1 shows, the fact that interest rates are likely to be higher the more restrictive the scenario describing access to credit means that education of children will be correspondingly lower. Thus, under the best scenario, borrowing from international credit markets, the interest rate will be r_w and education will be e_w. Compared to that, a competitive domestic credit market will result in an interest rate of r_c and a lower choice, e_c. Still higher will be the (implicit) interest rate r_b and lower the educational choice e_b when the household is subject to a binding borrowing constraint, $\bar{b}$. Finally, as the constraint gets tighter, r_b will rise and e_b will fall, until at a constraint of zero borrowing the implicit interest rate will be r_a and education e_a. Putting all three panels together, note the three-way association of higher interest rates with lower borrowing levels and lower educational choice.

The policy implication of Figure 17.1 is clear. Credit market reform which allows freer access to credit will result in higher incidences of schooling and lower child labour. The case of a domestic credit market is particularly interesting. For example, take a two-class society in which rich households send all their children to school while poor households send a fraction. Note that, in the economy under consideration, the only form of 'investment' is the education of children and that this is decided by each household independently of others. But the rich are up against a corner (that is, cannot increase e beyond unity) with respect to such investment. Indeed, given an analogous condition to equation (17.6) for rich households, it is likely that the marginal benefit to educating an extra child will exceed the marginal opportunity cost even in pecuniary terms alone.[16] A domestic credit market will thus allow the rich to increase indirectly their choice of e. This will be channelled via an increase in their 'savings' (broadly defined to include both their stock of loanable funds and the asset value of their children's education) and a resulting increase in poor households' investment in education.

Just as the conventional interpretation of credit markets is that they channel funds towards investment in physical capital, in our interpretation they also help channel funds towards education, part of a broader concept of investment which covers the formation of human capital. In Figure 17.1, imagine there is already a credit market which links poor and rich households but its functioning is improved by, say, a reform which enhances the banking infrastructure of rural areas. This would cause a rightward shift in the supply curve, which would lower the equilibrium interest rate, r_c, and promote greater educational choice. The difference, of course, is that the impact of an improvement in this form of credit exchange is not obvious. On the surface it would appear to involve the exchange of *consumption* loans between rich and poor households, and not something that promotes investment narrowly defined. It would thus be likely to escape policy makers' attention as they undertake credit market measures to increase flows into narrowly conceived categories of investment.[17]

A slightly different point from the one discussed so far can be made by appeal to the analogy between insurance and credit. In countries with practically non-existent markets either for private or for socially provided insurance, poor families might be able to offset negative shocks to their income by undertaking short-term borrowing on the credit market. When even this market is not present, they are left to their own devices in dealing with fluctuations in their incomes. Such fluctuations are especially pronounced in rural areas, where the bulk of the poor live and where the incidence of child labour is the greatest. Jacoby and Skoufias (1997) argue that, in this situation, households are likely to use children's work as a 'buffer' against uncertainty. In good times, children may be sent to school, but in bad ones they would be obliged to suspend study and supplement the family's income through their own labour. If credit were available, households could borrow on the market whenever they faced a downturn in income, repaying when income went up again. Hence children's school attendance would not be subject to the vagaries of parental income.

While empirical investigation of the role of credit markets in child labour has been quite limited, Jacoby and Skoufias (1997) did test their own hypothesis using village survey data from rural India.[18] They found evidence that fluctuations in children's school attendance acted as buffers against shocks to household income. Ilahi (1999) found supporting evidence. Using Living Standards Management Surveys (LSMS) panel data for Peru for the years 1994 and 1997, he found that external shocks such as sickness of family members or loss of employment by an adult were likely to affect children's school attendance, although the effect was greater on girls than on boys. The sickness of a child in the household forces girls to withdraw from work, while the sickness of an adult forces them into child labour. This is broadly consistent with Jacoby and Skoufias' (1997) hypothesis, although with the added twist of a gender dimension.

Apart from the direct impact of credit on educational choice, another important role of credit markets is that they can indirectly affect the efficacy of non-credit-related policy measures as means of influencing child labour and education decisions. In Jafarey and Lahiri (2000) and (2002), several policies are analysed: trade sanctions, food subsidies linked to educational attendance by a family's children and investment in improving school quality. We shall take up each in turn, using the model of this subsection as our analytical guide.

Taking trade sanctions first, it is relatively straightforward to extend the two-period model of this section to include two goods per period, one an exportable and the other an importable. Child labour is used to produce the exportable alone. A trade sanction against the import of this good into the developed world arises either through an official ban on the sale of goods produced by child labour or through an unofficial consumer boycott. An official ban on the import of goods produced by child labour would induce employers to hire adult labourers instead of children. It would also tend to depress the price of the exportable good in world markets, which would further discourage production of that good and of employment of workers in the industry which produces that good. The price effect would occur even if there was only an informal decision by consumers in the developed world to stop buying a good believed to have been produced by child labour. The upshot would be to discourage the demand for child workers by employers, which in turn would depress the wage of child labour.

While the above scenario would be relatively easy to model, it is more convenient to accept the premise that trade sanctions result in a lower wage for child work and use that as the starting point for the analysis, without formally expanding on the one good per period framework used so far. Referring to equation (17.6), imagine that it holds as an equality at an interior value of e, when w^c goes down. At the *original* value of e, the fall in w^c will have three effects: (i) a direct effect which pushes the left-hand side to become positive and thus induce a higher value of e (since $-w^c$ becomes smaller in magnitude); (ii) an income effect which counteracts this (since lower w^c means lower income and thus higher marginal utility of income, captured by a rise in u_1 in the third term of (17.6)); (iii) an intertemporal substitution effect which leads to a change in r (discussed in the paragraph after next), which appears in the first term on the left-hand side of equation (17.6).

Note that, even without the third effect, a fall in w^c can have ambiguous implications for the labour–education split. The direct effect of lower opportunity costs of education stimulates a desire for more education, but the negative income effect works against this. The irony is that the negative effect is likely to be bigger the poorer the household is to begin with; that is, the smaller e is to begin with.

It is through the intertemporal substitution effect of a fall in w^c, however, that the concomitant influence of credit markets is felt. Note that, while a fall in w^c lowers the present value of the family's income, the actual timing is such that it is income at $t = 1$ which actually falls (at the original value of e). This will lead to a greater *demand* for loans by the household. The effect of this on the equilibrium value of r depends on the credit market scenario. In the case of a perfect international credit market, the greater demand is met without any change in the interest rate and the intertemporal substitution effect is zero. But, when the supply of credit is not perfectly elastic, there will be an increase in r which will further discourage education.

Figure 17.2 below pulls together all the strands of the above argument. It depicts the comparative-static effect of a fall in w^c on e, b and r under two

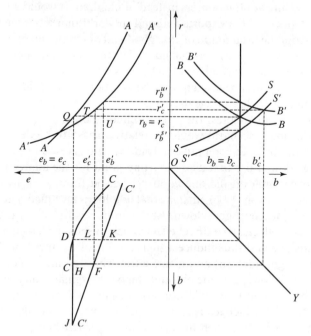

Figure 17.2   Trade sanctions

of the three credit scenarios discussed above, a domestic credit market and a borrowing constraint which, for comparison's sake, is assumed to be set at the level of borrowing which occurs at the original equilibrium.[19] The four panels of Figure 17.2 are analogous to the four panels of Figure 17.1. The first panel shows precisely this equilibrium, which results in an interest rate $r_b = r_c$. The second and third panels show that at the market interest rate the household chooses $e_b = e_c$ units of educations along AA and $b_b = b_c$ units of borrowing along CC, respectively.

A fall in w_c shifts the e–r relationship in the second panel from AA to $A'A'$. This shows how e changes at given values of r, that is, the sum of the direct and the income effects. At low values of e, the negative income effect prevails so that the e–r relationship shifts right (towards less e) along the upper portion of $A'A'$. At higher values of e, the positive direct effect prevails so that the e–r relationship shifts left along the lower portion of $A'A'$. The fall in w^c also leads to a greater demand for borrowing, and this is depicted by the upward shift from BB to $B'B'$ in the first panel (and from CC to $C'C'$ in the third panel). Equilibrium in the loan market depends on supply conditions. When the supply of loans can adjust along an upward-sloping supply curve, the resulting increase in the interest rate is to r_c', which is less than the interest rate that would arise, r_b', if the supply of loans could not adjust from the original equilibrium. While not explicitly considered here, imagine that, starting at the original equilibrium, the supply of loans could adjust in a perfectly elastic fashion. Then the interest rate would not change at all.

In Figure 17.2, as drawn, the *fall* in w^c leads to a *fall* in e (and an increase in child labour) even when r is held constant. This is a perverse effect given the intentions of those who initiate such sanctions. Of course, this perverse effect is not always going to arise, but, as stated above, the possibility that it does is greater for a poorer household. Besides, the increase that takes place in r makes this perverse outcome even stronger (or would dampen a non-perverse outcome). At the same time, access to credit is beneficial at the margin in the sense that the outcome is more strongly perverse when the supply of credit cannot adjust than when it can. The policy conclusions to be drawn are that trade sanctions can be counterproductive for reducing child labour, and that this possibility increases when they are directed towards countries with badly developed credit markets.

An example from Bangladesh provides support for these predictions. In 1993, under the threat of sanctions from the US Congress, employers in the garment industry of Bangladesh dismissed about 50 000 child workers, about 75 per cent of the children employed by the industry at the time. Follow-up studies found that very few of the dismissed children had gone into education; most had moved into even worse occupations:

leatherwork, brick-making, even child prostitution (see UNICEF, 1997). Thus, while trade sanctions imposed from overseas will lower the demand for child workers in export-oriented industries, they will not necessarily lower parents' decisions to have their offspring work. So long as opportunities for child labour exist elsewhere in the economy, both the incidence and, as happened in Bangladesh, the nature of child labour can easily be made worse. Indeed, given that the production of tradable goods employs only 5 per cent of child labourers, there is plenty of scope for other sectors to absorb whatever children are laid off from tradable sectors as a result of sanctions.

Note that trade sanctions, even should they work in terms of reducing child labour, are punitive in the sense that they make conditions worse, at least initially, for families with working children. One indication of this is the existence of a negative income effect from trade sanctions. Other examples of punitive measures would be compulsory education, or a ban on child labour, or the setting of labour standards which make it illegal to employ children in certain industries. We shall discuss some of these policies later, and show that there can indeed be some justification for certain types of punitive policy.

It is nonetheless useful to separate this entire class of policies from measures which provide positive incentive for families to educate their children.[20] Improvement in the supply of credit would be one such measure although, as the *Economist* (16 September 2000) noted, this is not something which receives great attention in policy circles. An example of a positive measure actually applied in practice is a programme, being tested in countries like Brazil, Mexico and Bangladesh by the World Bank, which pays families to send their children to school. This programme, known as Bolsa Escola in Brazil and PROGRESA in Mexico, gives poor families a means-tested income subsidy, typically in the form of food rations, for sending their children to school on a full-time basis. Another example would be investment in school reform which increases the educational wage premium. Our model can be used to address the impact of both these policies and, indeed, to compare them.

What 'food for schooling' and investment in school quality have in common is that they increase the present value of the beneficiary's lifetime income. This is precisely what distinguishes these policies from the punitive measures discussed above. Both these policies will also have direct effects which tilt incentives towards education.

A 'food-for-schooling' subsidy leads to the following budget constraint at $t = 1$:

$$c_1 = w^p + (1 - e)Nw^c + \sigma Ne + b,$$

where σ is the monetary value of the subsidy per child. The budget constraint at $t = 2$ in unaffected. The first-order condition for e (assuming an interior solution) now reads as:

$$\frac{(w^s - w^u)}{1 + r} - w^c + \sigma + \frac{g'(Ne)}{u_1} = 0,$$

with an extra positive term. An increase in σ would both directly increase the marginal benefit of educating a child and induce a positive income effect. Both effects increase the choice of e at given values of r. Further, since the extra income associated with a food-for-schooling subsidy is paid out at $t = 1$, it helps lower the family's demand for loanable funds. This results in a fall in the interest rate (assuming an imperfectly elastic supply of credit) applied to future income and makes it more attractive. This further stimulates an increase in e.

An improvement in school quality would have the effect of increasing the educational wage premium, $(w^s - w^u)$. In equation (17.6), this tilts incentives for greater schooling, not to mention the positive income effect which enhances this effect at given interest rates. But, unlike the subsidy, better schooling only pays off at $t = 2$. At given interest rates and given values of e, an increase in the educational wage premium would increase the demand for funds at $t = 1$, as the family attempts to smooth its consumption in anticipation of higher $t = 2$ income. This would result in *higher* interest rates unless the supply of credit were perfectly elastic. The last effect would dampen the increase in e, and could even offset the positive direct and income effects.

On the surface, comparing food for schooling with improvements in school quality may not appear to be a natural comparison to make. This is partly because we have so far conducted arbitrary comparative-static experiments regarding the two variables. But, from a policy point of view, there is a natural tradeoff between them, since they both require funding by governments or international donor agencies and are thus ultimately financed by general taxation. The question has been asked of donor agencies like the World Bank whether funds currently devoted to programmes like Bolsa Escola would be better spent on directly improving the quality and quantity of schools in order to make schooling more attractive.

We can think of two ways to consider this tradeoff. The first one controls for the effects of each policy on the recipient household's budget; the second considers the effects on the donor agency's budget. In the first case, consider a situation in which a donor agency can either improve school quality by an amount which leads to a given increase in the *present* value of the educational wage premium at $t = 1$ (at the interest rate prevailing before the policy is implemented) or devote enough funds to a food subsidy to increase a representative household's $t = 1$ income by the same amount.[21] In other words, consider two alternative programmes of assistance which have the same effect on the present value of the household's income.

$$\sigma = \frac{w^s - w^u}{1 + r}.$$

It is easy to show that both policies will have a positive effect of equal magnitude on e for given values of r. When access to borrowing is perfectly elastic, the overall effect will also be the same. But when access to credit is imperfectly elastic, the food subsidy will have an enhanced effect due to the fall in r while the increase in the educational wage premium will have a reduced effect due to the increase in r.

This argument is illustrated in Figure 17.3, where both policies under consideration cause the e–r relationship to shift left unambiguously and by the same amount. Under a perfect credit scenario, the two instruments would have the same effect on e. But since the increase in the education premium makes the demand for borrowing shift up, as shown, to $B'B'$ while an increased food subsidy would make the demand for borrowing shift down (not shown), under an imperfectly elastic supply of credit, the former increases the interest rate, while the latter decreases it. So, as far as the household is concerned, facing an imperfectly elastic supply of credit, it would increase its education choice more if given a food-for-schooling subsidy than if faced with an equivalent (in present value terms) increase in the educational wage premium. Indeed the gap between the effectiveness of the two policies would increase as the supply of credit became more inelastic.

The second type of comparison, taking the donor's budget into account, leads to analogous insights. Suppose that the donor agency has a fixed quantity of funds which it can allocate either to improvements in school quality or to financing a food-for-education subsidy to poor households. Its objective is to maximize school enrolment. Assuming that expenditures on school quality improvement yield positive but marginally diminishing increases in the educational wage premium, an allocation of the funds in which a positive amount is spent on each instrument can be found. The precise share going to each instrument, however, depends on the credit market scenario. Starting from a benchmark of a completely inelastic supply of credit, the optimal share of funds allocated to investment in school quality will rise as the supply elasticity of credit rises.[22] This is in accordance with the intuition already discussed: since a euro spent on increasing the educational wage premium will be more effective in encouraging greater education if, all else equal, families can borrow more easily

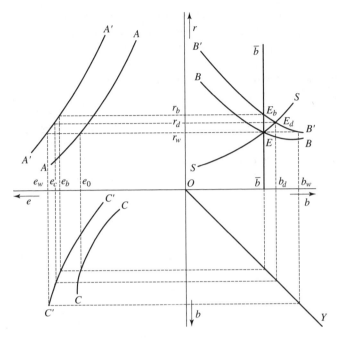

Figure 17.3   Policies for school enrolment

against the future wage of an educated child, it follows that the optimal share going to this instrument from a fixed pool of funds rises with the elasticity of the supply of credit.

Evaluation and critique   While the above analysis provides a compelling argument in favour of programmes such as food-for-schooling subsidies, Ravallion and Wodon (2000) have argued that programmes which stimulate educational enrolment will not ipso facto lower child labour. This is because of the third use of a child's time: leisure and the possibility that a family might respond to an incentive for greater schooling by reducing its children's leisure. Indeed, carrying out an empirical analysis of the food-for-schooling programme in Bangladesh, the authors found that, while it had indeed succeeded in stimulating greater school participation, it had not significantly reduced child labour among the target households. Their finding has to be placed in the context of other empirical studies, however, which report a significant negative relationship between school enrolment and child labour (for example, Drèze and Gandhi-Kingdon (2001)). In any case, it might be argued that encouraging school enrolment is desirable even if the effect on child labour is small. This is because of the beneficial effects of education on both household and aggregate income growth, not to mention the public benefits that educated citizens bring to society.

Another limitation of the policy analysis above is that it applied solely to the supply side of the credit market. An offsetting argument arises on the demand side, and concerns the motivation of parents to borrow in order to facilitate their children's school enrolment in the first place.[23] So far we have assumed the household to be a unitary decision maker: there has been no conflict of interest or of strategy between parents and children at any time. This would indeed be the case if parents and children were mutually altruistic, or at least if parents could effectively control their children's actions throughout their own lives. But suppose that neither is true: in particular, that parents cannot control their offspring beyond childhood. In that event, even if parents were altruistic towards their children, in the sense that they took the impact of their own decisions on their children's welfare into account, but that children did not reciprocate, then parents might be discouraged from using the credit market for supporting their children's education.[24] The reason for this is that any loan taken out by the household at $t = 1$ legally becomes the responsibility of the parent, even though it is for the child's education that the loan is used implicitly. In a unitary household model, this poses no problems, since the educated children will 'repay' the loan indirectly by providing old-age income support to their parents *if the latter wish for it*. The qualification is important, since it tells us that not all parents might expect to receive old-age support.

In the model used so far, this possibility is excluded by the assumption that parents have no direct source of income when they become old and, if they were net borrowers at $t = 1$, they would have no asset income either. Hence they must receive old-age support at $t = 2$, not just to help repay the loan which is nominally their burden, but also to share in family consumption. But this situation can be relaxed by assuming that parents receive an independent income, w_2^p, at $t = 2$. If w_2^p is high enough, their altruism might lead them to make positive income transfers (or bequests) to their children even during their own old age. In that event, they would adjust the implications of the debt burden incurred on behalf of their children's education in the amount of the bequest, so that the absence of any help from their grown-up children in repaying would not stop them from incurring the debt. Once again, the household would make full use of whatever debt facility was available to it.[25]

The problem arises when w_2^p is small or non-existent, so that parents cannot and, despite their innate altruism, will not make a positive bequest to their offspring. In this case, under the unitary household model of mutual altruism, the direction of the bequest would be *negative*, so that children would be the ones making an old-age payment to their parents.

When mutual altruism does not apply, however, children will have no motive for providing old-age support. Parents will have to use their meagre old-age income not just to provide for their own consumption but also to repay any debt they had incurred while their children were young. In fact, even if parents are altruistic towards their children, this lack of support later in life will discourage them from taking on credit to support their children.[26]

Note that the lack of demand for credit to 'finance' school enrolment arises, not because parental altruism is assumed to be any less in its intensity, but because it is not reciprocated. When parents expect to provide for themselves independently during their old age, and expect to have meagre resources at that point, they will be discouraged from undertaking debts on behalf of their children when the latter are still young. Ironically the lack of children's love rebounds back on them, because ultimately it is their schooling which is harmed by their unwillingness to help their parents later in life. The problem would not arise if children could undertake loans directly, since then their parents would not be saddled with the burden of repaying these loans out of their own old-age funds.

The argument is theoretically appealing. It is also consistent with the assumption of one-sided altruism made by macroeconomists who work on intergenerational issues such as the burden of public debt. But the debates on public debt tend to focus mainly on developed countries, while the present argument pertains to developing ones. There appears to be considerable evidence, albeit mostly casual, that in the latter type of countries parents receive considerable old-age support, both material and emotional, from their offspring. Whether this reflects differences in cultural norms or simply reflects the fact that developed countries enjoy higher levels of publicly provided old-age support, is debatable. But the observed prevalence of old-age support from children in the developing world does call into question the model on which the above argument is based. In any case, such a problem on the demand side of the credit market does not obviate the need for reforms on the supply side; indeed one that might be called for is a system which enables minors to take on debts directly under their own names.

To summarize the main policy implications of this section, credit markets are important not only in influencing the incidence of child labour directly, but also through their concomitant impact on the effectiveness of other policy measures. Thus trade sanctions are more likely to be counterproductive if imposed in an environment of restricted access to credit. Benign policies like food for education and investment in school quality will also vary in their effectiveness according to the precise credit market scenario. Investment in school quality will be less fruitful, both in absolute terms and in comparison with a scheme of direct subsidies to support school enrolment, with inelastic credit supply and will improve on both counts as the elasticity of this supply increases.

In the model used so far, all wages have been specified exogenously. In a literal sense, this makes it a partial equilibrium model. This is not a severe limitation, since the model could be easily interpreted as one in which output is produced with labour which has constant marginal productivity, as in the Ricardian model of international trade. Under this interpretation, the different wages would be proportional to the productivity of different types of labour. However a more illuminating way to endogonize wages is to follow the approach taken by Basu and Van (1998).

A labour market model
In a seminal paper, Basu and Van (1998) make a very interesting argument about the relationship between adult poverty and child labour. Since, as we shall see in greater detail, the focus of their study is on contemporaneous relationships, their model does not use a multi-period framework. Also they do not literally address the question of education, focusing instead on the tradeoff between child labour and child leisure. However, without any injustice to their argument, we can keep assuming that the alternative to child labour is child education and that the latter provides utility to the parents in its own right (subject to a qualification discussed below). In fact, we shall strengthen this role of education by assuming that, since there is no future period, a child's future earning capacity is not at all enhanced by education.

The other major assumptions we shall make are that (i) children and adults are perfect substitutes for each other in a competitive labour market, even though each child's productivity is a fraction, $\phi \leq 1$, of an adult's; and (ii) parents have a utility function which values household consumption in all cases, but values children's education if and only if household consumption exceeds a certain level (which could be interpreted as subsistence). This is the qualification referred to above: education is now a 'luxury' good in the economic sense of the word, unlike the case in the previous section, in which it was treated as a 'normal' good.

We shall make the following assumptions for ease of exposition. First, there are M households in total with N children and one adult per household. N is a large number. Second, each adult has one unit of time devoted exclusively to labour; each child has one unit of time which she can devote either to work or to schooling. The proportion of children who go to school full time is e. Third, the parental utility function is discontinuous in aggregate household consumption, c:

$$U = c - s, \ c < s$$
$$U = (c - s)(Ne)^{\alpha}, \ c \geq s, \ \alpha > N,$$

where s represents a subsistence level of consumption. This is what makes education a luxury good; a family does not derive any utility from education if it cannot collectively earn enough to meet a bare minimum level of consumption. Beyond that level of consumption, it derives utility from education in proportion to the number of children educated.[27]

In a competitive labour market, the wage paid to a child, w^c, will be proportional to the wage paid to an adult, w^p, according to the productivity difference between them. Thus, in general, $w^c = \phi w^p$. But it simplifies the exposition tremendously if we allow ourselves to assume that $\phi = 1$, that is, children have the same productivity as adults. This implies that children and adults will earn the same wage. Thus, depending on the number of children who work, the budget constraint of each household will be

$$c = [N(1 - e) + 1]w,$$

where the term in square brackets represents the total number of workers supplied by the household, each worker earning the same wage, w.

If we further assume that a neoclassical production function relates aggregate output, Y, to aggregate labour, L:

$$Y = f(L), \, f'(L) \geq 0, f''(L) \leq 0,$$

then the demand for labour by each firm is characterized by the equation $w = f'(L)$. As is well known in the literature, this will trace out a negative relationship between the market wage and the quantity of labour demanded.

To construct the supply curve of labour, note that, if $w < s/(1 + N)$, then $e = 0$ since, from the budget constraint, the consumption of each family will lie strictly below subsistence for any feasible value of e. This will in turn mean that education is neither valued nor sought, so that e is set at zero by each household. The total labour supplied per family will be $N + 1$ and the total labour force will be $L = M(N + 1)$.

If $w > s/(1 + n)$, it is possible for the family to enjoy consumption levels above subsistence for suitable choices of e. In this case, the family will choose e by maximizing

$$((N(1 - e) + 1)w - s)(Ne)^\alpha$$

with respect to e. The first-order condition for this problem, after some manipulation, can be written:

$$\alpha(Nw + w - s) - (\alpha + 1)Nwe \geq 0,$$

which implies that

$$e = \frac{\alpha(N+1)w - s}{(1+\alpha)Nw} \text{ if } \frac{s}{N+1} \le w \le \frac{\alpha s}{\alpha - N}$$

$$e = 1 \text{ if } w > \frac{\alpha s}{\alpha - N}.$$

Thus, if the market wage exceeds $\alpha s/(\alpha - N)$, every child is sent to school by its parents. In this case, which represents the opposite extreme, labour supply per household is 1 and total labour is $L = M$. In the intermediate case, where $e \in (0, 1)$, it can be shown that e is monotonically increasing in w, so that labour supply per household and on aggregate is falling as w increases. Note that this is quite distinct from conventional labour market models in which labour supply is typically found to be an increasing or a non-monotonic function of the wage, but not to decrease monotonically. This happens here because each adult's labour is assumed to be inelastically supplied, while children's labour is supplied only to the extent that it is needed to make up for household poverty. Thus, as the wage rises, parents earn more and buy out more of their children's time for education rather than work.

The supply of labour is depicted in Figure 17.4 by the set of loci labelled $SGBS$. At wages below $\underline{w}$ (equal to $s/(N+1)$), the labour supply curve is represented by the segment BS, which is vertical at $M(N+1)$ units of labour. At wages above $\bar{w}$ (equal to $\alpha s/(\alpha - N)$), the labour supply curve is given by SG, which is vertical at M units of labour. At wages that lie between these two extremes, the labour supply curve is represented by GB, which is downward sloping. With this labour supply curve and a conventional downward-sloping labour demand curve, multiple equilibria can arise in the labour market. Figure 17.4 shows an example. As drawn, the labour demand curve, DD, intersects the labour supply curve, SS, at three points. The highest intersection is labelled E_g. The lowest intersection is labelled E_b. The middle intersection is not labelled because it represents an unstable equilibrium.[28]

Figure 17.4 establishes the possibility that a given labour market can be consistent with the existence of both an equilibrium in which there is no child labour and one in which all children work instead of going to school. Labour-supplying households are unambiguously better off in equilibrium E_g than in equilibrium E_b. This is easily proved by an elementary application of the principle of revealed preference. In Figure 17.4, refer to the point labelled E', which is directly above E_b and directly to the right of E_g. If E' could (somehow) be implemented as an outcome, labouring households would unambiguously prefer it over E_b, since E' would offer them

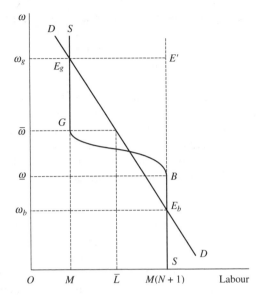

Figure 17.4   The Basu–Van model

higher wages for the same total supply of labour per household. Now compare E' to E_g. These points offer the same wage, but households choose to supply labour at a level consistent with E_g rather than with E'. Therefore E_g is revealed preferred to E' by these households. Since E' is unambiguously preferred to E_b, then so too must E_g. Accordingly we refer to E_g as a 'good' equilibrium and E_b as a 'bad' one.[29]

In the good equilibrium, adults face no competition from child workers, so each adult earns enough on his own to enrol his children willingly in full-time education. In the bad equilibrium, children competing with adults exert such a strong downward pressure on wages that each family's collective wages lie below what is needed for subsistence, thus completing the logical circle which sends children into work instead of school. Given that all other parents are sending their children to work, the individual parent finds himself too poor to choose otherwise. Thus, if the labour market ends up in a bad equilibrium, no individual parent will be able to break out of it.

An interesting implication of this model is that economic growth may not lead to progressively less child labour. Suppose that the overall productivity of labour is reflected in the position of the labour demand curve. As labour productivity increases, this curve shifts outwards. At very low levels of productivity, the labour demand curve might pass entirely below the segment *SG*. In this case, only a bad equilibrium is possible. At very high levels of productivity, the labour demand curve might pass entirely above the segment labelled *BS*. In this case, only a good equilibrium is possible. But at intermediate levels of labour productivity both equilibria are possible. Thus, while very poor economies will undoubtedly have high levels of child labour and very rich ones will have none, economies at an intermediate stage of growth could go either way. Within this group, it is possible for an economy with somewhat higher income per capita to experience more child labour than an economy with somewhat lower income per capita. The empirical implication is that cross-country analysis might find no clear-cut correlation between a country's per capita income and the incidence of child labour, depending on how many countries in the sample belong to the 'intermediate' stage.

While the Basu and Van model cautions against cross-country comparisons of per capita income in explaining child labour, it does imply that, at the household level, poverty and child labour are causally linked. This link has been the subject of numerous empirical studies using cross-sectional data from within a country. Note that Basu and Van are not alone in identifying a causal link between poverty and child labour. Their specific contribution is to endogenize the vicious circle between the two on the basis of their axiom that households prefer not to supply child labour only if their income without it exceeds a certain benchmark. In a specific test of this luxury axiom, Ray (2000) used household data from Peru and Pakistan to study whether child labour rose if adult household income fell below some benchmark level, equating that benchmark with each country's 'poverty line'.[30] For Pakistan, Ray used data from the Pakistan Integrated Household Survey of 1991 (PIHS). He found statistically compelling evidence that, when a 'Pakistani household falls into poverty . . . it significantly and substantially increases its children's involvement in outside, paid employment by about 500 hours annually for each child' (Ray, 2000). For Peru, where the data came from the Peru Living Standards Measurement Survey of 1994 (PLSS), Ray found the evidence to be statistically weak although it too was qualitatively consistent with the luxury axiom.

On the general link between household poverty and child labour, similar findings have been reported by Addison *et al.* (1997) for Ghana and Pakistan, Bhalotra (1999) for Pakistan, Ray (1999) for India, and Blunch and Verner (2001) for Ghana. Maitra and Ray (2002) compared the nature of the relationship between household poverty and child labour in Pakistan, Peru and Ghana and found that, while the effect varies markedly across the three countries, poverty leads children into child work and away from school enrolment. While a direct comparison of cross-country per capita income may be suspect, given the Basu–Van hypothesis, as a causal source of the variation in the incidence of child labour, an indirect use of cross-country data was made by Ranjan (2001), who used data from different countries and a variety of sources to study the relationship between the Gini coefficient measure of income inequality within a country and its incidence of child labour. He found that the Gini coefficient did have a significant and positive effect on the incidence of child labour. Since income inequality is known to be positively related to the incidence of poor households in a country, this provides indirect support for the household poverty–child labour relationship.

While the Basu and Van model identifies household income with wages and poverty with low wages, this identification may be challenged on the grounds that, in the rural areas of developing countries, many fairly poor households derive their income from family-run enterprise based on ownership of land, livestock and other farm assets. A theoretical contribution by Swinnerton and Rogers (1999) has challenged the identification of household income with market wages, not on the empirical grounds discussed above, but on the more academic grounds that some households can earn income from both wages and dividends based on share ownership.[31] They show that, if a country is developed enough to experience the possibility of multiple labour market equilibria, its share-owning households will not engage in child labour even in a bad equilibrium. This is because their low wages will be adequately compensated for by high profits should a bad equilibrium occur, making them rich enough to engage in the luxury of child education. This result therefore suggests that asset ownership might act as a barrier to child labour.

Returning, however, to the more realistic case of asset ownership based on family-run enterprise, as opposed to corporate share ownership, it is no longer clear that assets provide a natural brake on child labour. For example, in a study of child labour in rural Ethiopia, Cockburn (2001) found that, after controlling for other possible influences, children from families with some assets tend to work more than children from families with no assets. Children from the former type of families can work on family-run enterprises, while children from the latter type of families can only work on the child labour market, where wages are low and work conditions severe. Similar findings were also reported by Cain (1977) in his study of Bangladesh. He found that, whereas children from landless families worked only after the age of 12, when they became employable as wage labourers, those from small land-owning subsistence farming families worked on family plots from a much earlier age.

These findings also bear some interpretation in light of the general relationship between household poverty and child labour. They suggest that, in postulating this link, the source of income should be taken into account. For households that own no assets, and whose income is derived solely from wages, low income will straightforwardly contribute to the incidence of child labour. For households that own productive assets, the relationship between income and child labour will be more complex. While the pure income effect of asset ownership will work to discourage child labour, it is possible that, in environments where the available schools are of dubious quality and where children who work on the family enterprise might receive useful training for a future takeover of the family business, slightly better off families might engage in even more child labour and less schooling than poorer ones.

Policy implications   The most obvious policy implication of the Basu–Van model is a complete ban on child labour. Such a ban could deflect the economy from a bad equilibrium to a good one. To understand the mechanics of this process, let us go back to the essential difference between the two equilibria. In the bad equilibrium, there is a 'tragedy of the commons' in the labour market, which gets overcrowded by child workers to an extent that total (adult plus children) wages cannot even buy subsistence levels of consumption. A ban would prevent this overcrowding. As parents withdrew their children following the ban, the labour market would become less crowded and wages would rise. Eventually the remaining adult workers would all be earning enough not just for their households to enjoy more than subsistence levels of consumption but for their children to enjoy an education as well. All this would happen with no expenditure of any resources, save for those required to implement the ban in its early stages. Eventually, once the good equilibrium was reached, the ban would be self-liquidating in that it would no longer require outside enforcement. A ban is a *benign* intervention in this respect.

A ban will, however, be unambiguously benign only in an economy which is developed enough to allow for the possibility of multiple equilibria. If the economy is very poor, only a bad equilibrium is possible. In such a case, while a ban would force the withdrawal of child labour, it would not automatically bring about a good equilibrium. This would imply the need for keeping the ban in place forever. A ban imposed in these circumstances could also reduce family consumption. While it would increase adult wages, this might not be enough to compensate for the loss of child wages. Of course, it also might be enough, but this ambiguity just underscores the point that a ban imposed outside the framework of multiple equilibria is unlikely to produce clear-cut benefits. And, since it is difficult to predict exactly what level of development is required before multiple equilibria become possible, this suggests overall caution with the use of this policy.[32]

Given the relationship between child labour and education assumed in the model, one might be tempted to interpret a ban on child labour as equivalent to a law requiring compulsory school enrolment. That this will not be exactly so is because, as noted previously, the third use of a child's time is leisure. A compulsory education law would leave less opportunity for children to work, but it would not eliminate such an opportunity altogether, since families could still trade off child work for child leisure.

Despite this, it remains possible that compulsory education would do just as well as an outright ban. This point can be sketched with the help of Figure 17.4. Suppose the economy is at a bad equilibrium when a compulsory education law (or, for that matter, any other law which restricts the supply of labour only partially, such as a law which limits child work to a maximum number of hours per week) is enacted and enforced. Suppose that, at the wage paid in the bad equilibrium, this law leads to a partial withdrawal of child labourers, resulting in a fall in the total labour force from $M(N+1)$ to $\bar{L}$. Because of the fall in the number of workers, the market wage will rise from w_b to $\bar{w}$. At this wage, all parents will become willing to send their children to school in the first place.

Thus even a policy of compulsory education can potentially eliminate the bad equilibrium just as well as an explicit ban on all child labour. But, to do this, the initial withdrawal of child labour has to be sufficiently large; otherwise the policy fails to induce a good equilibrium. Nonetheless it will at least produce the result of having children enrolled in and attending school (provided it is properly enforced). Of course, if it does not cure the child labour problem, compulsory education might make the labouring families themselves worse off, but even this might be justifiable from the point of view of social welfare, given the positive externalities associated with education (for more on the externalities of education, see Chapter 6, by McMahon).

Another alternative to an outright ban is a ban on child labour in export industries. Such a ban might arise as a result of pressures from consumer groups, human rights campaigners and, for that matter, protectionist lobbies who care only for their own interests, in the developed countries. One form in which such a ban is being implemented is the requirement that goods originating in the developing countries are certified as 'child-labour free' before they are imported for sale in countries like the United States and Great Britain. Assuming, again, that such a policy does work effectively, it amounts to a ban on the use of child labour for the production of these goods.

Given that such a ban applies only to export industries it will also only enjoy partial scope in terms of how it affects child labour. And, unlike a policy of compulsory education, which is non-selective across industries, a ban on child labour in export industries leaves other industries free to hire as many children as they want. The implications of such a selective policy are quite numerous and depend on many contingencies.[33] For example, if the export industries are collectively large relative to the economy, even a selective ban might succeed in driving out the bad equilibrium. On the other hand, if they are collectively small, a selective ban would simply divert all child workers into non-export industries, and have no effect on wages or the decision to supply child labour.

At intermediate values of the relative size of the export sector, it is possible for the non-export industries to end up employing only children while the export ones employ only adults. In this case, children and adults will earn different wages, with the wages of adults rising relative to the pre-ban equilibrium and those of children falling. Aggregate household income may rise or fall. Thus, not only will the selective ban not only fail in terms of eliminating child labour from the economy (although it will drive it out of the target industries), it will also entail the risk of *lowering* aggregate household income even further below the subsistence level.

Two pieces of casual evidence are relevant to this point. First, UNICEF estimates that only 5 per cent of child labourers are employed in the exports sector worldwide (UNICEF, 1997). This suggests that selectively banning child labour in exports might not do much for the overall incidence of this problem in the developing world (although, by removing the evidence of its existence from the shopping malls of the rich countries, it might do wonders for liberal consciences). Second, there is the anecdotal evidence about the impact of precisely such a selective ban on children laid off from the garment industry in Bangladesh, discussed in the evaluation of trade sanctions in the previous section.

Since the Basu–Van model suggests that the reason for child labour's existence is its symbiotic relationship with low adult wages, an alternative to banning it might be a minimum adult wage law. One might conjecture that, if all adults are paid a minimum wage which exceeds the wage that they would receive in the bad equilibrium of the labour market, this would rule out that equilibrium.

There are problems, however, with this conjecture.[34] First, a minimum wage for adults but not for children will make employers strictly prefer child workers (should they be available) over adult ones. If the potential supply of child workers was high enough, children would compete away all jobs from adults. The latter would be unable to compete back, since they could not undercut the minimum wage in forming their own wage demands. Given mass adult unemployment, all households would be compelled to send children to work in order to survive, completing the logical circle between adult poverty and child labour again, this time not because adult wages are too low, but because they are too high for adults to find any jobs.

A similar, but not as vicious, circle may arise if the minimum wage is set above the 'good' market wage for adults. Any wage that exceeds the market-clearing wage creates some unemployment; while those adults who do find work would be quite happy not to send their children to work, those who are left unemployed would receive no income unless they sent their children to work. Ironically, perhaps, a minimum wage for children might help achieve a good equilibrium, by discouraging employers from hiring children and allowing the adult wage to rise in its wake. The irony is that such a policy might be perceived as *encouraging* children to work, rather than discouraging firms from hiring them.

Intergenerational persistence
The models studied so far have all implied that parental income exerts a positive influence on the decision to send a child to school. Parental income itself will undoubtedly be influenced by the parent's own schooling level as a child. This suggests that a dynamic link exists between an older generation's own schooling and that of the next generation. In this subsection, we shall present a model which analyses this link.[35]

To simplify the generalization to a dynamic model, we shall modify certain assumptions made so far. We shall restrict, N, the number of children per household, to equal unity. In order to keep allowing for interior solutions of education, we shall drop the assumption that it can only be undertaken on an all-or-nothing basis. Accordingly the variable which measures the intensity of education, e, will now be interpreted as the fraction of time that a child spends in school during her childhood; $1 - e$ will be the fraction spent in work. We shall also abstract from the issue of wages by assuming that households can apply their labour directly to production at home. Unlike previous sections, we assume that the economy does not end in one or two periods but goes on forever. Finally we abstract from the issue of total population size and assume that, at $t = 1$, when the economy starts, there is a solitary adult alive, who will live until the end of that period.

At the very start of $t = 1$, this adult begets one child. The child will live two periods. At $t = 2$, the child becomes an adult herself and begets her own child who also lives two periods, and so on. In this way, at the start of every period $t \geq 1$, one adult gives birth to one child. Each adult–child pair constitutes the household for that period. Because the child of an earlier household becomes the parent of the next, all households are linked together as a single *dynasty*. In each period, the parent of the household works full-time herself and also decides on the amount of time spent by her child in work.

Each household can produce a single type of output using its own labour, which can vary in its aggregate quantity and skill level depending on the current education choice of the child and the past educational level of the parent. Each child is born with a skill level normalized to unity. Education enhances her skill but with a lag of one period. A child who studies e_t units at time t acquires a skill level, $h_{t+1} (\geq 1)$, at time $t+1$. Assume that a function

$$h_{t+1} = H(e_t), \quad H' > 0, \; H(0) = 1, \; H(1) = \bar{h}$$

relates the time spend in education to future skills. This formulation implies that the skill level increases in the amount of education undertaken as a child, that without any education the individual remains with the bare minimum of skills (call this an 'unskilled' individual) and that there is a maximum skill level which can be attained by attending school full-time. Since, at time $t = 1$, there is an adult whose educational decision was made before the economy started, we assume that her skill level, h_1, lies arbitrarily between unity and $\bar{h}$.

Units of output are normalized so that one unit of output is produced with one unit of skills. A child who studies e units of time produces an output equal to $(1 - e)$, while an adult with skill h produces an amount equal to h, since she works full-time. The total output produced by the household of a given period represents its earning or income for that period. Each individual born in this dynasty gets to control one of its constituents, the household of which she is the adult member. Analogously her utility function is specified only over that single period:

$$U_t = u(c_t) + g(e_t),$$

where u and g are analogously interpreted and satisfy the same assumptions as on pages 747–50. The budget constraint facing the adult is

$$c_t = h_t + (1 - e_t).$$

Each household is assumed to consume its entire income within the period, implying an absence of saving or borrowing opportunities.[36]

Since saving or borrowing is not possible, the parent maximizes U_t by choosing e_t alone. The resulting first-order condition is

$$u'(h_t + 1 - e_t) = g'(e_t),$$

which states that e_t is chosen to equate the marginal utility from consumption with that from education. This condition is closely analogous to the ones derived on page 751. In particular, recall that an increase in parental income affects positively the value of e_t. The same will be true in the present case.[37] An increase in h_t lowers (at given e_t) the marginal utility of consumption, so the parent raises e_t in order to rebalance the two terms. We can express this relationship as

$$e_t = f(h_t), \quad f' > 0.$$

It is easy to find conditions such that, if a parent is 'fully' educated herself, she chooses to educate her child full-time and, if she is completely uneducated, she chooses not to educate her child at all. These restrictions would imply that $f(\bar{h}) = 1$ and $f(1) = 0$. Noting that the child's future skill level, h_{t+1} depends on e_t, we can express the former as

$$h_{t+1} = H(e_t) = H(f(h_t)) = G(h(t)) \ G' > 0, \ G(1) = 1, \ G(\bar{h}) = \bar{h},$$

where G is a composite function which combines the properties of $H(\cdot)$ and of $f(\cdot)$. Since H increases in e_t and f increases in $h(t)$, G increases in $h(t)$.[38] A link which was implicit in our previous models is now explicit: the higher the 'human capital' of an earlier generation the higher will be that of its successor.

The dynamic implications resulting from such a linkage are expressed in Figure 17.5. The vertical axis of Figure 17.5 measures h_{t+1} and the horizontal axis measures h_t. The 45-degree line represents *steady states* in which the skill level of successive generations is constant, that is, $h_t = h_{t+1}$. The curved line represents the G function, the dependence of h_{t+1} on h_t. Note that G coincides with the 45-degree line at the two extremes, $h_t = h_{t+1} = 1$ and $h_t = h_{t+1} = \bar{h}$. Given that it is upward sloping between these two extremes, it can

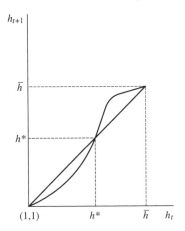

Figure 17.5   Poverty trap

intersect the 45-degree line at any number of intermediate points. As drawn, it intersects the 45-degree line at one intermediate point, labelled h^*. Thus there are three possible steady states, $h = 1$, $h = h^*$ and $h = \bar{h}$, representing a 'poverty trap', partial education and no child labour, respectively.[39]

But the partial education steady state is dynamically unstable. To see this, consider an adult who, at $t = 1$, starts off with $\bar{h} > h_1 > h^*$. Because the G function lies above the 45-degree line to the right of h^*, the next generation will have a skill level, $h_2 > h_1$. Because this child will grow up to 'earn' more than her parent, she will make her own child spend even more time in education than she did, so that $h_3 > h_2$. Thus, over time, successive generations will study more and more until the child-labour steady state $\bar{h}$ is reached. If, on the other hand, $1 < h_1 < h^*$, the child at $t = 1$ will end up with $h_2 < h_1$, since G is below the 45-degree line. Because she will earn less than her parent, her own child will study even less than she did, so that $h_3 < h_2$ and so on. Thus, except for the knife-edge case where $h_1 = h^*$, future levels of skill will head off either to the 'poverty trap' or the 'no-child-labour' steady state.

The model of intergenerational linkage suggests that the initial skill level of a dynasty's 'founder' is crucial for determining which steady state the dynasty heads off to. If the founder is herself sufficiently skilled, successive generations will study progressively more and work progressively less during their childhood, so that eventually the dynasty will eliminate child labour altogether. If the founder is insufficiently skilled, successive generations will acquire progressively less education until the entire dynasty is locked into a poverty trap. In other words, there is likely to be intergenerational persistence at both extremes of the labour–education choice.

Dessy (2000) and Hazan and Berdugo (2002) have extended the analysis of intergenerational persistence to encompass fertility choice. These articles make the number of children per family an endogenous variable, chosen optimally by the adults of each generation. What underpins this choice is that each parent has to spend a certain portion of her own time per child devoted to child care, and thus is taken out of income-earning activity. The greater the number of children, the less income is earned by the parent and the more the incentive to rely on child labour rather than send children to school. Parents with low skills (and low wages) have, on the one hand, less to lose by not working and taking care of children instead and, on the other, more to gain by having each child work. Hence a poverty trap develops with low parental skills, high fertility and child labour reinforcing each other through the generations.

Before going into the policy implications of these models, it is helpful to discuss some of the empirical studies that examine the issues of intertemporal persistence of child labour and/or endogenous fertility decisions. Emerson and de Souza (2003) have explicitly tested for the evidence of intertemporal persistence using survey data from Brazil. They found strong evidence of intergenerational persistence in child labour: if the parents had joined the workforce at an early age, this increased the likelihood of the child joining at an early age. Higher parental educational attainment lowers the probability of child labour. Grandparents' education also lowers the probability of child labour, but only in so far as it lowers the probability of the parent having been a child labourer.

Evidence that lack of parental education contributes to child labour is also provided by Ray (1999) for India and Grootaert (1999) for the Ivory Coast. Certain aspects of each of these papers are worthy of separate mention. Ray, for example, also finds that households with a large number of siblings are more likely to send children to work than to school. This is consistent with one of the predictions of Dessy's (2000) model. Grootaert (1999) finds one circumstance in which parental education can encourage child labour: he finds that an increase in a mother's education can positively affect the labour supply of daughters. This result may be explained by appeal to another of his findings, namely the existence of a bias against female education. Girls who do not engage in paid work are not sent to school in the first place; they are obliged to help their mother do housework. As a mother's labour market prospects improve with her own education, she does less housework and releases the girls into paid labour. As in Ilahi (1999), it appears that gender bias is an important part of the child labour story.

Apart from studying how parental education affects child labour, Emerson and de Souza (2003) also studied whether child labour in turn perpetuates poverty. They divided the effect of child labour on lifetime wages into two components: a direct one, which (essentially) gives the change in lifetime wages due to having worked instead of having played, and an indirect one, which gives the change in lifetime wages due to having worked instead of having gone to school. They found both effects to be negative. These findings are closely paralleled by Ilahi and Sedlacek (2000) who, using the same survey as Emerson and de Souza, report that the indirect effect of future wages of missing out on education is at least three times greater than the direct effect from early entry into the workforce. The latter effect, however, remains negative as in Emerson and de Souza. These studies together point to a very disturbing conclusion: children who work will earn less as adults than children who just stayed home and played: the benefits of gaining work experience are outweighed by the losses to physical and emotional well-being for child workers.

The question of interrelationship between fertility choice and child labour was the focus of analysis in the classic works of Cain (1977) and Rosenzweig and Evenson (1977). In fact Cain (1977) attempted to explain why poor families in the village of Char Gopalpur in Bangladesh have large families by examining the economic contributions of the children to their families. Rosenzweig and Evenson (1977) in contrast examine the simultaneous determination of fertility decision, school enrolment decision and child labour decision by estimating a structural model for India. Both studies find evidence that child labour decisions are closely related to the decision on fertility. The issue of intergenerational persistence, though not explicit in their analysis, is also part of the broader story told by these authors: abject poverty has a lot to do with high fertility and low school enrolment, and the latter makes it impossible for the children to avoid poverty when they are adults.

Policy implications   The model of intergenerational persistence provides an independent rationale for laws which restrict child labour and/or require compulsory education. As in the Basu–Van model, this law need not involve an absolute ban so long as it leads to a sufficiently large increase in schooling intensity: in this case, so long as an initial generation of children were able to get enough education to increase *their* skill level beyond h^*. It would also not need to be permanent since, after achieving the transition to whatever level of schooling was being aimed at, it could be withdrawn since, in fact, schooling choices would spontaneously rise above those mandated by the law (unless, of course, the law already required full-time schooling).

But there is a significant difference in welfare implications from the Basu–Van model. In that model, the existence of multiple equilibria means that a ban on child labour can make each (labouring) household better off. But in the model of intergenerational persistence, a ban on child labour would make the adult alive at the time the ban is enacted clearly worse off, since they would be denied the benefits of the child wage but would neither experience an increase in their own wage (since this model does not generate multiple labour market equilibria) nor live to share in the higher income of the child when the latter grows up. Of course, from a social welfare point of view, this might be an acceptable 'price' to pay for breaking the persistence of child labour through generations.[40]

In the model of intergenerational persistence, we had assumed that a single adult was alive initially, giving rise to a single dynasty. But this assumption can be easily relaxed.[41] In particular, suppose that, at $t = 1$, there are a large number of adults who differ in their skill levels and that their skills are distributed over the entire feasible range from unity to $\bar{h}$. Then the extended families of those adults with skill greater than h^* will go on to increase their educational attainment over time, while those of adults with skills below h^* will sink into the child labour trap. Thus, in the long run, a bipolar income distribution will emerge.

To take this point further, imagine that there are two economies with an identical number of adults alive at $t = 1$. In economy A, all adults have a skill level slightly above h^*. In economy B, half the adults have skills above h^* and the other half have skills below h^*, but the *average* skill level of adults in economy B equals that in economy A. At $t = 1$ itself, economy B will actually have somewhat higher income per capita than economy A, since more of its children will work. But, over time, economy B will become bipolar, with half its population trapped in child labour and relatively little (if any) growth in per capita income over time, while economy A will grow towards a high level of per capita income along with an equitable distribution of income and welfare. Distribution of income is therefore an important determinant, not just of economic growth, but of the long-run incidence of child labour.

Redistribution can thus help economy B escape its inequality trap. While skills cannot be redistributed, the income arising from skills can. So a redistributive tax from high-skill adults to low-skill ones at $t = 1$ could raise all incomes beyond the required threshold, h^*.[42] While such a redistributive tax would need to be applied only temporarily, it would make those adults who pay it at $t = 1$ worse off. But, as in the case of a temporary ban on child labour, policy makers might find this an acceptable price to pay.

4   Conclusions and extensions

This chapter has reviewed some of the leading economic models of the causes and cures of child labour, a phenomenon that deprives millions of children in the developing world from receiving education. Taken together, this literature emphasizes poverty, lack of credit opportunities, low pecuniary returns to schooling, coordination failures in labour markets and intergenerational transmission mechanisms for the persistence of child labour. Among the policy options for reducing child labour considered by this literature are absolute and partial bans on the employment of children, compulsory education laws, minimum wage laws, redistributive taxation, trade sanctions, subsidies for enrolling children in school rather than making them work and investments in improving school quality. As noted, not all these instruments are found to be equivalent in terms of their effectiveness; indeed certain measures, such as trade sanctions, might make things worse. The relative effectiveness of the instruments may depend on the specific circumstances, for example, the nature of the credit market. Even potentially effective measures such as providing subsidies linked to school enrolment beg the question of how they are to be financed.

Although the emerging literature on child labour and basic education has made significant headway in understanding the phenomenon of child labour, it is a relatively new literature and thus considerable scope remains in developing it further. For example, a common theme running through the models considered above is that, with rare exceptions, they are based on the unitary household assumption. This is justifiable partly as an analytical convenience which has allowed researchers to concentrate on factors arising outside the household and partly as a reflection of their reluctance to point the finger of blame at parents who are themselves mired in poverty and deprived of meaningful choices. Clearly some departure from this norm could lead to interesting insights into the problem, especially since evidence, some casual and some econometric, suggests that child labour might be interacting with household dynamics in interesting ways. For example, child welfare activists in developing countries often claim that one of the benefits, however small, to children who work is that their position within the household gets strengthened and their share in the intra-household allocation of resources goes up. This suggests that approaches based on household bargaining might be used as a complement to the unitary household model in studying intra-household allocation of resources. While some work has been done along these lines (see Basu, 1999, for a survey), this remains a largely undeveloped area, especially in terms of econometric work.

Another interesting departure from the framework of the unitary household model is suggested by the widespread finding that a bias exists against female education in all parts of the developing world. Again it is worth considering alternatives to the unitary household model in attempting to explain this finding. Recent work by Lahiri and Self (2003), which finds that inter-family externalities can lead to intra-household inequalities, is a step in this direction, but much more work remains to be done in this area as well.

Notes

1. See Chapter 4 by Stevens and Weale and Chapter 6 by McMahon.
2. This is one of the rights enshrined in the United Nations' 1989 Convention on the Rights of the Child. Visit www.unicef.org, for details.
3. The economic literature on child labour is not so new, although the focus of the literature has shifted over the years. For example, the classic study by Cain (1977) for the village of Char Gopalpur in Bangladesh was an attempt to explain high fertility rates among poor families of the village by pointing out, inter alia, that children's contributions to family income are an important factor behind high fertility. Rosenzweig and Evenson (1977) on the other hand estimated a three-way relationship between fertility, child labour and school enrolment in a simultaneous equation system using district-level data from India for the year 1961.
4. An important data source for many of the recent econometric studies is the Living Standards Measurement Surveys (LSMS) conducted by the World Bank.

5. When these excluded categories are added to those included in the definition of child labour, the resulting category is referred to as 'child work'.

6. Hazardous work is defined as work which by its nature or the circumstances in which it is carried out poses a danger to those who undertake it, plus any work which is carried out for an excessive amount of time. The unconditional worst forms of child labour are, if anything, more hazardous than those defined as hazardous, but they are treated as a separate category because of their illegal nature and the grave risks they pose even for adults who engage in them.

7. A heuristic explanation is as follows. Note that the right-hand side of (17.4) depends on e. At $e = 0$, the household will experience the highest possible (given all the wages) consumption at $t = 1$ and the lowest possible consumption at $t = 2$; thus the marginal rate of substitution between the two periods will be relatively low. Suppose that the wage of child labour and the educational wage premium are such that the left-hand side of (17.4) exceeds the right-hand side at $e = 0$. Then e will be chosen as positive, but, as e rises, income and consumption fall at $t = 1$ and rise at $t = 2$, so that the marginal rate of substitution and thus the right-hand side of (17.4) also rise, moving towards equality with the left-hand side.

8. This could be established algebraically by totally differentiating equation (17.4) with respect to w^p and e and deriving de/dw^p, which will have an unambiguously positive sign.

9. For example, a recent survey of six villages in India studied attitudes towards educating children. The survey found that a large number of respondents identified non-economic factors as important in motivating them to educate their children (Probe, 1999).

10. These calculations are made on the basis of extreme assumptions made for simplicity, notably that children who work earn the full adult unskilled wage and that the educational wage premium is enjoyed over an infinite horizon. To the extent that, in reality, children might earn less than unskilled adults, these calculations would have underestimated the pecuniary benefits of schooling over child labour. But to the extent that the educational wage premium accrues over a finite horizon, the benefits of schooling would be biased upwards. Whether the two biases cancel out is difficult to say. Thus these calculations should be seen as suggestive rather than conclusive.

11. Similarly low educational wage premiums were reported by Saha and Sarkar (1999) for India and Cohen and House (1994) for the Sudan. Drèze and Gandhi-Kingdon (2001) also found that in India the quality of education to a great extent affects the school enrolment decision. Of course, such localized survey findings do not contradict the possibility that, in the country as a whole, in particular in the modernized sectors of the economy, the discounted pecuniary returns to schooling are positive. See Chapter 1, by Psacharopoulos and Patrinos, for more evidence on returns to schooling.

12. This would be consistent with the empirical relationship between asset ownership, saving behaviour and income class in developing countries. Jafarey and Lahiri (2002) derive this type of credit exchange from a general equilibrium model with two classes, differentiated by the skill level of the parent.

13. The possibility that the saving curve may bend backwards at high interest rates is well known and indulging it would clutter up the discussion without changing anything of substance in it.

14. Note that, wherever u_1 and u_2 occur in these equations, their arguments would be c_1 and c_2, respectively, which would have to be replaced by the budget constraints to make b, e and r the indirect arguments of the subutility functions.

15. For purposes of exposition, either the supply curve can be interpreted as funds available per poor household, or M can be assumed to be unity.

16. The rich are likely to have access to better schools for their children and, thus, to a higher educational wage premium. Their greater current income will also make them discount future income less heavily than the poor in the absence of credit flows between them.

17. It is a sad fact of development that governments have done little to improve the access of poor sections of their population to credit, even as they have made vigorous attempts (such as national saving schemes) to improve the flow of funds *from* such households to larger-scale players in the economy. The creation of micro-credit institutions which lend

to the poor has been a step in the right direction, but so far their quantitative impact has been rather modest when it comes to the alleviation of credit constraints for poor, especially rural, households.

18. The data were obtained from the Village Level Studies survey, conducted by the International Crops Research Institute for the Semi-Arid Tropics (ICRISAT) and reported in Walker and Ryan (1990).

19. This would imply that the original borrowing constraint was quite generous so as not to bind initially. This fiction is necessary, however, if we are to distinguish between the level effects of various credit market scenarios and their comparative static effects.

20. See Grootaert and Kanbur (1995) who make a strong case for a gradualist approach to reduce child labour.

21. Note that the implications of these two policies for the donor's budget can be quite different.

22. A formal demonstration of this claim is beyond the scope of the present exposition. Readers are referred to Jafarey and Lahiri (2000).

23. The argument sketched here is based on Baland and Robinson (2000). Readers are referred to the paper itself for a formal exposition.

24. The utility function facing the household could no longer be written in the form used previously.

25. Similarly, if individuals lived three periods and received income during middle age which they partly saved for their own old age and partly set aside as a bequest, the presence of a positive bequest would imply that they have fully internalized the burden of any debt incurred on behalf of their children.

26. This problem was noted earlier by Parsons and Goldin (1989), who found evidence supporting its contribution to the incidence of child labour in nineteenth-century America.

27. This utility function is analogous to the one used previously, bearing in mind that, in the present model, there is only one period of consumption rather than two. Other differences are that consumption and education are no longer separable in the subutility function and that their interaction is represented by a specific functional form.

28. At any market wage that lies slightly below the one associated with the middle intersection, there will be an excess supply of labour, so the wage will fall away even further. For any wage slightly above that intersection, there is an excess demand of labour so the wage will rise even further.

29. The terms 'good' and 'bad' are used with reference to the welfare of households which derive income from labour alone. Families that derive income from profits alone will be worse off in the 'good' equilibrium and better off in the 'bad' one. We shall discuss this point in greater detail below.

30. Note, however, that nothing in the Basu and Van hypothesis suggests that the benchmark be set at the poverty line. In this respect, Ray's test is based on stronger assumptions than the hypothesis itself so the failure of his test would not necessarily falsify the hypothesis.

31. Since child labour is predominantly a phenomenon of rural and working-class urban populations in developing countries, who typically own few assets beyond those on which family enterprise is based, it is questionable how applicable this assumption is to the actual conditions facing households which potentially supply child labour.

32. Other problems with a ban include (i) the practical problem of enforcing it in its early stages, (ii) the effect it would have on children with no parents or adult guardians to make up for the loss of child income, (iii) the existence of informal and illegal sectors which often exploit the worst forms of child labour and would not easily fall under the purview of the ban.

33. The reader is referred to Basu and Van (1998) for a more detailed analysis of this policy.

34. This discussion is based on Basu (2000), which should be consulted for details.

35. The model presented here is based on Basu (1999). See also Emerson and de Souza (2003).

36. This restriction could be easily relaxed, without fundamentally altering the analysis.

37. The only difference is that an increase in e now reflects a given child attending school for a greater part of the time, instead of more children attending school full-time.

38. The other properties of G also follow from the assumed properties of f and H. If a parent has a skill level of unity, she chooses to make her child work full-time, so that the child's skill level is also unity. If the parent has skill $\bar{h}$, she makes her child attend school full-time so that the child's human capital is also $\bar{h}$.

39. The steady state with no education represents a 'poverty trap' because it implies that successive generations work full-time as children and therefore all generations remain unskilled.

40. In Hazan and Berdugo (2002), it is assumed that each generation lives three periods, childhood, adulthood and retirement, so that a ban on child labour followed one period later by an income transfer to the retired which is financed by taxes on their children can potentially make everyone better off. But this requires a more complicated intervention than simply banning child labour, which underscores the difficulty of obtaining an unambiguous welfare improvement in the case of intergenerational persistence.

41. This discussion is based on Ranjan (1999).

42. A word of caution about a redistributive policy is that it might discourage work effort by those who are paying the tax and, if they were already close to the threshold level, h^*, might actually tip them below it. This possibility does not arise in the formal model since adults are assumed to spend all their adulthood working, but it is worth noting.

References

Addison, T., S. Bhalotra and C. Heady (1997), 'Child labor in Pakistan and Ghana', mimeo, University of Warwick, UK.

Baland, J.-M. and J. Robinson (2000), 'Is child labor inefficient?', *Journal of Political Economy*, **108**, 663–79.

Basu, K. (1997), *Analytical Development Economics*, Boston: MIT Press.

Basu, K. (1999), 'Child labor: causes, consequences and cures, with remarks on international labor standards', *Journal of Economic Literature*, **37**, 1083–1119.

Basu, K. (2000), 'The intriguing relation between adult minimum wage and child labor', *Economic Journal*, **110**, C50–C61.

Basu, K. and P.H. Van (1998), 'The economics of child labor', *American Economic Review*, **88**, 412–27.

Bhalotra, S. (1999), 'Is child labor necessary?', mimeo, University of Bristol, UK.

Blunch, N. and D. Verner (2001), 'Revisiting the link between poverty and child labor: the Ghanaian experience', working paper no. 01-03, Centre for Labour Market and Social Research, Department of Economics, The Aarhus School of Business.

Cain, M.T. (1977), 'The economic activities of children in a village in Bangladesh', *Population and Development Review*, **3**, 201–27.

Cockburn, J. (2001), 'Child labor versus education: poverty constraints or income opportunities?', Discussion Paper 01-16, CREFA, Université Laral.

Cohen, B. and W. House (1994), 'Education, experience and earnings in the labor market of a developing country: the case of urban Khartoum', *World Development*, **22**, 1549–65.

Dessy, S.E. (2000), 'A defense of compulsory measures against child labor', *Journal of Development Economics*, **62**, 261–75.

Drèze, J. and G. Gandhi-Kingdon (2001), 'School participation in rural India', *Review of Development Economics*, **5**, 1–24.

Emerson, P.M. and A.P.F. de Souza (2003), 'Is there a child labor trap? Intergenerational persistence of child labor in Brazil', *Economic Development and Cultural Change*, **51**, 375–98.

Grootaert, C. (1999), 'Child labor in Côte d'Ivoire: incidence and determinants', in C. Grootaert and H. Patrinos (eds), *The Policy Analysis of Child Labor: A Comparative Study*, New York: St Martin's Press.

Grootaert, C. and R. Kanbur (1995), 'Child labor: an economic perspective', *International Labor Review*, **134**.

Hazan, M. and B. Berdugo (2002), 'Child labour, fertility and economic growth', *Economic Journal*, **112**, 810–28.

Ilahi, N. (1999), 'Children's work and schooling: does gender matter? Evidence from the Peru LSMS panel data', World Bank, Washington DC, USA.

Ilahi, N. and G. Sedlacek (2000), 'The effect of child labor on lifetime wages and poverty: retrospective evidence from Brazil', World Bank, Washington DC, USA.

ILO (2002), *A Future without Child Labour*, Geneva: International Labour Office.

Jacoby, H. and E. Skoufias (1997), 'Risk, financial markets and human capital in a developing country', *Review of Economic Studies*, **64**, 311–35.

Jafarey, S. and S. Lahiri (2000), 'Food for education versus school quality: a comparison of policy options to reduce child labour', discussion paper no. 00-03, Department of Economics, University of Wales, Swansea, UK.

Jafarey, S. and S. Lahiri (2002), 'Will trade sanctions reduce child labour? The role of credit markets', *Journal of Development Economics*, **68**, 137–56.

Lahiri, S. and S. Self (2003), 'Gender bias in education: the role of inter-household externalities, dowry, and other social institutions', Department of Economics, Southern Illinois University, Carbondale.

Maitra, P. and R. Ray (2002), 'The joint estimation of child participation in schooling and employment: comparative evidence from three continents', *Oxford Development Studies*, **30**, 41–62.

Parsons, D.O. and C. Goldin (1989), 'Parental altruism and self-interest: child labor among late nineteenth century American families', *Economic Inquiry*, **27**, 637–52.

PILER (1998), 'Child labour in hazardous industries', research report no. 2, Karachi, Pakistan.

The Probe team (1999), *Public Report on Basic Education in India*, New Delhi: Oxford University Press.

Ranjan, P. (1999), 'An economic analysis of child labor', *Economics Letters*, **64**, 99–105.

Ranjan, P. (2001), 'Credit constraints and the phenomenon of child labor', *Journal of Development Economics*, **64**, 81–102.

Ravallion, M. and Q. Wodon (2000), 'Does cheaper schooling mean less child labor? Evidence from behavioural responses to an enrollment subsidy', *Economic Journal*, **110**, C158–C175.

Ray, R. (1999), 'Poverty, household size and child welfare in India', mimeo, University of Tasmania, Australia.

Ray, R. (2000), 'Analysis of child labour in Peru and Pakistan', *Journal of Population Economics*, **13**, 3–19.

Rosenzweig, M. and R. Evenson (1977), 'Fertility, schooling and the economic contributions of children of rural India: an econometric analysis', *Econometrica*, **45**, 1065–79.

Saha, B. and S. Sarkar (1999), 'Schooling, informal experience, and formal sector earnings: a study of Indian workers', *Review of Development Economics*, **3**, 187–99.

Swinnerton, K. and C.A. Rogers (1999), 'The economics of child labor: comment', *American Economic Review*, **89**, 1382–5.

UNICEF (1997), *The State of the World's Children 1997*, Oxford: Oxford University Press.

Walker, T.S. and J.G. Ryan (1990), *Village and Household Economics in India's Semi-arid Tropics*, Baltimore, USA: Johns Hopkins Press.

18 Education and housing
William H. Hoyt

1 Introduction

There is an enormous literature, surveyed in this volume by Naylor and Smith (Chapter 11) and by Bradley and Taylor (Chapter 10) that examines links between educational inputs (expenditures, measures of staffing, demographic characteristics of students) and educational outcomes such as test scores, graduate rates and earnings. While undoubtedly these 'outputs' are related to the value of education, that is, how much households are willing to pay for various educational attributes, they are not, in themselves, measures of the value of educational inputs and therefore do not provide sufficient information to address normative issues regarding educational provision. Specifically, without knowledge of how educational outcomes are valued, it would seem to be impossible to address the question of whether public education is efficiently provided.

One explanation for the absence of measures of the value of educational outputs, offered by Samuelson (1954), is that the absence of a market for publicly provided goods meant that demands for these goods would not be revealed, making the determination of the efficient provision of them difficult, if not impossible. This argument, at least as made by Samuelson, applied to *pure public goods*, but would seemingly apply to goods such as publicly provided primary and secondary education which, while not pure public goods, share both the non-excludability and equal provision characteristics, though non-excludability in the case of education is a result of legislative fiat and not inherent in the nature of the good itself. Then given that public education is not explicitly purchased, following Samuelson's logic it seems reasonable to think that the value of publicly-provided education is not easily ascertained.

Tiebout (1956) is, in part, a response to Samuelson's assertion that the demands for public goods would not be revealed and, therefore, efficient provision is not likely to be obtained. Tiebout argued that for a class of public goods, *local public goods*, there was, in fact, a quasi-market. Local public goods are, following Tiebout's conception of them, goods for which there is a population for which the average cost is minimized and there are no external economies or diseconomies between communities.[1] Also critical are Tiebout's assumptions that households were mobile and based their choice of community on preferences for public services, and there were a number of alternative communities in which to reside. Within this setting, Tiebout argues that demands for local public goods are revealed with the mechanism for preference revelation being the choice of community in which the household resides. Tiebout further argues that this 'quasi-market' will lead to both the efficient provision of local public services and the efficient sorting of households based on their preferences for local public services.

Tiebout (1956) is an informal, loosely structured analysis, with the efficiency results better described as claims than theorems. Since this seminal piece, numerous articles have formalized Tiebout's analysis and considered what conditions might be necessary for the preference revelation and efficiency results to be obtained. While there may be some debate about whether primary and secondary education meets all of the conditions Tiebout had set out for local public goods, it would seem that public education, at least by implementation, meets most of these conditions.

In Tiebout's simple model the financing of the local public good was not explicitly stated, with Tiebout only mentioning taxes. The simplest tax system that would yield the efficiency results he sought would be a uniform head tax in each community in this setting. Then, at the optimum population, the tax would equal the marginal cost of providing another household with the local public good. The 'price' of the local public goods would simply be the increase in the tax rate due to an incremental increase in the local public good.

More complicated models of local public goods have explicitly incorporated land markets as well as different forms of taxes, primarily property taxes. In these models, the 'price' of the local public good may not be entirely reflected in taxes. Instead the quality or level of local public services may well influence property values; that is, the value of the local public services is capitalized into property values.

Here I discuss a significant literature that has examined how and the extent to which educational services, outcomes, inputs and reforms have influenced property values; that is, how public educational quality has been capitalized into property values. I divide this literature into two broad categories: a primarily theoretical literature focused on models of capitalization, and an empirical literature that focuses on estimating the capitalization of education into property values. In section 2 I discuss the theoretical literature on capitalization and develop a few simple models of capitalization as a way both of summarizing this literature and of suggesting the implications this literature has had for the empirical work that has primarily followed it. In section 3 I review a significant, but not voluminous, empirical literature on education and capitalization. In reviewing this literature, I provide an (imperfect) classification of these studies based on how they measure education. Specifically I consider, separately, studies that focus on the impact of measures of educational inputs, most frequently educational expenditures, on property values and studies that focus on what impact measures of educational outputs, most frequently a form of standardized test scores, have on property values. In addition, other studies have focused on how other characteristics of the education system, most frequently the racial composition of the students, affect property values, with a particular focus on the impact of integration on property values. A final component of this section is an examination of studies attempting to measure the impact of educational reforms including financial reform and school choice programmes on property values. While the majority of the empirical literature on education and housing prices has used data from the USA, recently several studies have examined the impact of education on housing prices in the UK. We discuss several of these studies in section 4. Section 5 offers some brief concluding remarks.

2 Capitalization versus no capitalization

In Tiebout's original article, communities are probably most accurately described as 'clubs' that households join to consume the services provided by the community. Communities are clubs in the sense that there is no spatial context: land is conspicuously absent from Tiebout's discussion. More sophisticated models of communities include modelling of land markets. Of course, it is the existence of land markets and rents accruing to land that make it possible to obtain some indication of the valuation of public services, in our case education, by households and to test whether there is evidence of the efficient provision and sorting asserted by Tiebout.

One of the earliest empirical studies of capitalization, Oates (1969), was motivated as a test of the Tiebout hypothesis. From Oates comes a summary of the decision facing households when choosing a residence:

> In terms of the Tiebout model, we can conceive of a utility-maximizing consumer who weighs the benefits stemming from the program of local public services against the cost of his tax liability and chooses as a residence that locality which provides him with the greatest surplus of benefits over costs. (Oates, 1969, p. 959)

Then Oates continues to devise a 'test' of whether, in fact, households appear to choose their community of residence following this cost–benefit approach:

> Moreover, this suggests a way to determine whether the Tiebout hypothesis of consumer location in accordance with preferences for local budgetary programs has any relevance to actual behavior. If consumers, in their choice of locality of

residence, do consider the available program of public services, we would expect to find that, other things being equal (including tax rates), gross rents (actual or imputed) and therefore property values would be higher in a community the more attractive its package of public goods. Individual families, desiring to consume higher levels of public output, would presumably tend to bid up property values in communities with high-quality programs of public services. (Ibid.)

Oates does not present a formal model of the capitalization described above. Here I briefly outline a simple model that captures the elements of Oates' argument in a more formal way.

A simple model of capitalization

A model of complete capitalization   We use a model closely following Epple and Zelenitz (1981) and Yinger (1982) to demonstrate conditions when capitalization might exist. Let there be N identical households each with utility functions $U(x,h,e)$ where x is private consumption, h is a measure of housing quality, and e is a (vector) of attributes of education. Let each household have income of y. Each of the J communities, $j = 1,...,J$, each with defined boundaries and land area L_j, provide educational services e_j financed by a property tax, a tax on the value of house, with the rate given by τ_j. Let the price of housing[2] be given by $p(\tau_j,e_j)$ making the budget constraint for a household in community j equal to $y = x_j + (p(\tau_j,e_j) + \tau_j)h_j$ with $p(\tau_j,e_j) + \tau_j$ the gross price of housing in community j. Then, given utility maximization subject to the budget constraint, we have the indirect utility function $V(p_j(1 + \tau_j),e_j)$.

Housing in community j is produced with capital and land. While capital is mobile among communities, land is immobile and fixed in supply to each community. Housing is assumed to be produced competitively with constant returns to scale. Then, given zero profits, we have $p_j = k_j + r_j l_j$ where k_j is capital per unit of housing in community j, l_j is land per unit of housing and r_j is rent per unit of land. Then housing supply in community j is given by $H(p_j)$ with $H'(p_j) > 0$. Then equilibrium conditions in this model are

$$n_j h_j(p_j(1 + \tau_j)) = H_j(p_j), \quad j = 1,...,J, \tag{18.1}$$

$$n_j l_j(r_j) = L_j, \quad j = 1,...,J, \tag{18.1'}$$

$$\sum_{j=1}^{J} n_j = N, \tag{18.2}$$

and

$$V(p_j(1 + \tau_j),e_j) = V(p_i(1 + \tau_i),e_i) = U^*. \tag{18.3}$$

Condition (18.1) or, equivalently (18.1'), is simply the requirement that the housing market (18.1) or land market (18.1') in each community clears. Condition (18.2) can be considered clearance for the housing market for the entire economy, as it literally requires that economy population (N) equals the sum of the populations of each of the J communities. As individuals are all identical and have the same income, mobility requires that all individuals have the same utility in equilibrium (18.3). That utility is given by U^* is intended to reflect the fact that, while utility is not exogenous to the economy, it is assumed to be exogenous to each of the communities. Essentially this is simply an assumption that the number of communities is large enough for the impact of any community's policies on the level of utility to be negligible. While this is a standard assumption (see, for example, Yinger, 1982), consistent with Tiebout's notion of 'competitive' communities, others have considered a framework in which, with a finite number of communities, the utility level is not exogenous to a single community (Epple and Zelenitz, 1981; Hoyt, 1991, 1992). Utility is not exogenous to a single community in this latter case because changes in a single community's policies (tax and public service), by causing significant changes in the population of other communities, change land rents in other communities and therefore the utility obtained in them). Still, for the examination of capitalization of education into property values, the 'competitive' model is a good starting point.

Then, given 'exogenous' utility, differentiation of (18.3) with respect to the tax rate yields

$$\frac{\partial p_j}{\partial \tau_j} = -\frac{p_j}{(1 + \tau_j)} \qquad (18.4a)$$

and, with respect to educational quality,

$$\frac{\partial p_j}{\partial e_j} = \frac{MRS_{ex}}{(1 + \tau_j)h_j}, \qquad (18.4b)$$

where MRS_{ex} is the marginal rate of substitution between educational services and the private good x. This model with costless mobility and identical residents generates 'full' capitalization – any increase or decrease in utility due to increases or decreases in either the tax rate or level of educational quality are completely offset by the changes in utility due to changes in the price of housing, the rate of capitalization.

This simple model provides a motivation for the Oates' (1969) 'test' of the efficient provision of educational expenditures. In addition to the equilibrium conditions (18.1)–(18.3), each community must maintain a balanced government budget. Then, in a community composed only of identical houses, we would have the balanced-budget condition

$$n_j \tau_j v_j = C(e_j, n_j),\qquad(18.5)$$

where $C(e_j, n_j)$ is the cost of providing education quality of e_j to the n_j households in community j. Then let

$$\frac{d\tau_j}{de_j} = \frac{C_e}{n_j p_j h_j},\qquad(18.6)$$

where C_e is the marginal cost of increasing the level of educational services. Then (18.6) gives the balanced-budget change in the property tax rate when education quality increases as defined by (18.6). Then from (18.4) and (18.6) a balanced budget change in property values in the community is

$$\frac{d[n_j v_j]}{de_j} = n_j h_j \left[\frac{\partial p_j}{\partial e_j} + \frac{\partial p_j}{\partial \tau_j}\frac{d\tau_j}{de_j} \right] = \frac{n_j^2}{(1 + \tau_j)}[n_j MRS_{ex} - C_e].\qquad(18.7)$$

Equation (18.7) states that whether property values in a community increase or decrease with a balanced-budget change in educational services and taxes depends on whether education is overprovided or underprovided. If underprovided ($n_j MRS_{ex} - C_e > 0$) property values would increase with a balanced-budget increase in educational services; if overprovided ($n_j MRS_{ex} - C_e < 0$) property values decrease. If educational services are efficiently provided, that is the sum of the marginal rates of substitutions in the community equals the marginal cost of increasing educational services ($n_j MRS_{ex} - C_e) = 0$ then a balanced-budget increase in educational services has no impact on property values in the community. Figure 18.1 provides an illustration of these different possibilities. Here we illustrate both the relationship between property value and educational services $p(e)$ and the relationship between property value and the property tax $p(\tau(e))$ where we relate the property tax rate to the level of educational services using the balanced budget condition. Then the slope of the curve $p(e)$ is simply $\partial p / \partial e$ and the slope of the curve $p(e(\tau))$ is $(\partial p / \partial \tau)$ $(\partial \tau / de)$. The level of services e_1 has $\partial p / \partial e > (\partial p / \partial \tau)$ $(d\tau / de)$, suggesting underprovision of educational services and level e_3 has $\partial p / \partial e < (\partial p / \partial \tau)$ $(d\tau / de)$, suggesting overprovision. At level e_2 we have $\partial p / \partial e = (\partial p / \partial \tau)$ $(d\tau / de)$, signifying the efficient provision of educational services.

A model of partial capitalization   While identical individuals and mobility generate full capitalization, other models with costless mobility can

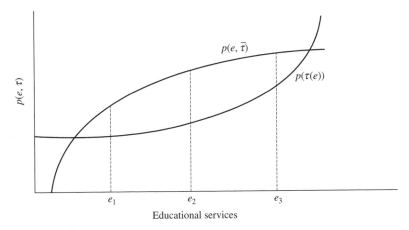

Figure 18.1

generate 'incomplete' capitalization. Suppose, for example, we modify our model by allowing identical tastes but an income distribution with $n(y)$ being the probability density function and $\underline{y}$ and $\bar{y}$ the minimum and maximum income levels, respectively. Different income levels and a tax on housing, with housing consumption varying with income, mean that different households will face different tax burdens in the same jurisdiction. Then rich households, with more valuable houses, subsidize poor households, with less valuable houses. This leads to the possibility of 'musical' suburbs (Hamilton, 1975) in which the poor 'chase' the rich. More generally, it may lead to no equilibrium existing. One solution to this problem suggested by Hamilton (1975) is the use of fiscal zoning in which minimum housing consumption (value) requirements lead to homogeneity in housing consumption within communities, thereby eliminating the cross-subsidization. In the absence of zoning, Epple *et al.* (1984) demonstrate that an equilibrium in this model requires that the 'single crossing' condition be satisfied. This condition, illustrated by two income classes $(y_2 > y_1)$ in Figure 18.2 ensures that households with higher incomes will 'outbid' lower-income households for housing in communities with higher taxes and public services.

Then, letting there be only two communities, the following conditions must be satisfied in equilibrium:

$$\int_{\underline{y}}^{\hat{y}} n(y)h(y, p_1(1 + \tau_1)) = H_1(p_1), \qquad (18.8a)$$

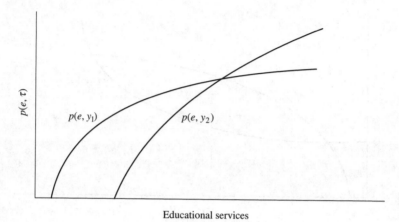

Figure 18.2

$$\int_{\hat{y}}^{\bar{y}} n(y)h(y, p_2(1 + \tau_2)) = H_2(p_2) \tag{18.8b}$$

and

$$V(\hat{y}, p_1(1 + \tau_1), e_1) = V(\hat{y}, p_2(1 + \tau_2), e_2) = U(\hat{y}). \tag{18.9}$$

Following Hoyt (1999) we can express the price gradients by

$$\frac{\partial p_1}{\partial \tau_1} = -\frac{p_1}{(1 + \tau_1)} - \frac{1}{h_1}\frac{d\hat{y}}{d\tau_1} < 0 \tag{18.10a}$$

and

$$\frac{\partial p_2}{\partial \tau_1} = -\frac{1}{h_2}\frac{d\hat{y}}{d\tau_1} > 0, \tag{18.10b}$$

where, with the increase in the tax rate of community 1, the population of the community decreases $(d\hat{y}/d\tau_1)$ and the marginal income decreases as well. Then, with the change in the income of the indifferent household, the utility level falls. Then capitalization does not fully offset the decrease in utility due to the increase in the tax rate in community 1. Analogously we have

$$\frac{\partial p_1}{\partial e_1} = \frac{p_1}{MRS_1 h_1} - \frac{1}{h_1}\frac{d\hat{y}}{de_1} > 0 \tag{18.11a}$$

and

$$\frac{\partial p_2}{\partial e_1} = -\frac{1}{h_2}\frac{d\hat{y}}{de_2} < 0 \qquad (18.11\text{b})$$

for the changes in property values related to changes in the level of educational services. In this case we have $d\hat{y}/de_1 > 0$; the income of the indifferent household increases, as does the population of community 1. Again, comparing (18.11a) to (18.4b), it is apparent that the capitalization of the educational service is incomplete: the decrease in utility in community 1 due to the increase in the price of housing does not fully offset the direct increase in utility due to increase in educational services.

Full capitalization of educational services or, for that matter, taxes, does not occur because the impacts of a policy in a single community influence the economy-wide utility level. In this case, it is because of changes in the income of the indifferent household. However, incomplete capitalization could also be obtained with identical households, both in income and tastes, if there is a small number of communities. Hoyt (1991, 1992) provides examples of models in which there is not full capitalization because of either a finite number of communities or a single large community (central city) with market power.

No capitalization

The simple models in the preceding subsection that generated capitalization had several attributes critical to obtaining capitalization of public services, in our case educational services. The first attribute is that political jurisdictions were of fixed land area, the economy was of limited land area, all of which was residential use (in contrast to an agricultural fringe). The second attribute is that there was a single or at least finite number of distinct types of consumers, at least with respect to their demands for educational services.

Epple *et al.* (1978) provide a formal model that illustrates the conditions under which no capitalization can be obtained consistent with the Hamilton (1975, 1976) and Edel and Sclar (1974) concept of long-run equilibrium in a Tiebout model. The model that Epple *et al.* (1978) develop is quite sophisticated, allowing for heterogeneity in both incomes and demands for the public service. In addition the level of public services and tax rates in this model is determined by majority voting within the community. However the critical assumption of the model, at least with respect to capitalization, is simply that there is a perfectly elastic supply of housing, that is, an elastic supply of both land and capital for housing. This perfectly elastic supply of housing means that in equilibrium the price of a unit of housing, property value, is determined entirely by the costs of land and capital and must be independent of any other attributes of the community in which the housing is located, including quality of education or the provision of public services. Essentially, if any individual or group of individuals did not receive the mix of taxes, public services and price of housing they desired (and satisfied budget constraints) they could move or create another community.

That all land and therefore housing, regardless of location, would be valued equally is clearly not true. However the proper interpretation of Epple *et al.* and other researchers arguing the 'no capitalization' viewpoint is that there should be no capitalization due to differences in mixes in public services or, in our case, educational quality or expenditures given that services are chosen by majority rule. One graphical interpretation of the no capitalization model is found in Figure 18.3. Here we have three different groups of consumers (1, 2 and 3) with different tastes for educational service. This generates three different relationships between educational services and housing prices and three different efficient levels of educational services. In all three cases there is no balanced-budget net or marginal capitalization of educational services as $\partial p/\partial e = (\partial p/\partial \tau)(d\tau/de)$.

While empirical studies of capitalization and capitalization as evidence of efficiency in educational provision received early criticism from the proponents of the 'no capitalization' viewpoint, the overwhelming evidence of capitalization of both taxes and measures of educational inputs and outputs makes it hard to dismiss theories that argue for the existence of capitalization. One way to reconcile the two views is that differences in land

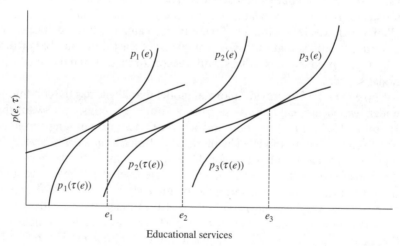

Figure 18.3

and housing prices due to factors other than the level or quality of public services allow for inefficient public service provision in those areas in which there are high property values thanks to attractive amenities or proximity to employment. Also critical to the view that educational services should affect property values would seem to be the need for some communities to provide these services inefficiently.

3 Empirical evidence on capitalization

In this section, I provide a review and discussion of what, over the past 35 years, has become a significant literature, at least in terms of quantity. My intention is to focus more on findings of this literature about the impact that education has had on property values and less on econometric techniques and data. However, as results are influenced by techniques and data, some discussion of both will be contained here. While it would be presumptuous to attempt to pass a verdict on what is known or not known about the impact of education on property values, I hope to suggest trends within this literature and what might be considered consensus where it appears to be emerging.

In discussing empirical studies of the capitalization of educational services, I consider two ways of categorizing these studies. First, studies might be categorized by what their purpose is in examining the capitalization of educational services into property values. This method of categorization is not altogether unrelated to the second method of categorization, the measure of educational services used in the study. For some studies, the purpose, rather than the measure of educational services, is of interest; for others, primarily more recent studies, the focus of the study is often the measure of educational service used.

The capitalization of educational services and the Tiebout hypothesis

Oates (1969), as discussed earlier, is the seminal early piece that examines the capitalization of educational services. Here, as discussed at some length earlier, the focus of the study is the so-called 'a test' of the Tiebout hypothesis, with the 'a test' of the Tiebout hypothesis being a test of whether there was evidence that households chose their residences according to fiscal variables, that is local taxes and public services. The theoretical motivation underlying this test as well as the theoretical objections to it were outlined in the preceding section. Since Oates' methodology is a starting point for numerous studies, it is worth reporting the form (and results) of his hedonic equation here. Using aggregate (community-level) data on 53 cities and townships in Northern New Jersey in 1960, Oates estimates a two-stage least squares equation with median house value as the dependent variable. From the two-stage estimate he finds

$$V = -29 - 3.6 \log T + 4.9 \log E - 1.3 \log M + 1.6R + 0.6N$$
$$ {}_{(2.3)} {}_{(3.1)} {}_{(2.1)} {}_{(4.0)} {}_{(3.6)} {}_{(3.9)}$$
$$+ 1.5Y + 0.3P, \quad R^2 = 0.93,$$
$$ {}_{(7.7)} {}_{(3.1)}$$

where V is median house value; T is effective percentage tax rate; E is current expenditures per pupil; M is linear distance from Manhattan; R is median number of rooms; N is percentage of houses built since 1950; Y is median family income in thousands of dollars; and P is percentage of homes with an annual income of less than \$3000 (Oates, 1969, p. 964). The numbers in brackets below the coefficients are *t-statistics*.

As the equation above shows, Oates (1969) did, in fact, find that educational spending per student (at the district level) had a positive and significant impact on property values for this sample. As Oates' purpose was less about the impact of educational services, per se, and more a test of the Tiebout hypothesis, the impact of property taxation was more of a focus than the impact of educational spending. Of course both were viewed as evidence supporting Tiebout's suggestion that public services and tax rates influence the location decisions of households. Oates, as did other early studies of capitalization, employed aggregated data. Specifically, in the case of Oates (1969), the level of observation was the community (township or city) and the dependent variable was the median value of owner-occupied housing, obtained from the 1960 Census of Housing.[3] That aggregate property value is the dependent variable raises concerns about endogeneity as the government budget, specifically the property tax rate and level of expenditures, depends on the property tax base. This being the case, Oates (1969) employs two-stage least squares estimation in an attempt to address these endogeneity issues.

While Oates (1969) can be viewed as the starting point and influence for numerous studies examining the capitalization of fiscal variables into house values, many of the studies following Oates (1969) were quite critical of it. Some, as discussed earlier, attacked Oates on the grounds that what he found was support for *disequilibrium*, not equilibrium, in a Tiebout model. These studies were primarily theoretical in nature (Hamilton, 1976; Pauly, 1976; Epple *et al.*, 1978). An exception is Edel and Sclar (1974), though Epple *et al.* (1978) also have an empirical component as well. Edel and Sclar essentially employ Oates' methodology to examine capitalization for Boston metropolitan area (MSA)[4] cities and townships using Census data from 1930 to 1970. Edel and Sclar estimate a hedonic equation for each of the Census years. They find evidence that the capitalization rate, the coefficient in the hedonic equation, on both the tax rate and educational expenditures, is diminishing from 1950 to 1970, with the coefficient on educational expenditures being statistically insignificant in 1960 and 1970. This is evidence, they suggest, that Oates' results using 1960 data might be viewed as short-run in nature and that capitalization of either tax rates or local public service expenditures is inconsistent with long-run Tiebout equilibrium.

Pollakowski (1973) also criticizes Oates' study but primarily for two different reasons. Pollakowski is particularly critical of Oates only including a single measure of local public services, educational expenditures, arguing that there are omitted variables and therefore the coefficient on educational expenditures is biased. Pollakowski argues that other municipal services should be included in the hedonic equation and that, if expenditures on these services are positively correlated with expenditures on education, the coefficient on educational spending in Oates' regression is positively biased; that is, it is too big. Pollakowski further argues that demand variables such as average income in the community should not be included in the hedonic equation if it is indeed the case that residents are mobile, since it is not solely the income in the community that should drive housing prices. Finally, Pollakowski argues that the instruments Oates uses, particularly demographic characteristics such as level of education, are themselves endogenous. Correcting for the deficiencies he sees in Oates (1969), Pollakowski estimates a similar hedonic equation to Oates, but using Census data on the San Francisco–Oakland–San Jose metropolitan area rather than New York–New Jersey. The results that he finds for both the tax rate and educational expenditures are quite sensitive to the specification of the hedonic equation. Educational expenditures are insignificant in the specification that essentially mirrors that of Oates but, once income and the percentage below the poverty line are excluded, as Pollakowski argues they should be, the coefficient on educational expenditures become rather large and statistically significant.

Sonstelie and Portney (1980), like Oates, wish to test the Tiebout hypothesis through the use of hedonic estimation. Writing after the criticisms of Oates by Hamilton (1975, 1976), Edel and Sclar (1974), Pauly (1976) and Epple *et al.* (1978), they propose an alternative structure for the hedonic equation. Instead of having, as a dependent variable, net of tax property value, Sonstelie and Portney argue that gross of tax property value is a more appropriate dependent variable. Gross of tax property value is created by determining a present value of taxes based on current taxes and a discount rate[5] and adding this to the value of the house. In contrast to the earlier studies of Oates (1969), Edel and Sclar (1974) and Pollakowski (1973), Sonstelie and Portney (1980) are among the first to use disaggregated data on individual housing sales usually obtained from real estate services such as the Multiple Listing Service (MLS). Sonstelie and Portney argue that educational services (or other municipal services) should be capitalized into gross property values regardless of whether there is a short-run (capitalization) Tiebout equilibrium or a long-run (no capitalization) equilibrium.[6] In addition to educational spending, Sonstelie and Portney (1980) are among the first to use an achievement measure, in this case the average district score for a third grade (age 8–9 year olds) reading test.

Sonstelie and Portney find that educational expenditures have a positive and significant impact on gross property value. Since, in addition to including educational spending per student, they include an interaction variable of spending per student and the number of bedrooms in the house, the impact of educational spending depends on the size of the home. Not surprisingly the rate of capitalization of educational spending is greater in homes with more bedrooms, presumably because these homes are more likely to be desired by households with larger families and more children likely to attend public schools.

Despite Sonstelie and Portney's assertion that gross property value is a more appropriate measure for purposes of testing Tiebout, no other studies of which I am aware have used this measure. One obvious problem with it is that the present value of future tax payments is sensitive to the discount rate chosen. Another factor that might make it unattractive is that it implicitly assumes full capitalization of property taxes. Of course one explanation of a positive relationship between educational expenditures and gross property value may have nothing to do with Tiebout: if taxes are higher in communities with greater educational expenditures, then, even if educational expenditures have no effect on net of tax property value, they would still have a positive impact on gross of tax property values.

Capitalization and the efficient provision of educational services
While Oates viewed his test of the Tiebout hypothesis in his 1969 *Journal of Political Economy* paper as a test of whether taxes and public services influence location decisions, a stronger conjecture made by Tiebout (1956) was that local public service provision with mobile residents should lead to efficient provision of these services. Oates (1969) offers an informal test of this aspect of the Tiebout hypothesis by considering the impact of a balanced-budget increase in educational spending on property values. By balanced-budget, Oates calculates the impact of raising the effective property tax rate from 2 per cent to 3 per cent on the median house value. He also determines how much additional revenue this will yield for education and what impact the additional revenue will have on educational spending per student. Then the impact of this increase in educational spending on property value, plus the impact of the tax increase, give the balanced budget increase. Oates finds that the two effects of a property tax increase roughly offset each other given his sample and the parameters of his regression model.

In two influential papers published in the *Journal of Public Economics*, Jan Brueckner (1979, 1982) also addresses the issue of whether local public services, specifically educational services, are efficiently provided or not. Referring to hedonic studies of property values such as Oates (1969, 1973), Pollakowski (1973) and Edel and Sclar (1974), Brueckner says,

> The present paper is based on the belief that none of the previous work in this area constitutes a test of the Tiebout hypothesis, and that a proper test would bear no resemblance to previous studies. In particular, results which show a relationship between public spending and property values only establish that consumers *value* [original italics] the public goods they consume. Such results say nothing whatever about the efficiency of public good provision, the ultimate implication of the Tiebout hypothesis. (Brueckner, 1979, pp. 223–4)

Of course, while this assertion ignores the informal 'test' offered by Oates (1969), it is certainly the case that the focus of that and other hedonic studies of property taxes and local public services that followed was on whether there was evidence of capitalization, and therefore evidence that consumers based choice of location on local fiscal factors and not on whether these services were efficiently provided. To examine what Brueckner asserts is a test of the Tiebout model, he begins with a bid-rent model similar to that discussed in section 2. Here, I give the basics of the model, which I have slightly modified to make exposition briefer. Assume that each household has enough residential options so that there is some other community in which they would receive the same level of utility. Then for household i we have

$$U^i(y^i - v^i(\tau, e, x)(1 + \tau), e, z) = \overline{U}^i, \qquad (18.12)$$

where $U^i(.,.,.)$ is household i's utility function; y^i is income; and v^i is the value of the house in which they reside. The terms τ and e refer to the tax rate and level of public services (educational spending) in the community, and z are attributes of the house. Again we follow the convention used in section 2 and express the value of a house in annual (rental) terms, meaning that the tax rate would be based on rental value, not actual property value, in this simple model. Then, if we differentiate this equal utility with respect to educational services, e, we obtain

$$\frac{\partial v^i}{\partial e} = \frac{1}{(1+\tau)} \frac{U_e^i}{U_x^i} = \frac{1}{(1+\tau)} MRS_{ex} \quad \text{and} \quad \frac{\partial v^i}{\partial \tau} = -\frac{1}{(1+\tau)} v^i. \quad (18.13)$$

Brueckner also considers business property. In this case, there is an equal profit condition with profits for firm j:

$$wl^j + rk^j + s^j(\tau, e)(1 + \tau) = \pi^j(e), \qquad (18.14)$$

where π^j are the profits for firm j, s^j is the value of its property and w is the wage rate in the community. Then, as with residential property, we have

$$\frac{\partial s^j}{\partial \tau} = -\frac{1}{(1+\tau)} s^j \quad \text{and} \quad \frac{\partial s^j}{\partial e} = \frac{1}{(1+\tau)} \frac{\partial \pi}{\partial e}. \qquad (18.15)$$

The community budget constraint can be given by

$$(1 + m)\tau \left[\sum_i v^i(\tau, e, x^i) + \sum_j s^j(\tau, e) \right] + T = C(e), \qquad (18.16)$$

where m is a matching grant (or tax) and T is other tax revenue. If we begin with the simple case with no business property, matching grants or other tax revenue, differentiating (18.16) yields

$$\frac{d\tau}{de} = \frac{1}{(1+\tau)} \frac{\left[C'(e) - \tau \sum_i \frac{\partial v^i}{\partial e} \right]}{\sum_i v^i}. \qquad (18.17)$$

Then, if we totally differentiate aggregate residential property value, we have

$$\frac{d\sum_i v^i}{de} = \sum_i \left(\frac{\partial v^i}{\partial \tau} \frac{d\tau}{de} + \frac{\partial v^i}{\partial e} \right) = (1+\tau) \sum_i \frac{\partial v^i}{\partial e} - C'(e) = \sum_i MRS^i_{ex} - C'(e). \qquad (18.18)$$

Then, if it is the case that education is efficiently provided, $d\sum v^i/de = \sum_i MRS^i_{ex} - C'(e) = 0$. On the basis of this result, using the budget constraint to define the tax rate as an implicit function of the level of education, Brueckner (1979) asserts there is no need to include the tax rate in the hedonic equation and the empirical test of efficiency is whether the coefficient on educational expenditures is equal to zero in a regression in which aggregate property value is the dependent variable. If we include business property and matching grants we have

$$\frac{d\left(\sum_i v^i + \sum_j s^j\right)}{de} = \sum_i \left(\frac{\partial v^i}{\partial \tau}\frac{d\tau}{de} + \frac{\partial v^i}{\partial e}\right) + \sum_j \left(\frac{\partial s^j}{\partial \tau}\frac{d\tau}{de} + \frac{\partial s^j}{\partial e}\right)$$

$$= (1+\tau)\left(\sum_i \frac{\partial v^i}{\partial e} + \sum_j \frac{\partial s^j}{\partial e}\right) - \frac{C'(e)}{(1+m)}$$

$$= \sum_i MRS^i_{ex} + \sum_j \frac{\partial \pi^j}{\partial e} - \frac{C'(e)}{(1+m)} \qquad (18.18')$$

If there is no matching grant, then $d(\Sigma v^i + \Sigma s^j)/de = 0$ and a coefficient of zero on aggregate community value still gives efficiency; however, if there is the use of a matching grant, for example, that subsidizes local public service provision, efficiency is not obtained when property value is maximized.

Brueckner (1979) employs this framework to determine whether education (and other local public services) were efficiently provided using the same data as Oates did in his 1969 article. However, as Oates used median property value as a dependent variable, a direct test as Brueckner envisioned was not possible. A study using data that is more amenable to this technique is Brueckner (1982). In this study, Brueckner uses data on aggregate property values for 54 Massachusetts communities in 1976. This sample has the desirable property of being 'equalized' property values in which the state government of Massachusetts engaged in a costly project to determine accurate measures of community aggregate property for the purposes of state aid to education. Brueckner uses two-stage least squares to estimate a hedonic equation of the form,

$$APV_i = \beta_0 + \beta_1 EE_i + \beta_2 ME_i + \beta_3 Units_i + \beta_4 Baths_i + \beta_5 Emp_i + \beta_6 Income_i + \beta_7 IGR_i + \beta_8 Location,$$

where *EE* is educational expenditures, *ME* is municipal spending, *Units* is the number of housing units in the community, *Baths* is average number of baths in housing units in the community, *Emp* is manufacturing employment in the community, *Income* is median income, *IGR* is intergovernmental revenue and *Location* is a locational dummy. Estimating this equation, Brueckner finds that the coefficient on educational spending, while positive, is not significantly different from zero. As Brueckner notes, the coefficient on educational spending could be zero because some communities underprovide education, $d\Sigma_i v^i/de > 0$, while other communities overprovide education, $d\Sigma_i v^i/de < 0$. Thus Brueckner argues this result might be interpreted as evidence that these communities do not systematically under- or over-provide education.

In the past 20 years, a number of studies have adopted Brueckner's framework and methodology. These include Deller (1990a, 1990b), Taylor (1995), Bates and Santerre (2003) and Barrow and Rouse (2003). The studies by Deller are the closest to Brueckner (1982) in methodology, data and the issues addressed. Deller (1990a) uses Brueckner's methodology to estimate whether total educational expenditures have any impact on total property value using educational expenditures aggregated to the county level for a sample of counties in Illinois in 1982, arguing that aggregating to the county level eliminates difficulties with overlapping jurisdictions. Deller finds no evidence of overexpenditure on education in this sample. In Deller (1990b), Brueckner's methodology is applied to looking at educational spending in small towns and cities (1000–5000) in rural Maine in 1986. Deller's interest in examining this sample is to determine whether the Tiebout hypothesis can apply to rural settings where mobility between communities might be more costly. Again he finds no evidence of overexpenditure on education.

Taylor (1995) examines the impact of educational spending on aggregate property value using community-level data from the 1980 Census for the Hartford, CT MSA. Taylor argues that earlier studies that use data from several labour markets (metropolitan areas) might be misspecified as some of the capitalization of educational services could be in wages, not housing prices. Focusing on this single metropolitan area, Taylor again finds no evidence of overexpenditure on education.

Bates and Santerre (2003) use Brueckner's framework to determine whether the Connecticut minimum educational expenditure requirement affects property values. Using a sample of 169 Connecticut communities in 1995, Bates and Santerre estimate a model almost identical to that found in Brueckner (1982). However, in addition, they include an interaction term, Bound*Educational Expenditures, where Bound equals 1 if the community is within 5 per cent of the minimum expenditure level and zero otherwise. Estimating this model, Bates and Santerre find positive coefficients on both Educational Expenditures and the interaction term, Bound*Educational Expenditures. They view this as evidence that minimum educational expenditure requirements imposed by state governments on school districts may increase property values and enhance efficiency by increasing the under-provided educational expenditures.

A final study we discuss that follows Brueckner's methodology, forthcoming in the *Journal of Public Economics*, is by Lisa Barrow and Cecilia Rouse. In this study, the authors again examine whether the level of school expenditures is inefficient. However, they do this by considering the impact of state aid on property values. From Barrow and Rouse (2003), aggregate property value is given by

$$P = \frac{1}{\delta}\left[\sum_{i=1}^{n} R(E, G, H_i; I_i) - CE(E, N) + S - CG(G, N)\right], \quad (18.19)$$

where $R(.,.,.,.)$ is the value of house i, $CE(E,N)$ is the cost of education quality E for N residents, S is state educational aid and $CG(G,N)$ is other local government expenditures (ibid., p. 5, eqn 7). The term δ is the discount rate. Totally differentiating (18.19) with respect to S gives

$$\frac{\partial P}{\partial S} = \frac{1}{\delta}\left[\sum_{i=1}^{n} R_E(E, G, H_i; I_i) - CE_E(E, N)\right] + \frac{1}{\delta}. \quad (18.20)$$

Then, if the educational spending is efficient, we have $\sum_{i=1}^{n} R_E(E, G, H_i; I_i) - CE_E(E, N) = 0$ and therefore $\partial P/\partial S = 1/\delta$. Then, rather than including a measure of educational expenditures in their hedonic equation, Barrow and Rouse only include a measure of state aid, state aid per student. They estimate their hedonic equation using school district-level data for 1980 and 1990. The dependent variable in this case is aggregate house values per pupil. Barrow and Rouse find a negative relationship between state aid and property value in OLS regressions using both cross-sectional analysis and first-differences of the data with the coefficient on state aid statistically different from $1/\delta$. However, with an IV estimator (replacing actual state aid per pupil with predicted state aid), Barrow and Rouse cannot reject the null that the coefficient on state aid is equal to $1/\delta$. Their most interesting results might be when they consider how the impact of predicted state aid on property value might vary with characteristics of the school district, specifically size, unionization and concentration. Defining concentration using the Herfindahl–Hirschman Index (HHI) with a market being defined as a county, they find that the coefficient on predicted state aid is highly positive when there is low concentration (the 'competitive' case) but not significantly different from zero when there is high concentration (the 'not competitive' case). Consistent with this is their finding that small districts (smallest 20 per cent) also have a highly positive and significant coefficient on predicted state aid but large districts (largest 20 per cent) have negative coefficients on predicted state aid. This, argue Barrow and Rouse, suggests that overspending might be occurring in larger districts and districts facing less competition.

While few studies of the capitalization of taxes and public services, including educational spending, into property values estimate equations following Oates (1969), the structure of the equations first estimated by

Brueckner (1982) still form the basis of studies as recent as 2003. While Brueckner (1979, 1982) was careful in outlining the role of business property in determining whether educational expenditures are inefficiently spent as well as carefully outlining the nature of the budget constraint, more recent studies have generally ignored business property. While ignoring business property (that is, using only aggregate residential housing as a dependent variable) still provides an indication of the balanced-budget change in educational spending on residential values, it does not offer any interpretation for efficiency. The same criticism can be applied to ignoring state aid, particularly state aid that has the form of a matching grant, as is frequently the case with the use of equalization plans in the United States. While Barrow and Rouse incorporate state aid into their budget constraint and analysis, in fact making it the focus of their analysis, they do not model aid as a matching grant. Essentially they argue that the additional impact of aid on aggregate property value can be expressed as

$$\frac{dP}{dS} = \underbrace{\left(\frac{\partial P}{\partial \tau} \frac{\partial \tau}{\partial e} + \frac{\partial P}{\partial e} \right) \frac{de}{dS}}_{(a)} + \underbrace{\frac{\partial P}{\partial \tau} \frac{\partial \tau}{\partial S}}_{(b)}, \tag{18.21}$$

where, if communities were efficiently providing educational services, in the absence of a matching grant we have term (a) equal to zero. This is not the case, as shown in (18.18′); when there is matching aid, a coefficient of zero on educational spending in a regression of aggregate property value means that the marginal rate of substitution is not equal to marginal cost but to the share of marginal cost borne by the community; when term (a) is equal to zero, educational services will be overprovided, not efficiently provided. We can re-express (18.21) as

$$\frac{dP}{dS} = \underbrace{\left(\sum_i MRS_{ex}^i - C_E \right) \frac{de}{dS}}_{(a)} + \underbrace{\frac{\partial P}{\partial \tau} \frac{\partial \tau}{\partial S}}_{(b)} + \underbrace{\frac{m}{(1+m)} C_E \frac{de}{dS}}_{(c)}, \tag{18.21′}$$

where it can be shown that $dE/dS > 0$. Then, while at the efficient level of public services (where term (a) equals zero) $dP/dS > 0$, this should also be the case if the community is maximizing its property value (terms (a) and (c) are equal to zero).

What aspects of education are capitalized: inputs or outputs?

As mentioned in the introduction to this chapter, a voluminous literature has developed on the relationship between inputs in the production of education (student–teacher ratios, teacher education, expenditures) and measures of educational 'outputs', typically scores on standardized tests, usually of reading or mathematics, given at a state level. Occasionally graduation rates or earnings have been used as well. As discussed in this volume by Averett and McLennan (Chapter 9) many of these studies, with the earliest and probably best known of these being those done by Eric Hanushek (1986), have found little evidence that increases in educational inputs, including expenditures, have much impact on performance on standardized tests.

While this extensive literature may have stimulated interest in the way outputs, specifically student scores on standardized tests, influence property values, the first study that uses an output measure, Rosen and Fullerton (1977), actually precedes the best known literature on the relationship between educational inputs and outputs. Rosen and Fullerton argue that it is the output or performance of the educational system that should influence property values, not expenditures, as presumably the quality of the schools is what consumer/residents value. In their study, Rosen and Fullerton essentially try to follow Oates (1969), replacing educational expenditures with one of several test scores (mean reading, maths and an average of the two for fourth grade students (9–11 years of age) in the school district) in the hedonic equation. Rosen and Fullerton begin by estimating a hedonic equation using educational expenditures and data on Northern New Jersey communities (following Oates, 1969) from the 1970 census. Using the 1970 census, Rosen and Fullerton found educational expenditures were insignificant in the hedonic equation. However, when they replaced educational expenditures with either the math or reading score or the average of the two, there was a positive and significant relationship between property values and educational output. Based on their estimates, being in the highest rather than the lowest decile in reading scores would increase the median property value by $4300 (in 1970 prices) or $20 699 (in 2003 prices)!

Following Rosen and Fullerton, a number of studies have included educational test scores as explanatory variables. Unlike Rosen and Fullerton, some of these studies also include educational expenditures along with test score measures (Sonstelie and Portney, 1980; Jud and Watts, 1981; Jud, 1985; Walden, 1990; Hayes and Taylor, 1996; Haurin and Brasington, 1996; Brasington, 1999, 2003; Downes and Zabel, 2002; Black, 1999; Gibbons and Machin, 2003). Many of these studies as well as other studies have included a measure of minority attendance, with the focus of some studies explicitly on the impact of integration of schools on property values (Clotfelter, 1975; Gill, 1983; Vandell and Zerbst, 1984; Bogart and Cromwell, 1997). We discuss these studies in more detail later.

The studies by Jud and Watts (1981), Jud (1985), Walden (1990), Haurin and Brasington (1996), Downes and Zabel (2002), and Gibbons and Machin (2003) essentially follow the framework of Rosen and Fullerton, replacing educational expenditures with some measure of performance, that is, some test score. Sonstelie and Portney (1980), as discussed before, differs from the basic framework of Oates (1969) by using a measure of gross of tax property value as a dependent variable. In contrast to Oates (1969) and Rosen and Fullerton (1977), these studies generally use individual housing sales data rather than aggregate or median property value in a community. Since these studies are not focused directly on whether education is provided efficiently, that is, whether property value in a community is maximized, use of individual housing sales affords more observations and less aggregation bias. In all of these studies, test scores were found to have a positive and significant impact on property values, sometimes quantitatively quite large. Jud and Watts (1981), using single family home sales in Charlotte, NC, find that the average third grade test scores at the school level significantly affect housing prices with a half-grade increase leading to an increase in house value of $675 (in 1977 prices). Jud (1985) is one of the few studies using aggregate property data and test scores, with the data coming from the 1980 census on towns and cities in the Los Angeles and San Francisco metropolitan area. Jud finds that that the average district test score for third grade reading has a positive impact on median owner-occupied house value, with a 4 per cent increase in district test score associated with a 2 per cent to 3 per cent increase in house value. Walden (1990) is one of the few studies to include measures of achievement for different grade levels using a score from a standardized test for elementary and middle schools (CAT) and a college admittance exam (SAT) for a measure of high school quality. Using data on sales of single family homes in the Raleigh, NC, MSA in 1987, he finds that capitalization of test scores is higher for high school (SAT) than for the elementary and secondary schools (CAT). Raleigh has a 'magnet' school programme which provides students with an opportunity to attend a school other than the one in which they were assigned according to residential location. Walden asserts that the lower capitalization rate for elementary and middle schools is consistent with the more extensive use of the magnet programme at these levels: if residential location is less relevant in determining the school in which a student attends, presumably the less the quality of the local school is capitalized into property values.

A number of studies have included both measures of educational inputs, usually expenditures per pupil, and educational output, test scores, as explanatory variables, often with the explicit purpose of determining which measure seems to have more of an effect on property values. Downes and Zabel (2002) use a panel of the American Housing Survey for the Chicago metropolitan area for 1987–1991 merged with data on Illinois schools that include expenditures, percentage minority and reading scores. They use a first difference approach, with the dependent variable being the difference in property value perceived by the owner. They emphasize three results from their study: first, that school-level attributes dominate district-level attributes in the estimation; second, that changes in spending seem to have no impact on changes in property values when changes in test scores are included in the regression; finally, they find the percentage minority, both African-American and Hispanic, has a negative impact on property values.

Two studies, Hayes and Taylor (1996) and Brasington (2003), follow suggestions by many, including Summers and Wolfe (1977) and Hanushek and Taylor (1990), that it is the 'value-added', not the level of performance or achievement, that should be capitalized into property values, though empirical measurement of value-added is quite different in the two studies. Weimer and Wolkoff (2001), while not referring explicitly to value-added, also employ an estimation procedure in which they attempt to control for achievement differences because of differences in the demographic composition of students.

Hayes and Taylor employ a two-stage procedure in which they attempt to distinguish how much of the difference in achievement scores, in their case average elementary maths scores in Dallas in 1987, is due to a school effect and how much is due to the demographic composition of the students, the peer group effect. To distinguish the school and peer group effect, Hayes and Taylor follow the approach described in Hanushek and Taylor (1990) in which they estimate an equation using data on individual students' test performance in which demographic characteristics of the student and his or her household and a dummy variable for the school that the student attended are explanatory variables. Then the school effect is the coefficient on the dummy variable for that school. The 'peer' effect is simply the difference between the mean score of students attending the school and the school effect. Hayes and Taylor find that, while spending has no effect on property values, test scores do. Further separating the test score into the school and peer effects, Hayes and Taylor find that the impact on property values is due to the school effect, not the peer effect.

In a similar vein, but a more direct approach, Weimer and Wolkoff (2001) include the demographic characteristics of the students, a measure of poverty (the percentage receiving free or reduced price lunches), a measure of student behaviour (the suspension rate from school) and measures of performance. For the elementary schools the measures of performance are exam scores in English; for high school, the measures are the graduation rate and advance placement rate on the ACT. Using data on Monroe County (Rochester, NY) single home house sales, Weimer and Wolkoff find positive impacts of test scores even controlling for demographics.

Brasington (1999) explicitly considers a number of measures of educational inputs and outputs in examining the impact of education on single family house sales price for Ohio metropolitan areas in 1991. However his measure of value-added is quite different from that of Hayes and Taylor (1996) or what is implicitly done by Weimer and Wolkoff (2001). Brasington measures value-added as the percentage change in the number of proficient students in the district between grades. Since the data are for a single year, this represents a difference in proficiency for two cohorts in the districts, not the change in proficiency for a single cohort. It also might be argued that it has not entirely separated, as Hayes and Taylor attempt to do, the difference in school and peer group effects, as different peer groups might progress at different rates. Given these concerns, it is perhaps not surprising that the value-added measure was not significant in the hedonic estimations. Brasington did find that several of the absolute test score measures, expenditures per pupil and teacher salary are positive.

Property values and integration   As mentioned earlier, a number of studies have examined the impact of the demographic composition of schools, specifically the percentage who are African-American or, less frequently, percentage who are Hispanic, on property values or, in a more dynamic setting, the impact of a change in minority composition on property value with this change associated with bussing (integration) policies. The earliest study of this nature is Clotfelter (1975). Using the Census of Population for 1960 and 1970 for the Atlanta MSA, Clotfelter examines how the change in percentage minority in schools from 1960 to 1970 affected the median property value of predominately White census tracts associated with those schools.[7] He found a negative and significant impact attributing a decrease in median house value of anywhere between 0 per cent to 25 per cent in some of the White census tracts. Gill (1983) examines the impacts of desegregation by comparing capitalization rate from 1975 to 1979 of single family homes in suburbs of Columbus, OH, where there was no desegregation to the capitalization rate of single family houses in the city of Columbus in which a desegregation plan was pursued. To estimate the impact of desegregation, Gill estimates a hedonic regression that uses single family house sales from 1975 to 1979. In addition to including the characteristics of the houses, the year the house was sold, and location (suburb or city) as explanatory variables, Gill included an interaction term of location (suburb) and year and another of suburb, year and house size (four bedrooms or larger). If desegregation adversely affects property values where it occurred (the city) then the interaction terms on time and suburb should be positive, as desegregation in the city should have increased over time. Gill includes the interaction terms of time, suburb and house size to determine whether larger houses, more likely to have more children, are differentially affected.

Bogart and Cromwell (2000), while not explicitly measuring the impact of the racial mix of students on housing values, do consider how housing values are affected by changing school districts primarily for the purpose of increasing racial integration. To consider this impact, they use data on a wealthy suburb of Cleveland Ohio, Shaker Heights, using housing sales between 1983 and 1994, a period during which boundaries of the schools were changed several times, primarily for the purpose of integration. The primary effect of the change of district was to reduce the number of students who attend a 'neighbourhood' school, that is, the public school that is geographically the closest to them. They find a significant impact of changes in districts on property values even when controlling for how these changes alter the racial mix of the schools. For houses that have changed districts, the loss in property values is reduced if the students residing in these houses have access to public transportation (buses). The impact of the percentage of non-white students, while negative, was not statistically significant in any of the hedonic estimates.

Separating effects of educational inputs from other government services
A frequent criticism of many hedonic estimates of the impact of educational services on property values is that the differences in educational inputs or outputs obtained by having property value data in distinct schools or school districts almost always mean that the properties will be in different jurisdictions with respect to the provision of other government services and certainly in distinct neighbourhoods. For example, Oates (1969) and Brueckner (1982) examined property values in distinct cities and townships in Northern New Jersey and metropolitan Boston, respectively. Not only did these communities vary in educational spending but they did so presumably in spending on and the quality of other public services, as education is not the only service provided by the local governments. Other characteristics and amenities of these communities presumably also vary. How, then, can the effects of differences in educational quality be parcelled out from all of these other differences among communities that will have an impact on educational quality?

One solution is to attempt to control for these differences in amenities and public services among communities as much as possible by inclusion of measures of them in the hedonic equation. Of course, this approach is always subject to the criticism of omitted variables. An alternative approach is taken in Black (1999) following earlier work by Kain and Quigley (1975) and Li and Brown (1980). Black, using micro-data on housing values in suburbs of Boston for the years 1993 to 1995, attempts to control for differences in unobserved amenities and variation at the district level by only considering houses along borders between elementary school catchment areas in the same district. Formally, she estimates a model,

$$\ln(price_{iab}) = \alpha + X'_{iab}\beta + K'_b\phi + \gamma test_a + \varepsilon_{iab},$$

where $price_{iab}$ is the price (value) of house i in district a along the border b, K_b is a vector of dummy variables indicating which border, and $test_a$ is a measure of test scores received by students in elementary school a (Black, 1999, p. 579). Then the vector K_b is designed to capture any differences in property values between borders with the assumption that, along a border (0.35 miles (600 yards) on each side), houses should be subject to the same district-level policies and are in essentially the same neighbourhood. Using this approach, Black finds a significant impact of test scores on property values: a 2.5 per cent increase in property value for a 5 per cent increase in the average test score found in the school.

Bogart and Cromwell (1997) follow an approach similar to Black (1999), using properties that are geographically close but have different schools associated with them. Specifically Bogart and Cromwell use an Oaxaca decomposition (Oaxaca, 1973) to decompose differences in housing prices between houses in different school districts but in overlapping jurisdictions for other services into an 'explained' variation in housing prices and an 'unexplained' variation. The explained variation is due to differences in the average attributes of the houses in the two districts. The unexplained differences, Bogart and Cromwell argue, must be due to differences in school quality, given that other public services and amenities should differ between the properties. Using data from 1976 to 1994 on housing sales in three school districts in the Cleveland, Ohio metropolitan area, they find that differences in school districts can lead to *annual* differences in housing costs of up to $2171 (in 1997 prices). However what they cannot find using this approach, in contrast to Black (1999), is what educational factors contribute to this difference in property values, as no attempt is made to measure any differences between the districts.

4   Education and housing prices in the United Kingdom
Perhaps not surprisingly, given its traditionally more decentralized system of government in which more variation in educational spending might be expected as well as more accessible data, particularly at the micro level, the vast majority of studies on education and housing prices have focused on the United States. The few published exceptions of which the author is aware focus on schooling in the United Kingdom.

Gibbons and Machin (2003) examine the relationship between property values and achievement in schools using a merged data set on single family sales prices and primary school performance, the percentage of students reaching 'target' level by age 11 as measured by performance on Key Stage 2 throughout the UK from 1996 to 1999. Gibbons and Machin employ sophisticated spatial econometric techniques to address the fact that there is a weaker link between residential location and school attendance in the UK than in the USA.[8] Even with this weaker link between where a student lives and where he attends school, Gibbons and Machin still find that school performance is capitalized into property values. In their study they found a 10 per cent increase in performance (10 per cent more students reaching target level) increases property values by 6.9 per cent.

In a series of papers, Paul Cheshire and Stephen Sheppard use hedonic equations to examine the influence of amenities in general on properties values in the UK, specifically in Reading and Darlington. While the focus of Cheshire and Sheppard (1995) is more generally to consider the impact of amenities on land values, one of the amenities they consider is school. The measure of property value they use is the list asking price for properties in Reading and Darlington (UK) provided by local estate agents. Using this sample they then estimate a hedonic equation for each town separately, including dummy variables for whichever school catchment area residents of the property would attend. Thus, like Bogart and Cromwell (1997), they can and do find significant differences in listed prices among the catchment areas; however, also like Bogart and Cromwell, they do not attempt to attribute these differences in housing prices to any particular aspect of educational production or quality. Cheshire and Sheppard (1998), using the same data as in their 1995 paper, estimate a demand equation for housing. While not explicitly addressing how education quality may affect housing prices, this paper provides estimates of hedonic equations that include a measure of education, the same dummy variable for school attendance, in order to estimate a price for housing to be used in the demand equation.

In Cheshire and Sheppard (2002), the authors more directly address the issue of how education, specifically test scores, affects housing prices. Confounding the relationship between educational quality and housing prices in the UK is the possibility of a student being granted the option to attend a state-supported school in another catchment area through an appeal to the local educational authority (LEA). While Cheshire and Sheppard document a relatively high rate of success in these appeals, the number of students who attend state-supported schools out of their catchment area remains relatively small, less than 2.5 per cent in Reading, the source of their data. Data on housing prices, the list price of property, were obtained by a survey of major estate agents in Reading for 17 months during 1999 and 2000. In total, list prices for 870 separate structures were obtained, with 490 of these observations usable in the estimation. Cheshire and Sheppard include measures of both primary and secondary school quality. The measure of primary school quality includes performance on Key Stage 2 exams (percentage of students passing the components of the test). For a measure of secondary school performance, they used the proportion of students obtaining five or more passes at grade C or better in the GCSE. Thus, in contrast to Gibbons and Machin (2003), they provide measures of educational quality for both primary and secondary schools.

Cheshire and Sheppard (2002) find that the hedonic price of secondary quality is higher than that for primary schools. However the variation in primary school quality is significantly greater than that for secondary schools. This being the case, they find that moving from worst to best secondary school would increase average house value by £23 763 (18.1 per cent), while moving from the worst to best primary school would increase value by £42 542 (33.5 per cent).

In contrast to the Cheshire and Sheppard work focused on a single housing market, Rosenthal (2000), like Gibbons and Machin (2003), examines the impact of school quality using a data set for all of England. The data include the selling price of approximately 350 000 individual dwellings for the period September 1995 to August 1998.[9] Unlike Gibbons and Machin, Rosenthal's focus is on secondary quality. As with Cheshire and Sheppard (2002) the measure of secondary educational quality he used was a transformation of the percentage of students passing the GCSE at a grade of C or better. As the focus of Rosenthal (2000) is on non-selective state-funded schools, the only individual dwellings included in the final sample were those ones in which the closest secondary school had non-selective admission. Using this sample and measure of school quality, Rosenthal estimates an elasticity with respect to quality of 0.05. He notes that, at an average dwelling price of £72 000, this means that a 5 per cent increase in the passing rate of the GCSE for the nearest school would increase property value by £450.

Leech and Campos (2003) also examine the impact of secondary education on housing prices but, in contrast to Rosenthal, they focus on a single city, Coventry, and similarly to the studies of Cheshire and Sheppard, use advertised list prices as a measure of house price. Their study, as they describe it, follows a case study approach in the sense that they focus on two schools in Coventry with excellent reputations and consistently oversubscribed. Then, similarly to Black (1999), and Bogart and Cromwell (1997), they focus on the price differentials along borders or, as they refer to it, within blocks between these two schools and the neighbouring schools. Unlike Black (1999), but along the lines of Bogart and Cromwell (1997), they make no attempt to measure what factors contribute to the differences in housing prices. However they do, in fact, find significant differences in housing prices between these houses in these two school catchment areas and the others in Coventry: for one school a 20 per cent premium in housing prices and for the other a 16 per cent premium.

5 Concluding comments

For over 30 years, the relationship between housing prices and education has been a topic of interest among urban economists and economists examining educational issues more generally. Not surprisingly, over this period both the methodology used in the research and the focus of the research have changed, although not dramatically as one might expect or as might be found in other areas of economic and education research. In general there has been a shift in focus from the relationship between educational spending and housing prices to relationship between educational performance, almost always measured by standardized test scores, and housing prices. One reason for this shift in research focus is the lack of evidence on a positive relationship between educational spending and educational outcomes, particularly scores on standardized tests. Another reason might be the significant reductions in inequities in educational spending that have occurred in both the USA and UK during the past 30 years.

While studies on the way educational spending affects housing prices generally find positive impacts, for those few studies that have examined this while also controlling for measures of educational quality the evidence seems weaker. The results may be considered more mixed when the efficiency of educational spending is examined.

Evidence on the impact of educational output, as measured by test scores, on house values is consistently positive and often represents a substantial component of the house value. That these measures of educational output do appear to matter in both the USA and, particularly, the UK suggests that families, and not only researchers, appear to pay attention to these measures and are in fact willing to pay for higher performance. Perhaps somewhat puzzling and contradictory is weak, albeit limited, evidence that what should matter, value-added performance, has much of an impact on house values. While households are choosing to live by and attend schools where test scores are higher, it is unclear that the premium they pay will necessarily translate into higher test scores for their children. Furthermore, while households evidently value quality as measured by test scores, the question of how educational quality can be improved is still unresolved. Here we obtain some measure of how much households value this quality; the benefits they would receive but which are yet to be determined are the cost of this quality.

Notes

1. See Tiebout (1956, p. 419) for a discussion of the assumptions of his model.
2. Here we use the convention of referring to the price of housing on an annual basis, that is the rental value, rather than purchase value. Of course this means that the property tax rate we are discussing is based on rental value, not purchase price.
3. In addition to being aggregated, the measure obtained from the Census of Housing is also based on value reported by homeowners, not upon actual sale prices.
4. The acronym MSA refers to metropolitan statistical area in the United States. It is a group of counties defined by the U.S. Census Bureau primarily based on population and commuting patterns of the workforce. Under 2000 Census guidelines, an MSA generally consists of a 'central' county of at least 10 000 residents and 'outlying' counties. For a county to be included in the MSA as an 'outlying' county at least 25 per cent of its workforce must commute to the central county.
5. Sonstelie and Portney (1980) chose 9 per cent as their discount rate.
6. Less relevant for our discussion, Sonstelie and Portney also argue that their approach is superior to Oates (1969) and similar studies, in that they are using tax payments and not tax rates and it is the tax payments, not rates, that should be capitalized.
7. Census tracts are small areas within US counties designated by the US Bureau of Census. These areas generally have between 2500 and 8000 residents with borders that usually follow features such as rivers, major highways or railways.
8. I discuss the issue of students attending school out of their catchment area in the UK more in my discussion of Cheshire and Sheppard (2002).
9. These data are from the Nationwide Building Society.

References

Barrow, L. and C. Rouse (2003), 'Using market valuation to assess public school spending', *Journal of Public Economics*, in press.

Bates, L. and R. Santerre (2003), 'The impact of a state mandated expenditure floor on aggregate property values', *Journal of Urban Economics*, **53**, 531–40.

Black, S. (1999), 'Do better schools matter? Parental valuation of elementary education', *Quarterly Journal of Economics*, **114**, 577–99.

Bogart, W. and B. Cromwell (1997), 'How much more is a good school district worth?', *National Tax Journal*, **50**, 215–32.

Bogart, W. and B. Cromwell (2000), 'How much is a neighbourhood school worth?', *Journal of Urban Economics*, **47**, 280–305.

Brasington, D. (1999), 'Which measures of school quality does the housing market value?', *Journal of Real Estate Research*, **18**(3), 395–413.

Brasington, D. (2003), 'The supply of public school quality', *Economics of Education Review*, **22**, 367–77.

Brueckner, J. (1979), 'Property values, local public expenditure, and economic efficiency', *Journal of Public Economics*, **11**, 223–45.

Brueckner, J. (1982), 'A test for allocative efficiency in the local public sector', *Journal of Public Economics*, **19**, 311–31.

Cheshire, P. and S. Sheppard (1995), 'On the price of land and the value of amenities', *Economica*, **62**, 247–67.

Cheshire, P. and S. Sheppard (1998), 'Estimating the demand for housing, land and neighbourhood characteristics', *Oxford Bulletin of Economics and Statistics*, **60**(3), 357–82.

Cheshire, P. and S. Sheppard (2002), 'Capitalising the value of free schools: the impact of land constraints', paper prepared for Conference on the Analysis of Urban Land Markets and the Impact of Land Market Regulation, Lincoln Institute of Land Policy, Cambridge, MA.

Clotfelter, C. (1975), 'The effect of school desegregation on housing prices', *The Review of Economics and Statistics*, **57**(4), 446–51.

Deller, S. (1990a), 'An application of a test for allocative efficiency in the local public sector', *Regional Science and Urban Economics*, **20**(3), 395–406.

Deller, S. (1990b), 'Pareto-efficiency and the provision of public goods within a rural setting', *Growth and Change*, **32**(1), 30–39.

Downes, T. and J. Zabel (2002), 'The impact of school characteristics on house prices: Chicago 1987–1991', *Journal of Urban Economics*, **52**, 1–25.

Edel, M. and E. Sclar (1974), 'Taxes, spending and property values: supply adjustment in a Tiebout model', *The Journal of Political Economy*, **82**(5), 941–54.

Epple, D. and A. Zelenitz (1981), 'The implications of competition among jurisdictions: does Tiebout need politics?', *The Journal of Political Economy*, **89**(6), 1197–217.

Epple, D., R. Filimon and T. Romer (1984), 'Equilibrium among local jurisdictions: toward an integrated treatment of voting and residential choice', *Journal of Public Economics*, **24**(3), 281–308.

Epple, D., A. Zelenitz and M. Visscher (1978), 'A search for testable implications of the Tiebout hypothesis', *The Journal of Political Economy*, **86**(3), 405–25.

Gibbons, S. and S. Machin (2003), 'Valuing English primary schools', *Journal of Urban Economics*, **53**, 197–219.

Gill, H. (1983), 'Changes in city and suburban house prices during a period of expected school desegregation', *Southern Economic Journal*, **50**, 169–84.

Hamilton, B. (1975), 'Zoning and property taxation in a system of local governments', *Urban Studies*, **12**, 205–11.

Hamilton, B. (1976), 'The effects of property taxes and local public spending on property values: a theoretical comment', *The Journal of Political Economy*, **84**(3), 647–50.

Hanushek, E. (1986), 'The economics of schooling: production and efficiency in the public schools', *The Journal of Economic Literature*, **24**(3), 1141–77.

Hanushek, E. and L. Taylor (1990), 'Alternative assessments of the performance of schools', *The Journal of Human Resources*, **25**(2), 179–201.

Haurin, D. and D. Brasington (1996), 'School quality and real house prices', *Journal of Housing Economics*, **5**, 351–68.

Hayes, K. and L. Taylor (1996), 'Neighbourhood school characteristics: what signals quality to homebuyers?', *Economic Review of Federal Reserve Bank of Dallas*, 4th Quarter.

Hoyt, W. (1991), 'Property taxation, Nash equilibrium, and market power', *Journal of Urban Economics*, **30**, 123–31.

Hoyt, W. (1992), 'Market power of large cities and policy differences in metropolitan areas', *Regional Science and Urban Economics*, **22**, 539–58.

Hoyt, W. (1999), 'Leviathan, local government expenditures, and capitalization', *Regional Science and Urban Economics*, **29**, 155–71.

Jud, G. (1985), 'A further note on schools and housing values', *AREAU Journal*, **13**(4), 452–61.

Jud, G. and J. Watts (1981), 'Schools and house values', *Land Economics*, **57**, 459–70.

Kain, J. and J. Quigley (1975), *Housing Markets and Racial Discrimination: A Microeconomic Analysis*, New York: National Bureau of Economic Research.

Leech, D. and E. Campos (2003), 'Is comprehensive education really free? A case study of the effects of secondary school admissions policies on house prices in one local area', *Journal of the Royal Statistical Society*, Series A (Statistics in Society), **166**(1), 135–54.

Li, M. and H. Brown, (1980), 'Micro-neighbourhood externalities and hedonic house prices', *Land Economics*, **56**, 125–41.

Oates, W. (1969), 'The effects of property taxes and local public spending on property values: an empirical study of tax capitalization and the Tiebout hypothesis', *The Journal of Political Economy*, **77**(6), 957–71.

Oates, W. (1973), 'The effects of property taxes and local spending on property values: a reply and yet further results', *The Journal of Political Economy*, **81**(4), 1004–8.

Oaxaca, R. (1973), 'Male–female wage differentials in urban labour markets', *International Economic Review*, **14**(3), 693–709.

Pauly, M. (1976), 'A model of local government expenditure and tax capitalization', *Journal of Public Economics*, **6**, 231–42.

Pollakowski, H. (1973), 'The effects of property taxes and local spending on property values: a comment and further results', *The Journal of Political Economy*, **81**(4), 994–1003.

Rosen, H. and D. Fullerton (1977), 'A note on local tax rates, public benefit levels, and property values', *The Journal of Political Economy*, **85**, 433–40.
Rosenthal, Leslie (2000), 'The value of secondary school quality', working paper, Department of Economics, University of Keele, Staffs, UK.
Samuelson, P. (1954), 'The pure theory of public expenditure', *Review of Economics and Statistics*, **36**(4), 387–9.
Sonstelie, J. and P. Portney (1980), 'Gross rents and market values: testing the implications of Tiebout's hypothesis', *Journal of Urban Economics*, **7**, 102–18.
Summers, A. and B. Wolfe (1977), 'Do schools make a difference?', *American Economic Review*, **67**, 639–52.
Taylor, L. (1995), 'Allocative inefficiency and local government', *Journal of Urban Economics*, **37**, 201–11.
Tiebout, C. (1956), 'A pure theory of local expenditures', *The Journal of Political Economy*, **64**(5), 416–24.
Vandell, K. and R. Zerbst (1984), 'Estimates of the effect of school desegregation plans on housing values over time', *AREUEA Journal*, **12**(2), 109–35.
Walden, M. (1990), 'Magnet schools and the differential impact of school quality on residential property values', *The Journal of Real Estate Research*, **5**(2), 221–30.
Weimer, D. and M. Wolkoff (2001), 'School performance and housing values: using non-contiguous boundaries and incorporating boundaries to identify school effects', *National Tax Journal*, **54**(2), 231–54.
Yinger, J. (1982), 'Capitalization and the theory of local public finance', *The Journal of Political Economy*, **90**(5), 917–43.

Index

A levels
    effect on degree outcome 415,
        419–20, 436, 443, 454, 456,
        478, 479
    effect on earnings 81, 82
    grade inflation in 473
    proportion of new university
        entrants with 432–3, 434, 453,
        454
    schools with A-level pupils 392, 395,
        396, 397, 398, 400, 401, 402,
        403, 405, 414
    scores achieved in 426–7, 433–4, 435,
        437, 441, 445, 450
    subjects taken 433, 435, 450
    targets relating to 467
    and university dropout rate 445, 449,
        450
Abbot, M. 607, 653, 655, 659, 671
Abbring, J. 129
ability, differential
    effect on earnings 9–10, 77–80, 84–5,
        91–3, 94, 97
    and exam performance 377, 382
    and school-to-work transition 487,
        490–91, 499, 503–6, 508,
        510–11, 514, 520
    and teaching participation rates
        539–40
Abraham, K. 150
absenteeism
    educated workers' 58, 81, 94
    school 383, 384–5, 386, 392, 395,
        396–7, 414, 752
    determinants of 397, 398–9, 407
    see also truancy
accommodation, family's 502, 504,
    507, 508, 511–12, 520
accommodation, student's 445, 457,
    458, 459, 469, 478, 479
accountability 25, 273–4, 371, 467, 527,
    545, 557, 561–2, 594
Acemoglou, D. 153, 207, 223, 224, 225

Achilles, C.M. 342, 345, 346, 364
Ackum, S. 142
active labour market policy (ALMP)
    102, 139
Addison, J.T. 18
Addison, T. 770
Adelaide Declaration 467
admissions procedures in UK
    universities 422–4, 449
Adnett, N. 407
adult retraining programmes 139
adverse selection 59
Africa
    externality component of social rate
        of return to education in 220,
        222, 223, 225, 226, 252
    non-market education
        externalities in 231–2, 234,
        238, 240, 241
    participation in higher education in
        581
    school finance in 277
    total social rate of return including
        non-market education
        externalities in 244
    total value of education externalities
        in 228
    university fees in 252–3
    see also Africa, North; Africa, Sub-
        Saharan
Africa, North
    child labour in 745
    returns to education in 16, 17
Africa, Sub-Saharan
    child labour in 744, 745
    non-market education externalities
        in 242
    returns to education in 16, 17
age
    distribution in higher education 301,
        304, 432, 434, 453, 454
    distribution in teaching profession
        567–8